RIGINAL
PEDIA
BOOK
ROES
UME ONE

featuring

MAN

The ORIGINAL ENCYCLOPEDIA *of* COMIC BOOK HEROES

VOLUME ONE

featuring

BATMAN

by **Michael L. Fleisher**

assisted by Janet E. Lincoln

BATMAN created by Bob Kane

To **PREAM**

THE ORIGINAL ENCYCLOPEDIA OF COMIC BOOK HEROES Volume One-Featuring BATMAN
Published by DC Comics.

DC Comics, 1700 Broadway, New York, NY 10019 A Warner Bros. Entertainment Company.
Printed in Canada. First Printing. ISBN: 1-4012-1355-3 ISBN 13: 978-1-4012-1355-8

The Encyclopedia of Comic Book Heroes

VOLUME **ONE**

BATMAN

VOLUME **TWO**

WONDER WOMAN

VOLUME **THREE**

SUPERMAN

FOREWORD BY PAUL LEVITZ

THINK OF IT AS A COLLAGE... an intricate picture, composed of hundreds, perhaps thousands, of images—each contributing to the overall impression. Then, focus more carefully, and try to isolate each individual image, evaluate it, and place it in context with all the rest. Now apply that process to the first thirty years of Batman's history, identifying each character who added meaning to the Gotham Guardian's life. And then imagine doing this before word processing, with all the data compiled in shoeboxes full of index cards, to be sorted by hand and typed in a final order.

It was still possible to read all the *Batman* stories ever published thirty-five years ago, when Michael Fleisher compiled this Encyclopedia (or even twenty-nine years ago, when I did a far less thorough reading of the whole canon to prepare myself to become the new editor of the *Batman* titles). But it was a massive task to not only read the tales, but also correlate their contents and make a useful reference work from them. Michael spent long months in the DC library, gathering the data for this and the seven companion volumes he originally conceived. The finished work has proved a useful resource—to writers, artists, editors, and even filmmakers—helping us find the moments in Batman's history that we wanted to build on. For one of the special joys of comics is how each generation of creative talent takes the legacy of its predecessors, refreshes and reimagines it, and passes it on, stronger and more complex. Making those legacies more accessible has been the contribution of Michael and of a host of index compilers since, many of whose works have become fingertip-searchable thanks to the web. But this particular reference work has long been out of print, and available only to those of us who kept our worn and well-used copies handy on our shelves. I'm pleased that it'll now be back in print, and available to all.

PAUL LEVITZ

PRESIDENT & PUBLISHER, DC COMICS

INTRODUCTION

THIRTY-EIGHT YEARS HAVE PASSED since that historic day in 1969 when Gerda Gattel, DC Comics' dedicated archivist and librarian, ushered me and my research assistant, Janet Lincoln, into the medium-sized, one-room library. Lined with floor-to-ceiling bookshelves, it served as the repository for bound volumes of the company's carefully preserved back issues, thousands upon thousands of them—two copies each of every single DC comic book ever published.

Janet and I spent five years in that library, taking painstakingly detailed notes on every single Batman comic book story produced in the character's first twenty-six years of publication—from the Caped Crusader's debut in *Detective Comics* No. 27, in November 1939, where his foe was murder-minded chemical company executive Alfred Stryker—to a trio of December 1965 stories, two of them in *Batman* No. 176 and one in *World's Finest Comics* No. 154.

The end result of our efforts was *The Encyclopedia of Comic Book Heroes Vol 1: Batman,* which was published in 1976 by Collier Books, a division of Macmillan Publishing Co., Inc.

As all of us who haven't spent our lives huddling in caves now know, of course, the Batman's comic book stock has skyrocketed over the course of the last 30 years. While in the mid-1970s you could have purchased a mint-condition *Detective Comics* No. 27 for a paltry $1,500, today you'd have to pony up more than $30,000 for a copy, as some gloriously happy fan did on eBay just this past November.

I wish I could report that copies of this Batman encyclopedia have appreciated in value that much in the past 31 years. They haven't. But they have become a lot scarcer and pricier than they used to be, with brand-new copies long since unavailable and used copies going for as high as $221 a pop on Amazon.com, fueled by ecstatically positive reader reviews in the 92% to 100% range. Let's face it! You practically have to be as rich as Bruce Wayne to own one!

But—whew!—not anymore! The spankin' new DC Comics collectors' reprint edition you've just purchased has set you back a mere fraction of that—which is cause for celebration, don't you think, fellow Batmaniac?

MICHAEL L. FLEISHER, March 2007

PREFACE

The Encyclopedia of Comic Book Heroes began as something of a lark, and ended as a labor of love.

In early 1969, I was working as a writer/editor for the Encyclopaedia Britannica, writing entries for an encyclopedia that the company intended to market overseas. One afternoon, as a humorous way of relieving the office tedium, one of the other writers composed a short biography of Clark Kent written in the same stuffy, pedantic style that characterized the biographies of real people in the encyclopedia we were working on. "KENT, CLARK," it began. "United States journalist who is secretly Superman. . . ."

As the bogus entry made its way around the room, the editorial office exploded with laughter. People laughed because, by using a serious, pseudoscholarly style in connection with subject matter generally regarded as frivolous, the author had successfully satirized the pomposity of our encyclopedia.

But I saw the Clark Kent entry in a different light. Already keenly interested in popular culture, I saw it as treating the comic book mythos as other, more "respectable" bodies of mythic literature have traditionally been treated, as a serious intellectual subject. I also saw that entry as a means of escape from my deadly dull job at the Britannica.

"Hey! This is a terrific idea," I exclaimed aloud in the midst of the merriment. "Somebody should do a whole book of these."

That idea seemed so ridiculous seven years ago that everyone started laughing all over again, but I was already out of the room, down the corridor, slamming that Clark Kent article onto the office copy machine, beginning to dream up the thousands of other articles I would write to go along with it.

I should say here and now that I was neither a comic book fan nor a comic book collector. I had not so much as glanced sideways at a comic book since the wise old age of fourteen, when, in what seemed at the time a decision born of maturity and sound judgment, I had sold my entire collection to a junk lady on Third Avenue for a penny a magazine.

Nevertheless, that night in 1969, using the Xeroxed Clark Kent article as my inspiration and the classic comic book stories reprinted in Jules Feiffer's *The Great Comic Book Heroes* as source material, I hammered out a half dozen sample entries and a two-page proposal for a one-volume encyclopedia of the comics. The following afternoon, I showed it all to an acquaintance in publishing, and within four hours he had called me on the telephone to say that his people loved the idea and that we had ourselves a deal.

Only then, after the commitment to write the book had actually been made, did I even begin to ponder the problem of how I was going to gain access to the many old comics that would be necessary to my research. Fortunately for me, the major comic book publishers were all willing to give me access to their extensive files of back issues. Later, a network of fans and collectors would help me acquire the various issues published by companies now defunct.

So it is that, one morning in March 1969, I walked into the offices of National Periodical Publications, Inc., publishers of DC Comics, and was introduced to Gerda Gattel, National's librarian, now retired. Her ring of keys jangling, Mrs. Gattel led me down a carpeted executive corridor to the locked door of the DC Comics Library. She knew that I intended to write a serious reference guide to the literature of the great comic book heroes, and she was proud that her precious library was at last to be used for serious research, rather than merely by client businessmen seeking out action pictures of super-heroes to laminate onto T-shirts and beach blankets.

As she swung open the library door and flicked on the light, I remember that I gasped a little. The library was only a medium-sized room, but its walls were lined with floor-to-ceiling bookshelves packed with neatly bound volumes of back-issue comic books, thousands upon thousands of them, two copies each of every single comic book National Periodicals has ever published. I had never imagined there would be so many.

Mrs. Gattel noticed my surprise, and her eyes twinkled with the slightly mischievous pleasure of a fabulously wealthy connoisseur showing an astounded visitor through the exquisitely stocked wine cellar. "You said you wanted to study *all* the heroes," she smiled benignly, taking in the entire room with a sweeping gesture of her arm. "We have dozens of them. Where would you like to begin?"

I decided to begin with Batman, because Batman had been my boyhood favorite. Between the ages of eight and fourteen I had been a comic book addict, and from the moment I opened that first bound volume of Batman stories I knew I was hooked again, transported despite my adulthood and education into an eerily garish world of magic and enchantment. On that first long day of "serious" research, I managed to take notes on exactly one comic book.

Few fictional characters of any kind, let alone comic book characters, have enjoyed the kind of hold over their readers that Batman has exerted for nearly four decades. His adventures are read by millions of young people in every state of the United States and in thirty-five foreign countries. Only one other character in the history of comic books — Superman — has been published continuously for so long a period. More people have thrilled to the exploits of Batman than have ever heard of Hamlet or seen a play by Shakespeare. He is the world's foremost fictional detective after Sherlock Holmes.

Yet the adventures of Batman, and the vast popular literature of which they are a part, are already all but lost to us. Destroyed on a massive scale during the paper drives of the 1940s – "Save your scrap to beat the Jap!" admonished one of the popular patriotic slogans appearing in the margins of many comics – and hysterically assailed during the 1950s as a root cause of juvenile delinquency, comic books have been almost universally derided as trash by adults and cherished only by their children.

In the entire world, not one library, university, or public or private institution of any kind has taken the trouble to acquire and preserve a complete set of Batman's adventures for posterity. Nowhere in the world is there a single research facility where the complete adventures of even one major comic book hero have been safely preserved and made available for study. Reasonable people may debate the value of the comics as art or literature, but no one can deny that they constitute the most widely read body of children's literature in the history of the world. Perhaps one day, there will be sufficient serious interest in the comics to warrant their widespread distribution on microfilm to libraries and universities, but as of this writing that day seems a long way off.

The writing of this volume required that Janet Lincoln and I have access to a complete file of Batman's adventures. Such a file is available in only one place – the corporate library at National Periodical Publications, Inc. – and it has been preserved there, along with complete files of the adventures of National's other comic book characters, partially through the foresight of the company's management, but mainly through the efforts of one determined woman.

At the time this project began, Gerda Gattel had been the guardian of the DC Comics archives for twelve years. During the long years when the comics were regarded as garbage even by most of their creators, when comic books and comic-book artwork were routinely destroyed and discarded by their publishers to eliminate the expense of storing them, she fought, and agitated, and cajoled to be allowed to maintain a real library at National, to be provided with bookshelves and storage space, and to be permitted to take occasional time off from her full-time job as the company proofreader in order to keep and maintain the library on her own.

Janet Lincoln and I spent seven full years working on *The Encyclopedia of Comic Book Heroes.* In that time, we examined more than 10,000 comic book stories and filled approximately 20,000 5" × 8" index cards with detailed notes on what we had read.

As the years passed, my original one-volume project expanded to encompass eight volumes, consuming in the process thirty-one reams of typing paper and producing, in the end, a completed typewritten manuscript of more than two million words. As the project grew in scope, my original publisher lost interest and eventually withdrew, and I am deeply grateful that the Macmillan Publishing Company has taken an interest in what, from a commercial standpoint, can only be regarded as a costly and risky project.

The *Batman* encyclopedia that you hold in your hands is the first volume of the eight-volume "labor of love" that I spoke of in my opening sentence. Other encyclopedias dealing with literary material, such as encyclopedias of Greek mythology or English literature, are able to refer their readers to the literature itself, but, with the exception of the occasional Batman stories reprinted in hardcover volumes, or the Batman comics still surviving in valuable private collections – a copy of Detective Comics No. 27, for example, the first comic book in which Batman ever appeared, currently brings a price of upwards of $1,500 on the collectors' market – the stories referred to in this volume are not available for examination.

For that reason, the material dealt with in this book has been covered in excruciating detail, retaining generous portions of the original dialogue and textual narrative and employing a style designed to present the material clearly while evoking what Jules Feiffer has termed the "florid pre-literacy" of the comics.

As you browse through the pages of this volume, renewing your acquaintance with such diabolical masters and mistresses of villainy as the Joker, the Penguin, and the Catwoman – and perhaps meeting for the first time such crafty lesser lights as the Thinker, an "arch criminal, whose wasted body houses a restless, writhing brain" – I hope you too find yourself transported into that world of magic and enchantment I spoke of earlier. And whether you're a serious student of sociology or popular culture – or just a stone Batmaniac with the smell of four-color ink in your nostrils and bits of cheap pulp paper floating like flotsam in your blood – I hope you have a real good time there.

New York City, 1976 MICHAEL L. FLEISHER

ACKNOWLEDGMENTS

The author would like to extend his heartfelt thanks to the management and staff of National Periodical Publications, Inc., publishers of DC Comics, without whose generous cooperation this volume could not have been written. In particular, the author would like to thank:

Carmine Infantino, Publisher, for generously extending the hospitality of his organization to the author and his assistant throughout the seven-year-long period during which *The Encyclopedia of Comic Book Heroes* was being researched and written.

Sol Harrison, Vice President-Director of Operations, for his generous advice, assistance, and support throughout the project, particularly in connection with the accumulation and reproduction of illustrative material.

Bernard Kashdan, Vice President-Business Manager, for generously granting permission for the use of the comic book illustrations reproduced in this volume.

Gerda Gattel, Librarian (ret.), whose devotion to the DC Comics Library, for nearly a quarter century, made possible the research on which this encyclopedia is based. For this devotion, and for the many personal kindnesses extended to the author and his assistant during the period of their research, the author would like to extend his special thanks.

Joe Kubert, Editor, and Denny O'Neil, Editor, for their advice and encouragement.

Joe Orlando, Editor, for his advice and encouragement, and for his generosity in sharing many insights born of a lifetime in comics.

Julius Schwartz, Editor, for generously sharing his many insights and anecdotes.

E. Nelson Bridwell, Associate Editor, for sharing with the author the broad reach of his knowledge.

Milton Snapinn, Head, Export Department, for his assistance in assembling the back-issue negatives used to produce many of the illustrations in this volume.

Lois Barker, Export Department, for her ready, affectionate wit, and for her assistance in assembling the back-issue negatives used to produce many of the illustrations in this volume.

Jack Adler, Production Manager, for generously using his technical expertise to review the illustrations in this volume to ensure their suitability for reproduction.

Wayne Seelal, Photographer, for giving generously of his time and technical knowhow to help photograph the comic book illustrations reproduced in this volume.

Joe Lederici, Morris Waldinger, and Debra Ulrich of the Production Department, for advising the author in connection with the retouching of the comic book illustrations reproduced in this volume.

The author would also like to extend his thanks to the following individuals, all of whom made significant contributions toward the preparation of this volume:

Neal Adams, Dick Giordano, and Frank McLaughlin, artists, and Mike Nolan, comic book fan, collector, and compiler of comic book indexes, for their encouragement and support, and for their help in putting the author in contact with other individuals who have made contributions toward the preparation of this volume.

Murphy Anderson, artist, for his encouragement and support, for giving generously of his time to retouch some of the comic book illustrations reproduced in this volume, and for his generous loan of rare comic books from his personal collection.

Jerry and Jean Bails, scholars, comic book collectors, and publishers of *The Who's Who of American Comic Books* and other publications; Otto Binder, writer; and Mike Friedrich, writer and comic book publisher, for their encouragement and support.

Linda Brown, for her generous help in preparing for publication many of the comic book illustrations reproduced in this volume.

Dagne Crowley, Ethan Roberts, Donald A. Whyte, and Len Wein, Editor, Magazine Management Company, Inc., Marvel Comics Group, for their generous loan of rare comic books from their personal collections.

Carol Fein, formerly secretary to the publisher of National Periodical Publications, Inc., for the numerous kindnesses extended to the author and his assistant during the period of their research.

Mark Hanerfeld, comic book collector and former publisher of *The Comic Reader;* Don and Margaret Thompson, authors, comic book collectors, and publishers of *Newfangles* and other publications; and Marvin Wolfman, Editor, Magazine Management Company, Inc., Marvel Comics Group, for their encouragement and support, and for their generous loan of rare comic books from their personal collections.

Earl Hokens, photographer, for giving generously of his time and technical knowhow to help photograph the comic book illustrations reproduced in this volume.

Mrs. Everett Larson, Acting Head, Reference Section, the Library of Congress, for giving unstintingly of her time to help the author and his assistant locate rare comic books in the library's archives.

Alan Light, publisher of *The Buyer's Guide for Comic Fandom* and other publications, for generously making space in *The Buyer's Guide* available to the author to help him in locating the owners of rare comic book materials necessary to his research.

William Morse, proprietor of the Adventure Bound Bookstore, and Phil Seuling, chairman of the New York

Comic Art Convention and proprietor of Phil Seuling's Comic Sales, for their generous loan of rare comic books from their respective inventories.

Byron Preiss, for his help in acquiring space in comic book fan publications in order to help the author locate the owners of rare comic book materials necessary to his research.

Keithe A. Sales, for giving generously of his time and expertise to help identify the various aircraft employed by Batman.

Roy Thomas, Editor, Magazine Management Company, Inc., Marvel Comics Group, and Jean Thomas for their advice, encouragement, and numerous personal kindnesses, including the generous loan of rare comic books from their personal collection.

Glynis Wein, Head, Coloring Department, Magazine Management Company, Inc., Marvel Comics Group, for advising the author in connection with the retouching of the comic book illustrations reproduced in this volume.

Marc Weinberger, for his friendship, encouragement, advice, and unstinting support.

In addition, the author would also like to acknowledge all of the gifted men and women who, by their work in the comics, have enriched the lives of all of us.

HOW TO USE THIS BOOK

The *Batman* encyclopedia is a comprehensive encyclopedic chronicle of the comic book adventures of Batman for the first twenty-seven years of his ongoing career. Comprised of more than 1,000 entries – assembled in a convenient A-Z format and ranging in length from a few short lines to more than 100 printed pages – it contains detailed accounts of more than 1,000 separate adventures. In addition, the encyclopedia contains 220 illustrations culled directly from the comics, including pictures of Batman and Robin, their friends and adversaries, elements of their famous crime-fighting arsenal, and charts and diagrams of such diverse places and items of interest as the batcave, the batplane, and the bat-signal.

The entries in the *Batman* encyclopedia are based on detailed notes taken by the author and his assistant on each of the comic books containing Batman's adventures. The entries contain a wealth of detail on the plot of each adventure, the weapons and equipment employed by Batman and his adversaries, the costumes worn by the many costumed characters, the major relationships and themes that emerge from Batman's collected adventures, and on every other topic of interest to followers of Batman.

No reference work can serve as a substitute for its subject, but a conscientious effort has been made to organize and record within this volume data pertaining to every aspect of Batman's life and adventures.

In studying the comic books containing Batman's adventures and in writing the entries in this encyclopedia, the author and his assistant made use of no outside sources whatever. Only the direct, firsthand evidence of the comic books themselves was used. Accordingly, the *Batman* encyclopedia is a detailed reference guide only to the comic book adventures of Batman. No information has been recorded here concerning the appearance of Batman in movies, on television, or as a newspaper comic strip. Indeed, it is in comic books that the character originated, and there that he has achieved his greatest renown.

Similarly, this book contains no information concerning either the literary and artistic genesis of the character or the various writers and artists who have, since 1939, been creatively responsible for shaping his destiny. Such a history deserves to be written, but when it is, it will probably fill another volume as large as this one. A few facts, however, bear mentioning:

To the literary historian looking back, Batman's name and costume would seem to have been inspired by the Black Bat, a vigilante hero of the pulp magazines who debuted in a series of popular detective stories in 1934. Batman's creators, however, have denied this, dismissing the similarities between the two bat-caped manhunters as a "weird coincidence" and citing instead such diverse influences as Sherlock Holmes, the Shadow, Doc Savage, Douglas Fairbanks, Sr., and the bat-costumed villain appearing in a 1926 film version of Mary Roberts Rinehart's *The Bat.*

Batman's alter ego, millionaire socialite Bruce Wayne, although described in the comic books as having been named after his distant cousin Bruce N. Wayne, was actually named by his creators after two historical figures, the fourteenth-century Scottish King Robert the Bruce, and the American Revolutionary War general "Mad Anthony" Wayne. Batman's young crime-fighting ally, Robin, described in the comic books as having been named after Robin Hood and the robin redbreast, was actually named after Jerry Robinson, an early Batman artist.

Definitions:

Throughout the encyclopedia, the word "text" is used to designate a single comic book story, and the word "texts" is used to designate two or more comic book stories, or, occasionally, as a synonym for "chronicles." The word "chronicles" is used to designate all the texts which, taken together, comprise the Batman legend. The word "chroniclers" is used to designate the artists and writers who have been collectively responsible for "recording" Batman's adventures for posterity.

In comic books, the thoughts and dialogue of the characters appear printed inside roughly ovular shapes called "word balloons." Other writing, usually narrative and frequently in the third person, appears at the opening of each story and above or below some of the pictures. In the *Batman* encyclopedia, these fragments of narrative writing, known as captions, are referred to as the "narrative text" or "textual narrative."

Treatment of Events:

In the writing of this encyclopedia, certain conventions were employed. Batman and all the other characters appearing in the chronicles were treated as though they were real people, and the adventures were treated as though they were actual historical events. The comic books containing the accounts of Batman's exploits were studied as though they were historical documents chronicling the lives and adventures of actual persons.

The legend of Batman is elaborate and complex. Individual comic book sources sometimes differ in recounting a given set of events, and sources can often be found to support conflicting sets of "facts." In cases where comic book sources were discrepant with regard to particular details of Batman's life and career, an effort was made to reconcile the discrepancies in light of the total data available. A fact attested to in several comic books was accorded more weight than a contradictory fact stated in only one comic book. A statement made in a comic book concerning a contemporary event in Batman's life was accorded more weight than a contradictory statement concerning that same event made years later in the form of a recollection or flashback. Wherever strong support exists in the texts for opposing sets of facts, the evidence for both is examined in detail in this encyclopedia.

Dating:

The events described in any given comic book were assumed to have taken place on the issue date of that comic book, except in those cases where the events were clearly described as past events or where internal textual evidence argued persuasively for a different dating, such as in the case of an adventure taking place at Christmastime in an issue dated February.

Most comic books bear issue dates of either a single month or a single season. A very few have been issued listing only the issue year. In the case of a comic book issued on a bimonthly basis, the issue is given a bimonthly dating, e.g., November–December 1957. When events are described in the encyclopedia as having occurred in a two-month period, e.g., in November–December 1957, it is because those events were recorded in a bimonthly comic book.

When an event is described as having taken place "in" a given month or season, it means that the event is described in the texts as taking place in the present, i.e., during the period of the issue date. When an event is described as having taken place "by" a particular month or season, it means that the event is described in the texts as having taken place in the past, prior to the period of the issue date.

If, for example, the Joker is described as breaking jail *in* November–December 1957, it means that the Joker is shown or described as breaking jail in a comic book dated November–December 1957. If, on the other hand, the Joker is described as having broken jail *by* November–December 1957, it means that the Joker is shown or described, in a comic book dated November–December 1957, as having broken out of jail sometime in the recent past.

Characters with Dual Identities:

In the case of characters with dual identities – e.g., Bruce Wayne and Batman, or Dick Grayson and Robin – actions and quotations are attributed in the encyclopedia to one identity or the other depending on which role the character is playing at the time he performs the action being described or recites the speech being quoted. Batman dressed in his crime-fighting costume is referred to as Batman. Batman dressed in his everyday attire is referred to as Bruce Wayne. Similarly, Robin dressed in his crime-fighting costume is referred to as Robin. Robin dressed in his everyday attire is referred to as Dick Grayson.

When Robin is described as saying something and Bruce Wayne as replying, it means that the text from which the dialogue is being quoted depicts a costumed Robin conversing with Bruce Wayne dressed in his everyday attire. When Robin is described as saying something and Batman as replying, it means that the text from which the dialogue is being quoted depicts a costumed Robin conversing with a costumed Batman.

The distinction is important. In the world of the chronicles, the fact that Bruce Wayne is Batman is a closely guarded secret. To their contemporaries, the millionaire and the crime-fighter are two different persons. Accordingly, they are often referred to in this encyclopedia as though they were two different people. Batman is a member of the Bullet-Hole Club, for example, but Bruce Wayne is not. Bruce Wayne is a member of the posh Millionaire's Club, but Batman is not. Batman always signs his name with his left hand, while Bruce Wayne always signs with his right.

Entries:

The vast majority of the entries in the *Batman* encyclopedia are articles about persons, but there are also numerous entries on animals, extraterrestrial and extradimensional aliens, distant planets and alien dimensions, aliases, and a host of other subjects.

At approximately 90,000 words, the article on Batman is the longest and most exhaustive entry in the entire encyclopedia. It contains a complete account of Batman's origin, an exhaustive inventory of his crime-fighting arsenal, a complete month-by-month chronology of the first twenty-seven years of his crime-fighting career, comprehensive analyses of the major themes and relationships of the chronicles, and many other features.

As such, the Batman entry is the hub of this encyclopedia. By reading the month-by-month chronology (*see* BATMAN [section L 2, Developments]) and then following up the various cross-references, the reader will eventually come upon every entry in the encyclopedia.

Any character appearing in two or more Batman stories has been accorded an entry of his own, as have all the famous historical personages – men and women such as Jules Verne, Leonardo da Vinci, and Cleopatra – with whom Batman has formed associations during his numerous journeys into the past.

Characters appearing in only one Batman story have sometimes been accorded entries of their own and sometimes not, depending on their importance within the single story in which they appear, their significance within the overall Batman legend, and other factors.

In general, one character from each story – usually the villain, but not always – has been chosen to serve as the vehicle for summarizing the plot of the story. The roles played by such subsidiary characters as Batwoman, Alfred, and Police Commissioner Gordon are summarized in their individual entries.

How To Use This Book

Titles:

The titles of individuals — e.g., Dr., Prof., Sgt., Count — are given in parentheses in the entry title after the individual's name, as indicated in the following examples:

EKHART (Dr.)
CRANE, JONATHAN (Prof.)
HAINER, HARVEY (Sgt.)
FELIX (Count)

Whether a title is spelled out (e.g., Doctor) or abbreviated (e.g., Dr.) depends on which form is employed most often in the actual text or texts in which the character appears.

In cases where a title reflects actual rank or status, or academic or professional standing, the entries have been inserted in alphabetical order in the encyclopedia under the last name of the individual, as in the four examples listed above.

Often, however, particularly in the case of villains, what would be a title in the case of an ordinary person is, in comic books, actually part of an individual's name. Here are some examples:

PROFESSOR RADIUM
MISTER X
DOCTOR DEATH
CAPTAIN LIGHTFOOT

In cases such as these, the entries have been inserted in alphabetical order in the encyclopedia under the individual's name *including* the title, as in the four examples listed above.

Doctor Death is not referred to as Doctor, after all, because he is a doctor of philosophy or a doctor of medicine. Doctor Death is merely a pseudonym employed by Dr. Karl Hellfern.

Similarly, Captain Lightfoot is not a captain of anything; the name is merely a pseudonym employed by Abel Adams. Sometimes, an abbreviated title precedes a name, as in the cases of Mr. Camera and Dr. Dreemo. In such cases, the entries have been inserted in alphabetical order in the encyclopedia as if the titles had been fully spelled out, so that Mr. Camera (read as Mister Camera) follows Mirror-Man and Dr. Dreemo (read as Doctor Dreemo) follows Doctor Death in the alphabetical ordering.

Extraterrestrial and Extradimensional Aliens:

Most extraterrestrial and extradimensional aliens in the comics have only one name (e.g., Than-Ar, Tlano, Quork). Some, however, have both a first name and a last name (e.g., Roh Kar). In such cases, each entry has been alphabetized in the encyclopedia as though it were one long name (i.e., as Roh Kar) to avoid the unnecessary confusion that would result from reversing two strange names that are unearthly and unfamiliar.

Quotations:

The *Batman* encyclopedia contains numerous quotations from the comic book literature, some of them quite lengthy. With rare exceptions, the words in comic books are all lettered by hand, and all the lettering is done in capitals. Hand lettering makes possible a wide variety of letter sizes and styles not readily duplicated in mechanically set type. Because all-capital lettering is jarring and confusing outside the comic book context, the quotations in this volume have all been translated into the more familiar form of small letters and capitals. Great care has been taken, however, and a wide range of type styles employed, to ensure capturing the flavor of the original hand-lettering as well as the essence and spirit of the comic book style. In every case, the quotations in this volume were carefully transcribed by hand from the original comic books and then set into type in a manner calculated to re-create as closely as possible the style of the original.

Cross-References:

Cross-references are indicated by capitals and small capitals, as in the following example:

CARDINE, "KNOTS." A ruthless "underworld chieftain" who attempts to capitalize on a visit to GOTHAM CITY by a group of famous foreign lawmen — including the KNIGHT and the SQUIRE from England, the MUSKETEER from France, the GAUCHO from South America, the RANGER from Australia, and the LEGIONARY from Rome — in order to carry out "the greatest scheme of his career": the assassination of BATMAN and the theft of an armored truckload of currency being transported to a new branch bank.

The cross-references in the above example, the first paragraph of the entry on "Knots" Cardine, indicate the existence of separate articles, elsewhere in the encyclopedia, on Gotham City, the Knight, the Squire, the Musketeer, the Gaucho, the Ranger, the Legionary, and of course Batman. Since the duplication of information in the various articles of the encyclopedia has been kept to a minimum, the articles indicated by the cross-references invariably contain new information not available in the entry in which the cross-reference appears.

Textual References:

In order to relate the innumerable statements and quotations in this encyclopedia to their precise sources in the chronicles, a system of textual references was devised, relating every single fact in the encyclopedia to its source in the collected comic book adventures of Batman.

A textual reference consists of the title of a comic book series (e.g., Detective Comics, Batman, World's Finest Comics); the issue number of a particular comic book in that series and the story number of the specific story being cited; the issue date, as stated on the comic book's indicia; the title of the story being cited, if it has a title; and, in cases where a story has been divided into parts or chapters, the titles of the individual parts or chapters where part or chapter titles exist.

For a complete listing of the abbreviations used in the textual references, consult the Table of Abbreviations at the end of this essay.

Textual references appear in the encyclopedia in parentheses, directly following the fact or group of facts which they are intended to substantiate. The shorter entries in the encyclopedia generally contain only one textual reference apiece, indicating that all of the information in any one such entry derives from a single textual source. In the case of entries containing two or more textual references, however, each textual reference applies to the information in that article following the textual reference that directly precedes it.

The following is a typical textual reference:

(BM No. 136/2, Dec '60: "The Town That Hated Batman")

The textual reference given above informs the reader that whatever quotation(s) or statement(s) preceded the reference can be found or substantiated in the Batman comic book series; issue number 136; the second Batman story in the issue; issue date December 1960; story title "The Town That Hated Batman."

Here is another example:

(WF No. 144, Sep '64: "The 1,001 Tricks of Clayface and Brainiac!" pts. I–II – no title; "The Helpless Partners!")

The textual reference given above informs the reader that whatever quotation(s) or statement(s) preceded the reference can be found or substantiated in the World's Finest Comics comic book series; issue number 144; the only story in the issue featuring Batman (indicated by the lack of story number); issue date September 1964; story title "The 1,001 Tricks of Clayface and Brainiac!"; the story is divided into two separate parts, the first of which has no title, the second of which is entitled "The Helpless Partners!"

In cases where a story lacks an overall title, the textual reference simply appears without one, as in the following examples:

(BM No. 1/4, Spr '40)
(WF No. 150, Jun '65: pts. I–II – "The Super-Gamble with Doom!"; "The Duel of the Super-Gamblers!")

In the cases of textual references pertaining to comic books containing more than one Batman story, a story number has been inserted in each textual reference – directly following the issue number and separated from it by a slash mark – to indicate the precise position in the comic book of the story being referred to.

This system of story numbering applies only to fully illustrated Batman stories. It does not apply to stories without illustrations or to those featuring the logo of some other major character. Where a textual reference refers to a comic book containing only one Batman story, a story number would be superfluous and has therefore not been included.

A typical issue in the Detective Comics series, for example, contains one story about Batman followed by one or more stories featuring other heroes or heroines. Textual references pertaining to comic books in the Detective Comics series therefore contain no story number, for no issue of Detective Comics has ever contained more than one story about Batman. Here is a typical textual reference to a comic book in the Detective Comics series:

(Det No. 142, Dec '48: "Crime's Puzzle Contest!")

Wherever a textual reference fails to contain a story number, the comic book which it cites may be understood to contain only one Batman story.

In the case of the Batman series, however, a single issue may contain as many as five illustrated Batman stories, and the Batman stories are occasionally interspersed with other illustrated features that do not include Batman.

Batman No. 22, for example, contains four illustrated stories, three of them Batman stories and the fourth, featuring an entirely different logo, a story initiating a new series of adventures about Batman's butler, Alfred. Since the story numbering system applies only to Batman stories, the story headlining Alfred is excluded from the system, and the three Batman stories in the issue are numbered consecutively from one to three, from the front of the comic book to the back. Here is a textual reference to one of the three Batman stories in Batman No. 22:

(BM No. 22/3, Apr/May '44: "The Cavalier Rides Again!")

This textual reference informs the reader that whatever quotation(s) or statement(s) preceded the reference can be found or substantiated in the Batman comic book series; issue number 22; the third Batman story in the issue; issue date April–May 1944; story title "The Cavalier Rides Again!"

Whenever information normally included in a textual reference is stated beforehand in the body of an entry, that information is omitted from the textual reference, as in the following two examples:

Glenn Farr and his henchmen are apprehended by Batman and Robin in September–October 1952 (WF No. 60: "The Richest Crook in the World!").

Detective Comics No. 73 describes Batman as an "ace criminologist" (Mar '43: "The Scarecrow Returns").

The following paragraph, taken from the article on Police Commissioner James W. Gordon, illustrates the extensive use of textual references in the major entries of the encyclopedia:

Police Commissioner Gordon is "Batman's closest friend" (BM No. 71/2, Jun/Jul '52: "Commissioner Gordon's Greatest Case!") and a "good friend" of Bruce Wayne (NYWF, 1940), but in spite of the fact that Gordon has expressed the view that Batman must be a member of his "inner circle of friends" (BM No. 71/2, Jun/Jul '52: "Commissioner Gordon's Greatest Case!"; *see also* WF No. 53, Aug/Sep '51: "The Private Life of Commissioner Gordon!"), he has never actually discovered that Bruce Wayne and Batman are one and the same man.

The unusual reference in the above example to NYWF, 1940, is to an obscure comic book series entitled

How To Use This Book

New York World's Fair Comics of which only two issues were ever printed, one dated 1939, the other dated 1940.

Occasionally, a textual reference will be followed, within the parentheses, by the words "and others," as in the following example:

(Det No. 72, Feb '43: "License for Larceny"; and others)

These added words indicate that evidence to substantiate whatever statement(s) preceded the reference can be found in the specific comic book issue cited, in this case Detective Comics No. 72, and in at least two other comic books as well. When such a textual reference follows a direct quotation, it means that the quotation itself was taken from the comic book issue cited, but that data supporting the substance of the quotation is available in at least two other Batman texts as well.

Using the Encyclopedia:

If you already know the entry you wish to look up, simply turn to that entry in the appropriate alphabetical listing. If more than one listing is possible and you are uncertain which listing has been employed – if you are uncertain, for example, whether Professor Radium has been listed under Professor Radium or under Radium (Professor) – it is suggested that you try both.

If you have no specific entry title in mind but would like to consult a month-by-month chronology of Batman's crime-fighting career, such a chronology is available in the Batman article (*see* BATMAN [section L 2, Developments]).

Similarly, if you would like to learn what Batman was doing during a particular time period – during September 1955, for example – merely consult the career chronology for that particular time period and follow the cross-references to the various articles dealing with Batman's adventures during the month and year that interest you. This is what the career chronology has to say about Batman's activities in September 1955:

In September 1955 Batman and Robin match wits with "BIG JIM" JARREL (Det No. 223: "The Batman Dime-Museum"); apprehend JOHN MARSTIN (BM No. 94/1: "The Sign of the Bat!"); humor ALFRED during his period of amnesia (BM No. 94/2: "The New Batman!"); and smash the racket run by JOHN GOSS (BM No. 94/3: "The Mystery of the Sky Museum!").

Separate entries may be found in the encyclopedia for all four of the names cross-referenced.

In Conclusion:

The *Batman* encyclopedia has been designed for both the browser and the researcher, the casual fan and the serious collector. Great care has been taken to make it enjoyable as well as functional, entertaining as well as definitive. Whether you are engaged in scholarly research or reading for pleasure, writing a thesis or preparing a trivia quiz, the *Batman* encyclopedia will provide you with the information you seek and with many pleasurable hours as well.

ABBREVIATIONS

Titles of comic book series:

AS	*All Star Comics*
BM	*Batman*
B&B	*The Brave and the Bold*
Det	*Detective Comics*
F	*The Flash*
NYWF	*New York World's Fair Comics*
S	*Superman*
WB	*World's Best Comics**
WF	*World's Finest Comics*

* Series was renamed World's Finest Comics beginning with issue #2

Months and seasons:

Jan	January
Feb	February
Mar	March
Apr	April
May	May
Jun	June
Jul	July
Aug	August
Sep	September
Oct	October
Nov	November
Dec	December
Win	Winter
Spr	Spring
Sum	Summer
Fall	Fall

Other abbreviations:

chs.	chapters
pts.	parts
No.	issue number

A

ABDULLAH. The "crafty magician" of ancient Baghdad who is the secret leader of the infamous FORTY THIEVES. Dispatched through the time barrier by PROFESSOR CARTER NICHOLS to the city of Baghdad in the tenth century A.D., BATMAN and ROBIN make the acquaintance of the legendary ALADDIN and, with SUPERMAN's help, recover the inheritance which the naïve lad has foolishly traded to the wily Abdullah in exchange for a worthless "magic" lamp and clear him of the groundless charge that he is one of the Forty Thieves. In addition, the three crime-fighters foil an attempt by Abdullah and his cohorts to loot the shops of Baghdad, and ultimately apprehend the villains after Superman has chased them from the city (WF No. 79, Nov/Dec '55: "The Three Magicians of Bagdad!").

ACADEMY, THE. A closely guarded estate in an outlying area of GOTHAM CITY which serves both as a training ground for master criminals and as the headquarters of "the greatest criminal organization in the world."

"Here at the Academy," explains its leader, ". . . we take the same approach to crime as the F.B.I. takes to crime-busting! We too take only the cream of manhood--and train them well--scientifically and intelligently!! All these men [i.e., the Academy's members] . . . have I.Q.'s of over 135! They're all athletes! They could be F.B.I. men, or army officers, but they chose crime!"

In April–May 1952, when the Academy prepares to hold its annual "all-around competition" to select the man who will lead it for the coming year, BATMAN infiltrates the Academy under an assumed name, successfully rises to leadership of the organization as part of his plan to recover the Academy's hoard of stolen loot, and ultimately apprehends the entire membership with the aid of the Gotham City Police Department (BM No. 70/2: "The Masterminds of Crime!").

ACE (the Bat-Hound). The courageous brown dog—owned first by engraver JOHN WILKER (BM No. 92/3, Jun '55: "Ace, the Bat-Hound!") and later by BRUCE WAYNE (BM No. 125/1, Aug '59: "The Secret Life of Bat-Hound") — that functions periodically, from June 1955 onward, as the canine crime-fighting companion of BATMAN and ROBIN (BM No. 92/3: "Ace, the Bat-Hound!"). For his role as Bat-Hound, Ace wears a tight-fitting black mask designed to conceal his distinctive forehead markings which, by betraying his true identity and therefore that of his owner, could severely jeopardize the secret identities of Batman and Robin.

In June 1955 Batman and Robin rescue a drowning dog from a river and then place an ad in a local newspaper in an effort to locate its owner. One night, when they leave the BATCAVE in response to a police call and the dog insists on coming with them, Robin conceals his distinctive forehead markings with a hastily fashioned black mask and affixes a small bat-insignia to his dog collar. Soon afterward, the courageous canine helps Batman and Robin capture escaped convict BERT BOWERS, who inadvertently gives the masked dog a new name when he cries out "Leggo, you--you **bat-hound!**"

"'Bat-Hound' is a good name for him, ***Batman!***" comments a police officer soon afterward. "He sure helped out this time!"

Not long afterward, Bruce Wayne and DICK GRAYSON learn that their new Bat-Hound is in reality a trained watchdog named Ace and that he belongs to John Wilker, a "skilled engraver" employed by the Gotham Printing and Engraving Company. Wilker, however, is nowhere to be found, and his small cottage in "an isolated suburb" of GOTHAM CITY shows signs of a struggle. Batman surmises that Ace was stunned by his master's abductors, and that he had fallen into the river where they had found him while trying to follow his master's scent.

When Ace growls menacingly upon entering the General Paper Company, where Batman is investigating the recent theft of some special paper used to print bonds, Batman is confirmed in his suspicions that Wilker has been abducted by criminals who intend to force him to use his skill as an engraver to counterfeit bonds for them, and that Ace's anger is related to his having smelled the scent of his master's abductors at the paper company.

On the hunch that the criminals will strike next at the Eastern Printing-Ink Company, Batman and Robin take Ace there, but the criminals knock Ace unconscious, capture Batman and Robin, and carry the Dynamic Duo captive to their hideout on the outskirts of the city, where they are kept tightly bound while Wilker is put to work counterfeiting bonds. By means of an improvised BAT-SIGNAL, however, Batman and Robin summon Ace, who has by now revived, to the scene. Once Ace has chewed through their bonds, Batman, Robin, and Ace capture the assembled criminals and free John Wilker from their clutches.

"He's sure a great dog, Mr. Wilker!" remarks Batman, after Wilker and his dog have been safely returned to their cottage. "It was *he* who really saved us!"

"And if you ever want to be a ***Bat-Hound*** again, Ace," adds Robin, "--the position is open!" (BM No. 92/3: "Ace, the Bat-Hound!").

In February 1956 John Wilker lends Ace to Batman and Robin so that he can help them track down a gang of criminals who are using a trained dog to help them commit crimes (*see* MILLEN, ROSS). At one point, Batman equips Ace's collar with a tiny two-way radio

Ace the Bat-Hound, 1959 © NPP 1959

which enables Batman and Robin to summon Ace over long distances and overhear the criminals' conversation after Ace has used his sense of smell to locate their hideout (BM No. 97/3: "The Return of the Bat-Hound!").

In October 1956, while John Wilker is in Europe and Ace is in the temporary care of Bruce Wayne and Dick Grayson, Bat-Hound helps Batman and Robin solve several cases, including the capture of fugitive criminal Baldy Gore. When Gore escapes from the Gotham Penitentiary and, in an effort to wreak vengeance on the Dynamic Duo, obtains a job as a prop man at the very Hollywood movie studio where Batman, Robin, and Bat-Hound are making a movie, it is Bat-Hound who, by means of his extraordinary sense of smell, "sees" through Gore's disguise and alerts the Dynamic Duo to his presence on the set (BM No. 103/3: "Bat-Hound, Movie Star!").

In April 1958, while John Wilker is on vacation and Ace is once again in the temporary custody of Bruce Wayne and Dick Grayson, Bat-Hound helps Batman and Robin recover a vial of powerful explosive stolen from the home of PROFESSOR DI PINA (Det No. 254: "One Ounce of Doom!").

Ace the Bat-Hound and Bat-Mite, 1960 © NPP 1960

In April 1959, while John Wilker is in Europe, Ace assumes the role of Bat-Hound long enough to help Batman and Robin capture the RED MASK MOB (BM No. 123/3: "The Fugitive Batman!").

By August 1959 John Wilker has accepted a new job which will keep him "traveling constantly" and has asked Bruce Wayne to provide Ace with a permanent home at the Wayne mansion. Both Wayne and Ace are enthusiastic about the new arrangement, for it will enable Ace to become Bat-Hound more often. By this time, Batman has constructed a special stand for Bat-Hound's mask, so that Ace can now slip into it alone, without any outside help. In addition, Batman has concealed a "tiny receiver" inside Bat-Hound's collar which, when activated by a signal from the tiny radio transmitter inside Batman's hollow boot heel, produces a high-pitched sound which only Bat-Hound can hear. Batman uses the high-pitched signal to summon Bat-Hound after he and Robin have been trapped inside an abandoned gold mine by the notorious Mr. Midas. Bat-Hound helps rescue the Dynamic Duo from the gold mine by summoning BATWOMAN to the scene, then helps Batman, Robin, and Batwoman capture Mr. Midas and his gang of gold thieves (BM No. 125/1: "The Secret Life of Bat-Hound").

In March 1960 Bat-Hound helps Batman and Robin apprehend GRAHAM and his henchmen (BM No. 130/2: "The Master of Weapons").

In April 1960 Bat-Hound develops a case of amnesia after his head has been creased by a gangster's bullet, and, because his most recent memory is of masked gunmen, he develops a fierce hatred of anyone wearing a mask, including Batman and Robin. At one point, criminals find Bat-Hound and use him as bait to lure the Dynamic Duo into a trap, but Batman tricks his captors into holding some handkerchiefs in front of their faces, causing the amnesiac Bat-Hound to attack them and giving Batman and Robin the opportunity to apprehend them. Afterward, Bat-Hound undergoes a surgical operation which successfully restores his memory, and he is once again united with Batman and Robin (BM No. 131/1: "The Dog That Betrayed Batman").

In August 1960 Bat-Hound uses his extraordinary sense of smell to help BAT-MITE trail some bank robbers to their warehouse hideaway. Soon afterward, when Batman, Robin, Batwoman, and all the criminals have been reduced to a few inches in height by Bat-Mite's mischievous magic, it is Bat-Hound, who has retained his normal size, who frightens the tiny criminals away from the warehouse doorway long enough to enable Batman to apprehend them, after which Bat-Mite restores them all to their normal size (BM No. 133/3: "Batwoman's Publicity Agent!").

In January 1961 Bat-Hound and Robin are frozen motionless inside "paralyzer beams" by Jhorl, an extraterrestrial alien, but they are ultimately rescued from the villain's clutches by Batman (Det No. 287: "The Raven and the Wasp!").

In October 1961 Bat-Hound helps Batman and Robin capture the Lippy Yates gang. The crime-fighters' lives are twice saved by a giant insect from outer space who is grateful to Bat-Hound for having rescued him from an animal trap. The creature is killed by a collapsing bridge after supporting it long enough for Batman, Robin, and Bat-Hound to get across safely (BM No. 143/3: "Bat-Hound and the Creature!").

In December 1962 Bat-Hound helps Batman and Robin smash a ring of renegade scientists and apprehend the criminals intending to market the scientists' illicitly manufactured, ultrapowerful explosive (BM No. 152/1: "Formula for Doom").

In August 1963, when Batman, Robin, and Batwoman are captured by the CAT-MAN and locked inside a sealed room from which there is apparently no escape, Batman uses the tiny transmitter hidden inside his boot heel to activate the supersonic signal device inside Bat-Hound's collar. Carefully homing in on the steady signal, Bat-Hound makes his way to the Cat-Man's hideout, slips through a narrow vent leading into the sealed room, and brings Batman the explosives he needs to blast his way out of the trap (Det No. 318: "The Cat-Man Strikes Back!").

In September 1963 Bat-Mite arrives in the batcave and mischievously endows Bat-Hound with super-powers: for a time, Bat-Hound can perform feats of super-strength, fly through the air at super-speed, melt blocks of ice with his "super-heat-vision," and shoot flame from his mouth like a legendary dragon. For a time, the effects of Bat-Mite's practical joke prove beneficial, as when Bat-Hound uses his super-powers to capture the notorious Logan Gang and rescue Batman and Robin from the whirling blades of a huge ice-shaving machine at the Gotham Ice Company. Later, however, it becomes apparent that Bat-Hound's acquisition of super-powers, combined with his accidental inhalation of some chemicals at the batcave, has made him sensitive to common coal gas in a bizarre way, so that in the presence of coal gas he obeys anyone who commands him. At one point, a gang of criminals capitalize on this fact by giving Bat-Hound a whiff of coal gas and ordering him to attack Batman and Robin. As Bat-Hound lunges toward the Dynamic Duo with flames shooting out of his mouth, Bat-Mite hastily uses his magical powers to protect Batman and Robin from Bat-Hound's vicious attack. Then, realizing what it is that has caused Bat-Hound's susceptibility to coal gas in the first place, he deprives Bat-Hound of his super-powers, thus neutralizing the influence of the coal gas and restoring Bat-Hound to normal. Now no longer under the hypnotic influence of the coal gas, Bat-Hound turns on the criminals and helps Batman and Robin apprehend them (BM No. 158/1: "Ace--the Super Bat-Hound!").

In March 1964 Bat-Hound plays a role in the capture of the evil ERIC BARROC by trailing one of Barroc's vicious "beast-humans" to the villain's hideout so that Batwoman and Robin can apprehend him (BM No. 162/1: "The Batman Creature!").

ADAMS, ABEL. The citizen of GOTHAM CITY in the eighteenth century who, according to Batman No. 79/2, was secretly the notorious highwayman known as CAPTAIN LIGHTFOOT (Oct/Nov '53: "The Batman of Yesterday!").

AGAR (Dr.). A revenge-mad scientist who attempts to wreak vengeance on the wealthy men who refused to finance his experiments with shrinking gas by placing his victims inside a gigantic room designed to trick them into believing that they have been reduced to the size of Pygmies so that he can extort large sums of money from them in return for restoring them to normal. BATMAN and ROBIN apprehend Dr. Agar in September 1947 (Det No. 127: "Pigmies in Giantland!").

AGATHA (Aunt). The bespectacled, white-haired old lady who is the aunt of Bruce Wayne, the man who is secretly BATMAN. Basically a "good-hearted" woman, Aunt Agatha tends to be somewhat motherly and overprotective, and to treat her nephew Bruce as though he were still a small boy.

In February 1955 Aunt Agatha appears at the door of the Wayne mansion and announces that she intends to visit there for "at least a week, possibly two!"

"But you can't," stammers Wayne, fearful that Aunt Agatha's presence in the house will impede his efforts, as Batman, to apprehend the notorious Rotor-Robbers, "--I mean--our cook-and-butler Alfred is on vacation! We've been shifting for ourselves--eating out of cans--you wouldn't like it!"

"Indeed!" exclaims Aunt Agatha. "Now I know I must stay! You need someone to look after you--give you some nourishing, home-cooked meals! Where is the kitchen?"

Batman, Aunt Agatha, and Robin, 1955 © NPP 1955

It is not long before Aunt Agatha's presence in the household creates some amusing dilemmas for the Dynamic Duo. For example, when Aunt Agatha falls asleep in a rocking chair positioned directly in front of the grandfather clock that disguises a secret entrance to the BATCAVE, Bruce Wayne and Dick Grayson are forced to change into their Batman and ROBIN costumes in the kitchen and then tiptoe out of the house in a vain attempt to avoid waking Aunt Agatha. "So! **I MIGHT HAVE KNOWN!**" cries Aunt Agatha sternly as, suddenly awakened from her nap, she spies her costumed nephew and his ward sneaking stealthily out of the house. "I might have known you'd try to sneak out to a masquerade party like this! You boys are all the same--never think of the weather!"

"Masquerade party?!?" thinks Batman in panic, caught completely off guard by Aunt Agatha's sudden tirade. **"Weather?!?"**

"Now you march right back in here and put on your rubbers!" continues Aunt Agatha, undeterred by the look of bewilderment on Batman's face. "Tsk-tsk! Such a cloudy-looking night! I won't have you coming home in the rain!"

"Rubbers?" thinks Batman, still dazed by his aunt's scolding. "**Batman** and **Robin** must put on rubbers?"

"Have a nice time at the party!" says Aunt Agatha soothingly, as the Dynamic Duo prepare to leave the house again. "And, Bruce, don't forget your umbrella!"

"Oh, sure," murmurs Batman, "--the umbrella! We mustn't forget the umbrella!"

"We look a little silly!" laughs Robin, after Aunt Agatha has shut the door behind them. "You should see yourself carrying that umbrella!"

"Ha! Ha!" laughs Batman. "As long as Aunt Agatha only thinks we are dressed for a costume party, it's worth it!"

As things turn out, Batman is fortunate indeed that he has been forced to carry his umbrella, because later that night, during a battle with the infamous Rotor-Robbers — "flying bandits" who propel themselves through the air by means of special one-man helicopter devices strapped to their backs — Batman is sent plummeting off the roof of the Pyramid Building, and it is only by snapping open his umbrella as he hurtles toward the pavement that he is able to check his fall sufficiently to enable him to land safely on a penthouse awning.

The Rotor-Robbers make good their escape, but Batman and Robin are pleased to learn that the rainy weather has resulted in the last-minute postponement of the masquerade ball which Aunt Agatha had assumed they were going to attend, thus providing them with an excuse for wearing their Batman and Robin costumes the following night, in spite of Aunt Agatha's continuing presence in the household.

The following night, after they have left Aunt Agatha at home on the pretext of setting out for the masquerade party, Batman and Robin make their way to the Rotor-Robbers' warehouse hideaway, only to be taken by surprise and captured in a large net. "Now, ***Batman***," gloats Raven, the leader of the Rotor-Robbers, "it's going to give me extreme pleasure to put a bullet into your heart!"

Suddenly, however, "a familiar, mocking figure" enters the hideout and calls a halt to the gangland execution. The intruder, apparently the notorious JOKER himself, points a pistol at the criminals and orders them to release their prisoners at once. No sooner have Batman and Robin been released, however, than their rescuer rips off a Joker-like face mask to reveal the bespectacled countenance of Aunt Agatha. "Are you all right, Bruce?" she asks.

"A dame!" cries the gang leader. "Wh-What is this? How come you called ***Batman*** 'Bruce'?"

"This boy--'**Batman'?**" exclaims Aunt Agatha, as she tears away Batman's cowl to reveal the angular features of Bruce Wayne. "Don't be idiotic! This is only my nephew, Bruce Wayne, dressed for the outdoor masquerade ball!"

For a moment, it appears that the secret of Batman's identity has been revealed at last, but slowly it becomes apparent that Aunt Agatha's ingenuous explanation has fooled even the Rotor-Robbers. "Boss," exclaims one of the criminals, "maybe it's a trick! It's gotta be **Batman!**" "Naw!" replies the gang boss. "If Wayne was really **Batman,** you don't really think his own aunt would have unmasked him, do you? Naw--we made a mistake, that's all!"

"Then how come they wuz snoopin' around?" insists the henchman.

"Foolish man!" replies Aunt Agatha. "If you were wearing a ***'Batman'*** costume, and saw a chance to capture a thief, wouldn't you do it? It's simply a case of my nephew trying to be like his idol--***Batman!***"

Suddenly, however, the leader of the gang gives Aunt Agatha a shove, straps one of his gang's pinwheel rotor blades to his back, and sails through an open window in a daring bid for freedom, but Batman dons another of the gang's rotor blades, pursues the fleeing criminal through the skies of GOTHAM CITY, and swiftly apprehends him while Aunt Agatha stands guard with her pistol over the Rotor-Robbers at the hideout.

"Now, Aunt Agatha," asks Batman, after the Rotor-Robbers have been placed safely in police custody, "suppose you tell us the reason for this [Joker] outfit!"

"It's simple!" replies Aunt Agatha with a smile. "I decided to go to the costume ball and surprise you! And since you went as **'Batman** and **Robin'** I thought it fitting to go along as the **'Joker'!** It was to be my joke on you! I followed you, of course! And good thing I did! Imagine you two trying to pretend to be the real **Batman** and **Robin!** I hope you learned your lesson!"

Days later, after Aunt Agatha's visit has ended and she has boarded a train for home, Dick Grayson asks Bruce Wayne why Aunt Agatha never suspected that Wayne is actually the real Batman. "She could never imagine me as being the famous ***Batman!***" replies Wayne with a grin. "In my aunt's eyes, I've never grown up! To her, I'm still her young nephew, a boy!" (BM No. 89/3: "Bruce Wayne's Aunt Agatha!").

ALADDIN. The hero of the story "Aladdin and the Wonderful Lamp," one of the tales of the *Arabian Nights.* BATMAN, ROBIN, and SUPERMAN make the acquaintance of Aladdin during a journey to tenth-century Baghdad (WF No. 79, Nov/Dec '55: "The Three Magicians of Bagdad!"). (*See* ABDULLAH.)

ALBREK, EDGAR. A cunning would-be murderer who concocts an elaborate scheme to strangle his wealthy uncle and then escape prosecution by claiming that his own hands were recently amputated in Africa because of a spreading gangrene infection and replaced, by means of a complex hand-grafting operation, with the hands of a deceased English murderer which now persist in exercising a murderous will of their own which is beyond Albrek's power to control. With ROBIN's help, however, BATMAN exposes Albrek's hand-grafting story as an elaborate hoax and apprehends the would-be killer before he can successfully carry out his uncle's murder (WF No. 41, Jul/Aug '49: "The Man with the Fatal Hands!").

ALCHEMIST, THE. An alias employed by SUPERMAN in June 1961 when, in collaboration with BATMAN, he poses as the inventor of a magic elixir guaranteed to protect anyone who drinks it from bodily harm as part of an elaborate plan to persuade four gangland assassins, hired by the underworld to destroy Batman, that their efforts to murder Batman must inevitably end in failure since Batman has already drunk the magic elixir. Although the plan goes somewhat awry when one of the assassins discovers the Alchemist's true identity, Batman and Superman nevertheless succeed in apprehending the four assassins and in thwarting their attempts on Batman's life (BM No. 140/2: "The Charmed Life of Batman!").

ALCOR. The far-distant planet which is the home of the alien crime-fighter TAL-DAR. BATMAN and ROBIN journey to Alcor in August 1960 in order to help Tal-Dar battle the villain Zan-Rak (Det No. 282: "Batman's Interplanetary Rival!").

ALFRED. The loyal English servant who has been Bruce Wayne's butler for more than three decades. Indeed, since his arrival in the United States in April–May 1943 (BM No. 16/4: "Here Comes Alfred!"), Alfred has functioned in the Wayne household as butler, chauffeur, cook, valet — i.e., as "major-domo and chief factotum of the household" (BM No. 29/2, Jun/Jul '45: "Heroes by Proxy!") — and, occasionally, as the courageous, albeit somewhat inept, crime-fighting ally of BATMAN and ROBIN.

"To Bruce Wayne and Dick Grayson, Alfred is more than their butler, for he is also a loyal friend entrusted with the knowledge that they are also **Batman** and **Robin!**" (Det No. 328, Jun '64: "Gotham Gang Line-Up!"). Batman has hailed Alfred as "the greatest gentleman's gentleman in the world!" (BM No. 110/2, Sep '57: "The Secret of Batman's Butler").

But Alfred is not merely a domestic servant of great dependability and skill; he is also, in his own words, "an amateur criminologist of little experience but much talent" (BM No. 16/4, Apr/May '43: "Here Comes Alfred!"); the author of the so-called "imaginary tales," a series of imaginative fictional accounts "of what possibly might happen . . . in the future" to Batman, Robin, their friends, and their descendants (BM No. 131/3, Apr '60: "The Second Batman and Robin Team!"; and others); and the inventor of several pieces of vital equipment which have found their way into the Dynamic Duo's crime-fighting arsenal (BM No. 68/2, Dec/Jan '51–'52: "The Secret Life of Batman's Butler!"; BM No. 110/2, Sep '57: "The Secret of Batman's Butler"). (For an exhaustive inventory of the Dynamic Duo's arsenal of crime-fighting equipment, *see* BATMAN [section E, the extraordinary abilities and the famous crime-fighting equipment].)

Since Alfred's full name is never actually stated in the texts, it constitutes one of the minor mysteries of the chronicles. In December 1956 Alfred employs the alias Thaddeus Crane when he poses as "a private investigator from upstate" as part of Batman's plan to apprehend "mobster czar" John Varden, and the text states explicitly that Thaddeus and Crane are Alfred's "middle names" (BM No. 104/1: "The Man Who Knew Batman's Secret!"). Furthermore, since Alfred has a brother named WILFRED PENNYWORTH (BM No. 216, Nov '69: "Angel--or Devil?"), it seems fairly safe to assume that Alfred's last name is also Pennyworth. Alfred's full name, then, is probably Alfred Thaddeus Crane Pennyworth. The question of Alfred's full name is complicated, however, by the fact that Alfred opens a private detective office in the town of Middleton in February 1945 under the name Alfred Beagle; it is impossible to determine from the text whether Beagle is a fictitious surname employed by Alfred, whether its appearance in the text represents a chronicler's error, or whether Beagle is actually intended to represent Alfred's last name (Det No. 96: "Alfred, Private Detective!").

Alfred, 1943 © NPP 1943

Alfred was born, raised, and educated in England, apparently in London (Det No. 110, Apr '46: "Batman and Robin in Scotland Yard!"). His father, a butler whose first name was Jarvis, served "for many years" as butler to DR. THOMAS WAYNE, Bruce Wayne's father, but Jarvis was already dead by April–May 1943, when Alfred first arrived in America (BM No. 16/4: "Here Comes Alfred!"). Alfred received at least part of his education at a school called Wheeton, where he apparently achieved something of a reputation as a rugby player (Det No. 82, Dec '43: "Quarterback of Crime!").

Both Alfred and his brother Wilfred began their careers in the theater. Wilfred eventually became a

Bruce Wayne, Alfred, and Dick Grayson, 1962 © NPP 1962

skilled Shakespearean actor, affiliated with a "traveling repertory company" known as the Avon Players (BM No. 216, Nov '69: "Angel--or Devil?"), but Alfred abandoned his theatrical career at the insistence of his dying father who, "heartbroken" at Alfred's having forsaken the "family calling" of domestic service, begged his son to "mend [his] ways," quit his life as "a music hall actor," and come to America to serve as Bruce Wayne's butler (BM No. 16/4, Apr/May '43: "Here Comes Alfred!").

Almost from the day of his arrival in the United States, Alfred has been far more than merely a butler to both Bruce Wayne and Dick Grayson: he cooks and serves their meals; washes, irons, and mends their crime-fighting costumes; cleans and dusts the trophies and equipment in the subterranean BATCAVE; and, in general, presides over the day-to-day domestic operation of the palatial Wayne mansion. On innumerable occasions, he has safeguarded the vital secret of Batman's dual identity, either by imitating Bruce Wayne's voice over the telephone to make it appear that Wayne was sitting quietly at home (BM No. 20/4, Dec/Jan '43–'44: "Bruce Wayne Loses the Guardianship of Dick Grayson!"), or by impersonating either Bruce Wayne or Batman so that Wayne and Batman could appear in two different places simultaneously (BM No. 87/1, Oct '54: "Batman's Greatest Thrills!"; and others).

Within a few months after his arrival in the United States, in fact, Alfred has become such an indispensable presence around the Wayne mansion that "there are times when a stranger might have trouble deciding which is servant and which is master of the household!"

In June–July 1943, for example, Alfred decrees a restful vacation for the Dynamic Duo, and takes pains to see to it that his orders for rest and relaxation are not violated: "Both you and the young mawster [i.e., Dick Grayson] have worn yourselves out battlin' footpads and scalawags," insists Alfred, "and it's my duty to see that you take a real rest!" Moreover, to ensure that Bruce Wayne and Dick Grayson comply with his instructions, Alfred has carefully hidden their crime-fighting costumes so that they will not be able to use them.

"So long, tyrant!" cries Wayne cheerfully, as he and Grayson drive away from the Wayne mansion.

"It's all very well to scoff, sir," replies Alfred, "--but you know as well as I, I'm acting for your own good! Mind you eat well and get lots of sleep!"

Unbeknownst to Alfred, however, Wayne and Grayson have taken the precaution of wearing spare Batman and Robin costumes under their civilian clothing, and before long, in the "historic" city of Santo Pablo somewhere in the American Southwest, they become embroiled in a deadly battle with the notorious DUCKY MALLARD gang. Ultimately, they defeat the criminals and return home, only to find themselves confronted by an infuriated Alfred. "I've read the public prints," sniffs Alfred, "and your deceit is known to me." When he shows them that he has packed his bags, Wayne and Grayson become terrified that Alfred is about to leave them.

"But, Alfred," pleads Wayne, "you can't leave us! You're like one of the family! We couldn't get along without you!"

"Indeed I'm going to leave, sirs," replies Alfred huffily, "--with you, on your very next out-of-town case! As a trained criminologist, I'll be invaluable to you" (BM No. 17/3: "Rogues' Pageant!").

In January 1944, after Alfred has embarked on a short vacation, Dick Grayson confides to Bruce Wayne that "It'll be a vacation for us, too! It's 'sir' and 'mawster' but Alfred does most of the bossing!"

"He's a tyrant in his own way," agrees Wayne with a smile, "--and he's clumsy as an elephant---but we'll miss him!" (Det No. 83: "Accidentally on Purpose!").

Batman No. 24/2 observes quite rightly that "Frustrated ambition burns in the soul of Alfred . . . for he dreams of being a great detective, following in the footsteps of his famed masters, **Batman** and **Robin** . . ." (Aug/Sep '44: "Convict Cargo!"). Indeed, Alfred regards himself as a "trained criminologist" (BM No. 17/3, Jun/Jul '43: "Rogues' Pageant!"), in spite of the fact that this training stems largely from his assiduous study of a book entitled *How to Be a Detective* (BM No. 16/4, Apr/May '43: "Here Comes Alfred!"; and others) and from the fact that he is a "graduate cum laude of Hives' Criminological Correspondence School" (Det No. 96, Feb '45: "Alfred, Private Detective!").

Inevitably, however, Alfred is tickled pink by the opportunity to play even a minor role in the crime-fighting activities of Batman and Robin. Particularly during his early years as Bruce Wayne's butler, Alfred frequently dons a special sleuthing outfit whenever he embarks on a crime-fighting errand, apparently so that no one will recognize him as Bruce Wayne's butler and thereby deduce the true connection between Bruce Wayne and Batman. The somewhat comical sleuthing outfit consists of a green or red deerstalker hat, dark glasses, a meerschaum pipe, and, occasionally, a large magnifying glass for studying clues (Det No. 86, Apr '44: "Danger Strikes Three!"; and others). By and large,

Alfred's crime-fighting efforts tend to deteriorate into ineptitude, but over the years he has proven himself sufficiently loyal and courageous that even the F.B.I. has on at least one occasion requested the use of his services (BM No. 81/2, Feb '54: "The Boy Wonder Confesses!"). "The mawsters," observes Alfred proudly in July 1945, "[have] dubbed me the buttling bloodhound!" (Det No. 101: "The Tyrannical Twins!").

Alfred is also the inventor of several devices that have found their way into the Dynamic Duo's renowned crime-fighting arsenal. One of these is the "sky sled," a red airplane-shaped object, roughly twelve feet long, on which one man can lie prone and soar through the air (BM No. 68/2, Dec/Jan '51–'52: "The Secret Life of Batman's Butler!"). Another is a pair of "life-saver inflatable costumes" for Batman and Robin. "If you fall in the river," explained Alfred proudly, after the costumes had just been completed, "just touch the valve, and compressed gas instantly inflates them!" The costumes ultimately proved to be far too clumsy to serve the purpose for which Alfred had intended them, but Batman and Robin did once use them as decoys to help them trap a ruthless band of "river pirates" (BM No. 110/2, Sep '57: "The Secret of Batman's Butler").

Alfred is also an accomplished writer, the author of a series of "imaginary tales" which appear in the chronicles periodically from April 1960 (BM No. 131/3: "The Second Batman and Robin Team!") onward. "Ah, what prose!" exclaims Alfred approximately two years later, as he puts the finishing touches on yet another of his imaginary tales. "Jack London couldn't have done better!" (BM No. 145/3, Feb '62: "The Son of the Joker!").

In June 1964 Alfred apparently loses his life while rescuing Batman and Robin from death at the hands of the notorious TRI-STATE GANG. It is in tribute to Alfred that Bruce Wayne establishes the Alfred Foundation, "a charitable organization that will contribute to the betterment of all mankind!" (Det No. 328: "Gotham Gang Line-Up!"). By October 1966, however, it becomes clear that Alfred has managed miraculously to survive, and he and his former employers are joyfully reunited. Because Alfred is not dead after all, the Alfred Foundation is renamed the Wayne Foundation (Det No. 356: "Inside Story of the Outsider!").

When Alfred first arrives in America in April–May 1943, he is a portly, clean-shaven man, bald except for some dark hair around his ears and at the back of his head (BM No. 16/4: "Here Comes Alfred!"). In January 1944, however, after reading that "The ideal detective is athletic, light and swift in movement, [and] graceful as a swan," Alfred decides to do something about his image. He spends his next vacation at a health resort, "cultivatin' a new figure," and then returns to the Wayne mansion a new man: now he is thin, has some strands of hair combed across his bald pate, and sports a narrow moustache. "I felt I lacked a certain dash and elegance that would enhance my value as your crime-fighting assistant," explains Alfred to Batman and Robin, who do not even recognize him at first due to his altered appearance (Det No. 83: "Accidentally on Purpose!"). Apparently, everyone concerned is pleased with Alfred's new image, for Alfred has maintained it since then.

In April–May 1943 Alfred arrives in GOTHAM CITY aboard a "small passenger vessel" and informs an astonished Bruce Wayne that he has come all the way from England to serve as his butler. Wayne is not pleased at the prospect of a stranger poking around the Wayne mansion, but he decides to allow Alfred to remain until he can find some means of sending Alfred away without hurting his feelings.

In the hours that follow, Batman and Robin become embroiled in a series of deadly encounters with a trio of ruthless criminals – led by "international crook" Manuel Stiletti – who are determined to steal a set of priceless crown jewels recently transported to America by the exiled Duke of Dorian. On one occasion, after Stiletti and his henchmen have taken the Dynamic Duo captive, it is the bumbling but well-meaning Alfred who finds them bound and gagged and sets them free. Indeed, by the time Batman and Robin have apprehended the criminals and restored the crown jewels to the Duke of Dorian, Alfred has, albeit accidentally, earned a large share of the credit.

"**Alfred's** pretty proud since we gave him full credit for this case!" remarks Bruce Wayne, as he and Dick Grayson peruse a nightly newspaper in the quiet of the Wayne mansion. "I really thought he'd done a great job of detecting, till it turned out he got all his information by accident!"

"For awhile," replies Grayson, "I was afraid he'd find out who we really are--but if we're careful, it will be safe to let him stay, since he isn't too bright!"

Both Wayne and Grayson are unaware, however, that Alfred has already accidentally stumbled on a secret entrance from the Wayne mansion to the BATCAVE, so that he already knows that his two wealthy employers are secretly Batman and Robin. No sooner has Grayson expressed his confidence in Alfred's lack of intelligence, than Alfred enters the living room carrying two Batman and Robin costumes slung over one arm. "Beg pardon, sirs," intrudes Alfred politely, ". . . you'll be going out directly, and I thought I might assist you with your uniforms!"

"What's this?" stammers Wayne.

"Huh?" exclaims Grayson. ". . . those cloaks . . . why, what does this mean?"

"The searchlight went on a few seconds ago!" replies Alfred calmly, pointing out a large picture window at the yellow beam of the BAT-SIGNAL stabbing across the night sky outside. "I believe it means the police require the **Batman's** services!"

"The signal!" stammers Grayson, almost paralyzed with disbelief. ". . . but--but what's that got to do with us?"

"You forget my deductive abilities!" replies Alfred. "I have known since last night that you were the **Batman** and **Robin**--but I saw no reason to mention it till now!"

"Well, you're one of us now, **Alfred!**" remarks Wayne, as he and Grayson climb into their crime-fighting costumes. "I hope you realize that if your knowledge leaked out, **Robin's** life and mine would be forfeit. Criminals would have an easier time of it!"

"I understand perfectly," replies Alfred, "and you may rely utterly on my discretion!"

Moments later, after Batman and Robin have roared forth from the batcave in their mighty BATPLANE, Alfred stares after them through a living-room window. "They are so impressed with me," muses Alfred to himself, "it would never do to tell them I learned their identity by sheer luck! Much better to act mysterious and say nothing!" (BM No. 16/4: "Here Comes Alfred!").

In May 1943 Alfred attempts to do some unauthorized sleuthing and is promptly taken captive – along with the wounded Batman – by the notorious ROBBER BARON. Ultimately, however, Alfred and Batman are rescued from the villains' clutches by Robin, who joins them in apprehending the Robber Baron and his henchmen (Det No. 75: "The Robber Baron!").

In August–September 1943, after Batman and Robin have been rendered unconscious by coal gas sprayed at them by one of the notorious Tweed cousins, (*see* TWEEDLEDUM AND TWEEDLEDEE), it is Alfred who revives them by artificial respiration (BM No. 18/1: "The Secret of Hunter's Inn!").

In December 1943, after he has been instructed to keep an eye out for the BLACKIE BLONDEEN gang, Alfred spies the criminals and then realizes, to his chagrin, that he has forgotten to bring along the special flashlight with which he was supposed to summon Batman and Robin. After a courageous, if somewhat comical, attempt to apprehend the criminals single-handedly, Alfred ultimately brings the Dynamic Duo rushing to the scene by accidentally detonating the time bomb which the criminals had intended to use in the robbery of a jewelry store (Det No. 82: "Quarterback of Crime!").

In Winter 1943 Alfred overhears a conversation on the Gotham City waterfront which leads him to believe that one of the men, an ex-convict named Slick Swade, is extorting money from a man named Squirrel. Because Bruce Wayne and Dick Grayson are away on a fishing trip and won't be home until later, Alfred takes matters into his own hands and attempts to arrest Slick Swade single-handedly, only to discover that Slade and Squirrel are partners in crime and that the money passing between them had to do with diamonds being smuggled into the United States aboard the *Northern Prince.* Taken captive by the criminals and left to suffocate inside a locked room, Alfred manages, albeit partly by accident, to summon the Dynamic Duo to his aid. Before long the smuggled diamonds have been recovered and the smugglers safely apprehended (WF No. 12: "Alfred Gets His Man!").

In December 1943–January 1944, when George and CLARA GRAYSON sue Bruce Wayne for the custody of Dick Grayson, Alfred testifies glowingly in Bruce Wayne's behalf. ". . . I've never seen Mr. Wayne deny the young lad anything!" swears Alfred. "He fair worships the boy!" Later, Alfred mimics Bruce Wayne's voice over the telephone so that GEORGE GRAYSON will not know that Wayne is not at home and thus become suspicious of Batman's true identity. When Batman is taken prisoner by the Fatso Foley gang and locked inside a divers' decompression chamber to die, Alfred and Robin race to the villains' hideout. After Alfred has rendered the criminals unconscious with the aid of a gas-shooting umbrella once owned by the PENGUIN, which he has borrowed from Batman's trophy room, he and Robin safely extricate Batman from the deadly chamber (BM No. 20/4: "Bruce Wayne Loses the Guardianship of Dick Grayson!").

In January 1944 Alfred spends his vacation at a health resort, "cultivatin' [the] new figure" that he is to retain throughout the chronicles. Later, when Batman and Robin are about to be shot by DR. GOODWIN and members of the Biff Bannister gang, Alfred, just returning from his vacation, charges clumsily into the room, giving the Dynamic Duo the momentary advantage they need to overwhelm and apprehend their captors (Det No. 83: "Accidentally on Purpose!").

By February–March 1944, Lord David Hurley Burleigh has discovered an inexpensive process for obtaining rubber from petroleum and has come to the United States in the hope of persuading an American oil company to deliver some sorely needed rubber to England in exchange for the process. However, Stevens, Lord Burleigh's unscrupulous assistant, has taken his employer prisoner and is determined to seize the priceless rubber process for himself.

Because Lord Burleigh had accepted an invitation to appear at a charity bazaar at the Gotham City home of Mr. and Mrs. C. L. J. Carruthers, Stevens has hired an actor to impersonate Lord Burleigh at the bazaar so that no one will realize that the real Lord Burleigh is being held prisoner. Meanwhile, because his second cousin once worked as a servant in the Burleigh home, Alfred, who has never met Lord Burleigh, decides to pay a brief visit to the Burleigh residence. When Alfred enters the Burleigh residence, Stevens, who assumes that Alfred is the actor he has hired, claims that he is Burleigh and asks Alfred to impersonate him at the upcoming charity bazaar. Alfred has heard that Lord Burleigh is somewhat eccentric, so his "spirit of prankishness" impels him to accept "Lord Burleigh's" proposition.

At the charity bazaar, Bruce Wayne and Dick Grayson are dumbfounded when they see their own butler being introduced as Lord Burleigh, and they decide to investigate by hitching a ride on the back of "Burleigh's" car as he speeds away from the party. Stevens, meanwhile, has discovered that Alfred is not his hired actor at all, and Batman and Robin are compelled to intervene to prevent Stevens's henchmen from killing Alfred.

When Batman and Robin pay a visit to the Burleigh residence, Stevens once again poses as Lord Burleigh, but the Dynamic Duo see through the impersonation and, although they are briefly taken captive by Stevens and his henchmen, they succeed in escaping from their captors, apprehending Stevens and his cohorts, and rescuing the real Lord Burleigh from the villains' clutches (BM No. 21/3: "His Lordship's Double!").

In April 1944, after Robin has been taken prisoner while trying to thwart a fur robbery by the GENTLEMAN JIM JOWELL gang, Alfred sets out to rescue him alone, in spite of the fact that "Mr. Wayne--the **Batman**--has warned me about goin' awfter criminals without him--." Before long, Alfred has been taken captive also and, to make matters worse, Batman is also taken prisoner while trying to prevent Gentleman Jim Jowell and his gang from stealing a shipment of platinum from a freighter in Gotham City Harbor.

Batman, Robin, and Alfred are left bound in a lonely tower, next to a hidden time bomb, while the criminals race off to hijack a planeload of commercial diamonds, but Batman uses Alfred's Sherlock Holmes-style magnifying glass to focus the heat of the sun's rays on his ropes, frees himself and his companions from their bonds, and then, with their help, apprehends the entire Gentleman Jim Jowell gang (Det No. 86: "Danger Strikes Three!").

In April–May 1944 Alfred begins a brief romance with a domestic named Belinda, unaware that she is secretly the notorious CATWOMAN (BM 22/1: "The Duped Domestics!").

In February 1945 Alfred, his pride injured over Batman's refusal to allow him to accompany the Dynamic Duo on their nightly patrol of the city, requests permission to begin his month-long vacation immediately, then promptly sets up a private detective office in the nearby town of Middleton, where he hopes to "show the mawsters . . . that Alfred is a better sleuth than they suspect!"

At about this same time, gangster Stoney Peters, boss of "the most dangerous gang of thieves in Gotham City," flees Gotham City for Middleton after a heated encounter with Batman and Robin and promptly concocts a scheme to dupe Alfred into helping him rob the local bank. Peters and his cohorts visit Alfred in his private detective office, tell him that they are suspicious that banker J. C. Willis is planning to rob his own bank, and commission him to follow the banker to learn what he is planning. Alfred surreptitiously tails Willis and reports to his clients that he has observed no suspicious behavior on the part of the banker, but Peters and his henchmen capitalize on the information Alfred has accumulated concerning Willis's habits in order to rob the Middleton bank themselves.

When Alfred learns of the robbery, he realizes that he may have unwittingly aided the thieves and promptly pays a visit to the local police, but banker Willis had observed Alfred shadowing him, and Alfred soon finds himself charged with the Middleton bank robbery and thrown into the local jail.

Back in Gotham City, Bruce Wayne and Dick Grayson read newspaper accounts of the Middleton bank robbery, deduce that Peters and his henchmen were responsible, and, as Batman and Robin, promptly set out for Middleton, where they find Alfred a prisoner in the local jail. After Alfred has told them his story, Batman and Robin set out in search of the criminals' hideout, which, from Alfred's account, they feel may be a shack on pier 60. After they have left, however, Alfred recalls that the criminals made mention of a houseboat and, anxious that Batman and Robin learn this additional information as soon as possible, he breaks out of jail and races to the dockside area where the criminals' houseboat is located. Just as he is wondering whether he should attempt to apprehend the criminals single-handedly, Alfred is taken captive, and moments later, when Batman and Robin approach the houseboat in search of Alfred, they are taken captive also.

Just as Stoney Peters is about to shoot Batman, however, Alfred manages to swing an oar at the criminals, throwing them off guard long enough for Batman and Robin to subdue and apprehend them. When local reporters gather round to hear the story, Batman gives Alfred all the credit, explaining that Alfred "not only led us to Stoney and his pals, but saved our lives when we crashed in to capture them!"

Soon afterward, a headline in the Gotham *News* proclaims Alfred's heroism – "Private Detective Saves Lives of Batman, Robin; Helps Smash Robber Ring!" – and Alfred promptly frames it as a memento. When Batman and Robin prepare to set out on their next nightly patrol, Alfred announces that he is going along. "Since I have proved beyond question my qualifications as a nemesis o' criminals," crows Alfred, "--where do **we** go tonight?" (Det No. 96: "Alfred, Private Detective!").

In April–May 1945 Alfred is punched in the nose when he attempts to prevent a masher from molesting a pretty blond girl in the park. The girl, however, is more than a match for the masher, and she swiftly apprehends the molester, rewards Alfred's gallantry with a kiss, and then introduces herself as policewoman Sgt. Shirley Holmes.

Not long afterward, after Shirley has, at Batman's request, infiltrated the underworld organization of a criminal known as the COUNT, Alfred – unaware of Shirley's undercover assignment – inadvertently exposes her to grave danger when he hails her on the street as "Sergeant." The criminals, now aware that their companion is a policewoman, are about to kill Shirley when Batman and Robin leap to the rescue. In the battle that follows, the criminals are completely defeated, and Alfred does his part by punching a hoodlum who is about to kill Shirley. When Batman suggests that they all go out together to celebrate their victory, Shirley declines. "I want Alfred all to myself!" insists Shirley. "He just saved my life!" (BM No. 28/2: "Shirley Holmes, Policewoman!").

In July 1945 Alfred is captured by the JOE BART gang, strung up by his feet, and is about to have his head crushed inside the mechanism of a giant printing press when Batman and Robin arrive on the scene. Although still hanging by his heels, Alfred manages to grab a criminal's gun during the ensuing battle and thereby prevent him from shooting Batman and Robin (Det No. 101: "The Tyrannical Twins!").

In November 1945, after Bruce Wayne and Dick Grayson have been left temporarily penniless as the result of a huge embezzlement from the Wayne Motor Company, Alfred gets a job mowing lawns in order to help support the crime-fighting activities of the now impoverished Batman and Robin. "There was never any doubt in my mind that they'd continue in action," explains Alfred sometime later, after the Wayne Motor Company's dishonest treasurer has been apprehended and Wayne's fortune has been restored to him, ". . . though I must confess I was a bit dismayed at the prospect of supporting them in their customary manner by pushing a lawn mower!" (Det No. 105: "The Batman Goes Broke!").

In April 1946 Alfred accompanies the Dynamic Duo to London to help them battle the infamous PROFESSOR MORIARTY. At one point, Alfred is taken prisoner by Moriarty and his henchmen, only to be rescued by Robin soon afterward. Later, Alfred is knocked unconscious by the criminals while attempting to capture them single-handedly, but Batman apprehends them before Alfred can come to any further harm (Det No. 110: "Batman and Robin in Scotland Yard!").

In April–May 1947, after Batman and Robin have been overpowered by the BEETLE BOLES gang, Alfred saves them from seemingly certain death by leaping through a skylight into the abandoned theater serving as the criminals' hideout. Alfred is knocked unconscious by the fall, but the incident gives Batman and Robin the momentary advantage they need to subdue and apprehend their captors (BM No. 40/2: "The Case of Batman II").

In April–May 1949 Alfred joins Batman in an elaborate plan to defeat the Thinker, a ruthless criminal "who employs super-human 'thinking machines' to plan every inch of his crimes. . . ." Batman's most immediate problem is that the Thinker has fed every known fact about Batman into one of his four "electronic 'automatic brains,'" and it is therefore only a matter of time before the machine matches these facts against every single citizen of Gotham City and discloses the vital secret of Batman's dual identity.

In order to stall the Thinker's search for his secret identity while he works furiously to bring the villain to justice, Batman arranges with Alfred to fake the death of Bruce Wayne so that, at least for the time being, it will appear to be impossible that Bruce Wayne and Batman are one and the same man. One afternoon, while Bruce Wayne and Alfred are sailing aboard the yacht *Carolina* on its gala maiden voyage, Alfred hurls a Bruce Wayne dummy over the side and then claims that Wayne fell overboard after accepting a childish dare to walk tightrope-style across the ship's narrow railing.

Bruce Wayne's "death" is now accepted as a fact, but events take an unexpected turn when Alfred is arrested and charged with Wayne's murder. In prison, however, Alfred shrewdly lets it be known that he is a hardened gangster responsible for innumerable crimes besides the murder of Bruce Wayne. When a fellow inmate informs Alfred that the Thinker is planning to break an entire group of them out of prison and that the Thinker could use a man of Alfred's talents, Alfred agrees to participate in the breakout and then promptly informs Batman of what he has learned. Batman, meanwhile, has been engaged in a frenzy of fighting the underworld so that it will appear to the Thinker that although Bruce Wayne is dead, Batman is still very much alive.

Before long, Alfred has been broken out of prison and transported to the Thinker's hideout, where he manages surreptitiously to pick up a monkey wrench and hurl it into the electronic calculator assigned the task of discovering Batman's secret identity. As the result of Alfred's tampering, however, the machine produces the startling answer that Batman is none other than Alfred himself, whereupon the Thinker and his henchmen turn on Alfred in the mistaken belief that their electronic brain has successfully discovered Batman's secret identity. Just as Alfred appears doomed, however, Batman and Robin arrive on the scene and, after a long battle, succeed in apprehending the Thinker and his cohorts with some occasional assistance from Alfred. Batman will arrange for Bruce Wayne to be discovered alive on some island in the Atlantic, and Alfred will therefore be exonerated of the murder charge against him (BM No. 52/1: "The Man with the Automatic Brain!").

In October–November 1949, after a series of coincidences have forced Bruce Wayne to temporarily assume the role of a rookie policeman, Alfred poses as Batman so that the secret of Batman's dual identity will not be placed in jeopardy (BM No. 55/2: "Bruce Wayne, Rookie Policeman!").

In December 1951–January 1952, when LONGHORN BELL and his cohorts discover the existence of a network of caves beneath the Wayne mansion and leap to the conclusion that they have uncovered the location of the batcave, Alfred helps Batman and Robin trick the criminals into believing that the cave they have found is only a subterranean cavern being used as a batcave set in the filming of a Batman movie (BM No. 68/1: "The Atom Cave Raiders!").

During this same period, Alfred receives the shock of his life when Bruce Wayne announces that he is dismissing him from his post as butler at the Wayne mansion. "Surely you're jesting!" cries Alfred, heartbroken and incredulous. "I've served you faithfully all these years! I'd gladly lay down my life for you and the young mawster [i.e., Dick Grayson]!" Wayne, however, remains adamant, and before long Alfred has packed his bags and departed the Wayne mansion for a dreary furnished room somewhere in Gotham City.

In an effort to lift his flagging spirits, Alfred pays a visit to the home of his new friend Willie Willis, where Willis and some of his friends are gathered for what appears to be some innocent merrymaking. Willis, who claims to be a professional polygraph operator, suggests that they all have some fun with a lie detector he owns, and before long Alfred finds himself hooked up to the complex apparatus.

Willis asks Alfred a few innocent questions, ostensibly in the spirit of good fun, and then asks Alfred the crucial question that he has been preparing to ask all along: "Isn't it true," asks Willis slyly, "that ***you're Batman's butler?***"

Unbeknownst to Willis, however, Alfred has just been fired from his job as Bruce Wayne's butler and is therefore in a position to answer truthfully that he is not Batman's butler. Indeed, the lie detector shows that Alfred's negative answer is the correct one. It is at that moment that Batman and Robin arrive on the scene and take Willis and his cohorts into custody.

Willis, Batman explains later, is in reality Slippery Willie Willis, a criminal wanted in Chicago on a robbery charge. When the Dynamic Duo observed Alfred innocently making friends with Willis, and learned of Willis's plan to test his theory concerning Batman's secret identity by getting Alfred to take a lie-detector test, they realized that they would have to fire Alfred since this "was the only way [Alfred] could answer Willis's question and tell the ***truth!*** It's impossible," explains Batman, "to deceive a lie detector!" Batman and Robin also explain that arresting Willis before he used the lie detector would have jeopardized the secret of Batman's identity, since "unless he used the lie detector, Willis would always suspect Bruce Wayne was ***Batman!***"

Now that Willis and his cohorts have been apprehended and Willis has been safely disabused of the notion that Bruce Wayne is Batman, Alfred, of course, may have his old job back. "Oh, please forget it, sir!" replies Alfred, when Batman apologizes for all the anguish the firing must have caused him. "The only thing that matters is that we are together again, like the Three Musketeers!" (BM No. 68/2, Dec/Jan '51–'52: "The Secret Life of Batman's Butler!").

In March–April 1952, during the period when Bruce Wayne allows the public to think that he is secretly the underworld czar known as the KINGPIN, Alfred plays the role of Wayne's bodyguard (WF No. 57: "Public Enemy Bruce Wayne!").

In December 1952–January 1953 Alfred, who bears an uncanny resemblance to convicted murderer Skid Turkel, is asked to portray Turkel in an upcoming film starring Batman and Robin. Alfred agrees, but the real Turkel escapes from his death cell at Gotham Prison, makes Alfred his prisoner, and then takes Alfred's place on the movie set in the hope of murdering Batman and Robin while the filming is in progress. Batman and Robin soon realize that the actor "portraying" Turkel is not really Alfred, however, and soon succeed in taking him into custody (BM No. 74/2: "The Movie That Killed Batman!").

In May–June 1953 Alfred poses briefly as Bruce Wayne in order to help Batman create the impression that Bruce Wayne and Batman are at the same place at the same time (WF No. 64: "Bruce Wayne . . . Amateur Detective!").

In July 1954, after Batman has been shot and wounded by the INVENTOR's henchmen, Alfred administers emergency first-aid to Batman in the safety of the batcave. Later, Alfred carries a Batman dummy toward the Inventor's firehouse hideout as part of Batman's plan to create a diversionary image on the villain's "magno-radarscope" while he and Robin close in from a different direction. Ultimately, it is Alfred who knocks the Inventor unconscious with his shoe as the villain attempts to flee his hideout (Det No. 209: "The Man Who Shadowed Batman!").

In October 1954, when television station GCTV presents Batman's life story on its "Your Life Story" program, Alfred poses briefly as Batman so that both Batman and his "friend" Bruce Wayne can appear on the program simultaneously (BM No. 87/1: "Batman's Greatest Thrills!").

In September 1955, after Batman and Robin have moved all of their possessions out of the batcave, Alfred helps Robin dam up the batcave's underground river and temporarily flood the batcave with water as part of Batman's plan to trick racketeer "BIG JIM" JARREL into believing that the cave would have no value as a potential hideout (Det No. 223: "The Batman Dime-Museum").

During this same period, Alfred receives an accidental blow on the head while trying on a spare Batman costume in the security of the batcave, lapses into unconsciousness, and awakens to find that he has suffered a complete loss of memory. Because he is wearing a Batman costume, Alfred assumes that he must secretly be Batman, and Bruce Wayne and Dick Grayson are reluctant to tell Alfred the truth for fear that the shock will retard his recovery, perhaps permanently.

Instead, Wayne and Grayson allow Alfred to think that he is Batman and that Bruce Wayne is the household butler while they search for a means to restore Alfred's memory. In the days that follow, Alfred, clad in his Batman costume, patrols the streets of Gotham City with Robin, and the Dynamic Duo's chief difficulty consists of getting Alfred safely out of harm's way so that Bruce Wayne can battle the underworld as Batman. Finally, after Batman has been asked to take part in the trial cruise of a new jet-motored yacht to protect it from thieves who may try to steal its valuable new motor, Wayne suggests that Alfred pose as the household butler while he poses as Batman so that, if anyone attempts to make off with the new jet motor, Alfred can take them by surprise. Alfred thinks that this is a capital idea, and Wayne's plan is promptly put into operation.

Aboard the yacht, criminals do indeed make an attempt to steal the new motor, and the real Batman and Robin succeed in apprehending them. During the fighting, moreover, Alfred receives another accidental blow on the head, which completely restores his memory and robs him of all recollection of his brief career as Batman. "A remarkable delusion, that I was ***Batman!***" exclaims Alfred, after Batman and Robin have told him the entire story. "But it seems that I did very well in that role, eh wot?" "Alfred," replies Batman with a grin, "you were a lot better ***Batman*** than ***Batman*** was a butler!" (BM No. 94/2, Sep '55: "The New Batman!").

In December 1956 Alfred assumes the fictitious role of Thaddeus Crane, "a private investigator from upstate," as part of Batman's plan to apprehend "mobster czar" John Varden. As Crane, Alfred pretends to have learned Batman's secret identity, then allows himself to be kidnapped by Varden, who hopes to force this out-of-town "detective" to reveal Batman's secret. Once in Varden's hideout, however, Alfred summons Batman and Robin to the scene via belt-radio and the Dynamic Duo swiftly apprehend the assembled criminals (BM No. 104/1: "The Man Who Knew Batman's Secret!").

In March 1957 Alfred poses as a criminal as part of Batman's plan to apprehend "underworld racket leader" GUY GRANEY, then helps Batman and Robin capture Graney and his cohorts (BM No. 106/3: "The Puppet Batman!").

In April 1957, after gangster BRAINY WALKER has tricked Robin into revealing the location of the batcave, Alfred poses briefly as Bruce Wayne as part of Batman's plan to persuade Walker that the cave beneath the Wayne mansion is not really the batcave after all (Det No. 242: "The Underworld Bat-Cave!").

In September 1957 a heartbroken and guilt-ridden Alfred packs his belongings and prepares to depart the Wayne mansion forever in the mistaken belief that he has inadvertently betrayed the secret of Batman's dual identity to an underworld character named Noyes. Many years before, according to this text, Alfred had been approached by Noyes and offered a large sum of money for information concerning Bruce Wayne's habits and activities. Alfred had angrily rebuffed Noyes's persistent requests for information, but now, many years later, Alfred has spied Noyes poking around in the batcave, and he assumes that some chance remark he made at the time must have now enabled Noyes to locate the batcave and learn the secret identities of Batman and Robin.

Embarrassed and ashamed at having brought this misfortune upon the Dynamic Duo, Alfred decides to pose as Batman to trick Noyes into thinking that he is secretly Batman, and then to leave the Wayne mansion forever in the hope that Batman's true identity may yet remain a secret. When Alfred confronts Noyes in the batcave, however, and begins his impersonation, Noyes removes some makeup and a false moustache to reveal that he is none other than Batman in disguise.

"Alfred, when I first hired you as butler," confesses Batman, "I wanted to test your loyalty--I disguised myself as *'Noyes'* and tried to bribe you! Thus I was convinced we could trust you!"

"But why didn't you tell me that, later, when you decided to hire me?" asks Alfred.

"Because you proved so loyal and dependable a friend," explains Batman, "I was ashamed to let you know I'd doubted you and tested you at first! I didn't mean for you ever to know!"

Recently, however, continues Batman, he had donned the old Noyes disguise as part of a plan to capture a desperate criminal. It was actually a disguised Batman, and not an underworld character named Noyes, whom Alfred had spied prowling around in the batcave.

"Thank goodness I won't have to play ***Batman*** and can be just a butler again!" exclaims Alfred happily.

"Not just a butler, Alfred," replies Batman, "--to us, you're the greatest gentleman's ***gentleman*** in the world!"

This account of Alfred's early days as Batman's butler is at odds with earlier texts. For one thing, this text states that Alfred applied for the post of Bruce Wayne's butler in response to an advertisement, rather than that he marched into the Wayne mansion and persuaded a reluctant Bruce Wayne to allow him to stay. Secondly, this text depicts a thin, moustached Alfred applying for the post of butler, as opposed to the portly, clean-shaven one. Thirdly, this text claims that Batman and Robin decided to take Alfred into their confidence regarding the secret of their dual identities, rather than that Alfred discovered their dual identities on his own, albeit by accident (BM No. 110/2: "The Secret of Batman's Butler").

During this same period, Alfred helps Robin restore Batman to normal after a freak electrical accident at the Gotham Electronics Company has "reversed the atoms of [Batman's] body" and transformed him into a negatively charged "phantom Batman," capable of passing through walls and solid objects (BM No. 110/3, Sep '57: "The Phantom Batman!").

In December 1957 Alfred poses as Bruce Wayne as part of Robin's plan to make it impossible for Batman to prove – even to himself – that he is really Batman (BM No. 112/3: "Am I Really Batman?"). (*See* MILO [PROFESSOR].)

In August 1958 Alfred poses briefly as Batman in order to help safeguard the secret of Batman's dual identity (BM No. 117/2: "Bruce Wayne--Batman").

In December 1958 Alfred poses briefly as Batman as part of Bruce Wayne's elaborate plan to persuade his great-uncle SILAS WAYNE that he is something more than a "rich idler," without simultaneously betraying the secret of his dual identity (BM No. 120/2: "The Failure of Bruce Wayne").

In October 1959 a freak accident in the trophy room

Alfred as the Eagle, 1959 © NPP 1959

of the batcave endows Alfred with "amazing strength," invulnerability, and the ability to "leap hundreds of feet" into the air. Alfred promptly dons a golden costume trimmed with brown feathers and, under the name the Eagle, attempts to establish himself as a coequal crime-fighting partner of Batman and Robin (BM No. 127/1: "Batman's Super-Partner"). (*See* JOKER, THE.)

In April 1960 Alfred composes his first "imaginary tale," an entirely fictional account "of what possibly might happen . . . in the future" to Batman and Robin, their friends, and their descendants. In it, an elderly Batman announces his retirement from crime-fighting and settles down to a life of relaxation with Kathy Kane, "whom he had long ago married. . . ." Dick Grayson, now a grown man, inherits Batman's mantle and continues the fight against crime as Batman II, while the Waynes' young son, Bruce Wayne, Jr., joins him as Robin II. At one point, Batman II and Robin II are taken captive by the Babyface Jordan gang, but Bruce Wayne and his wife Kathy, who once fought crime as BATWOMAN, climb into their old crime-fighting costumes and race to the rescue. Before long, Batman II and Robin II have been freed and the mobsters have been taken into custody (BM No. 131/3: "The Second Batman and Robin Team!").

In September 1962 Alfred disguises himself as a white-haired old man and claims to have come into possession of a magical sorcerer's flagon as part of Batman's elaborate plan to capture criminal JACK PINE and recover $2,000,000 in cash and gems stolen in a recent armored-car robbery (BM No. 150/2: "The Girl Who Stole Batman's Heart").

In August 1963, during Batman's battle with the notorious MIRROR-MAN, Alfred poses first as Bruce Wayne and then as Batman in order to safeguard the secret of Batman's dual identity (BM No. 157/2: "The Hunt for Batman's Secret Identity!").

In February 1964 – during a special award ceremony in honor of Batman, Robin, and SUPERMAN – Alfred poses as Batman in order to enable Bruce Wayne to persuade KATHY KANE that he and Batman are two entirely different persons (WF No. 139: "The Ghost of Batman!").

In June 1964 Alfred is taken captive by the notorious TRI-STATE GANG and locked inside an old prison cell to await a gangland-style execution after he has foolishly trailed a member of the gang to their headquarters inside an abandoned prison. When Batman and Robin follow Alfred to the prison, they are also taken captive, but are locked in a cell out of Alfred's sight. The Dynamic Duo manage to escape from their cell, and Alfred succeeds in overpowering his gangland guard and escaping also, but a fateful misunderstanding causes Batman and Robin to believe that their butler has been executed, and Alfred to believe that his two beloved employers have already been led to their doom. Independently, Alfred and the Dynamic Duo set out to capture the Tri-State Gang in order to avenge the "deaths" that they erroneously believe to have taken place.

By the time Alfred drives his motorcycle to the scene of the Tri-State Gang's next crime, Batman and Robin have already plunged into battle with them, and Alfred realizes with horror that the villains are about to use a steam shovel to drop a huge boulder on them. "I can never warn them in time!" thinks Alfred frantically. "Only one thing left to do--risk my life to save theirs!"

Furiously gunning the engine of his motorcycle, Alfred manages to knock Batman and Robin out of the path of the plummeting boulder in the nick of time, but Alfred is unable to save himself, and he falls tragic victim to the crushing weight of the mighty boulder.

Horrified and enraged at the death of their friend, Batman and Robin hurl themselves at the Tri-State Gang "like avenging angels," swiftly take them into custody, and then sadly carry Alfred's limp body to the waiting BATMOBILE. "He gave his life so that we might live!" says Batman sadly. "No friend could do more!"

"The house will be so empty without Alfred," remarks Dick Grayson, after arrangements have been made for Alfred's funeral. "I'll never forget what he did for us. . . ."

"Neither will I," replies Bruce Wayne, "--and I want to make certain the world doesn't forget! Alfred deserves a fine tribute--a memorial!" Later, Wayne decides to establish a philanthropic foundation in Alfred's honor – the Alfred Foundation, "a charitable organization that will contribute to the betterment of all mankind!" (Det No. 328: "Gotham Gang Line-Up!").

From December 1964 (Det No. 334: "The Man Who Stole from Batman!") through October 1966 (Det No. 356: "Inside Story of the Outsider!"), Batman and Robin find their lives continually menaced by a mysterious criminal mastermind known only as the Outsider, a man of extraordinary powers whose "mission in life is to destroy the great crime-fighter [i.e., Batman] and the **Boy Wonder!**" (Det No. 336, Feb '65: "Batman's Bewitched Nightmare").

Throughout his battles with the Dynamic Duo, the Outsider contrives to remain unseen, working his diabolical will through other criminals and communicating with his intended victims only by means of tape recordings and telephone calls. The deadly threat posed by the Outsider is all the more bizarre in that the villain seems privy to the Dynamic Duo's innermost secrets – the secret of their dual identities and the location of the subterranean batcave.

Finally, in October 1966, Batman and Robin learn, for the first time, that the Outsider is none other than their dear friend Alfred, who had never actually died at all.

Alfred it seems, had been laid to rest, unembalmed, in a refrigerated coffin in the Wayne family mausoleum at Gotham Cemetery. That night, scientific genius and recluse Brandon Crawford had passed by the mausoleum in pursuit of a rare insect, and his ultrasensitive "micro-audiometer" – a device capable of picking up the faint fluttering sound of the insect's wings – had registered a faint moaning from inside the mausoleum. Inside the refrigerated coffin, an astonished Crawford had found Alfred, still barely alive in spite of his massive injuries.

Crawford had quickly loaded Alfred into his automobile and carried him to his basement laboratory, "equipped with machines and inventions as yet unknown to the world."

"Although his body was very badly damaged," mused Crawford to himself, "his sheer will to live staved off death! I'm hoping my as yet untested experiment in cell regeneration will restore him to full life!"

Crawford's "regeneration machine," however, had not functioned properly, and a series of monstrous accidents had taken place: Crawford had slumped to the floor in a deathlike "catatonic trance," transformed by the regeneration machine into an exact look-alike for Alfred; and Alfred, although he had been brought back from the brink of death to full life, had been horribly transformed also, both mentally and physically. The new Alfred had no hair, chalk-white skin, and flesh hideously pocked with huge bumps or blisters. "I must save ***Batman*** and ***Robin*** from--no! ***No!*** That's wrong!" exclaimed the transformed Alfred as he arose from the table in Brandon Crawford's laboratory. "I don't want to save them--I want to ***kill Batman and Robin!*** I am no longer the man I was! I have been changed in mind and body--twisted into ***reverse!*** I don't even feel human any more! I am outside the human race! Yes! ***I--am--the--Outsider!!***"

Because Crawford now looked exactly as Alfred had looked prior to his transformation into the Outsider, the new, evil Alfred – i.e., the Outsider – placed Crawford in the refrigerated casket and returned him to the mausoleum, so that no one but he would ever realize that the real Alfred was still alive in the form of the Outsider. "Oddly enough," mused the Outsider grimly, as he settled into Crawford's elaborately equipped laboratory, "I feel at home here! My altered brain understands the principles of these ultra-scientific machines! With my increased mental power I can operate them--use them to destroy ***Batman and Robin!***"

For almost two full years, Alfred wages war against the Dynamic Duo as the Outsider, until finally, in October 1966, Batman and Robin invade his laboratory in a desperate attempt to apprehend him. During the battle that follows, the Outsider falls against the activation lever of Brandon Crawford's regeneration machine and is once again transformed into the real Alfred, the loyal friend and ally of Batman and Robin. As the bizarre transformation process nears its completion, Alfred tells Batman the full story of the Outsider, and then, when the transformation has ended, collapses on the floor, with all knowledge of his life as the Outsider erased completely from his memory.

"Poor Alfred!" thinks Batman sadly. "His very love for and devotion to ***Robin*** and myself became warped and twisted by this malevolent machine! But his story shall be my secret--***Alfred*** must never learn the truth!"

Moments later, Batman warns Robin that they must never allow Alfred to learn the story of his life as the Outsider. "I think the news of his treachery might kill him," explains Batman, "so great was his devotion to us!"

Soon afterward, Brandon Crawford is taken from the Wayne mausoleum and restored to normal with the regeneration machine, and Alfred returns to the Wayne mansion to resume his happy life with Bruce Wayne and Dick Grayson. The name of the foundation established by Bruce Wayne at the time of Alfred's apparent death is changed from the Alfred Foundation to the Wayne Foundation (Det No. 356: "Inside Story of the Outsider!").

ALFRED FOUNDATION, THE. A philanthropic foundation established by BRUCE WAYNE in June 1964, in honor of his butler ALFRED, after Alfred has apparently been killed during an encounter with the notorious TRI-STATE GANG. Wayne describes the foundation – which is also referred to as the Alfred Memorial Foundation – as "a charitable organization that will contribute to the betterment of all mankind!" (Det No. 328: "Gotham Gang Line-Up!").

In October 1966 Alfred – who has never really been dead at all – is reunited with the Wayne household, and the name of the foundation is changed from the Alfred Foundation to the Wayne Foundation (Det No. 356: "Inside Story of the Outsider!").

In December 1969, after DICK GRAYSON has set out for his first year of classes at Hudson University, Bruce Wayne abandons his palatial suburban mansion for a more unencumbered life in the city, establishing a new headquarters for himself in the executive offices atop the Wayne Foundation skyscraper, which he has had converted into a spacious penthouse suite. From this time onward, Wayne supervises the philanthropic activities of the Wayne Foundation by day and fights crime as BATMAN by night (BM No. 217: "One Bullet Too Many!").

ALI. The corpulent Arab proprietor of Ali's Health Resort and the leader of a gang of criminals who have kidnapped prominent persons, imprisoned them at the health resort, and replaced them with impersonators as part of a scheme to reap huge profits by capitalizing on their victims' positions of prominence in GOTHAM CITY society. For a time, even BRUCE WAYNE is held captive at Ali's Health Resort while an impostor takes his place at the Wayne mansion. Ali and his accomplices are exposed and apprehended by BATMAN and ROBIN in October–November 1943 (BM No. 19/4: "Collector of Millionaires").

ALLEN, TOD. A friend of Bruce Wayne and Dick Grayson and a member of the Sportsmen's Club – a man well known for his love of practical jokes – who, having deduced largely on the basis of circumstantial evidence that Wayne and Grayson are secretly BATMAN and ROBIN, is unable to resist the temptation to bedevil Bruce Wayne by mailing him a series of letters, all signed with the pseudonym Mr. X, in which he teases Wayne about having unraveled the secret of his dual identity. Batman and Robin ultimately deduce that Allen is their tormentor and decide to confront him to learn the exact nature of his evidence. Allen, however, dies in a plane crash, taking his knowledge of the Dynamic Duo's secret identities with him (BM No. 134/2, Sep '60: "Batman's Secret Enemy").

ALPHA (the Experimental Man). An "artificial man" who has been described by his creator, the scientist Dr. Burgos, as "a living creature made entirely of synthetic material!" In September 1962, endowed with superhuman strength but with the emotions of an infant, Alpha helps BATMAN and ROBIN apprehend the GREEN MASK BANDITS; goes on a destructive rampage when he imagines his friend Batman has turned against him; develops an adoring infatuation for BATWOMAN; and, ultimately, forced in a moment of crisis to choose between saving Batwoman's life and saving his own, willingly sacrifices his life for Batwoman and plunges to his doom over the edge of a cliff (Det No. 307: "Alpha, the Experimental Man!").

ALVAREZ (Don). An alias employed by DICK GRAYSON in February 1954 when he poses as the wealthy son of an Argentine jewel merchant as part of VICKI VALE's elaborate plan to trap the notorious PHANTOM BANDIT of GOTHAM CITY (BM No. 81/3: "The Phantom Bandit of Gotham City!").

ANANDA (Swami). An alias employed by BATMAN in November–December 1954 when he poses as a fortune-teller at a GOTHAM CITY carnival as part of his plan to apprehend the FANG (WF No. 73: "Batman and Superman, Swamis, Inc!").

ANDERSON (Professor). The inventor of a unique machine capable of transporting people into the world of literary fantasy. "If you were to sit in this chair and read this book," explains Anderson in Spring 1941, "by pressing a series of buttons I could send you into the world of the book you are reading!" At Anderson's request, the Dynamic Duo allow themselves to be transported into the world inside the *Anthology of Fairy Tales,* where they rescue Anderson's daughter Enid from the evil Black Witch before returning safely to the world of reality (BM No. 5/2: "Book of Enchantment").

ANDREWS. An unscrupulous assistant curator at the Gotham Museum who commits a series of spectacular crimes while pretending to be the mummy of an ancient Egyptian bandit come to life. Andrews is captured and unmasked by BATMAN and ROBIN in February–March 1950.

Andrews adopted the role of an ancient mummy, explains Batman, "because the mummy costume frightened his victims so thoroughly that robbery was easy! Also, because a regular mask wouldn't cover his ***oversized hearing aid!*** Otherwise it would be simple for the police to track down a crook with a hearing aid and a knowledge of Egyptology!" (BM No. 57/2: "The Walking Mummy!").

ANT-MAN. A tiny, foot-high man, clad in a bright red costume, who appears in GOTHAM CITY in June 1963, helps ROBIN apprehend a gang of criminals led by mobster Al Welles, and then, to Robin's surprise and consternation, makes off with a satchel full of the very jewelry that Welles had been trying to rob. Ant-Man is in reality Jumbo Carson, a "rival mobster" believed dead at the hands of the Welles mob, who actually escaped his own attempted gangland assassination and shrunk to his present size when he fell into the river running past Hanson's Research Laboratory – where Professor Hanson was experimenting to perfect a formula to "shrink living tissue" – and was bathed in the weird chemical discharge from Hanson's lab. Carson then assumed the identity of Ant-Man in order to strike back at the Welles gang for attempting to kill him. Ant-Man, who will probably remain small forever due to the lack of an antidote to the chemical mixture that affected him, is apprehended by Robin in June 1963 (BM No. 156/1: "The Secret of the Ant-Man").

ANTAL, PIERRE. A talented European painter who twice becomes embroiled, albeit innocently, in a series of bizarre murders.

By August 1940 "socially eminent" Mr. Wylie – a man "insane about paintings" and "the patron of many a starving [artistic] genius" – has returned from a trip to Europe with Antal, his latest artistic discovery. Unbeknownst to his wealthy friends and acquaintances, however, Wylie is deeply in debt and has concocted an elaborate scheme to recoup his fortune by making Antal so famous that the value of his own collection of Antal paintings, which he purchased from the artist in Europe at bargain prices, will skyrocket.

The plot involves transforming each of Antal's carefully executed portraits of prominent citizens, which the artist paints during his sojourn in the United States, into a grim depiction of the subject's impending death. After Antal has painted the portrait of one socialite, for example, Wylie, taking care to remain unseen, plunges a dagger into the portrait's heart, then murders the man who sat for the portrait in the gruesome manner depicted in the mutilated portrait. Because Wylie covers his face with a frightening skull-like mask when he commits the murders, and because he goes so far as to pretend that an attempt has been made on his own life, no one is able to deduce the identity of the murderer. Antal remains innocent of any wrongdoing, but the notoriety connected with his "prophetic pictures" will inevitably increase their value to collectors.

Finally, after Wylie has committed three successful murders and been prevented by ROBIN from committing a fourth, BRUCE WAYNE has his portrait painted by Antal in order to lure the murderer into a trap. When the mysterious murderer makes an attempt on Wayne's life, BATMAN captures him and unmasks him as art collector Wylie, but Wylie grabs a pistol and shoots himself rather than face trial and imprisonment. "He couldn't stand the disgrace!" murmurs Robin. "Much better this way!" agrees Batman (Det No. 42: "The Case of the Prophetic Pictures!").

In December 1946–January 1947 a broker named Jennings, a singer named Louisa Ponelle, and an unnamed lawyer are brutally murdered soon after having had their portraits painted by Pierre Antal. In each case, the portrait has been mutilated so as to depict the impending death of the subject, and Pierre Antal complains loudly to Batman and Robin that his artistic career is once again being threatened by a series of bizarre murders. Every detail of the new case, in fact, represents a bizarre re-creation of the old case (above), a case which Batman describes here as "our first really big case" and which he erroneously recalls as having been entitled "The Case of the Prophetic Murders."

Recalling that Wylie, the murderer of six years ago, was apprehended when he attempted to murder Bruce Wayne, Batman and Robin set a similar trap for their new antagonist. This time, however, they are taken prisoner and carried captive to the villain's house on the outskirts of GOTHAM CITY.

"I'm a psychologist," explains their captor, ". . . I have always thought that if your first big case had failed, you would not have become famous! So--I decided to prove that criminologists are successful **only** because of a good start--a lucky beginning! I chose you for the experiment . . . I picked your first famous case, reproduced it to prove that if you had failed to solve it, you would never have become famous! . . . By altering the pattern of your first case--producing a **failure** instead of a success--I expect to induce a failure psychosis in you--a loss of nerve!"

"He *is* mad!" exclaims Batman, after the villain has left them alone, locked inside an escape-proof room. "An egomaniac!"

Certain that they will be brutally murdered as soon as their captor has completed his maniacal psychological experiment, Batman settles on a daring plan which he feels "might unbalance an egomaniac completely" and give them a precious opportunity to escape.

When the villain returns, Batman and Robin pull off their masks, announce that they are not really Batman and Robin at all, and claim that they had merely been standing in for the real Batman and Robin, who are busy making a radio broadcast. When the murderer turns on the radio to confirm whether or not they are telling the truth, he actually hears the voices of Batman and Robin, who had prerecorded a radio broadcast sometime prior to their capture.

"It--it's true!" cries the villain, clearly staggered by the thought that his elaborate psychological attack has been directed against the wrong persons. "All my work--wasted! Wasted!"

As his mind snaps under the strain of his failure, the villain grabs a pistol and fires wildly at Batman and Robin, who somehow manage to avoid being hit. Finally, the tormented madman turns the gun on himself and pulls the trigger in an ironic reenactment of the death of the man whose brutal murders he had so cunningly re-created (BM No. 38/2: "The Carbon Copy Crimes!").

ARDELLO. A "weird, nonmetallic robot," the "chief of robot detectives" in some distant, alien dimension, who journeys to the earthly dimension in May 1960 accompanied by an incredible "electronic bloodhound" — an extradimensional "creature" that has been "trained to track down criminals by tuning in on their brain waves" — in a determined effort to apprehend BATMAN, whom Ardello mistakenly believes to have been responsible for invading his home dimension and making off with a powerful extradimensional weapon "designed to transform matter" and capable of "terrible damage."

For a time, Batman and ROBIN find themselves the objects of a deadly manhunt by Ardello and his electronic bloodhound, but the extradimensional lawman ultimately comes to the realization that Batman is a crime-fighter like himself and that the earthling responsible for the weapons theft could only have been an impostor in a Batman costume.

Working together, Batman, Robin, and Ardello finally recover the stolen weapon and apprehend the real thief — criminal Ed Collins, alias Gimlet — who had journeyed to Ardello's dimension disguised in a Batman costume with the aid of an experimental "dimensional machine" created by a prominent GOTHAM CITY scientist (Det No. 279: "The Creatures That Stalked Batman!").

ARISTO. The leader of a gang of criminals (the text describes Aristo as a "cunning international thief" and "slippery international character") who steal a magic lantern created by Larko the sorcerer from its place in the Gotham Museum and then transform BATMAN into a magic genie, doomed to remain imprisoned inside the lantern until he has fulfilled three wishes for the lamp's owner, by sprinkling him with mystic powder stolen from Larko's tomb. In his genie form, Batman possesses awesome magical powers and is an obedient slave to whomever holds the magic lantern, but, by working together, ROBIN and Bat-Girl (*see* BAT-GIRL [BETTY KANE]) succeed in outwitting Aristo until the three wishes have been completely exhausted. Then, with Batman liberated from his role as genie and transformed into a mere mortal again, the Dynamic Duo swiftly apprehend Aristo and his henchmen (Det No. 322, Dec '63: "The Bizarre Batman Genie!").

ARNOLD, HUGO (Professor). A scientist with an "over-inflated ego" who, bitter at having been overlooked by the Gotham City Historical Society in connection with its plans to stage a series of historical pageants honoring famed ancestors of GOTHAM CITY celebrities, resolves to "smash the Historical Society's pageants" and then "astound the world with a scientific wonder--so that no one will ever ignore me again!"

After using an ingenious "brain-stimulator" of his own invention to send "tremendous power surging through [his] brain" — thereby transforming himself into a scientific wizard of unparalleled genius while at the same time endowing himself with a cranium of "freakish size to accommodate the huge size of [his] brain" — Professor Arnold uses his astounding intellectual capabilities to create an arsenal of mind-boggling inventions, including a deadly "lightning cannon" and invisible flying robots, to enable him to disrupt the historical pageants and then cap his revenge with the scientific feat of creating a second moon for Earth, regardless of the fact that by colliding with the existing moon the new moon could literally cause the destruction of Earth. Professor Arnold and his henchmen are apprehended by BATMAN and ROBIN in August 1962 (Det No. 306: "The Wizard of 1,000 Menaces!").

ARTHUR (King). A British chieftain of the sixth century A.D., and the central figure of a large body of pseudohistorical and romantic literature. In legend he is the ruler of Camelot, the seat of his court and of the Round Table. He is the brother of MORGAN LE FAY and the father-uncle of the traitorous MORDRED. His wife, Queen Guinevere, betrays him by having an amour with SIR LANCELOT, his dearest knight.

In Batman No. 36/3, Mordred, a trusted but traitorous knight of the Round Table, and Morgan Le Fay, queen of a nearby realm and openly an enemy of King Arthur, are presented as coconspirators in an elaborate scheme to abduct the wizard MERLIN from Camelot and imprison him in Queen Morgan Le Fay's castle in order to make it appear that Merlin is a traitor.

Dispatched through the time barrier to Camelot, however, by PROFESSOR CARTER NICHOLS, BATMAN and ROBIN join forces with Sir Lancelot and the other knights of the Round Table to expose and apprehend the evil Mordred, overwhelm the forces of Queen Morgan Le Fay, and rescue Merlin from the villains' clutches. Morgan Le Fay manages to escape, and there are hints that Batman has deliberately allowed this, perhaps because the evil queen had earlier rescued him from death at the hands of Mordred, perhaps because of her uncanny resemblance to the CATWOMAN (Aug/Sep '46: "Sir Batman at King Arthur's Court!").

ARTISANS, THE. A gang of ruthless criminals secretly led by JACK "FIVE STAR" THORPE (BM No. 65/2, Jun/Jul '51: "Bruce Wayne—Crime Reporter!").

ARVIN, EDWARD (Dr.). The "brilliant scientist" who is secretly MR. BLANK (BM No. 77/1, Jun/Jul '53: "The Crime Predictor!").

ASHER. The unscrupulous owner of the Asher Lumber Company. By October-November 1941 Asher has murdered lumber magnate Matthew Powell as the first step in an elaborate scheme to seize control of Powell's extensive North Woods lumber holdings, but BATMAN outwits Asher at every turn and ultimately apprehends him (BM No. 7/3: "The North Woods Mystery").

ASHLEY, J. J. A promoter of Mardi Gras carnivals in cities across the United States, and the partner of Ed Burton in an elaborate scheme that entails purchasing stolen goods in various cities and then transporting them for resale in other cities inside the wax statues of mythological figures that accompany the traveling Mardi Gras. When Burton and escaped convict Mike Kelso attempt to double-cross Ashley in November 1962, Ashley murders them both, only to be apprehended by BATMAN and ROBIN soon afterward with the aid of a photograph taken by VICKI VALE (Det No. 309: "The Mystery of the Mardi Gras Murders!").

ASTRO. The underworld inventor who is the creator of the "crime satellite," an ingenious flying device, operated by remote control from Astro's hideout, which is capable of such feats as blasting open a bank wall with sheets of flame, melting pursuing police cars with a "searing wave of heat bursts" from one of its antennae, creating impassable fissures in the earth with powerful energy bolts, and creating an impenetrable "force field" around itself to protect itself from harm. Aided by the crime satellite, Astro and his henchmen commit a series of spectacular crimes in April 1959, until they are finally apprehended by BATMAN, ROBIN, and members of the Gotham City Police Department (Det No. 266: "The Satellite of Gotham City!").

ATKINS (1941). A stockholder of the Hobbs Clock Company who cunningly plays on the "warped senses" of deranged clockmaker Elias Brock in order to make Brock his dupe in a scheme to murder his fellow stockholders and thereby gain a controlling interest in Hobbs Clock.

Brock, a "fanatical old clock maker" suffering from the delusion that he is Father Time, murders two of the stockholders and attempts unsuccessfully to murder a third—each time by means of a booby-trapped clock that releases a deadly gas, fires a poisoned dart, or explodes—after Atkins has persuaded him that the intended victims are incorrigible time-wasters, "murderers of time" who are unfit to live.

Brock eventually kills Atkins for making him his dupe in the murderous stock-acquisition scheme, and then dies himself soon afterward when, during a scuffle with BATMAN and ROBIN, he plummets to his doom from atop the lofty clock tower of the Hobbs Clock Company, where he has planted a massive charge of TNT in hopes of blowing up the tower (BM No. 6/2, Aug/Sep '41: "The Clock Maker!").

ATKINS (1959). The co-owner, with a man named Bork, of the Atkins and Bork Curio Shop in GOTHAM CITY. In August 1959, with the aid of a map sold to them by a dying criminal, Atkins and Bork set out to recover four ancient objects, once owned by an ancient sorcerer and possessed of miraculous powers—a green box containing a fire-breathing dragon; a "magic prism" which "distorts light and deflects energy"; a "sorcerer's glove" which possesses the power to "dissolve inert matter"; and a "sorcerer's mantle" which possesses the power to render invisible anyone who wears it—with the apparent intention of using the objects' awesome powers for evil. Ultimately, BATMAN, ROBIN, and SUPERMAN defeat Atkins and Bork and recover the four objects, whereupon Superman hurls the objects into the air with such incredible velocity that the friction created by their passage through the atmosphere is certain to destroy them (WF No. 103: "The Secret of the Sorcerer's Treasure!").

ATLANTIS. A legendary island in the Atlantic Ocean which, according to Plato, was the site of a powerful kingdom more than 11,000 years ago before it sank to the bottom of the sea.

According to Batman No. 19/2, Atlantis and its scientifically advanced civilization survive to this day on the floor of the Atlantic, warmed and illuminated by an artificial sun and protected from the sea around it by a gigantic transparent dome. Its rulers are the boy emperor Taro and his sister, the girl empress Lanya. Atlantis is the scene of a battle that pits BATMAN and ROBIN against the forces of the Nazi ADMIRAL VON BURITZ in October-November 1943 ("Atlantis Goes to War!").

ATOMIC-MAN. A cunning criminal, clad in a green and yellow costume with the elliptical symbol of the atom emblazoned on his chest, who has succeeded in inventing a machine which endows him with the power to "alter the molecular structure of any object" merely by staring at it through special goggles with interchangeable colored lenses, different combinations of which "filter" his power differently and determine how that power will affect the objects he looks at: one lens combination, for example, enables Atomic-Man to transform objects into glass, while another combination enables him to change objects into water.

Atomic-Man is secretly Paul Strobe, a brilliant electrical engineer who is determined to revenge himself on his three former business partners, as well as on BATMAN, for having once sent him to prison for stealing the firm's platinum and gold supplies in order to finance the private atomic experiments that led ultimately to the creation of the machine that has endowed him with his special powers.

In June 1960 Atomic-Man and his henchmen commit a series of spectacular crimes aimed at the money and personal property of the three former partners, but the villains are ultimately apprehended through the heroic efforts of Batman and ROBIN (Det No. 280: "The Menace of the Atomic Man").

ATOM-MASTER, THE. A renegade scientist – also referred to as the Illusion-Master – who is defeated in May 1959 through the heroic efforts of BATMAN, ROBIN, and SUPERMAN (WF No. 101: "The Menace of the Atom-Master!").

AVIARY, THE. The PENGUIN's hideout during December 1951–January 1952 (WF No. 55: "The Bird Sayings Crimes!").

B

Ally Babble, Robin, and Batman, 1945 © NPP 1945

BABBLE, ALLY. An endlessly voluble fellow for whom incessant jabbering is both a valued hallmark and a way of life. Batman No. 30/3 refers to him as "that amazing man who is never down in the mouth . . . that original individual who was vaccinated with a phonograph needle . . . that human walkie-talkie . . ." (Aug/Sep '45: "Ally Babble and the Fourteen Peeves!").

In August–September 1945, after Ally Babble has successfully silenced a persistent tap dancer living directly above a man named Jasper Quinch, Quinch offers to pay Babble $5,000 to dispose of thirteen other pet peeves that have bothered him for ages, including a subway guard at a particular subway station who persists in pushing people into overcrowded subway cars (Babble gives the guard a taste of his own medicine by shoving *him* into a subway car) and motorists who drive in such a way as to splash muddy water on passing pedestrians (Babble hauls one such motorist from his vehicle and tosses him headlong into a large puddle).

As Ally Babble races about the city wreaking his zany vengeance on the perpetrators of Jasper Quinch's "fourteen peeves," a series of complaints flow into police headquarters, and the constabulary set out in search of the "lunatic" responsible for the damage. At one point, criminals Hoiman and Shoiman hear about Babble's antics and decide to capitalize on them. While one of Babble's angry victims is chasing him through the streets, Hoiman and Shoiman break into his home and rob it. Later, when Babble enters the Clown Club, a club for practical jokers, in order to continue his ridiculous reign of terror — practical jokers are one of Jasper Quinch's fourteen pet peeves — Hoiman and Shoiman invade the club and attempt to make off with its solid gold anniversary cup, only to be apprehended by BATMAN and ROBIN. Ally Babble returns to Jasper Quinch's house with the Dynamic Duo, but Batman, Robin, and Quinch become infuriated with Babble's incessant jabbering and finally boot him out the doorway and into the street (BM No. 30/3: "Ally Babble and the Fourteen Peeves!").

In April–May 1946, after a gypsy fortune teller has promised him that the four tea leaves in his cup will bring him financial reward, love, a voyage, and the ability to bring happiness to other people, Ally Babble puts each tea leaf in a separate envelope and lets the wind carry them away one at a time, on the assumption that following the windblown envelopes will enable him to find the various rewards promised by the gypsy.

The tea leaf bearing the promise of financial reward floats onto a trolley car which has been commandeered by a gang of criminals who hope to steal a briefcase full of valuable bonds from a passenger who is the president of a bond company. Batman and Robin thwart the theft and apprehend the criminals and, because the Dynamic Duo never accept rewards for their crime-fighting exploits, Ally Babble ends up with the meager $1 reward offered by the bond-company president.

Soon afterward, while he is racing through the streets in pursuit of the envelope containing his love tea-leaf, Ally Babble inadvertently saves the life of a young woman about to be run over by a car. The grateful girl rewards Babble with a kiss, and Babble assumes that he has fallen in love.

The envelope containing the voyage tea-leaf sails into a hospital whose therapeutic equipment includes a lounging area for patients resembling the deck of an ocean liner. Inside the hospital, Babble collides with some criminals who, disguised as doctors, are attempting to make off with the hospital's radium supply. When Batman and Robin arrive on the scene, a pitched battle begins, during which Babble becomes completely intoxicated after accidentally inhaling some pure oxygen. The battle concludes on the hospital's simulated boat deck — symbolizing Babble's promised voyage — and it is the zany antics resulting from Babble's oxygen-induced intoxication which ultimately facilitate the capture of the criminals and the recovery of the radium.

Later, after the radium thieves have been turned over to the authorities, Babble finds that he has grown suddenly hoarse. The hoarseness, Batman observes wryly, must be the legacy of the fourth tea leaf, since

Ally Babble has now brought happiness to others by losing his voice (BM No. 34/2: "Ally Babble and the Four Tea Leaves!").

BACON, ROGER. An English philosopher, scientist, and educational reformer (*ca.* 1220–*ca.* 1292) who strove to win a proper place for the sciences in university curricula.

According to Detective Comics No. 220, where he is described as the "greatest medieval scientist," Bacon had mastered, by the year 1255, a secret "hypnotic time-science" by which man could traverse time and had prevailed upon two of his most devoted pupils, Marcus and Guy Tiller, to travel through time to the twentieth century to discover the answers to the following questions: "Will the future world be worth working for? Will it be a good world?"

And so, after being dispatched through the time barrier by Roger Bacon to GOTHAM CITY in the year 1955, Marcus Tiller and his brother Guy make the acquaintance of BATMAN and ROBIN, help them apprehend a notorious gang of criminals known as the Speedboat Bandits, and ultimately depart for their home in the thirteenth century, having concluded that "though it [i.e., the modern world] still has a few wicked men in it, it is a good world worthy of [Bacon's] hopes!" (Jun '55: "The Second 'Batman and Robin' Team!").

BAFFLE, MICHAEL. A debonair "international thief" and wily "society burglar" who, after being sentenced to the firing squad for jewel theft "somewhere in dictator-trodden Europe," bribes his executioners into loading their rifles with blanks and then flees to GOTHAM CITY, where he matches wits with BATMAN and ROBIN in May 1942.

"Look how she wears those lights, like a beautiful, dazzling necklace!" exclaims Baffle, as he stands atop the observation deck of Gotham City's State Building and gazes out over the glistening nighttime skyline. "This is a rich city. A huge melting pot . . . of jewels and wealth! I'm going to dip my arms into it . . . right up to the elbows!"

LINDA PAGE has described Michael Baffle as "tall, handsome, [and] debonair," and Detective Comics No. 63 says that he is "clever as a fox, romantic as some buccaneer of old . . . [and a] gallant desperado."

With the aid of two henchmen named Fish-eye and Egg-head whom he acquires in Gotham City, Baffle compiles a list of "extremely rich people whose safes need opening" and then proceeds to rob them, sometimes outright, and sometimes by assuming the role of a newspaper society reporter, gaining access to the homes of the wealthy and surreptitiously photographing the layouts with a tiny camera concealed inside his boutonniere and then robbing them at a later date. Curiously, Baffle feels little real malice toward Batman – "I respect him!" exclaims Baffle at one point. "He has an uncanny knack for putting people in jail---and I detest jails!" – and, similarly, Baffle's agile mind, quick wit, and gallant manner soon earn him the grudging respect and reluctant admiration of Batman.

Together, Batman and Robin thwart most of Baffle's crimes, recover Baffle's stolen loot, and apprehend Baffle's two accomplices, but Baffle himself escapes from Batman and is never apprehended. "So long, fella!" cries Batman, as Baffle executes a final, spectacular escape. "I would have wanted you for my friend---but we're on opposite sides, so next time we meet, you've got a fight on your hands, Mr. Baffle!"

"Good-bye for now," calls out Baffle cheerfully, ". . . see you again sometime, **Batman!**" (Det No. 63: "A Gentleman in Gotham").

BAGLEY. A ruthless gangland chieftain who hatches an elaborate plot to destroy BATMAN's crime-fighting career and establish himself as undisputed "king of the underworld" by capturing Batman and then unmasking him at his hideout in full view of "all the top czars of crime." Batman and ROBIN thwart Bagley's scheme by allowing him to capture a Batman robot rather than the real Batman, and ultimately they apprehend Bagley and all his cronies (BM No. 109/1, Aug '57: "Three Crimes Against Batman").

BAILEY, NICK. A ruthless GOTHAM CITY gangster who kidnaps and then impersonates Shing Far, the mayor of Chinatown and the city's largest importer of Chinese curios, as part of an elaborate scheme to dispose of a fortune in Wyoming jade hijacked from a boxcar. Bailey is apprehended in September 1948 through the heroic efforts of BATMAN, ROBIN, and Chinese detective Ling Ho (Det No. 139: "Crimes of Jade!").

BAIN, MARTIN. A GOTHAM CITY gangster who impersonates PROFESSOR CARTER NICHOLS, well-known authority on time travel, as part of an elaborate scheme to persuade the authorities that a current wave of Gotham City gold thefts are actually being committed by famous villains from the past, including Jesse James, John Dillinger, Genghis Khan, and Captain Kidd.

After locking the real Professor Nichols inside a closet and donning an elaborate Carter Nichols disguise, Bain, as Nichols, informs BATMAN, ROBIN, and POLICE COMMISSIONER GORDON that his latest invention – a "time-ray machine" designed to "bring things out of the past" – has been stolen, thus leading the police and public alike to the inevitable but erroneous conclusion that the gold thieves running rampant in Gotham City are villains from the past, summoned to the present by whoever stole Professor Nichols's time-ray machine.

Ultimately, however, after Batman and Robin have apprehended the gold thieves with the aid of the Gotham City Police Department, Batman unmasks "Professor Nichols" as gangster Bain, exposes the so-called historical villains as modern criminals in disguise, and frees the real Carter Nichols from the closet where he has been held prisoner (BM No. 43/3, Oct/Nov '47: "The Four Horsemen of Crime!").

BAKER, BIG JACK. A GOTHAM CITY mobster, in prison awaiting trial for his underworld activities, who persuades his unscrupulous defense attorney, Verne Lever – described as "the best mouthpiece in the country" – to assume the leadership of his gang during his pretrial confinement, ostensibly so that the gang will have a leader during his absence, but in reality so that by threatening to make Lever's own underworld involvement public he can blackmail his attorney into doing his utmost to win him an acquittal. "With your own freedom at stake," gloats Baker, after lawyer Lever has become inextricably involved in the Baker gang's activities, "I **know** you'll try real hard to win an acquittal for me!"

BATMAN's efforts to preserve the secret of his dual identity during this period, as well as to carry out his role as the prosecution's star witness at Big Jack Baker's trial, are severely hampered by the fact that an accidental dousing by a vat of experimental radioactive dye has rendered him temporarily invisible, but the unseen Batman nevertheless manages to persuade the judge of his presence in the courtroom so that he may be permitted to testify, Big Jack Baker is ultimately convicted, and Verne Lever, incriminated on the spot by his gangland client, is apprehended by Batman while attempting to flee the courthouse with ROBIN as hostage (Det No. 199, Sep '53: "The Invisible Batman!").

BALFOR, GRIFFIN. A famous silent film director – known as "one of the greatest directors of silent films" – who disappeared from public view shortly after the advent of talking pictures. In August–September 1951, in a desperate effort to stage a comeback, Balfor kidnaps a crew of famous movie stars, transports them to an inaccessible valley, and sets them to work filming what he believes will be his greatest movie epic. BATMAN and ROBIN invade the valley and ultimately rescue the kidnapped actors from Balfor's clutches, but Balfor drowns when, after flooding the valley in an effort to kill Batman and Robin, he races back into the flood area in an attempt to rescue a reel of film from his personal library of great silent films (BM No. 66/2: "The Movie Stars Who Died Twice!").

BALKANIA. The "faraway kingdom" ruled by the lovely PRINCESS VARINA. Balkania is apparently European, but its exact location is impossible to determine due to the lack of data in the text (WF No. 85, Nov/Dec '56: "The Super-Rivals!").

BALLARD, BRAND. A "makeup artist and stage illusionist with a shady record" who, in concert with underworld elements, concocts an elaborate scheme to destroy BATMAN's career as a crime-fighter by persuading the citizens of GOTHAM CITY that Batman is secretly an alien from outer space.

As the manufactured evidence branding Batman an alien continues to mount, wary citizens – including POLICE COMMISSIONER GORDON and VICKI VALE – begin sifting through their personal recollections of Batman's countless heroic feats and wondering aloud whether those feats could actually have been performed by a crime-fighter who was merely human. "And come to think of it," muses Police Commissioner Gordon, "he ***has*** done things no ordinary man could. . . ."

Before long, fear and suspicion have seized hold of the population, the city's racketeers have become increasingly brazen, and Batman has begun to find his effectiveness as a crime-fighter severely diminished. "I hate being cagey with ***Batman,***" muses one police officer, after he has refused to cooperate with Batman in an investigation, "--but he could be getting ready to climax some alien scheme, now that he's been discovered!"

Eventually, however, Batman learns that Brand Ballard is the man responsible for branding him an alien and tricks Ballard into making a full confession. In the process, Batman and ROBIN also apprehend Ballard's accomplice and a gang of protection racketeers.

Soon afterward, Police Commissioner Gordon apologizes for having ever suspected Batman of being an alien. "Yes," chimes in Vicki Vale, "--but can you blame us for thinking ***Batman*** must be ***superhuman?***" (Det No. 251, Jan '58: "The Alien Batman!").

BANCROFT, BIG JACK. A ruthless gangster, "Public Enemy Number One," who attempts to hide from the police by having his men kidnap saxophonist Eddie Blinn, whom he resembles, and then taking Blinn's place in Kay Kyser's famous band. For a time, Bancroft eludes capture, but he is ultimately apprehended by members of the Gotham City Police Department through the heroic efforts of BATMAN, ROBIN, and bandleader Kyser (Det No. 144, Feb '49: "Kay Kyser's Mystery Broadcast!").

BAND OF SUPER-VILLAINS, THE. The name adopted by a trio of ordinary criminals after a visiting alien from a far-distant planet has provided them with a set of special belts capable of endowing them with "amazing powers," ostensibly because he wants to enable them to become wealthy super-criminals in return for their promise of future aid in establishing a dictatorship on his native planet, but in reality because the belts, which release "an alien element" into the air, are part of a fiendish alien scheme to poison Earth's atmosphere and annihilate its people in order to pave the way for an alien colonization. BATMAN, ROBIN, and SUPERMAN apprehend the Band of Super-Villains in June 1963, and the evil alien, finally cornered and defeated, blows himself and his spacecraft to smithereens as the self-imposed penalty for the failure of his mission (WF No. 134: "The Band of Super-Villains").

BARD, JASON. The man who achieves infamy as the TRAPPER (Det No. 206, Apr '54: "The Trapper of Gotham City!").

BARD, JONATHAN. A brilliant but unscrupulous puppet-master – described as a "wizard with puppets" – who, enraged at having been expelled from a puppeteering competition for attempting to sabotage the puppets of a fellow contestant, angrily "resolves to embark on a career of crime" in order to wreak revenge on the contest's judges while at the same time establishing himself beyond dispute as "the greatest puppetmaster of all!" Aided by a spectacular array of lifelike puppets, Bard commits a series of brazen robberies – all directed against property owned by the contest judges who expelled him – until he is finally apprehended by BATMAN and ROBIN (Det No. 212, Oct '54: "The Puppet-Master!").

BARDEN, CHARLES. A wealthy businessman and lover of children who purchases an entire amusement park situated at Gotham Beach and has it transported to a private island, renamed Playland Island, where he plans to make it available to children without charge.

When Barden is found murdered in the funhouse in February 1959, there are three prime suspects: Wilton, Barden's nephew, who had hated his uncle for spending his money on the amusement park instead of giving it to him to squander; Macklin, Barden's prospective son-in-law, who had been bitter at Barden for refusing him permission to marry his daughter until after Macklin had finished college; and Carter, an associate of Barden, who had resented Barden for having withdrawn his financing from Carter's careless business ventures. BATMAN ultimately deduces that the killer is Carter, who had murdered Barden after Barden had discovered that the robot clown inside the funhouse was being used as a drop-off point for stolen jewelry (Det No. 264: "Peril at Playland Isle!").

BARHAM, JAMES. A millionaire gun manufacturer and collector of ancient weapons who lives on a lonely island upriver from GOTHAM CITY in a medieval castle that he had transported from Europe stone by stone. When Barham is found murdered in August 1957, there are four likely suspects: Jay Sonderson, a gun smuggler and former racketeer; Adam Barham, the dead man's cousin and only heir; John Gorley, a businessman whom Barham had accused of fraud; and Robert Cray, vice-president of the Barham Gun Company. BATMAN ultimately proves that Cray committed the murder to conceal a large embezzlement, and he and ROBIN take the killer into custody (Det No. 246: "Murder at Mystery Castle!").

BARNABY, A. K. The fabulously wealthy BATMAN fan who is the owner of Batman Island, a private island off the coast of GOTHAM CITY where Barnaby maintains the world's largest collection of Batman trophies, films, and memorabilia. Barnaby, whom the text describes as "one of the richest men in the world," helps Batman and ROBIN apprehend a gang of diamond thieves on his island in October 1958 (BM No. 119/2: "The Secret of Batman Island!").

BARR, ELVA. An alias employed by the CATWOMAN in February–March 1943 when she poses as a beautician in a lavish beauty salon as part of an elaborate plot to enable her to gain access to the homes of the wealthy (BM No. 15/1: "Your Face Is Your Fortune!").

BARROC, ERIC. The villainous inventor of a diabolical "transformation machine" whose "electronic ray," focused on wild animals, has the power to transform them into terrifying "beast-humans," humanoid creatures who retain the basic facial characteristics – as well as other of the bestial attributes, such as "fantastic strength" – of the original wild animals. Barroc and his henchman, Roscoe, use their assortment of beast-humans to commit a series of spectacular crimes in GOTHAM CITY. They are finally defeated and apprehended in March 1964 through the heroic efforts of BATWOMAN, ROBIN, Bat-Hound (see ACE [THE BAT-HOUND]), and BATMAN, who is more a hindrance than a help throughout much of the adventure because Eric Barroc's transformation machine has temporarily transformed him into an apelike creature with no recollection whatever of his human existence (BM No. 162/1: "The Batman Creature!").

BARROW, "BOSS." The cunning master criminal who is the inventor of the "electrofaciograph," an ingenious device which, by means of "electronic rays," scans the face of anyone standing in front of its "recording unit" and then "not only blanks out his memory, but 're-writes' his features" onto the face of a second person selected by Barrow, with the astounding result that the two persons involved actually trade faces for a period of about twelve hours. Barrow and his henchmen use their machine to steal the faces of millionaires for brief periods of time so that they can profit from the undetectable impersonations, but they are apprehended in September 1964 by BATMAN and ROBIN, with some assistance from the ELONGATED MAN (Det No. 331: "Museum of Mixed-Up Men!").

BARROWS, BARNEY. A janitor at the headquarters of the Gotham City Police Department, possessed by a violent hatred of criminals and unhappy because he is not sufficiently intelligent to pass the "mental examinations" required for becoming a police officer, who is accidentally exposed to "a tremendous burst of strange radiation" as the result of "a freak explosion" in the police department laboratory and who regains consciousness hours later to discover that the "accidental burst of freak radiation" has somehow "stimulated [his] brain-cells" and transformed him into "the world's greatest mental giant."

Now gifted with "titanic brain-power" but still seized by the same unenlightened lust for vengeance against criminals that had characterized him as a "weak-minded" janitor, Barrows uses his newly acquired intellectual abilities to deduce the secret identities of BATMAN and ROBIN and then, by threatening to make his knowledge public, forces them to serve as his unwilling assistants in an all-out war against crime that has as its end the deliberate assassination, rather than the capture, of criminals.

Batman and Robin manage to outwit Barrows long enough to apprehend the Metals Mob – a gang of criminals specializing in the theft of rare metals – without allowing the former janitor to harm the crooks, and eventually the effects of Barrows's mind-expanding accident wear off and, lapsing into unconsciousness once again, he awakens bereft of his enormous mental powers – without any recollection whatever either of the Dynamic Duo's secret identities or of any of the events that took place following his accident – and returns to his janitorial duties at police department headquarters (Det No. 217, Mar '55: "The Mental Giant of Gotham City!").

BARSH. The leader of a gang of criminals who conspire with Mr. Dane, the owner of the Batmantown Safe

Storage Company, to lull the citizens of Batmantown (*see* PLAINVILLE) into believing that their town is crime-free and that Dane's storage company is the ideal place to store their valuables so that Barsh and his henchmen can steal the valuables while the community is preoccupied with its colorful Batman Pageant. BATMAN and ROBIN learn of the scheme, however, and apprehend the plotters in June 1956 (BM No. 100/1: "Batmantown, U.S.A.").

BART, JOE. A criminal who operates a print shop where fraudulent stock certificates are printed. In July 1945 Bart and his cohorts rob the jewelry store next door to their print shop and attempt to place the blame on ex-convict Roger Ranier, but BATMAN and ROBIN apprehend the real criminals and exonerate Ranier of any wrongdoing (Det No. 101: "The Tyrannical Twins!").

BARTOK. An underworld inventor, once sentenced to five years in prison for selling his inventions to criminals for use in the commission of crimes, who attempts, with the aid of giant remote-controlled robots that he has already created, to steal the vital electronic components necessary for the construction of an army of lifelike "self-thinking robots" programmed to loot and plunder until they have succeeded in making Bartok "the richest man in the world!"

In August 1958 BATMAN and ROBIN trail some of Bartok's robots to the huge cavern in the Eagle Mountain Range – approximately 125 miles northwest of GOTHAM CITY – which serves both as Bartok's headquarters and as the site of his elaborate robot production line, only to be taken prisoner by Bartok's powerful robot guards. Ultimately, however, with the aid of a Batman robot they have brought with them in the BATMOBILE, the Dynamic Duo succeed in overpowering Bartok, commandeering his robot control room, and capturing his henchmen (Det No. 258: "Prisoners of the Giant Robots!").

BARTON (Captain). An old seafaring man who is a member of the Stamp Club, a club for GOTHAM CITY stamp collectors each of whom specializes in stamps depicting scenes related to his particular hobby or occupation; Barton's collection, for example, features stamps containing pictures of ships.

Knowing that the monetary value of a stamp can be greatly increased by imbuing it with an air of notoriety, Barton begins buying up entire issues of stamps depicting scenes of violence, and then, one by one, attempts to murder his fellow club members in such a way that the manner of death reflects the victim's own stamp specialty as well as the particular issue which Barton has just purchased.

When BATMAN joins the Stamp Club in his Bruce Wayne identity in an effort to root out the would-be killer, for example, he presents himself as an amateur racing-car driver and as a collector of stamps containing pictures of racing cars. Soon afterward, Barton purchases a Mexican stamp series depicting a fiery auto accident during a running of the Pan American road race, then attempts to murder Wayne by tampering with Wayne's racing car during an automobile race. Ultimately, however, Batman exposes Barton as the killer and he and ROBIN take him into custody (BM No. 78/2, Aug/Sep '53: "The Sinister Stamps!").

BARTOR, BRAND. A small-time criminal, arrested in GOTHAM CITY for wearing a BATMAN costume in violation of a local ordinance prohibiting anyone from imitating Batman's famous uniform, who raises as his legal defense the assertion that Batman is himself imitating a Batman of ancient Babylon, as evidenced by a three-thousand-year-old wall painting, recently unearthed, which depicts a figure in a Batman costume battling a soldier.

This defense creates a serious dilemma for Batman, for he knows that the wall painting was made of him when, after having been dispatched through the time barrier by PROFESSOR CARTER NICHOLS, he and ROBIN overthrew the tyrannical King Beladin and restored the good King Lanak to the throne of Babylon. Because he and Robin journeyed to and returned from ancient Babylon as Bruce Wayne and Dick Grayson, however, they cannot reveal that Batman was the subject of the painting without betraying the secret of their dual identities.

Fortunately for Batman and Robin, however, the people of ancient Babylon revered a "hero-idol" named Zorn whose statue shows him in a costume almost identical to Batman's. Acting on this fact, the judge at Bartor's trial rejects Bartor's defense on the ground that the wall painting depicts a mythic figure and not a human being, and that therefore the Batman of Gotham City is not imitating a Batman of the ancient past (BM No. 102/2, Sep '56: "The Batman from Babylon").

BATBOY. A mysterious midget crime-fighter – clad in the uniform of a baseball player with his identity concealed by a catcher's mask – who helps ROBIN apprehend the Tapper Nolan mob in March 1955. Batboy, who operates from a secret cavern headquarters known as "the dugout" and employs a versatile arsenal of bat-weapons to aid him in his war against crime – including a "baseball bat-arang," a "jet-powered battering-ram bat," a "parachute-bat," a quill-shooting "porcupine bat," and a weapon that releases a large net, termed a "web bat" – is in reality Midge Merrill, a middle-aged midget acrobat, once a member of a three-midget circus acrobatic team known as the Mighty Mites, whose vendetta against Tapper Nolan began years ago, when Nolan, then a circus roustabout, deliberately set fire to the circus tent to divert attention while he robbed the gate receipts, as the result of which both of Merrill's midget partners died in the fire. With BATMAN away on a special assignment throughout most of the adventure, Robin joins forces with Batboy to apprehend the Nolan mob, after which Merrill happily abandons his career as a crime-fighter for a job as batboy with a hometown baseball team (BM No. 90/3: "The Adventures of Batboy!").

BATCAVE. The subterranean cavern, situated beneath

the mansion of millionaire BRUCE WAYNE, which serves as the secret crime-fighting headquarters of BATMAN and ROBIN. (*See* BATMAN [section D, the batcave].)

BATGIRL (Barbara Gordon). A lovely red-haired crime-fighter who functions periodically, from January 1967 onward, as the crime-fighting colleague of BATMAN and ROBIN (Det No. 359: "The Million Dollar Debut of Batgirl!"). Batgirl is in reality Barbara Gordon, once the head librarian of the Gotham City Public Library (Det No. 363, May '67: "The True-False Face of Batman!"), more recently a congresswoman from GOTHAM CITY. She is the daughter of POLICE COMMISSIONER JAMES W. GORDON, and therefore presumably the sister of TONY GORDON, though this latter fact is never actually stated.

Barbara is highly trained in both judo and karate (Det No. 369, Nov '67: "Batgirl Breaks Up the Dynamic Duo!"), holds a Ph.D. from Gotham State University, from which she graduated *summa cum laude* (Det No. 359, Jan '67: "The Million Dollar Debut of Batgirl!"), and is gifted with a photographic memory.

Barbara Gordon, 1969 © NPP 1969

For her role as Batgirl, Barbara wears a close-fitting black costume with a bat-eared blue cowl, a long blue cape, and a yellow stylized bat-insignia emblazoned across her breast. She also wears yellow finned gauntlets with matching high-heeled boots and a yellow "weapons belt" with a yellow bat-shaped buckle. Attached to the weapons belt is a red "weapons bag" decorated with a stylized bat-insignia in black. From beneath her cowl, her long flame-red hair flows out behind her. Her principal means of transportation is a carefully "restyled," specially equipped motorcycle called the "bat-bike" (Det No. 359, Jan '67: "The Million Dollar Debut of Batgirl!").

The texts refer to Batgirl as the Bat-Beauty, the Chic Crime-Fighter, the Dominoed Dare-Doll, and the Masked Maiden.

Batgirl, 1971 © NPP 1971

In January 1967 KILLER MOTH and his henchmen – the so-called "moth-mob" – launch a vicious protection racket in Gotham City, waylaying and beating up the city's millionaires and then demanding $100,000 each from their victims in return for calling the brutal beatings to a halt.

One evening, while librarian Barbara Gordon is on her way to the Policemen's Masquerade Ball in a colorful "Batgirl" costume that she has designed especially for the occasion, she sees the moth-mob bring Bruce Wayne's car to a stop by enmeshing it in powerful "glistening strands of gooey substance" fired from their special weapons, and then drag Wayne into the street.

The incident represents a moment of truth for Barbara Gordon, for up until this moment, in spite of her attractive figure and her undisputed educational and professional attainments, she has felt dissatisfied with her mundane life, unhappy that "the whole world thinks I'm just a plain Jane--a colorless female 'brain'!" Now, however, she leaps to Wayne's aid, calling out to him to run for safety while she bravely battles the ruthless criminals. "He's always regarded me as a mousey sort of person!" muses Barbara. "I wonder what he'd say if he knew who it was coming to rescue him!"

Wayne pretends to flee, but only long enough to enable him to change into his Batman costume and leap back into the fray. Some members of the moth-mob are taken prisoner, but Killer Moth escapes by hurling Barbara Gordon into the "cocoon-like folds" of the gooey substance surrounding Wayne's car, thus forcing Batman to abandon the chase in order to extricate his ally from the sticky trap.

Batman is disturbed that Killer Moth has escaped, but Barbara Gordon is ecstatic about the exciting turn her life has just taken: "Her eyes sparkle! Her breath comes faster! Her heart thumps with alarming speed! Babs Gordon is having the time of her life--fully alive to this new excitement and danger--and loving it! . . ."

Barbara explains to Batman that she was on her way to the Policemen's Masquerade Ball when she saw the moth-mob attack Bruce Wayne's car. Now that her costume has been ruined in the fighting, she continues, she will have to abandon her plans for the evening, but she refuses to tell Batman her true identity, particularly since he obviously has no intention of reciprocating by revealing his own. "For all I know," she thinks to herself, "this marks the debut and farewell appearance of ***Batgirl!*** It was fun while it lasted. . . ."

The next day, back at her post at the Gotham City Public Library, Barbara Gordon ponders the exciting events of the night before. "I almost wish I'd never made that ***Batgirl*** costume!" she muses. "Now my life seems empty and humdrum!"

Soon afterward, Bruce Wayne receives a threatening note from the moth-mob, informing him that unless he agrees to pay $100,000 in protection money, incidents like the one of the previous night will recur. By checking with other Gotham City millionaires, Wayne learns that nine other men are being similarly victimized. He instructs ALFRED to deliver a note to the payoff site announcing his refusal to pay the extortion money and his intention to remain closeted in the Wayne mansion, surrounded by policemen. Actually, however, the note is part of Batman's elaborate plan to lure Killer Moth and his henchmen into a carefully laid trap. Indeed, as Batman had expected, Killer Moth is enraged at

Batgirl on her bat-bike, 1969 © NPP 1969

Wayne's note, carefully watches the Wayne mansion until he is certain that there are no policemen on the scene, and then sets out with his moth-mob to murder Bruce Wayne.

Meanwhile, a rare edition of the Bay Psalm Book ordered by Bruce Wayne has arrived at the Gotham City Public Library, and Barbara Gordon, uncomfortable about leaving the valuable edition in the library overnight, decides to carry it out to the Wayne mansion after work. As she draws near the mansion, she hears the crackle of gunfire and, through an open window, sees what appears to be the body of Bruce Wayne crumpling under a fusillade of bullets.

Following the incident on the night of the masquerade party, however, Barbara Gordon had found herself unwilling to abandon her Batgirl career entirely. She

Batgirl in action, 1972 © NPP 1972

had kept in fighting shape through "intensive exercise" and a "special protein diet," and had created an elaborate new Batgirl costume — "just in case" the opportunity ever arose for her to become Batgirl again — which converts her normal-looking street clothes into the colorful Batgirl costume within a matter of seconds.

Now, having witnessed what appears to have been the murder of Bruce Wayne, Barbara Gordon changes to Batgirl and springs into action against the ruthless moth-mob. Inside the mansion, however, Batman and Robin, who are in places of concealment, are dismayed at Batgirl's interference in their trap. At an opportune moment in the battle, when the criminals have knocked Batgirl toward the Dynamic Duo's hiding place, Batman and Robin quietly grab her so that Killer Moth and his men will have the opportunity to escape. They explain to her that it was only a Bruce Wayne dummy which she had seen "murdered" at the window, and that they had hoped to follow the villains back to their Moth Mansion hideaway so that they could capture the entire gang and recover all of the money extorted from Gotham City's millionaires.

"Ohhh!" cries the dismayed Batgirl. "I've spoiled **everything!**"

Robin consoles her, however, by explaining that all is not lost. He has managed to bug the villains' "moth-mobile" with a "magnetic tracking device" which will enable them to track the criminals to their hideout. Batgirl insists on going with them, but Batman refuses. "No, ***Batgirl!***" he says firmly. "This is a case for ***Batman*** and ***Robin!*** I'm sorry--but you must understand that we can't worry ourselves about a girl. . . ."

In spite of Batman's admonition, however, Batgirl follows closely behind them on her bat-bike. "Worry about a girl, eh?" she muses wryly. "**Hah!** If they think they can cut me off from where the action is, they're mistaken!"

At the Moth Mansion, Batman and Robin are taken prisoner and locked inside a "gravity-free chamber" where they are doomed to float helplessly until Killer Moth and his henchmen are ready to kill them.

Although Batman later indicates that he had already concocted a plan for escaping from the gravity-free chamber, it is nevertheless Batgirl who arrives on the scene, frees the Dynamic Duo from the trap, and then locates Killer Moth — who is hiding behind a secret panel in the Moth Mansion's "moth-master control room" — by smelling the traces of her own perfume that have lingered on the villain since his encounter with her earlier that evening at the Wayne mansion.

"Looks as if you have a new member of the team, ***Batman!***" observes Police Commissioner Gordon, after Killer Moth and his henchmen have been safely imprisoned. "Or will she prove to be a crime-fighting ***rival?***"

"I'll welcome her aid, Commissioner Gordon," replies Batman, "--when and where the occasion arises! From what I've seen, she doesn't have to take a back seat to anybody!" (Det No. 359: "The Million Dollar Debut of Batgirl!").

BAT-GIRL (Betty Kane). A daring teen-aged crime-fighter who functions periodically as the crime-fighting colleague of BATMAN, ROBIN, and BATWOMAN. Bat-Girl is actually Betty Kane, the pretty blond niece of Kathy Kane, the "wealthy heiress" who is secretly Batwoman (BM No. 139/3, Apr '61: "Bat-Girl!"). Betty Kane lives somewhere other than in GOTHAM CITY (BM No. 153, Feb '63: chs. 1–3 — "Prisoners of Three Worlds!"; "Death from Beyond"; "Dimension of Doom"), and her appearances as Bat-Girl are apparently restricted to those occasions when she comes to Gotham City to visit her aunt.

For her role as Bat-Girl, Betty wears a short-sleeved, short-skirted red dress with matching ankle-length boots and a highly stylized red mask. Her dress is set off by a green cape with a scalloped edge; a green belt decorated with a stylized bat-insignia; green sleeve-trim; and, on occasion, a pair of green gloves.

On crime-fighting missions, Bat-Girl carries a silken rope, called a "bat-rope," and an ingenious "crime compact" containing such useful equipment as a huge "self-inflating balloon" with a frightening face on it to startle criminals (BM No. 139/3, Apr '61: "Bat-Girl!"), luminous ink (BM No. 144/3, Dec '61: "Bat-Mite Meets Bat-Girl!"), and a trick lipstick which shoots out wire tendrils to ensnare her villainous adversaries (BM No. 153, Feb '63: chs. 1–3 — "Prisoners of Three Worlds!"; "Death from Beyond"; "Dimension of Doom"). In December 1963 she rides a colorful "bat-scooter" and carries an ingenious "smoke screen hair spray" (Det No. 322: "The Bizarre Batman Genie!"). In each of her appearances, she displays a strong romantic interest in Robin, but Robin does not really begin to reciprocate this affection until February 1963 (BM No. 153: chs. 1–3 — "Prisoners of Three Worlds!"; "Death from Beyond"; "Dimension of Doom").

Betty Kane, 1961 © NPP 1961

By April 1961 Betty Kane, suitcase in hand, has arrived in Gotham City for a surprise visit with her aunt, Kathy Kane. "This will complicate things!" thought Kathy, as she cordially greeted her "unexpected visitor." "I'll be secretly going out so much as ***Batwoman,*** I hope it doesn't arouse her suspicion!"

"As days passed," notes the textual narrative, "Kathy's fear became well justified," as young Betty began to wonder about her aunt's frequent absences from the house. "I wonder where Aunt Kathy goes every night?" thought Betty, as she sat alone watching television. "If she's dating a special person, why doesn't he ever call for her here?"

Suddenly, the television screen began to flash live-action pictures of Batwoman in action against some thieves whom she had surprised in the act of "robbing the safe of a manufacturer of school supplies." Batwoman easily defeated her underworld adversaries, but during the fighting several cartons of little gold stars, of the type used in elementary schools, were sent plummeting from their neat stacks, and thousands of tiny paper stars were wafted about the room. "Golly! She's wonderful!" thought Betty, as she watched spellbound. "How I wish I could be like her!"

Sometime afterward, after Kathy Kane had returned home, Betty chanced to brush her hair with her aunt's brush and discovered, to her amazement, that the brush was filled with tiny gold stars which, she concluded correctly, could only have come from the office of the school supplies manufacturer where Batwoman had battled the criminals. Her own aunt, she realized, was none other than the world-famous Batwoman.

One night in April 1961, without informing her aunt that she has discovered her secret, Betty fashions a red and green Bat-Girl costume and follows her aunt out of the house when, as Batwoman, Kathy Kane begins her nightly crime patrol. At one point, as Batman, Robin, and Batwoman close in on several members of the notorious Cobra Gang at an exhibition hall housing "an exhibit of new scientific equipment," one criminal seizes one of the numerous inventions on display and uses it to trap the crime-fighting trio in a sizzling circle of high-voltage electricity.

"Suddenly--an astonishing visitor intervenes," as Bat-Girl, swinging through the open window of the exhibition hall on a huge curtain, hurtles feet-first into the villain operating the deadly "electronic-ring" invention and then, after deactivating the electrical gadget and releasing Batman and his companions from their high-voltage deathtrap so that they can apprehend the demoralized criminals, disappears back through the window as suddenly and mysteriously as she had first appeared. "She--she called herself ***Bat-Girl!***" stammers Robin to himself, as the strange figure vanishes into the night. "Gosh, I wonder who she is?"

The answer is not long in coming, for when Batwoman returns to the batcave beneath her house, she finds the costumed newcomer already there waiting for her. "Well--did I do all right, Aunt Kathy?" she asks. ***"Betty!"*** exclaims the astonished Batwoman. "So it's ***you!*** And you've learned my secret disguise!"

Betty hastily narrates the story of how she had uncovered her aunt's secret identity and then fashioned a colorful Bat-Girl costume in the hope of becoming her aunt's junior crime-fighting partner.

"You were very clever, Betty," concedes Batwoman, "--but you must never be **Bat-Girl** again!"

"If **you** can be **Batwoman,**" replies Bat-Girl, "**I** can certainly be **Bat-Girl!** Maybe we can be a team--like **Batman** and **Robin!**"

"She has no idea how dangerous fighting is!" thinks Batwoman to herself. "I'd better get **Batman's** advice on how to cope with Betty!"

Bat-Girl in action, 1961 © NPP 1961

Later that evening, a worried Batwoman meets with Batman and Robin in the hope of finding a way to dissuade Betty Kane from risking her life as Bat-Girl. Batman proposes that Batwoman inform Betty that she may become Bat-Girl, but only after a great deal of rigorous training. Batman feels that by keeping Betty preoccupied with her training program, it ought to be possible to prevent her from risking her life in battles with the underworld until her visit with Kathy Kane is over and it is time for her to return home.

"And so, the rigid training program gets under way," and "day after day, ***Batwoman*** adds to the girl's assignments [in order] to occupy almost every moment of her time. . . ."

Gradually, however, Betty comes to the realization that her aunt is "deliberately stalling" her, and never actually intends to let her fight crime as Bat-Girl. One evening, after she has been left alone in Batwoman's batcave, Betty analyzes some particles stuck inside a shoe taken from a captured member of the Cobra Gang and discovers that they consist of "cellulose acetate," a substance "used in the manufacture of gunpowder, rayon, and other products!"

"I'll bet their hideout is a place that once used cellulose!" thinks Betty, as she dons her Bat-Girl costume. "So Aunt Kathy thinks I'm 'not ready yet'--huh? I'll show her! **Bat-Girl** will search everywhere until she locates the **Cobra Gang's** hideout!"

Sometime later, after a relentless search, Bat-Girl finally locates the Cobra Gang's hideout — "an abandoned rayon plant" somewhere in Gotham City. Foolishly, however, she attempts to capture the criminals single-handedly, and she is soon taken captive and locked inside an unused room that once served as an office.

Completely ashamed of herself for having attempted to apprehend the criminals alone, Bat-Girl nevertheless retains the presence of mind to find a way to notify Batman, Robin, and Batwoman of her predicament: in the abandoned office room are some old sheets of carbon paper; working feverishly, Bat-Girl cuts them into crude bat-shapes and feeds them into a ventilator shaft until an updraft carries them out "the roof's exhaust vent" into the street. Soon after a passerby has seen them and notified the police, Batman, Robin, and Batwoman arrive on the scene and, with some last-minute assistance from Bat-Girl, who disarms the leader of the Cobra Gang with a well-placed karate-chop, apprehend the members of the notorious gang.

"I've learned my lesson!" confesses Bat-Girl, after all the criminals have been turned over to the police. "I'll never be so foolish again!"

"I'm glad of that!" replies Batwoman. "But you proved you **can** be a good crime-fighter! Maybe we **will** go out as a team some day!"

"Oh, I can hardly wait!" gushes Bat-Girl, eyeing Robin romantically. "And perhaps **Robin** and I can work on a case together, too! Well, **Robin**--is that a date?"

"Ulp," stammers Robin, blushing furiously (BM No. 139/3: "Bat-Girl!").

By August 1961 Betty Kane has returned to Gotham City to visit her aunt and has once again resumed her role as Bat-Girl. "Ever since she got a taste of crime-fighting on her last visit," explains Batwoman to Batman, "she's been anxious to prove she can be a good junior partner!"

At one point, when Batman, Robin, Batwoman, and Bat-Girl battle the MOTH and his henchmen at the Gotham Chemical Plant, Bat-Girl single-handedly captures the villain by means of a tricky judo flip in spite of Robin's warnings that she should not try to tackle him alone. After the fight has ended, Bat-Girl rewards an embarrassed Robin for his concern with a warm kiss. "***Robin,*** it was sweet of you to want to help me!" coos Bat-Girl. "You're a living doll!"

Later, eager newsmen snap Bat-Girl's picture for their morning editions as they record the story of the daring capture. "What a story!" exclaims one reporter. "The ***Moth***--kayoed by a teen-age girl! ***Bat-Girl*** made him the laughing stock of the underworld!"

Robin, however, does not seem happy. "What a worried look on ***Robin!***" thinks Bat-Girl. "Is it because he's jealous that I'll be sharing some of his glory from now on?"

Bat-Girl's success in apprehending the Moth makes her an instant celebrity, but soon afterward Batman receives word that the Moth has broken out of prison. "That's especially bad news for ***Bat-Girl!***" Batman warns Robin. "She humiliated the ***Moth!*** He'll want revenge--and tracking him down will be too dangerous for a beginner like ***Bat-Girl!*** We've got to see ***Batwoman*** without delay!"

Soon afterward, Batman informs Batwoman of the problem they face: ". . . and ***Bat-Girl's*** so headstrong and proud," concludes Batman, "--she'd want to be in on the capture of the ***Moth!***"

"*Hmm!*" murmurs Batwoman. "Maybe ***Robin*** is the answer to our problem! Betty likes him!"

"M-Me?" shudders Robin.

Soon afterward, Robin dutifully pays a call on Betty Kane and asks her to stay out of the coming fight. "I--I was thinking," stammers Robin, ". . . since you proved you're a good crime-fighter, don't--don't you think you ought to give up being ***Bat-Girl*** for awhile. . . ?"

Betty, however, leaps to the conclusion that Robin's visit has been motivated by personal jealousy. "So," she exclaims, "--you ***are*** jealous of me! You want me to quit so ***you*** can have all the glory again. Oh, ***Robin,***" she sobs, "--how could you?"

"Gosh!" thinks Robin, hurt and embarrassed. "If I could only tell her the truth. . . ."

Sometime later, Batman deduces that the Moth will strike next at a newly opened science exposition where some precious metals used in scientific research have been put on display. When Batman consults Robin about keeping Bat-Girl away from the scene, Robin replies that the Robin and Bat-Girl fan clubs are giving a joint dance and that he and Bat-Girl will be the guests of honor there on the night of the robbery.

As the hour of the showdown battle nears, Robin and Bat-Girl head for their fan-club dance while Batman and Batwoman set out after the Moth. The villain, however, subdues Batman and Batwoman with knockout gas and ties them to one of the science exhibits alongside a cache of dynamite timed to explode within a matter of minutes. Before he succumbs completely to the knockout gas, however, Batman manages to put through a radio message to Robin, who quietly slips away from the dance. Bat-Girl, however, sees Robin leaving and follows him. At the exposition hall, she deactivates the dynamite's timing device and frees Batman and Batwoman while Robin battles the Moth and his henchmen. Within seconds, Batman, Batwoman, Robin, and Bat-Girl have succeeded in subduing all the villains.

Later, Batman explains to Bat-Girl that Robin had approached her earlier out of genuine concern, and not out of jealousy. "He was afraid too much publicity might make you over-confident instead of careful," explains Batman.

"Oh, ***Robin,***" cries Bat-Girl, as she gives a blushing Robin a heartfelt kiss, "--now I ***know*** you really care for me!"

"Hmm!" muses Batwoman, as she ponders Bat-Girl's romantic strategy and then gives Batman a warm kiss. "Perhaps ***Bat-Girl's*** direct approach is the best way for a gal to get her guy! Come here, ***Batman*** . . ." (BM No. 141/3: "Batwoman's Junior Partner!").

In December 1961 POLICE COMMISSIONER GORDON summons Batman, Robin, Batwoman, and Bat-Girl to his office, informs them that Batman and Batwoman must leave for Washington, D.C., immediately to testify before a Senate crime committee, and announces that he wants Robin and Bat-Girl to patrol Gotham City together in their absence. "Oh, no!" thinks Robin to himself. "That's all I need . . . ***Bat-Girl*** hounding me wherever I go!"

Bat-Girl, however, has an entirely different attitude toward the prospect of working with Robin. "Working with you is what I've always dreamed of!" sighs Bat-Girl as she kisses Robin outside police headquarters. "Oh, ***Robin***--I think you're just adorable!"

"***B-Bat-Girl*** . . . please," stammers Robin, ". . . y-you've just got to stop doing that! It--it isn't right, especially since I'm . . . er . . . devoted to another woman!"

Bat-Girl is absolutely heartbroken. ***"Another woman?"*** she asks tearfully. "Oh, ***Robin*** . . . y-you can't mean that!"

Bat-Girl and Robin, 1963 © NPP 1963

The "lovestruck lass" is still crying back at Batwoman's batcave when suddenly BAT-MITE appears before her as if from out of nowhere. "If only ***Robin*** would forget the other woman and fall in love with me!" sobs Bat-Girl to her elfin visitor. "Is that all?" replies Bat-Mite cheerily. "Why, with my powers, it'll be a cinch . . . and boyoboyoboy--will I have fun doing it!"

Now Bat-Mite sets in motion an elaborate plan designed to make Robin fall in love with Bat-Girl. "My ***first*** step," he explains at one point, "[is] to make ***Robin*** admire your crime-fighting skill--my ***second*** step [is] to make him jealous of another boy . . . my ***third*** step is to make him ***worry*** about you!"

To make Robin admire Bat-Girl's crime-fighting skill, Bat-Mite uses his magical powers to make it appear that Bat-Girl has performed a series of incredible stunts while apprehending two criminals at the Gotham Playground Equipment Company. Robin is indeed impressed by Bat-Girl's apparent prowess, but he remains silent out of fear that his compliments might make her reckless and overconfident.

To make Robin jealous, Bat-Mite intentionally lets loose a tiger at the Spangler Brothers Outdoor Circus and, while invisibly riding the tiger and controlling it, makes it appear to menace Chip Danton, a handsome young movie star. When Bat-Girl captures the tiger and rescues Danton, Danton hugs and kisses her in gratitude while Robin looks on disgustedly.

To make Robin worry about Bat-Girl and come to realize how much he really cares for her, Bat-Mite plans to use his magical powers to enlarge some toy men and cars to life-size, to make it appear that Bat-Girl has been abducted by real criminals, and then to allow Robin to unearth a clue to the kidnapping and rescue her from their clutches. The plot goes awry, however, when Bat-Girl arrives at the "abduction" spot early and gets kidnapped by *real* criminals before Bat-Mite has the chance to go into his act. Horrified at what has taken place, Bat-Mite allows himself to become visible and hastily explains the entire story to Robin. Fortunately, Bat-Girl has left behind a trail of luminous ink, and soon afterward, with Bat-Mite's help, Robin is able to capture the kidnappers and rescue Bat-Girl from their clutches.

"***Robin,*** I was a fool to try to get you to care for me," confesses Bat-Girl, after the criminals have been turned over to the police, "--but I was so jealous of that other woman!"

It is only then that Robin explains that the "other woman" he had referred to is only the statue of Justice, personified as a woman, which stands in Gotham City. "Yes, you see," explains Robin, "***Batman*** has often told me that his crime-fighting career is a full-time job and that he can't risk a big romance now--not until he's ready to retire! If ***Batman*** can make that kind of sacrifice, I guess ***I'm*** man enough to do it, too!"

"***Robin,*** there's time enough for you to make that kind of decision and sacrifice, when you're really grown up!" says Batman, who has returned with Batwoman from his trip to Washington in time to overhear Robin's last remark. "Right now, you're still a teen-ager, you know. . . ."

"Oh, ***Robin,***" cries Bat-Girl, as she gives an embarrassed Robin a big kiss, "--then it's all right for me to kiss you now!"

Bat-Girl and Robin, 1963 © NPP 1963

"Well," muses Bat-Mite, ". . . it looks like ***my*** work is finished--so I might as well go home!" (BM No. 144/3: "Bat-Mite Meets Bat-Girl!").

In February 1963 Bat-Girl helps Batman, Robin, and Batwoman defeat the evil extradimensional scientist ZEBO and his ruthless accomplice Karn. At one point, after she and Robin have been temporarily stranded in Zebo's extradimensional world, Bat-Girl is overjoyed when Robin regains consciousness after having been accidentally knocked senseless by the tendril arm of a large alien plant. "Oh, I'm so glad you're all right!" coos Bat-Girl. "I was so worried about you. . . ."

"Gosh!" exclaims Robin. "You were? Gee, ***Bat-Girl*** . . . I--I. . . ." Bat-Girl stifles Robin's momentary bewilderment with a warm kiss.

Later, after Robin and Bat-Girl have returned to Earth and the villains have been defeated, the happy couple walk away together, hand in hand. Batman calls out something to Robin, but Robin is oblivious to Batman's voice. "I'm afraid he can't hear you . . . now!" says Batwoman softly. The incident represents the first time that Robin seems to reciprocate Bat-Girl's affection for him, without either discomfort or embarrassment (BM No. 153: chs. 1–3 – "Prisoners of Three Worlds!"; "Death from Beyond"; "Dimension of Doom").

In November 1963 Betty Kane is again in Gotham City visiting her aunt. At one point, Batman and Robin cruise by the Kane mansion in the BATMOBILE and stop to chat with Kathy and Betty.

"Well, **Robin,**" asks Kathy, "aren't you glad to see that my pretty niece is visiting me again?"

"Gosh! I sure am!" replies Robin. "H-Hello, Betty!"

"Robin," sighs Betty, "I can hardly wait to get into my ***Bat-Girl*** costume again! Won't it be terrific if we could [sic] go on a crime case together like the last time?"

"It sure would, Betty!" sighs Robin.

Later, after Robin has rescued her from serious injury during a furious battle with Clayface (*see* CLAYFACE [MATT HAGEN]), Bat-Girl throws her arms around Robin's neck. "Oh, ***Robin,***" she cries, as Robin tries to comfort her, "--I'm afraid you'll just have to hold me! I'm still so shaky after fighting **Clayface**--and you're so **strong!**"

"Smart girl!" remarks Batwoman to Batman. "She knows how to play up to a man! Maybe I should take a tip from her, eh, Batman?"

Batman ultimately apprehends Clayface singlehandedly, and Bat-Girl and Batwoman apprehend the JOKER as he attempts to flee the scene of a daring robbery at the Gotham Museum (BM No. 159/1: "The Great Clayface-Joker Feud!").

In December 1963, while Batwoman is "out of town," Bat-Girl helps Batman and Robin defeat the "cunning Continental thief" ARISTO (Det No. 322: "The Bizarre Batman Genie!").

BAT-HOUND, THE. *See* ACE (THE BAT-HOUND).

BATMAN, THE. A costumed crime-fighter and adventurer who has, for almost four decades, waged an unrelenting battle against the forces of crime, brutality, and evil. He is secretly Bruce Wayne, a millionaire socialite and philanthropist who, while still a young boy, vowed to dedicate his life to "warring on all criminals" after seeing his parents murdered by a hoodlum on a darkened city street (*see* section A, Origin).

In April 1940, approximately a year after the onset of his dramatic career, Batman trained a young orphan named Dick Grayson to be his partner, conferred on him the name ROBIN, and thus launched the career of a crime-fighting partnership whose feats have become the stuff of legend (Det No. 38).

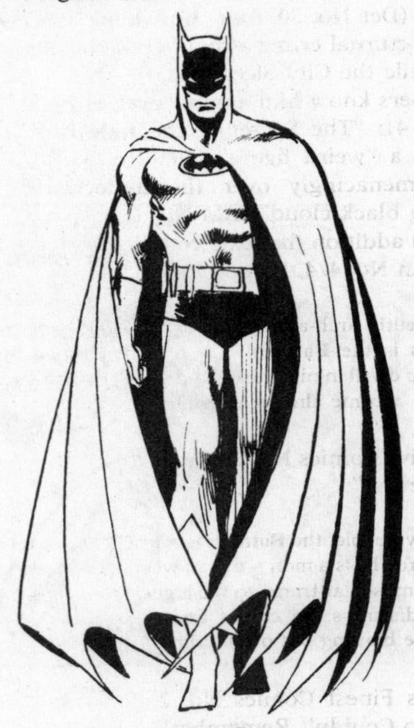

Batman, 1970 © NPP 1976

Batman is an "ace criminologist" (Det No. 73, Mar '43: "The Scarecrow Returns") and "master lawman" (BM No. 70/2, Apr/May '52: "The Masterminds of Crime!"), an "eerie figure of the night" (BM No. 1/4, Spr '40) and a "weird menace to all crime" (Det No. 31, Sep '39).

"He's a stunt man . . . an acrobat . . . a superb athlete . . . a lion-hearted fighter--and a sleuth . . . all rolled into one" (BM No. 14/1, Dec/Jan '42–'43: "The Case Batman Failed to Solve!!!"). He is a "dark warrior of the night" (BM No. 10/3, Apr/May '42: "The Princess of Plunder!") and a "dread scourge of evil" (BM No. 19/4, Oct/Nov '43: "Collector of Millionaires"), an "eerie nemesis of crime" (WB No. 1, Spr '41: "The Witch and the Manuscript of Doom!") and a "weird figure of the dark" (Det No. 33, Nov '39: "The Batman Wars Against the Dirigible of Doom") whose "cowled shadow . . . prowls through the night preying upon the criminal parasite, like the winged creature whose name he has adopted!" (Det No. 37, Mar '40).

He has "deep instincts of honesty and justice" (Det No. 83, Jan '44: "Accidentally on Purpose!"), but he is also a "deadly fighting machine" (Det No. 65, Jul '42: "The Cop Who Hated the Batman!") with a "physically perfect body" (BM No. 11/4, Jun/Jul '42: "Four Birds of a Feather!"), "the reflexes of . . . a wild animal" (Det No. 339, May '65: "Batman Battles the Living Beast-Bomb!"), fists "like twin sledgehammers" (BM No. 131/1, Apr '60: "The Dog That Betrayed Batman"), and "a punch like the kick of a Missouri mule!" (Det No. 54, Aug '41: "Hook Morgan and His Harbor Pirates").

He is "a creation of the night . . . elusive as a smear of smoke . . . dangerous as a striking panther . . ." (Det No. 47, Jan '41), and he is a "winged figure of vengeance" (Det No. 30, Aug '39) whose "unceasing vigil keeps nocturnal crime at bay" (BM No. 30/2, Aug/Sep '45: "While the City Sleeps!").

Evildoers know him as the "eyes of night" (Det No. 52, Jun '41: "The Secret of the Jade Box"; and others) – as a "weird figure" (Det No. 36, Feb '40) who hovers menacingly over the underworld "like an avenging black cloud" (BM No. 1/2, Spr '40).

And in addition the texts contain these descriptions:

Batman No. 4/4, Winter 1941:

> Supersleuth, arch-avenger of crime, foe of the underworld . . . this is the **Batman!**. . . . A dark-mantled fighter who seems to dwell in night itself and whose fame as a scourge of evil has become almost legendary.

Detective Comics No. 50, April 1941: "The Case of the Three Devils!":

> To many people, the **Batman** is a being of mystery, an eerie power. Yet, he is a man – a man who has developed his brain and his muscular frame to the highest degree. A living being of the darkness, he comes and goes unseen. His aim in life – the blotting out of all crime!

World's Finest Comics No. 2, Summer 1941: "The Man Who Couldn't Remember!":

> In great cities all over the world . . . from the flourishing capitals of the Western world to the arid deserts of the Far East, one name has become a symbol of justice . . . one name has struck fear into the hearts of men of crime----that is the name of the **Batman!** Master of darkness . . . foe of all evil, the **Batman,** with his young aide, **Robin** the Boy Wonder, has waged unceasing war against the denizens of the underworld and delivered a mortal blow to organized crime.

Detective Comics No. 190, December 1952: "How to Be the Batman!":

> Most dreaded of all crookdom's foes is the ***Batman!*** His brilliant genius in detective deduction, his marvelous acrobatic agility and skill, his limitless knowledge of crimesters' tricks, have made him and ***Robin*** the terror of the underworld!

Detective Comics No. 27, May 1939: "The Case of the Chemical Syndicate":

> The **'BAT-MAN,'** a mysterious and adventurous figure fighting for righteousness and apprehending the wrong doer, in his lone battle against the evil forces of society . . . his identity remains unknown.

Detective Comics No. 29, July 1939: "The Batman Meets Doctor Death":

> The **BAT MAN,** eery [sic] figure of the night, has become a legendary figure in the life of the teeming metropolis, righting wrongs and bringing justice where it has never been before. . . .

Friend and foe alike have paid tribute to his genius, and the texts have hailed him as "the greatest detective in the world" (Det No. 217, Mar '55: "The Mental Giant of Gotham City!"), as "a popular hero acclaimed by all right-thinking citizens" (Det No. 330, Aug '64: "The Fallen Idol of Gotham City!"), and as a dedicated warrior for justice whose life has been a "constant battle against crime and evil!" (Det No. 40, Jun '40).

POLICE COMMISSIONER GORDON once recalled his early appraisal of Batman as "the most gifted detective I had ever known" (WF No. 65, Jul/Aug '53: "The Five Different Batmen!"), and the Martian lawman ROH KAR has described Batman as "the greatest lawman of the universe!" (BM No. 78/1, Aug/Sep '53: "The Manhunter from Mars!").

"It's amazing," exclaims gangster "KNUCKLES" CONGER in February–March 1943, "how one man and a boy can terrorize the whole underworld!" (BM No. 15/2: "The Boy Who Wanted to Be Robin!").

Indeed, "no other man has ever rivaled **Batman** as champion of the law, nor matched his superb acrobatic skill, his scientific keenness, his mastery of disguise and detective skill!" (Det No. 233, Jul '56: "The Batwoman").

"In every field of endeavor there is a person whose name leads all the rest. In criminology, that distinction belongs to ***Batman***--the '***world's greatest*** detective'!" (Det No. 344, Oct '65: "The Crime-Boss Who Was Always One Step Ahead of Batman!").

The texts contain more than twenty alternate names for Batman, including the Ace of Detectives, the Black Knight, the Caped Champion, the Caped Crime-Buster, the Caped Crime-Fighter, the Caped Crusader, the Cloaked Crime-Fighter, the Cloaked Crusader, the Cowled Crusader, the Crime Crusader, the Dark Knight, the Darknight Detective, the Dynamic Detective, the Gotham City Gladiator, the Gotham City Sleuth, the Gotham Crusader, the Gotham Gladiator, the Gotham Goliath, the Mantled Manhunter, the Masked Manhunter, and the Mighty Manhunter.

In addition, the texts contain a similar number of alternate names for the crime-fighting team of Batman and Robin, including the Acrobatic Aces, the Caped Crime-Busters, the Caped Crime-Fighters, the Caped Crusaders, the Caped Manhunters, the Crime Crusaders, the Daring Duo, the Dynamic Detectives, the Dynamic Duo, the Fistic Furies, the Gotham Gangbusters, the Masked Manhunters, the Master Swordsmen of Justice, the Powerhouse Pair, the Sentinels of Justice, the Terrific Twosome, the Twin Defenders of Justice, and the Twin Terrors.

A. ORIGIN
1. The Original Account
2. Addenda and Revisions

B. THE SECRET IDENTITY
C. THE CRIME-FIGHTING COSTUME
  1. The Basic Costume and Accessories
  2. The Emergency and Special-Purpose Costumes
  3. The Utility Belt
D. THE BATCAVE
E. THE EXTRAORDINARY ABILITIES AND THE FAMOUS CRIME-FIGHTING EQUIPMENT
  1. The Abilities
  2. The Equipment
    a. *The Batmobile*
    b. *The Batplane and Other Aircraft*
      i. THE BATPLANE
      ii. THE OTHER AIRCRAFT
    c. The Bat-Boat and Other Seacraft
    d. The Bat-Rope, Batarang, and Other Equipment
      i. THE BAT-ROPE
      ii. THE BATARANG
      iii. THE OTHER EQUIPMENT
    e. The Bat-Signal
F. THE BATMAN COUNTERPARTS
G. THE MAN HIMSELF (as Bruce Wayne)
H. THE MAN HIMSELF (as Batman)
I. THE RELATIONSHIP WITH ROBIN
J. THE WOMEN OF THE CHRONICLES
  1. The Relationship with Julie Madison
  2. The Relationship with Linda Page
  3. The Relationship with Vicki Vale
  4. The Relationship with (the) Batwoman
  5. The Relationship with the Catwoman
K. THE RELATIONSHIP WITH THE LAW ENFORCEMENT ESTABLISHMENT
L. THE TEXTS
  1. Locales
  2. Developments
    a. *The Early Adventures*
    b. *The Wartime Adventures*
    c. *The Postwar Adventures*
    d. *The Later Adventures*

A. Origin. *1. The Original Account.* It was dusk in the city, and its skyscrapers glowed orange in the setting sun. The year was 1924 – or, to quote the text precisely, it was "some fifteen years" prior to November 1939.

THOMAS WAYNE and his wife (*see* WAYNE, MARTHA) and their young son Bruce were "walking home from a movie" when suddenly a gun-wielding hoodlum leaped from the shadows and blocked their path.

"W-What is this?" stammered Wayne.

"A stickup, buddy!" replied the gunman, reaching out to grab the necklace around Martha Wayne's neck. "I'll take that necklace you're wearin' lady!"

With a kind of instinctive, reckless bravery, Thomas Wayne stepped between his wife and the advancing gunman. "Leave her alone you . . ." he demanded.

"You asked for it!" snarled the gunman. And then he fired – a single shot – and Thomas Wayne slumped dead to the sidewalk.

"Thomas!" shrieked Martha Wayne, cradling her fallen husband in her arms. "You've killed him! *Help!* Police . . . *help!*"

"This'll shut you up!" barked the gunman. He fired again, and now Martha Wayne fell to the pavement, mortally wounded, as the Waynes' nameless assassin slipped silently away into the twilight shadows.

Now the street was silent, save for the quiet sobbing of Bruce Wayne, his eyes "wide with terror and shock" as he surveyed "the horrible scene" that lay "spread before him." For there, sprawled in the sickly yellow incandescence of a street light, both his parents lay dead.

Tears welled up in Bruce's eyes and streamed unimpeded across his cheeks. "Father . . ." he whispered, ". . . Mother!"

In that moment of horror, Bruce Wayne realized that what he had just seen had changed the face of his entire life. And so, days later, "a curious and strange scene" took place, as the orphaned youngster knelt by his bedside and made a solemn promise to himself. ". . . I swear by the spirits of my parents," he vowed, "to avenge their deaths by spending the rest of my life warring on all criminals."

> As the years pass Bruce Wayne prepares himself for his career. He becomes a master scientist. Trains his body to physical perfection until he is able to perform amazing athletic feats.

Finally, sometime in 1939, after many years of pain and sweat and almost unendurable dedication, Bruce Wayne knew that the time had come to embark on the fulfillment of his boyhood vow.

Late one night, in the drawing room of his lavish home, he sat in front of the fireplace and thought about the future.

"Dad's estate left me wealthy," he thought aloud. "I am ready . . . but first I must have a disguise."

For a moment there was silence as Wayne puffed heavily at his pipe, and then finally, he spoke again.

"Criminals are a superstitious cowardly lot, so my disguise must be able to strike terror into their hearts. I must be a creature of the night, black, terrible . . . a . . . a. . . ."

Suddenly, Wayne's thoughts were interrupted by "a huge bat," which flickered through an open window near Wayne's armchair as if in response to some silent, unconscious summons. As it whirled and fluttered about his head – its silken wings etched sharply against the full moon which silently asserted its wan dominion over the murky night sky outside – Bruce Wayne realized that his grim musings had found their fulfillment.

"A bat!" cried Wayne. "That's it! It's an omen. I shall become a **BAT!**"

And so a new creature of the night was born, a "weird figure of the dark" who cloaked himself in the murky mantle of a giant bat. Wherever there is evil, the blackhearted cower at his name, for he is a terrible "avenger of evil." He is the Batman! (Det No. 33: "The Batman Wars Against the Dirigible of Doom"; *reprinted*

© NPP 1968

© NPP 1968

The Origin of Batman © NPP 1968

in BM No. 1/1, Spr '40: "The Legend of the Batman – Who He Is and How He Came to Be!").

2. Addenda and Revisions. As the years passed, new Batman texts appeared which either supplemented or contradicted the original account of Batman's origin recounted above. Whereas the original asserts, for example, that both Thomas and Martha Wayne died of bullet wounds, later texts have asserted that only Thomas Wayne died from a bullet wound, while Martha Wayne – whose "weak heart could not stand seeing her husband shot down" – died of a heart attack at the scene (Det No. 190, Dec '52: "How to Be the Batman!"; *see also* BM No. 47/3, Jun/Jul '48: "The Origin of Batman!").

In June–July 1948, approximately twenty-four years after the death of his parents, Batman encounters the man who murdered them and grimly sets out to bring him to justice (BM No. 47/3: "The Origin of Batman!"). (*See* CHILL, JOE.)

In September 1956 another text appears which sheds further light on the murder of the Waynes and the origin of Batman. According to this text, Joe Chill, the man who perpetrated the Wayne murder, "only ***pretended*** to be a holdup man" when he waylaid the Waynes in 1924. Actually, it explains, Chill was a "hired killer" employed by LEW MOXON, a convicted bank robber whom Thomas Wayne had once helped send to the penitentiary.

This text also asserts that Bruce Wayne first adopted the guise of a giant bat not merely in symbolic imitation of the bat which had flown through his window, but because the sudden appearance of that bat somehow prodded his "subconscious memory" of an eerie "bat-man" costume his father had once worn to a masquerade ball (Det No. 235: "The First Batman!"). (*See* MOXON, LEW.)

B. The Secret Identity. "If the **Batman** is revealed as Bruce Wayne, his career as a nemesis of crime is finished!" (BM No. 1/5, Spr '40: "The Joker Returns").

Batman's identity is one of the world's most closely guarded secrets, and it is a truism of the chronicles, though the logic occasionally used to support it is never convincing, that "Once it is revealed that Batman is really Bruce Wayne . . . his role as the nation's leading crimefighter is ended for all time!" (Det No. 62, Apr '42: "Laugh, Town, Laugh").

The use of an alternate identity gives Bruce Wayne the advantage of surprise over the criminal element, enables him to "strike terror into their hearts" with his eerie batlike guise (Det No. 33, Nov '39: "The Batman Wars Against the Dirigible of Doom"), and serves to safeguard his friends and intimates against gangland reprisals.

AN ELECTRICAL ENGINEER DISAPPEARS... AN UNUSUAL "FOG" COVERS THE CITY... THE FIRST NAMES ON THE LITTLE BOOK'S LIST ARE ROBBED... AND A DYING MAN UTTERS THE SINISTER NAME OF PROFESSOR HUGO STRANGE... HMM....

Bruce Wayne, 1940 © NPP 1940

Because the secret of Batman's identity is one the underworld would pay any price to obtain, to say nothing of the countless law-abiding individuals who would like to solve the mystery for purely egotistical reasons, the protection of his dual identity remains one of Bruce Wayne's constant preoccupations.

Particularly during the first decade of his career as a crime-fighter, Wayne presents himself to others as a do-nothing playboy, devoid of ambition, too lazy to work, and generally bored with life.

"Everything bores that fellow!" remarks one of Wayne's acquaintances to a companion in August 1940. "If he ever got excited about anything I think they would declare a national holiday!"

"They say he is probably the laziest, most useless chap in our set!" replies the companion (Det No. 42: "The Case of the Prophetic Pictures!").

The advantages of the playboy pose are too obvious to belabor. "I, ***Batman?***" laughs Wayne in May 1950. "Ridiculous! Why, for me to be that fellow ***Batman*** would ruin my whole social schedule!" (Det No. 159: "Bruce Wayne – You Are Batman!").

There, are, however, numerous other devices that Bruce Wayne employs to safeguard his secret. As Batman, for example, he always signs his name with his left hand, while as Bruce Wayne he always signs with his right (BM No. 92/1, Jun '55: "Fan-Mail of Danger!"; and others). In addition, he has seen to it that there are no records anywhere of Batman's fingerprints (BM No. 83/1, Apr '54: "The Duplicate Batman!").

Indeed, the secret is so well protected that when SUPERMAN, who knows the secret, deliberately erases the knowledge from his mind with a "selective amnesia-inducer" and then attempts to solve the mystery on his own as a demonstration of his detecting skills, he is unable to do so. He becomes so piqued at his failure, in fact, that Batman and Robin finally let him "unravel" their secret merely to assure their super-friend's continued goodwill (WF No. 149, May '65: "The Game of Secret Identities!" pts. I–II – no title; "The Super-Detective!").

Fifteen months later, however, when Batman and Robin suffer complete losses of memory as the result of having been bombarded by the sonic-wave emissions of an "ultra-sonic beam projector," they manage to unravel the secret of their own dual identities, correctly deducing from a series of telltale facts – that Batman must be wealthy, have an aviator's license, and play polo – that millionaire Bruce Wayne is secretly Batman (Det No. 234, Aug '56: "Batman and Robin's Greatest Mystery"). (*See* CAIRD, JAY.)

Several individuals close to Batman have suspected his secret, or at least sought to discover it, but Batman has skillfully led them astray with ruses to prevent them from confirming their suspicions.

POLICE COMMISSIONER GORDON has expressed the view that Batman must be a member of his "inner circle of friends," but his suspicions have never actually focused on his close friend Bruce Wayne. And when Gordon makes an aggressive attempt to unravel the secret, Batman adroitly outwits him (BM No. 71/2, Jun/Jul '52: "Commissioner Gordon's Greatest Case!").

VICKI VALE has labored unceasingly to verify her strong suspicion that Bruce Wayne is Batman, but Batman has always managed to convince her that her suspicions were groundless, or at the very least not convincingly proven (BM No. 49/2, Oct/Nov '48: "The Scoop of the Century!"; and others).

Kathy Kane, the wealthy heiress and onetime circus daredevil who is secretly BATWOMAN, has never actually proven that Bruce Wayne is Batman, but she has long suspected it (Det No. 292, Jun '61: "The Colossus of Gotham City!").

Interestingly, two of Batman's most infamous foes have had perfect opportunities to unmask Batman, but have declined to do so on the ground that it would end Batman's career, thereby depriving them of the battles of wits they enjoy so much.

"Ha! Ha! No!" cries the JOKER in April 1942, as he declines the first of a series of opportunities to unmask a captive Batman. "It's too simple--unworthy of my intelligence! And I like these battles of wits! The hunt . . . the chase! . . . that's the breath of life to me!" (Det No. 62: "Laugh, Town, Laugh").

In a similar situation, KILLER MOTH adopts an identical attitude in February–March 1951. "I could remove your mask and reveal your identity right now," he muses aloud, ". . . but that would end our little game! And frankly, I enjoy torturing you this way! Ha! Ha!" (BM No. 63/3: "The Origin of Killer Moth!").

A number of trusted individuals are actually privy to the secret. A text for June 1940 describes Dick Grayson, the boy who is secretly ROBIN, as the "only living person" who knows that Bruce Wayne is Batman (Det No. 40), but ALFRED stumbles upon the secret accidentally in April–May 1943 (BM No. 16/4: "Here Comes Alfred!") and Superman and Batman learn each other's secret identities by accident in May–June 1952 (S No. 76/1: "The Mightiest Team in the World!").

Batman entrusts JIMMY OLSEN with the secret of his dual identity in September 1964 (WF No. 144: "The 1,001 Tricks of Clayface and Brainiac!" pts. I–II – no title; "The Helpless Partners!").

Bruce Wayne's AUNT AGATHA *should* know that Bruce Wayne is Batman, because she herself removes Batman's cowl and sees his face in February 1955. But Aunt Agatha cannot even *imagine* her nephew as Batman and assumes instead that Wayne has merely been masquerading as the famous lawman.

"In my aunt's eyes," explains Wayne to Dick Grayson privately soon afterward, "I've never grown up! To her, I'm still her young nephew, a boy!" (BM No. 89/3: "Bruce Wayne's Aunt Agatha!").

Other individuals or groups of individuals have learned Batman's secret, but they have invariably been inhabitants of other planets or time periods not likely to communicate their knowledge to contemporaries of Batman and Robin.

The inhabitants of MARS, including the scientist SAX GOLA, know that Bruce Wayne is Batman as the result of having "long observed Earth with X-ray telescopes . . ." (BM No. 41/3, Jun/Jul '47: "Batman, Interplanetary Policeman!").

The inhabitants of Venus know that Bruce Wayne is Batman as the result of having observed his crime-fighting exploits through their "TV space scanners" (Det No. 260, Oct '58: "The Mystery of the Space Olympics").

Batman reveals his identity to the inhabitants of the extradimensional planet PLAXIUS during a visit there in August 1959 (BM No. 125/3: "King Batman the First!").

Batman voluntarily reveals his secret identity to the JESTER and his other friends in ancient Rome during a time-journey that he makes there in August–September 1944. Since history shows that his identity was never betrayed as the result of knowledge from the past, explains Batman, this revelation involves no actual risk (BM No. 24/1: "It Happened in Rome").

All of the inhabitants of the twenty-sixth century A.D., including the villain KARKO, know that Bruce Wayne is Batman (Det No. 257, Jul '58: "Batman's Invincible Foe!").

Rak, a villain from the twenty-first century A.D., learns the secret identities of Batman and Robin during a time-journey to the twentieth century in August 1963, but he is apprehended and returned to the future before he has a chance to betray what he has learned to anyone in the twentieth century (WF No. 135: "The Menace of the Future Man!"). (*See* DURR, JON.)

More than a score of Batman's contemporaries have discovered or correctly deduced his identity, but they have all either taken their knowledge to the grave with them or developed amensia before they could betray the secret.

HARVEY HARRIS, the renowned police detective who was the crime-fighting idol of the teen-aged Bruce Wayne, correctly deduced that Bruce Wayne is Batman,

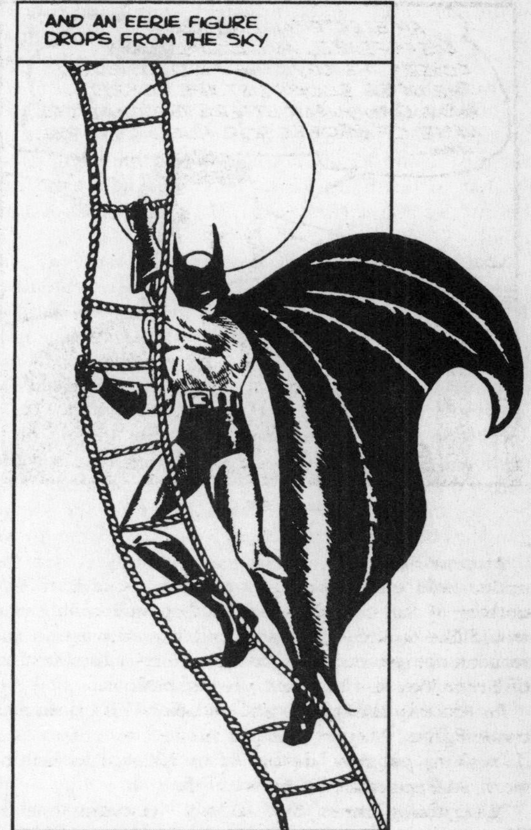

Batman descends the batplane's rope ladder, 1939
© NPP 1939

but reveals his deductions to Wayne only in a letter he arranges to have sent to Wayne after his death (Det No. 226, Dec '55: "When Batman Was Robin!").

QUEENIE, one of the Joker's accomplices, guesses Batman's secret after observing identical shaving nicks on the faces of Bruce Wayne and Batman, but she is shot to death soon afterward, in Spring 1941 (BM No. 5/1: "The Riddle of the Missing Card!").

Reporter SCOOP SCANLON deduces that Bruce Wayne is Batman in Summer 1942, but actor Mark Loring, who has also learned that Wayne is Batman but who has been shot and mortally wounded by gangsters, agrees to impersonate Batman long enough to persuade Scanlon that he has made a mistake (WF No. 6: "The Secret of Bruce Wayne!").

The evil mind reader CARLO learns Batman's identity by means of his paranormal powers, but he is shot and killed by one of his intended robbery victims before he can pass on the secret (Det No. 70, Dec '42: "The Man Who Could Read Minds!").

Dean of detectives DANA DRYE correctly deduced Batman's identity and recorded the fact in his personal diary. He voluntarily withheld the secret from the world, however, and ultimately committed suicide upon learning he was dying from "an incurable malady" (BM No. 14/1, Dec/Jan '42–'43: "The Case Batman Failed to Solve!!!").

Batman deliberately reveals his identity to JOE CHILL in June–July 1948 in an effort to shock him into confessing the murder of Thomas and Martha Wayne. Chill is shot to death by fellow hoodlums before he can betray the secret (BM No. 47/3: "The Origin of Batman!").

WOLF BRANDO, "Public Enemy Number One," invades the home of Bruce Wayne in August–September 1948 and stumbles upon the secret identities of Batman and Robin, but he perishes soon afterward when he loses his footing and topples into a whirlpool in the underground river that runs through the batcave (BM No. 48/2: "The 1,000 Secrets of the Batcave!").

Batman is forced to reveal his secret identity to a millionaire big-game hunter named Rogers in order to defeat mobster ACE RADKO in August–September 1950, but Rogers dies of a heart attack soon after the Radko gang has been apprehended (WF No. 47: "Crime Above the Clouds!").

KILLER MOTH stumbles upon the secret of Batman's identity in July 1951, but he is subsequently shot and critically wounded by a disguntled hoodlum and the surgical operation necessary for saving his life includes the removal of that part of his brain housing his memory of all recent events (Det No. 173: "Batman's Double!").

Ex-convict HARRY LARSON, a Bruce Wayne look-alike, accidentally learns the secret of Batman's identity in April 1954, but he is subsequently electrocuted while rescuing Batman from a gangland deathtrap (BM No. 83/1: "The Duplicate Batman!").

BARNEY BARROWS, a "weak-minded" janitor at Gotham City police headquarters, correctly deduces that Bruce Wayne is Batman after an "accidental burst of freak radiation" transforms him into "the world's greatest mental giant." Ultimately, however, the effects of Barrows's mind-expanding accident wear off and Barrows loses all recollection of Batman's identity (Det No. 217, Mar '55: "The Mental Giant of Gotham City!").

Bruce Wayne's former college classmate JOE DANTON discovers Batman's secret in December 1955, but he dies of a heart ailment soon afterward, taking Batman's secret with him (BM No. 96/2: "Batman's College Days").

Amateur Batman scholar FRANK DAVIS has successfully deduced that Bruce Wayne is Batman, but his knowledge dies with him when he is murdered by emcee JOE HARMON while appearing as a contestant on a television quiz show (BM No. 108/1, Jun '57: "The Big Batman Quiz").

When Bruce Wayne's great-uncle SILAS WAYNE is on his deathbed in December 1958, Wayne confides to him that he is secretly Batman so that the old gentleman will be able to die happily, knowing that his nephew is carrying on the Wayne family traditions of courage and valor (BM No. 120/2: "The Failure of Bruce Wayne").

ALEC WYRE, an "electronics genius who turned criminal," cunningly managed to locate the batcave and therefore presumably learned the identities of Batman and Robin, but he perished there after accidentally dropping his flashlight and slamming his head into a stalactite (BM No. 121/1, Feb '59: "The Body in the Bat-Cave").

Gurney, a criminal who happens to be on the extradimensional planet PLAXIUS at the same time as Batman and Robin, learns that Bruce Wayne is Batman when Batman reveals his secret to the Plaxians in August 1959. The journey back through the "time-warp" to Earth, however, causes Batman, Robin, and Gurney to forget their visit to Plaxius entirely, and Gurney retains no recollection whatever of the secret he learned there (BM No. 125/3: "King Batman the First!").

TOD ALLEN, a friend of Bruce Wayne and Dick Grayson with a fondness for practical jokes, has guessed that his friends are secretly Batman and Robin on the basis of evidence that is largely circumstantial. Allen causes them some uncomfortable moments by sending them a series of anonymous letters teasing them about his "knowledge" of their secret identities, but he dies in a plane crash soon afterward without passing his hunches on to anyone else (BM No. 134/2, Sep '60: "Batman's Secret Enemy").

DENNY KALE and Shorty Biggs capture Batman and Robin and unmask them as Bruce Wayne and Dick Grayson, but they lose all recollection of this and other recent events as the result of a freak accident in an alchemist's laboratory during a time-journey they make to fifteenth-century Florence (WF No. 132, Mar '63: "Batman and Robin, Medieval Bandits!").

Clayface (*see* CLAYFACE [MATT HAGEN]) learns Batman's secret identity in March 1964, but a complex series of circumstances robs him of his knowledge before he can carry out his intention to reveal it to the world (WF No. 140: "The Clayface Superman!").

Joe Meach learns Batman and Robin's secret identities when a freak accident transforms him into the COMPOSITE SUPERMAN, but Meach's powers ultimately vanish, leaving him with no recollection whatever of the secret he learned (WF No. 142, Jun '64: "The Origin of the Composite Superman!" pts. I–II – "The Composite Superman!"; "The Battle Between Titans!").

Throughout the years, numerous individuals have attempted to learn the secret of Batman's identity, or to confirm their suspicions that Bruce Wayne is Batman, only to be outwitted by the Dynamic Duo, through the use of elaborate ruses, often with the aid of Alfred.

The gambler STACY concludes that Bruce Wayne is Batman in Winter 1941, but Batman and Robin manage to deceive him into believing he has made a mistake (BM No. 4/4).

Nurse Noreen O'Day of Gotham Hospital, where Bruce Wayne is operated on for a knee injury in October–November 1946, attempts to verify her suspicion that Bruce Wayne is Batman by comparing separate "heart graphs" of Bruce Wayne and Batman. Batman outwits O'Day, however, by recalling his life's most dangerous moments while his graph is being

taken, thus speeding up his heartbeat sufficiently to make it appear different from that of Bruce Wayne (BM No. 37/1: "Calling Dr. Batman!").

Batman and Robin deliberately unmask before an unnamed "egomaniac" in December 1946–January 1947 as a ploy to persuade him that they are merely masquerading as Batman and Robin and not the actual famous crime-fighters (BM No. 38/2: "The Carbon Copy Crimes!"). (*See* ANTAL, PIERRE.)

Police officer Dan Grady, having concluded on the basis of a careful study of Batman's past cases that Bruce Wayne is Batman, confides his conclusion to mobster DUDS NEERY when the two men are marooned on a lifeboat together, apparently destined to perish. Both Grady and Neery are rescued by a passing ship, however, and return to the city, but Batman manages to trick both men into believing that they have erred in identifying Bruce Wayne with Batman (BM No. 42/2, Aug/Sep '47: "Blind Man's Bluff!").

Batman is forcibly unmasked before a host of underworld notables in November–December 1948, but since he has taken the precaution of wearing two face-masks beneath his cowl, the outer one a mask of Bruce Wayne's face and the inner one a mask of an anonymous face unknown to the criminals, the villains assume that the Wayne face, which they remove, is only a disguise and that the face they see beneath it, which they cannot recognize, is the face of the real Batman (WF No. 37: "The Underworld Museum of Crime!"). (*See* JONES, T-GUN.)

"Famed detective story writer" J. J. JASON, determined to solve "the biggest mystery of the day, purely for [his] own amusement," complies an impressive mass of evidence linking Bruce Wayne to Batman, but Wayne convinces Jason that he and Batman are two separate men by appearing in the writer's presence in the company of a Batman stand-in, a blind, deaf man whom Wayne has hired just for this occasion (WF No. 39, Mar/Apr '49: "The Conquest of Batman's Identity!").

The THINKER attempts to solve the secret of Batman's identity in April–May 1949 with the aid of an electronic "thinking machine," but Batman and Robin thwart the attempt by means of an elaborate ruse involving ALFRED (BM No. 52/1: "The Man with the Automatic Brain!").

The LONGSHOREMAN KID and his henchmen capture and unmask Batman in October–November 1949 during a period when Bruce Wayne is serving Gotham City as a rookie policeman. Batman succeeds, however, in duping his captors into believing that he is only patrolman Bruce Wayne masquerading as Batman (BM No. 55/2: "Bruce Wayne, Rookie Policeman!").

Crime czar T. WORTHINGTON CHUBB becomes convinced that Bruce Wayne is Batman in May 1950, but Batman and Robin employ a series of ingenious ruses to persuade the villain that he has made a mistake (Det No. 159: "Bruce Wayne – You Are Batman!").

"SHARK" MARLIN becomes suspicious that Bruce Wayne is Batman in August–September 1950, but the Dynamic Duo manage to trick the gang boss into believing his suspicions unfounded (BM No. 60/2: "The Counterfeit Batman!").

The PENGUIN forces Batman to unmask in October–November 1950, but Batman has managed to smear some makeup on his face, thereby convincing the Penguin that the Bruce Wayne face beneath his cowl is only a clever disguise (BM No. 61/2: "The Mystery of the Winged People!").

KILLER MOTH becomes suspicious that Bruce Wayne is Batman in April–May 1951, but Batman and Robin employ lifelike dummies of Bruce Wayne and Dick Grayson to dupe the villain into believing that his suspicions are unfounded (BM No. 64/3: "The Return of Killer Moth!").

Gangster LONGHORN BELL discovers the existence of a large cave beneath the Wayne mansion in December 1951–January 1952 and concludes that the cave must be the batcave and Bruce Wayne, Batman. Bell and his henchmen even tunnel into the cave to verify their suspicions, but Batman and Robin manage to fool the criminals into believing that the batcave is merely a set being used in the filming of a Batman movie (BM No. 68/1: "The Atom Cave Raiders!").

During this same period, SLIPPERY WILLIE WILLIS uses a lie detector on Alfred in an effort to confirm his suspicion that Bruce Wayne is Batman, but Batman outwits Willis through a ruse, thereby persuading the criminal his suspicion was unfounded (BM No. 68/2, Dec/Jan '51–'52: "The Secret Life of Batman's Butler!").

After a year of pondering the secret of Batman's identity, confidence man DEUCE CHALMERS has concluded that Bruce Wayne is Batman and concocted an elaborate scheme for cashing in on his knowledge. Batman outwits Chalmers, however, by making up a selected stand-in to impersonate Bruce Wayne while he himself plays the role of Batman. He hypnotizes the stand-in to assure that the stand-in will have no recollection whatever of his Bruce Wayne impersonation once the masquerade is over (Det No. 179, Jan '52: "Mayor Bruce Wayne!").

Batman's secret identity is seriously endangered in July 1952 when he loses his famed utility belt, containing a small metal disc inscribed with the secret of his dual identity. The lost utility belt passes through many hands, but Batman manages to recover it before his identity can be discovered (Det No. 185: "The Secret of Batman's Utility Belt!").

After fifteen years of probing the secret of Batman's identity, confidence man SLIM WHEELER has concluded that Bruce Wayne is Batman, and in September–October 1952 he sells his information to black marketeer GLENN FARR for $100,000. Farr attempts to confirm Wheeler's conclusion by comparing Batman's signature with that of Bruce Wayne, but the signatures are very different because Bruce Wayne always signs his name with his right hand, while Batman signs with his left (WF No. 60: "The Richest Crook in the World!").

Bank robber SAMMY SABRE almost learns Batman's secret identity in April 1953 when he stumbles upon a letter in Bruce Wayne's safety deposit box intended to reveal Batman's identity to Police Commissioner Gordon in the event of Batman's death. Sabre reads the contents of the letter but does not learn its vital secret since, by prearrangement with Police Commissioner Gordon, the important part of the letter is written in invisible ink on the outside of the envelope (Det No. 194: "The Stolen Bank!").

Verne Lever, lawyer for gangster BIG JACK BAKER, attempts to learn the secret of Batman's identity in order to blackmail Batman into refraining from testifying against his client. He ultimately narrows his list of Batman suspects down to five wealthy socialites including Bruce Wayne, but Batman nevertheless manages to thwart Lever's efforts to learn his identity (Det No. 199, Sep '53: "The Invisible Batman!").

After the villainous MR. CAMERA has allegedly obtained photographs of Bruce Wayne and Dick Grayson changing into their Batman and Robin costumes, the Dynamic Duo set in motion an elaborate ruse designed to convince the public that Bruce Wayne could not possibly be Batman in order to dampen the impact of the underworld film when it is finally released. The ruse, however, ultimately proves to have been unnecessary, since Mr. Camera's film was so badly underexposed that it represents no threat whatever to the Dynamic Duo's secret identities (BM No. 81/2, Feb '54: "The Boy Wonder Confesses!").

HARRY SHEPHERD devises an elaborate scheme to ruin Batman's career by tricking him into revealing his secret identity, but Batman successfully thwarts the scheme and Shepherd and his henchmen are apprehended (BM No. 84/3 Jun '54: "Ten Nights of Fear!").

In August 1954, after a freak laboratory accident has transferred the personality of the JOKER into the body of Batman, and vice versa, the Joker offers to reveal the face that is temporarily his – Batman's face – to the underworld for a fee of $1,000,000, but Batman apprehends the Joker and has their bodies and personalities restored to their proper places before the Joker can make good his offer (BM No. 85/1: "Batman – Clown of Crime!").

MIRROR-MAN uses an ingenious "two-way electronic mirror that X-rays anything covered by cloth" to peer beneath Batman's cowl and learn his identity in November 1954, but Batman tricks the villain's henchmen into believing that their boss has made a mistake. When Mirror-Man attempts to use his special mirror on Batman a second time to show the world what he has learned, Batman uses a special device concealed beneath his cowl to distort his features so that they are completely unrecognizable (Det No. 213: "The Mysterious Mirror-Man!").

VINCENT CRAIL, a "former handwriting expert" turned forger, attempts to uncover Batman's secret identity in June 1955 by comparing Batman's signature with those of Bruce Wayne and three other suspects, but Crail's efforts end in failure due to the fact that Batman always signs his name with his left hand, while Bruce Wayne always signs with his right (BM No. 92/1: "Fan-Mail of Danger!").

Underworld photographer "LENS" VORDEN attempts to penetrate the secret of Batman's identity by taking numerous photographs of Batman as he demonstrates disguises for students at the Kean School of Makeup so that, by creating a photo-composite of Batman's features, he can construct a photographic likeness of Batman's real face. The scheme is thwarted, however, by school director BARRETT KEAN, who, realizing the threat to Batman's identity posed by Vorden's photographs, counters it by impersonating Batman at one of the lectures, thus ruining Vorden's potential composite by contaminating it with some of Kean's own features (Det No. 227, Jan '56: "The 50 Faces of Batman!").

In April 1956 the villainous magician PARDU concocts an elaborate scheme to trick Batman into believing that he has learned his identity so that he can blackmail Batman by threatening to reveal it. Batman deduces, however, that Pardu has not really learned his identity and sets a trap for Pardu that enables the police to apprehend him (BM No. 99/3: "The Phantom of the Bat-Cave!").

Ex-convict and former scientist WALLACE WALEY devises a scheme for tricking Batman into revealing his secret identity, but Batman sees through Waley's scheme and apprehends him (Det No. 236, Oct '56: "The New-Model Batman!").

Racketeer GUY GRANEY attempts to force Batman to reveal his secret identity with the aid of an ingenious "mind ray" invention, but Batman, Robin, and Alfred successfully thwart the scheme in March 1957 (BM No. 106/3: "The Puppet Batman!").

During a visit to Gotham City in October 1957, private detective BRUCE N. WAYNE, a cousin of Bruce Wayne, becomes suspicious that Bruce Wayne and Dick Grayson are secretly Batman and Robin, but the Dynamic Duo use an elaborate ruse to convince the renowned detective that his suspicions are unfounded (BM No. 111/2: "The Other Bruce Wayne").

In August 1963 MIRROR-MAN breaks out of prison and sets out once again to convince the world that Bruce Wayne is Batman. This time, however, Batman arranges for Alfred to play the role of Batman, while he appears as Bruce Wayne, in order to convince the villain that he has made a mistake (BM No. 157/2: "The Hunt for Batman's Secret Identity!").

C. The Crime-Fighting Costume. "What is it that terrorizes crooks? What do they dread most? Yes, it is the flashing figure of ***Batman,*** clad in the shadowy colors of blue and gray" (Det No. 165, Nov '50: "The Strange Costumes of Batman!").

1. The Basic Costume and Accessories. As the young Bruce Wayne prepared to embark on his lifelong crusade against crime, he knew that he would need a disguise, one that would conceal his true identity and "strike terror" into the hearts of the underworld.

When suddenly a huge bat flickered through his open window, Wayne saw it as an omen. It conjured up an image of the "weird figure of the dark" he wished to become (Det No. 33, Nov '39: "The Batman Wars Against the Dirigible of Doom"), and, although he did

Batman clad in Dr. Thomas Wayne's "bat-man" costume, 1956 © NPP 1956

not realize it until seventeen years later, it prodded his "subconscious memory" of an eerie "bat-man" costume his father had once worn to a masquerade ball (Det No. 235, Sep '56: "The First Batman!").

And so, for his war against evil, Bruce Wayne cloaked himself in the costume of a giant bat. The basic costume is steel gray, with blue trunks, boots, and gauntlet-style gloves; a long, flowing blue cape with a deeply scalloped edge; and a bat-eared blue cowl that covers Wayne's entire head except for the lower half of his face. Around his waist he wears a yellow utility belt (*see* section C 3, the utility belt), and there is a stylized black bat-emblem emblazoned on his chest.

Batman's chroniclers have portrayed him in a variety of artistic styles, yet in the nearly four decades since his textual debut the basic details of his costume have gone substantially unchanged.

His cape, for example, stiff and angular in his earliest adventures (e.g., Det No. 27, May '39: "The Case of the Chemical Syndicate"), soon becomes soft and flowing, billowing out behind him when he leaps into action, but otherwise hanging more or less limply against his back. The cape retains these latter qualities today, except that in recent years an effort has been made to depict the cape more dramatically, so that it now tends to swirl about Batman even when he merely walks or gestures (e.g., BM No. 232, Jun '71: "Daughter of the Demon"), endowing him with an air of mystery lacking since the mid-1940s.

According to Detective Comics No. 150, Batman's cape is waterproof (Aug '49: "The Ghost of Gotham City!"), and according to World's Finest Comics No. 132 it contains a hidden pocket in its inner lining (Mar '63: "Batman and Robin, Medieval Bandits!"). Detective Comics No. 348 asserts that the cape can function as a serviceable parachute (Feb '66: "The Birdmaster of Bedlam!").

Batman's cowl—portrayed in some texts as permanently attached to his cape (e.g., BM No. 101/3, Aug '56: "The Great Bat-Cape Hunt!") and in others as a separate component of his costume entirely (e.g., BM No. 114/3, Mar '58: "The Bat-Ape!")—has also undergone a minor evolution, chiefly in terms of the length of the "ears." Long, distinctive, and highly pronounced in Batman's early adventures (e.g., Det No. 29, Jul '39: "The Batman Meets Doctor Death"), they have become noticeably deemphasized by the early 1940s (e.g., BM No. 5/3, Spr '41: "The Case of the Honest Crook") and even smaller by the mid-1950s (e.g., Det No. 235, Sep '56: "The First Batman!"). Only with the advent of the 1970s have they been restored to a size and prominence (e.g., BM No. 237, Dec '71: "Night of the Reaper!") reminiscent of the 1940s.

Batman's gloves, wrist-length and pale purple in color in his initial textual appearance (Det No. 27, May '39: "The Case of the Chemical Syndicate"), have become blue by August 1939 (Det No. 30), have become transformed into full-fledged gauntlets by September 1939 (Det No. 31), and by February 1940 have acquired the three fins on each forearm (Det No. 36) which, with some minor modification, they possess to this day. In a few early texts, Batman's gauntlets are equipped with short claws which protrude from the fingers (Det No. 33, Nov '39: "The Batman Wars Against the Dirigible of Doom"; Det No. 36, Feb '40), but this feature is extremely short-lived.

The stylized black bat-emblem on Batman's chest, small and somewhat crudely portrayed in Batman's earliest adventures (e.g., Det No. 32, Oct '39), soon becomes larger and more distinct. From May 1964 (Det No. 327: "The Mystery of the Menacing Mask!") onward, it has a more highly stylized design and is inscribed in a yellow oval on Batman's chest.

A feature of Batman's costume that has long since been discarded is the bulletproof vest which he wore, frequently if not always, during the first year and a half of his crime-fighting career. First mentioned in connection with Batman's struggle against the SCARLET HORDE in November 1939 (Det No. 33: "The Batman Wars Against the Dirigible of Doom"), the bulletproof vest is worn by Batman on at least two subsequent occasions (BM No. 1/2, Spr '40; BM No. 2/2, Sum '40) prior to Winter 1941, which is the very last time it appears in the chronicles (BM No. 4/3). Indeed, only a few months later, in Spring 1941, Batman No. 5/3 states unequivocally, if somewhat inaccurately, that "Long ago, the Batman . . . permanently discarded his bulletproof vest because it hampered freedom of movement" ("The Case of the Honest Crook").

Batman also carried a gun during the early days of his career, although he soon abandoned the practice, presumably for ethical reasons (*see* section H, the man himself [as Batman]). The cover of Detective Comics No. 33 shows Batman armed with an automatic pistol which he also carries throughout that issue's adventure (Nov '39: "The Batman Wars Against the Dirigible of Doom").

The page-one introductory illustration, known as the "splash panel," of Detective Comics No. 35 portrays Batman wielding a smoking automatic, but Batman neither carries nor uses a gun in that issue's adventure (Jan '40). In Winter 1941, although Batman deliberately wounds a gangster with a pistol dropped by his cohorts, the text carefully notes that "the Batman never carries or kills with a gun!" (BM No. 4/4).

Other items which may conceivably be regarded as costume accessories are the steel cutting blade built into Batman's boot, which appears in Detective Comics No. 33 (Nov '39: "The Batman Wars Against the Dirigible of Doom"), and the "apparatus for a small wireless" that Batman carries inside his boot heel in Detective Comics No. 54 (Aug '41: "Hook Morgan and His Harbor Pirates") as well as in a number of other early adventures (e.g., Det No. 95, Jan '45).

During the early days of his Batman career, Bruce Wayne stores his Batman costume inside a "small chest," like a sea chest, at the Wayne mansion when it is not in use (Det No. 29, Jul '39: "The Batman Meets Doctor Death"). A text for September 1939 shows Wayne's cape and cowl draped over a bedside valet (Det No. 31), but as late as November 1939 Wayne is still storing his costume inside the small chest (Det No. 33: "The Batman Wars Against the Dirigible of Doom").

Bruce Wayne, 1939 © NPP 1939

By May 1941 Bruce Wayne and Dick Grayson have taken to carrying their Batman and ROBIN costumes along with them in the trunk of their car even when they go out for a leisurely drive (Det No. 51: "The Case of the Mystery Carnival"), and by September 1942 they have adopted the habit of wearing their costumes underneath their street clothes (Det No. 67: "Crime's Early Bird!").

By June–July 1950, Batman has begun the practice of always wearing two uniforms, one beneath the other, a habit that proves useful when Batman needs to dress a suit of armor in one costume to use as a decoy (BM No. 59/2: "The Forbidden Cellar!").

As a precautionary measure, Batman always carries a spare costume in the batmobile (BM No. 49/1, Oct/Nov '48: "The Prison Doctor!"). Indeed, by May 1963 he has begun carrying several Batman costumes in the batmobile for use in special emergencies (BM No. 155/2: "The Return of the Penguin!").

2. The Emergency and Special-Purpose Costumes. Stored on a long pipe rack in the "costume room" of the batcave, along with Batman's supply of regular costumes, are the numerous Batman costumes designed for use in special emergencies. Their components — cape, cowl, boots, utility belt, and gauntlet-style gloves — are all similar to those of Batman's basic costume, but each possesses some unique capability that sets it apart from the others.

During an Arctic adventure in Fall 1942, Batman and Robin wear special costumes "interwoven with fine wires" connected to "small dynamos" in their utility belts designed to generate "radiating heat" to protect them from the subzero cold. They also employ a set of spare costumes dyed white as camouflage against the Arctic snow (WF No. 7: "The North Pole Crimes!").

Batman and Robin also use their snow costumes against the CATWOMAN in February–March 1947 (BM No. 39/3: "A Christmas Tale!"), and Batman dons his during the hunt for the notorious LECLERC BROTHERS in Canada in August–September 1953 (BM No. 78/3: "Batman of the Mounties!").

In August 1955, during their journey to the top of MOUNT K-4, "the world's most unclimbable peak," Batman and Robin wear special "heat-insulated costumes" (BM No. 93/1: "Journey to the Top of the World!"), but it is not clear whether these are the same as the heatable costumes that they used in Fall 1942.

By February–March 1948 Batman has developed a "compact plastic Batman suit" made out of "the same thin fabric used in the manufacture of the new folding rain coats," described as "so pliable it can be rolled into a ball" (BM No. 45/2: "A Parole for Christmas!").

Batman No. 47/2 describes the new costume as "the latest scientific miracle — a costume made of new plastic material so fine it can be folded into a thin packet" for concealment beneath a strip of flesh-colored bandage taped across Batman's chest (Jun/Jul '48: "The Chain Gang Crimes!").

By April 1951 Batman has taken to carrying the new compact costume in his boot heel (Det No. 170: "The Flying Dutchman II!"; and others), although he seems to change its location periodically from his boot heel (Det No. 236, Oct '56: "The New-Model Batman!") to his utility belt (BM No. 71/1, Jun/Jul '52: "The Jail for Heroes!"; and others). Detective Comics No. 165 describes this costume as manufactured out of "super-thin cellophane" rather than plastic, and notes that it can easily be destroyed with a match (Nov '50: "The Strange Costumes of Batman!").

In October 1956 Batman introduces a new "cape-parachute" (Det No. 236: "The New-Model Batman!") — a cape specially designed to double as a parachute — which he uses while performing an aerial stunt at the Gotham Police Show in January–February 1957 (WF No. 86: "The Super-Show of Gotham City") and again during a charity air-show in METROPOLIS in

January–February 1958 (WF No. 92: "The Boy from Outer Space!").

The device, alternatively referred to as a "parachute-cape," is apparently obsolete by February 1966, because a text for that period observes that Batman and Robin can use their regular costume capes as parachutes whenever the occasion requires (Det No. 348: "The Birdmaster of Bedlam!").

Batman's other special costumes include a "gold-cloth costume" once used to enable Batman to masquerade as a gold statue; a "luminous bat-costume which glows in the dark," once used to frighten a superstitious crook into submission; a "bat-space suit" for adventures in outer space; an "asbestos bat-costume" for use in fires; a "glider bat-costume" for soaring through the air or bailing out of aircraft; an "unique bat-costume which includes a supply of oxygen" for use underwater; an "air-costume" and "sub-costume" whose precise functions are never delineated; and an emergency foam-rubber costume, superficially identical to Batman's basic costume except for the red-breasted bird-symbol emblazoned on its chest, which has been specially molded to Robin's specifications and is designed to enable Robin to impersonate Batman (Det No. 165, Nov '50: "The Strange Costumes of Batman!").

In addition, Batman has a "thick rubber insulating bat-costume" for working with high-voltage electricity (Det No. 239, Jan '57: "Batman's Robot Twin!"); a bulletproof costume which he uses in March 1965 (BM No. 170/1: "Genius of the Getaway Gimmicks!"); and an array of costumes in a wide range of vivid colors – red, pale blue, gold, orange, green, black and white, and rainbow-striped – which he deliberately uses to draw attention to himself as a ploy to protect Robin's secret identity in March 1957 (Det No. 241: "The Rainbow Batman!").

Batman also has the special frogman suit pictured below (BM No. 68/3, Dec/Jan '51–'52: "The New Crimes of Two-Face!").

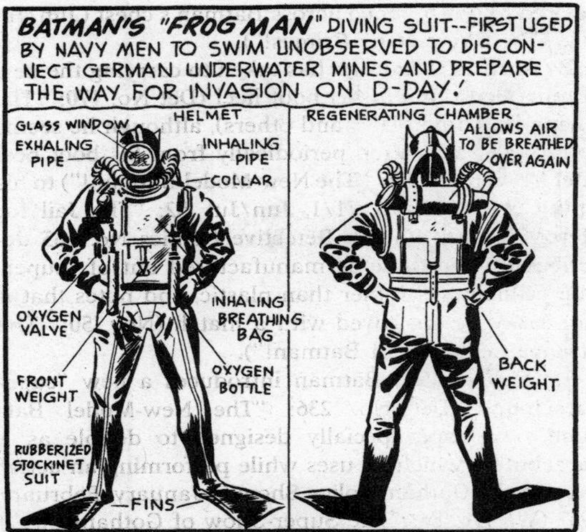

Batman's frogman suit © NPP 1954

ALFRED once invented a set of special "life-saver inflatable costumes" for Batman and Robin. Although they proved impractical for their intended use, the Dynamic Duo did once use them as decoys to trap a band of notorious river pirates (BM No. 110/2, Sep '57: "The Secret of Batman's Butler").

3. The Utility Belt. "The **Batman's** utility belt is an amazing miniature laboratory and tool kit, its metal compartments containing many mysterious objects . . ." (Det No. 86, Apr '44: "Danger Strikes Three!").

Batman's utility belt is an integral component of his costume as well as an indispensable feature of his crime-fighting arsenal. Colored alternately yellow (Det No. 27, May '39: "The Case of the Chemical Syndicate"; and others) and blue (Det No. 34, Dec '39; and others) during approximately the first year of Batman's career – and in one text colored sometimes blue and sometimes white (Det No. 32, Oct '39) – the utility belt is unvaryingly colored yellow from August 1940 (Det No. 42: "The Case of the Prophetic Pictures!") onward.

The buckle of the utility belt, round with a small round knob at its center in May 1939 (Det No. 27: "The Case of the Chemical Syndicate") – and varyingly round and square in June 1939 (Det No. 28) – is consistently square or rectangular from July 1939 (Det No. 29: "The Batman Meets Doctor Death") onward. It is fashioned from solid steel (Det No. 214, Dec '54: "The Batman Encyclopedia").

Cylindrical "pouches" (BM No. 128/1, Dec '59: "The Interplanetary Batman!") or "equipment containers" (BM No. 203, Jul/Aug '68), built into the leather utility belt along virtually its entire length, contain the various chemicals, tools, and other equipment so indispensable to Batman in his dangerous work. On the inside, the pouches are apparently lined with metal, for they are referred to as "metal compartments" in Detective Comics No. 86 (Apr '44: "Danger Strikes Three!").

In the early months of Batman's career, his silken rope (*see* section E 2 d i, the bat-rope) dangles lasso-style from his utility belt (Det No. 28, Jun '39; and others), but by October–November 1951 a special "super-thin emergency cord" has been installed on a tiny spool inside one of the equipment containers (BM No. 67/1: "The Mystery Rope!"), and by July 1952 the regular bat-rope has been secreted inside the belt's lining so that it may be drawn out almost instantly like a fisherman's line on a reel (Det No. 185: "The Secret of Batman's Utility Belt!"). By July–August 1968 the regular bat-rope has been transferred to an "automatic reel" inside one of the utility belt's equipment containers (BM No. 203).

In at least one early text, Batman carries a knife inside his belt (Det No. 37, Mar '40), but this is eventually abandoned in favor of a knife-blade concealed in the belt's lining (Det No. 211, Sep '54: "The Jungle Cat-Queen!").

Tucked behind the utility belt, where it may be extracted at a moment's notice, is Batman's famous batarang (Det No. 32, Oct '39; and others), and sometimes Batman's bat-bolo is carried there also (BM No. 111/3, Oct '57: "The Armored Batman!"; and others).

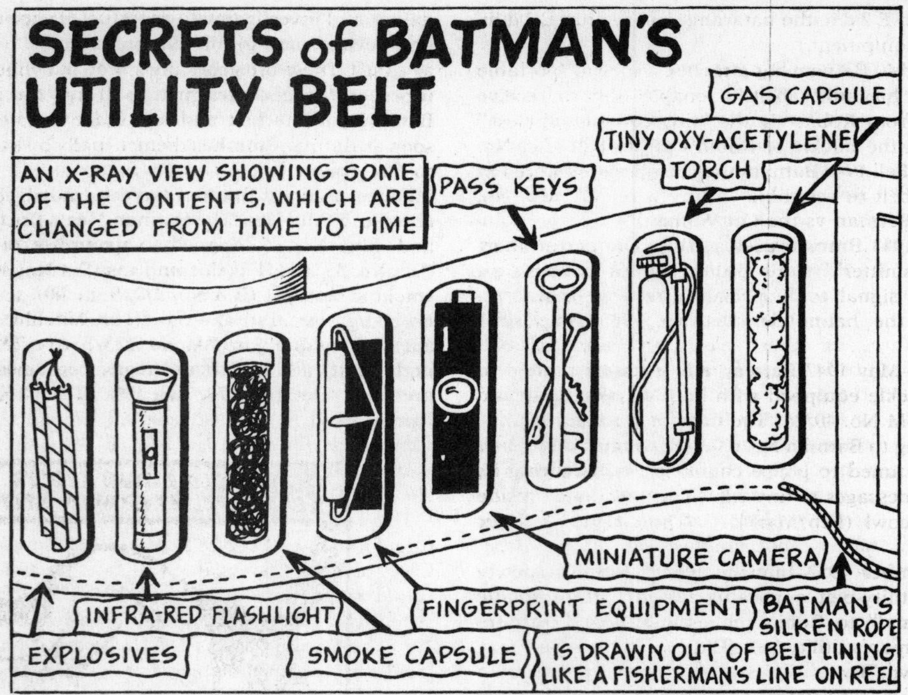

Batman's utility belt, 1961: contents of the equipment containers are changed periodically © NPP 1961

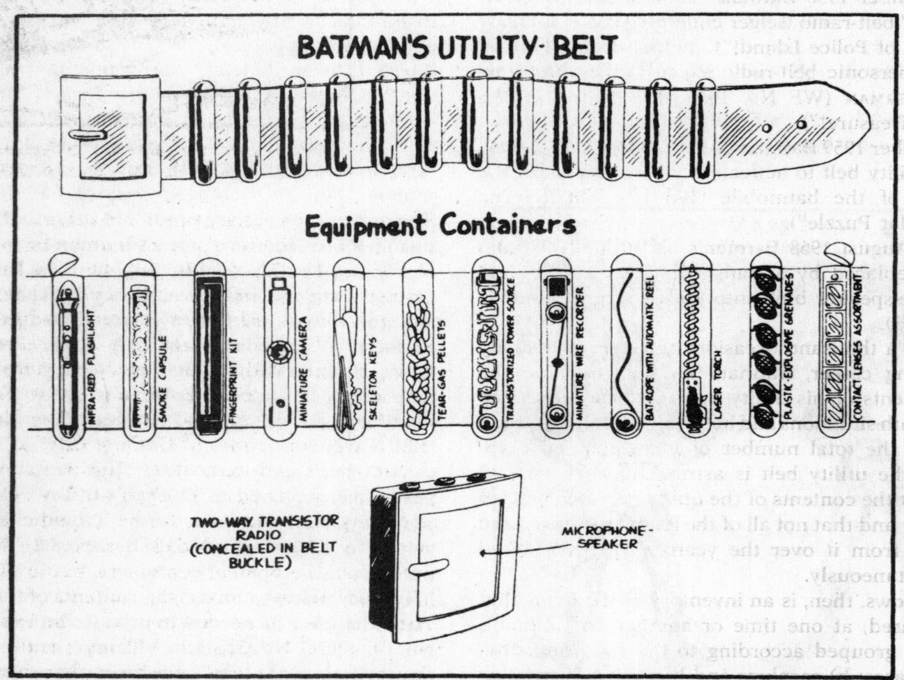

Batman's utility belt, 1968 © NPP 1968

(*See* section E 2 d ii, the batarang, *and* section E 2 d iii, the other equipment.)

By July 1940 Batman has attached a special "portable phone" to his utility belt to enable him to receive messages from Robin via the "tiny capable wireless" installed in the buckle of Robin's utility belt (Det No. 41), and in Fall 1940 Batman uses components stored in his utility belt to assemble "a tiny wireless" (BM No. 3/4: "The Batman vs the Cat-Woman!").

In July 1943 Batman uses a "tiny, low power short wave transmitter" in his utility belt to transmit an emergency signal to a special "direction finder" installed in the batmobile (Det No. 77: "The Crime Clinic!").

By April–May 1947 Batman has installed a radio in his belt buckle equipped with both a transmitter and receiver (BM No. 40/2: "The Case of Batman II").

According to Batman No. 63/3, "Batman's utility belt receiver is tuned to police channels," transmitting its incoming messages to tiny earphones concealed inside Batman's cowl (Feb/Mar '51: "The Origin of Killer Moth!").

In December 1952–January 1953 a piece of newly installed utility-belt apparatus radios "an automatic danger signal" to Robin the moment the JOKER removes Batman's utility belt (BM No. 74/1: "The Crazy Crime Clown!").

In February 1954 Batman and Robin transform their belt-radios into powerful electromagnets within a matter of seconds in order to escape from a deathtrap prepared by TWO-FACE (BM No. 81/1: "Two-Face Strikes Again!").

In September 1958 Batman makes a passing reference to his "belt-radio Geiger counter" (BM No. 118/1: "The Battle of Police Island!"), and in August 1959 he uses a "supersonic belt-radio signal" to summon his friend SUPERMAN (WF No. 103: "The Secret of the Sorcerer's Treasure!").

In December 1959 Batman uses an "electronic signal" from his utility belt to activate a tape recorder on the dashboard of the batmobile (BM No. 128/2: "The Million Dollar Puzzle").

By July–August 1968 Batman's old utility-belt radio has been replaced by a transistor radio with a dual microphone-speaker built into the face of the buckle (BM No. 203).

On easily a thousand occasions throughout his long and exacting career, Batman has depended on the varied contents of his utility belt to rescue him from life-and-death situations and help him apprehend criminals. Since the total number of items that have appeared in the utility belt is astronomic, it is safe to assume that the contents of the utility belt are changed periodically and that not all of the items that have been withdrawn from it over the years have been stored there simultaneously.

What follows, then, is an inventory of the items that have appeared, at one time or another, in Batman's utility belt, grouped according to the following categories: a) gases; b) earplugs and breathing apparatus; c) chemicals and explosives; d) tools; e) scientific, signaling, and investigatory apparatus; f) special weapons and devices; and g) miscellaneous items.

a) GASES. These are generally stored in cylindrical glass tubes, or "pellets," designed to fit into the pouches of Batman's utility belt and to release their contents as soon as Batman smashes them, usually by hurling them to the ground.

Gases used by Batman have included choking gas (Det No. 29, Jul '39: "The Batman Meets Doctor Death"; and others); gas designed to neutralize mustard gas (Det No. 35, Jan '40); sleeping gas (Det No. 36, Feb '40); smoke screen gas (BM No. 2/2, Sum '40); tear gas (BM No. 80/3, Dec/Jan '53–'54: "The Machines of Menace!"); laughing gas (BM No. 115/3, Apr '58: "Batman in the Bottle!"); and knockout gas, contained in special grenades (Det No. 270, Aug '59: "The Creature from Planet X!").

THE WOUNDED BATMAN EJECTS A GLASS PELLET FROM HIS BELT.

Batman extracts a pellet of choking gas from his utility belt, 1939 © NPP 1939

b) EARPLUGS AND BREATHING APPARATUS. These have included nose filters to protect Batman from the effects of toxic gases (Det No. 134, Apr '48: "The Umbrellas of Crime!"; and others); "emergency [gas] masks" (BM No. 151/2, Nov '62: "The Mystery Gadget from the Stars!"); a "miniature breathing apparatus" for providing Batman with an emergency oxygen supply (BM No. 164/2, Jun '64: "Batman's Great Face-Saving Feat!"); and conventional earplugs (Det No. 368, Oct '67: "7 Wonder Crimes of Gotham City!").

c) CHEMICALS AND EXPLOSIVES. The items in this category have appeared in Batman's utility belt in liquid, powder, pellet, and other forms. Liquid chemicals are stored in special glass vials designed to fit into the utility belt's equipment containers. In the early days of his career, Batman mixed the contents of two separate vials whenever he needed to produce an explosive (Det No. 84, Feb '44: "Artists in Villainy"; and others), but this technique has long since been superseded by more sophisticated explosives.

Chemicals and explosives employed by Batman have included a powerful acid for eating through locks (Det No. 45, Nov '40: "The Case of the Laughing Death!"; and others); "chemical fire-extinguishing powder" (BM No. 62/3, Dec/Jan '50–'51: "The Mystery of Millionaire Island!"; and others); grease solvent (BM No. 63/3, Feb/Mar '51: "The Origin of Killer Moth!"); smoke capsules (Det No. 185, Jul '52: "The Secret of Batman's Utility Belt!"); chemicals for mixing "xylil bromide," a "highly effective form of tear gas" (BM No. 80/3, Dec/Jan '53–'54: "The Machines of Menace!"); chemicals for transforming water into ice (BM No. 85/1, Aug '54: "Batman – Clown of Crime!"); shark repellent (BM No. 117/3, Aug '58: "Manhunt in Outer Space!"); gunpowder (Det. No. 261, Nov '58: "The Amazing Dr. Double X!"); miniature "bat-grenades" (BM No. 124/3, Jun '59: "The Mystery Seeds from Space!"; and others); a chemcal designed to emit "a strong aroma" to enable ACE THE BAT-HOUND to follow its scent (BM No. 130/2, Mar '60: "The Master of Weapons"); a pellet designed to "create intense heat when it hits the floor" (Det No. 279, May '60: "The Creatures That Stalked Batman!"); a special powder designed to temporarily blind adversaries with a "luminous dust cloud" as well as to leave luminous traces that Batman can follow with a special electronic device (BM No. 144/1, Dec '61: "The Alien Feud on Earth!"); "flame pellets" for starting fires (Det No. 299, Jan '62: "Prey of the Alien Hunters!"); "explosive capsules" (WF No. 132, Mar '63: "Batman and Robin, Medieval Bandits!"); "flare-capsules" for illuminating darkened places (BM No. 158/3, Sep '63: "Batman and Robin--Imposters!"); a "bat-freeze pill" which, taken internally, lowers the body temperature (Det No. 362, Apr '67: "The Night Batman Destroyed Gotham City!"); and miniature "plastic-explosive grenades" (BM No. 203, Jul/Aug '68).

d) TOOLS. The tools in Batman's utility belt have included a saw blade (WF No. 5, Spr '42: "Crime Takes a Holiday"); a miniature oxyacetylene torch (BM No. 12/1, Aug/Sep '42: "Brothers in Crime!"; and others); a screwdriver (WF No. 14, Sum '44: "Salvage Scavengers!" and others); a diamond-tipped boring tool (Det No. 89, Jul '44: "Laboratory Loot!"); a flashlight (BM No. 26/1, Dec/Jan '44–'45: "Twenty Ton Robbery!"); a special "utility-belt knife" (BM No. 162/1, Mar '64: "The Batman Creature!"; and others); and a highly sophisticated "laser torch" (BM No. 203, Jul/Aug '68).

e) SCIENTIFIC, SIGNALING, AND INVESTIGATORY APPARATUS. This category embraces a wide range of special equipment, including a makeup kit (BM No. 4/4, Win '41; and others); a skeleton key (WF No. 2, Sum '41: "The Man Who Couldn't Remember!"; and others); a magnifying glass (Det No. 167, Jan '51: "Bodyguards to Cleopatra!"); a miniature camera (Det No. 175, Sep '51: "The Underworld Bank!"; and others); an infrared flashlight and fingerprint equipment (Det No. 185, Jul '52: "The Secret of Batman's Utility Belt!"); a mirror (BM No. 110/3, Sep '57: "The Phantom Batman!"; and others); a miniature Geiger counter and a stethoscope-like "sound recorder" for listening to sounds on the ocean floor (BM No. 117/3, Aug '58: "Manhunt in Outer Space!"); heliographic signaling devices (WF No. 125, May '62: "The Hostages of the Island of Doom!"); a collapsible microscope (WF No. 136, Sep '63: "The Batman Nobody Remembered!"); "footprint powder" for bringing out faint footprints (Det No. 331, Sep '64: "Museum of Mixed-Up Men!"); a miniature tape recorder (WF No. 149, May '65: "The Game of Secret Identities!" pts. I–II – no title; "The Super-Detective!"); an assortment of contact lenses (Det No. 368, Oct '67: "7 Wonder Crimes of Gotham City!"); and a miniature wire recorder and transistorized power source (BM No. 203, Jul/Aug '68).

f) SPECIAL WEAPONS AND DEVICES. Included in this category are "steel rope hooks" used for grappling in conjunction with Batman's bat-rope (Det No. 214, Dec '54: "The Batman Encyclopedia"); a "tiny gadget" designed to ensnare an adversary in powerful "tendrils of thin, super-strong wire" (BM No. 144/1, Dec '61: "The Alien Feud on Earth!"); a "special lighting effects" device that Batman uses in October 1963 (Det No. 320: "Batman and Robin--the Mummy Crime-Fighters!"); and a powerful miniaturized "laser-weapon" (Det No. 359, Jan '67: "The Million Dollar Debut of Batgirl!"; and others).

g) MISCELLANEOUS ITEMS. Other utility-belt paraphernalia, not easily categorized, include a "small dynamo" designed to transmit heat through the special wire filaments in Batman's cold-weather costume (WF No. 7, Fall '42: "The North Pole Crimes!"); an ordinary marble which produces the sound of footsteps when rolled down a flight of stairs and, held tightly under the arm, serves to stop Batman's pulse temporarily when he wants to feign death (Det No. 173, Jul '51: "Batman's Double!"); a lightweight Batman costume for special emergencies (BM No. 71/1, Jun/Jul '52: "The Jail for Heroes!"; and others); a complete first-aid kit (BM No. 71/2, Jun/Jul '52: "Commissioner Gordon's Greatest Case!"); a seemingly blank disc which, when coated with a special chemical, will reveal the secret of Batman's identity (Det No. 185, Jul '52: "The Secret of Batman's Utility Belt!"); paper and ink (WF No. 72, Sep/Oct '54: "Fort Crime!"); flash powder, and a giant Batman balloon with capsules of "concentrated helium" for inflating it (BM No. 115/3, Apr '58: "Batman in the Bottle!"); and an ordinary crayon (BM No. 149/2, Aug '62: "The Invaders from the Past!").

D. The Batcave. "Beneath a harmless-looking Gotham City residence, a unique giant cavern lies hidden from the world! This is the famed **bat-cave**--nerve-center of the brilliant war against crime waged endlessly by the great **Batman** and **Robin** the **Boy Wonder!**" (Det No. 205, Mar '54: "The Origin of the Bat-Cave!").

Situated beneath Wayne Manor, the palatial GOTHAM CITY residence of millionaire Bruce Wayne, is the far-famed batcave, the secret subterranean headquarters of Batman and Robin and the storehouse for their extraordinary arsenal of crime-fighting equipment (*see* section E 2, the equipment). Here in this unique cavern, hidden from the outside world, are the fabulous Hall of Trophies, housing the hard-won memorabilia of more than a thousand cases; the criminological laboratory, with its array of apparatus unique in the annals of scientific crime detection; the crime-file room, containing "the most complete data on criminal activities and personalities ever compiled by any agency" (Det No. 205, Mar '54: "The Origin of the Bat-Cave!"); garage and repair facilities for the batmobile; hangar facilities for the batplane and other aircraft; mooring facilities for the bat-boat and other seacraft; and such other facilities as a special room for costumes and a fully equipped workshop.

Since to locate the batcave is to penetrate the secret of Batman's identity, its existence beneath Wayne Manor is "one of the most closely guarded secrets in the world" (WF No. 128, Sep '62: "The Power That Transformed Batman!").

The batcave is a gigantic natural cavern with a dirt floor (WF No. 39, Mar/Apr '49: "The Conquest of Batman's Identity!"), limestone walls (Det No. 240, Feb '57: "The Outlaw Batman!"; and others), and massive stalactites suspended from high-vaulted ceilings (BM No. 121/1, Feb '59: "The Body in the Bat-Cave"; and others) which are home to a multitude of fluttering bats (Det No. 205, Mar '54: "The Origin of the Bat-Cave!"; and others).

A swift-flowing underground stream, or river, containing at least one treacherous whirlpool, flows through the batcave to empty eventually into Gotham City's East River (BM No. 48/2, Aug/Sep '48: "The 1,000 Secrets of the Batcave!"; and others).

Branching outward from the batcave, a labyrinthine network of tunnels extends beyond the boundaries of Bruce Wayne's property (BM No. 92/2, Jun '55: "Batman's Guilty Neighbor!"; and others) and honeycombs the nearby mountain with limestone caves (BM No. 166/1, Sep '64: "Two-Way Deathtrap!"), although Batman has taken care to isolate the batcave by sealing off the various tunnels leading into it (Det No. 205, Mar '54: "The Origin of the Bat-Cave!").

The batcave enjoyed a colorful history even before becoming the secret headquarters of Batman and Robin. In the early Colonial period, it served as a subterranean base of operations for JEREMY COE, who courageously helped safeguard his fellow colonists against Indian attack by infiltrating the redmen's war councils disguised as an Indian (Det No. 205, Mar '54: "The Origin of the Bat-Cave!").

During the Civil War, when it was known as Anderson's Cave, it was a favorite hideout of Confederate spies (BM No. 64/2, Apr/May '51: "The Forgotten Men of Crime!"). And finally, in the early years of the twentieth century, before the mansion now known as Wayne Manor was constructed over it, the cave served as a hideout for gangster Whitey Weir, who died in prison many years later after confiding the cave's location to fellow convict "BIG JIM" JARREL. When Jarrel and his henchmen attempt to tunnel their way into the cave in September 1955 in hopes of using Weir's old hideout to elude the law, Batman and Robin have their hands full trying to prevent their discovering the batcave (Det. No. 223: "The Batman Dime-Museum").

When Bruce Wayne first purchased the mansion soon to be known as Wayne Manor, he was not even aware of the existence of the sprawling limestone cavern beneath it.

"Actually," he recalls years later, in March 1954, ". . . the **bat-cave** was first discovered by **accident!** . . . I had planned to use an old barn at the rear of the property as my secret headquarters. But one day, as I was testing the floor, it suddenly gave way!"

Indeed, as the rotted flooring of the old barn collapsed beneath his weight, Wayne had unexpectedly found himself in "a tremendous cave" filled with bats. It was, in Wayne's words, "an omen--if I ever saw one!" Then and there, Wayne decided that "This **cave** shall be my headquarters! I'll call it the **bat-cave!**" (Det No. 205: "The Origin of the Bat-Cave!").

In reality, however, Batman had no batcave in the early days of his career, and the secret subterranean headquarters that exists today is the product of a gradual evolution spanning many texts.

By September 1939 Batman has begun housing his batgyro, the early forerunner of the modern batplane, in a "secret hangar known only to himself," but the text contains no hint whatever as to the hangar's location (Det No. 31).

By November 1939 Bruce Wayne has installed a secret laboratory behind a hidden panel in one of the walls of the Wayne mansion. The laboratory contains a file of newspaper clippings (Det No. 33: "The Batman Wars Against the Dirigible of Doom") and apparently a certain amount of medical and surgical equipment as well, for in Summer 1940 Dick Grayson extracts a bullet from Batman's shoulder there (BM No. 2/2).

In Fall 1940, for the first time in the chronicles, mention is made of an underground passageway connecting the Wayne mansion with a deserted barn (BM No. 3/1: "The Strange Case of the Diabolical Puppet Master"), a barn which later texts describe as located "many yards away" from the mansion (Det No. 63, May '42: "A Gentleman in Gotham") "at the rear" of Wayne's property (Det No. 205, Mar '54: "The Origin of the Bat-Cave!").

In this early period, the primary function of the barn and passageway is to allow Batman unrestricted, unobserved access to the Wayne mansion to enable him to safeguard the secret of his dual identity.

"When the Batman darted into the barn," explains Batman No. 4/4, "he raised a cleverly hidden trapdoor which leads to a tunnel below. . . . This tunnel ran directly to the Wayne house where the **Batman** mounted steps and slipped through a secret panel into his home . . ." (Win '41).

Detective Comics No. 47 provides a more dramatic description of Batman's secret entry into the Wayne mansion, referred to here as "the lair of the Batman." To reach it, Batman

> enters what seems to be a deserted barn on a barren field. . . . Upon pressing a button, a section of the barn's floor slides away, revealing a flight of steps. . . . He pads silently through the tunnel below. . . . He ascends another flight of steps at the end of the long tunnel. . . . And steps

through another panel into a luxuriously furnished room! The secret labyrinth has led to the lair of the Batman! (Jan '41).

By February 1941 Batman has begun using the old barn as a garage for his batmobile (Det No. 48: "The Secret Cavern"), and by Summer 1942 it has begun to serve as a hangar for the batplane as well (WF No. 6: "The Secret of Bruce Wayne!").

A text for August–September 1942 contains the first actual description of a secret subterranean headquarters, referred to not as the batcave but as Batman's "secret underground hangars." An elevator connects the Wayne mansion with a single-level subterranean area consisting of a combination "repair and workshop"; a batmobile garage, housing two batmobiles; and a batplane hangar, housing three batplanes. A thick layer of reinforced concrete separates the floor of the Wayne mansion from the underground area beneath it, and a special chain and winch have been installed to haul the batplane – and presumably also the batmobile – up a steep subterranean incline to the old barn, where an "automatic door" swings open to allow the vehicles entry and exit (BM No. 12/2: "The Wizard of Words!").

During this same period, the chronicles make their first reference to Batman's "vast Hall of Trophies," described as a "secret chamber" housing "hundreds of odd souvenirs of the **Batman's** never-ceasing war against villainy!" Except for stating pictorially that one must descend a flight of stairs to reach it, the text containing this initial reference provides no clue whatever to the trophy hall's location, but the depiction of sunlight streaming through a window there argues for an aboveground, as opposed to a subterranean, location. Protected from intruders by a six-inch-thick steel door with combination lock, the Hall of Trophies already houses at least 897 separate trophies (BM No. 12/1, Aug/Sep '42: "Brothers in Crime!").

In April–May 1943, when Alfred, newly arrived at the Wayne mansion, accidentally releases a hidden spring and thereby discovers the existence of a sliding wall panel, he descends a "secret stairway" to an "underground hangar" and "criminological laboratory," this being the first explicit textual reference to a secret laboratory underground (BM No. 16/4: "Here Comes Alfred!").

In January 1944 the term "bat cave" is employed for the first time in the chronicles, and a fully equipped gymnasium is depicted as having been installed there. The subterranean headquarters is still depicted as a series of underground rooms, however, and not as a natural cave area (Det No. 83: "Accidentally on Purpose!").

In December 1945–January 1946 a cutaway diagram of the batcave depicts an added area for the storage of "secret files," but Batman's criminological laboratory has once again been moved to an aboveground location somewhere in the Wayne mansion (BM No. 32/2: "Dick Grayson, Boy Wonder!").

By July 1948 the secret laboratory has been restored to its former subterranean location. The Hall of Trophies, or trophy room, is depicted as being underground also. A spiral staircase connects the Wayne mansion with the batcave beneath it, reference to the elevator that once performed this function having been inexplicably omitted (Det No. 137: "The Rebus Crimes!").

In August–September 1948, for the first time in the chronicles, the batcave is depicted as a natural subterranean cavern rather than as a series of man-made rooms, and a natural grotto is depicted at the left of the cave area. A spiral staircase still connects the Wayne mansion with the batcave, and the batmobile and batplane still utilize the old barn as an exit after ascending a steep incline from the batcave by means of a winch and chain (BM No. 48/2: "The 1,000 Secrets of the Batcave!").

In April 1950 Batman and Robin add their thousandth and thousand and first trophies to the batcave's

Batcave cutaway diagram, 1948 © NPP 1948

burgeoning Hall of Trophies (Det No. 158: "The Thousand and One Trophies of Batman!").

In May 1950 a secret elevator is once again depicted as connecting the Wayne mansion with the batcave (Det No. 159: "Bruce Wayne – You Are Batman!").

By November 1950 a "costume room" has been added to the batcave (Det No. 165: "The Strange Costumes of Batman!").

By December 1952–January 1953 Batman has installed an emergency chute leading from a secret floor panel in Bruce Wayne's dressing room to the batcave beneath it (BM No. 74/2: "The Movie That Killed Batman!").

By July–August 1953 a secret new exterior entrance has been added to the batcave, making it possible for the batmobile and batplane to enter and leave the batcave through a natural cavern opening at ground level, rather than through the old barn (WF No. 65: "The Five Different Batmen!"). This new entranceway, which Dick Grayson refers to as the batcave's "emergency exterior entrance" (BM No. 80/2, Dec/Jan '53–'54: "Dick Grayson's Nightmare!"), soon becomes established as the standard exit and entranceway (BM No. 91/1, Apr '55: "The Living Batplane!"; and others), relegating the route up the incline and out the old barn to the status of a seldom-used emergency exit.

By March 1954 a second subterranean level has been added to the batcave, with the crime-lab on the upper subterranean level and a storeroom, garage and hangar facilities, and what appears to be a workshop on the level beneath it. A grandfather's clock in Bruce Wayne's study now conceals the secret stairway leading down to the batcave, although a cutaway diagram accompanying this text inconsistently depicts the secret staircase as originating in Wayne's living room. The Hall of Trophies is not depicted at all, suggesting that this cutaway represents only a partial view of the batcave (Det No. 205: "The Origin of the Bat-Cave!").

Secret entrance to the batcave, 1954 © NPP 1954

In December 1955, during a period when they are responding to fire calls in the batmobile to help publicize fire-prevention week, Batman and Robin install a firemen's pole beside the secret staircase connecting

Batcave cutaway diagram, 1954 © NPP 1954

SECRETS OF
THE BATMOBILE
1968
WAYNE
MANOR
TOP LEVEL OF BATCAVE
REPAIR SHOP
GARAGE
LAB
ELEVATOR
LOWER LEVEL OF BATCAVE
TROPHY ROOM
WORKSHOP
IN GOD WE TRUST
LIBERTY
1937

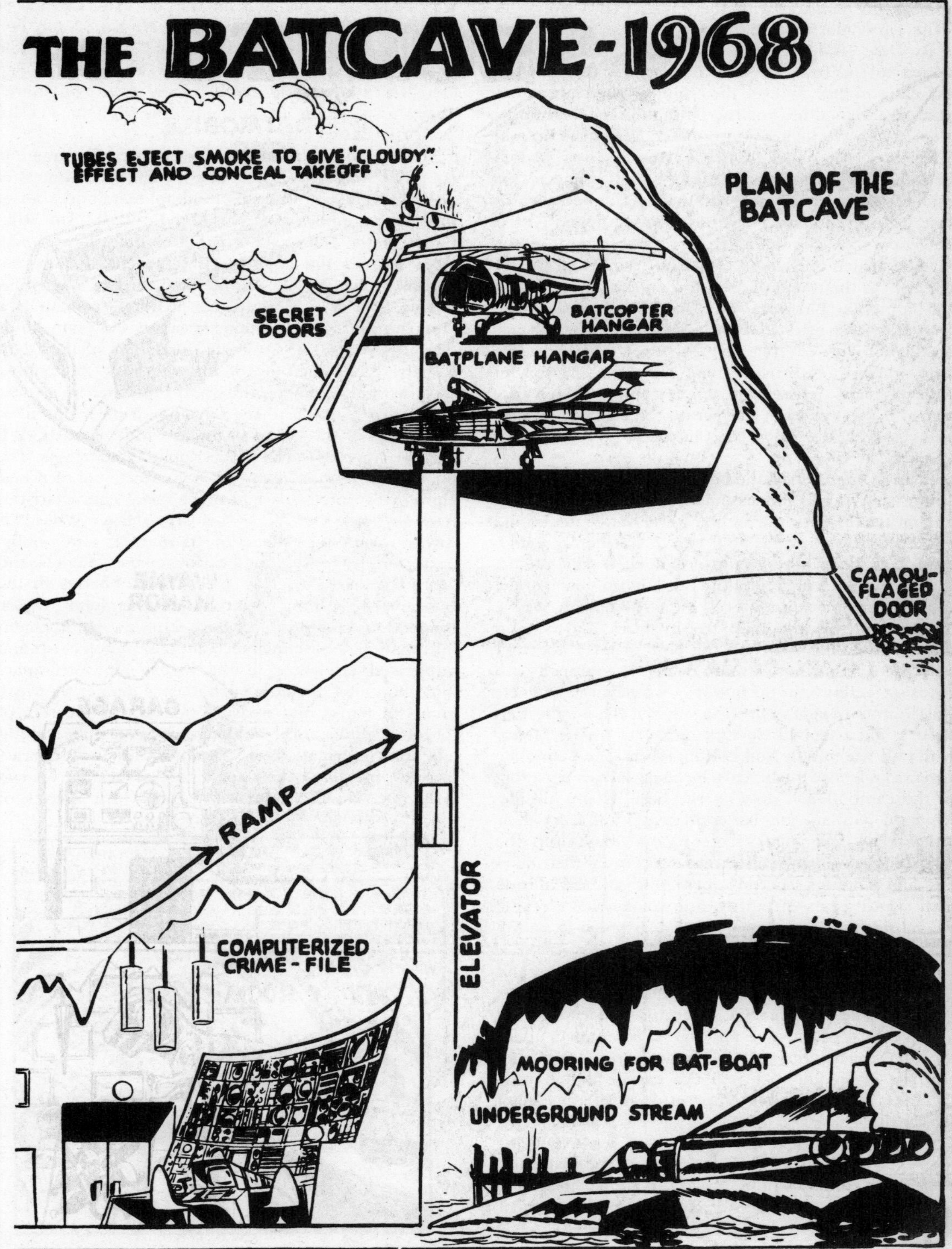

30 *Batcave cutaway diagram, 1968* © NPP 1968

the Wayne mansion with the batcave (BM No. 96/3: "The Third Alarm for Batman!").

By June 1964 a third subterranean level has been added to the batcave, with hangar facilities for the batplane on the top level, the criminological laboratory and garage facilities for the batmobile on the middle level, and a workshop and radio room on the bottom level. A secret panel in Bruce Wayne's living room conceals an "automatic elevator" that connects the mansion with the batcave, and the exterior batcave exit installed in the early 1950s has been equipped with a new doorway, camouflaged to resemble part of the hillside, which opens and closes by "remote electronic control" at the touch of a button on the dashboard of the batmobile (BM No. 164/1: "Two-Way Gem Caper!").

In May 1966, after Dick Grayson's AUNT HARRIET has accidentally discovered the existence of the secret batcave elevator, Bruce Wayne and Dick Grayson install a special "electronic remote-control device" designed to permit them to operate the elevator, but no one else (Det No. 351: "The Cluemaster's Topsy-Turvy Crimes!").

In July–August 1968 the batcave is again depicted as comprising three subterranean levels, with separate hangar facilities for the batplane and bat-copter on the top level, here shown as built into the interior of a high hillside above ground level overlooking Wayne Manor; the criminological laboratory and batmobile garage facilities on the middle level, directly beneath Wayne Manor; and the workshop, trophy room, and computerized crime-file room on the bottom level, together with the underground stream, which is equipped with mooring facilities for the bat-boat. An elevator connects the aircraft hangars with the other levels of the batcave, while a second elevator connects Wayne Manor with only the middle and bottom levels. The batmobile enters and leaves the batcave by a special ramp leading to the camouflaged door at the base of the hillside, while the batplane and bat-copter enter and leave their hangars by means of "secret doors" built into the hillside precisely at hangar level. To conceal their take-offs and landings, special tubes built into the hillside emit steady gusts of puffy white smoke that wreathe the hillside in what appear from a distance to be billowy clouds (BM No. 203).

To aid them in their war against crime, Batman and Robin have equipped the batcave with an extensive arsenal of files and special apparatus. What follows is an inventory of batcave apparatus, assembled under the following headings: 1) the criminological laboratory and the crime-file room; 2) the garage and hangar facilities; 3) miscellaneous apparatus; and 4) the Hall of Trophies.

1) The Criminological Laboratory and the Crime-File Room. These areas of the batcave house the maps and charts, files, and scientific apparatus indispensable to scientific crime detection and the apprehension of criminals.

The maps and charts include geological maps of GOTHAM CITY and environs (Det No. 122, Apr '47: "The Black Cat Crimes!"; and others); an extensive file of laundry and dry-cleaners' symbols (WF No. 32, Jan/Feb '48: "The Man Who Could Not Die!"); a "key profile chart" for identifying types of keys (Det No. 175, Sep '51: "The Underworld Bank!"); and cave and tunnel charts for Gotham City and environs (Det No. 233, Jul '56: "The Batwoman").

The files in the batcave include a microfilm mug-file (Det No. 165, Nov '50: "The Strange Costumes of Batman!"); a sample case of animal hairs and a set of hair-tonic samples (Det No. 177, Nov '51: "The Robberies in the Bat-Cave!"); a file of daily newspapers from around the country (BM No. 100/1, Jun '56: "Batmantown, U.S.A."); a file of theatrical and circus people (Det No. 233, Jul '56: "The Batwoman"); a "topographic file" containing specimens of many kinds of soil (Det No. 258, Aug '58: "Prisoners of the Giant Robots!"); a "microfile of known thugs" containing records of their fingerprints and other pertinent data (WF No. 102, Jun '59: "The Caveman from Krypton!"); recordings of the voices of underworld scientists (WF No. 141, May '64: "The Olsen-Robin Team versus 'The Superman-Batman Team!'"); a complete file of noses, chins, eyes, foreheads and other facial characteristics (Det No. 344, Oct '65: "The Crime Boss Who Was Always One Step Ahead of Batman!"); automobile-parts samples representing various makes, models, and years (Det No. 177, Nov '51: "The Robberies in the Bat-Cave!"); and an "electronic data analyzer" whose tremendous storehouse of top-secret law enforcement information — contained on computer punch-cards and duplicated elsewhere in the batcave in a compact microfilm file — includes such diverse data as the weak points of banks and treasure houses, the location of forgotten underworld hideouts, data on police methods, and information on criminals and their characteristics, including their addresses, associates, special skills (Det No. 229, Mar '56: "The 10,000 Secrets of

Batman and Robin consult the batcave's crime-files, 1954

Batman!"), and even such minutiae as the lengths of their thumbs (BM No. 108/2, Jun '57: "Prisoners of the Bat-Cave").

According to Detective Comics No. 271, the batcave's "electronic brain" can simultaneously assimilate the backgrounds and descriptions of as many as 30,000 men (Sep '59: "Batman's Armored Rival!").

The batcave's scientific apparatus and crime-detection equipment include one or more electron microscopes (Det No. 165, Nov '50: "The Strange Costumes of Batman!"; and others); a centrifuge, a casting kit for making moulages of footprints, a micrometer, a helixometer for examining the insides of gun barrels, a dactyloscope for viewing fingerprints, and an iodine fume gun for bringing out hidden fingerprints (Det No. 177, Nov '51: "The Robberies in the Bat-Cave!"); a "gamma ray machine" (WF No. 66, Sep/Oct '53: "The Proving Ground for Crime!"); a "spectroscope machine" for identifying "minute particles by their color-spectrum breakdown" (Det No. 205, Mar '54: "The Origin of the Bat-Cave!"); and a portable "magnetometer" for "measuring the magnitude [and] direction of a magnetic force" (BM No. 172/1, Jun '65: "Attack of the Invisible Knights!").

Batman at work in the batcave's criminological laboratory, 1952 © NPP 1952

2) *The Garage and Hangar Facilities.* The batcave's garage and hangar facilities include a lubricating car-hoist, oil pump, and all the tools and equipment necessary for the repair and maintenance of the batmobile, batplane, and other vehicles and aircraft (BM No. 91/1, Apr '55: "The Living Batplane!"); emergency snowmobile equipment – consisting of runners and tanklike treads – for enabling the batmobile to travel over snow (BM No. 98/3, Mar '56: "Secret of the Batmobile"); and a miniature wind tunnel for performing preliminary tests on scale models of the batplane (BM No. 72/3, Aug/Sep '52: "The Death-Cheaters of Gotham City!").

3) *Miscellaneous Apparatus.* Other batcave apparatus includes a barred cell for practicing escapes (BM No. 34/3, Apr/May '46: "The Master vs. the Pupil!"); a television set (Det No. 142, Dec '48: "Crime's Puzzle Contest!"; and others), reception for which necessitated the installation of "an intricate indoor antenna . . . hooked up in relay to the innocent-looking antenna on Bruce Wayne's roof" (Det No. 205, Mar '54: "The Origin of the Bat-Cave!"); a gigantic radar screen (BM No. 61/1, Oct/Nov '50: "The Birth of Batplane II!"; and others); a miniature scale model of Gotham City (BM No. 83/2, Apr '54: "The Deep-Sea Diver Mystery!"); a seismograph (BM No. 136/3, Dec '60: "The Challenge of the Joker"); and a radio for receiving standard police calls (WF No. 144, Sep '64: "The 1,001 Tricks of Clayface and Brainiac!" pts. I–II – no title; "The Helpless Partners!").

Perhaps one of the most intriguing items of batcave apparatus is Batman's "truth chamber," a tiny interrogation room with four mirrored walls "designed to crack a criminal's silence by making him watch fearful faces reflecting his own guilt multiplied many times!"

Strapped helplessly in a chair at the center of the room while Batman grimly accuses him of wrongdoing and demands confession, the criminal is forced to gaze at his own terrified reflections in the truth chamber's mirrored walls as a succession of colored lights play upon his face: first an "eerie red"; then yellow, "the sickly color of fear"; and finally green, imparting to the multiple reflections "an unhealthy green pallor, betraying the sickness of mind that has gripped the criminal!"

Batman uses his truth chamber for grilling one of the PENGUIN's henchmen in April 1948 (Det No. 134: "The Umbrellas of Crime!").

Other batcave apparatus is designed to alert Batman and Robin to the appearance of the bat-signal or to enable them to receive direct communications from POLICE COMMISSIONER GORDON. (*See* section E 2 e, the bat-signal.)

4) *The Hall of Trophies.* Inside the vast Hall of Trophies, "the strangest room" in the batcave (Det No. 158, Apr '50: "The Thousand and One Trophies of Batman!"), are the more than one thousand trophies that together form a collective "symbol of the Batman's victories over crime" (BM No. 12/1, Aug/Sep '42: "Brothers in Crime!").

The batcave's Hall of Trophies, 1952 © NPP 1952

The chronicles do not provide a complete inventory of Batman's many trophies, but the most famous ones, and those most frequently depicted, include a life-sized mechanical dinosaur from Batman and Robin's adventure on "Dinosaur Island!" (BM No. 35/2, Jun/Jul '46); a gigantic Lincoln-head penny from the case of "The Penny Plunderers!" (WF No. 30, Sep/Oct '47); and a huge, grinning face-mask of the JOKER (Det No. 158, Apr '50: "The Thousand and One Trophies of Batman!").

Other batcave trophies include a bulletproof vest taken from one of the RAFFERTY BROTHERS (BM No. 12/1, Aug/Sep '42: "Brothers in Crime!"); a two-headed silver dollar used by TWO-FACE (Det No. 80, Oct '43: "The End of Two-Face!"); a trick jail-cell used by the Joker (Det No. 340, Jun '65: "The Outsider Strikes Again!"); and at least one of the many trick umbrellas employed by the PENGUIN (Det No. 158, Apr '50: "The Thousand and One Trophies of Batman!").

Because it would be calamitous if the underworld were to penetrate the batcave, a network of alarms and security devices have been installed to safeguard Batman's subterranean headquarters against intruders. An alarm rings in Wayne Manor whenever an outsider steps into the batcave (Det No. 83, Jan '44: "Accidentally on Purpose!"), and an "ingenious automatic camera" photographs all who enter there (Det No. 158, Apr '50: "The Thousand and One Trophies of Batman!").

By April–May 1951 Batman has installed an elaborate "sliding-wall arrangement whereby plain stone-colored walls come down to conceal the bat-cave" in the event unauthorized persons attempt to approach it by means of one of the adjoining subterranean tunnels (BM No. 64/2: "The Forgotten Men of Crime!"). It is these walls that safeguard the batcave against the accidental flooding caused by the villain HYDRO in December 1952–January 1953 (BM No. 74/3: "The Water Crimes of Mr. Hydro!").

By May 1964 a special chandelier has been installed in the Wayne mansion which begins glowing as soon as an intruder enters the batcave (WF No. 141: "The Olsen-Robin Team versus 'The Superman-Batman Team!'"), and by May 1965 an ordinary-looking wall-lamp has been installed elsewhere in the mansion which flashes on suddenly to signal the presence of batcave intruders (WF No. 149: "The Game of Secret Identities!" pts. I–II – no title; "The Super-Detective!").

Visitors to the batcave are brought there blindfolded in the batmobile, while a concealed tape recorder plays misleading ambient sounds to prevent their retracing the route later by utilizing sound-clues (BM No. 108/3, Jun '57: "The Career of Batman Jones!").

Over the years, various mobile batcaves have appeared in the chronicles. Batman introduces "the flying batcave" in August 1952 as part of his plan to outwit gangster DIAMOND LANG (Det No. 186: "The Flying Bat-Cave!"). (*See* section E 2 b ii, the other aircraft.)

In October 1955, after police commissioners from around the country have asked Batman to help them publicize Anti-Crime Week by making appearances in their respective cities, Batman and Robin outfit a special "traveling bat-cave" – the so-called "bat-train" – in cooperation with the railroads and tour the country with it. The bat-train features a black locomotive decorated with a distinctive bat-head ornament; flatcars for the batmobile and batplane; a crime-laboratory car; and a Museum of Justice car filled with trophies from the batcave's Hall of Trophies (BM No. 95/2: "The Bat-Train").

In August 1960 Batman and Robin launch the S.S. *Batman*, a medium-sized vessel containing a well-equipped replica of the batcave, including a trophy room and seagoing crime-lab. Open to the public as it tours ports along the coastline, the S.S. *Batman* will accumulate admissions fees to be contributed to charity (BM No. 133/2: "The Voyage of the S.S. Batman").

In December 1969, after Dick Grayson has departed Wayne Manor for his freshman year at Hudson University, Batman closes up the batcave with all its crime-fighting paraphernalia and leaves Wayne Manor for a new home in a penthouse apartment atop the roof of the skyscraper housing his own Wayne Foundation in the heart of Gotham City (BM No. 217: "One Bullet Too Many!"). (*See* section H, the man himself [as Batman].)

E. The Extraordinary Abilities and the Famous Crime-Fighting Equipment. *1. The Abilities.* "To many people, the **Batman** is a being of mystery, an eerie power. Yet, he is a man – a man who has developed his brain and his muscular frame to the highest degree" (Det No. 50, Apr '41: "The Case of the Three Devils!").

Batman is a supremely gifted individual, the possessor of an "ingenious mind" (BM No. 14/1, Dec/Jan '42–'43: "The Case Batman Failed to Solve!!!") and of a body trained to such extraordinary "physical perfection" that he can perform "amazing athletic feats" (Det No. 33, Nov '39: "The Batman Wars Against the Dirigible of Doom").

He is not only an "ace criminologist" (Det No. 73, Mar '43: "The Scarecrow Returns") and the "world's greatest detective" (Det No. 344, Oct '65: "The Crime-Boss Who Was Always One Step Ahead of Batman!"; and others), but also a "scientific genius" and prolific inventor who has devised literally scores of "astonishing inventions" to aid him in his never-ending war against lawbreakers (BM No. 109/3, Aug '57: "The 1,000 Inventions of Batman!").

Possessed of an extraordinary "photographic memory" (Det No. 152, Oct '49: "The Goblin of Gotham City!"; and others), he once remarked that "I never forget a face in my crime-file . . ." (Det No. 246, Aug '57: "Murder at Mystery Castle!"), although that file contains data on literally thousands of criminals.

Batman is a "superb athlete" (BM No. 14/1, Dec/Jan '42–'43: "The Case Batman Failed to Solve!!!") whose "splendid physical condition" (Det No. 59, Jan '42: "The King of the Jungle!") enables him to run the mile in four minutes three seconds (BM No. 70/2, Apr/May '52: "The Masterminds of Crime!"), clear a six-foot fence with ease (Det No. 36, Feb '40), hold his breath for three minutes at a time (Det No. 169, Mar '51: "Batman--Boss of the Big House!"), and, when the situation requires it, "work for three days and nights without any sleep!" (WF No. 49, Dec/Jan '50–'51: "A White Feather for Batman!").

He is a world-renowned acrobat and gymnast who has mastered the conventional circus acrobatic routines (BM No. 81/1, Feb '54: "Two-Face Strikes Again!") and gone on to perfect his own "famous quadruple somersault, a feat no other acrobat has ever duplicated!" (BM No. 109/2, Aug '57: "Follow the Batman"). "The way that guy flies around," comments an awe-struck hoodlum in November 1940, "you'd think he was a bird!" (Det No. 45: "The Case of the Laughing Death!").

Batman is a "lion-hearted fighter" (BM No. 14/1, Dec/Jan '42–'43: "The Case Batman Failed to Solve!!!") whose lifelong war against the underworld has transformed him into a "deadly fighting machine" (Det No. 65, Jul '42: "The Cop Who Hated the Batman!"). He is an expert at boxing (Det No. 174, Aug '51: "The Park Avenue Kid!") and wrestling (BM No. 11/3, Jun/Jul '42: "Bandits in Toyland!"), not to mention judo (Det No. 28, Jun '39; and others), jujitsu (Det No. 95, Jan '45; and others), savate (Det No. 370, Dec '67: "The Nemesis from Batman's Boyhood!"), karate and kung fu (Det No. 399, May '70: "Death Comes to a Small, Locked Room!"; and others), and all the fighting arts.

He is a master swordsman (WF No. 82, May/Jun '56: "The Three Super-Musketeers!") and fencer who has worked to become proficient in "the use of all weapons!" (BM No. 4/2, Win '41: "Blackbeard's Crew and the Yacht Society"). He is probably unexcelled as a master of the boomerang (Det No. 244, Jun '57: "The 100 Batarangs of Batman!").

Batman's extensive knowledge of weapons includes a "wide knowledge of firearms." He can assemble a pistol, blindfolded, within sixty seconds (BM No. 73/1, Oct/Nov '52: "Guns for Hire!") and determine merely from hearing the report of a firearm the caliber of the pistol that fired the shot (BM No. 16/3, Apr/May '43: "The Adventures of the Branded Tree!").

Batman is also a champion swimmer and skin diver (BM No. 83/2, Apr '54: "The Deep-Sea Diver Mystery!"); an accomplished deep-sea diver (BM No. 86/1, Sep '54: "The Voyage of the First Batmarine!"), scuba diver (BM No. 81/1, Feb '54: "Two-Face Strikes Again!"), ice skater (BM No. 29/1, Jun/Jul '45: "Enemy No. 1"), and skier (BM No. 126/1, Sep '59: "The Mystery of the 49th Star"); an experienced polo player (Det No. 234, Aug '56: "Batman and Robin's Greatest Mystery") and mountain climber (BM No. 93/1, Aug '55: "Journey to the Top of the World!"); and a skilled automobile stunt driver (BM No. 60/3, Aug/Sep '50: "The Auto Circus Mystery!"), motorcycle stunt rider (Det No. 286, Dec '60: "The Doomed Batwoman!"), aviator (Det No. 234, Aug '56: "Batman and Robin's Greatest Mystery"; and others), and stunt man (BM No. 14/1, Dec/Jan '42–'43: "The Case Batman Failed to Solve!!!").

No man alive can compare with Batman as a "master of disguise" (Det No. 91, Sep '44: "The Case of the Practical Joker"; and others) and a genius at impersonation (BM No. 60/3, Aug/Sep '50: "The Auto Circus Mystery!"; and others). The chronicles attest repeatedly to his "unsurpassed skill at makeup" (Det No. 204, Feb '54: "The Man Who Could Live Forever!"; and others) and to his uncanny skill at mimicking voices (Det No. 349, Mar '66: "The Blockbuster Breaks Loose!"; and others).

In addition, Batman is an "expert ventriloquist" (Det No. 150, Aug '49: "The Ghost of Gotham City!"; and others) who, "through a thorough study of ventriloquism, can throw his voice in any direction he pleases" (WF No. 2, Sum '41: "The Man Who Couldn't Remember!").

BARRETT KEAN, the man who taught Batman all he knows about makeup, has called Batman "the greatest impersonator alive," although Batman has modestly insisted that the honor of that designation rightfully belongs to Kean himself (Det No. 227, Jan '56: "The 50 Faces of Batman!").

Batman is a skilled mechanic (Det No. 85, Mar '44: "The Joker's Double"; and others), locksmith, and picklock, who once noted that "A man can't catch crooks until he has learned all their tricks!" (Det No. 87, May '44: "The Man of a Thousand Umbrellas"; and others).

Batman is also an accomplished hypnotist (Det No. 179, Jan '52: "Mayor Bruce Wayne!"), magician (Det No. 207, May '54: "Batman the Magician!"), and escape artist (Det No. 360, Feb '67: "The Case of the Abbreviated Batman!") who has "mastered all of Houdini's famous handcuffs-escapes!" (Det No. 328, Jun '64: "Gotham Gang Line-Up!").

He may also be regarded as an expert whittler. Locked in a barred cell by the Joker in October 1964, Batman escapes by carving a serviceable key out of a stool leg (Det No. 332: "The Joker's Last Laugh!").

Batman is also a man with a wide-ranging linguistic facility. He has at least a working understanding of Arabic (BM No. 25/2, Oct/Nov '44: "The Sheik of Gotham City!"), Tibetan (BM No. 168/2, Dec '64: "How to Solve a Perfect Crime--in Reverse!"), Eskimo (BM No. 130/3, Mar '60: "The Hand from Nowhere!"), the language of the exploded planet KRYPTON, now spoken only in the bottle city of KANDOR (WF No. 143, Aug '64: "The Feud Between Batman and Superman!" pts. I–II – no title; "The Manhunters from Earth!"), and other languages.

Batman is also conversant with numerous types of slang and special dialects, including circus slang (Det No. 233, Jul '56: "The Batwoman"), carnival slang (BM No. 154/2, Mar '63: "The Amazing Odyssey of Batman and Robin"), the slang employed by television studio technicians (BM No. 108/1, Jun '57: "The Big Batman Quiz"), and the slang spoken by convicts at Joliet Prison (BM No. 129/1, Feb '60: "The Web of the Spinner!").

He has a knowledge of Morse code (Det No. 164, Oct '50: "Untold Tales of the Bat-Signal!"; and others), semaphore code (BM No. 167, Nov '64: "Zero Hour for Earth!"), heliographic code (WF No. 125, May '62: "The Hostages of the Island of Doom!"), and nautical symbols (BM No. 124/2, Jun '59: "The Return of Signalman").

He is also an "accomplished lip-reader" (BM No. 11/3, Jun/Jul '42: "Bandits in Toyland!"; and others), knows Braille (Det No. 300, Feb '62: "The Bizarre Polka-Dot Man!"; and others), and understands the standard American sign language employed by deaf-and-dumb persons (WF No. 18, Sum '45: "Specialists in Crime!"; and others).

Few men possess Batman's ready fund of specialized knowledge. He has an expert's familiarity with South American and African wildlife (Det No. 255, May '58: "Death in Dinosaur Hall!"; and others); can identify the various species of bats by sight (BM No. 88/1, Dec '54: "The Mystery of the Four Batmen!"); has a wide knowledge of soils and clays (Det No. 211, Sep '54: "The Jungle Cat-Queen!"; and others), and is enough of an ornithologist to identify species of birds by their eggs (BM No. 99/1, Apr '56: "The Golden Eggs!").

In addition, Batman is an expert on gems (BM No. 149/3, Aug '62: "Batman Tunes in on Murder"), has an "expert knowledge of graphology" (Det No. 167, Jan '51: "Bodyguards to Cleopatra!"), and enjoys the facility of a skilled mathematician with the laws of chance and the theory of games (WF No. 150, Jun '65: pts. I–II – "The Super-Gamble with Doom!"; "The Duel of the Super-Gamblers!").

2. The Equipment. "The whole world knows of the detective skill of ***Batman*** and ***Robin,*** but less well known is the scientific genius of the Dynamic Duo! That's because they have guarded the secret of the many astonishing inventions they have devised in their war against lawbreakers!" (BM No. 109/3, Aug '57: "The 1,000 Inventions of Batman!").

To aid them in their unending crusade against villainy, Batman and Robin have assembled a vast, formidable arsenal of vehicles, machinery, and special equipment, virtually all of it of their own design and invention. What follows is an inventory of this arsenal, along with the history and evolution of each major component.

a. THE BATMOBILE. "A black thunderbolt on wheels, a swift nemesis to lawbreakers, a mighty machine of justice . . . that's the ***batmobile!***" (BM No. 98/3, Mar '56: "Secret of the Batmobile").

The term "batmobile" designates the specially designed and equipped automobile employed by Batman and Robin. In the early days of Batman's career, however, there was no special batmobile. Throughout 1939 Batman drives a series of red sedans which vary slightly in design from text to text, including the "special built high-powered auto" pictured here from Detective Comics No. 30 (Aug '39).

Batman's "special built high-powered auto," 1939
© NPP 1939

By January 1940 Batman has begun driving a dark blue roadster (Det No. 35) which he continues to drive through Fall 1940 (BM No. 3/2: "The Ugliest Man in the World"). In one text, however, it is portrayed as red (Det No. 38, Apr '40). According to Batman No. 3/2, "the tires of the **Batman's** car are coated with radio-active substance which glows under an infra-red ray," thus making it possible for either Batman or Robin to follow

Batman's roadster, 1940 © NPP 1940

Batman's roadster, 1940 © NPP 1940

The first batmobile, February 1941 © NPP 1941

the invisible tracks left by the vehicle (Fall '40: "The Ugliest Man in the World").

In February 1941 Batman's roadster, here colored red, appears with a small batlike ornament adorning the hood, and for the first time in the chronicles the term "batmobile" is used. Detective Comics No. 48 notes that it "flashes through the street with bullet speed," to "the quiet purr of a supercharged motor" ("The Secret Cavern").

In March 1941 the batmobile is a red roadster for the very last time in the chronicles. It lacks the distinctive batlike hood ornament of the previous month and, in structure and design, more closely resembles the roadster driven by Batman throughout 1940 (Det No. 49: "Clayface Walks Again!").

Spring 1941 brings with it an array of fundamental changes in batmobile styling that are destined to endure for very nearly a decade. The new vehicle is a dark blue "super-charged car" with a hard, fully enclosed top; a distinctive bat-head front; and a single sharklike tail fin protruding backward from the rear portion of the roof (BM No. 5/1: "The Riddle of the Missing Card!").

It is a "car of weird design and blinding speed" (Det No. 94, Dec '44: "No One Must Know!"), the "fleetest car in the world" (Det No. 89, Jul '44: "Laboratory Loot!"), a "sleek, rakish vehicle" (BM No. 17/1, Jun/Jul '43: "The Batman's Biographer!") that "flashes through the streets [like] a runaway meteor of streamlined steel!" (BM No. 6/2, Aug/Sep '41: "The Clock Maker!").

Fashioned out of "special reinforced glass and steel" to enable it to smash through barriers and withstand collisions (WF No. 2, Sum '41: "The Man Who Couldn't Remember!"), it is equipped with "special tires" (Det No. 60, Feb '42: "Case of the Costume-Clad Killers"); has a "secret throttle for high-speed travel" to prevent criminals from commandeering it for high-speed getaways (BM No. 37/3, Oct/Nov '46: "The Joker Follows Suit!"); and, "buoyed up by air tanks and propelled by retractible [sic] props," can even travel through the water (Det No. 147, May '49: "Tiger Shark!").

By April–May 1946 Batman and Robin have installed "new rocket and jet-propulsion gadgets" in the batmobile to give it enough "extra power" to "overtake a comet" (BM No. 34/1: "The Marathon of Menace!"),

The batmobile, 1941 © NPP 1941

The batmobile, 1941 © NPP 1941

The batmobile, 1943–1944 © NPP 1968

and in June–July 1949 they equip the batmobile with closed-circuit television.

"It will mean faster and better identification of criminals," explains Batman. "Now, police can flash us pictures of wanted crooks, rather than just descriptions" (BM No. 53/1: "A Hairpin, a Hoe, a Hacksaw, a Hole in the Ground!").

By July–August 1949 Batman and Robin have installed a new handset in the batmobile to enable them to receive direct telephone communications from POLICE COMMISSIONER GORDON (WF No. 41: "The Man with the Fatal Hands!").

WARILY, BATMAN ENTERS... WHEN SUDDENLY THE BATMOBILE, LIKE A ROBOT GONE BERSERK, RUSHES AT ITS INVENTOR!
HAW! HAW! WHAT A LAUGH... BATMAN'S GONNA BE RUN OVER BY HIS OWN BATMOBILE!

The batmobile, 1948 © NPP 1948

Other batmobile equipment and accessories include a built-in makeup kit that flips into view at the touch of a secret button (BM No. 47/2, Jun/Jul '48: "The Chain Gang Crimes!"); a special "direction finder" for picking up the continuous emergency signal broadcast by the "tiny, low power short wave transmitter" in Batman's utility belt (Det No. 77, Jul '43: "The Crime Clinic!"); a spare Batman costume (BM No. 49/1, Oct/Nov '48: "The Prison Doctor!"); and "an inhalator, gas masks and other equipment!" (BM No. 50/1, Dec/Jan '48–'49: "Lights – Camera – Crime!").

In February 1942, and intermittently for two years thereafter, the batmobile is portrayed with red streaks on either side of the body (Det No. 60: "Case of the Costume-Clad Killers"; and others), but these streaks make their last appearance in February–March 1944 (BM No. 21/4: "The Three Eccentrics!"). From Spring 1941 onward the batmobile is always dark blue (BM No. 5/1: "The Riddle of the Missing Card!"; and others), but at least one text describes the vehicle as black (Det No. 74, Apr '43: "Tweedledum and Tweedledee!") and it is indeed possible to interpret the batmobile's coloring as black with dark blue highlights.

By August–September 1942 Batman has installed at least one spare batmobile in his subterranean "batmobile garage" (BM No. 12/2: "The Wizard of Words!").

The batmobile remains substantially unchanged for nearly a decade, the most distinctive change being in the evolution of the tail fin, which gradually grows larger, beginning on the top of the car at the center of the roof and extending backward to end in a distinctive, deeply scalloped edge (e.g., Det No. 122, Apr '47: "The Black Cat Crimes!").

In February 1950, however, after the batmobile has careened off a dynamited bridge during a high-speed auto chase and been completely demolished, Batman and Robin design and construct a new one. The new vehicle, dark blue and fully enclosed like its predecessor and retaining the distinctive bat-head front, features dramatically modern, streamlined styling; an enlarged, gently angular tail fin; a transparent "plastic bubble" top instead of a windshield; and a powerful roof-mounted searchlight.

The new batmobile has "blinding speed"; can "accelerate to 100 miles per hour in 100 feet, and stop on a dime"; and is "ten years ahead of anything else on wheels."

Its permanent fixtures include: closed-circuit television, including built-in monitor and portable camera; a built-in radar screen, serviced by radar antennae in the tail fin; a "built-in crime-lab," complete with "built-in cabinets, workbench, stool," and "everything necessary for making tests on the run"; and powerful "rocket tubes," installed in the fenders, which provide the vehicle with "bursts of tremendous speed for short distances," enable it to hurtle over obstacles, and make it possible for Batman and Robin to blanket the surrounding area with "chemical blackout fog" to blind and confuse their adversaries.

In addition, the distinctive bat-head front-ornament now houses a "knife-edge steel nose for cutting through barriers," and the roof-mounted searchlight has been equipped to throw either a bat-symbol or a powerful light beam (Det No. 156: "The Batmobile of 1950!").

Equipped with a special shock-bumper to enable it to withstand the impact of high-speed, front-end collisions (BM No. 82/3, Mar '54: "The Olympic Games of Crime!"), the new batmobile is "shockproof and waterproof" (BM No. 114/2, Mar '58: "The Mirage Maker"), features "crash-proof construction" (Det No. 325, Mar '64: "The Strange Lives of the Cat-Man!"), and is "tougher than an ordinary armored car" (WF No. 72, Sep/Oct '54: "Fort Crime!").

Powerful "emergency searchlights" have been installed in the headlights (BM No. 157/1, Aug '63: "The Villain of the Year!"). The turning radius of the vehicle is 40 feet (Det No. 214, Dec '54: "The Batman Encyclopedia").

Other special equipment installed in the new batmobile includes a "sonic range finder" (Det No. 253, Mar '58: "The Fox, the Shark, and the Vulture!"); an "emergency-cable" (BM No. 76/1, Apr/May '53: "The Danger Club!") and "power-hoist" (BM No. 76/2, Apr/May '53: "The Penguin's Fabulous Fowls!") for extricating the vehicle from ditches and quicksand; a fire extinguisher mounted on the outside wall, just behind the driver's seat (WF No. 60, Sep/Oct '52: "The Richest Crook in the World!"); a short-wave police radio (BM No. 81/3, Feb '54: "The Phantom Bandit of Gotham City!"); a Geiger counter which the Dynamic Duo install in June 1951 (Det No. 172: "The Outlaw Who Had Nine Lives!"); and a concealed tape recorder which

The batmobile, 1950 © NPP 1950

plays misleading ambient sounds to blindfolded visitors being brought to the batcave in order to prevent their retracing the route later by utilizing sound-clues (BM No. 108/3, Jun '57: "The Career of Batman Jones!").

Stored in the batmobile, along with its "traveling research files" (BM No. 90/1, Mar '55: "The Web of Doom!") and "black cloth toolbag" (BM No. 92/3, Jun '55: "Ace, the Bat-Hound!"), are several spare Batman costumes (BM No. 155/2, May '63: "The Return of the Penguin!"), asbestos suits for fighting fires (BM No. 76/2, Apr/May '53: "The Penguin's Fabulous Fowls!"), and special grappling equipment for latching onto fleeing getaway cars and forcing them to a halt (BM No. 106/3, Mar '57: "The Puppet Batman!").

By July 1958 a pair of whirly-bats (*see* section E 2 b ii, the other aircraft) have been installed in the batmobile's trunk (Det No. 257: "Batman's Invincible Foe!"; and others), and by December 1960 an inflatable "rubber bat-raft" (*see* section E 2 c, the bat-boat and other seacraft) has been stored there also (BM No. 136/3: "The Challenge of the Joker").

In special emergencies, the batmobile can be outfitted with "snowmobile equipment" to enable it to travel over snow; with a special "duck chassis" to enable it to move both on land and in water; or with heavy steel plates that transform it into an "armored batmobile," powerful enough to withstand a hurricane (BM No. 98/3, Mar '56: "Secret of the Batmobile"). Beginning in April 1955, the batmobile can also be operated by "radio remote-control" (BM No. 91/1: "The Living Batplane!").

At least one spare batmobile is housed in the batcave (BM No. 150/2, Sep '62: "The Girl Who Stole Batman's Heart"; and others). The flying batcave (*see* section E 2 b ii, the other aircraft) houses a smaller version of the batmobile called the "bat-racer" (Det No. 317, Jul '63: "The Secrets of the Flying Bat-Cave!").

The batmobile introduced in early 1950 remains substantially unchanged for fourteen years, the major changes being the deepening scalloping and increasing stylization of the tail fin, the squaring of the fronts of

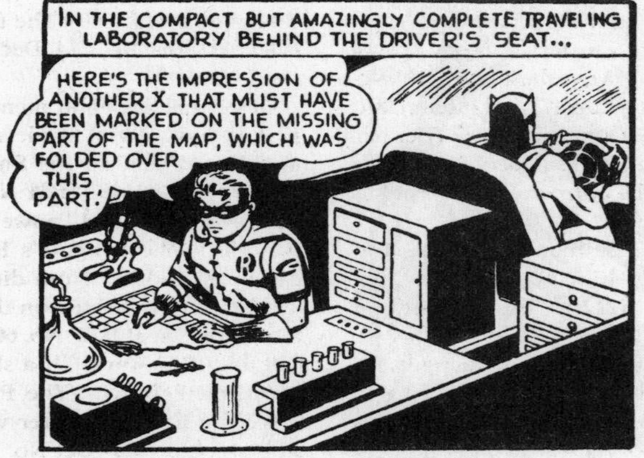

The batmobile (interior), 1950 © NPP 1950

The batmobile, 1953 © NPP 1953

the fenders, and the replacement of the doors by a plastic-bubble top that tilts back on a hinge to permit the passengers entry and exit (Det No. 316, Jun '63: "Double Batman vs. Double X"; and others).

In June 1964, however, realizing that "the trend now is toward sports cars--small, maneuverable jobs," Batman introduces an entirely different batmobile, a dark blue sports-car convertible with twin tail fins and a stylized black bat-head emblem painted on the hood (BM No. 164/1: "Two-Way Gem Caper!").

Smaller, sportier, and less cumbersome than its predecessor, the new batmobile features a "portable crime-lab" (Det No. 335, Jan '65: "Trail of the Talking Mask!"; and others) complete with microscope (BM No. 170/2, Mar '65: "The Puzzle of the Perilous Prizes!") and other equipment; a hot-line telephone to the office of POLICE COMISSIONER GORDON (BM No. 164/1, Jun '64: "Two-Way Gem Caper!"; and others); a "special sound effects gimmick that simulates the noise of a motor receding into the distance" (Det No. 344, Oct '65: "The

The batmobile, 1957 © NPP 1957

Crime-Boss Who Was Always One Step Ahead of Batman!"); a dashboard button for opening and closing the camouflaged entrance to the batcave by "remote electronic control" (BM No. 164/1, Jun '64: "Two-Way Gem Caper!"); a "special-filter windshield" for following the invisible infrared trail left by the chemically treated tires of ALFRED's motorcycle (Det No. 328, Jun '64: "Gotham Gang Line-Up!"); and a special "emergency signal" that sounds whenever Batman is needed by the Justice League of America, an organization of heroes of which he is a member (BM No. 172/2, Jun '65: "Robin's Unassisted Triple Play!").

In April 1965 Batman and Robin equip the batmobile with the newly invented "encephitector," a device that "picks out and filters the alpha waves that a human brain gives out," reacting whenever it receives wave-patterns that "show a person is thinking about committing a crime" and thereby facilitating Batman's task of locating and apprehending criminals (Det No. 338: "Batman's Power-Packed Punch!").

By July 1965 Batman has equipped the batmobile with an alarm that sets off a "screaming siren" and locks the ignition as a precaution against any attempted theft of the vehicle (Det No. 341: "The Joker's Comedy Capers!").

By May 1966 Batman and Robin have equipped the batmobile with a new "hydrofoil attachment" and rear-end propeller that enable the vehicle to travel over land or water on a cushion of compressed air (Det No. 351: "The Cluemaster's Topsy-Turvy Crimes!").

The sports-car batmobile remains substantially unchanged for approximately two and a half years, the major changes being the gradual increasing of the overall size of the vehicle, the enlarging of the tail fins in proportion to the size of the body, the substitution of bucket seats for the single front seat, the introduction of a new design for the bat-head emblem on the hood, and the addition of such accessories as a roof-mounted searchlight just behind the front seats.

By December 1966 the stylized black bat-head emblem painted on the batmobile's hood has been replaced by a metal bat-head affixed to the front of the vehicle (Det No. 358: "The Circle of Terror!"), and, in the year and a half that follows, the batmobile undergoes a series of minor design variations culminating in the 1968 dual-cockpit model at the bottom of the following page (BM No. 203, Jul/Aug '68).

Special equipment introduced during this period includes the "bat-tector," an ingenious sound-detecting device capable of distinguishing different types of sounds — from gunshots to bomb explosions — and pinpointing their sources (Det No. 364, Jun '67: "The Curious Case of the Crime-less Clues!"), and a sophisticated "amplifier" sensitive to human heartbeats.

"Ah!" thinks Batman to himself as he drives through the city. "My improved sound amplifier is picking up the thump of human heartbeats--in that dark building! Heartbeats that I've graphed as telltale signs of criminal activity!" (Det No. 366: "The Round-Robin Death Threats").

The batmobile, 1966 © NPP 1966

In December 1969, when Batman closes up the batcave and departs Wayne Manor for a new penthouse home in the heart of Gotham City, the batmobile is one of the pieces of equipment that remains left behind (BM No. 217: "One Bullet Too Many!"). In its place, Batman substitutes the sleek turbo-powered sports car pictured on the following page, equipped with "one-way mirrored windows and windshield" to enable him to see out while preventing passersby from seeing in (Det No. 394, Dec '69: "A Victim's Victim!"); bulletproof chassis and window glass; front-end "hydraulic impact-absorbers"; a device for creating smoke screens; and remote-control machinery operated by means of a tiny "micro-control" on Batman's utility belt (Det No. 396, Feb '70: "The Brain Pickers!").

b. THE BATPLANE AND OTHER AIRCRAFT. ***i. The Batplane.*** The term "batplane" designates the specially designed and equipped aircraft employed by Batman and Robin.

Batman's first aircraft, introduced in September 1939, is the so-called "batgyro" or "bat-plane," a powerful autogyro whose highly stylized batlike design gives it the appearance in flight of an eerie "monster bat."

Housed in a "secret hangar" whose location is known only to Batman, and equipped with "automatic con-

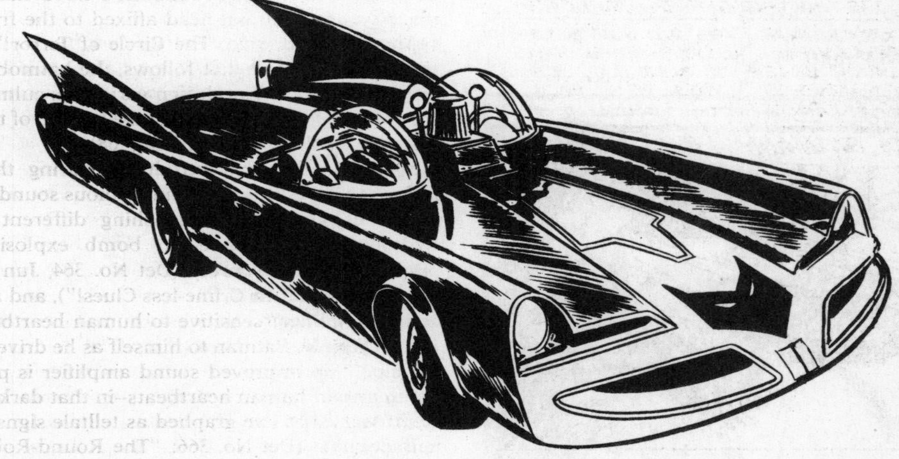

The batmobile, 1968 © NPP 1968

Batman's turbo-powered sports car, 1969 © NPP 1969

trols" that enable it to hover in mid-air or maintain a pre-set course automatically, the batgyro inspires awe and pandemonium as it passes overhead.

"The end of the world," cries one frightened onlooker. "We are attacked by Martians!" (Det No. 31).

In October 1939 the hyphen in "bat-plane" is dropped, and from this time onward the term "batplane" is used (Det No. 32).

By Spring 1940 Batman has replaced his autogyro with a new batplane, this one an open-cockpit, mid-wing, single-prop monoplane with a retractable undercarriage and a water-cooled machine gun mounted on the fuselage. In styling, the body of the new batplane is similar to that of the batgyro, except that the wings and bat-head front of the new aircraft are even more realistically batlike and the "ears" of the bat-head are considerably larger (BM No. 1/3).

By Fall 1940 the batplane has changed again, this time to an open-cockpit, low-wing, single-prop monoplane with an elliptical tail. This aircraft features gently scalloped, batlike wings with a conventional fuselage and tail assembly (BM No. 3/1: "The Strange Case of the Diabolical Puppet Master").

Batman with batgyro and batarang, 1939 © NPP 1939

The ensuing months bring with them a series of minor variations in the style of the batplane, the most significant being the acquisition of a gently rounded bat-head front in November 1940 (Det No. 45: "The Case of the Laughing Death!").

By Winter 1941 the batplane has become an enclosed-cockpit, low-wing, single-prop monoplane with delta tail and spats. At the touch of a button as the aircraft lands on the ocean, "the wheels are drawn in . . . the wings fold against the plane's side . . ." and the batplane is converted into a boat (BM No. 4/2: "Blackbeard's Crew and the Yacht Society").

From early 1942 through early 1946, the batplane – now characterized by a less fully rounded, more nearly heart-shaped bat-head front – is an enclosed-cockpit, low-wing, single-prop monoplane with non-swept tail and retractable undercarriage.

Other features include automatic pilot (WF No. 10, Sum '43: "Man with the Camera Eyes"); retractable autogyro (BM No. 14/4, Dec/Jan '42–'43: "Bargains in Banditry!"; and others) with "automatic gyroscope stabilizer" for hovering (BM No. 23/1, Jun/Jul '44: "The Upside Down Crimes!"); and pontoons (WF No. 20, Win '45: "King of Coins!").

The batgyro, 1939 © NPP 1939

The batplane has red stripes on its fuselage in the early months of 1942 (BM No. 9/1, Feb/Mar '42: "The Four Fates!"; and others), but these disappear after April–May 1942 (BM No. 10/4: "Sheriff of Ghost Town!"). A tail insignia consisting of a black bat-emblem inscribed in a yellow circle appears occasionally (BM No. 21/1, Feb/Mar '44: "The Streamlined Rustlers!").

Described as a "weird craft" (BM No. 21/4, Feb/Mar '44: "The Three Eccentrics!") and a "dread scourge of the skies" (BM No. 21/2, Feb/Mar '44: "Blitzkrieg Bandits!"), the aircraft is housed first in Bruce Wayne's barn (WF No. 6, Sum '42: "The Secret of Bruce Wayne!") and later in Batman's subterranean "batplane hangar" along with two spare batplanes (BM No. 12/2, Aug/Sep '42: "The Wizard of Words!").

Bruce Wayne gives Robin a smaller version of the batplane as a birthday present in April–May 1942 (BM No. 10/1: "The Isle That Time Forgot!").

Passersby react to the batgyro, 1939 © NPP 1939

The batplane, Spring 1940 © NPP 1940

By February 1946 the batplane has been outfitted with "jet tubes," thus increasing its speed by "an extra hundred miles an hour, at least," and transforming it into a non-swept-wing, jet-propelled aircraft with retractable autogyro (Det No. 108: "The Goat of Gotham City!") and "gyroscopic stabilizers" (Det No. 124, Jun '47: "The Crime Parade"; and others) for hovering. Although colored dark blue like the batplanes before it, it is described as black in at least one text (BM No. 37/3, Oct/Nov '46: "The Joker Follows Suit!").

By April–May 1946 Batman and Robin have equipped the batplane with "new rocket and jet-propulsion gadgets" designed to give the aircraft enough "extra power" to "overtake a comet" (BM No. 34/1: "The Marathon of Menace!").

In November–December 1946 they equip the batplane with engineer FRANK FOLLAND's ingenious "aeraquamobile devices," which enable the batplane to retract its wings partially and travel across land as a "sleek, three-wheeled automobile," or retract its wings completely and either skim across water in the style of a hydroplane or travel beneath the surface as a jet-propelled submarine.

"With Folland's new gadgets added to our jet propulsion," remarks Robin, "the **batplane** ought to rank among the wonders of the world!" (WF No. 25: "The Famous First Crimes!").

The batplane remains substantially unchanged until October–November 1950, when an air experiment gone awry allows it to fall into the hands of the notorious BOLEY BROTHERS, forcing Batman and Robin to design and construct Batplane II.

Batplane II is a non-swept-wing, jet-propelled aircraft with super-ramjet power plant, retractable autogyro with gyroscopic stabilizers, and retractable undercarriage featuring interchangeable wheels, skis, and pontoons.

The batplane, Fall 1940 © NPP 1940

The batplane, 1942 © NPP 1968

Other permanent features include a fully equipped crime-laboratory in the aircraft's cabin; human ejector tubes in the tail-section for emergency escapes; a storage area for spare costumes and other equipment; television, radio, and radar antennae housed in the wing structures; a "magnesium fired batbeam" in the nose area for momentarily blinding airborne adversaries with "a powerful flash of light" in the form of a giant bat; grappling hooks for seizing enemy aircraft in mid-flight; and an ingenious "vacuum blanket" which, activated in mid-air directly over an opposing aircraft, causes engine failure in the target aircraft, forcing its pilot to make an immediate emergency landing.

In addition, the wings and rudder assembly of Batplane II "fold into the fuselage" at the touch of a button, transforming the extraordinary aircraft into a "batmarine," i.e., a jet-propelled submarine (BM No. 61/1: "The Birth of Batplane II!").

The new batplane is also equipped with bomb-bay doors (BM No. 70/3, Apr/May '52: "The Parasols of Plunder"); remote-control piloting facilities (BM No. 81/2, Feb '54: "The Boy Wonder Confesses!"); "reserve jets" for extra power (BM No. 116/3, Jun '58: "The Winged Bat-People!"); and a "parachute brake" for rapid deceleration upon landing (Det No. 261, Nov '58: "The Amazing Dr. Double X!").

Batplane II can be used for skywriting (BM No. 92/1, Jun '55: "Fan-Mail of Danger!") and for reconnoitering hurricanes (BM No. 116/3, Jun '58: "The Winged Bat-People!"), even in cases when the storms are so tempestuous that ordinary "hurricane-hunter" aircraft are

AND, ATOP THE ROOF OF POLICE HEADQUARTERS...
A HAIRPIN AND A HACKSAW! WHAT IS THAT CRAZY CRIME-CLOWN UP TO NOW?!
I DON'T KNOW, COMMISSIONER-BUT WE MUST BE READY FOR ANYTHING!

The batplane, 1949 © NPP 1949

unable to penetrate their winds (BM No. 106/2, Mar '57: "Storm Over Gotham City!"). Its "super-powerful jets" can be used for such diverse purposes as forcing down opposing aircraft (Det No. 171, May '51: "The Menace of the Giant Birds!") and starting large fires (BM No. 91/1, Apr '55: "The Living Batplane!"; and others).

Equipment carried aboard the batplane includes the following items: fire extinguishers (WF No. 102, Jun '59: "The Caveman from Krypton!"); a microfilm rogues' gallery (BM No. 126/1, Sep '59: "The Mystery of the 49th Star"); parachutes and spare Batman and Robin costumes (BM No. 61/1, Oct/Nov '50: "The Birth of Batplane II!"); Batman and Robin dummies housed in a "secret floor-compartment" (BM No. 91/1, Apr '55: "The Living Batplane!"); a pair of whirly-bats (*see* section E 2 b ii, the other aircraft); and a special "emergency kit" containing candles and other useful items (BM No. 124/3, Jun '59: "The Mystery Seeds from Space!").

In place of the bat-head front that characterized its predecessor, Batplane II features a highly stylized black bat-emblem painted on the nose section, complemented by a special insignia – a stylized black bat-cowl inscribed in a yellow circle superimposed on a black lightning-flash – painted on either side of the fuselage directly beneath the cockpit (BM No. 61/1, Oct/Nov '50: "The Birth of Batplane II!"; and others).

Both the emblem and insignia are occasionally varied. In World's Finest Comics No. 61, for example, the circles on the fuselage are red, not yellow (Nov/Dec '52: "The Crimes of Batman!"), and in World's Finest Comics No. 92 the customary black bat-emblem on the batplane's nose is shown inscribed in a yellow circle (Jan/Feb '58: "The Boy from Outer Space!").

In August–September 1952 Batman and Robin discuss their intention to install new "wing modifications" to "improve the jet performance of the batplane" (BM No. 72/3: "The Death-Cheaters of Gotham City!"), and in December 1953–January 1954 Robin remarks that "those new jet engines we installed in the batplane certainly performed nicely" (BM No. 80/2: "Dick Grayson's Nightmare!"). The Dynamic Duo install even newer jets in the batplane in October 1955, thus endowing the aircraft with the "terrific speed" worthy of a "super-fast craft" (Det No. 224: "The Batman Machine!").

Following the introduction of Batplane II in late 1950, the batplane remains virtually unchanged for fourteen years, the sole changes consisting of minor, erratic stylistic modifications occurring occasionally from text

Batplane II, 1950 © NPP 1950

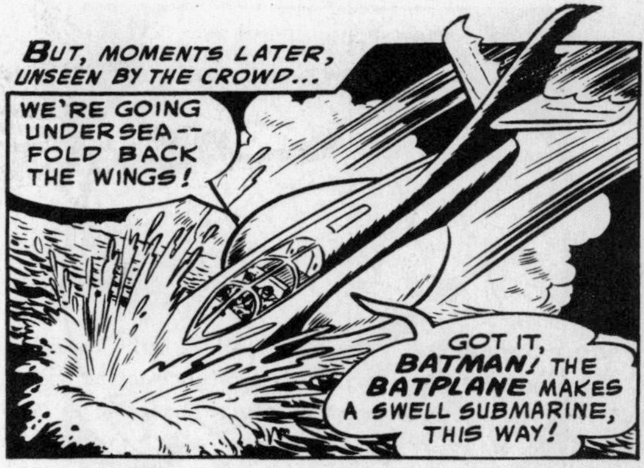

The batplane converting into a submarine © NPP 1956

to text. The batplane appears as a swept-wing, jet-propelled aircraft, for example, in April–May 1952 (BM No. 70/3: "The Parasols of Plunder"), only to appear with a delta configuration in December 1952 (Det No. 190: "How to Be the Batman!") and as a non-swept-wing aircraft in August 1954 (BM No. 85/2: "The Guardian of the Bat-Signal!").

By late 1964, however, the batplane has once again changed radically, this time into a non-swept-wing, jet-propelled aircraft with V.T.O.L. modification, decorative needle-nose, and long-range fuel tanks mounted on the wing-tips. Best described as a rough adaptation of the Lockheed F-104 Starfighter, the new batplane features a black bat-emblem insignia inscribed in a yellow circle on either side of the fuselage.

By mid-1968 the batplane has undergone yet another transformation, this time into a swept-wing, jet-propelled aircraft with V.T.O.L. modification, its design closely based on that of the McDonnell F-101 Voodoo. The new aircraft boasts two black bat-emblem insignia inscribed inside yellow ovals, one painted on a wing, the other on the fuselage (BM No. 203, Jul/Aug '68).

ii. The Other Aircraft. Batman and Robin have employed a number of aircraft besides the batplane in the course of their careers, although the batplane has remained by far the most important. These other aircraft have included *a)* the flying batcave, *b)* the bat-copter, *c)* the whirly-bats, and *d)* the bat-missile.

a) THE FLYING BATCAVE. In August 1952, after gangster DIAMOND LANG has forced them to pledge under duress not to "set foot" for a week in Gotham City, Batman and Robin take to the air in the so-called flying batcave, an airborne crime-fighting headquarters – in the form of a gigantic single-rotor helicopter – designed to enable them to fight crime in Gotham City without actually "setting foot" in it.

Colored dark blue and emblazoned with a black bat-emblem inscribed in a large white circle, the flying batcave features the following equipment and apparatus: four television monitors providing simultaneous views of the city as it would appear from heights of 200, 1,000, 5,000, and 10,000 feet; a huge "radar-observascope" providing panoramic aerial views of Gotham City, with a large magnifying lens which can be moved about the observascope screen for close-ups; selected trophies from the batcave's Hall of Trophies, including

Batplane II construction diagram, 1950 © NPP 1950

The batplane, April–May 1952 © NPP 1952

The batplane, August 1954 © NPP 1954

the giant Lincoln-head penny; closed-circuit television equipment; a "giant electromagnet" for disarming criminals from the air; and an ingenious bathysphere—the so-called "underwater bat-osphere"—which can be lowered into the harbor for underwater crime-fighting. It is also equipped with scuba gear, "delicate radio instruments . . . similar to the submarine-detecting devices on battleships," and other apparatus (Det No. 186: "The Flying Bat-Cave!").

In July 1963 Batman and Robin employ an "improved version" of the flying batcave featuring a small trophy room, a galley and sleeping quarters described as "compact but comfortable," and a "comination workshop-and-garage" housing, among other things, a smaller version of the batmobile called the "bat-racer."

Special equipment includes voice-amplifying apparatus for broadcasting directly to the ground, closed-circuit television equipment for communicating with the police headquarters of any large city, research files similar to those maintained in the batcave's crime laboratory, a telescoping metal hand for reaching down and seizing fleeing criminals, ingenious "glider bat-wings" for riding the air currents, and "special steam valves" for camouflaging the flying batcave to resemble a cloud (Det No. 317: "The Secrets of the Flying Bat-Cave!").

The batplane, December 1952 © NPP 1952

b) THE BAT-COPTER. By April 1958 Batman and Robin have begun to employ a helicopter—called the "bat-copter"—separate and distinct from the batplane with its retractable autogyro mechanism deployed (Det No. 254: "One Ounce of Doom!"). In its earliest appearances, however, the bat-copter closely resembles the batplane with its autogyro in place, but by March 1965 it has assumed the form depicted on page 66, that of a single-rotor transport helicopter with a semiretractable undercarriage (Det No. 337: "Deep-Freeze Menace!").

c) THE WHIRLY-BATS. By July 1958 Batman and Robin have completed construction of their first pair of whirly-bats, a "new one-man 'copter invention" which henceforth they carry along with them in the trunk of the batmobile (Det No. 257: "Batman's Invincible Foe!"; and others), in the batplane (BM No. 124/3, Jun '59: "The Mystery Seeds from Space!"), and even in the bat-missile (Det No. 270, Aug '59: "The Creature from Planet X!").

The whirly-bats are collapsible and can be placed on "automatic" and left to hover in mid-air (BM No. 124/3, Jun '59: "The Mystery Seeds from Space!"). They can be made to emit a smoke screen by stalling the engine (Det No. 266, Apr '59: "The Satellite of Gotham City!"), and are equipped with long, powerful "vacuum hoses" for snatching up criminals (BM No. 120/3, Dec '58: "The Airborne Batman!").

d) THE BAT-MISSILE. In August 1959, despite the fact that it "hasn't been completely flight-tested yet," Batman and Robin take to the air in their experimental bat-missile, an enclosed-cockpit aircraft in the form of a surface-to-air missile that is launched from a platform inside the batcave and brought to earth by means of a special "rocket chute" landing device (Det No. 270: "The Creature from Planet X!").

In addition to the various special aircraft enumerated above, Batman and Robin have employed the "sky sled," invented by ALFRED, a red airplane-shaped craft,

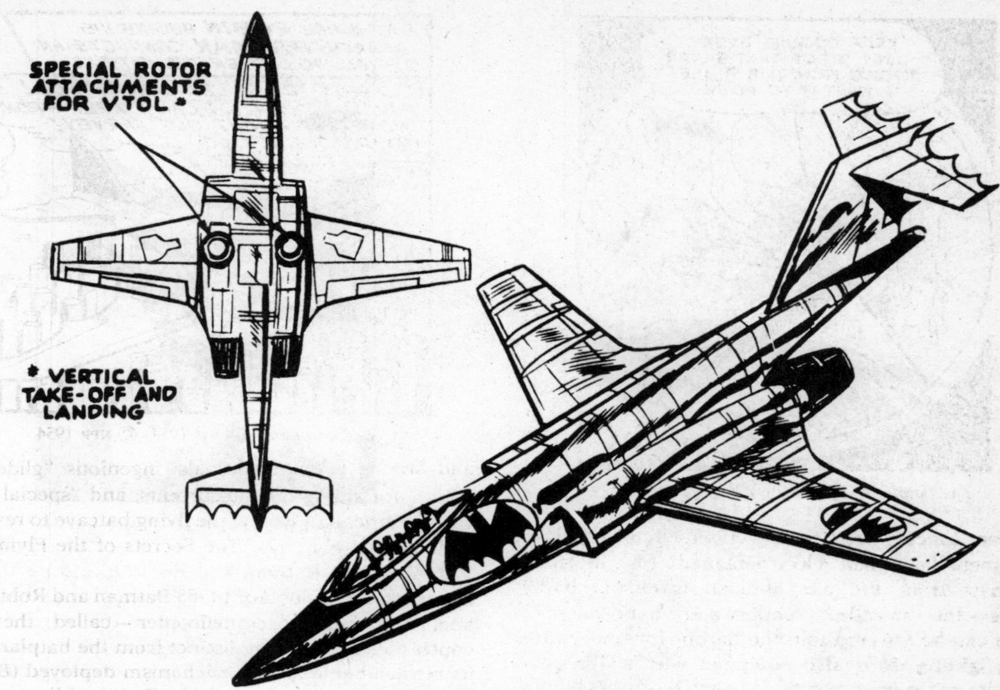

The batplane, 1968 © NPP 1968

roughly twelve feet long, on which one man lies prone while soaring through the air (BM No. 68/2, Dec/Jan '51–'52: "The Secret Life of Batman's Butler!"), and a flying-saucer-like aerodyne to serve as a temporary substitute for the batplane (Det No. 236, Oct '56: "The New-Model Batman!").

In December 1969, when Batman closes up the batcave and departs Wayne Manor for a new penthouse home in the heart of Gotham City, the batplane and other aircraft are among the items of equipment that remain left behind (BM No. 217: "One Bullet Too Many!").

A glimpse of what the future may hold for Batman's aircraft, however, is offered in Batman No. 59/3, which depicts the rocket-propelled "bat-ship" – a highly stylized, batlike spacecraft – employed by Batman and Robin during a time-journey they make to the world of 2050 A.D. (Jun/Jul '50: "Batman in the Future!").

C. THE BAT-BOAT AND OTHER SEACRAFT. Unlike the batmobile and batplane, which appear continually in the chronicles, Batman's seacraft play only a minor and occasional role. Cataloging them is difficult because of the capriciousness with which they are added to and subtracted from Batman's crime-fighting arsenal and because the terminology used to describe them is inconsistent.

The term "bat-boat," for example, with or without the hyphen, has been variously utilized to designate an inboard motorboat prepared for Batman's use by Scotland Yard during the Dynamic Duo's visit to London in April 1946 (Det No. 110: "Batman and Robin in Scotland Yard!"); a highly stylized black sailboat with an auxiliary motor that appears in a text for March 1963 (BM No. 154/2: "The Amazing Odyssey of Batman and Robin"); and a motorized craft with one or two fins that begins appearing in the texts in the 1960s (Det No. 334, Dec '64: "The Man Who Stole From Batman!"; and others).

Given that these difficulties exist, however, what follows is an inventory of Batman's seacraft, grouped according to the following general categories: i) motorized surface craft; ii) undersea craft; and iii) nonmotorized surface craft.

i. Motorized Surface Craft. The first seacraft ever employed by Batman is the red motor launch that he uses during his premiere encounter with the CATWOMAN in Spring 1940 (BM No. 1/4). Less than a year later, in Winter 1941, the batplane converts into a motorized boat for the very first time (BM No. 4/2: "Blackbeard's Crew and the Yacht Society").

In April 1946, when Batman and Robin visit London for their encounter with PROFESSOR MORIARTY, Scotland Yard provides them with a specially prepared "batboat" – an inboard motorboat equipped with "all [Batman's] inventions, including the batarang gun" – to use during their stay there (Det No. 110: "Batman and Robin in Scotland Yard!").

By April–May 1946 Batman and Robin have installed "new rocket and jet-propulsion gadgets" in the batboat to give it enough "extra power" to "overtake a comet" (BM No. 34/1: "The Marathon of Menace!"), but it is unclear whether this means that the Dynamic Duo have brought the Scotland Yard batboat home with them or whether the reference is to some other seacraft.

The flying batcave, 1963 © NPP 1963

By December 1957 Batman and Robin have acquired the "bat-launch," a sharp-nosed, high-finned seacraft (BM No. 112/1: "The Signalman of Crime") described as bulletproof in Batman No. 115/1 (Apr '58: "The Million-Dollar Clues").

The whirly-bats © NPP 1976

The bat-copter, 1965 © NPP 1965

In May 1963 Batman and Robin introduce the Batman patrol boat, a black patrol boat with a white cabin and a black bat-emblem painted on the bow. The craft, which flies a white flag emblazoned with a black bat-emblem, is equipped with a pair of ingenious "bat-torpedos," special manned torpedos, fired from torpedo tubes situated just above the waterline, which can be used to jettison Batman and Robin from the patrol boat and then independently operated like tiny one-man craft on the surface of the water (BM No. 155/1: "Batman's Psychic Twin!").

Another seacraft making its debut in the 1960s is the "bat-boat," a small, highly stylized surface craft with two blue fins and a sharply pointed bat-head front (Det No. 334, Dec '64: "The Man Who Stole from Batman!"; and others). The bat-boat undergoes a series of minor design modifications following its initial appearance, culminating in the single-finned model shown moored in the batcave in the batcave cutaway diagram that appears in July–August 1968 (BM No. 203). (*See* section D, the batcave.)

Batman's only other motorized surface craft is the S.S. *Batman*, a medium-sized vessel housing a replica of the batcave, that tours the coastline in August 1960 accumulating admissions fees to be contributed to charity (BM No. 133/2: "The Voyage of the S.S. Batman").

ii. Undersea Craft. Batman's first undersea vessel is actually the batplane, which, following the installation of FRANK FOLLAND's "aeraquamobile devices" in November–December 1946, can retract its wings and travel beneath the surface as a jet-propelled submarine (WF No. 25: "The Famous First Crimes!"). Later the term "batmarine" is employed to designate the batplane functioning as a submarine (BM No. 61/1, Oct/Nov '50: "The Birth of Batplane II!").

In May 1949, during their hunt for the villainous TIGER SHARK, Batman and Robin employ another undersea vessel, the "sub-batmarine," equipped with grappling hooks, periscope, batarang gun, diving gear, a net for ensnaring submarines, and other devices (Det No. 147: "Tiger Shark!").

In September 1954, when a prolonged deep-sea diving excursion to the bottom of the Gotham City River forces Batman and Robin to remain underwater for two full days as a precaution against the bends, the Dynamic Duo arrange for the temporary donation of a Navy surplus pocket-submarine – which they promptly dub the "batmarine" – and use it as a temporary crime-fighting headquarters until it is safe for them to return to the surface (BM No. 86/1: "The Voyage of the First Batmarine!").

In June 1960 Batman and Robin employ a new submarine, the so-called "bat-sub," equipped with a sophisticated "sound detector" and other specialized apparatus (BM No. 132/3: "The Lair of The Sea-Fox!"). Within less than a year, however, the design of the bat-sub has been radically altered, its newly acquired fins giving it the appearance of a gigantic fish (BM No. 138/3, Mar '61: "The Secret of the Sea Beast!").

Other undersea craft employed by Batman and Robin include the bathysphere they use in May 1949 (Det No. 147: "Tiger Shark!"); the "underwater bat-osphere" – also a bathysphere – stored in the flying batcave (Det No. 186, Aug '52: "The Flying Bat-Cave!"); and the "batosphere" – presumably a more sophisticated version of the underwater bat-osphere – whose special features include a "super-surface viewer," a "sub-surface viewer," and extravehicular "extension arms" for grasping and grappling (Det No. 189, Nov '52: "The Undersea Hideout!").

iii. Nonmotorized Surface Craft. These include the "bat-ship," a sailboat used by Batman and Robin when they fire the starting gun at the Gotham Regatta in April–May 1950 (BM No. 58/3: "The Black Diamond!"), and the "bat-boat," a black sailboat with matching bat-wing sails and a decorative bat-head front, which is, however, fitted with an auxiliary motor (BM No. 154/2, Mar '63: "The Amazing Odyssey of Batman and Robin").

Batman and Robin keep an inflatable "rubber bat-raft" stored in the trunk of the batmobile (BM No. 136/3, Dec '60: "The Challenge of the Joker"). In Detective Comics No. 314, where it is referred to as an "inflatable rubber bat-boat," the bat-raft is equipped with serrated sides designed to simulate bat-wings (Apr '63: "Murder in Movieland!").

In December 1969, when Batman closes up the batcave and departs Wayne Manor for a new penthouse home in the heart of Gotham City, his various seacraft are among the items of equipment that remain left behind (BM No. 217: "One Bullet Too Many!").

d. THE BAT-ROPE, BATARANG, AND OTHER EQUIPMENT. ***i. The Bat-Rope.*** Almost from the onset of his colorful career, a "tough silk rope" (Det No. 28, Jun '39) has been part of Batman's standard equipment. These special ropes – variously described as "silken ropes" (WF No. 18, Sum '45: "Specialists in Crime!"; and others); "traveling cords" and "silken cords" (BM No. 67/1, Oct/Nov '51: "The Mystery Rope!"; and others); "bat-lines" (BM No. 117/3, Aug '58: "Manhunt in Outer Space!"; and others); and, finally, "bat-ropes," either with the hyphen (Det No. 322, Dec '63: "The Bizarre Batman Genie!"; and others) or without (Det No. 340, Jun '65: "The Outsider Strikes Again!"; and others) – are light in weight but "strong as steel" (BM No. 24/3, Aug/Sep '44: "The Mayors of Yonville!"), powerful enough to tie down an elephant (Det No. 284, Oct '60: "The Negative Batman!") or halt the charge of an angry rhino (BM No. 100/2, Jun '56: "The Hunters of Gotham City").

With near unanimity, the texts describe Batman's bat-rope as made of silk; a description of the rope as "hempen" in one early text (Det No. 90, Aug '44: "Crime Between the Acts!") may therefore safely be regarded as a chronicler's error.

The bat-rope serves a multitude of functions. Batman has used it as a lasso, sometimes to lethal effect (Det No. 29, Jul '39: "The Batman Meets Doctor Death"; BM No. 1/3, Spr '40); as a harpoon line in conjunction with the "batpoon" (*see* section d iii, the other equipment); and as a grappling rope when tied to the special "steel rope hooks" he carries in his utility belt (Det No. 214, Dec '54: "The Batman Encyclopedia").

For the most part, however, Batman uses his bat-rope for scaling buildings and swinging from rooftops, propelling himself through the Gotham City canyons like a Tarzan in an urban jungle. Because he does not possess a limitless supply of bat-ropes, Batman sometimes returns the following day to retrieve any bat-ropes he may have been forced to leave behind the night before (BM No. 169/2, Feb '65: "A Bad Day for Batman!").

In the early months of Batman's career, the bat-rope

Rocket-powered bat-ship employed by Batman and Robin during a visit to the world of 2050 A.D. © NPP 1950

Batman casts his bat-rope, 1939 © NPP 1939

dangles lasso-style from his utility belt (Det No. 28, Jun '39; and others), but by October–November 1951 a special "super-thin emergency cord" has been installed on a tiny spool inside the utility belt (BM No. 67/1: "The Mystery Rope!"), and by July 1952 the regular bat-rope has been secreted inside the belt's lining so that it may be drawn out almost instantly like a fisherman's line on a reel (Det No. 185: "The Secret of Batman's Utility Belt!"). By July-August 1968 the regular bat-rope has been transferred to an "automatic reel" inside one of the utility belt's equipment containers (BM No. 203).

Over the years, Batman and Robin have developed many different kinds of bat-ropes, each one suited to some special purpose. These include hollow ropes designed for use as breathing tubes; white camouflage ropes for use in conjunction with their white snow-uniforms (*see* section C 2, the emergency and special-purpose costumes); and "self-disintegrating" ropes chemically treated to self-destruct after being exposed to the air for five minutes. The Dynamic Duo's bat-rope collection also includes an elastic rope, a cellophane rope, and a rope of spun gold donated to Batman by an admirer in the Near East (BM No. 67/1, Oct/Nov '51: "The Mystery Rope!"). According to Batman No. 83/3, Batman always wears an "emergency wire-centered silk rope" tied around his waist (Apr '54: "The Testing of Batman!").

ii. The Batarang. First introduced into Batman's crime-fighting arsenal in September 1939, the batarang – a batlike, scalloped-edged boomerang "modeled after the Australian Bushman's boomerang" (Det No. 31) – has been described as the Dynamic Duo's "strangest piece of equipment" (Det No. 244, Jun '57: "The 100 Batarangs of Batman!").

According to Detective Comics No. 244, the term "batarang" was coined by Australian circus performer and boomerang expert LEE COLLINS, who educated Batman in his mastery of the boomerang and then presented him with the world's first bat-shaped boomerang as a personal gift. "Now that you're as skillful as I am, ***Batman,***" said Collins, "I've made this special boomerang for you! It's a sort of **bat-arang,** with bat-like wings!" (Jul '57: "The 100 Batarangs of Batman!").

Tucked behind Batman's utility belt, from where it may be extracted at a moment's notice (Det No. 32, Oct '39; and others), the batarang was spelled "baterang," with an "e," in the earliest texts, before changing to "batarang," the form it retains today.

Batman and Robin can throw and retrieve their batarangs with an almost uncanny accuracy, but they have also developed a "batarang gun" for firing the batarang over longer distances (Det No. 110, Apr '46: "Batman and Robin in Scotland Yard!"), as well as a more easily portable "batarang pistol" (BM No. 40/2,

Batman with batarang (spelled baterang *in early texts), 1939* © NPP 1939

Batman reaches for his batarang, 1939 © NPP 1939

Batman hurls his batarang, 1939 © NPP 1939

Apr/May '47: "The Case of Batman II"; and others). By June 1954 they have managed to further perfect the batarang itself in order to give the device "greater range and more accuracy" (BM No. 84/3: "Ten Nights of Fear!").

Over the years, Batman and Robin have devised an arsenal of emergency batarangs, each one suited to some special purpose. These include the magnet or magnetic batarang, for disarming criminals and other uses; the seeing-eye batarang, equipped with a tiny camera; the flash-bulb batarang, for providing illumination or momentarily blinding an adversary; the bomb batarang, for delivering explosives to a target; the rope batarang, equipped with a length of rope wound around a small reel; the police whistle batarang, which makes a sound like that of a police whistle as it flies through the air; and batarang X, a gigantic batarang, launched from a catapult, which a man can use to soar through the air (Det No. 244, Jun '57: "The 100 Batarangs of Batman!").

Other special batarangs include the flashlight batarang, which emits a continuous beam of light (WF No. 104, Sep '59: "The Plot to Destroy Superman!"); the saw-tooth batarang, for escapes and other uses; the fire-prevention batarang, which sprays a fire-extinguishing chemical; the spinning batarang, which spins round and round in a tight circle, creating an effect similar to that of a powerful fan (BM No. 139/1, Apr '61: "The Blue Bowman"); the flare batarang, for sending up a flare (Det No. 300, Feb '62: "The Bizarre Polka-Dot Man!"); the sharp-edged cutlass batarang, for various types of cutting (Det No. 319, Sep '63: "The Fantastic Dr. No-Face!"); and the harpoon batarang, which Batman uses to puncture the tires on an underworld vehicle in December 1963 (BM No. 160/2: "The Alien Boss of Gotham City!").

iii. The Other Equipment. In addition to the vast arsenal of vehicles and equipment already described and enumerated in this article under various headings, Batman and Robin have employed a host of other apparatus in their never-ending war against crime. What follows is an inventory of this equipment, grouped according to the following categories: *a)* weapons and tools; *b)* gliding, scaling, skating, and water-crossing apparatus; *c)* scientific, investigatory, and communications apparatus; *d)* dummies, robots, and audio-animatrons; and *e)* apparatus for special emergencies.

a) WEAPONS AND TOOLS. Chief among the items in this category are the bat-bolo, an entangling weapon closely modeled after the bolas employed by South American gauchos, which Batman sometimes carries in his utility belt (BM No. 83/2, Apr '54: "The Deep-Sea Diver

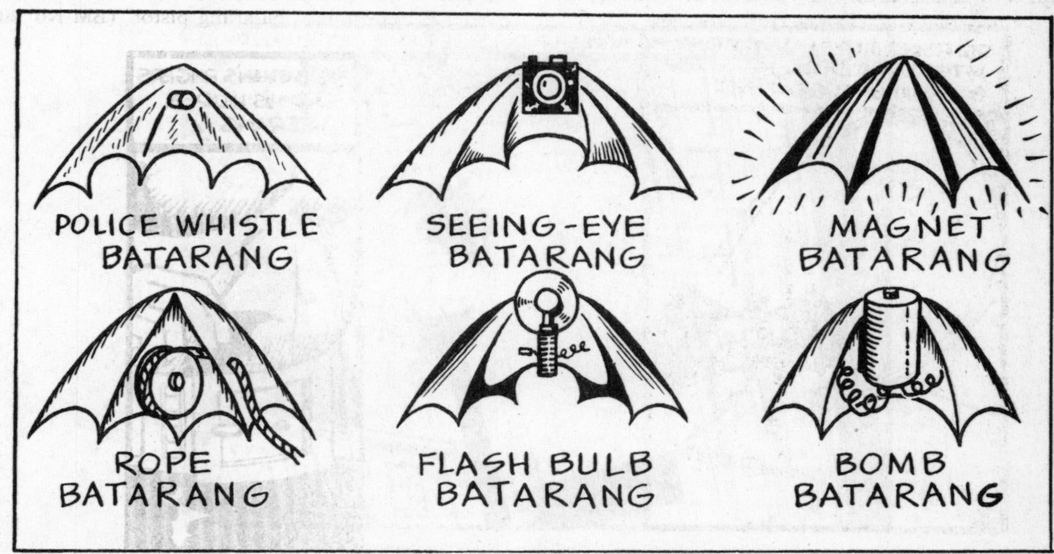

Batman's emergency batarangs © NPP 1961

Mystery!"; and others), and the batpoon, a small harpoon with a bat-rope attached (WF No. 9, Spr '43: "Crime of the Month"; and others).

Other weapons and tools include the glass cutter that Batman carries in July 1939 (Det No. 29: "The Batman Meets Doctor Death"); the knife blade that he carries in his boot heel in a number of early adventures (BM No. 6/4, Aug/Sep '41: "Suicide Beat!"; and others); the "bat-darts" that he uses in March 1958 (Det No. 253: "The Fox, the Shark, and the Vulture!"); and the "freeze gun" with which he unsuccessfully attempts to apprehend Clayface (*see* CLAYFACE [MATT HAGEN]) in June 1962 (Det No. 304: "The Return of Clay-Face!").

Batman carries an automatic pistol in the early days of his career (Det No. 33, Nov '39: "The Batman Wars Against the Dirigible of Doom"; and others), but he has abandoned the practice forever by early 1940. (*See* section H, the man himself [as Batman].)

b) GLIDING, SCALING, SKATING, AND WATER-CROSSING APPARATUS. Gliding apparatus employed by Batman includes the bat-scalloped "webbed wings" that he uses during an aerial acrobatic exhibition in October–November 1945 (BM No. 31/1: "Punch and Judy!"), and the "glider bat-wings," included among the equipment carried aboard the flying batcave in July 1963, with which he and Robin can "ride the air currents" (Det No. 317: "The Secrets of the Flying Bat-Cave!").

By August 1957 Batman and Robin have perfected a pair of "human jet-power units" which, strapped to their backs and used in conjunction with pairs of batlike "folding wings," enable them to soar through the air with blinding speed (BM No. 109/3: "The 1,000 Inventions of Batman!").

In September 1959 Batman uses a new pair of "inflatable batwings," still in the experimental stage, to apprehend henchmen of renegade scientist LEX LUTHOR. Described as "collapsible rubber wings--just like the new inflatable airplane used by the Air Force," the new bat wings are inflated by means of a "gas cartridge" in Batman's utility belt and powered by two tiny detachable jets (WF No. 104: "The Plot to Destroy Superman!").

For scaling the outer wall of a skyscraper in July 1939, Batman uses special "suction gloves" and "knee pads" with suction cups attached (Det No. 29: "The Batman Meets Doctor Death"), equipment which he employs again in August 1940 (Det No. 42: "The Case of the Prophetic Pictures!"). In November 1959 Batman and Robin tie special "magnetic footplates" to the soles of their boots to enable them to cling to an underworld armored vehicle used in a robbery at the Gotham Bank (WF No. 105: "The Alien Superman!").

Special skating equipment employed by Batman and Robin includes the "rocket-roller skates" used by Robin in April 1941 (Det No. 50: "The Case of the Three Devils!"), and the jet-propelled roller skates, called "bat-skates" or "collapsible jet-skaters," introduced by the Dynamic Duo in August 1958 (BM No. 117/3: "Manhunt in Outer Space!").

To enable them to walk on water, Batman and Robin employ specially developed "air-inflated raft-shoes" in April 1942 (Det No. 62: "Laugh, Town, Laugh").

c) SCIENTIFIC, INVESTIGATORY, AND COMMUNICATIONS APPARATUS. Particularly in the early years of his career, Batman frequently employs infrared equipment of various kinds to aid him in his work.

In March 1940 Batman uses a pair of green-tinted infrared glasses, or goggles, to enable him to see in the dark, although the term infrared is never actually employed in the text. Face to face in a room with a half dozen armed thugs, Batman flicks out the lights, plunging the room into darkness. And then:

> The ***Batman*** pulls over his eyes a queer type of glass from its almost invisible support upon [his] black cowl . . .

Aided by special suction gloves and knee pads, Batman scales a skyscraper, 1939 © NPP 1939

Though he himself cannot be seen with these glasses of his own invention, the ***Batman*** can now see in the dark as would a real **bat!**

As Batman moves deftly about the room, striking out from the blackness to outmaneuver and outfight his bewildered adversaries, the hoodlums "shudder in terror as they realize the 'supernatural' power of the **Batman!**"

"He can see in the dark!" cries one.

"Just like a real **bat!**" exclaims another.

"It's uncanny!" gasps a third.

"No wonder he's called the **Batman!**" shudders a fourth (Det No. 37).

In Summer 1941 these lenses for seeing in the dark are called "especially prepared glasses" (WF No. 2: "The Man Who Couldn't Remember!"), and in Fall 1943 they are referred to as "infra-red goggles" (WF No. 11: "A Thief in Time!").

In Spring 1940 Batman trails Robin with the aid of an infrared flashlight – referred to in the text as an "infra-red lamp" – designed to bring out traces of the invisible "luminous chemical" used to coat the soles of Robin's boots (BM No. 1/2). By Summer 1940 the luminous chemical has also been applied to the floor of Batman's automobile, enabling Robin to use the infra-red flashlight to follow the CATWOMAN after she has sat inside the car and unwittingly acquired traces of the chemical on the soles of her shoes (BM No. 2/1).

According to Batman No. 3/2, "the tires of the **Batman's** car are coated with radio-active substance which glows under an infra-red ray" (Fall '40: "The Ugliest Man in the World"), and Detective Comics No. 61 describes a past occasion when Robin used infrared glasses to trail a suspect after surreptitiously coating the suspect's shoes with a special luminous chemical (Mar '42: "The Three Racketeers!").

Other special glasses employed by Batman include the "magnifying goggles" he has in his possession in August 1963 (WF No. 135: "The Menace of the Future Man!").

Scientific instruments used by Batman include the "bat counter," a device for locating explosives that "will register even a minute quantity of explosive material in the area being tested" (BM No. 58/3, Apr/May '50: "The Black Diamond!"); a "pocket radio direction finder" for locating the source of radio signals (BM No. 62/3, Dec/Jan '50–'51: "The Mystery of Millionaire Island!"); a "super-sensitive Geiger counter" (Det No. 230, Apr '56: "The Mad Hatter of Gotham City!"); and a special "detonating ray" for detonating explosives from a safe distance. "The concentrated infra-red heat-ray," explains Batman, "detonates the explosives wherever it hits them" (BM No. 109/3, Aug '57: "The 1,000 Inventions of Batman!").

For investigative purposes, Batman and Robin have devised a wide array of ingenious apparatus. Their three-wheeled "sleuth machine," for example, is equipped with a special radar device which, "when locked onto any object, will make the machine automatically follow that object, while emitting radio-signals" which the Dynamic Duo can follow by means of the radios in the belt-buckles of their utility belts. To prevent criminals from destroying the machine, it has been equipped with special "photo-electric beams" that move the device out of harm's way in the event anyone but Batman or Robin attempts to approach it (BM No. 109/3, Aug '57: "The 1,000 Inventions of Batman!").

By August 1957 Batman and Robin have devised the "flying eye," the first in a series of remote-controlled spy devices designed to provide them with advance intelligence concerning underworld activities. Equipped with "televisor lens and microphones" and operated by means of a sophisticated remote-control panel located in the batcave, the flying eye is a silent, self-powered, spherical machine, slightly larger than a bowling ball, that can fly through the air, hover in place, and televise what it sees and hears back to a receiver mounted in the batcave (BM No. 109/3: "The 1,000 Inventions of Batman!").

By May 1965 Batman and Robin have perfected the "bat-eye," a spherical, remote-controlled spy device, equipped with a "miniature TV camera" and "tiny jet motor," which they describe as "a new, faster version of our flying eye" (WF No. 149: "The Game of Secret Identities!" pts. I–II – no title; "The Super-Detective!").

By June 1965 Batman and Robin have six "flying television cameras" circling Gotham City, relaying aerial views of the city to a half dozen monitors installed in the batcave (BM No. 172/2: "Robin's Unassisted Triple Play!").

For communication, Batman and Robin rely primarily on the radios in the buckles of their utility belts. Other communications devices employed by the Dynamic Duo, however, include the tiny transmitter in Batman's boot heel that enables him to summon ACE THE BAT-HOUND by transmitting a supersonic signal to a receiver concealed in Ace's collar (BM No. 125/1, Aug '59: "The Secret Life of Bat-Hound"; and others); the special "wrist-radios" used by Batman and SUPERMAN to communicate with one another during December 1959 (WF No. 106: "The Duplicate Man!"); and the emergency "signal-watch" that Superman lends Batman in the event Batman needs to summon a super-powered Superman robot from Superman's FORTRESS OF SOLITUDE (WF No. 135, Aug '63: "The Menace of the Future Man!").

Special signaling devices used by Batman have included the "bat-flash ring" which emits a blinding flash of light (Det No. 236, Oct '56: "The New-Model Batman!") and a "miniature flare gun" which shoots forth a bat-signal (BM No. 17/4, Jun/Jul '43: "Adventure of the Vitamin Vandals!"). (*See* section E 2 e, the bat-signal.)

An unusual piece of crime-fighting equipment with a variety of uses is the "bat-kite," invented in June 1956 by Gotham City high school student JEFF KEATING. The invention, which won Keating a four-year criminology scholarship in a competition sponsored by Batman, is a large, black, bat-shaped kite, maneuvered by means of "ingenious control-strings" and intended for such diverse uses as taking aerial photographs, dropping scaling ropes over the sides of buildings, and bumping into criminals and knocking them off balance (BM No. 100/3, Jun '56: "The Great Batman Contest").

d) DUMMIES, ROBOTS, AND AUDIO-ANIMATRONS. Throughout his daring career, Batman has employed dummies and robots of Bruce Wayne and Batman to help him apprehend criminals and safeguard the secret of his dual identity.

In Winter 1941 Batman and Robin use a specially constructed dummy that enables Robin to impersonate Bruce Wayne as part of a ploy to persuade the gambler STACY and his henchmen that Bruce Wayne and Batman are two different persons (BM No. 4/4).

In Spring 1945 Batman employs a bust of Bruce Wayne and a Batman dummy to protect the secret of his identity from the sinister DR. DREEMO (WF No. 17: "Crime Goes to College!").

In April–May 1949 ALFRED throws a Bruce Wayne dummy overboard during a yacht cruise as part of a deliberate plan by Batman to make it appear that Wayne has slipped over the railing and perished, but complications arise when Alfred is arrested and charged with Bruce Wayne's murder (BM No. 52/1: "The Man with the Automatic Brain!").

In July 1954 Alfred carries a Batman dummy through the streets of Gotham City as part of Batman's ploy to outwit the INVENTOR (Det No. 209: "The Man Who Shadowed Batman!").

In October 1955 Batman and Robin construct the first Batman robot – called "the Batman machine" – as part of an elaborate plan to apprehend the "BLAST" VARNER gang. Operated by remote control by means of a special "radio-control box," the robot is equipped with "electric-motored" arms and legs, television-camera eyes and microphone ears, and a concealed direction-signal transmitter designed to keep the Dynamic Duo continually apprised of the robot's location (Det No. 224: "The Batman Machine!").

In January 1957 PROFESSOR CARDEN creates an even more ingenious robot and, by means of a special "brain-wave helmet," transforms it into Batman's "robot twin," endowing it with a personality, knowledge, and capabilities identical to Batman's own. The robot is stolen soon afterward by the criminal DALL, only to be subsequently recovered and placed in the permanent custody of Batman and Robin (Det No. 239: "Batman's Robot Twin!").

In August 1957 Batman and Robin once again employ a Batman robot with television-camera eyes, this time to help them locate the hideout of gang boss BAGLEY (BM No. 109/1: "Three Crimes Against Batman").

By August 1958 Batman is able to summon and control his Batman robot by means of the radio installed in his utility belt. The Batman robot is quite powerful now, able to do battle with larger robots (Det No. 258: "Prisoners of the Giant Robots!") or smash heavy machinery (Det No. 261, Nov '58: "The Amazing Dr. Double X!"). Even as late as July 1960, however, its movements are somewhat jerky and not altogether lifelike (Det No. 281: "Batman, Robot!").

By October 1960, however, the Batman robot is sufficiently lifelike to impersonate Batman, at least for a few moments (Det No. 284: "The Negative Batman!"), and by March 1961 it has become so electronically sophisticated and psychologically complex that it is even capable of becoming temporarily evil and working against Batman (BM No. 138/1: "Batman's Master").

Indeed, by September 1962 Batman is able to send his Batman robot out socializing with an attractive young lady without onlookers becoming even fleetingly aware of the robot impersonation (BM No. 150/2: "The Girl Who Stole Batman's Heart"). And in March 1963, when Batman deliberately sends his robot into a death-trap set by gang boss ELLIOT MADDAN, Maddan never even suspects that he has captured only a robot (Det No. 313: "The Mystery of the $1,000,000 Treasure Hunt!").

By the late 1960s Batman and Robin have devised complex "audio-animatrons" to serve as their occasional surrogates, ingenious androids so utterly lifelike that only a detailed examination could betray them as robots (Det No. 364, Jun '67: "The Curious Case of the Crime-less Clues!"; and others).

e) APPARATUS FOR SPECIAL EMERGENCIES. On certain extraordinary occasions, when necessity has demanded it, Batman and Robin have proven adroit at devising new crime-fighting apparatus even beyond what is already contained in their already vast arsenal.

In October 1956, for example, after renegade scientist WALLACE WALEY has devised means of thwarting the use of their accustomed crime-fighting weapons, Batman and Robin devise an ingenious tanklike "bat-track" to replace the batmobile; "jumping-springs" to propel them through the streets in place of their bat-ropes; and a flying-saucer-like aerodyne to serve as a temporary replacement for the batplane (Det No. 236: "The New-Model Batman!").

In September 1957, when PROFESSOR MILO uses his diabolical "phobia liquid" to afflict Batman with a mortal fear of bats and anything batlike, Batman devises an entire new arsenal of equipment – employing the star as its unifying symbol instead of the bat – to carry him through the crisis until he can be cured of his phobia. During this difficult period, Batman becomes Starman, the batcave is replaced by the star-loft, the batplane is replaced by the star-plane, and Batman's batarangs are replaced by star-shaped starangs (Det No. 247: "The Man Who Ended Batman's Career!").

And in October 1961, after being struck temporarily blind by an injury to his optic nerve suffered in a battle with DR. PNEUMO, Batman fights on until his recovery with the aid of a pair of special electronic earplugs, one equipped with a radar device to alert him to obstacles, the other designed to vastly improve his hearing (BM No. 143/2: "The Blind Batman").

In December 1969, when Batman closes up the batcave and departs Wayne Manor for a new penthouse home in the heart of Gotham City, virtually all of the crime-fighting equipment inventoried above remains left behind (BM No. 217: "One Bullet Too Many!").

IN THE DARK HOURS WHEN CRIME INVADES THE STREETS OF GOTHAM CITY, A FATEFUL BEAM STABS THE MIDNIGHT SKY --THE BAT-SIGNAL!

The bat-signal over Gotham City, 1952 © NPP 1952

e. THE BAT-SIGNAL. "Suddenly a gigantic cone of light pierces the dusk of day and etches an eerie symbol against a black cloud--the silhouette of a giant bat!" (Det No. 60, Feb '42: "Case of the Costume-Clad Killers").

Since February 1942 POLICE COMMISSIONER GORDON of GOTHAM CITY has summoned Batman and Robin into action by means of the "bat-signal," a giant searchlight mounted on the roof of police headquarters that casts a circle of light against the sky containing the image of a giant black bat.

Detective Comics No. 164 describes it as an "eerie finger of brilliant light, which regularly chills the underworld as it sets in motion the Dynamic Duo . . ." (Oct '50: "Untold Tales of the Bat-Signal!").

As employed in the chronicles, the term bat-signal refers both to the searchlight that projects the light-summons and to the light-summons itself. By October 1950, the earliest date for which precise specifications are available, the bat-signal searchlight's principal features have come to include a hand-ground, bulletproof glass lens; a yellow fog-filter to enable the bat-signal to penetrate fog and heavy smoke; and super-carbon arc filaments which "produce a beam 100 times more powerful than the ordinary searchlight."

During wartime blackouts, the bat-signal was converted to infrared rays, and special infrared filters were installed in the windows of the batcave to enable Batman and Robin to see the signal (Det No. 164: "Untold Tales of the Bat-Signal!").

By August 1954 the bat-signal searchlight has undergone a radical design change, from the device depicted in the construction diagram below into the much larger mechanism pictured on the following page.

When Police Commissioner Gordon wants the bat-signal activated, he presses a button on his desk which lights a red blinker on the bat-signal's control unit, thus alerting the bat-signal attendant stationed on the roof. For more than twenty years, since August 1954, the bat-signal has been operated by SGT. HARVEY HAINER of the Gotham City police (BM No. 85/2: "The Guardian of the Bat-Signal!"; and others).

In 1964, when the bat-emblem on Batman's costume becomes more highly stylized, the bat-symbol projected by the bat-signal becomes more highly stylized too (Det No. 330, Aug '64: "The Fallen Idol of Gotham City!"; and others).

In the early days of the bat-signal, Batman and Robin must actually see the signal in the sky in order to respond to it (Det No. 60, Feb '42: "Case of the Costume-Clad Killers"; and others), but as time goes by they develop more sophisticated means of alerting themselves to the summons even when they are not in a position to observe it.

By June–July 1951 Batman and Robin have equipped the batcave with a special "electric eye alarm" that "sounds off" to signify the flashing of the bat-signal

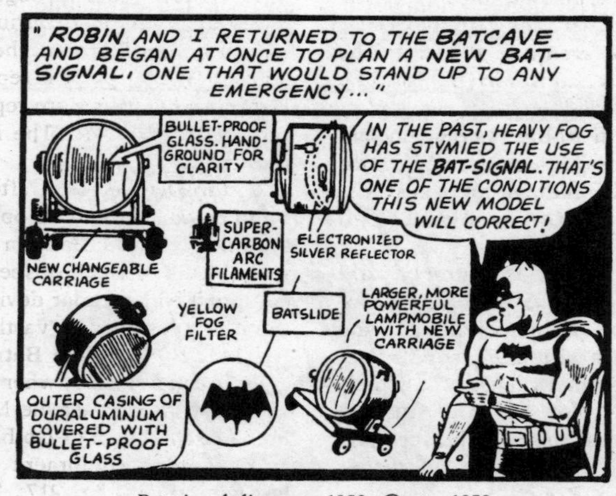

"ROBIN AND I RETURNED TO THE BATCAVE AND BEGAN AT ONCE TO PLAN A NEW BAT-SIGNAL, ONE THAT WOULD STAND UP TO ANY EMERGENCY..."
IN THE PAST, HEAVY FOG HAS STYMIED THE USE OF THE BAT-SIGNAL. THAT'S ONE OF THE CONDITIONS THIS NEW MODEL WILL CORRECT!
BULLET-PROOF GLASS. HAND-GROUND FOR CLARITY
SUPER-CARBON ARC FILAMENTS
ELECTRONIZED SILVER REFLECTOR
NEW CHANGEABLE CARRIAGE
YELLOW FOG FILTER
BATSLIDE
LARGER, MORE POWERFUL LAMPMOBILE WITH NEW CARRIAGE
OUTER CASING OF DURALUMINUM COVERED WITH BULLET-PROOF GLASS

Bat-signal diagram, 1950 © NPP 1950

The bat-signal, 1954 © NPP 1954

overhead, while at the same time a red bulb lights up on a special batcave alarm board (BM No. 65/1: "A Partner for Batman!").

"Suddenly," observes Batman No. 75/1, "a red lamp blinks--an electronic signal indicating that the rays of the ***bat-signal*** are piercing the skies!" (Feb/Mar '53: "Outlaw Town, U.S.A.!").

And Detective Comics No. 197 adds: "Suddenly a warning buzzer echoes through the **bat-cave,** as an electronic 'eye' atop the Wayne mansion picks up the beam of the **bat-signal** . . ." (Jul '53: "The League Against Batman!").

The closest thing to a technical explanation of the bat-signal alarm is offered by Detective Comics No. 205, which recalls Batman's early devising of a special "transmitter" designed to "beam a photoelectric cell directly over police headquarters."

"Any time the **bat-signal** flashes on," thought Batman, "it will interrupt the cell and illuminate [a] red bulb" installed in the batcave (Mar '54: "The Origin of the Bat-Cave!").

By May 1959, however, Batman and Robin have replaced the batcave's bat-signal alarm with a special wall-mounted "tele-screen" which alerts the Dynamic Duo to the appearance of the bat-signal by flashing a televised image of the bat-signal beaming over the Gotham City skyline (Det No. 267: "Batman Meets Bat-Mite!"). Detective Comics No. 272 refers to this device as a "special TV receiver" (Oct '59: "The Crystal Creature"), and Batman No. 142/1 describes it as a "unique receiver, tuned in to [police] headquarters" (Sep '61: "Batman's Robot-Guardian").

By March 1963 Bruce Wayne and Dick Grayson have installed a loud "buzzer alarm" on their bedside table to alert them to the flashing of the bat-signal on the tele-screen in the batcave (Det No. 313: "The Mystery of the $1,000,000 Treasure Hunt!"), and by June 1963 the appearance of the bat-signal on the batcave's tele-screen has begun to be accompanied by a loud buzzing sound (BM No. 156/2: "Robin Dies at Dawn!").

Batman and Robin respond to the summons of the bat-signal in its early years by reporting to police headquarters for instructions from Police Commissioner Gordon (BM No. 23/1, Jun/Jul '44: "The Upside Down Crimes!"; and others). By March 1955, however, they have begun responding to the bat-signal by proceeding in the direction indicated by the sweeping motion of the signal (BM No. 90/2: "City of Fantasy!").

"The **bat-signal**--and it's sweeping south-westward!" cries Dick Grayson as he spies the bat-signal in July 1956. And moments later, as the Dynamic Duo speed away in the batmobile, one of them remarks, "The signal was sweeping toward the new air terminal!

Bruce Wayne and Dick Grayson spy the bat-signal, 1952 © NPP 1952

Someone there must have phoned in an alarm!" (Det No. 233: "The Batwoman").

Similarly, in October 1956, Dick Grayson spies the bat-signal and exclaims, "Bruce, look . . . the ***bat-signal,*** pointing westward!"

"The police are warning us of trouble in west Gotham City!" replies Bruce Wayne (Det No. 236: "The New-Model Batman!").

On other occasions, however, the Dynamic Duo react differently to the bat-signal, sometimes speeding to the location indicated by the police shortwave radio in the batcave or batmobile (BM No. 94/2, Sep '55: "The New Batman!"; and others); sometimes contacting Police Commissioner Gordon for instructions via two-way radio (BM No. 156/2, Jun '63: "Robin Dies at Dawn!"; and others); and sometimes proceeding, as in former days, directly to police headquarters for a detailed briefing (BM No. 139/1, Apr '61: "The Blue Bowman"; and others).

In March 1954 the bat-signal blinks on and off, indicating "an extreme emergency" (BM No. 82/3: "The Olympic Games of Crime!"), and in September 1954, during a period when Batman and Robin are temporarily stranded underwater inside a Navy surplus pocket-submarine, the bat-signal flashes them messages in police code which they receive by peering at the signal through the submarine's periscope (BM No. 86/1: "The Voyage of the First Batmarine!").

On occasion, special bat-signals have been employed, including a "miniature flare gun" which sends forth a smaller version of the bat-signal, which Batman and Robin use to summon a sea rescue for themselves in June–July 1943 (BM No. 17/4: "Adventure of the Vitamin Vandals!"); the spare bat-signal mounted on the police department's floodlight truck in December 1951 (Det No. 178: "The Defeat of Batman!"); and the gigantic battery-powered bat-signal which SUPERMAN constructs in order to summon the aid of the Dynamic Duo in September–October 1955 (WF No. 78: "When Superman's Identity Is Exposed!").

By June 1964, however, after more than two decades of use, the bat-signal has been all but superseded by a sophisticated system of hot-line telephones linking Police Commissioner Gordon's office with the batcave — where a tape recorder is wired into the system to record all incoming messages (Det No. 328: "Gotham Gang Line-Up!") — as well as with a hot-line extension mounted in the batmobile (BM No. 164/1, Jun '64: "Two-Way Gem Caper!").

By July 1964 a hot-line extension has been installed in the Wayne mansion (Det No. 329: "Castle with Wall-to-Wall Danger!"), and a specially installed security device ensures that anyone answering it hears a signal that is understood only by Bruce Wayne and Dick Grayson (Det No. 331, Sep '64: "Museum of Mixed-Up Men!").

In December 1969, when Batman closes up the batcave and departs Wayne Manor for a new penthouse home in the heart of Gotham City, all the hot-line telephone apparatus remains left behind (BM No. 217: "One Bullet Too Many!"), and the bat-signal resumes its traditional function as Police Commissioner Gordon's principal means of contacting Batman.

F. The Batman Counterparts. "Lashing out at the lawless, crushing the cunning conspiracies of crime, shielding the innocent . . . it's small wonder that **Batman** and **Robin** are the world's most famous lawmen! But in other parts of the world are **other** crime-fighters who have taken **Batman** as their model!" (Det No. 215, Jan '55: "The Batmen of All Nations!").

Throughout the world, as well as in other eras and on at least one distant planet, the almost legendary fame of Batman as a nemesis of crime has led other crime-fighters to adopt his methods and emulate his example.

England has the KNIGHT and the SQUIRE, secretly the Earl of Wordenshire and his young son Cyril, who, clad in knightly raiment, roar into action astride their motorized "war horses" whenever the tolling of the bell in a nearby rectory warns them that their services are urgently needed (BM No. 62/2, Dec/Jan '50–'51: "The Batman of England!").

Batman and his counterparts, 1955 (clockwise, from left): the Gaucho, the Legionary, the Ranger, the Musketeer, the Knight, Batman, the Squire, Robin, and Police Commissioner Gordon © NPP 1955

Batman counterparts in other countries include the LEGIONARY of Italy, the MUSKETEER of France, the RANGER of Australia, and the GAUCHO of South America (Det No. 215, Jan '55: "The Batmen of All Nations!"). And in the Western United States, in the region inhabited by the Sioux, CHIEF MAN-OF-THE-BATS and his young son LITTLE RAVEN battle crime and injustice among the Sioux much as Batman and Robin battle crime in Gotham City (BM No. 86/3, Sep '54: "Batman--Indian Chief!").

Although Batman has given advice and encouragement to all these crime-fighters, some he has actually trained himself from scratch, such as Northern Europe's WINGMAN (BM No. 65/1, Jun/Jul '51: "A Partner for Batman!") and Latin America's Bat-Hombre (BM No. 56/1, Dec/Jan '49–'50: "Ride, Bat-Hombre, Ride!"). Bat-Hombre caused Batman grave disappointment, however, when he turned out to be a member of an outlaw band. (*See* PAPAGAYO, EL.)

In the year 3000 A.D., after being inspired by some action films of Batman and Robin they find in a time capsule, BRANE and his young companion Ricky become the Dynamic Duo of their own era long enough to liberate Earth from the domination of a ruthless Saturnian warlord (BM No. 26/2, Dec/Jan '44–'45: "The Year 3000!").

Later in the thirty-first century, BRANE TAYLOR and his young nephew launch crime-fighting careers as their own era's Batman and Robin after perusing some historical "micro-films" of Batman's exploits.

"I studied micro-films of . . . ***Batman's*** exploits in our museums," Taylor once explained to Robin, "and I trained myself and my young nephew to duplicate them--and thus another ***'Batman*** and ***Robin'*** team was born--in the thirty-first century!" (BM No. 67/3, Oct/Nov '51: "The Lost Legion of Space").

In February 1957 Batman and Robin receive an unexpected visit from yet another Batman counterpart, the "Batman of the far future," a crime-fighter from a distant but unspecified future era who has journeyed through the time barrier to see them after having

Brane Taylor and Batman, 1955 © NPP 1955

loaned them his own futuristic version of the batmobile – the so-called "bat-missile" – to help them in their search for a fugitive criminal.

". . . my thanks to ***you, Batman,*** " exclaims the visitor as he prepares to depart for his home in the future, "--for being the great example whose fame inspired ***my*** future career!" (BM No. 105/3: "The Mysterious Bat-Missile"). (*See* THARP, "GUNNER.")

The far-distant planet Zur-en-arrh also has its own Batman, the scientist TLANO, who has long observed Earth's Batman through a "powerful telescope" and modeled his career after Batman's own.

"I've observed your every action!" explains Tlano in February 1958, after he has teleported Batman to Zur-en-arrh. "It inspired me to play the same role here!" (BM No. 113/3: "Batman--The Superman of Planet X!").

In addition to those crime-fighters actually inspired or influenced by Batman, certain heroes of past eras and remote cultures have employed methods and techniques that seem to foreshadow Batman's own.

TIGER MAN, "probably the world's first lawman," was a caveman named Rog who fought evil in the Stone Age while concealing his true identity beneath a mask made from the head of a saber-toothed tiger (BM No. 93/3, Aug '55: "The Caveman Batman").

The people of ancient Babylon revered ZORN, a "hero-idol" whose statue, unearthed in September 1956, depicts him clad in a costume almost identical to Batman's. It is unclear, however, whether a man named Zorn ever actually existed (BM No. 102/2: "The Batman from Babylon").

JEREMY COE, an American colonist of the seventeenth century – and the first known man in history to have used the batcave as his headquarters (*see* section D, the batcave) – struggled courageously to safeguard his fellow colonists against surprise Indian attacks by disguising himself as an Indian and infiltrating their war councils (Det No. 205, Mar '54: "The Origin of the Bat-Cave!").

In the eighteenth century, Abel Adams, a citizen of Gotham City, adopted the secret identity of CAPTAIN LIGHTFOOT and confiscated shipments of contraband guns in order to help avert warfare between the colonists and Indians (BM No. 79/2, Oct/Nov '53: "The Batman of Yesterday!").

G. The Man Himself (as Bruce Wayne). The chief protagonist of the Batman chronicles is in one sense really two men. He is, of course, Batman, the world's greatest detective, but he is also Bruce Wayne, millionaire socialite and philanthropist, the master of Wayne Manor and one of GOTHAM CITY's most prominent citizens. In his role as Bruce Wayne, he is the guardian of Dick Grayson, the boy who is secretly ROBIN; the owner of Ace, the dog that is secretly Bat-Hound (*see* ACE [THE BAT-HOUND]); the employer of ALFRED, majordomo and chief factotum of the Wayne household; and a close personal friend of POLICE COMMISSIONER JAMES W. GORDON.

Bruce Wayne is a handsome, worldly, sophisticated man, and an impeccable dresser. Left "fabulously wealthy" (Det No. 185, Jul '52: "The Secret of Batman's Utility Belt!"; and others) by the estate of his deceased father, THOMAS WAYNE (Det No. 33, Nov '39: "The Batman Wars Against the Dirigible of Doom"), he is a man of vast holdings, a stockholder and trustee of numerous banks, corporations, and civic organizations, as well as a member of Gotham City's most exclusive clubs.

Bruce Wayne's most important relationship is the one he shares with his ward Dick Grayson (*see* section I, the relationship with Robin), but Wayne has also enjoyed his share of romantic involvements, including relationships with such beautiful, talented, and fascinating women as JULIE MADISON, LINDA PAGE, VICKI VALE, the CATWOMAN, and heiress Kathy Kane, secretly (the) BATWOMAN (*see* section J, the women of the chronicles).

Bruce Wayne has black hair and blue eyes (S No. 173/3, Nov '64: "The Triumph of Luthor and Brainiac!"). His height, usually given as 6'1" (Det No. 141, Nov '48: "The Gallery of Public Heroes!"; and others), is reported in one text as being an even 6 feet (WF No. 51, Apr/May '51: "The Academy for Gangsters!"), and his weight, usually given as 185 pounds (Det No. 141, Nov '48: "The Gallery of Public Heroes!"; and others), has been as low as 180 pounds (Det No. 214, Dec '54: "The Batman Encyclopedia") and as high as 187½ pounds (Det No. 174, Aug '51: "The Park Avenue Kid!").

Bruce Wayne is ambidextrous, always signing his name with his right hand as Bruce Wayne and with his left hand as Batman in order to help safeguard the secret of his dual identity (BM No. 92/1, Jun '55: "Fan-Mail of Danger!"; and others).

He has a chest measurement of 44" and a sleeve length of 33" (Det No. 169, Mar '51: "Batman--Boss of the Big House!"). There is a surgical silver plate implanted inside his left shoulder where, while he was fighting crime as Batman, his bone was once splintered by a gangster's bullet (Det No. 199, Sep '53: "The Invisible Batman!").

Bruce Wayne frequently smoked a pipe during 1939 and the 1940s (Det No. 27, May '39: "The Case of the Chemical Syndicate"; and others), but he had all but given up the habit by the beginning of the 1950s.

The son of Dr. Thomas Wayne and his wife Martha (*see* WAYNE, MARTHA), Bruce Wayne was born either in April or May (BM No. 22/2, Apr/May '44: "Dick Grayson, Telegraph Boy!"), within a few years, one way or the other, of 1914. The precise year of Wayne's birth has never been stated in the chronicles, but his parents are described as having been murdered by a gun-wielding hoodlum "some fifteen years" prior to November 1939 (i.e., *ca.* 1924), and young Bruce is clearly depicted in this account as a boy of no more than ten or eleven (Det No. 33, Nov '39: "The Batman Wars Against the Dirigible of Doom"). Efforts to fix the date of Bruce Wayne's birth more precisely, however, are frustrated by a number of later texts which assert that Wayne was already a teen-ager at the time his parents were murdered (Det No. 226, Dec '55: "When Batman Was Robin!"; and others).

Bruce Wayne, 1939 © NPP 1939

Little is known of the origins of Martha Wayne or her family, but Dr. Thomas Wayne was a prominent physician and onetime army doctor who had managed to amass a sizable fortune through judicious investment of the income he earned in his private practice (Det No. 235, Sep '56: "The First Batman!"). When Bruce Wayne was born, he was named after BRUCE N. WAYNE, a West Coast cousin of Thomas Wayne who has since acquired a reputation as "one of the greatest private detectives in the country" (BM No. 111/2, Oct '57: "The Other Bruce Wayne").

Indeed, the Waynes are the custodians of a centuries-long tradition of greatness, and their family history is replete with "brave adventurers" and men of lasting achievement (BM No. 120/2, Dec '58: "The Failure of Bruce Wayne").

Lancelot Wayne, one of Bruce Wayne's earliest known ancestors, experimented with homemade glider wings in an early attempt at flight, risking death by gliding from atop a high cliff into a river (Det No. 306, Aug '62: "The Wizard of 1,000 Menaces!").

General Horatio Wayne was a hero of the American Revolution (BM No. 120/2, Dec '58: "The Failure of Bruce Wayne"), and SILAS WAYNE was a Philadelphia silversmith during the 1780s (BM No. 44/3, Dec/Jan '47–'48: "The First American Detective!").

Caleb Wayne was a courageous frontier scout who led a wagon train through hostile Indian territory, and Cap'n Ismael Wayne was an intrepid New England whaler. Bruce Wayne's invalid great-uncle SILAS WAYNE, who took special pride in the Wayne family tradition, passed away in December 1958, but not before Bruce Wayne had entrusted him with the secret of his dual identity so that the old man could die happily, knowing that his nephew was secretly carrying on the Wayne tradition of courage and valor (BM No. 120/2: "The Failure of Bruce Wayne").

Bruce Wayne's living relatives include his AUNT AGATHA (BM No. 89/3, Feb '55: "Bruce Wayne's Aunt

Agatha!"); a cousin Jane (BM No. 93/2, Aug '55: "Batman, Baby-Sitter!"); his cousin Bruce N. Wayne (BM No. 111/2, Oct '57: "The Other Bruce Wayne"); and his young cousin VANDERVEER WAYNE, an approximate contemporary of Robin (BM No. 148/2, Jun '62: "The Boy Who Was Robin"). Bruce Wayne's descendants include the courageous BRANE, a distant descendant living in the year 3000 A.D. (BM No. 26/2, Dec/Jan '44–'45: "The Year 3000!").

Bruce Wayne was only a youngster when, as he and his parents were on their way home from a movie, a gun-wielding thug stepped from the shadows and murdered his father and mother in cold blood (*see* section A, Origin).

"In a single, searing moment," he recalled years later, "my childhood was gone, blasted by a cheap thug's bullets, and I was left alone in a world grown cold . . ." (BM No. 232, Jun '71: "Daughter of the Demon").

Now an orphan, Bruce Wayne was taken into the home of his Uncle Philip, who became his guardian (BM No. 208, Jan/Feb '69). Sometime during his boyhood, he joined the Sea Scouts, where he learned sewing and presumably other skills (Det No. 226, Dec '55: "When Batman Was Robin!").

Several texts assert that Bruce Wayne nurtured the ambition to become a detective even before his parents were murdered (Det No. 226, Dec '55: "When Batman Was Robin!"; and others), but whether or not this is actually true, there is no doubt that the traumatic event served to fix the orphaned youngster's resolve.

Detective Comics No. 265 states that Bruce Wayne attended "a school of criminology" (Mar '59: "Batman's First Case!") to prepare himself for his future career, but other texts assert, more plausibly, that he attended Gotham University (WF No. 59, Jul/Aug '52: "The Joker's Aces!"), or Gotham College, where he "worked hard to master the college's course in scientific criminal investigation" and "trained his body to muscular perfection on athletic teams" and through long, brutal hours in the college gymnasium (BM No. 96/2, Dec '55: "Batman's College Days").

Bruce Wayne, 1939 © NPP 1939

He worked long hours in the laboratory, until he had made himself a "master scientist" (Det No. 33, Nov '39: "The Batman Wars Against the Dirigible of Doom"), and he "trained his body to such physical and athletic perfection that he could perform any daredevil feat . . ." (BM No. 47/3, Jun/Jul '48: "The Origin of Batman!").

His college yearbook contained this entry: "Star athlete, honor student in criminology class. Most likely to succeed as a detective" (BM No. 96/2, Dec '55: "Batman's College Days").

Sometime prior to his twenty-first birthday, Bruce Wayne graduated. "I was not yet old enough to vote," he recalled years later, ". . . a totally devoted, almost fanatical young man . . . consumed with a need, but unable to focus it! Then, one night a ***bat*** chanced in my window--and my future was clear. . . ."

"It's an ***omen!***" he thought suddenly. "I shall become a ***bat!***" And so Bruce Wayne cloaked himself in the costume of a giant bat and, as Batman, embarked on the fulfillment of his boyhood vow, to avenge the murder of his parents and dedicate his life to "a relentless war against crime . . ." (BM No. 232, Jun '71: "Daughter of the Demon").

To help him conceal the fact that he is secretly Batman, Bruce Wayne has adopted the role of a "debonair society playboy" (BM No. 19/4, Oct/Nov '43: "Collector of Millionaires"), bored, lazy, apathetic, and frivolous. The texts contain a variety of short descriptions of Wayne, some more or less neutral, some mildly pejorative. He is a "bored young socialite" (Det No. 28, Jun '39); a "spendthrift, pleasure-loving society playboy" (Det No. 47, Jan '41); a "millionaire socialite" (BM No. 64/2, Apr/May '51: "The Forgotten Men of Crime!"); a "society blueblood" (BM No. 47/3, Jun/Jul '48: "The Origin of Batman!"); a "wealthy sportsman" (BM No. 16/3, Apr/May '43: "The Adventures of the Branded Tree!"); a "social butterfly" (Det No. 155, Jan '50: "Bruce Wayne, Private Detective!"); a "well-known philanthropist" (Det No. 357, Nov '66: "Bruce Wayne Unmasks Batman!"); and a "society man-about-town, debonair polo player, [and] rich idler" (BM No. 111/2, Oct '57: "The Other Bruce Wayne").

". . . Bruce Wayne is a nice young chap," muses Police Commissioner Gordon in May 1939, "--but he certainly must lead a boring life . . . seems disinterested in everything" (Det No. 27: "The Case of the Chemical Syndicate").

"He has no more brains in his head," comments an onlooker at a party in Winter 1941, "than the head of his walking stick has!" (BM No. 4/1: "The Case of the Joker's Crime Circus!").

"It's really too bad!" comments a woman at a society function in April 1951. "Bruce is rich, handsome--but that's all! Something's lacking. . . ."

"Ambition!" replies her companion knowingly. "He goes through life without any real purpose!" (Det No. 170: "The Flying Dutchman II!").

And at an exclusive club in March 1961, someone makes a similar comment. "Nice chap, that Bruce Wayne . . . but I wish he'd make his life worthwhile!" (Det No. 289: "The Bat-Mite Bandits!").

"Bruce is a nice, amiable fellow," muses Police Commissioner Gordon in February 1963, "--but it's a mystery to me why he seems to have no goal in life!" (BM No. 153: chs. 1-3 – "Prisoners of Three Worlds!"; "Death from Beyond"; "Dimension of Doom").

This reputation as a rich idler, however, is not without its disadvantages. In December 1943–January 1944, for example, Bruce Wayne temporarily loses custody of Dick Grayson in a court battle with GEORGE GRAYSON because of his reputation as a "nightclubbing, shiftless, cafe society playboy" (BM No. 20/4: "Bruce Wayne Loses the Guardianship of Dick Grayson!").

Even discounting Bruce Wayne's heroic role as Batman, however, a reading of the chronicles makes it clear that his public reputation as an idler is entirely undeserved. Even in his Bruce Wayne identity he is at the forefront of his community, a "well-known philanthropist" (Det No. 357, Nov '66: "Bruce Wayne Unmasks Batman!"), the chairman of the philanthropic Wayne Foundation (see ALFRED FOUNDATION, THE), a man who has donated large sums of money to orphanages (Det No. 101, Jul '45: "The Tyrannical Twins!") and headed innumerable charity drives (Det No. 306, Aug '62: "The Wizard of 1,000 Menaces!").

"He is no loose-living playboy, I assure you!" remarks Batman in February–March 1950, when circumstances force him to leap to the defense of his much-abused alter ego. "In his own quiet way, he has fought injustice and evil as much as I have!" (BM No. 57/1: "The Trial of Bruce Wayne!").

Indeed, even in his public life as a millionaire, Bruce Wayne is a uniquely talented, multifaceted individual who has served society with distinction in numerous ways: as acting mayor of Gotham City (Det No. 179, Jan '52: "Mayor Bruce Wayne!"), as a rookie policeman (BM No. 55/2, Oct/Nov '49: "Bruce Wayne, Rookie Policeman!"), as a private detective (WF No. 64, May/Jun '53: "Bruce Wayne . . . Amateur Detective!"), and as a journalist (BM No. 65/2, Jun/Jul '51: "Bruce Wayne – Crime Reporter!"). He has even gone to prison voluntarily to help thwart an underworld scheme (Det No. 249, Nov '57: "The Crime of Bruce Wayne!").

Bruce Wayne is "society's top polo player" (Det No. 141, Nov '48: "The Gallery of Public Heroes!") and the owner of several prize polo ponies (BM No. 48/2, Aug/Sep '48: "The 1,000 Secrets of the Batcave!") which he keeps in his own private stable (Det No. 157, Mar '50: "The Race of the Century").

He is also an amateur auto racer (BM No. 78/2, Aug/Sep '53: "The Sinister Stamps!"), aviator (Det No. 234, Aug '56: "Batman and Robin's Greatest Mystery"), and a boxer of considerable talent (Det No. 174, Aug '51: "The Park Avenue Kid!").

He is an avid operagoer (BM No. 40/3, Apr/May '47: "The Grand Opera Murders!") and theatergoer (Det No. 184, Jun '52: "The Human Firefly!"), and enjoys playing chess, particularly with his ward Dick Grayson (BM No. 2/1, Sum '40; and others).

Bruce Wayne, 1940 © NPP 1940

Bruce Wayne owns "quite a number of priceless antiques" (BM No. 22/1, Apr/May '44: "The Duped Domestics!"), a "rare collection of dime novels" (BM No. 54/1, Aug/Sep '49: "The Treasure Hunter!"), and a valuable art collection that includes a number of original Modiglianis purchased in Paris by his father (Det No. 368, Oct '67: "7 Wonder Crimes of Gotham City!").

Bruce Wayne is a member of the board of Gotham College (BM No. 59/2, Jun/Jul '50: "The Forbidden Cellar!") and a trustee of the Gotham Museum (Det No. 136, Jun '48: "The Dead Man's Chest!"; and others), the Natural History Museum (BM No. 86/1, Sep '54: "The Voyage of the First Batmarine!"), and the Gotham Scientific Foundation (BM No. 111/2, Oct '57: "The Other Bruce Wayne").

He is the chairman of the board of Ace Utilities (WF No. 34, May/Jun '48: "Killer for Hire!"), and the principal stockholder in the Wayne Motor Co. (Det No. 105, Nov '45: "The Batman Goes Broke!"), the Wayne Steel Foundries (WF No. 73, Nov/Dec '54: "Batman and Superman, Swamis, Inc!"), and the Gotham Steamship Company (BM No. 73/3, Oct/Nov '52: "The Joker's Utility Belt!").

He is on the board of directors of the State Bank (BM No. 20/1, Dec/Jan '43–'44: "The Centuries of Crime!"), the United Chemicals Corporation (BM No. 62/3, Dec/Jan '50–'51: "The Mystery of Millionaire Island!"), the International Chemical Company (WF No. 58, May/Jun '52: "The Murder of Bruce Wayne!"), the company which owns the Gotham *Gazette* (WF No. 80, Jan/Feb '56: "The Super-Newspaper of Gotham City"), and other of Gotham City's "largest banks and industries" (WF No. 52, Jun/Jul '51: "The $1,000,000 Star Club!").

The firms in which he is a major stockholder include the Hobbs Clock Company (BM No. 6/2, Aug/Sep '41: "The Clock Maker!"), the Seven Seas Insurance Company (BM No. 9/2, Feb/Mar '42: "The White Whale!"),

THE SANDS OF TIME DROP SLOWLY. BRUCE HAS ALREADY REACHED HOME AND WAITS IMPATIENTLY FOR ROBIN'S RETURN.
IT'S LATE... HE SHOULD HAVE BEEN BACK HOURS AGO...

Bruce Wayne, 1941 © NPP 1941

and an unnamed lens-grinding company (WF No. 16, Win '44: "The Mountaineers of Crime!").

Because his holdings are so extensive and his institutional responsibilities so great, Bruce Wayne's life is insured for $1,000,000 (WF No. 52, Jun/Jul '51: "The $1,000,000 Star Club!"). His entire estate is to be left to Dick Grayson in the event of his death (BM No. 20/4, Dec/Jan '43–'44: "Bruce Wayne Loses the Guardianship of Dick Grayson!").

As one of Gotham City society's most prominent members, Bruce Wayne holds membership in more than a dozen of the city's most exclusive clubs, including the Card Club, an "exclusive society salon" (Det No. 85, Mar '44: "The Joker's Double"); the Crocus Club (Det No. 109, Mar '46: "The House That Jokes Built!"); the Yacht Club (BM No. 49/2, Oct/Nov '48: "The Scoop of the Century!"); the Hobby Horse, a club for collectors (BM No. 54/1, Aug/Sep '49: "The Treasure Hunter!"); the Court Club (WF No. 57, Mar/Apr '52: "Public Enemy Bruce Wayne!"); the DEATH-CHEATERS' CLUB (BM No. 72/3, Aug/Sep '52: "The Death-Cheaters of Gotham City!"); the Explorers' Club (WF No. 60, Sep/Oct '52: "The Richest Crook in the World!"); the Troy Club (WF No. 64, May/Jun '53: "Bruce Wayne . . . Amateur Detective!"); the Stamp Club (BM No. 78/2, Aug/Sep '53: "The Sinister Stamps!"); the Gotham Beach Club (WF No. 66, Sep/Oct '53: "The Proving Ground for Crime!"); the Millionaire's Club, described as "the most exclusive club in the world" (BM No. 98/2, Mar '56: "The Desert Island Batman!"); the Sportsmen's Club (BM No. 134/2, Sep '60: "Batman's Secret Enemy"); and the Pharaoh Club, where Bruce Wayne serves on the rules committee (Det No. 304, Jun '62: "The Return of Clay-Face!").

Bruce Wayne's civic responsibilities have included serving as judge at the Gotham Arts Festival in October 1954 (Det No. 212: "The Puppet-Master!") and as vice-chairman of the Committee to Preserve Gotham Village in May 1964 (Det No. 327: "The Mystery of the Menacing Mask!").

An urbane, cosmopolitan man who was "once voted the best dressed male of Gotham City society" (WF No. 46, Jun/Jul '50: "Bruce Wayne, Riveter!"), Bruce Wayne is also a man with an eye for the ladies (BM No. 49/2, Oct/Nov '48: "The Scoop of the Century!"; and others). He has served as a beauty contest judge on at least two occasions, one at a contest for beauty salon operators in February–March 1943 (BM No. 15/1: "Your Face Is Your Fortune!"), and again at the Gotham Bathing Beauty Contest in September 1958 (Det No. 259: "The Challenge of the Calendar Man").

Interestingly, a number of men in various times and places have been perfect Bruce Wayne look-alikes, including reformed convict EDDIE ROGERS (BM No. 45/2, Feb/Mar '48: "A Parole for Christmas!"), tenth-century Viking OLAF ERICKSON (BM No. 52/2, Apr/May '49: "Batman and the Vikings!"), ex-convict and skilled diamond cutter Vinton Wells (BM No. 65/2, Jun/Jul '51: "Bruce Wayne – Crime Reporter!"), and reformed ex-convict HARRY LARSON (BM No. 83/1, Apr '54: "The Duplicate Batman!"). KILLER MOTH pays a "disreputable plastic surgeon" to transform his face into the exact image of Bruce Wayne's in July 1951, but it is ultimately mutilated beyond recognition by a gangster's bullets (Det No. 173: "Batman's Double!").

During the first thirty years of his career as Batman, Bruce Wayne resides at Wayne Manor (Det No. 368, Oct '67: "7 Wonder Crimes of Gotham City!"; and others), a "palatial" (WF No. 57, Mar/Apr '52: "Public Enemy Bruce Wayne!"; and others) mansion situated on a lavish estate (BM No. 12/3, Aug/Sep '42: "They Thrill to Conquer!"; and others) somewhere in the suburbs (Det No. 178, Dec '51: "The Defeat of Batman!"; and others) north of Gotham City (WF No. 39, Mar/Apr '49: "The Conquest of Batman's Identity!").

The exact address of Wayne Manor is uncertain, having been inconsistenly reported in the texts both as 224 Park Drive (Det No. 185, Jul '52: "The Secret of Batman's Utility Belt!"), and as 37 Gotham Boulevard (WF No. 66, Sep/Oct '53: "The Proving Ground for Crime!").

The grounds of the estate are large, with numerous trees (WF No. 60, Sep/Oct '52: "The Richest Crook in the World!"), a swimming pool (Det No. 310, Dec '62: "Bat-Mite's Super-Circus!"), and tennis courts (WF No. 140, Mar '64: "The Clayface Superman!").

The lavish facilities of the mansion include a well-equipped gymnasium (BM No. 72/2, Aug/Sep '52: "The Legion of Faceless Men!"; and others); a "private crime library" (WF No. 9, Spr '43: "Crime of the Month"); a darkroom (BM No. 175, Nov '65: "The Decline and Fall of Batman!"); and a set of trapezes located in the basement (Det No. 286, Dec '60: "The Doomed Batwoman!").

"Many yards away" from the mansion (Det No. 63, May '42: "A Gentleman in Gotham"), "at the rear" of Wayne's property (Det No. 205, Mar '54: "The Origin of the Bat-Cave!"), is the old barn that has served at various times as the secret entrance to an underground passageway leading to the mansion, as a secret hangar and garage for the batplane and the batmobile, and as a secret entrance to the batcave, the sprawling subterranean headquarters of Batman and Robin situated beneath the grounds of the Wayne estate (*see* section D, the batcave).

Several early texts contain references to Bruce Wayne's "room" (Det No. 27, May '39: "The Case of the Chemical Syndicate") or "apartment" (BM No. 10/3, Apr/May '42: "The Princess of Plunder!") – or to "the apartment of Bruce Wayne and Dick Grayson" (BM No. 5/1, Spr '41: "The Riddle of the Missing Card!") – but these references are few and scattered, and the evidence of the chronicles, taken as a whole, is overwhelming that Bruce Wayne has resided in his suburban mansion since the beginning of his career as Batman (Det No. 33, Nov '39: "The Batman Wars Against the Dirigible of Doom"; and others).

Dick Grayson begins living at Wayne Manor in April 1940, the month Bruce Wayne becomes his guardian (Det No. 38), and Alfred joins the household as its butler in April–May 1943 (BM No. 16/4: "Here Comes Alfred!").

In December 1969, after Dick Grayson has departed Wayne Manor for his freshman year at Hudson University, Bruce Wayne closes up Wayne Manor and the batcave beneath it and moves to a new home in a penthouse apartment atop the skyscraper housing his own Wayne Foundation in the heart of Gotham City (BM No. 217: "One Bullet Too Many!"). (*See* section H, the man himself [as Batman].)

In the years that follow, Wayne tends to foundation affairs by day, while by night he carries on his war against the underworld as Batman, alone, without Robin, much as he did in the initial year of his crime-fighting career. Away at Hudson University, Dick Grayson periodically dons his Robin costume to fight crime on his own, joining forces with Batman only for an occasional adventure.

***H. The Man Himself* (*as Batman*).** Batman, the crime-fighting alter ego of millionaire socialite Bruce Wayne, is the hero of the Batman chronicles and the veteran of more than a thousand adventures. He is the mentor and ally of ROBIN, the owner of the canine crime-fighter Bat-Hound (see ACE [the BAT-HOUND]), the close friend and frequent crime-fighting ally of SUPERMAN, and a close personal friend of POLICE COMMISSIONER JAMES W. GORDON.

In the course of a career spanning nearly four decades, he has fought such nemeses of justice as TWO-FACE, the JOKER, the PENGUIN, and the CATWOMAN, and time and again he has beaten them all.

His allies in the war against crime have included BATWOMAN, Bat-Girl (*see* BAT-GIRL [BETTY KANE]), ALFRED, and Batgirl (*see* BATGIRL [BARBARA GORDON]).

Batman is a man with seemingly limitless resources and uncounted abilities, a man hungry for action and "bored by inactivity" (BM No. 10/3, Apr/May '42: "The Princess of Plunder!"). He is sleuth, acrobat, fighter, and inventor. He is, quite simply, the world's greatest detective. (*See* section E 1, the abilities.)

It is common knowledge in the world of the chronicles that Batman has another identity, but the name of

Batman, 1972 © NPP 1976

the real person lurking beneath his cowl is one of the world's most closely guarded secrets (*see* section B, the secret identity).

Operating from the batcave, his secret subterranean headquarters sprawling beneath Wayne Manor (*see* section D, the batcave), Batman wages unrelenting warfare against the forces of evil, aided by Robin, the Boy Wonder, and by an extraordinary arsenal of crime-fighting equipment (*see* section E 2, the equipment).

Batman's most important relationship is the one he shares with Robin (*see* section I, the relationship with Robin), but Batman has also enjoyed his share of romantic involvements, including relationships with such beautiful, talented, and fascinating women as JULIE MADISON, LINDA PAGE, VICKI VALE, BATWOMAN, and the CATWOMAN (*see* section J, the women of the chronicles).

Batman has blue eyes (S No. 173/3, Nov '64: "The Triumph of Luthor and Brainiac!"), and beneath his bat-eared cowl his hair is black.

His height, usually given as 6'1" (Det No. 141, Nov '48: "The Gallery of Public Heroes!"; and others), is reported in one text as being an even 6 feet (WF No. 51, Apr/May '51: "The Academy for Gangsters!"), and his weight, usually given as 185 pounds (Det No. 141, Nov '48: "The Gallery of Public Heroes!"; and others), has been as low as 180 pounds (Det No. 214, Dec '54: "The Batman Encyclopedia") and as high as 187½ pounds (Det No. 174, Aug '51: "The Park Avenue Kid!").

Described as a man of "gigantic frame" and "massive figure" (Det No. 36, Feb '40), he has a chest measurement of 44" and a sleeve length of 33" (Det No. 169, Mar '51: "Batman--Boss of the Big House!").

Batman is ambidextrous, always signing his name with his left hand as Batman and with his right hand as Bruce Wayne in order to help safeguard the secret of his dual identity (BM No. 92/1, Jun '55: "Fan-Mail of Danger!"; and others). There are no existing records of Batman's fingerprints (BM No. 83/1, Apr '54: "The Duplicate Batman!"), but he can be identified beneath a fluoroscope by means of the silver plate once implanted inside his left shoulder after the bone had been splintered by a gangster's bullet (Det No. 199, Sep '53: "The Invisible Batman!").

The name and persona of Batman were adopted by Bruce Wayne sometime prior to his twenty-first birthday, as he prepared to embark on the fulfillment of his boyhood vow to avenge the murder of his parents by dedicating his life to "a relentless war against crime . . ." (BM No. 232, Jun '71: "Daughter of the Demon").

By all accounts, the cold-blooded murder of Bruce Wayne's parents was the seminal event in Batman's life, the event which, more than anything else, has been responsible for his long and brilliant career as a crime-fighter (*see* section A, Origin). As Bruce Wayne was the offspring of his parents' life together, so Batman is the offspring of his parents' death.

The sudden, violent death of his parents has left lasting scars upon Batman. Like many youngsters orphaned in childhood, he seems to have experienced the loss of his mother and father as a personal desertion. In the unconscious mind of the young Bruce Wayne, he was unworthy of his parents' love and so they deserted him. It is the deep inner feelings of worthlessness engendered by this unconsciously perceived desertion that drive Batman to strive for almost superhuman perfection in a field of endeavor where he must prove his self-worth constantly by risking his life against overwhelming odds. Moreover, the traumatic "desertion" of Bruce Wayne's parents has left the adult Batman with an abiding legacy of deep-seated anger, for just as criminals have broken faith with society, the young Bruce Wayne felt that his parents, by abandoning him, had broken faith with him.

This mortal anger at his parents for having deserted him, and at himself for having been unworthy of their lasting love, finds socially acceptable expression in Batman's hatred of the underworld and in his lifelong crusade against criminals. Seen in this light, the life of socially sanctioned violence in which Batman has embroiled himself is not a freely chosen occupation at all, but rather the acting out of an unconscious, violent compulsion, for Batman's war against the underworld is in reality a war against his parents. And, in the sense that the inner compulsion to wage this war has deprived Batman of his own freedom, in particular the joys of ordinary life that he claims to envy, it is also a war against himself.

Bruce Wayne acknowledges as much in September 1975. ". . . **the Batman seldom** enjoys himself!" he remarks. "I'm **certain** he **envies** those who can lead peaceful lives! He's **driven** . . . he's **burdened** with a **compulsion** to battle crime! It isn't **pretty**--it's simply what he **does** . . . what he **needs** to do!" (Det No. 451: "The Batman's Burden!").

What Wayne does not acknowledge on this occasion, however, probably because he has never acknowledged it to himself, is the significance of his compulsion as an expression of anger against his parents. Indeed, such an acknowledgement would be so traumatic that Wayne took the extreme step of creating a whole new identity, the persona of Batman, to act out his seething anger for him. Whatever Wayne does as Batman, he can at least take solace from the fact that he is not really being himself.

By his own account, Bruce Wayne was "not yet old enough to vote" when he first set out on his lifelong crusade against villainy, cloaked in the costume of a giant bat (BM No. 232, Jun '71: "Daughter of the Demon").

In the early days of his career, Batman was a vigilante avenger, an "'outside the law' racket-buster" (Det No. 65, Jul '42: "The Cop Who Hated the Batman!") hunted by the police for working beyond the pale of legitimate authority. He carried an automatic pistol (Det No. 33, Nov '39: "The Batman Wars Against the Dirigible of Doom"; and others) and wore a bulletproof vest (*see* section C 1, the basic costume and accessories); "borrowed" parked automobiles to chase down criminals (BM No. 6/4, Aug/Sep '41: "Suicide Beat!"; BM No. 7/1, Oct/Nov '41); extorted confessions from his adversaries by means of physical violence (BM No. 5/3, Spr '41: "The Case of the Honest Crook"; and others), the threat of violence (Det No. 28, Jun '39; and others), or the third degree (Det No. 134, Apr '48: "The Umbrellas of Crime!"; and others) and often deposited his bound captives and their confessions on the sidewalk in front of police headquarters (Det No. 28, Jun '39; and others) before racing away into the night to avoid confrontations with the police. Occasionally these nocturnal gifts to the officers of the law were accompanied by wry explanatory notes signed with the image of a small black bat (BM No. 3/4, Fall '40: "The Batman vs the Cat-Woman!"; and others).

One of his favorite ploys for terrifying criminals during this early period was to send them a live bat inside a cardboard box, frequently accompanied by a note warning them to get out of town (Det No. 38, Apr '40; and others). When Batman felt the situation war-

Crime czar "Boss" Zucco and his henchmen receive a warning from Batman, 1940 © NPP 1940

ranted it, he was not even averse to meting out death (BM No. 1/3, Spr '40; and others).

"If you can't beat them 'inside' the law," he commented in September 1940, "you must beat them 'outside' it--and that's where I come in!" (Det No. 43: "The Case of the City of Terror").

In October 1939, after melting down a silver statuette to form two silver bullets, Batman loads them into his automatic pistol and destroys the vampires DALA and the MONK by firing them into their bodies at point-blank range as they lie in their coffins (Det No. 32).

In November 1939 Batman is shown armed with an automatic pistol which he also wields on that issue's cover (Det No. 33: "The Batman Wars Against the Dirigible of Doom").

In January 1940, the page-one introductory illustration – known as the "splash panel" – of Detective Comics No. 35 portrays Batman wielding a smoking automatic, but Batman neither carries nor uses a firearm in that issue's adventure.

Batman's use of the automatic is short-lived, however. By Winter 1941, he has abandoned the practice of carrying a firearm entirely, although, while under fire from a fleeing criminal wielding a sub-machine gun during this period, he does scoop up a pistol dropped by one of the gangster's cohorts and wing the gunman in the arm, forcing him to drop his weapon. "Just want to wing him!" remarks Batman. Observes the textual narrative: "The **Batman** never carries or kills with a gun!" (BM No. 4/4).

In July 1942 state trooper TOM BOLTON remarks that "the **Batman** never uses a gun . . ." (Det No. 65: "The Cop Who Hated the Batman!"), and by March–April 1952 Batman's self-imposed ethical prohibition against carrying firearms has become such an article of faith in the chronicles that Dick Grayson even questions his carrying a pistol while disguised as a gangster.

". . . I want this disguise to be **complete!**" explains Batman. "However, the pistol's not loaded so I'm not really breaking my rule against firearms!" (WF No. 57: "Public Enemy Bruce Wayne!").

Although Batman's ethical aversion to firearms is alluded to frequently after 1940 (Det No. 217, Mar '55: "The Mental Giant of Gotham City!"; and others), there have been occasions in recent years when he has resorted to firearms briefly, such as when he holds a gang of criminals at bay with a gangster's pistol in May 1964 (Det No. 327: "The Mystery of the Menacing Mask!"), or uses a seaman's rifle aboard a yacht in November 1970 in an attempt to turn aside an assault by trained dolphins carrying plastic explosives (Det No. 405: "The First of the Assassins!").

During the first year of Batman's crime-fighting career, easily a score of criminals die by his hand, but the grim brutality of Batman's early period is soon replaced by what is described in the chronicles as Batman's deep-seated moral aversion to killing.

In May 1939 Batman seizes a hoodlum in a "deadly headlock" and hurls him bodily off the roof of a two-story house (Det No. 27: "The Case of the Chemical Syndicate"), and in June 1939 he flips a member of the

Batman with automatic pistol, 1939 © NPP 1939

FRENCHY BLAKE gang over the side of a building to his doom (Det No. 28).

In July 1939 Batman kills DOCTOR DEATH's giant Indian assistant, JABAH, by strangling him from behind with his lasso (Det No. 29: "The Batman Meets Doctor Death"), and in August 1939 he kills Doctor Death's second assistant, Mikhail, by kicking him in the head and breaking his neck (Det. No. 30).

In Spring 1940 Batman annihilates two of PROFESSOR HUGO STRANGE's man-monsters and several of his henchmen by blazing away at them with a water-cooled machine gun mounted on the fuselage of the batplane – "Much as I hate to take human life," he says grimly, "I'm afraid **this time** it's necessary!" – and strangling one of the man-monsters with his silken lasso (BM No. 1/3).

In May 1940, after invading the schooner hideout of the ruthless GREEN DRAGON tong, Batman overturns a gigantic green idol, crushing and killing many of the tong's members (Det No. 39).

In Summer 1940 Batman unleashes a mighty blow that sends pathetically deranged villain ADAM LAMB plummeting down a flight of stairs, breaking his neck. "This is the only time I was ever sorry to see a criminal die!" murmurs Batman grimly. "Medical attention might have cured him!" (BM No. 2/2).

By Winter 1941, however, Batman's attitude toward the taking of human life has changed radically. "Use only the **flat** of your sword, Robin!" he cries during a battle with BLACKBEARD and his pirate horde. "Remember, we never kill with weapons of any kind!" (BM No. 4/2: "Blackbeard's Crew and the Yacht Society").

Indeed, from this time onward, killing remains deeply repugnant to Batman's moral code.

During the early period of his career, Batman's behavior was characterized by the frequently brutal extortion of information and confessions from criminal suspects as well as gross violations of their individual rights, as when he devises a plan to abduct the JOKER

The BATMAN
THE BATMAN, WEIRD FIGURE OF DARKNESS AGAIN PROWLS FORTH TO STRIKE ANOTHER BLOW AGAINST CRIME...

Batman with automatic pistol, 1940 © NPP 1940

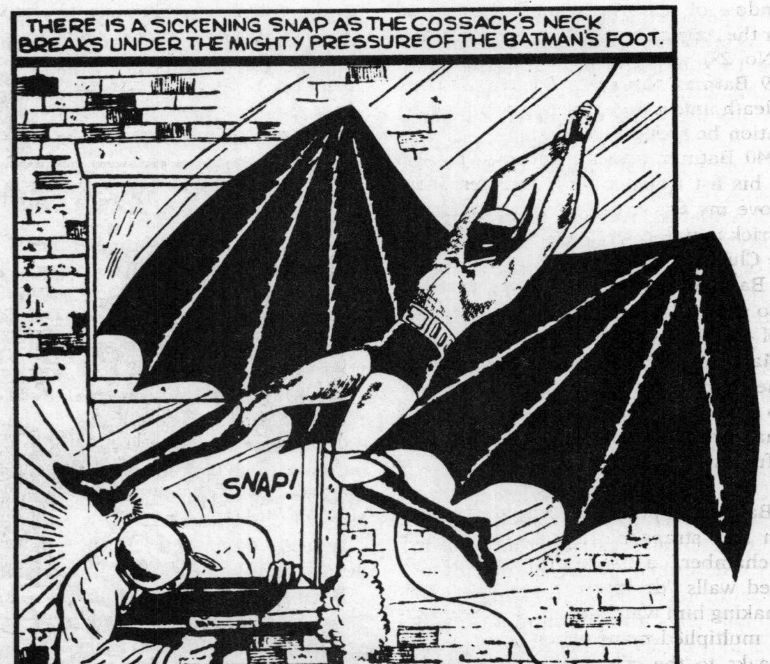

THERE IS A SICKENING SNAP AS THE COSSACK'S NECK BREAKS UNDER THE MIGHTY PRESSURE OF THE BATMAN'S FOOT.
SNAP!

Batman kills Mikhail, 1939 © NPP 1939

". . . out of the sky, spitting death . . . the Batman!" 1940
© NPP 1940

from a hospital in Summer 1940 and "take him to a famous brain specialist for an operation, so that he can be cured and turned into a valuable citizen" (BM No. 2/1).

Following are a few examples of particularly flagrant violations of civil liberties and due process perpetrated by Batman during the early years of his career.

In June 1939 Batman suspends FRENCHY BLAKE by a rope out the window of his apartment building and threatens to sever the rope unless Blake agrees to sign a confession (Det No. 28).

In August 1939 Batman threatens DOCTOR DEATH's henchmen with death unless they agree to provide him with the information he seeks (Det No. 30).

In Summer 1940 Batman seizes a criminal by the shirtfront, raises his fist threateningly, and demands, "Talk!--Or I'll shove my fist so far down your throat, they'll need a derrick to pull it up again!" (BM No. 2/3: "The Case of the Clubfoot Murders").

In Spring 1941 Batman beats SMILEY SIKES senseless until he agrees to sign a written confession (BM No. 5/3: "The Case of the Honest Crook").

In February–March 1942 Batman slams a wooden desk into Fritz the Fence, pinning him to the wall, and then threatens to give Fritz a beating unless he agrees to provide Batman with information on the whereabouts of some fugitive criminals (BM No. 9/1: "The Four Fates!").

In April 1948 Batman apprehends one of the PENGUIN's henchmen and straps him to a chair in the batcave's "truth chamber," a tiny interrogation room with four mirrored walls "designed to crack a criminal's silence by making him watch fearful faces reflecting his own guilt multiplied many times!"

As Batman speaks to the criminal from behind a two-way mirror, grimly accusing him of wrongdoing

Batman annihilates one of Professor Hugo Strange's man-monsters, 1940 © NPP 1940

and demanding confession, the henchman is forced to gaze at his own terrified reflections in the truth chamber's mirrored walls as a succession of colored lights play upon his face: first an "eerie red"; then yellow, "the sickly color of fear"; and finally green, imparting to the multiple reflections "an unhealthy green pallor,

Batman and gangster Roxy Brenner, 1940 © NPP 1940

Batman, 1939 © NPP 1939

betraying the sickness of mind that has gripped the criminal!" (Det No. 134: "The Umbrellas of Crime!").

In April–May 1948 Batman apprehends criminal Whitey Harlan, imprisons him in the batcave, and, after disguising himself to resemble his captive, turns himself in to the police for a robbery Harlan once committed and gets himself sentenced to a two-year term in the Gotham City Prison – all as part of a plan to infiltrate the prison as an inmate in order to uncover the explanation behind its low rate of recidivism. A week later, having obtained the information he seeks, Batman leaves the prison, forces the real Whitey Harlan to don the convict garb that was issued to him in the course of his impersonation, and returns Harlan to the prison to serve out the remainder of the bogus sentence.

"I got you a light sentence, Whitey, and I've served the first week of it for you!" smiles Batman, when Harlan protests the blatant illegality of the situation. "And I've started a good record for you! What more do you want?" (BM No. 46/2: "Big House Chaplain!").

Today Batman continues to violate the civil liberties of suspects in criminal cases, particularly when they are members of the criminal subculture and therefore unlikely to have any recourse to legitimate authority. Today's infractions, however, are infinitely less blatant than those of his early years and are generally limited to intimidation unaccompanied by the threat of lethal violence.

In October–November 1941 Batman's status as a vigilante crime-fighter is abruptly ended as Police Commissioner Gordon appoints him an honorary member of the Gotham City Police Department (BM No. 7/4: "The People vs. The Batman"). From this time forward, Batman's attitude toward law enforcement becomes ever more law-abiding. Even in August–September 1944, for example, after the villainous TWEEDLEDUM AND TWEEDLEDEE have gotten themselves elected mayor of the town of Yonville and railroaded Batman and Robin into prison on a trumped-up charge, Batman refuses to resist arrest.

"Whatever their game, **Robin**," he explains, "they've got the law behind them--and we never fight the law!" (BM No. 24/3: "The Mayors of Yonville!").

(For further information concerning Batman's changing relationship with the law-enforcement establishment, see section K, the relationship with the law-enforcement establishment.)

In addition to being dangerous, the life of Batman is arduous and demanding. As Bruce Wayne explains in November 1945:

> . . . There's a lot more to it than chasing crooks! **Batman** and **Robin** must constantly put in long hours of study of criminology, police methods, science. . . .
>
> Sometimes they must spend whole days and nights in the secret laboratory experimenting in search of clues . . . not to mention the daily workout in the gym, keeping in fighting shape! (Det No. 105: "The Batman Goes Broke!").

For Batman and Robin, each new day begins with a grueling workout in the gym (BM No. 23/1, Jun/Jul '44: "The Upside Down Crimes!") – frequently in time to music (BM No. 56/3, Dec/Jan '49–'50: "A Greater Detective Than Batman!") – practicing acrobatic routines, wrestling (BM No. 11/3, Jun/Jul '42: "Bandits in Toyland!"), boxing (BM No. 12/4, Aug/Sep '42: "Around the Clock with the Batman!"), and other skills.

"Yes, practice makes perfect!" explains the textual narrative of Batman No. 11/3. "That is the secret behind the daring deeds and phenomenal feats of the twin foes of crime!" (Jun/Jul '42: "Bandits in Toyland!").

Following their morning workout and breakfast on a typical day in August–September 1942, Batman and Robin test a "new wing placement" on the batplane; perform tests in their criminological laboratory on evidence linking a suspect to a crime; drill one another in identifying wanted criminals, "a daily routine that produces [Batman's] amazing photographic memory"; devote some time to selling war bonds; return to their civilian identities long enough for Dick Grayson to do his homework while Bruce Wayne works on Batman's forthcoming book, *Observation on Crime;* apprehend a gang of jewel thieves; put on an acrobatic display for infantile paralysis victims at a local hospital; and, finally, heading homeward from the hospital at 9:00 P.M., stop to thwart an attempted suicide, only to discover that the "suicide" attempt is actually a diversion designed to cover up a bank robbery in progress, whereupon they swing into action and apprehend the bank robbers (BM No. 12/4: "Around the Clock with the Batman!").

Late at night, while the city is asleep, Batman and Robin make their "regular midnight patrol" of the city (Det No. 131, Jan '48: "The Underworld Surgeon!"; and others). Batman No. 84/3 refers to the Dynamic Duo's "usual night patrol to every corner of the city" (Jun '54: "Ten Nights of Fear!"), but in September 1964 Batman examines a map of GOTHAM CITY in the batcave and refers to "my patrol sector for tonight" (BM No. 166/1: "Two-Way Deathtrap!"), suggesting that each nighttime patrol includes only a selected portion of the city.

Similarly, many texts describe the patrol as a nightly event (BM No. 121/1, Feb '59: "The Body in the Bat-Cave"; and others), but in September 1964 Robin refers

Batman and monster gorilla, 1939 © NPP 1939

to a specific night as "our patrol night" (BM No. 166/1: "Two-Way Deathtrap!"), implying that some nights are set aside for patrolling the city, but not others. Sometimes, when Robin is busy with schoolwork or other responsibilities, Batman patrols the city alone (BM No. 166/1, Sep '64: "Two-Way Deathtrap!"; and others).

Whenever some particularly dire menace threatens the people of Gotham City – such as the escape from prison of Clayface (*see* CLAYFACE [MATT HAGEN]) in June 1962 (Det No. 304: "The Return of Clay-Face!") – Batman and Robin abandon their customary patrol procedure in favor of a round-the-clock alert accompanied by a twenty-four-hour patrol of the city (BM No. 162/1, Mar '64: "The Batman Creature!"; and others). On occasion, Batman has worked for as long as three days and nights without any sleep (WF No. 49, Dec/Jan '50–'51: "A White Feather for Batman!").

It is only after the menace of the moment has been met and overcome, and the day's work is truly done, that Batman takes time out to record all the facts in his private casebook, containing detailed accounts of all his adventures (Det No. 148, Jun '49: "The Experiment of Professor Zero").

Batman possesses "deep instincts of honesty and justice" (Det No. 83, Jan '44: "Accidentally on Purpose!"), and much of his behavior is motivated by an abiding sense of honor and principle.

Among his deeply held convictions is the sacredness of human life, which, except for the first year of his crime-fighting career, forbids him from either carrying a gun (Det No. 65, Jul '42: "The Cop Who Hated The Batman!"; and others) or killing a criminal (BM No. 4/2, Win '41: "Blackbeard's Crew and the Yacht Society"; and others), even if that criminal is in a position to end his career as a crime-fighter.

In August–September 1948, for example, after WOLF BRANDO, Public Enemy Number One, has stumbled upon the secret of Batman's identity and then collapsed after accidentally inhaling some poison gas in the batcave, Batman hastens to administer an antidote, but only over the objections of Robin.

Batman, 1939 © NPP 1939

Batman, 1939 © NPP 1939

"Let him die!" insists Robin. "He's a killer! You'd only be saving him for the electric chair anyway! Why give him a chance to reveal your identity?"

"**Robin**, we've always followed a moral code," replies Batman, ". . . we must keep him alive . . . even though it will mean the finish of **Batman!**" (BM No. 48/2: "The 1,000 Secrets of the Batcave!").

Similarly, in July 1951, after KILLER MOTH has uncovered the secret of Batman's identity only to be riddled with bullets soon afterward by a disgruntled hoodlum, Batman insists on doing everything possible to save the villain even though, if he lives, he will be in a position to end Batman's career by revealing his secret.

"The only important thing now," remarks Batman, as he and Robin race the critically wounded criminal to the hospital in the batmobile, "is that a human being is in danger and we can help him!" (Det No. 173: "Batman's Double!").

Another of Batman's convictions is that ". . . **Batman** and **Robin** [must] never use their talents or equipment for winning money or personal glory!" (BM No. 34/1, Apr/May '46: "The Marathon of Menace!"). They never accept rewards for apprehending criminals (Det No. 48, Feb '41: "The Secret Cavern"; and others), and in cases where income is forthcoming from work they do—such as the royalties from Batman's book on crime (BM No. 12/4, Aug/Sep '42: "Around the Clock with the Batman!") or his fee for serving as technical advisor on the set of a Hollywood crime movie (BM No. 76/3, Apr/May '53: "The Man of 100 Murders")—it is, without exception, donated to charity.

Indeed, just as Batman's alter ego, millionaire Bruce Wayne, regularly donates large sums of money to worthy causes, so do Batman and Robin unstintingly donate large amounts of their time. Examples are their performance before an audience of infantile paralysis victims in August–September 1942 (BM No. 12/4: "Around the Clock with the Batman!") and the acrobatic display they put on each year at the Gotham City Charity Circus (BM No. 114/3, Mar '58: "The Bat-Ape!").

Criminals frequently attempt to capitalize on Batman's humanitarian instincts in order to delay or stymie him while they make good their escape. In every case, Batman puts the safety of victims and bystanders above the capture of the criminals, yet he always manages to catch the culprits in the end (Det No. 124, Jun '47: "The Crime Parade"; and others).

Batman's exciting career inevitably centers on his efforts to apprehend criminals, but Batman is also deeply committed to programs of crime prevention, particularly among young people, and to the rehabilitation of men and women convicted of crimes.

"Crooks are **yellow** without their guns!" he advises a group of youngsters in Spring 1940. "--Don't go around admiring them--rather do your best in fighting them--and <u>all their kind</u>!" (BM No. 1/4).

In recent years, he has taken to lecturing at the Gotham City Police Academy (BM No. 165/2, Aug '64: "The Dilemma of the Detective's Daughter!") and at other police academies across the country (BM No. 132/1, Jun '60: "The Martian from Gotham City") to press home his conviction that the prevention of crime must be among the top priorities of law enforcement.

". . . ***Robin*** and I do a job--we fight criminals!" he tells a gathering of law officers at the Center City police convention in July 1963. "But, like all of you, our greatest satisfaction is in ***preventing*** crime, and proving to youngsters that ***crime does not pay!***" (Det No. 317: "The Secrets of the Flying Bat-Cave!").

Batman wrecks an underworld casino, 1940 © NPP 1940

Even in the early years of his career, Batman spoke out forcefully in favor of providing increased opportunities for former convicts who have paid their debts to society.

"The great lesson of democracy is that all men are created equal," he tells a radio audience in April–May 1945, prior to testifying before the U.S. Senate on behalf of legislation to provide employment opportunities for ex-convicts. "Why then should anyone continue to suffer for a mistake after [his] debt has been paid? . . . for this great nation cannot allow prejudice to deprive it of the badly needed skills of these men!" (BM No. 28/3: "Batman Goes to Washington!").

Batman's first book, *Observation on Crime*, is "a file of [his] cases with notes on the psychological aspects of crime!" Its royalties are earmarked for donation to the Red Cross (BM No. 12/4, Aug/Sep '42: "Around the Clock with the Batman!").

Batman is a patriotic American (Det No. 48, Feb '41: "The Secret Cavern"; and others), a "great sports fan" (BM No. 169/2, Feb '65: "A Bad Day for Batman!"), and a firm believer in the lasting value of a good education: "A good education," he muses in August 1967, "is one thing that not even the cleverest criminal in the world can steal from you!" (Det No. 366: "The Round-Robin Death Threats").

Although Batman has always modestly shunned the spotlight of public acclaim, few individuals in history have been accorded such widespread honor and distinction.

He has been elected the mayor of one city (BM No. 24/3, Aug/Sep '44: "The Mayors of Yonville!"), the sheriff of another (BM No. 10/4, Apr/May '42: "Sheriff of Ghost Town!"), and even served as a frontier marshal in the Wild West of 1880 (BM No. 99/2, Apr '56: "Batman--Frontier Marshal").

He has been dubbed a knight by KING ARTHUR (BM No. 36/3, Aug/Sep '46: "Sir Batman at King Arthur's Court!"), appointed bodyguard to CLEOPATRA (Det No. 167, Jan '51: "Bodyguards to Cleopatra!"), deputized as a Mountie (BM No. 78/3, Aug/Sep '53: "Batman of the Mounties!"), and named an honorary citizen of Athens in the fifth century B.C. (BM No. 38/1, Dec/Jan '46–'47: "Peril in Greece!").

In his honor, the town of PLAINVILLE once changed its name to Batmantown (BM No. 100/1, Jun '56: "Batmantown, U.S.A.") and a pair of grateful parents named their newborn son Batman (BM No. 108/3, Jun '57: "The Career of Batman Jones!"). (*See* JONES, BATMAN.)

The exploits of Batman have been celebrated and immortalized in virtually every known medium: in music, in balladeer SAM STRONG's "Ballad of Batman" (BM No. 95/3, Oct '55: "The Ballad of Batman!") and composer Joseph Macklas's "The Batman and Robin March" (WF No. 48, Oct/Nov '50: "Song of Crime!"); on radio, on station WABX's adventure series "The True Adventures of Batman" (Det No. 64, Jun '42: "The Joker Walks the Last Mile!"); on television, on station GCTV's "Your Life Story" (BM No. 87/1, Oct '54: "Batman's Greatest Thrills!") and on station WPO's "Underworld, Incorporated," narrated by Batman and televised from the batcave (WF No. 57, Mar/Apr '52: "Public Enemy Bruce Wayne!"); and in the movies, in the Hollywood film *Crime Crushers*, in which Batman and Robin star in August–September 1951 (BM No. 66/2: "The Movie Stars Who Died Twice!").

Batman has been the recipient of numerous awards, trophies, citations, and other honors, including the bat-shaped, diamond-studded police badge presented to him by Police Commissioner Gordon at graduation exercises for Gotham City's rookie policemen in January 1945 (Det No. 95); the gold trophy, inscribed to "Batman and Robin, Globe-Trotters of the Law," presented to the Dynamic Duo by a group of law-enforcement officials from around the world in June 1950 (Det No. 160: "The Globe-Trotter of Crime!"); being honored as Man of the Year by the Big Six Club, a club comprised of America's six wealthiest and most influential men, in January 1952 (Det No. 179: "Mayor Bruce Wayne!"); the golden key to Gotham City presented to him by Police Commissioner Gordon on GCTV's "Your Life Story" program in October 1954 (BM No. 87/1: "Batman's Greatest Thrills!"); the key to the city presented to him by the mayor on Gotham City's annual Batman Day in December 1958 (BM No. 120/1: "The Curse of the Bat-Ring"); the collection of honorary police badges presented to him by countries around the world (BM No. 124/2, Jun '59: "The Return of Signalman"); and the "special citation signed by the president of the United States" that he receives in August 1964, thanking him and Robin for their success in smashing a foreign spy ring (Det No. 330: "The Fallen Idol of Gotham City!").

Statues and other artistic tributes to Batman abound, particularly in Gotham City, including the large stone statue of the Dynamic Duo unveiled at City Hall following a ticker-tape parade in their honor in August–September 1942 (BM No. 12/4: "Around the Clock with the Batman!"); the portrait of the Dynamic Duo by

Batman in action, 1941 © NPP 1941

Batman, 1941 © NPP 1941

"famed artist" Carl Marlin (BM No. 53/2, Jun/Jul '49: "The Portrait of Doom!") and the bust of Batman (BM No. 111/3, Oct '57: "The Armored Batman!") in the Gotham City Hall of Fame; the iron bust of Batman in the City Museum and the standing steel statue of Batman in City Park (BM No. 109/1, Aug '57: "Three Crimes Against Batman"); and the statue of a seated Batman in Gotham Park reminiscent of the statue of Abraham Lincoln in the Lincoln Memorial in Washington, D.C. (BM No. 107/1, Apr '57: "The Boy Who Adopted Batman"; BM No. 134/3, Sep '60: "The Deadly Dummy").

A monumental head of Batman has been carved into the side of Mt. Gotham (Det No. 319, Sep '63: "The Fantastic Dr. No-Face!"), and the gigantic Batman Lighthouse – "a towering tribute to [the] great lawman" – stands majestically in Gotham Bay. Sculpted in Batman's image, with an upraised arm grasping an incandescent torch beacon, the lighthouse is "a unique structure of steel, rearing 300 feet into the air--a towering figure that guides approaching ships" to safety with its ever-glowing beacon (BM No. 126/2, Sep '59: "The Batman Lighthouse").

A magnificent Batman statue clock, unveiled in Gotham City Park in March 1959, is destroyed at the unveiling by the CLOCK as an act of vengeance against Batman (Det No. 265: "Batman's First Case!").

Batman is indisputably Gotham City's most renowned citizen. Batman Day is celebrated there annually (BM No. 103/1, Oct '56: "The Broken Batman Trophies"; WF No. 140, Mar '64: "The Clayface Superman!"), and the city's famed BATMAN MUSEUM houses an extensive collection of Batman memorabilia (BM No. 119/2, Oct '58: "The Secret of Batman Island!"; and others).

A Batman Exposition opens in Gotham City in December 1956 (BM No. 104/2: "Robin's 50 Batman Partners"), and a Batman Sightseeing Bus regularly ferries tourists around the city to the sites of Batman and Robin's most exciting cases (BM No. 117/1, Aug '58: "The Mystery of the Batman Bus"). In March 1960 Gotham City holds a series of special celebrations to commemorate the anniversary of Batman's first case (BM No. 130/1: "Batman's Deadly Birthday").

The greatest single tribute ever paid to Batman by an individual is probably Batman Island off the coast of Gotham City. Owned by fabulously wealthy Batman fan A. K. BARNABY, it houses the world's largest collection of Batman trophies, films, and memorabilia (BM No. 119/2, Oct '58: "The Secret of Batman Island!").

Other important tributes to Batman and Robin have included the statue erected in their honor by the citizens of an unnamed United States city after the Dynamic Duo have put an end to gangland oppression (*see* GREER, HARLISS) there in September 1940 (Det No. 43: "The Case of the City of Terror"); the heroes' welcome they receive in Washington, D.C., in December 1941–January 1942 (*see* section K, the relationship with the law-enforcement establishment); and the statue of them placed on display in the Scotland Yard Museum following their capture of PROFESSOR MORIARTY in April 1946 (Det No. 110: "Batman and Robin in Scotland Yard!").

Batman is an honorary member of the Gotham City Police Department (BM No. 7/4, Oct/Nov '41: "The People vs. The Batman"; and others) and a member of the Gotham City Crime Commission (Det No. 175, Sep '51: "The Underworld Bank!").

He holds membership in the following clubs: the 13 Club (*see* JOKER, THE); the Voyager's Club (Det No. 147, May '49: "Tiger Shark!"); the BULLET-HOLE CLUB (WF No. 50, Feb/Mar '51: "Bullet-Hole Club!"); the Club of Heroes (*see* LIGHTNING-MAN); and the MYSTERY ANALYSTS OF GOTHAM CITY (BM No. 164/2, Jun '64: "Batman's Great Face-Saving Feat!"; Det No. 335, Jan '65: "Trial of the Talking Mask!").

He holds honorary membership in the following clubs: the Folklore Society (WF No. 38, Jan/Feb '49: "The Impossible People!"); the Maskers, a club for people who wear masks in their everyday work (BM No. 72/2, Aug/Sep '52: "The Legion of Faceless Men!"); the 50 Fathoms Club, a club for underwater specialists (BM No. 104/3, Dec '56: "The Creature from 20,000

Batman in action, 1941 © NPP 1941

Fathoms!"); and the Safari Club, a club for sportsmen (BM No. 111/1, Oct '57: "The Gotham City Safari"). Batman joins the DANGER CLUB in April–May 1953 to root out a murderer, but the club is dissolved at the conclusion of the adventure (BM No. 76/1: "The Danger Club!").

In December 1969, after nearly thirty years as Batman's inseparable crime-fighting partner, Dick Grayson, the boy who is secretly Robin, departs Wayne Manor to begin his freshman year of college at Hudson University.

Following his departure, Bruce Wayne closes up Wayne Manor and the batcave beneath it and moves to a new home in a penthouse apartment atop the skyscraper housing his own Wayne Foundation (*see* ALFRED FOUNDATION, THE) in the heart of Gotham City.

"It's time we **all** started a **new** way of life!" he tells a slightly bewildered Alfred as the two of them inspect the batcave for what may be the last time. "A new way of **everything!**"

"We're in danger of becoming--**outmoded!**" he adds moments later. "**Obsolete** dodos of the **mod world** outside! Our best chance for survival is to--**close up shop** here!

"Take a long--possibly **last** look, Alfred--the **batcave** is destined to join all the caves of history housing the **extinct past!**"

"Oh-h . . . **no,** master Bruce!" gasps Alfred. "H-How will--er--we function as the crime-fighters of old?"

"By becoming **new**---**streamlining** the operation!" replies Wayne. "By discarding the paraphernalia of the past . . . and functioning with the clothes on our backs . . . the wits in our heads!

"By re-establishing [the] **trademark** of the **'old' Batman**---to strike **new fear** into the new breed of gangsterism sweeping the world!

"Today this new breed of rat--uses the modern weapons of . . . '**phoney** respectability'---'big business **fronts**'--'legal **cover-ups**'--and hides in the fortress towers of **Gotham's** metropolis!

"We're moving out of this suburban sanctuary, to live in the heart of that sprawling urban blight---to dig them out where they live and fatten on the innocent!" (BM No. 217: "One Bullet Too Many!").

Beginning at this time, and continuing through the mid-1970s, Batman carries on his war against the underworld alone, without Robin, much as he did in the initial year of his crime-fighting career. Away at Hudson University, Dick Grayson periodically dons his Robin costume to fight crime on his own, joining forces with Batman for only an occasional adventure.

I. The Relationship with Robin. "The friendship of **Batman** and **Robin** is one that has stood steadfast as a rock! To **Batman, Robin** is like his own son--and **Robin** would brave any danger to keep **Batman** from harm!" (BM No. 156/2, Jun '63: "Robin Dies at Dawn!").

Of all the human relationships dealt with in the Batman chronicles, the most important is the one that exists between Bruce Wayne, the man who is secretly Batman, and his ward Dick Grayson, the boy who is secretly ROBIN.

Batman has described Robin as "my closest pal" (Det No. 166, Dec '50: "The Man with a Million Faces!") and as "the best friend I've got" (Det No. 49, Mar '41: "Clayface Walks Again!"), and Robin has referred to Batman as "my best friend" (BM No. 3/1, Fall '40: "The Strange Case of the Diabolical Puppet Master") and as "the greatest friend I ever had" (BM No. 118/3, Sep '58: "The Merman Batman!").

"Dick, though you're only my ward," remarks Batman in August–September 1951, "I couldn't love you more if you were my own son!" (BM No. 66/3: "Batman II and Robin, Junior!").

Indeed, since the day Batman first took the orphaned Dick Grayson under his wing in April 1940 (Det No. 38), "the mutual affection between this man and boy has been as strong as that between father and son!" (BM No. 20/4, Dec/Jan '43–'44: "Bruce Wayne Loses the Guardianship of Dick Grayson!").

Batman in action, 1962 © NPP 1962

The depth of this great relationship is one of the major themes of the Batman chronicles, and the chroniclers have described the great emotions that underlie it in numerous texts.

Batman No. 5/3, for example, describes Batman's reaction after he has found Robin brutally beaten and covered with blood after a run-in with the henchmen of gangster SMILEY SIKES:

> The **Batman,** man who has faced a thousand dangers, man of strength and willpower, now bends his head and weeps. Anguished sobs are torn from him!
>
> Slowly, his great frame straightens. Small veins stand out on his features. Muscles cord in his throat. His eyes become fires, his mouth a knife-edged line--
>
> For the first time, the **Batman** knows rage, bleak, grim rage. Woe to all criminals, for now, the **Batman** has become a terrible figure of **vengeance**!

Batman, 1964 © NPP 1976

Realizing that a spark of life still remains in the gravely injured Robin, Batman carries him to the batmobile and races through the night to the home of the nearest doctor. When the physician, roused unexpectedly from his sleep, appears momentarily hesitant about performing the necessary emergency operation, Batman seizes him roughly by the shirtfront and threatens him with death unless he operates. ". . . if this boy dies because you refused to operate," he intones grimly, his eyes glowering beneath his cowl, "—I'll come back and kill you with my bare hands!"

"I'll operate . . . but not because of your threats," replies the doctor, ". . . but because it is the duty of a doctor to come to the aid of anyone who needs his services!"

Soon afterward, having left Robin in the care of the physician, Batman storms into the hideout of the Smiley Sikes gang and, ignoring the three bullets that come slamming into his chest in the course of the ensuing battle, beats Sikes senseless and forces him to sign a full confession of his crimes.

"Did-did you see his face?" gasps an awestruck policeman after Batman has turned Sikes and his confession over to the authorities.

"Yeah!" replies his companion. "That's the first time I ever saw it look like that! It-it was terrible . . . like a demon's!" (Spr '41: "The Case of the Honest Crook").

In February 1942, after Robin has apparently been drowned by the JOKER, "a strange dullness grips Batman's heart--and black despair numbs his brain!"

"Robin, dead!" he murmurs distractedly. "I don't care what happens to me now!" Soon afterward, however, his "lethargy is replaced by a terrible rage," and he becomes bent on vengeance (Det No. 60: "Case of the Costume-Clad Killers").

In February–March 1944, with Batman near death after battling a gang of "black market rustlers" (*see* BRULE), Robin begins to cry uncontrollably. "He can't die! He can't!" thinks Robin desperately. "Golly, why couldn't it have been me, instead! Please don't let him die!"

Later, Batman recovers, and man and boy embrace. "Golly!" exclaims Robin, beside himself with joy. "I thought you . . . you . . . golly! Guess you think I'm a sissy bawling this way!"

"Heck," replies Batman reassuringly, "I'm doing a little bawling myself!" (BM No. 21/1: "The Streamlined Rustlers!").

In the entire history of the Batman chronicles, there is not the slightest hint of any kind that an overt homosexual relationship exists between Batman and Robin, although the two have managed to forge a world for themselves in which meaningful relationships with women are all but impossible. What the chronicles do portray is a highly idealized relationship between a perfect, loving father and a loyal, worshipping son.

Like many youngsters orphaned in early childhood, Robin seems to have experienced the death of his parents – aerialists murdered by protection racketeers – as a personal desertion. In Robin's mind, he was unworthy of his parents' love and so they deserted him. To alleviate the deep inner feelings of worthlessness engendered by this unconsciously perceived rejection, Robin must continually strive to attain an almost superhuman perfection, to prove his self-worth constantly by risking his life daily against overwhelming odds.

His mortal anger at his parents for having deserted him, and at himself for having been unworthy of their lasting love, finds socially acceptable expression in his

Batman and Robin, 1941 © NPP 1941

hatred of the underworld and in his lifelong crusade against criminals.

Batman's parents were also murdered by criminals. In many ways his psychological makeup is identical to Robin's. It is this common inner need for a life of socially sanctioned violence, this shared compulsion to prove their self-worth continually by living with their lives always hanging by a thread, that forms the eternal psychic bond between Batman and Robin.

The death of his parents left lasting scars upon Batman, but it did not make him a homosexual. Rather, it exerted a lasting detrimental influence on his capacity for loving and helped to determine the kind of women for whom he could feel affection and experience erotic feeling (*see* section J, the women of the chronicles).

The orphaning of young Dick Grayson has left Robin insecure and apprehensive. Now, like many orphans, he hungers for affection and is fearful lest he lose that which has already come his way. And, like many youngsters being raised by only one parent, he is unduly apprehensive about the possible loss of his parent, overly jealous and possessive, and thus hostile toward any person, man or woman, whom he perceives as an interloper and a threat to the relationship.

The chronicles deal extensively with threats, real and imagined, to the continued existence of the Batman-Robin relationship. In general, each such threat assumes one of three basic forms: (a) an outsider attempts to deprive Bruce Wayne of the legal custody of Dick Grayson; (b) Robin fears, invariably without justification, that Batman intends to replace him with a new crime-fighting partner; and (c) Robin fears that a woman is about to supplant him in Batman's affections, thus destroying his relationship with Batman and bringing an end to their "wonderful life together" (WF No. 110, Jun '60: "The Alien Who Doomed Robin!").

(a) Two attempts have been made to wrest the guardianship of Dick Grayson away from Bruce Wayne, the first by Dick Grayson's unscrupulous uncle GEORGE GRAYSON, who institutes the legal action as part of a scheme to bilk Bruce Wayne out of $1,000,000 (BM No. 20/4, Dec/Jan '43–'44: "Bruce Wayne Loses the Guardianship of Dick Grayson!"), and the second by ex-convict ED KOLUM who hopes to revenge himself on Bruce Wayne for having once exposed him as a charity swindler (BM No. 57/1, Feb/Mar '50: "The Trial of Bruce Wayne!"). (*See* ROBIN.)

(b) There are a number of occasions when Robin becomes convinced that Batman has been training a new partner to take his place in the Dynamic Duo.

In December 1948–January 1949, for example, Robin feels certain that he is on the verge of being replaced as Batman's partner when he learns that Batman has been giving crime-fighting training to a boy named Jimmy and even taking the new youngster out on patrol with him at night.

"Did I do something wrong?" thinks Robin anxiously. "Maybe **Batman** thinks I'm slipping . . . that I'm not a fit partner for him anymore!"

Ultimately, however, he learns that Jimmy is blind, and that Batman has been training him in criminology only in order to help him fulfill his ambition of becoming a criminologist when he gets older.

". . . as for replacing you as **Batman's** partner," exclaims Jimmy, "**nobody** could do that!"

"Jimmy's right, **Robin,**" adds Batman, ". . . there's only **one Boy Wonder** . . . and he's **you!**" (BM No. 50/3: "The Second Boy Wonder!").

In June–July 1951, after a broken leg has confined him temporarily to a wheelchair, Robin becomes intensely jealous of Batman's interim partner, a crime-fighter named WINGMAN, despite Batman's assurances that he is merely training Wingman for a career as a lawman in some Northern European country.

"I wish I could believe him," thinks Robin sadly, "but I've got a feeling I'm being eased out of the picture. . . ."

Ultimately, however, despite a series of ambiguous events that serve to fuel Robin's paranoia, Batman turns out to have been telling the truth all along.

"Golly," exclaims Robin ashamedly, "--what a fool ***I've*** been!"

"You got off on the wrong foot and let your imagination take you the rest of the way!" replies Batman. "But I don't think it'll happen again!"

"You bet!" promises Robin. "From now on, I won't listen to those green-eyed monsters! I'll put my trust in our friendship!" (BM No. 65/1: "A Partner for Batman!").

In May 1956 Robin becomes fearful that he is about to be replaced by JOHN VANCE, once known as Batman, Junior. On the basis of a photograph that has fallen from Batman's files, Robin leaps to the wholly erroneous conclusion that Vance was once Batman's regular partner.

"**Batman** once had another partner--and he never told me!" pines Robin. "I guess he didn't want me to know I was only his **second choice** as a partner!"

And when Batman becomes worried about Vance's safety due to the recent escape from prison of bank robber Birrel Bintner, whom Vance once helped send to the penitentiary, Robin sees this as proof that Batman intends to abandon him so that he can fight crime again alongside his "original partner."

Robin's fears are proved groundless, however, when Vance turns out merely to be a man who, while still a youngster, helped Batman solve a single criminal case many years ago (Det No. 231: "Batman, Junior!").

Although it is usually Robin who fears desertion by Batman, the reverse has also been true. In March–April 1955, for example, after Batman has been temporarily sidelined by a crime-fighting mishap, Robin joins forces with SUPERMAN, for the first time in his career, to help apprehend the infamous PURPLE MASK MOB.

"After working with **Superman,** I wonder if **Robin** will find it **dull** working with me again?" thinks Batman anxiously. "After all, I don't have any super-powers!"

And the following day he muses, "They certainly make a great team! ***Superman*** and ***Robin*** . . . that's a team that could make everyone forget about ***Batman*** and ***Robin!*** I wonder if that would ever happen. . . ?"

Later, after the Purple Mask Mob has been apprehended and the temporary Superman-Robin partnership dissolved, Batman looks hesitantly to Robin for some needed reassurance. "Uh . . . wouldn't you rather be working as a team with ***Superman*** than with me?" he asks. "It must have been more exciting for you!"

"Oh, it was fun for awhile," replies Robin, "--a new novelty. . . . But it isn't the same as working with you, ***Batman!*** Golly, you taught me all I know . . . we'll ***always*** be a team!"

"Of course we will!" exclaims Batman proudly. "Nobody will ever see the end of ***Batman*** and ***Robin!***" (WF No. 75: "The New Team of Superman and Robin!").

Bruce Wayne and Dick Grayson, 1960
© NPP 1960

In February 1961 an extraterrestrial alien calling himself MR. MARVEL forces Robin to become his partner, and abandon Batman, by threatening to kill Batman if Robin refuses. Ultimately, Mr. Marvel is defeated and Batman and Robin are reunited, but Batman, who has not been told the reason for Robin's abrupt defection, suffers some anxious moments until he learns that Robin had only pretended to abandon him in order to safeguard his life (BM No. 137/1: "Robin's New Boss!").

(c) Robin becomes seized by unhappiness and anxiety whenever it appears that a woman is vying with him for Batman's affections.

In February–March 1943, after Bruce Wayne has announced his intention to marry Elva Barr despite his being fully aware that she is secretly the CATWOMAN, Robin is dismayed. "But, **Bruce,** you can't do this! That Elva's the Catwoman! What's got into you? What about Linda [LINDA PAGE]? What about . . . us?" (BM No. 15/1: "Your Face Is Your Fortune!").

In October–November 1953, when it appears that Batman may be forced to marry VICKI VALE against his will, Robin becomes decidedly gloomy, but not entirely over the prospect of Batman's acquiring a wife he does not really want. "It looks like we're sunk, ***Batman!***" says Robin dejectedly. "And that means ***everything*** changes! You won't have much time to pal around with me---not with a wife around . . ." (BM No. 79/1: "The Bride of Batman!").

In October 1954 Robin becomes mournful once again, this time over Batman's apparent romance with "international beauty" MAGDA LUVESCU. "***Batman*** hardly has time for me anymore!" complains Robin to Vicki Vale. "I never thought anyone could come between us . . . I see now that I was dead wrong!" (BM No. 87/3: "Batman Falls in Love!").

In March 1959 Bruce Wayne dons his tuxedo for a date with Kathy Kane, the lovely heiress who is secretly BATWOMAN.

"Hmm-mm! Bruce certainly is fond of Kathy!" muses Dick Grayson. "Gosh--what if he should fall in love and marry her? Boy, would that break up our partnership?"

Moments later, alone in the house, Dick Grayson falls asleep and has a dream which, more than any event in the chronicles, betrays the true extent of the anxiety and resentment he feels for the women in Bruce Wayne's life. In it, Kathy Kane becomes the wife of Bruce Wayne – and therefore the wife of Batman – and stubbornly pursues her crime-fighting career in defiance of Batman's admonition that "one crime-fighter in the family is enough" and that "a wife's place is in the home!"

The dream reaches a tragic climax when Kathy's recklessness results in the betrayal of Batman's secret identity to the underworld. Despite this disastrous turn of events, Batman retains his outward calm, but Robin becomes nearly hysterical with rage.

"Kathy, do you know what you've done?" he cries, his brow dripping with perspiration. "You've wrecked ***Batman's*** career! He's finished, Kathy--and it's all your fault because you wouldn't listen! You did it--you did it. . . ."

Seconds later, Grayson awakens to find Bruce Wayne standing over him, shouting to him to wake up and trying desperately to shake him back to reality. "Fine thing!" cries Wayne. "I come back from a date and instead of finding you in bed, I find you asleep in a chair!"

"Ohh!" moans Grayson, still somewhat dazed. "Then it didn't happen! It was all a ***dream!*** You didn't marry Kathy!"

"I--marry Kathy?" muses Wayne. "I expect some day I will marry! Kathy, eh? Well, she's a nice girl! Who knows--who knows?"

"Golly!" thinks Grayson. "What if Bruce ***does*** marry Kathy some day? Will my dream come ***true?*** Oh, gosh--gosh!" (BM No. 122/3: "The Marriage of Batman and Batwoman!").

There are a number of occasions in the chronicles when Batman and Robin actually go their separate ways, albeit only for a short time.

In October–November 1942 Batman parts company with Robin in order to protect him from a gangster called the THUMB, but Robin, who has not been told the reason for his abrupt dismissal, suffers through a great deal of anxiety and heartbreak until the Thumb is finally apprehended and the Dynamic Duo are once again reunited (BM No. 13/1: "The Batman Plays a Lone Hand!").

In November 1956, after Bruce Wayne is publicly believed to have been murdered, Bruce Wayne and Dick Grayson are forced to part company to prevent its becoming known that Wayne is really alive, a discovery that, because of the complex circumstances surrounding the "murder," could expose the secret of Batman's identity. During this period, Wayne moves into a furnished room, adopts the pseudonym Barney Warren, and becomes a cab driver, but a way is finally found whereby Wayne can safely admit his existence, and he and Grayson are once again reunited (Det No. 237: "Search for a New Robin!"). (*See* ROBIN.)

J. The Women of the Chronicles. "Beneath the dark denim of that stern figure of the night . . . **Batman!** . . . beats a tender, generous heart! A heart that can be moved by sorrow, that can be merciful to the unfortunate . . . and that can soften to the whispers of love!" (BM No. 15/1, Feb/Mar '43: "Your Face Is Your Fortune!").

The sudden, violent loss of his mother while he was still a boy, during the period of his childhood when his psyche was grappling with the complexity of his affectional and erotic feelings for her, left Bruce Wayne with a deep reservoir of unconscious hostility toward women. Like many orphaned children, he saw the death of his mother as a personal desertion. He loved and needed his mother, and yet she left him. The death of a loved one, particularly a parent, is always painful, but for the young Bruce Wayne the unconsciously perceived desertion was an unendurable agony.

The world of the adult Batman is one from which women have been all but excluded, one in which meaningful relationships with them are all but impossible. In the violent, male world of crime-fighting, women are unwelcome, even as allies, for Batman "feels that no girl should pursue the dangerous occupation of crime-fighting!" (BM No. 116/2, Jun '58: "Batwoman's New Identity").

Women are also unwelcome as partners in committed relationships. ". . . ***Batman*** has often told me," remarks Robin in December 1961, "that his crime-fighting career is a full-time job and that he can't risk a big romance now--not until he's ready to retire!" (BM No. 144/3: "Bat-Mite Meets Bat-Girl!").

These and other, similar rationalizations serve to safeguard Batman against the pain of adult romantic involvement and the emotional suffering that another loss of a cherished woman might bring.

Throughout the chronicles, Batman's most meaningful human relationship is the idealized father-son relationship he shares with Robin. In that relationship there is emotional safety. Relationships with women, on the other hand, bring only anxiety and uncertainty.

"Women are unpredictable, ***Robin,***" explains Batman in November 1960, ". . . men can never tell what they'll do next!" (Det No. 285: "The Mystery of the Man-Beast!").

Five women play important roles in the Batman chronicles during the first three decades of Batman's career. The following pages are devoted to an examination of Batman's relationships with these women, both in his role as Bruce Wayne and in his role as Batman.

1. The Relationship with Julie Madison. Beautiful black-haired JULIE MADISON makes her textual debut as Bruce Wayne's fiancée in September 1939 (Det No. 31) and remains his fiancée until March 1941, when she abruptly terminates their engagement because of Wayne's refusal to "find [himself] a career instead of being the public's number one playboy!" (Det No. 49: "Clayface Walks Again!"). Throughout this period, she remains completely unaware that the man she is engaged to marry is secretly Batman.

The chronicles provide little real information on the background of Julie Madison, but the available data suggest that she is a woman of some means, probably a member of Bruce Wayne's social set. The dissolution of their relationship results from Julie's increasing tendency to compare Wayne unfavorably with Batman, and from Batman's first encounter and fascination with the CATWOMAN.

Bruce Wayne and Julie Madison, 1939 © NPP 1939

Julie first encounters Bruce Wayne in his Batman identity in September 1939, the month of her textual debut (Det No. 31), when, after a series of action-filled encounters, he finally rescues her from the clutches of the diabolical villain known as the MONK.

"I don't know who you are," exclaims Julie, throwing her arms around him, "but you saved my life and I shall be forever grateful!" (Det No. 32, Oct '39).

Julie Madison and Batman, 1939 © NPP 1939

In Spring 1940 Batman meets the Catwoman for the first time in the chronicles and, having finally apprehended her, deliberately allows her to escape.

". . . Lovely girl!" he sighs aloud, obviously bedazzled. "--What eyes!--Say--mustn't forget I've got a girl named Julie!--Oh well--she still had lovely eyes!--Maybe I'll bump into her again sometime . . ." (BM No. 1/4).

The implication is unmistakable that the appeal of Julie Madison has been all but eclipsed by the erotic allure of the Catwoman.

Similarly, for Julie, the lackluster life of Bruce Wayne has begun to pale beside the electrifying derring-do of Batman. "What an exciting character, that **Batman**," she exclaims to Wayne in May 1940, after scanning some headlines trumpeting news of Batman's exploits, ". . . why can't **you** be that sort of man?!" (Det No. 39).

And in June 1940, after an encounter with Batman and Robin she comments, "They're what I call a pair of **real** heroes . . . if only Bruce was so dashing!" (Det No. 40).

Finally, in March 1941, after having successfully launched herself on the road to stardom as a motion-picture actress, Julie Madison abruptly breaks her engagement to socialite Bruce Wayne.

"Oh, Bruce if only you would do something!" she cries. "If only you'd find yourself a career instead of being the public's number one playboy!"

"Sorry, honey," replies Wayne. "I'm having too good a time to be bothered with anything remotely connected with work!" ("You'd be mighty surprised," he thinks to himself, "if you knew I had a career – as the **Batman!**").

"Then I'm sorry, Bruce," continues Julie. "Until you decide to make something of yourself, I'm afraid our engagement is off."

"I-I see," stammers Wayne.

"I'm not walking out on you, Bruce," insists Julie. "Anytime you decide to change your ways, I'll come back to you gladly!"

Soon afterward, after hearing Batman decline an offer to become a movie actor because of his commitment to crime-fighting, Julie remarks, "That's the sort of career I wish Bruce would pick for himself! But I guess that's wishing for the impossible!" (Det No. 49: "Clayface Walks Again!").

Although it is Julie Madison who has ostensibly dissolved the relationship, the responsibility for the breakup is clearly Bruce Wayne's. Had he chosen to share with her the secret of his dual identity, it is clear that Julie would not have left him. In the end, however, Bruce Wayne's career as a crime-fighter – or, more specifically, the rationalization of needing to preserve the secret identity he had already shared with Robin – provides Wayne with the excuse he needs for terminating his involvement with Julie Madison. Perhaps more significantly, the affection that Wayne undeniably feels for his fiancée, a beautiful, talented woman engaged in a socially acceptable field of endeavor (movie acting), has been rendered all but insignificant by the infinitely more erotic allure of the Catwoman, a thief (*see* section J 5, the relationship with the Catwoman).

2. The Relationship with Linda Page. Lovely LINDA PAGE, "a society girl who has become a nurse in order to make something of herself" (WF No. 2, Sum '41: "The Man Who Couldn't Remember!"), is Bruce Wayne's girlfriend from Spring 1941 (BM No. 5/4) through December 1945–January 1946 (BM No. 32/1: "Rackety-Rax Racket!"), after which her name disappears from the chronicles entirely. She represents

Linda Page and Bruce Wayne, 1941 © NPP 1941

Bruce Wayne's first romantic involvement following the abrupt termination of his engagement to JULIE MADISON in March 1941 (Det No. 49: "Clayface Walks Again!").

Like Julie Madison, Linda — the daughter of a wealthy oilman (BM No. 6/3, Aug/Sep '41: "The Secret of the Iron Jungle!") and the niece of an airplane manufacturer (Det No. 55, Sep '41: "The 'Brain Burglar!' ") — is a beautiful, intelligent woman of high social standing who has devoted herself to a socially constructive field of endeavor. Like Julie, however, Linda Page quickly develops a fascination for Batman and an inclination to compare Bruce Wayne unfavorably with his costumed alter ego. The relationship between Bruce Wayne and Linda Page is never actually terminated, but the intimation is unmistakable that Wayne can never fully win her love without revealing he is Batman. Once again, by rationalizing his need to keep his identity secret, Bruce Wayne brings about the dissolution of a meaningful relationship with a woman.

In Spring 1941, while walking along a GOTHAM CITY street, Bruce Wayne accidentally collides with a lovely redhead who turns out to be an old friend.

"Linda Page!" exclaims Wayne. "Well, well! I haven't seen you in a dog's age. The whole crowd has been asking about you!"

"Tell the crowd I woke up one day to realize there are more important things than cafe society," replies Linda, "— so-o-o . . . I've moved out and become a nurse!"

"A nurse?" cries Wayne, ever faithful to his role of frivolous socialite. "You . . . you gave up a place in society to work for a living? It's . . . it's stupid!"

"**You're** the one who's stupid---wasting your life as the great society playboy," retorts Linda sharply. "You've got talent. If you wanted to, you--"

"Ah-ah!" scolds Wayne, cradling Linda's chin in his hand. "Don't try to reform me. I'm having too good a time to kill myself with work!"

Soon afterward, Linda gets her first glimpse of Batman in action as the Dynamic Duo battle a gang of criminals.

"Was that fellow with the boy the famous **Batman** I've heard so much about?" she asks a policeman after the famed crime-fighters have left the scene.

"That was him all right," replies the policeman. "Quite a guy, isn't he?"

"I should say so!" sighs Linda, clearly infatuated. "He--**he's wonderful!**"

That very evening, Linda has a dinner date with socialite Wayne.

"Look," says Wayne finally, "you've been talking about the **Batman** all evening. What's he got that I haven't got? I've got money, good looks. . . ."

"A girl isn't always interested in in [sic] that . . ." replies Linda. "He . . . he represents excitement, color, daring . . . I can't exactly explain it."

Then, for a moment, both Wayne and his date lapse into thought.

"Bruce is nice," thinks Linda, ". . . and I do like him a lot, but if he only were a little more like the **Batman**. But I guess that's asking too much!"

"Ho-ho!" laughs Wayne to himself meanwhile. "It looks very much like the **Batman** will be seeing more of Linda Page in the future. I'll see to that!" (BM No. 5/4).

In the months that follow, the relationship continues, but Wayne really makes no effort whatever to court Linda as Batman. In August 1941 Bruce Wayne brings Linda a bouquet of flowers and takes her out shopping (Det No. 54: "Hook Morgan and His Harbor Pirates").

In August–September 1941, after Linda has expressed fears for her father's safety, Bruce Wayne and Dick Grayson travel to Texas to protect Linda's father, TOM PAGE, against the sinister machinations of his unscrupulous business partner. It is Batman and Robin who actually defeat the villains, however, while Wayne pretends to have been fast asleep elsewhere throughout the action-packed proceedings.

Later, when Wayne offers to drive Linda back to Gotham City, she petulantly refuses. "Thanks a lot," she replies, "— but there couldn't be any excitement driving with you. Weren't you man enough to help Dad? I'd like you a little better if you took a leaf out of **Batman's** book!"

"Poor Linda--she'll never know!" muses Wayne aloud as he and Dick Grayson drive toward Gotham City alone. "Sometimes I kind of wish she could know."

"Aw gee!" replies Grayson. "The **Batman's** job is to hunt criminals!" (BM No. 6/3: "The Secret of the Iron Jungle!").

In September 1941 Linda takes Bruce Wayne on a tour of an airplane factory owned by her uncle.

"I see you want me to get interested in aviation so I'll find myself some sort of occupation!" remarks Wayne. "Sorry —"

"I don't know why I bother to try to make something of you!" snaps Linda.

"Maybe it's because you like me huh?" suggests Wayne.

Soon afterward, Bruce Wayne pretends to have been knocked unconscious so that he can surreptitiously change to Batman to battle saboteurs running amok in the factory.

"The **Batman** — that guy again?" exclaims Wayne afterward, after being told the tale of Batman's latest exploit.

" 'That guy' probably saved your life and my uncle's plant from being ruined!" scolds Linda. "Which is more than you did!" (Det No. 55: "The 'Brain Burglar!' ").

On Christmas 1941, Batman, Robin, and Linda Page are guests at the home of POLICE COMMISSIONER GORDON, marking the only time in the chronicles that Linda is shown socializing with Batman rather than Bruce Wayne (BM No. 9/4, Feb/Mar '42).

In May 1942 Bruce Wayne escorts Linda Page to a lavish society party which is subsequently looted by debonair "international thief" MICHAEL BAFFLE. Not long afterward, at another society function, Baffle manages to dupe Linda and the other wealthy guests into entrusting him with their valuable jewelry by persuading them that he, Baffle, is secretly Batman.

"Batman," cries Linda, overjoyed at the opportunity

of at last meeting her hero in his civilian identity, "you're just what I always imagined you looked like--tall, handsome, debonair!"

Within moments, however, Linda has seen through Baffle's masquerade and realized that he is actually a criminal, but it is interesting to note that Linda readily projected her fantasy of Batman – "tall, handsome, debonair" – onto society burglar Michael Baffle, while apparently ignoring these identical qualities in socialite Bruce Wayne (Det No. 63: "A Gentleman in Gotham").

In June–July 1942, as he leaves the house, Bruce Wayne asks Dick Grayson to take a phone message from Linda in the event she calls later to confirm a date. "Love! Ah, love!" sighs Grayson teasingly (BM No. 11/1).

In November 1942 Bruce Wayne takes Linda Page on a date to an amusement park (Det No. 69: "The Harlequin's Hoax!").

In February–March 1943 a crisis occurs in the relationship between Bruce Wayne and Linda Page, resulting, interestingly, from Wayne's attentions to the CATWOMAN.

The Catwoman falls in love with Wayne during this period when, having entered a beauty contest under an alias, she comes in contact with Wayne, who is one of the judges. Upon learning of the Catwoman's love for him, Wayne begins to court her, telling himself that by playing on her affections he may be able to persuade her to give up her life of crime. Before long, Wayne has proposed marriage and the couple have announced their engagement.

"But, **Bruce,** you can't do this!" exclaims Dick Grayson. ". . . What's got into you? What about **Linda?** What about . . . us?"

"Patience, m'lad," replies Wayne casually, "you're too young to understand! [sic] these things!"

Linda Page, on the other hand, is heartbroken. "And I thought **Bruce** loved me!" she cries aloud. "Oh, I hate him . . . **I hate him!** I don't care who he's engaged to!"

The Catwoman, however, fearful that Wayne may actually be in love with Linda Page, disguises herself as Linda and pays a call on Bruce Wayne, determined to discover which of them Wayne really loves.

"Now, listen, **Linda,**" stammers Wayne, unaware that the woman in his presence is really an impostor, "please understand! I--I'm doing a favor for the **Batman!** He asked me to do this!" A moment later, he adds: "You must trust me, **Linda!** My engagement won't be for long!"

"So he really doesn't love me!" thinks the Catwoman bitterly. "He loves **Linda!** And he's just doing this because the **Batman** asked him!"

Feeling justifiably embittered and betrayed, the Catwoman retaliates by returning to crime, only to be swiftly apprehended by Batman and Robin.

"Glad that's over!" sighs Bruce Wayne afterward. "I hope **Linda** will forgive me now!" (BM No. 15/1: "Your Face Is Your Fortune!").

Wayne's idea of proposing marriage to the Catwoman in order to help her reform is clearly irrational. Carried to its logical conclusion, the scheme could only alienate Linda Page, ostensibly the true object of Wayne's affections, and embitter the Catwoman, whose only crime was falling in love with him. Since the scheme of declaring a false love for the Catwoman could not conceivably have been expected to achieve its stated objective, the moral reform of the Catwoman, the real motive for the plan must be sought in Bruce Wayne's unconscious. Indeed, the real motive behind the ill-conceived scheme lies in the forbidden, but overpowering, allure of the Catwoman. Like Julie Madison before her, Linda Page is, in the final analysis, overshadowed completely by the tantalizing villainess (*see* section J 5, the relationship with the Catwoman).

In March 1943 Bruce Wayne accompanies Linda Page to an exclusive millinery salon to help her select some expensive hats (Det No. 73: "The Scarecrow Returns"), and by December 1945–January 1946 he has purchased a beautiful star sapphire as a gift for her birthday (BM No. 32/1: "Rackety-Rax Racket!"). This latter episode marks the last time Linda Page is mentioned in the chronicles.

3. The Relationship with Vicki Vale. Noted news photographer VICKI VALE makes her textual debut in October–November 1948 (BM No. 49/2: "The Scoop of the Century!") and, in the course of the ensuing fifteen years, becomes romantically linked with both Bruce Wayne and Batman. Throughout this period, she makes repeated attempts to verify her suspicion that Bruce Wayne and Batman are one and the same man. From October 1958 onward, Vicki Vale is the rival of BATWOMAN for the affections of Batman (BM No. 119/1: "The Arch-Rivals of Gotham City"; and others). She represents the first romantic involvement of either Bruce Wayne or Batman following the abrupt disappearance from the chronicles of LINDA PAGE after December 1945–January 1946 (BM No. 32/1: "Rackety-Rax Racket!").

Like JULIE MADISON and Linda Page before her, Vicki Vale is a beautiful, intelligent woman who has dedicated herself to a career in a socially constructive field – in her case, photojournalism. Unlike her predecessors, however, who were primarily upper-class women who embarked on careers in order to give their lives meaning, Vicki is a woman of the middle class whose career is her livelihood. Her career is less glamorous than that of Julie Madison, the movie star, but more glamorous than that of Linda Page, the nurse.

Like Julie Madison and Linda Page, Vicki is primarily a girlfriend of Bruce Wayne who develops a fascination for Batman, and like them she attempts to persuade Wayne to do something significant with his life and tends to compare him unfavorably with his costumed alter ego. There, however, the similarities end, for Vicki Vale is the first important woman in Bruce Wayne's life to make an aggressive attempt to become the wife of Batman. She is also the first important woman of the chronicles to suspect that Bruce Wayne is Batman and to make a serious effort to unravel his secret.

Most significantly, Vicki Vale is the first woman to perceive, albeit subconsciously, the link between winning Batman as a love partner and learning his identity, for, as Batman's other relationships demonstrate, it is the rationalization of needing to preserve his secret identity that enables him to close himself off from meaningful relationships with women. In perceiving this link, however, and in making repeated, determined attempts to penetrate Batman's secret, Vicki Vale becomes the most destructive of Batman's women and his potential emasculator.

It is a truism of the chronicles, however irrational, that the revelation of Batman's secret identity will end his crime-fighting career forever (*see* section B, the secret identity). By refusing to share his secret with Julie Madison and Linda Page, Batman kept them at a distance, assured that they would eventually become dissatisfied with socialite Bruce Wayne. In contrast, however, Vicki Vale suspects Batman's secret and is determined to prove it. Indeed, by her own admission, she intends not only to prove it, but to publish it as well, thereby achieving for herself "the scoop of the century" (BM No. 49/2, Oct/Nov '48: "The Scoop of the Century!"; and others). Were she to succeed, she would end Batman's career — there would no longer be a Batman — and thus symbolically destroy him. Since the existence of Batman is the very reason why Bruce Wayne cannot "risk a big romance now" (BM No. 144/3, Dec '61: "Bat-Mite Meets Bat-Girl!"), the publication of his secret identity by Vicki Vale would shatter the sole obstacle to a relationship between them, but since Wayne's masculinity and sense of self are inextricably bound up with his heroic life as Batman, Vicki's partner would be an emasculated Bruce Wayne rather than the virile Batman.

The chronicles contain no suggestion whatever that Bruce Wayne harbors either erotic feeling or abiding affection for the aggressive Vicki Vale. Rather, the relationship with Vicki Vale is, for Batman, a flirtation with emasculation, a battle of wits and manhood in which both Wayne and Batman tantalize Vicki with their attentions and subtle displays of interest, daring her to attempt to unravel their secret and then bending every effort toward seeing that she fails. It is in the daring and the thwarting — and in the occasional, exquisite anxiety that she may at last be on the verge of learning his secret — that the excitement of this relationship exists for Batman.

What follows is a chronological listing of the textual data relating to Vicki Vale's relationships with Bruce Wayne and Batman. (*See also* VALE, VICKI.)

In October–November 1948 Vicki approaches Bruce Wayne at the Gotham City Yacht Club and asks him to pose for a photograph.

"Hmm-m!" replies Wayne. "You make quite a nice picture yourself!" ("Being **Batman** is tough work," explains the textual narrative, "and once in a while Bruce Wayne deserves to take time off for romance!")

"Puh-lease, Mr. Wayne," replies Vicki, ". . . I'm here to get a picture, not a **date!**"

Wayne proceeds to request a date for the following evening, but Vicki declines on the ground that she may have to work.

Not long afterward, Vicki gamely tags along as Batman pursues the villainous MAD HATTER.

"Batman," she remarks, "I hope it doesn't injure your pride to get help from an ordinary girl!"

"There's nothing ordinary about you!" replies Batman.

When Batman predicts that the Mad Hatter will strike next at the Gotham City Horse Show, Vicki telephones Bruce Wayne and asks him to escort her there, but her motive is less to spend an evening with Wayne than to be on the scene when Batman swings into action. Indeed, when the Mad Hatter appears at the horse show as Batman had anticipated, Vicki leaps over the ringside railing after him with her camera at the ready.

Bruce Wayne and Vicki Vale, 1963 © NPP 1963

"The female camera fiend has forgotten me already!" thinks Wayne.

In the course of this adventure, which marks Vicki Vale's textual debut, Vicki attempts to prove that Bruce Wayne is Batman, but Batman is alert to her suspicions and successfully outwits her.

"Now that I've fooled her," thinks Bruce Wayne finally, "there'll be no harm in seeing her again!"

But Vicki is still not entirely convinced that her suspicions were unfounded. "I have a feeling he tricked me!" she muses. "Mr. Bruce Wayne, you'll be seeing more of me!" (BM No. 49/2: "The Scoop of the Century!").

In April–May 1949, aboard the pleasure yacht *Carolina* on its maiden voyage, Vicki snaps a series of photographs of socialite Bruce Wayne.

"Methinks Miss Vicki Vale doth take too many pictures of our handsome playboy, Bruce Wayne!" comments a blond onlooker cattily. "Are they for *Picture* magazine — or your diary?"

"Meow!" replies Vicki (BM No. 52/1: "The Man with the Automatic Brain!").

In June–July 1949 Batman becomes temporarily transformed into a merman during an adventure undersea, although whether the adventure is fact or fantasy is left ambiguous by the text.

"Uh . . . in your surface world, were . . . were you ever in love?" asks a lovely mermaid scientist, smitten by Batman. "Did . . . did you have a sweetheart?"

"No . . . but there was a girl . . . Vicki Vale," replies Batman hesitantly, ". . . I used to like her!" (BM No. 53/3: "Batman Under the Sea!").

In October 1949, after Batman has been wounded in the scalp during an encounter with the GOBLIN, Vicki stands over him, soothingly stroking his head. "Ohh, you wonderful man!" she sighs. "Does your head hurt? Just relax . . . while I stroke it . . . like this . . . hmmm."

"Ahhhhh . . ." replies Batman contentedly.

Not long afterward, Vicki pays a call on Bruce Wayne, who has wrapped his head in a towel and pretends to have come down with a cold in order to prevent Vicki from seeing the bandages on his wounded head and thus deducing the secret of his dual identity. Vicki affectionally strokes Wayne's head exactly as she had earlier stroked Batman's. "Ahhhhh . . ." says Bruce Wayne (Det No. 152: "The Goblin of Gotham City!").

In January 1950 Bruce Wayne takes Vicki to dinner, only to discover with chagrin that her "sole topic of conversation is--his secret identity!"

"Bruce, you're hopeless!" she remarks. "Now take ***Batman*** . . . there's a **man**!"

At a subsequent dinner date, however, after Wayne has performed admirably during a brief stint as a private detective, Vicki congratulates him on the quick thinking he displayed during a scuffle with criminals. "But let's not kid ourselves," she adds, ". . . you're no **Batman!**" (Det No. 155: "Bruce Wayne, Private Detective!").

In March 1950 Bruce Wayne takes Vicki horseback riding, only to have her again express her suspicions about his secret identity. On this occasion, however, Wayne successfully diverts Vicki's attention with flattery. "That horse is a beauty!" he remarks. "I admire beauty . . . especially a beauty like you!"

"Flattery will get you no place! Tee-hee!" replies Vicki playfully (Det No. 157: "The Race of the Century").

In October 1950 a crime reporter for the Gotham City *Gazette* refers to Vicki Vale as "Bruce Wayne's girl friend" (Det No. 164: "Untold Tales of the Bat-Signal!").

In October–November 1950 Bruce Wayne takes Vicki out for an evening of dancing (BM No. 61/3: "The Wheelchair Crimefighter!").

In April–May 1951 Bruce Wayne and Dick Grayson are at a photography exhibition when they spy Vicki Vale walking toward them.

"It's no use, Bruce--you're trapped!" remarks Dick Grayson quietly. "Your ardent admirer, magazine photographer Vicki Vale, has that love-light in her eyes again!"

Just as Vicki is asking Wayne to escort her to a club, however, Wayne realizes he must leave immediately to change to Batman, and he hastily turns her down with the excuse that he is tired. "You're a real deadhead, Bruce!" remarks Vicki. "I wish I knew why you were so attractive!"

Soon afterward, when Batman decides he needs to obtain some information from Vicki, he decides to "call on her as her old boy friend, Bruce Wayne," unaware that she is being held prisoner in her home by deranged criminal GREGORY BOTA.

"It's Bruce Wayne--an old boy friend of mine . . ." Vicki tells Bota when she spies Wayne approaching her house.

"It ***would*** be Bruce!" she thinks ruefully to herself. "I love him, but a lot of help ***he'll*** be!"

Indeed, Vicki's thoughts indicate that she regards Wayne as "just a handsome mug who hasn't a serious thought in his head" (BM No. 64/1: "The Candid Camera Killer!").

The quotations cited above would seem to indicate that Vicki Vale's romantic relationship with Bruce Wayne is already at an end, but subsequent texts do not bear this out. Eighteen months later, for example, in October–November 1952, Batman No. 73/2 describes Vicki Vale as a "cute society photographer with a pert nose for news, and a yen for Bruce Wayne" ("Vicki Vale's Secret!").

Batman, Vicki Vale, and Robin, 1962 © NPP 1962

In October–November 1953 the Shah of Nairomi falls in love with Vicki Vale and unwittingly sets in motion a bizarre chain of events that threatens to force Batman to take Vicki as his bride (BM No. 79/1: "Bride of Batman!"). This text is the first in which Vicki Vale is portrayed as being in love with Batman and eager to become his wife, as opposed to nurturing romantic feelings for socialite Bruce Wayne. (*See* VALE, VICKI.)

On the question of exactly where Vicki Vale's affections lie, the chronicles remain somewhat inconsistent. In October 1954, for example, when Gotham City television station GCTV presents Batman's life story on its "Your Life Story" program, Vicki Vale appears on the show and gives Batman an affectionate peck on the cheek. "Bruce Wayne isn't here to see this, ***Batman,***" remarks Vicki, "--but I'm sure he wouldn't mind his girl kissing ***you!***" (BM No. 87/1: "Batman's Greatest Thrills!").

During this same period, however, Vicki expresses a powerful romantic yearning for Batman. "I know why I'm so in love with him!" she sighs at one point. "He's the one man Magda [MAGDA LUVESCU] will never get her hooks into, that's for sure! Golly--if I could only make him go for me!"

And soon afterward, she warns Batman, ". . . listen, you handsome heel . . . if you ever break down and start thinking about romance--it'd better be with me, and not Magda! Or so help me!"

When it appears that Batman has begun an ardent courtship of the beautiful Magda Luvescu, Vicki becomes jealous and resentful, only to learn sometime later that the apparent romance was only part of a ruse by Batman to lure a notorious Devil's Island escapee out of hiding.

Chastened somewhat at having been jealous over nothing, Vicki remains nonetheless determined to win Batman for herself. Her thoughts make it plain that "she won't stop trying till she's ***Mrs. Batman!*** So--watch out, ***Batman*** . . . all's fair in love and war!" (BM No. 87/3, Oct '54: "Batman Falls in Love!").

In February 1955, when it becomes temporarily necessary for BRANE TAYLOR to impersonate Batman, Vicki's suspicions are aroused immediately by Taylor's gallant behavior and flowery language. "That doesn't sound like **Batman,**" she thinks, "--he never got so romantic before!" (Det No. 216: "The Batman of Tomorrow!").

In November–December 1956 Vicki Vale and LOIS LANE become jealous and upset – and make a determined effort to intervene – when it appears that both Batman and SUPERMAN have fallen in love with the beautiful PRINCESS VARINA, ruler of the "farway kingdom of Balkania" (WF No. 85: "The Super-Rivals!").

In October 1958 the rivalry between Vicki Vale and Batwoman for the affections of Batman begins as both women vie for the honor of being named GOTHAM CITY's Woman of the Year, a title that brings with it a special award plus a date with Batman (BM No. 119/1: "The Arch-Rivals of Gotham City"). (*See* VALE, VICKI.)

Vicki Vale then remains absent from the chronicles until November 1962, when she runs into Batman and Robin at a gala Mardi Gras festival.

"Vicki Vale!" exclaims Batman. "My favorite gal photographer! So you finally got back from that European assignment **View** magazine sent you on!"

"Oh, ***Batman,***" cries Vicki, giving him a warm hug and kiss, "--I missed you so much! ***MMMMmmm!***"

"Phew!" thinks Robin. "It's a good thing **Batwoman** isn't around to see that!"

Batman is subsequently elected king of the Mardi Gras and Batwoman his queen, but Batman suggests that Vicki be allowed to share the queenly honors because of her role in the capture of J. J. ASHLEY.

"Imagine ***Batman*** choosing ***her*** to share this honor with ***me!***" fumes Batwoman jealously. "Hmmmph!"

"Batwoman's fuming!" thinks Robin to himself. "Looks like there'll be a big ***Batwoman-Vicki Vale feud*** in the days ahead!" (Det No. 309: "The Mystery of the Mardi Gras Murders!").

In August 1963 Vicki Vale – described in the textual narrative as "a woman in love" – sets out to make Batman fall in love with her. "I'll need more than just a pretty face," she muses, "if I'm to make ***Batman*** prefer me to ***Batwoman. . . .***"

Vicki feels handicapped in her rivalry with Batwoman because Batwoman is in the unique position of being able to help Batman apprehend criminals. "A man always cares for a woman who is a help to him!" thinks Vicki. "That's why ***Batwoman*** has a better chance for ***Batman's*** love than I have. . . ."

When Vicki learns that the villain MIRROR-MAN suspects that Bruce Wayne is Batman, she decides to show Batman that "I can even be a greater help to [him] than ***Batwoman*** . . ." by helping him preserve the secret of his dual identity.

Vicki's meddling, however, leaves Batman with the doubly difficult problem of apprehending Mirror-Man and his henchmen while at the same time safeguarding his identity against both the villain and Vicki (BM No. 157/2: "The Hunt for Batman's Secret Identity!").

The "Batwoman-Vicki Vale feud" predicted by Robin (Det No. 309, Nov '62: "The Mystery of the Mardi Gras Murders!") never really takes hold as a major theme of the chronicles, and Vicki Vale soon disappears from the texts entirely, leaving the field completely to Batwoman.

4. The Relationship with (*the*) *Batwoman.* The lovely raven-haired crime-fighter known as (the) BATWOMAN makes her textual debut in July 1956 (Det No. 233: "The Batwoman") and, in the course of the ensuing decade, becomes romantically linked with both Bruce Wayne and Batman. From October 1958 onward, she is the rival of VICKI VALE for the affections of Batman (BM No. 119/1: "The Arch-Rivals of Gotham City"; and others).

Batwoman is in reality Kathy Kane, a wealthy heiress and onetime circus daredevil noted for her outstanding abilities both as a trapeze artist and motorcycle stunt rider. She is enamored sometimes of Bruce Wayne and sometimes of Batman. For the most part, however, she is involved with Bruce Wayne as heiress Kathy Kane, and involved with Batman in her role as Batwoman.

Like her predecessors, she is beautiful, talented, and intelligent. Her former career as a circus performer imbues her with the glamour of movie actress JULIE MADISON, while her work as a crime-fighter ensures her a socially constructive life akin to those of nurse LINDA PAGE and news photographer Vicki Vale. However, whereas Julie Madison and Linda Page were women of means who embarked on careers to give their lives meaning, Batwoman is a former circus performer transformed by inherited wealth into a woman of leisure. And, whereas Vicki Vale is an aggressive career woman who must work for a living, Batwoman can easily afford not to work but has chosen instead a life of danger and excitement. Armed with the glittering, gaudy glamour of her former life in the circus, the social refinement she has acquired in her life as an heiress, and the commitment to adventure implicit in her life as a crime-fighter, she represents Batman's most serious total romantic involvement, and the most serious threat to his unconscious determination to exclude meaningful involvements with women from his life.

If Batwoman yet lacks the powerful erotic allure of the CATWOMAN, she still possesses, more than any other woman of the chronicles, the combination of qualities most likely to make her a realistic mate for Bruce Wayne and Batman.

Batman and Batwoman, 1963 © NPP 1963

Like the other women in Bruce Wayne's life, Batwoman, in her role as Kathy Kane, develops a tendency to compare Wayne unfavorably with the more glamorous Batman. Yet, more than her predecessors, she holds this tendency in check and tends to like and accept Bruce Wayne for the qualities he exhibits.

Similarly, Batwoman attempts on occasion to unravel Batman's secret identity, but solving the riddle never becomes an obsession with her as it does with Vicki Vale, and the question of Batman's identity soon becomes all but irrelevant to the relationship. "***Batman*** knows that I'm secretly ***Batwoman,***" thinks Kathy Kane to herself in June 1961, ". . . but I only ***suspect*** that he's Bruce Wayne!" (Det No. 292: "The Colossus of Gotham City!"). There the situation remains, and, by and large, Batwoman seems content to accept it.

Just as Batman attempts to exclude women from his emotional life by rationalizing that "he can't risk a big romance . . . until he's ready to retire" (BM No. 144/3, Dec '61: "Bat-Mite Meets Bat-Girl!"), so he attempts to exclude them from the world of crime-fighting on the ground that it is a "dangerous occupation" that should be off-limits to women (BM No. 116/2, Jun '58: "Batwoman's New Identity"; and others).

Batwoman is the first of Batman's romantic involvements to invade the male preserve of crime-fighting as an ally and an equal. Consequently, Batman's efforts to reject her take the form of attempting to persuade her to retire from crime-fighting, ostensibly for her own protection, but in reality as a means of excluding her from the world of his career, to help him evade the emotional dangers of romantic involvement.

When Batwoman first appears on the scene as a costumed crime-fighter, Batman attempts to force her into retirement much as Vicki Vale had sought to force him into his, by penetrating the secret of her dual identity, his argument being that if he could learn her identity, the underworld could also (Det No. 233, Jul '56: "The Batwoman").

This is shaky reasoning at best when one considers that Batman is the world's greatest detective and therefore presumably capable of detecting feats of which the underworld is not. In this connection, it is worth noting that on one of the occasions when Batwoman attempts, albeit unsuccessfully, to learn the secret of Batman's identity, it is not so that she can expose the secret publicly and thus end Batman's career, but so that she can even the score – learn Batman's identity as he has already learned hers – and thereby prevent him from continuing to use his knowledge of her secret as an excuse for insisting that she retire from crime-fighting (WF No. 90, Sep/Oct '57: "The Super-Batwoman!").

When Batwoman's motive for attempting to uncover Batman's secret identity (to enable her to continue to fight alongside him as an equal) is contrasted with Vicki Vale's (to achieve the scoop of the century), it becomes clear that the rivalry that develops between the two women is less a rivalry for Batman's affections than it is a struggle between a woman who loves Batman (Batwoman) and another who seeks to destroy him (Vicki Vale).

Interestingly, Batman vacillates on the issue of Kathy Kane's continuing her crime-fighting career as Batwoman, on occasion insisting that she give it up, at other times relenting and welcoming her as an ally (WF No. 90, Sep/Oct '57: "The Super-Batwoman!"; and others). A telling example of this ambivalence occurs in June 1958, when Batman and Robin rescue her from the clutches of the FUNNY FACE GANG just as its leader, Al Talley, is on the verge of removing her disguise and ascertaining her identity.

"Don't you know crime-fighting is too dangerous for a girl?" scolds Batman after the criminals have been subdued and apprehended. "Sometimes, I wish your secret identity ***would*** be exposed so you'd have to quit being ***Batwoman!***"

"Someone almost did! Talley, remember?" replies Batwoman coyly. "But you interrupted him!"

"Ohh--n-o-o!" groans Batman (BM No. 116/2: "Batwoman's New Identity").

This acceptance of Batwoman as a crime-fighting ally, however grudging it may seem, is one of the principal indications of the extent to which Batwoman has successfully intruded herself into Batman's emotions and begun to break down the wall of rationalizations and defenses which he has characteristically used to defend himself against meaningful involvements with women.

What follows is a chronological listing of the textual data relating to the relationships between Kathy Kane and Bruce Wayne and between Batwoman and Batman. (*See also* BATWOMAN, THE.)

In July 1956 Batwoman makes her first appearance in GOTHAM CITY, dazzling onlookers with her daring crime-fighting exploits and even rescuing Batman himself on two separate occasions. When Bruce Wayne attends a lavish party at the home of heiress Kathy Kane one night soon afterward, he is completely unaware that his hostess is secretly the "mysterious and glamorous" Batwoman.

In the course of the evening, after hearing a radio news announcement concerning Batwoman's recent exploits, Kathy turns to Bruce Wayne and wonders aloud "how . . . any woman [could] ever equal the great ***Batman!***"

Kathy Kane and Bruce Wayne, 1960 © NPP 1960

"You have to admire this ***Batwoman's*** courage, though!" replies Wayne.

Then, for a moment, both Bruce Wayne and Kathy Kane are left alone with their thoughts.

"So she admires ***Batman!***" muses Wayne. "If only I could tell her I'm ***Batman***--but I can't!"

"Bruce is so good-looking," thinks Kathy, "--and he admires ***Batwoman!*** If--sigh--he only knew ***I'm Batwoman!***"

Some time later, when Batman, Robin, and Batwoman arrive at a nightclub in response to a call about a gunman loose on the premises, Batman tries to dissuade Batwoman from taking part in the capture. "This is no place for a girl," he insists, "--please let me handle it!"

"No, I'll stay, ***Batman,***" replies Batwoman. "I might have to save ***you*** again!"

"Batwoman," urges Batman impatiently, "to you this is just a thrill--you don't realize that fighting crime is a dangerous business!"

Batwoman insists on participating, however, and, in the battle that follows, it is really she who captures the criminal.

Soon afterward, Batman succeeds in uncovering Batwoman's secret identity and in persuading her to retire from her career as a crime-fighter. As a gift, Batwoman presents Batman with the gigantic Batwoman portrait which had stood at the entrance to her subterranean headquarters. Batman later claims that he accepted the portrait only as an "interesting trophy," but there is a strong hint that he really wants to own it for sentimental reasons (Det No. 233: "The Batwoman").

In February 1957, as Kathy Kane sets out for a masquerade party, she thinks, "I hope Bruce Wayne will be at the party! He's so good-looking!"

Not long afterward, Kathy visits Wayne at his home and, seeing that he has an injured ankle, asks him how he happened to sprain it. To conceal the fact that he injured it as Batman during a battle with criminals, Wayne replies that he sprained it while dancing.

"Dancing . . . *hmph!*" sniffs Kathy. "I'll bet if ***Batman*** ever got an injury, it would be because he was doing something ***heroic!***" Then she sighs and adds, "I wish you could be more like him, Bruce!" (BM No. 105/1: "The Challenge of Batwoman!").

In September–October 1957 Batwoman makes a determined effort to uncover the secret identities of Batman, Robin, and SUPERMAN in retaliation for their insistence that she abandon her career as a crime-fighter. The effort ultimately ends in failure, but Batman finally concedes that she "showed such cleverness and courage" that she ought to be allowed to continue her career as Batwoman (WF No. 90: "The Super-Batwoman!"). (*See* BATWOMAN, THE.)

In November 1957, while Bruce Wayne is in prison, Batwoman joins forces with Robin to apprehend the Collector. ". . . from what **Robin** tells me," remarks Bruce Wayne afterward, "he couldn't have cracked this case without your fine help! **Batman himself** couldn't have done better!" (Det No. 249: "The Crime of Bruce Wayne!"). (*See* BATWOMAN, THE.)

In June 1958, Batman No. 116/2 observes that "There's only one **Batwoman**--and it's **Batman's** opinion that's one too many--for he feels that no girl should pursue the dangerous occupation of crime-fighting!"

At one point, when Batwoman proposes a strategy for apprehending the FUNNY FACE GANG, Batman replies, "That might be dangerous! Besides, not so long ago, you promised to give up crime-fighting!"

"Why, ***Batman,***" replies Batwoman coyly, "--you know a lady has the right to change her mind!"

Later, after the entire gang, including their leader, Al Talley, has been brought to justice, Batwoman says, "Well, **Batman**--we certainly made a nice team, didn't we? Let's do it again some time!"

"Don't you know crime-fighting is too dangerous for a girl?" scolds Batman. "Sometimes, I wish your secret identity ***would*** be exposed so you'd have to quit being ***Batwoman!***"

"Someone almost did!" replies Batwoman. "Talley, remember? But you interrupted him!"

"Ohhh--no-o-o!" groans Batman (BM No. 116/2: "Batwoman's New Identity").

In October 1958 the rivalry between Batwoman and Vicki Vale for the affections of Batman begins as both women vie for the honor of becoming Gotham City's Woman of the Year, a title that brings with it a special award plus a date with Batman (BM No. 119/1: "The Arch-Rivals of Gotham City"). (*See* VALE, VICKI.)

In March 1959 Bruce Wayne dons his tuxedo and informs Dick Grayson, "I've got a date with beautiful Kathy Kane!"

"Kathy?" exclaims Grayson. "But you always said she annoys you by interfering in our cases as ***Batwoman!***"

"True!" replies Wayne. "But Kathy's a lovely girl--and a lovely girl can be forgiven almost anything! I hope she likes this corsage. . . ."

When Wayne leaves the house, Grayson falls asleep in an armchair and dreams that Kathy Kane has become the wife of Bruce Wayne, and therefore also the wife of Batman.

"I--marry Kathy?" remarks Wayne later that evening, after Grayson has related the dream to him. "I expect some day I will marry! Kathy, eh? Well, she's a nice girl! Who knows--who knows?" (BM No. 122/3: "The Marriage of Batman and Batwoman!").

In September 1959 Bruce Wayne and Dick Grayson attend a party together. "Wonder what happened to Kathy Kane?" asks Wayne. "She's the last guest to arrive!"

"Impatient, eh?" laughs Grayson. "I think you really like Kathy--even if she does give you some trouble as ***Batwoman!***"

"Sure--I like her," replies Wayne, ". . . but I wish she'd like ***Bruce Wayne*** as much as she does ***Batman!***"

Not long afterward, Wayne and Grayson run into Kathy on the street and invite her to walk with them, but she excuses herself to keep a date with Ted Carson, the man who is secretly the Firefly (*see* FIREFLY, THE [TED CARSON]), and moments later drives off with him.

"Well . . . looks like Carson has suddenly made a big hit with Kathy!" remarks Grayson. "You jealous, Bruce?"

"Perhaps--a little!" replies Wayne. "After all, Kathy ***is*** attractive!" And after a pause he adds, "Bah! . . . As if ***the Firefly*** isn't giving me enough trouble, now I've got a ***rival*** to worry about!"

Not long afterward, Bruce Wayne visits Kathy at her home, but she pleads a sudden headache and asks Wayne to leave.

"A sudden 'headache'?" thinks Wayne to himself. "Is she really so bored with me--or is she just using Carson to make me jealous?"

"Poor, dear Bruce," muses Kathy to herself after Wayne has departed, ". . . I do believe he's jealous!"

Indeed, during this period, Kathy Kane becomes embroiled in a whirlwind romance with Ted Carson after a series of coincidences has misled her into believing that Carson is secretly Batman. Ultimately, however, Kathy learns to her horror that the man she has come to love is actually an arch-villain.

"And I fell in love with him because I thought he was ***Batman!***" thinks Batwoman ruefully. "What a fool I've been! What a mistake I made . . ." (BM No. 126/3: "The Menace of the Firefly!").

In December 1960 Bruce Wayne takes Kathy Kane to dinner at a lavish supper club.

"I must admit you're a handsome man, Bruce," she remarks, "--but good looks aren't enough for me. . . ."

"I know!" interjects Wayne. "As you've told me a hundred times, you wish I were more like ***Batman!***"

In the course of the evening, Kathy becomes ill and Wayne is forced to take her home early. "I hope Kathy will be all right!" he tells Robin afterward. "She looked so pale--so fragile. . . ."

"*Hmm* . . . I've never heard you talk about any ***other*** woman with such concern!" remarks Robin. "I guess Kathy means more to you than you care to admit . . ." (Det No. 286: "The Doomed Batwoman!").

In August 1961, after Bat-Girl (*see* BAT-GIRL [BETTY KANE]) has given a blushing Robin an affectionate kiss, Batwoman leans over and gives Batman a kiss of her own. "*Hmm!* Perhaps ***Bat-Girl's*** direct approach is the best way for a gal to get her guy!" she remarks. "Come here, ***Batman*** . . ." (BM No. 141/3: "Batwoman's Junior Partner!").

In May 1962, during a period when it becomes necessary to keep Kathy Kane away from the Wayne mansion, Bruce Wayne uses a cutout silhouette of himself kissing a woman to make Kathy believe she is seeing the shadow of Wayne romancing another woman.

"That playboy! That kissing bug!" she fumes jealously. "I'll never set foot in this house again!"

"She's so angry, she'll stay away from here for quite a while!" remarks Wayne. "Later, I'll explain that the 'girl' she saw was a cousin!" (BM No. 147/3: "Batman Becomes Bat-Baby!").

In September 1962 ALPHA, THE EXPERIMENTAL MAN, "a living creature made entirely of synthetic material," falls in love with Batwoman.

"**Batwoman!**" he says. "You are--not un-nice to look at!"

"Did you hear that compliment, ***Batman?***" asks Batwoman. "I wish *you* could be as sweet to me!"

"Her face--her eyes," thinks Alpha, "--they grow soft--when she looks at **Batman!**" (Det No. 307: "Alpha, the Experimental Man!").

In November 1962 Batman is elected king of a gala Mardi Gras festival, and Batwoman is chosen to serve as his queen. When Batman suggests that Vicki Vale be allowed to share the queenly honors because of her role in the recent capture of J. J. ASHLEY, Batwoman fumes with jealousy.

"Imagine ***Batman*** choosing ***her*** to share this honor with ***me!***" she thinks. "Hmmmph!"

"***Batwoman's*** fuming!" thinks Robin. "Looks like there'll be a big ***Batwoman-Vicki Vale feud*** in the days ahead!" (Det No. 309: "The Mystery of the Mardi Gras Murders!").

In February 1963 Batman and Batwoman find themselves faced with seemingly certain death as the result of the gradual extinction of their "life-forces" in an alien dimension.

"Hold me close!" pleads Batwoman. "If I must die, I want it to be in your arms! *Oh,* ***Batman,*** you know I love you--dying wouldn't be so bad, if I knew you loved me, too. . . ."

"I--I ***do*** love you!" replies Batman. "I never wanted to admit it before. . . ."

"*Oh,* ***Batman*** . . ." sighs Batwoman, giving Batman a warm, loving kiss.

Ultimately, however, largely through Batman's resourcefulness, Batman and Batwoman manage to recover their waning life-forces and to draw back from the brink of death.

"I ***did*** hear you admit that you loved me!" remarks Batwoman triumphantly, once all danger is safely past.

"Whew!" thinks Batman, now placed in a position of having either to confirm or deny his earlier avowal of love. "I've always managed to escape death-traps--all kinds of danger! But how do I get out of ***this?***"

Batman and Batwoman, 1963 © NPP 1963

"Well--er--***Batwoman,***" he finally stammers, "--I thought we were going to die--and I wanted to make your last moments happy ones!"

"*Hmm* . . . I wonder . . ." replies Batwoman (BM No. 153: chs. 1–3 – "Prisoners of Three Worlds!"; "Death from Beyond"; "Dimension of Doom").

In August 1963 Vicki Vale becomes determined "to make ***Batman*** prefer me to ***Batwoman,***" believing that Batwoman has the upper hand in their rivalry because her work as a crime-fighter enables her to help Batman apprehend criminals.

"A man always cares for a woman who is a help to him!" muses Vicki. "That's why ***Batwoman*** has a better chance for ***Batman's*** love than I have. . . ."

When Vicki learns that the villain MIRROR-MAN suspects that Bruce Wayne is Batman, she decides to show Batman that "I can even be a greater help to [him] than ***Batwoman*** . . ." by helping him preserve the secret of his dual identity.

Vicki's meddling, however, inevitably misfires, leaving Batman with the dual problem of apprehending Mirror-Man and his henchmen while at the same time safeguarding his secret identity against both the villain and Vicki (BM No. 157/2: "The Hunt for Batman's Secret Identity!").

The "Batwoman-Vicki Vale feud" once predicted by Robin (Det No. 309, Nov '62: "The Mystery of the Mardi Gras Murders!") never really takes hold as a major theme of the chronicles, and before long Vicki Vale has disappeared from the texts entirely, leaving the field completely to Batwoman.

In August 1963, while having lunch with Bruce Wayne, Kathy Kane thinks, "Bruce is a dear, but just not my type!"

Soon afterward, Batman and Batwoman stage a lovers' quarrel in public as part of a ploy to help them apprehend the CAT-MAN. A local newspaper runs the story of the quarrel beneath the headline "Batman and Batwoman Split Up," a strong indication that, by this date, Batwoman has become firmly established in the public mind as Batman's girlfriend (Det No. 318: "The Cat-Man Strikes Back!").

In November 1963, after a rousing battle with the villain Clayface (*see* CLAYFACE [MATT HAGEN]), Batwoman's niece, Bat-Girl (*see* BAT-GIRL [BETTY KANE]), plays up to Robin by assuming the role of a helpless female.

"Oh, ***Robin,***" she cries, "--I'm afraid you'll just have to hold me! I'm still so shaky after fighting **Clayface**--and you're so **strong!**"

"Smart girl!" remarks Batwoman in an aside to Batman. "She knows how to play up to a man! Maybe I should take a tip from her, eh, Batman?" And then, in a mock-serious, singsong voice she adds, "Oh, **Batman**--I'm afraid you'll just have to hold me! I'm still shaky after fighting **Clayface**--and you're so **STRONNN-G!**"

Later, after Clayface has been apprehended, Robin thanks Bat-Girl for soothing his nerves during an anxious moment earlier when he was worried about Batman.

". . . why don't you follow **Robin's** example," remarks Batwoman to Batman with a smile, "and let me soothe you?"

"Gulp," replies Batman (BM No. 159/1: "The Great Clayface-Joker Feud!").

Although Batman's relationship with Batwoman would seem to have been the most meaningful and well-rounded of his various relationships, and the only one in which he might conceivably have hoped to find any real measure of happiness, Batwoman disappears from the chronicles in the mid-1960s, thus bringing the relationship to an end.

Of all the women with whom Batman has become involved, Batwoman appears to have exercised the strongest hold over his affections. She is not, however, the women who has achieved the strongest hold over his emotions. That role in the chronicles is reserved to the Catwoman.

5. The Relationship with the Catwoman. The sultry

sloe-eyed villainess known as the CATWOMAN – the country's "cleverest, most dangerous--and most beautiful lady of crime" (BM No. 62/1, Dec/Jan '50–'51: "The Secret Life of the Catwoman") – makes her textual debut in Spring 1940 (BM No. 1/4) and launches a relationship with Batman of such unique intensity that it has endured for more than three decades. Of the five women who have enjoyed long-standing relationships with Bruce Wayne and Batman, the Catwoman is the only villainess. And of all five relationships, it is the one with the Catwoman that has proven the most enduring.

It is no accident that the Catwoman remains to this day the most enduring woman of the chronicles while Batman's other romantic involvements have disappeared from the texts, because it is the Catwoman who arouses in Batman his strongest erotic feelings.

Batman is unconsciously torn between two types of women, "good" women and "bad" women, both types representing conflicting aspects of his own mother as he unconsciously perceives her. Good women, like JULIE MADISON and LINDA PAGE, represent the kind, loving, dependable mother who fulfilled young Bruce Wayne's every childhood need. Bad women, like the Catwoman, represent the wicked, irresponsible, unloving mother who, by dying, "deserted" him in childhood when he needed her most. It is to safeguard his psyche against the anguish of another emotional dependency and another desertion that Batman has withdrawn into a violent, male-centered world from which women are excluded, surrounding himself with a wall of rationalizations, or plausible excuses, for not becoming involved with them.

When Batman does fall in love, despite his best efforts not to, it is invariably with the bad mother, represented by the Catwoman or some other villainess. Batman as much as acknowledges the fact in May–June 1974, although he describes his predilection as a personal "curse" rather than as a deeply rooted psychological need.

"As for me," he remarks after having once again defeated the Catwoman, ". . . whenever I meet a woman I can **care** for, she's an **enemy!** . . . that's **my** curse!" (BM No. 256/1: "Catwoman's Circus Caper!").

Seen in the light of this unconscious conflict, Batman's long-standing relationship with the Catwoman becomes readily understandable. The Catwoman excites and exhilarates Batman, yet he knows he cannot have her. Being a villainess makes her the most desirable of women, but it also makes her, like the mother he lost in childhood, completely unattainable.

Whenever the Catwoman commits a crime, Batman must pursue her. Indeed, the excitement and exhilaration of the relationship lie largely in the chase. Ultimately, inevitably, Batman overtakes and apprehends her, for she wants to be caught, and, just as inevitably, she offers herself to Batman as his reward, suggesting that they join forces as the "king and queen of crime" (BM No. 1/4, Spr '40; *see also* BM No. 39/3, Feb/Mar '47: "A Christmas Tale!"). The symbolism of king and queen admits of only one interpretation: now that Batman has apprehended the sultry villainess, she offers him intercourse.

Batman is sorely tempted. On the conscious level, he knows that he desires the Catwoman, but he also knows that he cannot surrender to the siren song of his lust without at the same time denying everything that it means to be Batman.

On a deeper, unconscious level, Batman desires the Catwoman as a young boy desires his mother. The prize is tempting, yet forbidden. Indeed, the moral force within Batman that struggles against succumbing to the lure of the Catwoman parallels the universal taboo against having sex with one's mother.

For Batman, the tension is agonizing, but the end result of his agony is always the same: either he deliberately lets the Catwoman go free, so that the delicious pursuit may begin anew, or he takes her to jail, confident that, as she always has, she will find the means to make good her escape.

In capturing the Catwoman and letting her go free – or putting her in prison, from which she is certain to escape – Batman is re-creating and reenacting, with every fresh encounter, the "desertion" of his mother and the forbidden effort that must always fail to claim her for his own.

However unconsciously, the Catwoman seems to perceive this conflict. Even Batman realizes that she is not really a criminal at heart (BM No. 69/3, Feb/Mar '52: "The King of the Cats!"), and periodically she makes what appear to be sincere efforts to reform. It is only as a villainess, however, that the Catwoman can capture Batman's attention, hold his interest, and thus reassure herself that he really cares for her. A reformed Catwoman, after all, is of no interest to Batman; it is only as a criminal that she can get him to pursue her. Yet, tragically, having embarked once again upon the criminal life, she becomes for Batman a love object beyond the pale, however much she fascinates him.

What follows is a chronological listing of the textual data relating to the Catwoman's relationships with Bruce Wayne and Batman. (*See also* CATWOMAN, THE.)

In Spring 1940 Batman and Robin meet the Catwoman for the first time in the chronicles when they foil an attempt by the villainess and her accomplice Denny to steal a priceless emerald necklace from wealthy Martha Travers aboard the pleasure yacht *Dolphin*.

". . . why don't you come in, as a partner with me!" suggests the captured Catwoman seductively, placing her arms around Batman's neck. "**You** and **I** together! **You** and **I**--king and queen of crime!--We'd make a great team!"

"Sorry," replies Batman, "your proposition tempts me but we work on different sides of the law!"

Moments later, after the Catwoman's accomplice has been locked in a cabin aboard the yacht so that he can be turned over later to the police on shore, Batman and Robin climb into their motor launch with the captive Catwoman and begin speeding toward shore. The Catwoman asks Batman why he has decided to take her to the police himself, instead of leaving her on board the yacht with Denny, but a terse "I've got my reasons!" is Batman's only reply.

Suddenly, without warning, the Catwoman leaps overboard in a desperate dash for freedom, and when Robin starts to leap after her, Batman bumps him aside with seemingly calculated clumsiness.

"Too late," cries Robin, staring dejectedly out over the water, "--she's gone!"

And then the truth behind Batman's decision to take the Catwoman aboard the launch begins to dawn on Robin. "--and--**say**," he exclaims, "--I'll bet you bumped into me on purpose!--That's why you took her along with us--so she might try a break!"

"Why, Robin, my boy," smiles Batman wryly, "whatever gave you such an idea! . . . Hmm--nice night, isn't it? . . . Lovely girl!--What eyes!--Say--mustn't forget I've got a girl named Julie [*see* MADISON, JULIE]!--Oh well--she still had lovely eyes!--Maybe I'll bump into her again sometime . . ." (BM No. 1/4).

In Fall 1940 Batman and Robin apprehend the Catwoman and a group of other criminals, in the process rescuing the lovely villainess from a double-crossing accomplice. When the Dynamic Duo tie up their captives, however, Batman pointedly fails to bind the Catwoman.

"Well, **Cat**," he remarks, ". . . I'm sorry, but I guess you've got to go along to the police too!"

"It doesn't matter!" replies the Catwoman sweetly. "You saved my life! I'd like to thank you for that!"

The Catwoman embraces Batman warmly and kisses him, then suddenly gives him a hard backward shove, darts out the doorway to a waiting automobile, and roars away into the night.

Robin starts to pursue her, but Batman holds him back. "Take it easy!" he says quietly. "She's too far away for you to catch up."

"I guess you're right about that," replies Robin, ". . . but it's too bad a crook like that has to get away, even if she **is** a girl!"

"Yes," sighs Batman, "and it's too bad she has to be a crook! What a night! . . . A night for romance, eh, **Robin?**"

"Romance?" exclaims Robin. "**BAH. . . .**"

Meanwhile, behind the wheel of her getaway car, the Catwoman is thinking of romance also. "I sort of wish the **Batman** were driving this car – and I were sitting beside him . . . and we were just another boy and girl out for a ride on a moonlight [sic] night. That would be sort of . . . of . . . nice!!" (BM No. 3/4: "The Batman vs the Cat-Woman!").

In April–May 1942 Batman and Robin match wits with the Catwoman again, and once again the lovely villainess finds herself thinking fondly of Batman. "How brave and strong he is!" she muses. "If only he would team up with me---nobody would be able to stop us---nobody!"

Later, after Batman and Robin have captured the Catwoman and her cohorts – and Batman has rescued her from death at the hands of a disgruntled henchman – the Catwoman throws her arms around Batman and gives him a warm kiss. Then, without warning, "before the startled **Batman** can recover his wits," the wily villainess races out the door and escapes.

The Catwoman and Batman, 1940 © NPP 1940

Moments later, a policeman arriving on the scene asks Batman what become of the Catwoman.

"She---er---she got away," stammers Batman, "---slipped through my fingers. . . ."

Later, however, when he and Bruce Wayne are alone, Dick Grayson advances a theory of his own. "You know, Bruce," remarks Grayson, "I've a feeling you **let** the **Cat-Woman** escape!"

"Why, Dick," replies Wayne with a wry grin, "how can you say a thing like that! She's clever and beautiful, yes---and it's a shame that we both work on opposite sides of the law but I hope--I mean I know we'll meet again--soon! And then it will be my round!" (BM No. 10/3: "The Princess of Plunder!").

In Summer 1942, while listening to an interview with Batman on the "Racket-Smashers" radio and television program, the Catwoman thinks aloud, "What a man! Some times I want to kiss him . . . and some times I want to scratch his eyes out!" (WF No. 6: "The Secret of Bruce Wayne!").

In February–March 1943, having entered and won a beauty contest under the alias Elva Barr, the Catwoman finds herself falling in love with Bruce Wayne, one of the judges.

"My heart's fluttering . . . **I'm falling in love!**" she thinks to herself. "And he seems interested in me, too!"

Unaware that Bruce Wayne is secretly Batman, the Catwoman does not realize that what she perceives as Wayne's romantic interest in her is actually nothing but Wayne's silent recognition of the fact that Elva Barr is the fugitive Catwoman.

Not long afterward, after Batman and Robin have captured the villainess and her henchmen in the midst of a robbery, the Catwoman begs Batman not to turn her over to the authorities.

"I'm in love, **Batman,**" she pleads, ". . . in love with a fine, decent man! You've probably heard of him . . . **Bruce Wayne!** Oh! If only you'd let me go, **Batman** . . . if I knew I had a chance with him, I'd give up my life of crime!"

Moved by the Catwoman's plea, and hopeful that her love for Bruce Wayne will enable him to help her reform, Batman allows her to escape and then, in the days that follow, begins a whirlwind romance with Elva Barr that soon culminates in their engagement.

"I'm through, men!" announces the Catwoman to her henchmen, after her engagement to Bruce Wayne has been formally announced. "No more crime! You read the papers--I'm engaged now! I'm going straight!"

"Aw, that guy **Bruce Wayne** ain't in love with you!" replies one of the henchmen disdainfully. "He's sweet on **Linda Page!** Everybody knows . . ."

The Catwoman cuts the henchman short with a vicious slap, but she remains haunted by the fear that he may have been right. "Maybe . . . maybe he's right!" she muses. "Maybe I'm just a silly fool!"

To determine once and for all which of them, she or Linda Page, Bruce Wayne really loves, the Catwoman decides to pay a call on Wayne disguised as Linda Page.

"Now, listen, **Linda,**" stammers Wayne, unaware that the woman in his presence is really an impostor, "please understand! I--I'm doing a favor for the **Batman!** He asked me to do this!" A moment later, he adds: "You must trust me, **Linda!** My engagement won't be for long!"

"So he really doesn't love me!" thinks the Catwoman bitterly. "He loves **Linda!** And he's just doing this because the **Batman** asked him!"

Moments later, feeling bitter and betrayed, she leaves Wayne's home, vowing revenge. "This is the **Batman's** fault!" she thinks angrily. "He wanted to refom [sic] me! Well, I'll show him!"

In an effort to retaliate against Bruce Wayne and Batman, the Catwoman resumes her life of crime, only to be apprehended soon afterward by Batman and Robin.

"Glad that's over!" sighs Bruce Wayne afterward. "I hope **Linda** will forgive me now!" (BM No. 15/1: "Your Face Is Your Fortune!"). (*See also* section J 2, the relationship with Linda Page.)

Bruce Wayne's idea of proposing marriage to the Catwoman in order to help her reform – particularly when he planned to terminate the engagement at the earliest opportunity – was clearly irrational and could not possibly have been expected to bring about the achievement of its stated objective, renunciation by the Catwoman of her life of crime. Since declaring a false love for the Catwoman could only have been expected to embitter her, not reform her, the real explanation for the scheme must be sought in Bruce Wayne's unconscious.

Why the Catwoman falls in love with Bruce Wayne in the first place is easy to understand. The Catwoman is in love with Batman, and since Bruce Wayne and Batman are the same person, she unconsciously perceives in Wayne the same qualities that draw her to Batman.

Although the text would have us believe that what the Catwoman perceives as Wayne's romantic interest is really only his unspoken realization that beauty contestant Elva Barr is actually the Catwoman, a more plausible explanation is that the Catwoman correctly perceives in Wayne that which he makes manifest as Batman, i.e., a strong erotic interest in the Catwoman.

Since being a villainess makes the Catwoman taboo as a love object both for Bruce Wayne and for Batman, the only way he can hope to possess her is by rationalizing that his courtship of her is not a genuine display of ardor or affection, but merely a cunning ruse designed to attain some secret objective.

Wayne speaks of his courtship of the Catwoman as "a favor for the Batman," but of course a favor Wayne does for Batman is really a favor he does for himself.

Wayne, in fact, never actually breaks the engagement. The Catwoman does, and for good reason, after learning that Wayne was acting in bad faith when he asked her to marry him.

Wayne's real motive for the ill-conceived, ill-fated scheme is twofold: (1) it enables him to court the Catwoman and declare his love for her while concealing from himself his desire to possess her; and (2) because the scheme is foolhardy and doomed to failure, it ensures that the Catwoman will not reform, but will return to a life of crime and thus retain her sexual allure.

In June–July 1946, after the Catwoman has plummeted from atop a floating dirigible to seemingly certain doom, Batman is visibly distressed. "She's dead, **Robin!**" he murmurs. "She was a criminal--but somehow . . . well, now she's dead!" (BM No. 35/1: "Nine Lives Has the Catwoman!").

In late 1946, at Christmastime, just as her henchman is about to shoot Batman as he lies unconscious and helpless, the Catwoman intervenes, savagely whipping the gun from his hand with a lash of her cat-o'-nine-tails.

"What's de idea?" asks the henchman, bewildered. "You soft for dis guy?"

"N-No," stammers the Catwoman, ". . . but why have a murder rap hanging over us?"

Inside, however, the Catwoman is torn by silent doubts. "Why **did** I save him?" she asks herself. "Maybe I **am** soft . . . oh . . . I'm all confused!"

Later, after Batman and Robin have apprehended the Catwoman and her henchmen at the lavish Moon Valley Winter Resort, Batman and the Catwoman pass beneath some mistletoe hanging in the hotel.

"That's **mistletoe** above us!" exlaims the Catwoman, throwing her arms around Batman. "Well, don't stand there – **kiss me!**" Batman, however, does not respond.

"Don't turn me in, **Batman!**" pleads the Catwoman. "Join up with me instead! Together, we can rule the underworld! We can be king and queen of crime! You and I – together!"

"Together?" replies Batman with a smile. "How could we – with me **outside** and you **inside** a jail cell!"

"You . . . I hate you!" cries the Catwoman, suddenly furious. "I-I'll scratch your eyes out!" (BM No. 39/3, Feb/Mar '47: "A Christmas Tale!").

In April 1947, during a dramatic chase up the circular staircase inside the Statue of Liberty, the Catwoman hurls a loose block of stone at Batman, momentarily stunning him and knocking him out of the fight. And moments later, with Robin her captive, she makes good her escape in a helicopter flown by her henchmen.

"**Batman** wasn't hurt, was he?" she asks Robin anxiously back at her hideout. "I only meant to scare him back when I dropped that block!"

"It only grazed him!" replies Robin. "You sort of like him, don't you?"

"Of course not!" snaps the Catwoman. "We're sworn enemies!" (Det No. 122: "The Black Cat Crimes!").

In June–July 1948 the Catwoman disguises herself in a blond wig and, under the alias Madame Moderne, begins publishing a high-fashion magazine called *Damsel.* At one point, after having borrowed a valuable mink coat from a furrier for a fashion show in her Madame Moderne disguise, and then having stolen the coat from the fashion show as the Catwoman despite the efforts of Batman and Robin to apprehend her, she returns to the scene as Madame Moderne and, informed of Batman's heroic attempt to thwart the robbery, throws her arms around him and kisses him passionately, ostensibly out of gratitude for his having attempted to protect the mink coat.

"Nice going, honey!" she muses aloud to herself when she is finally alone. "You stole a mink coat . . . and a kiss from the **Batman!**" (BM No. 47/1: "Fashions in Crime!").

In December 1950–January 1951 the Catwoman plunges into battle with Batman and Robin, only to find herself torn by conflicting feelings when she sees the crumbling brick wall of an abandoned building toppling toward Batman.

"Batman will be killed!" she thinks at first. "I'll be able to escape now! I'll be free!" But then suddenly she hesitates, abruptly changes direction, and rescues Batman from certain death by shoving him out of the path of the plummeting bricks.

In saving Batman, however, the Catwoman is herself knocked unconscious by a falling brick. This accidental blow on the head restores her memory and rescues her from the near-total amnesia concerning her past that has plagued her for over a decade (BM No. 62/1: "The Secret Life of the Catwoman"). (*See* CATWOMAN, THE.)

In January 1954, following the appearance of a newspaper article detailing the Catwoman's previous defeats at the hands of Batman and Robin, Batman becomes concerned that, after three years as a law-abiding citizen, the Catwoman may decide to return to crime.

"She misses the old excitement, the daring that made her so dreaded in crime!" he confides to Robin. "And I'm afraid this publicity may turn her back to her old life!"

"You're really worried about her, aren't you?" asks Robin. "Or maybe I shouldn't say that!"

Indeed, the Catwoman does return to crime, but soon afterward she intervenes to prevent her henchmen from murdering an unconscious Batman. "No, don't shoot!" she cries. "I couldn't bear to see him killed! I---mean we'll take him along---as a hostage!"

At the Catwoman's hideout, Batman regains consciousness and asks his captor why she allowed his life to be spared. "Only because you're a valuable hostage!" snaps the Catwoman.

Later, after Batman has escaped from the Catwoman's clutches, Robin comments on her strange behavior. "Those angry crooks surely would have killed you if she hadn't intervened, ***Batman!*** It's strange, her feeling toward you!"

"No use talking about that," replies Batman, "---she's got to be stopped!" (Det No. 203: "The Crimes of the Catwoman!").

In September 1954 Batman and Robin pursue the Catwoman to a lonely tropical island, only to be captured there by a gang of criminals with whom the Catwoman has formed an uneasy alliance. The criminals want to murder the Dynamic Duo, but the Catwoman forbids it.

"I want the pleasure of hunting them down," she insists, "as they hunted me!"

After confiscating their costumes and utility belts – leaving them attired only in their identity-concealing masks and primitive animal-skin clothing – the Catwoman sets Batman and Robin free in the jungle with a ten-minute head start, then sets out after them with her pet leopard, lion, and panther.

At one point, Batman and Robin attempt to elude the Catwoman by hiding in shallow water and breathing through hollow reeds. After the Catwoman has passed them by, Robin remarks that she must not have discerned their hiding place.

"Didn't she, ***Robin?***" replies Batman. "I wonder!"

Soon afterward, Batman is recaptured by the Catwoman's ruthless underworld allies. After returning his costume and utility belt, which the Catwoman claims to have emptied of its tools and other contents, the Catwoman and her cohorts bind Batman with rope and hurl him into a river flowing swiftly toward a waterfall. With the aid of a knife and a silken rope which he finds intact inside his utility belt, however, Batman succeeds in escaping from his bonds and reaching the riverbank, although, for a time, he allows his adversaries to believe he has perished.

"***Batman*** . . . gone," thinks the Catwoman ruefully. "And I thought he'd save himself--he always has in the past. . . ."

"Funny, that she accidentally left that knife-blade and silken cord in your utility belt," remarks Robin to Batman soon afterward, ". . . ***or was*** it an accident? She's always been soft on you!"

"That was no accident, ***Robin,***" replies Batman.

"Murder isn't in the ***Catwoman's*** heart. Sentiment is her weakness--and that's why we'll catch her the next time!" (Det No. 211: "The Jungle Cat-Queen!").

Following the above-mentioned encounter, the Catwoman remains absent from the chronicles for thirteen years, only to reemerge in November 1967, bitterly jealous over Batman's having publicly paid Batgirl (*see* BATGIRL [BARBARA GORDON]) an innocuous compliment.

"Looks to me like ***Batgirl*** is making a play for ***Batman!***" fumes the Catwoman. "She has her nerve--trying to cut herself in ***on my man!***

"I've known ***Batman*** a lot longer than that Jill-come-lately! If he belongs to anybody, he belongs to . . . ***Catwoman!!***" (Det No. 369: "Batgirl Breaks Up the Dynamic Duo!").

The statement is probably closer to the truth than Batman would ever acknowledge. As of the mid-1970s, the Catwoman's relationship with Batman has endured at least fifteen years longer than any of his other relationships with women described in the chronicles.

K. The Relationship with the Law-Enforcement Establishment. Nearly forty years as a costumed crime-fighter have made Batman one of the world's most prominent lawmen, an honored and respected member of the law enforcement fraternity. He is an honorary member of the Gotham City Police Department (BM No. 7/4, Oct/Nov '41: "The People vs. The Batman"; and others), a member of the Gotham City Crime Commission (Det No. 175, Sep '51: "The Underworld Bank!"), and a close personal friend of POLICE COMMISSIONER JAMES W. GORDON (BM No. 71/2, Jun/Jul '52: "Commissioner Gordon's Greatest Case!"; and others).

For years, he has worked hand in hand with the police, as well as the F.B.I. (BM No. 93/1, Aug '55: "Journey to the Top of the World!"; and others); Scotland Yard (Det No. 110, Apr '46: "Batman and Robin in Scotland Yard!"; and others); the Royal Canadian Mounted Police (BM No. 78/3, Aug/Sep '53: "Batman of the Mounties!"); the French Sûreté (Det No. 160, Jun '50: "The Globe-Trotter of Crime!"); and a myriad of law-enforcement agencies around the globe.

He has been the recipient of countless awards, trophies, citations, and other honors, including gifts of honorary police badges from countries around the world (BM No. 124/2, Jun '59: "The Return of Signalman"). Nearly a dozen statues and monuments have been erected in his honor, including the gigantic head of Batman carved into the side of Mt. Gotham (Det No. 319, Sep '63: "The Fantastic Dr. No-Face!") and the statue of a seated Batman erected in Gotham Park (BM No. 107/1, Apr '57: "The Boy Who Adopted Batman"; BM No. 134/3, Sep '60: "The Deadly Dummy"). (*See also* section H, the man himself [as Batman].)

As an identifying emblem as well as a token of the city's esteem, Batman has been presented with a special bat-shaped police badge, made of platinum and set with diamonds (Det No. 105, Nov '45: "The Batman Goes Broke!"; and others). To discourage either criminals or hucksters from impersonating Batman, "a law was passed [in GOTHAM CITY] which forbids anyone appearing as the **Batman** except the **original Batman** of Gotham City or with his permission!" (Det No. 195, May '53: "The Original Batman!"; and others). The SECRET STAR, an elite five-man organization chosen by Police Commissioner Gordon and trained by Batman and Robin, is already in the wings, ready to carry on the Batman legend in the event of his death or long-term disability.

Batman has not always enjoyed the approval of the law-enforcement establishment, however, although he has generally enjoyed the admiration of the common man (Det No. 36, Feb '40) and of the cop on the beat (Det No. 50, Apr '41: "The Case of the Three Devils!"; and others). In the early days of his career, Batman was a vigilante avenger, an "'outside the law' racket-buster" (Det No. 65, Jul '42: "The Cop Who Hated the Batman!") who "borrowed" parked automobiles to chase down criminals (BM No. 6/4, Aug/Sep '41: "Suicide Beat!"; BM No. 7/1, Oct/Nov '41); extorted confessions from his adversaries by means of physical violence (BM No. 5/3, Spr '41: "The Case of the Honest Crook"; and others) or the third degree (Det No. 134, Apr '48: "The Umbrellas of Crime!"; and others); and then deposited his bound captives and their signed confessions on the sidewalk in front of police headquarters before racing away into the night (Det No. 28, June '39; and others). When he felt the situation warranted it, he was not even averse to meting out death (BM No. 1/3, Spr '40; and others).

"If you can't beat them 'inside' the law," he commented in September 1940, "you must beat them 'outside' it--and that's where I come in!" (Det No. 43: "The Case of the City of Terror").

Pursued by the police during this early period (Det No. 27, May '39: "The Case of the Chemical Syndicate"; and others) – and on occasion even forced to battle them in order to make good his escape (BM No. 1/5, Spr '40: "The Joker Returns"; and others) – Batman was sought as a fugitive less for having committed any actual crime than for the audacity he displayed in repeatedly humiliating the authorities with his spectacular successes against the underworld.

"That Batman," cries an exasperated Police Commissioner Gordon in January 1940. "He's done it again! He's making the police department look ridiculous. I wish I could get my hands on him" (Det No. 35).

As Bruce Wayne, however, Batman was a close friend of Police Commissioner Gordon even in the vigilante stage of his career. Unable to acquire vital information as Batman through official police channels, he often hung around police headquarters as socialite Wayne (BM No. 4/4, Win '41; and others), affecting his practiced bored-playboy pose and accompanying Police Commissioner Gordon on criminal cases on the pretext of having "nothing else to do" (Det No. 27, May '39: "The Case of the Chemical Syndicate"; and others).

As time passed, however, Gordon came to view Batman as "the most gifted detective I had ever known" (WF No. 65, Jul/Aug '53: "The Five Different Batmen!"). In October–November 1941, after delivering a stirring courtroom defense of Batman's extralegal

Bruce Wayne and Police Commissioner Gordon, 1939 © NPP 1939

activities, he appointed Batman an honorary member of the Gotham City Police Department (BM No. 7/4: "The People vs. The Batman"), thus ushering in an era of mutual cooperation between Batman and the law-enforcement establishment that has endured for more than three decades.

What follows is a chronological listing of the textual data relating to the relationship between Batman and the law-enforcement establishment. (*See also* GORDON, JAMES W. [POLICE COMMISSIONER].)

By May 1939, the date of the premier text of the Batman chronicles, Batman is apparently already being sought by the police for battling crime outside the law.

"It's the Bat-Man! Get him!" shouts Police Commissioner Gordon to his officers as he spies Batman atop a nearby roof. Batman, however, escapes to his red sedan and roars safely away (Det No. 27: "The Case of the Chemical Syndicate").

In January 1940, after being mistaken for a thief by the police, Batman is forced to punch an officer in order to make good his escape.

"I tell you Bruce," comments an agitated Police Commissioner Gordon to his friend Bruce Wayne, "if I ever catch the Batman!"

And later he remarks in exasperation, "That Batman . . . . He's making the police department look ridiculous. I wish I could get my hands on him" (Det No. 35).

In February 1940 Batman is examining a murder victim for identification when police, arriving on the scene, mistake him for the murderer and force him to flee.

Later, however, after news of Batman's capture of PROFESSOR HUGO STRANGE has been broadcast over the radio, a youngster asks his father, "Who is the **Batman,** Daddy?"

"A great man, son," replies his father, "a **great** man!" (Det No. 36).

In Spring 1940 the police find Batman lying on the floor of the Drake Museum after being knocked unconscious during a battle with the JOKER.

"The Batman!" exclaims one officer. "Well, we have caught somebody! Now I'm going to do something I've wanted to do for a long time--take off the **Batman's mask** and see who he really is!"

"Sorry boys," cries Batman, leaping suddenly to his feet and fighting his way to freedom through a phalanx of police, "but I'm not quite ready for jail!"

Even later, after having apprehended the Joker, Batman and Robin flee at the approach of the police (BM No. 1/5: "The Joker Returns").

In July 1940, after Dick Grayson has informed Bruce Wayne of the recent murder of the superintendent of a boys' school, Wayne comments, ". . . I think we should lend a little support to the police, on the sly, of course!" (Det No. 41).

In August 1940 police come upon Batman in the presence of a murder victim and accuse him of having committed the crime.

"Surely you don't believe I had anything to do with this!" replies Batman. "My methods may be--er--different. But I've always worked on the side of the law!"

"He's right!" thinks one of the policemen to himself. "I don't believe he did it!" (Det No. 42: "The Case of the Prophetic Pictures!").

In Fall 1940 Batman is forced to elude the police after robbing Martier's jewelry salon while under the hypnotic control of the diabolical PUPPET MASTER. Ultimately, Batman and Robin apprehend the villain, exonerating Batman of the charges against him (BM No. 3/1: "The Strange Case of the Diabolical Puppet Master").

In Fall 1940 the bumbling, bombastic DETECTIVE MCGONIGLE makes a series of attempts to apprehend Batman, only to find himself repeatedly outwitted (BM No. 3/2: "The Ugliest Man in the World"; BM No. 3/4: "The Batman vs the Cat-Woman!").

In Winter 1941 Batman and Robin flee the scene of one of their battles with criminals to avoid capture by the police (BM No. 4/4).

In January 1941, as policemen approach, Batman remarks, "Police! — My exit cue!" and swiftly makes his escape (Det No. 47).

In February 1941 Batman and Robin thwart an attempt by criminals to loot the U.S. Government gold reserve at Kentucky's Fort Stox.

"You've done your country a great service!" declares the Fort Stox commander. "I'll see that the president hears of this and gives you both a suitable reward!"

"That's not necessary," replies Batman. "Being Americans is enough of an award!" (Det No. 48: "The Secret Cavern").

In Spring 1941, after a climactic battle with a gang of bank robbers, Batman and Robin leap through a window into the river to escape the arriving police. "You boys can take over now," cries Batman. "Our job is finished!"

"Was that fellow with the boy the famous **Batman** I've heard so much about?" inquires LINDA PAGE of one of the policemen.

"That was him all right," replies the officer. "Quite a guy, isn't he?" (BM No. 5/4).

In April 1941 Batman, still a fugitive from the law, is finally apprehended by a patrolman named Riley.

"T'is a funny thing, Mr. Batman," remarks Riley, "but I have a lot of respect for ye – even though your methods ain't exactly peaceful! Ye know, if you was ta be hittin' me once, I guess then I couldn't hold ye – and I'd still be carryin' out me dooty!"

"Say, you're okay!" replies Batman, whereupon he obliges Patrolman Riley with a resounding punch to the jaw and then hastily departs (Det No. 50: "The Case of the Three Devils!").

In June 1941 Batman is pursued by the police after battling henchmen of the evil LOO CHUNG (Det No. 52: "The Secret of the Jade Box").

In August–September 1941 Batman and Robin are forced to fight their way past some policemen in order to avoid arrest. "The police," remarks Batman wryly, "aren't as yet exactly too fond of my slightly different way in fighting crime!"

Soon afterward, however, a Gotham City policeman, seeing Robin in the clutches of a criminal, expresses this attitude: "I don't want to see that boy killed! Even though he does work outside the law, still he does fight crime!" (BM No. 6/1: "Murder on Parole").

In October–November 1941 Batman and Robin apprehend GRANDA THE MYSTIC and his cohorts with the aid of Police Commissioner Gordon and members of his police department. At the time of this adventure, Batman and Robin are still technically fugitives from the law – "Better leave before the police arrive!" comments Robin at one point – but after the criminals have been taken into custody, Police Commissioner Gordon shakes Batman's hand and congratulates him personally for the first time in the chronicles. "The police department, [and] the people of the city," he says, "thank you and Robin for the swell job you did!" (BM No. 7/2: "The Trouble Trap!"). Even after this precedent-setting event, however, Batman continues to be hunted by the police as a fugitive from justice (BM No. 7/4, Oct/Nov '41: "The People vs. The Batman").

It is still October–November 1941 when Bruce Wayne is arrested and charged with murder after being framed for the shooting death of rackets boss HORATIO DELMAR by gangster Freddie Hill, Delmar's principal underworld lieutenant. With Wayne in jail awaiting trial, Hill moves to discredit any potential testimony by Batman and Robin by having one of his henchmen disguise himself in a Batman costume and make an attempt on the life of a material witness to the Delmar murder.

Soon afterward, however, Robin breaks Bruce Wayne out of jail so that he can function as Batman and, after successfully apprehending gang chief Freddie Hill, the Dynamic Duo burst into a crowded Gotham City courtroom where a district attorney is denouncing Bruce Wayne to the jury, insisting that Wayne has "proved his guilt" in the Delmar murder case by breaking out of jail.

When Batman intervenes to plead Wayne's innocence, the indignant district attorney turns on Batman:

"**Batman,** I accuse you of aiding and abetting Bruce Wayne to escape jail," he cries, "--and attempting to murder a court witness--and obstructing justice with your infernal meddling and your absurd crime theories! **Police, arrest this man!**"

It is at this moment, however, that Police Commissioner Gordon leaps to his feet, coming to Batman's defense with a stirring courtroom speech:

> I speak for the **Batman**--the friend of the people! Yes---he works "outside the law," as you call it, but the legal devices that hamper us are hurdled by this crime-fighter so he may bring these men of evil to justice . . . The eminent district attorney calls him a meddler with a theory---
>
> Washington, the Wright Brothers, Lincoln, Edison and others, they were "meddlers," too--who proved their theories. They made sacrifices so that we might enjoy the security and comfort we do. The **Batman** has done that, too!
>
> This man who has saved a nation's gold reserve, fought fifth columnists and saboteurs, beaten the Joker, the Puppet Master, and other crime geniuses. . . .
>
> This man who daily risks his life to save others--who never carries a gun-- who is aided by his young friend, **Robin,** fights crime with the courage and zeal born of love for his follow [sic] man. This is . . . the **Batman!**

"Perhaps this comes a little late," concludes Police Commissioner Gordon finally, putting his hand on Batman's shoulder and shaking his hand, "but I, the police commissioner of Gotham City, appoint you an **honorary member of the police department!** From now on, you work hand in hand with the police!" (BM No. 7/4: "The People vs. The Batman").

These events mark the end of Batman's period as a fugitive and usher in an era of lasting cooperation between Batman and the law-enforcement establishment.

In December 1941 Batman becomes a fugitive from justice once again, due to the sinister machinations of the PENGUIN, but ultimately he succeeds in establishing his innocence (Det No. 58).

In December 1941–January 1942 Bruce Wayne and Dick Grayson are relaxing at home, when the following announcement comes over the radio:

> Calling the **Batman** and **Robin** wherever they may be . . . you are requested to come to Washington, D.C. . . . G. Henry Mover, the head of the F.B.I., will meet [you] . . . and will personally deliver the good wishes of the people and the president for your efforts in ridding this country of crime . . . the president himself requests your appearance. . . .

Arriving in Washington, D.C., Batman and Robin "lead a great triumphal procession into the city as the people cheer wildly." G. Henry Mover, head of the F.B.I., greets the Dynamic Duo personally. "It's indeed a pleasure to meet you two---" he says proudly.

"Robin and I can never hope to be as thorough as your G-men, Mr. Mover!" replies Batman.

The festivities are rudely interrupted, however, when the JOKER fires a single shot at Batman from somewhere within the crowd, missing Batman but wounding Mover in the shoulder (BM No. 8/4: "The Cross Country Crimes!").

In February 1942 Police Commissioner Gordon summons Batman and Robin into action with the bat-signal for the first time in the chronicles, although at this early date it is referred to only as a "searchlight on the roof of police headquarters!" (Det No. 60: "Case of the Costume-Clad Killers"). (*See* section E 2 e, the bat-signal.)

In August–September 1942 Batman and Robin are feted with a ticker-tape parade through the streets of Gotham City, and a large stone statue of them – a "monument to their ceaseless crime crusade" – is unveiled in ceremonies at City Hall.

"Never in history," proclaims the mayor proudly, "has there been such a record as this . . . 120 arrests . . . 118 convictions . . . 70 confessions . . . encountered and defeated the **Joker** six times, the Penguin, etc. etc. . . ." (BM No. 12/4: "Around the Clock with the Batman!").

In February–March 1944 Batman and Robin are briefly hospitalized after being subjected to a "severe dose" of the PENGUIN's "new kind of knockout gas."

"Whew! What amazing vitality!" exclaims an attending physician. "They're coming out of it!"

"Th-Thank heavens!" cries the police officer who brought them in for treatment. "The police department would rather have Batman and Robin alive . . . than a thousand Penguins captured!" (BM No. 21/4: "The Three Eccentrics!").

In January 1945, at graduation exercises for Gotham City's rookie policemen, Police Commissioner Gordon presents Batman with a "diamond-studded **Batman** badge as a token of our respect!" (Det No. 95). Despite the fact that this special bat-shaped police badge – described in a later text as made of platinum as well as set with diamonds (Det No. 105, Nov '45: "The Batman Goes Broke!") – is officially presented to Batman on the occasion of the rookies' graduation, Batman has already had it in his possession in at least two previous texts (Det No. 70, Dec '42: "The Man Who Could Read Minds!"; BM No. 19/4, Oct/Nov '43: "Collector of Millionaires").

In March 1947 Police Commissioner Gordon is abruptly removed from his post as commissioner and demoted to the rank of patrolman, and Batman is ordered to surrender the special bat-shaped badge that identifies him as an honorary member of the Gotham City Police Department. "From now on," warns the new commissioner, "the police will handle cases without your help!"

Ultimately, however, Gordon is restored to the commissioner's post through the heroic efforts of the Dynamic Duo, and Batman is reinstated as an honorary member of the department (Det No. 121: "Commissioner Gordon Walks a Beat!").

In June 1950 Police Commissioner Gordon and a group of law-enforcement officials from around the world present the Dynamic Duo with a gold trophy in honor of their crime-fighting exploits. Inscribed to "Batman and Robin, Globe-Trotters of the Law," the trophy consists of gold statuettes of Batman and Robin standing atop a gold globe (Det No. 160: "The Globe-Trotter of Crime!").

In April–May 1952 Police Commissioner Gordon orders Batman into retirement after an inventor named MR. WEIR has presented the police department with an electronically controlled robot which, in addition to being invulnerable to bullets and hand grenades, appears to possess all the crime-fighting prowess of Batman himself. Ultimately, however, the "robot cop" proves seriously deficient, and Batman resumes his duties as Gotham City's most intrepid lawman (BM No. 70/1: "The Robot Cop of Gotham City").

By June–July 1953 Police Commissioner Gordon has organized the SECRET STAR, an organization of five hand-picked men whose duty it will be to carry on the Batman legend in the event of Batman's death or long-term disability (BM No. 77/2: "The Secret Star").

During this same period, with Police Commissioner Gordon away from Gotham City attending a "big police convention on the Coast," Batman and Robin experience firsthand the life of ordinary patrolmen when the acting commissioner forbids them from concentrating on the department's important, glamorous cases, insisting instead that they perform such tedious routine chores as handing out traffic tickets and apprehending fruit-stand pilferers (BM No. 77/3, Jun/Jul '53: "Batman Pounds a Beat!"). (*See* KERN, "DANCER.")

In October 1954, when television station GCTV presents the story of Batman's life on its "Your Life Story" program, Police Commissioner Gordon appears on the program to present Batman with a "golden key to the city" as "a gift from the people of Gotham City . . .!" (BM No. 87/1: "Batman's Greatest Thrills!").

In July–August 1956 Batman and Robin – and their friend SUPERMAN – are "honored guests" at Gotham City's annual police ball (WF No. 83: "The Case of the Mother Goose Mystery!").

In August 1956 a text – inconsistent with earlier accounts cited above – appears which purports to recapitulate the origins of Batman's relationship with Police Commissioner Gordon and the Gotham City law-enforcement establishment.

"I was working late that night," reminisces Gordon, recalling what he here describes as his initial meeting with Batman, "and I looked up suddenly in amazement . . ." to see a mysterious, cowled figure standing silently in his office.

"That queer costume," stammered Gordon, "--that mask--who are you?"

"My real name, no one will ever know!" replied the bat-caped visitor. "But you can call me--***Batman!*** And I want to help the police in their work! I've trained myself thoroughly, and want to help enforce the law!"

"I appreciate your spirit," replied Gordon skeptically, "--but police work isn't for amateurs!"

"Even after you'd successfully solved a few cases," recalls Gordon, as he describes his feelings concerning this early encounter to Batman, "I doubted your ability!"

When a mysterious robbery occurred at a local museum, Batman appeared on the scene to help solve it. "A really tough case," thought Gordon at the time, "will teach him that police work is too much for him!"

Batman successfully solved the case, however, and when Gordon saw him at work and observed his acrobatic skills firsthand he decided that the costumed newcomer could indeed make a valuable contribution to law enforcement.

"We ***can*** use your help, ***Batman!***" he said finally. "But it's a hard job you've taken on, devoting your life to fight crime!"

"Yes," replied Batman solemnly, "--but I've suffered from crime and I ***want*** to fight it!" (Det No. 234: "Batman and Robin's Greatest Mystery").

In February 1957 crime syndicate chief BURT WEVER sets in motion an elaborate scheme to ruin Batman's reputation and destroy his effectiveness as a crime-fighter by framing him for a series of old unsolved crimes. Arrested, booked, and even brought to trial for crimes he did not commit, Batman succeeds ultimately in establishing his innocence – and in bringing Burt Wever to justice – with the aid of loyal members of the Gotham City Police Department and of "citizens of all classes who have faith in **Batman's** integrity!" (Det No. 240: "The Outlaw Batman!").

In January 1958 Batman is denied the cooperation of Police Commissioner Gordon and his department after the citizens of Gotham City have been duped into believing that Batman is secretly an alien from outer space. Ultimately, however, Batman succeeds in exposing the hoax and in apprehending its perpetrators (Det No. 251: "The Alien Batman!"). (*See* BALLARD, BRAND.)

In September 1959 Police Commissioner Gordon informs Batman and Robin that they have been appointed to the honor guard accompanying the Liberty Train, a "rolling exhibition of our country's most precious documents!"

"Thanks, commissioner," replies Batman, ". . . there is no higher honor than to be made guardians of our nation's democratic declarations!" (Det No. 271: "Batman's Armored Rival!").

In June 1960 Batman and Robin refer to their recent "lecture tour of police academies in other cities" (BM No. 132/1: "The Martian from Gotham City").

In July 1963 Batman and Robin are honored guests at a police convention in Center City (Det No. 317: "The Secrets of the Flying Bat-Cave!").

In August 1964 Batman appears as guest speaker at the annual graduation exercises at the Gotham City Police Academy (BM No. 165/2: "The Dilemma of the Detective's Daughter!").

In August 1964, after having smashed a ring of foreign spies (*see* MOLNEY), Batman and Robin are honored by the mayor of Gotham City and presented with a "special citation signed by the president of the United States . . ." (Det No. 330: "The Fallen Idol of Gotham City!").

L. The Texts. *1. Locales.* In the course of a career spanning nearly four decades of adventure, Batman has traveled to the four corners of the earth; to distant planets and alien dimensions; back into the past and forward into the future; and throughout his own country, the United States of America.

Foreign countries visited by Batman have included France (Det No. 31, Sep '39; and others); Hungary, or Hungaria (Det No. 32, Oct '39); England (Det No. 110, Apr '46: "Batman and Robin in Scotland Yard!"; and others); Canada (Det No. 157, Mar '50: "The Race of the Century"; and others); Scotland (Det No. 198, Aug '53: "The Lord of Batmanor!"); Switzerland (BM No. 167, Nov '64: "Zero Hour for Earth!"); Holland, Italy, Austria, Greece, Algeria, Siam (now Thailand), and Mexico (Det No. 248, Oct '57: "Around the World in 8 Days!"); Central America (BM No. 142/3, Sep '61: "Ruler of the Bewitched Valley!"); South America (BM No. 134/1, Sep '60: "The Rainbow Creature!"; and others); and Asia (BM No. 167, Nov '64: "Zero Hour for Earth!").

Distant planets and alien dimensions visited by Batman have included the planets TORA (Det No. 256, Jun '58: "The Captive Planet!"), ALCOR (Det No. 282, Aug '60: "Batman's Interplanetary Rival!"), ZUR-EN-ARRH (BM No. 113/3, Feb '58: "Batman--The Superman of Planet X!"), and MARS (BM No. 41/3, Jun/Jul '47: "Batman, Interplanetary Policeman!"), and the extra-dimensional world inhabited by the BAT-PEOPLE (BM No. 116/3, Jun '58: "The Winged Bat-People!").

Past and future eras visited by Batman have included ancient Rome (BM No. 24/1, Aug/Sep '44: "It Happened in Rome"); seventeenth-century France (BM No. 32/3, Dec/Jan '45–'46: "All for One, One for All!"); the court of KING ARTHUR (BM No. 36/3, Aug/Sep '46: "Sir Batman at King Arthur's Court!"); thirteenth-century England (Det No. 116, Oct '46: "The Rescue of Robin Hood!"); fifth-century B.C. Athens (BM No. 38/1, Dec/Jan '46–'47: "Peril in Greece!"); eighteenth-century Philadelphia (BM No. 44/3, Dec/Jan '47–'48: "The First American Detective!"); fifteenth-century Milan (BM No. 46/3, Apr/May '48: "The Batman That History Forgot!"); nineteenth-century Europe (Det No. 135, May '48: "The True Story of Frankenstein!"); the seventeenth-century Caribbean (Det No. 136, Jun '48: "The Dead Man's Chest!"); ancient Baghdad (BM No. 49/3, Oct/Nov '48: "Batman's Arabian Nights!"); tenth-century Norway (BM No. 52/2, Apr/May '49: "Batman and the Vikings!"); thirteenth-century China (WF No. 42, Sep/Oct '49: "The Amazing Adventure of Batman and Marco Polo!"); the era of the California gold rush (BM No. 58/2, Apr/May '50: "The Brand of a Hero!"); twenty-first-century A.D. GOTHAM CITY (BM No. 59/3, Jun/Jul '50: "Batman in the Future!"); ancient Egypt (Det No. 167, Jan '51: "Bodyguards to Cleopatra!"); eighteenth-century Gotham City (BM No. 79/2, Oct/Nov '53: "The Batman of Yesterday!"); seventeenth-century Gotham City (Det No. 205, Mar '54: "The Origin of the Bat-Cave!"); the Mississippi River, 1854 (BM No. 89/1, Feb '55: "River Rogues"); the Stone Age (BM No. 93/3, Aug '55: "The Caveman Batman"); early twentieth-century France (BM No. 98/1, Mar '56: "The Return of Mr. Future!"); the Wild West (BM No. 99/2, Apr '56: "Batman--Frontier Marshal"); ancient Babylon (BM No. 102/2, Sep '56: "The Batman from Babylon"); the eighth-century Middle East (BM No. 115/3, Apr '58: "Batman in the Bottle!"); seventeenth-century Venice (BM No. 125/2, Aug '59: "The Last Days of Batman"); ancient Macedonia (WF No. 107, Feb '60: "The Secret of the Time Creature!"); fifteenth-century Florence (WF No. 132, Mar '63: "Batman and Robin, Medieval Bandits!"); ancient Norseland (WF No. 135, Aug '63: "The Menace of the Future Man!"); and the prehistoric era of the fiftieth milennium B.C. (WF No. 138, Dec '63: "The Secret of the Captive Cavemen!").

Areas of the United States visited by Batman have included West Virginia (Det No. 85, Mar '44: "The Joker's Double"); Tennessee and Arkansas (Det No. 59, Jan '42: "The King of the Jungle!"); Kentucky (Det No. 48, Feb '41: "The Secret Cavern"); Alaska (WF No. 7, Fall '42: "The North Pole Crimes!"; and others); Louisiana (WF No. 20, Win '45: "King of Coins!"); Texas (BM No. 6/3, Aug/Sep '41: "The Secret of the Iron Jungle!"); New Jersey, Ohio, Kansas, Delaware, and Rhode Island (BM No. 8/4, Dec/Jan '41–'42: "The Cross Country Crimes!"); Florida (BM No. 11/4, Jun/Jul '42: "Four Birds of a Feather!"; and others); Hawaii (BM No. 145/1, Feb '62: "Hunt for Mr. 50"); California (BM No. 17/4, Jun/Jul '43: "Adventure of the Vitamin Vandals!"; and others); the West (BM No. 21/1, Feb/Mar '44: "The Streamlined Rustlers!"; and others); the Southwest (BM No. 17/3, Jun/Jul '43: "Rogues' Pageant!"); the North Woods (BM No. 7/3, Oct/Nov '41: "The North Woods Mystery"); the Ozarks (BM No. 16/1, Apr/May '43: "The Joker Reforms!"); and the towns of Yonville (BM No. 24/3, Aug/Sep '44: "The Mayors of Yonville!"); Hillvale (BM No. 170/2, Mar '65: "The Puzzle of the Perilous Prizes!"); Glass Town (WF No. 28, May/Jun '47: "Crime Under Glass!"); Waterville (WF No. 60, Sep/Oct '52: "The Richest Crook in the World!"); and Ghost Gulch City (Det No. 56, Oct '41: "The Stone Idol!").

By and large, however, the adventures of Batman take place in and around GOTHAM CITY, the resident city of Batman and Robin and the site of Wayne Manor, the place where they make their home as Bruce Wayne and Dick Grayson. The textual evidence is overwhelming that Gotham City is modeled after, and fully intended to represent, the city of New York. (*See* GOTHAM CITY.)

2. Developments. a. THE EARLY ADVENTURES. In May 1939 Batman makes his textual debut and matches wits with the villainous ALFRED STRYKER (Det No. 27: "The Case of the Chemical Syndicate").

In June 1939 Batman apprehends jewel thief FRENCHY BLAKE (Det No. 28).

In July 1939 Batman battles DOCTOR DEATH (Det No. 29: "The Batman Meets Doctor Death").

In August 1939 Batman renews his battle with DOCTOR DEATH (Det No. 30).

In September 1939 Batman matches wits with the MONK (Det No. 31).

In October 1939 Batman's battle with the MONK continues (Det No. 32).

In November 1939, in a text which offers the first account of Batman's origin (*see* section A, Origin), Batman battles the SCARLET HORDE (Det No. 33: "The Batman Wars Against the Dirigible of Doom").

In December 1939 Batman encounters the nefarious DUC D'ORTERRE (Det No. 34).

In January 1940 Batman faces death at the hands of SHELDON LENOX (Det No. 35).

In February 1940 Batman matches wits with PROFESSOR HUGO STRANGE (Det No. 36).

In March 1940 Batman battles COUNT GRUTT (Det No. 37).

In April 1940 Batman takes the orphaned Dick Grayson under his protection and presides over his emergence as ROBIN, THE BOY WONDER (Det No. 38).

In Spring 1940 Batman's origin is recapitulated (BM No. 1/1); Batman and Robin battle the JOKER (BM No. 1/2); Batman matches wits with PROFESSOR HUGO STRANGE (BM No. 1/3); Batman and Robin meet the CATWOMAN (BM No. 1/4); and Batman and Robin renew their battle with the JOKER (BM No. 1/5: "The Joker Returns").

In May 1940 Batman and Robin smash the GREEN DRAGON (Det No. 39).

In June 1940 Batman and Robin match wits with Clayface (*see* CLAYFACE [BASIL KARLO]) (Det No. 40).

In Summer 1940 Batman and Robin battle the JOKER and the CATWOMAN (BM No. 2/1); unravel the bizarre mystery of ADAM LAMB (BM No. 2/2); apprehend attorney WARD (BM No. 2/3: "The Case of the Clubfoot Murders"); and match wits with the wily HACKETT AND SNEAD (BM No. 2/4: "The Case of the Missing Link").

In July 1940 Batman and Robin apprehend the evil GRAVES (Det No. 41).

In August 1940 Batman and Robin meet artist PIERRE ANTAL (Det No. 42, "The Case of the Prophetic Pictures!").

In September 1940 Batman and Robin battle "crafty politician" HARLISS GREER (Det No. 43: "The Case of the City of Terror").

In Fall 1940 Batman and Robin match wits with the PUPPET MASTER (BM No. 3/1: "The Strange Case of the Diabolical Puppet Master"); battle the Ugly Horde (*see* CARLSON) (BM No. 3/2: "The Ugliest Man in the World"); smash the BIG BOY DANIELS mob (BM No. 3/3: "The Crime School for Boys!!"); and match wits with the CATWOMAN (BM No. 3/4: "The Batman vs the Catwoman!").

In October 1940 Robin dreams that he and Batman have somehow entered the fourth dimension, a bizarre world inhabited by giants and midgets (Det No. 44: "The Land Beyond the Light!").

In November 1940 Batman and Robin battle the JOKER (Det No. 45: "The Case of the Laughing Death!").

In December 1940 Batman and Robin match wits with PROFESSOR HUGO STRANGE (Det No. 46).

Sometime during 1940, Batman and Robin attend the New York World's Fair and battle the evil DR. HUGO VREEKILL (NYWF).

In Winter 1941 Batman and Robin match wits with the JOKER (BM No. 4/1: "The Case of the Joker's Crime Circus!"); apprehend the villainous BLACKBEARD (BM No. 4/2: "Blackbeard's Crew and the Yacht Society"); find themselves caught in the midst of a bloody gang war (*see* MCCOY, JIMMY "RED") (BM No. 4/3); and battle a gang of criminals led by the gambler STACY (BM No. 4/4).

In January 1941 Batman and Robin help teach multimillionaire banker Harvey Midas and his wife that money can't buy happiness (Det No. 47).

In February 1941 Batman and Robin lend a helping hand to millionaire HENRY LEWIS (Det No. 48: "The Secret Cavern").

In March 1941 Batman and Robin match wits with Clayface (*see* CLAYFACE [BASIL KARLO]) (Det No. 49: "Clayface Walks Again!").

In Spring 1941 Batman and Robin battle the JOKER (BM No. 5/1: "The Riddle of the Missing Card!"); meet PROFESSOR ANDERSON (BM No. 5/2: "Book of Enchantment"); apprehend SMILEY SIKES (BM No. 5/3: "The Case of the Honest Crook"); battle a "mysterious band of bank robbers" (*see* GROGAN, MIKE) (BM No. 5/4); and fight against the sinister machinations of the ruthless fifth columnist WRIGHT (WB No. 1: "The Witch and the Manuscript of Doom!").

In April 1941 Batman and Robin defeat the THREE DEVILS (Det No. 50: "The Case of the Three Devils!").

In May 1941 Batman and Robin apprehend the MINDY gang (Det No. 51: "The Case of the Mystery Carnival").

In June 1941 Batman and Robin match wits with the evil LOO CHUNG (Det No. 52: "The Secret of the Jade Box").

In Summer 1941 Batman and Robin meet AMBROSE TAYLOR (WF No. 2: "The Man Who Couldn't Remember!").

In July 1941 Batman and Robin lend a helping hand to aspiring actress VIOLA VANE and apprehend the TOOTHY HARE gang (Det No. 53).

In August 1941 Batman and Robin battle HOOK MORGAN's harbor pirates (Det No. 54: "Hook Morgan and His Harbor Pirates").

In August–September 1941 Batman and Robin battle the evil ATKINS (BM No. 6/2: "The Clock Maker!"); meet TOM PAGE (BM No. 6/3: "The Secret of the Iron Jungle!"); apprehend ALDERMAN SKIGG (BM No. 6/4: "Suicide Beat!"); and expose an unscrupulous parole-board member who has been using his influence to obtain paroles for specially selected convicts and then forcing the freed men to join the underworld gang that he himself heads as compensation for the parole he has obtained for them (BM No. 6/1: "Murder on Parole").

In September 1941 Batman and Robin match wits with DOCTOR DEREK (Det No. 55: "The 'Brain Burglar!'").

In Fall 1941 Batman and Robin meet the SCARECROW (WF No. 3: "The Scarecrow!").

In October 1941 Batman and Robin smash a ruthless scheme masterminded by MAD MACK (Det No. 56: "The Stone Idol!").

In October–November 1941 Batman and Robin battle the JOKER (BM No. 7/1); match wits with GRANDA THE MYSTIC (BM No. 7/2: "The Trouble Trap!"); apprehend the evil ASHER (BM No. 7/3: "The North Woods Mystery"); and exonerate Bruce Wayne of the charge that he murdered HORATIO DELMAR (BM No. 7/4: "The People vs. The Batman").

In November 1941 Batman and Robin meet RICHARD SNEED (Det No. 57: "Twenty-Four Hours to Live!").

b. THE WARTIME ADVENTURES. In December 1941 Batman and Robin battle the PENGUIN (Det No. 58).

In Winter 1941 Batman and Robin match wits with the GHOST GANG (WF No. 4: "The Ghost Gang Goes West!").

In December 1941–January 1942 Batman and Robin smash an elaborate scheme masterminded by BIG MIKE RUSSO (BM No. 8/1: "Stone Walls Do Not a Prison Make"); battle PROFESSOR RADIUM (BM No. 8/2: "The Strange Case of Professor Radium!"); apprehend JOHNNY GLIM (BM No. 8/3: "The Superstition Murders!"); and match wits with the JOKER (BM No. 8/4: "The Cross Country Crimes!").

In January 1942 Batman and Robin battle the PENGUIN (Det No. 59: "The King of the Jungle!").

In February 1942 Batman and Robin match wits with the JOKER (Det No. 60: "Case of the Costume-Clad Killers").

In February–March 1942 Batman and Robin take up the trail of four fugitive criminals (*see* JAFFEER) (BM No. 9/1: "The Four Fates!"); make the acquaintance of RADBEY, secretary of the Seven Seas Insurance Company (BM No. 9/2: "The White Whale!"); battle the JOKER (BM No. 9/3: "The Case of the Lucky Law-Breakers!"); and lend a helping hand to young TIMMY CRATCHIT (BM No. 9/4).

In March 1942 PROFESSOR POST and "CRAFTY" CAL CLATE recall their past encounters with Batman and Robin (Det No. 61: "The Three Racketeers!").

In Spring 1942 Batman and Robin smash an elaborate gangland scheme masterminded by BRAINS KELLEY (WF No. 5: "Crime Takes a Holiday").

In April 1942 Batman and Robin match wits with the JOKER (Det No. 62: "Laugh, Town, Laugh").

In April–May 1942 Batman and Robin meet GUY "BIG GUY" MARKHAM (BM No. 10/1: "The Isle That Time Forgot!"); capture some criminals with the aid of TOMMY TRENT (BM No. 10/2: "Report Card Blues!"); match wits with the CATWOMAN (BM No. 10/3: "The Princess of Plunder!"); and battle the "FIVE ACES" FROGEL gang (BM No. 10/4: "Sheriff of Ghost Town!").

In May 1942 Batman and Robin meet MICHAEL BAFFLE (Det No. 63: "A Gentleman in Gotham").

In June 1942 Batman and Robin match wits with the JOKER (Det No. 64: "The Joker Walks the Last Mile!").

In June–July 1942 Batman and Robin battle the JOKER (BM No. 11/1); apprehend JOE DOLAN (BM No. 11/2: "Payment in Full"); get the goods on HENRY BURTON (BM No. 11/3: "Bandits in Toyland!"); and match wits with the PENGUIN (BM No. 11/4: "Four Birds of a Feather!").

In Summer 1942 Batman and Robin meet SCOOP SCANLON (WF No. 6: "The Secret of Bruce Wayne!").

In July 1942 Batman and Robin meet state trooper TOM BOLTON (Det No. 65: "The Cop Who Hated the Batman!").

In August 1942 Batman and Robin battle TWO-FACE (Det No. 66: "The Crimes of Two-Face!").

In August–September 1942 Batman and Robin recall their past encounters with the notorious RAFFERTY BROTHERS (BM No. 12/1: "Brothers in Crime!"); match wits with the JOKER (BM No. 12/2: "The Wizard of Words!"); capture JOE KIRK (BM No. 12/3: "They Thrill to Conquer!"); and give their readers a glimpse of a typical action-packed day in the life of the Dynamic Duo, including such activities as a morning workout in their gym, tests on the batplane, experimental work in their laboratory, entertaining infantile paralysis patients at a local hospital, and capturing several gangs of criminals (BM No. 12/4: "Around the Clock with the Batman!").

In September 1942 Batman and Robin match wits with the PENGUIN (Det No. 67: "Crime's Early Bird!").

In Fall 1942 Batman and Robin battle the Snow Man Bandits (*see* BIGBEE, "ANGLES") (WF No. 7: "The North Pole Crimes!").

In October 1942 Batman and Robin apprehend TWO-FACE (Det No. 68: "The Man Who Led a Double Life!").

In October–November 1942 Batman and Robin meet the THUMB (BM No. 13/1: "The Batman Plays a Lone Hand!"); match wits with the JOKER (BM No. 13/2: "Comedy of Tears!"); battle ROCKY GRIMES (BM No. 13/3: "The Story of the Seventeen Stones!"); and protect the life of JOHN KEYES (BM No. 13/4: "Destination Unknown!").

In November 1942 Batman and Robin match wits with the JOKER (Det No. 69: "The Harlequin's Hoax!").

In December 1942 Batman and Robin meet the amazing CARLO (Det No. 70: "The Man Who Could Read Minds!").

In Winter 1942 Batman and Robin match wits with LITTLE NAP BOYD (WF No. 8: "Brothers in Law!").

In December 1942–January 1943 Batman and Robin investigate the death of DANA DRYE (BM No. 14/1: "The Case Batman Failed to Solve!!!"); apprehend "PILLS" MATTSON (BM No. 14/2: "Prescription for Happiness!"); smash the Nazi spy ring headed by COUNT FELIX (BM No. 14/3: "Swastika over the White House!"); and battle the PENGUIN (BM No. 14/4: "Bargains in Banditry!").

In January 1943 Batman and Robin match wits with the JOKER (Det No. 71: "A Crime a Day!").

In February 1943 Batman and Robin battle LARRY THE JUDGE (Det No. 72: "License for Larceny").

In February–March 1943 Batman and Robin match wits with the CATWOMAN (BM No. 15/1: "Your Face Is Your Fortune!"); apprehend "KNUCKLES" CONGER (BM No. 15/2: "The Boy Who Wanted to Be Robin!"); and battle the DIRK DAGNER gang (BM No. 15/4: "The Loneliest Men in the World").

In March 1943 Batman and Robin match wits with the SCARECROW (Det No. 73: "The Scarecrow Returns").

In Spring 1943 Batman and Robin thwart the sinister machinations of BRAMWELL B. BRAMWELL (WF No. 9: "Crime of the Month").

In April 1943 Batman and Robin meet TWEEDLEDUM AND TWEEDLEDEE (Det No. 74: "Tweedledum and Tweedledee!").

In April–May 1943 Batman and Robin battle the JOKER (BM No. 16/1: "The Joker Reforms!"); expose WINTHROP as the mastermind behind the "early bird" crimes (BM No. 16/2: "The Grade A Crimes!"); match wits with SQUIDGE (BM No. 16/3: "The Adventures of the Branded Tree!"); and meet ALFRED (BM No. 16/4: "Here Comes Alfred!").

In May 1943 Batman and Robin battle the ROBBER BARON (Det No. 75: "The Robber Baron!").

In June 1943 Batman and Robin match wits with the JOKER (Det No. 76: "Slay 'em with Flowers").

In June–July 1943 Batman and Robin meet B. BOSWELL BROWNE (BM No. 17/1: "The Batman's Biographer!"); battle the PENGUIN (BM No. 17/2: "The Penguin Goes A-Hunting"); apprehend the DUCKY MALLARD gang (BM No. 17/3: "Rogues' Pageant!"); and match wits with ARCHIE GIBBONS's "phantom raiders" (BM No. 17/4: "Adventure of the Vitamin Vandals!").

In Summer 1943 Batman and Robin meet OLIVER HUNT (WF No. 10: "Man with the Camera Eyes").

In July 1943 Batman and Robin battle DOCTOR MATTHEW THORNE (Det No. 77: "The Crime Clinic!").

In August 1943 Batman and Robin apprehend BARON VON LUGER (Det No. 78: "The Bond Wagon").

In August–September 1943 Batman and Robin match wits with TWEEDLEDUM AND TWEEDLEDEE (BM No. 18/1: "The Secret of Hunter's Inn!"); Batman orders ROBIN to stay at home and give up crime-fighting until he has made some improvement in his failing report card (BM No. 18/2: "Robin Studies His Lessons!"); Batman and Robin battle DOCTOR MATTHEW THORNE (BM No. 18/4: "The Crime Surgeon!"); and the Dynamic Duo spend a day answering calls with the police emergency squad, the first in a series of adventures designed to familiarize the famed crime-fighters and their readers with the activities and operations of "our various police services," those "living, human people who keep a daily vigil to make the United States safe for you and 130,000,000 others!" (BM No. 18/3: "The Good Samaritan Cops").

In September 1943 Batman and Robin apprehend a gang of criminals led by Diamond Pete Ransome and help aspiring actress Judy O'Casson and has-been actor Tremaine Wentworth launch successful careers in the legitimate theater (Det No. 79: "Destiny's Auction!").

In Fall 1943 Batman and Robin match wits with ROB CALLENDER (WF No. 11: "A Thief in Time!").

In October 1943 Batman and Robin battle TWO-FACE (Det No. 80: "The End of Two-Face!").

In October–November 1943 Batman and Robin apprehend the BIG BEN ROLLING gang (BM No. 19/1: "Batman Makes a Deadline!"); battle ADMIRAL VON BURITZ (BM No. 19/2: "Atlantis Goes to War!"); match wits with the JOKER (BM No. 19/3: "The Case of the Timid Lion!"); and smash an elaborate underworld scheme concocted by the ruthless ALI (BM No. 19/4: "Collector of Millionaires").

In November 1943 Batman and Robin meet the CAVALIER (Det No. 81: "The Cavalier of Crime!").

In December 1943 Batman and Robin match wits with BLACKIE BLONDEEN (Det No. 82: "Quarterback of Crime!").

In Winter 1943 Batman and Robin apprehend some criminals with the aid of ALFRED (WF No. 12: "Alfred Gets His Man!").

In December 1943–January 1944 Batman and Robin battle the JOKER (BM No. 20/1: "The Centuries of Crime!"); apprehend SLICK FINGERS (BM No. 20/2:

"The Trial of Titus Keyes!"); spend a day and night with the harbor patrol, the second in a series of adventures dealing with the various law-enforcement agencies of the United States (BM No. 20/3: "The Lawmen of the Sea!"); and agonize over the dilemma that confronts them when Bruce Wayne loses legal custody of Dick Grayson (*see* ROBIN) (BM No. 20/4: "Bruce Wayne Loses the Guardianship of Dick Grayson!").

In January 1944 Batman and Robin match wits with DR. GOODWIN (Det No. 83: "Accidentally on Purpose!").

In February 1944 Batman and Robin battle IVAN KRAFFT (Det No. 84: "Artists in Villainy").

In February–March 1944 Batman and Robin apprehend a gang of cattle rustlers led by the evil BRULE (BM No. 21/1: "The Streamlined Rustlers!"); battle the CHOPPER GANT mob (BM No. 21/2: "Blitzkrieg Bandits!"); unravel a complex mystery with the aid of ALFRED (BM No. 21/3: "His Lordship's Double!"); and match wits with the PENGUIN (BM No. 21/4: "The Three Eccentrics!").

In March 1944 Batman and Robin battle the JOKER (Det No. 85: "The Joker's Double").

In Spring 1944 Batman and Robin apprehend SWAMI PRAVHOR (WF No. 13: "The Curse of Isis!").

In April 1944 Batman and Robin match wits with GENTLEMAN JIM JOWELL (Det No. 86: "Danger Strikes Three!").

In April–May 1944 Batman and Robin battle the CATWOMAN (BM No. 22/1: "The Duped Domestics!"); apprehend the "ghost gang" (*see* OPTIK, MIKE) (BM No. 22/2: "Dick Grayson, Telegraph Boy!"); and match wits with the CAVALIER (BM No. 22/3: "The Cavalier Rides Again!").

In May 1944 Batman and Robin battle the PENGUIN (Det No. 87: "The Man of a Thousand Umbrellas").

In June 1944 Batman and Robin apprehend a gang of thugs headed by BIG-HEARTED JOHN (Det No. 88: "The Merchants of Misery!").

In June–July 1944 Batman and Robin match wits with the JOKER (BM No. 23/1: "The Upside Down Crimes!"); battle the BUGS CONKLIN gang (BM No. 23/2: "Damsel in Distress!"); and apprehend the SKINNER SHORT gang with the aid of the Royal Canadian Mounted Police (BM No. 23/3: "Pelt Plunderers!").

In Summer 1944 Batman and Robin battle salvage racketeer JIB BUCKLER (WF No. 14: "Salvage Scavengers!").

In July 1944 Batman and Robin match wits with the CAVALIER (Det No. 89: "Laboratory Loot!").

In August 1944 Batman and Robin apprehend the CAPTAIN BEN gang (Det No. 90: "Crime Between the Acts!").

In August–September 1944 Batman and Robin journey to ancient Rome for a battle with Roman racketeer PUBLIUS MALCHIO (BM No. 24/1: "It Happened in Rome"); match wits with TWEEDLEDUM AND TWEEDLEDEE (BM No. 24/3: "The Mayors of Yonville!"); and, with the aid of the U.S. Coast Guard, apprehend a gang of criminals who have been charging wealthy embezzlers exorbitant sums to smuggle them out of the country by ship, safely beyond the reach of the law, then callously hurling their human cargo overboard as soon as the escape vessel is far out at sea (BM No. 24/2: "Convict Cargo!").

In September 1944 Batman and Robin match wits with the JOKER (Det No. 91: "The Case of the Practical Joker").

In Fall 1944 Batman and Robin apprehend the villainous MENNEKIN (WF No. 15: "The Men Who Died Twice!").

In October 1944 Batman and Robin apprehend BRAINY BULOW (Det No. 92: "Crime's Man-Hunt").

In October–November 1944 Batman and Robin battle the JOKER and the PENGUIN (BM No. 25/1: "Knights of Knavery"), and, with the aid of two linemen employed by the Rocky Dam Light and Power Company, apprehend a gang of criminals who have been hijacking the company's valuable copper wire (BM No. 25/3: "The Kilowatt Cowboys!"). Another text for this period recalls the Dynamic Duo's past encounter with the villainous OMAR EL KOBRA (BM No. 25/2: "The Sheik of Gotham City!").

In November 1944 Batman and Robin apprehend the murderers of gangster "TIGER" RAGLAND (Det No. 93: "One Night of Crime!").

In December 1944 Batman and Robin apprehend confidence men Lefty Goran and Slats Macer (Det No. 94: "No One Must Know!").

In Winter 1944 Batman and Robin apprehend NOCKY JOHNSON (WF No. 16: "The Mountaineers of Crime!").

In December 1944–January 1945 Batman and Robin match wits with the CAVALIER (BM No. 26/1: "Twenty Ton Robbery!") and visit the mysterious LOST MESA pueblo (BM No. 26/3: "Crime Comes to Lost Mesa!"). Another text for this period describes the battle pitting BRANE and his young companion Ricky against the Saturnian warlord Fura (BM No. 26/2: "The Year 3000!").

In January 1945 Batman and Robin match wits with the BLAZE (Det No. 95).

In February 1945 ALFRED sets himself up in business as a private detective (Det No. 96: "Alfred, Private Detective!").

In February–March 1945 Batman and Robin battle the PENGUIN (BM No. 27/1: "The Penguin's New Apprentice!"); locate the hidden fortune of JOHN SVENSON (BM No. 27/2: "Voyage into Villainy!"); and apprehend HAPPY HOGGSBY (BM No. 27/3: "A Christmas Peril!").

In March 1945 Batman and Robin apprehend NICK PETRI (Det No. 97: "The Secret of the Switch!").

In Spring 1945 Batman and Robin match wits with DR. DREEMO (WF No. 17: "Crime Goes to College!").

In April 1945 Batman and Robin lend a helping hand to CASPER THURBRIDGE (Det No. 98: "The King of the Hoboes!").

In April–May 1945 Batman and Robin battle the JOKER (BM No. 28/1: "Shadow City!"); smash an epidemic of "short-confidence rackets" masterminded by MICHAEL STRAIT (BM No. 28/2: "Shirley Holmes, Policewoman!"); and apprehend JOHN SKYE (BM No. 28/3: "Batman Goes to Washington!").

In May 1945 Batman and Robin match wits with the PENGUIN (Det No. 99: "The Temporary Murders!").

In June 1945 Batman and Robin apprehend DIGGES and his band of smugglers (Det No. 100: "The Crow's Nest Mystery!").

In June–July 1945 Batman and Robin match wits with ADAM FRANK (BM No. 29/1: "Enemy No. 1"); apprehend CATSPAW CARLIN (BM No. 29/2: "Heroes by Proxy!"); and battle the SCUTTLER (BM No. 29/3: "The Mails Go Through!").

In Summer 1945 Batman and Robin match wits with PROFESSOR L. M. BRANE (WF No. 18: "Specialists in Crime!").

In July 1945 Batman and Robin apprehend the JOE BART gang (Det No. 101: "The Tyrannical Twins!").

In August 1945 Batman and Robin battle the JOKER (Det No. 102: "The House That was Held for Ransom!").

In August–September 1945 Batman and Robin match wits with the PENGUIN (BM No. 30/1: "Back to the House!"); apprehend the HUSH-HUSH BODIN mob (BM No. 30/2: "While the City Sleeps!"); and meet the vociferous ALLY BABBLE (BM No. 30/3: "Ally Babble and the Fourteen Peeves!").

In September 1945 Batman and Robin meet DEAN GRAY, retired dean of Gotham University (Det No. 103: "Trouble, Incorporated!").

In Fall 1945 Batman and Robin battle the JOKER (WF No. 19: "The League for Larceny!").

In October 1945 Batman and Robin match wits with the FAT FRANK gang (Det No. 104: "The Battle of the Billboards!").

In October–November 1945 Batman and Robin meet PUNCH AND JUDY (BM No. 31/1: "Punch and Judy!"); apprehend KNUCKLES DONEGAN and SLICK (BM No. 31/2: "Vanishing Village!"); and expose MRS. DALLING as a criminal mastermind (BM No. 31/3: "Trade Marks of Crime!").

In November 1945 Batman and Robin apprehend SIMON GURLIN (Det No. 105: "The Batman Goes Broke!").

In December 1945 Batman and Robin battle fanatical bibliophile TODD TORREY (Det No. 106: "The Phantom of the Library!").

In Winter 1945 Batman and Robin match wits with LEW CRONIN (WF No. 20: "King of Coins!").

In December 1945–January 1946 Batman and Robin battle the JOKER (BM No. 32/1: "Rackety-Rax Racket!") and journey into the past to meet the THREE MUSKETEERS (BM No. 32/3: "All for One, One for All!"). Another text for this period recapitulates ROBIN's origin and recalls events that occurred very early in his crime-fighting partnership with Batman (BM No. 32/2: "Dick Grayson, Boy Wonder!").

C. THE POSTWAR ADVENTURES. In January 1946 Batman and Robin match wits with BUGS SCARPIS (Det No. 107: "The Mountain of the Moon!").

In February 1946 Batman and Robin help restore the good name and self-confidence of Ed Gregory, a bright young detective who has been duped by criminals into believing himself responsible for sending an innocent man to the electric chair (Det No. 108: "The Goat of Gotham City!").

In February–March 1946 Batman and Robin battle the PENGUIN (BM No. 33/1: "Crime on the Wing!"); match wits with the JACKAL (BM No. 33/2: "The Looters!"); and help put three bitter old men on the path to brighter, happier lives (BM No. 33/3: "The Search for Santa Claus!").

In March 1946 Batman and Robin battle the JOKER (Det No. 109: "The House That Jokes Built!").

In March–April 1946 Batman and Robin match wits with SAM GARTH (WF No. 21: "Crime's Cameraman!").

In April 1946 Batman and Robin visit London for an encounter with the evil PROFESSOR MORIARTY (Det No. 110: "Batman and Robin in Scotland Yard!").

In April–May 1946 Batman and Robin thwart the machinations of GEORGE KALE (BM No. 34/1: "The Marathon of Menace!"); renew their acquaintance with ALLY BABBLE (BM No. 34/2: "Ally Babble and the Four Tea Leaves!"); and break off an elaborate crime-detecting exercise, in which Robin is given twenty-four hours to locate and "apprehend" Batman, long enough to capture a gang of criminals attempting to hijack a truckload of antiques (BM No. 34/3: "The Master vs. the Pupil!").

In May 1946 Batman and Robin teach a much-needed lesson to mine owner JULIUS REED (Det No. 111: "Coaltown, U.S.A.").

In May–June 1946 Batman and Robin battle NAILS FINNEY (WF No. 22: "A Tree Grows in Gotham City!").

In June 1946 Batman and Robin recall the time they investigated the apparent theft of $99 from the cash register at Papa Brugel's Costume Shop, only to discover that the cash discrepancy was actually the result of customer Bruce Wayne's having been accidentally given a $100 bill instead of a $1 bill as change for a purchase (Det No. 112: "The Case Without a Crime!").

In June–July 1946 Batman and Robin match wits with the CATWOMAN (BM No. 35/1: "Nine Lives Has the Catwoman!"); meet MURRAY WILSON HART, "master showman and specialist in the spectacular" (BM No. 35/2: "Dinosaur Island!"); and lend a helping hand to BIG ED CONROY (BM No. 35/3: "Dick Grayson, Author!").

In July 1946 Batman and Robin battle the oyster racketeer BLACKHAND (Det No. 113: "Crime on the Half-Shell!").

In July–August 1946 Batman and Robin match wits with GOLDPLATE GORNEY (WF No. 23: "Champions Don't Brag!").

In August 1946 Batman and Robin battle the JOKER (Det No. 114: "Acrostic of Crime!").

In August–September 1946 Batman and Robin match wits with the PENGUIN (BM No. 36/1: "The Penguin's Nest!"); meet JERRY MCGLONE (BM No. 36/2: "Stand-In for Danger!"); and journey through the time barrier to the court of the legendary KING ARTHUR (BM No. 36/3: "Sir Batman at King Arthur's Court!").

In September 1946 Batman and Robin apprehend BASIL GRIMES (Det No. 115: "The Man Who Lived in a Glass House!").

In October 1946 Batman and Robin journey into the past for an adventure with ROBIN HOOD (Det No. 116: "The Rescue of Robin Hood!").

In October–November 1946 Batman and Robin apprehend LOU DARRELL (BM No. 37/1: "Calling Dr. Batman!"); thwart the film-theft scheme of Hollywood director E. J. LORING (BM No. 37/2: "Hollywood Hoax!"); and match wits with the JOKER (BM No. 37/3: "The Joker Follows Suit!").

In November 1946 Batman and Robin put an end to the villainous careers of Logan and Red, a pair of unscrupulous steeplejacks who have been working at legitimate jobs for the Skyline Steeplejack Co. by day and then using the company's steeplejack equipment to loot empty office buildings by night (Det No. 117: "Steeplejack's Showdown!").

In November–December 1946 Batman and Robin lend a helping hand to engineer FRANK FOLLAND (WF No. 25: "The Famous First Crimes!").

In December 1946 Batman and Robin match wits with the JOKER (Det No. 118: "The Royal Flush Crimes!").

In December 1946–January 1947 Batman and Robin battle the Persian villain BYRUS in fifth-century B.C. Athens (BM No. 38/1: "Peril in Greece!"); renew their acquaintance with artist PIERRE ANTAL (BM No. 38/2: "The Carbon Copy Crimes!"); and match wits with the PENGUIN (BM No. 38/3: "The Penguin on Parole!").

In January 1947 Batman and Robin apprehend WILEY DEREK (Det No. 119: "The Case of the Famous Foes!").

In January–February 1947 Batman and Robin apprehend the SPARKS FARRELL mob (WF No. 26: "His Highness, Prince Robin!").

In February 1947 Batman and Robin battle the PENGUIN (Det No. 120: "Fowl Play!").

In February–March 1947 Batman and Robin match wits with ROGER RYALL (BM No. 39/1: "The Frightened People!"); meet IRON-HAT FERRIS (BM No. 39/2: "The Man in the Iron Mask!"); and battle the CATWOMAN (BM No. 39/3: "A Christmas Tale!").

In March 1947 Batman and Robin lend a helping hand to POLICE COMMISSIONER GORDON (Det No. 121: "Commissioner Gordon Walks a Beat!").

In March–April 1947 condemned murderer WHEELS MITCHUM recalls his past encounters with Batman and Robin (WF No. 27: "Me, Outlaw!").

In April 1947 Batman and Robin match wits with the CATWOMAN (Det No. 122: "The Black Cat Crimes!").

In April–May 1947 Batman and Robin battle the JOKER (BM No. 40/1: "The 13 Club!"); apprehend the BEETLE BOLES gang and get the goods on HENRY BUSH (BM No. 40/2: "The Case of Batman II"); and investigate a series of grisly murders at the Gotham City Opera (*see* VANNING, COLIN) (BM No. 40/3: "The Grand Opera Murders!").

In May 1947 Batman and Robin apprehend the SHINER (Det No. 123: "The Dawn Patrol Crimes!").

In May–June 1947 Batman and Robin battle the GLASS MAN (WF No. 28: "Crime Under Glass!").

In June 1947 Batman and Robin match wits with the JOKER (Det No. 124: "The Crime Parade").

In June–July 1947 Batman and Robin battle the PENGUIN (BM No. 41/1: "The Bird Cage Bandits!"); apprehend the "MOOSE" MILLER gang (BM No. 41/2: "The Bandits of Tiny Town!"); and journey to Mars for an encounter with the Martian villain SAX GOLA (BM No. 41/3: "Batman, Interplanetary Policeman!").

In July 1947 Batman and Robin match wits with the THINKER, an "arch criminal, whose wasted body houses a restless, writhing brain!" (Det No. 125: "The Citadel of Crime!").

In August 1947 Batman and Robin battle the PENGUIN (Det No. 126: "Case of the Silent Songbirds!").

In August–September 1947 Batman and Robin match wits with the CATWOMAN (BM No. 42/1: "Claws of the Catwoman!"); battle the DUDS NEERY mob (BM No. 42/2: "Blind Man's Bluff!"); and thwart the nefarious schemes of DOCTOR HERCULES (BM No. 42/3: "The Robot Robbers!").

In September 1947 Batman and Robin match wits with DR. AGAR (Det No. 127: "Pigmies in Giantland!").

In September–October 1947 Batman and Robin apprehend JOE COYNE (WF No. 30: "The Penny Plunderers!").

In October 1947 Batman and Robin battle the JOKER (Det No. 128: "Crime in ƎSЯƎVƎЯ !).

In October–November 1947 Batman and Robin match wits with the PENGUIN (BM No. 43/1: "The Blackbird of Banditry!"); battle gangsters JIM BRADY and Al Rorick (BM No. 43/2: "Next Stop – Danger!"); and apprehend MARTIN BAIN (BM No. 43/3: "The Four Horsemen of Crime!").

In November 1947 Batman and Robin apprehend the Diamond Dan mob when they attempt to seize control of the peaceful island town of Goodwinville, where all modern inventions are prohibited and life remains just as it was in the America of the Gay Nineties (Det No. 129: "The Isle of Yesterday!").

In November–December 1947 Batman and Robin meet wartime aerial ace EDDIE BRAND (WF No. 31: "The Man with the X-Ray Eyes!").

In December 1947–January 1948 Batman and Robin match wits with the JOKER (BM No. 44/1: "Gamble with Doom!"); battle the GLOBETROTTER (BM No. 44/2: "Born for Adventure!"); and journey into the past, to Philadelphia in the year 1787, for a meeting with SILAS WAYNE (BM No. 44/3: "The First American Detective!").

In January 1948 Batman and Robin battle "TRIGGER JOE" TRAVERS (Det No. 131: "The Underworld Surgeon!").

A text for January–February 1948 relates the story of Batman and Robin's encounter with the villainous LUCKY STARR (WF No. 32: "The Man Who Could Not Die!").

In February 1948 Batman and Robin meet the HUMAN KEY (Det No. 132: "The Human Key!").

In February–March 1948 Batman and Robin match wits with the CATWOMAN (BM No. 45/1: "The Lady Rogues!"); lend a helping hand to EDDIE ROGERS (BM

No. 45/2: "A Parole for Christmas!"); and apprehend the MATCH (BM No. 45/3: "The Match!").

In March 1948 Batman and Robin meet ARTHUR LOOM (Det No. 133: "The Man Who Could See the Future!").

In March–April 1948 Batman and Robin match wits with JAMES HARMON (WF No. 33: "The 5 Jewels of Doom!").

In April 1948 Batman and Robin battle the PENGUIN (Det No. 134: "The Umbrellas of Crime!").

In April–May 1948 Batman and Robin match wits with the JOKER (BM No. 46/1: "'Guileful Greetings!' or 'The Joker Sends Regrets!'"); quell a convict revolt at Gotham City Prison and establish that the uniquely low rate of recidivism there is due to the ability of the prison's chaplain to inspire his charges with "hope and ambition" (BM No. 46/2: "Big House Chaplain!"); and journey into the past, to fifteenth-century Milan, for an encounter with the world-famed LEONARDO DA VINCI (BM No. 46/3: "The Batman That History Forgot!").

In May 1948 Batman and Robin journey into the past for a meeting with BARON FRANKENSTEIN (Det No. 135: "The True Story of Frankenstein!").

A text for May–June 1948 relates the story of Batman and Robin's encounter with the villainous JIM DURFEE (WF No. 34: "Killer for Hire!").

In June 1948 Batman and Robin journey into the past to meet the pirate HENRY MORGAN (Det No. 136: "The Dead Man's Chest!").

In June–July 1948 Batman and Robin match wits with the CATWOMAN (BM No. 47/1: "Fashions in Crime!"); apprehend WARDEN BELTT (BM No. 47/2: "The Chain Gang Crimes!"); and meet JOE CHILL (BM No. 47/3: "The Origin of Batman!").

In July 1948 Batman and Robin battle the JOKER (Det No. 137: "The Rebus Crimes!").

In July–August 1948 Batman and Robin match wits with the PENGUIN (WF No. 35: "Crime by the Book!").

In August 1948 Batman and Robin battle the JOKER (Det No. 138: "The Invisible Crimes!").

In August–September 1948 Batman and Robin match wits with the PENGUIN (BM No. 48/1: "The Fowls of Fate!"); battle WOLF BRANDO (BM No. 48/2: "The 1,000 Secrets of the Batcave!"); and apprehend MORTON, secretary to the chairman of the "World of the Future" fair (BM No. 48/3: "Crime from Tomorrow!").

In September 1948 Batman and Robin match wits with NICK BAILEY (Det No. 139: "Crimes of Jade!").

In October 1948 Batman and Robin meet the RIDDLER (Det No. 140: "The Riddler").

In October–November 1948 Batman and Robin match wits with the MAD HATTER (BM No. 49/2: "The Scoop of the Century!") and journey to ancient Baghdad to battle the CRIER (BM No. 49/3: "Batman's Arabian Nights!"). Another text for this period tells how, sometime in the recent past, Batman joined forces with Gotham Penitentiary physician Paul Taber to let Death Row inmate Jeff "Nitro" Blake cheat death in the electric chair and escape from the prison as part of an elaborate ruse to trick Blake into leading Batman to $500,000 in unrecovered bank loot (BM No. 49/1: "The Prison Doctor!").

In November 1948 Batman and Robin match wits with CHARLES "BLACKIE" NASON (Det No. 141: "The Gallery of Public Heroes!").

In November–December 1948 Batman and Robin apprehend T-GUN JONES (WF No. 37: "The Underworld's Museum of Crime!").

In December 1948 Batman and Robin battle the RIDDLER (Det No. 142: "Crime's Puzzle Contest!").

In December 1948–January 1949 Batman and Robin apprehend the STILTS TYLER gang (BM No. 50/1: "Lights—Camera—Crime!"); match wits with TWO-FACE (BM No. 50/2: "The Return of Two-Face!"); and battle the GLOVES gang (BM No. 50/3: "The Second Boy Wonder!").

In January 1949 Batman and Robin meet the PIED PIPER (Det No. 143: "The Pied Piper of Peril!").

In February 1949 Batman and Robin match wits with BIG JACK BANCROFT (Det No. 144: "Kay Kyser's Mystery Broadcast!").

In February–March 1949 Batman and Robin battle the PENGUIN (BM No. 51/1: "Pee-Wee, the Talking Penguin!"); match wits with RUFUS LANE (BM No. 51/2: "The Stars of Yesterday!"); and apprehend the WARTS gang (BM No. 51/3: "The Wonderful Mr. Wimble!").

In March 1949 Batman and Robin battle the YELLOW MASK MOB (Det No. 145: "Robin, the Boy Failure!").

In March–April 1949 Batman and Robin match wits with J. J. JASON (WF No. 39: "The Conquest of Batman's Identity!").

In April 1949 Batman and Robin apprehend NUMBERS (Det No. 146: "Three's a Crime!").

In April–May 1949 Batman and Robin battle the THINKER (BM No. 52/1: "The Man with the Automatic Brain!"); journey to tenth-century Norway for a meeting with OLAF ERICKSON (BM No. 52/2: "Batman and the Vikings!"); and match wits with the JOKER (BM No. 52/3: "The Happy Victims!").

In May 1949 Batman and Robin battle TIGER SHARK (Det No. 147: "Tiger Shark!").

In May–June 1949 Batman and Robin launch an intense manhunt for JUMPY PETERS and three other escaped condemned killers, each of whom has been sentenced to a different form of execution in a different part of the country (WF No. 40: "4 Killers Against Fate!").

In June 1949 Batman and Robin match wits with PROFESSOR ZERO (Det No. 148: "The Experiment of Professor Zero").

In June–July 1949 Batman and Robin battle the JOKER (BM No. 53/1: "A Hairpin, a Hoe, a Hacksaw, a Hole in the Ground!"); apprehend FRANK FABIAN (BM No. 53/2: "The Portrait of Doom!"); and meet MR. PHAETON (BM No. 53/3: "Batman Under the Sea!").

In July 1949 Batman and Robin match wits with the JOKER (Det No. 149: "The Sound-Effect Crimes!").

In July–August 1949 Batman and Robin apprehend EDGAR ALBREK (WF No. 41: "The Man with the Fatal Hands!").

In August 1949 Batman and Robin match wits with DR. PAUL VISIO (Det No. 150: "The Ghost of Gotham City!").

In August–September 1949 Batman and Robin battle the TREASURE HUNTER (BM No. 54/1: "The Treasure Hunter!"); meet JOHN DELION (BM No. 54/2: "The Door Without a Key!"); and match wits with JOHN FOSTER (BM No. 54/3: "The Amazing Masquerade!").

In September 1949 Batman and Robin apprehend HOMER DAVIS (Det No. 151: "I.O.U. My Life!").

In September–October 1949 Batman and Robin journey into the distant past for encounters with MARCO POLO and KUBLA KHAN (WF No. 42: "The Amazing Adventure of Batman and Marco Polo!").

In October 1949 Batman and Robin match wits with the GOBLIN (Det No. 152: "The Goblin of Gotham City!").

In October–November 1949 Batman and Robin battle the JOKER (BM No. 55/1: "The Case of the 48 Jokers!"); apprehend the LONGSHOREMAN KID (BM No. 55/2: "Bruce Wayne, Rookie Policeman!"); and match wits with the GONG (BM No. 55/3: "The Bandit of the Bells!").

In November 1949 Batman and Robin apprehend SLITS DANTON (Det No. 153: "The Flying Batman!").

In December 1949 Batman and Robin apprehend HATCH MARLIN (Det No. 154: "Underground Railroad of Crime!").

In December 1949–January 1950 Batman and Robin match wits with COUNT FLORIAN (WF No. 43: "The Man with a Thousand Eyes!"); apprehend EL PAPAGAYO (BM No. 56/1: "Ride, Bat-Hombre, Ride!"); battle the PENGUIN (BM No. 56/2: "The Riddle of the Seven Birds!"); and capture "SPECS" ROSE (BM No. 56/3: "A Greater Detective Than Batman!").

In January 1950 VICKI VALE talks Bruce Wayne into putting in a temporary stint as a private detective (Det No. 155: "Bruce Wayne, Private Detective!").

In February 1950 Batman and Robin apprehend SMILEY DIX (Det No. 156: "The Batmobile of 1950!").

In February–March 1950 Batman and Robin match wits with JACQUES VENTA (WF No. 44: "The Confession of Batman!"); outwit ED KOLUM (BM No. 57/1: "The Trial of Bruce Wayne!"); apprehend ANDREWS (BM No. 57/2: "The Walking Mummy!"); and battle the JOKER (BM No. 57/3: "The Funny Man Crimes!").

In March 1950 Batman and Robin match wits with BART GILLIS (Det No. 157: "The Race of the Century").

In April 1950 Batman and Robin battle DR. DOOM (Det No. 158: "The Thousand and One Trophies of Batman!").

In April–May 1950 Batman and Robin apprehend HECTOR SIMMONS (WF No. 45: "The Historian of Crime!"); match wits with the PENGUIN (BM No. 58/1: "The State-Bird Crimes!"); journey into the past, to 1850s California, for an encounter with JOAQUÍN MURIETA (BM No. 58/2: "The Brand of a Hero!"); and battle the BLACK DIAMOND (BM No. 58/3: "The Black Diamond!").

In May 1950 Batman and Robin match wits with T. WORTHINGTON CHUBB (Det No. 159: "Bruce Wayne – You Are Batman!").

In June 1950 three law-enforcement officers from around the world recount the story of Batman and Robin's encounter with the Globe-Trotter (*see* GLOBE-TROTTER, THE [HENRY GUILE III]) (Det No. 160: "The Globe-Trotter of Crime!").

In June–July 1950 Batman and Robin match wits with CHARLEY STARK (WF No. 46: "Bruce Wayne, Riveter!"); thwart the machinations of DEADSHOT (BM No. 59/1: "The Man Who Replaced Batman!"); get the goods on PROFESSOR VINCENT (BM No. 59/2: "The Forbidden Cellar!"); and, after apprehending THE JOKER, journey 100 years into the future for an encounter with the evil ERKHAM (BM No. 59/3: "Batman in the Future!").

In July 1950 Batman and Robin match wits with BILL WATERS (Det No. 161: "The Men Who Died on Time!").

In August 1950 Batman and Robin accompany a railroad policeman on his accustomed beat to enable Robin to acquire firsthand knowledge of the duties and activities of the railroad protective association (Det No. 162: "The Law of the Iron Road!").

In August–September 1950 Batman and Robin battle the ACE RADKO mob (WF No. 47: "Crime Above the Clouds!"); apprehend the SMITHERS gang (BM No. 60/1: "Crime Through the Ages!"); match wits with "SHARK" MARLIN (BM No. 60/2: "The Counterfeit Batman!"); and meet LUCKY HOOTON (BM No. 60/3: "The Auto Circus Mystery!").

In September 1950 Batman and Robin battle SLIPPERY JIM ELGIN (Det No. 163: "The Man Who Feared Metal!").

In October 1950 Batman helps ace crime reporter Dave Purdy apprehend TIGER BISHOP, "one of the coldest killers in the history of crime!" (Det No. 164: "Untold Tales of the Bat-Signal!").

In October–November 1950 Batman and Robin match wits with the JOKER (WF No. 48: "Song of Crime!"); apprehend the BOLEY BROTHERS (BM No. 61/1: "The Birth of Batplane II!"); battle the PENGUIN (BM No. 61/2: "The Mystery of the Winged People!"); and get the goods on DOCTOR CHUBB (BM No. 61/3: "The Wheelchair Crimefighter!").

In November 1950 Batman and Robin battle DR. ROBERT DARCY (Det No. 165: "The Strange Costumes of Batman!").

In December 1950 Batman and Robin lend a helping hand to JOHN GILLEN, "the man with a million faces" (Det No. 166: "The Man with a Million Faces!").

In December 1950–January 1951 Batman and Robin match wits with the PENGUIN (WF No. 49: "A White Feather for Batman!"); learn the origin of the CATWOMAN (BM No. 62/1: "The Secret Life of the Catwoman"); journey to England to battle gangster MATT THORNE (BM No. 62/2: "The Batman of England!"); and apprehend PORTER WEST (BM No. 62/3: "The Mystery of Millionaire Island!").

In January 1951 Batman and Robin journey to ancient Egypt to meet the legendary CLEOPATRA (Det No. 167: "Bodyguards to Cleopatra!").

In February 1951 Batman and Robin encounter the JOKER (Det No. 168: "The Man Behind the Red Hood!").

In February–March 1951 Batman and Robin apprehend JOE FLINT (WF No. 50: "Bullet-Hole Club!"); match wits with the JOKER (BM No. 63/1: "The Joker's Crime Costumes!"); battle EROBT and his henchmen (BM No. 63/2: "The Case of the Flying Saucers"); and meet KILLER MOTH (BM No. 63/3: "The Origin of Killer Moth!").

In March 1951 Batman and Robin match wits with JOHN "SQUINT" TOLMAR (Det No. 169: "Batman--Boss of the Big House!").

In April 1951, aided by the U.S. Navy and Coast Guard, Batman and Robin apprehend a gang of modern-day pirates who have been preying on merchant shipping (Det No. 170: "The Flying Dutchman II!").

In April–May 1951 Batman and Robin match wits with BOSTON BURNS (WF No. 51: "The Academy for Gangsters!"); apprehend GREGORY BOTA (BM No. 64/1: "The Candid Camera Killer!"); battle the NINE OLD MEN (BM No. 64/2: "The Forgotten Men of Crime!"); and thwart the evil machinations of KILLER MOTH (BM No. 64/3: "The Return of Killer Moth!").

In May 1951 Batman and Robin match wits with the PENGUIN (Det No. 171: "The Menace of the Giant Birds!").

In June 1951 Batman and Robin meet PAUL GREGORIAN (Det No. 172: "The Outlaw Who Had Nine Lives!").

In June-July 1951 Batman and Robin become embroiled in an adventure involving the INSURANCE CLUB (WF No. 52: "The $1,000,000 Star Club!"); meet WINGMAN (BM No. 65/1: "A Partner for Batman!"); battle the Artisans (*see* THORPE, JACK "FIVE STAR") (BM No. 65/2: "Bruce Wayne – Crime Reporter!"); and match wits with the CATWOMAN (BM No. 65/3: "Catwoman – Empress of the Underworld").

In July 1951 Batman and Robin battle KILLER MOTH (Det No. 173: "Batman's Double!").

In August 1951 Batman and Robin match wits with the DAGGER (Det No. 174: "The Park Avenue Kid!").

In August–September 1951 Batman and Robin work to safeguard the life of POLICE COMMISSIONER GORDON (WF No. 53: "The Private Life of Commissioner Gordon!"); battle the JOKER (BM No. 66/1: "The Joker's Comedy of Errors!"); match wits with GRIFFIN BALFOR (BM No. 66/2: "The Movie Stars Who Died Twice!"); and apprehend the Foxy Fenton gang (BM No. 66/3: "Batman II and Robin, Junior!").

In September 1951 Batman and Robin close down KANGAROO KILEY's underworld bank (Det No. 175: "The Underworld Bank!").

In October 1951 Batman and Robin match wits with MR. VELVET (Det No. 176: "The Underworld Crime Committee!").

In October–November 1951 Batman and Robin rescue PETER DODSON (WF No. 54: "The Carbon Copy Batman!"); apprehend JINX BOLEY (BM No. 67/1: "The Mystery Rope!"); battle the JOKER (BM No. 67/2: "The Man Who Wrote the Joker's Jokes!"); and meet BRANE TAYLOR (BM No. 67/3: "The Lost Legion of Space").

In November 1951 Batman and Robin investigate a series of mysterious thefts in the batcave and apprehend MONROE PEEL (Det No. 177: "The Robberies in the Bat-Cave!").

In December 1951 Batman and Robin battle BARTON SWANE (Det No. 178: "The Defeat of Batman!").

In December 1951–January 1952 Batman and Robin match wits with the PENGUIN (WF No. 55: "The Bird Sayings Crimes!"); apprehend LONGHORN BELL (BM No. 68/1: "The Atom Cave Raiders!"); outwit Slippery Willie Willis (*see* ALFRED) (BM No. 68/2: "The Secret Life of Batman's Butler!"); and battle TWO-FACE (BM No. 68/3: "The New Crimes of Two-Face!").

In January 1952 Batman and Robin match wits with confidence man DEUCE CHALMERS (Det No. 179: "Mayor Bruce Wayne!").

In January–February 1952 Batman and Robin battle BIG DAN HOOKER (WF No. 56: "The Crimes in Double").

In February 1952 Batman and Robin match wits with the JOKER (Det No. 180: "The Joker's Millions!").

In February–March 1952 Batman and Robin apprehend W. W. HAMMOND (BM No. 69/1: "The Batman Exposé!"); battle JIM GARTH (BM No. 69/2: "The Buttons of Doom!"); and match wits with the KING OF THE CATS (BM No. 69/3: "The King of the Cats!").

In March 1952 Batman and Robin meet the HUMAN MAGNET (Det No. 181: "The Crimes of the Human Magnet!").

In March–April 1952 Batman and Robin battle the KINGPIN (WF No. 57: "Public Enemy Bruce Wayne!").

In April 1952 Batman and Robin match wits with MAESTRO DORN (Det No. 182: "The Human Puppets").

In April–May 1952 Batman and Robin meet MR. WEIR and apprehend the "Barker" Dawes gang (BM No. 70/1: "The Robot Cop of Gotham City"); close down the ACADEMY (BM No. 70/2: "The Masterminds of Crime!"); and battle the PENGUIN (BM No. 70/3: "The Parasols of Plunder").

In May 1952 Batman and Robin match wits with JOHN COOK (Det No. 183: "Famous Names Crimes!").

In May–June 1952 Batman and Robin thwart the twisted vengeance of ROGER J. KEEP (WF No. 58: "The Murder of Bruce Wayne!"), and Batman and Superman apprehend JOHN SMILTER (S No. 76/1: "The Mightiest Team in the World!").

In June 1952 Batman and Robin battle the Firefly (*see* FIREFLY, THE [GARFIELD LYNNS]) (Det No. 184: "The Human Firefly!").

In June–July 1952 Batman and Robin apprehend SCAR BRINK (BM No. 71/1: "The Jail for Heroes!"); match wits with the MASKED MYSTIC (BM No. 71/2: Commissioner Gordon's Greatest Case!"); and battle the bizarre MR. CIPHER (BM No. 71/3: "The Mask of Mr. Cipher!").

A text for July 1952 tells of a recent occasion when Batman accidentally lost his utility belt, relating the belt's strange odyssey as it passes from hand to hand, affecting and often saving the lives of the people who come into possession of it, until Batman and Robin succeed finally in recovering it (Det No. 185: "The Secret of Batman's Utility Belt!").

In July–August 1952 Batman and Robin battle the JOKER (WF No. 59: "The Joker's Aces!").

In August 1952 Batman and Robin match wits with DIAMOND LANG (Det No. 186: "The Flying Bat-Cave!").

In August–September 1952 Batman and Robin find themselves pitted against the SINISTER 8 (BM No. 72/1: "The Jungle Batman!"); apprehend BIFF (BM No. 72/2: "The Legion of Faceless Men!"); and unravel a mystery involving the DEATH-CHEATERS' CLUB (BM No. 72/3: "The Death-Cheaters of Gotham City!").

In September 1952 Batman and Robin match wits with TWO-FACE (Det No. 187: "The Double Crimes of Two-Face!").

In September–October 1952 Batman and Robin apprehend GLENN FARR (WF No. 60: "The Richest Crook in the World!").

In October 1952 Batman and Robin match wits with WILLIAM MILDEN (Det No. 188: "The Doom in the Bat-Cave!").

In October–November 1952 Batman and Robin meet the RENTER (BM No. 73/1: "Guns for Hire!"); apprehend "KEYS" BENNETT and outwit VICKI VALE (BM No. 73/2: "Vicki Vale's Secret!"); and battle the JOKER (BM No. 73/3: "The Joker's Utility Belt!").

In November 1952 Batman and Robin find themselves pitted against the villainous STYX (Det No. 189: "The Undersea Hideout!").

In November–December 1952 Batman and Robin match wits with the JOKER (WF No. 61: "The Crimes of Batman!").

In December 1952 Batman and Robin meet DR. SAMPSON (Det No. 190: "How to Be the Batman!").

In December 1952–January 1953 Batman and Robin battle the JOKER (BM No. 74/1: "The Crazy Crime Clown!"); apprehend Skid Turkel (*see* ALFRED) (BM No. 74/2: "The Movie That Killed Batman!"); and match wits with HYDRO (BM No. 74/3: "The Water Crimes of Mr. Hydro!").

In January 1953 Batman and Robin meet the EXECUTIONER (Det No. 191: "The Man with a License to Kill!").

In January–February 1953 Batman and Robin battle the BLACK ROGUE (WF No. 62: "Sir Batman and the Black Knight").

In February 1953 Batman and Robin apprehend NAILS RILEY (Det No. 192: "The Phantom Eye of Gotham City").

In February–March 1953 Batman and Robin visit OUTLAW TOWN (BM No. 75/1: "Outlaw Town, U.S.A.!"); meet MR. ROULETTE (BM No. 75/2: "Mr. Roulette's Greatest Gamble"); and battle the gorilla recipient of GEORGE "BOSS" DYKE's transplanted brain (BM No. 75/3: "The Gorilla Boss of Gotham City!").

In March 1953 Batman and Robin match wits with the JOKER (Det No. 193: "The Joker's Journal!").

In March–April 1953 Batman and Robin apprehend BIX GELBY (WF No. 63: "The Crime Capsule!").

In April 1953 Batman and Robin meet SAMMY SABRE (Det No. 194: "The Stolen Bank!").

In April–May 1953 Batman and Robin unravel a mystery at the DANGER CLUB (BM No. 76/1: "The Danger Club!"); battle the PENGUIN (BM No. 76/2: "The Penguin's Fabulous Fowls!"); and match wits with FERRIS HEDRANT (BM No. 76/3: "The Man of 100 Murders").

In May 1953 Batman and Robin meet HUGO MARMON (Det No. 195: "The Original Batman!").

In May–June 1953 Batman and Robin outwit BOLEY WEBB (WF No. 64: "Bruce Wayne . . . Amateur Detective!").

In June 1953 Batman and Robin apprehend FRANK LUMARDI (Det No. 196: "City Without Guns!").

In June–July 1953 Batman and Robin match wits with DR. EDWARD ARVIN (BM No. 77/1: "The Crime Predictor!"); meet TED BLAKELY (BM No. 77/2: "The Secret Star"); and apprehend the "DANCER" KERN mob (BM No. 77/3: "Batman Pounds a Beat!").

In July 1953 Batman and Robin meet the WRECKER (Det No. 197: "The League Against Batman!").

A text for July–August 1953 recounts the events surrounding Batman and Robin's encounter with the BLASTER (WF No. 65: "The Five Different Batmen!").

In August 1953 Batman and Robin travel to Scotland to receive the bequest of ANGUS MCLAUGHLIE (Det No. 198: "The Lord of Batmanor!").

In August–September 1953 Batman and Robin match wits with QUORK (BM No. 78/1: "The Manhunter from Mars!"); apprehend CAPTAIN BARTON (BM No. 78/2: "The Sinister Stamps!"); and battle the LECLERC BROTHERS (BM No. 78/3: "Batman of the Mounties!").

In September 1953 Batman and Robin thwart the schemes of BIG JACK BAKER (Det No. 199: "The Invisible Batman!").

In September–October 1953 Batman and Robin match wits with BRASS HADLEY (WF No. 66: "The Proving Ground for Crime!").

In October 1953 Batman and Robin apprehend BRAND KELDEN (Det No. 200: "Radio Station C-R-I-M-E!").

In October–November 1953 Batman and Robin become embroiled in a complex predicament involving photographer VICKI VALE (BM No. 79/1: "Bride of Batman!"); get the goods on WALTER FRALEY and journey into the past for an encounter with CAPTAIN LIGHTFOOT (BM No. 79/2: "The Batman of Yesterday!"); and battle LARS VEKING, "notorious modern-day pirate" (BM No. 79/3: "Batman---Gang Boss!").

In November 1953 Batman and Robin meet the HUMAN TARGET (Det No. 201: "Human Target!").

In November–December 1953 Batman and Robin match wits with the ZERO (WF No. 67: "The Millionaire Detective!").

In December 1953 Batman and Robin thwart the sinister machinations of JOLLY ROGER (Det No. 202: "Millionaire Island!").

In December 1953–January 1954 Batman and Robin battle the JOKER (BM No. 80/1: "The Joker's Movie Crimes!") and meet ERIC GOLAR (BM No. 80/3: "The Machines of Menace!"). During this same period, while Batman is away in Chicago attending a murder trial, Robin apprehends five criminals in the act of robbing a warehouse (BM No. 80/2: "Dick Grayson's Nightmare!").

In January 1954 Batman and Robin match wits with

the CATWOMAN (Det No. 203: "The Crimes of the Catwoman!").

In January–February 1954 Batman and Robin battle the CRIMESMITH (WF No. 68: "The Secret Weapons of the Crimesmith!").

In February 1954 Batman and Robin thwart the schemes of ODO NEVAL (Det No. 204: "The Man Who Could Live Forever!"); match wits with TWO-FACE (BM No. 81/1: "Two-Face Strikes Again!"); outwit MR. CAMERA (BM No. 81/2: "The Boy Wonder Confesses!"); and battle the PHANTOM BANDIT (BM No. 81/3: "The Phantom Bandit of Gotham City!").

In March 1954 Batman and Robin meet JEREMY COE (Det No. 205: "The Origin of the Bat-Cave!"); battle the GRAVIO family (BM No. 82/1: "The Flying Batman"); match wits with LEW FARNUM (BM No. 82/2: "The Man Who Could Change Fingerprints!"); and thwart the sinister machinations of "DIMPLES" DREW (BM No. 82/3: "The Olympic Games of Crime!").

In March–April 1954 Batman and Robin match wits with TOM BECKETT (WF No. 69: "The Man Who Wanted to Die with Batman!").

In April 1954 Batman and Robin meet the TRAPPER (Det No. 206: "The Trapper of Gotham City!"); battle the "FISH" FRYE gang (BM No. 83/1: "The Duplicate Batman!"); apprehend the opposing factions of a major counterfeiting ring and recover a large store of stolen government currency paper (BM No. 83/2: "The Deep-Sea Diver Mystery!"); and match wits with rackets boss "HATCHET" MARLEY (BM No. 83/3: "The Testing of Batman!").

In May 1954 Batman and Robin meet MERKO THE GREAT (Det No. 207: "Batman the Magician!").

In May-June 1954 Batman and Robin apprehend JAY VARDEN (WF No. 70: "The Crime Consultant!").

In June 1954 Batman and Robin match wits with GROFF (Det No. 208: "The Nine Worlds of Batman!"); thwart the schemes of the CATWOMAN (BM No. 84/2: "The Sleeping Beauties of Gotham City!"); and apprehend HARRY SHEPHERD (BM No. 84/3: "Ten Nights of Fear!"). During this same period, while trailing thieves who have raided a sugar warehouse, Batman accidentally falls, knocks himself unconscious, and dreams that gigantic bees have enslaved humans through hypnosis and are forcing them to steal vast quantities of sugar for their hive (BM No. 84/1: "The Valley of Giant Bees!").

In July 1954 Batman and Robin match wits with the INVENTOR (Det No. 209: "The Man Who Shadowed Batman!").

In July–August 1954 Batman and Robin join forces with Superman to apprehend a gang of criminals and prevent LOIS LANE from learning the secret of Superman's identity (WF No. 71: "Batman — Double for Superman!").

In August 1954 Batman and Robin smash an underworld plot revolving around executed criminal "BRAIN" HOBSON (Det No. 210: "The Brain That Ruled Gotham City!"); battle the JOKER (BM No. 85/1: "Batman — Clown of Crime!"); meet SGT. HARVEY HAINER (BM No. 85/2: "The Guardian of the Bat-Signal!"); and apprehend HUBERT HALL (BM No. 85/3: "The Costume of Doom!").

In September 1954 Batman and Robin thwart the schemes of the CATWOMAN (Det No. 211: "The Jungle Cat-Queen!"); apprehend the "SLANT" STACY gang (BM No. 86/1: "The Voyage of the First Batmarine!"); battle the JOKER (BM No. 86/2: "The Joker's Winning Team!"); and meet CHIEF MAN-OF-THE-BATS (BM No. 86/3: "Batman--Indian Chief!").

In September–October 1954 Batman and Robin match wits with the HEAVY WEAPONS GANG (WF No. 72: "Fort Crime!").

In October 1954 Batman and Robin meet JONATHAN BARD (Det No. 212: "The Puppet-Master!"); thwart the schemes of the JOKER (BM No. 87/1: "Batman's Greatest Thrills!"); apprehend PROFESSOR VILMER (BM No. 87/2: "The Synthetic Crime King!"); and match wits with JACQUES TERLAY (BM No. 87/3: "Batman Falls in Love!").

In November 1954 Batman and Robin meet MIRROR-MAN (Det No. 213: "The Mysterious Mirror-Man!").

In November–December 1954 Batman, Robin, and Superman battle the FANG (WF No. 73: "Batman and Superman, Swamis, Inc!").

In December 1954 Batman and Robin meet HERBERT SMIRT (Det No. 214: "The Batman Encyclopedia"); smash "an international theft-ring" (BM No. 88/1: "The Mystery of the Four Batmen!"); pursue the elusive MR. MYSTERY (BM No. 88/2: "Three Letters to Batman!"); and apprehend BIG JIM GARVER (BM No. 88/3: "The Son of Batman!").

In January 1955 Batman and Robin match wits with "KNOTS" CARDINE (Det No. 215: "The Batmen of All Nations!").

In January–February 1955 Batman, Robin, and Superman help an extraterrestrial youngster stranded on Earth find his way home again (WF No. 74: "The Contest of Heroes!").

In February 1955 Batman and Robin renew their acquaintance with BRANE TAYLOR (Det No. 216: "The Batman of Tomorrow!"); journey into the past for an encounter with CAPTAIN JOHN GORDON (BM No. 89/1: "River Rogues"); match wits with VINCE VARDEN (BM No. 89/2: "The Seven Wonders of the Underworld!"); and receive an unexpected visit from AUNT AGATHA (BM No. 89/3: "Bruce Wayne's Aunt Agatha!").

In March 1955 Batman and Robin meet BARNEY BARROWS (Det No. 217: "The Mental Giant of Gotham City!"); lend a helping hand to DR. PETER DRISCOLL (BM No. 90/1: "The Web of Doom!"); match wits with AL FRAMM (BM No. 90/2: "City of Fantasy!"); and meet BATBOY (BM No. 90/3: "The Adventures of Batboy!").

In March–April 1955 Batman, Robin, and Superman apprehend the PURPLE MASK MOB (WF No. 75: "The New Team of Superman and Robin!").

In April 1955 Batman and Robin meet DR. RICHARD MARSTEN (Det No. 218: "Batman, Junior and Robin, Senior!"); apprehend "SLANT" STAFFORD (BM No. 91/1: "The Living Batplane!"); match wits with BLINKY GROSSET (BM No. 91/2: "Batman's Publicity Agent!"); and thwart the schemes of RAND BLANNING (BM No. 91/3: "The Map of Mystery!").

In May 1955 Batman and Robin battle MARTY MANTEE and his cohorts (Det No. 219: "Gotham City's Strangest Race!").

In May–June 1955 Batman and Robin engage in a contest with Superman (*see* VOHR [PROFESSOR]) (WF No. 76: "When Gotham City Challenged Metropolis!").

In June 1955 Batman and Robin meet two pupils of ROGER BACON (Det No. 220: "The Second 'Batman and Robin' Team!"); thwart the schemes of VINCENT CRAIL (BM No. 92/1: "Fan-Mail of Danger!"); investigate CAL TREMONT (BM No. 92/2: "Batman's Guilty Neighbor!"); and apprehend escaped convict BERT BOWERS with the aid of the brown dog that achieves renown as Bat-Hound (*see* ACE [THE BAT-HOUND]) (BM No. 92/3: "Ace, the Bat-Hound!").

In July 1955 Batman and Robin match wits with PAUL KING (Det No. 221: "The Thousand-and-One Escapes of Batman and Robin!").

In July–August 1955 Batman, Robin, and Superman match wits with PROFESSOR PENDER (WF No. 77: "The Super Bat-Man!").

In August 1955 Batman and Robin lend a helping hand to NED JUDSON (Det No. 222: "The Great Batman Swindle!"); scale MOUNT K-4 (BM No. 93/1: "Journey to the Top of the World!"); baby-sit with the infant son of Bruce Wayne's cousin Jane (BM No. 93/2: "Batman, Baby-Sitter!"); and journey through the time barrier to the Stone Age for an encounter with TIGER MAN (BM No. 93/3: "The Caveman Batman").

In September 1955 Batman and Robin match wits with "BIG JIM" JARREL (Det No. 223: "The Batman Dime-Museum"); apprehend JOHN MARSTIN (BM No. 94/1: "The Sign of the Bat!"); humor ALFRED during his period of amnesia (BM No. 94/2: "The New Batman!"); and smash the racket run by JOHN GOSS (BM No. 94/3: "The Mystery of the Sky Museum!").

In September–October 1955 Batman, Robin, and Superman apprehend the VARREL MOB (WF No. 78: "When Superman's Identity Is Exposed!").

In October 1955 Batman and Robin match wits with "BLAST" VARNER (Det No. 224: "The Batman Machine!"); become embroiled in an adventure involving a spool of wire from the "WIRES" WELKEN case (BM No. 95/2: "The Bat-Train"); and meet mountain minstrel SAM STRONG (BM No. 95/3: "The Ballad of Batman!").

In November 1955 Batman and Robin thwart an attempted jailbreak by JOHN LARROW (Det No. 225: "If I Were Batman!").

In November–December 1955 Batman, Robin, and Superman journey into the distant past for an encounter with the legendary ALADDIN (WF No. 79: "The Three Magicians of Bagdad!").

In December 1955 Batman and Robin receive a mysterious package from HARVEY HARRIS (Det No. 226: "When Batman Was Robin!"); apprehend MAYNE MALAN (BM No. 96/1: "His Majesty, King Batman"); and spend some time responding to fire calls in the batmobile — temporarily renamed the "firemobile" — in order to help Gotham City's fire chief publicize Fire Prevention Week (BM No. 96/3: "The Third Alarm for Batman!"). During this same period, Batman has a run-in with former college classmate JOE DANTON (BM No. 96/2: "Batman's College Days").

In January 1956 Batman and Robin match wits with "LENS" VORDEN (Det No. 227: "The 50 Faces of Batman!").

In January–February 1956 Batman, Robin, and Superman apprehend the MOLE (WF No. 80: "The Super-Newspaper of Gotham City").

In February 1956 Batman and Robin thwart the schemes of SPADE STINSON (Det No. 228: "The Outlaw Batman!"); battle the JOKER (BM No. 97/1: "The Joker Announces Danger"); recapture MARTY KIRK (BM No. 97/2: "Doom on Channel 14"); and lend a helping hand to dog-lover ROSS MILLEN (BM No. 97/3: "The Return of the Bat-Hound!").

In March 1956 Batman and Robin match wits with MART MATHERS (Det No. 229: "The 10,000 Secrets of Batman!"); meet JULES VERNE and defeat SIMAK (BM No. 98/1: "The Return of Mr. Future!"); and apprehend the RACER (BM No. 98/3: "Secret of the Batmobile").

In March–April 1956 Batman, Robin, and Superman meet KA THAR (WF No. 81: "The True History of Superman and Batman!").

In April 1956 Batman and Robin battle the MAD HATTER (Det No. 230: "The Mad Hatter of Gotham City!"); match wits with the PENGUIN (BM No. 99/1: "The Golden Eggs!"); journey into the past to apprehend HARRIS HARPER and meet BAT MASTERSON (BM No. 99/2: "Batman--Frontier Marshal"); and outwit the villainous PARDU (BM No. 99/3: "The Phantom of the Bat-Cave!").

In May 1956 Batman and Robin become embroiled in an adventure with BATMAN, JUNIOR (Det No. 231: "Batman, Junior!").

In May–June 1956 Batman, Robin, and Superman journey into the past for an encounter with the THREE MUSKETEERS (WF No. 82: "The Three Super-Musketeers!").

In June 1956 Batman and Robin match wits with BART DAVIS (Det No. 232: "The Outlaw Who Played Batman!"); visit PLAINVILLE and apprehend the gangster BARSH (BM No. 100/1: "Batmantown, U.S.A."); thwart the schemes of RALPH KIER (BM No. 100/2: "The Hunters of Gotham City"); and meet JEFF KEATING (BM No. 100/3: "The Great Batman Contest").

In July 1956 Batman and Robin meet BATWOMAN (Det No. 233: "The Batwoman").

In August 1956 Batman and Robin apprehend JAY CAIRD (Det No. 234: "Batman and Robin's Greatest Mystery"); match wits with PACK PURDY (BM No. 101/1: "The Vanished Batman"); battle the JAY JANDRON mob (BM No. 101/2: "The Six Strangest Sleuths"); and finally recover a lost bat-cape, blown off Batman's costume in the midst of a hurricane, which, were it to be examined closely by an outsider, would betray the secret of Batman's identity (BM No. 101/3: "The Great Bat-Cape Hunt!").

In September 1956 Batman and Robin pursue LEW MOXON (Det No. 235: "The First Batman!"); apprehend MAYNE MALLOCK (BM No. 102/1: "The House of Batman"); meet BRAND BARTOR (BM No. 102/2: "The Batman from Babylon"); and battle the temporarily deranged actor CARLIN (BM No. 102/3: "The Caveman at Large").

In September–October 1956 Batman, Robin, and Superman apprehend the THAD LINNIS gang (WF No. 84: "The Super-Mystery of Metropolis!").

In October 1956 Batman and Robin match wits with WALLACE WALEY (Det No. 236: "The New-Model Batman!"); apprehend RALPH BELLOWS (BM No. 103/2: "The League of Ex-Convicts"); and recapture an escaped convict with the aid of ACE THE BAT-HOUND (BM No. 103/3: "Bat-Hound, Movie Star!").

In November 1956 a bizarre set of circumstances forces Batman to temporarily dissolve his crime-fighting partnership with ROBIN (Det No. 237: "Search for a New Robin!").

In November–December 1956 Batman, Robin, and Superman meet the lovely PRINCESS VARINA (WF No. 85: "The Super-Rivals!").

In December 1956 Batman and Robin escape the terrible vengeance of CHECKMATE (Det No. 238: "The Doors That Hid Disaster!"); apprehend a ruthless "mobster czar" with the aid of ALFRED (BM No. 104/1: "The Man Who Knew Batman's Secret!); and expose the villainy of DEVOE (BM No. 104/3: "The Creature from 20,000 Fathoms!"). During this same period, Robin single-handedly apprehends "SPARKLES" GRADY (BM No. 104/2: "Robin's 50 Batman Partners").

d. THE LATER ADVENTURES. In January 1957 Batman and Robin match wits with the villain DALL (Det No. 239: "Batman's Robot Twin!").

In January–February 1957 Batman, Robin, and Superman appear at the Gotham Police Show at the behest of POLICE COMMISSIONER GORDON (WF No. 86: "The Super-Show of Gotham City").

In February 1957 Batman and Robin match wits with BURT WEVER (Det No. 240: "The Outlaw Batman!"); apprehend a gang of thieves with the aid of BATWOMAN (BM No. 105/1: "The Challenge of Batwoman!"); and battle fugitive mobster "GUNNER" THARP (BM No. 105/3: "The Mysterious Bat-Missile"). During this same period, ROBIN temporarily assumes a new identity in an effort to prove that his skill at disguises is as great as Batman's (BM No. 105/2: "The Second Boy Wonder!").

In March 1957 Batman and Robin battle the KEENE HARNER gang (BM No. 106/2: "Storm Over Gotham City!") and match wits with GUY GRANEY (BM No. 106/3: "The Puppet Batman!"). During this same period, after Dick Grayson has injured his left arm while rescuing a young girl about to be run over by an automobile, Batman begins wearing a series of brightly colored Batman costumes in a wide array of vivid colors – red, pale blue, gold, orange, green, black and white, and rainbow-striped – whenever he and Robin appear in public so that onlookers will be too distracted by his own dazzling costumes to notice that Robin, like Dick Grayson, has an injured left arm and thus deduce that Dick Grayson is secretly Robin (Det No. 241: "The Rainbow Batman!").

In March–April 1957 Superman narrates the story of a past encounter that he, Batman, and Robin had with the villainous ELTON CRAIG (WF No. 87: "The Reversed Heroes!").

In April 1957 Batman and Robin match wits with BRAINY WALKER (Det No. 242: "The Underworld Bat-Cave!"); apprehend BEN KEEFE (BM No. 107/2: "Robin Falls in Love"); and battle the DAREDEVILS (BM No. 107/3: "The Grown-Up Boy Wonder!").

In May 1957 Batman and Robin defeat JAY VANNEY (Det No. 243: "Batman the Giant!").

In May–June 1957 Batman, Robin, and Superman match wits with Lex Luthor and the JOKER (WF No. 88: "Superman's and Batman's Greatest Foes!").

In June 1957 Batman and Robin battle the JAY GARRIS mob and recall Batman's early meeting with LEE COLLINS (Det No. 244: "The 100 Batarangs of Batman!"); match wits with JOE HARMON (BM No. 108/1: "The Big Batman Quiz"); rescue JOHN RODDY (BM No. 108/2: "Prisoners of the Bat-Cave"); and become embroiled in an adventure with young BATMAN JONES (BM No. 108/3: "The Career of Batman Jones!").

In July 1957 Batman and Robin smash a crook-smuggling ring with the aid of POLICE COMMISSIONER GORDON (Det No. 245: "The Dynamic Trio!").

In July–August 1957 Batman, Robin, and Superman become embroiled in an adventure involving the amazing LIGHTNING-MAN (WF No. 89: "The Club of Heroes!").

In August 1957 Batman and Robin investigate the murder of JAMES BARHAM (Det No. 246: "Murder at Mystery Castle!"); match wits with the villainous BAGLEY (BM No. 109/1: "Three Crimes Against Batman"); and apprehend "criminal-scientist" CURT MATHIS (BM No. 109/3: "The 1,000 Inventions of Batman!").

In September 1957 Batman and Robin match wits with PROFESSOR MILO (Det No. 247: "The Man Who Ended Batman's Career!"); battle the JOKER (BM No. 110/1: "Crime-of-the-Month Club!"); calm the fears of ALFRED, who believes that he has unwittingly betrayed the secret of Batman's identity (BM No. 110/2: "The Secret of Batman's Butler"); and apprehend the LEN LANDERS mob (BM No. 110/3: "The Phantom Batman!").

In September–October 1957 Batman, Robin, and Superman find themselves forced to cope with a super-powered BATWOMAN (WF No. 90: "The Super-Batwoman!").

In October 1957 Batman and Robin smash an international ring of radium and platinum thieves and recover the supply of sorely needed "miracle drug" the thieves have inadvertently stolen from Gotham Hospital (Det No. 248: "Around the World in 8 Days!"); apprehend ALEC JUDSON (BM No. 111/1: "The Gotham City Safari"); meet BRUCE N. WAYNE (BM No. 111/2: "The Other Bruce Wayne"); and recover a supply of "radioactive atomic fuel" stolen from the Gotham Scientific Foundation (*see* GRAEME, BLAIR) (BM No. 111/3: "The Armored Batman!").

In November 1957, with Bruce Wayne on Death Row facing imminent execution, Batwoman joins forces with Robin to apprehend the COLLECTOR (Det No. 249: "The Crime of Bruce Wayne!").

In November–December 1957 Batman, Robin, and Superman apprehend RICK HARBEN and match wits with ROHTUL (WF No. 91: "The Three Super-Sleepers!").

In December 1957 Batman and Robin thwart the schemes of JOHN STANNAR (Det No. 250: "Batman's Super-Enemy!"); meet SIGNALMAN (BM No. 112/1: "The Signalman of Crime"); journey to ancient Rome to rescue PROFESSOR CARTER NICHOLS (BM No. 112/2: "Batman's Roman Holiday!"); and thwart the vengeful machinations of "renegade scientist" PROFESSOR MILO (BM No. 112/3: "Am I Really Batman?").

In January 1958 Batman and Robin apprehend BRAND BALLARD (Det No. 251: "The Alien Batman!").

In January–February 1958 Batman, Robin, and Superman meet SKYBOY (WF No. 92: "The Boy from Outer Space!").

In February 1958 Batman and Robin lend a helping hand to film producer CORY BLANE (Det No. 252: "The Creature from the Green Lagoon!"); match wits with FALSE FACE (BM No. 113/1: "The Menace of False Face"); and meet FATMAN (BM No. 113/2: "Batman Meets Fatman"). During this same period Batman is transported to the far-distant planet Zur-en-arrh for an encounter with the alien crime-fighter TLANO (BM No. 113/3: "Batman--The Superman of Planet X!").

In March 1958 Batman and Robin battle the TERRIBLE TRIO (Det No. 253: "The Fox, the Shark, and the Vulture!"); match wits with the MIRAGE MAKER (BM No. 114/2: "The Mirage Maker"); and apprehend RALPH RODER (BM No. 114/3: "The Bat-Ape!").

In March–April 1958 Batman, Robin, and Superman thwart the schemes of VICTOR DANNING (WF No. 93: "The Boss of Batman and Superman").

In April 1958 Batman and Robin meet PROFESSOR DI PINA (Det No. 254: "One Ounce of Doom!"); match wits with the PHANTOM BANK BANDIT (BM No. 115/2: "Batman for Hire"); and journey through the time barrier to the Middle East *ca.* 700 A.D. for an encounter with TANG, chief of the Zotos (BM No. 115/3: "Batman in the Bottle!").

In May 1958 Batman and Robin investigate the murder of PROFESSOR HALE and apprehend FINGERS NOLAN (Det No. 255: "Death in Dinosaur Hall!").

In May–June 1958 Batman, Robin, and Superman battle the villainous LEX LUTHOR (WF No. 94: "The Origin of the Superman-Batman Team!").

In June 1958 Batman and Robin journey to the planet TORA (Det No. 256: "The Captive Planet!"); battle the FUNNY FACE GANG (BM No. 116/2: "Batwoman's New Identity"); and meet the BAT-PEOPLE (BM No. 116/3: "The Winged Bat-People!").

In July 1958 Batman and Robin match wits with KARKO (Det No. 257: "Batman's Invincible Foe!").

In July–August 1958 Batman, Robin, and Superman fall under the baleful influence of a pair of aliens from the planet XLYM (WF No. 95: "The Battle of the Super-Heroes!").

In August 1958 Batman and Robin match wits with BARTOK (Det No. 258: "Prisoners of the Giant Robots!"); battle the Red Gloves Gang (*see* CARSON, BENNETT) (BM No. 117/1: "The Mystery of the Batman Bus"); and thwart the schemes of "the notorious space raider" GARR (BM No. 117/3: "Manhunt in Outer Space!").

In September 1958 Batman and Robin meet CALENDAR MAN (Det No. 259: "The Challenge of the Calendar Man"); apprehend GAVIN (BM No. 118/1: "The Battle of Police Island!"); match wits with CARL SMARTE (BM No. 118/3: "The Merman Batman!"); and, with Superman's assistance, lend a helping hand to a band of extraterrestrial aliens who have journeyed to the planet Earth (WF No. 96: "The Super-Foes from Planet X").

In October 1958 Batwoman and VICKI VALE vie for the honor of becoming Gotham City's Woman of the Year (BM No. 119/1: "The Arch-Rivals of Gotham City"); Batman and Robin meet A. K. BARNABY (BM No. 119/2: "The Secret of Batman Island!"); Robin apprehends AL HACKETT (BM No. 119/3: "Rip Van Batman!"); and Batman, Robin, and Superman battle the CONDOR GANG (WF No. 97: "The Day Superman Betrayed Batman!"). During this same period, after having been transported to an "olympic asteroid" in outer space to represent Earth in the Universal Olympics, Batman and Robin thwart an elaborate scheme by the representatives of Pluto to humiliate and discredit the representatives of Venus and thereby make inroads into the Venusians' lucrative interplanetary trade (Det No. 260: "The Mystery of the Space Olympics").

In November 1958 Batman and Robin battle the amazing DOUBLE X (Det No. 261: "The Amazing Dr. Double X!").

In December 1958 Batman and Robin match wits with JACKAL-HEAD (Det No. 262: "The Jackal of the Underworld!"); concoct an elaborate scheme to lighten the last remaining days of Bruce Wayne's great-uncle SILAS WAYNE (BM No. 120/2: "The Failure of Bruce Wayne"); and, with Superman's help, battle the MOONMAN (WF No. 98: "The Menace of the Moonman!"). During this same period, after Batman has broken both his legs while protecting a circus crowd from a charging elephant, the Dynamic Duo fight crime from the air, using their one-man helicopter units, the so-called whirly-bats, to move about from place to place until finally it is time to remove Batman's leg casts so that he can fight crime on the ground again (BM No. 120/3: "The Airborne Batman!").

In January 1959 Batman and Robin match wits with a "master criminal" referred to only as PROFESSOR (Det No. 263: "The Secret of the Fantastic Weapons!").

In February 1959 Batman and Robin investigate the murder of CHARLES BARDEN (Det No. 264: "Peril at Playland Isle!"); probe the mysterious death of ALEC WYRE (BM No. 121/1: "The Body in the Bat-Cave"); accompany a railroad policeman on his daily rounds to help familiarize themselves with the work of the railroad police (BM No. 121/2: "Crime Rides the Rails"); match wits with MR. ZERO (BM No. 121/3: "The Ice Crimes of Mr. Zero!"); and, with Superman, become embroiled in an adventure involving the bizarre last will and testament of eccentric millionaire CARL VERRIL (WF No. 99: "Batman's Super-Spending Spree!").

In March 1959 Batman and Robin match wits with the CLOCK (Det No. 265: "Batman's First Case!"); apprehend HIJACK (BM No. 122/2: "The Cross-Country Crimes!"); and, with the help of Superman, battle LEX LUTHOR (WF No. 100: "The Dictator of Krypton City!"). During this same period, Dick Grayson dreams a disturbing dream in which Bruce Wayne marries Kathy Kane (*see* ROBIN) (BM No. 122/3: "The Marriage of Batman and Batwoman!").

In April 1959 Batman and Robin meet ASTRO (Det No. 266: "The Satellite of Gotham City!"); battle the JOKER (BM No. 123/2: "The Joker's Practical Jokes!); and match wits with the RED MASK MOB (BM No. 123/3: "The Fugitive Batman!").

In May 1959 Batman and Robin meet BAT-MITE (Det No. 267: "Batman Meets Bat-Mite!") and, with Superman's help, battle the ATOM-MASTER (WF No. 101: "The Menace of the Atom-Master!").

In June 1959 Batman and Robin apprehend the "BIG JOE" FOSTER gang (Det No. 268: "The Power That Doomed Batman!"); match wits with SIGNALMAN (BM No. 124/2: "The Return of Signalman"); successfully destroy three dangerous podlike objects which invade Earth from outer space (BM No. 124/3: "The Mystery Seeds from Space!"); and, with Superman's help, battle the JO-JO GROFF gang (WF No. 102: "The Caveman from Krypton!"). During this same period, Batman is forced to suffer through a period of temporary invisibility when he is accidentally subjected to the bizarre ray-emissions of an experimental device in the laboratories of the Aladdin Lamp Company in Gotham City. Ultimately, however, Batman's invisibility wears off and he returns to normal once again (BM No. 124/1: "The Invisible Batman").

In July 1959 Batman and Robin meet the DIRECTOR (Det No. 269: "The Thousand Deaths of Batman!").

In August 1959 Batman and Robin thwart the schemes of BART TRAVERS (Det No. 270: "The Creature from Planet X!"); are sent into the past by PROFESSOR CARTER NICHOLS (BM No. 125/2: "The Last Days of Batman"); journey to the extradimensional planet PLAXIUS (BM No. 125/3: "King Batman the First!"); and, together with Superman, match wits with ATKINS and Bork (WF No. 103: "The Secret of the Sorcerer's Treasure!"). During this same period, Ace the Bat-Hound recalls the events surrounding Batman and Robin's battle with MR. MIDAS (BM No. 125/1: "The Secret Life of Bat-Hound").

In September 1959 Batman and Robin meet the CRIMSON KNIGHT (Det No. 271: "Batman's Armored Rival!"); apprehend the BRADY BROTHERS (BM No. 126/1: "The Mystery of the 49th Star"); match wits with the Firefly (see FIREFLY, THE [TED CARSON]) (BM No. 126/3: "The Menace of the Firefly!"); and, together with Superman, thwart the schemes of LEX LUTHOR (WF No. 104: "The Plot to Destroy Superman!").

In October 1959 Batman and Robin encounter an incredible "crystal creature" (*see* CRYSTAL CREATURE, THE) (Det No. 272: "The Crystal Creature"); battle the JOKER (BM No. 127/1: "Batman's Super-Partner"); test a new machine invented by PROFESSOR CARTER NICHOLS (BM No. 127/2: "The Second Life of Batman"); and meet HENRY MEKE (BM No. 127/3: "The Hammer of Thor!").

In November 1959 Batman, Robin, and Superman match wits with the evil KHALEX (WF No. 105: "The Alien Superman!"), and Police Commissioner Gordon relates the story of Batman and Robin's battle with the DRAGON SOCIETY to graduates of the Gotham City Police Academy (Det No. 273: "Secret of the Dragon Society!").

In December 1959 Batman and Robin match wits with NAILS LEWIN (Det No. 274: "The Hermit of Mystery Island!"); battle the "space pirate" KRAAK (BM No. 128/1: "The Interplanetary Batman!"); apprehend HILLERY (BM No. 128/2: "The Million Dollar Puzzle"); thwart the schemes of BARON KARL (BM No. 128/3: "The Batman Baby"); and, with the help of Superman, defeat the DUPLICATE MAN (WF No. 106: "The Duplicate Man!").

In January 1960 Batman and Robin meet the ZEBRA-MAN (Det No. 275: "The Zebra Batman!").

In February 1960 Batman and Robin cope with the mischievous antics of BAT-MITE (Det No. 276: "The Return of Bat-Mite!"); battle the SPINNER (BM No. 129/1: "The Web of the Spinner!"); apprehend the ART COLBY gang (BM No. 129/2: "The Man from Robin's Past"); and, together with Superman, annihilate an awesomely destructive "creature of energy" spawned by the "alien gases" of a "strange fireball" from outer space (WF No. 107: "The Secret of the Time Creature!").

In March 1960 Batman and Robin battle the extraterrestrial creature known as the "kraal" (*see* KRAAL) (Det No. 277: "The Jigsaw Menace From Space"); apprehend GRAHAM (BM No. 130/2: "The Master of Weapons"); match wits with LEX LUTHOR (BM No. 130/3: "The Hand from Nowhere!"); and, together with Superman, meet an alien movie producer from the planet KZOTL (WF No. 108: "The Star Creatures!").

In April 1960 Batman and Robin match wits with PROFESSOR SIMMS (Det No. 278: "The Man Who Became a Giant!"); cope with the dilemma posed by Bat-Hound's amnesia (*see* ACE [THE BAT-HOUND]) (BM No. 131/1: "The Dog That Betrayed Batman"); and investigate the murder of CLAYBER (BM No. 131/2: "The Case of the Deadly Gems"). During this same period, ALFRED composes his first "imaginary tale" (BM No. 131/3: "The Second Batman and Robin Team!").

In May 1960 Batman and Robin meet the robot ARDELLO (Det No. 279: "The Creatures That Stalked Batman!") and, with Superman, become embroiled in a bizarre adventure involving a centuries-old trap set by the sorcerer FANGAN (WF No. 109: "The Bewitched Batman!").

In June 1960 Batman and Robin battle ATOMIC-MAN (Det No. 280: "The Menace of the Atomic Man"); match wits with BIG JIM MASTERS (BM No. 132/2: "The Three Faces of Batman"); and thwart the schemes of the SEA-FOX (BM No. 132/3: "The Lair of the Sea-Fox!"). During this same period, Batman and Superman battle and defeat an extraterrestrial alien who has stolen part of Robin's life force (WF No. 110: "The Alien Who Doomed Robin!").

In July 1960 Batman and Robin match wits with EDDIE CHILL (Det No. 281: "Batman, Robot!").

In August 1960 Batman and Robin meet the alien lawman TAL-DAR (Det No. 282: "Batman's Interplanetary Rival!"); battle the KITE-MAN (BM No. 133/1: "Crimes of the Kite-Man"); cope with the mischievous antics of BAT-MITE (BM No. 133/3: "Batwoman's Publicity Agent!"); and, together with Superman, apprehend FLOYD FRISBY (WF No. 111: "Superman's Secret Kingdom!").

In September 1960 Batman and Robin meet the PHANTOM (Det No. 283: "The Phantom of Gotham City!"); battle the RAINBOW BEAST (BM No. 134/1: "The Rainbow Creature!"); are plagued by TOD ALLEN's last practical joke (BM No. 134/2: "Batman's Secret Enemy"); match wits with DANNY THE DUMMY (BM No. 134/3: "The Deadly Dummy"); and apprehend the WRECKERS (WF No. 112: "The Menace of Superman's Pet!").

In October 1960 Batman and Robin match wits with HAL DURGIN (Det No. 284: "The Negative Batman!"); apprehend FRANK "WHEELS" FOSTER (BM No. 135/1: "Crimes of the Wheel"); and battle the SKY CREATURE (BM No. 135/3: "The Menace of the Sky Creature!").

In November 1960 Batman and Robin apprehend HARBIN (Det No. 285: "The Mystery of the Man-Beast!") and, together with Superman, endure the magical mischief of BAT-MITE and Mr. Mxyzptlk (WF No. 113: "Bat-Mite Meets Mr. Mxyzptlk!").

In December 1960 Batman and Robin battle STAR-MAN (Det No. 286: "The Doomed Batwoman!"); cope with the mischief of BAT-MITE (BM No. 136/1: "The Case of the Crazy Crimes"); match wits with aliens from the planet VORDA (BM No. 136/2: "The Town That Hated Batman"); thwart the schemes of the JOKER (BM No. 136/3: "The Challenge of the Joker"); and, together with Superman, journey to the planet Zoron for an encounter with the evil CHORN (WF No. 114: "Captives of the Space Globes!").

In January 1961, with the aid of Ace the Bat-Hound, Batman and Robin thwart the efforts of two rival extraterrestrial aliens to gain control of the various fragments of a weird meteor that has landed on Earth so that they may be used to create a diabolical "hypnotic machine" capable of hypnotizing entire populations and therefore of transforming anyone who possesses it into a potential "dictator--of any planet in the universe!" (Det No. 287: "The Raven and the Wasp!").

In February 1961 Batman and Robin battle the MULTICREATURE (Det No. 288: "The Menace of the Multiple Creature!"); match wits with MR. MARVEL (*see also* ROBIN) (BM No. 137/1: "Robin's New Boss!); apprehend the BRAND (BM No. 137/2: "The Bandit with 1,000 Brands"); and, together with Superman, thwart an elaborate scheme by a gang of criminals to steal $500,000 in contributions earmarked for the Children's Charity Fund (WF No. 115: "The Curse That Doomed Superman!").

In March 1961 Batman and Robin cope with the magical mischief of BAT-MITE (Det No. 289: "The Bat-Mite Bandits!"); battle one of their own Batman robots when it temporarily turns against them (BM No. 138/1: "Batman's Master"); match wits with SIMPLE SIMON (BM No. 138/2: "The Simple Crimes of Simple Simon"); thwart the schemes of HAL TORSON (BM No. 138/3: "The Secret of the Sea Beast!"); and, together with Superman, encounter the weirdly transformed VANCE COLLINS (WF No. 116: "The Creature from Beyond!").

In April 1961 Batman and Robin match wits with "GADGETS" BLORE (Det No. 290: "Robin's Robot!"); meet the Blue Bowman (*see* SIGNALMAN) (BM No. 139/1: "The Blue Bowman"); and witness the emergence of Bat-Girl (*see* BAT-GIRL [BETTY KANE]) (BM No. 139/3: "Bat-Girl!").

In May 1961 Batman and Robin encounter a creature from the planet SHARL (Det No. 291: "The Creature from the Bat-Cave!") and, together with Superman, thwart the evil machinations of LEX LUTHOR (WF No. 117: "The Super-Batwoman and the Super-Creature!").

In June 1961 Batman and Robin battle the "ROCKETS" ROGAN gang (Det No. 292: "The Colossus of Gotham City!"); match wits with the JOKER (BM No. 140/1: "The Ghost of the Joker!"); find themselves temporarily transformed into aliens after a visit to the planet XLUR (BM No. 140/3: "The Eighth Wonder of Space!"); and, together with Superman, thwart a series of attempts by gangland assassins to murder Batman (*see* ALCHEMIST, THE) (BM No. 140/2: "The Charmed Life of Batman!") and thwart the dictatorial ambitions of VATHGAR (WF No. 118: "The Creature That Was Exchanged for Superman!").

In July 1961 Batman and Robin apprehend EDDIE STARK (Det No. 293: "Prisoners of the Dark World!").

In August 1961 Batman and Robin meet the ELEMENTAL MAN (Det No. 294: "The Villain of 100 Elements!"); match wits with the CLOCKMASTER (BM No. 141/1: "The Crimes of the Clockmaster"); battle the MOTH (BM No. 141/3: "Batwoman's Junior Partner!"); and, together with Superman, thwart the sinister schemes of GENERAL GRAMBLY (WF No. 119: "The Secret of Tigerman!").

In September 1961 Batman and Robin battle the ruthless TORG (Det No. 295: "The Secret of the Beast Paintings!"); receive a bizarre gift from the alien lawman TAL-DAR (BM No. 142/1: "Batman's Robot-Guardian"); match wits with HARTLEY (BM No. 142/3: "Ruler of the Bewitched Valley!"); and, together with Superman, defeat an unnamed criminal who has managed to bring to life three enchanted beings, all originally created by the ancient alchemist Albertus, who proceed to temporarily steal several of Superman's super-powers (WF No. 120: "The Challenge of the Faceless Creatures!").

In October 1961 Batman and Robin meet the PLANET-MASTER (Det No. 296: "The Menace of the Planet Master!"); match wits with DR. PNEUMO (BM No. 143/2: "The Blind Batman"); and encounter a bizarre creature from outer space (*see* ACE [THE BAT-HOUND]) (BM No. 143/3: "Bat-Hound and the Creature!").

In November 1961 Batman and Robin apprehend SPENCE (Det No. 297: "The Beast of Koba Bay!") and, together with Superman, battle the villainous XANU (WF No. 121: "The Mirror Batman!").

In December 1961 Batman and Robin match wits with Clayface (*see* CLAYFACE [MATT HAGEN]) (Det No. 298: "The Challenge of Clay-Face"); battle the JOKER (BM No. 144/2: "The Man Who Played Batman!"); and, together with Superman, thwart the dictatorial ambitions of the villainous KLOR (WF No. 122: "The Capture of Superman!"). During this same period, zany complications develop when Bat-Mite decides to play Cupid between Robin and Bat-Girl (*see* BAT-GIRL [BETTY KANE]) (BM No. 144/3: "Bat-Mite Meets Bat-Girl!").

In January 1962 Batman and Robin help overthrow the ruthless emperor KAALE (Det No. 299: "Prey of the Alien Hunters!").

In February 1962 Batman and Robin meet MR. POLKA-DOT (Det No. 300: "The Bizarre Polka-Dot Man!"); match wits with MR. 50 (BM No. 145/1: "Hunt for Mr. 50"); apprehend JOE BURR (BM No. 145/2: "The Tiniest Villain in the World"); and, together with Superman, attempt to cope with the magical mischief of BAT-MITE and Mr. Mxyzptlk (WF No. 123: "The Incredible Team of Bat-Mite and Mr. Mxyzptlk!").

In March 1962 Batman and Robin battle the "BRAINS" BELDON gang (Det No. 301: "The Condemned Batman!"); endure the antics of BAT-MITE (BM No. 146/1: "Batman and Robin's Magical Powers"); match wits with KEITH LARSEN (BM No. 146/3: "The Deadly Curse of Korabo!"); and, together with Superman, thwart the evil machinations of HROGUTH (WF No. 124: "The Mystery of the Alien Super-Boy!").

In April 1962 Batman and Robin battle the gang of criminals who have been misusing the "secret discoveries in suspended animation" made by scientist HENRY WINNS (Det No. 302: "The Bronze Menace!").

In May 1962 Batman and Robin investigate the murder of WALLY DODD (Det No. 303: "Murder in Skyland!"); match wits with the heirs of millionaire architect BRIGGS (BM No. 147/2: "The Secret of Mystery Island!"); apprehend NAILS FINNEY (BM No. 147/3: "Batman Becomes Bat-Baby!"); and, together with Superman, thwart the sinister schemes of JUNDY (WF No. 125: "The Hostages of the Island of Doom!").

In June 1962 Batman and Robin battle Clayface (*see* CLAYFACE [MATT HAGEN]) (Det No. 304: "The Return of Clay-Face!"); teach a much-needed lesson to VANDERVEER WAYNE (BM No. 148/2: "The Boy Who Was Robin"); match wits with the JOKER (BM No. 148/3: "The Joker's Greatest Triumph!"); and, together with Superman, thwart the evil schemes of LEX LUTHOR (WF No. 126: "The Negative Superman!").

In July 1962 Batman and Robin meet the extraterrestrial aliens HYORO and Goga (Det No. 305: "Targets of the Alien Z-Ray!").

In August 1962 Batman and Robin match wits with PROFESSOR HUGO ARNOLD (Det No. 306: "The Wizard of 1,000 Menaces!"); battle the MAESTRO (BM No. 149/1: "The Maestro of Crime"); apprehend "international gem thieves" BEN RYDER and Slick Ronson (BM No. 149/2: "The Invaders from the Past!"); and, together with Superman, thwart the schemes of the evil ZERNO (WF No. 127: "The Sorcerer from the Stars!").

In September 1962 Batman and Robin meet ALPHA THE EXPERIMENTAL MAN (Det No. 307: "Alpha, the Experimental Man!"); apprehend JACK PINE (BM No. 150/2: "The Girl Who Stole Batman's Heart"); match wits with BIFF WARNER (BM No. 150/3: "Robin, the Super Boy Wonder!"); and, together with Superman, thwart the schemes of MOOSE MORANS (WF No. 128: "The Power That Transformed Batman!").

In October 1962 Batman and Robin apprehend PETER DALE (Det No. 308: "The Flame-Master!").

In November 1962 Batman and Robin match wits with J. J. ASHLEY (Det No. 309: "The Mystery of the Mardi Gras Murders!"); apprehend the HARRIS BOYS (BM No. 151/2: "The Mystery Gadget from the Stars!"); and, together with Superman, thwart the sinister schemes of Lex Luthor and the JOKER (WF No. 129: "Joker-Luthor, Incorporated!").

In December 1962 Batman and Robin endure the magical mischief of BAT-MITE (Det No. 310: "Bat-Mite's Super-Circus!"); smash a ring of renegade scientists and apprehend the criminals who intend to market the scientists' illicitly manufactured ultrapowerful explosive (BM No. 152/1: "Formula for Doom"); match wits with the JOKER (BM No. 152/2: "The False Face Society!"); and give a dazzling acrobatic performance for the inhabitants of the far-distant planet Unxor when members of a traveling interplanetary acrobatic troupe are suddenly stricken by an attack of space measles (WF No. 130: "The Riddle of the Four Planets!").

In January 1963 Batman and Robin match wits with the CAT-MAN (Det No. 311: "The Challenge of the Cat-Man!").

In February 1963 Batman and Robin battle Clayface (*see* CLAYFACE [MATT HAGEN]) (Det No. 312: "The Secret of Clayface's Power!"); thwart the sinister schemes of ZEBO (BM No. 153: chs. 1–3 — "Prisoners of Three Worlds!"; "Death from Beyond"; "Dimension of Doom"); and, together with Superman, match wits with the OCTOPUS (WF No. 131: "The Mystery of the Crimson Avenger!").

In March 1963 Batman and Robin match wits with gang boss ELLIOT MADDAN (Det No. 313: "The Mystery of the $1,000,000 Treasure Hunt!"); apprehend the evil KARDO (BM No. 154/2: "The Amazing Odyssey of Batman and Robin"); meet DR. DORN (BM No. 154/3: "The Strange Experiment of Dr. Dorn!"); and, together with Superman, capture DENNY KALE and his partner, Shorty Biggs (WF No. 132: "Batman and Robin, Medieval Bandits!").

In April 1963 Batman and Robin match wits with ROGER CARLYLE (Det No. 314: "Murder in Movieland!").

In May 1963 Batman and Robin meet JUNGLE-MAN (Det No. 315: "The Jungle Man of Gotham City!") and battle the PENGUIN (BM No. 155/2: "The Return of the Penguin!").

In June 1963 Batman and Robin defeat DOUBLE X (Det No. 316: "Double Batman vs. Double X"); battle the GORILLA GANG (BM No. 156/2: "Robin Dies at Dawn!"); and, together with Superman, defeat and apprehend the BAND OF SUPER-VILLAINS (WF No. 134: "The Band of Super-Villains"). During this same period, Robin captures ANT-MAN (BM No. 156/1: "The Secret of the Ant-Man").

In July 1963 Batman and Robin match wits with the CONDOR GANG (Det No. 317: "The Secrets of the Flying Bat-Cave!").

In August 1963 Batman and Robin battle the CAT-MAN (Det No. 318: "The Cat-Man Strikes Back!"); thwart the schemes of MIRROR-MAN (BM No. 157/2: "The Hunt for Batman's Secret Identity!"); and, together with Superman, journey into the future to meet JON DURR (WF No. 135: "The Menace of the Future Man!").

In September 1963 Batman and Robin match wits with DR. NO-FACE (Det No. 319: "The Fantastic Dr. No-Face!"); become embroiled in a bizarre adventure involving ACE THE BAT-HOUND and Bat-Mite (BM No. 158/1: "Ace--the Super Bat-Hound!"); and apprehend BOBO CULLEN (BM No. 158/3: "Batman and Robin--Imposters!"). During this same period, Batman journeys to an extradimensional parallel world where he participates in the capture of the infamous RED RAVEN gang (WF No. 136: "The Batman Nobody Remembered!").

In October 1963 Batman and Robin successfully protect the secret of their dual identities from the prying eyes of VICKI VALE (Det No. 320: "Batman and Robin--the Mummy Crime-Fighters!").

In November 1963 Batman and Robin battle the TERRIBLE TRIO (Det No. 321: "The Terrible Trio!"); match wits with Clayface (*see* CLAYFACE [MATT HAGEN]) and the JOKER (BM No. 159/1: "The Great Clayface-Joker Feud!"); and, together with Superman, thwart the malevolent schemes of LEX LUTHOR (WF No. 137: "Superman's Secret Master!").

In December 1963 Batman and Robin match wits with ARISTO (Det No. 322: "The Bizarre Batman Genie!"); apprehend BART CULLEN (BM No. 160/2: "The Alien Boss of Gotham City!"); and, together with Superman, defeat GENERAL GROTE (WF No. 138: "The Secret of the Captive Cavemen!").

In January 1964 Batman and Robin meet the ZODIAC MASTER (Det No. 323: "The Zodiac Master!").

In February 1964 Batman and Robin apprehend ERNST LARUE (Det No. 324: "Menace of the Robot Brain!"); match wits with the MAD HATTER (BM No. 161/1: "The New Crimes of the Mad Hatter"); endure the mischief of BAT-MITE (BM No. 161/2: "The Bat-Mite Hero!"); and, together with Superman, battle the SPHINX GANG (WF No. 139: "The Ghost of Batman!").

In March 1964 Batman and Robin match wits with the CAT-MAN (Det No. 325: "The Strange Lives of the Cat-Man!"); apprehend ERIC BARROC (BM No. 162/1: "The Batman Creature!"); and, together with Superman, thwart the nefarious schemes of Clayface (*see* CLAYFACE [MATT HAGEN]) (WF No. 140: "The Clayface Superman!"). During this same period, ROBIN temporarily adopts a new identity (BM No. 162/2: "Robin's New Secret Identity!").

In April 1964 Batman and Robin match wits with the extraterrestrial alien KHOR (Det No. 326: "Captives of the Alien Zoo!").

In May 1964 Batman and Robin apprehend SMILER (Det No. 327: "The Mystery of the Menacing Mask!") and battle the JOKER (BM No. 163/2: "The Joker Jury!"). During this same period, with the aid of Robin and JIMMY OLSEN, Batman and Superman apprehend a pair of criminals who have kidnapped a prominent physicist and stolen his newly invented "invisibility de-visors" so that they can use the devices to render themselves invisible while they commit crimes (WF No. 141: "The Olsen-Robin Team versus 'The Superman-Batman Team!' ").

In June 1964 Batman and Robin battle the TRI-STATE GANG (*see also* ALFRED) (Det No. 328: "Gotham Gang Line-Up!"); apprehend MR. DABBLO (BM No. 164/1: "Two-Way Gem Caper!"); and, together with Superman, find themselves pitted against the COMPOSITE SUPERMAN (WF No. 142: "The Origin of the Composite Superman!" pts. I–II – "The Composite Superman!"; "The Battle Between Titans!").

In July 1964 Batman and Robin meet ALBERT MAUNCH (Det No. 329: "Castle with Wall-to-Wall Danger!").

In August 1964 Batman and Robin match wits with MOLNEY (Det No. 330: "The Fallen Idol of Gotham City!"); cope with the fearsome menace of the "mutated man" (*see* WARNER, ANDREW [GOVERNOR]) (BM No. 165/1: "The Man Who Quit the Human Race!"); meet the lovely PATRICIA POWELL (BM No. 165/2: "The Dilemma of the Detective's Daughter!"); and, together with Superman, become embroiled in an adventure involving the Kandorian official THAN-AR (WF No. 143: "The Feud Between Batman and Superman!" pts. I–II – no title; "The Manhunters from Earth!").

In September 1964 Batman and Robin match wits with "BOSS" BARROW (Det No. 331: "Museum of Mixed-Up Men!"); apprehend a gang of criminals with the aid of PATRICIA POWELL and her father (BM No. 166/2: "A Rendezvous with Robbery!"); and, together with Superman, thwart the nefarious schemes of Clayface (*see* CLAYFACE [MATT HAGEN]) and Brainiac (WF No. 144: "The 1,001 Tricks of Clayface and Brainiac!" pts. I–II – no title; "The Helpless Partners!"). During this same period, some criminals lure Batman into a seemingly inescapable deathtrap – a tightly enclosed concrete room which fills rapidly with water while a machine gun simultaneously sprays the room with automatic gunfire – but Batman escapes the trap and apprehends his captors (BM No. 166/1: "Two-Way Deathtrap!").

In October 1964 Batman and Robin battle the JOKER (Det No. 332: "The Joker's Last Laugh!").

In November 1964 Batman and Robin defeat "RED" LOFTUS (Det No. 333: "Hunters of the Elephants' Graveyard!"); apprehend KARABI and battle HYDRA, the "international crime cartel" (BM No. 167: "Zero Hour for Earth!"); and, together with Superman, thwart the schemes of conquest of the masters of the planet VOR (WF No. 145: "Prison for Heroes!" pts. I–II – no title; "The Revenge of Superman!").

In December 1964 Batman and Robin meet MR. MAMMOTH (BM No. 168/1: "The Fight That Jolted Gotham City!"); apprehend PROF. RALPH VERN (BM No. 168/2: "How to Solve a Perfect Crime--in Reverse!"); battle and defeat a pair of criminals known as the Grasshoppers, only to discover that their adversaries were merely agents of the Outsider (*see* ALFRED) (Det No. 334: "The Man Who Stole from Batman!"); and, together with Superman, learn the incredible story of DR. THOMAS ELLISON (WF No. 146: "Batman, Son of Krypton!" pts. I–II – no title; "The Destroyer of Krypton!").

In January 1965 Batman and Robin match wits with the MAKE-UP MAN (Det No. 335: "Trail of the Talking Mask!").

In February 1965 Batman and Robin match wits with the PENGUIN (BM No. 169/1: "Partners in Plunder!") and battle and defeat a witchlike villainess gifted with extraordinary "paranormal powers," only to discover that their fearsome adversary was merely another agent of the Outsider (*see* ALFRED) (Det No. 336: "Batman's Bewitched Nightmare"). During this same period, the minds of both ROBIN and JIMMY OLSEN are "taken over and possessed" by some weirdly glowing jewels from a distant planet, but Batman and Superman manage ultimately to rescue them (WF No. 147: "The Doomed Boy Heroes!" pts. I–II – "The New Terrific Team!"; "The Doom of Jimmy Olsen and Robin!").

In March 1965 Batman and Robin meet KLAG THE HUNTER (Det No. 337: "Deep-Freeze Menace!"); match wits with ROY REYNOLDS (BM No. 170/1: "Genius of the Getaway Gimmicks!"); and conduct an investigation of CAP'N BEN'S WILD ANIMAL ACT (BM No. 170/2: "The Puzzle of the Perilous Prizes!"). During this same period, Batman and Superman are temporarily catapulted into a bizarre "parallel world . . . a world that's almost like Earth in every way, but in which history had a different course than on Earth!" On this parallel world, the counterparts of Batman and Superman are master criminals, and Lex Luthor and Clayface (Matt Hagen), notorious villains on the world inhabited by the real Batman and Superman, are renowned champions of law and justice. During their stay on the parallel world, Batman and Superman help their fellow lawmen apprehend the evil Batman and Superman before departing for home (WF No. 148: "Superman and Batman--Outlaw!" pts. I–II – "The Evil Superman and Batman"; "The Incredible New Super-Team!").

In April 1965 Batman and Robin battle the "BULL" FLEMING gang (Det No. 338: "Batman's Power-Packed Punch!").

In May 1965 Batman and Robin meet WALTER HEWITT (Det No. 339: "Batman Battles the Living Beast-Bomb!") and match wits with the RIDDLER (BM No. 171: "Remarkable Ruse of the Riddler!"). During this same period, when, as a means of testing the security of his secret identity, Superman uses a "selective amnesia-inducer" to erase from the minds of Batman and Robin the knowledge that Clark Kent is secretly Superman, the Dynamic Duo are nevertheless able to deduce Superman's secret on their own. When the roles are reversed, however, and the selective amnesia-inducer is used to erase Superman's knowledge of the Dynamic Duo's identities, Superman is unable to discover, try though he might, that Batman and Robin are secretly Bruce Wayne and Dick Grayson. ". . . Though he's the mightiest man in the world," remarks Robin privately to Batman, "he's not the greatest detective!" (WF No. 149: "The Game of Secret Identities!" pts. I–II – no title; "The Super-Detective!").

In June 1965 Batman and Robin battle the Outsider (*see* ALFRED) (Det No. 340: "The Outsider Strikes Again!") and match wits with WILBUR JENKINS (BM No. 172/1: "Attack of the Invisible Knights!"). During this same period, Robin apprehends the FLOWER GANG (BM No. 172/2: "Robin's Unassisted Triple Play!"), and Batman and Superman match wits with Rokk and Sorban on the planet VENTURA (WF No. 150: pts. I–II – "The Super-Gamble with Doom!"; "The Duel of the Super-Gamblers!").

In July 1965 Batman and Robin battle the JOKER (Det No. 341: "The Joker's Comedy Capers!").

In August 1965 Batman and Robin apprehend AL CRAIG (Det No. 342: "The Midnight Raid of the Robin Gang!") and match wits with ELWOOD PEARSON (BM No. 173/1: "Secret Identities For Sale!").

In September 1965 Batman and Robin battle GENERAL VON DORT (Det No. 343: "The Secret War of the Phantom General"); thwart the schemes of the BIG GAME HUNTER (BM No. 174/1: "The Human Punching Bag!"); and, together with Superman, attempt to cope with the magical mischief of BAT-MITE and Mr. Mxyzptlk (WF No. 152: "The Colossal Kids!" pts. I–II – no title; "The Magic of Bat-Mite and Mr. Mxyzptlk!").

In October 1965 Batman and Robin match wits with JOHNNY WITTS (Det No. 344: "The Crime-Boss Who Was Always One Step Ahead of Batman!").

In November 1965 Batman and Robin apprehend EDDIE REPP (BM No. 175: "The Decline and Fall of Batman!").

In December 1965 Batman and Robin battle the ED "NUMBERS" GARVEY gang (BM No. 176/1: "Two Batmen Too Many!") and apprehend LATHROP and his henchmen (BM No. 176/2: "The Art Gallery of Rogues!").

BATMAN, JUNIOR. A pseudonym briefly employed by JOHN VANCE years ago, when, as a youngster, before BATMAN had met ROBIN, he helped Batman identify and apprehend a pair of fugitive bank robbers (Det No. 231, May '56: "Batman, Junior!").

BATMAN MUSEUM, THE. A museum in GOTHAM CITY, open to the public, which houses an extensive collection of BATMAN memorabilia; the chronicles contain several references to a Batman Museum, but it is not possible to determine whether one museum, or several museums, are intended.

In September 1956, following the apprehension of fugitive criminal MAYNE MALLOCK, Batman turns Mallock's House of Batman over to Gotham City so that it may be converted into a Batman Law Enforcement Museum. The name of the proposed museum suggests that it will contain a wide range of law-enforcement exhibits, and not merely souvenirs of Batman's famous cases (BM No. 102/1: "The House of Batman").

A Batman text for October 1958 contains a specific reference to a Batman Museum in Gotham City (BM No. 119/2: "The Secret of Batman Island!"), but it is impossible to determine whether this is the same as the Batman Law Enforcement Museum mentioned above.

The Gotham City of the twenty-first century A.D. will also have a Batman Museum, filled with trophies commemorating the spectacular exploits of that "famous manhunter of [the] past" (WF No. 11, Fall '43: "A Thief in Time!").

In September 1955 traveling showman "Breezy" Lane and his young son Johnny open a Batman Dime Museum on a downtown Gotham City side street, but BRUCE WAYNE buys the museum from the Lanes and shuts it down soon afterward (Det No. 223: "The Batman Dime-Museum").

BATMANTOWN. *See* PLAINVILLE.

BATMANUS. The name which the citizens of ancient Rome bestow upon BATMAN during a time-journey he makes there in August–September 1944 (BM No. 24/1: "It Happened in Rome").

BAT-MITE. A "mischievous mite from another dimension" (Det No. 276, Feb '60: "The Return of Bat-Mite!") who possesses "unearthly," magical powers, and looks like "an elf dressed in a crazy-looking Batman costume!" (Det No. 267, May '59: "Batman Meets Bat-Mite!"). ROBIN has called him an "imp" and a "gremlin" and BATMAN has called him a "pest" (Det No. 267, May '59: "Batman Meets Bat-Mite!"), but Bat-Mite sees himself only as Batman's "greatest fan," and his periodic visits to the earthly dimension as exciting opportunities to "see [his] favorite crime-fighting hero in spectacular action . . ." (BM No. 161/2, Feb '64: "The Bat-Mite Hero!").

To ensure that the action he sees will indeed be "spectacular," Bat-Mite uses his extraordinary extra-dimensional powers to prolong and enliven Batman's battles with the underworld, thus forcing the Dynamic Duo to ever greater heights of skill and ingenuity. In December 1962, for example, Bat-Mite intentionally endows three small-time criminals with superhuman powers so that "Batman and Robin [will] have to use sensational tricks to defeat them!" (Det No. 310: "Bat-Mite's Super-Circus!").

It is impossible to define the extent and limits of Bat-Mite's powers with any real precision, but his powers are similar if not identical to those of the incredible MR. MXYZPTLK. Among other things, Bat-Mite can make himself visible and invisible at will, animate inanimate objects (Det No. 267, May '59: "Batman Meets Bat-Mite!"), shrink or enlarge either people or objects (BM No. 133/3, Aug '60: "Batwoman's Publicity Agent!"), levitate people or objects (Det No. 289, Mar '61: "The Bat-Mite Bandits!"), and endow either people (Det No. 310, Dec '62: "Bat-Mite's Super-Circus!") or animals (BM No. 158/1, Sep '63: "Ace--the Super Bat-Hound!") with super-powers.

Bat-Mite, 1959 © NPP 1959

The chronicles do not provide precise data concerning the name or location of Bat-Mite's home dimension; in most cases, the texts refer to Bat-Mite simply as a visitor from "another dimension" (Det No. 267, May '59: "Batman Meets Bat-Mite!"; and others). In December 1963 Batman calls Bat-Mite "that 5th-dimensional imp" (BM No. 160/1: "The Mystery of the Madcap Island"), but the accuracy of this assertion is open to serious question since numerous texts refer to Mr. Mxyzptlk as "the imp from the fifth dimension" (WF No. 113, Nov '60: "Bat-Mite Meets Mr. Mxyzptlk!"; and others) and at least one text states unequivocally that Bat-Mite's home dimension is not the same as Mr. Mxyzptlk's (WF No. 152, Sep '65: "The Colossal Kids!" pts. 1–2 – no title; "The Magic of Bat-Mite and Mr. Mxyzptlk!").

Bat-Mite has been described as a "pesky pixie" (Det No. 276, Feb '60: "The Return of Bat-Mite!") and as an "elfin character from another dimension whose greatest pleasure is using his zany powers to make things tough for Batman and Robin" (WF No. 113, Nov '60: "Bat-Mite Meets Mr. Mxyzptlk!"), but these descriptions hardly jibe with Bat-Mite's somewhat less jaundiced view of himself. "I'm not a pest at all," he insists in November 1960, ". . . I help Batman and Robin! Because I admire them so, I want them to do their best feats and stunts! That's why I use my magic!" (WF No. 113: "Bat-Mite Meets Mr. Mxyzptlk!").

In May 1959, as Batman and Robin prepare to set out on their nightly patrol of GOTHAM CITY, they notice that someone has apparently been rummaging about in the BATCAVE: Batman's UTILITY BELT is on the floor instead of in its customary place inside a closet, Robin's belt-radio has been tampered with, and equipment on a laboratory table has been left in uncharacteristic disorder.

"Could there have been a **stranger** down here, in the **bat-cave?**" asks Robin aloud with an anxious "gulp."

"Dear me--I'm sorry!" replies a disembodied voice, speaking from somewhere behind Robin. "I was examining your equipment, and I'm afraid I got careless!"

"What--?" cries Robin, whirling around. "A voice . . . but I can't see anyone!"

"In that case," replies the voice, "I'd better make myself visible!" There is a sudden "pop," and Batman and Robin find themselves confronted by a strange little man in a costume modeled after Batman's own.

"It's an elf," exclaims Robin, ". . . an **elf dressed in a crazy-looking Batman costume!**"

"I'm not an elf!" replies the little man. "I come from **another dimension,** where all men are my size! ***Batman,*** I've observed and admired your exploits for years--so I decided to help you fight crime with my unearthly powers! Won't that be ***fun?***

"I made myself a costume--and I'm calling myself ***Bat-Mite!***" continues the odd little man. "Oh boy, will we have fun! ***Batman, Robin*** . . . and ***Bat-Mite!*** What a trio!"

I MADE MYSELF A COSTUME--AND I'M CALLING MYSELF BAT-MITE! OH BOY, WILL WE HAVE FUN! BATMAN, ROBIN... AND BAT-MITE! WHAT A TRIO!
YOU-- A CREATURE FROM ANOTHER DIMENSION-- WANT TO WORK WITH US? B-BUT THAT'S IMPOSSIBLE!

Bat-Mite, Batman, and Robin, 1959 © NPP 1959

"You," replies Batman, still somewhat taken aback, "--a creature from another dimension--want to work with us? B-But that's impossible! We'd have a hard time explaining your presence to people . . . you'd only be in the way! Besides, it takes a lot of training to become a crime-fighter!"

"Oh, this is very disappointing!" replies Bat-Mite resignedly. "In that case, I'd better leave. . . ." There is another "pop," and the strange little man disappears from view.

"He's disappeared," cries Robin, "--gone back to his own dimension!"

"Cute little fellow," remarks Batman, ". . . I hated to hurt his feelings--but we certainly couldn't have him around!"

However, the wily Bat-Mite has not given up so easily, and when the powerful BATMOBILE roars out of the batcave to begin its nightly patrol of the city, Bat-Mite is an invisible passenger atop the transparent cockpit.

Soon afterward, at the Gotham City waterfront, Batman and Robin spot the notorious Tipper Neely gang racing toward a getaway car and move swiftly to cut off their escape. With their escape route blocked by the batmobile, the criminals attempt to flee on foot across a wide metal bridge, but Batman and Robin close in on them and their capture seems imminent.

Suddenly, however, the bridge begins to bend and buckle like a giant rubber band, and Batman, Robin, and the members of the Tipper Neely gang have all they can do to retain their balance on the wildly undulating bridge.

"To the quick-thinking ***Batman,***" however, "there is only one possible answer. . . ."

"Bat-Mite!" cries Batman. "Remember he said he has strange powers? He's responsible for this! But--but ***why?***"

Batman and Robin ultimately apprehend the fleeing criminals and, for their benefit, provide them with a hastily concocted but sufficiently plausible explanation to explain away the bizarre occurrence on the bridge, but back at the batcave, Batman demands a more substantial explanation from the now-visible Bat-Mite.

"Gosh, ***Batman,***" replies Bat-Mite brightly, "you went after those crooks so quickly, I hardly got to see you in action--so I prolonged the fight a little! I just wanted to have some ***fun!***"

"Crime-fighting isn't fun," scolds Batman, ". . . it's serious business! Now please--***go home!*** All you're doing is making problems for us!"

"Spoilsport!" cries Bat-Mite. Then, there is another "pop," and Bat-Mite fades away into invisibility once again.

"Whew," exclaims Robin. "He's gone back to his own dimension! What a relief!"

"Yes," concurs Batman, ". . . maybe the little imp means well--but he's a ***pest!***"

Bat-Mite, however, has retreated into invisibility only temporarily in order to be on hand when the crime-fighting action begins again in earnest. Soon afterward, when Batman and Robin receive word of an attempted holdup at a hi-fi exhibition, they race to the scene and swiftly apprehend the criminals, but Bat-Mite, who is watching invisibly nearby, is disappointed at the dearth of exciting action. "Gee . . . and I was looking forward to some spectacular action!" muses Bat-Mite sadly. "I guess I'll just have to ***create*** some!"

Within seconds, Bat-Mite has used his extradimensional powers to animate a giant phonograph record associated with the hi-fi display and send it whirling up into the air, like a giant flying saucer, with the criminals perched safely atop it. Once again, Batman is forced to summon additional skill and ingenuity in order to capture the criminals, and then to concoct a plausible explanation for the phonograph-record phenomenon.

"Listen, you little scamp," scolds Batman, after he and Robin have returned to the batcave and Bat-Mite has once again made his presence known, "you've got to cut out all this mischief! You hear me? . . . Cut it out or I ***will*** spank you!"

"Aw, gee, ***Batman,***" replies Bat-Mite forlornly, "--where's your sense of humor?"

"Furthermore, I . . ." continues Batman in his scolding tone, but Bat-Mite merely "pops" away into his protective aura of invisibility.

Soon afterward, Bat-Mite overhears Batman and Robin discussing their plan to trap the Yellow Gloves Gang inside an empty warehouse that the gang is certain to race through while fleeing the scene of their next robbery.

"An ***empty*** warehouse?" muses Bat-Mite silently. "No objects for spectacular action? I'll have to do something about that!"

Indeed, before Batman and Robin arrive at the warehouse to lie in wait for the criminals, Bat-Mite fills it with gigantic props, including a stagecoach, a life-size model of an ancient Viking ship, a huge sphinx, and a giant statue of Batman. "There," exclaims Bat-Mite, after his mischievous work has been completed, ". . . with these props borrowed from a movie lot, I've provided a perfect backdrop for sensational ***Batman*** stunts! I can hardly wait for the fun to begin!"

At one point during the ensuing battle with the Yellow Gloves Gang, the criminals gain the upper hand and it appears they will succeed in making good their escape. Bat-Mite attempts to use his magical powers to intervene on behalf of the Dynamic Duo, but his ineptitude only makes matters worse. Within moments, the criminals have fled the warehouse.

"Guess I--uh--overdid my powers a bit!" confesses Bat-Mite sadly, after rendering himself visible to Batman and Robin. "Just a little mistake. . . ."

"***You're*** the little mistake!" scolds Batman. "***You*** rigged up this action set so you'd have some **fun**--and now your **fun** has allowed those bandits to escape! But maybe it's not too late to catch them yet--if you use your powers exactly as I tell you! Understand?"

"Y-Yessir!" replies Bat-Mite brightly, eager for the opportunity to redeem itself.

Following Batman's instructions, Bat-Mite animates the giant statue of Batman and, after the Dynamic Duo have taken up positions inside the pouches of the statue's utility belt, sends it racing after the fleeing bandits. Within moments, the Yellow Gloves Gang has been apprehended and its members have been turned over to the authorities for prosecution.

Later, back at the batcave, Batman scolds the impish Bat-Mite for the last time. "Ever since you arrived," declares Batman angrily, "you've caused us nothing but trouble! Now you've had your ***fun***--so please leave us alone and go back to your own dimension!"

"All right, ***Batman,***" replies Bat-Mite, "--I guess it's time I went home! Good-bye--for now!"

"'For now?'" cries Batman, as Bat-Mite disappears into nothingness. "You mean you'll be back? Oh, no!"

"Don't come back," cries Robin, "--please! We're moving--going to China--Mars. . . ."

"Golly, ***Batman,***" exclaims Robin, after Bat-Mite has vanished completely, "--do you realize what it'll mean if that little gremlin ever comes back?"

"Yes, ***Robin,***" replies Batman with a sigh, ". . . trouble . . . more trouble--and ***'fun'!***" (Det No. 267: "Batman Meets Bat-Mite!").

In February 1960, after Bat-Mite has returned to the earthly dimension and used his magical powers to prolong a battle between Batman, Robin, BATWOMAN, and criminals in the employ of the notorious Hobby Robber, a villain who "steals rare items for his own collections from honest hobbyists," Batman and Robin angrily berate him for his mischievous intervention.

Annoyed at the Dynamic Duo's failure to appreciate what he regards as his positive contribution to their crime-fighting effort, Bat-Mite approaches Batwoman, who does not yet know about his penchant for mischief, and complains that Batman is always sending him away, even though his only desire is to help the Dynamic Duo fight crime.

"How could ***Batman*** be so ungrateful?" exclaims Batwoman. ". . . and you're such a cute little fellow, too. . . ."

"Gosh, ***Batwoman,***" replies Bat-Mite eagerly, "you're nice--and you're beautiful! I've admired your crime-fighting, too! I think I'll be seeing more of it!"

And so, soon afterward, when Batwoman encounters some of the Hobby Robber's henchmen while standing guard over a "valuable collection," Bat-Mite uses his magical powers to prolong and enliven the ensuing battle. When Batwoman realizes what Bat-Mite has done, however, she becomes furious, threatens to spank him, and admonishes him to ". . . go bother somebody else!"

Not long afterward, Bat-Mite listens invisibly as Batman and Robin discuss their plan to apprehend the Hobby Robber by hiding inside a crate of rare books and then tricking the Hobby Robber into attempting to steal them. Batman and Robin agree, however, to keep their plan a secret from Batwoman so that she will not be exposed to the coming danger.

Realizing that Batwoman will not want to be excluded from the coming fighting, Bat-Mite races to Batwoman with the details of the Dynamic Duo's plan, hoping that this will make her like him once again. Batwoman listens to the plan intently and then gives Bat-Mite a warm hug. ***"Bat-Mite,"*** she exclaims happily, "you're a doll!"

Meanwhile, Batman and Robin have enticed the Hobby Robber into attempting to steal the crate of rare books by planting a story about them in a local newspaper. The villain, however, discovers their hiding place, takes them prisoner, and then places them inside a seemingly escape-proof deathtrap.

Suddenly, Batwoman arrives on the scene and creates a diversion with a smoke bomb long enough for Batman and Robin to secure their freedom. "Well," admits Batman, after he has learned that it is Bat-Mite who has been responsible for Batwoman's timely arrival, "for once I'm glad that little fellow poked his inquisitive nose into our business!"

Moments later, when Batman, Robin, and Batwoman

are having difficulty apprehending the Hobby Robber and his henchmen because they are blazing away at them with a machine gun, Bat-Mite uses his magical powers to animate the Hobby Robber's collection of puppets and send them marching about the room, a ploy which panics the criminals and enables Batman, Robin, and Batwoman to apprehend them.

"Well, I certainly had a wonderful time!" exclaims Bat-Mite, as he prepares to depart for his own dimension. "I'll have plenty to think about when I return home!"

Out of gratitude, Batwoman gives Bat-Mite a warm kiss, which so embarrasses Bat-Mite that he flees homeward immediately.

"Well," laughs Batman, "that's one way of getting rid of him!" (Det No. 276: "The Return of Bat-Mite!").

In August 1960 Bat-Mite arrives in the earthly dimension with the startling announcement that he has decided to become Batwoman's new partner. "Since ***Batman*** has ***Robin*** to help him fight crime," explains Bat-Mite, "--I've decided it's time ***Batwoman*** had an assistant, too--so I'm going to become ***Batwoman's new partner!***"

"Now look here!" exclaims Batwoman, somewhat stunned by this unwelcome piece of news. ". . . I don't want your help! You'll only want to have 'fun' again, and make trouble for me!"

"No-no," insists Bat-Mite, ". . . honest--I'll behave myself, ***Batwoman!*** Please?"

"Well . . . all right," replies Batwoman finally, ". . . but the minute you start acting up--out you go!"

"Batwoman--you'll be ***sorry!"*** sing out Batman and Robin in unison.

For a time, Bat-Mite remains faithful to his promise to remain out of mischief, and before long his magical powers have established the crime-fighting team of Batwoman and Bat-Mite as "a formidable foe of crime" in Gotham City. After their second successful foray against the underworld, however, Batwoman makes the fateful mistake of rewarding Bat-Mite for his cooperativeness with an affectionate kiss on the cheek. "This is for keeping your promise," she tells Bat-Mite, "--and for being so cute!"

This kiss, however, quickly goes to Bat-Mite's head; he decides that he is in love with Batwoman and that an ideal way for him to prove his affection would be for him to "use [his] unusual powers to make her the most sensational crime-fighter of all time!"

When Bat-Mite learns that policemen are on the lookout for a gang of criminals who have just robbed the Gotham Bank, he uses Bat-Hound (*see* ACE [THE BAT-HOUND]) to track the criminals to their hideout in an old warehouse, then telephones its location to Batwoman so that she will be able to capture the criminals single-handedly and claim full credit for apprehending them.

Batman and Robin, however, have located the criminals' hideout independently, and they arrive at the scene in time to join Batwoman in breaking down the warehouse door and plunging into battle with the assembled criminals.

"Shucks!" exclaims Bat-Mite, who has perched himself comfortably, but invisibly, inside the warehouse to watch the coming action. "Who invited ***Batman*** and ***Robin?*** Now the crooks will be captured so easily, there won't be any chance for some spectacular action by ***Batwoman***--unless I do something about it!"

Within seconds, Bat-Mite has used his magical powers to shrink Batman, Robin, Batwoman, and the criminals to a few inches in height, providing the criminals with a million places in which to hide and making their capture infinitely more difficult. "I know I'm breaking my promise to [Batwoman]," thinks Bat-Mite to himself, "but gosh--a fella's got to have a ***little*** fun!"

Bat-Mite in love, 1960 © NPP 1960

As the battle rages between the tiny crime-fighters and the tiny criminals, however, Bat-Mite accidentally leaps onto a fireplace bellows. The resulting blast of air knocks Batman, Robin, and Batwoman off their feet, giving the frightened criminals an opportunity to escape.

"Oh, well," thinks Bat-Mite, "--that accident made things even better! The crooks will try to escape--and ***Batman*** and ***Robin*** will be forced to use some sensational stunt to block them!"

At the warehouse door, however, the criminals encounter Bat-Hound, who has retained his normal size and is therefore many times larger than the fleeing criminals. The criminals are so terrified by their encounter with the "giant dog" that Batman is able to apprehend them easily. "All right, ***Bat-Mite,***" cries Batman, "the fun's over! You might as well restore us to our normal size now!"

Bat-Mite promptly restores the crime-fighters and the criminals to their normal size, but he escapes to the safety of his own dimension before Batman, Robin, and Batwoman can manage to give him a well-deserved bawling out (BM No. 133/3: "Batwoman's Publicity Agent!").

In November 1960, shortly after Bat-Mite has mischievously used his magical powers to prevent SUPERMAN from capturing some criminals so that he will have the opportunity of watching his heroes, Batman and

Robin, go into action against the villains instead, Mr. Mxyzptlk materializes in the earthly dimension and launches into a zany, pixilated rivalry with his extradimensional counterpart in order to prove to Bat-Mite that his "weird magic" is greater than Bat-Mite's, that he is a far greater pest than Bat-Mite, and that Superman is strictly off-limits to Bat-Mite since the Man of Steel is, in Mr. Mxyzptlk's view, his own private preserve for pestering purposes. The rivalry produces both danger and mayhem for Batman, Robin, and Superman until finally bôth imps tire of the battle and whisk themselves away voluntarily to their respective dimensions (WF No. 113: "Bat-Mite Meets Mr. Mxyzptlk!").

In December 1960 Bat-Mite uses his magical powers to embroil Batman and Robin in a bizarre adventure entirely of his own design — complete with a menacing robot, an imaginary criminal mastermind named Mr. X, strange pink sea creatures, and a castle full of gorillas — purely for the thrill of being able to watch his crime-fighting idols in action. Ultimately, however, Batman discovers what Bat-Mite has done. Threatened with a spanking, Bat-Mite returns hastily to his own dimension (BM No. 136/1: "The Case of the Crazy Crimes").

In March 1961 gangster Willy Wile tricks Bat-Mite into believing that he and his henchmen are filming a movie about Batman, its proceeds earmarked for charity, but that Batman is such a modest person that the filming must be done in secret. "If you use your powers to help us get movies of ***Batman*** in unusual action," explains Wile, "the picture will be a smash success, and the more money it makes, the more [Batman's] charities will get!"

In the days that follow, Wile's henchmen stage a series of spectacular robberies in Gotham City. On each occasion, Bat-Mite — who believes that Wile's cohorts are only movie actors and that the robberies are being staged with the full cooperation of the victims — uses his powers to prolong and enliven the Dynamic Duo's battle with the criminals to provide Wile with the spectacular action footage he says he requires, then whisks the criminals away before Batman and Robin can apprehend them. Before long, the Dynamic Duo have become convinced that Bat-Mite has become a criminal. ". . . ***Bat-Mite*** obviously thinks it's more fun working ***against*** us," observes Batman grimly, "than ***with*** us!"

Ultimately, however — in spite of the fact that Wile has actually been filming the robberies in order to keep Bat-Mite fully persuaded of his honest intentions — Bat-Mite learns that he is being duped and, at the scene of the criminals' next robbery, allows Batman and Robin to apprehend them. "***Bat-Mite***--you really meant well," remarks Batman, after Wile and his henchmen have been taken into custody, ". . . so you're forgiven!" (Det No. 289: "The Bat-Mite Bandits!").

In December 1961 Bat-Mite meets Bat-Girl (*see* BAT-GIRL [BETTY KANE]) and agrees to use his magic powers to make Robin fall in love with her, but events do not proceed precisely as Bat-Mite had anticipated (BM No. 144/3: "Bat-Mite Meets Bat-Girl!").

In February 1962 Bat-Mite and Mr. Mxyzptlk renew their extradimensional rivalry, to the everlasting chagrin of Batman, Robin, and Superman. Serious complications arise, however, when the combined magical powers of the two super-pests somehow creates a rampaging monster which even their magic cannot control or destroy. Their rivalry quickly forgotten in the face of this magical menace, the two imps join forces in an effort to undo their mischief. Indeed, by the time they finally find a way to obliterate the monster with the aid of Batman, Robin, and Superman, it appears that the extradimensional mischief-makers have become fast friends (WF No. 123: "The Incredible Team of Bat-Mite and Mr. Mxyzptlk!").

In March 1962 a "student of magic" named Antura rewards Batman and Robin for saving his life by reciting a "strange and ancient verse" which, he promises, will endow them with magical power over objects made either of steel, rope, wood, or rubber. Although his intentions are honest, Antura does not really possess any magical powers, but Bat-Mite, who has been standing invisibly nearby, decides to have some fun at Batman's expense by using his own magical powers to make it appear that Antura's charm actually works. Before long, as the result of Bat-Mite's mischievous meddling, Batman and Robin have become convinced that they have actually become endowed with the ability to exercise magical control over steel, rope, wood, and rubber.

Bat-Mite's practical joke backfires, however, when Antura is kidnapped by criminals who want him to confer some of his magical powers upon them. When Batman deduces that Antura's captors have taken him to Gotham City's hippodrome, Bat-Mite, who feels guilt-stricken at what he has done, beats the Dynamic Duo to the hippodrome and arrives in time to see Antura attempting to confer magical powers on the hoodlums holding him prisoner.

Using his own magic, Bat-Mite first makes it appear that Antura has actually given the criminals magical powers, then whisks Antura safely to his home so that he will be out of harm's way. Bat-Mite intends to have some additional fun at the Dynamic Duo's expense by making it appear that they are using magical powers against criminals who also possess magical powers, but Batman has no sooner arrived at the hippodrome than he realizes that only Bat-Mite could have been the culprit behind the recent bizarre events. After bringing a halt to Bat-Mite's mischievous intervention, Batman and Robin apprehend the assembled kidnappers, then force Bat-Mite to come with them to Antura to admit his part in the recent hoax (BM No. 146/1: "Batman and Robin's Magical Powers").

In December 1962 Bat-Mite attempts to have some fun at the Dynamic Duo's expense by endowing three fugitive criminals with superhuman powers "so that **Batman** and **Robin** [will] **have** to use sensational tricks to defeat them!" The joke backfires, however, when an accidental blow on the head deprives Bat-Mite of "the ability to project [his] unearthly powers," thus enabling the Dynamic Duo's "super-opponents" to gain the upper hand and capture Batman, Robin, and even Bat-Mite himself.

"Your crazy powers got us into this jam," chides Batman angrily, "--now get us out of it!"

"I--I can't!" confesses Bat-Mite sadly. "I got hit on the head--and it's affected that part of my brain that enables me to project my powers!"

By the time the three companions have escaped from the watery deathtrap in which the criminals have placed them, the three criminals have split up, but Bat-Mite and the Dynamic Duo remain together to track them down one at a time. After they have apprehended one of the criminals and have begun to battle the second, Bat-Mite receives another blow on the head and regains his powers, but he keeps this development a secret so that he will not be compelled to bring the crime-fighting action to a speedy conclusion. After the third criminal has been apprehended, however, with the aid of some timely magical assistance from Bat-Mite, Bat-Mite makes a slip of the tongue which reveals to Batman that he had recovered his magical powers much earlier, but had deliberately kept it a secret. "You little imp!" scolds Robin angrily. "You didn't tell us because it might have spoiled your 'fun'!"

"Aw, gee whiz!" whines Bat-Mite. "Don't you guys have a sense of humor?" (Det No. 310: "Bat-Mite's Super-Circus!").

In September 1963 Bat-Mite decides to have some fun by endowing Bat-Hound with super-powers, but this joke, like Bat-Mite's other pranks, goes awry in a bizarre and unpredictable way (BM No. 158/1: "Ace--the Super Bat-Hound!"). (*See* ACE [THE BAT-HOUND].)

In February 1964, after Bat-Mite has capriciously intervened to prolong a battle between the Dynamic Duo and some criminals who have just looted a baseball stadium box office, Batman gives his extradimensional fan an angry dressing-down. "Catching criminals is no game, little feller!" scolds Batman. "You'd better learn that fast!"

"Oh gee-golly, ***Batman,***" replies Bat-Mite contritely, "--I just wanted to see my favorite crime-fighting hero in spectacular action. . . ."

"Well, since you can't control your emotions," retorts Batman sternly, "go and find yourself another hero, ***Bat-Mite!***"

"Humph!" muses Bat-Mite, as he stalks away in a self-righteous huff. "Fine way for a hero to treat his greatest fan! 'Go and find yourself another hero!' Hmm . . . maybe that's just what I'll do! I'll show him . . . he's got no monopoly on being a crime-fighter!"

Bat-Mite decides to create a hero of his own to steal the crime-fighting spotlight away from Batman and Robin. His first choice is Jerome Withers, a skinny fellow whom he promptly outfits in a stunning red costume with a picture of Bat-Mite emblazoned on the chest. Bat-Mite's plan is to use his magical powers to turn ordinary Jerome Withers into Gotham City's most spectacular crime-fighter, but after Withers has fallen off a high ledge while pursuing some criminals and Batman has been forced to intervene to rescue him, Bat-Mite concludes that Withers is not sufficiently athletic to serve as his hero.

The next wearer of Bat-Mite's heroic red costume is a muscular but brainless professional wrestler known as the Blond Bombshell. He possesses the athletic prerequisites of a crime-fighter, but his stupidity leads him to apprehend several criminals whom Batman and Robin had intentionally allowed to escape in order to locate their leader and the loot from their previous robberies, and Bat-Mite soon abandons his second hero as insufficiently intelligent.

Bat-Mite is despondent about his failure to produce a successful hero until he is approached by Frank Collins, who claims to have located a perfect hero for Bat-Mite to experiment with—a former Olympic champion, college graduate, and private detective named Bill Strong.

Bat-Mite promptly seizes upon this latest opportunity and makes Bill Strong his next hero, unaware of the fact that Collins is really a gangster, that Strong is one of his henchmen, and that Collins's real motive is to ensure the success of his gang's next robbery by having the costumed Strong pretend to apprehend them in order to forestall intervention by the Dynamic Duo.

Soon afterward, when Bat-Mite overhears a police radio broadcast summoning Batman and Robin to the Clean-All Soap Factory, where Collins's henchmen are stealing the payroll, he races there with Strong, eager to see his own hero swing into action before the Dynamic Duo arrive. Strong pretends to apprehend the fleeing criminals, but Batman, arriving moments afterward, hears Strong make a passing reference to "the decathlon medal in basketball" and realizes immediately that Strong is a criminal, not a former Olympic champion.

When Batman attempts to apprehend the criminals, however, Bat-Mite assumes that Batman is acting only out of jealousy and swiftly intervenes with his magical powers to prevent the Dynamic Duo from taking the criminals into custody. Seconds later, however, when he sees that his own hero is freeing the captive criminals and racing off with them, Bat-Mite realizes that he has been duped and quickly helps Batman and Robin capture them.

"Gol-lee gee . . . I've been stupid!" confesses Bat-Mite, after Strong and the other criminals have been safely taken into custody. "Can you ever forgive me, ***Batman?***"

"Well," replies Batman, "if you'll pop off into your dimension now and give us all a little time, ***Bat-Mite***. . . ."

Bat-Mite promptly disappears, promising to return another day (BM No. 161/2: "The Bat-Mite Hero!").

By September 1965 Bat-Mite and Mr. Mxyzptlk have returned to the earthly dimension and magically transformed themselves into colorfully costumed adolescents with superhuman powers, using the pseudonyms Speed Kid and Force Boy, as part of a wager they have made as to whether, if they wreak their customary mischief in these forms, Batman will be intelligent enough to deduce their actual identities.

The extradimensional imps lead Batman, Robin, and Superman a merry chase, leaving a trail of magical havoc in their wake and forcing the famed crime-fighters to speculate whether the newly arrived troublemakers are powerful androids, super-powered survivors from KRYPTON, or perhaps even the destructive advance guard of some impending alien invasion. Bat-Mite's undying faith in Batman is upheld, however, and he wins his wager with Mr. Mxyzptlk when Batman correctly deduces their identities.

"I appreciate your loyalty, **Bat-Mite,**" replies Batman with a pained expression after Bat-Mite has congratulated him, ". . . but won't you find someone else to admire? . . . **Please** . . ." (WF No. 152: "The Colossal Kids!" pts. I–II – no title; "The Magic of Bat-Mite and Mr. Mxyzptlk!").

BATMOBILE. The unique automobile, specially designed and equipped, which is the principal land vehicle employed by BATMAN and ROBIN. (*See* BATMAN [section E 2 a, the batmobile].)

BAT-PEOPLE, THE. A cunning race of elfin, batwinged people who, in their colorful costumes and batlike wings, bear a striking resemblance to the famous BATMAN. They inhabit "another dimension," somewhere beyond the "sonic barrier," where they stage repeated mass attacks on the peace-loving human civilization which inhabits the same dimension.

In June 1958, while piloting the BATPLANE through the pounding winds near the eye of a turbulent hurricane, Batman and ROBIN suddenly shatter the sonic barrier "at a speed ten times greater than was ever thought possible," only to find that their "high acceleration through the sonic barrier" has catapulted them into the extradimensional world of the evil bat-people and their peace-loving human adversaries. Mistaken for bat-people by the fearful humans, they are swiftly taken captive, dragged before the people's queen, and sentenced to imprisonment in a dank castle dungeon.

Before long, however, they have successfully proved their good intentions, established themselves as heroes in the eyes of their captors, and created a fiery natural barrier designed to prevent the bat-people from staging any further forays against the human stronghold. In addition, they help apprehend a band of traitors led by an unscrupulous royal minister named Arko, who have been secretly in league with the bat-people to overthrow the city and enslave its inhabitants. Finally, their work done, Batman and Robin pilot the batplane back through the sonic barrier to the safety of their own dimension (BM No. 116/3: "The Winged Bat-People!").

BATPLANE. The unique airplane, specially designed and equipped, which is the principal aircraft employed by BATMAN and ROBIN. (*See* BATMAN [section E 2 b i, the batplane].)

BAT-SIGNAL. The powerful searchlight, with the symbol of a bat silhouetted against its lens, which is situated atop the roof of police headquarters in GOTHAM CITY and used by POLICE COMMISSIONER GORDON to summon the services of BATMAN and ROBIN. (*See* BATMAN [section E 2 e, the bat-signal].)

BATWOMAN, THE. A lovely raven-haired crimefighter who functions periodically, from July 1956 onward, as the crime-fighting colleague of BATMAN and ROBIN. Batwoman is in reality Kathy Kane, a wealthy heiress and onetime "circus daredevil performer" noted for her outstanding ability both as a trapeze artist and motorcycle stunt rider (Det No. 233: "The Batwoman").

Kathy Kane, 1956 © NPP 1956

Kathy Kane is the aunt of Betty Kane, the "pretty teen-ager" who makes her crime-fighting debut as Bat-Girl (*see* BAT-GIRL [BETTY KANE]) in April 1961 and who functions periodically as Batwoman's crime-fighting partner from that time onward (BM No. 139/3: "Bat-Girl!").

For her role as Batwoman, Kathy wears a close-fitting yellow costume with red gloves, red ankle-length boots, a long red cape, a red pointed collar, and a red and yellow belt with a diamond-shaped buckle. Her highly stylized face-mask is sometimes red (Det No. 233, Jul '56: "The Batwoman"; and others) and sometimes yellow (BM No. 133/3, Aug '60: "Batwoman's Publicity Agent!"; and others).

The red "shoulder-bag utility-case" that Batwoman carries slung across her shoulder contains an extensive array of ingenious crime-fighting equipment, including "a large powder-puff" filled with sneezing powder, a "perfume flask" filled with tear gas, a special "hairnet" which expands rapidly to form a large net for ensnaring criminals (Det No. 233, Jul '56: "The Batwoman"), a smoke-bomb lipstick, a necklace of imitation pearls which Batwoman scatters across the floor like marbles to throw her opponents off balance (Det No. 276, Feb '60: "The Return of Bat-Mite!"), a telescoping "periscope lipstick" which enables Batwoman to peer around corners and over obstacles (Det No. 321, Nov '63: "The Terrible Trio!"), and a special device which Batwoman refers to as her "powder-puff smoke screen" (WF No. 139, Feb '64: "The Ghost of Batman!"). Batwoman's handsome "charm bracelets are really disguised steel handcuffs," and her "shoulder-bag strap . . . has weighted ends," which enables her to detach it from her utility case and use it as a serviceable "bat-bolo." Her principal means of transportation is a high-powered red motorcycle called the "bat-cycle" (Det No. 233, Jul '56: "The Batwoman").

Kathy Kane's opulently appointed suburban mansion stands directly over a "forgotten old mine-tunnel" which Kathy has transformed into her own personal "bat-cave," complete with a modern "crime-laboratory" and an all-inclusive set of crime files. A secret

Batwoman, 1956 © NPP 1956

stairway connects the bat-cave with the mansion above it (Det No. 233, Jul '56: "The Batwoman"), and "the old mine door" serves as a "secret entrance" connecting the cave with the outside world (BM No. 116/2, Jun '58: "Batwoman's New Identity"). One text refers to Kathy's bat-cave as her "batcavern" (BM No. 105/1, Feb '57: "The Challenge of Batwoman!"), but bat-cave is by far the most common rendering.

Only Batman, Robin, and Bat-Girl know that heiress Kathy Kane is also Batwoman. For her part, Kathy has never actually proven that BRUCE WAYNE is Batman, but she has long suspected it (Det No. 292, Jun '61: "The Colossus of Gotham City!"). As Kathy Kane, she has often been linked romantically with Bruce Wayne, while as Batwoman she has often been linked romantically with Batman. (*See* BATMAN [section J 4, the relationship with (the) Batwoman].)

The texts have referred to Batwoman as the Girl-Gangbuster.

Long before her first appearance as Batwoman, Kathy Kane was a skilled circus performer, renowned for her ability both as a trapeze artist and trick motorcycle-rider. Yet Kathy was not satisfied with her career as a performer. ". . . I wish I could be like ***Batman,*** the greatest acrobat of all!" she thought, as she swung gracefully from a high trapeze beneath the big top. "He uses **his** skill, not for shows, but against crime!"

Then, one day, an unexpected inheritance gave Kathy the opportunity to realize her life's ambition. "I inherit my uncle's entire fortune!" she thought happily, as she perused the letter informing her of her inheritance. "Now I **can** use my skills as **Batman** does! I, too, will fight crime--I'll be a **Batwoman!**"

After supervising the construction of a new mansion in the suburbs of GOTHAM CITY, carefully outfitting the bat-cave beneath it, designing a colorful costume to conceal her identity, and undergoing a long and arduous period of self-training, Kathy was finally ready to begin her crime-fighting career as Batwoman.

In July 1956 Batwoman appears in Gotham City for the first time, subdues two gunmen attempting to steal the "fare receipts" from the "new air terminal," and then races away into the night on her bat-cycle before Batman and Robin can either stop her or learn her identity.

"Wait!" cries Batman. "Whoever you are--***you*** can't crusade against crime! The law of Gotham City says that nobody can wear a ***Batman*** costume!"

"You're wrong, ***Batman,*** cries the fleeing Batwoman. "The law says 'no ***man*** can wear it.' I'm a woman!"

As the Dynamic Duo race to their BATMOBILE, Batman calls out his plan to Robin. "We'll trail her home," he exclaims, "and find out who she is--that way we can stop her interference!"

"***Batman,*** I give you fair warning," calls out Batwoman, as her bat-cycle roars away into the darkness, "--if you ever should penetrate **my** secret, you'll be automatically revealing your **own** identity!"

Batman and Robin give chase in the batmobile, but Batwoman eludes them by racing through a narrow alley, where the batmobile cannot follow.

On the following night, the mysterious Batwoman appears in Gotham City once again. On two separate occasions, she intervenes to rescue Batman from ruthless mobsters, thus enabling the Dynamic Duo to apprehend them, and then roars away on her bat-cycle before Batman and Robin can question her about her identity. Before long, Batwoman's heroic exploits have become the talk of Gotham City.

"She doesn't realize that she's been successful thus far because of **good luck!**" observes Batman grimly. "And she's so reckless that some criminal is bound to find out her identity. Then, when that happens, she'll be in bad danger!"

"Yet," replies Robin, "she said that if we exposed her, it would expose you, too!"

"I've got to risk that," replies Batman, "and reveal her identity--to prove to her she can't keep this up! If we only knew where her secret base is--."

That night, Bruce Wayne attends a lavish party at the home of Kathy Kane, unaware that his hostess is none other than the "mysterious and glamorous" Batwoman. At one point, after a news announcement about Batwoman's exploits has played over the radio, Kathy turns to Bruce Wayne and wonders aloud "how . . . any woman [could] ever equal the great ***Batman!***"

"You have to admire this ***Batwoman's*** courage, though!" replies Wayne.

Then, for a moment, both Bruce Wayne and Kathy Kane are left alone with their thoughts. "So she admires ***Batman!***" muses Wayne. "If only I could tell her I'm ***Batman***--but I can't!"

"Bruce is so good-looking," thinks Kathy to herself, "--and he admires ***Batwoman!*** If--sigh--he only knew ***I'm Batwoman!***"

Later, as the party breaks up, Wayne sees the pale glow of the BAT-SIGNAL lighting up the nighttime sky and hastily changes into his Batman costume under cover of some nearby shrubbery. At the same moment, Kathy races into her bat-cave and changes into her Batwoman costume in response to the same alarm, and before long both Batwoman and the Dynamic Duo have arrived at the Tomorrow Club, a "futuristic nightclub outside town" which, for no apparent reason, is being terrorized by an armed hoodlum.

In the battle that follows, Batwoman cries out a warning to Batman just in time to save him from being crushed by a falling statue and, moments later, Batman returns the favor by knocking Batwoman out of the way of a blow aimed at her by one of the nightclub's huge robotlike decorations, which has been activated by the gunman wreaking havoc at the club. The robot's mighty arm misses Batwoman completely, but Batman is knocked unconscious by a glancing blow. Working alone, however, Batwoman captures the fleeing gunman and then returns to tend to the fallen Batman.

"While he's unconscious," thinks Batwoman, "--I could lift his mask and see who he is--no--I can't do it! He got stunned only because he tried to save me from a blow! I'm to blame for his plight. It wouldn't be fair for me to unmask him!"

Within moments, Batman has revived, but although he quickly recognizes the captured gunman as "one of Hugo Vorn's mob," the hoodlum refuses to explain his reason for terrorizing the Tomorrow Club. "Vorn would only have one reason to order this place wrecked," reasons Batman, "--to draw **us** here while he committed some robbery **elsewhere!**"

Suddenly, Batman spies a large advertising blimp, which "normally cruises over the city every night," dropping suspiciously "toward the East Side section--toward the [Gotham City] mint!"

Racing swiftly to the mint, Batwoman and the Dynamic Duo soon learn that Batman's suspicions were well-founded – that Hugo Vorn and his gang have commandeered the advertising blimp and are using it to stage a surprise raid on the mint. Working together, the three crime-fighters quickly thwart the attempted raid on the mint and take the Vorn gang into custody, but Batman allows Batwoman to turn the criminals over to the police by herself while he returns to the BATCAVE with Robin to ponder the secret of Batwoman's dual identity.

In recent conversations with the Dynamic Duo, Batwoman has employed a number of "circus terms," leading Batman to deduce that "***Batwoman*** must be an expert circus performer" capable of the stunts that Batman and Robin have seen her perform during her encounters with criminals. Before long, the batcave's "file of theatrical and circus people" has yielded up the name and photograph of Kathy Kane. Then, a quick check of the batcave's "cave and tunnel charts" reveals the existence of "an old mine-tunnel leading to where Kathy's house now stands!"

Later that night, when Batwoman returns to the subterranean bat-cave situated beneath the Kane mansion, she finds Batman and Robin waiting there to greet her. "Hello--Kathy!" says Batman quietly.

"So you found me out!" replies Batwoman. "All right--but you've given away your **own** identity by doing so!"

"Listen, Kathy," continues Batman, "--if ***I*** found you out, crooks could do so, too, eventually! Once they learned your real identity, you'd be in mortal danger!"

"I--I never thought of that!" replies Kathy. "I guess you're right! I--I'll quit my career as ***Batwoman*** . . . !" Kathy goes on to explain, however, that she could also uncover the secret of Batman's identity, if she so chose, for hidden behind the huge Batwoman portrait which guards the entrance to her bat-cave "are cameras and instruments which take photos, X-ray pictures, and record the height and weight of everyone who comes in here!"

"Then you have enough data there to trace my real identity!" remarks Batman.

"I could," replies Kathy, "--but I won't. Here are the films and record-tapes--I won't look at them! I--I could never harm you, ***Batman!***"

"Thanks, Kathy!" replies Batman.

On the way home, however, Batman reveals to Robin that there was never actually any danger of Kathy's uncovering the secret of his dual identity. "Then you **knew** about that automatic X-ray and data device?" asks Robin. "Yes," replies Batman, "the camera-lenses concealed in her portrait's *'eyes'* made them the wrong color, and I investigated! I over-exposed her films of me before she came!"

Sometime later, "a new trophy is added to Batman's batcave" – it is the gigantic color-portrait that used to guard the bat-cave beneath the Kane mansion.

". . . she gave me the portrait now that her career's over!" remarks Batman. "I thought it would be an--er--interesting trophy!" (Det No. 233: "The Batwoman").

In February 1957 Kathy Kane recalls how, some seven months earlier, Batman had uncovered the secret of her dual identity and made her promise to abandon her career as a crime-fighter. "If only I could wear this [Batwoman] costume once again," muses Kathy longingly, "just once!" Suddenly, she is seized by an inspiration. "***Hmm*** . . . maybe I can--and without breaking my promise to ***Batman!*** I can wear it to the masquerade ball tonight!"

Later, on her way to the masquerade party, the costumed Kathy passes the scene of a just-completed battle between the Dynamic Duo and a gang of criminals who specialize in the theft of valuable art treasures. In the course of the fighting, a complex series of events have taken place: Batman has severely sprained his ankle and is momentarily out of sight, and Curt Briggs, the athletic proprietor of a physical culture school who has been, up to now, the secret leader of the gang, has developed amnesia as the result of a blow on the head. Briggs has removed the cowl with which he had formerly concealed his true identity, even from his own henchmen, but an outline etched on his face in black soot, the result of a recent chase with Batman and Robin across the top of a moving railroad car, reveals that Briggs had been accustomed to wearing a cowl to cover his face.

When Batwoman arrives on the scene and sees Robin with the unmasked Briggs, she leaps to the conclusion that Briggs, because of the sooty cowl-like outline across his face, must really be the unmasked Batman. When it becomes apparent that Briggs has become the victim of amnesia, Batwoman proposes that she and Robin take Briggs to her bat-cave in order to retrain him thoroughly as a crime-fighter, so the underworld will not learn that Batman has developed amnesia.

Robin plays along with Batwoman, thinking that the secret of Batman's identity will be jeopardized if Batwoman discovers that both Batman and Bruce Wayne have injured ankles. Batman encourages Robin to retrain the amnesiac Briggs as a Batman so that the underworld will not realize that the real Batman is temporarily out of action because of an injury.

After a period of arduous training in Batwoman's bat-cave, Briggs, clad in a Batman costume, actually begins to function as the crime-fighting companion of Robin and Batwoman. At one point, however, unbeknownst to either Robin or Batwoman, a magazine picture jars Briggs's memory and snaps him out of his amnesia. He decides to continue as Batman, pretending that he is still suffering from a loss of memory, until he can lure Robin and Batwoman into a trap.

Finally, after Robin, Batwoman, and the Batman-clad Briggs have raced to the Chinatown Museum to prevent Briggs's former cohorts from stealing a valuable jade Buddha there, Briggs turns on his crime-fighting companions and takes them prisoner. The real Batman, however, has discovered that Briggs has regained his memory and, taking care to conceal his injured ankle, he arrives on the scene in time to rescue Robin and Batwoman from their captors and join them in apprehending Briggs and his henchmen.

Later, Robin apologizes to Batwoman for having deceived her about Briggs's true identity, and expresses his hope that she will forgive him.

"I do," replies Batwoman with a sigh, "and it was fun while it lasted . . . but it looks like the ***Batwoman*** is going into retirement again!" (BM No. 105/1: "The Challenge of Batwoman!").

In September–October 1957, after the notorious ELTON CRAIG has broken out of the Metropolis Prison, Kathy Kane decides to resume her career as a crime-fighter. "I, who was once **Batwoman,** could help **Batman** and **Superman** in this emergency!" thinks Kathy. "Even though **Batman** discovered my identity and insisted I give up my career, he'd surely welcome my help now!" "If **I** could catch him," she thinks to herself as she races toward Elton Craig's former hideout, ". . . it would show **Batman** what I can do!"

At the abandoned hideout, Batwoman encounters Batman, Robin, and SUPERMAN and explains to them that she felt certain that they would not mind her helping them. "We **do** mind," insists Batman, "--it's too big a risk! Remember, **I** discovered your identity, **Batwoman,** and crooks could do the same!"

"Oh--all right!" retorts an angry Batwoman. "I'll go back home again!"

On the way home, however, Batwoman passes an abandoned chemical factory and, on a hunch, steps inside to look for Elton Craig. Ultimately, Batwoman apprehends Craig, but not before she has become endowed with temporary super-powers as the result of swallowing a special "radioactive capsule" invented long ago by the Kryptonian scientist JOR-EL, Superman's father.

After returning Craig to the Metropolis Prison, Batwoman — whose super-powers will not fade away for about twenty-four hours — rejoins Batman, Robin, and Superman at Craig's old hideout and tells them about what has happened to her.

"--but super-powers can be **dangerous!**" insists Batman. "You must go home and stay safely quiet until your powers have faded away!"

"Batman," replies Batwoman, "I'm tired of your bossing me! Just because you found out my identity, you think you're superior and keep lecturing me!"

"But it's only for your own good--" insists Batman.

"I'm going to find out **your** secret identities!" exclaims Batwoman to the assembled crime-fighters. "I won't tell anyone, but **that'll** keep you from bossing me!"

Batwoman attempts to use her newly acquired X-ray vision to peer through the Dynamic Duo's face-masks, but Batman has already taken the precaution of asking Superman to line their masks with lead, which X-ray vision cannot penetrate. When Superman makes a remark to the effect that Batman has outwitted her once again, Batwoman becomes furious. "I've got super-powers for twenty-four hours," she declares, "and I'll use those to discover your secret identities somehow! From now on, I'm out to learn your secrets!"

For the next twenty-four hours, the temporarily super-powered Batwoman makes a determined effort to uncover the secret identities of Batman, Robin, and Superman, but the three crime-fighters manage to outwit her at every turn. "All right," confesses Batwoman, after the twenty-four hours have elapsed and her super-powers have finally disappeared, "--you [i.e., Superman] and **Batman** have won--I'll go back home and never be **Batwoman** again!"

"No, **Batwoman,**" replies Batman, "we think you've **won!** You showed such cleverness and courage that I can't ask you to drop your career completely. Just be careful!"

"Oh, **Batman--Superman,**" cries Batwoman happily, "--you're darlings after all!" (WF No. 90: "The Super-Batwoman!").

In November 1957 POLICE COMMISSIONER GORDON summons Bruce Wayne to his office and asks him to accept a dangerous undercover assignment. He explains that "dangerous convict" Squint Neely has somehow obtained a copy of "the builder's blueprint of **Gotham Prison!**" With it, continues Gordon, Neely and other imprisoned convicts "could find an escape route out of prison!"

Gordon asks Wayne to allow himself to be unmasked as the Collector, a notorious criminal currently being sought by the Gotham City police. According to the plan, Wayne would allow himself to be arrested, tried, and convicted of the Collector's crimes so that he could become Squint Neely's cellmate at the Gotham Prison and, hopefully, discover where Neely has hidden the important blueprint. "I warn you, it's risky," concludes Gordon, "--because, for security reasons, no one else--not even the warden--will know the truth! Will you do it?"

"When do I start?" replies Wayne.

In the days that follow, Bruce Wayne is "unmasked" as the notorious Collector, tried and convicted on the basis of false evidence carefully manufactured by Police Commissioner Gordon, and then sentenced to a term in Gotham Prison as Squint Neely's cellmate.

By promising Neely $50,000 if he will help him escape from prison, Wayne persuades Neely to let him take part in the mass breakout attempt scheduled for the following night. Then, on the day of the escape attempt, Wayne waits until Neely has recovered the blueprint from its hiding place inside a vat of soap flakes in the prison laundry, then seizes the blueprint and rings a nearby alarm to summon the warden and the prison guards. Before the guards have arrived on the scene, however, Neely, enraged at Wayne for having double-crossed him, seizes a heavy laundry iron and rushes at Wayne, only to slip in a puddle of soap flakes and die almost instantly after striking his head on the concrete floor.

When the guards arrive, the other convicts, bitter at Wayne for having thwarted their escape attempt, accuse him of having masterminded it and then of having murdered Neely when Neely attempted to sound the alarm. Within seconds the plot has taken a bizarre turn as Bruce Wayne is charged with the murder of Squint Neely.

"Wait!" cries Wayne, as a prison guard starts to lead him away to his cell. "Call up Police Commissioner Gordon! He'll clear me!"

"Gordon?" exclaims the warden. "That's impossible! He was in an auto accident--and has been in a coma ever since!"

In the words of the textual narrative, "The machinery of the law grinds swiftly--and Bruce soon finds himself in that place of last hopes . . . the **DEATH HOUSE,**" awaiting execution for the first-degree murder of Squint Neely.

When a tearful DICK GRAYSON visits him in prison, Wayne suggests that he call on Batwoman and ask for her help in establishing his innocence. Later, when Robin pays a visit to the Kane mansion, Kathy Kane agrees to help Bruce Wayne in any way she can, but only on the condition that Robin agree to work out of her bat-cave, and follow her orders, just as he would Batman's.

In the days that follow, Batwoman and Robin engage in a series of battles with the Collector and his henchmen on the theory that only by apprehending the real Collector can they establish that Wayne is not the Collector and lend credibility to his claim that he had allowed himself to be tried and convicted as the Collector only as part of an undercover mission for Police Commissioner Gordon.

Ironically, although Batwoman is the self-appointed leader of their crime-fighting effort, it is Robin's quick thinking and fine detective work which ultimately enable them to apprehend the Collector and his cohorts and establish Bruce Wayne's innocence just as Wayne is being led down the infamous last mile to his doom in the Gotham Prison execution chamber. Time and again, Batwoman overlooks important clues, only to have Robin correctly interpret the physical evidence.

Later, after the real Collector has been jailed and Bruce Wayne has been released from prison, Batwoman apologizes for her somewhat arbitrary behavior. "I shouldn't have been so smug about those clues!" she confesses. "I've been a fool. . . ."

"No, Batwoman," replies Wayne, "--from what **Robin** tells me, he couldn't have cracked this case without your fine help! **Batman himself** couldn't have done better!" (Det No. 249: "The Crime of Bruce Wayne!").

In June 1958 Batwoman poses as a blond photographer at the Tally Ho Club as part of a plan to apprehend the infamous FUNNY FACE GANG. When one of the gang members sees through her disguise, Batwoman is taken prisoner and carried captive to the gang's warehouse hideout on the Gotham City waterfront. She manages, however, to summon Batman and Robin, who swiftly invade the warehouse hideaway, rescue Batwoman, and, with her help, apprehend the entire Funny Face Gang (BM No. 116/2: "Batwoman's New Identity").

In October 1958 Batwoman and VICKI VALE are chosen as the finalists in Gotham City's annual Woman of the Year contest. Because the judges are unable to agree on a final decision, they give Batwoman and Vicki six additional hours "in which to prove who is more talented in her chosen field," in order to give them a basis for selecting the final winner (BM No. 119/1: "The Arch-Rivals of Gotham City").

In March 1959 Dick Grayson, the boy who is secretly Robin, falls asleep in an armchair and dreams that Kathy Kane has become the wife of Bruce Wayne, and therefore the wife of Batman. The dream reaches a tragic climax when Kathy's careless interference in her husband's crime-fighting affairs results in the exposure of his secret identity to the underworld (BM No. 122/3: "The Marriage of Batman and Batwoman!").

In August 1959 Batwoman, summoned to the rescue by a frantically barking Bat-Hound (*see* ACE [THE BAT-HOUND]), uses a steam shovel to dig Batman and Robin out of an abandoned gold mine after they have been trapped there by the notorious Mr. Midas. Then she joins forces with Batman, Robin, and Bat-Hound to apprehend Mr. Midas and his entire gang of gold thieves (BM No. 125/1: "The Secret Life of Bat-Hound").

In September 1959 Batwoman joins forces with Batman and Robin to apprehend the Firefly (*see* FIREFLY, THE [TED CARSON]). For a time, as Kathy Kane, she becomes embroiled in a romance with Ted Carson, the man who is secretly the Firefly, after a series of coincidences has led her to the erroneous conclusion that Ted Carson is secretly Batman.

"C-Carson is . . . ***the Firefly!***" shudders Batwoman, after Carson has revealed his true colors and taken her prisoner. "And I fell in love with him because I thought he was ***Batman!*** What a fool I've been! What a mistake I made. . . ."

Batwoman manages to escape from her bonds, however, in time to help Batman and Robin capture the villain and his henchmen as they attempt to flee the scene of a daring robbery at the Gotham Museum of Natural History (BM No. 126/3: "The Menace of the Firefly!").

During this same period, Batwoman helps foil a plot by the evil LEX LUTHOR to destroy Superman (WF No. 104, Sep '59: "The Plot to Destroy Superman!").

In February 1960 Batwoman – who is helped, and occasionally hindered, by the mischievous BAT-MITE – joins forces with Batman and Robin to apprehend the notorious Hobby Robber (Det No. 276: "The Return of Bat-Mite!"). During this same period, Batwoman joins forces with Batman and Robin to apprehend the cunning villain known as the SPINNER (BM No. 129/1, Feb '60: "The Web of the Spinner!").

In April 1960 ALFRED composes his first "imaginary tale," an entirely fictional account "of what possibly might happen . . . in the future!" In it, an elderly Batman announces his retirement from crime-fighting and settles down to a life of relaxation with Kathy Kane, "whom he had long ago married. . . ." Dick Grayson, now a grown man, inherits Batman's mantle and continues the fight against crime as Batman II, while the Waynes' young son, Bruce Wayne, Jr., joins him as Robin II. At one point, Batman II and Robin II are taken captive by the Babyface Jordan gang, but Bruce Wayne and his wife climb into their old crime-fighting costumes and race to the rescue, and before long Batman II and Robin II have been freed and the mobsters taken into custody (BM No. 131/3: "The Second Batman and Robin Team!").

In August 1960 Batwoman finds that she has taken on more trouble than she has bargained for when she agrees, albeit reluctantly, to allow BAT-MITE to become her "new partner" (BM No. 133/3: "Batwoman's Publicity Agent!").

In November 1960, when a prehistoric "man-beast" – kept alive in a state of suspended animation inside a block of ice at the Gotham Museum – comes alive, flees the museum, and runs amok in Gotham City, it is Batwoman who eases the man-beast's ravenous hunger with a roast chicken and thus enables Batman and Robin to return him to a cage at the museum. Later, after the man-beast has been released from his cage by a murderer who hopes to blame the man-beast for his own crime, the man-beast leaps to Batwoman's rescue when she is attacked by a mountain lion and dies when he and the struggling mountain lion plummet over the edge of a cliff. "He--he sacrificed his life for me!" sobs Batwoman. "Perhaps it's better this way!" suggests Batman softly. "The world he knew died ages ago! Had he lived, he would have been a freak in our time!" (Det No. 285: "The Mystery of the Man-Beast!").

By December 1960 Kathy Kane has purchased an unusual Tibetan belt from Carter's Curio Shop, unaware of the fact that the belt is endowed with bizarre powers and that, when reunited with its two missing parts – a gold buckle and a red star which fits inside it – it will endow its wearer with super-strength, the ability to defy gravity, immortality, and other fabulous powers.

During this period, Batwoman joins forces with Batman and Robin to battle a mysterious costumed villain named Star-Man, who is determined to possess the three vital parts of the fabulous Tibetan belt. For a time, it appears that Batwoman will weaken and die as a result of a "strange force" associated with the interaction of the belt's parts, but she and the Dynamic Duo ultimately defeat Star-Man, reunite the belt's three parts long enough to banish the mysterious force that has sapped her strength, and then destroy it because, in Batwoman's words, "It's far too dangerous for a mortal to possess!" (Det No. 286: "The Doomed Batwoman!").

In April 1961, the month which marks the textual debut of Bat-Girl (*see* BAT-GIRL [BETTY KANE]), Batwoman joins forces with Batman, Robin, and Bat-Girl to apprehend the notorious Cobra Gang (BM No. 139/3: "Bat-Girl!").

In May 1961 Batwoman becomes accidentally endowed with superhuman powers and falls under the control of the evil scientist LEX LUTHOR. She is rescued from his clutches, however, through the heroic efforts of Batman, Robin, and Superman (WF No. 117: "The Super-Batwoman and the Super-Creature!").

In June 1961 Batwoman helps Batman and Robin apprehend the "ROCKETS" ROGAN gang (Det No. 292: "The Colossus of Gotham City!").

In August 1961 Batwoman joins forces with Batman, Robin, and Bat-Girl to apprehend the criminal known as the Moth (BM No. 141/3: "Batwoman's Junior Partner!"). (*See* BAT-GIRL [BETTY KANE].)

In December 1961 Batwoman and Batman leave Gotham City for Washington, D.C., where they are scheduled to testify before a Senate crime committee. In their absence, Police Commissioner Gordon asks Robin and Bat-Girl to patrol Gotham City on their own, but he does not reckon on the mischievous intervention of Bat-Mite (BM No. 144/3: "Bat-Mite Meets Bat-Girl!"). (*See* BAT-GIRL [BETTY KANE].)

In April 1962 Batwoman helps Batman and Robin apprehend the gang of criminals headed by the villain Vulcan (Det No. 302: "The Bronze Menace!"). (*See* WINNS, HENRY.)

In September 1962 ALPHA, THE EXPERIMENTAL MAN, falls in love with Batwoman and ultimately sacrifies his life to save her after she has become trapped on the crumbling ledge of a rocky cliff (Det No. 307: "Alpha, the Experimental Man!").

In November 1962 Batman is elected king of a gala Mardi Gras festival, and Batwoman is chosen to serve as his queen. When Batman insists that Vicki Vale be allowed to share the regal honors because of her role in solving two recent murders, Batwoman becomes furious, but has no choice but to grant Batman's request. "Imagine," fumes Batwoman jealously, "***Batman*** choosing ***her*** to share this honor with ***me!*** Hmmmph!" (Det No. 309: "The Mystery of the Mardi Gras Murders!").

In January 1963 Batwoman joins forces with Batman and Robin in an attempt to apprehend the CAT-MAN. Batwoman's role in the battle is somewhat complicated by the fact that the Cat-Man has fallen in love with her (Det No. 311: "The Challenge of the Cat-Man!").

In February 1963 Batwoman joins forces with Batman, Robin, and Bat-Girl (*see* Bat-Girl [Betty Kane]) to defeat the evil extradimensional scientist ZEBO (BM No. 153: chs. 1–3 – "Prisoners of Three Worlds!"; "Death from Beyond"; "Dimension of Doom").

Batwoman and Batman, 1963 © NPP 1963

In August 1963 Batwoman once again becomes embroiled in a deadly battle with the villainous CAT-MAN (Det No. 318: "The Cat-Man Strikes Back!").

In November 1963 Batwoman rescues the Dynamic Duo just as it appears that they have been hopelessly doomed to a grisly death in outer space by the TERRIBLE TRIO (Det No. 321: "The Terrible Trio!").

During this same period, Batwoman and Bat-Girl (*see* Bat-Girl [Betty Kane]) apprehend the JOKER as he attempts to flee the scene of a daring robbery at the Gotham Museum (BM No. 159/1, Nov '63: "The Great Clayface-Joker Feud!").

In February 1964 – the month in which Batman, Robin, and Superman join forces to apprehend the SPHINX GANG – a series of events occur which convince Batwoman that she has been correct all along in assuming that Bruce Wayne is secretly Batman. Wayne ultimately succeeds in persuading Batwoman that she has made a mistake, however, by means of an elaborate ruse involving the complicity of Superman, Robin, and Alfred (WF No. 139: "The Ghost of Batman!").

In March 1964 Batwoman joins forces with Batman and Robin in another battle with the diabolical CAT-MAN (Det No. 325: "The Strange Lives of the Cat-Man!").

During this same period, after the evil ERIC BARROC has transformed Batman into a gorillalike "beast-human" with his diabolical "transformation ray," it is Batwoman who befriends the bestial "Batman creature" by offering it some fruit to eat. Later, after Batwoman, Robin, and Bat-Hound have finally made their way to the villain's hideout, Barroc attempts to destroy them by loosing his collection of wild animals from their cages. The Batman creature, however, sees its friend Batwoman in danger and uses its strength to defeat the ferocious animals, thus enabling Batwoman and Robin to apprehend Barroc and his accomplice and, with the aid of the transformation ray, to restore Batman to his normal human condition (BM No. 162/1, Mar '64: "The Batman Creature!").

World's Finest Comics No. 154 contains an "imaginary tale" in which Kathy Kane appears as the wife of Bruce Wayne and the mother of their son, Bruce Wayne, Jr., while LOIS LANE appears as the wife of CLARK KENT and the mother of their son, Kal-El, Jr. After the youngsters have had a childish quarrel over whose father is the most impressive hero, their mothers take up the argument and refuse to allow their sons to play with one another anymore. Bruce Wayne, Jr. and Kal-El, Jr. ultimately reunite their warring families by pretending to leave home. At one point, they are kidnapped by an escaped convict named Nappy Klains, the so-called "Napoleon of crime," but they join forces as a sort of junior Batman-Superman team and apprehend their abductor (Dec '65: "The Sons of Superman and Batman!" pts. 1–2 – no title; "The Junior Super-Team").

BECKETT, TOM. An explorer who is secretly the adopted son of "Grey Mike" Riggs, a notorious criminal executed at Baxter Prison north of GOTHAM CITY in March–April 1954 after being apprehended by BATMAN and ROBIN.

Soon after Riggs's execution, Beckett is stricken by a rare jungle malady contracted during a recent expedition and informed by his physician that he has only a month to live. "Crazed by the fear of death" and tortured by the memory of his foster father's recent execution, Beckett – his sanity fading – vows to devote his final month of life to the destruction of Batman. "If I must die," muses Beckett, "I will not die in vain! The man who **killed** my father--**Batman**--dies with me! This will be my revenge!"

In the days that follow, Beckett makes a series of elaborate but unsuccessful attempts at murder-suicide, each designed to bring a violent end to his own terminal illness while simultaneously destroying Batman.

Ultimately, however, Batman provides Beckett's doctors with a little-known native remedy that cures Beckett of his disease and completely restores his sanity, so that he is no longer possessed by the senseless desire to kill Batman in order to avenge his foster father's death (WF No. 69: "The Man Who Wanted to Die with Batman!").

BELDON, "BRAINS." The leader of a gang of criminals who concoct an elaborate scheme to make off with $20,000,000 being transported to the new headquarters of the Gotham National Bank in a convoy of armored trucks. The Dynamic Duo's efforts to apprehend the Beldon gang — and, in fact, all of their crime-fighting efforts during this period — are severely hampered by the fact that a freak accident in a synthetic gem factory has so altered BATMAN's bodily structure that regular air is poisonous to him and he can breathe only methane. In addition, Batman's body has begun to radiate heat of such extreme intensity that he represents a continual hazard to all life around him.

In order to combat this dilemma, Batman orders the immediate construction of a special one-man hovercraft, powered by compressed air, fitted with a heatproof dome of transparent plastic, equipped with special telescoping arms and pincers which can be operated from within, and supplied continually with cylinders of methane gas to enable Batman to breathe inside it without difficulty.

For a time, Batman fights crime successfully from within his transparent prison, but nevertheless, by means of a cunningly contrived diversion, Beldon and his henchmen succeed in luring the city's policemen away from the bank convoy long enough to loot the currency-laden trucks and flee with the $20,000,000. Batman gives chase and, in the course of attempting to apprehend them, is accidentally struck by a falling power line; somehow, the "tremendous jolt of electricity" that surges through his body counteracts Batman's "strange condition" and restores him to normal, and he and ROBIN apprehend the "Brains" Beldon gang soon afterward (Det No. 301, Mar '62: "The Condemned Batman!").

BELINDA. An alias employed by the CATWOMAN in April–May 1944 when she poses as a maid in the lavish home of her accomplice Craven in order to enable her to mingle with the servants of local wealthy families and learn where their valuables are hidden. ALFRED becomes quite smitten with Belinda until he learns that she is secretly the Catwoman (BM No. 22/1: "The Duped Domestics!").

BELL, LONGHORN. The leader of a gang of criminals who, aided by a geologist named Duane, successfully plunder a series of subterranean "atom caves" — i.e., lead-lined caves used by institutions and wealthy individuals to safeguard their art treasures and other valuables in the event of an atomic attack — until they are finally apprehended by BATMAN and ROBIN in December 1951–January 1952. At one point, after Duane's sensitive geological instruments have disclosed the existence of a large, sprawling cave beneath the Wayne mansion — a cave whose specifications do not conform to those characteristic of an atom cave — Bell and his cohorts tunnel their way into the BATCAVE, certain that they have inadvertently stumbled upon the secret identities of Batman and Robin. Aided by ALFRED, however, Batman and Robin trick the criminals into believing that the cave they have uncovered is only an elaborately equipped subterranean set being used in the filming of a Batman movie (BM No. 68/1: "The Atom Cave Raiders!").

BELLOWS, RALPH. An unscrupulous GOTHAM CITY businessman who attempts to capitalize on the fact that an honest ex-convict named Ed Stinson has just opened an employment agency for ex-convicts by robbing the firms which employ Stinson's clients and then abducting the ex-convicts themselves so that the missing ex-convicts will appear to have absconded with the loot and consequently be blamed for the thefts. Bellows and his henchmen are apprehended by BATMAN and ROBIN in October 1956 (BM No. 103/2: "The League of Ex-Convicts").

BELTT (Warden). The brutal warden of an out-of-state prison farm and the secret leader of the so-called Whiskers Mob, a gang of criminals who pull daring robberies and then vanish before they can be apprehended. Actually, the Whiskers Mob is comprised of prison farm inmates who, in concert with their warden and his corrupt prison staff, sneak away from the prison farm to commit robberies and then quickly return to the prison farm to establish perfect alibis for themselves. After apprehending the Whiskers Mob in the act of committing a robbery at a local oil field, BATMAN and ROBIN return to the prison farm with the local sheriff and his deputies and take Warden Beltt and his staff into custody (BM No. 47/2, Jun/Jul '48: "The Chain Gang Crimes!").

BELVOS. The far-distant planet which is the home of the evil KLOR. BATMAN, ROBIN, and SUPERMAN visit Belvos in December 1961 (WF No. 122: "The Capture of Superman!").

BENNETT, "KEYS." A wanted criminal who has considered the key his lucky symbol ever since he received an unusual key-shaped scar on his face. Bennett and his henchmen are apprehended by BATMAN and ROBIN in October–November 1952 (BM No. 73/2: "Vicki Vale's Secret!"). (*See* VALE, VICKI.)

BENTLEY. The head of the Argus Motion Picture Company, the company which produces the horror film *Dread Castle* in June 1940. "Stay with me," insists Bentley, after BATMAN and ROBIN have defeated the maniacal Clayface (*see* CLAYFACE [BASIL KARLO]), "and you have a career in the movies!" "Sorry!" replies Batman. "Our career is our constant battle against **crime** and **evil!**" (Det No. 40).

By March 1941 *Dread Castle* has been released, and the "rave notices" that JULIE MADISON has received for her role in it have made her a star. Convinced that Julie's new fame calls for a more glamorous name, Bentley instructs his publicity manager, Gabby Fest, to come up with an exciting stage name, and Fest conceives the name Portia Storme. During this period, Bentley again offers Batman a career in films, but once again Batman feels compelled to decline (Det No. 49: "Clayface Walks Again!").

BIFF. An elevator operator at the building which houses the Maskers, a club for people who wear masks in their everyday work. In August–September 1952, in order to accumulate the equipment he needs to launch a projected counterfeiting operation, Biff stages a series of spectacular thefts while clad in costumes similar to those worn by members of the Maskers, such as a deep-sea diver's uniform or a set of knightly armor. Through this elaborate masquerade, Biff hopes to cast suspicion elsewhere while at the same time concealing his thick prescription eyeglasses which, were they to be seen by witnesses, would quickly lead to the discovery of his identity. Ultimately, however, BATMAN deduces the identity of the mysterious thief, and he and ROBIN take him into custody (BM No. 72/2: "The Legion of Faceless Men!").

BIGBEE, "ANGLES." The former GOTHAM CITY gang chief who is the leader of the Snow Man Bandits, a gang of criminals, headquartered in an elaborate hide-out built into the side of Bikou Glacier, somewhere in the Arctic, who prey on trading posts and fur shipments in Alaska, Greenland, and the Baffin Bay area until they are finally apprehended by BATMAN, ROBIN, and the aroused citizens of North Town – a settlement in the vicinity of the Alaskan Klondike – in Fall 1942. Bigbee is crushed to death when, during a final battle with Batman, he falls into an icy crevasse which closes again before he can escape (WF No. 7: "The North Pole Crimes!").

BIG GAME HUNTER, THE. A ruthless villain who, with the grudging assistance of ROY REYNOLDS, concocts an elaborate plot to capture BATMAN in September 1965. The Big Game Hunter's real name is apparently B. G. Hunter, but it is not possible to state this with certainty based on the textual evidence. "For **B. G. Hunter**," observes the text, "who has tramped the African veldt for lions--who has climbed the peaks of frozen Himalaya mountains to capture the horned ibex--there is one hunting thrill still untasted--the bagging of **Batman!** For only then will he be able to claim the laurel wreath of victory as the world's greatest **huntsman!**"

By September 1965 the Big Game Hunter has broken Roy Reynolds out of prison and imprisoned him in a barred cage at his hideout. "My racket is big game hunting," explains the Big Game Hunter, "--at which I'm the world's best! But when it comes to crime, I'm a ***big zero!*** And I need a spectacular crime with a perfect getaway to bag ***Batman*** . . . the biggest game of all!

"Killing is not for me," continues the villain, ". . . I want to take ***Batman*** alive! As my prisoner, he'll be so brainwashed, that when I turn him loose, he'll be a 'tamed animal'--with no knowledge of who 'broke' him--and no ability to function as ***Batman*** again! It'll be my ***greatest triumph!***"

Reynolds, who believes that any effort to defeat Batman is doomed to failure, is reluctant to help the Big Game Hunter with his plan, but under the circumstances he appears to have little real choice. Soon afterward, acting on Reynolds's crime plan, the Big Game Hunter's henchmen steal some jewelry from GOTHAM CITY's Riverside Museum, then intentionally leave a trail for Batman to follow. Batman pursues the thieves to the Big Game Hunter's mansion hideaway, only to find himself hurtling through a trapdoor into a huge plastic bag suspended from the ceiling of one of the rooms. Suddenly, other henchmen rush forward and begin punching Batman in an effort to keep him hyperactive so that he will exhaust his supply of oxygen in the bag and lapse into unconsciousness, after which the Big Game Hunter intends to transfer him to a barred cage.

Batman, however, deduces the Big Game Hunter's intention, feigns unconsciousness, and apprehends the villain and his henchmen as soon as they release him from the plastic bag (BM No. 174/1: "The Human Punching Bag!").

BIG-HEARTED JOHN. A corpulent, cigar-smoking loan shark who orders his victims beaten up and even killed if they fail to pay the exorbitant interest he demands. During a climactic battle with BATMAN and ROBIN, Big-Hearted John is apparently killed when he accidentally topples from an elevator on a construction site (Det No. 88, Jun '44: "The Merchants of Misery!").

BIRD HOUSE, THE. A combination nightclub and gambling casino which the PENGUIN opens in Florida in June–July 1942 with the aid of three "old compatriots" – Buzzard Benny, Joe Crow, and a lovely blond singer named CANARY (BM No. 11/4: "Four Birds of a Feather!").

BISHOP, TIGER. "One of the coldest killers in the history of crime." Bishop is apprehended in October 1950 by ace crime reporter Dave Purdy, who, with a bit of secret assistance from BATMAN, blinds Bishop with the glaring beam of the BAT-SIGNAL and then knocks the villain unconscious before he can recover (Det No. 164: "Untold Tales of the Bat-Signal!").

BLACKBEARD. The leader of a ruthless band of modern-day pirates who, in Winter 1941, board and loot the private yacht carrying the wealthy members of the Yacht Society on their annual outing and then carry their victims back to their pirate galleon, intending to hold them for ransom. BATMAN and ROBIN defeat the pirates, rescue their wealthy captives, and unmask Blackbeard as Thatch, a small-time criminal (BM No. 4/2: "Blackbeard's Crew and the Yacht Society").

BLACK DIAMOND, THE. A ruthless GOTHAM CITY "gang lord" who has devoted his life to accumulating the world's most fabulous gems, because, in his words, "rare gems have ***always*** been a source of wealth and power." In April–May 1950 the Black Diamond establishes an "underworld braintrust" – consisting of Bulls-Eye Kendall, "the underworld's keenest trigger-man"; the Barracuda brothers, "most feared pirates since the days of sailing ships"; and "Nitro" Nelson, "master of high-powered explosives" – and instructs them to assassinate BATMAN and ROBIN in order to pave the way for future crimes. The Dynamic Duo thwart the ensuing attempts on their lives, however, and ultimately apprehend the Black Diamond with the aid of the Gotham City Police Department (BM No. 58/3: "The Black Diamond!").

BLACKHAND. The leader of a band of ruthless "oyster pirates" who terrorize local oyster fishermen by boarding their ships at the end of each fishing day and making off with their day's oyster catches. "See this hand?" exclaims Blackhand at one point, indicating the horribly burned hand that has given rise to his bizarre name. "I was handcuffed to a detective. I shoved both our hands into a fire! The copper fainted and I got the cuff key!" Blackhand and his henchmen are finally apprehended in July 1946 through the heroic efforts of BATMAN, ROBIN, and Josephine Jibbs, a courageous lady oyster fisherman (Det No. 113: "Crime on the Half-Shell!").

BLACK PATCH. The leader of a gang of criminals who attempt to capitalize on the existence of "the crystal creature" (*see* CRYSTAL CREATURE, THE), a bizarre crystalline creature that feeds on metal, by dressing one of their members to resemble the creature and then stealing some valuable metal statuettes and gold bullion in the hope that the thefts will be attributed to the creature's appetite. BATMAN sees through the ruse, however, and he and ROBIN take the criminals into custody (Det No. 272, Oct '59: "The Crystal Creature").

BLACK ROGUE, THE. A cunning criminal, clad in a black costume and plumed hat similar to those reputedly worn by the legendary Black Knight, who matches wits with BATMAN and ROBIN in January–February 1953. He is actually Felix Dunn, a "scholarly criminal" and longtime fan of the Black Knight who has adopted his underworld pseudonym and knightly regalia as a tribute to the legendary villain he so greatly admires.

The Dynamic Duo's efforts to apprehend the Black Rogue and recover the set of priceless crown jewels he has recently stolen become complicated when, as the result of an accidental blow on the head, the villain "suddenly goes mad--his mind snapping like a twig," and he becomes convinced that he is actually the very Black Knight he has long sought to emulate. Fearful that the villain may forget where he has buried the crown jewels if his sanity is abruptly restored by any sudden shock, Batman and Robin and the police force go to great lengths to humor their quarry, even to the point of masquerading as Arthurian knights while they pursue him.

Ultimately, however, Batman tricks the villain into revealing the hiding place of the jewels by posing as Merlin the Magician, and the captured Black Rogue is promptly consigned to a mental institution (WF No. 62: "Sir Batman and the Black Knight").

BLAKE, DON. An alias employed by ROBIN in February–March 1952 when he poses as a movie actor in order to obtain the role of Robin in W. W. HAMMOND's film *The Batman Story* (BM No. 69/1: "The Batman Exposé!").

BLAKE, FRENCHY. The dapper, monocled leader of a gang of jewel thieves who match wits with BATMAN in June 1939. Batman corners Blake in his apartment, extorts a written confession from him by dangling him out the window at the end of a rope and threatening to cut the rope unless Blake cooperates, and then turns both Blake and the confession over to the authorities (Det No. 28).

BLAKE, GEORGE. The manager of the Gotham Theater. In September 1952 Blake disguises himself as TWO-FACE and commits a series of spectacular crimes in the hope that Harvey Kent, because of his prior career as the original Two-Face, will be blamed for them. Batman, however, ultimately apprehends Blake and exonerates Harvey Kent of any wrongdoing (Det No. 187: "The Double Crimes of Two-Face!").

BLAKE, TOM. The renowned trapper of wild jungle cats who turns to crime as the CAT-MAN (Det No. 311, Jan '63: "The Challenge of the Cat-Man!").

BLAKELY, TED. The "brightest young man in the FBI," and one of the charter members of the SECRET STAR, an elite five-man organization, chosen by POLICE COMMISSIONER GORDON and trained by BATMAN and ROBIN, whose members are intended to serve as replacements for Batman in the event of his death or disability. What Blakely has confided to no one, however, is that he has been financially supported since infancy by Matt "Sugar" Kroler, a GOTHAM CITY rackets czar who once shared a prison cell with Blakely's now-deceased convict father. Torn between his duty as a lawman and his gratitude to Kroler when Batman is temporarily trapped in a mine shaft and he is called upon to serve as Batman's interim replacement, Blakely wavers at first, but then moves heroically to apprehend Kroler and his henchmen (BM No. 77/2, Jun/Jul '53: "The Secret Star").

BLANE, CORY. A film producer and friend of BATMAN who, while filming a movie on Skull Island in the Pacific Ocean in February 1958, finds his shooting schedule continually disrupted by a gigantic dinosaur-like creature that appears repeatedly to terrorize his production staff and demolish his equipment. Summoned to the scene by a frightened Blane, Batman and ROBIN soon discover that the rampaging monster is in reality a robot-controlled mechanical creature created and operated by Tod Martin, Blane's production assistant. After Martin has been taken into custody, Batman explains that Martin had discovered a bed of rare black-pearl oysters in the island's Green Lagoon and had become determined to sabotage the filming and frighten away the film crew in order to prevent anyone else from discovering the oyster bed and sharing his find (Det No. 252: "The Creature from the Green Lagoon!").

BLANNING, RAND. A member of the Gotham City Exploration Club who is determined to plunder the gold-laden ruins of "a lost city of the ancient Incas" – situated deep in the Peruvian jungles near the banks of the Rio Solin – which was recently discovered by archaeologist and fellow club member Guy Hawtree. After learning the location of the lost city, which Hawtree had attempted to keep secret in order to discourage would-be looters, Blanning flies to Peru to plunder it, but BATMAN and ROBIN pursue him in the

BATPLANE and ultimately apprehend him (BM No. 91/3, Apr '55: "The Map of Mystery!").

BLASTER, THE. A "Western criminal" who – with the aid of underworld accomplice "Spots" Derrow and unscrupulous explosives company executive Guy Banning, who helped the pair obtain illicit supplies of high-powered explosives – "ruthlessly wrecked trains and buildings" until he was finally apprehended by BATMAN and ROBIN sometime prior to July–August 1953. Within minutes after the Blaster's capture, "Spots" Derrow lost his footing atop a high cliff while attempting to shoot Batman with a pistol and fell to his doom on the rocks below. Banning is taken into custody soon afterward when Batman, disguised as the recently deceased Derrow, visits him in his office at the Samson Explosive Works and tricks him into making a full confession of his role in providing Derrow and the Blaster with the powerful "concentrated explosive" used in a recent armored-car robbery (WF No. 65: "The Five Different Batmen!").

BLAZE, THE. A ruthless criminal with red hair, moustache, and beard whose name derives from his frequent use of fire and smoke to defeat the forces of law and order.

In January 1945, after BATMAN and members of the Gotham City Police Department have halted a rising crime wave and apprehended a "motley horde of criminals," the Blaze and his henchmen hijack the special train transporting them to prison and set the criminals free. "Today marks the beginning of a new regime in the underworld!" gloats the Blaze, and he proceeds to announce the formation of an underworld organization "that will strike so efficiently that all America will be ours for the looting! That is why I have rescued you from the law!" At one point, the Blaze lures Batman into a trap by assuming the alias Baron Von Peltz and approaching Batman on the pretext of requiring protection from personal enemies, but Batman and ROBIN ultimately apprehend the Blaze and his cohorts in the act of robbing the City Museum (Det No. 95).

BLONDEEN, BLACKIE. The leader of a gang of criminals who attempt to apply the techniques of football – such as elaborately diagrammed "plays," numbered signals, and practice sessions with dummies – to the commission of crimes. The gang – whose other members include Glassjaw Greegan, Curly, and Skeets – is apprehended by BATMAN and ROBIN in December 1943 (Det No. 82: "Quarterback of Crime!").

BLORE, "GADGETS." A ruthless underworld inventor – the text describes him as a "warped genius, who has turned his talents to crime" – who commits a series of spectacular crimes in April 1961 with the aid of a formidable arsenal of "crime tools [which] depend on high-voltage electricity" for their power, including a powerful "electronic cannon" which can melt safe doors, and an "ultra-sonic gun" capable of splitting an entire tree in half. The Dynamic Duo's efforts to apprehend the Blore gang are severely hampered by the fact that a series of electrical accidents involving Blore's electronic cannon have left BATMAN's body bathed in a powerful "positive charge" and ROBIN's body bathed in an equally powerful "negative charge" so that the two crime-fighters cannot draw close enough to one another to fight crime effectively as a team. In order to combat this dilemma, the Dynamic Duo create a lifelike Robin robot to function as Batman's partner while the real Robin operates it via remote-control from a safe distance away. Eventually, however, after an unexpected electrical shock has eradicated Robin's electrical charge, he and Batman apprehend the "Gadgets" Blore gang and confiscate their awesome weapons arsenal. Batman's electrical charge soon dissipates of its own accord, so that both he and Robin have been restored to normal by the time the adventure draws to a close (Det No. 290: "Robin's Robot!").

BLUE BOWMAN, THE. An identity assumed by SIGNALMAN in April 1961 (BM No. 139/1: "The Blue Bowman").

BODIN, HUSH-HUSH. The leader of a gang of criminals, called Hush-Hush because of his extreme aversion to loud noises. Bodin and his henchmen are apprehended by BATMAN and ROBIN in August–September 1945 (BM No. 30/2: "While the City Sleeps!").

BODIN, PAUL. The famous circus escape artist, now retired, who is secretly the HUMAN KEY (Det No. 132, Feb '48: "The Human Key!").

BOLES, BEETLE. An escaped convict and cop killer, described in the text as a "master of savage underworld strategy," who is apprehended along with his henchmen by BATMAN and ROBIN, with some timely assistance from ALFRED, in April–May 1947 (BM No. 40/2: "The Case of Batman II").

BOLEY, JINX. An escaped convict, known for his habit of wearing a bulletproof vest and for his superstitious belief in the good-luck qualities of the number seven, who attempts to steal some valuable jewels on display at the Gotham Historical Society only to be trapped and apprehended when his metal vest becomes magnetized to an electromagnet planted on the premises beforehand by BATMAN (BM No. 67/1, Oct/Nov '51: "The Mystery Rope!").

BOLEY BROTHERS, THE. Three smugglers – Slats, Dave, and Bull – who come into unexpected possession of the BATPLANE when they find it nestled in a clump of trees north of GOTHAM CITY shortly after a sudden equipment failure has forced BATMAN and ROBIN to bail out in mid-flight. With the aid of the batplane – and with the aid of the two additional batplanes which they build soon afterward so that each brother will have his own – the Boley brothers embark on a series of spectacular crimes designed to enable them to "rule the crime world," but Batman and Robin defeat and apprehend them with the aid of a new, improved batplane, Batplane II, which they build to replace the one they were forced to abandon (BM No. 61/1, Oct/Nov '50: "The Birth of Batplane II!"). (*See also* BATMAN [section E 2 b i, the batplane].)

BOLTON, FRANK (Dr.). A "famed physicist" who, while working to develop a "device to refract light in a special way," accidentally invents an "illus-o-ray," a bizarre device whose "twin gemlike globes," spinning on a single shaft, make the surrounding environment "seem to shatter into fantastic shifting patterns," as if it were reflected in a giant prism, so that unless one wears a pair of specially designed goggles it is impossible to tell whether one is looking at a real skyscraper, for example, or merely an illusory one created by the illus-o-ray. In March 1955 Bolton's unscrupulous assistant, Parker, conspires with gangster Al Framm and his henchmen to steal the illus-o-ray and use its optical powers to facilitate a series of spectacular crimes. The criminals – who quickly become known as the Illus-o-raiders – are finally apprehended by BATMAN and ROBIN with the aid of a special "radar-sonar guide," installed in the BATMOBILE by Batman, which enables the Dynamic Duo to overcome the perplexing effects of the illus-o-ray (BM No. 90/2: "City of Fantasy!").

BOLTON, TOM. A courageous state tropper in one of the northern states who is secretly the son of Mike Nolan, a member of the Nick Rocco gang who was shot and killed by Nick Rocco himself in the year 1937 just as Nolan was about to make a full confession to BATMAN. Because Tom Bolton has come to believe that it was Batman, and not Nick Rocco, who killed his father, he has developed a bitter hatred of Batman and a misguided conviction that Batman is secretly a spineless coward. In July 1942, however, Batman, ROBIN, and Tom Bolton join forces to apprehend the Nick Rocco gang and, after having seen Batman in action and after having learned the true circumstances of his father's death, Bolton abandons his grudge against Batman and enthusiastically agrees to become Batman's friend (Det No. 65: "The Cop Who Hated the Batman!").

BONIFACE (Mr.). An alias employed by the PENGUIN in December 1941 as part of his scheme to steal a valuable jade idol from himself so that he can collect the insurance on it. His plot is thwarted by BATMAN (Det No. 58).

BOTA, GREGORY. A South American millionaire now residing in GOTHAM CITY who, by pretending to be merely a wealthy hobbyist interested in photographs having to do with crime, has acquired, from underworld sources, a vast collection of incriminating photographs showing criminals in the act of committing crimes as part of an elaborate scheme to blackmail four of the city's most powerful mobsters into crowning him king of the Gotham City underworld. When BATMAN and ROBIN apprehend the four crime chiefs in a rousing battle and Bota's photographs are destroyed in a resulting fire, Bota – driven insane by the collapse of his blackmail scheme – becomes obsessed with the desire to murder the Dynamic Duo with a diabolical "camera-gun" designed to slay its victims with bullets while simultaneously recording the act for posterity, but he is apprehended by Batman and Robin in April–May 1951 (BM No. 64/1: "The Candid Camera Killer!").

BOURDET. In World's Finest Comics No. 82, an "evil chancellor" in the court of Louis XIV of France (1638–1715) who, unbeknownst to his king, has illegally abducted the benevolent Count Ferney, "a noble friend of the people," and locked him away in Pignerol Castle, and then later in the Bastille, imprisoned in an iron mask. However, at the urging of PROFESSOR CARTER NICHOLS – who hopes to solve the enigma of the identity of the Man in the Iron Mask – BATMAN, ROBIN, and SUPERMAN return through the time barrier to France in the year 1696, where they trade places with the THREE MUSKETEERS – all of whom have been badly wounded by Bourdet's guardsmen – and, aided by the musketeers' comrade D'Artagnan, expose the treachery of the evil Bourdet and free Count Ferney from the iron mask. Bourdet, ordered imprisoned by the king, will remain shut away in the Bastille for the rest of his days, forced to wear the iron mask himself (May/Jun '56: "The Three Super-Musketeers!").

BOWERS, BERT. An escaped convict, hiding out in the Stevens Warehouse, who is captured by BATMAN and ROBIN in June 1955 with the aid of a courageous brown dog they have recently fished out of a nearby river. Bowers inadvertently provides the valiant canine with a new name when he cries out "Leggo, you--you **Bat-Hound!**" (BM No. 92/3: "Ace, the Bat-Hound!"). (*See* ACE [THE BAT-HOUND].)

BOYD, LITTLE NAP. A ruthless gangland chieftain, known also as the Little Corporal, who emulates the style and manner of Napoleon and formulates elaborate schemes for the commission of crimes "just like a general planning a campaign." After staging a series of spectacular crimes in GOTHAM CITY, Boyd is finally apprehended in Winter 1942 through the heroic efforts of BATMAN, ROBIN, and Tim and Nick O'Brien, the two sons of U.S. special agent John O'Brien, who was recently shot to death by Boyd while attempting to take him into custody (WF No. 8: "Brothers in Law!").

BRADEN, WALTER "SLUG." An alias employed by Batman in March 1951 when he allows himself to be incarcerated in the penitentiary as an inmate in an effort to investigate the suspicious behavior of convict JOHN "SQUINT" TOLMAR (Det No. 169: "Batman--Boss of the Big House!").

BRADY, JIM. A GOTHAM CITY racketeer who, with his cohort Al Rorick, commandeers an early-morning subway train in October–November 1947 in a desperate effort to escape from BATMAN and ROBIN. Rorick is shot and apparently killed when he accidentally gets in the way of a bullet Brady has intended for one of the subway passengers, and Brady is electrocuted when a metal hammer which he swings at Batman accidentally strikes the deadly third rail (BM No. 43/2: "Next Stop – Danger!").

BRADY BROTHERS, THE. Three notorious criminals – Matt, Will, and Bart – who make off with the "fabulous gift" which Chalmers, a wealthy Alaskan miner and "old friend" of BATMAN, had intended to present to the Alaskan government in honor of Alaska's newly acquired statehood – forty-eight valuable diamonds, each representing a star in the flag of the United States, plus an even larger forty-ninth diamond symbolizing the recent addition of Alaska, the forty-ninth state to be admitted to the Union. One by one, in various parts of Alaska, Batman and ROBIN track down the Brady Brothers and recover forty-eight of the missing diamonds. They recover the forty-ninth diamond when they apprehend Atkins, a guard at the

Chalmers mining plant who had received the giant diamond from the Brady Brothers in return for his complicity in the theft of the other forty-eight (BM No. 126/1, Sep '59: "The Mystery of the 49th Star").

BRAINIAC. A ruthless extraterrestrial villain – in reality an ingenious humanoid computer designed and manufactured on a distant planet – who has been an implacable foe of SUPERMAN since mid-1958. It was Brainiac who literally stole the city of KANDOR by reducing it to microscopic size with a diabolical shrinking ray, preserving it aboard his spacecraft inside a large glass bottle until it was finally recovered by Superman and placed for safekeeping inside his FORTRESS OF SOLITUDE. Brainiac forms a temporary alliance with the diabolical Clayface (*see* CLAYFACE [MATT HAGEN]) in September 1964 (WF No. 144: "The 1,001 Tricks of Clayface and Brainiac!" pts. 1–2 – no title; "The Helpless Partners!"). (For a complete account of the villainous carreer of Brainiac, consult *The Encyclopedia of Comic Book Heroes: Volume VI – Superman.*)

Brainiac and his alien pet, Koko © NPP 1976

BRAMWELL, BRAMWELL B. A "famous mystery writer" and author of best-selling crime novels who invites the four top "crime bosses of Gotham City" – Bright Guy Warner, Slim Ryan, Chopper Gant, and Muscles Hardy – to a "literary tea" at his gloomy castle residence and brazenly challenges them to an incredible "crime of the month" contest to determine which of them is capable of planning and executing the most spectacular crime, with the winner to receive the accumulated loot from all the robberies. As the crime contest gets under way, GOTHAM CITY finds itself subjected to a series of elaborately conceived gangland escapades, but BATMAN and ROBIN ultimately apprehend Bramwell when he attempts to rob the wealthy guests at a lavish society benefit for the Allied War Relief Fund. The fate of the four gangland chieftains is not stated in the text (WF No. 9, Spr '43: "Crime of the Month").

BRAND, EDDIE. A former World War II flying ace, seriously injured in the crash of an experimental jet plane in November–December 1947, who undergoes an emergency operation to save his sight only to discover that the circumstances of the crash have somehow endowed him with "X-ray eyes" – the ability to see through all solid substances except lead.

In the beginning, Brand uses his newly acquired power to earn a living in vaudeville, but the bitterness that he feels when people shun him because of his strange power, combined with the psychological trauma of the plane crash, soon leads him to seek out Milt, an underworld accomplice, and to begin using his bizarre power for crime, as when he loots a locked safe by using his X-ray eyes to read the tumblers of the combination lock.

For a time, Brand "makes criminal history" as he and Milt commit one spectacular crime after another, but Milt is ultimately electrocuted when he accidentally touches a high-voltage electrical wire while attempting to shoot BATMAN and ROBIN, and Brand collapses in a state of nervous exhaustion in response to the elaborate psychological ploy that Batman and Robin have devised to apprehend him. When Brand recovers, he finds that the traumatic circumstances of his capture have robbed him of his X-ray vision and restored his sight to normal, and Batman assures him that he will not be prosecuted for his crimes since his short-lived criminal career was obviously the result of World War II "battle fatigue" combined with the traumatic effects of his recent plane crash (WF No. 31: "The Man with the X-ray Eyes!").

BRAND, THE. A cunning criminal, clad in Western-style clothes, who attempts to tunnel his way into the vault of the Gotham Bank from the abandoned subway tunnel which runs beneath it in order to make off with $100,000 in youth center contributions being stored there pending the public ceremony at which BATMAN is scheduled to present the money to the mayor of GOTHAM CITY. When it becomes apparent that his tunnel will not be completed on schedule, the Brand sets in motion an elaborate scheme designed to delay the ceremony and forestall the removal of the money from the bank vault until he has had the opportunity to steal it. Batman deduces the existence of the tunneling project however, and, with ROBIN's help, apprehends the Brand in February 1961 (BM No. 137/2: "The Bandit with 1,000 Brands").

BRANDO, WOLF. "Public Enemy Number One," a condemned killer who escapes from prison in GOTHAM CITY and ends up seeking refuge in the home of Bruce Wayne and Dick Grayson, where, by accident, he discovers the hidden spiral staircase leading to the BATCAVE and realizes that he has inadvertently stumbled upon the secret identities of BATMAN and ROBIN. Pursued relentlessly through the batcave's passageways by the Dynamic Duo, Brando dies when, startled abruptly by some bats, he plunges to his doom in an underground whirlpool (BM No. 48/2, Aug/Sep '48: "The 1,000 Secrets of the Batcave!").

BRANE. A citizen of Earth in the year 3000 A.D. who, with his young companion Ricky, revives the twentieth-century legend of BATMAN and ROBIN in order to free Earth from the oppressive domination of the ruthless Saturnian warlord Fura. Brane is apparently a descendant of Bruce Wayne, for he states that he is "the twentieth direct descendant of [his] family" to bear Wayne's name; the name Brane is the result of a thirty-first-century custom whereby individuals are known by contractions of their first and last names, so that Bruce Wayne has yielded the contraction Brane (BM No. 26/2, Dec/Jan '44–'45: "The Year 3000!"). There seems little doubt that Brane provided later chroniclers with the inspiration that led to the emergence of the thirty-first-century A.D. crime-fighter known as BRANE TAYLOR (BM No. 67/3, Oct/Nov '51: "The Lost Legion of Space"), but there is ample textual evidence that Brane and Brane Taylor are not identical. (*See* TAYLOR, BRANE.)

In the year 3000 A.D., the entire planet Earth is invaded and subjugated by a mighty army of Saturnian conquerors who, it later develops, are actually robot warriors under the control of the brutal Saturnian warlord Fura. Soon afterward, while Earth suffers under the oppressive dominion of the Saturnian conquerors, Brane and his companion Ricky happen upon a time capsule, buried in the earth at the time of the 1939 New York World's Fair, which contains motion-picture footage of Batman and Robin in action.

Inspired by these action films from the twentieth century, Brane and Ricky dón Batman and Robin costumes and revive the legend of Batman and Robin in their own time in order to inspire their fellow earthmen to instigate a revolution against their Saturnian masters. Before long, led by Brane and Ricky, the enslaved people of Earth have retaken Earth from the Saturnian robots and carried the fight to Saturn, where they obliterate the control tower which regulates the activities of the robot warriors.

In a desperate effort to evade capture, Fura flees into space aboard a rocket ship, but Brane races after him and, in the battle that follows, rips a hole in Fura's space suit with a blast from his ray gun. Now unprotected from the freezing temperatures of space, Fura freezes to death, thus ending forever his threat to the freedom of Earth (BM No. 26/2, Dec/Jan '44–'45: "The Year 3000!"). (*See also* BATMAN [section F, the Batman counterparts].)

BRANE, L. M. (Professor). The theatrical booking agent who is the leader of the so-called "specialists in crime," a gang of criminals who employ men with highly specialized talents and abilities to aid them in their carefully planned crimes, as when they cause a partial blackout in GOTHAM CITY by sabotaging the municipal power plant so that their blind accomplices — who are accustomed to moving about in the "darkness" — can steal a gold shipment from the Gotham City Bank while BATMAN and ROBIN stumble about in the near-total blackness. Brane is finally apprehended by Batman and Robin in Summer 1945, along with a band of deaf henchmen whose talents he had hoped to use to rob a chestful of donations to the Allied war effort (WF No. 18: "Specialists in Crime!").

BRANN, NED. The GOTHAM CITY gambling czar who is secretly the DAGGER (Det No. 174, Aug '51: "The Park Avenue Kid!").

BRIGGS. A millionaire architect and secret leader of a gang of criminals whose private hobby involves purchasing buildings of all kinds and then having them disassembled, transported to a private island, and rebuilt. On his deathbed in May 1962, Briggs provides his henchman Catlin with a key to a safe, containing a letter, which in turn guides Catlin to the first in a series of complex clues which Briggs has promised will lead ultimately to a valuable "treasure." Because they feel certain that Briggs was secretly a criminal, BATMAN and ROBIN become embroiled in the treasure hunt themselves. Ultimately, they apprehend Catlin — along with two other Briggs henchmen, Hoke and Danny, who had hoped to seize the treasure for themselves — and recover the hidden treasure, a fortune in valuable art stolen by Briggs from the world's great museums (BM No. 147/2: "The Secret of Mystery Island!").

BRINK, SCAR. The warden of a bizarre underworld prison, situated "on a desolate stretch of marshland near Gotham City," where Brink and his henchmen stand guard over an inmate population consisting entirely of captured law-enforcement personnel. By June–July 1952 BATMAN and ROBIN have been taken captive by Brink and his henchmen and incarcerated inside the underworld prison, but Batman finally defeats Brink and initiates a successful inmate revolt which ends with the criminals locked in jail cells and the law-enforcement officials securely in command (BM No. 71/1: "The Jail for Heroes!").

BROWNE, B. BOSWELL. BATMAN's biographer, an elderly gentleman who has devoted much of his life to the collection and preservation of Batman memorabilia in addition to having written an exhaustive book about them "for the inspiration of future generations!" "I flatter myself," Browne has said, "that I know more about them than any other person . . .!" In June–July 1943 a villain called the CONJURER poses as a journalist and, under the pretense of interviewing Browne about Batman, plies the old scholar for information about Batman's habits and weaknesses. Although fooled for a time, Browne ultimately plays a major role in the capture of the Conjurer and his henchmen (BM No. 17/1: "The Batman's Biographer!").

BRUCE, JOHN. An alias employed by Bruce Wayne, the man who is secretly BATMAN, when he obtains employment as a riveter at the Gotham Shipyard in an effort to solve the recent murder of the yard's night watchman (WF No. 46, Jun/Jul '50: "Bruce Wayne, Riveter!"). (*See* STARK, CHARLEY.)

BRULE. A prosperous Western cattle rancher, and the secret leader of a gang of black-market cattle rustlers who are captured by BATMAN and ROBIN in February–March 1944 with the aid of local ranchers. Brule is shot and apparently killed by the local sheriff just as he is about to shoot Robin (BM No. 21/1: "The Streamlined Rustlers!").

BUCKLER, JIB. An ex-convict who has devised an elaborate underwater salvage racket. First Buckler surreptitiously torpedoes a vessel in Gotham Harbor and races to the scene to claim salvage rights; then, on the pretext of lacking the heavy equipment to perform the salvage task himself, he sells the salvage rights to someone else; then, before the firm to which he has sold the salvage rights can arrive on the scene to begin operations, he loots the sunken vessel of its cargo with the aid of an underwater vehicle called a "submobile" and then destroys the sunken vessel with explosives to prevent the cause of the original sinking from being discovered. While attempting to escape from BATMAN and ROBIN in his submobile in Summer 1944, Buckler crashes into his stockpile of torpedoes on the harbor floor and apparently perishes in the ensuing explosion (WF No. 14: "Salvage Scavengers!").

BULLET-HOLE CLUB. A unique club for law-enforcement personnel located in GOTHAM CITY, membership in which is restricted to lawmen who have been wounded by a bullet in the line of duty and who have presented the extracted bullets to the club as certification of their right to membership. Status within the club is determined by the number of bullet wounds received, making BATMAN the club's president with a total bullet count of nine (WF No. 50, Feb/Mar '51: "Bullet-Hole Club!").

BULOW, BRAINY. The leader of a trio of criminals, captured by BATMAN and ROBIN and then released from prison after serving their sentences, who go into the business of capturing wanted criminals and turning them in for the reward money. When they run out of criminals to capture, however, they decide to engineer a series of prison breaks and turn in the escapees for the rewards, but they are ultimately apprehended by Batman and Robin (Det No. 92, Oct '44: "Crime's Man-Hunt").

BURNS, BOSTON. A cunning ex-convict who, convinced that criminals must be trained as thoroughly as policemen if they are to compete effectively against modern crime-fighting techniques, establishes an elaborate training academy for criminals on deserted Devers Island so that criminals may receive rigorous instruction in the most modern underworld techiques. "When my class graduates," gloats Burns, "I'll have the most efficient criminal organization in the world! ***No one will stop me!***" BATMAN infiltrates the underworld academy in April–May 1951 by posing as a fugitive criminal and, although an accidental explosion eventually tears away his hoodlum disguise and betrays the presence of his Batman costume beneath his clothing, he nevertheless succeeds, with the aid of ROBIN and a contingent of Coast Guardsmen, in apprehending Burns and his gangland associates (WF No. 51: "The Academy for Gangsters!").

BURR, JOE. A fugitive criminal who abducts the scientist Professor Norenz and makes off with his latest invention – a fabulous "shrinking machine" capable of reducing a man to a height of three inches – as part of a scheme to have himself reduced in size and smuggled out of the United States inside a shipment of toys. Burr and his henchmen are apprehended by BATMAN and ROBIN in February 1962 (BM No. 145/2: "The Tiniest Villain in the World").

BURTON, HENRY. The unscrupulous manager of Thompson's Luxury Shop, who has been stealing gems and jewelry from the store's jewelry department, hiding the loot inside toys in the toy department, and then smuggling the toys out of the store by selling them to members of the "Muscles" Malone gang. Burton and his gangland confederates are apprehended by BATMAN and ROBIN in June–July 1942 (BM No. 11/3: "Bandits in Toyland!").

BUSH, HENRY. An unscrupulous attorney who is in charge of BRUCE WAYNE's legal affairs until April–May 1947, when Wayne exposes him as a forger and embezzler by faking his own death in an auto accident and then listening from hiding at the reading of his own will long enough to ascertain that Bush has secretly altered the document to channel a large portion of Wayne's estate into a dummy foundation which Bush himself controls (BM No. 40/2: "The Case of Batman II").

BYRUS. A Persian villain of the fifth century B.C. who attempts to sow riot and dissension among the Greeks attending the Olympic games at Athens in order to pave the way for a Persian conquest of Greece. Dispatched through the time barrier by PROFESSOR CARTER NICHOLS to the city of Athens in the fifth century B.C., BATMAN and ROBIN defeat Byrus and his henchmen with the aid of various members of the Athenian Olympic team (BM No. 38/1, Dec/Jan '46–'47: "Peril in Greece!").

C

CAIRD, JAY. A renegade scientist, once sentenced to prison for espionage and now recently released, who attempts to use the revolutionary "ultra-sonic beam projector" he has stolen from the Gotham Research Center to stun armed guards and passersby into unconsciousness by bombarding them with "sonic waves" so that he and his henchmen can loot a payroll truck belonging to the Gotham Trust. The robbery is thwarted, however, and Caird and his henchmen are apprehended, by BATMAN and ROBIN in August 1956, even though the Dynamic Duo's efforts to apprehend the villains, and indeed all of their activities during this period, are severely hampered by the fact that a burst of the beam projector's sonic-wave emissions leveled at them by the evil Caird has afflicted them with temporary amnesia, even to the extent of forgetting their own secret identities, so that before they can attempt to capture the criminals they must first solve the riddle of who they are (Det No. 234: "Batman and Robin's Greatest Mystery").

CALENDAR MAN. A cunning criminal who publicly challenges BATMAN to a battle of wits and then brazenly commits four spectacular crimes, each having as its theme one of the four seasons of the year, before he is finally apprehended by Batman and ROBIN in September 1958. Calendar Man, who wears a different costume during the commission of each crime to further accentuate the seasonal theme, is in reality Maharajah the Magician, a stage magician appearing at GOTHAM CITY's Bijou Theater for a five-day engagement. Calendar Man's carefully orchestrated crime plan had originally included a fifth crime symbolizing the fifth season – the Indian monsoon, or rainy, season – but the Dynamic Duo deduce his true identity and apprehend him before he can actually commit it (Det No. 259: "The Challenge of the Calendar Man").

CALLENDER, ROB. An "obscure laboratory worker" in twenty-first-century A.D. GOTHAM CITY who, while absentmindedly performing his routine laboratory chores, accidentally causes an explosion which produces a "temporary warp in space-time" and propels him back through time to the twentieth century, where he quickly hires a gang of criminals to help him steal a series of seemingly worthless objects which, because they are destined to become a part of BATMAN's private trophy collection, will acquire great value in the future and hence make Callender a wealthy man if he can succeed in carrying them back to his own era. Batman and ROBIN deduce Callender's true origins and ultimately apprehend him, but whereas Callender's twentieth-century henchmen are promptly turned over to the authorities for prosecution, Callender suddenly vanishes into thin air – "A space-time warp," he had noted, "can't last indefinitely . . ." – and arrives back in his own era safe but empty-handed (WF No. 11, Fall '43: "A Thief in Time!").

CANARY. A lovely blond nightclub singer who – along with Buzzard Benny and Joe Crow – is an accomplice of the PENGUIN in June–July 1942, until she finally decides to abandon her life in the rackets in favor of a career as a Red Cross nurse.

In June–July 1942 Canary travels to Florida in the company of Buzzard Benny, Joe Crow, and the Penguin and, with them, launches a combination nightclub and gambling casino called the Bird House, where she performs as a singer.

Not long afterward, when Canary is attacked by a squid while swimming in the Florida surf, she is rescued by BATMAN, who, in his Bruce Wayne identity, is enjoying a short Florida vacation. Soon afterward, after Canary has related the incident to her cohorts, Buzzard Benny warns her against becoming sentimental about Batman. "You can't stop me from dreaming!" replies Canary wistfully.

Later, after the villains have kidnapped ROBIN, Batman barges into the Bird House and demands to know where his young companion has been taken. Buzzard Benny quickly provides Batman with an address, but Canary interrupts, warns Batman that he will be walking into a trap, and begs him not to go there.

Enraged at Canary's betrayal, Buzzard Benny draws his pistol and fires at her, but Batman leaps in the path of the oncoming bullets, receiving two serious wounds in the chest, and barely manages to knock Buzzard Benny unconscious before staggering weakly out of the Bird House to rescue Robin.

Batman makes his way to the Penguin's hideout and rescues Robin before collapsing into unconsciousness and, when a doctor is not immediately available to treat Batman's bullet wounds, it is Canary – who was once a doctor's assistant – who operates on Batman, extracts the two bullets, and, for the second time in the space of a few hours, saves his life.

Later, after the villains have been defeated and Batman has somewhat recuperated from his operation, he asks Canary what she plans to do next. Canary replies that she is quitting the rackets for a life as a Red Cross nurse. "This is good-bye, **Batman!**" cries Canary, as she throws her arms around him and gives him a parting kiss. "I'll never forget you!" (BM No. 11/4: "Four Birds of a Feather!").

CAP'N BEN'S WILD ANIMAL ACT. A traveling animal act performed on a showboat and operated by three criminals who commit robberies in towns along the showboat's route and hide their loot beneath the floors of the act's animal cages as a means of smuggling it to fences in other cities. The perpetrators of this scheme – Stilts, Ed, and Pete – are apprehended by BATMAN and ROBIN in March 1965 (BM No. 170/2: "The Puzzle of the Perilous Prizes!").

CAPTAIN BEN. The captain of a Mississippi River showboat which plies the Mississippi with a troupe of performers, entertaining audiences at towns along the riverbanks. During showtime intermissions, however, while the performers are ostensibly enjoying a few minutes' rest, Captain Ben and his cohorts sneak away from the riverboat and loot the nearby towns, until they are finally apprehended by BATMAN and ROBIN in August 1944 (Det No. 90: "Crime Between the Acts!").

CAPTAIN LIGHTFOOT (1775–1822). The pseudonym employed by Michael Martin, a notorious highwayman, born in Ireland, who immigrated to the United States to avoid capture in 1818 and plied his trade throughout the New England states until he was finally caught and hanged as a horse thief in Cambridge, Massachusetts.

According to Batman No. 79/2, however, Captain Lightfoot was actually Abel Adams, a courageous citizen of GOTHAM CITY in the year 1753 who, having learned that unscrupulous merchant Hugo Vorney was inciting the Indians to war so that he could make a fortune selling guns and ammunition to them, assumed the unpopular role of a highwayman in an effort to avert open warfare between the colonists and Indians by intercepting and confiscating Vorney's shipments of contraband guns.

Dispatched through the time barrier to the eighteenth century by PROFESSOR CARTER NICHOLS, BATMAN and ROBIN help Captain Lightfoot apprehend Vorney and his henchmen and establish a peace between the colonists and the Indians. In addition, they unearth evidence that enables them to apprehend hijacker WALTER FRALEY once they have returned to the twentieth century (Oct/Nov '53: "The Batman of Yesterday!").

CARDEN (Professor). The inventor of an incredible robot which, with the aid of a special "brain-wave helmet," can be instantaneously transformed into the "robot twin" of any selected individual, endowed with that person's personality, knowledge, and capabilities. Professor Carden endows his robot with BATMAN's personality and attributes in January 1957, only to have it stolen soon afterward by the criminal DALL (Det No. 239: "Batman's Robot Twin!").

CARDINE, "KNOTS." A ruthless "underworld chieftain" who attempts to capitalize on a visit to GOTHAM CITY by a group of famous foreign lawmen – including the KNIGHT and the SQUIRE from England, the MUSKETEER from France, the GAUCHO from South America, the RANGER from Australia, and the LEGIONARY from Rome – in order to carry out "the greatest scheme of his career": the assassination of BATMAN and the theft of an armored truckload of currency being transported to a new branch bank. The scheme involves having Cardine kidnap and impersonate the Legionary so that he can lure Batman into a deathtrap and then, with Batman dead, volunteer to guard the currency shipment in Batman's stead, but Batman and ROBIN thwart the scheme and apprehend Cardine and his henchmen in January 1955 (Det No. 215: "The Batmen of All Nations!").

CARDINE, PAYNE. The embittered concert pianist who launches a career in crime as the MAESTRO (BM No. 149/1, Aug '62: "The Maestro of Crime").

CARLATHAN MOUNTAINS. A mountain range of far-off HUNGARIA. When BATMAN journeys to Hungaria to battle the diabolical villain known as the MONK, he stays at a hotel situated somewhere in the Carlathan Mountains. The Monk's towering castle stronghold, which is not too far distant, stands "in the lost mountains of Cathala by the turbulent river Dess," but it is not possible to discern from the narrative whether "the lost mountains of Cathala" are part of the Carlathan range, or whether the Carlathan Mountains represent a separate range entirely (Det No. 32, Oct '39).

CARLIN. A "great actor" who receives a blow on the head while playing the role of a caveman and falls victim to the delusion that he is actually a prehistoric caveman named Goth. Quite by accident, he stumbles upon the BATCAVE and defends it as his personal preserve until another blow on the head, received during a battle with BATMAN and ROBIN, shatters his delusion and restores him to his proper frame of mind. Fortunately for the Dynamic Duo, Carlin regains his true personality away from the batcave and retains no recollection whatever of his short-lived caveman career, thus ensuring that the location of the batcave will remain a closely guarded secret (BM No. 102/3, Sep '56: "The Caveman at Large").

CARLIN, CATSPAW. One of a pair of criminals – his accomplice is Corky Huggins – who loot the Wayne mansion in June–July 1945 while BRUCE WAYNE, DICK GRAYSON, and ALFRED are away on a fishing trip. They are apprehended soon afterward by BATMAN and ROBIN in spite of the somewhat comical intervention of two private detectives named Hawke and Wrenn, who have decided to garner some publicity for their failing detective agency by posing as Batman and Robin and apprehending Carlin and Huggins themselves (BM No. 29/2: "Heroes by Proxy!").

CARLO. A vaudeville mind-reader who turns to crime when he discovers that the delicate brain surgery he underwent following an automobile accident actually endowed him with the miraculous ability to read minds. At one point, Carlo reads BATMAN's mind and learns his secret identity, but he is shot and killed by Pete Jorgen, one of his intended robbery victims, before he can reveal the secret to anyone else (Det No. 70, Dec '42: "The Man Who Could Read Minds!").

CARLSON. The leader of a gang of horribly ugly criminal fanatics known as the Ugly Horde, a once-handsome man who, as the result of having been accidentally injected with a haphazard mixture of chemicals during a college fraternity initiation many years ago, became hideously transformed into "a man who is undoubtedly the ugliest man in the world."

Consumed with bitterness and rage by the tragedy that had befallen him, Carlson labored for years to duplicate the weird chemical mixture responsible for his tragic transformation, until finally, having succeeded in developing a serum able "to paralyze the thyroid gland and cause a form of disease known as myxedema or cretinism" — and thus render those injected with it as frighteningly ugly as Carlson himself — he gathered about him a band of horribly ugly men, the so-called Ugly Horde, and set out to wreak a twisted vengeance upon the world in general and, more particularly, upon the fraternity men who had unintentionally maimed him and the fiancée who had abandoned him because of his ugliness.

Led by Carlson, the Ugly Horde embarks on a senselessly savage campaign aimed at destroying things of beauty — a campaign that includes the killing of a beauty queen, the bombing of a museum, and the destruction of paintings, statues, and other fine objects — while Carlson himself, disguised in a rubber face-mask to give him a handsome appearance, cunningly gains access to his former fraternity brothers and transforms them into ugly creatures like himself with injections of his hideous serum.

BATMAN and ROBIN finally apprehend the Ugly Horde in Fall 1940, and Carlson is shot to death by DETECTIVE MCGONIGLE just as he is on the verge of stabbing Batman in the midst of a climactic battle. Fortunately for the victims of Carlson's serum, they will be able to regain their good looks with the aid of an antidote recently developed by a scientist named Dr. Ekhart (BM No. 3/2: "The Ugliest Man in the World").

CARLYLE, ROGER. A "great character actor," his acting ability seriously impaired as the result of brain damage suffered in a recent auto accident, who became enraged when the three owners of Monarch Pictures — Austin, Bates, and Harmon — suggested that he take a short vacation and enter a hospital for a checkup. "Are you hinting that I'm through?" cried Carlyle. "I, Roger Carlyle, the greatest character actor of all time? Such a slur calls for ***vengeance! Vengeance!***" In April 1963 Carlyle murders Austin and Bates and only narrowly misses killing Harmon owing to the timely intervention of BATMAN and ROBIN. All the while, Carlyle cleverly contrives to make it appear that he is the victim of a frame-up by the real murderer, who, he intimates, is capitalizing on his angry outburst in order to murder the movie executives for reasons of his own. Ultimately, however, Batman deduces that Carlyle is indeed guilty, lures him into a trap, and apprehends him (Det No. 314: "Murder in Movieland!").

CARSON, BENNETT. The secret leader of a gang of criminals known as the Red Gloves Gang and, ironically, the chairman of a citizens' committee recently appointed to investigate the gang's activities. When Carson develops amnesia during a battle with members of his own gang — who have learned of Carson's attempt to cheat them out of their fair share of some bank loot — BATMAN and ROBIN are faced with the task of restoring Carson's memory so that they can learn exactly why the Red Gloves Gang is so anxious to harm him. Eventually, Carson's memory returns, and Batman and Robin learn the true story of his involvement with the gang. Carson attempts to murder the Dynamic Duo, but ultimately they succeed in apprehending both Carson and his vengeful henchmen (BM No. 117/1, Aug '58: "The Mystery of the Batman Bus").

CARSON, JUMBO. The GOTHAM CITY mobster who is secretly ANT-MAN (BM No. 156/1, Jun '63: "The Secret of the Ant-Man").

CARSON, SLUG. An alias employed by BATMAN in October–November 1952 when he poses as a member of the underworld in order to obtain employment in the RENTER's secret gun factory (BM No. 73/1: "Guns for Hire!").

CARSON, TED. The debt-ridden gold-mine heir who is secretly the Firefly (BM No. 126/3, Sep '59: "The Menace of the Firefly!"). (*See* FIREFLY, THE [TED CARSON].)

CAT, THE. *See* CATWOMAN, THE.

CATHALA. A geographical place-name designating either a region or a mountain range of far-off HUNGARIA. The castle stronghold of the diabolical villain known as the MONK is situated in the vicinity.

According to Detective Comics No. 32, the Monk's stronghold lies somewhere "in the lost mountains of Cathala by the turbulent river Dess. . . ." The lofty peaks of the Carlathan Mountains rise somewhere nearby, but it is not possible to discern from the narrative whether "the lost mountains of Cathala" are part of the Carlathan range, or whether the Carlathan Mountains represent a separate chain entirely (Oct '39).

CAT-MAN, THE. A cunning villain whose costume, special equipment, and choice of crimes all revolve around a feline theme, suggested to him by the spectacular criminal career of the notorious CATWOMAN. The Cat-Man is in reality Tom Blake, a renowned trapper of wild jungle cats, now retired, who turns to crime in January 1963 both to alleviate his boredom and to recoup the sizable fortune that he made as a trapper and then squandered gambling (Det No. 311: "The Challenge of the Cat-Man!"). The texts refer alternatively to the Cat-Man as the Feline Free-booter.

As the Cat-Man, Blake wears a yellow cat-costume with orange boots, gauntlets, cape, and belt, and an

Tom Blake, 1963 © NPP 1963

The Cat-Man makes a getaway, 1963 © NPP 1963

orange "CM" emblazoned across his chest. A catlike hood conceals his true identity, although BATMAN succeeds in deducing it in January 1963 (Det No. 311: "The Challenge of the Cat-Man!"). The villain's special equipment includes an orange "kit-bag" for carrying his loot, a "cat-line" ("oil field slang for a hoist rope") for climbing (Det No. 311, Jan '63: "The Challenge of the Cat-Man!"), a catamaran boat, and a boomerang with serrated edges called a "catarang" (Det No. 318, Aug '63: "The Cat-Man Strikes Back!"). He drives a high-powered catlike automobile – the so-called "cat-car" – equipped with special springs to enable it to make "short, cat-like leaps" over obstacles and with a specially prepared front seat which, at the touch of a button, can "catapult" him high into the air (Det No. 311, Jan '63: "The Challenge of the Cat-Man!"). The Cat-Man possesses the uncanny ability to command the behavior of all feline creatures (Det No. 325, Mar '64: "The Strange Lives of the Cat-Man!").

By January 1963, apathy and boredom have caused Tom Blake to abandon the career as an animal trapper that had brought him fame and fortune: ". . . I've retired!" he explains to BRUCE WAYNE, as the two men chat in the lavishly appointed rooms of one of GOTHAM CITY's gentlemen's clubs. ". . . When I first went into the business of capturing **big cats**, and selling them to circuses and zoos, it was dangerous, exciting! . . . But now I know the habits of big cats so well, that outwitting them has become dull routine! Life can be so boring!" sighs Blake.

Another member of the club, having overheard Tom Blake and Bruce Wayne discoursing together on the meaninglessness of life, suggests sarcastically that the two men might alleviate their boredom by becoming crime-fighters. Although he does not reveal his true feelings at the time, Blake finds the member's remark intriguing: "Maybe I **should** become a crime-fighter?" thinks Blake soon afterward. "But there's only **one Batman**--I'd be just another rival crime-fighter!

"Hmm . . . what if I became **Batman's adversary?**" muses Blake. "To pit my wits against his would be exciting . . . thrillingly dangerous! But I must be a unique criminal, like the **Joker**--my crimes must have a theme. . . ."

Then, suddenly, a glance at his own pet black panther Felina reminds Blake of the notorious Catwoman: "But she was a mere woman!" thinks Blake. "Think what I, a **man** could do! Imagine what I with my knowledge of cat lore can do! Yes--**cats** will be my **cat**egory of crime! I shall become--**the Cat-Man!"**

Soon afterward, now disguised in the colorful garb of the Cat-Man, Blake launches a spectacular series of cat-crimes, beginning with the theft of a priceless statue of an Egyptian cat-goddess from the Gotham Museum. "Hmm!" muses Blake. "I wonder if I **really** turned to crime to escape boredom? Maybe I've been hiding the truth from myself . . . [maybe] I secretly **wanted** to steal, to regain the wealth people still think I have!"

While fleeing the scene of another of his robberies, the Cat-Man is attacked by BATWOMAN, who attempts unsuccessfully to take him into custody. The Cat-Man defeats Batwoman and binds her with rope so that she cannot pursue him further, but in the process he becomes completely smitten by her womanly charms: "I've seen your photograph in newspapers," remarks the Cat-Man admiringly, "--but in person you're beautiful--especially when you're angry! What fire!--what spirit! You're gorgeous! What a team we'd make," he continues enthusiastically, "--**Cat-Man** and **Batwoman!** Together we'd rule the underworld--become the king and queen of crime! What do you say?"

"I say you're a conceited fool," replies Batwoman contemptuously, "and that **Batman** will put you behind bars where you belong!"

Batwoman's words prove prophetic, for Batman and ROBIN have already deduced that the Cat-Man must be Tom Blake, and before long they have trailed him to the abandoned mine shaft that serves as the villain's "catacomb" hideaway. After successfully thwarting several attempts by the Cat-Man to destroy them, Batman and Robin pursue their quarry through the labyrinthine mine tunnels to an underground river, only to look on in horror as the Cat-Man slips and falls into an underground cataract, hurtling to his apparent doom before the Dynamic Duo can save or apprehend him (Det No. 311: "The Challenge of the Cat-Man!").

By August 1963, however, it has become apparent that the Cat-Man managed somehow to survive his fall into the underground river, for he has returned to Gotham City and set up new headquarters in an abandoned subway tunnel, complete with a huge portrait of Batwoman and a special Cat-Woman costume, a female version of his own costume, which he intends to hold in readiness for the day when he can persuade Batwoman to abandon her role as a crime-fighter and join him.

During this period, the Cat-Man launches a series of daring crimes, all having as their theme the famous felines of fiction, such as "Puss in Boots" and "Dick Whittington's Cat." This crime theme, and much of the actual story, is based upon an encounter between Batman and the Catwoman first chronicled in Batman No. 42/1 (Aug/Sep '47: "Claws of the Catwoman!"). At one point, Robin asks Batman why the Cat-Man would return to Gotham City to commit his crimes knowing that Batman was constantly on patrol there. "He's in love with ***Batwoman,*** remember!" replies Batman. "I think he hopes to win her by proving he's a better man than I am!"

Sometime afterward, as the Cat-Man flees the scene of one of his robberies in his high-powered cat-car, he catches sight of Batwoman pursuing him on her "bat-cycle." "***Batwoman!*** Hmm!" muses the Cat-Man. "I'll make that woman respect me yet, by proving I'm superior to her--right now!" Moving swiftly, the Cat-Man uses the special leaping capabilities of his cat-car to make it leap across a wide ravine, then rescues Batwoman from seemingly certain doom when she and her bat-cycle, unable either to stop or turn in time, plummet headlong into the chasm.

"***Batman*** will never marry you!" cries the Cat-Man as he drives off again following the rescue. "You're a fool to waste your time on him! Someday, you'll change your mind and join me! Together we'll rule the underworld as ***king and queen of crime!***"

Later, Batwoman tells Batman about how the Cat-Man rescued her from plunging to her doom in the ravine. "What a strange man he is," muses Batwoman, "--good-looking, intelligent--yet a criminal! What a waste!"

"I agree!" replies Batman. "I wish he'd use his talents lawfully--but until he does, we must think of him as a criminal! You must not sentimentalize him!"

"I can't help having mixed feelings about him!" sobs Batwoman, on the verge of tears. "After all, he ***did*** save my life!"

"Gosh!" exclaims Robin, after Batwoman has departed. "I hope ***Batwoman*** isn't starting to go for ***Cat-Man. . . .***"

"She's too sensible for that!" replies Batman. "She knows only too well that he's an egocentric with a warped, criminal mind! Yet, there's no telling what a woman will do. . . ."

Batman and Batwoman subsequently concoct a plan to apprehend the Cat-Man by pretending to have had a falling out, so that Batwoman can gain the villain's confidence, join his gang, and then guide Batman and Robin to his hideout with a secretly transmitted radio signal. For a time, the plan succeeds, but when Batman and Robin invade the Cat-Man's hideout they are taken captive by the Cat-Man and his henchmen and locked, along with Batwoman, in a sealed room from which there appears to be no escape. Batman, however, uses the tiny transmitter hidden in his boot heel to summon ACE THE BAT-HOUND, who races to the hideout, slips through a small vent leading to the sealed room, and brings Batman the explosives he needs to blast his way out of the trap. In the battle that follows, the Cat-Man attempts to escape in his catamaran, only to have it ram into a large buoy and explode in a pillar of flame, apparently ending both the Cat-Man's life and his criminal career (Det No. 318: "The Cat-Man Strikes Back!").

In March 1964, however, the Cat-Man is once again at large in Gotham City, and an explanation quickly begins to emerge for the villain's uncanny ability to cheat death: sometime in the past, as Tom Blake, the Cat-Man had purchased a native cat-carving wrapped in orange cloth. According to legend, the orange cloth had been imbued with magical properties which enabled it to protect the cat-idol from harm and to endow the wearer of the cloth with the proverbial nine lives cats are said to possess. The Cat-Man had scoffed at the legend, but he had used the orange cloth to make the orange parts of his own costume, as well as the orange parts of the Cat-Woman costume that he had made in the hope that Batwoman might one day join him. In March 1964, when he narrowly escapes from seemingly certain death while attempting to escape from Batman and Robin, the Cat-Man becomes convinced that the legend of the orange cloth is true, and that his recent escape from Batman and Robin, combined with his previous escapes from the underground cataract and the exploding catamaran, indicates that he has six lives left before the power of the magic cloth vanishes forever. At one point, as he escapes from Batman and Robin by leaping onto a high-voltage power line, the Cat-Man cries out, "Ha, ha. He who wears the Cat-Man suit also wears many lives!" and later, at police headquarters, Batman repeats the strange taunt to Batwoman.

In her hidden sanctuary, Batwoman has preserved the Cat-Woman costume which the Cat-Man once fashioned for her, and inside it she finds a cryptic message attesting to the strange legend: "The cloth that protects the idol shall nine lives on the wearer bestow."

Realizing that the nine lives bestowed by the orange cloth are probably cumulative — i.e., if she were to use up some of the lives by risking her own life in the Cat-Woman costume, she would reduce the number of lives available to the Cat-Man — Batwoman dons the Cat-Woman costume and sets out after the villain.

In his ensuing encounters with Batman and Robin, the Cat-Man enjoys the obvious advantage of being invulnerable to death in any form, and on one occasion Batwoman is forced to intervene to save her friends from a raging oil fire. Finally, after consuming a number of the nine lives so that only one life remains, Batwoman, garbed in the Cat-Woman uniform, confronts the Cat-Man high inside the huge, globe-shaped structure housing the World Trades Fair. As the Cat-Man prepares to make good his escape by leaping to the street below, Batwoman informs him that the huge leap will mean his doom, for the miraculous nine lives endowed by the magical orange cloth have by now been completely exhausted. Cornered, the Cat-Man prepares to hurl Batwoman out a high window to her doom rather than face capture and imprisonment. "I love you," cries the Cat-Man, "--but I love freedom more! I cannot allow you to capture me!"

At that moment, however, Batman and Robin arrive on the scene, rescue Batwoman, and apprehend the Cat-Man (Det No. 325: "The Strange Lives of the Cat-Man!").

CATWOMAN, THE. A daring and beautiful arch-villainess whose costumes, special equipment, and choice of crimes all revolve around a feline theme. She is GOTHAM CITY's "most-dreaded female figure" (Det No. 203, Jan '54: "The Crimes of the Catwoman!"), its undisputed "queen of crime" (BM No. 10/3, Apr/May '42: "The Princess of Plunder!"; and others), and, in the words of an underworld colleague, ". . . the cleverest, most dangerous--and most beautiful lady of crime in the country . . .!" (BM No. 62/1, Dec/Jan '50–'51: "The Secret Life of the Catwoman"). Early texts call her the Cat (BM No. 1/4, Spr '40; and others) – or employ the forms Cat Woman (BM No. 2/1, Sum '40; and others) or Cat-Woman (BM No. 2/1, Sum '40; and others) – but Catwoman has long since emerged as the only authentic rendering.

During the course of a career that has spanned three decades and embraced more than twenty separate encounters with BATMAN and ROBIN, the Catwoman has established and discarded several alternate identities – including that of Marguerite Tone, high-society hostess (BM No. 10/3, Apr/May '42: "The Princess of Plunder!"), Elva Barr, beautician (BM No. 15/1, Feb/Mar '43: "Your Face Is Your Fortune!"), and Madame Moderne, publisher of the high-fashion magazine *Damsel* (BM No. 47/1, Jun/Jul '48: "Fashions in Crime!") – in an effort to outwit the law and gain access to the homes and social circles of the wealthy. In reality, however, she is Selina Kyle, a onetime airline stewardess and daughter of a pet shop proprietor, who turned to crime as the Catwoman sometime prior to mid-1940, after a disastrous airline crash had completely obliterated her memory of past events and left her afflicted with a total amnesia that was to persist for more than a decade.

In December 1950–January 1951, after an accidental blow on the head has restored her memory, she abandons her life of crime, becomes "plain Selina Kyle" once again (BM No. 62/1: "The Secret Life of the Catwoman"), and opens a "tiny pet shop" specializing in cats "in the heart of Gotham City," emerging from semiretirement only long enough to help Batman and Robin defeat gangland czar "Whale" Morton (BM No. 65/3, Jun/Jul '51: "Catwoman – Empress of the Underworld") and to persuade her brother Karl to abandon his villainous career as the KING OF THE CATS (BM No. 69/3, Feb/Mar '52: "The King of the Cats!"). In January 1954, however, furious over what she regards as a humiliating newspaper account of her past defeats at the hands of Batman, she dons her famous feline costume and returns to crime as the Catwoman (Det No. 203: "The Crimes of the Catwoman!").

Batman and Robin hold a briefing on the Catwoman for the Gotham City Police Department, 1954 © NPP 1954

Because the early texts were not always consistent regarding the color of the Catwoman's hair, it appears variously in the early chronicles as either black (BM No. 1/4, Spr '40; and others), brown (BM No. 22/1, Apr/May '44: "The Duped Domestics!"), or blond (BM No. 35/1, Jun/Jul '46: "Nine Lives Has the Catwoman!"; BM No. 39/3, Feb/Mar '47: "A Christmas Tale!"). Since April 1947, however, it has been consistently rendered an inky black (Det No. 122: "The Black Cat Crimes!"; and others).

The Catwoman began her career as a jewel thief (BM No. 1/4, Spr '40), and by Summer 1940 had established a reputation as "the slickest and prettiest jewel thief in the business . . ." (BM No. 2/1). By April–May 1942, however, she had extended her range of interests to include valuables of all kinds (BM No. 10/3: "The Princess of Plunder!"), and by June–July 1946 her criminal activities had begun to reflect the deep-seated preoccupation with feline imagery and paraphernalia for which she has become so widely noted (BM No. 35/1: "Nine Lives Has the Catwoman!").

THANKS, BATMAN, FOR PROTECTING ME! DID YOU COME TO GLOAT OVER YOUR PAST VICTORY OVER CATWOMAN?
SELINA, I CAME TO TELL YOU I HAD NOTHING TO DO WITH THAT NEWSPAPER SERIES! I'D NEVER HAVE PERMITTED IT, FOR I KNOW YOU WANT TO FORGET ALL ABOUT YOUR CATWOMAN PAST!

Selina Kyle and Batman, 1954 © NPP 1954

In the early days of her career, the Catwoman frequently employed aliases and disguises to aid her in her crimes: in Spring 1940, for example, using the name Miss Peggs, she poses as a lame old lady as part of a plot to steal a priceless emerald necklace from wealthy Martha Travers (BM No. 1/4). In Summer 1940, while the JOKER is undergoing medical treatment at Vesalius Hospital, the Catwoman appears on the sidewalk outside, disguised as an elderly chewing-gum vendor (BM No. 2/1). And in April–May 1944, using the name Belinda, she poses as a maid as part of a plot to trick the servants of Gotham City's wealthy households into betraying confidential information regarding the whereabouts of their employers' valuables (BM No. 22/1: "The Duped Domestics!").

Although one text refers to the Catwoman as "that silken, beautiful and deadly queen of crime" (Det No. 122, Apr '47: "The Black Cat Crimes!"), while another portrays her as carrying a pistol (BM No. 3/4, Fall '40: "The Batman vs the Cat-Woman!"), there is no evidence whatever that the Catwoman is really "deadly" or that she has ever actually committed a murder. On the contrary, the picture of the Catwoman that emerges from the chronicles is of a woman unalterably opposed to killing and extremely ambivalent regarding her own role as a criminal.

The most dramatic expression of this ambivalence – and the one which continues to hold the greatest fascination for Batman scholars – is the Catwoman's undeniable love for Batman, a love which has as its partial basis the Catwoman's subconscious belief that, of all men, only Batman might be powerful enough to wrest her from the sordid web of crime in which she has allowed herself to become enmeshed: "I sort of wish the **Batman** were driving this car – and I were sitting beside him," she muses wistfully in Fall 1940 as her getaway car roars away into the night, ". . . and we were just another boy and girl out for a ride on a moonlight [sic] night. That would be sort of . . . of . . . nice!!" (BM No. 3/4: "The Batman vs the Cat-Woman!").

In February–March 1952, after Selina Kyle has abandoned her role as the Catwoman in favor of a more subdued life as a pet shop proprietor, Batman offers a possible explanation for the Catwoman's characteristic ambivalence toward crime: ". . . Selina [Kyle] was an amnesia victim during her Catwoman career!" he remarks. "She wasn't really a criminal at heart!" (BM No. 69/3: "The King of the Cats!"). The explanation loses much of its persuasiveness two years later, however, when Selina, at this point no longer suffering from loss of memory, once again returns to crime as the Catwoman (Det No. 203, Jan '54: "The Crimes of the Catwoman!").

Whatever the ultimate causes of the Catwoman's criminal leanings, evidence of her unwillingness to commit murder abounds. In Summer 1940, for example, she pleads with the Joker to spare the life of Robin (BM No. 2/1), and in December 1950–January 1951 the evil MISTER X, eager to avoid ever having to face a murder charge, deliberately chooses her as an accomplice because of her reputation as a criminal who will "always rob without killing" (BM No. 62/1: "The Secret Life of the Catwoman"). In September 1954, after the Catwoman has, through an apparent oversight, enabled Batman and Robin to escape from a waterfall deathtrap, Batman assures Robin that their escape "was no accident." "Murder isn't in the ***Catwoman's*** heart," observes Batman. "Sentiment is her weakness--and that's why we'll catch her the next time!" (Det No. 211: "The Jungle Cat-Queen!").

Occasionally, even the Catwoman has pondered the danger-filled life that she has chosen for herself and wondered what is likely to become of her. "I wonder," she muses quietly in April–May 1942, ". . . I wonder if this time I'm not flirting once too often with danger and death?" (BM No. 10/3: "The Princess of Plunder!").

Although the Catwoman wears a catlike mask as early as Fall 1940 (BM No. 3/4: "The Batman vs the Cat-Woman!"), it is not until mid-1946 that she begins to exhibit the "mania for cat-crime tricks" (Det No. 203, Jan '54: "The Crimes of the Catwoman!") and feline paraphernalia with which her name has become inextricably associated.

In June–July 1946, for example, she constructs a labyrinthine hideaway called the "cat-acombs" (BM No. 35/1: "Nine Lives Has the Catwoman!"), and in February–March 1947 she brandishes her versatile cat-o'-nine-tails for the first time (BM No. 39/3: "A Christmas Tale!").

In April 1947 the Catwoman unveils the "kitty car," a high-powered black roadster whose highly stylized body resembles the body of a crouching cat. The kitty car is fitted with special "rocket-jets" to enable it to leap over obstacles (Det No. 122: "The Black Cat Crimes!"), and Batman has been moved to observe that the kitty car "is almost the equal of the batmobile!" (BM No. 84/2, Jun '54: "The Sleeping Beauties of Gotham City!").

In January 1954 the Catwoman uses a specially prepared "cat-apult" to launch herself into the air toward a passing mail helicopter, employs an ingeniously woven "cat's-cradle" as a bridge between two rooftops, and later flees from the Dynamic Duo in a tiny "catboat" (Det No. 203: "The Crimes of the Catwoman!").

In September 1954 the Catwoman unveils a special cat-shaped airplane, and at one point uses its "great retractable steel claws" to damage the wings of the BATPLANE to force Batman and Robin to make an emergency landing (Det No. 211: "The Jungle Cat-Queen!").

She is frequently surrounded by pet cats, particularly a black cat named HECATE, who makes appearances in approximately half a dozen separate texts (BM No. 35/1, Jun/Jul '46: "Nine Lives Has the Catwoman!"; and others).

Detective Comics No. 211 observes that the Catwoman "strikes as fast as the cats she loves" (Sep '54: "The Jungle Cat-Queen!"), and some texts have suggested, without explanation, that she is endowed with a cat's extraordinary ability to see in the dark (BM No. 47/1, Jun/Jul '48: "Fashions in Crime!"; and others).

Throughout the years, the Catwoman's colorful costumes have reflected her preoccupation with feline themes:

In Spring 1940 the Catwoman wears a long-sleeved green dress with a yellow mandarin collar and a matching belt (BM No. 1/4). In Summer 1940 she wears another green dress, but this one lacks the yellow collar and belt of the dress that preceded it (BM No. 2/1).

In Fall 1940 the Catwoman wears a real cat costume for the first time in the chronicles: it consists of a brown cat's-head mask that covers her entire head, complemented by an orange dress, a red cape, and high-heeled shoes (BM No. 3/4: "The Batman vs the Cat-Woman!").

In April–May 1942 the Catwoman wears a black cat's-head mask – similar in design, but not in color, to the one she wore previously – complemented by a black dress, purple cape, and purple belt (BM No. 10/3: "The Princess of Plunder!").

In February–March 1943 the Catwoman again wears the black cat's-head mask, this time with a green dress, green boots, and a red cape (BM No. 15/1: "Your Face Is Your Fortune!").

In April–May 1944 the Catwoman wears the black cat's-head mask, complemented by a black dress, purple cape, and purple boots (BM No. 22/1: "The Duped Domestics!").

In June–July 1946 the Catwoman wears a short-sleeved purple dress with light purple gloves and boots, a green cape, and a purple cowl that covers the upper part of her face and allows her hair to flow out the back at her neck (BM No. 35/1: "Nine Lives Has the Catwoman!"). In February–March 1947 her costume is virtually identical, except that her belt doubles as a menacing cat-o-nine-tails (BM No. 39/3: "A Christmas Tale!").

During the next seven years, the Catwoman's costume undergoes only minor variations from one text to the next. In April 1947 the Catwoman wears a long-sleeved dress for the first time – thus initiating a feature which is to persist for several years – and adds a pair of special "claw gloves" (Det No. 122: "The Black Cat Crimes!") which "enable her to climb like the feline creature for which she is named!" (BM No. 45/1, Feb/Mar '48: "The Lady Rogues!"). In December 1950–January 1951 the Catwoman appears in a costume with long sleeves extending past her wrists, but without gloves (BM No. 62/1: "The Secret Life of the Catwoman"), features which persist in the chronicles for some time afterward.

In the texts, the Catwoman is alternatively referred to as the Crime-Queen, the Empress of the Underworld, the Feline Felon, the Mistress of Menace, the Princess of Plunder, the Queen of Crime, the Ruthless Queen of Roguery, the Tigress of Crime, and the Tigress Queen.

According to Batman No. 36/3, QUEEN MORGAN LE FAY, the treacherous sister of KING ARTHUR, was a perfect look-alike for the Catwoman. Batman and Robin observe the uncanny resemblance firsthand during a time-journey to Arthur's Camelot that they make in August–September 1946 ("Sir Batman at King Arthur's Court!").

Counting backward from the date of her first encounter with Batman, Selina Kyle – the raven-haired, green-eyed girl who achieves infamy as the Catwoman – can have been born no later than 1922 (BM No. 1/4, Spr '40). Her father's name is not known, but he "once owned a pet shop" and at one time or another taught his young daughter "all about cats" (BM No. 62/1, Dec/Jan '50–'51: "The Secret Life of the Catwoman"). Selina also has a brother named Karl, who, under the pseudonym the King of the Cats, commits a rash of cat-related crimes in Gotham City in February–March 1952, only to abandon his criminal career soon afterward and disappear from the chronicles altogether (BM No. 69/3: "The King of the Cats!").

Sometime before the onset of her career as the Catwoman, presumably while she was still in her late teens, Selina became a stewardess with Speed Airlines. One day, an airliner in which she was flying crashed in a wooded area, and the impact of the landing sent Selina careening through a doorway into the side of a tree. Miraculously, she escaped serious physical injury, but she suffered a total loss of memory that was to plague her for over a decade.

Shaken by her involvement in the crash and with no memory whatever of her former life, Selina fell into a life of crime (BM No. 62/1, Dec/Jan '50–'51: "The Secret Life of the Catwoman"). It is not certain exactly when her criminal career began, but by Spring 1940 her beauty and her daring had apparently earned her a certain infamy, for Batman remarks at that time that he has "heard tales about the Cat[woman] before in the underworld!" (BM No. 1/4).

Although the Catwoman wears a catlike mask as early as Fall 1940 (BM No. 3/4: "The Batman vs the Cat-Woman!"), it is not until mid-1946 that a preoccupation with cat-related crimes and feline paraphernalia begins to dominate her career. Selina has traced this phenomenon to her father and to the pet shop which he once owned: "I learned all about cats from him!" she tells Batman in December 1950–January 1951, after her memory has been suddenly restored to her by a blow on the head from a falling brick. "I guess, subconsciously, I remembered about cats even while having amnesia!" (BM No. 62/1: "The Secret Life of the Catwoman").

The Catwoman's first battle of wits with Batman and Robin occurs in Spring 1940, when she concocts a scheme to steal a priceless emerald necklace from wealthy Martha Travers. During this period, when Martha Travers sets out on a cruise aboard her pleasure yacht *Dolphin* with a group of invited guests, the Catwoman – who has entered into a conspiracy with Mrs. Travers's spendthrift nephew Denny to steal Mrs. Travers's priceless emerald necklace – mingles with the other cruise guests, under the alias Miss Peggs, disguised as an elderly lady with a pronounced limp. Soon after the yacht sets sail, DICK GRAYSON – who has obtained a post as a steward aboard the yacht for the express purpose of guarding Mrs. Travers's necklace – learns that the Catwoman is somewhere on board and that a conspiracy is afoot to steal the necklace, but he is unable to move into action swiftly enough to prevent the theft of the necklace from Mrs. Travers's stateroom.

At one point, after an anguished Mrs. Travers has discovered the loss of her necklace, a gang of criminals overtake the yacht by boat and board it, only to discover to their chagrin that the necklace they have come to steal has already been stolen. "Can you imagine that!" exclaims one of them. "Someone stole it before we did! Whatta crook! Ya can't trust anybody these days!" The criminals attempt to console themselves by stealing cash and other valuables from the yacht's wealthy guests, but Batman and Robin appear on the scene, capture the criminals, and recover the stolen loot before the bandits can make good their escape.

Not long afterward, after Batman has returned the stolen valuables to the guests aboard the Travers yacht, he and Robin set into motion their plan to expose the thief responsible for the theft of Mrs. Travers's necklace. From a place of concealment, Robin activates the yacht's fire alarm, producing instant pandemonium in the yacht's ballroom, where a masquerade party is in progress. As the panic-stricken guests flee for the exits, Batman observes that Miss Peggs, supposedly elderly and lame, is running with the nimble swiftness of a young woman. When the Catwoman realizes that there is in fact no fire on board the yacht, she attempts to flee, fearing that Batman may have somehow penetrated her disguise, but Robin apprehends her moments afterward and Batman rips off her disguise to reveal the face of the dark-haired Catwoman. Inside the bandage protecting her supposedly lame ankle, Batman discovers Mrs. Travers's stolen emerald necklace.

At that moment, Mrs. Travers's nephew Denny bursts into the room with a drawn pistol and demands that the necklace be handed over to him, but Batman knocks him unconscious with a well-timed punch.

". . . why don't you come in, as a partner with me!" offers the Catwoman seductively, folding her arms tenderly around Batman's neck. "**You** and **I** together! **You** and **I**--king and queen of crime!--We'd make a great team!"

"Sorry," replies Batman, "your proposition tempts me but we work on different sides of the law!"

The Catwoman, Spring 1940 © NPP 1940

Then, after Mrs. Travers has been given back her necklace and Denny has been locked in his cabin so that he can be turned over later to the police on shore, Batman and Robin climb into their own launch with the captive Catwoman and begin the journey toward shore. When the Catwoman asks Batman why he has decided to take her to the police himself, instead of merely leaving her on board the Travers yacht with Denny, a terse "I've got my reasons!" is Batman's only reply.

Suddenly, without warning, the Catwoman leaps overboard in a daring bid for freedom, and when Robin starts to leap after her, Batman deliberately bumps him aside, feigning clumsiness.

"Too late," cries Robin dejectedly, as he stares out over the water, "--she's gone!" And then the truth behind Batman's decision to take the Catwoman aboard the launch begins to dawn on him. "--and--**say,**" exclaims Robin, "--I'll bet you bumped into me on purpose!--That's why you took her along with us--so she might try a break!"

"Why, Robin, my boy," smiles Batman wryly, "whatever gave you such an idea! . . . Hmm--nice night, isn't it? . . . Lovely girl!--What eyes!--Say--mustn't forget I've got a girl named Julie [*see* MADISON, JULIE]!--Oh well--she still had lovely eyes!--Maybe I'll bump into her again sometime. . ." (BM No. 1/4).

In Summer 1940, while the Joker is undergoing medical treatment at Vesalius Hospital, Batman devises a plan to abduct the villain from the hospital and "take him to a famous brain specialist for an operation, so that he can be cured and turned into a valuable citizen." By the time he and Robin arrive at the hospital to put their plan into effect, however, the Joker has already been abducted by the members of Crime Syndicate Inc., a gang of criminals who intend to make the Joker their new leader.

Outside the hospital, Batman encounters the Catwoman who, in the guise of an elderly chewing-gum vendor, has witnessed the Joker's recent departure.

When Batman seizes the Catwoman and drags her to his waiting automobile, she assumes that he intends to turn her over to the police, but Batman offers to set her free if she will provide him with information concerning the Joker's whereabouts.

The Catwoman informs Batman that the members of Crime Syndicate Inc. intend to make the Joker their leader, that they plan to keep him airborne in a hospital plane until he has recuperated from his recent operation at Vesalius Hospital, and that their regular hideout is a hunting lodge belonging to a hoodlum named Weasel. Batman sets the Catwoman free, but a radioactive substance on the floor of his car – now transferred to the soles of the Catwoman's shoes – will enable Robin to follow her footprints with a special flashlight while he himself sets out after the Joker.

Not long afterward, the Catwoman makes her way to the lonely castle sanctuary of millionaire E. S. Arthur, owner of the fabulous Pharaoh Gems. The Catwoman has managed to seduce Arthur into inviting her to visit his castle, and she plans to steal the Pharaoh Gems sometime during her stay there. At the castle, however, she finds Arthur lying on the floor dead, killed by a poison-tipped needle planted in one of his shoes by the Joker's henchmen. She is about to make off with the Pharaoh Gems when suddenly the Joker – who had ordered Arthur murdered to facilitate his own theft of the jewels – appears on the scene and demands that the Catwoman turn the gems over to him. "Hand over that **jewel** cask, my pretty!" cries the Joker. "Or must I kill you first?"

At that moment, Robin, who has been trailing the Catwoman, invades the castle and plunges into battle with the Joker. The Joker, however, knocks Robin unconscious and is about to inject the Boy Wonder with a chemical solution which will "reduce [him] to nothingness inside of five minutes," when the Catwoman intervenes desperately in his behalf. "Stop, **Joker!**" she pleads. "Spare the boy and the **jewels** are yours!"

At that moment, Batman arrives at the castle and leaps into battle with the Joker, but the villain subdues Batman temporarily and then sets fire to the castle library in an effort to smoke out the Catwoman, who has barricaded herself inside with Robin and the Pharaoh Gems.

Batman returns to the fray and knocks the Joker unconscious, but the castle is already a roaring inferno, and he is forced to throw the unconscious Robin over his shoulder and flee with the Catwoman to the safety of the waiting batplane, leaving the fallen Joker behind in the blazing castle. Halfway up the rope ladder toward the hovering batplane, however, the Catwoman leaps into the river below in a daring bid for freedom, with E. S. Arthur's jewel cask still in her possession. Batman, however, has already managed to remove the jewels from the cask, leaving the Catwoman with her freedom but without the Pharaoh Gems (BM No. 2/1).

In Fall 1940, after staging at least one daring jewel robbery, the Catwoman is hired by Messrs. Darral (also Darrel) and Hoffer, two of the three partners in a major diamond syndicate, to steal a shipment of fabulous diamonds that their firm has recently received so that they can use the money from the sale of the gems to cover their losses in the stock market while their firm collects the insurance on the diamonds.

After donning a blond wig and posing as one of the jewelry models in the firm's lavish salon, the Catwoman blinds the salespeople and onlookers with magicians' flash powder and escapes with the jewels, only to be taken captive outside the salon by Hoffer's henchmen, who, acting on Hoffer's instructions, intend to murder the Catwoman and double-cross Darral so that they can keep the stolen diamonds for themselves.

Ultimately, however, Batman and Robin learn the details of the plot to steal the diamonds and collect the insurance, and they invade Hoffer's hideout in time to apprehend Hoffer and his henchmen and rescue the Catwoman from their clutches.

Batman has no sooner untied the Catwoman, however, than she leaps at Hoffer, "her long nails slashing like the claws of a tiger!" "I'll scratch his eyes out!" cries the Catwoman. Batman restrains the Catwoman and smiles broadly. "You certainly live up to your name, Cat!" he remarks.

Batman and Robin tie up their captives, but Batman pointedly fails to bind the Catwoman. "Well, **Cat,**" he says finally, when the time has come to turn the criminals over to the authorities, ". . . I'm sorry, but I guess you've got to go along to the police too!"

"It doesn't matter!" replies the Catwoman sweetly. "You saved my life! I'd like to thank you for that!" The Catwoman embraces Batman and gives him a tender kiss, then suddenly gives him a hard backward shove, darts out the door, and roars away in the car belonging to Hoffer and his henchmen. Robin starts to pursue her, but Batman holds him back. "Take it easy!" says Batman quietly. "She's too far away for you to catch

The Catwoman, Fall 1940 © NPP 1940

Batman, the Catwoman, and Robin, Fall 1940 © NPP 1940

up." "I guess you're right about that," replies Robin, ". . . but it's too bad a crook like that has to get away, even if she **is** a girl!" "Yes," sighs Batman, "and it's too bad she has to be a crook! What a night! . . . A night for romance, eh, **Robin?**" "Romance?" exclaims Robin. **"BAH. . . ."**

Meanwhile, behind the wheel of her getaway car, the Catwoman is thinking of romance also: "I sort of wish the **Batman** were driving this car – and I were sitting beside him . . . and we were just another boy and girl out for a ride on a moonlight [sic] night. That would be sort of . . . of . . . nice!!" (BM No. 3/4: "The Batman vs the Cat-Woman!").

In April–May 1942 the Catwoman reappears, this time in the guise of Marguerite Tone, a "popular party hostess" and "toast of high society" whose "palatial home" is the scene of frequent parties attended by the city's wealthy social set.

During one of her parties, Marguerite Tone organizes a scavenger hunt, ostensibly for the entertainment of her guests but in reality to enable her henchmen to gain access to the homes of the wealthy on the pretext of searching for items required by the hunt. At one point, for example, Batman and Robin see two men climbing through an open window and apprehend them, only to be told that the men are merely innocent participants in Marguerite Tone's scavenger hunt. Batman telephones Marguerite Tone for verification of the men's story and then lets them go, but he has managed to recognize the sound of her voice. "That voice!" exclaims Batman. "I could never forget it! It was--the **Cat-Woman's!"**

For her next party, Marguerite Tone invites each of her guests to come dressed in the costume of his or her favorite character. The Catwoman plans for her henchmen to come to the party in Batman costumes and then fan out across the city on a looting spree, each criminal gaining easy access to a different wealthy home by claiming to be the real Batman.

Batman, however, receives an invitation to the party in his Bruce Wayne identity and attends the party clad in his Batman costume. At the party, he sneaks unrecognized into a final briefing for Marguerite Tone's

The Catwoman as Marguerite Tone, 1942 © NPP 1942

Batman-clad henchmen, only to be exposed as an outsider when too many men in Batman costumes show up at the secret meeting. Batman and Robin battle the criminals and ultimately apprehend them, but they have insufficient evidence to enable them to arrest Marguerite Tone. "Your round, **Batman!**" she exclaims. "But you can't prove I committed any crime! You spoiled my scheme, though---and I won't forget that!" Moments later, after Batman and Robin have left, the Catwoman finds herself still thinking about Batman. "How brave and strong he is!" she muses. "If only he would team up with me---nobody would be able to stop us---nobody!"

The Catwoman's next scheme involves setting up an employment agency for domestic servants, still utilizing her Marguerite Tone identity. Because many of Marguerite Tone's house guests have admired her own servants, they are eager to employ servants recommended by her agency, unaware that the Catwoman's real intention is to place her henchmen in wealthy homes as servants and then rob all of the infiltrated homes simultaneously, on a single prearranged night.

While dining at a friend's home as Bruce Wayne, however, Batman recognizes the newly hired butler there as a known criminal, but although he moves swiftly to smash the Catwoman's latest plot, she and most of her henchmen nevertheless succeed in making good their escape.

Soon afterward, the Catwoman establishes a "lost and found" bureau where, in return for exorbitant fees paid to her by victims of her own recent burglaries, she agrees to "find" the stolen loot and return it to them. Batman and Robin invade the lost-and-found agency and plunge into a furious battle with the Catwoman and her henchmen. As the sound of approaching police sirens begins to be heard in the distance, one of the Catwoman's own henchmen turns on her with gun in hand. "You're responsible for getting me in this jam, **Cat-Woman!**" he cries. "Now the cops are gonna get us---but here's a souvenir from me, first!" Batman, however, swiftly intervenes and disarms the henchman before he can do any harm to his erstwhile leader.

With the battle over, the Catwoman throws her arms around Batman and gives him a warm kiss, presumably in gratitude for having saved her life. Then suddenly, "before the startled **Batman** can recover his wits," the wily villainess races out the door and escapes.

Moments later, after having thanked Batman for capturing the Catwoman's henchmen and recovering a hoard of stolen loot, a policeman asks Batman what has become of the Catwoman. "She---er---she got away," stammers Batman. "---slipped through my fingers. . . ."

Later, however, when he and Bruce Wayne are alone, Dick Grayson advances a theory of his own. "You know, Bruce," remarks Grayson, "I've a feeling you **let** the **Cat-Woman** escape!"

"Why, Dick," replies Wayne with a wry grin, "how can you say a thing like that! She's clever and beautiful, yes---and it's a shame that we both work on opposite sides of the law but I hope---I mean I know we'll meet again--soon! And then it will be my round!" (BM No. 10/3: "The Princess of Plunder!").

In February–March 1943 the Catwoman reappears, this time in the guise of Elva Barr, a beauty operator at the lavish Manon's Beauty Salon. By recording the voices of her wealthy clients with a hidden tape recorder so that she can learn to mimic them, as well as molding lifelike masks of their faces with the aid of a special hardening ingredient added to their mudpacks, the Catwoman is able to impersonate her wealthy customers to aid her in her crimes.

At one point, the Catwoman enters a beauty contest for beauticians as Elva Barr and is declared the winner. One of the judges at the contest is Bruce Wayne, and the Catwoman soon finds herself falling in love with him. "My heart's fluttering . . **I'm falling in love!**" she thinks to herself. "And he seems interested in me, too!" She does not realize that Bruce Wayne is also Batman, and that what she interprets as Wayne's romantic interest in her is really nothing more than Wayne's silent recognition that Elva Barr is also the fugitive Catwoman.

Not long afterward, the Catwoman makes a lifelike mask of the face of newspaper society editor Grace Arnold, and then poses as Grace Arnold in order to gain entrance to a lavish wedding party accompanied by a group of her henchmen, who pose as newspaper photographers. Batman and Robin appear on the scene and capture the Catwoman and her henchmen before they can make off with the valuable wedding gifts on display there, but the Catwoman begs Batman not to turn her over to the authorities. "I'm in love, **Batman,**" pleads the Catwoman, ". . . in love with a fine, decent man! You've probably heard of him . . . **Bruce Wayne!** Oh! If only you'd let me go, **Batman** . . . if I knew I had a chance with him, I'd give up my life of crime!"

Moved by the Catwoman's plea, and hopeful that her love for Bruce Wayne will enable him to find a way to persuade her to reform, Batman allows her to escape and then, in the days that follow, begins a whirlwind romance with Elva Barr in his Bruce Wayne identity that soon culminates in their engagement.

"I'm through, men!" announces the Catwoman to her henchmen, after her engagement to Bruce Wayne has been formally announced. "No more crime! You read the papers--I'm engaged now! I'm going straight!"

"Aw, that guy **Bruce Wayne** ain't in love with you!" replies one of the henchmen disdainfully. "He's sweet on **Linda Page!** Everybody knows . ."

The Catwoman cuts the henchman's sentence short with a vicious slap, but soon afterward she is haunted by the fear that her henchman may have been right. "Maybe . . . maybe he's right!" she muses. "Maybe I'm just a silly fool!"

Meanwhile, however, a heartbroken LINDA PAGE reads the announcement of Bruce Wayne's engagement to Elva Barr and decides to visit Manon's Beauty Salon to take a firsthand look at her rival. However, while the Catwoman – in her beauty parlor role as Elva Barr – administers a beauty treatment to Linda Page, she suddenly decides to make a mudpack mask of Linda Page's face in order to be able to discover which of them Bruce Wayne really loves.

Later, disguised as Linda Page, the Catwoman pays a call on Bruce Wayne and pretends to be annoyed and upset at the news of Wayne's engagement to Elva Barr.

"Now, listen, **Linda,**" stammers Wayne, unaware that the woman in his presence is the disguised Catwoman, "please understand! I--I'm doing a favor for the **Batman!** He asked me to do this!" A moment later, he adds, "You must trust me, **Linda!** My engagement won't be for long!"

"So he really doesn't love me!" thinks the Catwoman bitterly. "He loves **Linda!** And he's just doing this because the **Batman** asked him!" Moments later, she leaves Wayne's home in a huff, plotting her revenge. "This is the **Batman's** fault!" thinks the Catwoman. "He wanted to refom [sic] me! Well, I'll show him!"

Sometime later, Bruce Wayne discovers that the woman who visited him earlier was not the real Linda Page at all, but the Catwoman in disguise. By then, however, it is too late to salvage his plan to lead the Catwoman away from her life of crime.

In the days that follow, the Catwoman launches a new wave of spectacular crimes in the city. At one point, she poses as a well-known animal lover as part of a plan to steal some valuable pets from the Fairview Pet Show so that she and her henchmen can hold them for ransom, but she and her cohorts are ultimately apprehended through the heroic efforts of Batman and Robin (BM No. 15/1: "Your Face Is Your Fortune!").

By April–May 1944 the Catwoman has apparently regained her freedom, because she and an accomplice named Craven have installed themselves in a rented mansion – with Craven posing as the master of the house, and the Catwoman posing as his maid under the name Belinda – as part of a plot to burglarize the wealthy homes of the area. By throwing a lavish ball for the neighborhood's domestic servants, Craven entices the servants of all the local gentry to his mansion. There the Catwoman, posing as Craven's maid, mingles with the servants — the text says that she plays "fast and loose" with them — cleverly tricking them into betraying confidential information regarding the habits of their employers and the whereabouts of their valuables so that she and Craven can later burglarize their homes.

It is during this period that Bruce Wayne's butler ALFRED, who does not suspect that Craven's maid Belinda is really the Catwoman, meets Belinda and falls in love with her. For a time, Alfred's romantic state of mind leads him to neglect his duties at the Wayne mansion, much to the chagrin of Bruce Wayne and Dick Grayson.

One afternoon, during one of his frequent trysts with Belinda in Gotham Park, Alfred attempts to impress Belinda by boasting of his close friendship with Batman. When Belinda remains skeptical, Alfred attempts to make good his boast by promising Belinda that he will send Batman to the park to meet her. Alfred races home, dons one of Batman's spare costumes, and then returns to Gotham Park to keep his promise to Belinda, unaware that he is walking unprotected into the clutches of the Catwoman.

Back in the park, the Catwoman and her henchmen are lying in wait to capture the arriving "Batman," and although the Catwoman observes that Batman seems to have lost a lot of weight since she saw him last, she and her henchmen pounce on Alfred and take him prisoner, believing that they have captured the real Batman.

Meanwhile, at the Wayne mansion, Bruce Wayne and Dick Grayson enter Alfred's room and, coming upon a love poem he has written about Belinda, surmise that Alfred is in love with the girl in the poem and that this explains his recent inattention to his duties as their butler. Suddenly, however, Wayne realizes that the description of the girl in the poem sounds suspiciously like that of the Catwoman, and he begins to suspect the real explanation behind the recent goings-on at the Craven mansion.

Under the pretext of being neighborly, Wayne and Grayson pay a visit to the Craven mansion, hoping to solve the mystery of Alfred's disappearance and to gather the evidence they need to apprehend Craven and the Catwoman, but the Catwoman and her henchmen take them prisoner, lock them in a refrigeration room with the costumed Alfred, and then race off to loot the Wayne mansion at their leisure.

After the criminals have gone, however, Wayne, Grayson, and Alfred escape from the refrigeration room and race back toward the Wayne mansion to battle the Catwoman and her henchmen. Batman and Robin arrive on the scene ahead of Alfred and apprehend all of the criminals except for the Catwoman, who manages to escape.

Outside the Wayne mansion, however, the Catwoman is captured by the still-costumed Alfred, who gives his prisoner a sound spanking before bringing her back to the Wayne mansion to await the arrival of the police. "I still think, Alfred," remarks Bruce Wayne afterward, "that you were rather drastic with her!"

"Perhaps so, sir," replies Alfred. "But think of my wounded affections and the effect of my romance on your digestions! Er — by the way, If I may be so bold," adds Alfred, "I think I make rather a good **Batman,** sir!" (BM No. 22/1: "The Duped Domestics!").

In June–July 1946 the Catwoman escapes from State Prison by hypnotizing a guard with a cat's-eye gem, but when she returns to Gotham City and attempts to recruit a gang, she finds that local criminals are reluctant to join her because, in the words of one of them, "the **Batman** always stops you cold!"

Batman and the Catwoman, 1946 © NPP 1946

Realizing that she cannot possibly hope to "rebuild [her] crime empire" without henchmen to help her, the Catwoman sets out to regain the confidence of the underworld by proving to them that she possesses the nine lives of the proverbial cat and can therefore never be permanently defeated. With the aid of two faithful cohorts, Mike and Pete, the Catwoman stages a series of elaborately contrived incidents in which she appears to cheat death and emerge unscathed. Thus fooled into believing that their leader is virtually invincible, the minions of the underworld willingly join forces with her once again.

In the days that follow, the Catwoman and her henchmen stage a series of spectacular crimes, and at the scene of each one the Catwoman seems to defy death. One such crime involves an attempt to loot a dirigible transporting a shipment of valuable industrial diamonds. When Batman and Robin appear on the scene and plunge into battle with the criminals, the Catwoman's henchmen flee, leaving their leader to battle Batman alone atop the giant dirigible. The Princess of Plunder appears doomed when, in the midst of the battle, she topples over the side of the dirigible and plummets toward the ground, but somehow she manages to survive to continue her spectacular criminal career.

At one point, Batman and Robin trail one of the Catwoman's henchmen to her labyrinthine hideout — the so-called "cat-acombs" — only to be taken prisoner and locked inside a series of mazelike passageways.

Ultimately, they escape from the cat-acombs and make their way to the castle home of millionaire Carl Gibbs, situated atop a high precipice overlooking a waterfall, where the Catwoman and her cohorts are attempting to make off with Gibbs's valuable weapons collection. The Dynamic Duo battle the Catwoman's henchmen and swiftly defeat them, but the Catwoman leaps atop a Caterpillar tractor and attempts to escape. Suddenly, however, the tractor strikes a hidden boulder, sending the Catwoman hurtling over the nearby cliff into the foaming waters of the thundering cataract far below. Whether she has managed to survive remains seriously in doubt (BM No. 35/1: "Nine Lives Has the Catwoman!").

In the Batman text for February–March 1947, which purports to describe events which took place during Christmas, 1946, the Catwoman steals three pet cats to aid her in some future crimes: a Manx cat from a little boy, a red Persian cat from an old lady, and a white mouser from a frozen foods factory.

After attaching a phony tail filled with knockout gas to the tail of the Manx cat, the Catwoman lets it loose near the guards at the Gotham Museum. When the guards pet the cat, the false tail comes off, the gas is released, and the guards are knocked unconscious, enabling the Catwoman and her henchman to begin stealing jewels from the museum's Egyptian room. Batman and Robin arrive on the scene and attempt to apprehend them, but the Catwoman and the lone cohort with her manage to make good their escape.

Later, at the lavish Moon Valley Winter Resort – the scene of an annual dog-sled racing competition with a purse of $10,000 to be awarded the winner – the Catwoman's henchmen release the white mouser directly in front of the sled dogs, which, in their eagerness to catch the cat, upset their sleds and cause general pandemonium while the Catwoman's cohorts make off with the prize money. Inside the resort, meanwhile, the Catwoman tricks the hotel detective into opening the hotel vault by claiming that she wants to deposit some jewels in it, then knocks the detective unconscious so that she can freely loot the safe by allowing the red Persian cat, whose claws she has coated with a special knockout drug, to scratch him. Batman and Robin arrive at the resort, however, capture the Catwoman's henchmen, and ultimately apprehend the Catwoman herself.

"Don't turn me in, **Batman!**" pleads the Catwoman. "Join up with me instead! Together, we can rule the underworld! We can be king and queen of crime! You and I – together!"

"Together?" replies Batman incredulously. "How could we – with me **outside** and you **inside** a jail cell!" (BM No. 39/3: "A Christmas Tale!").

In April 1947 the Catwoman escapes from prison with the aid of a pair of special "claw gloves" which enable her to scale the prison walls and make her way to a waiting getaway car manned by members of her gang. Back at her hideout, when a superstitious henchman makes a remark to the effect that he is frightened of the Catwoman's pet black cat, Hecate, because all black cats are unlucky, the Catwoman is inspired with an idea for a new series of spectacular cat-crimes.

First she mails letters to three wealthy men – "fur magnate" John Ross, circus owner Sam Slade, and shipowner Bill Drew – informing them that unless each of them agrees to pay her $50,000, black cats will cross their paths and bring them bad luck. Then, when her three letters are ignored, she sets out to make good her threat.

At Gotham City's Central Airport, where a shipment of furs is coming in by plane for John Ross, the Catwoman uses a *black Cat*erpillar tractor to haul a dirigible into the path of the approaching fur plane and then, with the aid of her henchmen, loots the plane after it has crashed into the dirigible and makes good her escape in her high-powered "kitty car."

Later, the Catwoman and her henchmen create pandemonium at Sam Slade's circus by setting a black panther – i.e., a *black* jungle *cat* – loose in the circus ring, apparently with the intention of robbing the circus box-office in the ensuing confusion, but Batman and Robin recapture the panther so swiftly that the Catwoman and her henchmen barely manage to flee in the Catwoman's kitty car.

Soon afterward, when one of Bill Drew's ships sets sail with a particularly rich cargo, the Catwoman and her henchmen – posing as fishermen – deliberately allow the freighter to ram their tiny *cat*boat so that the crew of the freighter will be compelled to take them aboard. Once aboard the freighter, the Catwoman and her henchmen attempt to hijack the cargo, but Batman and Robin appear on the scene and swiftly apprehend the Catwoman's cohorts. The Catwoman, however, leaps overboard and swims to the nearby Statue of Liberty, with Batman and Robin in hot pursuit.

As the Dynamic Duo pursue the Catwoman up the circular staircase inside the gigantic statue, the Catwoman hurls a loose block at Batman, stunning him and knocking him temporarily out of the fight. Then, with the aid of her claw gloves, the Catwoman climbs up the outside of the statue to the hand grasping the torch, where her henchmen are waiting in a helicopter to carry her to safety. Robin battles valiantly to prevent the Catwoman's henchmen from rescuing their leader, but one of the henchmen knocks him unconscious and Robin soon finds himself a captive in the Catwoman's hideout.

The Catwoman sends Batman a note offering to exchange Robin for her own captive henchmen, but Batman ultimately locates the Catwoman's hideout, captures another of the Catwoman's henchmen, and frees Robin.

The Catwoman, however, flees to her waiting kitty car and roars off into the night, with Batman and Robin close behind her in the high-powered BATMOBILE. Suddenly, as the Catwoman races toward a drawbridge, it rises unexpectedly, and the Catwoman, apparently unable to stop the kitty car in time, "roars ahead – straight into the black void!" Even Batman and Robin are uncertain whether the kitty car has plunged headlong into the murky bay or landed safely on the other side of the wide embankment (Det No. 122: "The Black Cat Crimes!").

In August–September 1947 the Catwoman breaks out of jail by fashioning a homemade bomb from the specially prepared, chemically treated pages of a seemingly innocuous book mailed to her by her henchmen. Now safely reunited with her gang once again, she maps a campaign for a series of spectacular crimes having as their theme the "famous felines of fiction," such as "Puss in Boots," "Dick Whittington's Cat," and "The Cat and the Fiddle."

For their "Puss in Boots" crime, the Catwoman and her gang make off with the ticket receipts from a local rodeo after the Catwoman has disguised herself as a rodeo cowboy (thereby transforming herself into a *puss* [cat] *in boots* [cowboy boots]) in order to gain entrance to the box office.

For their "Dick Whittington's Cat" crime, the Catwoman and her henchmen steal a payroll from the headquarters of the White Cat Coal Company. (The real Dick Whittington, explains Batman, made his fortune in the coal business, and a "cat" is a type of boat used for hauling coal.) When Batman and Robin attempt to thwart this crime, they are taken captive by the Catwoman and her henchmen and left trapped inside a walled-up room, but they escape from their prison soon afterward with the aid of a local policeman and subsequently apprehend the Catwoman when she attempts to flee the scene of a robbery at The Cat and the Fiddle, a Gotham City nightspot described in the text as a "jive spot for hep-*cats*" (BM No. 42/1: "Claws of the Catwoman!").

In February–March 1948 the Catwoman escapes from prison again and sets out to avenge what she regards as a humiliating slight — the failure of author Neil Weston to include any mention of her in *The Lady Rogues*, his recently published book about the famous women criminals of history and legend. Movie rights to the book have already been acquired by Paragon Pictures of Hollywood, and movie actress Gala Kazon has been hired to publicize the forthcoming movie by playing the roles of all the villainesses in a series of performances for theater and television.

At each of Gala Kazon's performances, the Catwoman appears on the scene to commit a spectacular crime as a pointed reminder to author Weston, and to all of Gotham City, that she, and not any of the villainesses in Weston's book, is the greatest woman criminal of all time. While Gala Kazon is playing the sorceress Circe at the Gotham Island Amphitheater, for example, the Catwoman swoops onto the stage, seizes a valuable string of pearls from around the actress's neck, and makes good her escape despite the best efforts of Batman and Robin to apprehend her. Soon afterward, when Gala Kazon appears on television as the wicked queen in *Snow White*, telecast from the castle home of millionaire J. B. Vanders, the Catwoman appears on the scene and attempts to make off with Vanders's renowned collection of miniature paintings, although the text is vague on the question of whether or not she actually succeeds in escaping with the loot. Batman and Robin ultimately apprehend the Catwoman and her henchmen when they attempt to disrupt a rehearsal of Gala Kazon's performance as the biblical villainess Delilah.

"Why don't you reform, **Catwoman?**" asks Batman, as he prepares to turn his captive over to the authorities.

"Oh, stop crowing!" snaps the Catwoman. "You men are all alike! Take me to jail and shut up!"

Another blow awaits the Catwoman, however, when Neil Weston, author of *The Lady Rogues*, visits her in prison. **"You!"** she cries accusingly. "You're to blame for all of this! Why didn't you include ***me*** in your list of lady rogues?"

"Because ***your*** exploits are so terrific," replies Weston, "that I was writing a book about ***you alone!***"

". . . ***ooohhh!***" moans the Catwoman (BM No. 45/1: "The Lady Rogues!").

Batman, and the Catwoman as Madame Moderne, 1948 © NPP 1948

In June–July 1948, after her loyal pet cat Hecate has found its way to her prison cell, the Catwoman breaks out of jail by utilizing a skeleton key and gas capsules concealed inside Hecate's "utility collar." Back in Gotham City, she dons a blond wig and, under the alias Madame Moderne, establishes herself as the publisher of *Damsel*, a high-fashion magazine, in order to help her gain easy access to the wealthy and their possessions.

At one point, for example, she approaches furrier A. J. Nixon in her Madame Moderne identity and persuades him to lend her a valuable mink coat for use in an upcoming televised fashion show sponsored by *Damsel*. On the day of the actual show, however, the Catwoman appears out of nowhere, seizes the mink coat, and races from the scene despite the best efforts of Batman and Robin to apprehend her.

Later, as Madame Moderne, the Catwoman flatters wealthy Mrs. Van Tyler into allowing her fabulous diamond necklace to be photographed for an upcoming article in *Damsel*. While the necklace is being photographed, however, and before it has been replaced inside Mrs. Van Tyler's wall safe, the Catwoman coats the jewelry case in which it is kept with a special chemical designed to release a powerful sleeping gas inside the wall safe as soon as it dries. That evening, when Mrs. Van Tyler attempts to return some other items to the safe, the sleeping gas inside knocks her unconscious, enabling the Catwoman to enter the house and steal the necklace.

Not long afterward, Madame Moderne invites Gotham City's wealthiest women to a special fashion exposition sponsored by her magazine, with the intention of appearing on the scene as the Catwoman and robbing the assembled guests. Batman and Robin, however, have managed to deduce that Madame Moderne is really the Catwoman, and they appear at the fashion exposition in time to apprehend the Catwoman and her henchmen as they attempt to make off with their victims' jewelry and other valuables (BM No. 47/1: "Fashions in Crime!").

In December 1950–January 1951 an underworld figure known only as MISTER X arranges for the Catwoman to be broken out of prison to become his accomplice. "I've got many jobs lined up for my mob," explains Mister X, "but in order to work them, the boys might have to kill guards or watchmen! That, I don't want . . . I don't ever want a murder rap hanging over my head! ***Catwoman,*** you always rob ***without killing,*** by using your knowledge of cats! So here's my offer-- ***you do the jobs for me,*** and we'll share the loot!"

The Catwoman agrees, and soon afterward sets out to reconnoiter the scene of the first robbery. At one point, she spies Batman and Robin following her through the streets and plunges into battle with them, only to find herself torn by conflicting feelings when she sees the crumbling brick wall of an abandoned building toppling toward Batman. For an instant, she thinks only of her personal freedom – "***Batman will be killed!*** I'll be able to escape now! I'll be free!" – but then she hesitates, abruptly turns back toward Batman, and rescues him from certain death by shoving him out of the path of the plummeting bricks, only to be knocked unconscious by a falling brick herself.

Batman and Robin carry the unconscious Catwoman to the BATCAVE, where she soon revives, but without any recollection whatever of her long career as the Catwoman. She explains that her name is really Selina Kyle, that she was once a stewardess with Speed Airlines, and that sometime in the past she injured her head when her airplane crashed.

Realizing that this early head injury must have given Selina Kyle temporary amnesia, Batman shows her a series of newsreel clips showing her in action as the Catwoman in the hope that seeing them may somehow restore her recollection of her criminal escapades.

"***No! No! Don't*** show me any more!" cries Selina finally, shaken and distraught at the idea that she had become a criminal while suffering from a loss of memory. "Now I understand . . . while I had amnesia, I became a criminal! Ohh . . . how horrible . . . horrible. . . ."

When Batman expresses bewilderment over the Catwoman's obsession with cat crimes, Selina offers this explanation: "My dad once owned a ***pet shop!*** I learned all about cats from him! I guess, ***subconsciously,*** I remembered about cats even while having amnesia!"

Finally, Selina begins to recall her career as the Catwoman and the details of her recent agreement with Mister X. After she has told her full story to POLICE COMMISSIONER GORDON, Gordon asks her to become the Catwoman again, and to resume her partnership with Mister X, long enough for Batman and Robin to apprehend him.

"No . . . please!" begs Selina, severely shaken by Gordon's request. "I want to put my criminal past behind me!"

When Batman informs her that she would be performing a valuable public service by helping the authorities capture Mister X, however, Selina finally relents. Soon afterward, she dons her Catwoman costume and helps Mister X's gang stage a spectacular robbery. "The scoundrels!" thinks the Catwoman bitterly. "During my amnesia, I'd have gloried in this robbery! Now it just sickens me!"

Later, when she makes her report to Batman and Police Commissioner Gordon, she again expresses reluctance to continue in her Catwoman role, even to serve the cause of law and order. "But must I go on with this?" she asks. "I find stealing so hateful . . . so horrible!"

Together, Batman and the Catwoman work out a final plan for the capture of Mister X. At the scene of the Catwoman's next robbery, the Dynamic Duo allow themselves to be captured and carried captive to Mister X's hideout in an abandoned farmhouse on the outskirts of Gotham City. There, Mister X locks Batman and Robin in an abandoned grain mill alongside a time bomb and then, having learned of the Catwoman's recent defection to the police, ties his former ally to a tractor and sends it hurtling toward the edge of a towering cliff. In the nick of time, however, Batman and Robin escape from the deathtrap, rescue Selina Kyle, and apprehend Mister X and his henchmen.

Later, at police headquarters, Selina surrenders her Catwoman costume to Police Commissioner Gordon and vows never to use it again. "That's that," promises Selina. "From now on I'm plain Selina Kyle! The ***Catwoman*** has ***retired!***"

"I wonder!" muses Batman. "Somehow, I think the law will again need the services of ***Catwoman--police operative*** . . . and it may be sooner than you think!" (BM No. 62/1: "The Secret Life of the Catwoman").

By June–July 1951 Selina Kyle has opened a "tiny pet shop" specializing in cats "in the heart of Gotham City," and has settled quietly into a new life as a pet shop proprietor. During this period, however, gangland czar "Whale" Morton, who is determined to recruit the Catwoman as his partner in crime, attempts to cajole, and then to trick, Selina into emerging from retirement to become the Catwoman once again.

Over a period of several days, Morton and his henchmen stage a series of spectacular crimes, each based upon a feline theme. Their aim appears twofold: first, to coax Selina out of retirement by persuading both the authorities and the public that the Catwoman has returned to crime; and second, to persuade Selina that her role as the Catwoman has such a compelling hold on her psyche that she has already committed a rash of Catwoman crimes without even being consciously aware of it.

For a time, Selina does indeed worry that perhaps, without realizing it, she has been responsible for the recent wave of cat-related crimes. Finally, she decides to don her Catwoman costume and pretend to join forces with Morton long enough to bring about his capture.

In the days that follow, the Catwoman commits a series of crimes with the aid of Morton's henchmen while Morton himself directs their operations from a nearby parked car. On one occasion, while the Catwoman and Morton's henchmen are attempting to steal a valuable necklace at the Gotham International Airport, the Catwoman hastily improvises a makeshift "cat-signal" in the hope that it will attract Batman and Robin to the scene to thwart the robbery.

Batman and Robin spot the signal and arrive at the airport in time to prevent the theft, although the Catwoman has fled the scene by the time they arrive, but they do not realize that the Catwoman had summoned them intentionally, and both Batman and Robin leap to the erroneous conclusion that the Catwoman has emerged from retirement and returned to crime.

Before long, the Catwoman has come to realize that Morton will never be apprehended unless he can be lured directly to the scene of a crime, and that the only thing that might tempt him to forgo his usual caution and appear at the scene would be the prospect of witnessing the murder of Batman and Robin. At the scene of her next robbery, the theft of a gem-encrusted Egyptian cat-idol from the ZBC television studios, the Catwoman again lures Batman and Robin to the scene with a cat-signal, then lures them into a trap in a darkened television studio, takes them prisoner, and places them atop a camera dolly rigged to carry them directly into the whirling blades of a giant studio wind machine.

As the Catwoman had anticipated, Morton races eagerly to the scene in the belief that he is about to witness the deaths of Batman and Robin. Unbeknownst to Morton, however, the Catwoman has carefully rigged her wind-machine deathtrap to prevent it from killing the Dynamic Duo, and has activated a studio television camera in the hope that the police will spot the crime-in-progress on television and race to the scene. It is not clear whether Batman and Robin realize that they are in no actual danger, but Batman has apparently begun to realize that the Catwoman is their ally in this encounter, and not their enemy. In any event, the Catwoman's safety measures prove unnecessary because Batman and Robin cleverly engineer their own escape from the deathtrap and plunge into battle with the criminals. Seconds later the police arrive, and "Whale" Morton and his henchmen are apprehended. Batman now realizes that the Catwoman never actually intended to return to crime, and the Catwoman is relieved to have learned for certain that the early rash of cat-crimes were "Whale" Morton's and not her own (BM No. 65/3: "Catwoman – Empress of the Underworld").

In February–March 1952 Gotham City is rocked by yet another series of cat-related crimes, this time committed by a bizarre villain calling himself the KING OF THE CATS. Because Selina Kyle is obviously the expert on this type of crime, and because Batman and Robin know that Selina has recently received a bouquet of flowers from the villain, the Dynamic Duo visit Selina at her pet shop in order to ask her help in bringing the villain to justice.

Selina, however, is visibly shaken by Batman's request and obviously ambivalent. "Oh, ***Batman,***" cries Selina, "I don't know what to do! I want to work with the law, but . . . this makes things different! Please go and let me think this out! I'll give you my answer tomorrow!"

"Good grief," thinks Batman to himself, as he and Robin prepare to leave the shop, ". . . look at her weeping! Why . . . why, I think she's actually ***fallen in love*** with the ***Cat King!***"

Batman, however, has leaped to an erroneous conclusion, for Selina's reluctance to assist in the apprehension of the King of the Cats is not due to the fact that he is her lover, but to the fact that he is her brother Karl.

Batman and Robin have no sooner left Selina's pet shop, than they spy the King of the Cats going inside to see Selina. Inside the shop, the King of the Cats is attempting to persuade Selina to join him in a life of crime, when suddenly Batman and Robin hurl themselves into the shop and make the King of the Cats their prisoner. Heartbroken, Selina pleads with Batman not to turn the villain over to the law, but Batman insists that he has no alternative. Suddenly, Selina hits Batman and Robin over the head with a heavy vase and then ties them up with the aid of her brother. "I saved you only so you'd have a chance to come to your senses!" says Selina to her brother. "I want you to return what you've stolen and go straight! Promise me!"

The King of the Cats leaves, promising only that he will think over what Selina has asked of him. Once he is safely out the door and out of sight, Selina unties the Dynamic Duo and sets them free.

"Selina, you sure love that guy, don't you?" asks Robin.

"Well," replies Selina, incorrectly assuming that both Batman and Robin realize that the King of the Cats is her brother, "isn't it natural?"

"Natural?" thinks Batman to himself. "I suppose she think [sic] it's natural to love a criminal who is so much like she used to be! It's so eerie . . . a ***Catwoman*** . . . in love with a ***Cat King!***"

"You understand why I let him escape, don't you?" asks Selina hopefully, as Batman and Robin leave the pet shop. "I want him to make his own decision! That's the only way he'll ever reform!"

Not long afterward, when the King of the Cats attempts to steal a rare black lion from the private zoo of a local millionaire – with the intention of holding it for ransom – Batman and Robin appear on the scene and attempt to apprehend him. In the battle that follows, Robin is knocked unconscious, and Batman and the King of the Cats fall against some faulty fencing in the private zoo and find themselves hopelessly trapped inside separate tiger cages, each menaced by a snarling tiger.

It is at that moment that Selina Kyle arrives on the scene in her Catwoman costume, seizes the special animal-tranquilizing rifle which her brother has dropped on the ground, and races to the tiger cages. She is confronted, however, by an agonizing decision, because the tranquilizing rifle contains only one anaesthetizing gas pellet, and she can therefore subdue only one of the two tigers, either the one about to kill Batman, or the one about to kill her brother.

After a moment of painful hesitation, the Catwoman shoots the lone anesthetizing pellet at her brother's tiger, then leaps into the tiger cage where Batman is trapped and courageously distracts the snarling tiger with her cape long enough to enable Batman to ensnare it with his silken rope so that both of them can climb out of the cage to safety. "Great Scott!" exclaims Batman. "The ***Catwoman*** deliberately risked her own life to save me!"

For his part, the King of the Cats is remorseful that his criminal activities very nearly caused the death of his sister. "Selina, you saved my life!" exclaims the villain. "It's only fair that I give it to you to do with as you choose! If you want me to, I'll give myself up and take my medicine!"

It is only now that Batman and Robin learn that the King of the Cats is in reality Selina's brother; both are extremely surprised, and a little ashamed of themselves for having misjudged Selina's intentions (BM No. 69/3: "The King of the Cats!").

In January 1954 the editor of a Gotham City newspaper decides to run a series of feature articles describing Batman's greatest cases. The first article infuriates Selina Kyle with its descriptions of her previous defeats at the hands of Batman, and her anger and humiliation are only intensified when a group of small-time hoodlums enter her pet shop and begin to tease her about it. Batman arrives moments later and drives the hoodlums away, but he cannot eradicate the sting of the Gotham *Gazette* newspaper article.

"Did you come to gloat over your past victory over ***Catwoman?***" asks Selina accusingly.

"Selina," replies Batman, "I came to tell you I had nothing to do with that newspaper series! I'd never have permitted it, for I know you want to forget all about your ***Catwoman*** past!"

"Do I?" wonders Selina aloud. "I wonder! They say a leopard never changes its spots---and a leopard is a member of the cat family!"

"Don't talk like that!" replies Batman. "Unless you forget your former life as ***Catwoman,*** there's no future for you, ever!"

Batman leaves the pet shop, but he confides to Robin that he is worried. "She misses the old excitement, the daring that made her so dreaded in crime!" observes Batman grimly. "And I'm afraid this publicity may turn her back to her old life!"

"Indeed," observes the text, "the ex-**Catwoman's** long-smoldering emotions finally burst into fateful action!" For the first time in approximately two years, she dons her colorful Catwoman costume and gazes at herself in a full-length mirror. "No one laughed at me when I wore ***this!***" she muses aloud. "And I'll wear it again! I'll stun Gotham City with such cat-crimes that they'll never ridicule ***Catwoman*** again!"

Soon afterward, by silhouetting a cat against a powerful searchlight, the Catwoman projects an eerie cat-signal over Gotham City to announce her intention to return to crime.

"How could she do it?" murmurs a heartbroken Bruce Wayne. "I've done everything to keep her away from crime! Too late now---she's chosen her path, and we have to stop her at any cost!"

For her first crime, the Catwoman forces down a helicopter carrying a valuable shipment of iridium and then escapes with the loot before Batman and Robin can apprehend her. "Now," vows the Catwoman, after she has outfitted a new secret hideaway and constructed a new high-powered kitty car, "I'll make Gotham City dread the very name of ***cat. . . !***"

Meanwhile, at police headquarters, Police Commissioner Gordon consults with Batman about the Catwoman's return to crime. "***Batman,*** you seemed so interested in this girl, the way you tried to get her to go straight," remarks Gordon, "---perhaps you'd rather stay out of this ***Catwoman*** case?"

"No," replies Batman firmly, "I tried to help her, but she chose to return to crime! I must bring her to justice!"

Soon afterward, during a performance by lion-tamer Gus Vaney at the Gotham Garden Circus, the Catwoman and her cohorts place the entire audience in a "*cat*-aleptic" sleep by releasing a special gas into the air-conditioning system as part of a plot to loot the circus safe. Batman, who is on the scene and among those overcome by the gas, nevertheless manages to thwart the robbery by crawling to the open safe, slamming its door shut, and setting off a burglar alarm before lapsing into unconsciousness. The Catwoman's henchmen are about to murder the unconscious Batman when their leader intervenes. "No," she cries, "don't shoot! I couldn't bear to see him killed! I---mean, we'll take him along---as a hostage!"

Later, at the Catwoman's catacomb hideaway, Batman regains consciousness and asks the Catwoman why she allowed his life to be spared. "Only because you're a valuable hostage!" snaps the Catwoman.

Soon afterward, the Catwoman and her henchmen leave their hideaway and set out to steal the priceless collection of "cat's-eye jewels" that "millionaire collector" Horace Braham has taken aboard his yacht for safekeeping. Batman escapes from the catacomb and, with Robin, arrives at the yacht in time to thwart the robbery, but the Catwoman flees in a tiny catboat. Batman and Robin set out in hot pursuit, but all they ever find is the catboat wrecked on a marshy shore, and

The Catwoman in action, 1954 © NPP 1954

no trace whatsoever of the Catwoman (Det No. 203: "The Crimes of the Catwoman!").

In June 1954 the Catwoman returns to Gotham City, this time as the cunning mastermind behind an elaborate plot to smuggle "a fortune in diamonds" from Europe into the United States.

In her Selina Kyle identity, the Catwoman enters the local "Queen for a Day" beauty contest, sponsored by the W. Ross Cosmetic Company of Gotham City, and is selected as one of the four finalists. Officially, the Catwoman is still a fugitive from justice, but Batman observes that the Catwoman's fingerprints have never been recorded and that there is no actual documentary proof that Selina Kyle and the Catwoman are one and the same person.

After she has been chosen as a finalist, Selina intentionally places herself in a mysterious, trancelike coma with special gas designed to induce temporary sleeping sickness. When Selina is discovered in the strange coma, the officials of the cosmetic company – partly out of a desire for free publicity, and partly out of a desire to further the cause of science – place Selina on display in a glass display case so that she may be viewed by the medical profession as well as the public.

Soon afterward, however, Selina awakens and, after carefully using trick mirrors and 3-D motion-picture projectors to create the illusion that she is still inside the glass case, transforms herself into the Catwoman to carry out the next phase of her plan. As the Catwoman, she uses her special sleep gas to place all three of the other finalists into the same temporary coma from which she herself has just emerged, thus making it appear that all four of the finalists have fallen victim to the same mysterious malady.

Then, after transforming herself back into her Selina Kyle identity, she resumes her place inside the glass display case and, in full view of onlookers, pretends to awaken from her trance. Because all the other finalists are fast asleep, the judges of the beauty contest have no choice but to declare Selina the winner.

During the coronation ceremonies for Gotham City's new Queen for a Day, a messenger arrives with a bottle of special perfume for the new queen. Batman, his suspicions aroused, climbs onto the stage and, feigning clumsiness, knocks the perfume bottle to the floor, revealing to the astonished onlookers that it is filled not with perfume, but with a cache of valuable diamonds.

Batman explains that Selina had known beforehand that the winner of the Queen for a Day contest was to receive a special gift of French perfume, and she had arranged for "her agents in Europe" to substitute a flask containing the diamonds for the regular perfume flask being transported by the regular courier, knowing that the gift perfume for the contest would easily pass through customs without being carefully inspected. The elaborate sleeping-sickness ruse had merely been Selina's way of ensuring that she – and not one of the other finalists – would win the contest and therefore become eligible to receive the gift from France. On the basis of these revelations, Selina Kyle is promptly taken into custody by the Gotham City police (BM No. 84/2: "The Sleeping Beauties of Gotham City!").

The Catwoman makes a getaway, 1954 © NPP 1954

By September 1954 the Catwoman has somehow regained her freedom and returned to Gotham City, where, accompanied by a black panther and other wild cats that she has stolen from a local circus, she steals a shipment of diamonds that have just arrived by plane at the Gotham City airport and then makes good her escape aboard a special cat-shaped aircraft.

Batman and Robin pursue the Catwoman in the batplane, but she swoops down on them in her special aircraft, severely damaging the batplane's wings with her craft's "great retractable steel claws," and forces the Dynamic Duo to make an emergency landing on a lonely tropical island, where they are swiftly taken captive by John Jarrow, a ruthless criminal. Jarrow and his henchmen – who have apparently formed an uneasy alliance with the Catwoman – have been recutting stolen diamonds on the island and then selling them on the world market by claiming to have mined the diamonds themselves. Jarrow and his henchmen want to kill Batman and Robin, but the Catwoman forbids it. "I want the pleasure of hunting them down," she insists, "as they hunted me!" After she has confiscated their costumes and utility belts – leaving them attired only in their masks and primitive animal-skin clothing – the Catwoman sets Batman and Robin free in the jungle with a ten-minute head start, then sets out after them with her pet leopard, lion, and panther.

At one point, Batman and Robin attempt to elude the Catwoman by hiding in shallow water and breathing through some hollow reeds. After the Catwoman has passed them by, Robin observes, with obvious relief, that the Catwoman must not have discerned their hiding place. "Didn't she, ***Robin?***" replies Batman skeptically. "I wonder!"

A short while later, the Dynamic Duo come upon the Catwoman's lair in the ruins of an ancient temple and quickly make the Catwoman their prisoner. Jarrow, however, unleashes a huge gorilla against the trio, ruthlessly indifferent to the fact that the gorilla may also kill his ally, the Catwoman. Robin is stunned by the gorilla, but Batman manages to force it back into its cage, only to be taken prisoner by Jarrow once again.

After tying Batman with rope – but after returning his costume and allowing him to put on his UTILITY BELT, whose contents they say they have discarded – Jarrow and the Catwoman hurl Batman into a river flowing swiftly toward a waterfall. With the aid of a knife and a silken rope which he finds intact inside his utility belt, however, Batman succeeds in escaping from his bonds and in making his way to the riverbank, although, for a time, he continues to allow his enemies to think that he has perished.

"***Batman***... gone," thinks the Catwoman regretfully. "And I thought he'd save himself--he always has in the past...."

Moments later, however, Batman captures the Catwoman, binds her to a tree, and then, with Robin, apprehends John Jarrow and all his henchmen. When they return to the tree where Batman left the Catwoman, however, they find that their quarry has escaped, having successfully cut through her bonds with the aid of her pet leopard.

"Funny, that she accidentally left that knife-blade and silken cord in your utility belt," muses Robin aloud, "... or ***was*** it an accident? She's always been soft on you!"

"That was no accident, ***Robin,***" replies Batman. "Murder isn't in the ***Catwoman's*** heart. Sentiment is her weakness--and that's why we'll catch her the next time!" (Det No. 211: "The Jungle Cat-Queen!").

CAVALIER, THE. A gallant and courtly villain who speaks in flowery phrases and dresses in the colorful garb of a seventeenth-century musketeer. "Chivalry," explains the Cavalier in November 1943, "is my entire code of honor!" Indeed, on one occasion, he halts in his headlong rush toward the scene of his next crime long enough to help an elderly lady carry some heavy packages (Det No. 81: "The Cavalier of Crime!"). In everyday life, the Cavalier is secretly Mortimer Drake, "a playboy in Bruce Wayne's own social set" (BM No. 26/1, Dec/Jan '44–'45: "Twenty Ton Robbery!"), but BATMAN solves the mystery of the Cavalier's secret identity as early as July 1944 (Det No. 89: "Laboratory Loot!"). The texts alternatively refer to the Cavalier as the Romantic Rogue and the Swashbuckling Swordsman of Crime.

The Cavalier © NPP 1944

In the early stages of his career, the Cavalier steals only curios and pieces of bric-a-brac that are of little value to anyone but him. Detective Comics No. 89 describes him as "a crime collector" who is laboring to fill a private museum with interesting gadgets, trophies, and souvenirs (Jul '44: "Laboratory Loot!"). By December 1944–January 1945, however, he has graduated to the theft of more conventional valuables (BM No. 26/1: "Twenty Ton Robbery!").

The Cavalier's weaponry consists of the plume on his hat, which is actually a deadly steel-tipped dart; an "electrical sword" that emits barrages of electrical bolts (Det No. 81, Nov '43: "The Cavalier of Crime!"); a colorful kerchief attached to a heavy lead pellet; and debilitating "snuff" which he blows in his victims' faces

(BM No. 22/3, Apr/May '44: "The Cavalier Rides Again!").

In November 1943 the Cavalier sets in motion an elaborate scheme to gain possession of "a collection of sports miniatures" — a set of relatively valueless silver trophy cups owned by former baseball pitcher Berry Berrigan. The Cavalier and his henchmen have just opened the safe in Berrigan's sporting goods store when they are surprised by Batman and ROBIN. The henchmen are soon apprehended, but the Cavalier makes good his escape — albeit without the loot — by pinning Batman's cape to the wall with his plumed dart and riding to safety on a waiting motorcycle (Det No. 81: "The Cavalier of Crime!").

In April–May 1944 the Cavalier sets out to avenge his previous defeat at the hands of Batman by making Batman the laughingstock of GOTHAM CITY. ". . . I shall even the score!" vows the Cavalier. "I'll make him appear a veritable buffoon! I shall have my triumph!"

Not long afterward, the Cavalier lures Batman and Robin into an antique shop, traps Robin in a Murphy bed, and locks Batman in an old trunk. Soon afterward, however, Batman and Robin surprise the Cavalier and his henchmen in the act of stealing a relatively worthless curio, the model of a priceless diamond made by a stonecutter preparatory to cutting the actual stone. The henchmen are quickly taken into custody, but the Cavalier makes good his escape (BM No. 22/3: "The Cavalier Rides Again!").

In July 1944 the Cavalier attempts to steal another item for his private museum, the first working model of an old typewriter invented by Dr. Helmar Helstrom. At Helstrom's laboratory, the Cavalier is surprised by Batman and Robin, who are on the verge of taking him into custody when suddenly the laboratory is invaded by the Stinger Sloane gang, who have come there to steal a new invention created by Dr. Helstrom for the U.S. Government.

Batman, Robin, and the Cavalier abruptly break off their battle with each other and join forces to battle the intruders, but all three are soon taken captive. Batman and Robin ultimately turn the tables on the Sloane gang, but when they turn their attention back to the Cavalier, they find that he has already fled with Dr. Helstrom's early-model typewriter. Batman and Robin successfully lure the Cavalier back to the laboratory by having Dr. Helstrom announce that the typewriter stolen by the Cavalier was not really the first working model he sought, but only an early production model. Another battle at Dr. Helstrom's laboratory soon follows, during which Batman announces that he has deduced the Cavalier's real identity, but the villain nevertheless makes good his escape. In the hope that the Cavalier might stop at the home of his alter ego, Mortimer Drake, in order to salvage some belongings before fleeing the city, Batman and Robin race to the Drake home, but the Romantic Rogue is nowhere to be found (Det No. 89: "Laboratory Loot!").

In December 1944–January 1945 the Cavalier returns again, this time in quest of conventional wealth as opposed to the "miniature booty-trinkets and gadgets and odd bric-a-brac" that have occupied his attention in the past. After Batman and Robin have foiled an attempt by the Cavalier and his henchmen to rob the patrons attending a "socialite masquerade ball," the criminals invade the city's whaling museum and make off with a huge tank containing the museum's live whale with the intention of holding it for ransom. Ultimately, Batman and Robin apprehend the Cavalier and his henchmen and recover the stolen whale, and when finally Batman turns the Cavalier over to POLICE COMMISSIONER GORDON, it is with evident satisfaction: "The Cavalier, Commissioner," announces Batman, "--first time he was ever captured!" (BM No. 26/1: "Twenty Ton Robbery!").

CAVE, CARL C. The man who achieves infamy as NUMBERS (Det No. 146, Apr '49: "Three's a Crime!").

CHALMERS, DEUCE. A wily confidence man who impersonates BATMAN as part of an elaborate scheme to kidnap the six wealthiest and most influential men in America and hold them for $6,000,000 in ransom. Batman's efforts to thwart Chalmers's scheme are hampered by the fact that Bruce Wayne has been chosen to serve as mayor of GOTHAM CITY for an entire week, thus making it difficult for Wayne to appear as Batman in order to expose Chalmers as an imposter. Ultimately, however, Batman captures Chalmers and rescues his six wealthy captives (Det No. 179, Jan '52: "Mayor Bruce Wayne!").

CHECKMATE. A cunning criminal mastermind who is doomed to die from radioactive poisoning as the result of having unwittingly concealed himself inside "a lead-lined container for radioactive materials" while successfully attempting to evade capture by BATMAN and ROBIN. Checkmate concocts an elaborate scheme to wreak vengeance on the Dynamic Duo from beyond the grave by having his henchmen lure the famed lawmen into a huge GOTHAM CITY amphitheater filled with a series of diabolical deathtraps, any one of which could spell their doom and the last of which consists of a sealed room, filled with "deadly radioactive materials," which is designed to inflict upon Batman and Robin the same grisly death that Checkmate unwittingly inflicted upon himself. In December 1956, after their ruthless leader has died, Checkmate's henchmen lure Batman and Robin to the booby-trapped amphitheater and set in motion Checkmate's twisted scheme of vengeance, but Batman and Robin escape from each of the diabolical deathtraps and ultimately take Checkmate's entire gang into custody (Det No. 238: "The Doors That Hid Disaster!").

CHILL, EDDIE. The leader of the infamous Night Owl Gang, a gang of criminals who conceal their true identities with hoods resembling the heads of owls. In order to draw Chill out of hiding and accumulate the evidence necessary to apprehend him, BATMAN devises an elaborate ruse to lull the gang chief into a false sense of security by making him believe that Batman is dead. Then, with Chill's guard down, Batman impersonates Chill's trusted gangland lieutenant, Wedge Dixon, and tricks Chill into leading him to the gang's hoard of hidden loot, whereupon he and ROBIN swiftly apprehend the entire Night Owl Gang with the aid of a Batman robot (Det No. 281, Jul '60: "Batman, Robot!").

CHILL, JOE. The killer of Bruce Wayne's parents, and the man therefore directly responsible for the emergence of Bruce Wayne as BATMAN. Chill is shot to death by vengeful hoodlums in June–July 1948, approximately twenty-four years after the brutal act of murder which first launched Batman on his fabled crime-fighting career (BM No. 47/3: "The Origin of Batman!"). In Detective Comics No. 235, Joe Chill is referred to as Joey Chill (Sep '56: "The First Batman!").

Joe Chill, 1948 © NPP 1948

In the year 1924 – or, to quote the text precisely, "some fifteen years" prior to November 1939 – THOMAS WAYNE and his wife (*see* WAYNE, MARTHA) and their young son Bruce were on their way home from a movie when suddenly an unidentified gunman leaped from the shadows, announced a holdup, and reached out to grab the necklace around Martha Wayne's neck. When Thomas Wayne attempted to intervene, the gunman shot him dead with a single bullet, then murdered the shrieking Martha Wayne before fading away into the deepening twilight shadows (Det No. 33: "The Batman Wars Against the Dirigible of Doom"; *reprinted in* BM No. 1/1, Spr '40: "The Legend of the Batman – Who He Is and How He Came to Be!").

Later texts asserted that Thomas Wayne died of a bullet wound while Martha Wayne – whose "weak heart could not stand seeing her husband shot down" – died of a heart attack (Det No. 190, Dec '52: "How to Be the Batman!"; *see also* BM No. 47/3, Jun/Jul '48: "The Origin of Batman!"), but the texts are unanimous in their assertion that the dread event marked a crucial turning point in Bruce Wayne's life and fired him with the grim determination to eradicate evil that led to his emergence as Batman. (*See* BATMAN [section A, Origin].)

In June–July 1948 Batman and ROBIN learn that wanted criminals are being smuggled out of the state inside transport trucks owned and operated by the Land, Sea, Air Transport Company of GOTHAM CITY. When, at police headquarters, Batman is shown a photograph of the firm's owner, Joe Chill, he recognizes him instantly as the unidentified gunman who murdered his parents twenty-four years before. Having obtained POLICE COMMISSIONER GORDON's authorization to assume command of the crook-smuggling investigation, Batman informs Robin that he intends to handle this case alone. "I don't have to explain," he remarks grimly, "– you can understand why!"

Soon afterward, Batman dons a trucker's disguise in an attempt to obtain a job as one of Joe Chill's drivers, but the wily Chill will hire only truckers with whom he is personally acquainted. Thus thwarted, Batman devises another ploy: together with members of the Gotham City Police Department, he conducts a surprise raid on an underworld gambling ship and intentionally allows its proprietor to escape in the hope that he will flee to Chill's trucking firm to obtain safe passage out of the state. Chill, however, sees Batman trailing the gambler – a racketeer named Monty Julep – shoots Julep to prevent him from providing the authorities with information about his crook-smuggling operation, and then tells Batman that he was forced to shoot Julep in self-defense when Julep pulled a gun on him for refusing to smuggle him out of the state.

"There's only one way," muses Batman awhile later, as he grimly ponders his next move against the crafty Joe Chill. "It's a desperate move . . . but I **must** take it . . . even if it means **the end of Batman's career!**"

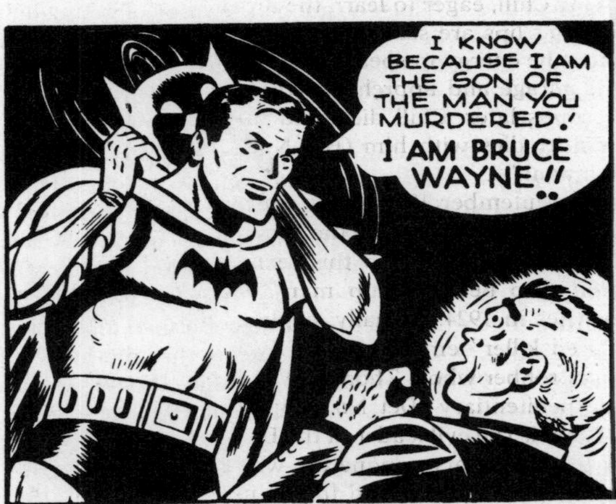

Batman and Joe Chill, 1948 © NPP 1948

And so, soon afterward, at the offices of the Land, Sea, Air Transport Company, a determined Batman confronts the killer of Bruce Wayne's parents, narrates the story of their murder, and coldly assures the frightened Chill that the passing years have not lessened Bruce Wayne's ability to identify his parents' killer. "I became **Batman** because of what you did," cries Batman, yanking off his batlike cowl to reveal the angular features of Bruce Wayne, "and I swore I'd arrest you for it some day! I can't prove your guilt, but I'll never stop hounding you until I do . . . whatever you do, I'll be watching . . . wherever you go, I'll be watching . . . I'll **always** be watching . . . and someday you'll make a mistake . . . and I'll be there . . . waiting! Remember that," he concludes menacingly, snapping a vicious punch off Joe Chill's jaw, "— and this!"

Then Batman stalks off, leaving behind him a shaken and terrified Chill. "What'll I do?" cries Chill. "**Batman** means everything he said! He proved it by revealing his identity! He'll get me . . . unless I kill him first!"

Panic-stricken, Chill races into his transport company's repair garage and begs his gangland cronies to help him. "Listen boys . . . I need help bad!" cries Chill. "Years ago, I knocked off a guy . . . an' now his son is after me! That guy's son is the **Batman!** He just told me! . . . **Batman** just told me who he is! He became **Batman** because I killed his father!"

"You mean," exclaims one of the hoodlums incredulously, ". . . **you're** the reason for **Batman. . . .**"

An electric tension fills the air as the hoodlums realize that the man in their midst is almost singlehandedly responsible for the creation of the Batman legend. "Almost as one man," notes the narrative text, "the hate-crazed thugs [draw their pistols and] mete vengeance to the criminal responsible for their dreaded nemesis!"

Only after Chill has been gunned mercilessly to the floor do his executioners realize that they have slain the only man who might have told them the secret of Batman's dual identity. Hastily they bend over the dying Chill, eager to learn the dread secret before their victim's lips are sealed forever. Before Chill can summon the energy to speak, however, Batman bursts into the garage and apprehends the assembled hoodlums. Seconds later, Chill dies, and the secret of Batman's identity dies with him (BM No. 47/3: "The Origin of Batman!").

In September 1956 a text appears which sheds new light on the murder of the Waynes and the origin of Batman. According to this text, Joe Chill "only ***pretended*** to be a holdup man" when he waylaid the Waynes in 1924. Actually, explains the text, he was a "hired killer" employed by LEW MOXON, a convicted bank robber whom Thomas Wayne had helped send to the penitentiary (Det No. 235: "The First Batman!").

CHORN. The evil leader of the Baxians, a ruthless band of interplanetary conquerors who have seized control of the planet Zoron and forced its peace-loving populace into grueling slave labor. On Zoron, a planet whose alien environment endows BATMAN and ROBIN with super-powers identical to SUPERMAN's while it renders Superman as powerless as an ordinary mortal, the three heroes combine their talents to defeat Chorn and his cohorts and deliver the Zorians from the yoke of Baxian oppression (WF No. 114, Dec '60: "Captives of the Space Globes!").

CHUBB (Doctor). An underworld physician and plastic surgeon who, having secretly taken pre- and post-operative photographs of all the underworld figures on whom he has performed face-altering plastic surgery, is now blackmailing his former patients by threatening to reveal their new facial descriptions to the police. Called upon to treat an injury to BATMAN's legs in October–November 1950, Dr. Chubb tricks the famed crime-fighter into believing that both his legs have been broken so that he can encase them in plaster casts and hide the tiny film canister containing the incriminating before-and-after photographs inside one of them to ensure that they will not be recovered and destroyed by one of his erstwhile gangland clients. Batman's crime-fighting efforts are therefore severely hampered in the ensuing period by the fact that he must battle gangsters from a motorized wheelchair and by the need to conceal the casts on BRUCE WAYNE's legs for fear of betraying the secret of his dual identity, but ultimately, with ROBIN's help, he discovers that his legs are not broken, finds the tiny film canister encased in his cast, and apprehends the wily Dr. Chubb along with a gang of vengeful hoodlums who have invaded the doctor's home in search of the incriminating film (BM No. 61/3: "The Wheelchair Crimefighter!").

CHUBB, T. WORTHINGTON. A GOTHAM CITY "crime-czar" who correctly deduces that BRUCE WAYNE and DICK GRAYSON are secretly BATMAN and ROBIN and then threatens to expose them if they attempt to interfere with his gang's activities. By means of a series of elaborate ruses, however, Batman succeeds in persuading Chubb that he has made a mistake, and Chubb and his gang are ultimately apprehended by Batman, Robin, and members of the Gotham City Police Department (Det No. 159, May '50: "Bruce Wayne — You Are Batman!").

CLATE, "CRAFTY" CAL. The leader of a gang of criminals who successfully lured policemen away from the scenes of their intended crimes by sending out false police calls on a transmitter hidden inside a laundry truck, until they were finally apprehended by BATMAN and ROBIN sometime prior to March 1942 (Det No. 61: "The Three Racketeers!").

CLAYBER. A partner in the Gotham Gem Company — a GOTHAM CITY jewelry concern which is secretly a front for a lucrative gem-smuggling operation — who is murdered by his fellow partners, John Wilcox, Henry Stubbs, and Ed Carder, in April 1960. For a while, the three killers succeed in focusing suspicion for the slaying on Ted Greaves, an ex-convict once convicted of a holdup at the gem company who vowed revenge against the firm's partners at his trial, but BATMAN and ROBIN ultimately uncover the truth — that Clayber, the last of the four partners to join the firm, had originally blackmailed his three colleagues into accepting him as their fourth partner by threatening to expose their smuggling racket, and that the three partners had murdered Clayber when he demanded too large a share of their illicit profits — and apprehend the three guilty partners (BM No. 131/2: "The Case of the Deadly Gems").

CLAYFACE (Matt Hagen). A diabolical villain who possesses the incredible power to transform his body into any form he chooses, merely by issuing a silent, mental command: ". . . all I need do is concentrate," muses Clayface to himself in June 1962, "--and my mental command can mold my body like pliable clay . . . and turn it into any shape and color I wish!" (Det No. 304: "The Return of Clay-Face!"). In the moments between transformations, after Clayface has abandoned one bodily form but not yet assumed another, his body is a brown, earthy color and "his 'flesh' [is]--soft and malleable . . . just like clay!" (Det No. 298, Dec '61: "The Challenge of Clay-Face"). In reality, Clayface is Matt Hagen, an unscrupulous skin diver whose amazing powers are the result of his inadvertent discovery of a secret pool that "shimmers like a trapped rainbow" and is filled with "a strange liquid protoplasm" whose "freakish properties defy analysis" (Det No. 304, Jun '62: "The Return of Clay-Face!"). It is only after Hagen has committed his first spectacular robbery — and engineered an astounding getaway by assuming, in rapid succession, the forms of a giant python, a buzz-saw, and a huge eagle — that an amazed newspaper editor in the city room of the Gotham *Gazette* bestows on him the name Clayface (Det No. 298, Dec '61: "The Challenge of Clay-Face").

Matt Hagen, 1961 © NPP 1961

In December 1961, while skin diving for sunken treasure in hopes of sparing himself the odious necessity of working for a living, Matt Hagen surfaced for a brief rest, only to find himself "in an undiscovered grotto," standing before "a natural pool" that seemed "to bubble up colors of every shade!" Determined to have a closer look at the strange pool, Hagen stepped to the edge, but a wet stone slid beneath his weight and sent him plunging into the depths of the strange rainbow-colored liquid.

"This isn't water!" thought Hagen, his mind racing wildly as he thrashed about beneath the surface of the pool. "It's a kind of protoplasm--clinging to me . . . sending some strange energy through my body!"

Finally Hagen emerged from the pool and stood once again in the grotto, only to reel with "shock and terror" as he realized that his body had somehow become transformed into a lumpy mound of brown, earthy clay. "If only I could be as I used to be," sobbed the anguished Hagen, "--if only I could look as I did before. . . ."

Then suddenly, as if in response to Hagen's ardent wish, a strange change began to take place in Hagen's brown claylike body: "Strange," thought Hagen, "--I felt as if my brain were sending energy through my body--commanding my body . . . making it change!"

"It **is** changing!" realized Hagen with a start. "My body's soft and pliable now! It's as if my mind is molding my body like soft clay. . . ."

And finally, after anxious moments, Hagen found himself transformed back into his human self again. "I'm myself again!" he thought gratefully. "My body is hard again--because the change is now complete!"

In the moments that followed, Hagen experimented with his new powers, transforming himself, by mental commands, into a mythological centaur and other forms as well. ". . . I can change to ***anything,***" thought Hagen exultantly, "--just by ***concentrating!*** I can even duplicate ***colors!*** With this power, I can ***do*** anything I want--***take*** anything I want . . . ***ha, ha, ha.***"

With the aid of his newly acquired powers, Hagen — who soon becomes known as Clayface — commits a series of spectacular crimes in GOTHAM CITY. After awhile, however, Clayface's chameleonlike powers fade, then disappear entirely, and Hagen is forced to return to the hidden grotto to renew his powers in the secret pool. At the grotto, Hagen vows to keep a close "time-check" on his powers so that he can learn exactly how long his powers will remain potent between renewals. In this way, reasons Hagen, he will be able to renew his powers at the pool in enough time to avoid being apprehended away from the pool after his powers have left him.

Unfortunately for Hagen, however, his powers fade and vanish exactly forty-eight hours later, while he is

Clayface, 1962 © NPP 1962

embroiled in a deadly battle with BATMAN and ROBIN. In a desperate effort to defeat the Dynamic Duo, Clayface has transformed himself into a horrible monster – "part lion--part dinosaur--part unicorn" – but as his powers begin to fade, the monster becomes slowly, irrevocably transformed into the relatively helpless form of Matt Hagen, and Batman and Robin easily take him into custody. Hagen is sent to prison for his crimes, but he retains his knowledge of the secret pool, and he knows now that its powers retain their potency for exactly forty-eight hours. "One day," vows Hagen, standing alone in his cell, "I'll escape, return to the secret pool--and renew my power! One day--***Clay-Face will return!***" (Det No. 298: "The Challenge of Clay-Face").

By June 1962 Matt Hagen has escaped from prison, and he loses no time in renewing his Clayface powers in the special protoplasm of the secret pool. "The pool has done it again," thinks Clayface, "--changed my body to a hard, claylike consistency for 48 hours. . . !"

By posing as a member of Gotham City's exclusive Pharaoh Club, Clayface obtains permission for a "friend" of his to use the club's facilities. Then, under the alias John Royce, Clayface pretends to be the friend of the member he had recently impersonated and mingles with the club's wealthy members, greedily accumulating the kind of private information and careless gossip that will enable him to rob them of their valuables. At one point, he steals a priceless Rembrandt painting owned by a club member named Phipps and escapes with it by transforming himself into a giant locust despite Batman's desperate efforts to apprehend him.

Ultimately, however, Batman becomes suspicious of John Royce, tricks Royce into transforming himself into a giant bat, thereby betraying his Clayface identity, and then freezes the villain into a state of temporary suspended animation with the aid of a special "freeze gun" that he has invented for the purpose (Det No. 304: "The Return of Clay-Face!").

Clayface as a winged horse, and Batman, 1962 © NPP 1962

In February 1963 Matt Hagen escapes from Gotham Prison, renews his special powers at the hidden pool, and returns to Gotham City as Clayface. This time he poses as Batman in order to rob a local bank and then poses as a valuable statue in order to gain entrance to a room of priceless art treasures in the home of the wealthy Mrs. Vanderhoeft. Ultimately, Batman trails Clayface to his hidden grotto where, during a furious battle, both men fall into the rainbow-hued pool and emerge with Clayface powers. After a great battle, in which both Batman and Clayface assume numerous forms and attributes in an effort to defeat one another, Batman emerges victorious and promptly places Clayface under heavy sedation until forty-eight hours have elapsed and his powers have vanished. Batman informs Hagen that he has set off an explosion designed to bury his hidden pool under tons of rock so that he will never again be able to assume the awesome powers of Clayface, but Hagen knows that he has hidden a supply of the special liquid protoplasm in another section of the grotto and that he has only to escape from prison once again in order to resume his career as Clayface (Det No. 312: "The Secret of Clayface's Power!").

By November 1963 Matt Hagen has escaped from prison, and although Batman has destroyed his secret pool, he has not uncovered the bottle of the liquid that Hagen had managed to conceal in a hidden corner of the grotto. By analyzing it, Hagen is able to produce a synthetic protoplasm capable of endowing him with Clayface powers for a period of five hours.

During this period, the JOKER becomes enraged at a fellow criminal's assertion that "**Clayface** is the top criminal in the country," and he and Clayface become embroiled in a violent feud over which of them is the most spectacular criminal. "My **cunning** has made me **Batman's** greatest foe!" insists the Joker. "Without his freak powers, **Clayface** is a blundering third-rater--incapable of matching crimes of my calibre!"

Aided by Batman and Robin, BATWOMAN and Bat-Girl (*see* BAT-GIRL [BETTY KANE]) ultimately apprehend the Joker as he attempts to flee the scene of a daring robbery at the Gotham Museum, and Batman apprehends Clayface soon afterward by posing as the Joker, suggesting that he and Clayface end their feud and join forces, and then knocking Clayface unconscious while his attention is momentarily diverted. Matt Hagen is returned to prison, but he has hidden away a cache of his synthetic protoplasm and he is confident that Clayface will once again return (BM No. 159/1: "The Great Clayface-Joker Feud!").

Anticipating the possibility of capture during his previous encounter with Batman and Robin (above), Matt Hagen had buried a vial of his synthetic protoplasm in the yard of Green Walls, a maximum security prison. By March 1964 Hagen has managed to have himself transferred to Green Walls as punishment for his "obstinate behavior" in the city prison, and now he digs up his vial of synthetic protoplasm, transforms himself into a vulture, and soars over the prison walls to freedom.

Soon afterward, Clayface embarks on a series of spectacular crimes, occasionally transforming himself into the invulnerable image of SUPERMAN in order to render himself virtually undefeatable. Ultimately, however, Batman, Robin, and the real Superman defeat the Clayface Superman by exposing him to the rays of red KRYPTONITE, thus causing the villain to behave erratically long enough for his Clayface powers to fade and vanish before he has had the opportunity to return to his hideout for another dose of his synthetic protoplasm (WF No. 140: "The Clayface Superman!").

In September 1964 Matt Hagen escapes from prison when a barrage of destructive rays unleashed over Gotham City by BRAINIAC inadvertently smashes apart the walls of the Gotham City prison where Hagen is incarcerated. Not long afterward, after Hagen has renewed his Clayface powers with a dose of his synthetic protoplasm, Clayface joins forces with Brainiac in an effort to annihilate Superman, Batman, and Robin. Both villains, however, are ultimately defeated through the heroic efforts of Superman, Batman, Robin, and JIMMY OLSEN (WF No. 144: "The 1,001 Tricks of Clayface and Brainiac!" pts. 1–2 – no title; "The Helpless Partners!").

CLAYFACE (Basil Karlo). A maniacally cunning murderer who matches wits with BATMAN and ROBIN in June 1940 (Det No. 40) and again in March 1941 (Det No. 49: "Clayface Walks Again!"). Clayface is in reality Basil Karlo, a renowned character actor and makeup artist who turns to murder as a demented means of attaining his former stardom. As Clayface, Karlo wears a purple cloak and a matching wide-brimmed hat. A special wax makeup, splotched with pieces of either brown (Det No. 40, Jun '40) or green (Det No. 49, Mar '41: "Clayface Walks Again!") clay, gives his face a hideous claylike appearance. The idea for the grotesque appearance and personality of Clayface came easily to Karlo, for Karlo once played a maniac named Clayface in an old horror movie (Det No. 40, Jun '40).

Clayface © NPP 1940

In June 1940 the Argus Motion Picture Company prepares to begin the filming of *Dread Castle,* a remake of an old horror film that originally starred Basil Karlo as a maniacal murderer known as the Terror. Enraged because another actor, Kenneth Todd, has been chosen to play the role of the Terror in his stead, Karlo stalks the set of *Dread Castle* in the guise of the horror-movie maniac Clayface and attempts to annihilate each actor at the precise point in the filming when the script calls for that actor to be "murdered" by the Terror. In this way, Karlo transforms the filming of *Dread Castle* from a cinematic exercise into a real-life horror story, with Karlo himself in the murderer's starring role.

As Clayface, Karlo murders movie star Lorna Dane on the set of *Dread Castle,* then murders Lorna's former sweetheart, Fred Walker, at his home after Walker has discovered the identity of Lorna's murderer and demanded money from Karlo in return for keeping his knowledge secret. Back on the set, Clayface attempts to murder actress JULIE MADISON, but Batman thwarts the attempt and, with Robin, captures Clayface and unmasks him as Basil Karlo.

"He had played so many **horror roles** in pictures," explains Batman, "that they had **taken possession** of his **mind** and **soul!** He made up as Clayface, one of his old roles, and then **followed** the **plot** of *Dread Castle* and killed off each one [of the actors] as they 'died' in the **picture!**

"In the last reel," continues Batman, "[Kenneth] Todd, as the Terror, was supposed to 'die' . . . **that's** when [Karlo] intended to kill **him!!** In this way Basil Karlo would again be the real Terror! Once more **he** would **star!**" (Det No. 40).

In March 1941 the prison ambulance transferring Basil Karlo to the state asylum for the criminally insane crashes on the road during a violent thunderstorm, and Karlo succeeds in making good his escape. After viciously attacking the owner of a makeup store, Karlo steals some makeup and transforms himself into his hideous Clayface identity before setting out to wreak vengeance on Batman, Robin, and actress Julie Madison, who, under her new stage name Portia Storme, is already engaged in the shooting of another film.

At one point, Clayface attempts to crush Batman under the wheels of a heavy truck, and at another he attempts to murder an unconscious Robin by dropping him in the midst of a wooden movie set and then setting it afire. **"Ha ha – burn!"** cackles Clayface manially." – Like the hate in my heart! Burn! Ha ha ha!"

Miraculously, however, the Dynamic Duo manage to survive, and ultimately they apprehend Clayface by having Robin change costumes with Julie Madison and then waiting for Clayface to make an attempt on Julie's life. As Batman's final fistfight with Clayface moves toward its climax, Batman's "right fist whistles through the air, there is a sharp crack like that of a rifle shot" as Batman's fist smashes into the villain's jaw, "and Clayface drops like a felled steer!" (Det No. 49: "Clayface Walks Again!").

CLEOPATRA. The name of several queens and princesses of the Ptolemaic dynasty in Egypt, the most notable of these being Cleopatra VII (69–30 B.C.), the queen of Egypt from 51 B.C. until her death by suicide twenty-one years later, who, largely through her personal involvement with Julius Caesar and Mark Antony, two of the chief Roman statesmen of her time, exerted a powerful influence in the ancient world. BATMAN and ROBIN meet Cleopatra, serve as her personal bodyguards, and apprehend a would-be assassin in her entourage (see KA-RA) during a time-journey to ancient Egypt in the first century B.C. (Det No. 167, Jan '51: "Bodyguards to Cleopatra!").

CLOCK, THE. A cunning criminal – clad in a hooded yellow costume with a white clock emblazoned on his chest, complemented by black trunks and purple gloves, belt, cape, and boots – whose crimes revolve around clocks and watches, or around the more general theme of time. The Clock is in reality Kyle, an ex-convict who claims – although the validity of the claim must be regarded as extremely doubtful – to have been the first criminal ever sent to prison by BATMAN.

In prison, Kyle's fellow convicts had all studied trades in preparation for the time when they would become free men, but Kyle had spent all his time learning about clocks, because, in his words, "***Batman*** made me do ***time*** in prison!"

"Other cons used to kid me because I was the ***first*** criminal ***Batman*** arrested!" recalls Kyle bitterly. "I'll show them! I was ***Batman's first case***--and ***I'll be his last, too!***"

In March 1959 the Clock brazenly announces his intention to commit a series of spectacular clock crimes, to be climaxed by the killing of Batman at precisely 3:00 P.M., the time when, long ago, Kyle was brought to prison after having been apprehended by Batman. For a time, the clock crimes continue unabated, but the Clock is ultimately apprehended by Batman and ROBIN (Det No. 265: "Batman's First Case!").

CLOCKMASTER, THE. A cunning criminal who hopes to steal the "fortune in gems" on display at the Gems in the News exhibit with the aid of a bogus gem which he has planted among the real gems and which is designed to emit clouds of sleeping gas at a prearranged time so that he and his henchmen can make off with the jewels. In order to ensure that BATMAN and ROBIN will be preoccupied elsewhere at the time and thus unable to interfere with the theft, the Clockmaster begins providing them with a series of elaborate clues, each leading them to a real crime being committed by other criminals, so that Batman and Robin will be busy foiling a decoy crime while the Clockmaster and his henchman rob the gem exhibit. The Clockmaster's scheme is thwarted, however, and he and his henchman are apprehended, when Batman arrives at the scene of the gem heist at the same time that Robin is busy foiling the decoy crime at a local bakery (BM No. 141/1, Aug '61: "The Crimes of the Clockmaster").

COBB, PHIL. The "small-time crook with big ideas" who achieves infamy as SIGNALMAN (BM No. 112/1, Dec '57: "The Signalman of Crime").

COE, JEREMY. An American colonist of the seventeenth century who, operating from a secret headquarters in the gigantic subterranean cavern now known as the BATCAVE, struggled courageously to safeguard his fellow colonists against surprise Indian attacks by disguising himself as an Indian and infiltrating their war councils to learn their plans. Dispatched through the time barrier by PROFESSOR CARTER NICHOLS to what is now GOTHAM CITY in the middle years of the seventeenth century, BATMAN and ROBIN rescue Jeremy Coe from pursuing Indians, tour the underground headquarters which even Coe has dubbed the batcave because of its plethora of bats, and ultimately accumulate intelligence which enables them to warn a nearby colonial fort of an impending massive Indian attack (Det No. 205, Mar '54: "The Origin of the Bat-Cave!").

COLBY, ART. The owner of the Green Anchor Nightclub in the United States town of Midville and the leader of a gang of jewel thieves who rob a Midville jewelry store in February 1960 and hide the loot in the tent of Sando, a circus strongman. When one of the stolen jewels is discovered in Sando's tent, Sando is placed under arrest, charged with the crime, and then released on bail pending his trial on a charge of jewel theft. With Sando's help, however, BATMAN and ROBIN apprehend Colby and his henchmen, recover the missing portion of the stolen loot, and exonerate Sando, an old friend of DICK GRAYSON since Grayson's early days with the FLYING GRAYSONS (BM No. 129/2: "The Man from Robin's Past").

COLLECTOR, THE. A masked bandit who specializes in the theft of priceless art treasures for his own private collection. The Collector and his henchmen are apprehended by ROBIN and BATWOMAN in November 1957 (Det No. 249: "The Crime of Bruce Wayne!"). (*See* BATWOMAN, THE.)

COLLINS, LEE. The Australian circus performer and boomerang expert who, according to Detective Comics No. 244, taught BATMAN to use the boomerang and created the world's first bat-shaped boomerang, i.e., the first batarang, which he presented to Batman as a personal gift.

Batman first became aware of the boomerang's potential as a crime-fighting weapon when, on the grounds of a traveling circus, Collins used a skillful boomerang throw to help him apprehend a wanted criminal. "Your boomerangs interest me, Collins," exclaimed Batman, ". . . I'll bet I could put them to good use!"

"Why, I'd be happy to show you all I know about boomerangs, ***Batman!***" replied Collins. "I know the great work you do as a lawman!"

In the days that followed, Collins taught Batman "every detail of the device" and patiently helped him master its use. "I want to have absolute control," insisted Batman, "--since I'm going to use this not as a weapon, but as a sort of extension-**arm!**"

When Batman's instruction was finally completed, Collins presented him with a specially made boomerang with scalloped edges, like the wings of a bat. "Now that you're as skillful as I am, ***Batman,***" said Collins, "I've made this special boomerang for you! It's a sort of

bat-arang, with bat-like wings!" (Jun '57: "The 100 Batarangs of Batman!").

From that day forward, the batarang has been an indispensable feature of Batman's crime-fighting arsenal. (*See* BATMAN [section E 2 d ii, the batarang].)

COLLINS, VANCE. A reformed ex-convict, once sent to prison by BATMAN and ROBIN but now working honestly as an employee at a hot-dog stand, who is accidentally struck by a bizarre purple ray from outer space as it bounces off a billboard advertising a horror movie, and who, as a result, from that time onward, becomes periodically transformed into a living version of the horrifying creature depicted vividly on the billboard. "That weird ray must have hit Vance after it burnt the creature's picture from the billboard!" explains SUPERMAN. "A freak reaction caused him to **become** the creature! He's like a Jekyll and Hyde character now!"

In his monster form, Collins leads a gang of criminals known as the Jackson Mob on a series of spectacular robberies, only to lose all recollection of his monstrous metamorphosis once the effects of the purple ray have temporarily exhausted themselves and Collins has temporarily reverted to his human form. Eventually, however, the effects of the purple ray wear off completely, and a horrified and guilt-ridden Collins readily joins forces with Batman, Robin, and Superman to apprehend his former underworld allies (WF No. 116, Mar '61: "The Creature from Beyond!").

COMPOSITE SUPERMAN, THE. A ruthless, power-hungry villain – endowed with all the super-powers of SUPERMAN as well as with all the extraordinary powers possessed by the various members of the Legion of Super-Heroes – who sets out, in June 1964, to "use [his] unmatchable powers to humiliate Superman and Batman before the world, and end their careers forever," as the first phase of his plan to conquer Earth and other worlds as well. The Composite Superman is in reality Joe Meach, the curator of the Superman Museum in METROPOLIS, a onetime high-diver, embittered by his failure to achieve fame and fortune, who received his museum job from Superman after the Man of Steel had rescued him from a dive off a tall building into an inch-deep pool of water that would certainly have caused his death, but who nevertheless feels that "Superman humiliated me, by making me a lowly sweeper!"

As the Composite Superman, Meach – who acquires his unbelievable multiplicity of powers when a fateful bolt of lightning strikes a metal table in the museum containing lifelike statuettes of the Legion of Super-Heroes – has green skin, but otherwise resembles a weird composite of Superman and BATMAN, as though one half of his body were Superman's and the other half Batman's, divided vertically down the middle. By employing his seemingly endless arsenal of super-powers, the Composite Superman is able to humiliate Batman, ROBIN, and Superman, and even to defeat them. Ultimately, however, Meach's powers fade and vanish, leaving him with no recollection whatever of his short-lived career as a super-villain (WF No. 142: "The Origin of the Composite Superman!" pts. I–II – "The Composite Superman!"; "The Battle Between Titans!").

The Legion of Super-Heroes is an organization of teen-aged crime-fighters and adventurers – representing Earth and more than a score of far-flung planets and consisting, all in all, of several dozen active members, honorary members, and reservists – each of whom possesses some unique super-power distinct from those possessed by every other member of the group. The Legion makes its headquarters in the city of Metropolis in the thirtieth century A.D., where it is primarily active.

CONDOR GANG, THE (1958). A gang of criminals led by a dark-robed villain known only as the Condor, who is in reality John Titus, a respected GOTHAM CITY millionaire. In October 1958 BATMAN, ROBIN, and SUPERMAN join forces in an intricately convoluted scheme to apprehend the Condor and his henchmen by having Superman assume the wholly fictitious identity of Professor Milo, self-proclaimed inventor of "a mechanical brain that can predict the future," and then carefully building up a reputation for the machine's accuracy by contriving to make a series of its improbable "predictions" come true. Ultimately, "Professor Milo" and his so-called "predictor" are ushered into the presence of the Condor himself, whereupon Superman, Batman, and Robin join forces to apprehend the Condor Gang and unmask the Condor as millionaire Titus (WF No. 97: "The Day Superman Betrayed Batman!").

CONDOR GANG, THE (1963). A gang of ruthless criminals, headquartered in Center City and distinguished by the colorful condor headgear worn by its members, who have been absorbing other underworld organizations at a ferocious pace and forging them into a nationwide crime syndicate with branches in cities throughout the United States. In July 1963, with BATMAN and ROBIN in Center City as honored guests at a police convention there, the Condor Gang concocts an elaborate scheme to humiliate Batman and enhance its own prestige among the nation's underworld by blowing up the Dynamic Duo's flying batcave (*see* BATMAN [section E 2 b ii, the other aircraft]) at the site of the police convention and making off with the proceeds of the policemen's fund. The entire Condor Gang is ultimately apprehended, however, through the heroic efforts of Batman, Robin, and a resourceful rookie policeman named Joseph Arno (Det No. 317: "The Secrets of the Flying Bat-Cave!").

CONGER, "KNUCKLES." "The slickest criminal in town," a gifted boxer, track athlete, and acrobat who attempts to emulate the techniques of BATMAN and ROBIN, in reverse, by training a boy companion to help him commit spectacular crimes. Under the pretense of wanting to launch a new crime-fighting team modeled after the Dynamic Duo, Conger tricks a homeless shoeshine boy named Bobby Deen into becoming his companion. For a time, Conger succeeds in duping Deen into believing that the two of them are fighting crimes rather than committing them, but Deen ultimately realizes that he has been deceived and helps Batman apprehend his underworld mentor (BM No. 15/2, Feb/Mar '43: "The Boy Who Wanted to Be Robin!").

CONJURER, THE. A "self-styled worker of miracles of crime," so named because he uses the time-tested devices of the skilled magician – deception and misdirection – to aid him in his crimes. The Conjurer and his henchmen are apprehended by BATMAN and ROBIN in June–July 1943 with the aid of B. BOSWELL BROWNE, Batman's biographer (BM No. 17/1: "The Batman's Biographer!").

CONKLIN, BUGS. A ruthless "underworld kingpin," shot and wounded during a gun battle with police, whose henchmen force Dr. R. Davenport to treat their leader and then kidnap Davenport's daughter Marjory (*see* DAVENPORT, MARJORY) in order to prevent the physician from reporting the gunshot wound to the police. BATMAN and ROBIN apprehend the Conklin gang and rescue young Marjory from their clutches. Bugs Conklin's bullet wound, however, has become badly infected despite Dr. Davenport's best efforts, and the gang leader will probably die within a few days (BM No. 23/2, Jun/Jul '44: "Damsel in Distress!").

CONROY, BIG ED. A former convict, recently released from prison and anxious to go straight, who establishes a payroll messenger service so that he can earn a living himself as well as provide gainful employment for other honest ex-convicts. Crime czar Duke Ryall, furious that his own henchmen have been deserting his gang to join Conroy's company, attempts to put Conroy out of business by stealing his payroll shipments and pinning the blame for the thefts on Conroy's own messengers, but BATMAN and ROBIN apprehend Ryall and his henchmen and exonerate Conroy and his messengers of any wrongdoing (BM No. 35/3, Jun/Jul '46: "Dick Grayson, Author!").

COOK, JOHN. The vice-chairman of the Namesake Club, a club for people whose surnames are the same as those of famous historical personages. In May 1952 Cook murders two club members and attempts to kill several others as part of a scheme to seize control of the large bequests which some of the members have made to the club, but BATMAN and ROBIN apprehend Cook and expose him as the murderer (Det No. 183: "Famous Names Crimes!").

COUNT, THE. A cunning criminal who, having organized all of GOTHAM CITY's bunco rackets into one vast underworld organization, is now responsible for the "regular epidemic of ['short-confidence'] rackets" sweeping the city. The Count's real name is Michael Strait. BATMAN and ROBIN apprehend the Count and his cohorts in April–May 1945, aided by ALFRED and the undercover detective work of policewoman SGT. SHIRLEY HOLMES (BM No. 28/2: "Shirley Holmes, Policewoman!").

COURTLY, CHARLES. An alias employed by "international thief" MICHAEL BAFFLE when he obtains a job as a newspaper society reporter in order to help him gain access to the homes of the wealthy (Det No. 63, May '42: "A Gentleman in Gotham").

COYNE, JOE. A ruthless criminal, known also as "the penny plunderer" because of his obsession with pennies, who vows a bizarre form of vengeance against both pennies and policemen after a policeman arrests him for attempting to rob a cash register that turns out to have contained only pennies: "Pennies . . . and coppers!" muses Coyne bitterly as he sits alone in his prison cell. "They did this to me! **Pennies . . . coppers . . . copper pennies!** I hate them all! When I get out, I'll get back at coppers and pennies! I'll fight coppers – with pennies! Every job I pull will involve pennies! **My crime symbol will be pennies!**" Upon his release, Coyne forms a company dealing in penny slot-machines as a front for his criminal activities and then embarks on a series of crimes reflecting his obsession with pennies, as when he attempts to steal a priceless British stamp known as the "one-penny black." Coyne is apprehended by BATMAN and ROBIN in September–October 1947 (WF No. 30: "The Penny Plunderers!").

CRAIG, AL. The proprietor of a gymnasium in GOTHAM CITY and the organizer of a gang of juvenile delinquents, all dressed in ROBIN costumes, who stage a serious of simultaneous crimes during a night in August 1965, only to be apprehended soon afterward by BATMAN and Robin (Det No. 342: "The Midnight Raid of the Robin Gang!").

CRAIG, ARCHIE. An alias employed by BATMAN in November 1963 when he poses as an escaped convict as part of his plan to apprehend the TERRIBLE TRIO (Det No. 321: "The Terrible Trio!").

CRAIG, ELTON. A ruthless criminal whose various encounters with BATMAN, ROBIN, SUPERMAN, and BATWOMAN are described in World's Finest Comics No. 87 (Mar/Apr '57: "The Reversed Heroes!") and in World's Finest Comics No. 90 (Sep/Oct '57: "The Super-Batwoman!").

In March–April 1957 Superman narrates the story of his first encounter with the villainous Craig, which evidently took place sometime in the past. Superman recalls that, years ago, his father Jor-El had foreseen the imminent destruction of the planet KRYPTON and had made arrangements to transport himself and his family to Earth to begin a new life. Jor-El had also created some special "radioactive capsules" which he hoped to bring to Earth with him. "Krypton is doomed," Jor-El had announced grimly, "--but when we migrate to Earth, we'll have super-powers there, because of the lesser gravity, and should anything on Earth make our powers fade away, these capsules will ***renew*** our super-powers temporarily!"

Even at that moment, however, the death of Krypton was at hand, and Jor-El barely had time to launch the infant Superman toward Earth in a tiny rocket before the entire planet exploded with a titanic roar. The metal box containing the radioactive capsules was never placed in the rocket, and when Krypton exploded it was sent hurtling into outer space, eventually to find its way to Earth embedded in a meteoric fragment.

Years after the death of Krypton, Elton Craig came upon the box of capsules while examining fallen meteors in hopes of finding some KRYPTONITE to use against Superman. When Craig read the inscription on the metal box — "These radioactive capsules to be used only if needed to renew our super-powers on Earth. [signed] Jor-El" — and realized what he had found, he promptly swallowed one of the capsules and endowed himself with temporary super-powers which would last (according to World's Finest Comics No. 90 [Sep/Oct '57: "The Super-Batwoman!"]) for a period of twenty-four hours.

When Superman became temporarily incapacitated by kryptonite during an encounter with the now super-powered Craig, he summoned Batman and Robin to Craig's hideout and asked them to swallow some of Craig's capsules to endow themselves with super-powers temporarily so that they could take up the battle against Craig while Superman recovered from the effects of the kryptonite. Because it was Craig who had swallowed the first capsule, his super-powers faded first, thus enabling the super-powered Batman and Robin to capture him with relative ease. Soon afterward, Superman recovered his full powers, enabling Batman and Robin, whose temporary super-powers had by then faded, to return to their home in GOTHAM CITY (WF No. 87: "The Reversed Heroes!").

In September–October 1957 Elton Craig, the "most dangerous prisoner" at the Metropolis Prison, breaks out of jail and makes his way to the General Chemical Company, Inc., where he had managed to secrete one of Jor-El's special super-power capsules prior to his capture by Batman and Robin. Batman, Robin, and Superman all set out in search of the escaped Craig, but it is Batwoman who deduces that Craig may have hidden his super-power capsule at the General Chemical Company. Inside the plant, having come upon Craig about to swallow his capsule, she snatches it out of his hand and hastily swallows it herself in order to prevent him from getting it away from her. Then, aided by her temporary super-powers, Batwoman apprehends Craig and returns him to Metropolis Prison (WF No. 90: "The Super-Batwoman!").

CRAIL, VINCENT. A "former handwriting expert now wanted for forgery" who, realizing that "there are racketeers who'll pay a fortune to know who ***Batman*** is," attempts to uncover the secret of BATMAN's identity by comparing his handwriting with that of four men — Howard Dane, Ted Stevens, Guy Wilford, and Bruce Wayne — who have in the past been suspected of being Batman. Crail and his henchmen are ultimately apprehended by the Dynamic Duo, and Crail's scheme to learn Batman's identity fails when none of the four signatures he has collected matches that of Batman. "He couldn't guess," whispers ROBIN to Batman, "that as a security measure we always sign our ***Batman*** and ***Robin*** names with the ***left*** hand, so the signatures can't ever be traced!" (BM No. 92/1, Jun '55: "Fan-Mail of Danger!").

CRANE, JONATHAN (Prof.). The spindly psychology professor who turns to crime as the SCARECROW (WF No. 3, Fall '41: "The Scarecrow!").

CRANE, THADDEUS. An alias employed by ALFRED in December 1956 when he poses as "a private investigator from upstate" as part of BATMAN's plan to apprehend "mobster czar" John Varden. According to this text, Thaddeus and Crane are Alfred's "middle names" (BM No. 104/1: "The Man Who Knew Batman's Secret!").

CRATCHIT, TIMMY. A youthful inhabitant of a local orphanage, whose father, Bob Cratchit, has been sentenced to a life term in prison for the murder of a night watchman. BATMAN, who discovers that Bob Cratchit has been framed for the murder, apprehends the real killer and reunites Cratchit with his son in time for Christmas (BM No. 9/4, Feb/Mar '42).

CRAWFORD, BRANDON. The scientific genius and recluse who is inadvertently responsible for transforming ALFRED into the OUTSIDER (Det No. 356, Oct '66: "Inside Story of the Outsider!").

CRIER, THE. A villain of ancient Baghdad "who always weeps as he steals." The Crier is a perfect look-alike for the JOKER, but whereas the Joker uses mirth to aid him in his crimes, the Crier uses sadness. Dispatched through the time barrier to ancient Baghdad by PROFESSOR CARTER NICHOLS, BATMAN and ROBIN apprehend the Crier and thwart his plans to plunder Baghdad. At one point, they soar over the city in a makeshift glider which they have covered with a hand-woven rug, prompting Batman to observe that it is this very feat "that started the flying carpet legend!" (BM No. 49/3, Oct/Nov '48: "Batman's Arabian Nights!").

CRIMESMITH, THE. A "dangerous criminal" with a "genius for mechanics and invention" who creates fantastic mechanical devices to enable his underworld clients to commit spectacular crimes, as when he creates a gigantic "mechanical mole" to help gangland allies loot a heavily guarded warehouse containing a hoard of precious platinum. The Crimesmith is in reality Rand Garrow, a criminal once sent to prison by BATMAN and ROBIN for robbing a theater, but then granted a parole by prison authorities after he had used his "mechanical genius" to help rebuild the prison workshops. After allowing several underworld gangs to commit crimes with his devices in return for 50 percent of their loot, the Crimesmith unleashes his secret "super-weapon" on GOTHAM CITY — a simulated robot invasion designed to throw the populace into a mindless panic while his gangland cohorts plunder the city. While Robin calms the frightened masses with a reassuring skywritten message from the BATPLANE, however, Batman and members of the Gotham City Police Department apprehend the Crimesmith and his underworld entourage (WF No. 68, Jan/Feb '54: "The Secret Weapons of the Crimesmith!").

CRIMSON KNIGHT, THE. A mysterious costumed crime-fighter — clad in a red suit of knightly armor and equipped with such colorful paraphernalia as a bullet-proof shield, an electrically charged "broadsword," and a "jet-propelled steed" — who appears in GOTHAM CITY in September 1959 and swiftly establishes a reputation as a crime-fighter by thwarting a series of robberies and apprehending a large number of criminals. He is secretly Dick Lyons, a Gotham City gang chief who, unbeknownst even to his own henchmen, has assumed the identity of the Crimson Knight as part of an elaborate scheme to have himself appointed to the honor guard accompanying the Liberty Train – a "rolling exhibition of our country's most precious documents" – so that he can steal the documents and then ransom them back to the U.S. Government. As Lyons, he plans a series of crimes for members of his own gang, then treacherously apprehends them as the Crimson Knight – or helps BATMAN and ROBIN apprehend them – in order to enhance his reputation as a crime-fighter. Ultimately, in recognition of his seemingly heroic efforts on behalf of law enforcement, the Crimson Knight is assigned, along with Batman and Robin, to the Liberty Train's honor guard. Batman, however, has already succeeded in deducing the Crimson Knight's true identity, and he and Robin apprehend the villain as he attempts to make off with the priceless documents which form such an important part of the American heritage (Det No. 271: "Batman's Armored Rival!").

CRONIN, LEW. An escaped convict and coin counterfeiter who, having successfully recovered $2,000,000 in stolen gold bullion hidden away by a former cellmate, concocts an elaborate scheme to dispose of the bullion by minting it into counterfeit copies of ancient gold coins, burying it in areas where famous lost treasures are supposed to be located, and then, posing as a wheelchair-ridden coin dealer under the alias Mark Medalion, offering maps to the "ancient" treasure to unsuspecting treasure-seekers in return for a promise of half their find. BATMAN and ROBIN expose and apprehend Lew Cronin in Winter 1945, along with a gang of criminals led by gangster "Lucky" Smith who have taken to stealing the treasure maps offered by coin dealer "Medalion" and hijacking the treasure unearthed by his customers (WF No. 20: "King of Coins!").

CRYSTAL CREATURE, THE. The term used to describe a bizarre crystalline creature, vaguely humanoid in form, which digests metal with two "green rays" fired from its head, and sets objects on fire with a red "heat-ray" fired from its hand, apparently as a display of anger. One scientist has theorized that "the crystal creature" came into being when an underwater volcanic eruption cracked open a thick lead container housing abandoned atomic waste, thus allowing radiation to pour forth which ultimately "caused some ordinary fish to mutate into the ***crystal creature!***" In October 1959 the crystal creature wreaks havoc in GOTHAM CITY, voraciously consuming all the metal in its path until ROBIN finally lures it out of the city by dropping it appetizing steel cubes to eat from the back of a moving truck. BATMAN ultimately destroys the creature by bombarding it with high-frequency sound waves from a large radio transmitter until finally, "like a bursting prism, the crystal creature shatters into thousands of faceted fragments!" "And so," concludes the textual narrative, "the menace that once threatened to wipe out a city, a country--the whole world, perhaps--now lies in a mass of glittering rubble!" (Det No. 272: "The Crystal Creature").

CULLEN, BART. A GOTHAM CITY gang boss who, having stumbled upon an abandoned, crash-landed alien spaceship filled with all sorts of advanced weaponry from some distant planet, disguises himself as a green-skinned extraterrestrial alien and, after passing himself off to Tod Garret, his principal gangland rival, as an alien fugitive from outer space, joins forces with the Garret gang to form the so-called Gimmick Gang and, with their help, uses the alien weaponry to commit a series of spectacular crimes, all as part of an elaborate scheme to profit from a series of successful crimes while awaiting a convenient opportunity to rid himself of his underworld competitors by betraying Garret and his henchmen to the police. As a result of Cullen's intricate double cross, Garret and his cohorts are indeed taken into custody, but Cullen is exposed as an earthman and apprehended by BATMAN and ROBIN soon afterward, in December 1963 (BM No. 160/2: "The Alien Boss of Gotham City!").

CULLEN, BOBO. A GOTHAM CITY gangster who managed to steal BATMAN'S UTILITY BELT when his gang clashed with Batman and ROBIN sometime "last week." In order to lure Cullen into the open and recover the belt, which contains Batman's fingerprints and could therefore serve as a clue to his secret identity, Batman devises an elaborate ruse in which he and Robin, employing the aliases Spence and Li'l Red, hire themselves out to a pair of underworld figures – Hugh Bradford and his partner Wilks – as impersonators of Batman and Robin. When Cullen comes forward with an offer to lend the "bogus" Dynamic Duo the utility belt, for a price, to help make their "impersonation" more realistic, Batman and Robin swing into action and take the criminals into custody (BM No. 158/3, Sep '63: "Batman and Robin--Imposters!").

CYRIL. The young son of the Earl of Wordenshire, and the boy who is secretly the SQUIRE (BM No. 62/2, Dec/Jan '50–'51: "The Batman of England!").

D

DABBLO (Mr.). A cunning criminal who devises a complex scheme to enable him to steal the million-dollar Pearl of the Orient from an exhibition of rare treasures from around the world scheduled to go on public display at the Gotham Square Museum in GOTHAM CITY. Working according to a carefully prearranged timetable, Dabblo overcomes the museum's elaborate security precautions, grabs the pearl, and flees to the city's waterfront district, only to be apprehended along with an underworld cohort soon afterward through the heroic efforts of BATMAN and ROBIN (BM No. 164/1, Jun '64: "Two-Way Gem Caper!").

DAGGER, THE. An elusive, knife-throwing criminal, his true identity concealed by a red hood, who commits his crimes aided by a gang of red-hooded henchmen. The Dagger is secretly Ned Brann, a ruthless gambling czar who controls prizefighting in GOTHAM CITY. Certain that some link exists between the Dagger and the boxing profession, BRUCE WAYNE becomes a professional prizefighter in the hope of obtaining a lead to the Dagger's true identity. Ultimately, BATMAN and ROBIN take Brann and his cohorts into custody and prove that Brann and the Dagger are one and the same man (Det No. 174, Aug '51: "The Park Avenue Kid!").

DAGNER, DIRK. A ruthless underworld chieftain who decides to "make some dough and at the same time give the **Batman** the worst Christmas he ever had," by committing a series of daring Christmas Eve crimes right under the nose of BATMAN. Batman and ROBIN finally apprehend Dagner and his henchmen before sitting down to a sumptuous meal with lighthouse keeper Tom Wick, one of the several lonely citizens whose lives they had decided to brighten with Christmas Eve visits. It is Dirk Dagner who should really be considered lonely, observes BRUCE WAYNE on Christmas Day. "He'll never have a friend because he's all greed and hatred . . . he's completely bad---a wild beast to be kept caged!" (BM No. 15/4, Feb/Mar '43: "The Loneliest Men in the World").

DALA. The beautiful raven-haired vampire who is the accomplice of the diabolical villain known as the MONK. Dala murders JULIE MADISON — apparently transforming her into a vampire — by sinking her fangs deep into Julie's throat, but BATMAN destroys both Dala and the Monk, thereby restoring Julie to life and rescuing her from vampirism, by firing silver bullets into the villains' bodies as they lie resting in their coffins (Det No. 32, Oct '39).

DALE, PETER. A wanted criminal who, pursued by BATMAN and ROBIN into the ruins of a long-abandoned Indian pueblo somewhere in the American Southwest, becomes miraculously endowed — by virtue of his accidental exposure to a strange gas developed by some long-dead medicine man — with absolute mastery over "the ancient four elements" — earth, air, fire, and water — as well as with the ability to transform himself into four awesomely powerful manifestations: (1) that of a man made of earth, called Earth-Man, who can create earthquakes by stamping his foot; (2) that of a whirling Cyclone-Man, who can leave the devastation of a cyclone in his wake; (3) that of a man of fire, called Flame-Master, who can "make all fire obey [his] commands"; and (4) that of a watery Liquid-Man, who can escape his pursuers by flowing into a lake or river. Vowing to use his cataclysmic powers to "make myself the king of crime for one month and then retire," Dale attempts to rob a bank in GOTHAM CITY, only to be defeated and apprehended by Batman and Robin (Det No. 308, oct '62: "The Flame-Master!").

AND SO THE BATMAN AND DALA DEPART ON THEIR WEIRD MISSION

Dala and Batman, 1939 © NPP 1939

DALL. A cunning criminal who, by posing as a fellow scientist, dupes PROFESSOR CARDEN into transforming his newly created robot into BATMAN's "robot twin," then makes off with the robot as part of a scheme to use its unique personality, knowledge, and capabilities for crime. Because Professor Carden's robot has been successfully endowed with attributes and abilities identical to Batman's own — and because Dall fixes its "control relays" so that it will obey only the sound of Dall's own voice — the robot represents a potential disaster for Batman, and for law enforcement in general, because it now possesses every ounce of Batman's agility, skill, and specialized knowledge, including the closely guarded secret of Batman's dual identity. Ultimately, however, by luring the robot into the midst of high-voltage wiring at the Gotham Power Company, Batman succeeds in bombarding the robot with the "high-voltage electric shock" necessary for eradicating Batman's distinctive "brain-wave pattern" from its electronic brain and thereby depriving it of the special knowledge, skills, and attributes with which it has been endowed. Then, with the robot no longer an adversary, Batman easily apprehends Dall and his henchmen (Det No. 239, Jan '57: "Batman's Robot Twin!").

DALLING (Mrs.). An elderly scrubwoman at GOTHAM CITY police headquarters who studies the department's "colossal catalogue of criminals and crime technique" and then uses her newly acquired knowledge to mastermind a series of spectacular crimes. Mrs. Dalling is exposed and apprehended in October–November 1945 through the heroic efforts of BATMAN and ROBIN (BM No. 31/3: "Trade Marks of Crime!").

DAMSEL. A high-fashion magazine published by the CATWOMAN – under the alias Madame Moderne – as a front for her criminal activities during June–July 1948 (BM No. 47/1: "Fashions in Crime!").

DANGER CLUB, THE. A club in GOTHAM CITY for men whose occupations are so hazardous that no life insurance company will write policies on their lives. The club provides a measure of financial security for its members' families, since all members "contribute to an accident-fund we [the members] keep in case one of us gets killed!"

In April–May 1953 the club's secretary, an experimental jet pilot named Milding, sets out to murder his fellow members in an effort to prevent them from discovering that he has been embezzling money from the club's accident fund to support a life of lavish partying. At the same time, Milding attempts to focus suspicion on Mack Thorn, a man who, bitter over the fact that his younger brother had taken up auto racing and then died in a racetrack accident while attempting to qualify for Danger Club membership, had recently made what could easily be construed as a veiled threat against the lives of the club members.

In order to root out the real killer, BATMAN applies for Danger Club membership, is initiated as a new member, and ultimately exposes Milding as the murderer.

"We'll dissolve the **Danger Club**," remarks one club member, as Milding is led away by members of the Gotham City Police Department, ". . . the club itself proved the biggest danger we ever faced!"

"There's always danger when greedy men break the law," replies Batman, ". . . and for such lawbreakers, there's always doom!" (BM No. 76/1: "The Danger Club!").

DANIELS, BIG BOY. The ruthless leader of a gang of criminals who is the sponsor of a "crime school for boys" where youngsters from the city's slums are tutored in the ways of crime and groomed for positions in Daniels's own mob. Aided, however, by DICK GRAYSON and the reformed pupils of the crime school, who have finally come to "hate crime and evil" thanks to a vigorous "campaign for fair play and honesty" waged by BATMAN, Batman apprehends the Big Boy Daniels mob and closes down the crime school in Fall 1940 (BM No. 3/3: "The Crime School for Boys!!").

DANNING, VICTOR. A scientist turned criminal, at one time a specialist in mechanical engineering, who attempts to steal an as yet unperfected "brain-amplifying ray" – a device designed to "increase any man's mental power 100 times" – from the laboratory of its inventor, Dr. John Carr, with the intention of using it to endow himself with a super-intellect to aid him in the planning and execution of spectacular crimes. Danning does not actually succeed in stealing the machine, but efforts to apprehend him receive a severe setback when, during a scuffle in Carr's laboratory, Danning and ROBIN become accidentally transformed into supergeniuses while SUPERMAN becomes transformed into a mindless dullard. Although they are generally more hindered than helped by the slow-witted behavior of the intellectually impoverished Superman, the quick-witted BATMAN and the superingenious Robin ultimately succeed in apprehending Danning and his henchmen and in using Dr. Carr's "brain-amplifier" to restore Danning, Robin, and Superman to normal (WF No. 93, Mar/Apr '58: "The Boss of Batman and Superman").

DANNY THE DUMMY. A midget ventriloquist whose hilarious vaudeville act with a man-sized dummy named Matt has been hailed as "one of the newest and funniest acts in show business." Danny's unique talent lies in his ability to make it appear that he is the dummy and Matt the ventriloquist, and, at the conclusion of each performance, Danny smilingly announces the truth to his astonished audience. In spite of Danny's repeated explanations, however, fans and passersby persist in referring to him as Danny the Dummy, a salutation that infuriates the pint-sized ventriloquist: ***"Fools!"*** mutters Danny angrily. "Why do they keep calling ***me*** the dummy? I'm the ***boss*** of the act . . . ***I*** manipulate ***Matt!*** Why don't they remember that?"

As the days pass, this angry thought "becomes an obsession--until, one day, [Danny's] mind cracks," and he explodes in a fit of maniacal laughter. "I know what I'll do!" he cries. "I'll manipulate ***people*** like dummies! Yes . . . I'll use dummies for ***crime!*** That'll show 'em who's ***really*** the dummy!"

Operating from a secret hideaway in a "dummy" Western town – a mock Western town used in the filming of television Westerns – Danny the Dummy launches a series of spectacular crimes, each of which involves the use of dummies in some form, as when he arranges for his henchmen to conceal themselves inside the Gotham Department Store after closing time by posing as mannequins. For a time, the dummy crimes continue unabated, but Danny the Dummy and his henchmen are ultimately apprehended by BATMAN and ROBIN in September 1960 (BM No. 134/3: "The Deadly Dummy").

DANTON, JOE. A former college classmate of Bruce Wayne, shunned by his college teammates because of his selfish, unsportsmanlike behavior, who deeply resented Bruce Wayne because of Wayne's greater popularity and athletic prowess. Danton once lashed out at

Wayne during a college fencing match by removing the protective rubber cap from the tip of his own foil and inflicting an oddly shaped scar on Bruce Wayne's wrist.

Years later, in December 1955, still bitter over the rejection by his college teammates and determined to wreak a paranoiac's revenge, Danton invites a group of them, including Bruce Wayne, for a three-day cruise aboard his yacht with the intention of steering the vessel into the path of underwater mines and blowing them all to kingdom come. During a scuffle with BATMAN on board the yacht, Danton spies the old fencing scar on Batman's wrist, realizes that his old college classmate Wayne is secretly Batman, and decides to reveal his accidental discovery to all the passengers aboard his yacht.

After seeing Batman heroically risk his life to save the ship and its passengers from the deadly underwater mines, however, Danton repents his obsession with vengeance and, suddenly stricken by the long-standing heart ailment that he always knew might prove fatal at any time, he dies quietly, willingly taking the secret of Batman's identity with him to the grave (BM No. 96/2: "Batman's College Days").

DANTON, SLITS. An escaped convict who has vowed to murder BATMAN in retaliation for Batman's having once been responsible for sending him to prison. During a rousing battle with the villain in a lecture hall, where BRUCE WAYNE and DICK GRAYSON have come to attend a lecture on bats, Batman is knocked unconscious, but ROBIN succeeds in apprehending Danton single-handedly (Det No. 153, Nov '49: "The Flying Batman!").

DARCY, ROBERT (Dr.). An "expert chemist and technician" who organizes a "sinister new corporation of crime" in November 1950. "Why should I waste my scientific genius in a cheap laboratory job," Darcy asks his henchmen, "when it can reap millions for us!" When Darcy shoots BATMAN and puts him out of action for a week, ROBIN impersonates Batman by donning a special "emergency bat-costume" designed expressly for that purpose and ultimately succeeds in chasing Darcy and his cohorts into the waiting arms of members of the Gotham City Police Department (Det No. 165: "The Strange Costumes of Batman!"). (*See* BATMAN [section c 2, the emergency and special-purpose costumes].)

DAREDEVILS, THE. "Three circus acrobats . . . turned bandits" who are apprehended by BATMAN and ROBIN in April 1957 (BM No. 107/3: "The Grown-Up Boy Wonder!"). (*See* ROBIN.)

DARRELL, LOU. An unscrupulous worker at Gotham Hospital who steals the hospital's valuable radium supply with the intention of using the proceeds from his theft for the construction of a new type of "radiotherapy machine" with which he feels certain he can make a fortune. BATMAN and ROBIN apprehend Darrell and recover the stolen radium in October–November 1946 (BM No. 37/1: "Calling Dr. Batman!").

DAVENPORT, MARJORY. The pretty blond girl who is a classmate of DICK GRAYSON and the daughter of Dr. R. Davenport, "the best surgeon in Gotham City." Grayson, who has a crush on Marjory during June–July 1944, has described her as "the smartest girl in school – and the prettiest in the whole world!" For a time, it appears that Marjory may reciprocate Dick Grayson's affections, but after the Dynamic Duo have rescued her from the clutches of the BUGS CONKLIN gang, Marjory has eyes only for the far more glamorous ROBIN. "A fine thing!" thinks Grayson bitterly. "I'm my own rival – and I can't do a thing about it!" (BM No. 23/2: "Damsel in Distress!").

DAVIS, BART. A cunning criminal, once sent to prison for impersonating BATMAN, who, in June 1956, is among the many men who apply for the role of Batman in Excelsior Studios' upcoming movie based on the adventures of Batman and ROBIN. Having promised movie producer Herb Denison that he will personally select the winning Batman candidate, Batman intentionally selects Davis in the hope that Davis will revert to his old habits, begin impersonating Batman once again in order to extort money from his fellow criminals, and perhaps ultimately lead him to the missing loot from the "million dollar stickup" of a Fields Armored Car, still unsolved after three weeks.

Sure enough, as Batman had anticipated, Davis begins using his Excelsior Studios Batman costume and other Batman paraphernalia created for the movie to frighten GOTHAM CITY criminals into surrendering large quantities of their stolen loot to him. "My authentic ***Batman*** equipment will lead us to some real big dough!" gloats Davis to his henchmen. "There isn't a crook who isn't scared to death of ***Batman!***"

Ultimately, however, after Davis has fulfilled Batman's highest expectations by leading him to the hideout of the gang responsible for the Fields Armored Car theft – thus enabling Batman to effect the complete recovery of the stolen armored car loot – Batman apprehends Davis and his henchmen and, because Herb Denison's filming schedule has been disrupted by Batman's crime-fighting activities, offers to play the role of Batman himself in the upcoming Batman epic (Det No. 232: "The Outlaw Who Played Batman!").

DAVIS, FRANK. An amateur BATMAN scholar and expert on the career of Batman whose years-long fascination with the world's foremost detective has actually enabled him to deduce Batman's secret identity. Davis's secret knowledge dies with him, however, when he is murdered by emcee JOE HARMON while appearing on a television quiz show (BM No. 108/1, Jun '57: "The Big Batman Quiz").

DAVIS, HOMER. A GOTHAM CITY banker, deeply in debt to an architect named Peter Chaney, who concocts an elaborate scheme to murder Chaney while placing the blame on a loudmouth named Ben Kole who has recently threatened to kill Davis, Chaney, and BATMAN. Davis murders his own butler in the course of the adventure, but Batman and ROBIN thwart his effort to murder Chaney and ultimately apprehend him (Det No. 151, Sep '49: "I.O.U. My Life!").

DEADSHOT. A tuxedo-clad crime-fighter, his true identity concealed by a black face-mask, whose incredible virtuosity with firearms enables him to apprehend criminals with the aid of his guns, but without ever killing or wounding them or even shooting at them directly. He is secretly Floyd Lawton, a GOTHAM CITY millionaire whose emergence as Deadshot is part of a cunning scheme to eliminate BATMAN and establish himself as Gotham City's most powerful crime boss.

By June–July 1950 Deadshot's dazzling crime-fighting virtuosity has won him the enthusiastic support of POLICE COMMISSIONER GORDON and the Gotham City Police Department and established him as a rival of Batman for the mantle of Gotham City's foremost crime-fighter. "Each day," gloats Lawton to his butler, "**Batman** loses more face with Commissioner Gordon while I, and my guns, rise in his esteem!" "Ahh, Mr. Lawton!" replies the butler. "Soon you will replace **Batman!** And then you'll run this city the way you've dreamed--as its ***greatest crime lord!***"

From the beginning, Batman is leery of the newly emergent Deadshot, but his suspicions, unsupported by hard evidence, tend to appear like the jealous reservations of a prima donna who has enjoyed the limelight unchallenged for too long. Ultimately, however, Batman uses a clever psychological ploy to destroy Deadshot's self-confidence and trick him into making a full confession of his scheme to Police Commissioner Gordon (BM No. 59/1: "The Man Who Replaced Batman!").

DEATH (Dr.). *See* DOCTOR DEATH.

DEATH-CHEATERS' CLUB, THE. A private club in GOTHAM CITY whose members were, at one time or another, all pronounced legally dead and then miraculously brought back to life. One member, for example, was once bitten by a cobra and pronounced dead by a physician, only to be revived eleven minutes later with the aid of a potent native serum.

By August–September 1952 Jeff Sievers, an unscrupulous accountant who is both a member of the club and "the personal accountant of all the club members," has "managed to embezzle thousands of dollars" of the members' personal funds. Fearful that these embezzlements are on the verge of being discovered, Sievers begins the systematic murder of his fellow members while carefully contriving to focus suspicion on Little Dougy, a notorious gangster, pronounced legally dead after a gangland shoot-out and then brought miraculously back to life by emergency heart massage, who had sworn vengeance on the club members after being denied membership in the Death-Cheaters' Club because of his long criminal record.

In order to root out the real killer, BRUCE WAYNE deliberately swallows a deadly, swift-acting poison so that, after DICK GRAYSON has brought him back to life by means of artificial respiration, he may join the Death-Cheaters' Club as a bona fide member. Before long, BATMAN deduces the identity of the murderer, and he and ROBIN take accountant Sievers into custody (BM No. 72/3: "The Death-Cheaters of Gotham City!").

DEEMS, DARBY. The expert in the science of dreams who achieves infamy as DR. DREEMO (WF No. 17, Spr '45: "Crime Goes to College!").

DELION, JOHN. A sixteenth-century Spanish explorer who, having come upon the fabled fountain of youth in a lush valley somewhere in the Florida Everglades, built a medieval Spanish-style castle at the gateway to the valley, with a massive golden door leading directly into the valley proper, so that, as each of his descendants reached the age of sixty, he might pass through the gold door into the valley to drink from the "spring of immortality" and dwell for all eternity beside the generations of DeLions who had preceded him into the valley. Once a DeLion had entered the valley, however, and drunk the water of the enchanted spring, he could never again leave the valley without dying from the water's effects.

In August–September 1949 Bruce Wayne and Dick Grayson come upon the castle and, passing through the golden doorway as BATMAN and ROBIN, discover that the notorious Dan Morgan gang has entered the tranquil valley sometime before them, seized control of the valley's only village, and driven John DeLion and his various immortal descendants into the nearby hills. Pursued by Batman and Robin, the criminals — who have not yet partaken of the enchanted water — attempt to flee the valley for the outside world, unaware that a drink they unsuspectingly accept from John DeLion during their flight toward the valley's rim is actually water from the fountain of youth. As they reach the outer edge of the valley, with the Dynamic Duo in close pursuit, the criminals topple over dead, avenged by the immortal valley residents they had sought to terrorize. Because of the similarity of their names, the text suggests that the John DeLion encountered by Batman and Robin may actually have been the noted Spanish explorer JUAN PONCE DE LEÓN (BM No. 54/2: "The Door Without a Key!").

DELMAR, HORATIO. A seemingly respectable professional man who is in reality "head of the rackets" in one of the wards of GOTHAM CITY. In October–November 1941 triggerman Weasel Venner murders Delmar and frames BRUCE WAYNE for the crime on the orders of "gang chief" Freddie Hill, Delmar's principal underworld lieutenant, who hopes by eliminating Delmar to assume control of his boss's gangland fiefdom. Freddie Hill and his henchmen are ultimately apprehended by BATMAN and ROBIN, and a dying Weasel Venner, viciously double-crossed by Hill to prevent him from disclosing his role in Delmar's murder, clears Bruce Wayne of the charges against him by making a dramatic courtroom confession (BM No. 7/4: "The People vs. The Batman").

DE NIL, B. C. An alias employed by the JOKER in July 1965, when he poses as a movie producer as part of his plot to rob the home of the "incredibly rich" Cornelius Van-Van (Det No. 341: "The Joker's Comedy Capers!").

DENT, HARVEY. *See* KENT, HARVEY.

DENT, PAUL (Dr.). The inventor of the experimental "skin rejuvenation ray," designed to "heal flesh scars in seconds," which accidentally transforms fugitive criminal Bart Magan into the hideous DR. NO-FACE (Det No. 319, Sep '63: "The Fantastic Dr. No-Face!").

DEREK (Doctor). A ruthless FIFTH COLUMNIST and saboteur who is the leading figure behind a series of vicious spy-plots which rock America in September 1941, including a plot to kidnap America's key scientists, inventors, and military men and compel them to disclose defense secrets involuntarily by subjecting them to the ingenious "brain machine" recently developed by kidnapped American scientist Jon Henry; a plot to kidnap the foreman of a major steel mill so that he can be forced to divulge secret information concerning a formula for "new type steel" recently developed by the United States; and a plot to utilize Prof. Henry's new "theory . . . about radio beams," i.e., "if a man has a sliver of metal put in his head at the base of his brain, jangled radio waves passing through it could drive that man crazy!"

Derek reasons that by implanting the metal slivers in the heads of willing Axis agents, obtaining jobs for them in key defense plants, and then driving them insane with the radio beams, it will be possible to wreak unparalleled havoc in vital industries since "madness-induced havoc would be more destructive than ordinary sabotage." BATMAN and ROBIN thwart all of Derek's schemes, however, and apprehend Derek and his cohorts (Det No. 55: "The 'Brain Burglar!'").

DEREK, WILEY. An escaped convict and master makeup artist, now employed as a guard at a local insane asylum, who capitalizes on the delusions of inmates who believe they are famous historical personages — such as George Washington, Abraham Lincoln, and Benjamin Franklin — by posing as Lafayette and duping them into helping him commit a series of crimes. Derek is apprehended by BATMAN and ROBIN in January 1947 (Det No. 119: "The Case of the Famous Foes!").

DEVOE. A deep-sea diver and member of the 50 Fathoms Club — a club for underwater specialists — who, having discovered a "fire-breathing creature of the dinosaur age" in the waters off an isolated island, concocts an elaborate scheme to kill the creature — while ostensibly taking part in an expedition to capture it alive — so that he can seize the creature's only egg and, once it has hatched, amass a fortune by exhibiting the infant creature as the only surviving example of an all-but-extinct species. When BATMAN thwarts Devoe's attempts to kill the sea creature, Devoe attempts to murder Batman, but Batman survives the attempt on his life and, with ROBIN's help, captures the sea creature alive, exposes Devoe's plot, and recovers the sea creature's unhatched egg intact. Ironically, Devoe's scheme was doomed to failure from the outset, because the rare egg — now on display in the trophy room of the BATCAVE — is not due to hatch for another 100 years (BM No. 104/3, Dec '56: "The Creature from 20,000 Fathoms!").

DIBNY, RALPH. The hero with elastic powers who is best known as the ELONGATED MAN (Det No. 331, Sep '64: "Museum of Mixed-Up Men!"; and others).

DIGGES. The butler to Reginald Scofield — a noted mystery writer who inhabits a "strange old house with a tower" on Crow's Nest, "a lonely point of rock" approximately "twenty miles up the coast" from GOTHAM CITY — and the secret leader of a band of smugglers who use Scofield's residence as the headquarters for an elaborate gem-smuggling operation until they are apprehended by BATMAN and ROBIN in June 1945 (Det No. 100: "The Crow's Nest Mystery!").

DILLON, JOHN V. (Dr.). The GOTHAM CITY doctor who is personal physician to Bruce Wayne and Dick Grayson, the man and boy who are secretly BATMAN and ROBIN. It is Dr. Dillon who first diagnoses BRASS HADLEY's rare heart ailment in September–October 1953 (WF No. 66: "The Proving Ground for Crime!").

DI PINA (Professor). A GOTHAM CITY scientist who has invented an explosive so powerful that one ounce of it can blow up an entire city block. In April 1958 a lead cylinder containing one ounce of the explosive is stolen by Bates, a hobo who does not realize what he is stealing, only to begin a strange and fateful odyssey that carries it through the successive hands of two boy scouts, a pair of ex-convicts named Burton and Hegan, and two escaped convicts, one of whom is named Burns. Meanwhile, BATMAN, ROBIN, and Bat-Hound (*see* ACE [THE BAT-HOUND]) have desperately taken up the trail of the stolen explosive in an effort to recover the cylinder before someone accidentally detonates its contents. Ultimately, the Dynamic Duo and their canine companion apprehend the escaped convicts and recover the explosive only moments before it is about to explode as the result of inadvertent tampering by Burns (Det No. 254: "One Ounce of Doom!").

DIRECTOR, THE. The proprietor of a bizarre "underworld theater," located in a huge arena on a private island in Gotham Bay, which is the scene of a series of nightly theatrical extravaganzas entitled "The Thousand Deaths of Batman," in which, for the price of admission, gangland audiences may watch actors in BATMAN and ROBIN costumes "dying" in some new exotic way every single night of the week. In July 1959 Batman and Robin infiltrate the island, take the places of the underworld actors hired to portray them, and, with the aid of the harbor police, ultimately apprehend the Director and his entire gangland audience, including the new boss of the GOTHAM CITY underworld, a criminal known as the Big Guy (Det No. 269: "The Thousand Deaths of Batman!").

DIX, SMILEY. The leader of an underworld trio who rob the Van Ness mansion and then escape from BATMAN and ROBIN by dynamiting a bridge and demolishing the BATMOBILE. The Dynamic Duo ultimately apprehend Dix and his henchmen with the aid of the new features incorporated in a brand-new batmobile, which they build to replace the one that has been destroyed (Det No. 156, Feb '50: "The Batmobile of 1950!"). (*See* BATMAN [section E 2 a, the batmobile].)

DOCTOR DEATH. A cunning and diabolical villain who matches wits with BATMAN in July 1939 (Det No. 29: "The Batman Meets Doctor Death") and again in

Doctor Death © NPP 1939

August 1939 (Det No. 30). Doctor Death, whose real name is Dr. Karl Hellfern, is bald, has a goatee, and wears a monocle.

By July 1939 the fiendish Doctor Death has devised a means of causing "death by pollen extract," and is now ready to launch a campaign of terror against the world's wealthy. "I am ready to exact my tribute from the wealthy of the world," announces Doctor Death grimly. "They will either pay tribute to me or **die**. . . ."

In an effort to forestall any possible interference by Batman, Doctor Death lures Batman into an ambush, but Batman, wounded in the right shoulder by a bullet fired by Doctor Death's "giant Indian" assistant JABAH, escapes from his would-be assassins, kills Jabah soon afterward, and ultimately corners Doctor Death in his laboratory, where the villain arms himself with a tube filled with volatile incendiary chemicals. When Batman hurls a fire extinguisher at Doctor Death, the villain drops the tube and the laboratory goes up in flames, trapping Doctor Death in the midst of the fiery inferno. As the flames swirl ever higher, Doctor Death, his mind shattered, begins to laugh maniacally. Batman flees the burning laboratory, leaving his apparently doomed adversary behind him in the flames (Det No. 29: "The Batman Meets Doctor Death").

In August 1939 it becomes apparent that Doctor Death managed to survive the fire in his laboratory by escaping through a secret doorway. His face, however, now a ghastly brown color, has been virtually "destroyed" by the flames, leaving him with no lips and almost no nose.

When Doctor Death's assistant MIKHAIL attempts to steal some jewels from the widow of John Jones – a man whom Doctor Death murdered for refusing to pay him $500,000 in extortion money – Batman intervenes and knocks Mikhail unconscious, only to allow him to escape soon afterward in the hope that Mikhail will lead him to the hideout of Doctor Death.

Batman pursues Doctor Death to his secret laboratory . . . © NPP 1939

. . . and knocks the vial of incendiary chemical from the villain's hand © NPP 1939

Trapped in the inferno, Doctor Death goes mad . . . © NPP 1939

. . . and Batman grimly departs, leaving his foe to die in the flames, 1939 © NPP 1939

Mikhail, however, leads Batman only as far as the headquarters of an underworld fence named Ivan Herd, and Batman kills Mikhail soon afterward without learning anything further about the whereabouts of Doctor Death. "First Jabah, now you," observes Batman grimly, after his mighty foot has broken Mikhail's neck with a sickening snap, ". . . and yet Doctor Death lives on!"

In an effort to exploit his only remaining lead, Batman pays a call on Ivan Herd, demands to be told the whereabouts of Doctor Death, and then lassos Herd by the throat when he attempts to flee. The violent jerk of Batman's lasso sends a false hairpiece flying off Herd's head, and Batman realizes to his astonishment that Ivan Herd is none other than Doctor Death himself, his identity concealed behind a clever disguise. After binding his captive with rope, Batman hands him over to the police, thus bringing to a close Doctor Death's brief but diabolical career (Det No. 30).

DR. DOOM. A ruthless smuggler who conceals himself inside a mummy case after a narrow escape from BATMAN and ROBIN, only to have the Dynamic Duo transport the mummy case to the BATCAVE's trophy room and place it on display there, unaware that Dr. Doom is hiding inside it. After surreptitiously emerging from the mummy case and making a series of unsuccessful attempts to murder Batman and Robin by booby-trapping the batcave's other trophies, Dr. Doom hurls a live hand grenade at the Dynamic Duo and then leaps back inside the mummy case to shield himself from the impact of the impending blast. Batman and Robin manage to escape injury, but the explosion seals the mummy case shut so tightly that Dr. Doom dies of suffocation before Batman and Robin can pry it open (Det No. 158, Apr '50: "The Thousand and One Trophies of Batman!").

DR. DREEMO. The stage name employed by Darby Deems, the unscrupulous scholar and expert in the science of dreams who is the host of the "Nightmare Hour," a radio program on which guests are invited to recite their nightmares, ostensibly so that Dr. Dreemo can entertain his audience with innocuous interpretations, but in reality so that he can use his expertise in nightmare analysis to discern the secret, subconscious fears of his unsuspecting guests and exploit them later to his own advantage, as when he correctly discerns that one guest feels guilty about having committed a murder and then later blackmails the guest into handing over the money that constituted the motive for the killing. Dr. Dreemo and his henchmen are apprehended by BATMAN and ROBIN in Spring 1945 (WF No. 17: "Crime Goes to College!").

DR. NO-FACE. A mysterious man who possesses no face—whose eyes, ears, and nose have been totally obliterated—and who embarks on a seemingly "senseless rampage of destruction" in September 1963, destroying statues, clocks, masks, and anything else that may be regarded as having a face.

Dr. No-Face is widely believed to be Dr. Paul Dent, the inventor of an experimental "skin rejuvenation ray" designed to "heal flesh scars in seconds," whose facial features are thought to have been obliterated due to a malfunctioning of his machine during a recent public demonstration, and who, the theory continues, has "lost his senses" as the result of the traumatic episode and is now striking out at other "faces" in a sort of pathetic dementia.

Dr. No-Face is indeed a man who has lost his face as the result of a malfunctioning of Dr. Dent's rejuvenation ray, but Dr. No-Face is not Dr. Dent. He is Bart Magan, a wanted criminal who accidentally suffered the loss of his facial characteristics while trying to obliterate a telltale facial scar with Dr. Dent's machine, and who, following the mishap, concocted an elaborate scheme to enable him to profit from his own hideous misfortune.

Magan's complex scheme has involved establishing two erroneous ideas in the mind of the public: (1) that the faceless man calling himself Dr. No-Face is Dr. Dent, and (2) that Dr. No-Face's senseless destruction of objects with faces represents Dr. Dent's deranged response to his own tragic maiming. The truth, however, is that Dr. No-Face is Bart Magan, that Magan's henchmen have been surreptitiously stealing valuable objects with faces and replacing them with worthless duplicates, and that Magan's seemingly insane destruction of these duplicates has in fact been a cunning ploy designed to conceal the theft of the valuable originals.

Dr. No-Face and his henchmen are apprehended by BATMAN and ROBIN in September 1963 (Det No. 319: "The Fantastic Dr. No-Face!").

DOCTOR X. The creator of the evil energy being known as DOUBLE X (Det No. 261, Nov '58: "The Amazing Dr. Double X!").

DODD, WALLY. The proprietor of Skyland, a futuristic amusement park floating on a specially constructed platform high over GOTHAM CITY and featuring such novel attractions as a "toys of the future" display and an interplanetary zoo where imaginary beasts from distant worlds are exhibited. When Dodd is found murdered in May 1962, BATMAN and ROBIN launch an investigation and pinpoint the killer: he is Blinky Cole, a crime syndicate strongarm man who killed Dodd after Dodd had obtained movie film of Cole performing acts of sabotage in Skyland in retaliation for Dodd's having steadfastly refused to pay protection money to Cole's underworld employers (Det No. 303: "Murder in Skyland!").

DODSON, PETER. A young, reclusive, former millionaire, now fallen upon hard times, who is widely remembered in GOTHAM CITY as "the No. 1 Batman fan," a man who, while he had wealth, "contributed liberal sums to the cause of law and order" and was "the galvanizing force behind many of the tributes paid Batman by Gotham City." In October–November 1954 Dodson and his well-known idolization of BATMAN figure in an elaborate scheme by gangster Henry Stoll to preoccupy Batman and ROBIN with trivial diversions while he and his henchmen loot Gotham City.

After kidnapping Dodson from his home and replacing him with an underworld look-alike, Stoll summons Batman and Robin to the scene and, posing as Dodson's physician, informs them that Dodson has suffered a mental breakdown accompanied by the delusion that he is actually Batman and that if Batman and Robin will only help humor him in this delusion, a cure will follow in a matter of weeks. While the Dynamic Duo are busy helping the supposedly ailing Dodson, however, providing him with a Batman costume and equipment and generally keeping an eye on him as he "patrols" Gotham City, Stoll and his henchmen stage a series of spectacular robberies until finally Batman and Robin see through the complex ruse, apprehend Stoll and his cohorts, and rescue the real Peter Dodson from their clutches (WF No. 54: "The Carbon Copy Batman!").

DOLAN, JOE. A vicious robber and murderer who is captured by BATMAN and ROBIN in June–July 1942, and then subsequently recaptured by them with the aid of a district attorney, once Dolan's boyhood pal, after he has strangled a guard and broken out of jail (BM No. 11/2: "Payment in Full").

DOLAN, JOHN. The man who launches an incredible criminal career as the ELEMENTAL MAN (Det No. 294, Aug '61: "The Villain of 100 Elements!").

DONEGAN, KNUCKLES. A fugitive gang chieftain who is apprehended in Florida by BATMAN and ROBIN in October–November 1945 (BM No. 31/2: "Vanishing Village!").

DORN (Dr.). A scientist who, as the result of a freak accident that occurred in his laboratory while he was experimenting with "methods to reactivate dormant microbes he found in a meteorite," becomes periodically transformed, for brief periods of time that remain blanks in his memory, into a hideous green alien monster possessed of awesome strength and unearthly powers, including the ability to communicate telepathically and to surround itself with an aura of "eerie energy" to safeguard itself against attack. In March 1963 the bizarre creature goes on a series of destructive rampages in GOTHAM CITY and environs, thwarting the efforts of BATMAN and ROBIN either to stop it or destroy it, until finally Batman deduces that the creature is actually Dr. Dorn and finds a way to destroy the creature while seeing that Dr. Dorn remains unharmed (BM No. 154/3: "The Strange Experiment of Dr. Dorn!").

DORN (Maestro). An ingenious criminal mastermind and master puppeteer who plans each of his gang's crimes in painstaking detail and then uses puppets to "enact [each] fantastic crime in miniature," as a sort of rehearsal, so that his henchmen will know exactly what functions they are to perform during the commission of the actual crime. Maestro Dorn and his henchmen are captured by BATMAN and ROBIN in April 1952 (Det No. 182: "The Human Puppets").

D'ORTERRE (Duc). A diabolical Parisian villain, headquartered in an "unearthly den in the Paris sewers," who is known and feared as "master of the Apaches," members of the Parisian underworld noted for their crimes of violence. By December 1939 Duc D'Orterre has become determined to marry lovely Karel Maire and seize control of the inheritance that has been bequeathed to Karel and her brother Charles, and has responded to Charles's strenuous objections to the courtship by viciously obliterating Charles's facial features with a "terrible ray." Finally, Duc D'Orterre places the captive Karel in an automobile and speeds toward his chateau in the French region of Champagne, but BATMAN overtakes the vehicle and rescues the frightened Karel from the villain's clutches. During the ensuing struggle, however, Duc D'Orterre's car is sent hurtling out of control, and it careens crazily off a high bridge, carrying the villain to his doom (Det No. 34).

DOUBLE X. The diabolical energy duplicate of the ingenious Doctor X. BATMAN has described Double X as "energy in human form" (Det No. 261, Nov '58: "The Amazing Dr. Double X!"), and BRUCE WAYNE has referred to him as the "dangerous energy form" of Doctor X (Det No. 316, Jun '63: "Double Batman vs. Double X"). Double X – who is occasionally referred to as Dr. Double X – is living proof of Doctor X's "theory that you could isolate a man's personality and invent a

Doctor X and Double X, 1963 © NPP 1963

machine . . . to give it form. . . ." In order to see to it that Double X does not "vanish from existence," Doctor X must continually fuel the machine which created him with a special "chemical solution" (Det No. 261, Nov '58: "The Amazing Dr. Double X!").

The texts are somewhat inconsistent regarding the nature of the relationship between Doctor X and his diabolical energy creation. Detective Comics No. 261 presents Doctor X as a well-meaning, if misguided, scientist and Double X as the powerful energy duplicate of Doctor X's "other self," i.e., the powerful energy duplicate of Doctor X's evil, normally repressed side. While Double X is present, he completely dominates his well-intentioned creator and forces him to commit acts of evil. Occasionally, Doctor X tries to resist the demands of his evil energy creation, but the overpowering personality of Double X is invariably too strong for him. Whenever Double X vanishes from the scene temporarily, Doctor X is left dazed and confused, with no recollection whatever of the evil events which took place while Double X was present. At one point, after he has been placed in a prison cell after an attempted robbery at the Tick Tock Watch Works, he is bitter and resentful, for he has no recollection of the attempted robbery or of his part in it (Nov '58: "The Amazing Dr. Double X!").

Detective Comics No. 316, however, presents Doctor X as an evil scientist, and Double X as the powerful energy duplicate of his entire personality. In this text, Doctor X is the leader rather than the follower, an ingenious criminal mastermind fully in command of his diabolical energy creation. The dizzy spells and the lapses of memory that characterized Doctor X during his first textual appearance are no longer evident (Jun '63: "Double Batman vs. Double X").

By November 1958, after a series of daring experiments conducted in his "secret mountain laboratory," Doctor X has succeeded in creating the fearsome energy duplicate known as Double X. Double X is dependent on his creator for the frequent infusions of chemical fuel needed to maintain the machine which ensures his continued existence. Double X leads Doctor X into a life of crime, apparently so that the two of them can accumulate sufficient plunder to enable Doctor X to continue with his daring scientific experiments. As the narrative reaches its climax, Double X has seized Batman and is about to destroy him when suddenly, in the nick of time, Batman orders his Batman robot to demolish the diabolical machine which has endowed Double X with life. With the machine hopelessly smashed, Double X begins to fade into nothingness, and within moments it appears that he "has vanished into oblivion . . . forever!" Doctor X, left dazed and confused following the disappearance of Double X, will, according to Batman, "be placed in a sanitarium where he'll be cured!" (Det No. 261: "The Amazing Dr. Double X!").

In June 1963 Doctor X escapes from GOTHAM CITY's Happydale Sanitarium and makes his way to a house on the city's outskirts, where, four and a half years ago, he had managed to conceal a duplicate of the machine which first gave life to the evil energy being known as Double X. Then, after re-creating the diabolical Double X, Doctor X leads his fearsome energy duplicate on a renewal of their whirlwind career in crime. At one point, Batman and ROBIN come upon Doctor X's machine and use it to create a Double Batman – a benevolent and powerful energy duplicate of Batman – to aid them in their battle with Doctor X and Double X. Eventually, Batman, Robin, and Double Batman defeat the villains: Double Batman destroys Double X by demolishing the ingenious machine which sustains his existence, and Doctor X is taken to jail, where he will be unable to do further harm.

Later, back in the BATCAVE, Double Batman announces that it is time for him to disappear too. "You created me to equalize your battle against the infamous **Dr. Double X!**" explains Double Batman. "And now, it is only right that I depart . . . forever!"

". . . I feel as if I'm losing a part of my self!" says Batman sadly, as Double Batman fades away. "We sure will miss him!" (Det No. 316: "Double Batman vs. Double X").

DRAGON SOCIETY, THE. A nationwide underworld organization – its members' identities concealed, even from each other, by bizarre dragon-headed costumes – whose battle with BATMAN is the subject of a speech by POLICE COMMISSIONER GORDON to recent graduates of the Gotham City Police Academy in November 1959.

The adventure, which reportedly took place sometime in the past, pitted Batman and ROBIN against the leader of the Dragon Society, known as the Chief Dragon, and his principal subordinates from other cities, i.e., Dragon One from GOTHAM CITY, Dragon Two from Chicago, Dragon Three from Houston, and Dragon Four from San Francisco.

For a time, even Batman was discouraged by his inability to apprehend the members of the Dragon Society, but ultimately he succeeded in apprehending antique dealer Harvey Straker, the man who was secretly Dragon One, and in infiltrating a top-level Dragon Society meeting in Straker's dragon-headed costume. The Chief Dragon soon discovered that "Dragon One" was an impostor, but Batman had already summoned Robin and the police via belt-radio, and the criminals were quickly apprehended.

"And that's the story of the ***Dragon Society,*** " concludes Gordon finally, "--a gang so cunning that even ***Batman*** began to feel they could not be stopped. . . . But ***Batman*** never gave up--because he knew that a lawman must fight--and keep on fighting--until he wins the battle against crime!" (Det No. 273: "Secret of the Dragon Society!").

DRAKE, MORTIMER. The wealthy playboy who turns to crime as the CAVALIER (BM No. 22/3, Apr/May '44: "The Cavalier Rides Again!").

DREW, "DIMPLES." The gangland chieftain who is the organizer of the Olympic Games of Crime, an underworld Olympics competition – held inside an abandoned airplane hangar near the town of Orville, about an hour's drive from GOTHAM CITY – in which criminals from throughout the United States vie for the honor of being acclaimed the most accomplished criminal in a series of underworld categories, such as safecracking, shoplifting, and the like.

Confident that BATMAN will eventually learn about the Olympics and attempt to infiltrate the competition disguised as one of the contestants, Drew announces a "special event" in which the winners of the various Olympics categories will compete to see which of them can correctly identify the disguised Batman in their midst, with the winner receiving the approximately $1,000,000 in entrance fees contributed by the underworld contestants.

By surreptitiously rigging the special event so that one of his own henchmen is certain to win it, Drew hopes to garner the accumulated entrance fees for himself while destroying Batman at the same time. However, in spite of the fact that Batman has indeed infiltrated the Olympics as Drew had anticipated he would — and in spite of the fact that he is ultimately exposed — Batman still manages, with ROBIN's help, to apprehend Drew and his underworld cohorts (BM No. 82/3, Mar '54: "The Olympic Games of Crime!").

DREXEL, TOM. An alias employed by BATMAN in April–May 1952 when he poses as a criminal in order to gain entrance to the infamous crime ACADEMY (BM No. 70/2: "The Masterminds of Crime!").

DRISCOLL, PETER (Dr.). A "famed research scientist" who loses his memory following an accidental blow on the head and, as a result, forgets where in the city he has dropped a package containing deadly disease germs which will imperil the entire metropolis if the package is inadvertently opened. After employing an elaborate ruse to jar Dr. Driscoll out of his amnesia, BATMAN and ROBIN safely recover the sealed package in March 1955 (BM No. 90/1: "The Web of Doom!").

DRYE, DANA. A world-famous detective — in BATMAN's words, the "dean of detectives, greatest of them all" — who, on November 18, 1942, is guest of honor at a "conference of the world's greatest detectives" where, in full view of the other conferees, including Batman and ROBIN, he is suddenly shot dead by an unseen assassin. Although all the conference guests attempt to solve the bizarre murder, only Batman and Robin are able to uncover the truth, that Drye's death was not murder at all but a bizarre form of suicide. "Drye knew he was to die shortly of an incurable malady," explains Batman to Robin, "so he staged this mystery to baffle us all, hoping we'd never be able to solve it!"

Among the dead detective's papers is yet another surprise, a diary entry stating that Drye had correctly solved the mystery of Batman's identity, but resolved not to betray it for fear of doing harm to his career. Later, Batman tells the assembled detectives that he and Robin have failed to solve Drye's murder. "Since Drye kept **our** secret, **Robin,**" he explains soon afterward, "I think it only fair that we keep **his.** Let his 'murder' remain the mystery he wanted [it] to be!" (BM No. 14/1, Dec/Jan '42–'43: "The Case Batman Failed to Solve!!!").

DUNN, FELIX. The "scholarly criminal" and admirer of the legendary Black Knight who achieves infamy as the BLACK ROGUE (WF No. 62, Jan/Feb '53: "Sir Batman and the Black Knight").

DUPLICATE MAN, THE. A cunning, ingenious criminal, clad in an orange and blue costume, who has somehow devised a scientific means of transforming himself into twins and then merging the twins into one man again, so that if one twin is captured he can easily "dematerialize" like a wraith from the grasp of his captors to rejoin the body of the second twin some distance away. Determined to "steal the world's greatest inventions, and become the most powerful criminal on earth," the Duplicate Man perpetrates a series of spectacular thefts only to be finally apprehended by BATMAN, ROBIN, and SUPERMAN in December 1959 (WF No. 106: "The Duplicate Man!").

DURFEE, JIM. A contract killer who, while fleeing from BATMAN and ROBIN after an unsuccessful attempt to assassinate BRUCE WAYNE, was shot dead by a policeman who leaped to the erroneous conclusion that Durfee was fleeing from a jewel robbery. The story of Durfee's life — from his childhood obsession with guns and killing to his adult life as a hired killer — is recounted in detail in World's Finest Comics No. 34 (May/Jun '48: "Killer for Hire!").

DURGIN, HAL. A cunning scientist turned criminal who commits a series of spectacular crimes in GOTHAM CITY with the aid of an ingenious cameralike device that enables him to imprison an object, such as a truckload of furs, inside his camera merely by taking its picture so that he can transport it to his hideout, "project" it back to its full size, and loot it at his leisure.

"My invention," explains Durgin in October 1960, "is a kind of atomic-'camera!' When I keep it focused on an object, it breaks down the object's atomic structure--and three things happen in rapid succession. . . . The object turns black and white, like a photographic negative--shrinks down until it vanishes--and becomes imprisoned within my 'camera,' like a photograph!"

The Dynamic Duo's efforts to apprehend the Durgin gang are complicated by the fact that a freakish malfunctioning of Durgin's camera — caused when ROBIN jars Durgin's arm at the precise instant the villain is attempting to "photograph" BATMAN in order to imprison him inside the atomic-camera — has resulted in Batman's transformation into a living black-and-white negative of his former self — a so-called "negative-Batman" — and doomed him to become continually weaker through exposure to sunlight until eventually his strength leaves him entirely and he dies. Ultimately, however, through an elaborate ruse, Batman tricks Durgin into using the atomic-camera to restore him to normal, whereupon he and Robin swiftly apprehend the villain and his henchmen with the aid of a Batman robot (Det No. 284: "The Negative Batman!").

DURIM. The far-distant planet which is the home of the heroic Logi and the villainous HROGUTH (WF No. 124, Mar '62: "The Mystery of the Alien Super-Boy!").

DURR, JON. The Secretary of Science in the ruling Government Council headquartered in New Gotham

City in the twenty-first century A.D., and the inventor of a revolutionary, "experimental time-machine." When Rak, Jon Durr's evil assistant and twin brother, discovers that the fusion of KRYPTONITE with a fragment of the legendary hammer of Thor yields a new substance "with fantastic powers" which, accumulated in sufficient quantities, would enable him to establish himself as dictator of the entire planet Earth, he steals Jon's time machine and travels into the past, to GOTHAM CITY in the year 1963 and then to ancient Norseland in the year 522 A.D., to obtain the kryptonite he needs and to steal the fabled hammer belonging to the Norse tribal chieftain Thor. For a time, Rak's scheme succeeds, but he and his henchmen are ultimately defeated and apprehended through the heroic efforts of BATMAN, ROBIN, and SUPERMAN (WF No. 135, Aug '63: "The Menace of the Future Man!").

DYKE, GEORGE "BOSS." A cunning and vicious criminal, executed in the gas chamber in February–March 1953, who has arranged beforehand to have his body claimed by his henchmen and transported to the laboratory of Doc Willard, a brilliant surgeon expelled from his profession for malpractice, who promptly transfers Dyke's brain into the body of "the world's largest gorilla," which has been captured in the Congo and transported to GOTHAM CITY for the bizarre operation.

Animated by Dyke's malevolent brain, the gorilla launches a brutal crime wave in Gotham City, ultimately amassing $1,000,000 in stolen loot. Then, as the crime rampage nears its climax, the gorilla captures BATMAN and carries him to Doc Willard's laboratory, intending to have Willard transfer Batman's brain into the body of the gorilla and Dyke's brain into the body of Batman. Batman, however, secures his freedom, escapes the operation, and apprehends all of Dyke's henchmen. The giant gorilla, which still contains Dyke's brain, dies after plummeting from the top of a tall building while being pursued by ROBIN, and a hair-raising experience with the gorilla drives Doc Willard hopelessly insane, so that he will remain forever incapable of recalling the techniques that made the original brain transplant possible (BM No. 75/3: "The Gorilla Boss of Gotham City!").

DYNAMIC DUO, THE. An alternate name for the crime-fighting team of BATMAN and ROBIN.

E

EAGLE, THE. A name assumed by ALFRED in October 1959 after a freak accident in the trophy room of the BATCAVE has temporarily endowed him with "amazing strength," invulnerability, and the ability to "leap hundreds of feet" into the air. The Eagle's super-powers fade suddenly during a battle with the JOKER, but BATMAN and ROBIN soon apprehend the Joker and Alfred emerges from the experience unharmed (BM No. 127/1: "Batman's Super-Partner").

EKHART (Dr.). The "famous plastic surgeon" who performs plastic surgery on Harvey Kent in order to restore the handsome appearance that Kent enjoyed prior to his emergence as TWO-FACE (Det No. 80, Oct '43: "The End of Two-Face!").

In August 1942, when a vial of acid hurled by gangster "Boss" Moroni leaves the left side of Harvey Kent's face hideously scarred, it is said that only the skilled hands of Dr. Ekhart might be capable of undoing the damage. Yet Ekhart had gone to Germany to visit his brother sometime prior to the onset of World War II, and by August 1942 had been incarcerated in a German concentration camp (Det No. 66: "The Crimes of Two-Face!").

By October 1943, however, Dr. Ekhart has escaped from Germany and returned to the United States, and two months later he performs the ingenious plastic surgical operation that ends the grotesque career of Two-Face — at least for the time being (Det No. 80: "The End of Two-Face!").

In February 1954, however, an accidental explosion destroys Dr. Ekhart's carefully wrought plastic surgery, and Kent returns to crime as Two-Face. "This **proves** I was **meant** to be a criminal!" cries Kent bitterly. "Fate has decreed it! My doctor warned me against any future accidents--said plastic surgery couldn't be performed a second time! I'm doomed to look this way for the rest of my life!" (BM No. 81/1: "Two-Face Strikes Again!").

ELEMENTAL MAN, THE. A fearsome criminal who commits a series of spectacular crimes before he is finally apprehended by BATMAN in August 1961. He is in reality John Dolan, a man who, while assisting a GOTHAM CITY scientist in the construction of a machine designed to "alter the molecular structure of elements," became exposed to a prolonged energy-leak from the machine's power source, which drove him "criminally insane" and endowed him with the awesome power to control the molecular structure of his own body so long as he wears a special control-belt. Batman has described the Elemental Man as "the most dangerous, most bizarre villain we've ever fought!"

The Dynamic Duo's efforts to defeat the Elemental Man and drain him of his elemental powers with a special new machine receive a severe setback when the accidental explosion of the new machine afflicts Batman with a "mild dose of the same affliction as Dolan's" and causes his body to become continually and uncontrollably transformed from one basic element to another. Ultimately, however, after a new, improved power-draining machine has been constructed, Batman lures the Elemental Man into a trap, drains every last vestige of elemental energy from both the villain's body and his own, and apprehends the Elemental Man's two gangland accomplices (Det No. 294: "The Villain of 100 Elements!").

ELGIN, SLIPPERY JIM. An underworld disguise artist, known as the "man of 1000 faces," who is forced to avoid all metal as the result of an accidental explosion at the Baxter Experimental Laboratory which lodged a sliver of magnetic metal deep inside his head, so close to his brain that a movement by the sliver of as little as one-half inch will prove instantly fatal. Elgin is killed in September 1950 when, in a desperate attempt to escape from BATMAN and ROBIN, he grabs an opera hat from a passerby in an effort to meld into the ranks of a passing parade, not realizing that the hat contains a metal spring to make it collapsible (Det No. 163: "The Man Who Feared Metal!").

ELLISON, THOMAS (Dr.). An American scientist and astronomer — once a close friend and neighbor of BRUCE WAYNE's father, DR. THOMAS WAYNE — who, according to World's Finest Comics No. 146, studied the planet KRYPTON for years prior to its destruction by means of a revolutionary "monitor-type telescope" of his own invention, an optical device of such "unprecedented power" that it enabled him to observe events on the far-off planet as though they were happening merely a few feet away.

As time passed, Ellison studied Krypton's culture, mastered its language, and began to wile away the hours at home by showing the infant Bruce Wayne, with whom he often baby-sat, photographs of Krypton and initiating him into the wonders of Kryptonian lore. When Ellison learned that Krypton faced imminent extinction due to an atomic reaction building up within the core of the planet, he beamed an "atomic-neutralizing ray" of his own invention at the distant world in hopes of neutralizing the atomic reaction and thereby averting the cataclysm, but when Krypton exploded anyway, in spite of his efforts, Ellison was beset by unbearable guilt, believing, erroneously, that his ray had somehow been responsible for stimulating Krypton's atomic disturbance "to the critical point," thereby causing the death of the planet.

In December 1964, however, when SUPERMAN uses a special "time-space viewer" from his FORTRESS OF

SOLITUDE — a device which "picks up light and sound waves from the past" and thus enables one to view selected historical events — to re-create the end of Krypton, Ellison learns that his valiant effort to save Krypton merely came too late, and that he played no part whatever in bringing about the planet's destruction ("Batman, Son of Krypton!" pts. I–II — no title; "The Destroyer of Krypton!").

ELONGATED MAN, THE. A costumed crime-fighter and adventurer who possesses the extraordinary ability to stretch his body "almost indefinitely," as though it were an endlessly stretchable elastic band. The Elongated Man, whose real name is Ralph Dibny, is the husband of Sue Dibny, formerly Sue Dearbon. The texts refer to him as the Ductile Detective and as the Stretching Sleuth.

Years ago, when he was only nine years old, Ralph Dibny spent a day at a traveling sideshow. He became fascinated by the India rubber man and made it his life's ambition to master the secret of stretching his body like the man in the sideshow. As he grew older, Dibny traveled throughout the country, interviewing India rubber men in sideshows everywhere, but none would reveal the secret behind their incredible powers.

Dibny noticed, however, that all India rubber men drank a variety of soft drink called Gingold, and he resolved to make a thorough study of its properties. Learning that the principal ingredient of the Gingold drink was "the juice of a little-known tropical fruit," Dibny isolated the "essence of that fruit" and drank it. To his amazement, he found that the Gingold fruit essence, combined with "an exertion of will power," enabled him to elongate his body almost indefinitely. Dibny designed a special costume for himself out of a material similar to stretch nylon, but a great deal stronger and more elastic, assumed the name the Elongated Man, and "vowed I would only use my ability in emergencies or to help people!" (F No. 112, Apr/May '60: "The Mystery of the Elongated Man!").

In September 1964 the Elongated Man helps BATMAN and ROBIN apprehend the "Boss" BARROW gang (Det No. 331: "Museum of Mixed-Up Men!").

In September 1965 the Elongated Man helps Batman and Robin capture a gang of Nazis led by the "brilliant but evil" GENERAL VON DORT (Det No. 343: "The Secret War of the Phantom General").

In December 1965 the Elongated Man helps Batman and Robin perpetrate an elaborate ruse that results ultimately in the capture of the Ed "Numbers" Garvey gang and the recovery of the stolen Kimber Gem Collection (BM No. 176/1: "Two Batmen Too Many!").

The further exploits of the Elongated Man have been extensively chronicled in a comic-book literature separate and distinct from that of Batman and Robin; these adventures are not treated in this volume.

ERGON. The far-distant planet which is the home of the "space pirate" KRAAK (BM No. 128/1, Dec '59: "The Interplanetary Batman!").

ERICKSON, OLAF. A tenth-century A.D. Viking who is a perfect look-alike for Bruce Wayne, the man who is secretly BATMAN. Sent into the past by PROFESSOR CARTER NICHOLS, Batman and ROBIN rescue Erickson from imprisonment in far-off Byzantium; accompany him on an expedition to Vinland (the continent of North America) to rescue a contingent of Vikings, led by Erickson's cousin, who have established a fort there only to find themselves under attack by hostile Indians; and help Erickson regain his self-confidence and overcome his undeserved reputation as a coward (BM No. 52/2, Apr/May '49: "Batman and the Vikings!").

ERKHAM. The chief engineer at the Comet spacecraft company in twenty-first-century GOTHAM CITY. While visiting the world of the twenty-first century A.D., BATMAN and ROBIN expose Erkham as an industrial saboteur who has been hired by the owners of the competing Meteor spacecraft company to sabotage Comet ships before they leave the assembly plant (BM No. 59/3, Jun/Jul '50: "Batman in the Future!").

EROBT. The leader of a gang of criminals who pose as spies from Saturn as part of an elaborate scheme to extort one hundred tons of gold from the U.S. Government by threatening a Saturnian invasion if the authorities fail to comply. BATMAN and ROBIN apprehend Erobt and his henchmen and expose them as ordinary earthmen in February–March 1951 (BM No. 63/2: "The Case of the Flying Saucers").

EXECUTIONER, THE. A ruthless modern-day bounty hunter, clad in a hooded maroon robe with a white "E" emblazoned on his chest, who murders wanted criminals in cold blood and then turns in their bodies for the proffered rewards. He is in reality Willy Hooker, a penny-arcade shooting-gallery proprietor who has created the role of the Executioner as part of an elaborate conspiracy in which, in return for half of the $2,000,000 in loot once stolen by convict Big Cal Davis but never recovered, Hooker has agreed to engineer Davis's escape from prison and then fake his death at the hands of the Executioner so that the authorities will think him dead and abandon their search for him.

After uncovering the Executioner's true identity and learning of the impending prison break, BATMAN disguises himself as Big Cal Davis, takes Davis's place in prison, and then follows the escape instructions that have been smuggled in to him from the outside. The plot is complicated even further, however, when the Executioner discovers a map to Davis's hidden loot among Davis's personal possessions and decides to shoot Davis with real bullets and keep the entire $2,000,000 for himself, instead of shooting him with blanks and splitting the loot as agreed. Fortunately, Batman is alerted to the impending double cross in time to escape death by donning a bulletproof vest, and the Executioner is apprehended soon afterward by members of the Gotham City Police Department (Det No. 191, Jan '53: "The Man with a License to Kill!").

F

FABIAN, FRANK. A professional artist's model, distinguished by his singularly noble, honest face, who brutally murders "famed artist" Carl Marlin in June–July 1949 in order to steal a portrait for which he sat that Marlin refused to sell him. "You . . . you may deceive the world with your harmless face," gasps the dying artist, "but your portrait will show your real self . . . your evil soul!"

Watching in helpless horror from a place of concealment, Marlin's wife resolves to frighten Fabian into confessing her husband's murder by sneaking periodically into Fabian's home and, in fulfillment of her husband's prophecy, gradually altering Fabian's stolen portrait to reflect his evil character. The handsome Fabian, meanwhile, has abandoned his model's profession for a career in crime, employing the alias the Dapper Bandit.

Indeed, as the days pass and Fabian's crimes continue unabated, "more lines of evil sear the portrait's hideous face – depicting greed, hypocricy [sic], violence!" Although Mrs. Marlin's surreptitious tampering with the portrait does not, in and of itself, frighten Fabian into making a confession, it does sufficiently rattle him so that when BATMAN takes the additional step of restoring the painting to its original, handsome state while Fabian is unconscious – and of using makeup to transform Fabian's real face into the image of hideous evil into which Mrs. Marlin had transformed the painting – Fabian, upon regaining consciousness, becomes so terror-stricken by what he sees in the mirror that he blurts out a full confession of his crimes, whereupon Batman and ROBIN promptly apprehend him (BM No. 53/2: "The Portrait of Doom!").

FALSE FACE. "A versatile disguise expert" who impersonates wealthy and prominent people to facilitate the commission of a series of spectacular crimes. At one point, for example, he poses as eccentric uranium millionaire P. S. Smithington, purchases some valuable jewelry ostensibly on credit, and then absconds with his loot before anyone realizes that the jewelry has been given to an impostor. False Face and his henchmen are apprehended by BATMAN in February 1958 (BM No. 113/1: "The Menace of False Face").

FANG, THE. A buck-toothed, bespectacled gang chief, described by BATMAN as "a serious believer in the supernatural," whose most prized possession is a "Chinese lucky sword," a sort of "super-rabbit's foot," which he scrupulously carries with him on each of his gang's many robberies. According to the Fang, the lucky sword "was forged 1,000 years ago in the ancient East--and brings luck and success to whoever uses it!" In November–December 1954, after the Fang has been forced to abandon his sword at the scene of a robbery, Batman, ROBIN, and SUPERMAN attempt to use the sword as bait in an elaborate scheme to lure the villain into a trap. The scheme goes somewhat awry when the Fang makes Batman and Robin his prisoners, but Superman ultimately appears on the scene, captures the Fang and his cohorts, and rescues the Dynamic Duo from their clutches (WF No. 73: "Batman and Superman, Swamis, Inc!").

FANGAN. An English sorcerer of the twelfth century A.D. who once set a trap for a knight he hated consisting of a flagon of mystic potion, hidden inside a cave, whose fumes were designed to hypnotize anyone entering into becoming obsessed with the desire to fulfill three commands – to fight a dragon, to dress as a jester and obey the commands of the townspeople for an hour, and to do battle with the most powerful man on Earth – which one way or another, Fangan reasoned, were likely to end in his victim's death. Fangan died and the knight never blundered into his trap, but 800 years later, while attending a police convention in England, BATMAN enters the cave alone and becomes obsessed with the desire to fulfill Fangan's three commands. To enable Batman to carry out the sorcerer's directives without coming to any harm, SUPERMAN exposes him to a ray-machine in his FORTRESS OF SOLITUDE designed to give a man super-powers for twenty-four hours, then brings him a dragonlike beast to fight from outer space, watches over him during the "jester" period to ensure that criminals will not profit from Batman's compulsion to carry out people's commands, and then lets Batman defeat him, the strongest man on Earth, so that, Fangan's commands finally fulfilled, Batman can recover unharmed from the sorcerer's curse (WF No. 109, May '60: "The Bewitched Batman!").

FARNUM, LEW. An escaped convict who masterminds an elaborate scheme to trick criminals into believing that his physician accomplice has discovered a technique for changing both faces and fingerprints through plastic surgery, rendering police identification impossible. Actually, fingerprints cannot be altered through plastic surgery, but Farnum hopes to collect a fortune in surgical fees from his underworld clientele and then murder his customers before they discover that the surgery they have received is worthless. Farnum and his cohorts are apprehended by BATMAN and ROBIN in March 1954 (BM No. 82/2: "The Man Who Could Change Fingerprints!").

FARR, GLENN. "A greedy, unscrupulous black marketeer," – "one of the richest men in the world" after ten years of dealing on the black market – who retires to his lonely castle estate in the hills north of GOTHAM CITY, determined to devote his great wealth to acquiring the great "art treasures of the world" to transform his bare, empty castle into "one of the nation's showplaces!" Enraged upon learning that many of the fabulous *objets d'art* he covets are unavailable to him at any price — because their owners refuse to part with them or because they have been promised to museums — Farr returns again to the world of crime, vowing to use his vast fortune to "accomplish feats no other criminal before me could accomplish" — as when he purchases an entire town and installs his own henchmen as the new municipal government as part of a scheme to hijack a priceless jade collection — in order to acquire through theft the great objects of art he has been unable to purchase. Farr and his henchmen are apprehended by BATMAN and ROBIN in September–October 1952 (WF No. 60: "The Richest Crook in the World!"). (*See* WHEELER, SLIM.)

FARRELL, SPARKS. The leader of a gang of criminals who are hired by the unscrupulous Baron Ferric, a Valonian nobleman, to kidnap Valonia's PRINCE STEFAN during his visit to the United States so that the baron can seize power in his home country by proclaiming himself regent. BATMAN and ROBIN foil the vicious kidnap plot in January–February 1947 and, with the aid of the young prince, apprehend the Sparks Farrell mob and arrest the evil Baron Ferric (WF No. 26: "His Highness, Prince Robin!").

FAT FRANK. The leader of a gang of criminals who, having come unexpectedly into possession of a billboard advertising business, hit upon the ingenious idea of using their billboards for blackmail by threatening to use them to publicize damaging or embarrassing information about their victims unless the victims agree to pay them large sums of money, ostensibly for billboard advertising space but in reality to ensure that the scurrilous "advertisements" will not be posted. Moreover, since all that is theoretically involved is a transaction involving the sale of billboard space, the Gotham City Police Department finds itself powerless to intervene.

"We can't let that blackmail gang flourish, Bruce," complains DICK GRAYSON to Bruce Wayne, the man who is secretly BATMAN. "Maybe the law's hands are tied, but what about us?"

"Until the law can act, Dick," replies Wayne grimly, "we're going to smash those billboards whenever Fat Frank puts a blackmail ad up!"

After Batman and ROBIN have destroyed some of the damaging billboard signs, Fat Frank attempts to have them arrested for destroying his private property, but the police pointedly ignore Fat Frank's complaint and refuse to make the appropriate arrests.

Eventually, although Fat Frank and his henchmen are, according to the text, guilty of no real crime, Batman and Robin arouse the citizens of GOTHAM CITY against them by posting their pictures and past criminal records on a huge billboard, and then swiftly escort the criminals to the city limits before an angry mob of citizens can seize them and lynch them (Det No. 104, Oct '45: "The Battle of the Billboards!").

FATMAN. A fat, jolly circus clown who, clad in a BATMAN costume, performs a circus routine in which he spoofs Batman (BM No. 113/2, Feb '58: "Batman Meets Fatman").

FELINA. The CAT-MAN's pet black panther (Det No. 311, Jan '63: "The Challenge of the Cat-Man!").

FELIX (Count). The leader of a Nazi spy ring — described as "the most dangerous band of spies and saboteurs thus far discovered in America" — whose goal is the "systematic sabotage of America's war effort!" Count Felix and his cohorts, including the young spy FRITZ HOFFNER, are captured by BATMAN and ROBIN in December 1942–January 1943 (BM No. 14/3: "Swastika over the White House!").

FERRIS, IRON-HAT. A GOTHAM CITY criminal who has an iron mask welded tightly over his head by vindictive gangsters as punishment for his having informed on underworld activities to the Gotham City police. In February–March 1947, however, while Ferris is still imprisoned in the iron mask, Henry Kendall, an unscrupulous aspirant to the office of district attorney, kidnaps Ferris, imprisons him in his basement, and then proceeds to commit a series of brazen robberies while clad in Ferris's iron mask, all as part of an elaborate scheme to castigate the incumbent D.A. for his failure to apprehend the notorious "Ferris," whom police and public alike hold responsible for Kendall's wave of crimes.

To climax his evil scheme, Kendall plans to murder the captive Ferris and then claim that he succeeded in stopping Ferris where the incumbent D.A. failed, but BATMAN and ROBIN rescue Ferris in the nick of time and Kendall dies when, still wearing the iron mask, he races outside in a desperate bid for escape and is electrocuted by a bolt of lightning striking his iron mask (BM No. 39/2: "The Man in the Iron Mask!").

FERRIS, PAUL. An alias employed by the villainous Clayface (see CLAYFACE [MATT HAGEN]) in February 1963 when he rents a mansion in GOTHAM CITY (Det No. 312: "The Secret of Clayface's Power!").

FIFTH COLUMNIST. "Worst of all menaces--worst of all criminals is the **fifth columnist!** Treacherous, dangerous as a snake, he burgles the secrets of a peace-loving people in an attempt to smash American democracy!" (Det No. 55, Sep '41: "The 'Brain Burglar!'").

FINGERS, SLICK. The criminal responsible for burglarizing various safes originally manufactured by the Titus Keyes Safe Company and then framing company owner Titus Keyes for the burglaries. Fingers's real name is George Collins, but it is as Slick Fingers that he is best known. When testimony at Titus Keyes's trial pinpoints Fingers as the real culprit, Fingers attempts to flee the courtroom, only to be apprehended by BATMAN (BM No. 20/2, Dec/Jan '43–'44: "The Trial of Titus Keyes!").

FINNEY, NAILS (1946). The leader of a gang of radium thieves, called "Nails" because of his habit of continually biting his fingernails. Among Finney's accomplices are Dr. James Martin, a tree surgeon who hollowed out a giant cavity in a huge oak tree on the estate of wealthy Francis Van Orsdell in order to prevent the tree from dying, then camouflaged the hollow area with a zinc cover — instead of filling it with the customary cement — so that the Finney gang could use the cavity as a hiding place for their stolen loot. After committing a series of daring radium thefts in May–June 1946,

Finney and his cohorts return to the oak tree to recover their loot, only to be confronted there by BATMAN and ROBIN. In the ensuing battle, two of Finney's henchmen are knocked unconscious and taken into custody, but Finney and Martin are crushed to death when the giant oak tree, weakened by its unfilled cavity and struck suddenly by lightning, topples over on them before they can leap out of its path (WF No. 22: "A Tree Grows in Gotham City!").

FINNEY, NAILS (1962). A GOTHAM CITY gang chief who, having hired a "renegade scientist" named Garth to help him wreak vengeance on BATMAN, lures Batman into a trap and uses one of Garth's inventions – a machine designed to "reverse growth" – to transform Batman into a baby.

"Other gangsters tried to **kill Batman,**" gloats Finney to his henchmen, "--but, with Garth's help, I stopped him in a better way!"

"Instead of making a dead **Batman** into a martyr," adds Garth, "--we've made a **live Batman** into a **laughing stock**. . . ."

Although Batman now requires a new costume to accommodate his greatly reduced size, his mental processes and physical strength remain those of an adult, and he continues to fight crime as Bat-Baby with remarkable success. Ultimately, during a showdown battle at Finney's hideout, Batman restores himself to normal size by reversing Garth's ray-machine, and then, with ROBIN's help, apprehends Garth, the entire Finney gang, and an underworld fence named Swap Smith who has come to the hideout to do business with them (BM No. 147/3, May '62: "Batman Becomes Bat-Baby!").

FIREFLY, THE (Ted Carson). A costumed criminal who is apprehended in September 1959 through the heroic efforts of BATMAN, ROBIN, and BATWOMAN. The Firefly is secretly Ted Carson, a debt-ridden but ostensibly wealthy gold-mine heir who has turned to crime in an effort to accumulate the money he needs to pay his sizable gambling debts (BM No. 126/3: "The Menace of the Firefly!").

FIREFLY, THE (Garfield Lynns). A costumed criminal who uses his extensive knowledge of light to commit spectacular crimes. He is in reality Garfield Lynns, a theatrical "lighting-effects genius" turned criminal whose knowledge of light is the product of years of "secret lighting experiments" conducted in a hidden cave on the outskirts of GOTHAM CITY.

By June 1952 the lighting technician at the Gotham Theater has decided to embark upon a life of crime. "I am ***merely*** Garfield Lynns, world's foremost lighting-effects genius!" muses the technician bitterly, as yet another audience files into the theater for a performance of the new hit musical *Aqua-Melodies of 1952*. "Yes, I exist on a meager salary while those idiots in the audience come here in their limousines, their fur coats--flashing rare gems!"

In the midst of the performance, Lynns uses his incredible skill with theatrical lighting to create the illusion of a huge fire on stage. While the audience mills about in a state of near-panic, Lynns's henchmen, disguised as ushers, move through the theater helping themselves to the spectators' wallets and jewelry. Unbeknownst to Lynns, however, BATMAN and ROBIN are in the audience in their Bruce Wayne and Dick Grayson identities, and, after changing into their crime-fighting costumes and successfully calming the panicky crowd, they leap into the BATMOBILE and race off into the night in pursuit of the escaping Lynns.

When Lynns's car crashes near the riverfront, it seems virtually certain that Lynns will be apprehended, but Lynns is saved when a tiny firefly – which Batman and Robin assume must be Lynns's cigarette, glowing in the darkness – lures the Dynamic Duo off Lynns's trail long enough for him to reach the river and make good his escape.

"Ha!" laughs Lynns. "So a simple little ***firefly*** saved me! . . . Ha, ha! A real twist of fate! Perhaps that's my lucky symbol . . . ***the firefly!*** For centuries that little fellow has baffled science! Like me, it is a ***lighting*** genius! And now--it saved my life! Ha! What an inspiration it has given me! Garfield Lynns is gone--forever! But in his place is one they shall ***never*** forget! . . . One whom they shall know as ***the Firefly!***"

For his new life of crime, Lynns designs a colorful costume modeled after the tiny insect which provided him with his inspiration. Around his waist he wears a complex "light belt capable of producing varied and amazing lighting effects." In the days that follow, the Firefly and his henchmen commit a series of staggering crimes, each aided and abetted by the Firefly's extraordinary knowledge of light and its effects. At one point, the Firefly captures Batman and Robin and locks them in the cellar of a lighthouse with a diabolical "cyclops light," a powerful lighting device whose "blinding colors" are certain either to kill the Dynamic Duo or drive them "raving mad" within three days, but Batman and Robin escape from the lighthouse and apprehend the Firefly and his henchmen soon afterward (Det No. 184: "The Human Firefly!").

FLAGG, TIM. The bespectacled escaped convict who achieves infamy as HYDRO (BM No. 74/3, Dec/Jan '52–'53: "The Water Crimes of Mr. Hydro!").

FLAMEBIRD. An alternate identity employed by JIMMY OLSEN on those occasions when he and SUPERMAN, employing the name NIGHTWING, participate in adventures together inside the bottle city of KANDOR. The bright red and yellow colors of Jimmy's Flamebird costume are reminiscent of the brilliant plumage of the flamebird, a Kandorian bird.

FLEMING, "BULL." The leader of a gang of criminals who are apprehended by BATMAN and ROBIN in April 1965. Batman's crime-fighting efforts are somewhat hampered during this period by the fact that a freak chemical accident has temporarily transformed his fists into super-powered "lethal weapons," thus forcing Batman to employ extreme caution to assure his apprehending his adversaries without accidentally killing them (Det No. 338: "Batman's Power-Packed Punch!").

FLINT, JOE. A GOTHAM CITY private detective, secretly the mastermind behind a counterfeiting scheme, who contrives to join the BULLET-HOLE CLUB by having one of his own henchmen shoot and wound him in the leg as part of a scheme to murder F.B.I. agent Terry Collins, a member of the club, who is on the trail of the counterfeiters but does not yet know that Flint is their secret leader. Thwarted and finally cornered by BATMAN and ROBIN, Flint attempts a suicidal leap out an open window when "his mind suddenly snaps" under the strain of exposure, but Batman takes him into custody. Flint will be incarcerated in a mental institution (WF No. 50, Feb/Mar '51: "Bullet-Hole Club!").

FLORIAN (Count). A cunning "international spy" – characterized by a European-style monocle, a neatly trimmed goatee, and an ever-present cigarette holder – who is the leader of a vast underworld spy network specializing in the use of international spy techniques to further the cause of crime. Because many of the count's agents brazenly display their "contempt for the law" by wearing special stickers, in the form of a third eye, pasted to the center of their foreheads, the count has become known as "the man with a thousand eyes," a villain whose stark symbol is an all-seeing "'eye' that [sees] into a thousand secrets!" ROBIN has described Count Florian as "the man without a country," and BATMAN has observed darkly that "For money, he'd sell his services to anyone!"

By December 1949–January 1950 Count Florian has placed his vast spy network at the disposal of the underworld, offering its members secret instruction in espionage techniques and providing the use of his agents, for a price, to criminals requiring specialized help in the commission of crimes. Batman ultimately locates Count Florian by posing as one of the count's former pupils, and before long he and Robin have apprehended Count Florian and all of the members of his underworld spy organization (WF No. 43: "The Man with a Thousand Eyes!").

FLOWER GANG, THE. A gang of criminals whose members use flowers to aid them in their crimes, as when they melt their way through the glass front door of the Morrow Art Gallery by placing a dittany (fraxinella) plant – a Eurasian perennial herb (*Dictamnus albus*) of the family *Rutaceae* whose flowers exude "a highly volatile gas that ignites easily and burns with a hot flame" – in front of the door and setting it afire. All three members of the Flower Gang are single-handedly apprehended by ROBIN in June 1965 (BM No. 172/2: "Robin's Unassisted Triple Play!").

FLYING GRAYSONS, THE. A troupe of circus trapeze performers, formerly employed by the Haly Circus, which consisted of John and Mary Grayson and their young son Dick. The career of the Flying Graysons came to a tragic end in April 1940 when, in retaliation for the circus owner's steadfast refusal to pay protection money to "Boss" ZUCCO and his gang of racketeers, the racketeers weakened the Graysons' trapeze ropes with acid, sending John and Mary Grayson hurtling to their doom and making an orphan of their young son Dick. The tragic incident led directly to the emergence of Dick Grayson as ROBIN, THE BOY WONDER (Det No. 38). (*See* ROBIN.)

FOLLAND, FRANK. A brilliant young engineer who, in November–December 1946, organizes a series of so-called "famous firsts" exhibitions – in which he reenacts famous vehicular events, such as the first balloon ascension, and displays models of famous vehicles, such as the first submarine and the first steamboat – in hopes of attracting publicity and financial backing for his new invention, the "aeraquamobile," a carlike vehicle capable of traveling in the air, on land, and in the water. When the unscrupulous George Sellman, Folland's "estranged former partner," hires a gang of thugs to sabotage the various exhibitions, murder Folland, and make off with the aeraquamobile, BATMAN and ROBIN apprehend them all. Folland soon receives backing for his invention from a prestigious manufacturing firm (WF No. 25: "The Famous First Crimes!").

FORBES, FREDDY. A well-known television comedian, stage name the Joker, who inhabits the extradimensional parallel world visited by BATMAN in September 1963. Dressed in his stage makeup, Forbes is a perfect look-alike for Batman's infamous foe, the JOKER (WF No. 136: "The Batman Nobody Remembered!").

FORROW, DWIGHT. The man who is secretly the WRECKER (Det No. 197, Jul '53: "The League Against Batman!").

FORTRESS OF SOLITUDE, THE. The impenetrable secret sanctuary, carved out of a mountainside amid the barren Arctic wastes, which serves both as a retreat and a headquarters for SUPERMAN. Superman maintains a laboratory there, along with his robots, personal mementos, and an array of specialized equipment. The bottle city of KANDOR has been placed there for safekeeping. (For a complete description of the Fortress of Solitude, including its uses, history, and equipment, consult *The Encyclopedia of Comic Book Heroes: Volume VI – Superman.*)

FORTY THIEVES, THE. A band of robbers appearing in the story "Ali Baba and the Forty Thieves," one of the tales of the *Arabian Nights.* BATMAN, ROBIN, and SUPERMAN apprehend the Forty Thieves during a time-journey to tenth-century Baghdad (WF No. 79, Nov/Dec '55: "The Three Magicians of Bagdad!"). (*See* ABDULLAH.)

FOSTER, ALBERT. An alias employed by the CAVALIER in December 1944–January 1945 when he disguises his face with makeup in order to conceal his true features from the gangsters whom he recruits to serve him (BM No. 26/1: "Twenty Ton Robbery!").

FOSTER, "BIG JOE." The leader of a gang of criminals, who, having learned that BATMAN's very life depends upon his locating an eccentric scientist named Professor Blake, kidnaps the professor in an attempt to hold him captive until Batman is beyond help.

In June 1959, while Batman is testing an experimental jet aircraft for the Eagle Aircraft Co., a falling comet crosses its path and "bathes the jet in its eerie yellow radiance." Upon landing, Batman discovers that he has somehow acquired superhuman strength and that his body has begun to radiate a strange yellow glow, like the glow of the comet's tail through which he has just passed.

"We have bad news, ***Batman!***" explains a company scientist soon afterward. "Our tests show that the day that the glow dies, ***you*** die--and I'm afraid it will happen within a week! You're like a normal star that suddenly becomes a ***nova***--flaring in a temporary burst of energy--and then burns out and dies! When your glowing super-strength fades, your life will fade, too!"

Batman's only hope for survival lies in locating Professor Blake, an eccentric scientist whose research on gases would enable him to cure Batman if only he could be contacted in time. Unfortunately, Blake often goes into hiding for weeks while he works on his experiments, and locating him will not be an easy matter.

In the days that follow, Batman uses his newly acquired super-strength to fight crime and otherwise aid the citizens of GOTHAM CITY while Eagle Aircraft officials press a relentless search for Professor Blake. The search is complicated, however, by gang chief "Big Joe" Foster, who, upon learning that only Professor Blake stands between Batman and certain death, kidnaps Blake in an attempt to hold him captive until Batman is beyond all help. Through a ruse, however, Batman manages to uncover Blake's whereabouts and apprehend his abductors in time to receive the life-giving serum that will restore him to normal (Det No. 268: "The Power That Doomed Batman!").

FOSTER, FRANK "WHEELS." The proprietor of a restaurant, secretly a front for an illegal gambling den, who is sent to prison by BATMAN and ROBIN, only to escape soon afterward when a laundry truck careens wildly out of control in the prison yard as the result of a blowout and smashes down the prison gate. "A wheel was responsible for freeing me," thinks Foster exultantly, "so it must be an omen of my future! I'll organize a gang and use wheels for crimes!" Foster adopts a colorful yellow and orange costume with wheel insignia emblazoned on his chest and cape, recruits a gang of underworld followers, and launches a wave of spectacular "wheel crimes" characterized by the use of wheels to facilitate both the crimes themselves and the subsequent escapes. Despite a series of initial reverses, Batman and Robin finally apprehend Foster and his henchmen in October 1960 (BM No. 135/1: "Crimes of the Wheel").

FOSTER, JOHN. A ruthless criminal who, having discovered that he is a perfect look-alike for noted architect George C. Hudson, murders Hudson, takes over his architectural practice, and then adds secret roof panels to the blueprints for homes which Hudson had designed for his wealthy clients so that at a later date he will be able to sneak into them and rob them. BATMAN discovers that architect "Hudson" is an impostor, however, and ultimately tricks him into confessing the architect's murder (BM No. 54/3, Aug/Sep '49: "The Amazing Masquerade!").

FOX, THE. A member – along with the Shark and the Vulture – of the TERRIBLE TRIO.

FRALEY, WALTER. A cunning criminal who, with the aid of an unnamed accomplice, hijacks a gold shipment, melts the stolen gold into antique-looking gold bars, and then attempts to escape prosecution by claiming that the gold is actually a hitherto unrecovered treasure buried more than 200 years ago by the infamous highwayman CAPTAIN LIGHTFOOT. Sent into the past by PROFESSOR CARTER NICHOLS, however, BATMAN and ROBIN soon learn that Captain Lightfoot was not a highwayman at all, but rather a colonial crime-fighter who fought to avert war between the colonists and Indians. Confronted with this evidence, Fraley's accomplice makes a full confession, thus ensuring that both he and Fraley will be prosecuted for the gold hijacking (BM No. 79/2, Oct/Nov '53: "The Batman of Yesterday!").

FRANK, ADAM. A "well known character about town," renowned for his fanatical desire to be "first" in everything, who becomes furious when book collector A. H. Evans refuses to sell him a valuable Shakespeare first edition and resolves to steal the book from Evans instead. "After all," muses Frank, "why not? I'll be first again! The first in my family to become a criminal!" In the days that follow, Frank recruits a gang and embarks on a series of spectacular "first" crimes, as when he and his henchmen steal the gate receipts from the premiere performance of a gala ice show. The villains are ultimately apprehended through the heroic efforts of BATMAN and ROBIN (BM No. 29/1, Jun/Jul '45: "Enemy No. 1").

FRANKENSTEIN (Baron). In the novel *Frankenstein* by Mary Wollstonecraft Shelley (1797–1851), a scientist who creates a monster out of charnel fragments and is ultimately destroyed by it. Completed in 1818, *Frankenstein* remains one of the great classic horror stories as well as the most widely known pseudoscientific novel.

In May 1948 PROFESSOR CARTER NICHOLS uses his "powers of time-hypnosis" to transport himself across the time barrier to nineteenth-century Europe in the hope of verifying the claim of an old document that the fictional Baron Frankenstein and his monster actually existed. Welcomed as a guest at Baron Frankenstein's castle, Nichols is being shown a "crude electrostatic machine" recently developed by the baron when suddenly the baron's assistant, a gentle giant named Ivan, accidentally receives a jolting electric shock that sends him slumping to the floor in a deep coma. Nichols hastily administers an adrenalin serum to revive Ivan, but the dosage is insufficient for Ivan's massive frame, and when finally Ivan rises dazedly to his feet, he is a mindless robot, powerful in body but completely lacking any will of his own.

Hoping to capitalize on Ivan's pathetic condition in order to eliminate Baron Frankenstein and inherit his estates, the baron's ruthless cousin, Count Mettern, orders Ivan to murder Baron Frankenstein, and although the baron is rescued from Ivan in the nick of time through the intervention of Professor Nichols and some of the baron's household servants, the mindless giant responds by fleeing to the nearby village and embarking on a hideous rampage of death and destruction.

Realizing that additional help is needed at once if the hulking behemoth is to be stopped, Nichols "projects his weird powers of hypnosis across the years" to the twentieth century, and by so doing transports BATMAN and ROBIN back into the past to help him. Ultimately, the Dynamic Duo subdue the giant, enabling Nichols to administer an additional dose of adrenalin sufficient to restore Ivan to full control over both his body and his mind.

But Ivan is sickened and remorseful over the senseless acts of violence he committed while under the influence of the evil Count Mettern. Seizing Count Mettern and warning all others to evacuate the castle, Ivan locks his victim and himself in the castle's chemical storeroom and then blows the castle to kingdom come.

"It wouldn't be believed!" comments the "Englishwoman writer" Mary Shelley, after Batman has told her the entire grisly story. "I'll have to write it as fiction!" (Det No. 135: "The True Story of Frankenstein!").

FRANKLIN, BENJAMIN (1706–1790). One of the founding fathers of the United States, an extraordinarily versatile and complex man who, in the course of a long and varied career, was a printer, author, publisher, scientist, inventor, and diplomat. BATMAN and ROBIN meet Benjamin Franklin during a time-journey to Philadelphia in the year 1787 (BM No. 44/3, Dec/Jan '47–'48: "The First American Detective!").

FRISBY, FLOYD. A fugitive racketeer who is finally apprehended in the jungles of South America by BATMAN, ROBIN, and SUPERMAN in August 1960, despite the complications that arise when Superman, in the midst of his hunt for Frisby, becomes afflicted with temporary amnesia after absorbing the full force of a volcanic explosion and is persuaded by local natives that he is in reality their legendary king, returned to rebuild and rule over their crumbling ancient city (WF No. 111: "Superman's Secret Kingdom!").

FROGEL, "FIVE ACES." The leader of a gang of criminals who terrorize the peaceful Western community of Sunshine City until BATMAN – summoned by the desperate townspeople and elected to the office of sheriff – arrives on the scene and, with ROBIN's help, apprehends them all (BM No. 10/4, Apr/May '42: "Sheriff of Ghost Town!").

FRYE, "FISH." A fugitive GOTHAM CITY "gang chief" who, having inadvertently intercepted a radio distress call sent out by the injured BATMAN after he has crashed alone in the BATPLANE in the mountains outside the city, blackmails reformed ex-convict Harry Larson into agreeing to impersonate Batman so that, with the real Batman helpless to intervene or expose the impersonation, he and his henchmen can loot Gotham City unimpeded. Events take a complex turn, however, when the reluctant Larson, by coincidence a perfect BRUCE WAYNE look-alike, develops amnesia as the result of a blow on the head. After being led back to the Wayne mansion by an unsuspecting ROBIN and ALFRED, he concludes that he must really be Batman and launches a serious effort to apprehend the Frye gang. Ultimately, however, Larson's memory returns, and, after intervening heroically to rescue the real Batman from death at the hands of the criminals, he falls against some high-tension wires and is accidentally electrocuted. "Fish" Frye and his cohorts are apprehended, apparently by the Gotham City police (BM No. 83/1, Apr '54: "The Duplicate Batman!").

FUNNY FACE GANG, THE. A gang of armored-car bandits, so called because of their habit of wearing funny-face masks to conceal their identities whenever they pull a robbery. Al Talley, owner of a GOTHAM CITY nightclub known as the Tally Ho Club, is their secret leader. Talley and his confederates are apprehended in June 1958 through the heroic efforts of BATMAN, ROBIN, and BATWOMAN (BM No. 116/2: "Batwoman's New Identity").

G

GAIGE (Dr.). The renowned oceanographer who is secretly TIGER SHARK (Det No. 147, May '49: "Tiger Shark!").

GANT, CHOPPER. The leader of a "notorious gang" of criminals who dupe brilliant but somewhat naïve amateur military strategist Hannibal Bonaparte Brown into helping them plan a series of complex crimes by claiming to be newspaper reporters interested in certain specialized military-strategical "problems." Gant and his henchmen are ultimately apprehended through the heroic efforts of BATMAN, ROBIN, and a sadder but wiser Brown (BM No. 21/2, Feb/Mar '44: "Blitzkrieg Bandits!").

GARR. A "notorious space raider" and self-styled "king of the interplanetary underworld" who joins forces with Earth criminal Eddie Marrow in August 1958. After a long chase across the length and breadth of PLANETOID X, Garr and Marrow are finally apprehended through the heroic efforts of BATMAN, ROBIN, and the alien lawman Tutian, Chief Inspector of the Universal Police Corps (BM No. 117/3: "Manhunt in Outer Space!").

GARRIS, JAY. The leader of a gang of criminals who steal newsreel footage of BATMAN using his batarang from Batman admirer Elmer Mason, teach themselves how to make and throw the batarang until they have become expert, and then manufacture a supply of specially designed "bomb batarangs" – batarangs fitted with explosive devices – for use in the commission of crimes.

After Elmer Mason has identified the newsreel thieves as members of the Garris gang, and Batman and ROBIN have located the gang's hideout on a deserted offshore island, Batman gains access to the island – to defuse the criminals' entire supply of bomb batarangs – by propelling himself through the air atop "batarang X," a giant batarang, capable of supporting a man, which is fired from a large catapult.

The following day, Garris and his henchmen confront Batman unaware that their supply of batarangs have been disarmed, thus enabling Batman to apprehend them easily (Det No. 244, Jun '57: "The 100 Batarangs of Batman!"). (*See* BATMAN [section E 2 d ii, the batarang].)

GARROW, RAND. The "dangerous criminal" with a "genius for mechanics and invention" who achieves his greatest infamy as the CRIMESMITH (WF No. 68, Jan/Feb '54: "The Secret Weapons of the Crimesmith!").

GARTH. A ruthless "renegade scientist" who constructs a machine designed to "reverse growth" and then uses it to transform BATMAN into a baby (BM No. 147/3, May '62: "Batman Becomes Bat-Baby!"). (*See* FINNEY, NAILS [1962].)

GARTH, JIM. A deranged arsonist, his face left hideously scarred by a fire which destroyed his home and killed his only son, whose twisted mind has led him to blame his personal tragedy on the brave volunteer firemen who attempted unsuccessfully to quell the blaze. Armed with a powerful flamethrower and clad in an asbestos suit which protects him from fire and effectively conceals his true identity, Garth – who soon becomes known and feared as the Blaze – sets out to wreak his twisted vengeance on the members of the now-defunct "suburban volunteer fire service" who fought the original fire at his home several years ago. One by one, Garth tracks them down according to the bizarre logic of a popular children's rhyme – "Rich man, poor man, beggar man, thief/doctor, lawyer, Indian chief" – and then attempts either to burn them alive with his flamethrower or set fire to their homes or offices. Finally, however, while attempting to escape from BATMAN and ROBIN, Garth accidentally ignites a cache of dynamite with his flamethrower and perishes in the ensuing explosion (BM No. 69/2, Feb/Mar '52: "The Buttons of Doom!").

GARTH, SAM. A cunning criminal who uses forged credentials identifying him as a member of the prestigious Camera Scoops Club – an exclusive GOTHAM CITY photographic society whose members "are privileged to take pictures even inside police lines" – to enable him to gain access to, and photograph, the places that he and his henchmen intend to rob at a later date. Garth and his cohorts are apprehended by BATMAN and ROBIN in March–April 1946 with the aid of the Camera Scoops Club's junior members, who help the Dynamic Duo by obtaining photographic evidence linking Garth with the robberies committed by his two accomplices (WF No. 21: "Crime's Cameraman!").

GARVER, BIG JIM. The leader of a gang of criminals who match wits with BATMAN and ROBIN in December 1954.

The Dynamic Duo's efforts to apprehend the Garver gang are greatly complicated by the fact that a recently paroled convict named Ed Wilson has foolishly chosen to conceal the real reason for his prolonged absence from home by telling his young son Tommy that he is secretly Batman, that he has been away from home fighting crime, and that he has now decided to retire permanently and allow another Batman to take his place and carry on his role as a crime-fighter. While posing in a Batman costume in an effort to make his lie more persuasive, Wilson is gunned down by gangsters and now lies perilously near death in a GOTHAM CITY hospital.

For Tommy's benefit, Batman agrees to pose as Wilson and help maintain Wilson's falsehood, at least until young Tommy can be prepared emotionally to accept the real reason for his father's prolonged absence from home. At one point, Tommy is kidnapped by the Garver gang – who believe that they have actually succeeding in kidnapping the son of Batman – but Batman ultimately apprehends the criminals and rescues young Tommy from their clutches. Ed Wilson rallies and is reunited with his son, and Tommy "understandingly accepts the truth" about his father's prison past (BM No. 88/3: "The Son of Batman!").

GARVEY, ED "NUMBERS." The leader of a gang of criminals who are apprehended by BATMAN and ROBIN in December 1965 (BM No. 176/1: "Two Batmen Too Many!").

GAUCHO, THE. A South American crime-fighter whose methods and techniques are modeled after those of America's BATMAN.

In January 1955, in response to Batman's personal invitation, the Gaucho and other foreign lawmen – including the RANGER, the LEGIONARY, the MUSKETEER, and the KNIGHT and the SQUIRE – arrive in GOTHAM CITY to study Batman's techniques firsthand, only to find themselves embroiled in a deadly battle of wits with "underworld chieftain" "KNOTS" CARDINE (Det No. 215: "The Batmen of All Nations!").

In July–August 1957 the Gaucho visits the United States once again, this time in response to a summons from "well-known philanthropist" John Mayhew, who wishes to award the Gaucho and other world-famous crime-fighters – including Batman and ROBIN, SUPERMAN, the Musketeer, the Legionary, and the Knight and the Squire – charter membership in his newly formed Club of Heroes (WF No. 89: "The Club of Heroes!"). (*See also* BATMAN [section F, the Batman counterparts]; LIGHTNING-MAN.)

GAVIN. The leader of a group of four convicts – the others are Gee-Gee, Moore, and Dalton – who break out of the Gotham State Prison in September 1958, only to become contaminated by deadly radiation when, in the course of their escape, Gavin conceals himself inside a large container recently used by a government atomic plant to transport "radio-active specimens." Confronted with the dual problem of capturing the escapees before they die of radiation poisoning or contaminate others, BATMAN and ROBIN pursue their quarry to Police Island – site of a Police World's Fair not yet open to the public – where, with the aid of the crime-fighting equipment included in the various displays and exhibits, they ultimately succeed in apprehending the criminals without ever touching them, thus avoiding the potential hazard of becoming contaminated themselves (BM No. 118/1: "The Battle of Police Island!").

The Gaucho, 1957 © NPP 1957

GELBY, BIX. A cunning criminal who concocts an elaborate scheme to extort $1,000,000 from the nation's top gangsters by tricking them into contributing mementos of their exploits and written accounts of their most spectacular unsolved crimes for ostensible inclusion in a special "crime capsule" – a time capsule similar to the capsule buried at the New York World's Fair in 1940, but devoted entirely to gangland memorabilia – and then threatening to turn the accumulated documents over to the authorities unless the contributors agree to pay him $1,000,000 to destroy the capsule and its incriminating contents. Gelby finally collects the $1,000,000 from the underworld and destroys the capsule, but BATMAN and ROBIN have successfully extracted the documents from the capsule prior to its destruction, and they swiftly apprehend Gelby and his gangland associates (WF No. 63, Mar/Apr '53: "The Crime Capsule!").

GETAWAY GENIUS, THE. *See* REYNOLDS, ROY.

GHOST GANG, THE. A gang of criminals – clad in cowboy clothes, mounted on horses, and active in the Western United States – whose name derives from their uncanny ability to rob two places 100 miles apart within the space of ten minutes. The gang's "ghostly" ability to appear in two different places almost simultaneously is made possible by a giant autogyro, kept carefully hidden from their victims, with which they transport both men and horses from one robbery site to the next. In Winter 1941 BATMAN and ROBIN expose prominent rancher Lafe Brunt as the secret leader of the Ghost Gang and provide the local sheriff with information which leads to the ultimate apprehension of all of Brunt's accomplices (WF No. 4: "The Ghost Gang Goes West!").

GIBBONS, ARCHIE. A fish wholesaler specializing in the buying and selling of soupfin sharks, a fish whose livers are highly valued because of their high vitamin A content, and the secret leader of the "phantom raiders," a gang of criminals who swoop down on homeward-bound fishing vessels, steal their catches of soupfin sharks, and then make good their escape by blimp. "Robbing honest hard-working fishermen is bad enough," exclaims BRUCE WAYNE, ". . . but this hits our government! We need vitamins to keep our soldiers healthy!" BATMAN and ROBIN apprehend the phantom raiders and expose Gibbons as their leader in June–July 1943 (BM No. 17/4: "Adventure of the Vitamin Vandals!").

GIBLING, WILLIS. The ex-convict who is secretly the ZERO (WF No. 67, Nov/Dec '53: "The Millionaire Detective!").

GIBSON. An assistant to Dr. Coombs, an Egyptologist affiliated with the Gotham Museum. Gibson is secretly the villainous JACKAL-HEAD (Det No. 262, Dec '58: "The Jackal of the Underworld!").

GILDA. The lovely brunette sculptress who is the fiancée (Det No. 66, Aug '42: "The Crimes of Two-Face!"), and later the wife (BM No. 50/2, Dec/Jan '48–'49: "The Return of Two-Face!"), of Harvey Kent, the man who achieves infamy as TWO-FACE.

GILDED CAGE BIRD SHOPPE. A bird shop which serves as the PENGUIN's base of operations during September 1942. The Gilded Cage Bird Shoppe is destroyed when, in a desperate effort to escape from BATMAN and ROBIN, the Penguin sets it ablaze with "liquid fire" sprayed from one of his many trick umbrellas (Det No. 67: "Crime's Early Bird!").

GILLEN, JOHN. A professional circus impersonator, the so-called "man with a million faces," who long ago served time in prison for an unspecified crime. In December 1950 two assistant prop men named Carey and Withers threaten to reveal Gillen's past to the circus management unless Gillen agrees to impersonate famous people in order to help them commit crimes, but BATMAN and ROBIN ultimately apprehend the blackmailers, and Gillen's employers and co-workers agree to stand by him in spite of his past (Det No. 166: "The Man with a Million Faces!").

GILLIS, BART. A Canadian highwayman, captured by BATMAN and ROBIN during a visit to Canada, who escapes from prison and attempts to kill a horse, now owned by Robin, which could link him with the murder of a Canadian Mountie named Atkins. Batman recaptures Gillis and, with the aid of a fluoroscope, discovers a bullet lodged in the horse's neck, which will incriminate Gillis in Atkins's murder (Det No. 157, Mar '50: "The Race of the Century").

GIMMICK GANG, THE. "The trickiest trio of bandits in Gotham City." The Gimmick Gang is captured by BATMAN and ROBIN in June 1958 (BM No. 116/1: "The City of Ancient Heroes").

GLASS MAN, THE. A ruthless murderer, his true identity concealed by a "strange mask of faceted glass that distorts the features beneath," who commits a series of brutal murders by sending his victims attractive glass sculptures whose razor-sharp edges have been coated with a deadly poison. The Glass Man is in reality an automobile manufacturer named Judson, the owner of Judson's Comet Cars, who has assumed the identity of the Glass Man in order to murder Horace Manders, a wealthy amateur astronomer whose decision to withdraw his financial support from Judson's automobile manufacturing enterprise would ruin Judson. In May–June 1947 the Glass Man murders Manders and two other men while attempting to focus suspicion on George Stevens, a local glass manufacturer who, in a moment of anger, had once threatened to kill Manders and the Glass Man's other victims for withdrawing their patronage from his glass-making concern. Ultimately, however, BATMAN and ROBIN apprehend the Glass Man and his henchmen and unmask the Glass Man as Judson. At the last moment, Judson makes a last, desperate bid for freedom, only to die horribly when he plummets accidentally into a fiery glass furnace (WF No. 28: "Crime Under Glass!").

GLIM, JOHNNY. An ambitious playwright who sells his play outright to a theatrical producer for a very low price, only to learn that a Hollywood movie company would have paid him a fortune for the movie rights. Because the original sales contract stipulates that all rights revert to the author of the play if it fails to remain open for two full weeks, Glim murders several of the leading players in an effort to force his play to close prematurely. He is exposed and apprehended by BATMAN and ROBIN in December 1941–January 1942 (BM No. 8/3: "The Superstition Murders!").

GLOBETROTTER, THE. An "infamous fugitive" who has committed crimes throughout the world. In December 1947–January 1948 the Globetrotter and his henchmen invade the Natural History Museum in an attempt to steal some priceless inlaid gems from the giant statue of the deity Kwaidan, but BATMAN and ROBIN – aided by young museum worker Bill Jordan – apprehend the criminals before they can flee the scene (BM No. 44/2: "Born for Adventure!").

GLOBE-TROTTER, THE (Henry Guile III). An embittered thespian turned criminal who used his ability at acting and impersonation to commit a series of spectacular crimes in England and France before he was finally apprehended at the Eiffel Tower by BATMAN and ROBIN. The story of the Dynamic Duo's battle with the Globe-Trotter is recounted in June 1950, at a special gathering of international law-enforcement officials held to celebrate the Globe-Trotter's successful apprehension.

The Globe-Trotter was in reality Henry Guile III, "a wealthy society figure who loved three things only-- ***himself, money,*** and the ***theater!***" Lambasted by the critics for his failings as an actor, the embittered Guile established his own repertory company, financed its productions with his own money, and led it on a tour of the United States and Europe. The repertory venture was a critical and financial disaster, however, and Guile returned forlornly to the United States, penniless except for a single dime. "I'll show the ***world!***" cried Guile. "With this ***dime*** I'll start on a tour of the globe and I'll return made ***rich*** again . . . by my ***acting!*** The world will be my stage and it will see a new real life drama titled ***'The Globe-Trotter of Crime!'*** . . . and ***I will play the title role!***"

After using his dime for a ride on a local subway train, Guile stole aboard an airliner bound for England and then, by means of a variety of intricate disguises and impersonations, committed a series of spectacular crimes – first in England, then in France – before he was finally apprehended by Batman and Robin (Det No. 160: "The Globe-Trotter of Crime!").

GLOVES. The leader of a gang of criminals who murder GOTHAM CITY gang chief Waxey Wilson in a bid for control over Wilson's lucrative underworld territory, only to be finally apprehended in December 1948–January 1949 through the heroic efforts of BATMAN, ROBIN, and a blind youngster named Jimmy, whom Batman has been training privately for a career in criminology (BM No. 50/3: "The Second Boy Wonder!").

GOBLIN, THE. A notorious safecracker who conceals his true identity beneath a grotesque face mask and a beat-up old hat. He is secretly Martin Tate, the owner of the Tate Jewelry Shop. The Goblin is apprehended in October 1949 through the heroic efforts of BATMAN, ROBIN, and members of the Gotham City Police Department (Det No. 152: "The Goblin of Gotham City!"). (*See* VALE, VICKI.)

GOLAR, ERIC. A "famous inventor" who, sometime in the recent past, retired to a secluded island laboratory to begin work on a completely automated city, where all work would be performed by complex, remote-controlled machines. Golar had intended to present working models of his machines to American manufacturers so that they could eventually be mass-produced, but by December 1953–January 1954 the Nero Thompson gang has invaded the island, imprisoned Golar, and begun sending Golar's machines into GOTHAM CITY to plunder and rob by remote control. After one such robbery, however, BATMAN and ROBIN follow the remote-controlled machine – a so-called "flying umbrella" – to Golar's island where, ultimately, they succeed in freeing the captive Golar and in apprehending the entire Nero Thompson gang (BM No. 80/3: "The Machines of Menace!").

GOLD COAST KID, THE. An alias employed by BATMAN in Spring 1942 when he poses as a criminal in order to infiltrate the "Big John" Waller gang (WF No. 5: "Crime Takes A Holiday"). (*See* KELLEY, BRAINS.)

GONG, THE. A ruthless criminal who uses bells to aid him in his crimes. He is in reality Ed Peale, a man whose entire life has been marked by a "morbid hatred" of all bells.

"I will rebel against bells!" decided Peale finally. "I won't obey bells . . . I'll make bells obey **me!** I'll make them do evil, criminal things! . . . yes . . . I'll become a bandit . . . and I'll call myself – ***the Gong!***"

For a time, the Gong electrifies the nation with his diabolical "bell crimes," but he and his henchmen are finally apprehended in October–November 1949 by BATMAN, ROBIN, and local police (BM No. 55/3: "The Bandit of the Bells!").

GOODWIN (Dr.). The inventor of a diabolical chemical formula which, when administered to an unsuspecting victim, "puts the [victim's] will to sleep" and forces him, in Goodwin's words, to "remember and obey whatever orders I give him!"

In January 1944, in collusion with members of the Biff Bannister gang, Goodwin drugs several prominent businessmen and orders them to rob their own places of business, surrender the loot to his underworld allies, and then completely forget everything that they have done. At one point, Goodwin even succeeds in drugging BATMAN, but Batman's "deep instincts of honesty and justice grapple with the insidious spell put upon him by Dr. Goodwin" and enable him to overcome the almost overpowering effects of the drug. Dr. Goodwin and his gangland cohorts are ultimately apprehended by BATMAN and ROBIN, with the aid of some crucial last-minute assistance from ALFRED (Det No. 83: "Accidentally on Purpose!").

GORDON (Police Commissioner). *See* GORDON, JAMES W. (POLICE COMMISSIONER).

GORDON, BARBARA. The lovely red-haired young woman who is secretly Batgirl (*see* BATGIRL [BARBARA GORDON].) Barbara Gordon is a congresswoman from GOTHAM CITY and the daughter of POLICE COMMISSIONER JAMES W. GORDON. She is presumably the sister of TONY GORDON, although this is never actually stated in the texts.

GORDON, JAMES W. (Police Commissioner). The dedicated police official who has served as police commissioner of BATMAN's resident city – identified as New York City from May 1939 (Det No. 27: "The Case of the Chemical Syndicate") to December 1940 (Det No. 46), and as GOTHAM CITY from Winter 1941 (BM No. 4/4) onward – for nearly four decades. Excepting only Batman and ROBIN, he has appeared in more texts than any other character in the Batman chronicles.

James W. Gordon was born on January 5, 1900 and graduated from law school on June 6, 1924. On October 11, 1926 he married a gracious, attractive woman known to the chronicles only as Mrs. Gordon (*see* GORDON, JAMES W. [MRS.]), and "a few years" later, while Gordon was still pounding a beat as a rookie policeman, his wife gave birth to an infant son, TONY GORDON, who is an approximate contemporary of Robin. By 1931 Gordon had attained the rank of police lieutenant and earned a reputation as "the pride of the force," both for his great skill at crime detection and his unshakable devotion to the department (WF No. 53, Aug/Sep '51: "The Private Life of Commissioner Gordon!"). Before long, Gordon had become "the crack detective of [his] era" and had risen through the ranks of the police department to become chief of police (BM No. 71/2, Jun/Jul '52: "Commissioner Gordon's Greatest Case!") and, by May 1939, police commissioner (Det No. 27: "The Case of the Chemical Syndicate").

Barbara Gordon, the lovely red-haired young woman who makes her textual debut as Batgirl (*see* BATGIRL [BARBARA GORDON]) in January 1967, is Gordon's daughter (Det No. 359: "The Million Dollar Debut of Batgirl!"). Gordon's great-grandfather, CAPTAIN JOHN GORDON, was a showboat captain on the Mississippi River during the middle years of the nineteenth century (BM No. 89/1, Feb '55: "River Rogues").

Police Commissioner Gordon is a perfect look-alike for Takeloth, the man who, according to Detective Comics No. 167, was chief of the royal police in the court of the legendary CLEOPATRA. Batman and Robin observe the uncanny resemblance firsthand during a time-journey to ancient Egypt that they make in January 1951 ("Bodyguards to Cleopatra!").

Police Commissioner Gordon is "Batman's closest friend" (BM No. 71/2, Jun/Jul '52: "Commissioner Gordon's Greatest Case!") and a "good friend" of Bruce Wayne (NYWF, 1940), but in spite of the fact that Gordon has expressed the view that Batman must be a member of his "inner circle of friends" (BM No. 71/2,

Jun/Jul '52: "Commissioner Gordon's Greatest Case!"; *see also* WF No. 53, Aug/Sep '51: "The Private Life of Commissioner Gordon!"), he has never actually discovered that Bruce Wayne and Batman are one and the same man.

On a number of occasions, Gordon has been seized with the desire to unravel the secret of Batman's dual identity (e.g., in BM No. 71/2, Jun/Jul '52: "Commissioner Gordon's Greatest Case!"), but his suspicions have never actually focused on his friend Bruce Wayne. In September–October 1952, for example, after "unscrupulous black marketeer" GLENN FARR has tried unsuccessfully to prove that Bruce Wayne is Batman, Police Commissioner Gordon shakes his head in amused disbelief: "Can you beat it!" he exclaims. "**Another** crook tries to link up Bruce Wayne with **Batman!** Poor Bruce! Why **him** all the time?" (WF No. 60: "The Richest Crook in the World!").

Other people in Bruce Wayne's social circle have suspected that Wayne is secretly Batman, although they have never been able to prove it, but Police Commissioner Gordon has apparently been taken in completely by Wayne's carefully cultivated socialite pose. ". . . Bruce Wayne is a nice young chap," muses Gordon in May 1939, "--but he certainly must lead a boring life . . . seems disinterested in everything" (Det No. 27: "The Case of the Chemical Syndicate"). In November 1955, after Wayne has been chosen "Batman for a Day" as the result of his philanthropic efforts on behalf of the police department's widows and orphans fund, Gordon makes a similar remark: "You're a nice young chap," he tells Wayne frankly, "but as ***Batman,*** you're just hopelessly miscast!" (Det No. 225: "If I Were Batman!"). And in February 1963, Gordon echoes these sentiments once again: "Bruce is a nice, amiable fellow," thinks Gordon, "--but it's a mystery to me why he seems to have no goal in life!" (BM No. 153: chs. 1–3 — "Prisoners of Three Worlds!"; "Death from Beyond"; "Dimension of Doom").

In the event of Batman's untimely death, Gordon will receive the surprise of his life, for a secret letter, addressed to Gordon and hidden safely away in Bruce Wayne's safety deposit box, will inform him that Bruce Wayne and Batman were one and the same man (Det No. 194, Apr '53: "The Stolen Bank!").

Perhaps like most police commissioners, Police Commissioner Gordon is extremely sensitive about the prestige of his department and fiercely loyal to the men and women who serve under him. In October–November 1941, for example, after the JOKER has flooded Gotham City with taunting notes declaring that the "blundering police . . . will be unable to stop me," Gordon becomes livid with rage. "Take it easy, Gordon!" urges Bruce Wayne. "You're likely to burst a blood vessel!" "How can I take it easy," cries Gordon, "while the **Joker** laughs at the whole police force?" (BM No. 7/1).

It is probably this pride, more than anything else, which accounts for the adversary relationship that existed between Police Commissioner Gordon and the brash "'outside the law' racket-buster" (Det No. 65, Jul '42: "The Cop Who Hated the Batman!") known as Batman during the early days of Batman's crime-fighting career. "That Batman," cries an exasperated Gordon in January 1940, after a particularly daring display of courage and ingenuity by the Caped Crusader. "He's done it again! He's making the police department look ridiculous. I wish I could get my hands on him" (Det No. 35).

Ultimately, however, Gordon came to the realization that Batman "was the most gifted detective I had ever known" (WF No. 65, Jul/Aug '53: "The Five Different Batmen!"), and in October–November 1941, after delivering a stirring speech in defense of Batman's extra-legal activities, he appointed Batman "an honorary member of the [Gotham City] police department" (BM No. 7/4: "The People vs. The Batman"), thus ushering in an era of mutual cooperation between Batman and the Gotham City law-enforcement establishment that has persisted for more than thirty years. (*See* BATMAN [section K, the relationship with the law-enforcement establishment].)

Police Commissioner Gordon is a member of the Gotham City Crime Commission (WF No. 53, Aug/Sep '51: "The Private Life of Commissioner Gordon!"), the honorary chairman of the Police Athletic League (BM No. 168/1, Dec '64: "The Fight That Jolted Gotham City!"), a member of the MYSTERY ANALYSTS OF GOTHAM CITY (BM No. 164/2, Jun '64: "Batman's Great Face-Saving Feat!"), and the originator and organizer of the SECRET STAR, an organization of five hand-picked men who will serve as replacements for Batman in the event of Batman's death or long-term disability (BM No. 77/2, Jun/Jul '53: "The Secret Star"). Gordon may also be something of a writer, for he has indicated that when he retires he plans to write a book about the Gotham City Police Department entitled *Gotham City Guardians* (BM No. 140/3, Jun '61: "The Eighth Wonder of Space!").

Police Commissioner Gordon wears glasses, sports a moustache, and smokes a pipe. Prior to January 1952 (Det No. 179: "Mayor Bruce Wayne!"), Gordon's hair is variously portrayed as gray (Det No. 27, May '39: "The Case of the Chemical Syndicate"; and others), brown (BM No. 1/5, Spr '40: "The Joker Returns"; and others), black (BM No. 2/1, Sum '40), and white (BM No. 3/2, Fall '40: "The Ugliest Man in the World"; and others); but from January 1952 onward it is consistently portrayed as white.

In spite of the fact that Police Commissioner Gordon appears in the chronicles more often than almost any other character, with Batman and Robin the sole exceptions — and in spite of the fact that Gordon is the only supporting character to have appeared in the chronicles since their inception in May 1939 (Det No. 27: "The Case of the Chemical Syndicate") — the overwhelming majority of his appearances are minor. Consequently, the article which follows shall deal only with those adventures in which Police Commissioner Gordon plays at least a minimally significant role.

In May 1939, in the premiere text of the Batman chronicles, Police Commissioner Gordon makes his textual debut. On this occasion, as on numerous others during the early days of Batman's crime-fighting career, Gordon invites his friend Bruce Wayne to accompany him on his criminal investigations, and Wayne accepts, presumably so that he will be able to gather information to aid him in his role as Batman (Det No. 27: "The Case of the Chemical Syndicate").

In October–November 1941 Batman infiltrates the hideout of GRANDA THE MYSTIC, disguised as one of Granda's henchmen, after instructing Robin to summon police help to the scene. The arrival of the police is delayed, however, when the car carrying Police Commissioner Gordon to the scene becomes involved in a minor traffic accident, thus forcing Batman and Robin to become embroiled in a premature showdown battle with Granda and his hirelings. Batman, Robin, and LINDA PAGE – whom the criminals have been holding captive – are ultimately rescued through the timely arrival of Police Commissioner Gordon and members of his department, who swiftly take Granda's cohorts into custody while Batman and Robin apprehend the fleeing Granda.

These events take place during the period when Batman is still technically a fugitive from the law, but after the criminals have been safely apprehended, Police Commissioner Gordon shakes Batman's hand and congratulates him personally for the first time in the chronicles, saying: "The police department, [and] the people of the city thank you and Robin for the swell job you did!" (BM No. 7/2: "The Trouble Trap!").

During this same period, after gang chief Freddie Hill has framed Bruce Wayne for the murder of HORATIO DELMAR, Police Commissioner Gordon is forced to arrest Wayne and charge him with murder even though he continues to have faith in Wayne's innocence. Ultimately, Wayne is exonerated, and the man who ordered the Delmar murder, Freddie Hill himself, is brought to justice.

At one point, after a local district attorney has denounced Batman as a criminal and ordered his arrest on a series of criminal charges, Police Commissioner Gordon leaps to his defense and, in a stirring speech before a hushed and crowded courtroom, hails Batman as a "friend of the people" and as a "man who daily risks his life to save others."

Police Commissioner Gordon, 1939 © NPP 1939

"Perhaps this comes a little late," concludes Gordon proudly, "but I, the police commissioner of Gotham City, appoint you an **honorary member of the police department!** From now on, you work hand in hand with the police!"(For the complete text of this speech, *see* Batman [section K, the relationship with the law-enforcement establishment].) These events mark the end of Batman's period as a fugitive and usher in an era of complete cooperation between Batman and the law-enforcement establishment of Gotham City (BM No. 7/4, Oct/Nov '41: "The People vs. The Batman").

In December 1941 Batman once again becomes a fugitive from justice, this time due to the sinister machinations of the PENGUIN. "The **Batman**--turned criminal," laments Police Commissioner Gordon, "—I can't believe it! Why did he do it--why?" Ultimately, Batman establishes his innocence and Police Commissioner Gordon insists that he knew it all along: "Er---cough---we're sorry we suspected you, Batman," stammers Gordon, "but of course I felt all the time that you were innocent!" (Det No. 58).

On Christmas 1941 Police Commissioner Gordon hosts an informal get-together at his home for Batman, Robin, and Linda Page (BM No. 9/4, Feb/Mar '42).

In February 1942 Police Commissioner Gordon summons Batman and Robin with the BAT-SIGNAL for the first time in the chronicles, although in this early text it is referred to only as a "searchlight on the roof of police headquarters!" (Det No. 60: "Case of the Costume-Clad Killers").

In July 1942 Police Commissioner Gordon decides to spend a short vacation at a state troopers barracks in one of the northern states, and invites Batman and Robin to accompany him. It is during this vacation that Batman and Robin meet state trooper TOM BOLTON and battle underworld figure Nick Rocco (Det No. 65: "The Cop Who Hated the Batman!").

In Fall 1945 Police Commissioner Gordon is one of the numerous prominent citizens of Gotham City whose homes are robbed while they are busy attending a meeting of the newly organized Citizens' Committee for Law and Order, hosted by the Velvet Kid (WF No. 19: "The League for Larceny!"). (*See* JOKER, THE.)

In August–September 1946 the Penguin snatches a purse in full view of Police Commissioner Gordon in a deliberate attempt to get himself arrested for purse-snatching and sentenced to a short term in the Gotham Penitentiary. When Batman and Robin, their suspicions aroused by the Penguin's bizarre behavior, intervene to prevent him from being arrested, Gordon becomes absolutely furious, but he accepts Batman's advice to allow the Penguin to roam free until they can learn exactly why he seems so eager to be arrested for a petty crime (BM No. 36/1: "The Penguin's Nest!").

In March 1947 Batman and Robin are summoned to police headquarters to hear some shocking news: Police Commissioner Gordon has been removed from his post as commissioner and demoted to the rank of patrolman; an officer named Vane, the former chief inspector of the department, has been elevated to the rank of commissioner; and the mayor has instructed Vane to smash the famous bat-signal and confiscate the "special badge" that identifies Batman as an honorary member of the Gotham City Police Department. "From now on," Commissioner Vane warns Batman, "the police will handle cases without your help!"

Stunned by their interview with the new police commissioner, Batman and Robin swiftly seek out former commissioner Gordon, who is now walking a beat as a uniformed patrolman after some twenty years of service to the Gotham City Police Department. The mayor had asked Gordon to retire completely, but Gordon refused, and, because civil service regulations had made it impossible to fire him, a drastic demotion in rank had been the mayor's only alternative.

Gordon is understandably downhearted, but Batman and Robin vow to help Gordon uncover the real reason behind his sudden demotion. "We've worked together too long," observes Batman grimly, "to quit without a struggle."

Interviews with Mayor Carfax and his son Chadwick quickly reveal the true explanation behind Gordon's dismissal: "Sure Thing" Smiley, a Gotham City racketeer with a fondness for gambling and a knack for winning large wagers through underhanded tricks, had bet young Chadwick $100,000 that he could drive a golf ball a mile, then had won the wager by hitting the ball downhill on a paved stretch of highway. In order to settle the wager, Chadwick had been forced to sign a series of promissory notes totaling $100,000 and Smiley had threatened to use these notes to embarrass the mayor and ruin his political career unless he agreed to remove Gordon from the police commissioner's office and dismiss Batman as an honorary member of the Gotham City Police Department. Now, with Gordon a patrolman and Batman and Robin denied the official cooperation of the department, Smiley feels confident that he and his racketeers will be able to plunder Gotham City unhampered.

Ultimately, however, Batman defeats Smiley by beating him at his own game. He offers to use a pistol provided by Smiley to fire a bullet directly at Gordon's heart. If Gordon dies, promises Batman, he will pay Smiley $100,000 in cash and turn himself in on the murder charge arising from Gordon's murder, but if Gordon lives, Smiley must surrender young Carfax's promissory notes so that Gordon may be restored to his post as Gotham City's police commissioner.

Certain that Batman's wager offers him a chance to make $100,000 while at the same time eliminating Batman, Smiley agrees to the bet, and Batman quickly accumulates the $100,000 he needs to cover the wager by soliciting donations from Gotham City's loyal policemen, promising them that Gordon will be back in the commissioner's office if only he can win his bet with Smiley.

That afternoon, Batman meets Smiley at a street corner on Gordon's beat and, after Smiley has handed Batman a pistol and a bullet and satisfied himself that Gordon is not wearing a bulletproof vest, Batman fires the bullet straight at Gordon's heart. Batman, however, has erected a bulletproof plastic shield between himself and Gordon, and since Gordon remains completely unscathed, a horrified Smiley loses the wager. Gordon promptly arrests Smiley for the series of robberies that he and his henchmen have pulled during the period of Gordon's absence from the commissioner's office, and Batman and Robin apprehend Smiley's henchmen, who are in the act of robbing a piano company.

With Smiley and his men in jail and the promissory notes returned, Gotham City returns to normal once again: the bat-signal is returned to service, Batman's special police badge is returned to him, and Gordon is restored to his post as police commissioner. Vane, the hard-working police official who had been promoted to police commissioner in Gordon's absence, steps down without regrets. "I **like** working for Gordon!" explains Vane. "As chief inspector, my salary's the same as his – so I don't lose anything!" (Det No. 121: "Commissioner Gordon Walks a Beat!").

In October–November 1949, during a period when, as the result of a series of coincidences, Bruce Wayne is serving as a rookie policeman with the Gotham City Police Department, Police Commissioner Gordon, Patrolman Jack Bennett, and Bruce Wayne are captured by the LONGSHOREMAN KID and his henchmen and imprisoned inside a locked room at their garage hideout. Wayne, however, manages to pick the lock on the door, seize a pistol, and hold the criminals at bay until "Batman" (in reality ALFRED posing as Batman in order to safeguard the secret that Bruce Wayne is Batman), Robin, and members of the Gotham City Police Department can arrive to take the villains into custody (BM No. 55/2: "Bruce Wayne, Rookie Policeman!").

In June 1950 Police Commissioner Gordon and law-enforcement officials from around the world gather to celebrate Batman and Robin's successful apprehension of an international criminal known as the Globe-Trotter (*see* GLOBE-TROTTER, THE [HENRY GUILE III]) and to present the Dynamic Duo with a gold trophy inscribed to "Batman and Robin, Globe-Trotters of the Law." While they are waiting for Batman and Robin to arrive, Police Commissioner Gordon, Inspector Chisolm of Scotland Yard, and Inspector Bertrand of the French Sûreté narrate the story of the Dynamic Duo's battle with the Globe-Trotter, which carried the famed lawmen from the United States, to England, and finally to France (Det No. 160: "The Globe-Trotter of Crime!").

In June–July 1950 Police Commissioner Gordon welcomes the emergence of a new crime-fighter known as DEADSHOT and sharply rebukes Batman for regarding Deadshot so suspiciously. "You seem awfully anxious to discredit **Deadshot!**" chides Gordon. "It's not like ***you*, Batman,** to be afraid of competition. . . ." Ultimately, however, it becomes clear that Deadshot's real ambition is to become Gotham City's "greatest crime lord," and Gordon is compelled to acknowledge that Batman's suspicions were well-founded ones (BM No. 59/1: "The Man Who Replaced Batman!").

By August–September 1951 Sheik Hanson – a ruthless bandit and murderer apprehended by Police Commissioner Gordon many years ago, during his days as a rookie policeman – has escaped from Butler Penitentiary while serving a life term, and Gordon is fearful that Hanson will attempt to make good an old vow to wreak vengeance on the man who apprehended him. Gordon is particularly apprehensive that Hanson will strike – perhaps successfully – before he has had the opportunity to present some important testimony to an upcoming session of the local grand jury. "I've finally dug up evidence that links Big Dave Ravage with half the rackets in this town," explains Gordon to Batman. "I'm the one eye-witness who can go before a grand jury and cut Big Dave down to size!"

In order to safeguard Gordon's life until Sheik Hanson can be safely reapprehended, Batman prevails upon Gordon to go into hiding at an upstate rooming house while he disguises himself as Gordon and takes Gordon's place as police commissioner of Gotham City. "**Batman's** done a lot for me in his time," muses Gordon to himself, as he settles in for his stay at Mrs. Clancy's Rooming House somewhere north of Gotham City, "but this is his greatest favor! Somehow, I'm almost sure that in his real-life identity, he's one of my friends. I wonder which one he is?"

In the days that follow, Sheik Hanson makes a series of attempts to assassinate the man he believes to be Police Commissioner Gordon. The attempts are unsuccessful, but on each occasion Batman fails to apprehend his attacker. He does, however, begin to suspect that Gordon's would-be assassin is not Sheik Hanson at all, and a trip to Butler Penitentiary, where he finds Hanson's corpse hidden in the underbrush outside the prison walls, confirms his suspicion that the man who has been attempting to kill Police Commissioner Gordon is actually racketeer Big Dave Ravage, who has been impersonating Sheik Hanson in the hope of preventing Gordon from testifying before the grand jury while at the same time making it appear that Hanson has murdered Gordon in fulfillment of an old vow.

In order to accumulate the evidence he needs to convict Ravage of the villainous masquerade, Batman anonymously informs Ravage of the whereabouts of Gordon's hideaway, then tips off Gordon that the killer is on his way. Although Batman fails to trap the would-be murderer after he has made yet another unsuccessful attempt on Gordon's life, the fact that "Sheik Hanson" had found his way to the rooming house even though only Ravage had been informed of its location – combined with the discovery of Ravage's fingerprints on Gordon's rooming-house window sill – provides Batman with the evidence he needs to take Ravage into custody.

Ravage, explains Batman, had come upon the dying Hanson, who had been shot and mortally wounded by prison guards while attempting to flee the prison, and had seized upon the idea of impersonating Hanson during his attempts to assassinate the police commissioner. Now, with Hanson dead and Ravage behind bars, Gordon can resume his everyday role as police commissioner (WF No. 53: "The Private Life of Commissioner Gordon!").

In April–May 1952 Police Commissioner Gordon puts the bat-signal in storage and orders Batman into retirement after an inventor named Weir has presented the Gotham City Police Department with an electronically controlled robot which, in addition to being invulnerable to bullets and hand grenades, appears to possess all the crime-fighting prowess of Batman himself.

"But aren't you acting a little hastily?" protests Batman, when Gordon informs him that he must step down to make way for the so-called "robot cop."

"Be reasonable, ***Batman,*** " replies Gordon, "--I'm only thinking of you! Why should I risk your life any more when I can send the robot out to accomplish the same ends at ***no*** risk?

"We still need you, ***Batman***--we've plenty for you to do!" continues Gordon reassuringly, as he leads Batman to the wood-paneled office that has been set aside for him. "You'll be of invaluable aid in our research and compilation department. See--you'll even have a private secretary!"

"However you say it," retorts Batman angrily, "it adds up to one thing: a desk job! I never thought I'd come to this!"

Later, in the seclusion of the BATCAVE, Batman expresses his keen disappointment to Robin. "Put out of business by a machine! I still can't believe it! And to think they want me in a desk job!"

It soon develops, however, that the robot cop is subject to a serious mechanical deficiency in that exposure to X-rays renders it totally inoperative, a fact on which the Gotham City underworld would inevitably capitalize. Therefore, it is the robot cop who is forced into "retirement" while Batman resumes his rightful place as Gotham City's most intrepid lawman (BM No. 70/1: "The Robot Cop of Gotham City").

In May–June 1952 Batman is assigned to protect the lives of four trustees of the International Chemical Company who have been threatened with death by deranged invalid ROGER J. KEEP. Faced with the dual problem of protecting the trustees and apprehending Keep and his henchmen, Batman ingeniously thwarts each successive murder attempt while at the same time allowing Keep to think that his hired killers have succeeded, in this way hoping to forestall repeated attempts against the life of each man.

Police Commissioner Gordon, however, is unaware of Batman's plan, and after each successive "murder" he loses more and more faith in Gotham City's top lawman. "This is serious, ***Batman!*** " chides Gordon, after Keep's hirelings have apparently carried out the successful execution of trustee Donald Penn. "An insane killer has made good his boast--before your very eyes! This never happened before! It must never happen again! We must stop this killer--[and] protect the rest of the trustees!"

After the second apparent murder, this time of trustee Holmes Caffrey, Gordon's patience grows even thinner. ***"Batman,"*** scolds Gordon, "--things have come to a showdown! Two men you were protecting have been killed--and the killer is still at large! This time you have failed me miserably!"

After the third "murder," this time of trustee John Keith-Dudley, an angry and disillusioned Gordon removes Batman from a crime-fighting assignment for the first time in the chronicles. "I never thought I'd do this, ***Batman,*** remarks Gordon grimly, "--but I must! As of now, you are ***relieved*** of your ***present assignment!*** You leave me no other choice! That you have not yet unearthed the killer's hideout is understandable--those things take time. But failure to prevent murder ***three times***--there is no excuse for that!"

Ultimately, however, Batman and Robin apprehend Keep and his henchmen and reveal to an astonished Gordon that the three "murdered" trustees are still very much alive. Batman apologizes for leading Gordon astray but explains that absolute secrecy was necessary if his plan was to be carried out successfully (WF No. 58: "The Murder of Bruce Wayne!").

In June–July 1952 Police Commissioner Gordon becomes obsessed with the idea of discovering the secret of Batman's dual identity. It all begins late one evening, when Batman and Robin enter his office at police headquarters and ask permission to use his private bathroom in order to attend to some cuts and bruises that Batman has received during a recent battle with the MASKED MYSTIC gang.

Unbeknownst to the Dynamic Duo, however, a painting in Gordon's office conceals a two-way mirror which enables Gordon to spy on anyone using the private bathroom, and Gordon feels sorely tempted to use the mirror to learn the secret of Batman's dual identity when Batman removes his cowl to tend to the bruises on his face.

"For years," muses Gordon silently, "I've yearned to know who ***Batman*** really is! No harm could come from my knowing . . . I'd keep the secret! ***Batman's*** career could go on! After all, who has a better right to know the secret than ***I***???"

After a moment's pause, however, Gordon decides against using his secret mirror to uncover Batman's secret. "No!" he decides. "Not ***this*** way! I won't take ***advantage*** of ***Batman!*** If I'm to learn his identity, I'll do it the right way . . . by sheer brainwork! Then, when I'm sure, I'll lure ***Batman*** back to this mirror . . . and confirm my guess!"

Police Commissioner Gordon, 1952 © NPP 1952

"After all!" thinks Gordon to himself, after he has left headquarters and returned home. "Who would be better equipped to solve ***Batman's*** secret than myself? Wasn't I the crack detective of my era, before being appointed chief and then commissioner?? Yes . . . it will be a diverting problem! And I shall tackle it immediately! ***Batman's*** identity! I'm excited already!"

Proceeding from the reasonable assumption that Batman must be a member of his "inner circle of friends," Gordon sets out to unravel the secret of Batman's dual identity. He invites a large group of his friends, including Bruce Wayne, to his home for dinner, and then, after they have all arrived, has a member of his headquarters staff activate the bat-signal so that he can observe which of his guests makes a hasty excuse to leave the gathering. Wayne solves his dilemma by surreptitiously starting a small fire in Gordon's home and then changing to Batman during the ensuing turmoil, but the incident alerts him to Gordon's scheme and he realizes that he will have to be on his guard in the future.

In the days that follow, Gordon makes a series of attempts to trick Batman into providing him with data which could enable him to track down the secret of Batman's identity, but Batman successfully outwits the police commissioner at every turn. At one point, for example, Gordon attempts to obtain a sample of Batman's handwriting by insisting that Batman fill out a conventional police report, but Batman counters this ploy by claiming that his right hand has been slightly injured and then proceeding to fill out the form somewhat shakily with his left. At another point, Gordon lures Batman to his home and then instructs his butler to telephone all his close friends and invite them to dinner, hoping thereby to determine which of his Batman "suspects" is not at home to receive his invitation. Robin has countered this ploy, however, by luring all of Gordon's prospective dinner guests away from their homes with phony telephone calls so that not a single one of them is at home when Gordon's butler calls.

Finally, a few days later, when Batman and Robin arrive at police headquarters covered with soot and again request permission to use the private bathroom, Police Commissioner Gordon can restrain himself no longer. "I once said I wouldn't use this trick mirror to learn ***Batman's*** identity," thinks Gordon, ". . . but he's been too clever for me . . . outwitted me at every turn! Now I'm obsessed with learning his secret . . . I ***must*** take a look at him!!"

As Gordon stares through the two-way mirror, he sees the unmasked features of Batman for the first time: they are the features of his close friend James Bartley, a noted historian who is high on the list of the Masked Mystic's intended victims.

When Batman emerges from the private bathroom, Gordon tells him about the secret mirror and confesses that he has peered through it to uncover the secret of his dual identity. "And so I finally know who you are, ***Batman!***" concludes Gordon. "But don't worry! The secret is mine alone! Your career won't suffer one bit!"

"You shouldn't have done it Commissioner!" replies Batman sternly. "However good your intentions, you've placed ***Robin*** and me in jeopardy! One slip on your part . . . and we're through!"

Despite his assurances, however, Gordon becomes obsessed with the forbidden knowledge which he thinks he possesses. When his wife informs him that he has been mumbling about Batman's secret identity in his sleep, he becomes overwrought and hastily sends her away on a short vacation to visit their son in college. Later, as he is driving absentmindedly along a road, totally preoccupied with the forbidden knowledge of Batman's secret identity, he becomes involved in an auto accident, becomes dazed by a blow on the head, and wanders about the scene of the accident mumbling about Batman's secret identity and the fact that he has learned it.

A hoodlum standing nearby overhears Gordon's mumblings and relays the story to the Masked Mystic, who promptly invades Gordon's home and threatens to murder Gordon's wife and son unless he agrees to divulge Batman's secret. Desperate to save his family, Gordon reluctantly tells the Masked Mystic that Batman is secretly James Bartley.

Moments after the Masked Mystic and his men have departed, Batman and Robin appear on the scene and a contrite Gordon tells them what he has just done. Batman sternly assures Gordon that he is not James Bartley and then hastily departs with Robin after promising Gordon that he will explain the error later.

At the home of James Bartley, where the Masked Mystic and his henchmen have gone intending to murder the man they believe to be Batman, the Dynamic Duo swiftly apprehend the assembled criminals. The Masked Mystic accuses Batman of being James Bartley, but when the real James Bartley appears on the scene moments later, the Masked Mystic realizes that Batman is not James Bartley at all.

"You see, commissioner," explains Batman later, after the criminals have been taken into custody, ". . . I knew Bartley was in danger of being killed [by the Masked Mystic]. As I had done many times before on previous cases, I sent him into hiding and took over his identity . . . hoping to trap" the Masked Mystic. When Gordon stared through the trick mirror into the private bathroom, he had merely seen Batman's face with James Bartley's features molded onto it with makeup.

A week later, when Batman and Robin depart on their silken ropes through the window of Gordon's office, Gordon sees a bank deposit slip fall out of Batman's pocket. "If I were to read the name on it," thinks Gordon, "I'd know ***Batman's*** identity!" He pauses a moment and then makes his decision. "Oh, no!" he exclaims, as he sets the deposit slip afire. "Never again! If there's **one** thing I **don't** want to know, it's **Batman's** identity! I'll destroy my mirror, too! I've learned my lesson!" (BM No. 71/2: "Commissioner Gordon's Greatest Case!").

In January–February 1953, after a villain known as the BLACK ROGUE has been driven insane by a blow on the head and fallen victim to the delusion that he is the legendary Black Knight, it becomes apparent that the Black Rogue's hidden loot will be lost forever if his bizarre delusion is suddenly shattered. Therefore, when the Black Rogue and his henchmen attempt to steal a rich payroll from the movie set of the film *Charlemagne*, Police Commissioner Gordon poses as the legendary KING ARTHUR and, with the aid of Batman, Robin, and a contingent of mounted policemen – all of them dressed in the garb of Arthurian knights – attempts to take the criminals into custody. This particular attempt to apprehend the criminals ends in failure, although the payroll robbery itself is successfully thwarted, but Batman ultimately recovers the Black Rogue's hidden loot by posing as MERLIN the magician and threatening to unleash his evil sorcery against the villain unless he agrees to reveal where it is hidden (WF No. 62: "Sir Batman and the Black Knight").

By June–July 1953 Police Commissioner Gordon has organized the SECRET STAR, an organization of five hand-picked men whose job it will be to carry on the Batman legend in the event of Batman's death or long-term disability.

"Constant threats to his life . . . prompted **Batman** to urge me to think about a replacement for him," observes Gordon, ". . . that's why we've formed the ***Secret Star! Batman*** feels whatever happens to him, the ***Batman*** legend must go on! I realize that no ***one*** man could ever replace him . . . but ***five*** men might be able to!"

All five members of the Secret Star are to be thoroughly trained by Batman and Robin, and, in the event their services are ever needed, Police Commissioner Gordon will decide which of them would be the most appropriate Batman for each particular crime-fighting assignment.

One of the potential weaknesses of the Secret Star becomes painfully apparent, however, when one of its members, F.B.I. agent TED BLAKELY, is discovered to have underworld connections which, despite Blakely's basic honesty, render him inappropriate for Secret Star membership. Gordon insists that his idea is, nevertheless, basically a sound one: ". . . my ***Secret Star*** is still a good idea," he remarks, after Blakely's connections have been discovered, ". . . with another man to replace Blakely! But to tell you the truth . . . I hope I never have to use it!" (BM No. 77/2: "The Secret Star").

In October 1954, when television station GCTV presents the story of Batman's life on its "Your Life Story" program, Police Commissioner Gordon appears on the program long enough to present Batman with a "golden key to the city" as "a gift from the people of Gotham City. . . !" (BM No. 87/1: "Batman's Greatest Thrills!").

In February 1955, shortly after the Gotham *Gazette* has published a century-old picture of Police Commissioner Gordon's great-grandfather, CAPTAIN JOHN GORDON, locked in a jail cell, along with an article describing him as the "central figure" in a series of daring river crimes perpetrated during the mid-1850s, Bruce Wayne and Dick Grayson journey into the past, to the year 1854, in an effort to clear Captain Gordon's name and alleviate the embarrassment that the story has caused to Police Commissioner Gordon. ". . . some enemy of mine dug this [old photograph] up to make me the laughing-stock!" observes Gordon sadly, shortly after the story breaks. "I'll have to resign as police commissioner!"

During their visit to the year 1854, however, Batman and Robin succeed in establishing Captain Gordon's innocence and in apprehending Baird Hawes, the real river bandit. Then they return to the twentieth century where, aboard Captain Gordon's old showboat, now on display at a local museum, they find a copy of an 1854 newspaper proclaiming Captain Gordon's innocence of the earlier charges against him (BM No. 89/1: "River Rogues").

In November 1955, when it is announced that Batman will leave Gotham City for a few days to address a criminologists' convention in Pacific City, Martin Wayne, the editor of the Gotham *Gazette*, proposes that the city hold a "Batman for a Day" fund-raising contest in which the citizens who raise the most money on behalf of the police department's windows and orphans fund receive the honor of serving as Batman for a Day during Batman's absence. Batman agrees to the idea, since the contest will probably stimulate sizable contributions to the worthy police department charity.

After bookkeeper Jasper Smively and film star Rodney Random have had their turns at being Batman for a Day, Police Commissioner Gordon decides that he would like to be a Batman, too. "Why not admit it to myself," muses Gordon, "--I've always wished I could be like him--free to go into action, not tied to a desk! I brought in big contributions to the fund--if I claimed credit for them, **I** could be **Batman** for a day! Why not? . . . Yes--I **will** be **Batman!**"

During his day as Batman, Gordon joins Robin in an effort to gather information on convict JOHN LARROW, whom Gordon suspects is planning something illegal. "Mustn't hurt Gordon's feelings," thinks Robin, as he and the Batman-clad police commissioner set out together on patrol, "but he seems a bit old for our kind of action!"

Soon afterward, however, Gordon proves his mettle when he swings down from a rooftop on a silken rope in order to question some of Larrow's cohorts. "Look," cries one, "it's an old man ***Batman***. . . ! Haw, haw--let's show him!"

"Old man, am I?" cries Gordon, as he lights into the astonished criminals. "Maybe so, but I was learning how to handle characters like you 20 years ago!"

"Ouch! Lay off!" cries one of the hoodlums. "Let's get out of here--we shouldn't have tackled him!"

Indeed, it is partly through Gordon's efforts as Batman for a Day that the real Batman accumulates the information he needs to thwart a carefully planned attempt by John Larrow's henchmen to break their leader out of prison (Det No. 225: "If I Were Batman!").

In January–February 1957 Police Commissioner Gordon presides over the spectacular Gotham Police Show, the proceeds from which are to be donated to the Police Welfare Fund. In order to attract large crowds to the show and thereby aid the cause of charity, Batman, Robin, and SUPERMAN agree to perform a series of dramatic reenactments of their most exciting cases, and Superman chisels a huge amphitheater out of a solid rock cliff in order to accommodate the overflow crowds expected to attend. Swindler Henry Bartle hatches a plot to capture the dramatic reenactments on movie film and then cash in on the film by presenting it in theaters throughout the country as actual footage of Batman, Robin, and Superman in action against dangerous criminals. The three lawmen thwart Bartle's scheme, however, and see to it that their awe-inspiring feats of skill create a financial windfall only for the Police Welfare Fund, and not for swindler Bartle (WF No. 86: "The Super-Show of Gotham City").

In February 1957, while Police Commissioner Gordon is on a safari in Africa, crime syndicate chief BURT WEVER sets in motion an elaborate scheme to destroy Batman's effectiveness as a crime-fighter by framing him for a series of old unsolved crimes. Because Gordon is the only man who could immediately exonerate Batman, Wever bribes Gordon's native guides to keep him hopelessly lost in darkest Africa so that he cannot return to Gotham City. Aided by loyal members of the Gotham City Police Department, however, Batman succeeds in establishing his own innocence and in bringing Burt Wever to justice (Det No. 240: "The Outlaw Batman!").

In May 1957, after Batman has been accidentally transformed into a thirty-foot giant by DR. GREGGSON's incredible "maximizer," Police Commissioner Gordon provides Batman with a police siren to wear on his belt so that he will be able to warn citizens of his impending approach. Later, when Batman's titanic weight causes the destruction of the roadway leading onto the Gotham Bridge, Gordon reluctantly exiles his friend from Gotham City. "I'm sorry, ***Batman,***" explains Gordon, "--but in your present size you're too ***dangerous*** for Gotham City! I must order you to stay out of the city from now on!" Batman sadly departs for the seclusion of the batcave, but ultimately he regains his normal size and resumes residence in Gotham City (Det No. 243: "Batman the Giant!").

In July 1957 an angry mayor of Gotham City confronts Police Commissioner Gordon in his office at police headquarters. Somehow, fugitive criminals are being smuggled out of Gotham City to safe havens in foreign countries, and the mayor insists that the "crook-smugglers" be apprehended immediately. In spite of Gordon's assurances that his department is very close to cracking the case, the mayor demands that Batman and Robin be assigned to it at once.

Soon afterward, a mysterious costumed crime-fighter, known only as Mysteryman, appears in Gotham City to help Batman and Robin investigate the mystery of the disappearing fugitives. Mysteryman wears a light-green costume with green trunks, green boots, green gloves, and a green cape. A green hood covers his face and head and there is a red "M" emblazoned on his chest.

As Batman, Robin, and Mysteryman relentlessly pursue their investigations, magazine photographer VICKI VALE becomes more and more intrigued by Mysteryman and obsessed with the desire to uncover the secret of his identity. At first, convinced that Mysteryman must be some sort of robot, she arranges to bump into him "accidentally," only to discover that Mysteryman is not a robot at all, but human. Later she decides that Mysteryman is probably Batman's friend Superman, but when a pin she jabs into Mysteryman fails to bend, she realizes that this theory is also incorrect.

Through careful detective work, Batman, Robin, and Mysteryman establish that the fugitive criminals are being smuggled out of Gotham City inside huge hollowed-out pieces of fake industrial machinery, and before long the three heroes have smashed the entire smuggling ring and apprehended its members and clients. Vicki Vale, however, still has not succeeded in deducing the true identity of Mysteryman.

As Batman and Robin prepare to drive Mysteryman home in the BATMOBILE, however, Vicki notices that the trunklike "deck" of the batmobile has been left slightly open, apparently by accident, thus enabling her to stow away inside and learn exactly where Mysteryman lives.

The next day, at police headquarters, a grateful mayor of Gotham City congratulates Batman and Robin on their fine work in smashing the elusive crook-smuggling ring. "Give our thanks to ***Mysteryman,***" concludes the mayor, "whoever he may be!"

It is then that Vicki Vale announces that she has uncovered Mysteryman's true identity: Mysteryman, she charges, is none other than Police Commissioner Gordon himself. "But--but no one was ever supposed to find that out!" stammers Gordon.

"You, Gordon?" asks the mayor, perplexed. "But why?"

"I can explain that, your honor!" interjects Batman. "When you ordered the commissioner to turn that smuggling case over to me--I found that Gordon had already worked out a method of finding the smugglers!"

Batman had asked Gordon to help him on the case since it was he who had conceived the plan for apprehending the smugglers, but Gordon had felt compelled to decline. "No," Gordon had replied, "the mayor officially ordered me to turn the case over to you--***I*** can't appear personally in it now without seeming to disregard orders!" It was then that Batman had suggested that Gordon could participate anonymously, without seeming to disobey the mayor's instructions, by assuming the identity of Mysteryman.

"I'm sorry," says Gordon to the mayor, "--I didn't mean to disregard your orders, but--"

"**I'm** the one to apologize, for my impatience, Gordon!" insists the mayor. "Even though you had to work secretly, you did a splendid job!"

Later, outside police headquarters, Vicki Vale voices her latest suspicion to Batman. ". . . you ***wanted*** me to expose ***Mysteryman,*** didn't you?" she asks. "That's why you left the ***batmobile*** deck open for me to hide in?"

"Yes, Vicki," replies Batman, "--you see, I didn't want to hurt Gordon's reputation by succeeding where he'd seemingly failed! But I'd promised him I wouldn't expose him, so I let ***you*** do it!"

"You deliberately tricked me," scolds Vicki, as she kisses Batman's chin, "--but you're a darling, ***Batman!***" (Det No. 245: "The Dynamic Trio!").

In November 1957 Police Commissioner Gordon asks Bruce Wayne to accept a top-secret undercover assignment inside the walls of Gotham Prison. The plot takes a bizarre turn, however, when Bruce Wayne is charged with a murder he did not commit, and Police Commissioner Gordon, the only man who might clear him, is in a coma following a near-fatal automobile accident (Det No. 249: "The Crime of Bruce Wayne!"). (*See* BATWOMAN, THE.)

Police Commissioner Gordon, 1964 © NPP 1964

In January 1958 Police Commissioner Gordon is one of the many citizens of Gotham City who begin to fear and distrust Batman after they have been duped into believing that Batman is secretly an alien from outer space. Later, however, after the alien hoax has been finally exposed, Gordon offers Batman his profoundest apologies. "Yes," chimes in Vicki Vale, who had also been taken in by the hoax, "--but can you blame us for thinking ***Batman*** must be ***superhuman?***" (Det No. 251: "The Alien Batman!"). (*See* BALLARD, BRAND.)

In April 1959 Police Commissioner Gordon announces that Batman has committed an unspecified crime and become a fugitive from justice, but the announcement is only part of Batman's plan to infiltrate the RED MASK MOB and learn the identity of its leader (BM No. 123/3: "The Fugitive Batman!").

In November 1959, in a speech to recent graduates of the Gotham City Police Academy, Police Commissioner Gordon narrates the story of Batman's battle with the notorious DRAGON SOCIETY in order to illustrate the all-important principle that a lawman "must fight--and keep on fighting--until he wins the battle against crime!" (Det No. 273: "Secret of the Dragon Society!").

In August 1961, after Batman has received a "mild dose of the . . . affliction" recently responsible for transforming John Dolan into the ELEMENTAL MAN, Police Commissioner Gordon reluctantly locks Batman in a prison cell in the belief that Batman, like Dolan, will soon be driven "criminally insane" by the weird malady. Batman, however, escapes from the cell and, with the help of scientist Professor Higgins, ultimately restores both himself and the Elemental Man to normal (Det No. 294: "The Villain of 100 Elements!").

Police Commissioner Gordon, 1971 © NPP 1971

By June 1964 Police Commissioner Gordon has established a special twenty-four-hour "hot-line" linking his office with the subterranean batcave (Det No. 328: "Gotham Gang Line-Up!").

In January 1967 Police Commissioner Gordon's red-haired daughter, Barbara Gordon, makes her textual debut as Batgirl (Det No. 359: "The Million Dollar Debut of Batgirl!"). (*See* BATGIRL [BARBARA GORDON].)

GORDON, JAMES W. (Mrs.). The gracious, attractive woman who is the wife of POLICE COMMISSIONER JAMES W. GORDON, the mother of TONY GORDON (WF No. 53, Aug/Sep '51: "The Private Life of Commissioner Gordon!"), and, presumably, the mother of Barbara Gordon (*see* BATGIRL [BARBARA GORDON]), although this fact is never actually stated in the texts.

The chronicles contain few actual references to Mrs. Gordon, and those that do contain only scanty data concerning her. Detective Comics No. 72 refers to a necklace owned by Police Commissioner Gordon's wife, thus providing the first textual indication that Gordon is a married man (Feb '43: "License for Larceny").

According to World's Finest Comics No. 53, Mrs. Gordon married her husband on October 11, 1926, approximately two years after his graduation from law school. "A few years" later, while Gordon was still pounding a beat as a rookie policeman, Mrs. Gordon gave birth to an infant son, Tony Gordon, who is about ROBIN's age, or a little older. In this text, Mrs. Gordon is portrayed as an attractive white-haired woman with considerable poise and charm (Aug/Sep '51: "The Private Life of Commissioner Gordon!").

In August–September 1951, when BATMAN poses as Police Commissioner Gordon in order to guard against an anticipated attempt on the commissioner's life while the real commissioner goes into hiding, Mrs. Gordon leaves the city for a visit with her sister Martha (WF No. 53: "The Private Life of Commissioner Gordon!").

In June–July 1952, after Mrs. Gordon has informed her husband that she has heard him mumbling in his sleep about Batman's secret identity, Gordon becomes so overwrought that he hastily sends his wife away to visit their son in college. In this text, Mrs. Gordon is portrayed as a blonde. The son in college is presumably Tony Gordon, but this is never actually stated (BM No. 71/2: "Commissioner Gordon's Greatest Case!").

GORDON, JOHN (Captain). The captain of the Mississippi River showboat *River Queen* and the great-grandfather of POLICE COMMISSIONER JAMES W. GORDON. Sent into the past — to the year 1854 — by PROFESSOR CARTER NICHOLS, BATMAN and ROBIN clear Captain Gordon of the charge that he was once the "central figure" in a series of daring river crimes and apprehend the real villain, Baird Hawes, the director of the *River Queen*'s acting troupe, who had deliberately worn a captain's uniform during each of the robberies in order to cast suspicion on Captain Gordon (BM No. 89/1, Feb '55: "River Rogues").

GORDON, TONY. The teen-aged son of POLICE COMMISSIONER JAMES W. GORDON and his wife (*see* GORDON, JAMES W. [MRS.]) (WF No. 53, Aug/Sep '51: "The Private Life of Commissioner Gordon!") and, presumably, the brother of Barbara Gordon (*see* BATGIRL [BARBARA GORDON]), although this fact is never actually stated in the texts.

According to World's Finest Comics No. 53, Mrs. Gordon married her husband on October 11, 1926, and gave birth to Tony Gordon "a few years" later. In this text, Tony is portrayed as an approximate contemporary of ROBIN (Aug/Sep '51: "The Private Life of Commissioner Gordon!").

In June–July 1952, after Mrs. Gordon has informed her husband that she has heard him mumbling in his sleep about BATMAN's secret identity, Gordon becomes overwrought and hastily sends his wife away to visit their son in college. The son in college is presumably Tony Gordon, but this is never actually stated (BM No. 71/2: "Commissioner Gordon's Greatest Case!"). Because Dick Grayson, the boy who is secretly Robin, is still a high school student during this period, it seems safe to assume that Tony Gordon, at least in this text, is a few years Robin's senior.

GORILLA GANG, THE. A three-man gang of criminals, all clad in gorilla costumes, who commit a series of spectacular crimes in GOTHAM CITY in June 1963 before they are finally apprehended by BATMAN and ROBIN. The Dynamic Duo's efforts to capture the Gorilla Gang are severely hampered by the fact that Batman's recent participation in a demanding "space medicine" experiment – designed to help anticipate the effects of prolonged isolation on astronauts – has had the undesirable aftereffect of leaving Batman temporarily susceptible to a terrifying, recurring hallucination – filled with alien monsters and tentacled, man-eating plants – that periodically overwhelms him, causing him to become terror-stricken and irrational, and making it virtually impossible for him to fight crime effectively until the effects of the debilitating hallucination have passed (BM No. 156/2: "Robin Dies at Dawn!").

GORMAN, DUKE. An alias employed by BATMAN in February 1952 when he poses as an underworld figure as part of his plan to trap the JOKER (Det No. 180: "The Joker's Millions!").

GORNEY, GOLDPLATE. A "high-powered crook," sent to prison by BATMAN and ROBIN three times in the past and therefore likely to be sentenced to a life term if ever captured again, who concocts an elaborate scheme to kidnap Robin and then murder both members of the Dynamic Duo when Batman attempts to secure his young partner's release.

Acting on the logical assumption that Robin is a top high school athlete in his civilian identity, Gorney and his henchmen attend GOTHAM CITY's all-city high school track meet with the intention of kidnapping the youngster who emerges from the competition as all-city champion. As the criminals had anticipated, Robin, in his Dick Grayson identity, has indeed entered the competition, but because Grayson intentionally compromises his own performance to avoid betraying the true extent of his athletic prowess and thus endangering the secret of his dual identity, the criminals end up abducting higher-scoring youngster Hugh Ross and leaping to the wholly erroneous conclusion that Ross's father is secretly Batman.

Ultimately, however, Batman and Robin rescue young Ross and apprehend his abductors, leaving them as ignorant as ever concerning their true identities (WF No. 23, Jul/Aug '46: "Champions Don't Brag!").

GOSS, JOHN. The assistant curator of the Sky Museum, a museum on the outskirts of GOTHAM CITY housing "the world's greatest collection of ancient airships and planes." Using his job as a cover, Goss has been charging wanted criminals large sums of money to smuggle them out of Gotham City inside a large zeppelin from the museum's collection, but BATMAN and ROBIN apprehend Goss in September 1955, along with an airship full of criminals whom Goss is attempting to smuggle to safety (BM No. 94/3: "The Mystery of the Sky Museum!").

GOTHAM CITY. The resident city of BATMAN and ROBIN and the scene of the vast majority of the Dynamic Duo's adventures. Although the name Gotham City is itself fictional, Gotham City as it is described in the texts is modeled after, and fully intended to represent, the city of New York. New York is, in fact, explicitly cited in the earliest texts (Det No. 31, Sep '39; and others) as the resident city of Batman until the name Gotham City is introduced into the chronicles in the early months of 1941 (BM No. 4/4, Win '41; Det No. 48, Feb '41: "The Secret Cavern"). For the writer of Detective Comics No. 53, the sprawling megalopolis held an almost mystical fascination:

> Glittering, irresistible – that vast magnet which is **Gotham City,** draws to itself an army of millions yearly from every town and village in America. There is no withstanding its lure----for here is a city where you may touch the clouds atop some towering skyscraper--or go down deep in the earth to ride aboard its roaring subway trains! To **Gotham City** they come--to carve their names in foot-high letters on the famous sidewalks. Some succeed---some fail! Some leave---some stay! Some curse the city, others love it! But every one of them has something to say about **Gotham City**---for no one may ignore this gigantic ant heap! (Jul '41).

The evidence identifying Gotham City with the city of New York is overwhelming, even disregarding the fact that Gotham is itself a nickname for New York. Situated on the East Coast of the United States (BM No. 68/1, Dec/Jan '51–'52: "The Atom Cave Raiders!"), the largest city in Gotham State (BM No. 18/4, Aug/Sep '43: "The Crime Surgeon!"; and others), it is a major seaport with a large waterfront (Det No. 113, Jul '46: "Crime on the Half-Shell!"; and many others) populated by "eight-million faceless people" (BM No. 217, Dec '69: "One Bullet Too Many!"). The "symbol of Gotham City" is Father Knickerbocker (Det No. 368, Oct '67: "7 Wonder Crimes of Gotham City!"), and the world-famed Statue of Liberty stands vigilant in the city's harbor (Det No. 63, May '42: "A Gentleman in Gotham"; and others).

Gotham City's mightiest skyscraper is variously referred to as the State Building (BM No. 120/2, Dec '58: "The Failure of Bruce Wayne"; and others), the Great State Building (Det No. 63, May '42: "A Gentleman in Gotham"), the Capital State Building (Det No. 50, Apr '41: "The Case of the Three Devils!"), the Monarch State Building (Det No. 165, Nov '50: "The Strange Costumes of Batman!"), and the Gotham State Building (BM No. 162/1, Mar '64: "The Batman Creature!"), but, whatever its name, the structure is more than 100 stories tall (Det No. 53, Jul '41), features an outdoor observation deck with viewing telescopes (BM No. 89/3, Feb '55: "Bruce Wayne's Aunt Agatha!" and others), and is the "highest point in Gotham's skyline" (BM No. 42/3, Aug/Sep '47: "The Robot Robbers!").

Visitors to Gotham City may ride a sightseeing bus through the Bowery (Det No. 58, Dec '41) or past the city's "sprawling wharf district" (BM No. 118/3, Sep '58: "The Merman Batman!"); enjoy an Oriental meal in Chinatown (BM No. 48/1, Aug/Sep '48: "The Fowls of Fate!"; and others); take in a movie in the midtown area (BM No. 9/3, Feb/Mar '42: "The Case of the Lucky Law-Breakers!"); tour the bustling financial district (Det No. 72, Feb '43: "License for Larceny"); stroll through picturesque Gotham Village with its Bohemian atmosphere and sidewalk cafés (Det No. 327, May '64:

"The Mystery of the Menacing Mask!"); or perhaps just spend time familiarizing themselves with Gotham City's other famous neighborhoods, including the East Side (BM No. 50/3, Dec/Jan '48–'49: "The Second Boy Wonder!"), the Lower East Side (BM No. 14/2, Dec/Jan '42–'43: "Prescription for Happiness!"), Chelsea (BM No. 50/3, Dec/Jan '48–'49: "The Second Boy Wonder!"), and fashionable Park Avenue (Det No. 66, Aug '42: "The Crimes of Two-Face!").

Those interested mainly in recreation and relaxation will enjoy strolling past Gotham City's famed Fifth Avenue shops (Det No. 53, Jul '41); visiting the Gotham City Navy Yard (BM No. 72/1, Aug/Sep '52: "The Jungle Batman!"); taking in a concert at Tarnegie Hall (Det No. 80, Oct '43: "The End of Two-Face!") or a sporting event at Gotham Square Garden (Det No. 206, Apr '54: "The Trapper of Gotham City!"; and others); touring the Natural History Museum (BM No. 86/1, Sep '54: "The Voyage of the First Batmarine!") or visiting the public library to view its famous stone lions (WF No. 138, Dec '63: "The Secret of the Captive Cavemen!"); and buying gifts for friends at Spiffany's (BM No. 34/3, Apr/May '46: "The Master vs. the Pupil!") or Stacey's Department Store (BM No. 125/1, Aug '59: "The Secret Life of Bat-Hound"). On a warm day one can stroll through Central Park (BM No. 31/1, Oct/Nov '45: "Punch and Judy!"), take a boat ride on the park's lake (BM No. 86/1, Sep '54: "The Voyage of the First Batmarine!"), or just relax on a park bench with a copy of the Gotham *Times* (BM No. 171, May '65: "Remarkable Ruse of the Riddler!"). At night one can enjoy the majestic view of Gotham's East River (BM No. 8/1, Dec/Jan '41–'42: "Stone Walls Do Not a Prison Make").

Gotham City's most renowned citizen is indisputably Batman, and it is for him that the city has reserved its greatest honors. Batman Day is celebrated annually in Gotham (BM No. 103/1, Oct '56: "The Broken Batman Trophies"; WF No. 140, Mar '64: "The Clayface Superman!"), and the famed BATMAN MUSEUM houses an extensive collection of Batman memorabilia (BM No. 119/2, Oct '58: "The Secret of Batman Island!"; and others).

Statues and other artistic tributes to Batman abound in Gotham City. There is a bust of Batman in the Gotham City Hall of Fame (BM No. 111/3, Oct '57: "The Armored Batman!") and there are iron busts of both Batman and Robin on display in the City Museum (BM No. 109/1, Aug '57: "Three Crimes Against Batman"). There is a standing steel statue of Batman in City Park (BM No. 109/1, Aug '57: "Three Crimes Against Batman"), and a statue of a seated Batman in Gotham Park reminiscent of the statue of Abraham Lincoln in Washington, D.C.'s famed Lincoln Memorial (BM No. 107/1, Apr '57: "The Boy Who Adopted Batman"; BM No. 134/3, Sep '60: "The Deadly Dummy"). Standing majestically in Gotham Bay is the Batman Lighthouse, "a towering tribute to [the] great lawman" in the form of a gigantic lighthouse sculpted in Batman's image, with an upraised arm grasping an incandescent torch beacon. Batman No. 126/2 describes it as "a unique structure of steel, rearing 300 feet into the air--a towering figure that guides approaching ships" to safety with its ever-glowing beacon (Sep '59: "The Batman Lighthouse").

In order to discourage either criminals or hucksters from impersonating Batman, "a law was passed [in Gotham City] which forbids anyone appearing as the **Batman** except the **original Batman** of Gotham City or with his permission!" (Det No. 195, May '53: "The Original Batman!"; and others).

GRADY, "SPARKLES." The leader of a gang of criminals who waylay ROBIN at the site of GOTHAM CITY'S newly opened Batman Exposition—an open-air exposition featuring more than fifty memorials to BATMAN created by his admirers—in an effort to steal the fortune in diamonds which Robin is holding for the Rajah Punjab. Unable to rely upon the real Batman, who is temporarily out of action with a broken ankle, Robin employs the various Batman exhibits as crime-fighting weapons and, with their help, single-handedly apprehends Grady and his henchmen (BM No. 104/2, Dec '56: "Robin's 50 Batman Partners").

GRAEME, BLAIR. An alias employed by BATMAN in October 1957 when he poses as a fanatic making violent threats against Batman so that he and ROBIN will have a ready-made excuse for wearing full suits of armor in public. A panic might result were the public to learn that a supply of dangerously radioactive "atomic fuel" has been stolen and is somewhere in the city, a secret which could well leak out if Batman and Robin were to be seen openly wearing the special radiation-proof clothing that they are now able to conceal beneath the more ostentatious armor. The elaborate ruse is abandoned as soon as Batman and Robin have recovered the stolen atomic fuel and apprehended the thieves at their waterfront warehouse (BM No. 111/3: "The Armored Batman!").

GRAHAM. A technical expert at Paragon Pictures, responsible for the construction of ancient weapons replicas used in the studio's movies, who becomes mentally unbalanced as the result of an accidental blow on the head and, clad in medieval garb and a purple hood which covers his entire head, commits a series of spectacular robberies with the aid of replicas of such ancient weapons as the ballista and the catapult. Graham and his henchmen are finally apprehended in March 1960 through the heroic efforts of BATMAN, ROBIN, and ACE THE BAT-HOUND (BM No. 130/2: "The Master of Weapons").

GRAMBLY (General). The cunning criminal mastermind and self-styled "Napoleon of crime" who is the leader of the Purple Legion, a gang of criminals whose members wear purple military-style uniforms, function in the manner of a military unit, and carry out ingeniously complex crimes with practiced military precision.

In August 1961 BATMAN, ROBIN, and SUPERMAN join forces in an elaborate scheme to apprehend General Grambly and defeat the Purple Legion by replacing Superman with a lifelike Superman robot while the real Superman dons a colorful tiger-striped costume and assumes the fictitious identity of Tigerman, a hopelessly inept crime-fighter who seems to enjoy some sort of mysterious hold over Batman, Robin, and Superman. Eventually, as the three heroes had anticipated, General Grambly becomes eager to learn exactly why Batman, Robin, and Superman seem so willingly subservient to the bungling Tigerman. When Grambly's henchmen capture Tigerman and usher him into the general's secret mobile headquarters for questioning, Batman and Robin appear on the scene and apprehend General Grambly and his Purple Legionnaires (WF No. 119: "The Secret of Tigerman!").

GRANDA (the Mystic). An unscrupulous fortune-teller who hypnotizes his clients into revealing their innermost secrets, then uses these secrets to blackmail them. Granda and his henchmen are apprehended by BATMAN and ROBIN in October–November 1941, with the aid of POLICE COMMISSIONER GORDON and the GOTHAM CITY police (BM No. 7/2: "The Trouble Trap!").

GRANEY, GUY. A notorious "underworld racket leader" who, having stolen an ingenious "mind ray" invention designed to enable its operator to control the minds of others, offers a prize of $100,000 to whichever of his cohorts is "strong-willed enough" to control the mind of BATMAN and force him to reveal his secret identity in public. The efforts to control Batman's mind all end in failure, however, and Graney and his henchmen are ultimately apprehended by Batman, ROBIN, and ALFRED (BM No. 106/3, Mar '57: "The Puppet Batman!").

GRAVES (1940). An art teacher at the exclusive Blake School for Boys and a "master engraver" who, in partnership with Blake, the head of the Blake School, runs an elaborate counterfeiting operation headquartered in an abandoned dwelling not far from the school. Although Graves murders Blake to prevent him from talking, BATMAN and ROBIN ultimately apprehend the counterfeiters and unmask Graves as their leader (Det No. 41, Jul '40).

GRAVES (1942). The announcer on the "Racket-Smashers" radio and television program, a show which dramatizes near-perfect crimes culled from police department files, and the secret leader of a gang of criminals who study the scripts scheduled for use on the program and then actually commit the crimes on which the scripts are based, taking care to avoid the mistakes that resulted in the capture of the original gangs that committed them. Graves and his henchmen are exposed and apprehended by BATMAN and ROBIN in Summer 1942 (WF No. 6: "The Secret of Bruce Wayne!").

GRAVIO. The surname of a cruel, tyrannical family—inhabitants of the so-called "lost valley of the birdmen," situated somewhere "on another continent"—who, having discovered the means, generations ago, of grafting huge birdlike wings onto their bodies to endow them with the power of flight, and having successfully limited access to the rare "serum alpha" necessary for the operation to their own clan, have established an iron grip over the other residents of the valley, who, lacking wings of their own, are "powerless to cope with the slashing attacks of the winged Gravios."

In March 1954 BATMAN and ROBIN are abducted from GOTHAM CITY by Sandago Gravio, a member of the Gravio clan who, disenchanted with his family's evil ways, is determined to use force if necessary to persuade the Dynamic Duo to defeat the Gravios and bring justice to the valley. At Sandago's urging, Batman allows a pair of gigantic batlike wings to be temporarily grafted to his body so that he can meet the Gravios on their own terms, and before long, with Robin's help, he succeeds in defeating the Gravios and ending their tyranny over the valley's inhabitants. Returned to Gotham City while under the influence of anesthesia, however, Batman and Robin awaken with the thought that perhaps the entire adventure was only a vivid dream (BM No. 82/1: "The Flying Batman").

GRAY (Dean). The dean of Gotham University, long noted for his ability to help students in trouble, who, upon retirement, establishes Trouble, Inc., a confidential counseling service for people in trouble. In September 1945 gangster Sam Slick and his henchmen rent office space adjoining Trouble, Inc., eavesdrop on Gray's clients, and attempt in various ways to capitalize on the confidential information that they overhear. They are ultimately apprehended by BATMAN and ROBIN (Det No. 103: "Trouble, Incorporated!").

GRAYSON, CLARA. The alias employed by GEORGE GRAYSON's young female accomplice. The fact that Clara Grayson wears an elaborate disguise designed to make her appear much older than she actually is, apparently for the purpose of lending added respectability to George Grayson's custody suit, suggests that she is not really Grayson's wife and that her real name is not Clara Grayson. However, her real name and the true nature of her relationship with George Grayson are never stated in the chronicles (BM No. 20/4, Dec/Jan '43–'44: "Bruce Wayne Loses the Guardianship of Dick Grayson!").

GRAYSON, DICK. The teen-aged boy who is secretly ROBIN, the inseparable crime-fighting companion of BATMAN. Dick Grayson is the ward of socialite Bruce Wayne, the man who is secretly Batman.

Dick Grayson is the orphaned son of John and Mary Grayson, a husband-wife team of circus trapeze artists who, with their young son Dick, comprised the FLYING GRAYSONS until they were murdered by protection racketeers in April 1940 (Det No. 38). It was Batman who took the young orphan under his wing, helped him avenge the deaths of his parents, trained him for his new life as a crime-fighter, and, as Bruce Wayne, took the legal steps necessary to establish himself as Dick Grayson's "legal guardian" (BM No. 213/1, Jul/Aug '69: "The Origin of Robin!").

It is not possible to establish Dick Grayson's age with any real precision. There were fourteen candles on his birthday cake in April–May 1942, indicating that he turned fourteen during this period, or, if one of these candles was only a "good luck" candle, thirteen. On this same occasion, curiously enough, Bruce Wayne ceremoniously spanks his young ward eight times, plus "one for good measure" and another "to grow on," but it seems absurd to suggest that Grayson was only eight years old at this time (BM No. 10/1: "The Isle That Time Forgot!"). The chronicles, at any rate, treat Grayson as a student of high school age until December 1969, at which time, having apparently attained college age, he departs GOTHAM CITY to attend his first year of classes at Hudson University (BM No. 217: "One Bullet Too Many!").

Dick Grayson's living relatives include an unscrupulous uncle named GEORGE GRAYSON, who wins legal custody of his young nephew in December 1943–January 1944 as part of an elaborate scheme to extort $1,000,000 from Bruce Wayne (BM No. 20/4: "Bruce Wayne Loses the Guardianship of Dick Grayson!"), and a well-meaning if somewhat overprotective aunt named AUNT HARRIET (Det No. 328, Jun '64: "Gotham Gang Line-Up!"; and others). (*See* ROBIN.)

GRAYSON, GEORGE. The brother of JOHN GRAYSON, now deceased, and the uncle of Dick Grayson, the boy who is secretly ROBIN. In December 1943–January 1944 George Grayson – aided by a female accomplice who poses as his wife and calls herself CLARA GRAYSON – attempts to win legal custody of Dick Grayson as part of a scheme to extort 1,000,000 dollars from BRUCE WAYNE, but the scheme is ultimately thwarted through the heroic efforts of BATMAN, Robin, and ALFRED (BM No. 20/4: "Bruce Wayne Loses the Guardianship of Dick Grayson!"). (*See* ROBIN.)

GRAYSON, JOHN. The husband, now deceased, of Mary Grayson, and the father of Dick Grayson, the boy who is secretly ROBIN. Prior to the tragic deaths of John and Mary Grayson in April 1940, John Grayson and his wife and son comprised the daring trapeze troupe known as the FLYING GRAYSONS (Det No. 38). GEORGE GRAYSON, the man who attempts to win legal custody of Dick Grayson in December 1943–January 1944 as part of a scheme to bilk BRUCE WAYNE out of $1,000,000, is John Grayson's brother (BM No. 20/4: "Bruce Wayne Loses the Guardianship of Dick Grayson!").

GRAYSON, MARY. The wife, now deceased, of JOHN GRAYSON, and the mother of Dick Grayson, the boy who is secretly ROBIN. Prior to the tragic deaths of John and Mary Grayson in April 1940, John Grayson and his wife and son comprised the daring trapeze troupe known as the FLYING GRAYSONS (Det No. 38).

GREAT EAGLE. The Sioux Indian who is secretly CHIEF MAN-OF-THE-BATS. His son, Little Raven, is an almost perfect look-alike for ROBIN (BM No. 86/3, Sep '54: "Batman--Indian Chief!"). (*See also* BATMAN [section F, the Batman counterparts].)

GREAT SWAMI, THE. The nightclub mind-reader whose real name is "Muggsy" Morton. He is secretly the PHANTOM BANDIT (BM No. 81/3, Feb '54: "The Phantom Bandit of Gotham City!").

GREEN, DICK. An alias employed by ROBIN in August 1955 when he and BATMAN join a mountain-climbing expedition up the side of MOUNT K-4 as part of their plan to recover a vital roll of microfilm for the F.B.I. (BM No. 93/1: "Journey to the Top of the World!").

GREEN DRAGON, THE. A hatchet-wielding Chinese tong whose members "work many wicked enterprises" in the city, including murder, opium smuggling, and the kidnapping of wealthy men for ransom. BATMAN's friend WONG is murdered by tong agents in May 1940. "You are stubborn, eh?" smirks the tong's leader, when a captured ROBIN refuses to reveal the whereabouts of Batman. ". . . you know, I like to see things wriggle. You shall wriggle before me . . . with pain! . . Hee! Hee! Hee!"

Moments later, however, Batman intervenes, and he and Robin apprehend the tong leader and kill or capture all his henchmen (Det No. 39).

GREEN MASK BANDITS, THE. A gang of criminals – named for their green masks and noted for their habit of making their getaways by blimp – who are apprehended by BATMAN and ROBIN in September 1962 with the aid of ALPHA, THE EXPERIMENTAL MAN (Det No. 307: "Alpha, the Experimental Man!").

GREER, HARLISS. A "crafty politician" and city council president in an unnamed United States city who succeeds to the mayoralty upon the sudden death of the elected mayor and, under the patronage of racketeer "Bugs" Norton, ousts all honest public officials, forces the city's policemen into retirement and replaces them with hired hoodlums, and transforms the city into a "racketeer's paradise" where gambling and the drug traffic function openly, without fear of official interference.

With City Hall clearly in the hands of the mob, honest government seems doomed, but BATMAN is not yet ready to admit defeat: "If you can't beat them 'inside' the law," he explains to a local citizen, "you must beat them 'outside' it--and that's where I come in!"

After he and ROBIN have staged a series of daring commando raids on "Bugs" Norton's underworld operations and embroiled themselves in a series of skirmishes with the city's bogus cops, Batman calls a public meeting, "skillfully . . . urges the people to battle against the racketeers who have enslaved them," and then helps an aroused citizenry capture Harliss Greer, "Bugs" Norton, and their cohorts and restore honest government to the city (Det No. 43, Sep '40: "The Case of the City of Terror").

GREGGSON (Dr.). The GOTHAM CITY scientist who is the inventor of the two incredible "projectors" known as the "maximizer" and the "minimizer." "My **maximizer,**" explains Greggson, "enlarges any object by drawing cosmic electricity to expand its atoms! My **minimizer** diminishes an object by the reverse process!" Dr. Greggson's minimizer is stolen by underworld figure JAY VANNEY in May 1957 (Det No. 243: "Batman the Giant!").

GREGORIAN, PAUL. A successful magician, banned from the stage after some difficulties with the police, who has spent ten years perfecting new illusions and escape devices in preparation for a triumphant comeback under a new name, Gregorian. His real last name is apparently Martin, for he is described as the brother of gangster Hoofer Martin.

To pave the way for his comeback, Gregorian presents himself to the public as a man with nine lives, then involves himself in a series of spectacular stunts in which he escapes seemingly certain death by means of his special illusions and escape devices. However, by threatening to reveal certain aspects of Gregorian's unsavory past to the police, Hoofer Martin forces his brother to use his elaborate stage illusions to help his gang commit a series of spectacular crimes. Ultimately, BATMAN, ROBIN, and members of the Gotham City Police Department close in on Martin's hideout and capture the assembled criminals, but Gregorian dies when, in a desperate effort to evade capture, he hurls himself through an open window and smashes his head against a brick wall (Det No. 172, Jun '51: "The Outlaw Who Had Nine Lives!").

GRIMES, BASIL. An unscrupulous architect, once the partner of honest architect Ray Arliss in the development of an experimental house made entirely of shatterproof glass. Grimes enters into a conspiracy with an unscrupulous steel magnate to construct a steel house right next to Arliss's glass house and then hire gangsters to destroy the glass house as a means of publicizing the superiority of steel houses over glass ones. BATMAN and ROBIN thwart several attempts to demolish the glass house and finally apprehend Grimes and his henchmen in September 1946 (Det No. 115: "The Man Who Lived in a Glass House!").

GRIMES, ROCKY. A convicted felon, released from prison after serving a twenty-year term for bank robbery and murder, who vows revenge against his former gangland confederates for betraying him to the police and forcing him to stand trial alone for the bank robbery and murder they all committed together. Cornered by BATMAN and ROBIN after murdering two former accomplices and attempting to kill three others, Grimes accidentally falls off a high bridge and plummets to his doom (BM No. 13/3, Oct/Nov '42: "The Story of the Seventeen Stones!").

GROAT, "KNUCKLES." An alias employed by BATMAN in March 1953 when he poses as a fugitive criminal in order to obtain employment on the *JOKER'S JOURNAL* (Det No. 193: "The Joker's Journal!").

GROFF. One of a group of volunteers who have been undergoing space-medicine tests at the Space Research College near GOTHAM CITY to determine the adaptability of man to the conditions of space and to the hostile environments of the various planets. In June 1954, when criminals in Gotham City blast open the vault of a local bank with the aid of a guided missile powered by R-17, "the most secret and powerful rocket fuel in existence," BATMAN and ROBIN visit the Space Research College to learn how the top-secret rocket fuel found its way into criminal hands. Almost from the beginning, suspicion focuses on the various space-medicine volunteers. Ultimately Batman and Robin discover that Groff is the villain and take him into custody (Det No. 208: "The Nine Worlds of Batman!").

GROFF, JO-JO. The leader of a gang of criminals who commit a series of spectacular crimes with the aid of a mighty caveman from KRYPTON, a Stone Age survivor of SUPERMAN's home planet endowed with superhuman powers identical to Superman's, who awakens to renewed life after arriving on Earth in a state of suspended animation in the heart of a meteor, and whom the criminals dupe into becoming their friend. BATMAN, ROBIN, and Superman finally apprehend the villains in June 1959, and the lumbering caveman – hopelessly out of place on an alien planet in an alien era – dies moments afterward from the combined effects of his recent exposure to KRYPTONITE and the bombardment of cosmic rays he endured during his journey through space (WF No. 102: "The Caveman from Krypton!").

GROGAN, MIKE. One of a "mysterious band of bank robbers" who have been terrorizing GOTHAM CITY, and the older brother of Tommy Grogan, a youngster who idolizes his older brother and has consequently accompanied the gang on some of its holdups. When Tommy is wounded by gunfire during a midtown bank robbery, the gang kidnaps nurse LINDA PAGE to treat Tommy at their hideout, but when Tommy's condition threatens to imperil their getaway, and Mike Grogan refuses to abandon his kid brother, another member of the gang shoots the elder Grogan, mortally wounding him. BATMAN and ROBIN apprehend the criminals soon afterward, aided by Linda Page and the timely arrival of the Gotham City police, and Tommy Grogan promises to abandon his short-lived life of crime after his older brother Mike, with his dying breath, begs him to go straight from now on (BM No. 5/4, Spr '41).

GROSSET, BLINKY. A wily gangster who anonymously donates a large sum of money to GOTHAM CITY to finance a publicity campaign for BATMAN, ostensibly because he believes that publicizing Batman's exploits will discourage would-be evildoers, but actually because he hopes that Batman's various publicity activities will provide him with opportunities for committing a series of spectacular crimes. Although duped at first into cooperating with the publicity effort, Batman and ROBIN ultimately apprehend Grosset and his henchmen and expose Grosset as the anonymous donor (BM No. 91/2, Apr '55: "Batman's Publicity Agent!").

GROTE (General). The leader of a gang of power-mad rebels on a far-distant planet who kidnap a group of primitive cavemen from Earth's distant past for use as slave laborers on their native planet as part of a diabolical scheme to assassinate the leaders of their own government and then use their home planet as a base from which to carry out the bloody conquest and colonization of twentieth-century Earth. The plot is ultimately thwarted, and General Grote and his henchmen are apprehended, through the heroic efforts of BATMAN, ROBIN, and SUPERMAN (WF No. 138, Dec '63: "The Secret of the Captive Cavemen!").

GRUTT (Count). A ruthless international spy who attempts to create an international incident by having his henchmen blow up the foreign liner *Ronij* while making the United States appear responsible. Count Grutt's aliases include the name Elias Turg and the enigmatic title the Head. BATMAN thwarts the attempted sabotage, and Count Grutt dies soon afterward when, during a battle with Batman, he accidentally impales himself on his own sword (Det No. 37, Mar '40).

GUILE, HENRY, III. The embittered thespian who

achieves infamy as the Globe-Trotter (*see* GLOBE-TROTTER, THE [HENRY GUILE III]) (Det No. 160, Jun '50: "The Globe-Trotter of Crime!").

GURLIN, SIMON. The leader of a gang of criminals who match wits with BATMAN and ROBIN in November 1945. The Dynamic Duo's efforts to apprehend the Gurlin gang are severely hampered by the fact that a huge embezzlement from the Wayne Motor Co. has left Bruce Wayne and Dick Grayson – the man and boy who are secretly Batman and Robin – completely penniless, and therefore without the necessary funds to carry on their crime-fighting.

Dick Grayson suggests that he and Wayne obtain full-time jobs in order to help them continue their fight against the underworld, but Wayne explains that that is impossible. "You forget, fella," he reminds Grayson, "that being **Batman** and **Robin** is almost a full-time job in itself! There's a lot more to it than chasing crooks! **Batman** and **Robin** must constantly put in long hours of study of criminology, police methods, science. . . . Sometimes they must spend whole days and nights in the secret laboratory experimenting in search of clues . . . not to mention the daily workout in the gym, keeping in fighting shape!"

Reluctantly, Batman and Robin decide to apprehend the Simon Gurlin gang and then give up crime-fighting altogether in the face of their almost total lack of funds. Indeed, in the days that follow, Dick Grayson is forced to work as a newsboy and ALFRED is compelled to mow lawns merely to provide the Dynamic Duo with enough money to buy gasoline for the BATMOBILE. When the batmobile breaks down and requires $20 worth of minor repairs, Batman and Robin put on a paid acrobatic exhibition at a country fair in order to raise the money to pay for them.

In spite of these travails, however, Batman and Robin finally apprehend Gurlin and his henchmen in the town of Lansboro. Later, upon returning to GOTHAM CITY, they learn that police detectives have successfully apprehended the dishonest treasurer who absconded with the Wayne Motor Co. funds, thus ensuring that the Dynamic Duo will be able to continue their crime-fighting careers after all.

"There was never any doubt in my mind that they'd continue in action . . ." sighs a relieved Alfred. "Though I must confess I was a bit dismayed at the prospect of supporting them in their customary manner by pushing a lawn mower!" (Det No. 105: "The Batman Goes Broke!").

H

HACKETT, AL. A fugitive criminal who is the object of an intensive manhunt by BATMAN and ROBIN in October 1958.

While Robin searches for Hackett at his waterfront hideout, Batman drives to Hackett's mountain lodge where, after accidentally inhaling the hallucinogenic fumes of one of Hackett's exotic Amazon plants, he lapses into unconsciousness and dreams that, like the legendary Rip Van Winkle, he has awakened after a sleep of many years to find that he is now an old man and that the once-familiar world has completely passed him by. In the dream, GOTHAM CITY is a futuristic space-age metropolis and Dick Grayson, now a grown man, battles crime as Batman alongside a new, blond Robin.

When Batman finally awakens from his bizarre dream, he finds Robin leaning over him, excitedly telling him about his successful capture of Hackett at the waterfront hideout (BM No. 119/3: "Rip Van Batman!").

HACKETT AND SNEAD. The unscrupulous owners of the Hackett and Snead Circus, who hire a gangster named Grimes to murder Professor Drake and make off with Goliath – a fifteen-foot-tall giant, described as the "missing link" between ape and man, whom Drake recently brought to this country from Africa – so that they can feature the gigantic man-ape as an attraction in their circus. Hackett and Snead are ultimately apprehended through the heroic efforts of BATMAN and ROBIN. Goliath – who goes on a berserk rampage at the sight of Grimes in a crowd of circusgoers – is killed by a pellet from Robin's slingshot, but not before the gargantuan man-ape has taken murderous revenge on the villainous Grimes by bashing his head open against a circus pole "with a sickening thud" (BM No. 2/4, Sum '40: "The Case of the Missing Link").

HADLEY, BRASS. A "ruthless criminal," wanted for murder by the police, who, after suffering a heart attack and being informed by a physician that he is afflicted with a rare heart ailment shared by only four other men in GOTHAM CITY, decides to kidnap the four men and force them to undergo a series of exacting physical tests, like human guinea pigs, so that he can determine, without danger to himself, whether or not it will be safe for him to undertake a series of elaborate crime schemes involving strenuous physical exertion.

Late at night, Hadley sneaks into the doctor's office, copies down the names and addresses of the four heart patients, and then arranges for the kidnapping of all four. Fate has intervened, however, in the form of a misplaced file in the doctor's office, and, because of the mix-up, Bruce Wayne – the man who is secretly BATMAN – soon finds himself in Hadley's clutches along with three of the real heart patients, even though he is actually in perfect health.

Ultimately, Batman and ROBIN rescue the heart patients from the villain's clutches and take Hadley's henchmen into custody. Hadley, however, confident that strenuous swimming is completely safe for him after having recently watched Bruce Wayne swimming energetically at the Gotham Beach Club to no apparent ill effect, leaps into the water and swims desperately toward his one-man submarine in a last-ditch effort to escape, only to die from a heart seizure brought on by the sudden overexertion.

"Ironic, isn't it?" muses Batman aloud, after he and Robin have dragged Hadley's lifeless body from the water. "A killer who dreamed up the cruel scheme of using human guinea pigs--and the scheme itself was responsible for his death! A strange justice, Robin--but justice all the same!" (WF No. 66, Sep/Oct '53: "The Proving Ground for Crime!").

HAGEN (Dr.). The "well-known expert on foreign weapons" who is secretly the RENTER (BM No. 73/1, Oct/Nov '52: "Guns for Hire!").

HAGEN, MATT. The unscrupulous skin diver who achieves infamy as Clayface (Det No. 298, Dec '61: "The Challenge of Clay-Face"). (*See* CLAYFACE [MATT HAGEN].)

HAINER, HARVEY (Sgt.). A veteran GOTHAM CITY police officer – afflicted with steadily worsening eyesight as the result of an old bullet wound – who, as an alternative to early retirement from the police force, is assigned the relatively undemanding duty of operating the BAT-SIGNAL from the roof of police headquarters

Police Commissioner Gordon and Sgt. Harvey Hainer, 1954 © NPP 1954

(BM No. 85/2, Aug '54: "The Guardian of the Bat-Signal!"), a job he has held now for more than twenty years (BM No. 265, Jul '75: "Batman's Greatest Failure!").

HALE (Professor). The head curator of GOTHAM CITY's Mechanical Museum of Natural History, a vast museum housing a series of colorful exhibits featuring lifelike mechanical animals, all of them "robot-controlled so that they seem to be almost alive!" When Hale is found murdered among the dinosaur exhibits in May 1958, BATMAN and ROBIN are confronted with four prime suspects: Albert Linke, the museum's taxidermist, who had been "Hale's rival for the love of a girl they both knew"; Mario Nazzara, a museum official who had been "envious and bitter" because Hale, and not he, had been appointed to the post of head curator; John Logan, the museum's master electrician, who had "quarreled with Hale about technical details of [the exhibits'] robot-controls"; and Carl Danton, the museum's secretary, who had "quarreled with Hale over [the] mounting expenses of exhibits." An investigation by the Dynamic Duo, however, swiftly pinpoints the real killer, Carl Danton, who had murdered Hale in order to prevent him from disclosing that Danton had been embezzling large sums from the museum's treasury (Det No. 255: "Death in Dinosaur Hall!").

HALL, HUBERT. A cunning criminal who has painstakingly trained himself to perform many of BATMAN's acrobatic and crime-fighting stunts in order to win the role of Batman in Gotham Movie Studios' upcoming film version of Batman's life so that he and his gangland confederates, members of the "Twisty" Rhodes gang, can rob the Gotham Mint while one of the film sequences is being shot there. When Hall is threatened with dismissal from the movie because of his uncommonly poor acting ability, he launches a series of savage attacks on the other prospective candidates for the Batman role, hoping to injure them sufficiently to prevent their participation in the movie. Batman and ROBIN thwart most of these attacks, however, and ultimately apprehend Hall and his confederates inside the Gotham Mint (BM No. 85/3, Aug '54: "The Costume of Doom!").

HAMMOND, W. W. The unscrupulous scriptwriter who is the author of *The Batman Story*, a movie filmed by Gotham City Movie Studios in February–March 1952. Because all rights to the script will revert to Hammond if the studio fails to complete the film within one year – thereby enabling Hammond to sell the script to still another buyer – Hammond hires the "Spaghetti" Thompson gang to terrorize the cast and crew and sabotage the production effort. To counter this threat, BATMAN and ROBIN pose as ordinary movie actors, obtain the leading roles in the film, and then carefully husband *The Batman Story* through its entire production phase while thwarting the efforts of Hammond's hirelings to disrupt the filming. Ultimately, the Dynamic Duo apprehend the entire "Spaghetti" Thompson gang and expose Hammond as the man who hired them (BM No. 69/1: "The Batman Exposé!").

HARBEN, RICK. An escaped convict who lures BATMAN, ROBIN, and SUPERMAN to his hideout in a "lonely mountain range," renders them unconscious with knockout gas and a chunk of KRYPTONITE, and then shuts them inside glass cases, in states of suspended animation, where they remain until the year 2957 A.D., when they are finally discovered by mine workers searching the area for lead deposits. In the futuristic world of the thirtieth century A.D., Batman, Robin, and Superman defeat the villainous ROHTUL before returning to their own time – with the aid of a futuristic "time-ray apparatus" – to take the ruthless Harben into custody (WF No. 91, Nov/Dec '57: "The Three Super-Sleepers!").

HARBIN. An assistant curator at the Gotham Museum who has been pilfering valuable gold curios from the museum's Mexican Room, replacing them with gold-plated lead duplicates, and then selling the originals to private collectors through Drager, a crooked curio-shop proprietor. When a curator discovers the thefts, Harbin kills him, but Harbin and Drager are both ultimately apprehended through the heroic efforts of BATMAN and ROBIN (Det No. 285, Nov '60: "The Mystery of the Man-Beast!").

HARDI LE NOIR (Sir). "The bold black knight," the title bestowed upon BATMAN by KING ARTHUR when he dubs Batman a knight in legendary Camelot in gratitude for his having cleared MERLIN the magician of the charge of treason and exposed the evil MORDRED as a spy for QUEEN MORGAN LE FAY and a traitor to the throne (BM No. 36/3, Aug/Sep '46: "Sir Batman at King Arthur's Court!").

HARE, TOOTHY. The leader of a gang of criminals who are captured by BATMAN and ROBIN after they have stolen some furs and jewelry from VIOLA VANE (Det No. 53, Jul '41).

HARMON, JAMES. The curator of rare gems at the Gotham City Museum, credited with having assembled "the world's finest collection of precious stones," who is abruptly dismissed from his post in March–April 1948 when it is discovered that he has mistakenly purchased an imitation blue sapphire for the museum's collection.

Enraged at the museum's five directors for having separated him from his beloved gems, Harmon decides to wreak vengeance on all of them by sending them deadly, elaborately contrived booby traps in the form of gigantic replicas of their own birthstones, each designed to deal death in a manner somehow related to a legend or superstition associated with the birthstone involved: one director, for example, receives a replica in the form of a huge ruby, and, in accordance with the Oriental legend that a fire burns inside each ruby, Harmon's ruby has been booby-trapped with a deadly incendiary bomb.

Harmon successfully murders two of the five directors before BATMAN and ROBIN finally corner him in his hideout in a Broadway pottery shop. Harmon dies when, during the battle which follows, he falls from the top of a huge diamond replica and impales himself on his own jeweled dagger (WF No. 33: "The 5 Jewels of Doom!").

HARMON, JOE. The master of ceremonies of a popular big-money television quiz show, "The Big Quiz," on which contestants compete for enormous cash prizes by answering questions in specialized categories. When contestant FRANK DAVIS, whose self-chosen quiz category is the career of BATMAN, refuses an illicit offer by Harmon to provide him with the answers to his questions beforehand in return for a share of the prize money and threatens to expose Harmon's illegal offer over nationwide television, Harmon murders Davis with poison gas in the show's isolation booth and attempts to frame a convict named Garth for the crime, only to be apprehended soon afterward by Batman in June 1957 (BM No. 108/1: "The Big Batman Quiz").

HARNER, KEENE. The leader of a gang of criminals who pose as disaster-fighters in order to loot stores and businesses during a raging hurricane in GOTHAM CITY. They are apprehended by BATMAN and ROBIN in March 1957, while attempting to loot the vault of the Gotham Branch Bank (BM No. 106/2: "Storm over Gotham City!").

HARPER, HARRIS. An unscrupulous cattle buyer in the nineteenth-century Western United States town of Plain City who has been systematically sabotaging the operations of the local railroad so that he can buy cattle at rock-bottom prices from ranchers who have been stymied in their efforts to ship their cattle out of Plain City by rail. Dispatched through the time-barrier by PROFESSOR CARTER NICHOLS to Plain City in the year 1880, BATMAN and ROBIN expose and apprehend Harris Harper along with his gang of hired henchmen. For a time, Batman agrees to serve as Plain City's marshal, and at one point, during a crucial battle with some of Harper's henchmen, his life is saved by the famous Bat Masterson, who has just arrived from the state capital to replace him as marshal (BM No. 99/2, Apr '56: "Batman--Frontier Marshal").

HARRAH (Mr.). The owner of the Harrah Construction Company, a firm which has contracted to build a network of storm sewers beneath GOTHAM CITY. Mr. Harrah is secretly the escaped convict known as the MOLE (WF No. 80, Jan/Feb '56: "The Super-Newspaper of Gotham City").

HARRIET (Aunt). DICK GRAYSON's middle-aged aunt. Aunt Harriet is warmhearted and well-intentioned, but she tends to be somewhat overprotective and to treat her nephew and his guardian BRUCE WAYNE as though they were "helpless boys" (Det No. 328, Jun '64: "Gotham Gang Line-Up!").

In June 1964, after ALFRED has been declared dead following an encounter with the notorious TRI-STATE GANG, Aunt Harriet informs Bruce Wayne and Dick Grayson that she has come to the Wayne mansion to take care of them both. "When I heard of Alfred's death," explains Aunt Harriet, "I knew you'd need somebody to take care of you--so I've decided to look after you both. . . ."

"B-But Aunt Harriet . . ." stammers Dick Grayson.

"You youngsters are so helpless," continues Aunt Harriet firmly, "you'll need someone to see to it that you take care of your health!"

"It's no use, Bruce!" sighs Dick Grayson, after further efforts to dissuade Aunt Harriet from moving in have proved fruitless. "Aunt Harriet still thinks of us as helpless boys! She's here for good!"

Aunt Harriet's continued presence in the Wayne household poses some serious dilemmas for Wayne and Grayson, not the least of which is maintaining the secrecy of their dual identities (Det No. 328: "Gotham Gang Line-Up!").

In March 1965 Aunt Harriet makes a series of somewhat ambiguous insinuations which lead BATMAN and ROBIN to worry that she has somehow penetrated their secret identities. "I still can't shake the feeling that Aunt Harriet knows that we're secretly ***Batman*** and ***Robin!***" remarks Batman uneasily. "She seemed to insinuate something in her remarks. . . ." On the whole, however, the Dynamic Duo's fears seem somewhat exaggerated, and the text contains no hard evidence that Aunt Harriet has actually stumbled upon their closely guarded secret (BM No. 170/2: "The Puzzle of the Perilous Prizes!").

While housecleaning in May 1966, however, Aunt Harriet accidentally opens the sliding wall panel which conceals the secret elevator connecting the Wayne mansion with the subterranean BATCAVE beneath it. Descending in the secret elevator, Aunt Harriet soon finds herself in the labyrinthine batcave and realizes with a start that her nephew and his guardian must secretly be Batman and Robin. When Wayne and Grayson deny the charge, Aunt Harriet places hidden cameras near the secret panel and on the access road leading to and from the batcave as part of an elaborate effort to confirm her suspicions, but Wayne and Grayson outwit Aunt Harriet by replacing the film shot by one of the hidden cameras with a specially contrived sequence showing Batman and Robin emerging from the secret panel and being greeted by their "friends" Bruce Wayne and Dick Grayson (Det No. 351: "The Cluemaster's Topsy-Turvy Crimes!").

In October 1966, after Alfred has emerged alive from his experience as the OUTSIDER and returned to the Wayne mansion for a happy reunion with Bruce Wayne and Dick Grayson, Aunt Harriet sadly announces her impending departure. "I--I'll go and p-pack my things!" murmurs Aunt Harriet. "N-Now that your trusty butler has re-returned, y-you won't n-need me anymore. . . ."

"Nonsense, Aunt Harriet!" replies Bruce Wayne. "We all need you!"

"Holy relations! I'll say!" chimes in Dick Grayson.

"Indeed we do, ma'am!" adds Alfred. "May I venture to say that I--need you most of all--since I'm not entirely well yet, and your cooking will speed my recovery!"

"Oh, bless you all!" cries Aunt Harriet happily (Det No. 356: "Inside Story of the Outsider!").

HARRIS, HARVEY. A renowned police detective who, according to Detective Comics No. 226, was the crime-fighting idol of the teen-aged Bruce Wayne, gave young Wayne what may well have been his first practical instruction in solving crimes and apprehending criminals, and, although he never admitted it to Bruce

Wayne during his lifetime, was one of the few people ever to deduce correctly that millionaire Bruce Wayne is secretly BATMAN. In a letter he arranges to have mailed to the Wayne mansion after his death, Harris admits that he solved the secret of Batman's identity and describes his former pupil as "the greatest detective of all," but Batman insists privately to Robin that his early mentor was "a greater detective than I!"

According to Detective Comics No. 226, Bruce Wayne approached Harris while he was still a teen-ager and begged Harris to instruct him in the art of detection, taking care to conceal his true identity from the great detective by wearing a bright red costume almost identical to the one that would one day be worn by Batman's young partner, ROBIN. According to this text, it was Harris who coined the name Robin: ". . . since you're brilliant as a robin redbreast in that costume," he told the disguised Bruce Wayne, "I'll call you--**Robin!**"

In the days that followed, Harris and his young pupil apprehended a gang of protection racketeers secretly led by wealthy Arthur Mellen, a collector of valuable ship-models whose henchmen were attempting to intimidate wealthy collectors into buying "collector's insurance" for their various collections and sabotaging the collections of those who refused to pay.

"Someday, you're going to be a great detective!" Harris told Wayne, after the criminals had finally been apprehended. "But until you're a man, you need to study and learn in preparation. I want you to wait until you've trained yourself fully, before you start a career that can be great!"

Young Wayne promised to abide by his mentor's advice, and soon afterward, as a sign of his sincerity, he made Harris a gift of the bright red Robin costume that he had worn throughout their investigation, confident that although he had made one or two detecting blunders during their work together he had nevertheless managed to keep his true identity a secret from Harris.

Years later, however, in December 1955, a package arrives at the Wayne mansion addressed to Bruce Wayne, containing the old Robin costume and a letter from Harris, explaining that he had long ago deduced that Bruce Wayne is Batman and had "left orders for this sealed package, your old **Robin** costume, to be sent to you at your Bruce Wayne home--after my death!

"I realized that if you were aware that I had learned your identity," explains the letter, "you'd always feel insecure, so I never told you--and I was right, for you've since become the greatest detective of all!"

"He was wrong, ***Robin!***" remarks Batman as he puts down the letter. He . . . was a greater detective than I!" ("When Batman Was Robin!").

HARRIS, HENRY. An alias employed by VINCENT CRAIL in June 1955 when, as part of his scheme to uncover the secret of BATMAN's identity, he writes a letter to Batman asking for his autograph (BM No. 92/1: "Fan-Mail of Danger!").

HARRIS BOYS, THE. A gang of criminals who are apprehended by BATMAN and ROBIN in November 1962. Their capture is delayed somewhat by a series of misadventures that befall the Dynamic Duo as they desperately attempt to recover a strange superscientific device – evidently abandoned in the distant past by some alien race during a visit to the planet Earth and now recently discovered by accident by a man out gathering herbs – which has the power to drastically accelerate the natural evolution of plants, animals, and geological formations, thus posing a potentially severe threat to GOTHAM CITY, or indeed the entire Earth, if used carelessly. Batman and Robin finally recover the device and apprehend the Harris Boys soon afterward (BM No. 151/2: "The Mystery Gadget from the Stars!").

HART (Mr.). A Fayetteville, West Virginia, businessman who commits a series of robberies and murders while masquerading as the JOKER. He is ultimately unmasked by the real Joker – who is enraged at what he regards as the sullying of his reputation by a clumsy amateur – and then taken into custody by BATMAN and ROBIN (Det No. 85, Mar '44: "The Joker's Double").

HART, MURRAY WILSON. The "master showman and specialist in the spectacular" who presides over Dinosaur Island, an island amusement park filled with robot cavemen and gigantic robot dinosaurs.

When, as a means of raising money for charity, BATMAN and ROBIN agree to participate in a friendly "touch tag" hunting competition which pits their skills against the island's mechanical dinosaurs, Chase, a would-be crime czar, kidnaps the man operating the dinosaurs' robot control box, surreptiously takes his place at the controls, and transforms the supposedly friendly hunt into a real one, attempting to destroy the Dynamic Duo with the mechanical monsters while making his murderous attacks appear accidental.

Batman and Robin thwart Chase at every turn, however, and ultimately defeat him by short-circuiting the master control panel with which he has been controlling the actions of the mechanical dinosaurs (BM No. 35/2, Jun/Jul '46: "Dinosaur Island!").

HARTLEY. A cunning "renegade scientist" who operates a secret hideout for wanted criminals inside an ancient Mayan temple somewhere in Central America. By posing as Tezcatlipoca, ancient Mayan god of witchcraft and destruction – and with the aid of a giant mechanical jaguar and flying serpent which he has invented to terrorize the local populace – Hartley has successfully frightened the local peasants into providing free food for himself and his cohorts. In September 1961, however, BATMAN and ROBIN arrive on the scene in search of Regan, a missing detective friend, capture the assembled criminals, and free the captive Regan – who had come to Central America in search of a fugitive criminal – from the villains' clutches (BM No. 142/3: "Ruler of the Bewitched Valley!").

HARTLEY, SPOTSWOOD. The wealthy and prominent citizen of GOTHAM CITY who is secretly the KINGPIN (WF No. 57, Mar/Apr '52: "Public Enemy Bruce Wayne!").

HASSEL, CHIPS. The leader of a gang of criminals who are apprehended by BATMAN and ROBIN in March

1961. Batman subsequently impersonates Hassel as part of his plan to capture HAL TORSON and Lester Guinn (BM No. 138/3: "The Secret of the Sea Beast!").

HEAD, THE. One of COUNT GRUTT's aliases (Det No. 37, Mar '40).

HEAVY WEAPONS GANG, THE. A gang of criminals, headquartered in an old fort on the outskirts of METROPOLIS, who commit a series of brazen crimes in both GOTHAM CITY and Metropolis with the aid of "powerful automatic weapons" capable of crushing an armored car "like an eggshell" before they are finally apprehended in September–October 1954 through the heroic efforts of BATMAN, ROBIN, and SUPERMAN (WF No. 72: "Fort Crime!").

HECATE. The CATWOMAN's pet black cat (BM No. 35/1, Jun/Jul '46: "Nine Lives Has the Catwoman!"; and others). In April 1947 the appearance of swamp mud on Hecate's paws and pine needles in Hecate's fur provides BATMAN with a vital clue to the location of the Catwoman's hideout (Det No. 122: "The Black Cat Crimes!"). In June–July 1948 the Catwoman breaks jail by utilizing a skeleton key and gas capsules concealed inside Hecate's "utility collar" (BM No. 47/1: "Fashions in Crime!").

HEDRANT, FERRIS. A famous Hollywood "villain," once renowned for his compelling film portrayals of ruthless killers but now fallen upon a period of declining popularity at the box office, who becomes insane with rage when Triumphant Pictures refuses to renew his contract and begins the systematic reenactment, in real life, of the murderous roles which he played in his various films, this time using innocent citizens as his hapless victims. Hedrant commits two brutal murders before he is finally apprehended by BATMAN in April–May 1953 (BM No. 76/3: "The Man of 100 Murders").

HELLFERN, KARL (Dr.). The real name of the villain who is best known as DOCTOR DEATH (Det No. 29, Jul '39: "The Batman Meets Doctor Death").

HERCULES (Doctor). An evil scientist who constructs three giant robots designed to commit spectacular crimes, then breaks three expert criminals – precious metals thief Whitey Drebs, museum thief George "Four-Eyes" Foley, and jewel thief Jawbone Bannon – out of State Prison to help him operate his crime robots by remote control. Hercules murders Foley for failing in his attempt to commit a successful robot crime, but BATMAN and ROBIN ultimately locate the villains' hideout and take Hercules and his surviving cohorts into custody (BM No. 42/3, Aug/Sep '47: "The Robot Robbers!").

HERD, IVAN. An alias employed by DOCTOR DEATH when he poses as an underworld fence in August 1939 (Det No. 30).

HEWITT, WALTER. An avid student of the "new science of bionics" – described in the text as "the study of living creatures and the attempt to duplicate their special properties" – and the inventor of an ingenious machine, the "bioniformer," designed to "draw out the special properties of an animal and by a shower of irradiated light transfer them into a human being!" Having already used his machine successfully to endow himself with the eyesight of an eagle, the speed of a cheetah, and other much-admired animal qualities, Hewitt was attempting to endow himself with the strength of a gorilla when an unexpected malfunctioning of his apparatus caused Hewitt's own intellectual abilities to become transferred to the gorilla being employed in the experiment. In May 1965 the gorilla, Karmak, embarks on an orgy of looting and "wanton destruction" fired by his deep-seated resentment of human beings ("Humans took me from the jungle! Humans made me do tricks in circus--so they could laugh at me! Karmak make humans pay!"), but he is ultimately defeated and apprehended by BATMAN and ROBIN (Det No. 339: "Batman Battles the Living Beast-Bomb!").

HIJACK. The leader of a gang of "highway pirates" who prey upon the cargoes of cross-country trucks. His personal trademark is the jack of spades, and he wears a costume resembling that of a jack in a deck of playing cards. He is secretly Jack Spade, an ex-convict recently released from prison. Hijack and his henchmen are apprehended by BATMAN and ROBIN in March 1959 (BM No. 122/2: "The Cross-Country Crimes!").

HILLERY (Mr.). The unscrupulous assistant to Mr. Logan, millionaire Thaddeus Moore's lawyer. When Moore dies in an automobile crash, leaving behind him $1,000,000 in cash hidden somewhere in the city with clues to its location concealed inside his collection of working models of mankind's great inventions, Hillery becomes determined to steal the models, recover the clues, and ultimately gain possession of the million-dollar treasure trove, but he and his henchmen are apprehended by BATMAN and ROBIN in December 1959 (BM No. 128/2: "The Million Dollar Puzzle").

HOBSON, "BRAIN." A "great criminal mastermind" who is executed in the electric chair of North Gotham Prison in August 1954, only to have his principal gangland lieutenants steal his corpse from the prison morgue soon afterward, transport it to their hideout in the "extreme northern suburbs" of GOTHAM CITY, and utilize it in an elaborate scheme to assemble "the biggest mob in history" by deceiving the underworld into believing that Hobson's ingenious brain has survived his execution and is masterminding their gang's activities.

After pretending to extract Hobson's brain from his skull, surreptitiously substituting a plastic brain for Hobson's real one, and then placing the plastic substitute in a tank of chemicals allegedly designed to preserve its capacity to function, Hobson's lieutenants set about persuading their underworld colleagues that Hobson's brain is still alive and capable of conceiving fantastic crimes, that it can communicate vocally through a "scientifically constructed loud-speaker" and emit a "powerful hypnotic force" that enables it to exact complete obedience from its followers, and that it can read the "thought-waves" of its underlings and root out and destroy potential informers.

Aided by the fear and awe inspired among the underworld by the carefully nurtured myth of Hobson's living brain, the plotters recruit a mammoth underworld organization and brazenly launch one of the most spectacular crime waves in the history of Gotham City. Ultimately, however, BATMAN and ROBIN locate the gang's hideout, capture the criminals with the aid of the Gotham City Police Department, and expose the so-called living brain as an elaborate gangland hoax (Det No. 210: "The Brain That Ruled Gotham City!").

HOFFNER, FRITZ. A young Nazi spy in COUNT FELIX's spy ring. Under the name Fred Hopper, Fritz obtains employment as a newsreel cameraman as a means of gaining access to America's defense plants, but he is apprehended in December 1942–January 1943 through the heroic efforts of BATMAN and ROBIN (BM No. 14/3: "Swastika over the White House!").

HOGGSBY, HAPPY. A ruthless gangland chieftain who corners the Christmas-tree market, raises prices to three or four times their normal level, and terrorizes any seller of Christmas trees who dares to undersell him. Sickened by the toll in human suffering exacted by Hoggsby's fir monopoly, BATMAN and ROBIN apprehend Hoggsby and his cohorts and turn them over to the authorities (BM No. 27/3, Feb/Mar '45: "A Christmas Peril!").

HOLMES, SHIRLEY (Sgt.). A lovely blond policewoman who helps BATMAN and ROBIN smash an organization of GOTHAM CITY racketeers headed by the COUNT. Shirley enjoys a brief romance with ALFRED in April–May 1945 (BM No. 28/2: "Shirley Holmes, Policewoman!").

HOOKER, BIG DAN. A cunning criminal who attempts to establish himself as "the most powerful crime king ever" by conducting a nationwide crime contest to select and recruit members for a highly specialized "all-star gang" consisting of the leading practitioners in all the major areas of crime, i.e., bank robbery, counterfeiting, armored-car robbery, forgery, arson, confidence racketeering, smuggling, jewel theft, and murder.

After conducting a coast-to-coast balloting among the underworld to determine the two foremost contenders in each crime category, Hooker assigns each pair of contestants the task of committing two virtually identical crimes in separate areas of GOTHAM CITY, with a place on the all-star gang to be awarded to the man who commits his assigned crime successfully without being apprehended by BATMAN. Soon Gotham City is rocked by a series of brazen "double crimes" arising from Hooker's contest, with the final event, murder — to see which of the country's top killers can capture and execute Batman — still in the offing.

Batman finally infiltrates the contest's auditorium headquarters by posing as one of the gangland contestants, and although he is exposed as an impostor and suffers a series of near-fatal setbacks, he ultimately apprehends Hooker and his entire gangland assemblage with the aid of the Gotham City Police Department, thus effecting a spectacular mass arrest that POLICE COMMISSIONER GORDON hails as "the greatest haul of crooks I've ever had during my administration!" (WF No. 56, Jan/Feb '52: "The Crimes in Double").

HOOKER, WILLY. The penny arcade shooting-gallery proprietor who achieves infamy as the EXECUTIONER (Det No. 191, Jan '53: "The Man with a License to Kill!").

HOOTON, LUCKY. The owner and star performer of a famous "auto circus" whose members travel from town to town performing spectacular exhibitions of trick driving amid the colorful trappings of a circus. Four clowns in Hooton's circus who have been using their circus jobs to conceal their involvement in a series of elaborate car thefts are apprehended by BATMAN and ROBIN in August–September 1950 (BM No. 60/3: "The Auto Circus Mystery!").

HOPPER, FRED. The alias employed by Nazi spy FRITZ HOFFNER when he obtains employment as a newsreel cameraman to gain access to America's defense plants (BM No. 14/3, Dec/Jan '42–'43: "Swastika over the White House!").

HROGUTH. A green-skinned alien from the far-distant planet Durim, an "eccentric scientist" who several years ago acquired superhuman powers similar to SUPERMAN's as the result of being inadvertently exposed to the rays of a mysterious fallen meteor while hiking on his native planet, and who then embarked on a diabolical new career as a ruthless super-criminal.

In March 1962, accompanied by two henchmen, Hroguth journeys to Earth to steal a supply of copper, an element not available on Durim, for the construction of a special machine designed to permanently drain away the super-powers of the teen-ager Logi, another native of Durim, who had also acquired superhuman powers after exposure to the meteor but who had, in contrast, devoted his life to the cause of justice and become Hroguth's mortal foe on their native planet.

On Earth, Hroguth steals the copper he needs and constructs his machine, only to be apprehended along with his henchmen soon afterward — and permanently robbed of his super-powers by forced exposure to his own device — through the heroic efforts of BATMAN, ROBIN, Superman, and the alien crime-fighter Logi (WF No. 124: "The Mystery of the Alien Super-Boy!").

HUDSON UNIVERSITY. The university in which DICK GRAYSON enrolls as a freshman beginning in December 1969 (BM No. 217: "One Bullet Too Many!").

HUMAN KEY, THE. A mysterious, hooded thief who uses his incredible skill at picking locks and opening safes to commit ten spectacular crimes. The Human Key is in reality Paul Bodin, a retired circus escape artist who has been forced to commit the crimes by two criminals — Burly Graham and his accomplice Sleepy — who kidnapped his daughter and threatened to kill her unless Bodin agreed to cooperate with them. With Bodin's help, however, BATMAN and ROBIN finally apprehend Graham and his henchman and rescue Bodin's daughter from their clutches (Det No. 132, Feb '48: "The Human Key!").

HUMAN MAGNET, THE. A ruthless criminal with extraordinary magnetic powers – his right hand attracts metals and his left hand repels them – who matches wits with BATMAN and ROBIN in March 1952. He is secretly David Wist, an expert watch repairman by day and small-time safecracker by night who becomes endowed with magnetic powers after running into high-tension wires on the grounds of the Ultra-Nuclear Fission Commission while trying to escape from Batman and Robin, who had surprised him at the scene of a burglary.

After donning a colorful green and yellow costume and assuming the name the Human Magnet, Wist embarks on a series of spectacular crimes, ingeniously utilizing his magnetic powers to do such things as repel policemen's bullets, cause electrical machinery to run wild while he and his henchmen grab a factory payroll, and stymie Batman and Robin by repelling the metal objects in their utility belts. Capitalizing on the fact that the opposite poles of a magnet attract one another, however, Batman traps the Human Magnet by releasing some mosquitoes into the air; when the villain claps his hands together in an impulsive attempt to swat them, his hands become locked together and Batman easily apprehends him (Det No. 181: "The Crimes of the Human Magnet!").

HUMAN TARGET, THE. The pseudonym employed by onetime impersonator Fred Venable in November 1953, when, in order to accumulate the necessary funds for a series of vital operations for his crippled daughter, he offers to impersonate, for a fee, individuals who believe their lives in jeopardy, such as "famed European statesman" Prince Michael Gruyere, recently threatened with assassination, and noted art collector Perry Davison, who fears the vengeance of an escaped convict he once helped send to prison. After Venable has earned all the money he needs and retired from his short-lived career as the Human Target, however, GOTHAM CITY gangster Blinky Grove – who has been marked for death by the syndicate – has Venable's daughter kidnapped in order to force Venable to play the role of the Human Target for the benefit of the syndicate's hit-men. Aided by the genuinely heroic Venable, however, as well as by the Gotham City Police Department, BATMAN and ROBIN intervene to rescue Venable's daughter from her captors and apprehend the Blinky Grove gang along with the syndicate triggermen who have been hired to assassinate Grove (Det No. 201: "Human Target!").

HUNGARIA. The far-off country, apparently situated somewhere in Europe, which – according to Detective Comics No. 32 – is the site of the MONK's towering castle stronghold and the scene of a series of battles between BATMAN and the Monk (Oct '39). Detective Comics No. 31 places the Monk's castle in Hungary (Sep '39), a strong indication that Hungaria is intended to represent Hungary and not some wholly fictional country. Detective Comics No. 32 further situates the Monk's castle "in the lost mountains of Cathala by the turbulent river Dess" (Oct '39).

HUNT, OLIVER. A pudgy little man with an astounding photographic memory who agrees to join forces with GOTHAM CITY gang boss Dude Fay and use his extraordinary mnemonic talents for crime in hopes of accumulating enough money to abandon his career as a vaudeville performer and "devote [himself] to psychological research." Aided by Hunt's phenomenal memory, Fay and his henchmen commit a series of crimes involving the theft of such things as unpublished songs and unsold patents – and even go so far as to build themselves a duplicate of the BATPLANE after Hunt has memorized the details of its construction – until finally Hunt comes to realize the error of his ways and courageously helps BATMAN and ROBIN apprehend the villains in Summer 1943 (WF No. 10: "Man with the Camera Eyes").

HUNTER, B. G. *See* BIG GAME HUNTER, THE.

HYDRA. An "international crime cartel" named after "the fabled monster which grew a new head every time one head was lopped off!" Moving into action against Hydra in November 1964, BATMAN and ROBIN apprehend a group of Hydra gangsters using a windmill as a cache for stolen diamonds in Holland, capture another group in possession of a fortune in counterfeit money in Greece, and pursue and apprehend a third Hydra gang after they have robbed a Swiss bank (BM No. 167: "Zero Hour for Earth!").

HYDRO. A cunning costumed criminal who uses water to aid him in his crimes. He is in reality Tim Flagg, an unassuming, bespectacled escapee from Gotham State Penitentiary – where he was the water boy for the prison baseball team and therefore the object of continuous ridicule by his fellow convicts – who assumes the name Hydro after he has successfully used the prison water tower to facilitate his dramatic escape. "Yes," muses Flagg, as he prepares to enjoy his newly won freedom, "--[I'll launch] a crime-reign--with ***water*** as my weapon! I'll call myself ***Hydro***--and no one will stop me!"

After staging a series of spectacular water-crimes – including an attempt to blow up a dam so that he can loot the entire countryside at will – Hydro finally decides to eliminate BATMAN and ROBIN by making his way up the underground river leading to the BATCAVE and then blowing up the batcave with a charge of nitroglycerine. When the explosive charge detonates prematurely, however, the underground river channel becomes clogged with debris and the batcave begins to fill with water, although the cave structure itself remains intact. Batman and Robin protect the batcave from water damage by lowering special walls into place to contain the sudden flooding, and, soon afterward, Batman apprehends Hydro and removes the debris blocking the river channel to restore the water flow to normal. Because Hydro's voyage to the batcave was made entirely underwater, he remains ignorant of its precise location (BM No. 74/3, Dec/Jan '52–'53: "The Water Crimes of Mr. Hydro!").

HYORO. One of a pair of extraterrestrial aliens – Hyoro's companion is named Goga – who crash-land on the planet Earth in July 1962, only to have their spacecraft's vital "control unit" stolen by two fugitive bank robbers who attempt to coerce the aliens into destroying BATMAN and ROBIN with their deadly "Z-ray" in exchange for the safe return of the control unit. While pretending to have acceded to the criminals' demand, however, Hyoro and Goga manage to avoid harming the Dynamic Duo while at the same time providing the famed lawmen with an easily visible trail which enables them ultimately to apprehend the criminals and recover the control unit (Det No. 305: "Targets of the Alien Z-Ray!").

I

INSURANCE CLUB, THE. An exclusive club whose membership consists of all the people in GOTHAM CITY whose lives or other physical assets are insured for $1,000,000. Its members, all of whom have been insured by the Gotham Insurance Company, include world-famous magician Lorenzo Dumont, renowned pianist Paul Bond, atomic physicist Curt Alderson, lovely model Olga Craig, pitcher Lefty Stone, dancer Tony Cutler, and millionaire philanthropist and corporate board member BRUCE WAYNE. An attempt on the lives of the club members by "demented artist" JAN MARKI is thwarted by BATMAN and ROBIN, with the aid of the club members themselves, in June–July 1951 (WF No. 52: "The $1,000,000 Star Club!").

INVENTOR, THE. An ingenious "new gangland boss" in GOTHAM CITY whose easily portable "revolutionary electro-magnet" – powered by a "huge dynamo" in the basement of his gang's abandoned-firehouse hideout – enables him and his henchmen to "force the tumblers" of massive vaults and prevent any electrically operated burglar alarm from ringing. The efforts of the Dynamic Duo to apprehend the Inventor are severely hampered by the fact that the villain has managed to trick BATMAN into pocketing an unusual-looking key in the belief that it might be a clue, whereas in reality it is a sophisticated tracking device which transmits Batman's image and exact location to the screen of a giant "magno-radarscope" in the Inventor's hideout, thus enabling the villain and his cohorts to shadow the Dynamic Duo's every move and thereby elude capture. Ultimately, however, with some assistance from ALFRED, Batman and ROBIN apprehend the Inventor and his henchmen in July 1954 (Det No. 209: "The Man Who Shadowed Batman!").

J

JABAH. The fearsome "giant Indian" (i.e., from India) who serves as DOCTOR DEATH's assistant during July 1939. He achieves the distinction of being the first villain ever to shoot BATMAN when he fires a bullet into Batman's right shoulder, but he dies soon afterward when Batman lassos him from behind with his silken rope and jerks the noose tight around the villain's neck (Det No. 29: "The Batman Meets Doctor Death").

Jabah © NPP 1939

JACKAL, THE. The leader of the Looters, a gang of villainous "human scavengers" who swoop down on areas gutted by flood, earthquake, or hurricane in order to loot and plunder while citizens and authorities alike are too preoccupied with human suffering to adequately protect private property.

When the Jackal learns that PROFESSOR DOREMUS LEAF has developed a special seismograph designed to predict impending earthquakes, he dupes the professor into revealing the time and location of the next quake, forcibly prevents him from broadcasting a warning to the local authorities, and then races to the scene with his gang to begin an orgy of looting.

During a battle at the scene of the quake with BATMAN and ROBIN, the Jackal's henchmen topple into a gigantic fissure and plummet to their doom, and Batman manages to avoid a similar fate only by grabbing onto the fissure's edge and hanging on for dear life. Indeed, the Jackal is about to send Batman plunging into the abyss when Professor Leaf arrives on the scene and hurls a rock at the villain, sending him hurtling into the yawning fissure (BM No. 33/2, Feb/Mar '46: "The Looters!").

JACKAL-HEAD. A cunning criminal, his identity concealed by a jackal-headed mask of Anubis, ancient Egyptian god of the underworld, who commits a series of spectacular "underground crimes" – crimes which, in keeping with Anubis's fabled role as "emperor of the underworld," take place either underground or underwater – before he and his henchmen are finally apprehended by BATMAN and ROBIN in December 1958. For a time, speculation as to Jackal-Head's true identity focuses on Dr. Coombs, the Gotham Museum Egyptologist whose recent expedition to Egypt uncovered, in an ancient temple, the very jackal-headed Anubis mask which Jackal-Head now wears. When Jackal-Head is finally apprehended, however, he proves to be Gibson, Dr. Coombs's assistant (Det No. 262: "The Jackal of the Underworld!").

JAFFEER. A fortune-teller, shot and mortally wounded by four criminals intent on stealing the giant ruby in his turban, who, in his dying moments, calls down upon his murderers "the terrible curse of the four fates," telling one that he will die by lightning, the second that he will die by having the "air . . . choked from [his] lungs," the third that he will be killed by metal, and the fourth that he will be killed by water. BATMAN and ROBIN pursue the fleeing killers in February–March 1942, but all four die accidentally in the manner predicted by the fortune-teller (BM No. 9/1: "The Four Fates!").

JANDRON, JAY. The leader of a gang of criminals who steal $100,000 in gate receipts from the Vaudeville Relief Fund's benefit show, a vaudeville extravaganza featuring "some of the biggest vaudeville stars." BATMAN and ROBIN apprehend Jandron and his henchmen in August 1956 with the aid of six vaudevillians, including Scortini the magician, Elmo the impersonator, Leo the strongman, Victor Voice the ventriloquist, Carey the tightrope walker, and an unnamed India rubber man (BM No. 101/2: "The Six Strangest Sleuths").

JARREL, "BIG JIM." A GOTHAM CITY rackets chief who, having learned of the existence of a great cave beneath the mansion of millionaire BRUCE WAYNE, decides to buy property nearby and dig a tunnel into the cave so that he and his henchmen can use it as a hideout, unaware that the cave he seeks to utilize is actually the BATCAVE. BATMAN's dilemma, once he has learned of the scheme, is that apprehending the criminals in the midst of their project might make them suspicious of the truth, while allowing them to complete their tunnel would enable them to enter the batcave. Batman and ROBIN finally resolve this dilemma by temporarily transferring the batcave's crime-fighting apparatus to another location, temporarily flooding the batcave with water from an underground river to make it appear not only innocuous but unusable as a hideout, and then apprehending Jarrel and his henchmen within moments after they have finished digging their tunnel (Det No. 223, Sep '55: "The Batman Dime-Museum").

JASON, J. J. A "famed detective story writer" and author of numerous books on crime who, now bored with writing mysteries and in quest of "a problem that will challenge my mind," resolves to devote his considerable skills at armchair detection to unraveling the secret of BATMAN's identity. Through a ruse, Jason succeeds in tricking the Dynamic Duo into providing him with sufficient evidence to establish that Bruce Wayne is Batman, but Batman manages to deceive the crafty writer into believing he has made an error by employing a blind and deaf stand-in to impersonate him as Batman – presumably so that the stand-in will not become privy to the secret of his dual identity – while he appears in Jason's presence simultaneously as millionaire Bruce Wayne (WF No. 39, Mar/Apr '49: "The Conquest of Batman's Identity!").

JENKINS, WILBUR. An "evil genius" who has "perfected a way of beaming magnetism--similar to the way light is beamed in a laser!" He is the brother of Thomas Jenkins, a guard at the Gotham City Museum. In June 1965 the Jenkins brothers concoct an elaborate scheme to steal the museum's priceless Opals of Ealing and then cover their tracks by using Wilbur's ingenious magnetic device to make it appear that three suits of armor on display in the museum have come to life and destroyed the opals in fulfillment of a twelfth-century prophecy. Jenkins and his brother are apprehended by BATMAN and ROBIN shortly following the jewel theft (BM No. 172/1: "Attack of the Invisible Knights!").

JESTER, THE. A jester employed by PUBLIUS MALCHIO, the ruthless "Roman racketeer" who is defeated by BATMAN and ROBIN during their visit to ancient Rome in August–September 1944. Except for the fact that his face is flesh-colored, instead of white, the Jester is an exact double for the JOKER (BM No. 24/1: "It Happened in Rome").

JOHNSON, NOCKY. A ruthless criminal, wanted by the police in six states, who provokes a renewed outburst of fighting in the long-standing feud between the Chatfields and the McKees in the sleepy mountain town of Red Gulch as part of an elaborate scheme to steal two valuable lens-grinding machines from a local factory – engaged in the production of vital lenses for the U.S. Army – so that he and his two cohorts can hold the machines for ransom while blaming the theft on the feuding McKees. Johnson and his cohorts are apprehended by BATMAN and ROBIN in Winter 1944 (WF No. 16: "The Mountaineers of Crime!").

JOKER, THE. The arch-villain of the BATMAN chronicles, a maniacal harlequin whose bizarre appearance, unparalleled arrogance, and unerring instinct for absurdity have earned him a reputation as "the cleverest and the most dangerous criminal in the annals of crime . . ." (BM No. 4/1, Win '41: "The Case of the Joker's Crime Circus!").

Bruce Wayne, the man who is secretly Batman, has described the Joker as "a very unusual man. . . . shrewd, subtle, and above all ruthless" (BM No. 1/5, Spr '40: "The Joker Returns"), and Batman No. 8/4 describes him as a "grim jester, arch-criminal, [and] master fiend" (Dec/Jan '41–'42: "The Cross Country Crimes!").

By his own account, he is "the greatest criminal on Earth" (Det No. 388, Jun '69: "Public Luna-tic Number One!") and "the world's greatest clown" (BM No. 53/1, Jun/Jul '49: "A Hairpin, a Hoe, a Hacksaw, a Hole in the Ground!"), as well as "the greatest comedian of all--the caliph of crime clowns, the grand mogul of mountebanks, the king of jesters . . . the one and only Joker! Ha, ha, ha!" (BM No. 57/3, Feb/Mar '50: "The Funny Man Crimes!").

For over thirty years, the chronicles have resounded with his "mocking, spine-chilling laughter" (Det No. 91, Sep '44: "The Case of the Practical Joker"), and his

The Joker, 1952 © NPP 1952

"changeless, mask-like face" — with its chalk-white skin, rouge-red lips, and "burning, hate-filled eyes," all topped by a wavy mass of green hair — has become a visual synonym for evil. In moments of triumph, he wears a wide grin, but it is "a smile without mirth . . . a smile of death! The awesome, ghastly grin of . . . the Joker!" (BM No. 1/2, Spr '40).

If the Joker's villainy is great, then his conceit is colossal, for he is a man of unmatched arrogance and unmitigated gall whose dearest possession is a bound volume of newspaper clippings attesting to the notoriety of his numerous felonious exploits (Det No. 114, Aug '46: "Acrostic of Crime!").

"Of all the criminals Batman and Robin have faced," observes Batman No. 136/3, "none is more conceited than . . . the Joker" (Dec '60: "The Challenge of the Joker"), yet, fittingly, it is this very conceit which so often becomes the Joker's undoing. "The Joker is tricky, [and] cunning," remarks Batman in January 1943, but he is also "a supreme egoist advertising his crimes like a fool . . . [and he] leaves clues . . clues that defeat him! And so I always win, while he loses . . . all because of his conceit!" (Det No. 71: "A Crime a Day!").

Three decades of crime have netted the Joker a king's ransom in gold, silver, money, and jewels (BM No. 53/1, Jun/Jul '49: "A Hairpin, a Hoe, a Hacksaw, a Hole in the Ground!"; and others), so it is more than a lust for wealth that has motivated him to risk his freedom in more than seventy separate battles with Batman. "Bah!" snarls the Joker in December 1946, after his henchmen have expressed their eagerness to cash in on their leader's "royal flush crimes." "Always thinking of money! My royal flush crimes will be **artistic** first of all!" (Det No. 118: "The Royal Flush Crimes!"). On another occasion, years later, after he has forged a temporary alliance with the villainous mastermind LEX LUTHER, the Joker chides his colleague for his artless, mercenary approach: "Matching wits with a worthy opponent [Batman] makes crime a pleasure," explains the Joker, "--and not just a money-grubbing chore!" (WF No. 129, Nov '62: "Joker-Luthor, Incorporated!").

The Joker has been called the Harlequin of Hate, but like all great harlequins he unsettles because he mirrors society, not because he hates it: "Who raises one corner of his red mouth in mockery of the law, the other side in sarcasm at his fellow man? Yes, it's that nefarious crime clown — the Joker!" (BM No. 40/1, Apr/May '47: "The 13 Club!").

In the early days of his career, the Joker was a cold-blooded murderer — noted far more for his fiendishness than his hilarity — and his crimes reflected a miser's lust for priceless jewelry. In Spring 1940 alone, the Joker murdered more than half a dozen men, most of them with a grisly venom which, as it snuffed the life out of each gasping victim, contracted the muscles of the doomed man's face into a "repellent, ghastly grin, the sign of death from the Joker!" (BM No. 1/2; BM No. 1/5, Spr '40: "The Joker Returns").

It is during this period, for example, that the Joker cuts in on a commercial radio broadcast in order to announce to a million unbelieving listeners that "at precisely twelve o'clock midnight" he intends to murder Henry Claridge and steal the Claridge Diamond. "Do not try to stop me!" warns the rasping voice of the diabolical crime-clown. "The **Joker** has spoken!"

That night, "an inflexible cordon" of determined policemen forms about Henry Claridge in an effort to forestall his inevitable doom, but even as the clock tolls midnight Claridge utters a strangled gasp and pitches over dead, the muscles of his face frozen into a ghastly grin. "It's . . . it's horrible!" gasps a stunned policeman. "Grotesque!" echoes a fellow officer. "The Joker brings death to his victims with a smile!" (BM No. 1/2, Spr '40).

By mid-1941, however, the Joker has tempered his fascination with precious jewelry and murder and extended his range of criminal activity to embrace virtually every other form of crime. By mid-1942 he has murdered the last man he will kill until the 1970s, and in June–July 1942, when the Joker's henchmen confidently ask their leader for permission to kill the captive Batman, the Joker hastily demurs: "No!" he replies firmly. "Let him live! He is so amusing when he tries to match wits with me! Ha! Ha!" (BM No. 11/1).

In the months and years that follow, the Joker makes countless attempts to lure Batman into a mind-boggling array of diabolical deathtraps, but time and time again he seems to fabricate excuses for allowing a cornered Batman to survive. "You shoulda let me plug 'im!" protests a puzzled henchman, after a golden opportunity to shoot Batman has quickly come and gone. "No!" replies the Joker. "Anyone can kill with a gun! But I'm not anyone! I'm the Joker! When I kill it must be with imagination" (BM No. 12/2, Aug/Sep '42: "The Wizard of Words!").

Within a few years, in fact, even the carefully preserved secret of Batman's dual identity has lost its fascination for the crafty Joker: "Ha! Ha! No!" he cries in April 1942, as he makes a decision not to unmask a captive Batman. "It's too simple--unworthy of my intelligence! And I like these battles of wits! The hunt . . . the chase! . . . that's the breath of life to me!" (Det No. 62: "Laugh, Town, Laugh").

Seven years later, another opportunity presents itself to unmask Batman, but the Joker flatly turns it down: "I could unmask you now, Batman," he remarks, "but that would only take away what little fun is left to me — the **fun-loving Joker!** Yes, **Batman,** I will let your identity remain a secret. For you afford me the thrill of a supreme battle of wits each time we meet!" (BM No. 53/1, Jun/Jul '49: "A Hairpin, a Hoe, a Hacksaw, a Hole in the Ground!").

At the scenes of his early depredations, the Joker would often leave a calling card in the form of a mocking playing-card joker (BM No. 1/2, Spr '40; and others), but by the middle of 1942 this rather colorful eccentricity has all but disappeared from the chronicles. Throughout virtually his entire career, however, the Joker has retained his mania for announcing his crimes in advance, whether brazenly over the radio or by distributing a series of intricate clues. "Any fool can pull a surprise job," he remarks in February–March 1942, "but it takes the Joker to do the expected in spite of [the] odds!" (BM No. 9/3: "The Case of the Lucky Law-Breakers!").

Because the Joker is a past master at the art of disguise and impersonation (BM No. 1/2, Spr '40; and others), he frequently employs aliases in order to achieve his villainous ends. In the past, these have included inversions of his own name – A. Rekoj (Det No. 45, Nov '40: "The Case of the Laughing Death!") and I. Rekoj (BM No. 7/1, Oct/Nov '41) – as well as plainly fictitious contrivances such as B. C. De Nil (Det No. 341, Jul '65: "The Joker's Comedy Capers!").

Interestingly, other times and places have Jokers of their own: the Jester, an ancient Roman jester who allies himself with Batman and ROBIN in their battle with the "Roman racketeer" PUBLIUS MALCHIO, closely resembles the Joker, except that the Jester's skin is flesh-colored while the Joker's is chalk-white (BM No. 24/1, Aug/Sep '44: "It Happened in Rome"). The CRIER, a villain of ancient Baghdad "who always weeps as he steals," resembles the Joker in every respect except that he uses sadness to aid him in his crimes, while the Joker uses mirth (BM No. 49/3, Oct/Nov '48: "Batman's Arabian Nights!"). CHIEF ROKEJ, GOTHAM CITY's police chief in the twenty-first century A.D., is the Joker's direct descendant, as well as a perfect look-alike for his villainous ancestor (BM No. 59/3, Jun/Jul '50: "Batman in the Future!"). And, in a bizarre extradimensional parallel world which Batman visits in September 1963, the Joker is a stage name employed by television comic Freddy Forbes, who, in his clownlike theatrical make-up, could easily pass for the Joker's double (WF No. 136: "The Batman Nobody Remembered!").

During the past thirty years, the chroniclers have employed more than forty separate alternate names for the Joker, including: the Ace of Knaves, the Arch Buffoon of Banditry, the Bandit Buffoon, the Brazen Buffoon, the Brazen Buffoon of Crime, the Burglar Buffoon, the Clown of Crime, the Clown-Prince of Crime, the Comic of Crime, the Crafty Clown of Crime, the Crime Clown, the Crime Jester, the Cunning Crime-King, the Fearsome Fakir, the Fiendish Funster, the Funny Man of Felony, the Grim Jester, the Grinning Gargoyle of Greed, the Harlequin of Crime, the Harlequin of Hate, the Hilarious Harlequin, the Hoodlum Harlequin, the Jaunty Jester, the Jeering Jackanapes, the Jeering Jester of Crime, the Jester of Crime, the Jocund Jack of All Crimes, the King of Jesters, the Leonardo of the Larcenous Laugh, the Mad Buffoon, the Mad Maestro of Mirth, the Madman of Mirth, the Mad Master of Mirth, the Mad Merrymaker, the Malevolent Mime, the Malicious Mountebank, the Man of a Thousand False Fronts, the Master of Mockery, the Mephistopheles of Mirth, the Mirthful Menace, the Mirthful Mountebank, the Mocking Mountebank, and the Prince of Pranksters.

In addition, the texts have described the Joker as a "cunning caliph of crime" (BM No. 28/1, Apr/May '45: "Shadow City!"), a "macabre master of mirth" (Det No. 332, Oct '64: "The Joker's Last Laugh!"), a "mad manager of menace" (BM No. 86/2, Sep '54: "The Joker's Winning Team!"), a "maestro of malevolent mirth" (Det No. 388, Jun '69: "Public Luna-tic Number One!"), a "merry madcap of mayhem" (Det No. 332, Oct '64: "The Joker's Last Laugh!"), a "mirthful mountebank of mischief and menace" (BM No. 28/1, Apr/May '45: "Shadow City!"), a "mocking mountebank of menace" (BM No. 32/1, Dec/Jan '45–'46: "Rackety-Rax Racket!"), a "ringmaster of riotous robbery" (Det No. 388, Jun '69: "Public Luna-tic Number One!"), a "spinner of sinister skeins" (BM No. 37/3, Oct/Nov '46: "The Joker Follows Suit!"), and a "tycoon of teasing terror" (Det No. 388, Jun '69: "Public Luna-tic Number One!").

According to Detective Comics No. 168, the Joker was once an ordinary laboratory worker who decided to turn to crime long enough to steal $1,000,000, and then disappear into retirement. To ensure that he would never be identified and apprehended, he assumed the name the Red Hood and donned a disguise consisting of a black tie and tuxedo, white gloves, a red cape, and a red metal hood that covered his entire face and head.

For more than a month, the Red Hood robbed and pillaged, successfully eluding Batman and the other law enforcement authorities of Gotham City, until one night, just after he had achieved his goal of $1,000,000 by robbing the headquarters of the Monarch Playing Card Company, he finally found himself cornered by Batman and Robin on one of the factory's outdoor catwalks.

In a daring bid to avoid capture, the Red Hood dove headlong into "the catch basin for all the waste chemicals from [the] plant" and, aided by an oxygen tube built into his metal hood, swam beneath the surface of the chemical wastes until he reached the freedom of the open river.

When he arrived home and doffed his metal hood, however, he discovered that he had not emerged from the chemical wastes unscathed. Staring into a full-length mirror, he realized, with mounting horror, that the "chemical vapor" from the catch basin had somehow turned his hair green, his lips rouge-red and his skin chalk-white. "I look like an **evil clown!**" he cried aloud. "What a joke on me!"

Then the Red Hood realized that his bizarre new appearance had the power to "terrify people," and he decided to resume his criminal career in a new guise and under a new name. "And because the playing card company [had] made my new face," he explained years later, "I named myself after the card with the face of a clown--**the Joker!**"

The account goes on to assert that it is not until February 1951 — a full ten years after the incident at the Monarch Playing Card Company — that Batman deduces that the Red Hood and the Joker are one and the same man ("The Man Behind the Red Hood!").

As of the mid-1970s, the above account of the Joker's origin remains the only one extant, but internal chronological discrepancies — as well as the presence in the text of several highly implausible elements — may reasonably lead one to question the validity of the account.

In Spring 1940 the Joker commits a quartet of grisly murders before he is finally apprehended by Batman and Robin. The victims include Henry Claridge, owner of the famed Claridge Diamond; Jay Wilde, owner of the priceless Ronkers Ruby; Brute Nelson, a rival gangster; and Judge Drake, who once sentenced the Joker to a term in prison.

"The **Joker** was a clever but diabolical killer!" observes Bruce Wayne, after the Joker has been safely incarcerated. "Too clever and too deadly to be free!"

In his cell at the state prison, however, the Joker is already plotting his escape. "I know of a way out," promises the villain grimly, "--the **Joker** will yet have the last laugh!" (BM No. 1/2).

Soon afterward, the Joker makes good his boast by creating a powerful explosive from chemicals hidden inside two false teeth and blasting his way to freedom. In the days that follow, he commits a series of spectacular thefts that occasionally involve murder; kills a local police chief with a poison dart concealed inside the receiver of the police chief's telephone; and murders reformer Edgar Martin – who has angered the Joker by making public speeches calling for his capture – by poisoning the edges of the playing cards in Martin's home.

During a climactic battle with Batman and Robin, the Joker draws a dagger, only to stab himself accidentally when Batman deftly sidesteps a lethal lunge. **"Ha! Ha! Ha!"** laughs the Joker maniacally. **"The Joker is going to die ha! Ha! The laugh is on the Joker! Ha! Ha! Laugh clown laugh! Ha!** Ha! Ha! Ha-ha-ha-ha." Then the Joker falls silent and sinks lifelessly to the floor.

With the arrival of the police, Batman and Robin depart, believing that their nemesis is dead. As an ambulance speeds the wounded Joker toward a hospital, however, an attending physician remarks that the Joker is still alive and that he is going to recover (BM No. 1/5, Spr '40: "The Joker Returns").

By Summer 1940 Batman has concocted a plan to "abduct the Joker from the hospital before he becomes strong and wily enough to slip through the hands of the police. Then," he explains to Robin, "we'll take him to a famous brain specialist for an operation, so that he can be cured and turned into a valuable citizen."

Before Batman can move to carry out his plan, however, the members of Crime Syndicate Inc., who have recently lost their leader, invade Vesalius Hospital, where the Joker is being treated, force the physicians there to operate on the Joker immediately, and then escape with him in a waiting car, intending to keep him airborne in a hospital plane until he has recovered, and then to install him as their new crime leader.

When the Joker recovers, however, he double-crosses the syndicate members and races to the castle sanctuary of millionaire E. S. Arthur, owner of the fabulous Pharaoh Gems. There he encounters the CATWOMAN, who also intends to steal the jewels, as well as Batman and Robin, who arrive soon afterward. In the battle that follows, Arthur's castle is set afire, and Batman, carrying an unconscious Robin, is forced to flee up a rope ladder with the Catwoman toward the safety of the BATPLANE, leaving an unconscious Joker behind in the roaring inferno. Halfway up the rope ladder, the Catwoman makes a daring leap to the river below, and freedom, but the Joker has seemingly perished in the flaming castle (BM No. 2/1).

In November 1940 the Joker returns, this time under the guise of an elderly music store proprietor named A. Rekoj. As the bespectacled Rekoj, the Joker recruits a gang of criminals and plans a series of elaborate crimes for them without ever telling them that he is in reality the Joker. Later, after the henchmen have committed a robbery, the Joker, having shed his Rekoj disguise, appears on the scene and steals their accumulated loot, leaving the hapless henchmen with the impression that the loot they stole for Rekoj has been hijacked by the Joker. "The idiots!" gloats the Joker to himself. "I make them do all the dirty work, gather all the jewels to-gether . . . then I step in and take it away from them! Now I don't have to divide it with them! Ha ha! The fools! The utter fools! **Ha ha ha ha ha.**"

Later, however, during a long battle with Batman aboard the S.S. *Oriental* – where the Joker has come in hopes of stealing a jade Buddha worth $500,000 – the Joker topples overboard and plummets into the icy sea, leaving Batman to wonder aloud whether, this time, the Joker has actually perished (Det No. 45: "The Case of the Laughing Death!").

In Winter 1941 the Joker returns, this time as the leader of a troupe of circus performers who entertain at parties given by the city's wealthy. Disguised as a clown in the "miniature circus," the Joker carefully analyzes the layout of each mansion so that he can return to rob it at a later time.

Batman and Robin ultimately apprehend all of the Joker's accomplices and pursue their leader to the "seemingly deserted, gloomy old mansion" on "the edge of town" which serves as the Joker's hideaway. There, in the midst of a vicious battle with Batman, the Joker plummets through an open trapdoor into the sewage water running beneath the hideout, leaving Batman and Robin with the erroneous impression that their diabolical adversary has perished at last (BM No. 4/1: "The Case of the Joker's Crime Circus!").

The Joker survives, however, by swimming through the sewer system to the open bay, where he is fished from the water by three criminals – QUEENIE, Diamond Jack Deegan, and Clubsy. With the Joker as their leader, the four set up a lavish gambling ship just outside the three-mile limit where they ply their wealthy clientele with liquor and gather information likely to facilitate the burglarizing of their homes at a later date.

After spending some time aboard the gambling ship as Bruce Wayne – and discovering, to his astonishment, that an elderly man on board is really the Joker in disguise – Batman sets out to smash the Joker's burglary racket. Ultimately he succeeds. In a final battle with Robin, the Joker plunges over the side of a lighthouse railing and plummets into the icy sea below (BM No. 5/1, Spr '41: "The Riddle of the Missing Card!").

In October–November 1941 the Joker stages a spectacular diamond theft after tricking Batman and Robin – and a goodly number of what the Joker refers to as Gotham City's "blundering police" – into throwing a protective cordon around the home of one of his own henchmen, who poses as a panicky gem collector fearful of being robbed by the Joker. Later, the Joker incapacitates European nobleman Duke Michael with knockout gas and impersonates him at a banquet at which the duke is scheduled to receive $10,000 in war aid from the people of Gotham City. Pursued by Batman and Robin as he flees from the banquet hall, the Joker soon finds himself battling Batman atop a moving railroad car as it passes across the edge of a towering cliff. Suddenly, recoiling from one of Batman's terrific blows, the Joker loses his footing and plunges over the side of the cliff to seemingly certain doom (BM No. 7/1).

In December 1941–January 1942, while Batman and Robin are in Washington, D.C., to meet with F.B.I. chief G. Henry Mover – who has been asked by the President to extend the Dynamic Duo "the good wishes of the people and the President for [their] efforts in ridding this country of crime" – the Joker, who has concealed himself inside a huge throng of citizens cheering Batman's arrival, accidentally wounds Mover with a bullet intended for Batman. The nation is stunned by the attack, and "the President himself . . . orders the nation's police force to bring in the **Joker.**"

"And so," explains the text, "begins the greatest manhunt of all time as one great, rising cry sweeps across the country like a prairie fire . . . 'Get the **JOKER!**'"

Fleeing Washington after his unsuccessful attempt to assassinate Batman, the Joker embarks on a spectacular series of crimes which take him from state to state, leaving in his wake sinister clues pointing the way to a subtle pattern of state initials which gradually spell out the name Joker. After stealing some diamonds in New **J**ersey, the Joker commits a second crime in **O**hio, after which he murders two cohorts with poisoned cigars containing a mixture of Joker venom and laughing gas so that he will not have to share his loot with them. Realizing that the final state on the Joker's schedule will be **R**hode Island, Batman cunningly lures him into a trap and takes him into custody in the city of Providence (BM No. 8/4: "The Cross Country Crimes!").

In February 1942 the Joker and his henchmen commit a long series of crimes in which they impersonate uniformed officials of various kinds, such as soldiers, policemen, firemen, mailmen, railroad conductors, and Coast Guardsmen. They are ultimately apprehended, however, by Batman and Robin, who trail them to the costume shop which serves as their hideaway (Det No. 60: "Case of the Costume-Clad Killers").

In February–March 1942 the Joker breaks out of jail and commits a series of crimes with the aid of exconvicts recently released from prison. Then, in order to establish alibis to explain the sudden acquisition of wealth by his accomplices, he intimidates theater owners, radio programming officials, and other operators of raffles and promotional games into arranging for his cohorts to "win" the stolen loot in ostensibly legitimate ways. After a series of indecisive encounters, Batman and Robin finally surprise the Joker in the act of robbing an armored car. During the struggle that follows, the Joker falls directly into the path of an oncoming train and appears certain to be crushed to death. By the time the train has passed, however, the Joker is nowhere to be seen, and it is clear that he has somehow managed to make good his escape (BM No. 9/3: "The Case of the Lucky Law-Breakers!").

In April 1942 famed comedian Happy Hanson dies, leaving behind a great fortune and a bizarre will. According to its provisions, each of the nation's great comedians – Freddie Banter, Claude S. Tilley, Denny Jackson, Ted Allenby, and Buster Parks – is to receive a single clue to the location of Hanson's fortune. Then a contest is to be held in which the comedian who tells the funniest joke will be designated the "King of Jesters" and rewarded with the entire collection of clues, thus enabling him to locate and possess the entire missing fortune.

After escaping from jail, the Joker becomes enraged at having been excluded from participating in Hanson's contest. "King of Jesters," exclaims the Joker angrily. "How dare they? I--I am the king of all jesters---I---the **Joker**, himself. And they dare hold a contest of this nature without inviting me! Hah! I'll invite myself! Ha! Ha! Ha!"

Immediately the Joker sets out to murder the competing comedians and steal their clues, each time dealing death in such a way as to create a morbid twist on some famous joke. He murders comedian Freddie Banter, for example, by hanging him with a pair of suspenders, and then, in a book of Banter's favorite jokes, crosses out the conventional punch line to the old joke "Why does a fireman wear red suspenders?" (i.e., "To hold his pants up!") and adds in its place a grisly punch line of his own: "To hang this fool up, ha! Ha!"

After a series of murders and attempted murders, the Joker accumulates all of the clues and recovers the Hanson fortune, only to be apprehended moments afterward by Batman and Robin (Det No. 62: "Laugh, Town, Laugh").

By June 1942 the Joker has somehow regained his freedom, but he is angry and embittered at having to remain in hiding. "What good is money?" he exclaims. "Can I spend it like other people? Can I go to movies and ball games? No! The only way I can leave this hideout is in disguise. . . . I'm doomed to a living death. . . ." Suddenly, in mid-sentence, the Joker is seized by an astounding inspiration, an inspiration centering around the idea of death. "Now that may be a way out for me," reasons the Joker. "That's it . . . The **Joker** must die!"

Moving swiftly to implement his latest brainstorm, the Joker surrenders to the authorities, makes a full confession of all his dastardly crimes, and is promptly sentenced to death in the electric chair. Immediately following the execution, however, his body is removed from the prison morgue by his henchmen and, according to a prearranged plan, brought back to life by means of a special serum he has created. Now, having been legally tried and executed, the Joker is free to walk the streets at his leisure without fear of being apprehended by the police. "I've already paid the penalty for my crimes," explains the Joker. "The law says a man cannot be placed in double jeopardy for the same crimes!"

In order not to risk his newly won freedom while continuing to live a life of crime, the Joker communicates with his henchmen in code by flashing a light atop the Hotel Bockley while he himself remains clear of the actual robberies they commit. Ultimately, however, Batman and Robin crack the secret of the hotel-sign code and trick the Joker into revealing his complicity in the crimes of his henchmen, but the Joker leaps to freedom from his hotel window and flees by commandeering a passing Army jeep. Batman and Robin overtake the villain, but, during a battle with Robin, the Joker loses his grip on a wire strung out over the ocean and plummets into the icy waters. He survives and makes his way to safety, but he is once again a wanted criminal (Det No. 64: "The Joker Walks the Last Mile!").

In June–July 1942 the Joker stages yet another series of spectacular crimes in Gotham City. He places an advertisement in a local newspaper offering to buy antique vehicles, then robs a jewelry store and escapes down a narrow street while the crowds of clumsy old buggies and other vehicles which have clogged the streets in response to his ad render pursuit by the authorities virtually impossible. He impersonates a magician and makes off with the jewels of three wealthy ladies after requesting their permission to use the gems in a disappearing trick. Finally, he robs a jewelry store and attempts to escape by posing as a sign painter. Batman sees through the sign-painter impersonation, however, apprehends the Joker, and leaves him on the courthouse steps for the police after giving him a terrific beating for having attempted to kill Robin by trapping him in a room filled with burning sulphur.

"Puzzled police found a bruised, battered **Joker** lying on the court steps," reports a radio news announcer soon afterward. "He was taken to prison hospital for treatment . . ." (BM No. 11/1).

In August–September 1942 the Joker commits a series of elaborate crimes all of which involve acting out slang expressions in a literal way. After sending a note to POLICE COMMISSIONER GORDON announcing that he and his henchmen intend to "paint the town red," for example, the Joker travels around the city splashing red paint everywhere, including on the roof of a local bank. The paint used on the bank roof, however, contains a powerful acid, and after the acid has had time to eat through the roof, the Joker and his gang attempt to loot the bank. After a series of indecisive encounters, Batman finally battles the Joker atop a huge Army "barrage balloon" high over the city. In the midst of the struggle, however, the Joker suddenly loses his grip and plummets into the waters of a raging river below (BM No. 12/2: "The Wizard of Words!").

In October–November 1942 the Joker and his henchmen steal a series of seemingly trivial documents—including a child's report card, a local citizens' petition, and a chauffeur's written references—in order to use the signatures of wealthy men, contained in the documents, to facilitate a series of spectacular crimes. Batman and Robin finally lure the Joker into a trap, but the villain grabs Robin and threatens to kill him unless he receives assurances of freedom and $100,000 from the millionaire who had helped the Dynamic Duo spring their trap. Batman complies and Robin is released, but when the Joker finally flees and opens the envelope containing his $100,000, he finds that it is in the form of a personal check, which he could never cash without being arrested (BM No. 13/2: "Comedy of Tears!").

In November 1942 the Joker blackmails the manager of a department store, the superintendent of a camera company, an employee of a fur company, and a worker at an aircraft factory into helping him rob their employers' headquarters by threatening to reveal potentially damaging information about their pasts. Batman and Robin ultimately intercept the Joker at the aircraft factory and attempt to apprehend him, but the villain escapes by commandeering a recently completed aircraft (Det No. 69: "The Harlequin's Hoax!").

In January 1943 the Joker becomes enraged when he sees that he has become the subject of a biting editorial cartoon in a local newspaper and reads that Batman has described him as ". . . a supreme egoist advertising his crimes like a fool," certain always to be defeated "because of his conceit!"

". . . I must defeat the **Batman** at his own game!" cries the Joker angrily. "I'm going to make **Batman** the fool . . . I'm going to shame him . . . shame him into **quitting!** Ha! Ha! Ha!"

In the days that follow, the Joker makes Batman the laughingstock of Gotham City by staging a spectacular crime a day and making a fool out of Batman each time Batman attempts to apprehend him. When the city's newspapers begin to make Batman the butt of their sarcastic editorial cartoons, a shaken Batman contemplates resigning his career as a crime-fighter: "Maybe . . . maybe they're right!" he murmurs to Robin. "Maybe I **am** slipping! Maybe I ought to quit. . . ! Maybe. . . ."

"Maybe **nothing!**" cuts in Robin. "Golly, you never yelled quits before! You're taking this too seriously. C'mon, don't let it get the best of you!"

"You're right!" replies Batman. "I'm not quitting! **I'll get him!** I guess even a **Batman** finds it tough sledding once in awhile! Thanks, Robin, for putting me straight!"

Indeed, by week's end, Batman has apprehended the Joker in time to display him as a caged exhibit at one of his public lectures on crime-fighting (Det No. 71: "A Crime a Day!").

By April–May 1943 a plane bearing the Joker and three of his henchmen has crash-landed in the Ozarks, and while the three henchmen have all parachuted to safety, the Joker has emerged from the crash with total amnesia and has stumbled into the nearby town of Farr

Corners, a sleepy mountain community whose citizens are completely ignorant of the fact that the Joker is a wanted criminal. When Batman and Robin arrive in Farr Corners in search of the villain, they find that the amnesiac Joker – who has completely forgotten that he was ever a dangerous criminal – has become something of a local hero by turning some stolen loot over to the town constable, unaware that he stole it himself during a robbery spree in Gotham City.

The Joker's three henchmen, however, convinced that their boss is attempting to double-cross them, decide to kidnap him in order to force him to reveal where he has hidden the loot from their Gotham City robberies. During a scuffle, the Joker receives a blow on the head which completely restores his memory, and moments later Batman and Robin arrive on the scene and apprehend the Joker and his henchmen (BM No. 16/1: "The Joker Reforms!").

In June 1943 the Joker and his henchmen kidnap a florist named Pettle and assume control of his flower shop. Inside the dirt of the potted plants which they sell to the shop's wealthiest patrons, the Joker and his men bury tiny tubes of chloroform designed to knock everyone in the immediate area unconscious after a certain amount of time has elapsed. With their victims thus rendered unconscious, it becomes a simple matter for the Joker and his gang to enter their homes and rob them. Ultimately, however, Batman and Robin unravel the secret of the Joker's crime technique, trail the criminals to their hideout, knock them unconscious with some of their own chloroform, and notify the police to take them into custody (Det No. 76: "Slay 'em with Flowers").

In October–November 1943 a man named Lyon commits a series of crimes and attempts, by mimicking the Joker's zany crime-style and leaving behind the Joker's traditional calling cards, to pin the blame on the Joker. Furious at the thought of his reputation being sullied by an imitator, the Joker sets out after Lyon with a vengeance and ultimately locks him in a lion's cage at a local zoo along with Batman and Robin. The Dynamic Duo escape from the lion's cage, however, turn Lyon over to a zoo keeper for surrender to the authorities, and, with the aid of a cheetah which they employ as a bloodhound, ultimately apprehend the Joker and his lone accomplice (BM No. 19/3: "The Case of the Timid Lion!").

In December 1943–January 1944, with the aid of bogus scientist Ecla Tate and fraudulent mystic Swami Meera Kell, the Joker uses a group of abandoned movie sets – containing mock-ups of cities both past and future – in order to swindle greedy businessman Percival Pruitt and fugitive criminal Kid Glove Mixter into believing that, for a fee, he can transport them safely into the distant future, where, allegedly, Pruitt will be able to realize a fortune from money he has invested in the present, and Mixter will be able to evade the law. After rendering his "time travelers" unconscious with knockout gas and transporting them to a futuristic movie set, the Joker and his accomplices set in motion an elaborate scheme to extort additional money from their victims, but Batman and Robin smash the plot and apprehend the Joker, along with Ecla Tate, Swami Meera Kell, and a gang of the Joker's assorted accomplices (BM No. 20/1: "The Centuries of Crime!").

In March 1944 Fayetteville, West Virginia, businessman Hart murders a businessman and a bank president – and robs their respective businesses – while disguised as the Joker, taking care to leave a playing card joker at the scene of each crime so that the real Joker will be implicated.

From the outset, Batman is skeptical that the real Joker is the man he is after, but the Joker, meanwhile, is absolutely outraged. "The impudence of that cheap crook!" he cries. "Using my name to cover up his own clumsy jobs . . . daring to masquerade as **me,** the **Joker!** Holding up my sterling reputation for cleverness to scorn and contempt!"

When a thorough search of his personal files fails to yield up a clue to the impostor's identity, the Joker decides to launch a personal search for the culprit in order to expose him: "Very well, then!" he muses. "Even if it means that I must now fight on the side of law and order, I'll smash this cheap imitation and expose him! No sacrifice is too great to maintain the honor of the **Joker!**"

In the series of confusing encounters that follow – between Batman, Robin, the real Joker, and the bogus Joker – the Joker finds himself in the ironic position of fighting on the side of his twin nemeses, the Dynamic Duo: "The **Batman** and **Robin** in danger!" he cries at one point, as the bogus Joker is about to pour molten lead on Batman and Robin. "I can't let them die . . . this time! They've got to witness my innocence. . . ."

During a final, climactic battle, the real Joker unmasks the phony Joker as businessman Hart and leaves Batman and Robin to apprehend him while he himself makes a hasty escape (Det No. 85: "The Joker's Double").

In June–July 1944 the Joker and his henchmen stage a series of crimes revolving around the theme of being upside-down: the clues with which the Joker advertises his crimes are either upside-down or backward, and the crimes themselves invariably employ the upside-down theme in their fulfillment. After a series of indecisive battles – including a duel between Batman and the Joker while they hang suspended, with the aid of magnetized shoes, from the metal ceiling of the Joker's hideout – Batman and Robin capture the Joker's henchmen and recover their stolen loot. The Joker, however, escapes (BM No. 23/1: "The Upside Down Crimes!").

By September 1944 the Joker has apparently been apprehended, for the opening of the text finds him in prison, serving a life term. Soon afterward, after engineering a brilliant escape, the Joker embarks on a series of spectacular crimes featuring practical jokes as their common theme. During the attempted theft of a gem-encrusted model of Gotham City, for example, the Joker and his henchmen stymie the pursuing police by strewing their escape route with slippery banana peels. Batman and Robin ultimately apprehend the Joker's henchmen, and the Joker, attempting to escape in what he believes to be an empty van, is captured by policemen who, at Batman's suggestion, have been hiding inside it (Det No. 91: "The Case of the Practical Joker").

In October–November 1944, behind the gray walls of Gotham Penitentiary, the Joker and the PENGUIN become embroiled in a heated argument over which of them is the most ingenious criminal:

". . . you giggling ghoul," cries the Penguin. "Why, you couldn't pick a blind man's pocket on a foggy night!"

"Now look here, you umbrella-toting underworld upstart," retorts the Joker angrily, "--this town isn't big enough for both of us to operate in! We've got to settle who goes and who stays!"

To settle the question, the two villains decide to hold a crime contest, with whoever succeeds in stealing the priceless Van Landorpf Emerald winning "exclusive control of the Gotham City territory." After breaking out of jail together, the two arch-criminals go their separate ways to carry out their competition for the Van Landorpf Emerald and the honor of being Gotham City's cleverest criminal.

Soon afterward, however – after a disastrous three-way battle at the Van Landorpf mansion between the Joker's gang, the Penguin's gang, and the Dynamic Duo – the Joker and the Penguin decide to join forces and forget their differences. "After all," observes the Penguin, "**Batman** is our real enemy!"

"You're right!" replies the Joker. "From now on let bygones be bygones! We're partners!"

"Together," chimes in the Penguin, "we can pick Gotham City clean!"

The fragile alliance does not last long, however, and soon the Joker and the Penguin are embroiled in a heated argument over how best to destroy Batman and Robin, whom they have managed to capture during a payroll robbery. The Penguin favors a diabolical water torture, while the Joker insists on an overdose of laughing gas. While the battle rages, Batman and Robin free themselves from their bonds and apprehend both of the startled criminals.

"A fine partner you turned out to be!" accuses the Joker. "If you hadn't been so vain we'd never have been caught!"

"And I suppose you had nothing to do with it!" retorts the Penguin angrily. "Well, from now on, I'm operating alone!" (BM No. 25/1: "Knights of Knavery").

In April–May 1945 the Joker launches an elaborate swindle centering around Shadow City, a bogus movie-set "city" which he has established in an abandoned Gotham City warehouse. By tricking wealthy individuals into believing that Shadow City is an exciting, little-known section of Gotham City where their private fantasies will be fulfilled, the Joker is able to lure victims to the phony city, populated only by his own henchmen, and to cheat or intimidate them into leaving large sums of money behind them when they leave. The Joker promises wealthy gambling enthusiast "Bet-A-Million" Bannister, for example, that Shadow City features a fabulous gambling casino, then cheats Bannister unmercifully when he comes to gamble there. Batman and Robin ultimately locate Shadow City, however, capture the Joker, and put an end to his racket (BM No. 28/1: "Shadow City!").

In August 1945 the Joker and his henchmen literally steal an "historic old mansion" belonging to millionaire J. Bullion Stinckney, float it down the Kiddiwah River, and then hide it deep in the woods, intending to ransom it back to Stinckney for a huge sum of money. Batman and Robin ultimately locate the missing mansion, however, escape from a quicksand bog into which the Joker has thrown them, and apprehend the Joker and his henchmen (Det No. 102: "The House That was Held for Ransom!").

In Fall 1945 the Joker escapes from prison and makes his way to the hideout of the Velvet Kid, a criminal who, on the pretext of being "a reformed crook and an expert on thief-catching devices," gains access to the homes of prominent families to demonstrate his thief-catching devices so that he can analyze the layouts of the homes and burglarize them later.

Together the Joker and the Velvet Kid concoct an elaborate scheme in which the Velvet Kid, on the pretext of organizing a Citizens' Committee for Law and Order, invites Gotham City's most prominent citizens and public officials to a series of planning conferences, during which the Joker and his henchmen rob their unguarded homes. After a series of battles, however – both with the Velvet Kid and with the Joker – Batman and Robin learn the details of the scheme, apprehend the Velvet Kid, and take the Joker and his henchmen into custody (WF No. 19: "The League for Larceny!").

The following summer, after having somehow regained his freedom, the Joker spies bands of college freshmen roaming the streets performing various wacky stunts as part of their fraternity initiation ceremonies and decides to use similar stunts as the theme for a whole new series of crimes. At one point, after he and his henchmen have robbed a jewelry store while posing as a band of zany college students, the Joker captures Batman, imprisons him at his hideout, and then informs Robin that he will set Batman free only if Robin agrees to perform a series of humiliating stunts, such as selling winter mufflers and earmuffs on a street corner in the middle of summer.

"One thing I'd enjoy more than killing the **Batman**," the Joker tells Robin, "--and that's to make both of you look ridiculous!"

Unbeknownst to Robin, the zany stunts he is forced to perform are all designed to facilitate a series of spectacular crimes by the Joker and his henchmen, but ultimately, after Batman has escaped from the Joker's hideout, the Dynamic Duo join forces to apprehend the Joker and his gang (BM No. 32/1, Dec/Jan '45–'46: "Rackety-Rax Racket!").

In March 1946 the Joker robs the safe of investment broker Herbert Swail; picks the pocket of Titus Drumm, the "richest and meanest man in Gotham City," who, because he is distrustful of banks, always carries large sums of money on his person; and robs the patrons at the exclusive Crocus Club after incapacitating them with a special gas. At one point, after the Joker has taken Robin captive, Batman is forced to track down an elaborate series of clues and evade a cunning array of diabolical deathtraps before he is finally able to locate the Joker's hideout and, with Robin's help, to apprehend him (Det No. 109: "The House That Jokes Built!").

In August 1946 the Joker challenges Batman and Robin to an elaborate "crime acrostic contest" in which each crime involves the use, in triplicate, of key letters which, taken together, will spell out the name Joker once the acrostic has been completed: in quick succession, the Joker steals evidence from Gotham City's **J**ustice Building, where **j**udges sentence criminals to **j**ail terms; robs the patrons at the **O**rpheum **O**pera, where Shakespeare's *Othello* is playing; steals the **K**ing of Moravia's **K**han Ruby from **K**night Jewelers; and attempts to make off with some radar equipment from the headquarters of **E**lectrical **E**ngineering **E**nterprises, where he is finally apprehended by Batman.

In prison, the Joker feels humiliated at having failed to complete his crime acrostic, but his spirits rise when he spies a newspaper headline proclaiming that "Joker's Crime Acrostic Ends with 'R' for Robin, Who Helped Set Trap!"

"Huh?" cries the Joker, astonished at having actually fulfilled his acrostic, albeit inadvertently. ". . . I've **done** it! Another gem for my scrapbook! Ha-ha-ha-ha-ha-ha-ha-ha-ha!" (Det No. 114: "Acrostic of Crime!").

By October–November 1946 the Joker has escaped from prison and concocted yet another of his elaborate crime schemes. "Only one person stands in my way," explains the Joker, "--the Batman! He has outwitted me consistently thanks to the batmobile, batplane, bat signal and other revolutionary devices . . . but no more! The same weapons he has used against me, I can turn against him--with such improvements as only my genius could devise! Ho, ho, ho, ho!"

To aid him in his new war against Batman, the Joker has designed a "jokermobile" and a "jokergyro" and has placed special "Joker signals" in front of every store in Gotham City. Soon a special handbill is making its way through the underworld, announcing the Joker's new "insurance plan" for criminals: "MAKE CRIME PAY THE JOKER WAY!" trumpets the handbill. "Employ the one infallible intellect of the underworld on a percentage basis – plans for plunder – rescues on request – escapes engineered – alibis invented!"

Before long, criminals of every stripe have flocked to the Joker's banner, begging him to plan their crimes for them and bail them out of trouble, when necessary, with his heavily armed jokermobile or his fleet jokergyro.

Batman and Robin ultimately apprehend the Joker, however, and put him out of business (BM No. 37/3: "The Joker Follows Suit!").

In December 1946 the Joker perpetrates the dazzling "royal flush crimes," a series of spectacular criminal escapades centering on the theme of a royal flush in diamonds: he steals some gems from the "diamond jubilee" celebration of the Cottonworth **10**-Cent Stores; makes off with the gate receipts from a baseball game between the Gotham Goliaths – owned by "Diamond **Jack**" Barnes – and the Metropolis Mammoths; attempts, unsuccessfully, to steal a diamond tiara scheduled to be awarded to a beauty **queen;** and tries to make off with a gem collection belonging to Rupert Dazel, known as "the match **king**" because of his hobby of building things out of matches. Ironically, Batman and Robin finally apprehend the Joker at the Diamond X Dude Ranch – owned by ex-Air Force **ace** Eddie Hoyle – where the villain has been hiding out (Det No. 118: "The Royal Flush Crimes!").

In April–May 1947 a group of men known as the 13 Club launch a "strange new television program" on which they intentionally violate various traditional superstitions in order to demonstrate to the public the foolishness of being superstitious. In an effort to capitalize on the theme of the program, however, the Joker commits a series of crimes involving bizarre variations on the superstitions violated by the club members. After club member Ray Standish has allowed a black cat to cross his path on the program in order to demonstrate the foolishness of the superstition concerning black cats, for example, the Joker and his henchmen let a black panther loose in the Standish mansion and then loot it while Standish cowers in fear. After committing a long string of these crimes, however, the Joker is finally apprehended by Batman and Robin (BM No. 40/1: "The 13 Club!").

In June 1947 the Joker launches his spectacular "crime parade," a series of daring crimes based on the day's most frequently requested popular song on the "Tune Parade" radio program, although, in practice, the Joker controls the title of the most frequently requested song by flooding the radio station with anonymous song requests. When "Smoke Gets in Your Eyes" is the selection, for example, the Joker and his gang plug up the chimney of a warehouse, causing it to fill up with smoke, and steal the precious silk stored there. The Joker and his henchmen attempt four such crimes before they are finally apprehended by Batman and Robin (Det No. 124: "The Crime Parade").

In October 1947 the Joker escapes from prison and stages a series of spectacular crimes in reverse, all of which involve announcing the crime before it has actually been committed and then capitalizing on the reactions of the people who assume that the evil deed has already been done. At the Gotham Horse Show, for example, a henchman posing as an insurance investigator approaches wealthy Mrs. Tyler Vanderkill and tells her that he has received word that her priceless emerald necklace has been stolen. When Mrs. Vanderkill removes the necklace from her neck to prove that the necklace has not been stolen after all, the henchman seizes it and disappears with it into the crowd. The strange crimes in reverse proceed like clockwork until the Joker is finally apprehended by Batman and Robin (Det No. 128: "Crime in ƎSЯƎVƎЯ!").

In December 1947–January 1948, after he has broken

YES, ONCE AGAIN THE MIRTHFUL MOUNTE-BANK IS BEHIND BARS...
CRIME IN REVERSE? WHY NOT? HA, HA! WHAT A JOKE THAT WOULD BE! BUT I'LL HAVE TO GET OUT OF HERE FIRST...

The Joker in prison, 1947 © NPP 1947

the bank at an underworld gambling casino, the Joker decides to make gambling an integral part of his next diabolical scheme. "I'm so thrilled with gambling that I'm going to play a super-game," he exclaims. "**Batman** will be my opponent and ***real lives*** will be the stakes!"

After capturing a pair of fugitive radium thieves, the Joker lures Batman and Robin to his mansion hideout on a secluded island and forces Batman to participate in a "diabolical game of death" to preserve the lives of Robin and the two radium thieves. The games which Batman must master are giant games of chance – including a gigantic pinball machine and a huge pair of dice – any one of which will destroy Robin and the two radium thieves unless Batman overcomes seemingly insurmountable odds and wins according to the Joker's rules. Batman ultimately wins out over the Joker's games of death and sets out after the Joker, but the villain eludes him by leaping off a high cliff into an angry sea. The two radium thieves, repentant at having stolen radium from a hospital, promise to surrender to the authorities and accept their punishment (BM No. 44/1: "Gamble with Doom!").

By April–May 1948 the Joker has apparently been apprehended, for he escapes from jail early in the text. Later, at a lavish underworld party held to celebrate his return, the Joker becomes poetically inspired by the huge greeting cards with which his fellow criminals have decorated the hall. Vows the Joker: "Vast riches I'll grab with droll pictures and rhymes, as I make the world gasp with – my greeting card crimes!"

In the days that follow, the Joker commits a series of spectacular greeting-card crimes, robbing affairs which would ordinarily serve as the subject of greeting cards, such as birthday parties or wedding receptions, and forewarning both Batman and the intended victims by sending them greeting cards containing a few cryptic lines of greeting-card verse. The Joker is apprehended by Batman and Robin, however, while attempting to make off with the receipts of a charity masquerade ball (BM No. 46/1: "'Guileful Greetings!' or 'The Joker Sends Regards!'").

In July 1948 the Joker decides to stage a "rebus-riddle crime campaign," in which his clues to the authorities take the form of rebus riddles, messages which utilize pictures in place of words. By deciphering the ingenious rebus riddles, Batman and Robin successfully thwart the Joker's attempt to steal the Millman sapphire collection, then apprehend him when he attempts to flee the scene of an unsuccessful gold bullion robbery (Det No. 137: "The Rebus Crimes!").

In August 1948 the Joker kidnaps Dr. Walter Timmins, inventor of a fabulous "elixir of invisibility," and after sending extortion letters to three wealthy Gotham City business tycoons threatening to sabotage their business operations unless they agree to pay him protection money, uses the elixir to render himself invisible and sets out to ruin the business operations owned by his three intended victims. For a time, the Joker wreaks havoc among the businesses and other interests owned by the three tycoons, but, after Robin has freed Timmins from the Joker's hideout, Batman renders himself invisible with some of Timmins's elixir, locates the Joker by the sound of his bragging voice, and finally apprehends him (Det No. 138: "The Invisible Crimes!").

In April–May 1949 the Joker commits a series of spectacular robberies in such an outrageously funny manner that they become known as his "funny robberies"; the victims, in fact, claim to have been so overjoyed at the Joker's antics that they are unwilling to register complaints with the police.

In reality, however, the Joker has secured the complete cooperation of his "victims" by approaching them in advance, claiming that he wants to rob them only as part of a jovial game of wits with Batman and Robin and promising to repay their cooperation by returning double the amount of whatever he steals. The Joker's idea of "double," however, is not the same as their own: after he has stolen a valuable ermine coat from wealthy Mrs. Carlin, for example, he repays her by giving her two live ermines. The funny robberies are an uproarious success until the Joker is finally apprehended through the heroic efforts of Batman and Robin (BM No. 52/3: "The Happy Victims!").

In June–July 1949 the Joker gazes about him at his vast treasure-trove of ill-gotten riches and decides that material wealth is not his only goal. "I have everything I need," he exclaims, "– except that which I want the most, ***fame as the world's greatest clown!*** Yes, ha-ha! I am the **Joker,** and it must be as a great comedian that the world remembers me. Ha-ha! Ho-ho! I must be remembered for my **laughs!**"

Then, moments later, the Joker is seized by one of his egomaniacal inspirations: "I will write a book," he exclaims, "– a whole volume of books! I will become the authority on comedy!"

The Joker becomes so inspired by the first portion of his book, a chapter on "laughs," that he decides to steal a series of insignificant objects the first two letters of which, taken together, spell out the letters of his famous laugh, i.e., ha-ha, ho-ho. After he has stolen these objects (a **ha**irpin, a **ha**cksaw, a **ho**e, and a **ho**le in the ground), he commits a more serious crime, the last letters of whose key words spell out the letters of his famous laugh, in reverse: this crime consists of the theft of some golden golf clubs from the Maharajah of Nimpah at the Winne-koh-toh Golf Club. The zany "laugh crimes" are an undisputed aesthetic success, but the Joker is ultimately apprehended through the heroic efforts of Batman and Robin (BM No. 53/1: "A Hairpin, a Hoe, a Hacksaw, a Hole in the Ground!").

In July 1949 the Joker and his henchmen commit a series of spectacular crimes revolving around the ingenious use of sound effects. By creating the sound of cracking timbers, for example, the Joker fools the patrons of the Globe Theater into thinking that the roof is collapsing and then makes off with the ticket receipts in the ensuing confusion. When Batman and Robin give chase in the BATMOBILE, the Joker ties up the traffic behind him on his cliffside getaway route by broadcasting the sounds of an avalanche, with the result that the Dynamic Duo become so completely ensnarled in clogged traffic that they are forced to abandon their pursuit. The incredible sound-effects crimes continue unabated until finally Batman and Robin track the villain down with the aid of a "wartime sound-detector" and apprehend the Joker and his henchmen (Det No. 149: "The Sound-Effect Crimes!").

In October–November 1949 the Joker organizes an underworld "college of clowns" for the purpose of training an entire syndicate of Jokers who, under his personal direction, will commit simultaneous crimes in every state in the Union. After the authorities have apprehended the so-called New Jersey Joker, Batman impersonates him and infiltrates the clown college in hopes of apprehending the Joker, but the Joker penetrates Batman's disguise, imprisons Robin, and then, by threatening to murder Robin, forces Batman to don a poorly fitting, clownlike Batman costume and play the buffoon to the delight of the Joker's guffawing students. Ultimately, however, Batman frees Robin from the Joker's clutches and, with his help, apprehends the Joker and his underworld colleagues (BM No. 55/1: "The Case of the 48 Jokers!").

In February–March 1950, after a group of his fellow prison inmates have disparaged his skills as a comedian, the Joker breaks jail and sets out to become "the country's most famous – and richest – comedian, as well as the star performer of the underworld!" After committing a series of daring "funny man crimes," all designed to promote his reputation as an uproarious comedian as well as a master criminal, the Joker dashes off to Gotham City's Club Comique, which is holding a competition to select the city's funniest amateur comedian. The Joker expects to win the contest – and the platinum trophy being awarded to the winner – with what he calls his "side-splitting imitation of the Joker," but Batman, who has beaten the Joker to the Club Comique and secretly taken the place of the judge there, intentionally infuriates the Joker by informing him that his Joker "imitation" is decidedly unimpressive. When Batman and Robin leap to the attack, the Joker flees, but the Dynamic Duo give chase and apprehend him soon afterward (BM No. 57/3: "The Funny Man Crimes!").

In June–July 1950 Batman and Robin visit the Joker in prison in an effort to ascertain why he persists in using his extraordinary talents "to commit crazy humorous crimes."

"I guess I inherited that [tendency] from my ancestors a century ago," replies the Joker, "--they were famous clowns!"

". . . if we went back into the past and studied the Joker's ancestors," remarks Batman, after he and Robin have left the prison, "we might learn what hereditary influence affected him, and maybe reform him!"

Hoping to solve the riddle of the Joker's zany, larcenous personality, Bruce Wayne and Dick Grayson ask PROFESSOR CARTER NICHOLS to send them back 100 years into the past, but Nichols inadvertently dispatches them 100 years into the future, and Wayne and Grayson soon find themselves in the Gotham City of the twenty-first century A.D. They learn nothing there likely to help them reform the Joker, but they do meet CHIEF REKOJ, a law-abiding descendant of the Joker who is Gotham City's chief of police (BM No. 59/3: "Batman in the Future!").

By October–November 1950 composer Joseph Macklas has completed "The Batman and Robin March," and Batman has been invited to serve as guest conductor for its premiere performance at the Gotham City Concert Hall. In the midst of the performance, however, a huge drum tumbles out onto the stage and the Joker pops out of it to deliver a brash taunt to the astonished audience: ". . . soon," cries the Joker, "all of Gotham City will hear the notes of my ***'Song of Crime'***!"

In the days that follow, the Joker commits a series of spectacular crimes in a complex pattern based on the notes of the song "Laugh, Clown, Laugh," while attired in colorful circus-clown regalia. The villain and his henchmen are ultimately apprehended, however, through the heroic efforts of Batman and Robin (WF No. 48: "Song of Crime!").

In February 1951 the Joker dons the colorful garb of the Red Hood – thereby reassuming the villainous identity with which, according to Detective Comics No. 168, he first began his criminal career approximately a decade previously – although why the Joker would want to resume the use of a long-forgotten identity is never explained in the text. In the guise of the Red Hood, the Joker invades the campus of State University in an unsuccessful attempt to steal a payroll from the college bursar's office. The Red Hood successfully eludes Batman and Robin, but he is waylaid and held captive by Earl "Farmerboy" Benson, a twenty-two-year-old ex-convict employed as the campus gardener, who poses as the Red Hood while committing a series of campus robberies in the hope of pinning the blame on the real Red Hood, the Joker. Ultimately, however, with the help of a group of college criminology students, Batman and Robin apprehend the bogus Red Hood, unmask him as Earl "Farmerboy" Benson, and then force him to lead them to the ramshackle shed where he has been holding the Joker captive ("The Man Behind the Red Hood!").

In February–March 1951, inspired by a recent exhibition of Batman's famous crime-fighting costumes, the Joker commits a series of spectacular crimes based on the famous comedy characters of fiction – Falstaff, Mr. Pickwick, the Connecticut Yankee, Old King Cole, and Simple Simon – while wearing, during the commission of each crime, the costume of the particular comedy character around whom the crime revolves. The cunning costume crimes are successful for a time, but the Joker is finally apprehended by Batman and Robin (BM No. 63/1: "The Joker's Crime Costumes!").

In August–September 1951 the Joker shuts off the electric power at the headquarters of the electric company as part of his scheme to steal the company's payroll, only to discover, to his horror and chagrin, that by cutting off the electric power he has made it impossible to escape from the building by elevator. After a stairway battle with Batman and Robin, the Joker manages to escape, albeit without his loot, but the newspapers make him the laughingstock of Gotham City by publicizing his hilarious "boner" at the electric company building.

The news accounts, however, provide the Joker with one of his infamous inspirations, and he proceeds to commit a series of spectacular crimes based on the great boners of history. By tampering with buoys in the Gotham River, for example, and forcing the S.S. *Capetownia* to run aground so that they can steal the priceless diamond shipment on board, the Joker and his henchmen re-create a famous historical boner, i.e., the day the battleship *Missouri* got stuck in the mud. The Joker's greatest coup comes when he appears to have made fools of Batman and Robin by drawing their BATPLANE several thousand miles off course with a phony aircraft directional beam, but the Dynamic Duo have only pretended to pull a hilarious boner in order to pinpoint the location of the Joker's hideout by computing the transmission point of the phony beam, and they apprehend the Joker in the midst of an underworld party celebrating the Joker's supposed victory over Batman (BM No. 66/1: "The Joker's Comedy of Errors!").

In October–November 1951 a disconsolate Joker, fearful that he may be "going stale" after three full weeks without a successful crime, decides to appropriate a technique long used by professional comedians, i.e., to hire a team of underworld gag writers to plan a series of spectacular crimes designed to enable him to acquire wealth while at the same time making fools out of Batman and Robin.

When the first two crimes plotted by the newly hired gagmen are only partially successful, however, the Joker decides that he must somehow force Batman to plan his crimes for him, since crimes conceived by Batman would undoubtedly be the most ingenious crimes of all. After taking Robin captive, the Joker threatens to kill him unless Batman agrees to design a foolproof crime whose execution will make Batman the laughingstock of Gotham City. Batman obediently plans such a crime – a payroll theft from the Gotham Chewing Gum Company whose execution is supposed to entail Batman's becoming hopelessly enmeshed in a huge mass of chewing gum – but Batman double-crosses the Joker by pouring the chewing gum over the Joker and his henchmen instead, and Robin, who has managed to escape from the Joker's hideout, appears on the scene with the police to help apprehend the criminals (BM No. 67/2: "The Man Who Wrote the Joker's Jokes!").

In February 1952 the Joker resigns from his life of crime after inheriting a vast fortune in cash and other valuables from the estate of William "King" Barlowe, a wealthy underworld czar who was once the Joker's hated enemy. The Joker begins to live sumptuously and spend lavishly, only to discover soon afterward, to his horror and chagrin, that only a fraction of his inherited fortune consists of real cash and valuable jewelry, while the remainder is counterfeit.

"I should have suspected trickery when King Barlowe left me his fortune!" exclaims the Joker. "He hated me and this was his way of getting revenge on me! He wanted me to get used to riches and then humiliate me before the underworld by making me a laughingstock!"

When a Federal income tax collector informs the Joker that he will have to pay a $2,000,000 inheritance tax on his newly acquired fortune, the Joker finds himself on the horns of a cruel dilemma: unless he wants to make a fool of himself by admitting that his entire fortune is counterfeit, he must somehow accumulate $2,000,000 to pay his taxes, and yet he must avoid letting it become known that he has returned to crime, lest the world realize that he is actually poverty-stricken.

To solve his problem, the Joker embarks on a series of crimes deliberately lacking in his customary flair and artistry. "This is a stick-up! Hand over all the dough!" cries the Joker, his face carefully hidden, as he robs the box office at the Gotham Opera House while inwardly congratulating himself on the studied crudeness of his technique: "Ha, ha! How's that for a corny line! No imagination! No originality! Nobody could guess this is coming from the brilliant Joker!"

After a time, however, Batman begins to suspect the Joker's real plight, and he mischievously alters the circumstances of each crime just enough to make it seem a product of the Joker's peculiar genius. After the holdup at the Gotham Opera House, for example, Batman secretly makes off with all the tickets to "I Pagliacci," an opera about a clown, a typical Joker stunt which serves only to implicate the Joker in a crime he has in fact committed.

Ultimately, after a series of such incidents, Batman poses as an underworld figure and tricks the Joker into making a full confession that ultimately leads to his apprehension and imprisonment (Det No. 180: "The Joker's Millions!").

In July–August 1952 the Joker commits a series of seemingly "impossible" crimes with the aid of a team of highly skilled criminal specialists, each of whom has a talent or characteristic peculiarly suited to the particular crime. One of the crimes, for example, takes place at a jewel exhibit, where some of the Joker's henchmen begin a diversionary fistfight while the specialist for the occasion, a sword swallower, calmly swallows a bejeweled dagger and walks past the armed guards to freedom.

The Joker, 1952 © NPP 1952

At one point, the Joker and his henchmen kidnap Dick Grayson on his way home from school in order to force Bruce Wayne, who apparently achieved a degree of renown as a slingshot champion in college, to use his esoteric skill to help the Joker and his henchmen smuggle some stolen diamonds into the country. Wayne, however, manages to notify the authorities, who promptly apprehend the Joker's henchmen and free Dick Grayson from the Joker's hideout, enabling Batman and Robin to capture the Joker soon afterward (WF No. 59: "The Joker's Aces!").

In October–November 1952, after Batman has bested the Joker during one of their frequent encounters by employing a gas capsule from his famous UTILITY BELT, the Joker designs a utility belt of his own – complete with a hand buzzer, snake pellets, sneezing powder, itching powder, a water-squirting police badge, a jumping jack concealed inside a cigarette pack, a tiny pocket telescope which gives anyone who looks through it a black eye, Mexican jumping beans, pellets which burst into bouquets of flowers, playing cards, a pack of exploding cigarettes, and a common cork – and

The Joker and his henchmen, 1952 © NPP 1952

promptly embarks on an uproarious crime spree in which he uses the "jokes and trick novelties" in his utility belt to commit zany crimes and stymie the police. Ironically, after Batman and Robin have been captured by the Joker and carried captive to the villain's hideout, Batman seizes his captor's utility belt and uses its wacky arsenal of weapons to take the Joker and his henchmen into custody (BM No. 73/3: "The Joker's Utility Belt!").

In November–December 1952, by which time the Joker has been released from prison, Batman plants a tiny electronic listening device inside the Joker's automobile and, soon afterward, as the result of information unwittingly provided by the Joker, apprehends fugitive criminal Dink Devers. When the local newspapers sarcastically refer to the Joker as a "cop" and a "Sherlock" for having aided in the apprehension of a notorious criminal, the Joker becomes outraged. "**Batman** has made a fool of me, before **all** of Gotham City!" he cries. "Imagine! Using **me** to solve a crime! Turning the **Joker** into a **lawman!** I must **save face**--by **turning the tables on Batman!** I must make **Batman a criminal! Ha-ha!** That would even the score!"

Not long afterward, after he and his henchmen have kidnapped Robin, the Joker informs Batman that unless he agrees to "cheat, steal, and kill--in that order" – thus transforming himself into a criminal just as he has already transformed the Joker into a policeman – he will order his henchmen to execute Robin.

In the hours that follow, Batman obeys the Joker's instructions, but not in a way that pleases the Joker: he stages a phony accident with the batplane so that he can appear to have *cheated* death; he *steals* the Joker's thunder by thwarting his attempted robbery of Farley's Department Store; and finally, in the midst of a circus performance at Gotham Square Garden, he *kills* time with the Joker on the high trapeze while the circus guards apprehend his henchmen, *kills* the audience with laughter, and, finally *kills* the unscheduled trapeze routine by bringing it to a hasty conclusion. Then, having fulfilled his promise to the Joker, albeit not as the villain had intended, he returns to the Joker's hideout with the police, captures the remainder of the Joker's gang, and frees Robin from their clutches (WF No. 61: "The Crimes of Batman!").

In December 1952–January 1953 the Joker steals a series of worthless objects – such as a picture of the Mona Lisa painted on a billboard – and exhibits other bizarre behavior as part of a plot to get himself committed to Gotham City's Institute for the Insane, where James Derek, a mentally unbalanced bank clerk who embezzled and then hid $1,000,000 in cash, has recently been incarcerated. Before long, a psychiatrist has diagnosed the Joker's condition as "hebophrenic [sic] schizophrenia" – "an insanity marked by extremely foolish behavior" – and an elated Joker has been dispatched to the insane asylum, where he quickly succeeds in learning the location of the stolen bank loot from the sleep-talking James Derek. Batman, however, has entered the insane asylum under an assumed name in order to keep an eye on the Joker, and, with Robin's help, he thwarts the Joker's attempt to escape from the asylum, recovers the bank money stolen by James Derek, and takes the Joker into custody (BM No. 74/1: "The Crazy Crime Clown!").

In March 1953 the Joker escapes from prison, where he had been forced to undergo the excruciating humiliation of editing the prison newspaper, a chore that had entailed writing editorials praising the police and printing news stories in support of the theme that crime does not pay. Capitalizing on this odious prison experience, the Joker launches the *Joker's Journal*, an underworld newspaper featuring a comic strip which pokes fun at Batman and Robin; display advertisements promoting the services of fences, gun dealers, and other underworld businessmen; and classified advertisements offering such things as "complete, foolproof plans" for the commission of crimes.

In an effort to apprehend the newspaper's underworld advertisers, who include some of the city's major criminals, Batman poses as a member of the underworld, obtains a post on the *Joker's Journal* as an ad salesman, and uses the inside information available to him in his new capacity to apprehend, or to enable Robin and the police to apprehend, some of the newspaper's major underworld advertisers.

After a time, however, the Joker and his henchmen discover their new employee's true identity and, in order to humiliate him, they force him to perform the menial functions of a copyboy in the offices of the *Joker's Journal.* When the Joker photographs Batman wearing a dunce cap for the front page of the latest edition, however, Batman outwits him by seeing to it that subtle clues appear in the finished photograph which reveal the location of the Joker's hideout to Robin and the police. Before long, Batman is rescued, the Joker and his henchmen are apprehended, and the *Joker's Journal* is put permanently out of business. In addition, Batman tampers with the Joker's files in such a way that the criminals who attempt to commit the perfect crimes featured in his advertisements will walk directly into the waiting hands of the police (Det No. 193: "The Joker's Journal!").

In December 1953–January 1954 the Joker launches Joker Film Productions, Inc. to make "educational films for criminals." In this way, hopes the Joker, he and his henchmen will not only profit from their crimes directly, but will reap the additional profits stemming from the sale of live-action films of the crimes to their underworld colleagues. However, after attending a showing of *The Return of Batman and Robin*, a Hollywood movie in which an actor playing the Joker is defeated and humiliated by actors portraying the Dynamic Duo, the Joker decides to devote his energies to the making of a Batman and Robin film entitled *How to Handle Batman and Robin*, in which the real Joker, playing himself, will make fools of Batman and Robin, who the Joker hopes can be fooled into unwittingly portraying themselves in the film.

In the days that follow, the Joker lures Batman and Robin into a series of cleverly prearranged battles during which, through the cunning use of booby traps and other devices, the Dynamic Duo are made to appear foolish while the Joker habitually emerges victorious. Unbeknownst to the Joker, however, Batman and Robin have intentionally been allowing the Joker to complete his film in the hope of obtaining a complete list of the film's potential buyers, which would invariably lead the Dynamic Duo "to every important crook in the land." Indeed, once the film has been completed and the buyers list compiled, Batman and Robin invade the Joker's hideout and apprehend the Joker and his henchmen (BM No. 80/1: "The Joker's Movie Crimes!").

In August 1954, while Batman is pursuing the Joker through a building housing valuable radium, the two men suddenly find themselves in the experimental laboratory of Dr. Tom Rayburn, where they are inadvertently exposed to "the smashing force of the epsilon rays" emanating from Rayburn's latest invention. Miraculously, both Batman and the Joker escape serious injury, but their personalities have somehow been exchanged, and until Rayburn can accumulate the rare isotopes he needs to make the necessary repairs to his ray machine, Batman will remain imprisoned in the body of the Joker, and the Joker will remain imprisoned in the body of Batman.

In the days that follow, the Joker, trapped in the body of Batman, commits a series of crimes in Gotham City, while Batman, trapped in the body of the Joker, attempts both to apprehend the Joker and to perform his normal crime-fighting functions in the city. Perhaps the greatest threat to Batman posed by the personality changeover lies in the fact that the Joker, now residing in Batman's body, need only remove the cowl covering his face in order to reveal to the world at large that Bruce Wayne and Batman are one and the same man. For a time, it appears that the Joker will indeed reveal Batman's identity to the underworld for a fee of $1,000,000, but Dr. Rayburn manages to repair his ray machine and restore the personalities of Batman and the Joker to their proper bodies before the Joker can learn or reveal Batman's secret (BM No. 85/1: "Batman – Clown of Crime!").

In September 1954, while attending a baseball game in Gotham City, the Joker overhears a team manager speaking of trading players in order to fill his team's needs. Inspired by the ingenuity of the "trading" concept, the Joker and his henchmen commit a series of spectacular robberies by shrewdly trading with other underworld gangs in the city to obtain the precise criminal talent they need in order to execute each crime successfully.

"The **Joker**'s got a team of crime specialists," observes Batman grimly, "--and he trades them whenever the job requires a different sort of criminal talent!" For a time, the trading concept aids the Joker immeasurably, but he and his henchmen are ultimately apprehended through the heroic efforts of Batman and Robin (BM No. 86/2: "The Joker's Winning Team!").

In October 1954, when Gotham City's television station GCTV celebrates the life and career of Batman on its "Your Life Story" program, the Joker, who is believed to be safely behind bars, crashes out onto the stage — determined "to supply the last laugh to ***Batman's*** life story! Ha, ha, ha!" — and floods the theater's ventilation system with laughing gas in an effort to add "a crowning touch to ***the Joker's*** final funny victory over ***Batman!***" He is apprehended soon afterward, however, through the heroic efforts of Batman and Robin (BM No. 87/1: "Batman's Greatest Thrills!").

In February 1956 the Joker, infuriated by Batman's appearance as a guest announcer on a television law-enforcement program, launches a new wave of crimes centering around the theme of announcing. At one point, for example, he sends a ruse radio dispatch to the crew aboard an express train, informing them that Batman has warned of an impending attempt by the Joker to rob the train's jewel shipment and instructing them to make an unscheduled stop in order to take on additional armed guards. Then, after boarding the train disguised as the new "guards," the Joker and his men steal the jewel shipment and escape. For a time, the sensational "announcement" robberies proceed unabated, but the Joker and his henchmen are finally apprehended by Batman and Robin (BM No. 97/1: "The Joker Announces Danger").

In May–June 1957 the Joker sets up a manufacturing plant in METROPOLIS in partnership with LEX LUTHOR, ostensibly for the legitimate manufacturing and marketing of "mechano-men," ingenious robots made out of a "super-strong metal" developed by Luthor. "Because they [the mechano-men] are invulnerable to any amount of heat and pressure," explains Luthor solemnly, "they can be used for tasks impossible to ordinary workmen!"

The Joker and Lex Luthor, 1957 © NPP 1957

The real purpose of the mechano-men, however, is to make it possible for the Joker and Luthor to stage an elaborately planned heist at the Subtreasury Building, but Batman, Robin, and SUPERMAN discover the plot, lull the criminals into false complacency by making it appear that they are occupied elsewhere, and then appear at the Subtreasury Building to apprehend the Joker and Luthor before they can flee with their loot (WF No. 88: "Superman's and Batman's Greatest Foes!").

In September 1957 the Joker launches his Crime-of-the-Month Club, an organization of criminals whose membership entitles them to bid for ingenious crime plans concocted by the Joker, each appropriate to the month in which it is offered. "Each month," explains the Joker to an audience of underworld colleagues, "I create another perfect crime plan . . . your membership fee entitles you to bid for that plan!" Each month, the highest bidder in the club earns the right to put the "crime-of-the-month" into practice. For a time, the Crime-of-the-Month Club is a profitable endeavor, but it is ultimately put out of business by Batman and Robin (BM No. 110/1: "Crime-of-the-Month Club!").

In April 1959 the Joker is both amused and inspired when he overhears a workman poking fun at an inexperienced apprentice by ordering him to fetch a "left-handed monkey wrench."

"Ha! Ha!" laughs the Joker. "What a wonderful practical joke--sending that green kid for a fictitious tool! That gives me an idea for a series of challenging crimes that should nettle **Batman!**"

In the days that follow, the Joker commits a series of crimes based on the similar practical jokes of other industries and occupations. Seasoned sailors, for example, often poke fun at a new hand by ordering him to stand "anchor watch." For his anchor watch crime, the Joker ties an inflated rubber whale to the anchor of a large freighter and then loots the safe of a nearby passenger liner while its passengers are busily clustered on deck, excitedly "watching the anchor" with the rubber whale attached to it. This particular crime is successful, but the Joker is apprehended soon afterward by Batman and Robin (BM No. 123/2: "The Joker's Practical Jokes!").

In October 1959 the Joker and his henchmen commit a series of crimes in Gotham City, only to become embroiled in a series of battles with Batman, Robin, and a newly emergent super-hero known as the Eagle, who, as a result of having not yet mastered the art of controlling his newly acquired super-powers, tends to be more of a hindrance than a help to Batman and Robin. Unbeknownst to the Joker, the Eagle is really ALFRED, who, as the result of a freak accident in the trophy room of the BATCAVE, has become temporarily endowed with "amazing strength," invulnerability, and the ability to "leap hundreds of feet" into the air. In the midst of a final battle with the Joker, however, the Eagle's super-powers fade and vanish, leaving him completely at the villain's mercy, but Batman and Robin leap to the rescue and apprehend the Joker and his henchmen. Alfred returns to his duties as Bruce Wayne's butler, apparently none the worse for his brief career as a super-hero (BM No. 127/1: "Batman's Super-Partner").

In December 1960, in a television broadcast celebrating the anniversary of the founding of the Gotham City Police Department, Batman discusses the early days of scientific crime detection and how far the science of criminology has come. Long ago, observes Batman, people believed that earth, air, fire, and water were the only elements. Just as modern science has disproved this ancient view, continues Batman, so has it revolutionized police procedures, so that today no criminal can really hope to outwit the "scientific policeman" for long.

The broadcast infuriates the Joker, who promptly embarks on a series of spectacular crimes based on the four ancient elements. He steals a shipment of **air**mail from the **air**port by pulling it off the mail carts with a powerful **air** suction gadget. He creates a tiny artificial **earth**quake at the Gotham Amusement Park as part of a scheme to loot it. And he appears at a **fire**works factory and traps the Dynamic Duo in a ring of blazing **fire**balls in an effort to incapacitate them while he stages his "water" crime, the theft of a valuable necklace from singer Jenny Linden, who is performing at the **Aqua**-Stage in Gotham Bay. Batman and Robin appear on the scene, however, thwart the water crime, and apprehend the Joker (BM No. 136/3: "The Challenge of the Joker").

In June 1961 the Joker escapes from Gotham Penitentiary, only to be presumed dead when, fleeing from pursuing prison guards, he races onto a blast area at a nearby construction site and is apparently trapped in a huge dynamite explosion. The Joker escapes injury, however, by hiding in a tunnel prepared for him by his henchmen, and, after coating his body with phosphorescent paint, he reappears in Gotham City posing as the "ghost of the Joker" and stages a series of spectacular crimes having ghosts as their theme. He makes off with the box-office receipts from the play *Return of the Phantom,* steals the ticket receipts from the Ghost Town Amusement Park, steals the winner's purse of a horse race won by a horse named Poltergeist, and attempts to make off with a solid gold yachting trophy to be awarded to the winner of a yacht race in which the *Flying Dutchman* is the favored yacht. Batman and Robin thwart the attempted theft of the yachting trophy, however, capture the Joker's henchmen, and apprehend the Joker himself soon afterward (BM No. 140/1: "The Ghost of the Joker!").

In December 1961 the Joker constructs a movie-set model of Gotham City and sets out to recruit a "Batman-proof" gang to help him commit spectacular crimes. To gain membership in the new gang, prospective members must pass a series of tests in which they attempt to commit "crimes" in the Joker's model city while the Joker, clad in a Batman costume, attempts to "apprehend" them in an effort to establish how each prospective member would fare against the real Batman in the real Gotham City.

By disguising his features to resemble those of underworld figure "Gum-Ball" Burke, Batman gains entrance to the Joker's model city and participates in a series of test crimes. Ultimately, however, his identity is discovered, and it is only with the last-minute assistance of Robin and the Gotham City police that Batman finally apprehends the Joker and his henchmen (BM No. 144/2: "The Man Who Played Batman!").

In June 1962 the Joker commits a series of brazen crimes based on the names of famous ships, each time sending Batman a model of the ship on whose name he intends to base the next crime. After mailing Batman a small scale model of the fabled *Flying Dutchman,* for example, the Joker races to Gotham Airport to steal some valuable jewels from Hendrik Van Voort, a Dutch jewel merchant who has just gotten off a plane there.

At one point, the Joker succeeds in removing Batman's cowl and it appears that the villain has it within his power to end Batman's career as a crime-fighter by revealing the secret of his dual identity. After Batman and Robin have captured the Joker and his henchmen, however, it turns out that the Joker had seen Batman's face only in the direct glare of an airport beacon whose blinding light had made recognition of Batman's features impossible (BM No. 148/3: "The Joker's Greatest Triumph!").

In November 1962 the Joker and LEX LUTHOR join forces in an elaborate plot to steal $5,000,000 in gems from an exhibition at Wilson Park, a "new outdoor exhibit grounds" in the city of Metropolis. In order to overcome the elaborate security precautions that have been devised for the exhibit, the two villains kidnap Hilton Webb, Wilson Park's master of ceremonies, and replace him with a carefully disguised Luthor well in advance of the gem exhibit.

The villains' complex preparations for the heist involve them in a series of skirmishes with Batman, Robin, and Superman, during which Luthor incapacitates Superman with his newly developed "kryptonite X-beam" — a special pistol, described as "an atomic disperser with a kryptonite base" (*see* KRYPTONITE) which enables Luthor to transform Superman temporarily "into an electronic stream utterly incapable of action" — while the Joker busies himself subduing or stymying his arch-nemeses Batman and Robin.

By the evening of the gem exhibit, however, Superman's X-ray vision has informed him that Luthor is the master of ceremonies, and so Superman swiftly apprehends him while Batman and Robin subdue the Joker and his henchmen — who have staged a mock invasion of the gem exhibit in order to provide Luthor with an opportunity to make off with the gems — and confiscate the kryptonite X-beam which the Joker had intended to use against Superman (WF No. 129: "Joker-Luthor, Incorporated!").

In December 1962 the Joker reappears, this time as the secret leader of the False Face Society, an underworld organization. Even the society's members do not realize that their masked leader is actually the Joker, but under his aegis they launch a spectacular crime contest in which each member must commit a daring crime while employing the "false face" of a specific era or occupation: one criminal, for example, poses as a knight in armor, while another dons the occupational uniform of a deep-sea diver. According to the rules of the contest, all the loot accumulated from the robberies — minus a small percentage which is to be allocated to the leader of the society as his fee for administering the sweepstakes — is to be awarded to the man who, in the judgment of his fellows, has committed the group's most sensational crime.

Since the rules of the contest are specifically designed to prevent a member from voting in favor of his own crime, the Joker feels confident that his own secret accomplice within the group — who plans to steal a valuable violin from a world-famous violinist while disguised as Batman — will win the contest and collect the accumulated loot, which the Joker and his accomplice plan to divide between them.

In an effort to infiltrate the False Face Society, however, Batman impersonates the Joker's Batman-clad henchman and makes his way to the secret meeting place inside an abandoned lighthouse, where the winner of the contest is to be decided. Things begin to look grim for Batman when, through a verbal slip, he reveals to the assembled criminals that he is the real Batman and not one of their "false face" colleagues, but Robin arrives on the scene in the nick of time with members of the Gotham City Police Department. Together they apprehend the assembled members of the False Face Society and unmask their secret leader as the notorious Joker (BM No. 152/2: "The False Face Society!").

In November 1963 the Joker becomes enraged at a fellow criminal's assertion that "**Clayface** is the top criminal in the country!" and he and Clayface (*see* CLAYFACE [MATT HAGEN]) soon become embroiled in a violent feud over which of them is the most spectacular criminal. "My **cunning** has made me **Batman's** greatest foe!" insists the Joker. "Without his freak powers, **Clayface** is a blundering third-rater--incapable of matching crimes of my calibre!"

Aided by Batman and Robin, BATWOMAN and Bat-Girl (*see* BAT-GIRL [BETTY KANE]) ultimately apprehend the Joker as he attempts to flee the scene of a daring robbery at the Gotham Museum, and Batman apprehends Clayface soon afterward by posing as the Joker, suggesting that he and Clayface end their feud and join forces, and then knocking Clayface unconscious while the villain's attention is momentarily diverted (BM No. 159/1: "The Great Clayface-Joker Feud!").

In May 1964 the Joker and his henchmen embark on a series of spectacular crimes based on the names and functions of the various municipal departments. For their Department of Health crime, for example, the Joker and his gang pose as Department of Health physicians and attempt to make off with a fortune in charity receipts by hastily clearing a charity benefit of spectators on the pretext that the room has become infected with contagious disease germs and must be carefully fumigated before anyone can be permitted to reenter.

At one point, the Joker and his henchmen capture Batman and Robin and force Batman to undergo a bizarre trial in their castle hideaway on charges of "interfering with the rights of individuals to commit crimes." With the Joker as judge, and his henchmen — all dressed as Jokers — serving as prosecutor and jury, a guilty verdict is a foregone conclusion, but Batman and Robin manage to escape from their captors and apprehend the Joker and his cohorts before the sentence of the underworld court can be meted out to them (BM No. 163/2: "The Joker Jury!").

In October 1964 the Joker commits a series of crimes by incapacitating onlookers with "laughing dust," a loco-weed pollen spray that leaves his would-be pursuers helplessly doubled over with laughter and unable to apprehend him. When Batman and Robin render themselves immune to the laughing dust with large doses of antihistamine, the Joker retaliates with a special gas which leaves them weeping uncontrollably.

When Batman and Robin finally give chase in the batmobile, the Joker deliberately allows himself to be apprehended not far from a phony police station that he has constructed especially for the occasion. When Batman and Robin attempt to lock him in a cell there, a special revolving-door apparatus switches automatically into operation, leaving the Dynamic Duo locked inside a barred cell and the Joker free as a bird outside it. The Joker rushes off to commit another of his spectacular crimes, but Batman and Robin free themselves from the Joker's jail cell and apprehend the villain and his henchmen soon afterward (Det No. 332: "The Joker's Last Laugh!").

In July 1965 the Joker puts into operation an elaborate scheme to rob the home of Cornelius Van-Van, a Gotham City millionaire famous for his great love of old-time movie comedies. Because he has seen each of the famous old-time comedies over and over again, however, Van-Van has decided to commission the filming of some new comedies of his own. After reviewing a series of submitted filmscripts, Van-Van decides to finance the scripts submitted by B. C. De Nil, each of which deals with some hilarious form of slapstick crime. B. C. De Nil, however, is none other than the Joker, who is determined to commit each slapstick crime called for in his scripts while at the same time filming them for Van-Van as part of his plot to gain access to Van-Van's lavish home.

In the days that follow, the Joker stages a series of daring slapstick crimes, each time dressed in the costume of a famous old-time comedian, while his henchmen record the crimes for posterity. One film features two of the Joker's henchmen in the roles of Batman and Robin, while another film features the real Dynamic Duo, desperately attempting to apprehend the Joker, playing themselves.

When the films have been completed, Cornelius Van-Van invites the Joker to his home for an informal "award ceremony," at which time the Joker and his henchmen hope to rob Van-Van's home. Batman and Robin are also on the scene, however, and although Robin is taken prisoner by the Joker, Batman single-handedly overwhelms the Joker's six henchmen and then apprehends the Joker as he attempts to escape in the batmobile (Det No. 341: "The Joker's Comedy Capers!").

JOKER, THE (Freddy Forbes). The stage name employed by Freddy Forbes, a well-known television comedian who inhabits the extradimensional parallel world visited by BATMAN in September 1963. Dressed in his stage makeup, Forbes is a perfect look-alike for Batman's infamous foe, the JOKER (WF No. 136: "The Batman Nobody Remembered!").

JOKER FILM PRODUCTIONS, INC. A film company formed by the JOKER to make "educational films for criminals." Joker Film Productions, Inc. is put out of business by BATMAN and ROBIN in December 1953–January 1954 (BM No. 80/1: "The Joker's Movie Crimes!").

JOKER'S JOURNAL. An underworld newspaper founded by the JOKER in March 1953. The newspaper features a comic strip which pokes fun at BATMAN and ROBIN; display advertisements promoting the services of fences, gun dealers, and other underworld businessmen; and classified advertisements offering such things as "complete, foolproof plans" for the commission of crimes. *Joker's Journal* is put out of business by Batman and Robin in March 1953 (Det No. 193: "The Joker's Journal!").

JOLLY ROGER. The leader of a band of smugglers who, clad in the colorful costume of an old-time pirate, directs an elaborate smuggling operation from his headquarters in an old pirate cave on an island off the coast of GOTHAM CITY, site of the multimillion-dollar Jolly Roger hotel. Jolly Roger is in reality Thomas Wexley, the hotel's manager. Convinced that the smugglers are using the island as their base, Bruce Wayne and Dick Grayson visit the island in the guise of vacationers and, as BATMAN and ROBIN, ultimately apprehend Jolly Roger and his henchmen (Det No. 202, Dec '53: "Millionaire Island!").

JONES, BATMAN. A young boy, probably a few years younger than ROBIN, who was named Batman by his parents in gratitude for BATMAN's having saved their lives when the brakes on their automobile failed as they were driving home from the hospital with their then newborn son. In June 1957 young Batman Jones, attired in his own Batman costume and eager to become a great criminologist like his namesake, pesters Batman and Robin into letting him accompany them on a criminal investigation and actually uses his ingenuity to solve a pair of baffling crimes. Just when the Dynamic Duo have begun to fear that they may be stuck with Batman Jones for good, however, Jones, like many a youngster, loses interest in criminology and develops a passion for stamp collecting (BM No. 108/3: "The Career of Batman Jones!").

JONES, T-GUN. A notorious underworld triggerman, called "T-Gun" because of his deadly facility with a tommy gun and eagerly sought as a member by two competing GOTHAM CITY gangs, who agrees finally to align himself with whichever of the two gangs — one headed by mobster Stogie Bevans, the other by rackets chief Neon Syne — can acquire, within a twenty-four-hour period, the best souvenirs of BATMAN for the Underworld Museum of Crime, a gangland museum housing a vast collection of trophies and memorabilia commemorating the exploits of the great underworld gangs. Syne and his henchmen win the competition hands down when they capture Batman himself and put him on display in the museum, but Batman manages to escape from his captors and together he and ROBIN apprehend T-Gun Jones and the two mobs competing for his membership, along with the host of underworld notables who have been invited to the museum to witness the unmasking of the supposedly defeated Batman (WF No. 37, Nov/Dec '48: "The Underworld's Museum of Crime!").

JOR-EL. The father of SUPERMAN, and the foremost scientist of the planet KRYPTON prior to its destruction. It was Jor-El who dispatched the infant Superman toward Earth in an experimental rocket moments before Krypton exploded into fragments as the result of a cataclysmic chain reaction originating at the planet's core. (For a detailed account of the life and career of Jor-El, consult *The Encyclopedia of Comic Book Heroes: Volume VI — Superman.*)

JOWELL, GENTLEMAN JIM. A ruthless gentleman criminal described in the texts as "the crook deluxe." Jowell and his three henchmen — Herman, Tapper, and Shank — are apprehended in April 1944 through the heroic efforts of BATMAN, ROBIN, and ALFRED (Det No. 86: "Danger Strikes Three!").

JUDSON (Mr.). The owner of the automobile manufacturing concern known as Judson's Comet Cars, and the man who is secretly the GLASS MAN (WF No. 28, May/Jun '47: "Crime Under Glass!").

JUDSON, ALEC. The "millionaire sportsman" and founder of the Safari Club who is secretly the head of "an international crime cartel." In October 1957 Judson murders Ed Yancey — who had been blackmailing Judson by threatening to expose his criminal activities — and attempts to place the blame on Markham, a former hunting partner. BATMAN unravels the mystery of Yancey's murder, however, and ultimately takes Judson into custody (BM No. 111/1: "The Gotham City Safari").

JUDSON, NED. A GOTHAM CITY millionaire and avid BATMAN fan who is duped by four Batman-costumed swindlers into joining the so-called Brotherhood of the Batman, an organization whose elite handful of members, claim the swindlers, are responsible for having given birth to the Batman legend and now fight crime in relays in order to keep alive the myth that there is only one Batman. "***Batman*** is really ***four Batmen!***" claims one of them to Judson. "One man couldn't survive so many dangers and get about to so many places--so we ***pretend*** there is only one ***Batman***--to awe the underworld!" By initiating Judson into their brotherhood and pretending to groom him for a career as a fellow Batman, the swindlers hope to con the unsuspecting millionaire into laying out tens of thousands of dollars for such crime-fighting equipment as his own BATMOBILE and BATPLANE, but Batman and ROBIN ultimately alert Judson to the swindle and join him in apprehending the criminals in August 1955 (Det No. 222: "The Great Batman Swindle!").

JUNDY. An unscrupulous, power-hungry individual who, having come into possession of an ancient manuscript detailing the exact locations of the remote hiding places of the three pieces that make up the now-disassembled "Sorcerer King's sceptre" — an ancient mystic device said to confer "awesome powers" on whomever possesses it — kidnaps BATMAN and ROBIN and makes them captive on a tiny island as part of his scheme to force SUPERMAN to use his super-powers to retrieve the three hidden pieces of the magic sceptre as the ransom for the safe release of Batman and Robin. Jundy is ultimately apprehended and the sceptre destroyed through the heroic efforts of Batman, Robin, and Superman (WF No. 125, May '62: "The Hostages of the Island of Doom!").

JUNGLE-MAN. A "jungle wild-man" from darkest Africa who possesses the uncanny ability to communicate with animals and make them do his bidding. He does not realize that he is really Tommy Young, an American who became lost in the African wilds as a youngster fifteen years ago, who survived to grow up alone and savage in the jungle.

In May 1963 "notorious Gotham [City] criminal" Eli Mattock befriends Jungle-Man in Africa, arouses him to a fierce hatred of BATMAN by teasing and tormenting him while clad in a Batman costume, and then returns with him to GOTHAM CITY, where he and his henchmen capitalize on Jungle-Man's power over animals and hatred of Batman to stage a series of spectacular crimes, as when they get Jungle-Man to command a rhinoceros to overturn an armored car and charge the BATMOBILE when Batman and ROBIN attempt to intervene.

Ultimately, however, after Batman has discovered Jungle-Man's true identity and persuaded him that he is his friend and not his enemy, Jungle-Man turns on the gangsters who have duped him and uses his wild animals to apprehend the Mattock gang (Det No. 315: "The Jungle Man of Gotham City!").

K

KAALE. The cruel, despotic emperor of a far-distant planet who entertains himself by kidnapping the inhabitants of other planets and forcing them to serve as both hunter and hunted in vicious gladiatorial hunts – with only the victor to be returned alive to his home planet – while Kaale himself views the festivities with the aid of a floating "eye" television device which broadcasts the proceedings to a screen inside his lavish palace. Forcibly transported to Kaale's planet in January 1962 and compelled to serve as the unwilling quarry for three alien hunters who have been similarly abducted, BATMAN and ROBIN nevertheless manage to elude capture and ultimately to topple Kaale from his throne with the aid of the three alien hunters and a group of native freedom-fighters who have "sworn to dedicate [their] lives to deposing the emperor!" (Det No. 299: "Prey of the Alien Hunters!").

KALE, DENNY. One of a pair of escaped convicts, both former actors, who, by impersonating BATMAN and ROBIN, dupe PROFESSOR CARTER NICHOLS into transporting them into the past, to the city of Florence in the year 1479, where they establish themselves as the leaders of a band of ruthless medieval bandits. Followed into the past by SUPERMAN, and then by the real Batman and Robin, Denny Kale and his partner, Shorty Biggs, are apprehended by the three famous crimefighters, along with all their fifteenth-century henchmen, after an unsuccessful attempt to loot the treasure-laden strongroom of the Medici Palace (WF No. 132, Mar '63: "Batman and Robin, Medieval Bandits!").

KALE, GEORGE. The unscrupulous president of Lightning Motors, Inc., and the uncle of Glenda West, a contestant in a cross-country race involving planes, boats, automobiles, and other means of transportation. Kale's efforts to sabotage the efforts of the various contestants in order to ensure a victory by Glenda and the consequent publicity this will mean for his company are thwarted by BATMAN and ROBIN in April–May 1946 (BM No. 34/1: "The Marathon of Menace!").

KANDOR. A city of the planet KRYPTON which survived the destruction of its native planet as the result of having been stolen sometime prior to the cataclysm by the space-villain BRAINIAC, who reduced the city to microscopic size and preserved it, people and buildings alive and intact, inside a glass bottle aboard his spacecraft, where it remained for many years until it was finally recovered by SUPERMAN and placed for safekeeping inside the FORTRESS OF SOLITUDE.

Inside the bottle city, life goes on much as it did prior to the destruction of Krypton, yet although restoration to their normal size remains the heartfelt wish of all Kandorians, Superman has not yet succeeded, despite years of effort, in finding a way to enlarge the city safely. He has, however, on occasion managed to reduce himself in size temporarily for the purpose of visiting the bottle city and undertaking adventures there. (For detailed information concerning Kandor and its inhabitants, consult *The Encyclopedia of Comic Book Heroes: Volume VI – Superman.*)

KANE, BETTY. The pretty blond teen-ager who is secretly Bat-Girl (*see* BAT-GIRL [BETTY KANE]), and the niece of Kathy Kane, the "wealthy heiress" who is secretly BATWOMAN (BM No. 139/3, Apr '61: "Bat-Girl!").

KANE, KATHY. The wealthy heiress and onetime "circus daredevil performer" who is secretly BATWOMAN (Det No. 233, Jul '56: "The Batwoman"). Kathy Kane is the aunt of Betty Kane, the "pretty teen-ager" who is secretly Bat-Girl (*see* BAT-GIRL [BETTY KANE]) (BM No. 139/3, Apr '61: "Bat-Girl!").

KA-RA. In Detective Comics No. 167, the chief irrigation engineer in the court of CLEOPATRA (69–30 B.C.), and the man secretly responsible for a series of unsuccessful attempts on the life of the famed Egyptian queen. Dispatched through the time barrier by PROFESSOR CARTER NICHOLS to the land of Egypt in the first century B.C., BATMAN and ROBIN thwart repeated attempts to murder Cleopatra, pinpoint Ka-Ra as the would-be assassin, and ultimately apprehend him. They are aided throughout by Takeloth, the chief of Cleopatra's royal police, who is, coincidentally, a perfect look-alike for POLICE COMMISSIONER GORDON of GOTHAM CITY (Jan '51: "Bodyguards to Cleopatra!").

KARABI. A sinister, power-hungry villain, headquartered in an abandoned temple somewhere in Asia, who is the mastermind behind a scheme to precipitate a bloody war between two Asian countries so that, once an ever-widening group of allied nations have been drawn into the spreading conflict, he can "form a group of malcontents that will form the nucleus of a band like Hitler's S.S. elite--and . . . try to seize as much power as he can!" The plot is foiled by BATMAN and ROBIN, who apprehend Karabi and his henchmen in their Asian temple stronghold in November 1964 (BM No. 167: "Zero Hour for Earth!").

KARDO. A onetime circus magician turned criminal, also known as the Great Kardo, who is apprehended by BATMAN and ROBIN in March 1963 when he attempts to steal $100,000 in prize money earmarked for a television contest winner (BM No. 154/2: "The Amazing Odyssey of Batman and Robin").

KARKO. A cunning villain from the twenty-sixth century A.D. who journeys to the twentieth century by time machine to steal such seemingly ordinary items as automobiles, furniture, and inexpensive paintings by aspiring artists, knowing that these items will be regarded as priceless antiques and *objets d'art* in his own era. Karko is finally apprehended, however, through the heroic efforts of BATMAN, ROBIN, and Chief Inspector Mahan of the Universal Police, a twenty-sixth-century lawman who has traveled to the twentieth century to launch a manhunt for Karko (Det No. 257, Jul '58: "Batman's Invincible Foe!").

KARL (Baron). The unscrupulous cousin of King Rudolph, aged monarch of the tiny kingdom of Morania, who, now that the king is on his deathbed, is determined to seize the Moranian throne by arranging for the assassination of Rudolph's rightful heirs, the prince and princess, who have fled to America with their infant son to escape his vengeance.

Fearful that they will be assassinated before they can ascend the throne, and determined that their son survive to succeed them in the event of their untimely deaths, the prince and princess abandon their son on the steps of the Gotham Orphanage along with a written request that he be hidden in the home of a trustworthy citizen until his rightful parents are free to reclaim him. Somewhat ironically, the baby is left for safekeeping with prominent citizen Bruce Wayne, the man who is secretly BATMAN.

Although the infant's origins are a mystery at first, Batman ultimately deduces the child's true identity and, with ROBIN's help, defeats both of Baron Karl's hired assassins — "notorious foreign agent" Bruno Croft, and Lekkey, the secretary to the Moranian ambassador to the United States — before returning the infant prince to his parents (BM No. 128/3, Dec '59: "The Batman Baby").

KARLO, BASIL. The renowned character actor and makeup artist who launches a career of murder and mayhem as Clayface (Det No. 40, Jun '40). (*See* CLAYFACE [BASIL KARLO].)

KA THAR. A historian and author of the sixtieth century A.D. who journeys to the twentieth century in his "time-thrust projector" for the purpose of verifying the accuracy of his greatest book, *The History of Superman and Batman.* When his written explanations of how the famous heroes performed certain of their feats turn out not to be accurate, Ka Thar threatens to disclose their secret identities to the people of the twentieth century unless BATMAN, ROBIN, and SUPERMAN agree to reenact their great feats exactly as described in his history book. Bowing to Ka Thar's threat, the three crime-fighters set to work reenacting some of their past feats in order to justify Ka Thar's erroneous descriptions of them. Ultimately, however, Batman realizes that Ka Thar dares not reveal their secret identities for fear of jeopardizing another statement in his history book — that the crime-fighters' secret identities were not publicly revealed until many centuries after their deaths — whereupon Ka Thar, his bluff called, returns to his own time (WF No. 81, Mar–Apr '56: "The True History of Superman and Batman!").

KEAN, BARRETT. The world's greatest master of disguise, makeup, and impersonation — once the "greatest makeup and impersonation artist on the stage" and now the director of the Kean School of Makeup, a school he founded to teach actors the art of makeup. Years ago, when BATMAN was just setting out on his career as a crime-fighter, it was Kean who taught him the myriad skills that have since led him to dub his famous pupil "the greatest impersonator alive!" In January 1956, during a period when Batman is giving a series of lectures at the Kean School of Makeup, Kean helps thwart a scheme by underworld photographer "LENS" VORDEN to penetrate the secret of Batman's identity (Det No. 227: "The 50 Faces of Batman!").

KEATING, JEFF. The GOTHAM CITY high school student who is the inventor of the "bat-kite," a large, black, bat-shaped kite — maneuvered by "ingenious control-strings" and intended for aerial photography and other uses — which ultimately assumes a permanent place in the Dynamic Duo's famous arsenal of crime-fighting equipment. With his invention, Keating becomes the winner of a four-year criminology scholarship offered by BATMAN to the high school student who invents the best new "bat-weapon" (BM No. 100/3, Jun '56: "The Great Batman Contest"). (*See also* BATMAN [section E, the extraordinary abilities and the famous crime-fighting equipment].)

KEEFE, BEN. A jewel thief who is apprehended by BATMAN and ROBIN in April 1957, during the period of Robin's involvement with teen-age ice-skating star VERA LOVELY (BM No. 107/2: "Robin Falls in Love").

KEEP, ROGER J. A trustee of the International Chemical Company, afflicted with "a very nasty persecution complex" and the paranoid delusion that his fellow trustees are engaged in a conspiracy to force him out of the company, who vows to wreak vengeance on his fellow trustees — Holmes Caffrey, Donald Penn, John Keith-Dudley, and BRUCE WAYNE — after an accidental laboratory explosion, which Keep's twisted mind construes as a deliberate murder attempt, leaves him hopelessly paralyzed from the waist down. "Yes--they must **die!**" vows Keep. "But that is not enough! I must **see** them die! The **revenge** is no good unless I **see** them die with my **own eyes! This** will be my greatest pleasure!"

From a secluded hideaway on Crabshell Island, "an isolated island in Gotham Sound," Keep sends forth a series of gloating death-notes, promising death to the trustees when they least suspect it and vowing that despite his paralysis "I shall witness [each] execution with pleasure!"

"An egomaniac, who warns his victims in advance!" murmurs BATMAN as he surveys the first death-note. "They're always the most dangerous!"

In the days that follow, Keep's hired assassins make a series of brazen attempts on the lives of the trustees, executing each attempt in such a way as to enable Keep to witness it from his sanctuary on Crabshell Island: one trustee is attacked during a television appearance so that Keep can witness the murder on television, another is shot at with a gun concealed inside a movie camera so that Keep can witness the murder on film, and another is attacked while flying his private plane so that Keep can watch him go down in flames.

In each case, however, Batman manages to thwart Keep's lust for vengeance by anticipating the murder method in advance and taking steps to ensure that the intended victim escapes unscathed. Before long, Batman and ROBIN have located Keep's island hideaway, apprehended Keep's hired assassins, and taken the invalid Keep into custody (WF No. 58, May/Jun '52: "The Murder of Bruce Wayne!").

KELDEN, BRAND. The former radio engineer, once employed by the Gotham City Police Department but dismissed from his position on the suspicion that he was leaking secret information to the underworld, who operates radio station CRIME, a clandestine radio station for criminals which broadcasts from the back of a moving truck. In return for a percentage of their stolen loot, subscribing criminals are entitled to receive coded radio information concerning the safest possible escape routes, the location of pursuing police cars, and other useful data. Kelden obtains his inside information by focusing a high-powered telescope at police headquarters and reading the lips of the men inside. Despite his many ingenious precautions, however, Kelden is apprehended by BATMAN in October 1953 (Det No. 200: "Radio Station C-R-I-M-E!").

KELLEY, BRAINS. The operator of a "lavish night club" who is one of "the three crime lords of Gotham City," the other two being "Big John" Waller, a "notorious gambling house owner," and Dude Davis, a gang chief with headquarters in "an elaborate poolroom."

In Spring 1942 the three men enter into an elaborate conspiracy to bring crime to a standstill in GOTHAM CITY—so that they will cease being the objects of continual police suspicion and surveillance—while they and their gangs launch spectacular crime waves in other cities while disguised as members of the prominent gangs in those cities. In this way, hope the gang chiefs, they will be able to dispose of their stolen loot quietly in Gotham City while the local gangs in other cities receive the blame for the crimes.

By infiltrating the "Big John" Waller gang, however, BATMAN soon discovers that Kelley, Waller, and Davis are behind the current wave of crimes in other cities, and, through an elaborate ruse, he and ROBIN succeed in recovering the mobsters' stolen loot and in luring the members of their three gangs into a Gotham City Police Department trap (WF No. 5: "Crime Takes a Holiday").

KENT, CLARK. The mild-mannered journalist who is secretly SUPERMAN.

KENT, HARVEY. A handsome district attorney who, after the left side of his face has been hideously scarred by a vial of acid hurled at him in a GOTHAM CITY courtroom by gangster "Boss" MORONI, launches a spectacular career in crime as the incredible TWO-FACE (Det No. 66, Aug '42: "The Crimes of Two-Face!"). From December 1948–January 1949 onward, due to what can only be regarded as a chronicler's error, the texts repeatedly refer to Harvey Kent as Harvey Dent (BM No. 50/2: "The Return of Two-Face!"; and others).

KERN, "DANCER." The leader of a gang of criminals who have bribed carpenter Ralph Edney to build secret panels in the walls of selected buildings so that they can rob the buildings, hide the loot inside the secret panels, and then escape without fear of being apprehended in possession of the loot.

The Dynamic Duo's efforts to apprehend the Kern mob are severely hampered by the fact that Captain Harby, the veteran police officer who is serving as acting police commissioner of GOTHAM CITY during the temporary absence of POLICE COMMISSIONER GORDON, has decided to punish BATMAN and ROBIN for what he regards as their glory-seeking escapades by forbidding them to concentrate on the department's most important and glamorous cases and insisting instead that they perform the tedious routine chores of ordinary foot patrolmen, such as handing out traffic tickets and apprehending fruit-stand pilferers.

Although their time is consumed by the drudgery of everyday police work, Batman and Robin nevertheless manage to track down and apprehend the Kern gang without ever actually disobeying Captain Harby's strict orders. It is only then that Harby realizes that he has seriously misjudged the Dynamic Duo: "And you cracked this mystery [the "Dancer" Kern case] while I kept you busy carrying out my petty assignments!" exclaims Harby apologetically. "***Batman,*** I've learned a lesson! I know now it wasn't just opportunity that made you great--you ***made*** your opportunities!"

"***Robin*** and I have had a lesson, too, Captain Harby," replies Batman, "--we appreciate now how tough a regular policeman's job can be!" (BM No. 77/3, Jun/Jul '53: "Batman Pounds a Beat!").

KERSWAG, JOE. A fictitious name employed by the JOKER when he mails some stolen loot to himself in care of an express office in the sleepy Ozark town of Farr Corners, intending to collect it at a later date. The name Joe Kerswag wryly states the true nature of the packages mailed to the express office: Joker's swag (BM No. 16/1, Apr/May '43: "The Joker Reforms!").

KEYES, JOHN. An innocent man, convicted and sentenced to the gas chamber for a murder he did not commit, who escapes from the authorities long enough to accumulate exculpatory evidence sufficient to ensure him a new trial, only to be recaptured soon afterward. When Trigger Yurk and Biff Bolton, the real murderers, attempt to kill Keyes during his extradition to California to prevent his disclosing the new evidence he has uncovered, BATMAN and ROBIN intervene to prevent the murder and apprehend the criminals (BM No. 13/4, Oct/Nov '42: "Destination Unknown!").

K-4 (Mount). A Himalayan mountain peak which is described as "the world's most unclimbable peak." In August 1955 BATMAN and ROBIN become the first human beings to reach the summit when, under the aliases Bruce Martin and Dick Green, they join an expedition up the side of K-4 as part of their plan to recover a vital roll of microfilm for the F.B.I. (BM No. 93/1: "Journey to the Top of the World!"). (*See also* SMYTHE, SIDNEY.)

KHALEX. An escaped convict from a far-distant planet who arrives on Earth in November 1959 and joins forces with "notorious gang chief" Midge Martin and his henchmen. Together they concoct an elaborate scheme to trick BATMAN and ROBIN into helping them destroy a recently landed meteor whose presence on Earth robs Khalex of his awesome extraterrestrial powers, with which he could annihilate SUPERMAN and conquer the Earth. The scheme is ultimately thwarted and the villains apprehended through the heroic efforts of Batman, Robin, and Superman (WF No. 105: "The Alien Superman!").

KHOR. One of a pair of yellow-skinned, birdlike, extraterrestrial aliens – both keepers of a zoo on a far-distant planet – who capture BATMAN and ROBIN in April 1964 during an expedition to Earth in search of wildlife and transport them by spaceship to their native planet, where the Dynamic Duo are put on display in an alien zoo and forced to perform like seals in an alien circus in order to earn their daily food. Ultimately, however, Batman and Robin escape from the zoo and, after finally persuading some of the planet's inhabitants that they are intelligent beings and not merely zoo animals, they expose and apprehend Khor, who has been secretly using his trained zoo animals to help him commit spectacular crimes (Det No. 326: "Captives of the Alien Zoo!").

KIER, RALPH. The unscrupulous assistant to John Barly, a supplier of animals to American zoos. In June 1956 Kier attempts to smuggle some diamonds into the United States inside the collar of an ape bound for the Gotham Zoo, but BATMAN becomes suspicious of Kier, recovers the diamonds, and takes Kier into custody (BM No. 100/2: "The Hunters of Gotham City").

KILEY, KANGAROO. The president of an incredible "underworld bank" in GOTHAM CITY, where criminals may make loans, deposit stolen money and other valuables, and exchange "hot" money being sought by the authorities for "cool" money now deemed safe enough to return to circulation. Kiley and his cohorts are retired from the banking business by BATMAN and ROBIN in September 1951 (Det No. 175: "The Underworld Bank!").

KILLER MOTH, THE. A ruthless "guardian of the underworld" (Det No. 173, Jul '51: "Batman's Double!") who battles on behalf of crime as zealously as BATMAN and ROBIN battle in the name of law and order. Batman No. 64/3 describes him as "the most ingenious rogue ever to defy the Dynamic Duo" (Apr/May '51: "The Return of Killer Moth!").

By day, Killer Moth is Cameron Van Cleer, a wealthy GOTHAM CITY socialite whose palatial home adorns "one of Gotham's swank suburbs" (BM No. 64/3, Apr/May '51: "The Return of Killer Moth!"). At night, however, whenever the pale infrared glow of the "moth signal" flashes across the Gotham City skyline with its urgent message of criminals in trouble, Cameron Van Cleer dons the grotesque mothlike costume of Killer Moth, climbs into his ingeniously equipped "mothmobile," and roars forth from his subterranean "moth-cave" to answer the call of crime and injustice.

The man who achieves infamy as Killer Moth was once an obscure convict known only as inmate number 234026. Even while in prison, however, inmate 234026

Killer Moth, 1951 © NPP 1951

was formulating the concepts that were to find their fulfillment in the sinister career of Killer Moth. When the convict regained his freedom, he assumed the fictitious identity of Cameron Van Cleer and used a carefully hidden cache of ill-gotten wealth to build a lavish home in the suburbs of Gotham City. As Cameron Van Cleer, he constructed a "wall of respectability" designed to conceal his convict past from the respectable citizens who now surrounded him. Beneath his home, Van Cleer excavated an elaborate moth-cave, equipped with a modern crime lab in which he hoped to "develop the most scientific methods for making a crime impossible to solve," and a trophy room, where he hoped eventually to display the famous batlike cowl of Batman himself.

Inside the moth-cave sits the mothmobile, a supercharged automobile equipped with "antennae which warn of approaching danger on the dashboard radar screen" as well as with "exhaust gas control" devices which enable Killer Moth to disable the drivers of pursuing vehicles with irritants and anesthetics.

The eerie mothlike costume of Killer Moth includes a cleverly equipped utility belt and a pair of antennae, mounted on his costume's headgear, which "pick up police radio calls and transmit them to earphones inside [his] helmet!" Killer Moth also carries a gun, and a powerful "steel strand" – analogous to Batman's silken rope – that enables him to swing from rooftop to rooftop.

The bizarre services of Killer Moth are available only to those members of the underworld who have agreed in advance to pay for his protection. Each of these criminals has a moth signal – an ordinary-looking flashlight which emits an infrared distress signal visible only to Killer Moth through special glasses concealed in the lining of his helmet.

In February–March 1951 — the period in which Cameron Van Cleer is invited to sit, along with BRUCE WAYNE and other prominent citizens of Gotham City, on the board of directors of the Gotham Museum — Killer Moth knocks Batman and Robin unconscious with a powerful anesthetic fired through the exhaust of his mothmobile and carries them captive to his moth-cave, where he offers to trade Robin's life in exchange for an immediate visit to the BATCAVE. "There are," explains Killer Moth, "still a few secrets I need to make the ***moth cave*** complete!"

Batman agrees, but on the way to the batcave he receives a radio call from Robin informing him that Robin has escaped successfully from the moth-cave on his own and that Batman therefore need not feel compelled to show Killer Moth the secret location of the batcave. Killer Moth, however, picks up the radio call by means of the antennae on his costume, realizes he has lost his hold over Batman, and is soon racing on foot across a large suspension bridge with Batman in hot pursuit. As Killer Moth races across one of the bridge's large wire cables, however, he loses his footing and topples into the murky waters below. As the text draws to a close, his fate remains in doubt (BM No. 63/3: "The Origin of Killer Moth!").

By April–May 1951 it is clear that Killer Moth has managed to survive, but his decisive defeat at the hands of Batman has demolished his reputation as a guardian of the underworld and left him, for weeks now, without a single underworld call for his services.

"I spent a fortune building up ***Killer Moth,*** " muses the villain disconsolately, "but since losing face with the underworld, I've no way of profiting from my enterprise! I must prove that the ***Moth*** is ***Batman's*** master!"

In his role as Cameron Van Cleer, member of the board of directors of the Gotham Museum, Killer Moth uses his influence to bring about the purchase of the so-called Moth Collection, an assortment of moth idols recently unearthed in Mexico. Then, while the valuable idols are being stored in a secret museum vault pending their official purchase by the museum, Killer Moth successfully resuscitates his failing underworld image by stealing one idol and making two daring attempts to steal another, both of which, however, are thwarted through the timely intervention of Batman and Robin. At one point, Killer Moth becomes convinced that Bruce Wayne is secretly Batman, but a ruse by Batman involving dummies of Bruce Wayne and Dick Grayson persuades Killer Moth that he has made a mistake. Ultimately, Batman deduces that Killer Moth is Cameron Van Cleer, and he and Robin apprehend the villain when he returns to his suburban mansion (BM No. 64/3: "The Return of Killer Moth!").

In July 1951 Killer Moth escapes from prison and sets out to resume his career as guardian of the underworld. Because his Cameron Van Cleer identity is now useless to him, however, and because he no longer has sufficient funds to establish a new identity for himself in Gotham City, the villain decides to kidnap and impersonate some wealthy and influential citizen. Ironically, Killer Moth finally settles on Bruce Wayne, and after successfully abducting Wayne and locking him inside an abandoned safety deposit vault, he has a "disreputable plastic surgeon" transform his facial features into those of Bruce Wayne so that he can take Wayne's place in Gotham City.

Because Dick Grayson fails to see through the impersonation, Killer Moth quickly learns that Bruce Wayne is secretly Batman. "How ironic," he thinks, "that with a whole city to pick from, I chose to live the life of my **mortal enemy**! What a delicious revenge for **Killer Moth!**"

In the days that follow, Killer Moth capitalizes on the fact that he is now both Bruce Wayne and Batman in order to shore up his image among the denizens of the underworld. At one point, for example, he makes it appear that Batman is afraid of Killer Moth by retreating in his Batman costume as soon as the leader of a band of hijackers flashes the moth signal. Ultimately, however, Bruce Wayne escapes from the abandoned safety deposit vault, dons a spare Batman costume, and, with Robin, sets out in pursuit of Killer Moth. They come upon the villain just as he is being riddled with bullets by hijacker Whitey Casey, who has been led, through a series of complicated coincidences, to the erroneous conclusion that Killer Moth has double-crossed him.

As Batman and Robin rush Killer Moth to the hospital in the BATMOBILE, Robin remarks on the irony of their trying to save the life of a man who, if he lives, will destroy their crime-fighting careers by revealing the secret of their dual identities. "Let's not think about it, **Robin!**" replies Batman grimly. "The only important thing now is that a human being is in danger and we can help him!"

Miraculously, Killer Moth survives, but his face has been so badly disfigured by bullet wounds that it is nearly unrecognizable — thus concealing forever the fact that he had recently been impersonating Bruce Wayne — and a stray bullet, lodged in his head, has necessitated the surgical removal of the portion of his brain housing his memory of recent events, so that he will retain no recollection whatever of Batman and Robin's secret identities (Det No. 173: "Batman's Double!").

In January 1967 Killer Moth and his henchmen launch a vicious protection racket in Gotham City, but he and his henchmen are ultimately apprehended through the heroic efforts of Batman, Robin, and Batgirl (*see* BATGIRL [BARBARA GORDON]), who makes her textual debut in this adventure (Det No. 359: "The Million Dollar Debut of Batgirl!"). (*See* BATGIRL [BARBARA GORDON].)

KING, PAUL. A dapper criminal who describes himself as "the man the newspapers call Public Enemy Number One — the king of crime." In July 1955 King and his henchmen capture BATMAN and ROBIN and prepare to destroy them in an "escape-proof trap," but Robin manages to stall for time – long enough for Batman to strip a telephone cable in the hideout and tap out a Morse code message to the police – by telling King a series of stories about how he and Batman have escaped from diabolical deathtraps in the past. Before King can even activate his deathtrap, the Dynamic Duo have been rescued by the police, and within moments King and his henchmen have been apprehended (Det No. 221: "The Thousand-and-One Escapes of Batman and Robin!").

KING OF THE CATS, THE. A cunning criminal whose catlike costume, special equipment, and choice of crimes all revolve around a feline theme. The texts refer to him both as the King of the Cats and as the Cat King, but his real name is Karl (presumably Karl Kyle, although this is never explicitly stated), and he is the brother of Selina Kyle, the raven-haired, green-eyed girl best known as the CATWOMAN.

The King of the Cats © NPP 1952

The King of the Cats commits a rash of cat-related crimes in GOTHAM CITY in February–March 1952 and attempts to persuade his sister to return to crime with him as the Catwoman. She refuses and ultimately prevails upon him to abandon his role as the King of the Cats and surrender himself to the authorities (BM No. 69/3: "The King of the Cats!"). (*See* CATWOMAN, THE.)

KINGPIN, THE. The underworld boss of GOTHAM CITY, a cunning gangland czar – his true identity concealed from even his closest underworld associates by a white hood – whose capture by BATMAN and ROBIN in March–April 1952 comes as the culmination of an elaborate ruse in which BRUCE WAYNE deliberately cultivates the public impression that he is a hardened rackets czar, and secretly the Kingpin, so that ultimately he can infiltrate the gangsters' meeting place and apprehend the real Kingpin and his cohorts. Finally unmasked, the Kingpin stands revealed as Spotswood Hartley, a wealthy, prominent citizen of Gotham City who is a close friend of Bruce Wayne (WF No. 57: "Public Enemy Bruce Wayne!").

KIRK, JOE. A stunt men's theatrical agent and racketeer who extorts protection money from his stunt-man clientele and murders those who refuse to pay by arranging for them to die, ostensibly by accident, while performing dangerous stunts. Kirk is exposed and apprehended by BATMAN and ROBIN in August–September 1942 (BM No. 12/3: "They Thrill to Conquer!").

KIRK, MARTY. A "notorious public enemy," apprehended by BATMAN and ROBIN and now awaiting execution on Death Row, whose henchmen attempt to secure his release by seizing control of a television studio where a live dramatization of Kirk's life is being performed and threatening to murder the entire cast and crew unless their leader is promptly released. In response to a plea from Batman, the governor orders Kirk set free, but Batman and Robin apprehend Kirk's henchmen soon afterward, and then recapture Kirk when he attempts to retrieve the $100,000 in cash which he stole from the Federal Savings Bank and hid prior to his capture (BM No. 97/2, Feb '56: "Doom on Channel 14").

KITE-MAN, THE. A cunning criminal mastermind who uses an arsenal of complex kites to aid him in his crimes, including a remote-controlled box-kite for unleashing tear-gas bombs, a jet-powered kite to enable him to fly through the air, a "flash-bulb kite" which emits a blinding glare, and a "net-kite" which releases a large net. The Kite-Man commits a series of spectacular crimes – including the daring rescue of some fellow criminals from the Gotham Bay Prison – before he is finally apprehended by BATMAN and ROBIN in August 1960 (BM No. 133/1: "Crimes of the Kite-Man").

KLAG (the Hunter). A Cro-Magnon hunter who was trapped inside a deep crevasse and frozen into a state of suspended animation while pursuing Brugg, a Stone Age thief, during approximately the fiftieth millennium B.C. Klag awakens from his long sleep in March 1965 and, endowed with extraordinary powers – including the power of flight and complete control over "natural forces," such as lightning – somehow imparted to him by the action of stalactite minerals dripping for centuries onto his ice-encrusted body, goes on a destructive worldwide rampage in a futile search for the long-dead Brugg until he is finally defeated and captured by BATMAN and ROBIN (Det No. 337: "Deep-Freeze Menace!").

KLOR. A green-skinned alien from the far-distant planet Belvos who, having discovered that certain gems available on Earth could endow him with extraordinary powers, concocts an elaborate scheme to impersonate SUPERMAN and frame him for a series of crimes on the planet Belvos so that, while Superman is busy defending himself in a Belvos courtroom, he can stage a spectacular gem theft on Earth as a prelude to seizing dictatorial power on his native planet. The scheme is thwarted and Klor apprehended through the heroic efforts of BATMAN, ROBIN, and Superman (WF No. 122, Dec '61: "The Capture of Superman!").

KNIGHT, THE. An English crime-fighter who, with his youthful companion the Squire, fights crime in England much as BATMAN and ROBIN fight crime in the United States. Indeed, the crime-fighting career of the Knight and the Squire has been closely inspired by the almost legendary exploits of the Dynamic Duo. "We've learned a lot," explains the Squire in December 1950–January 1951, "by studying their cases and imitating them!"

The Knight and the Squire, 1955 © NPP 1955

In everyday life, the Knight and the Squire are secretly the Earl of Wordenshire and his young son Cyril, who inhabit stately Wordenshire Castle just outside the quiet English village of Wordenshire. However, when the ringing of the bell in the Wordenshire village rectory warns them that their services are needed, they swiftly don knightly raiment and roar into action astride their motorized "war horses" — the so-called "motorcycle-horses" — which are actually powerful motorcycles decked out like mighty medieval war horses.

In December 1950–January 1951, in England, the Knight and the Squire join forces with Batman and Robin to apprehend the notorious MATT THORNE gang (BM No. 62/2: "The Batman of England!").

In January 1955, in response to Batman's personal invitation, the Knight and the Squire and other foreign lawmen — including the RANGER, the LEGIONARY, the GAUCHO, and the MUSKETEER — arrive in GOTHAM CITY to study Batman's techniques firsthand, only to find themselves embroiled in a deadly battle of wits with "underworld chieftain" "KNOTS" CARDINE (Det No. 215: "The Batmen of All Nations!").

In July–August 1957 the Knight and the Squire visit the United States once again, this time in response to a summons from "well-known philanthropist" John Mayhew, who wishes to award the Knight and the Squire and other world-famous crime-fighters — including Batman and Robin, SUPERMAN, the Gaucho, the Legionary, and the Musketeer — charter membership in his newly formed Club of Heroes (WF No. 89: "The Club of Heroes!"). (*See also* BATMAN [section F, the Batman counterparts]; LIGHTNING-MAN.)

KOBRA, OMAR EL. "He of the evil name," a ruthless Arab villain, usurper of the throne to an Arabian desert sheikdom, who arrived in the United States with his henchmen sometime prior to October–November 1944 to assassinate Sidi ben Hassen, the rightful heir to the throne, then employed as a cab driver in GOTHAM CITY. Due to a series of unlikely coincidences, the would-be assassins mistook BATMAN for their intended victim and were apprehended by the Dynamic Duo before they could fulfill their villainous mission (BM No. 25/2: "The Sheik of Gotham City!").

KOLUM, ED. An unscrupulous press agent and ex-convict who attempts to deprive BRUCE WAYNE of the legal custody of DICK GRAYSON in retaliation for Wayne's having once exposed him as a charity swindler (BM No. 57/1, Feb/Mar '50: "The Trial of Bruce Wayne!"). (*See* ROBIN.)

KORMO. The far-distant planet which is the home of Tharn and the villainous bandit chieftain Rawl (WF No. 92, Jan/Feb '58: "The Boy from Outer Space!"). (*See* SKYBOY.)

KRAAK. A ruthless "space pirate" from the far-distant planet Ergon who, having fled to Earth to escape prosecution on his home planet, embroils BATMAN and ROBIN in a conflict with the Ergon police when he tricks them into helping him escape from the interplanetary lawmen who have been pursuing him. Finally apprehended along with Kraak by the Ergon police and sentenced to imprisonment as Kraak's accomplices on Ergon's lonely "moon prison," Batman and Robin ultimately establish their credentials as lawmen to the satisfaction of the Ergon authorities by joining forces with them in a daring scheme to recover Kraak's stolen loot and apprehend his space-pirate accomplices (BM No. 128/1, Dec '59: "The Interplanetary Batman!").

KRAAL. A bizarre creature from outer space — composed of three entirely separate, jigsawlike entities, called "kraals," each of which is capable of surviving independently of the others — which wreaks havoc on the planet Earth after an alien spacecraft, manned by the interplanetary explorer who recently captured it on some distant planet, crash-lands near GOTHAM CITY, enabling it to escape.

Separately, the three kraals are extremely dangerous — one feeds on electrical energy and shoots "bolts of electricity" from its hands, another has an "aura of flame" about its body and feeds on heat, and the third absorbs large quantities of water — but once united into a single being the three kraals become quite harmless because, in BATMAN's words, "Somehow, when the three kraals fuse, they neutralize each other's power--and the united kraal becomes harmless!"

Ultimately, Batman and ROBIN succeed in capturing the three kraals and in reuniting them in their harmless form, thus enabling the stranded space explorer, his spacecraft now repaired, to continue his journey toward his home planet with the kraal safely locked away on board (Det No. 277, Mar '60: "The Jigsaw Menace from Space").

KRAFFT, IVAN. The proprietor of the Happy Valley Gentlemen's Sporting Club, a private men's club which is actually an employment agency for the underworld where Krafft trains and houses "crime specialists" – such as demolitions experts, safecrackers, and machine-gun specialists – whom he hires out to gangs of criminals. The Happy Valley Gentlemen's Sporting Club is put out of business by BATMAN and ROBIN in February 1944 (Det No. 84: "Artists in Villainy").

KRYPTON. The far-distant planet which was the home world of SUPERMAN until it exploded into fragments as the result of a cataclysmic chain reaction originating at the planet's core. Fragments of the exploded planet, called KRYPTONITE, are generally toxic to Superman. (For detailed information concerning Krypton, its civilization, and its inhabitants, consult *The Encyclopedia of Comic Book Heroes: Volume VI – Superman.*)

KRYPTONITE. The term used to designate any surviving fragment of the exploded planet KRYPTON, home world of SUPERMAN. There are five distinct varieties of kryptonite (blue, white, green, red, and gold), the latter three toxic to Superman. Green kryptonite, the only variety potentially fatal to Superman, induces lassitude and inertia followed by death if not removed in time from Superman's presence. Red kryptonite inflicts bizarre and unpredictable – albeit temporary and nonfatal – symptoms, as when it divides Superman into twins or transforms him into an infant or a giant ant. Gold kryptonite would permanently rob Superman of his superhuman powers were he ever to be exposed to its radiations. (For further information concerning kryptonite, consult *The Encyclopedia of Comic Book Heroes: Volume VI – Superman.*)

KUBLA KHAN. The founder of the Mongol dynasty in China, and one of the great rulers of history. A son of Genghis Khan and the greatest of his successors, he rose to become the Great Khan of the Mongol Empire, the undisputed sovereign of all China and the master of an immense dominion extending from Korea to the Arabian Desert and eastern Poland. For many years he was gracious host and employer to the Venetian traveler MARCO POLO.

Arriving at the palace of Kubla Khan (1215–1294) during a time-journey to China in the year 1275, BATMAN and ROBIN expose a plot by ruthless provincial governor Bahung and traitorous court adviser Wong Tso to topple Kubla Khan from the throne of his empire, apprehend Wong Tso, and, by transmitting their early warning to the Great Khan, enable his army to rout the forces of Bahung marching against the capital (WF No. 42, Sep/Oct '49: "The Amazing Adventure of Batman and Marco Polo!").

KYLE. An ex-convict who claims to have been the first criminal ever apprehended by BATMAN. In March 1959 Kyle returns to plague Batman as the CLOCK (Det No. 265: "Batman's First Case!").

KYLE, KARL. *See* KING OF THE CATS, THE.

KYLE, SELINA. The raven-haired, green-eyed girl who has achieved infamy as the CATWOMAN (BM No. 62/1, Dec/Jan '50–'51: "The Secret Life of the Catwoman").

KZOTL. The far-distant planet which is the home of an alien movie producer who, in March 1960, tricks BATMAN, ROBIN, and SUPERMAN into battling robots designed to resemble extraterrestrial aliens so that he can obtain exciting movie footage of Earth's greatest heroes in action (WF No. 108: "The Star Creatures!").

L

LAMB, ADAM. A timid museum custodian and avid reader of mystery stories who embarks upon a bizarre double life — that of timid custodian Adam Lamb by day, and vicious criminal Wolf by night — after an accidental blow on the head unbalances his mind and transforms him into "a psychological Jekyll and Hyde!"

In Summer 1940 Adam Lamb trips on a rug and falls down a small flight of stairs just after finishing a mystery novel entitled *The Crime Master.* Lamb is apparently unhurt, but at midnight the following night, "a startling, dreadful change comes over his cherubic features . . . his mouth twists into a vicious, slitted leer. . . . A strange wild light flames with fury in his eyes! His form straightens [and] becomes like that of a wild caged and restless animal! . . . **Lamb** has become a **wolf!** . . . A beast . . . a snarling, cunning beast!"

That night, Lamb kills a man he meets on the street. In the nights that follow, he assumes the name Wolf, becomes the leader of a gang of criminals, and begins systematically perpetrating the savage crimes recounted in *The Crime Master.* By day, he remains the mild-mannered Lamb, completely unaware of the savage transformations he undergoes each night at midnight.

Ultimately, in a late-night confrontation at the museum where Lamb works, BATMAN unleashes a terrific blow that sends Wolf hurtling down the same flight of stairs responsible for Lamb's original transformation. As Lamb lies dying, his neck broken by the fall, he becomes consciously aware, for the first time, of the dual life he has been leading and tells Batman about the original accident.

"This is the only time I was ever sorry to see a criminal die!" murmurs Batman grimly. "Medical attention might have cured him!" (BM No. 2/2).

LANCELOT (Sir). In Arthurian legend, the bravest and most famous of the knights of the Round Table, and the lover of Guinevere, KING ARTHUR's queen. BATMAN and ROBIN fight alongside Sir Lancelot when they help smash a conspiracy against Arthur during a time-journey to Arthur's Camelot that they make in August–September 1946 (BM No. 36/3: "Sir Batman at King Arthur's Court!").

LANDERS, LEN. The leader of a gang of criminals who are apprehended by BATMAN and ROBIN in September 1957 during an attempted robbery of the Gotham Bank. Batman's crime-fighting activities throughout most of this period are severely hampered by the effects of a freak accident at the Gotham Electronics Company which has temporarily transformed him into a "phantom," capable of literally walking through walls but incapable of seizing any solid object (BM No. 110/3: "The Phantom Batman!").

LANE, LOIS. The persistent, curious, impulsive, intelligent, hard-working, ambitious, lovely woman reporter for the METROPOLIS *Daily Planet* who is, second only to SUPERMAN himself, the single most important person in the chronicled adventures of Superman, fulfilling as she does the tripartite role of Clark Kent's journalistic colleague, Superman's romantic pursuer, and the person most tirelessly determined to verify her long-held suspicion that Clark Kent is secretly Superman. (For a complete account of the life and career of Lois Lane, consult *The Encyclopedia of Comic Book Heroes: Volume VI — Superman.*)

LANE, LUCKY. A GOTHAM CITY gangster, described as the "one-time king of the underworld," who disappeared from view after being released from prison and who now directs the activities of the RED MASK MOB from a secret hideout inside an abandoned water tower. Lane and his gang are apprehended in April 1959 through the heroic efforts of BATMAN, ROBIN, and ACE THE BAT-HOUND (BM No. 123/3: "The Fugitive Batman!").

LANE, RUFUS. The leader of a gang of criminals who are captured by BATMAN and ROBIN in February–March 1949 with the aid of some elderly show-business people from the local old troupers' home (BM No. 51/2: "The Stars of Yesterday!").

LANG, DIAMOND. An underworld figure who obtains BATMAN's written pledge that neither he nor ROBIN will set foot in GOTHAM CITY for a full week, in exchange for the safe return of Robin, whom Lang's henchmen have captured. With the Dynamic Duo in exile, Lang and his henchmen — and their underworld associate Big-Time Gateson — look forward to a week of unrestrained criminality, but Batman and Robin thwart Lang at every turn, apprehend the entire Big-Time Gateson gang, and still manage to keep their pledge not to "set foot" in the city by operating from an ingenious flying headquarters known as "the flying bat-cave" (Det No. 186, Aug '52: "The Flying Bat-Cave!"). (*See* BATMAN [section E 2 b ii, the other aircraft].)

LARRIMORE, LARRY. An alias employed by CARLSON, the leader of the Ugly Horde, when he dons a handsome rubber face-mask to hide his ugly features as part of his scheme to wreak revenge on the college fraternity brothers who maimed him and the fiancée who spurned him (BM No. 3/2, Fall '40: "The Ugliest Man in the World").

LARROW, JOHN. An unscrupulous GOTHAM CITY businessman, indicted for fraud and jailed pending his trial, who hires a gang of criminals to break him out of prison by tunneling into his cell from a phony building excavation site adjoining the prison. With BATMAN out of town addressing a criminologists' convention in

Pacific City and ROBIN committed to playing nursemaid to a succession of inept, substitute Batmen – all winners of a citywide contest guaranteeing those who accumulate the largest contributions to the police department's widows and orphans fund the right to accompany Robin on his rounds as "Batman for a Day" – Larrow's escape scheme seems almost certain to succeed. In response to an urgent summons from Robin, however, the real Batman returns home ahead of schedule to help foil the jailbreak and apprehend Larrow's underworld cohorts (Det No. 225, Nov '55: "If I Were Batman!").

LARRY THE JUDGE. A "notorious underworld czar" who establishes a phony investment firm under the alias J. Spencer Larson, attracts large numbers of wealthy investors by promising, and then delivering, an unusually high rate of investment return, and then has his clients waylaid and robbed after they have left his office with their investments and added profits. With the lucrative proceeds from his bogus investment racket, Larry the Judge hires an army of hoodlums, seizes control of the GOTHAM CITY underworld, and decrees that henceforth no one may commit a crime in Gotham City unless he first obtains a license from Larry. In the days that follow, Larry the Judge issues licenses, dispenses advice on where and how to commit successful crimes, and studiously collects his share of the stolen loot, only to be finally apprehended along with his henchmen through the heroic efforts of BATMAN and ROBIN (Det No. 72, Feb '43: "License for Larceny").

LARSEN, KEITH. An unscrupulous "mountain-climbing adventurer" who, during a recent expedition to the summit of far-off Mount Rabachi, murdered fellow climber Cliff Amory so as to be able to seize possession of the so-called "hand of Korabo," a large, gem-encrusted golden hand which local natives had placed atop the summit to stand guard over their sacred mountain. Larsen has attempted to dismiss Amory's death as a mountain-climbing accident, but in March 1962 BATMAN and ROBIN – aided by mountain climbers Hampden and Dunne – use an elaborate ruse to frighten Larsen into making a full confession (BM No. 146/3: "The Deadly Curse of Korabo!").

LARSON, HARRY. A reformed ex-convict and BRUCE WAYNE look-alike who, in April 1954, is blackmailed by "gang chief" "FISH" FRYE into impersonating BATMAN (BM No. 83/1: "The Duplicate Batman!").

LARUE, ERNST. A cunning criminal mastermind who, by feeding specially prepared "brain-tapes" into a diabolical "robot brain," is able to establish complete mental control over certain selected individuals and force them to do his bidding. By mentally dominating a jewelry firm executive, an armored car driver, and an employee in the Rare Coin Exchange, Larue is able to commit a series of spectacular crimes by commanding his victims to steal for him and then forcing them to forget all that they have done in his behalf. Larue is apprehended by BATMAN and ROBIN in February 1964 (Det No. 324: "Menace of the Robot Brain!").

LATHROP. The proprietor of the Lathrop Gallery of Art in GOTHAM CITY and the secret leader of a gang of art thieves and swindlers who are exposed and apprehended by BATMAN and ROBIN in December 1965 (BM No. 176/2: "The Art Gallery of Rogues!").

LAWTON, FLOYD. The GOTHAM CITY millionaire who achieves renown as DEADSHOT (BM No. 59/1, Jun/Jul '50: "The Man Who Replaced Batman!").

LEAF, DOREMUS (Professor). A professor at Pacific Coast University in Coast City, U.S.A., who is "the world's [leading] authority on earthquakes" and the inventor of a special seismograph designed to calculate, in advance, the time and location of impending quakes. Leaf rescues BATMAN from seemingly certain death at the hands of the JACKAL in February–March 1946 (BM No. 33/2: "The Looters!").

LECLERC BROTHERS, THE. Two escaped Canadian convicts – Remy LeClerc, "the greatest knife-thrower in all Canada," and Pierre LeClerc, who "can shoot the whiskers off a wolf at 200 yards" – who become the objects of an intense manhunt by BATMAN and ROBIN in August–September 1953.

After spending some time as guests of the Royal Canadian Mounted Police, who had invited them to Canada to put on an exhibition of their famed crime-fighting techniques in honor of Canada's national law-enforcement week, Batman and Robin are homeward bound in the BATPLANE when they spy the limp body of Mountie Bob Jason, shot and badly wounded by the LeClercs while attempting to apprehend them. To ensure that Batman will be appropriately authorized to carry on the hunt, Jason deputizes him as a temporary Mountie, and the Dynamic Duo apprehend the LeClercs soon afterward.

In the course of this adventure, Batman employs his emergency white "snow uniform" to enable him to blend unseen into the snowy Canadian landscape (BM No. 78/3: "Batman of the Mounties!"). (*See* BATMAN [section C 2, the emergency and special-purpose costumes].)

LEGIONARY, THE. An Italian crime-fighter whose methods and techniques are modeled after those of America's BATMAN.

In January 1955, in response to Batman's personal invitation, the Legionary and other foreign lawmen – including the RANGER, the GAUCHO, the MUSKETEER, and the KNIGHT and the SQUIRE – arrive in GOTHAM CITY to study Batman's techniques firsthand. Soon after his arrival, however, the Legionary is kidnapped and then impersonated by "underworld chieftain" "KNOTS" CARDINE as part of an elaborate plot to destroy Batman (Det No. 215: "The Batmen of All Nations!").

In July–August 1957 the Legionary visits the United States once again, this time in response to a summons from "well-known philanthropist" John Mayhew, who wishes to award the Legionary and other world-famous crime-fighters – including Batman and ROBIN, SUPERMAN, the Musketeer, the Gaucho, and the Knight and the Squire – charter membership in his newly formed Club of Heroes (WF No. 89: "The Club of Heroes!").

The Legionary in action, 1955 © NPP 1955

(*See also* BATMAN [section F, the Batman counterparts]; LIGHTNING-MAN.)

LENOX, SHELDON. An unscrupulous "globe-trotter and explorer" who, having returned from India with a ruby statuette of Kila, the Hindu god of destruction, sells the statuette to a collector named Weldon and then steals the idol back from Weldon, contriving to place the blame for the theft on angry Hindu worshipers determined to recover the idol for their sacred shrine. Lenox dies when, during a battle with BATMAN, he falls through an open window to his doom (Det No. 35, Jan '40).

LEONARDO DA VINCI. A Florentine artist and scientist whose seemingly infinite curiosity and inventiveness — exemplified by his paintings, drawings, scientific and technical diagrams, and notes on a wealth of diverse subjects — combined with his uncanny modernity of vision have established him firmly in modern thought as the archetypal Renaissance man. Popularly, he is best known for his legendary universality and for his paintings of the "Mona Lisa" and "The Last Supper."

Dispatched through the time barrier by PROFESSOR CARTER NICHOLS to the city of Milan in the year 1499, BATMAN and ROBIN rescue Leonardo da Vinci (1452–1519) from death at the hands of the French forces currently in command of the city and ultimately facilitate his safe return to Florence (BM No. 46/3, Apr/May '48: "The Batman That Time Forgot!").

LEWIN, NAILS. One of four GOTHAM CITY gang chiefs — the others are Lew Gadge, Joe Keno, and Ed Mapes — who have recently joined forces in the successful theft of $1,000,000 from a Gotham City bank truck. In December 1959 Lewin concocts an elaborate scheme to seize the entire $1,000,000 for himself by either killing his accomplices or betraying them into the hands of the authorities without their becoming aware of who is plotting their downfall. For a time, Lewin's scheme is successful, as one after another of his cohorts is taken into custody by BATMAN and ROBIN. Ultimately, however, the Dynamic Duo see through the scheme, recover the stolen money, and take Lewin and his accomplices into custody (Det No. 274: "The Hermit of Mystery Island!").

LEWIS, HENRY. A prominent millionaire and amateur surveyor who, in Kentucky in February 1941, stumbles upon a huge limestone cavern — larger than either Mammoth Cave or the Carlsbad Caverns — extending directly beneath the famous Fort Stox gold reserve. Soon afterward, having learned of the existence of the cave but not its exact location, a gang of criminals headed by Renaldo, an unscrupulous nightclub owner, cleverly trick Lewis's daughter Linda into believing that she has committed a murder, and then blackmail Lewis into revealing the cave's location by threatening to report his daughter's "crime" to the authorities. Ultimately, however, BATMAN and ROBIN learn of Renaldo's scheme and race to Fort Stox in time to apprehend Renaldo and his cohorts in the act of looting the nation's largest gold vault.

"You've done your country a great service!" declares the Fort Stox commander after Batman and Robin have explained the story of Renaldo's plot. "I'll see that the President hears of this and gives you both a suitable reward!"

"That's not necessary," replies Batman. "Being Americans is enough of an award!" (Det No. 48: "The Secret Cavern").

LIDO. An alias employed by GOTHAM CITY gang boss BART CULLEN in December 1963 when he poses as an extraterrestrial alien criminal as part of an elaborate scheme to eliminate his principal gangland competitor and commit a series of spectacular crimes (BM No. 160/2: "The Alien Boss of Gotham City!").

LIGHTNING-MAN. A mysterious super-hero, his true identity unknown, who appears in METROPOLIS in July–August 1957 and performs a series of mind-boggling super-feats during a period when the world's greatest crime-fighters — including SUPERMAN, BATMAN and ROBIN, the KNIGHT and the SQUIRE, the MUSKETEER, the LEGIONARY, and the GAUCHO — are gathered in the city to accept a valuable gift from "well-known philanthropist" John Mayhew, a lavish Club of Heroes which he has constructed to serve as their Metropolis headquarters.

Since the land and building included in the gift are "worth a fortune" and Mayhew has decided to award the chairmanship of the club and the valuable deed to its property to whichever of the assembled crime-fighters performs the most impressive array of feats during the next several days, Superman becomes fearful that Lightning-Man is a criminal attempting to win control of the deed for himself. Lightning-Man does indeed win the chairmanship, but Batman ultimately establishes that Lightning-Man is in reality Superman himself and that the role of Lightning-Man was one the Man of Steel had unwittingly concocted during recurring short-lived periods of temporary amnesia brought on by the overhead orbiting of a meteoric KRYPTONITE fragment (WF No. 89: "The Club of Heroes!").

LI'L RED. An alias employed by ROBIN in September 1963 when he and BATMAN pose as underworld impersonators of Batman and Robin as part of Batman's plan to apprehend BOBO CULLEN and recover his stolen UTILITY BELT (BM No. 158/3: "Batman and Robin--Imposters!").

LINNIS, THAD. A cunning criminal who, by persuading SUPERMAN that he has solved the secret of his dual identity and threatening to expose it to the world, attempts to force Superman to remain outside METROPOLIS for two full weeks while he and his henchmen loot the city with a powerful "super-tank" which can be stopped only by Superman. With BATMAN's help, however, Superman eventually comes to realize that Linnis is only bluffing – the villain has no knowledge of Superman's secret identity – whereupon he and the Dynamic Duo apprehend Linnis and his henchmen before they can put their "tremendous theft-plan" into effect (WF No. 84, Sep/Oct '56: "The Super-Mystery of Metropolis!").

LITTLE RAVEN. The son of Great Eagle, the Sioux Indian who is secretly CHIEF MAN-OF-THE-BATS. Little Raven is an almost perfect look-alike for ROBIN (BM No. 86/3, Sep '54: "Batman--Indian Chief!").

LOFTUS, "RED." An unscrupulous big-game hunter who uses a weird mineral chunk possessing eerie hypnotic powers to gain "hypnotic control" over elephant lover Evan Bender – and, through Bender, control over a herd of East African elephants – so that he can force Bender to stampede the elephants through ivory storehouses and diamond mines to enable his native hirelings to loot the places in the ensuing mayhem. In East Africa in November 1964, BATMAN and ROBIN apprehend Loftus and free Evan Bender from his baleful hypnotic control (Det No. 333: "Hunters of the Elephants' Graveyard!").

LONGSHOREMAN KID, THE. A fugitive killer and leader of a gang of criminals who are apprehended by Bruce Wayne in October–November 1949 during a period when Wayne is serving a brief stint as a GOTHAM CITY policeman in fulfillment of a promise he made to a dying patrolman. Wayne's efforts to apprehend the Longshoreman Kid and his henchmen are hampered by the fact that, as a policeman, he must perform with distinction, without betraying abilities that might reveal he is secretly BATMAN, but Wayne manages to capture the criminals and then resign from the force without endangering the secret of his dual identity (BM No. 55/2: "Bruce Wayne, Rookie Policeman!").

LOO CHUNG. The unscrupulous Chinese-American who succeeds BATMAN's friend WONG as "unofficial mayor of Chinatown" following Wong's brutal murder by agents of the GREEN DRAGON tong in May 1940 (Det No. 39). In June 1941 Loo Chung gains possession of Wong's ornate serpent ring – once owned by Genghis Khan himself and used traditionally by the khan's descendants as a symbol of the khan's power and as a means of exacting tribute from the people of small towns – and uses it to instigate a ruthless protection racket among the merchants of GOTHAM CITY's Chinatown. Batman and ROBIN apprehend Loo Chung and his henchmen, however, and announce their intention to destroy the ring to prevent its further misuse (Det No. 52: "The Secret of the Jade Box").

LOOM, ARTHUR. A ruthless GOTHAM CITY gang chief who poses as a clairvoyant, "predicts" the impending deaths of two men who have refused to pay his gang blackmail money, and then arranges for his henchmen to murder the two men in the manner he had predicted, all as part of an elaborate scheme to enhance the credibility of his predictions and escape prosecution for his crimes. At one point, for example, Loom predicts the imminent collapse of the ceiling at the Palace movie theater, has his men steal the ticket receipts in the ensuing panic and confusion, and then surreptitiously causes the actual collapse of the ceiling in order to make his prophecy come true. While fleeing the scene of a "predicted" robbery aboard the ocean liner *Queen Helen*, however, Loom's henchmen are killed when their tiny getaway craft is accidentally crushed by the liner. Loom is taken into custody soon afterward when BATMAN, ROBIN, and POLICE COMMISSIONER GORDON trick him into making a full confession (Det No. 133, Mar '48: "The Man Who Could See the Future!").

LORING, E. J. A motion-picture director at Hollywood's Mammoth Studios who, fearful that his most recent film is of such poor quality that its release will ruin his reputation, hires a gang of criminals to steal the film and hold it for ransom so that the public will never be able to see it. Loring and his gangland hirelings are apprehended by BATMAN and ROBIN in October–November 1946 (BM No. 37/2: "Hollywood Hoax!").

LOST MESA. A secret Pueblo civilization, situated somewhere in the Southwestern United States and hidden from the world at large by towering cliffs and overhanging rocks, which was founded by Indians during the sixteenth century to escape the further depredations of the Spanish Conquistadors, who had killed and tortured them for their gold and treasure.

In December 1944–January 1945 two escaped convicts, Monk Bardo and Randy Roose, make their way to Lost Mesa and join forces with unscrupulous medicine man Mordu in an ill-fated effort to overthrow the good chief Tolto and loot the city. The villains are ultimately defeated, however, and the escaped convicts apprehended, through the heroic efforts of BATMAN, ROBIN, Chief Tolto, and an Indian youth named Nachee. Mordu dies after being hit by a stray bullet in the midst of some savage fighting (BM No. 26/3: "Crime Comes to Lost Mesa!").

LOUIS XIV (King). The king of France from 1643 until his death in 1715. BATMAN, ROBIN, and SUPERMAN meet Louis XIV (1638–1715) and expose the treachery of his "evil chancellor" BOURDET during a time-journey to France in the year 1696 (WF No. 82, May/Jun '56: "The Three Super-Musketeers!").

LOVELY, VERA. The pretty blond fourteen-year-old, the star of the Ice Capers ice-skating show, who enjoys a serious but short-lived romance with ROBIN during April 1957. His preoccupation with Vera causes Robin to make a series of careless crime-fighting blunders, and it is therefore not long before the Boy Wonder decides that women are simply not worth the trouble they cause and the time they consume. ". . . from now on," he promises Batman, "I'm keeping my mind on criminals, not ***girls!***" (BM No. 107/2: "Robin Falls in Love").

LOYD, FREDDY. An alias employed by Robin in February 1957 when he assumes a new identity in an effort to prove to Batman that his skill at disguises is as great as Batman's own (BM No. 105/2: "The Second Boy Wonder!"). (*See* Robin.)

LUMARDI, FRANK. A Gotham City gang chief who flees to England and, capitalizing on the fact that English policemen do not carry firearms, uses guns to commit a series of spectacular crimes and "start a reign of terror in London." On vacation in London in their Bruce Wayne and Dick Grayson identities, however, Batman and Robin apprehend Lumardi's newly recruited English henchmen, and Batman captures Lumardi himself soon afterward on the campus of Oxford University. Throughout their London adventure, the Dynamic Duo employ an imitation batmobile and other special equipment placed at their disposal by Chester Gleek, their "foremost English admirer" (Det No. 196, Jun '53: "City Without Guns!").

LUTHOR, LEX. The "warped scientific genius" who has been Superman's "most dangerous enemy" for more than three decades (WF No. 88, May/Jun '57: "Superman's and Batman's Greatest Foes!").

In May–June 1957 Luthor forms a temporary alliance with the nefarious Joker (WF No. 88: "Superman's and Batman's Greatest Foes!").

In May–June 1958 Luthor breaks out of Metropolis Prison by blasting his way through the prison wall with an awesomely destructive "ray device" fashioned secretly in prison and sets out to wreak revenge on both Superman and Metropolis. He is apprehended soon afterward, however, through the heroic efforts of Batman, Robin, and Superman (WF No. 94: "The Origin of the Superman-Batman Team!"). (*See* Power-man.)

By March 1959 Luthor has devised a set of ingenious belts that enable their wearers to reduce themselves drastically in size, and has concocted an elaborate

Lex Luthor © NPP 1959

scheme to rid himself of Superman. The scheme involves tricking Superman into reducing himself to microscopic size with one of the special belts and then following Luthor and his henchmen into the bottle city of Kandor, where, because the artificially controlled atmosphere is identical to that of Krypton, Superman's home planet, Superman becomes instantly deprived of his superhuman powers. In Kandor, the villains over-power Superman and confiscate his size-changing belt with the intention of leaving him stranded forever inside the tiny bottle city, but soon afterward, after Luthor and his henchmen have looted Kandor of its valuable super-scientific inventions and fled the city for the outside world, they are apprehended through the heroic efforts of Batman, Robin, and Superman (WF No. 100: "The Dictator of Krypton City!").

In September 1959 Luthor, employing an alias and a cunning disguise, poses as the inventor of an as yet unperfected "atomic transporter" — a device designed to transport individuals from place to place, almost instantaneously, by disassembling them into their component atoms and transmitting them to a distant "receiver" where their "atoms will be reassembled" — as part of an elaborate scheme to destroy Superman by disintegrating his atomic structure. Luthor and his henchmen are ultimately apprehended, however, through the heroic efforts of Batman, Robin, Batwoman, and Superman (WF No. 104: "The Plot to Destroy Superman!").

By March 1960 Luthor has constructed a gigantic lifelike mechanical hand — its movements secretly controlled by a henchman concealed inside the mammoth thumb — and disguised several of his henchmen as extradimensional aliens as part of an elaborate scheme to hijack a fortune in platinum while making it appear that the platinum theft is the work of an extradimensional giant extending his titanic hand into the earthly dimension. Luthor and his henchmen are apprehended, however, and the complex hoax exposed, through the heroic efforts of Batman and Robin (BM No. 130/3: "The Hand from Nowhere!").

By May 1961 Luthor has used his "scientific genius to devise [an] indestructible creature with super-powers . . . which takes its direction from radio waves emanating from [a] helmet" worn by Luthor. "All I need do is give it a task," gloats Luthor, "and its own electronic brain works out a solution!"

Aided by his awesome creation, a hideous mechanical monster somewhat resembling a gigantic starfish, Luthor and his henchmen commit a series of spectacular robberies in both Gotham City and Metropolis. The efforts of Batman, Robin, Batwoman, and Superman to halt the crime wave receive a severe setback when, as the result of a freak accident at Luthor's hideout, Batwoman becomes temporarily endowed with superhuman strength and the power of flight, but only at the cost of falling completely under Luthor's mental control whenever she is anywhere near his creature. Ultimately, however, Batwoman's superhuman powers fade and vanish, the creature is reduced to "a lifeless hulk," and Luthor and his henchmen are apprehended through the heroic efforts of Batman, Robin, and Superman (WF No. 117: "The Super-Batwoman and the Super-Creature!").

By June 1962 Luthor has devised a diabolical weapon designed to "re-arrange [Superman's] molecules so that he has no more substance than a shadow! Superman," gloats Luthor, "will become a living ghost!" Hair-raising complications arise, however, when a freak accident – the result of Superman's simultaneous exposure to two bizarre rays, the first emitted by Luthor's weapon and the second by an experimental ray-device undergoing development in a nearby laboratory – has the totally unanticipated effect of bringing into existence a so-called Negative Superman, a black and white super-powered being with all the strength and powers of Superman but with a personality that is "negative" where Superman's is "positive," so that whereas Superman uses his powers for good, the Negative Superman is determined to use his powers for evil.

For a time the Negative Superman wreaks havoc in Metropolis, sheltering Luthor and his henchmen whenever Superman tries to apprehend them and deliberately aggravating catastrophes whenever Superman tries to ameliorate their effects. Batman and Robin ultimately devise a means of destroying the Negative Superman, however, thus enabling them to apprehend Luthor and his henchmen (WF No. 126: "The Negative Superman!").

In November 1962 Luthor once again forms a partnership in crime with the nefarious JOKER (WF No. 129: "Joker-Luthor, Incorporated!").

In November 1963 Luthor enlists the aid of two evil extraterrestrial aliens in an elaborate scheme to lure Superman away from Earth on an interplanetary wild goose chase so that, in Superman's absence, he can use a lifelike super-powered Superman robot to commit a series of spectacular crimes and blame the crimes on the absent Superman. For a time, the people of Metropolis are actually duped into believing that their greatest hero has become a super-powered criminal, but ultimately Superman is exonerated – and Luthor and his alien accomplices are apprehended – through the heroic efforts of Batman, Robin, and Superman (WF No. 137: "Superman's Secret Master!").

(For a complete account of the villainous career of Lex Luthor, consult *The Encyclopedia of Comic Book Heroes: Volume VI – Superman.*)

LUVESCU, MAGDA. A glamorous "international beauty" with whom BATMAN initiates a whirlwind romance in October 1954 as part of his plan to apprehend Magda's former boyfriend, the "famous political prisoner" JACQUES TERLAY (BM No. 87/3: "Batman Falls in Love!").

LYNNS, GARFIELD. The theatrical "lighting-effects genius" who achieves infamy as the Firefly (Det No. 184, Jun '52: "The Human Firefly!"). (*See* FIREFLY, THE [GARFIELD LYNNS].)

LYON (Mr.). A criminal who commits a series of crimes in GOTHAM CITY and attempts, by mimicking the JOKER's zany crime-style and leaving behind the Joker's traditional calling cards, to pin the blame on the Joker. Furious at the very thought of his reputation being sullied by an imitator, the Joker takes Lyon prisoner and locks him in a lion's cage at a local zoo, along with BATMAN and ROBIN, whom he has also captured. The Dynamic Duo escape from the lion's cage, however, turn Lyon over to a zoo keeper for surrender to the authorities, and ultimately apprehend the Joker (BM No. 19/3, Oct/Nov '43: "The Case of the Timid Lion!").

LYONS, DICK. The GOTHAM CITY gang chief who is secretly the CRIMSON KNIGHT (Det No. 271, Sep '59: "Batman Armored Rival!").

M

McCOY, JIMMY "RED." The "king of rackets," a GOTHAM CITY crime boss who spent his boyhood in the city's slums, delivered bootleg liquor as a youth to earn extra money for himself and his mother, and, when he was finally apprehended and sentenced to a term in a reformatory for his crime – and his mother died of shock in the courtroom upon hearing the sentence pronounced – became a confirmed criminal for life in the twisted belief that it was the law that bore the responsibility for his mother's death. After rising to the top of the underworld hierarchy and serving ten years in prison on a conviction for income tax evasion, McCoy is released from custody in Winter 1941, determined to reorganize his mob and resume control of the rackets, in spite of the fact that gangster Big Costello has seized control of his territory in the interim. BATMAN and ROBIN play only a peripheral role in the events that follow: a bloody gang war which ends with McCoy shot to death by Costello and his bodyguards, Costello shot and perhaps killed by McCoy, and various members of both gangs taken into custody by the Dynamic Duo and the police (BM No. 4/3).

McCOY, MIDGE. An alias employed by ROBIN when he helps BRANE TAYLOR, the BATMAN of the thirty-first century A.D., battle the ruthless "solar system bandit" Yerxa (BM No. 67/3, Oct/Nov '51: "The Lost Legion of Space"). (*See* TAYLOR, BRANE.)

McCOY, MUSCLES. An alias employed by BRANE TAYLOR, the BATMAN of the thirty-first century A.D., as part of his plan to apprehend the villain Yerxa (BM No. 67/3, Oct/Nov '51: "The Lost Legion of Space"). (*See* TAYLOR, BRANE.)

McCURDY, SOUPY. An alias employed by BATMAN in October 1944 when he poses as a wanted criminal as part of his plan to apprehend the BRAINY BULOW gang (Det No. 92: "Crime's Man-Hunt").

McGLONE, JERRY. A Hollywood stunt man who commits a series of spectacular daredevil crimes after a head injury he suffers while performing a movie stunt robs him of his memory and leaves him with the delusion that he is actually Phantom Phelan, the fictional villain he was portraying when his accident occurred. After finally cornering McGlone, BATMAN and ROBIN rescue him from seemingly certain death when the cable he is swinging on snaps. McGlone recovers his memory soon afterward and will soon be completely well again (BM No. 36/2, Aug/Sep '46: "Stand-In for Danger!").

McGONIGLE (Detective). The bumbling, bombastic police detective who makes a series of clownishly futile attempts to apprehend BATMAN in Fall 1940, during a period when Batman – still in the early stages of his crime-fighting career – is being sought by the police for

Detective McGonigle © NPP 1940

working outside the law. The thickly moustached McGonigle speaks with an Irish brogue, wears a derby, and smokes an ever-present cigar.

In Fall 1940 Detective McGonigle is attacked by the Ugly Horde when he surprises them in the act of setting fire to a museum. Batman leaps to McGonigle's aid, helps him beat off his attackers, and then listens intently to McGonigle's account of the Ugly Horde's activities. Suddenly, however, McGonigle comes to the somewhat belated realization that the man he has been talking to is none other than the notorious Batman. "Whoosh!" cries McGonigle, pulling out his pistol. ". . . And what am I talkin' to you like this for? Hands up, **Batman**. . . . I've got ye covered!" Batman, however, merely grabs McGonigle's gun, pushes his would-be captor unceremoniously in the face, and makes good his escape.

Back at police headquarters, McGonigle attempts to regale his fellow officers with the tall tale of how he would have succeeded in apprehending Batman if only three of Batman's henchmen hadn't brutally attacked him. The police only laugh, however, for they know that Batman has no henchmen and that his only companion is ROBIN.

"I'd give a pretty penny to know who the **Batman** really is!" mutters McGonigle bitterly. "But as sure as me name is McGonigle . . . one of these days I'm going to find out!"

Later, while Batman and Robin are battling the Ugly Horde in an effort to prevent them from destroying a beautiful statue which the people of Boravia have shipped to the United States for safekeeping while they battle an enemy invasion at home, McGonigle intervenes to save Batman from a criminal who is about to shoot him. Again, McGonigle attempts to take Batman into custody, but Batman pushes McGonigle off a pier and escapes.

Not long afterward, during yet another battle with the Ugly Horde, McGonigle saves Batman's life a second time by shooting CARLSON, the leader of the Ugly Horde, just as he is about to stab Batman with a knife. This time Batman escapes from McGonigle by pulling McGonigle's derby down over his eyes. McGonigle receives the lion's share of the credit for capturing the Ugly Horde, however, credit that rightfully belongs to Batman and Robin (BM No. 3/2: "The Ugliest Man in the World").

It is still Fall 1940 when the notorious CATWOMAN invades a lavish penthouse apartment, makes off with some valuable jewels, and successfully thwarts every effort by the police to apprehend her. Fearful that his police department will soon become "the laughing stock of the country," and mindful of Detective McGonigle's alleged success in rounding up the Ugly Horde, POLICE COMMISSIONER GORDON assigns McGonigle the task of bringing in the Catwoman.

Ultimately, Batman and Robin recover the stolen jewels and apprehend the Catwoman, along with a group of other criminals involved in a plot to steal a valuable shipment of diamonds from a major diamond syndicate. The Catwoman escapes, but that night, as Detective McGonigle is walking toward police headquarters, Batman tosses him a small package containing the stolen jewels and a roll of film containing photographic evidence incriminating the captured criminals. Also included is a short note addressed to McGonigle: "Here are the missing gems," begins the note. "Develop the film. It will explain the reason for the men trussed up at 14 Chatham Road! Sorry I couldn't deliver the Cat[woman] too! Your old pal. . . ." The note is signed with a tiny drawing of a black bat.

"'Pal' is it!" fumes McGonigle. "Just because he delivers the jewels, I'm to be his 'pal'! As sure as me name is McGonigle, if I ever see the **Batman,** I'll . . . . bla . . . . bla . . . . bla . . . etc. . . . etc. . . etc. . ." (BM No. 3/4: "The Batman vs the Cat-Woman!"). (*See also* BATMAN [section K, the relationship with the law-enforcement establishment].)

McLAUGHLIE, ANGUS. The patriarch of Scotland's McLaughlie clan and the lord of Batmanor, a medieval castle so named because of the hordes of bats that fly over it from their caves in the nearby hills. Because a lord of Batmanor during the sixteenth century was entrusted with a fortune in gold for safekeeping by the king, and then died before he could pass along the secret of its hiding place to anyone else, the McLaughlies were widely suspected of having stolen the gold and the clan name has therefore been tarnished ever since. On his deathbed in August 1953, therefore, with the hiding place of the treasure still undiscovered, Angus McLaughlie bequeathes Batmanor to BATMAN in the hope that, as the new Lord of Batmanor, the famous detective will feel personally obligated to locate the missing gold and clear the McLaughlie name.

Indeed, arriving at Batmanor immediately following the bequest, Batman and ROBIN soon uncover the cache of gold – which had been camouflaged with a lead coating and installed as the weights of a gigantic tower clock adjacent to the castle – and apprehend a gang of criminals led by "Smoothy" Mathers, an American gangster who, posing as a private detective attempting to recover the gold for the McLaughlies, has already located the hiding place of the treasure and formulated plans to steal it (Det No. 198: "The Lord of Batmanor!").

MADDAN, ELLIOT. A GOTHAM CITY gang chief who concocts an elaborate scheme to reap a financial reward from the underworld and catapult himself to the coveted leadership of a nationwide crime syndicate by luring BATMAN into a cunningly devised deathtrap. After faking his own death at sea, Maddan entices the Dynamic Duo into an elaborately contrived treasure hunt for the $1,000,000 in stolen loot that he has allegedly left behind, all as part of a ruthless plan to trap Batman inside an electrified steel cage. Batman deduces that Maddan is still alive, however, and cleverly lulls the gang chief into a sense of false security by allowing a Batman robot to fall into Maddan's trap. Soon afterward, at Maddan's country hideaway, Batman, ROBIN, and members of the Gotham City Police Department apprehend Maddan and the other high-level syndicate racketeers who have gathered to witness Maddan's final victory over Batman (Det No. 313, Mar '63: "The Mystery of the $1,000,000 Treasure Hunt!").

MAD HATTER, THE. A wily villain who matches wits with BATMAN and ROBIN on three separate occasions between 1948 and 1964. His real name is Jervis Tetch. During the early days of his career, the chroniclers portrayed him as closely resembling the famous Mad Hatter of Lewis Carroll's *Alice in Wonderland,* but this

Jervis Tetch, the Mad Hatter, 1956 © NPP 1956

rendering was ultimately abandoned, and the name the Mad Hatter came to reflect the villain's somewhat eccentric preoccupation with hats, as opposed to his appearance.

In October–November 1948 the Mad Hatter steals a valuable Yacht Club trophy, then makes an unsuccessful attempt to rob the wealthy spectators at a GOTHAM CITY horse show. Ultimately, Batman and Robin trace the Mad Hatter to his hideout in a "now disused summer theater" and, with some timely assistance from VICKI VALE, apprehend the villain and his henchmen (BM No. 49/2: "The Scoop of the Century!").

In April 1956 the Mad Hatter becomes determined to steal Batman's cowl to add to his collection of valuable hats, most of them stolen from local museums. Items in the villain's collection include a hat which once belonged to George Washington; a drum hat used in the Indian "walking drum" ceremony; stone hats from Yappa Island; a cage hat used by South American Indians for carrying hunting hawks; and a trick sombrero, containing a tiny derringer, which once belonged to Western badman Ned Dalton.

After a series of ill-fated attempts to steal Batman's cowl, the Mad Hatter succeeds finally in spraying it with a special chemical which causes it to become dangerously radioactive when Batman visits a building where atomic energy experiments are performed and becomes exposed to the cobalt fumes there. When Batman removes his cowl so that it can be safely decontaminated, the Mad Hatter and one of his henchmen seize it and make off with it, but, with the aid of a "super-sensitive Geiger counter" mounted in the BATPLANE, the Dynamic Duo follow the faint radiation trail left by the radioactive cowl and apprehend the Mad Hatter and his henchmen moments after the villain has proudly added it to his collection (Det No. 230: "The Mad Hatter of Gotham City!").

By February 1964 the Mad Hatter has escaped from prison and he set out to commit a series of elaborate crimes involving the use of trick hats and having as their themes the occupations of the jurors who sent him to prison after his previous encounter with Batman and Robin. One juror was a fireman: disguised as firemen and equipped with a stolen fire engine, the Mad Hatter and his henchmen evacuate a bank on the pretext that a faulty gas main may cause the entire building to blow up at any moment, then calmly load the bank's money aboard their fire engine and escape. At one point, the Mad Hatter uses a trick fireman's hat to shoot blinding smoke at Batman and Robin, prompting Batman to remark that the Mad Hatter "used to rob just to ***collect*** hats, but now he seems to be using trick hats to ***rob!***"

After a while, however, Batman and Robin deduce the pattern behind the Mad Hatter's crimes, lie in wait for the criminals, and apprehend them (BM No. 161/1: "The New Crimes of the Mad Hatter").

MADISON, JULIE. The beautiful black-haired girl who makes her textual debut in September 1939 as BRUCE WAYNE's fiancée (Det No. 31), and remains Wayne's

Julie Madison and Batman, 1939 © NPP 1939

fiancée until March 1941, when she abruptly cancels their engagement because of Wayne's refusal to "find [himself] a career instead of being the public's number one playboy!" (Det No. 49: "Clayface Walks Again!").

By September 1939 Julie Madison has fallen under the hypnotic sway of the diabolical villain known as the MONK. In an adventure that carries BATMAN across the Atlantic Ocean to Paris (Det No. 31), and from there to the villain's forbidding Hungarian sanctuary "in the lost mountains of Cathala by the turbulent river Dess," he is forced to intervene continually to rescue Julie from the horrifying life of vampirism which the Monk and his accomplice DALA have planned for her. Ultimately, however, the Monk and his accomplice are defeated (Det No. 32, Oct '39), and Batman places Julie safely on a vessel bound for America (Det No. 34, Dec '39).

Bruce Wayne, Julie Madison, and Bentley, 1940 © NPP 1940

By June 1940 Julie Madison, now a budding movie actress, has landed a subsidiary role in *Dread Castle*, a horror film produced by the Argus Motion Picture Company. ". . . if Julie keeps up her fine work," observes BENTLEY, the head of Argus Pictures, "she'll be a star in no time. . . ." In the course of the filming, Julie becomes the target of a murder attempt by the maniacal Clayface (*see* CLAYFACE [BASIL KARLO]), but Batman thwarts the attempt and, with ROBIN's help, captures the villain (Det No. 40).

By March 1941 *Dread Castle* has been released, and Julie's "rave notices" have made her a star. Believing that Julie's new fame calls for a more glamorous name, Bentley instructs publicity manager Gabby Fest to come up with an exciting stage name, and Fest suggests the name Portia Storme.

"You're on your way up," remarks Bruce Wayne proudly, "a new star, a new name!"

". . . and a new career!" adds Julie pointedly. "Oh, Bruce if only you would do something! If only you'd find yourself a career instead of being the public's number one playboy!"

"Sorry, honey," replies Wayne. "I'm having too good a time to be bothered with anything remotely connected with work!" "You'd be mighty surprised," thinks Wayne silently, "if you knew I had a career – as the **Batman!**"

"Then I'm sorry, Bruce," continues Julie. "Until you decide to make something of yourself, I'm afraid our engagement is off."

"I-I see," stammers Wayne.

"I'm not walking out on you, Bruce," adds Julie. "Anytime you decide to change your ways, I'll come back to you gladly!"

"I understand!" replies Wayne. "It's all right! In case you ever need me for anything, just holler. If ever there's anything I can do. . . ."

"Thank you, Bruce," answers Julie, "but I don't think I'll ever be in much trouble."

Julie Madison and Batman, 1939 © NPP 1939

During this period, Clayface escapes from the prison ambulance transporting him to the state asylum for the criminally insane and returns to wreak vengeance on Batman and Robin. At one point, Julie Madison, now busy shooting another motion picture, spies Clayface staring at her and anxiously informs Bentley. "He still hates you because he failed to kill you before!" comments Bentley grimly. "He'll try again!"

Clayface does indeed make a renewed attempt on Julie's life, but Robin has secretly outfitted himself in the hooded robe which Julie wears in the movie, and he and Batman apprehend Clayface moments after he appears on the set (Det No. 49: "Clayface Walks Again!"). (*See also* BATMAN [section J 1, the relationship with Julie Madison].)

MAD MACK. An old prospector who, having come upon a valuable vein of silver in a played-out mine near Ghost Gulch City, conspires with some traveling circus performers to frighten the local townspeople into evacuating the town so that they can seize the newly discovered silver lode for themselves. Mad Mack and his cohorts are killed when, during a battle at the mine with BATMAN and ROBIN, one of the circus performers falls against a supporting beam, causing a devastating cave-in from which the Dynamic Duo barely manage to escape alive (Det No. 56, Oct '41: "The Stone Idol!").

MAESTRO, THE. A cunning criminal, clad in a maroon costume emblazoned with black musical notes, whose crimes invariably involve the use of musical instruments as weapons of crime – as when he and his henchmen employ horns specially equipped to shoot bullets – and who unfailingly provides BATMAN and ROBIN with a clue to his next escapade in the form of a musical fragment, usually played to them as he escapes from the scene of his previous crime.

The Maestro is in reality Payne Cardine, a concert pianist with a "twisted, brilliant mind" who, stung by the critical reviews accorded him after a recent concert, embarked on a criminal career, bitterly vowing to "make my musical performances more famous than those of any other virtuoso!" The Maestro and his henchmen commit a series of spectacular crimes before they are finally apprehended by Batman and Robin with the aid of a costumed individual referred to as the SPARROW (BM No. 149/1, Aug '62: "The Maestro of Crime").

MAGAN, BART. The fugitive criminal who is secretly DR. NO-FACE (Det No. 319, Sep '63: "The Fantastic Dr. No-Face!").

MAHARAJAH (the Magician). The stage magician who is secretly CALENDAR MAN (Det No. 259, Sep '58: "The Challenge of the Calendar Man").

MAKE-UP MAN, THE. A cunning criminal – a genius at mimicry and master of makeup – who conceals his true identity beneath constantly changing makeup disguises in the belief that "if no one knows what I really look like--no eyewitnesses can ever accuse me of a crime!" In January 1965, with the aid of three underworld accomplices and three lifelike remote-controlled robots called "audio-animatrons," the Make-Up Man engineers a spectacular robbery of the Gotham City

Jewel Mart, only to be apprehended soon afterward by BATMAN and ROBIN, with the aid of Hugh Rankin, a GOTHAM CITY private investigator (Det No. 335: "Trail of the Talking Mask!").

MALAN, MAYNE. The leader of a gang of criminals who are determined to steal the jeweled crown and scepter belonging to King Eric of Norania, a visiting monarch who has come to GOTHAM CITY to request a loan from the United States Government. To protect the king and safeguard the crown jewels, BATMAN agrees to trade places with the king until such time as the criminals have been safely apprehended. After Batman, ROBIN, and King Eric have captured the Mayne Malan gang and the king has successfully secured his loan, Batman sheds his kingly raiment for his customary Batman garb, while King Eric abandons his role as Batman, albeit somewhat reluctantly, and resumes his role as Norania's king (BM No. 96/1, Dec '55: "His Majesty, King Batman").

MALCHIO, PUBLIUS. A ruthless "Roman racketeer" whose sinister machinations are thwarted repeatedly by BATMAN and ROBIN during a visit to ancient Rome. Dispatched through the time barrier to ancient Rome by PROFESSOR CARTER NICHOLS – and aided throughout by the JESTER, an almost perfect look-alike for the JOKER – Batman and Robin smash Malchio's protection racket, thwart his efforts to fix a chariot race, and ultimately succeed in having him exiled from the city (BM No. 24/1, Aug/Sep '44: "It Happened in Rome").

MALLARD, DUCKY. The leader of a gang of criminals who are apprehended by BATMAN, ROBIN, and local police while attempting to loot the banks in "historic Santo Pablo, one of the oldest cities of the Southwest," in the midst of the colorful pageant being held in celebration of the town's 300th anniversary (BM No. 17/3, Jun/Jul '43: "Rogues' Pageant!").

MALLOCK, MAYNE. A notorious safecracker who, under an assumed name, donates a large sum of money and a complete set of blueprints to GOTHAM CITY for the construction of a fabulous House of Batman – a special house, designed as a crime-fighting headquarters and equipped with all kinds of ingenious devices to help the Dynamic Duo in their crime-fighting work – which is to be presented as a gift to BATMAN and ROBIN, ostensibly as a gesture of gratitude on the part of the donor for the Dynamic Duo's contribution to law enforcement, but in reality as part of an elaborate scheme by Mallock to prevent his own capture by periodically sneaking into the House of Batman via the city's sewer system and hiding in the ventilating shafts to spy on Batman and Robin and obtaining advance knowledge of their various anticrime patrols and strategies. Mallock stages a series of spectacular robberies in Gotham City's financial district before he is finally apprehended by Batman and Robin in September 1956. The House of Batman is turned back to the city for use as a Batman Law Enforcement Museum (BM No. 102/1: "The House of Batman").

MAN-OF-THE-BATS (Chief). A Sioux Indian – although not actually a chief – who, aided by his son Little Raven, an almost perfect look-alike for ROBIN, battles crime and injustice in the mountainous Western region inhabited by the Sioux, much as BATMAN battles crime in GOTHAM CITY. Chief Man-of-the-Bats, whose crime-fighting career is modeled after Batman's and whose costume is an Indian version of Batman's own, is secretly the Sioux Indian Great Eagle.

In September 1954, after Great Eagle has been wounded in the shoulder during a raid on his village by the villainous Black Elk, the leader of a band of renegades who have been terrorizing the countryside, Batman and Robin dye their skins red and don the feathered crime-fighting regalia of their Indian counterparts long enough to apprehend Black Elk and his raiders and convince them that Great Eagle and Chief Man-of-the-Bats are two entirely different persons, thereby safeguarding the secret of Chief Man-of-the-Bats's dual identity (BM No. 86/3: "Batman--Indian Chief!").

(*See also* BATMAN [section F, the Batman counterparts].)

MANON'S BEAUTY SALON. The lavish beauty salon where, under the name Elva Barr, the CATWOMAN is employed as a beauty operator during February–March 1943 (BM No. 15/1: "Your Face Is Your Fortune!").

MANTEE, MARTY. One of three criminals – the others are Lefty Royl and Duke Wilton – who are determined to recover a fortune in platinum that was stolen by another criminal some forty years ago, then fashioned into an automobile gas tank as part of an ingenious plan to smuggle it out of the country. It has never been recovered, in spite of the fact that the man who originally stole the platinum was subsequently apprehended. In May 1955 Mantee and his accomplices attend the Ancient Auto Society Convention in the GOTHAM CITY suburb of Millville in the hope that the current owner of the forty-year-old car – who is blissfully unaware of the fortune in platinum lying within his grasp – will decide to put it on display there. BATMAN and ROBIN also attend the convention, however, and ultimately they succeed in recovering the stolen platinum and in apprehending Mantee, Royl, and Wilton (Det No. 219: "Gotham City's Strangest Race!").

MARKHAM, GUY "BIG GUY." A famous film director who, while shooting a jungle picture on a tropical island, complete with spear-wielding "natives" and a mechanical dinosaur, spots BATMAN and ROBIN landing their BATPLANE nearby and instructs his actors to attack the Dynamic Duo and goad them into exciting action so that he can obtain valuable footage of the famed crime-fighters without informing them they are being filmed or obtaining their consent. One actor, jealous of the Dynamic Duo's appearance in the movie, engineers a series of attempts on their lives, but Batman and Robin survive the attempts and thwart the murderous actor, proving, in Markham's words, that "a fearless man is more than a match for any combination of evil!" (BM No. 10/1, Apr/May '42: "The Isle That Time Forgot!").

This adventure may have been the source of the mechanical dinosaur prominently displayed in the

BATCAVE's trophy room, but there is no solid textual evidence to support this contention.

MARKI, JAN. An impoverished, "demented artist" – in his own view "one of the few great painters of the day," but in the view of others almost totally devoid of talent – who, enraged at the Gotham Insurance Company for refusing to insure his hands for $1,000,000, decides to wreak vengeance on the insurance company that spurned him and on the members of GOTHAM CITY's Insurance Club after his hands become hideously mutilated in an explosion that he accidentally touches off himself while attempting to rob a safe. After luring the INSURANCE CLUB members to a booby-trapped mansion with the doors and windows electrified to prevent their escape, Marki unsuccessfully attempts to murder them all with poison gas, only to be apprehended by BATMAN and ROBIN (WF No. 52, Jun/Jul '51: "The $1,000,000 Star Club!").

MARLEY, "HATCHET." A GOTHAM CITY rackets boss who, aided by other "evil kings of Gotham City's underworld," captures BATMAN and ROBIN in April 1954 and forces them to undergo a series of grueling endurance challenges – tests of their strength, speed, muscular coordination, and the like – any one of which could, if not successfully completed, mean violent death for the Dynamic Duo. As time passes, however, Batman deduces the real motive behind the grueling testing, for he realizes that one of the tests poses a series of challenges identical to those which would face a gang of criminals attempting to loot the massive vault at the Gotham Mint. By observing the manner in which the Dynamic Duo meet this challenge, the criminals hope to master the techniques necessary for a subsequent raid on the mint, but Batman and Robin turn the tables on their captors and apprehend them all before the villains can profit from what Batman and Robin have taught them (BM No. 83/3: "The Testing of Batman!").

MARLIN, HATCH. The ruthless mastermind behind the "underground railroad of crime," an underworld organization which, in return for 50 percent of a convicted criminal's hidden loot, will engineer his escape from prison and flight to safety in a foreign country. Marlin and his cohorts are apprehended by BATMAN and ROBIN in December 1949 (Det No. 154: "Underground Railroad of Crime!").

MARLIN, "SHARK." The leader of a gang of criminals who, having learned that Bruce Wayne played the role of BATMAN at a recent society masquerade party, invade the Wayne mansion and, unaware that Wayne is secretly Batman, force him to impersonate Batman in order to frighten the rival Duke Kelmer gang away from the scene of a series of potentially lucrative robberies. Both gangs are apprehended by Batman and ROBIN in August–September 1950 (BM No. 60/2: "The Counterfeit Batman!").

MARMON, HUGO. An old-time circus acrobat, longing to recapture the acclaim and admiration that were his when he thrilled audiences with his feats beneath the big top, who openly defies the GOTHAM CITY statute forbidding anyone from appearing in a BATMAN costume "except the original Batman of Gotham City or with his permission" on the ground that he was performing his circus act under the name Bat Man, in a costume amazingly similar, although not identical, to the real Batman's, long before Batman's crime-fighting career ever began. It is therefore he, claims Marmon, and not Batman, who is Gotham City's true, original Batman, although he does agree to grant the more famous Batman permission to wear his Batman costume also.

John Vulney, "Gotham City's biggest racketeer," attempts to capitalize on Marmon's thirst for adulation by posing as a member of a citizens' anticrime organization and persuading Marmon to enter the crime-fighting profession – all as part of an elaborate scheme to get Marmon to frighten away criminals in the midst of committing crimes by appearing in his Bat Man costume so that Vulney and his henchmen can hijack their loot – but Batman apprehends him.

The costume dispute is eventually resolved to the satisfaction of all parties – thanks to a certain amount of psychological and diplomatic ingenuity on Batman's part – with Marmon retiring from crime-fighting and reviving his old Bat Man circus act, and Batman returning to his accustomed work as the world's greatest detective.

Although the issue of who was actually Gotham City's original Batman has by now become largely irrelevant, ROBIN does manage to unearth evidence that although Marmon was indeed the first of the two men to appear in a Batman costume, it was Batman who first wore his within the Gotham City limits (Det No. 195, May '53: "The Original Batman!").

MARS. The fourth planet from the sun.

Mars is the scene of a battle pitting BATMAN and ROBIN against the Martian scientist SAX GOLA in June–July 1947 (BM No. 41/3: "Batman, Interplanetary Policeman!").

Mars is the home planet of the alien lawman ROH KAR and of the alien master criminal QUORK (BM No. 78/1, Aug/Sep '53: "The Manhunter from Mars!").

MARSTEN, RICHARD (Dr.). A "famed scientist" who, having finally discovered a way to "synthesize the age-principle and youth-principle" in gaseous form, is now capable either of making a person younger with a specially prepared youth gas, or older with a specially prepared aging gas.

In April 1955 "criminal ex-scientist" Wilton Winders knocks Marsten unconscious and steals a canister of youth gas and another of aging gas with the intention of charging lucrative fees to make people young again, although he does not plan to inform his eager customers of the youth gas's chief liability: it makes one forget everything learned during the years the gas eradicates.

The Dynamic Duo's efforts to apprehend Wilton and recover the stolen gases are severely hampered by the fact that, as the result of having been exposed to the gases during an early battle with the villain, BATMAN has become transformed into an "impulsive and reckless" teen-ager while ROBIN has become transformed into a wise and deductive adult. In spite of the handicaps imposed by this rather staggering role reversal, however, Batman and Robin ultimately apprehend Wilton and his accomplice and use the recovered gases to restore themselves and other affected persons to normal (Det No. 218: "Batman, Junior and Robin, Senior!").

MARSTIN, JOHN. The head of the Marstin Employment Agency and the secret leader of a gang of jewel thieves. Using his employment agency as a front, Marstin obtains jobs for his accomplices inside prominent homes and businesses, then loots the places with the aid of inside information obtained by his accomplices in the course of their employment. Marstin and his henchmen are apprehended by BATMAN and ROBIN in September 1955 (BM No. 94/1: "The Sign of the Bat!").

MARTIN, BRUCE. An alias employed by BATMAN in August 1955 when he and ROBIN join a mountain-climbing expedition up the side of MOUNT K-4 as part of their plan to recover a vital roll of microfilm for the F.B.I. (BM No. 93/1: "Journey to the Top of the World!").

MARVEL (Mr.). An alias employed by an extraterrestrial alien in February 1961 when he poses as a new crime-fighter as part of an elaborate scheme to prove to his alien companion that he can get ROBIN to become his crime-fighting partner for ten full days (BM No. 137/1: "Robin's New Boss!"). (*See* ROBIN.)

MASKED MYSTIC, THE. A ruthless criminal who matches wits with BATMAN and ROBIN in June–July 1952. "He's a man named Gil Golen . . . who was treasurer of the Amateur Magicians' Society until they threw him out for attempting to embezzle funds!" explains Batman. "Golen swore revenge against all members of the society, most of whom are wealthy men. He's been terrorizing them, one by one!" (BM No. 71/2: "Commissioner Gordon's Greatest Case!"). (*See* GORDON, JAMES W. [POLICE COMMISSIONER].)

MASTERS, BIG JIM. The leader of a gang of criminals who effect a series of drastic changes in BATMAN's personality – making him reckless on one occasion and cowardly the next – by shoving him against an experimental personality-changing machine undergoing development at the Gotham Science Laboratory. For a time, the bizarre effects of the personality machine make Batman erratic and unreliable, and ROBIN is compelled to patrol GOTHAM CITY alone. Ultimately, however, Batman cures himself of his debilitating condition with the aid of the scientist who has been developing the personality machine, and apprehends Big Jim Masters and his henchmen (BM No. 132/2, Jun '60: "The Three Faces of Batman").

MASTERSON, BAT. A famous lawman of the Old West. BATMAN and ROBIN meet Bat Masterson – who at one point saves Batman's life by shooting a wanted outlaw named Gila Bill – during a time-journey to the Western town of Plain City in the year 1880 (BM No. 99/2, Apr '56: "Batman--Frontier Marshal").

MATCH, THE. An arsonist who conspires with the owners of failing businesses to torch places of business so that they can collect the outstanding insurance. The Match is apprehended by BATMAN and ROBIN in February–March 1948 (BM No. 45/3: "The Match!").

MATHERS, MART. A cunning criminal, skilled in the use of makeup and electrical equipment, who impersonates one of a group of television technicians who have been transported to the BATCAVE for a televised interview with BATMAN and steals the tiny box that contains a microfilmed duplicate of the "tremendous storehouse of top-secret law information" contained on punch cards in the batcave's "crime-file room." The theft of the microfilm represents a potential disaster for law enforcement because it contains vital information on such sensitive subjects as "police methods" and the "weak points of banks and treasure-houses."

A careful investigation, however, soon pinpoints Mathers as the thief and discloses that he has stolen the microfilmed crime file for "big-time crook" John Creeden for a fee of $10,000. Ultimately, Batman and ROBIN apprehend Mathers, Creeden, and their cohorts as they are about to loot a wholesale jewelry firm with the aid of information contained in the stolen file (Det No. 229, Mar '56: "The 10,000 Secrets of Batman!").

MATHIS, CURT. A "criminal-scientist with a long record" who was once apprehended by BATMAN and ROBIN with the aid of their incredible "flying eye," an aerial reconnaissance device of their own invention equipped with a "televisor lens and microphones" and operated by remote control. Prior to his capture, however, Mathis succeeded in obtaining some photographs of the flying eye, and on his release from prison has used these photographs to construct his own flying eye to help him pinpoint the secret route of a currency truck headed toward GOTHAM CITY.

After discovering the exact aerial location of Mathis's flying eye, however, Batman and Robin disable its television camera so that it cannot perform its reconnaissance function; and, when Mathis summons the flying eye back to his hideout to effect the necessary repairs, the Dynamic Duo follow it and apprehend Mathis and his accomplices (BM No. 109/3, Aug '57: "The 1,000 Inventions of Batman!"). (*See also* BATMAN [section E, the extraordinary abilities and the famous crime-fighting equipment].)

MATTSON, "PILLS." A fugitive criminal, called "Pills" because of his hypochondria, who seizes control of a neighborhood drugstore and transforms it into his gangland headquarters until he and his henchmen are captured by BATMAN, ROBIN, and two courageous drugstore customers in December 1942–January 1943 (BM No. 14/2: "Prescription for Happiness!").

MAUNCH, ALBERT. The owner of an English castle where, at the close of World War II, a band of Nazis fleeing Germany are reported to have buried a fortune in gold. By July 1964 Maunch's cousin Vincent Maunch – a criminal wanted in the United States under the alias Frank Pragnel – has seized control of the castle and imprisoned Maunch's family so that he and his henchmen can search for the treasure unhindered. Vincent Maunch and his cohorts are apprehended in the castle by BATMAN and ROBIN (Det No. 329: "Castle with Wall-to-Wall Danger!").

MEACH, JOE. A former high-diver, now the caretaker of METROPOLIS's Superman Museum, who achieves infamy as the COMPOSITE SUPERMAN (WF No. 142, Jun '64: "The Origin of the Composite Superman!" pts. I–II – "The Composite Superman!"; "The Battle Between Titans!").

MEACHAM, ROLAND. The chairman of the Citizens' Committee to Preserve Gotham Village – a picturesque area of GOTHAM CITY inhabited by artists, bohemians and intellectuals, and noted for its espresso houses and sidewalk cafés – and the man who is secretly the underworld figure known as SMILER (Det No. 327, May '64: "The Mystery of the Menacing Mask!").

MEDALION, MARK. The alias employed by fugitive coin counterfeiter LEW CRONIN when he opens a coin shop in GOTHAM CITY as part of his scheme to dispose of $2,000,000 worth of stolen gold bullion by transforming it into counterfeit duplicates of ancient gold coins (WF No. 20, Win '45: "King of Coins!").

MEGAN, JIM. "An ex-con who changed his name and pretended to go straight" as a legitimate businessman. Megan is secretly the PHANTOM BANK BANDIT (BM No. 115/2, Apr '58: "Batman for Hire").

MEKE, HENRY. The curator of a small museum featuring replicas of mythological curios who becomes transformed into the villainous THOR (BM No. 127/3, Oct '59: "The Hammer of Thor!").

MENNEKIN. A theatrical makeup expert who is described as "the greatest makeup artist of all time." In Fall 1944 Mennekin impersonates a prison physician long enough to help three condemned killers survive their scheduled executions in the electric chair and smuggle them out of the prison. He keeps the escaped men drugged and captive while three of his own henchmen, ingeniously made up as the killers' look-alikes, rob the city's largest bank and loot the diamond exchange; and then cold-bloodedly arranges for his three drugged captives to be killed in a shootout with police, all as part of an elaborate scheme to enjoy the ill-gotten gains from two spectacular robberies while the authorities, believing the perpetrators dead and the case closed, abandon their search for the bandits. Mennekin and his henchmen are apprehended, however, by BATMAN and ROBIN. "I wanted more money than I was making," confesses Mennekin, "and the idea of a perfect crime tickled my vanity!" (WF No. 15: "The Men Who Died Twice!").

MERKO (the Great). A famous stage magician and escape artist who is kidnapped in May 1954 by an underworld gang boss who hopes to force him to use his skill to free him from the massive chainlike manacles – allegedly filled with high explosive to prevent anyone from tampering with them – in which he has been imprisoned by members of a rival gang. While working behind the scenes to find the missing Merko and apprehend his abductors, BATMAN impersonates Merko, performs stunning magical feats in Merko's place on the stage of the Gotham Theater, and ultimately apprehends Merko's gangland abductor and his henchmen and frees the captive Merko from their clutches. The massive manacles, it turns out, were never really filled with high explosive at all, but were merely ordinary chains – part of a grim underworld joke – which the rival gang had hoped would keep their enemy manacled indefinitely by making him too fearful of causing an explosion to attempt their removal (Det No. 207: "Batman the Magician!").

MERLIN. In Arthurian legend, a wizard, seer, and counselor to KING ARTHUR. BATMAN and ROBIN rescue Merlin from the castle of QUEEN MORGAN LE FAY – and clear him of a charge of treason against the Round Table – during a time-journey to Arthur's Camelot that they make in August–September 1946 (BM No. 36/3: "Sir Batman at King Arthur's Court!").

MERRILL, MIDGE. The middle-aged midget and former circus acrobat who is secretly BATBOY (BM No. 90/3, Mar '55: "The Adventures of Batboy!").

METROPOLIS. The East Coast United States city which is the resident city of SUPERMAN and the scene of most of his adventures. (For further information on Metropolis, consult *The Encyclopedia of Comic Book Heroes: Volume VI – Superman.*)

MIDAS (Mr.). A costumed criminal who "specializes in gold robberies." Mr. Midas and his henchmen are apprehended by BATMAN, ROBIN, BATWOMAN, and ACE THE BAT-HOUND in an adventure narrated by Bat-Hound in August 1959 (BM No. 125/1: "The Secret Life of Bat-Hound").

MIKHAIL. DOCTOR DEATH's assistant during August 1939. Mikhail wears a fez and appears to be of either Indian or Arabic extraction, but the text describes him only as "one of Doctor Death's cossacks, such as Jabah" (*see* JABAH). When BATMAN leaps out a window to escape a hail of bullets fired at him by Mikhail, Mikhail races to the window to see where Batman has gone. Suddenly, Batman hurtles past the window on his silken rope, sending the full weight of his body slamming into the villain's outstretched neck: "There is a sickening snap," observes the narrative text, "as the cossack's neck breaks under the mighty pressure of the Batman's foot." "First Jabah, now you," observes Batman grimly, ". . . and yet Doctor Death lives on!" (Det No. 30).

MILDEN, WILLIAM. A GOTHAM CITY importer and secret underworld fence who is in league with a gang of waterfront bandits led by "Hook" Deering. In October 1952, feeling that Deering has been demanding too large a share of their loot, Milden sets in motion an elaborate scheme to destroy BATMAN, ROBIN, and Deering with a time-bomb he has managed to conceal inside Deering's artificial arm. Batman and Robin ultimately thwart Milden's plot, however, and take both Milden and the Deering gang into custody (Det No. 188: "The Doom in the Bat-Cave!").

MILLEN, ROSS. A dog trainer who, under duress, uses his dog Whitey to help a gang of criminals commit a series of spectacular diamond thefts after the criminals have threatened to kill Whitey if Millen refuses. With the help of JOHN WILKER's dog Ace (*see* ACE [THE BAT-HOUND]), who tracks the villains to their hideout by following Whitey's scent, BATMAN and ROBIN apprehend the criminals and rescue Millen from their clutches (BM No. 97/3, Feb '56: "The Return of the Bat-Hound!").

MILLER, "MOOSE." The leader of a gang of criminals who seize control of Midget City – a prosperous town, built and inhabited by midgets, where everything is "one-fourth of normal size" – terrorize its midget population, and use the town as a secret hideout from which to make forays into GOTHAM CITY and environs. Miller and his henchmen are apprehended by BATMAN and ROBIN in June–July 1947 with the aid of the residents of Midget City (BM No. 41/2: "The Bandits of Toy Town!").

MILO (Professor). A cunning "renegade scientist" who, in September 1957, uses a diabolical "phobia liquid" to make BATMAN deathly "afraid of anything that resembles a bat" (Det No. 247: "The Man Who Ended Batman's Career!"). He may or may not be the same man as the Professor Milo who nearly kills Batman with "a gas made from a rare Amazon plant" in December 1957 (BM No. 112/3: "Am I Really Batman?").

By September 1957 Professor Milo has used his phobia liquid to create an artificial phobia in Batman, making Batman deathly "afraid of anything bat-shaped!" The result is that Batman becomes so terrified of his own bat-styled equipment – e.g., his BATMOBILE, batarang, and bat-costume – that he is unable to use it effectively against Milo and his henchmen. In fact, Milo and his cohorts are able to reduce Batman to a state of quivering, abject terror merely by releasing a live bat in his presence or confronting him with some bat-shaped object.

To counter the grave threat posed by this artificially induced phobia, Batman announces that he is retiring from crime-fighting and that ROBIN will carry on without him with the aid of a new partner named Starman. Unbeknownst to anyone but Robin, Starman is actually Batman himself, clad in an entirely new costume and equipped with an entirely new arsenal of crime-fighting apparatus – e.g., a "star-plane," "star-darts," and a "stararang" – none of which is characterized by a batlike shape. Thus, Batman hopes to divest himself of the various bat-symbols that have become so terrifying to him while at the same time tricking Professor Milo and his men into believing that the various "bat-scares" which have proven so effective against Batman would inevitably prove ineffective against the new Starman.

For a time, Batman's transformation into Starman proves an effective tactic, but Professor Milo soon realizes that Starman is actually Batman in disguise and prepares to take renewed advantage of Batman's artificial phobia.

In the interim, however, Robin cures Batman of his phobia by strapping him into a chair and forcing him, against his will, to stare at newsreels of past cases in which his various bat-styled devices saved his life or aided him in his battle against criminals. "You see how all these bat-shaped things helped you?" asks Robin, as scene after scene flashes across the movie screen. "There's nothing to be afraid of! How can you be afraid of things that **help** you?"

Now cured of his debilitating phobia, Batman, still attired in his Starman costume, joins Robin in a climactic battle with Professor Milo's henchmen. The criminals attempt to frighten Starman with a huge bat-shaped balloon, only to learn to their dismay that he has no fear of bat-shaped objects. Within moments the criminals have been apprehended, and, soon afterward, Batman captures Professor Milo in his secret laboratory (Det No. 247: "The Man Who Ended Batman's Career!").

A "renegade scientist" named Professor Milo is also featured in the Batman text for December 1957, but this Professor Milo bears only a scant resemblance to the inventor of the diabolical phobia liquid and it is impossible to determine whether the chroniclers intended for him to be regarded as the same man.

This Professor Milo was apprehended by Batman and Robin just prior to December 1957, but not before he had exposed Batman to the fumes of "a gas made from a rare Amazon plant." "The gas," Professor Milo had explained to Robin, just before the Boy Wonder had turned him over to the authorities, "has a unique effect on the person inhaling it . . . the person ***loses the desire to live!*** He lies about listlessly, refusing to eat, and eventually he dies! Ha, ha, ha!"

Some hasty research on the effects of Professor Milo's debilitating gas informed Robin that there was only one hope for Batman: ". . . if the patient can be given the desire to live, and is kept moving, at the end of 24 hours, he will recover!"

Robin hastily concocted a plan to save Batman and presented it to POLICE COMMISSIONER GORDON: ". . . you see," explained Robin, "we must give **Batman** a purpose for living, a problem to solve--a problem so shocking that he won't rest until he has the answer!"

The plan, executed with the cooperation of the Gotham City Police Department and the staff of a local mental institution, involved committing Batman to a mental institution and treating him as though he were a lunatic suffering from the delusion that he is Batman. When Batman awakens in a padded cell and is unable to persuade anyone around him that he is really Batman, he becomes desperate to prove his identity to a disbelieving world. After escaping from the mental institution, he makes his way to the Wayne mansion, only to confront DICK GRAYSON, and ALFRED disguised as BRUCE WAYNE, both of whom treat him as though he were mad and persistently deny that he actually lives there or that he is really Batman.

The challenge of having to prove that he is really Batman, despite the repeated denials of those around him, provides Batman with the motivation he needs to keep on the move for the twenty-four hours necessary to survive the effects of Professor Milo's debilitating gas. Ultimately, through persistence and keen detective work, he succeeds in proving that he is really Batman and that the man posing as Bruce Wayne is an impostor. By then, fortunately, the twenty-four hours have elapsed. Robin is now free to tell Batman about the rare gas to which he was exposed and about the necessity for concocting a scheme to keep him hyperactive during the twenty-four-hour period (BM No. 112/3: "Am I Really Batman?").

MINDY. The leader of a gang of criminals who kidnap amusement park owner Col. John Dawes, replace him with a look-alike, and then operate Dawes's amusement park for their own benefit – accumulating gate receipts, collecting commissions from the amusement park concessionaires, and operating a string of slot machines – until they are finally apprehended by BATMAN and ROBIN in May 1941 (Det No. 51: "The Case of the Mystery Carnival").

MINOS (the Mind Reader). An alias employed by BATMAN in December 1952–January 1953 when he feigns insanity and gets himself committed to the Gotham Institute for the Insane as part of his plan to trap the JOKER (BM No. 74/1: "The Crazy Crime Clown!").

MIRAGE MAKER, THE. A cunning villain who commits a series of spectacular crimes with the aid of an ingenious "mirage machine," a large machine that enables him to create deceptively realistic mirages anywhere he chooses. At one point, for example, he and his henchmen use the machine to make it appear that the City Bridge has collapsed into the river, then loot a vessel carrying a cargo of gold bullion after it has run aground while attempting to steer a safe course around the apparently wrecked bridge. The Mirage Maker and his henchmen are apprehended by BATMAN and ROBIN in March 1958 (BM No. 114/2: "The Mirage Maker").

MIRROR-MAN. A ruthless villain whose name derives from his use of mirrors to aid him in the commission of spectacular crimes. He is in reality Floyd Ventris, a convicted felon who assumes the role of Mirror-Man after successfully using a fragment of broken mirror to facilitate his escape from the penitentiary (Det No. 213, Nov '54: "The Mysterious Mirror-Man!").

In November 1954 penitentiary inmate Floyd Ventris smashes a mirror, pockets one of the fragments, and then escapes over the prison wall by using the fragment to reflect the bright glare of a prison searchlight into the eyes of one of the guards. "I broke a mirror--and it brought me good luck!" exclaims Ventris. "It's like an omen! I'll do a lot of research on mirrors--because from now on I'm going to use them for crime!"

In the days that follow, Ventris outfits an elaborate mirror-filled hideout and establishes himself as Mirror-Man. One of his special mirrors, stolen from among the belongings of a recently deceased scientist, is a "two-way electronic mirror that X-rays anything covered by cloth," which Mirror-Man hopes to use to discover the secret of BATMAN's dual identity.

At one point, Mirror-Man and his henchmen seize control of a huge "solar mirror" at a United States Army research station and use it to focus the sun's rays on the ice at a local ice-skating rink with the intention of looting the rink's box office in the ensuing confusion. Arriving on the scene in the BATPLANE, however, Batman and ROBIN foil the crime by shrouding the solar mirror in a cloud of smoke. Batman pursues Mirror-Man to a nearby "house of mirrors," but the villain escapes after attempting, and only narrowly failing, to

Mirror-Man and Batman, 1954 © NPP 1954

discern the features beneath Batman's cowl with his two-way electronic mirror.

Later, Mirror-Man and his henchmen steal a giant circular telescopic mirror destined for installation at the Mt. Malador Observatory. When Batman and Robin give chase in the BATMOBILE, the criminals hurl the giant mirror out of their truck in the hope that the Dynamic Duo will abandon their pursuit to save the mirror, but Robin merely leaps onto the runaway mirror and rides it to safety like a giant cartwheel while Batman pursues the criminals in the batmobile. By using a mirror to reflect the glare of the batmobile's headlights back into Batman's eyes, however, Mirror-Man and his cohorts succeed in sending Batman careening off the road to avoid what appears to him to be an oncoming vehicle. And, while Batman is still dazed from the experience, Mirror-Man uses his two-way electronic mirror to peer beneath Batman's cowl and learn his secret identity. Robin arrives with the police moments afterward, but Batman knows that Mirror-Man has uncovered his secret.

To protect his dual identity, Batman publishes an article in the Gotham *Gazette* under the name Bruce Wayne in which he describes the numerous occasions on which people have concluded erroneously that Bruce Wayne is Batman. The next morning, when Mirror-Man announces to his cohorts that Bruce Wayne is really Batman, his henchmen laughingly show him the newspaper article and assure Mirror-Man that he is only repeating a mistake that has been made many times before.

Enraged at having been tricked by Batman, Mirror-Man vows to prove to all of GOTHAM CITY that Batman and Bruce Wayne are indeed one and the same man. When the Apex Glass Works celebrates its 150th anniversary by manufacturing the world's largest mirror before live television cameras, Mirror-Man arrives on the scene to steal the precious silver used in the manufacturing process. And when Batman and Robin attempt to intervene, Mirror-Man unveils his two-way electronic mirror and holds it in front of Batman's face so as to broadcast Batman's facial features through the television cameras and into the living rooms of Gotham City. Batman has prepared for this eventuality, however, by wearing, beneath his regular cowl, a special hood "made of 'crazy' mirrors" which so distorts his features that they are totally unrecognizable. So stunned is Mirror-Man by this unexpected turn of events that Batman easily apprehends him (Det No. 213: "The Mysterious Mirror-Man!").

In August 1963 Mirror-Man escapes from prison and sets out once again to prove to the world that Bruce Wayne is Batman. Knowing that Wayne is scheduled to attend a luncheon at the Gotham Men's Club, Mirror-Man decides to commit a crime elsewhere at the same time while his henchman Harry Vance keeps a close watch on Wayne to see that he does not change to Batman in an effort to prevent the crime.

Overlooking a busy street in the heart of the city, Mirror-Man places two ordinary-looking billboards. Under the heat of the sun, however, the specially prepared billboard paper suddenly vaporizes, revealing two huge mirrors which reflect the sun's rays with such a brilliant glare that drivers on the street below are unable to see properly and traffic becomes hopelessly snarled. In the ensuing confusion, Mirror-Man invades the Gotham Museum to steal a valuable jade mirror on display there.

Meanwhile, Bruce Wayne notices Harry Vance following him and pretends to fall into an open manhole and knock himself out in order to provide himself with the opportunity to don his Batman costume and race through the sewer system to the scene of the robbery. After he and Robin have attempted, unsuccessfully, to apprehend Mirror-Man and his accomplices, Batman returns through the sewers to the manhole, pretends to have regained consciousness, and returns to the street. Later, Vance assures Mirror-Man that Bruce Wayne was unconscious in the manhole throughout the robbery and that he could therefore not possibly have appeared at the museum as Batman. Mirror-Man, however, feels certain that the manhole incident must have been concocted by Wayne as a ploy to protect his dual identity.

Mirror-Man next learns that Bruce Wayne will present the Gotham Book Society with a valuable first edition of Lewis Carroll's *Through the Looking Glass.* Mirror-Man thinks the theft of such a volume would be appropriate for him and would also provide him with an excellent opportunity to prove that Bruce Wayne is Batman.

Batman, however, has deduced that Mirror-Man will strike during the book presentation, and he arranges for ALFRED to impersonate Bruce Wayne at the ceremony while he and Robin lurk nearby to apprehend the criminals when they appear. The plot is complicated, however, by VICKI VALE, who also believes that Bruce Wayne is Batman and who hopes to ingratiate herself with Batman by hiring an actor to impersonate Wayne during the book presentation so that Batman will remain free to apprehend the criminals.

Fortunately, Alfred arrives late, and it is only Vicki Vale's hired actor, disguised as Bruce Wayne, who is on hand to make the actual presentation. When Mirror-Man and his men appear on the scene and tie up the bogus Bruce Wayne, Batman and Robin leap to the attack, but the criminals escape before the Dynamic Duo can apprehend them.

Mirror-Man is suspicious, however, that the Bruce Wayne at the presentation ceremony was not the real one, and he instructs Harry Vance to follow this "Bruce Wayne" and report what he learns. When Vance learns that the Bruce Wayne at the book presentation was only a hired impersonator, Mirror-Man is elated, for he sees this as vindication of his view that Bruce Wayne is Batman.

Robin, meanwhile, has been trailing Harry Vance in the hope that Vance would lead him to Mirror-Man's hideout. Moments later, he and Batman invade Mirror-Man's headquarters and apprehend the villain and his henchmen.

For Batman, however, the problem of protecting the secret of his dual identity remains. He instructs Alfred to pose as Batman at police headquarters while Mirror-Man is being booked there, while he himself remains at home as Bruce Wayne. Indeed, after he has been booked, Mirror-Man announces to Vicki Vale and the assembled newspaper reporters that Bruce Wayne is secretly Batman, explaining that the Bruce Wayne at the Gotham Book Society presentation was only a hired actor whom Vicki Vale had hired to impersonate Bruce Wayne in an effort to help Batman conceal his dual identity.

"No--***Batman*** didn't know about it!" cries Vicki Vale tearfully. "I--I did it all on my own. . . ."

Batman, actually Alfred in disguise, replies that Mirror-Man's story is nonsense and suggests that they call Bruce Wayne and ask him to come to police headquarters to settle the matter once and for all.

Indeed, when Bruce Wayne arrives, Vicki Vale and the assembled reporters are treated to the spectacle of what appears to be Batman and Bruce Wayne in the same room at the same time. Mirror-Man, certain that the recently arrived Bruce Wayne is an impostor, touches his face and tugs at his hair in an effort to prove that the man claiming to be Bruce Wayne is only an impersonator, but the effort ends in frustrating failure. No one suspects that the man who claims to be Batman is actually Alfred in disguise.

Mirror-Man will go to prison, and both he and Vicki Vale will remain ignorant of the fact that Bruce Wayne is Batman (BM No. 157/2: "The Hunt for Batman's Secret Identity!").

MR. BLANK. A ruthless criminal, his identity concealed beneath a white mask, who concocts an elaborate scheme to seize control of the GOTHAM CITY underworld. He is in reality Dr. Edward Arvin, a "brilliant scientist" who, in June–July 1953, announces the successful construction of an electronic "crime predictor" capable of predicting crimes in advance of their occurrence.

Arvin's machine has no real power to predict future crimes, but Arvin is able to endow his crime predictor with a stunning reputation for accuracy by obtaining advance knowledge of planned crimes through the underworld grapevine and then attributing his predictions to the crime predictor, with the result that numerous criminals who have refused to join forces with Mr. Blank soon find themselves arrested and imprisoned. Mr. Blank further terrorizes the underworld when he smashes the crime predictor, pretends to kidnap Dr. Arvin, and then announces that he will release Dr. Arvin to build another crime predictor unless the underworld agrees to accept him as its leader. For a time, Mr. Blank's scheme proceeds as he had anticipated, but he is ultimately apprehended and unmasked through the heroic efforts of BATMAN and ROBIN (BM No. 77/1: "The Crime Predictor!").

MR. CAMERA. A cunning criminal, noted for his use of photographic devices to aid him in his crimes, who was sent to prison approximately "one year ago" by BATMAN and ROBIN, but not before one of his own cameras, set to record him for posterity in the act of committing a crime, had accidentally recorded film footage of Bruce Wayne and Dick Grayson changing into their dual identities of Batman and Robin. Because Mr. Camera—who hid the film prior to his capture without having had time either to develop or view it, but who does know that it contains Batman's and Robin's secret identities—has threatened to have the film made public by a gangland crony immediately upon his henchman's imminent release from prison, Batman and Robin set in motion an elaborate ruse designed to mute the impact of the film when it is finally released by persuading the public beforehand that Bruce Wayne and Dick Grayson could not possibly be Batman and Robin. The ruse is successful but, ironically, Mr. Camera's film turns out to have been so badly underexposed that it could never have endangered the Dynamic Duo's secret identities anyway (BM No. 81/2, Feb '54: "The Boy Wonder Confesses!").

MR. CIPHER. An ingenious criminal mastermind, his true identity concealed beneath a green mask which entirely covers his face and head, who operates a secret "transformation mill" in the heart of GOTHAM CITY where, for a price, wanted criminals may receive new faces and fingerprints through the miracle of plastic surgery. "New crooks for old!" muses BATMAN at one point. "A mad, incredible idea . . . and it works! Wonder how many have already changed their faces and begun new criminal careers . . . as safe from past crimes as if they were dead?"

In June–July 1952 Mr. Cipher and his henchmen are cornered by Batman, ROBIN, and members of the Gotham City Police Department, and Mr. Cipher is shot and killed by police officers while attempting to resist arrest. Beneath the villain's green mask, the authorities find a hideous, shapeless face almost devoid of normal features. "Those scars explain it!" murmurs Batman grimly. "His face has been changed by plastic surgery so often, the muscles have quit working!" (BM No. 71/3: "The Mask of Mr. Cipher!").

MR. 50. A cunning criminal mastermind—his true identity unknown, even to his underworld subordinates—who presides over a vast international gem smuggling network headquartered on the Hawaiian island of Oahu. In his everyday identity he is Narkin, the foreman of a local sugar plantation. To smuggle stolen gems into the continental United States, Narkin hides them inside huge sacks of raw sugar which he ships to a cooperative "distributor" in GOTHAM CITY. Mr. 50 is apprehended by BATMAN and ROBIN in February 1962 (BM No. 145/1: "Hunt for Mr. 50").

MR. MAMMOTH. A "fabulous strong man" appearing with a local circus who, although he remains completely unaware of the cause of his strange affliction, becomes overwhelmed by an uncontrollable urge to fight and destroy whenever he hears the call-letter chimes of GOTHAM CITY radio station WGC, whose unique "vibrations" somehow awaken a "deep-seated fighting emotion--or instinct" lying dormant within his personality, transforming him into a fearsome creature of rage and destruction. BATMAN and ROBIN ultimately discover the cause of Mr. Mammoth's bizarre affliction and—although Batman is forced at one point into a rousing battle with the strongman—eventually arrange for station WGC to change the sound of its call-letter chimes, at least until the normally gentle Mr. Mammoth has had time to receive medical treatment for his problem (BM No. 168/1, Dec '64: "The Fight That Jolted Gotham City!").

MISTER X. A mysterious underworld figure—noted for his powerful build and for the black face-cloth that conceals his identity—who forms an alliance with the CATWOMAN in December 1950–January 1951. Mister X is in reality Mousey, a diminutive small-time hoodlum who uses stilts and an elaborate wooden frame concealed beneath his suit to make it appear that he is a much larger, more powerful man than he actually is. ". . . it was a good coverup!" explains Mister X, after he has finally been taken into custody. "The cops would be hunting for ***Mister X,*** not a punk named ***Mousey!*** Yeah . . . my name . . . Mousey . . . that was the real reason for everything. . . . No gangsters would take orders from a little guy they call Mousey! In the underworld you have to be ***impressive!*** So, by posing as a mystery man--a ***Big* man**--I got myself a gang! Mousey, the punk, became ***Mister* X,** the big shot!"

Mister X is apprehended by BATMAN and ROBIN with the aid of the Catwoman, who has agreed to cooperate with the authorities (BM No. 62/1: "The Secret Life of the Catwoman"). (*See* CATWOMAN, THE.)

MITCHUM, WHEELS. A condemned murderer, awaiting execution on Death Row for the murder of a lawyer named Kipley, who narrates the story of his sordid life in crime and ultimate defeat at the hands of BATMAN and ROBIN to a newspaper reporter who has come to collect a written version of Mitchum's story for publication in a newspaper. Having told his story, Mitchum hands the completed written manuscript to the newspaperman and walks his last mile to the electric chair (WF No. 27, Mar/Apr '47: "Me, Outlaw!").

MODERNE (Madame). An alias employed by the CATWOMAN in June–July 1948 when she establishes herself as the publisher of *Damsel*, a high-fashion magazine, in order to help her gain entree to people of wealth (BM No. 47/1: "Fashions in Crime!").

MOLE, THE. The nickname of a notorious criminal, "an expert miner and tunneler" unheard of since the day he successfully tunneled his way to freedom from inside a GOTHAM CITY prison, who has, under the alias Mr. Harrah, succeeded in obtaining a municipal contract to construct a network of storm sewers beneath the streets of Gotham City. Using the sewer construction project as a cover, the Mole and his henchmen have surreptitiously dug a network of underground tunnels leading to and from Gotham City's major banks, so that they can loot the banks and make a hasty subterranean getaway. Ultimately, however, BATMAN, ROBIN, and SUPERMAN discover the ingenious tunneling scheme. Working at super-speed, Superman diverts the direction of the Mole's tunnels so that the villain and his henchmen, intending to tunnel their way into the Gotham Bank, emerge instead inside the grounds of the Gotham City Jail (WF No. 80, Jan/Feb '56: "The Super-Newspaper of Gotham City").

MOLNEY. The leader of a ring of foreign spies who, by August 1964, have managed to steal a top-secret chemical weapon, in pill form, developed by the U.S. Army. "Anyone who swallows the chemical," explains an Army representative to BATMAN, "soon arouses in other people . . . a ***homicidal hatred*** against him! The effect is automatic, overwhelming!"

"All our scientists have to do," gloats Molney meanwhile, "is analyze these pills--make enough of them! Then drop them in a city's water supply. . . !

"In a few hours, the whole city would be in a fury! Everybody attacking everybody else! Our soldiers could just march in and take over!"

Batman and ROBIN smash the spy ring, recover the pills, and turn Molney and his cohorts over to the F.B.I. (Det No. 330: "The Fallen Idol of Gotham City!").

MONK, THE. A cunning and diabolical villain – the texts describe him both as a werewolf and a vampire – whose battles with BATMAN are recorded in Detective Comics No. 31 (Sep '39) and Detective Comics No. 32 (Oct '39). Batman ultimately destroys the Monk and his raven-haired accomplice DALA by firing silver bullets into their bodies as they lie resting in their coffins in the Monk's castle stronghold in far-off Hungaria (Det No. 32, Oct '39).

The chronicles depict the Monk as a "gaunt figure" (Det No. 31, Sep '39) clad in a red robe and full hood with a yellow skull and crossbones emblazoned on the forehead. His precise status in the dark world of the occult remains uncertain: he explicitly refers to Dala and himself as werewolves, but Batman describes them both as vampires and, in fact, the weight of the textual evidence tends to support the latter designation.

Detective Comics No. 31 describes the Monk as "an opponent worthy of [Batman's] metal [sic]. A strange creature, cowled like a monk, but possessing the powers of a Satan! A man whose powers are uncanny.

The Monk © NPP 1939

Whose brain is the product of years of intense study and seclusion!" (Sep '39).

Somewhere in far-off Hungary (Det No. 31, Sep '39) – or Hungaria (Det No. 32, Oct '39) – nestled "in the lost mountains of Cathala by the turbulent river Dess," stands the Monk's towering castle stronghold. The lofty peaks of the Carlathan Mountains rise nearby, but it is not possible to discern from the narrative whether "the lost mountains of Cathala" are situated somewhere in the Carlathan Mountains or whether they represent an entirely separate range of mountains (Det No. 32, Oct '39).

By September 1939 the Monk has placed JULIE MADISON under his hypnotic control, and Batman only narrowly prevents the hypnotized Julie from murdering a man whom the Monk has marked for death. In an effort to uncover the cause of Julie's bizarre behavior, Batman, in his Bruce Wayne identity, takes her to a physician named Dr. Trent for a medical examination, unaware that he, too, has fallen under the Monk's hypnotic control.

Trent informs Wayne that Julie is the victim of hypnosis and recommends a restful ocean voyage – to Paris, and perhaps later to Hungary – to cure her affliction.

Julie promptly boards a ship for Paris, while Batman follows cautiously overhead in his batgyro. At one point, after Batman has descended momentarily from his batgyro to chat with Julie aboard the ocean liner, the Monk appears and attempts to hypnotize them both, and Batman barely manages to escape un-

SUDDENLY A BARRED DOOR DROPS BETWEEN THE BATMAN AND THE MONK...
DIE HERE, YOU FOOL, WHILE I SEND THE GIRL JULIE ON TO MY CASTLE IN HUNGARY TO FEED MY WEREWOLVES

Batman and the Monk © NPP 1939

affected. Later, in Paris, Batman is taken captive by the Monk and left to perish in a grisly deathtrap. He escapes, however, sets out after Julie once again, and soon rescues her from a speeding automobile carrying her toward the Monk's Hungarian castle stronghold, where the villain intends to use her as food for his werewolves.

Grimly, Batman "plans [his] vengeance" against the Monk and, with Julie safe at last, sets out for Hungary in the batgyro (Det No. 31).

Before long, Batman and Julie have arrived in what is now referred to as Hungaria and have rented rooms in a hotel somewhere in the Carlathan Mountains. At one point, Batman pursues a horsedrawn carriage in the mistaken belief that it contains the Monk, only to find a beautiful raven-haired girl named Dala seated inside. To protect Dala from the Monk and his minions, Batman locks her in a hotel room with Julie while he stands guard outside their door. During the night, however, Dala steps into the hallway in a deep trance, with traces of blood on her lips, and Batman races into the hotel room to find Julie Madison lying dead in her bed.

As Batman examines the "two red spots" on her throat which the textual narrative describes as the "marks of the vampire," Dala strikes Batman over the head and flees the hotel room, only to be recaptured by Batman moments later. Dala insists that she is frightened of the Monk and offers to lead him to the villain's sanctuary "in the lost mountains of Cathala by the turbulent river Dess. . . ."

Soon afterward, as the batgyro bearing Batman and Dala hovers over the Monk's stronghold, the Monk forces it to the ground, then hypnotizes Batman and leads him into his towering castle, intending to put him to death.

"Wait," cries Dala, ". . your vengeance must be perfect. First you must bring Julie here! Make the Batman suffer knowing to what fate [vampirism] the girl is doomed!"

The Monk agrees and, "by a tremendous concentration of will . . . forces his [occult] power through space," compelling Julie to rise from her deathbed in the hotel room and make her way to his castle stronghold.

"Soon your Julie will be as we are," gloats the Monk, "—werewolves to ravish on [sic] all living men. . . ."

Seconds later, the Monk transforms himself into a howling wolf to summon a horde of "mountain wolves" to his castle, then transforms himself back into his human form and hurls the hypnotized Batman into a wolf pit.

As Batman falls among the sharp-fanged wolves, however, his "senses return to their full power," and he soon engineers a daring escape from the pit.

Later, during the daytime, as the Monk and Dala lie resting in their coffins, Batman melts down a silver statuette and molds two bullets from the molten silver. Loading the bullets into an automatic pistol, he approaches the villains' coffins and fires point-blank into their bodies. With the Monk dead, his "spell is broken and life returns, once again, to Julie," thus freeing her forever from the awful vampirism the Monk had planned for her.

"I don't know who you are," cries Julie, embracing Batman warmly, "but you saved my life and I shall be forever grateful!" (Det No. 32, Oct '39).

MOON. The only known natural satellite of the Earth.

BATMAN, ROBIN, and SUPERMAN apprehend the villain ROHTUL on the moon in the year 2957 A.D. (WF No. 91, Nov/Dec '57: "The Three Super-Sleepers!").

MOONMAN, THE. A costumed criminal, possessed of awesome magnetic powers which enable him to attract objects with his right hand and repel them with his left, who commits a series of spectacular crimes having the moon as their general theme, as when he steals a precious moonstone from a local museum and an ancient silver chariot, representing the moon chariot of the goddess Diana, from an exhibition of historical vehicles. Unbeknownst even to himself, the Moonman is an astronaut named Rogers, the pilot of the world's "first manned rocket" to the moon, whose simultaneous exposure to the light of the moon and the eerie glow of a passing comet while his craft was still in moon orbit somehow produced the bizarre "chemical reaction" that now transforms him into a cunning super-criminal whenever he becomes exposed to the light of the moon.

"The glow of that strange comet," explains SUPERMAN, "plus the moon's light, must have had a chemical reaction that affected Rogers--which makes him a criminal only at night when moonlight touches him! During the day, he's normal and doesn't remember what happened the night before!"

Rogers commits a series of spectacular crimes as the Moonman before he finally realizes, to his horror, that the notorious Moonman is none other than himself. Before the well-meaning Rogers can turn himself over to the authorities, however, he is abducted by a gang of harbor pirates who hope to force him to use his Moonman powers to aid them in their crimes.

Ultimately, Rogers's Moonman powers permanently

fade and vanish, and Rogers earns an amnesty for the crimes he unintentionally committed by helping BATMAN, ROBIN, and Superman apprehend the harbor pirates who had hoped to profit from his powers (WF No. 98, Dec '58: "The Menace of the Moonman!").

MORANS, MOOSE. A "reputed . . . inventor of ingenious, secret crime devices" who is – along with Silky Steve, a "lone wolf" and "daring plotter," and Sparkles Garnet, a "master of explosives" and "connoisseur of gems" – one of "the country's three biggest crime moguls," all of whom are currently in GOTHAM CITY to attend a major "crime conference." Each is so fanatically determined to "dominate crime" that he is willing to go to almost any lengths to impress his underworld colleagues by staging a successful crime under the noses of BATMAN, ROBIN, and SUPERMAN. The Man of Steel and the Dynamic Duo apprehend the three crime czars in September 1962, however, despite the handicap that has been imposed on them by a freak occurrence that has temporarily transferred Superman's KRYPTONITE vulnerability to Batman, causing Batman to undergo a series of bizarre transformations as the result of his exposure to a red kryptonite sample stored in the BATCAVE (WF No. 128: "The Power That Transformed Batman!").

MORDRED. In Arthurian legend, the slayer of KING ARTHUR – a traitorous knight of the Round Table who is both Arthur's son and nephew by virtue of his having been fathered by Arthur in unconscious incest with his own half-sister. BATMAN and ROBIN smash a conspiracy against Arthur by Mordred and the treacherous QUEEN MORGAN LE FAY during a time-journey to Arthur's Camelot that they make in August–September 1946 (BM No. 36/3: "Sir Batman at King Arthur's Court!").

MORGAN, HENRY. The most famous of the seventeenth-century buccaneers who, knighted eventually by Charles II of England and appointed governor of Jamaica (1674), held this post intermittently until his death in 1688. A born leader and tactician who rapidly achieved top rank among the buccaneers and privateers who plundered the Caribbean in his day, he was probably never guilty of the barbaric cruelty commonly ascribed to him, as in Detective Comics No. 136, where he is portrayed as a murderous pirate chieftain and leader of a band of cutthroats.

Dispatched through the time barrier by PROFESSOR CARTER NICHOLS to the deck of the merchant ship *Spartan* on April 16, 1667, the day it is attacked and looted by Morgan (*ca.* 1635–1688) and his pirates, BATMAN and ROBIN are imprisoned as galley slaves on Morgan's ship. They defeat and outwit the pirates in a series of skirmishes and ultimately blow up Morgan's ship off the Florida Keys before returning to the safety of the twentieth century (Jun '48: "The Dead Man's Chest!").

MORGAN, HOOK. The leader of a gang of ruthless harbor pirates, called "Hook" because his amputated right hand has been replaced by a hook. Morgan and his henchmen – who steal merchandise being unloaded at the waterfront and then sell it through an ostensibly legitimate merchandising firm owned by a confederate – are apprehended by BATMAN and ROBIN in August 1941 (Det No. 54: "Hook Morgan and His Harbor Pirates").

MORGAN LE FAY (Queen). In Arthurian legend, the treacherous sister of KING ARTHUR, and one of the three queens who bore Arthur away to Avalon after he had been mortally wounded by MORDRED on the field of Camlan, in Cornwall. BATMAN and ROBIN smash a conspiracy against Arthur by Mordred and Queen Morgan Le Fay – who in the text is portrayed as a perfect look-alike for the CATWOMAN – during a time-journey to Arthur's Camelot that they make in August–September 1946 (BM No. 36/3: "Sir Batman at King Arthur's Court!").

MORIARTY (Professor). A diabolical English villain who takes his name from a cunning criminal mastermind in the fictional adventures of Sherlock Holmes. "A great criminal, that namesake of mine . . .!" gloats Moriarty. "Holmes himself was in awe of him! Who can outwit me if I adapt his methods?"

In April 1946, after Moriarty and his henchmen have stunned all of London with a "series of breathtaking robberies," Scotland Yard summons the Dynamic Duo to England to aid in the villains' capture. Indeed, BATMAN and ROBIN ultimately apprehend Moriarty and his cohorts with the aid of some somewhat inept assistance from ALFRED (Det No. 110: "Batman and Robin in Scotland Yard!").

MORONI, "BOSS." The gangster, on trial for murder in a GOTHAM CITY courtroom, who hurls a vial of acid at District Attorney Harvey Kent, hideously scarring Kent's face and thus paving the way for Kent's subsequent emergence as the incredible TWO-FACE. Soon afterward, when Kent turns to crime as Two-Face, it is Moroni's two-headed silver dollar, originally intended as an exhibit at his trial, which becomes the lucky coin which Two-Face habitually flips to determine each twist and turn on his grotesque criminal career (Det No. 66, Aug '42: "The Crimes of Two-Face!"). "Boss" Moroni's last name is alternately rendered as Morony (Det No. 187, Sep '52: "The Double Crimes of Two-Face!").

MORTON. The secretary of GOTHAM CITY's "World of the Future" fair, soon to be opened to the general public, and the secret leader of a gang of criminals who use futuristic vehicles and equipment from the fair's exhibits to commit a series of spectacular crimes. Because the bandits employ futuristic costumes and equipment, it is widely believed that they are men from the future who have journeyed back through time to plunder the city, but BATMAN and ROBIN apprehend the criminals and expose Morton as their leader (BM No. 48/3, Aug/Sep '48: "Crime from Tomorrow!").

MORTON, "MUGGSY." One of the cleverest crooks in the country. Morton is secretly the ingenious burglar known as the PHANTOM BANDIT (BM No. 81/3, Feb '54: "The Phantom Bandit of Gotham City!").

MOTH, THE. The leader of a gang of criminals who are apprehended in August 1961 through the heroic efforts of BATMAN, ROBIN, BATWOMAN, and Bat-Girl (*see* BAT-GIRL [BETTY KANE]). The Moth wears a mothlike costume with green wings, a mask equipped with twin antennae and large insectlike eyes, black trunks, and a green-and-yellow striped top (BM No. 141/3: "Batwoman's Junior Partner!"). (*See* BAT-GIRL [BETTY KANE].) The Moth is not to be confused with KILLER MOTH.

MOUSEY. The small-time hoodlum who is secretly MISTER X (BM No. 62/1, Dec/Jan '50–'51: "The Secret Life of the Catwoman").

MOXON, LEW. The racketeer, ex-convict, and onetime bank robber who hired JOE CHILL to murder THOMAS WAYNE, the father of Bruce Wayne, thereby setting in motion the grim chain of events which led ultimately to the emergence of Bruce Wayne as BATMAN. Moxon is killed in September 1956 when he races into the path of a speeding truck while attempting to escape from Batman (Det No. 235: "The First Batman!").

In 1924 — or, to quote the text precisely, "some fifteen years" prior to November 1939 — Thomas Wayne and his wife (*see* WAYNE, MARTHA) and their young son Bruce were on their way home from a movie when suddenly an unidentified gunman leaped from the shadows, announced a holdup, and reached out to grab the necklace around Martha Wayne's neck. When Thomas Wayne attempted to intervene, the gunman shot him dead with a single bullet, then murdered the shrieking Martha Wayne before fading away into the deepening twilight shadows (Det No. 33: "The Batman Wars Against the Dirigible of Doom"; *reprinted in* BM No. 1/1, Spr '40: "The Legend of the Batman — Who He Is and How He Came to Be!").

Later texts asserted that Thomas Wayne died of a bullet wound while Martha Wayne — whose "weak heart could not stand seeing her husband shot down" — died of a heart attack (Det No. 190, Dec '52: "How to Be the Batman!"; *see also* BM No. 47/3, Jun/Jul '48: "The Origin of Batman!"), but the texts are unanimous in their assertion that the dread event marked a crucial turning point in Bruce Wayne's life and fired him with the grim determination to eradicate evil that led to his emergence as Batman. (*See* BATMAN [section A, Origin].)

In June–July 1948, approximately twenty-four years after the death of his parents, Batman encounters their murderer — a criminal named Joe Chill — and grimly sets out to bring him to justice. Chill, however, is shot to death by vengeful hoodlums before Batman can accumulate the hard evidence he needs to take him into custody (BM No. 47/3: "The Origin of Batman!").

In September 1956, while Bruce Wayne and DICK GRAYSON are cleaning out the attic of the Wayne mansion, Grayson accidentally touches a "hidden spring" on Thomas Wayne's old desk, and a "secret drawer" springs suddenly open, revealing an eerie, batlike costume, a can of movie film, and an old diary once kept by Thomas Wayne.

The film, which was made "long, long ago," while Bruce Wayne was still a very young boy, turns out to have been shot at a lavish masquerade ball at which every guest attending was costumed as some sort of "flying creature." Thomas Wayne had won first prize for his spooky "bat-man" costume, now lying in the drawer, while his wife Martha had come costumed as a colorful butterfly.

The old film grinds on, showing the festivities suddenly interrupted by two gunmen who abduct Thomas Wayne from the ballroom, threatening to fire their guns into the crowd if he refuses to join them. At this point, the old film flickers to an end, but Wayne's diary contains entries which shed further light on the violent episode at the masquerade ball:

"Tonight," reads one entry, "Martha and I are going to the annual masquerade ball! Our little boy [Bruce] seems fascinated by my costume. . . ."

Previously, Bruce Wayne had thought that the inspiration for his own Batman costume had been the huge bat which had flown through an open window at the precise moment he was pondering exactly what sort of crime-fighting identity he should assume. Now, however, Wayne realizes that "when that bat flew into my room, it must have prodded my subconscious memory of my father's costume! Now I realize that I adopted a ***Batman*** costume because I remembered my father wearing one!"

Continuing his perusal of the old diary, Wayne learns what happened to his father following his abduction from the masquerade ball: "The gunmen took me to an old warehouse where their boss was in hiding. . . ." There, Wayne had encountered Lew Moxon, a fugitive bank robber who required medical attention after having been wounded by a policeman's bullet. But Thomas Wayne, still clad in his batlike party costume, knew that if he performed the necessary operation on Moxon it would be his last. "I knew," observes the diary, "that once I removed the bullet, Moxon would never let me live to reveal his whereabouts to the police. . . ."

Courageously, the costumed physician had leaped into action, overturning Moxon's chair and disarming his two henchmen with a flurry of rapid-fire punches. Before long, Moxon and his cronies had been turned over to the police, and Moxon had been "sentenced to ten years for armed robbery. . . ."

At his trial, however, Moxon vowed revenge on the man who had helped send him to prison. "You did this to me!" he shouted at Wayne. "I'll get you for this . . . **I'll get you!**"

In the words of Thomas Wayne's diary, "Ten years rolled by! I'd invested my savings wisely and became [sic] wealthy! I'd almost forgotten Moxon until today. . . ."

And then, on the fateful day referred to in the diary, Wayne had encountered Lew Moxon, newly released from prison, walking down a city street. **"Moxon,"** cried Wayne, **"--free!"**

"Yeah," replied Moxon with a sneer, "--I served my ten years in jail--where **you** put me! I swore I'd get you, and I will! But I'm too smart to do it myself! The police would arrest me on suspicion fast! I'll get someone else to do it for me!"

On that menacing note, Thomas Wayne's diary ends, but even now its revelations hold a grim significance for Bruce Wayne. "This means Joey Chill only ***pretended*** to be a holdup man," exclaims Wayne, "--actually he was Moxon's ***hired killer!*** Moxon must have ordered Chill **not** to kill me, too--so I'd be alive to testify that my parents were killed by a robber!"

"Gosh, Bruce," exclaims Dick Grayson, "--Moxon used **you** as his **alibi!**"

"He used me as a coverup for his deliberate murder of my parents!" observes Wayne angrily. "Put on your [Robin] costume, Dick--**we've just reopened the Wayne murder case!**"

Later, after POLICE COMMISSIONER GORDON has helped Batman and ROBIN uncover Lew Moxon's current whereabouts, the Dynamic Duo head "out west," to Coastal City, where their quarry is now engaged in "the billboard blimp business," — the use of dirigibles to carry advertising messages. With him in the BATPLANE, Batman carries his father's old bat-man costume, for it gives him "the feeling that my father is with me on this case!"

After a furious battle with Moxon and his gunmen at the headquarters of the Moxon Sky-Hi Advertising Co., Batman and Robin apprehend Moxon and take him to police headquarters, but Moxon denies any connection with Thomas Wayne's murder and offers to undergo a lie-detector test to prove it. Indeed, to Batman's surprise and chagrin, a polygraph test establishes beyond a doubt that Moxon is telling the truth when he insists that he has never heard of Joe Chill, known Thomas Wayne, or had any involvement whatever in Thomas Wayne's murder. Batman is forced to look on helplessly as Moxon is set free for lack of incriminating evidence.

A chance remark by Robin, however, gives Batman a hunch and inspires him to put through a long-distance telephone call to Police Commissioner Gordon in GOTHAM CITY. Sure enough, as Batman had suspected, Moxon had injured his head in an automobile accident shortly after the Wayne murder and had wandered away from the hospital and disappeared soon after receiving treatment. **"Robin,"** exclaims Batman, "that head injury gave Moxon **amnesia, loss of memory!** He doesn't remember my father or anything that happened before the auto accident!"

"Golly! What'll we do now?" asks Robin.

"Keep after Moxon!" replies Batman. "He must be involved in something shady--otherwise his men wouldn't have jumped us! Tonight we're going to trail his [advertising] blimp!"

That night, Batman's hunch pays off again. Moxon's advertising blimp, they discover, is being used at night for a series of "sky-high burglary jobs," and the Dynamic Duo soon apprehend Moxon's henchmen in the act of descending the blimp's rope ladder toward the roof of a lavish penthouse. Now, with at least a burglary charge to pin on Moxon, Batman sets out for Moxon's headquarters to arrest the gang boss again. His costume, however, has been badly torn in the recent fighting, and all his spare costumes are back in Gotham City. "Say," suggests Robin, "--how about wearing **your father's costume?**" "Yes--it would be appropriate!" replies Batman. "It'd be almost as if Dad were arresting Moxon!"

"Later, alone in his office, Moxon looks up to see a grim figure framed in the doorway!" It is Batman, wearing the eerie bat-man costume that his father had worn to that fateful masquerade party many years before.

As the startled Moxon stares at the strange figure framed in his doorway, a dim memory begins to stir deep in the subconscious recesses of his mind. "That costume," he murmurs uncertainly, "--I've seen it before--long ago! I'm beginning to remember--a doctor--Doc Wayne--he wore that costume!"

"Great Scott!" realizes Batman with a start. "I didn't realize the shock of seeing this costume would jar Moxon's memory!"

By now, Moxon's memory of those long-ago events has returned completely, and he stares transfixed with terror at the grim-faced figure before him. "Go away!" cries Moxon. "You're dead! I had Joey Chill kill you! Leave me alone!"

"Fear-ridden, Moxon wrenches open a side-door and rushes out into the night. . . ."

"He's come back to haunt me!" shrieks the panic-stricken Moxon. "I've got to get away--**get away!** . . ."

Consumed with guilt and terror, Moxon is blind to the bright red truck speeding toward him down the busy street. Before Batman can intervene, there is "a screech of brakes--a cry--and Moxon's career of violence ends in violence. . . ."

"I wanted to take him alive," muses Batman, ". . . to stand trial for his crimes . . . but his own guilt convicted him!" (Det No. 235: "The First Batman!").

MULTICREATURE, THE. A bizarre creature which possesses the uncanny ability to evolve, instantaneously and continually, into whatever forms of life are most likely to ensure its survival from moment to moment. "The normal evolutionary process is gradual," explains BATMAN, "over thousands of years . . . but this freak creature apparently can evolve ***instantly!*** It's able to adapt to a more defensive shape to meet any new threat!"

The "multicreature" first comes into being in February 1961, when "a lightning bolt strikes a pool of water seeping up from an underground pipe carrying waste materials from a chemical plant. . . . As the electricity courses through the chemical mixture, a freakish thing occurs--a new form of life is born. . . . While the storm snarls and screams overhead, the tiny form of life begins to grow--and **grow** . . . until, as the storm subsides, the creature begins to **walk!**"

For a time, it appears that efforts to defeat the multicreature are doomed to futility, but Batman ultimately succeeds in transforming the creature back into its original form — a harmless pool of water — by striking it with a harpoon wired to an electrical dynamo (Det No. 288: "The Menace of the Multiple Creature!").

MURIETA, JOAQUÍN. A ruthless desperado active in California during the days of the California gold rush, a "scourge of the gold fields" who is described in Batman

No. 58/2 as "California's most notorious outlaw of all time."

Dispatched through the time barrier by PROFESSOR CARTER NICHOLS to Columbia, California, in the year 1854, BATMAN and ROBIN capture Murieta and his gang with the aid of a local posse and solve the century-old mystery surrounding the disappearance of the great-grandfather of a close friend of BRUCE WAYNE, who struck it rich in the heyday of the gold rush and then vanished without a trace while en route eastward with a fortune in gold and $250,000 in cash (Apr/May '50: "The Brand of a Hero!").

MUSKETEER, THE. A French crime-fighter whose methods and techniques are modeled after those of America's BATMAN.

In January 1955, in response to Batman's personal invitation, the Musketeer and other foreign lawmen – including the RANGER, the LEGIONARY, the GAUCHO, and the KNIGHT and the SQUIRE – arrive in GOTHAM CITY to study Batman's techniques firsthand, only to find themselves embroiled in a deadly battle of wits with "underworld chieftain" "KNOTS" CARDINE (Det No. 215: "The Batmen of All Nations!").

The Musketeer in action, 1955 © NPP 1955

In July–August 1957 the Musketeer visits the United States once again, this time in response to a summons from "well-known philanthropist" John Mayhew, who wishes to award the Musketeer and other world-famous crime-fighters – including Batman and ROBIN, SUPERMAN, the Gaucho, the Legionary, and the Knight and the Squire – charter membership in his newly formed Club of Heroes (WF No. 89: "The Club of Heroes!"). (*See also* BATMAN [section F, the Batman counterparts]; LIGHTNING-MAN.)

MXYZPTLK (Mr.). A mischievous imp from the fifth dimension, endowed with extraordinary extra-dimensional powers similar if not identical to those possessed by BAT-MITE, who has for more than three decades been making periodic forays into the earthly dimension to pester, bedevil, and infuriate SUPERMAN.

Superman's only means of ridding himself of this pesky fifth-dimensional sprite is to trick him into pronouncinghisownname – Mxyzptlk – backwards,which has the effect of temporarily returning Mr. Mxyzptlk to his home dimension. Mxyzptlk is pronounced Mix-yez-pitel-ick. Mxyzptlk backwards – Kltpzyxm – is pronounced Kel-tipz-yex-im.

In November 1960 (WF No. 113: "Bat-Mite Meets Mr. Mxyzptlk!"), February 1962 (WF No. 123: "The Incredible Team of Bat-Mite and Mr. Mxyzptlk!"), and again in September 1965 (WF No. 152: "The Colossal Kids!" pts. I–II – no title; "The Magic of Bat-Mite and Mr. Mxyzptlk!"), Mr. Mxyzptlk visits the earthly dimension for a series of encounters with the mischievous Bat-Mite. (*See* BAT-MITE.) (For a complete account of Mr. Mxyzptlk's entire mischievous career, consult *The Encyclopedia of Comic Book Heroes: Volume VI – Superman.*)

Mr. Mxyzptlk © NPP 1976

MYSTERY (Mr.). The pen name of a mysterious correspondent who writes a series of letters to BATMAN in December 1954 which indicate that he has been secretly following the Dynamic Duo everywhere and has managed to unravel his secret identity. Ultimately, however, ROBIN deduces that Batman must have written the letters himself, for only he could have possessed the firsthand knowledge contained in them.

"Yes--I wrote the letters!" admits Batman finally. "The whole plan was a test case to see if you could ***really*** find a person trying to shadow us! Your deductions ruled out everybody but me--the culprit!" (BM No. 88/2: "Three Letters to Batman!").

MYSTERY ANALYSTS OF GOTHAM CITY, THE. An exclusive club whose members are "experts at the business of solving bizarre mysteries."

"Solution to exceptional mysteries," explains POLICE COMMISSIONER GORDON in June 1964, "is an essential qualification for membership . . ." (BM No. 164/2: "Batman's Great Face-Saving Feat!").

Its members meet monthly (BM No. 174/2, Sep '65: "The Off-Again On-Again Lightbulbs!") on a "sprawling estate" somewhere in or near GOTHAM CITY (BM No. 168/2, Dec '64: "How to Solve a Perfect Crime--in Reverse!"). The members of the club – which is occasionally referred to as the Mystery Analysts Club – include BATMAN; Police Commissioner Gordon; State University professor Ralph Vern, "whose laboratory sleuthing [has] led to the conviction of a score of criminals"; newspaper reporter Art Saddows, "winner of the ***'Front Page Award'*** for his successes in cracking unsolved crime cases"; mystery novelist Kaye Daye, "whose fictional version of Judge Blader's strange disappearance led to the solution of that real-life mystery" (BM No. 164/2, Jun '64: "Batman's Great Face-Saving Feat!"); District Attorney Danton; and "armchair sleuth" Martin Tellman (BM No. 168/2, Dec '64: "How to Solve a Perfect Crime--in Reverse!").

PROF. RALPH VERN is presumably dismissed from the club in December 1964, after the careful sleuthing of Batman and ROBIN has led to his arrest on a charge of jewel theft (BM No. 168/2: "How to Solve a Perfect Crime--in Reverse!").

MYSTERYMAN. A mysterious costumed crime-fighter who appears in GOTHAM CITY in July 1957 and helps BATMAN and ROBIN apprehend a gang of criminals who have been smuggling fugitive criminals out of the city. Mysteryman is none other than POLICE COMMISSIONER GORDON (Det No. 245: "The Dynamic Trio!").

N

NAIROMI, SHAH OF. The ruler of a country which "contains the single largest source of uranium in the world." The Shah precipitates a major crisis in BATMAN's life in October–November 1953, when he announces that he has fallen in love with photographer VICKI VALE (BM No. 79/1: "Bride of Batman!"). (See VALE, VICKI.)

NAKOR. The far-distant planet, located somewhere "far beyond [Earth's] solar system," which is the home of the villainous TORG (Det No. 295, Sep '61: "The Secret of the Beast Paintings!").

NAMTAB, I. A fictitious name which BATMAN inserts into a phony newspaper story in December 1941–January 1942 as part of his plan to trap the JOKER (BM No. 8/4: "The Cross Country Crimes!"). Namtab is Batman spelled backwards.

NARKIN. The foreman of a sugar plantation on the Hawaiian island of Oahu. Narkin is secretly MR. 50 (BM No. 145/1, Feb '62: "Hunt for Mr. 50").

NASON, CHARLES "BLACKIE." A "mysterious bandit," captured by BATMAN sometime in the past after he had eluded the police for more than two years, who has escaped from prison, had his face remodeled by a plastic surgeon, and compiled an extensive "cops' gallery" – the underworld counterpart of the police department's rogues' gallery – containing photographs and descriptions of virtually every important law-enforcement officer and private investigator in the country. For a time, Nason becomes prosperous by charging underworld figures fat fees for checking photographs of their new members against the photographs in the cops' gallery as a means of preventing infiltration of their mobs by law-enforcement agents. Ultimately, however, while attempting to escape from Batman and ROBIN, he is struck on the head and killed by the wheel of an airplane (Det No. 141, Nov '48: "The Gallery of Public Heroes!").

NEERY, DUDS. The leader of a gang of criminals who are apprehended by BATMAN and ROBIN in August–September 1947, during a period when Batman is suffering through three days of temporary but total blindness resulting from his recent rescue of a young girl from a raging fire while in his Bruce Wayne identity. Since Neery has already become convinced that Bruce Wayne is secretly Batman, Batman finds himself compelled not only to battle Neery and his henchmen while straining under the weight of his devastating handicap, but to do so without revealing his blindness for fear of betraying his secret identity. Batman and Robin ultimately apprehend the criminals, however, while successfully persuading them that they have erred in believing Bruce Wayne is Batman (BM No. 42/2: "Blind Man's Bluff!").

NEST, THE. A lavish restaurant opened by the PENGUIN in August–September 1946 as part of his scheme to accumulate the signatures of wealthy men so that he can have a famous forger copy them onto blank checks (BM No. 36/1: "The Penguin's Nest!").

NEVAL, ODO. A cunning criminal who, with his accomplice Marden, concocts an elaborate scheme to persuade the underworld that Neval is in reality a scientist of ancient ATLANTIS who has survived for centuries with the aid of a fabulous "elixir of immortality" which has rendered him invulnerable to the aging process and impervious to physical harm. Together, Neval and Marden hope to dupe the "crime-kings" of GOTHAM CITY into paying $100,000 each to sample their elixir, but BATMAN soon discovers that the elixir is fraudulent and, with ROBIN's help, apprehends Neval, Marden, and various members of their underworld clientele (Det No. 204, Feb '54: "The Man Who Could Live Forever!").

NICHOLS, CARTER (Professor). The renowned GOTHAM CITY scientist, historian (WF No. 82, May/Jun '56: "The Three Super-Musketeers!"), and "student of the mysteries of the subconscious mind" (Det No. 116, Oct '46: "The Rescue of Robin Hood!") who has come to be regarded as "the world's foremost authority on time-travel" (BM No. 36/3, Aug/Sep '46: "Sir Batman at King Arthur's Court!").

Professor Carter Nichols, Dick Grayson, and Bruce Wayne, 1946 © NPP 1946

On more than thirty separate occasions, beginning in August–September 1944 (BM No. 24/1: "It Happened in Rome"), Professor Nichols has used his "weird powers of hypnosis" (Det No. 135, May '48: "The True Story of

Frankenstein!") and incredible time-traveling apparatus to transmit BATMAN and ROBIN across the time barrier, either into the distant future or the misty past. He is completely unaware of the fact that his friends Bruce Wayne and Dick Grayson are secretly Batman and Robin.

In August–September 1944 Professor Nichols performs a daring "hypnotic experiment" which enables him to "project" his friends Bruce Wayne and Dick Grayson across the time barrier to the days of ancient Rome, where, as Batman and Robin, they battle ruthless "Roman racketeer" PUBLIUS MALCHIO (BM No. 24/1: "It Happened in Rome").

In December 1945–January 1946 Professor Nichols uses his ingenious hypnotic technique to transport Bruce Wayne and Dick Grayson to seventeenth-century France, during the time of the THREE MUSKETEERS, "when swords were deciding whether King Louis XIII or Richelieu was the real ruler of France!" (BM No. 32/3: "All for One, One for All!").

In August–September 1946 Professor Nichols uses his "special hypnosis" to send Bruce Wayne and Dick Grayson back into the past, to the court of KING ARTHUR, to verify an account, contained in a recently discovered historical document, of SIR HARDI LE NOIR, a knight reported to have performed some feats that "smack of modern science" (BM No. 36/3: "Sir Batman at King Arthur's Court!").

In October 1946 Professor Nichols uses hypnosis to send Bruce Wayne and Dick Grayson to Sherwood Forest in thirteenth-century England where, as Batman and Robin, they meet the legendary ROBIN HOOD and match wits with the evil Sheriff of Nottingham (Det No. 116: "The Rescue of Robin Hood!").

In December 1946–January 1947 Professor Nichols uses his hypnotic powers to transport Bruce Wayne and Dick Grayson to Athens, Greece, in the fifth-century B.C. where, as Batman and Robin, they thwart attempts by the evil BYRUS to disrupt the Olympic games (BM No. 38/1: "Peril in Greece!").

In October–November 1947 Professor Nichols is imprisoned in his own home and then impersonated by gang leader MARTIN BAIN, but Batman and Robin, aided by members of the Gotham City Police Department, ultimately apprehend Bain and his henchmen and rescue Nichols from their clutches (BM No. 43/3: "The Four Horsemen of Crime!").

In December 1947–January 1948 Professor Nichols uses hypnosis to transport Bruce Wayne and Dick Grayson to Philadelphia in the year 1787, where, as Batman and Robin, they accumulate evidence to help them clear the name of SILAS WAYNE, an ancestor of Bruce Wayne accused of having been a highwayman (BM No. 44/3: "The First American Detective!").

In April–May 1948 Professor Nichols uses his "special hypnotic technique" to send Bruce Wayne and Dick Grayson to the city of Milan in the year 1499 to verify an account, contained in an ancient document, of a mysterious Batman alleged to have performed some remarkable feats of magic there. In fifteenth-century Milan, Batman and Robin make the acquaintance of LEONARDO DA VINCI (BM No. 46/3: "The Batman That History Forgot!").

In May 1948 Professor Nichols uses his "powers of time-hypnosis" to transport himself back through time to the Europe of 150 years ago, where he hopes to verify the claim of an old document that the fictional BARON FRANKENSTEIN and his monster actually existed. When Nichols encounters difficulties in the past, he "projects his weird powers of hypnosis across the years" to summon Batman and Robin to his aid (Det No. 135: "The True Story of Frankenstein!"). This adventure marks the first occasion that Nichols has himself traveled into the past.

In June 1948 Professor Nichols transports Bruce Wayne and Dick Grayson back into the past – to the deck of the merchant ship *Spartan* on April 16, 1667 – to verify the authenticity of a controversial treasure map allegedly left behind by HENRY MORGAN and his band of pirates (Det No. 136: "The Dead Man's Chest!").

In October–November 1948 Professor Nichols uses his "weird hypnosis" to transport Bruce Wayne and Dick Grayson into the past, to the ancient city of Baghdad, where they hope to learn how the image of the JOKER came to be woven into a thousand-year-old Oriental rug they recently purchased at a public auction. The picture, they learn, is not of the Joker at all, but of an ancient villain known as the CRIER (BM No. 49/3: "Batman's Arabian Nights!").

In April–May 1949 Professor Nichols uses hypnosis to transport Bruce Wayne and Dick Grayson to Norway in the year 990 A.D., where they hope to prove that Viking OLAF ERICKSON – a Bruce Wayne look-alike – was unjustly accused of cowardice by his fellow Norsemen. In this text, time-travel is described as "a sensation of falling through darkness," followed by "a shock of blinding light . . ." (BM No. 52/2: "Batman and the Vikings!").

In September–October 1949 Professor Nichols uses hypnosis to send Bruce Wayne and Dick Grayson to China in the year 1275 A.D., where they hope to solve the mystery of an ancient fireworks rocket which, when found and exploded in the twentieth century, blazed into a fireworks portrait of Batman. In ancient China, Batman and Robin make the acquaintance of KUBLA KHAN and MARCO POLO (WF No. 42: "The Amazing Adventure of Batman and Marco Polo!").

In April–May 1950 Professor Nichols sends Bruce Wayne and Dick Grayson back into the past, to Columbia, California, in the year 1854, where they encounter JOAQUIN MURIETA, the "scourge of the gold fields" (BM No. 58/2: "The Brand of a Hero!").

In June–July 1950 Professor Nichols attempts to send Bruce Wayne and Dick Grayson back 100 years into the past, but accidentally transports them 100 years into the future instead, to the year 2050 A.D., where they make the acquaintance of CHIEF ROKEJ, a direct descendant of the JOKER who is Gotham City's chief of police. Because Professor Nichols had recently been contemplating the question of whether his hypnotic technique could successfully transport his subjects into the future as well as into the past, his mental preoccupation with the future had caused Bruce Wayne and Dick Grayson to be transported into the future by mistake (BM No. 59/3: "Batman in the Future!"). The adventure represents the Dynamic Duo's first journey into the future.

In January 1951 Professor Nichols sends Bruce Wayne and Dick Grayson back into the past, to ancient Egypt during the reign of CLEOPATRA, where they hope to learn how a picture of the BAT-SIGNAL came to be inscribed on an ancient Egyptian frieze recently unveiled at the Gotham City Museum (Det No. 167: "Bodyguards to Cleopatra!").

In October–November 1953 Professor Nichols – here described as the "scientific master of an hypnosis time-travel technique" – transports Bruce Wayne and Dick Grayson back to Gotham City in the year 1753, where they hope to prove that a fortune in gold in the possession of a hijacker named WALTER FRALEY is not, as he claims, gold buried in 1753 by a highwayman, but rather gold that Fraley and a cohort have recently hijacked from a modern gold train (BM No. 79/2: "The Batman of Yesterday!").

In March 1954 Professor Nichols – here described as "a scientist whose unique methods have succeeded in penetrating the **time barrier** . . ." – transports Bruce Wayne and Dick Grayson to the site of Gotham City in the seventeenth century, where they hope to learn the origin of a mysterious fragment of Indian pottery, unearthed in the BATCAVE, which bears the strange inscription "Death to the man of two identities!" In the past, Batman and Robin meet JEREMY COE, a courageous Colonial spy who poses as an Indian to obtain advance warning of impending Indian attacks.

This adventure marks the first occasion that Professor Nichols hypnotizes Wayne and Grayson and then exposes them to the black lightninglike rays emanating from a complex "time machine" which he operates from a special console in his "strange laboratory." The precise functions of the hypnosis and the time machine are not disclosed. Bruce Wayne and Dick Grayson experience "a weird ringing in their ears--the sensation of dropping off into a bottomless abyss, [and the feeling of] being caught up in a giant whirlpool of blackness . . . [as they] begin their fantastic trip back through the centuries!" (Det No. 205: "The Origin of the Bat-Cave!").

In February 1955 Professor Nichols transports Bruce Wayne and Dick Grayson back into the past, to the year 1854, where they hope to clear the name of CAPTAIN JOHN GORDON, a Mississippi showboat captain and ancestor of POLICE COMMISSIONER GORDON accused of having been the "central figure" in a series of daring robberies. In this text, Professor Nichols employs his hypnotic technique exclusively, enhanced only by some elaborate spotlights that play upon the faces of Wayne and Grayson (BM No. 89/1: "River Rogues").

In August 1955 Professor Nichols – here described as a man whose "scientific genius has mastered time" – transports Bruce Wayne and Dick Grayson to the Stone Age, where they hope to establish the authenticity of a controversial cave painting recently unearthed by Dr. William Sayre, which portrays the historically unlikely scene of a tyrannosaurus chasing some cavemen. It is during this time-journey that Batman and Robin encounter the incredible TIGER MAN. In this text, Wayne and Grayson experience "a moment of darkness, [and] a strange sense of falling . . ." as they cross the time barrier into the past (BM No. 93/3: "The Caveman Batman").

In November–December 1955, after Professor Nichols has placed Bruce Wayne and Dick Grayson in "an hypnotic trance" and propelled them back into the past, to the Baghdad of 1,000 years ago, to verify the authenticity of an ancient tradition concerning a "magnetic mountain" near the city, Batman and Robin find that "the terrific magnetic forces" of the magnetic mountain "interfere with [Nichols's] time-force" and prevent him from returning them to their own time. Nichols, however, calls on SUPERMAN, who uses "his full awesome speed to break through the barriers of time and space" and return Batman and Robin to the present. While they are in the past, Batman, Robin, and Superman meet the legendary ALADDIN (WF No. 79: "The Three Magicians of Bagdad!").

In March 1956 Professor Nichols uses hypnotism to transport Batman and Robin to Paris, France, in the year 1900, where they hope to make contact with author JULES VERNE. Eventually, Verne returns with Batman and Robin to the present, although exactly how he is able to do this is never explained. Later, after Verne's work in the twentieth century has been completed, Professor Nichols returns him to his own time by means of hypnosis. In this text, for the first time, Nichols informs Batman and Robin that they will have only three hours in the past, after which they will be returned automatically to the present (BM No. 98/1, "The Return of Mr. Future!").

In April 1956 Professor Nichols – here described as a scientist who has "mastered the secret of the time-space barrier" – transports Bruce Wayne and Dick Grayson to the Western frontier town of Plain City in the year 1880, where they hope to solve the questions raised by an old newspaper, recently uncovered in a Gotham City curio shop, which seems to indicate that Batman was once a marshal in the Old West and that he used a pistol to apprehend an outlaw. During this time-journey, Batman and Robin make the acquaintance of the legendary BAT MASTERSON. In this text, Wayne and Grayson lie flat on special tables in Professor Nichols's laboratory while special lamplike objects shoot bolts of yellow lightninglike energy at them and Nichols stands over them muttering, "Back . . . back to the frontier of 1880 . . ." (BM No. 99/2: "Batman--Frontier Marshal").

In May–June 1956 Professor Nichols – here described as a "famous historian and scientist of Gotham City" – transports Bruce Wayne, Dick Grayson, and CLARK KENT to France in the year 1696 in the hope that they will be able to uncover the answer to "history's greatest riddle," the identity of the famous "man in the iron mask." In the course of this adventure, Batman and Robin once again make the acquaintance of the THREE MUSKETEERS.

In this text, ". . . the great scholar [Nichols] employs

his secret, powerful **time-ray**" to propel his subjects into the past. The three time-travelers sit in large chairs beneath a single large light — evidently the "time-ray" — while Nichols stands over them, waving his arms hypnotically (WF No. 82: "The Three Super-Musketeers!").

In September 1956 Bruce Wayne and Dick Grayson recall a past adventure — not previously recorded in the chronicles — which took place when Professor Nichols transported them back into the past, to ancient Babylon to uncover the truth behind a mysterious tradition which holds that the Babylon of 3,000 years ago was ruled by a monarch known only as the "king who never existed." Now, however — because they traveled into the past as Bruce Wayne and Dick Grayson, and not as Batman and Robin — their secret identities have been jeopardized by archaeologist Horace Halley's recent discovery of an ancient Babylonian wall painting showing Batman battling a soldier (BM No. 102/2: "The Batman from Babylon"). (*See* BARTOR, BRAND.)

In December 1957 Bruce Wayne and Dick Grayson arrive in Carter Nichols's laboratory to witness the unveiling of what Nichols describes as "my greatest achievement . . . the time-ray I developed from my time hypnosis technique!" It is not clear exactly how this time-ray differs from the one unveiled in May–June 1956, but the text describes its initial testing by Nichols as "his most dangerous experiment."

Nichols announces that he intends to send himself back to ancient Rome to enable him to view the city with his own eyes. "This machine," explains Nichols, "includes an automatic control, which, in exactly 10 days, will turn the [time] ray on and draw me back here--provided I'm in the exact same place it sends me to!"

Bruce Wayne protests that the trip through time is too dangerous an undertaking for Nichols and insists that he and Dick Grayson make the journey instead. Nichols, however, remains adamant. Moments later, after he has seated himself in a special chair, "a mighty

Professor Carter Nichols, Bruce Wayne, and Dick Grayson, 1957 © NPP 1957

force streams from the projector" of the time-ray and Professor Nichols vanishes into the past.

Ten days later, Wayne and Grayson return to Nichols's laboratory to witness his return, but Nichols fails to materialize despite the fact that his "return time-ray" appears to be functioning normally. Fearful that some mishap may have befallen their friend, Batman and Robin set the time-ray's automatic controls to return them to Nichols's laboratory in ten days and then activate the time-ray to transport them to ancient Rome.

In Rome, the Dynamic Duo discover that Nichols has been carried captive to the castle of King Phorbus of Rhodes, who hopes to force the professor to "make magic weapons" for himself and his army. On Rhodes, Batman and Robin are also taken captive, but King Phorbus promises to grant his three prisoners their freedom if they will agree to manufacture "future-type weapons" for him. Batman agrees, but under the guise of constructing a new weapon, he and his companions build a giant balloon to carry them back to Rome, where the self-activating time-ray emerges to propel them back into the twentieth century.

"You saved me, ***Batman,***" says Nichols gratefully, "--but ***I*** never want to go into the past again! I'll send Bruce Wayne and his ward, instead!" (BM No. 112/2: "Batman's Roman Holiday!").

In April 1958 Professor Nichols transports Batman and Robin to the Middle Eastern valley stronghold of the ancient Zotos in the year 700 A.D., where they hope to solve the mystery behind the strange underground huts, giant lookout pole, and gigantic sling that modern archaeologists have discovered at the site. In the past, Batman and Robin help TANG and his fellow Zotos defend themselves against "the terrible river canyon giants." In this text, Professor Nichols employs new time-traveling equipment closely resembling a set of professional hair dryers (BM No. 115/3: "Batman in the Bottle!").

In August 1959, after a curator at the Gotham Art Museum has been accused of deliberately purchasing a forged painting attributed to the seventeenth-century Venetian painter Verillo, Professor Nichols sends Batman and Robin into the past to verify the authenticity of the disputed painting. In seventeenth-century Venice, the Dynamic Duo quickly establish the painting's authenticity, but when they attempt to return to the present, a momentary malfunction in Professor Nichols's time machine — produced by a bolt of lightning striking a high-voltage electrical line leading to Nichols's laboratory — causes Batman to arrive safely in Nichols's laboratory, while Robin is transmitted to a point in time three days farther into the future.

Within moments, Nichols has repaired his machine and returned Robin to the present, but during his brief sojourn in the near-future Robin saw a newspaper story telling of Batman's violent death, and now he feels certain that Batman is fated to die within the next three days. After three days have elapsed, the dreaded obituary does indeed appear in print, but Batman is still very much alive. The newspaper story was an inaccurate one, called in to a local newspaper prematurely by a reporter who thought Batman had been

Professor Carter Nichols, Dick Grayson, and Bruce Wayne, 1959 © NPP 1959

killed in an encounter with a criminal (BM No. 125/2: "The Last Days of Batman").

In October 1959 Professor Nichols unveils a new invention designed to reveal the future as it might have been if past events had been different from what they actually were. The subject need only don the special headgear and think of a past event which greatly influenced his life, and the machine "will reveal to [his] mind's eye the life [he] ***might*** have had!"

When Bruce Wayne steps beneath the machine, he thinks back to the brutal murder of his parents and wonders what his life would have been like had they died in an automobile accident instead. The machine informs him that he still would have become Batman, although under different circumstances (BM No. 127/2: "The Second Life of Batman").

In February 1960 Professor Nichols transports Batman and Robin back into the past, to the time just after Alexander the Great had been crowned king following the death of his father, Philip of Macedonia.

"I've made several improvements on my time-machine!" explains Nichols. One of these is a portable "time-box": by pushing a button on the time-box, a time-traveler "can return to the present whenever [he's] ready," and the time-box will transport not only its wearer, but anyone who happens to be standing "within the box's time-field." Another new development is the "time-scanner," a televisionlike device in Nichols's laboratory which enables him to observe the activities of his time-travelers firsthand.

At one point, after Batman's time-box has become damaged and he and Robin have been marooned in the past, Nichols summons Superman to his laboratory. "If anything goes wrong with the time-box," explains Nichols, "it automatically starts my ***time-scanner***--and it shows ***Batman*** and ***Robin*** are trapped, unable to return!"

After Nichols has shown Superman how to repair the time-box, the Man of Steel travels swiftly into the past, repairs Batman's time-box, and returns with Batman and Robin to the present (WF No. 107: "The Secret of the Time Creature!").

In September 1961 Professor Nichols transports Batman and Robin to ancient Egypt to unravel the mystery behind two recently unearthed Egyptian wall paintings: one shows Batman and Robin in red costumes, speaking with a pharaoh in an ancient throne room, while the other portrays Batman battling two huge beasts. In ancient Egypt, Batman and Robin encounter a band of aliens from the planet NAKOR under the command of the villainous TORG. In this text, Professor Nichols makes the observation that ". . . my frail body can't withstand the strain of time-travel . . ." (Det No. 295: "The Secret of the Beast Paintings!").

By March 1963, escaped convicts DENNY KALE and Shorty Biggs have imprisoned and impersonated Batman and Robin and tricked Professor Nichols into transporting them into the past, to the city of Florence in the year 1479, where they think their twentieth-century knowhow will enable them to amass wealth rapidly. When the two time-travelers fail to return to the present, Superman journeys to fifteenth-century Florence to search for them, but Kale and Biggs capture Superman and leave him to die with a piece of synthetic KRYPTONITE chained to his chest. Ultimately, however, Batman and Robin escape from their place of imprisonment and have Professor Nichols send them into the past, where they rescue Superman and, with his help, take Kale and Biggs into custody (WF No. 132: "Batman and Robin, Medieval Bandits!").

A text for August 1963 describes an adventure – purported to have taken place during June 1963 – in which Professor Nichols used his time-machine to transport Batman and Robin to ancient Norseland in the year 522 A.D., where they made the acquaintance of the legendary Thor (WF No. 135: "The Menace of the Future Man!"). (*See* DURR, JON.)

In December 1963 Professor Nichols uses his time machine to transport Batman and Robin 50,000 years into the past, where they hope to learn how to save Earth from an impending alien invasion (WF No. 138: "The Secret of the Captive Cavemen!"). (*See* GROTE [GENERAL].)

NIGHTWING. An alternate identity employed by SUPERMAN on those occasions when he and JIMMY OLSEN, employing the name FLAMEBIRD, participate in adventures together inside the bottle city of KANDOR. The Prussian-blue color of Superman's Nightwing costume is reminiscent of the plumage of the nightwing, a Kandorian bird.

NIGMA, EDWARD. The man who achieves infamy as the RIDDLER (Det No. 140, Oct '48: "The Riddler").

NINE OLD MEN, THE. A gang of elderly criminals organized and led by Pop Davies, a bitter, hateful old man who forms the Nine Old Men following his release from Northern Penitentiary after serving a thirty-year term, when he finds that because of his advanced age he is unable to obtain membership in any established underworld gang. By capitalizing on the arcane knowledge that their old age has given them, however – e.g., their familiarity with abandoned sewer systems, forgotten subterranean rivers, and the like – the Nine Old Men commit a series of spectacular crimes which establish them as the most successful gang in GOTHAM CITY.

At one point, BATMAN finds his secret identity in jeopardy when the Nine Old Men decide to rob BRUCE WAYNE by tunneling into the Wayne mansion through the long-forgotten Anderson's Cave running directly beneath it. Unknown to Davies and his henchmen, however, Anderson's Cave is now the BATCAVE, and one glimpse of the crime-fighting equipment now housed there would betray the secret identities of Batman and ROBIN.

Ultimately, however, special security devices installed by Batman succeed in maintaining the batcave's secrecy, and the Dynamic Duo apprehend the criminals in April–May 1951 (BM No. 64/2: "The Forgotten Men of Crime!"). (*See also* BATMAN [section D, the batcave].)

NOLAN, FINGERS. A jewel thief who returns to GOTHAM CITY's Mechanical Museum of Natural History in May 1958 in an effort to recover a stolen pearl necklace he hid previously in one of the exhibits. Nolan is apprehended by BATMAN and ROBIN, who have come to the museum to investigate the murder of PROFESSOR HALE (Det No. 255: "Death in Dinosaur Hall!").

NORBET (Professor). The eminent scientist who achieves infamy as the PLANET-MASTER (Det No. 296, Oct '61: "The Menace of the Planet Master!").

NOYES. An alias employed – according to Batman No. 110/2 – by BATMAN shortly after hiring ALFRED as his butler when he posed as an underworld character seeking confidential information concerning BRUCE WAYNE's habits and activities to help him ascertain whether Alfred would be a trustworthy butler (Sep '57: "The Secret of Batman's Butler"). (*See* ALFRED.)

NUMBERS. A wily criminal who, convinced that three is his lucky number, commits a series of spectacular crimes revolving around the number three. Numbers is in reality Carl C. Cave; his three initials are all "C," the third letter of the alphabet, and he was born on the third day of March, the third month of the year.

After winning a large sum of money by betting heavily on the third horse in the third race, Cave decides that three must be his lucky number and quickly confirms this feeling by winning even more money on a gambling ship by betting heavily on the number three and on multiples of three. When BATMAN and ROBIN appear on the scene but are helpless to put a stop to the ship's wide-open gambling operations because it is anchored outside the three-mile limit, Cave is exultant: "The **three** mile limit! It really **is** my lucky number!" he cries. "Why, I'm immune to the law as long as I stick to **threes!**"

In the days that follow, Cave forms a three-man gang and commits a series of spectacular robberies revolving around the number three, as when he and his henchmen rob a musical trio or steal the payroll from a tricycle factory. Before long, the city's newspapers have ceased calling Cave by his real name and have substituted the gangland pseudonym "Numbers." He is apprehended by Batman and Robin in April 1949 (Det No. 146: "Three's a Crime!").

O

OCTOPUS, THE. The cunning master criminal who is the leader of the Octopus Gang, a band of ruthless criminals—each clad in a gray hood emblazoned with an emblem in the form of an octopus—who commit a series of spectacular crimes before they are finally apprehended in February 1963 through the heroic efforts of BATMAN, ROBIN, SUPERMAN, and a strictly amateur costumed crime-fighter calling himself the Crimson Avenger. The Crimson Avenger is in reality Albert Elwood, a "crackpot inventor" who has designed a whimsical arsenal of crime-fighting weaponry which he feels certain will make him the "nemesis of all crimedom." The capture of the Octopus Gang is repeatedly—albeit unintentionally—thwarted by the Crimson Avenger's crackpot gadgetry and ceaseless bungling, but, at a point when the villains appear to have gained the upper hand, it is his courage and resourcefulness that make the final capture possible (WF No. 131: "The Mystery of the Crimson Avenger!").

OLSEN, JIMMY. The fledgling journalist and friend of SUPERMAN who is the junior colleague of CLARK KENT and LOIS LANE on the METROPOLIS *Daily Planet.* On occasion, Jimmy Olsen and Superman undertake adventures together, with Jimmy aiding Superman much as ROBIN aids BATMAN.

In May 1964 Jimmy Olsen and Robin establish a secret headquarters together in an abandoned observatory which they quickly dub the Eyrie (WF No. 141: "The Olsen-Robin Team versus 'The Superman-Batman Team!' "). The Eyrie is intended to serve as their base of operations on those occasions when they undertake joint adventures as the so-called Robin and Olsen team.

In August 1964 Jimmy Olsen and Superman help Batman and Robin defeat a gang of villains led by the evil Jhan-Ar (WF No. 143: "The Feud between Batman and Superman!" pts. I–II—no title; "The Manhunters from Earth!"). (*See* THAN-AR.)

In September 1964 Jimmy Olsen helps Batman, Robin, and Superman defeat the diabolical partnership of Clayface (*see* CLAYFACE [MATT HAGEN] and BRAINIAC (WF No. 144: "The 1,001 Tricks of Clayface and Brainiac!" pts. 1–2—no title; "The Helpless Partners!").

In February 1965 the minds of Jimmy Olsen and Robin are "taken over and possessed" by some weirdly glowing jewels from a far-distant planet which Superman has presented to Jimmy as a gift, unaware of the fact that the strange gems are really alien "living things with super-telepathic powers." Under the baleful influence of the extraterrestrial jewels, Jimmy and Robin turn against Batman and Superman, but the famed crime-fighters soon succeed in freeing their young pals from the jewels' telepathic clutches, thus enabling Superman to return them safely to the alien planet that spawned them (WF No. 147: "The Doomed Boy Heroes!" pts. 1–2—"The New Terrific Team!"; "The Doom of Jimmy Olsen and Robin!"). (For a complete account of the life and career of Jimmy Olsen, consult *The Encyclopedia of Comic Book Heroes: Volume VI—Superman.*)

OPTIK, MIKE. The leader of a gang of criminals who seize control of an astronomical observatory on the outskirts of GOTHAM CITY and, with the aid of its long-range telescope, read the lips of prosperous and highly placed individuals throughout the city and thus accumulate secret information to help them plan their crimes. Because no one can fathom how the criminals manage to secure their confidential information, they become known as the "ghost gang." Aided by Professor Hendricks, the scientist normally in charge of the commandeered observatory, BATMAN and ROBIN apprehend Optik and his henchmen in April–May 1944 (BM No. 22/2: "Dick Grayson, Telegraph Boy!").

OUTLAW TOWN. A United States town, situated somewhere in the mountains overlooking Death Valley, California, which was nothing but an abandoned mining town called Silver Vein until it was taken over by gangsters, renamed Outlaw Town, and transformed into a haven for wanted criminals. Now, however, because of an archaic state law guaranteeing complete local autonomy to mining towns, the authorities find themselves powerless to invade the burgeoning criminal haven.

In February–March 1953 BATMAN and ROBIN are dispatched unofficially to Outlaw Town to apprehend the notorious Jenko brothers—Matt, Phil, and Carl—who have taken refuge there after murdering a policeman in GOTHAM CITY. In Outlaw Town, Batman and Robin are taken captive and incarcerated in the local jail, but ultimately they escape, apprehend the Jenko brothers, and return them to Gotham City to stand trial. POLICE COMMISSIONER GORDON assures the Dynamic Duo that Outlaw Town will not be a gangland sanctuary much longer; a new law, just passed, will enable the National Guard to invade the town and apprehend its entire underworld population (BM No. 75/1: "Outlaw Town, U.S.A.!").

OUTSIDER, THE. A mysterious criminal mastermind who matches wits with BATMAN and ROBIN from December 1964 (Det No. 334: "The Man Who Stole from Batman!") through October 1966, when his reign of villainy is finally ended. The Outsider is in reality ALFRED, brought back from the brink of death and transformed into a twisted, malevolent version of his true self by the inadvertent malfunctioning of Brandon Crawford's incredible "regeneration machine" (Det No. 356: "Inside Story of the Outsider!"). (*See* ALFRED.)

OWLMAN. An identity assumed by ROBIN in April 1957 after a "strange gas" from outer space has temporarily transformed him into a full-grown adult (BM No. 107/3: "The Grown-Up Boy Wonder!").

P

PAGE, LINDA. The lovely society girl-turned-nurse who is BRUCE WAYNE's girlfriend from Spring 1941 (BM No. 5/4) through December 1945–January 1946 (BM No. 32/1: "Rackety-Rax Racket!"), after which she disappears from the chronicles entirely. She represents Bruce Wayne's first romantic involvement following the abrupt cancellation of his engagement to JULIE MADISON in March 1941 (Det No. 49: "Clayface Walks Again!"). She is usually portrayed as a redhead, but she has also been portrayed as a blonde (BM No. 15/1, Feb/Mar '43: "Your Face Is Your Fortune!").

Linda Page is the daughter of TOM PAGE, a wealthy oilman who owns a controlling interest in the Texas-based Page Oil Company (BM No. 6/3, Aug/Sep '41: "The Secret of the Iron Jungle!"). By Spring 1941 Linda has renounced her role as a frivolous society girl in favor of a more meaningful career in nursing (BM No. 5/4). World's Finest Comics No. 2 describes her as "a society girl who has become a nurse in order to make something of herself" (Sum '41: "The Man Who Couldn't Remember!"). By the end of 1941, the chroniclers have ceased portraying Linda as a nurse, but there is never any explicit indication that she has actually abandoned this occupation.

Linda lives in a "modest apartment building" somewhere in GOTHAM CITY (BM No. 5/4, Spr '41). Her birthday apparently occurs either in December or January (BM No. 32/1, Dec/Jan '45–'46: "Rackety-Rax Racket!"), but the precise year of her birth is never stated.

Linda is extremely fond of Bruce Wayne, but it is inevitably BATMAN who most excites her imagination: "Bruce is nice," muses Linda to herself in Spring 1941, ". . . and I do like him a lot, but if he only were a little more like the **Batman**" (BM No. 5/4). (*See* BATMAN [section J 2, the relationship with Linda Page].)

In Spring 1941, on a Gotham City street, Bruce Wayne accidentally collides with a lovely redhead who turns out to be an old friend. **"Linda Page!"** exclaims Wayne. "Well, well! I haven't seen you in a dog's age. The whole crowd has been asking about you!"

"Tell the crowd I woke up one day to realize there are more important things than cafe society," replies Linda, "—so-o-o . . . I've moved out and become a nurse!"

"A nurse?" cries Wayne, remaining faithful to his role of frivolous socialite. "You. . . . you gave up a place in society to work for a living? It's . . . it's stupid!"

"**You're** the one who's stupid---wasting your life as the great society playboy," retorts Linda sharply. "You've got talent. If you wanted to, you--"

"Ah-ah!" scolds Wayne, cradling Linda's chin in his hand. "Don't try to reform me. I'm having too good a time to kill myself with work!"

Soon afterward, Linda is abducted from her apartment by a gang of bank robbers who take her to their hideout and force her to treat a gunshot wound suffered by one of their members during a recent holdup at a midtown bank. Meanwhile, however, because Batman and ROBIN know that Linda is acquainted with MIKE GROGAN and his brother Tommy — two members of the "mysterious band of bank robbers" who have been terrorizing Gotham City — they pay a visit to Linda's apartment in the hope of securing her help in apprehending them, only to find a note scrawled in lipstick, left behind by Linda, indicating that she has been taken captive.

Ultimately, Batman and Robin locate the criminals' hideout and rescue Linda just as she is about to be murdered by one of the gunmen, and, moments later, Linda repays her debt to Batman by hitting another gunman with her shoe just as he is about to shoot Batman. Finally, the police arrive on the scene in time to rescue Batman from yet another gunman and take the assembled criminals into custody (BM No. 5/4).

In Summer 1941, after AMBROSE TAYLOR — the wealthy businessman and civic crusader who is secretly the leader of the notorious West Side Mob — has been shot and wounded by members of the rival East Side Mob, Batman carries him to the home of Linda Page to receive emergency first aid. Linda is taken captive by members of the East Side Mob soon afterward, but Batman and Robin capture the criminals and rescue Linda from their clutches (WF No. 2: "The Man Who Couldn't Remember!").

In August–September 1941, after Linda has expressed fears for her father's safety, Bruce Wayne and Dick Grayson journey to Texas, headquarters of the Page Oil Company, where Tom Page's unscrupulous partner, Graham Masters, is attempting to intimidate Page into selling him his stock in the company in advance of an anticipated gusher which will send the price of the company's stock soaring. At one point, Masters and his henchmen make Linda their prisoner, but Batman and Robin rescue her, defeat the villains, and restore Tom Page to control of his company (BM No. 6/3: "The Secret of the Iron Jungle!").

In September 1941 Bruce Wayne accompanies Linda Page on a tour of an airplane factory owned by her uncle. When agents of the ruthless fifth columnist DOCTOR DEREK run amok in the plant, destroying airplanes and smashing valuable machinery, Wayne changes secretly to Batman to stop the sabotage and apprehend the saboteurs (Det No. 55: "The 'Brain Burglar!'").

In October–November 1941 Linda is kidnapped by henchmen of GRANDA THE MYSTIC, who hopes to force her to provide him with inside information about Batman and his habits. Although Batman infiltrates Granda's hideout by posing as one of his henchmen, things take a turn for the worse when he and Robin are forced into a premature showdown battle. They are rescued, however, by the timely arrival of POLICE COMMISSIONER GORDON and members of the Gotham City Police Department, who take the henchmen into custody while Batman and Robin apprehend the fleeing Granda (BM No. 7/2: "The Trouble Trap!").

On Christmas 1941 Batman, Robin, and Linda Page are guests at the home of Police Commissioner Gordon (BM No. 9/4, Feb/Mar '42).

In May 1942 one of MICHAEL BAFFLE's henchmen seizes Linda long enough to prevent Batman and Robin from interfering with their attempt to loot the safe at the home of the wealthy Mrs. Davies. Later, during a lavish society party at Random Castle, Linda is taken captive by the criminals when she discovers that newspaper society reporter Charles Courtly is really Michael Baffle. Batman and Robin arrive on the scene, apprehend Baffle's henchmen, and rescue Linda, but Baffle manages to escape (Det No. 63: "A Gentleman in Gotham").

In February–March 1943 Linda becomes heartbroken when she learns that Bruce Wayne has become engaged to attractive beauty operator Elva Barr. She does not realize that Elva Barr is really the CATWOMAN, and that Wayne's whirlwind courtship of Elva Barr is only part of his plan to lure her away from a life of crime (BM No. 15/1: "Your Face Is Your Fortune!"). (*See* CATWOMAN, THE.)

In March 1943 Linda forces Bruce Wayne to accompany her to an expensive millinery shop – Mme. Chapeau Hats – where a valuable collection of antique hats is on display. "I'm bringing you to this hat show!" insists Linda. "You've made so much fun of mine, I'm going to let you do the picking for a change!"

While they are examining the hats, the SCARECROW and his henchmen invade the millinery shop and make off with the valuable hat collection. Wayne, unable to change to Batman without exposing his secret identity, attempts to intervene as Bruce Wayne, but the criminals knock him out and escape (Det No. 73: "The Scarecrow Returns").

By December 1945–January 1946 Bruce Wayne has purchased a beautiful star sapphire to give to Linda for her birthday (BM No. 32/1: "Rackety-Rax Racket!").

PAGE, TOM. The father of LINDA PAGE, and the co-owner, along with unscrupulous Graham Masters, of the Page Oil Company in Texas. In August–September 1941, with a valuable gusher of oil expected at almost any time, Masters and his henchmen resort to murder threats and then kidnapping in an attempt to terrorize Page into relinquishing his share of the company, but BATMAN and ROBIN defeat the criminals and rescue Page from their clutches. Masters dies when he accidentally shoots himself in the head during a climactic struggle with Robin (BM No. 6/3: "The Secret of the Iron Jungle!").

PAPAGAYO, EL. Spanish for "the Parrot," a "ruthless outlaw" whose bloodthirsty band has for years been terrorizing the tiny Latin American republic of Mantegua. Beseeched by Mantegua's president, the aging José Camaran, to equip and train a BATMAN counterpart – a so-called Bat-Hombre – to rid Mantegua of El Papagayo, Batman and ROBIN visit the Latin American republic in December 1949–January 1950, select a qualified candidate to play the role of Bat-Hombre, and then proceed to train and equip him for the coming war against El Papagayo, unaware that the man they have selected, Luis Peralda, is secretly a member of El Papagayo's band. Soon afterward, having finally discovered their grievous error, the Dynamic Duo decide that Batman should don the costume of Bat-Hombre and set out after El Papagayo himself, rather than cause Mantegua's aging president the heartbreak of learning that his dream of a heroic Bat-Hombre has become something of a national humiliation. Ultimately, Luis Peralda, the turncoat Bat-Hombre, is killed by a fall from a cliff; El Papagayo and his henchmen are apprehended through the heroic efforts of Batman, Robin, and Mantegua's police; and the elderly José Camaran dies happily, unaware of Peralda's treachery, knowing only that the Bat-Hombre he has so long hoped for has come finally to his country's aid (BM No. 56/1: "Ride, Bat-Hombre, Ride!"). (*See* BATMAN [section F, the Batman counterparts].)

PARDU. A wily stage magician who attempts to trick BATMAN into believing that he has penetrated the secret of his dual identity so that he can extort $10,000 from Batman as his price for keeping the knowledge secret. Although Batman is deceived at first, he soon realizes that the wily magician is only bluffing and has him arrested on a charge of blackmail (BM No. 99/3, Apr '56: "The Phantom of the Bat-Cave!").

PARK AVENUE KID, THE. The ring name bestowed on BRUCE WAYNE when he embarks upon a brief career in professional boxing, partly to raise money for charity, and partly to help him apprehend the sinister criminal known as the DAGGER (Det No. 174, Aug '51: "The Park Avenue Kid!").

PEALE, ED. The man who achieves infamy as the GONG (BM No. 55/3, Oct/Nov '49: "The Bandit of the Bells!").

PEARSON, ELWOOD. An unscrupulous free-lance photographer and the inventor of an ingenious process for taking photographs through solid objects by using a device called an "X-camera" to produce photographs which, when reflected in a "special mirror," reveal what Pearson describes as "the interior view of the photo," i.e., the scene hidden from an ordinary camera or the naked eye by whatever opaque object was blocking its view.

In August 1965, after taking a series of "X-photos" of BATMAN and ROBIN – as well as of a wanted criminal known as Mr. Incognito, a "mysterious masked mastermind" whose true identity is unknown to the authorities – Pearson attempts to blackmail the city into paying him $1,000,000 for a photographic glimpse behind the mask of Mr. Incognito and then asks Mr. Incognito for an identical sum in exchange for an X-photo of Batman and Robin.

Mr. Incognito and photographer Pearson are apprehended soon afterward by Batman and Robin, and although Mr. Incognito has already paid Pearson his $1,000,000, and both he and Pearson have actually glimpsed the unmasked faces of Bruce Wayne and Dick Grayson in Pearson's X-photo of the Dynamic Duo, neither Pearson nor his client is familiar with Wayne or Grayson, and so neither has really learned the Dynamic Duo's secret identities (BM No. 173/1: "Secret Identities for Sale!").

PEEL, MONROE. The murderer of Rudley Bates, who claimed to be an orchid grower but who secretly grew penicillin for sale on the European black market. Peel killed Bates and made off with his valuable penicillin supply, but BATMAN solves the Bates murder – and he and ROBIN apprehend Peel – in November 1951 (Det No. 177: "The Robberies in the Bat-Cave!"). (*See also* ROBIN.)

PEGGS (Miss). An alias employed by the CATWOMAN in Spring 1940 when she poses as a lame old lady in an effort to steal a priceless emerald necklace from wealthy Martha Travers (BM No. 1/4).

PENDER (Professor). A "renegade scientist" who has used his "warped scientific genius" to construct a powerful "super-charging machine" which, when properly activated, "will charge any human being with such electric energy that he'll have ***super-powers*** for 24 hours."

"With it," gloats Pender to his henchmen, "I'll make myself invulnerable and we'll loot all of Metropolis!"

The efforts of BATMAN, ROBIN, and SUPERMAN to apprehend Pender and destroy his machine before he can successfully endow himself with super-powers – superhuman strength, X-ray vision, the power of flight, and invulnerability – are somewhat hampered by the fact that, as the result of a series of complex coincidences, Batman has stepped beneath Pender's ray-machine and become endowed with super-powers which will endure for twenty-four hours, while Superman has been deprived of his super-powers altogether as the result of Pender's having sprayed his costume with minute particles of KRYPTONITE dust.

Eventually, Superman realizes that he can regain his powers through the simple expedient of donning a spare costume which has not been impregnated with kryptonite dust and, soon afterward, Superman, Robin, and the super-powered Batman invade Professor Pender's hideout and apprehend Pender and his henchmen before Pender can use the machine's awesome powers on himself. As the twenty-four-hour deadline arrives, Batman's super-powers fade and vanish. "I'm not sorry," sighs Batman with relief, "--being a super-***Batman*** is too much for me!" (WF No. 77, Jul/Aug '55: "The Super Bat-Man!").

PENGUIN, THE. "The odd little man with the peculiar rolling gait" and "fertile--but twisted--brain" (Det No. 59, Jan '42: "The King of the Jungle!") who ranks second only to the JOKER as the arch-nemesis of BATMAN and ROBIN. His name derives from his appearance, which resembles that of an oversized penguin.

The Penguin is noted for his outrageous vanity, his high-flown language, and his fondness for Shakespeare and Keats (Det No. 58, Dec '41), but he has been made

The Penguin © NPP 1976

most infamous by his passion for birds and bird-related crimes and for his ingenious use of the umbrella, which he has transformed from a harmless everyday device into a versatile implement of terror and destruction and which, more than anything else, has become his personal trademark.

The Penguin is a chubby little man – "surprisingly nimble, in spite of his fat . . ." (Det No. 59, Jan '42: "The King of the Jungle!") – with a pointy nose, a "waddling gait," a "cherubic face" (BM No. 11/4, Jun/Jul '42: "Four Birds of a Feather!"), and a monocle. He wears a black coat, a white shirt, gray trousers, a high silk hat, and a pair of gloves colored either white, green, yellow, or purple. He rarely appears in public without at least one of his trusty trick umbrellas, and he sometimes carries an entire arsenal of umbrellas slung over his shoulder inside a special umbrella quiver (BM No. 33/1, Feb/Mar '46: "Crime on the Wing!"; and others).

In the early days of his career, the Penguin was a cold-blooded murderer who dealt death with weapons ranging from bullets (Det No. 58, Dec '41) to psittacosis germs (Det No. 67, Sep '42: "Crime's Early Bird!"), but by early 1943 he has murdered his last victim and entered upon a career of comparatively benign criminality. In December 1949–January 1950, in fact, a prison guard erroneously describes him as a villain who has "never killed anybody!" (BM No. 56/2: "The Riddle of the Seven Birds!").

Whatever the crime, however, the Penguin has always committed it with the instinct and dedication of a master craftsman, for he is a man who feels strongly that "a perfect crime is a work of art!" In September 1942, for example, after having perpetrated a particularly artful robbery and murder, he informs his henchmen, with characteristic immodesty, that the job bore "the earmarks of genius!" (Det No. 67: "Crime's Early Bird!").

Such unrestrained self-confidence, however, has been known to contain pitfalls for the unwary, and despite his frequent characterization of Batman as an "overrated athlete in fancy dress" (WF No. 49, Dec/Jan '50–'51: "A White Feather for Batman!"; and others), the Penguin has been defeated by Batman on more than thirty separate occasions. "Every criminal has his weak spot," observes Batman dryly in October–November 1947, "— and vanity is the Penguin's!" (BM No. 43/1: "The Blackbird of Banditry!").

Throughout his career, the Penguin has felt most at home among his beloved birds and prized umbrellas, and when the time has come to move to a new hideout or select a new base of operations, he has frequently chosen either a local bird store (Det No. 67, Sep '42: "Crime's Early Bird!"; BM No. 41/1, Jun/Jul '47: "The Bird Cage Bandits!") or a neighborhood umbrella shop (Det No. 87, May '44: "The Man of a Thousand Umbrellas"; BM No. 70/3, Apr/May '52: "The Parasols of Plunder"; and others).

In a way, it is somewhat curious that the Penguin's fame has come to rest as much upon his birds as upon his umbrellas, for the Penguin has seldom actually employed live birds in the commission of his crimes. His occasional avian accomplices have, however, included a parrot, a falcon, jackdaws, eagles (Det No. 67, Sep '42: "Crime's Early Bird!"), a saw-whet owl, wood hens (Det No. 120, Feb '47: "Fowl Play!"), a pelican, gulls, umbrella birds, an India vulture, and nightingales (BM No. 56/2, Dec/Jan '49–'50: "The Riddle of the Seven Birds!").

More often, however, the Penguin has committed his crimes with the aid of his bizarre arsenal of ingenious umbrellas, some of which are lethal weapons while others are complex crime-tools or escape devices. "Haven't you heard," he remarks disdainfully in December 1942–January 1943, after a fellow criminal has clearly underestimated the potential of the umbrella as a weapon to be reckoned with, "that any of my umbrellas is more dangerous than a rapier in the hand of a champion fencer?" (BM No. 14/4: "Bargains in Banditry!").

Indeed, in the course of his long and colorful career, the Penguin has employed a formidable array of diabolical umbrellas, including umbrellas which fire bullets, squirt acid, or unleash clouds of debilitating gas (Det No. 58, Dec '41); a sword-handled umbrella and a lead-handled umbrella used as a club (Det No. 59, Jan '42: "The King of the Jungle!"); an umbrella which "shoots a small explosive shell" (BM No. 11/4, Jun/Jul '42: "Four Birds of a Feather!"); umbrellas which "explode a smoke cartridge," squirt "liquid fire," or unleash clouds of "sneeze powder" (Det No. 67, Sep '42: "Crime's Early Bird!"); umbrellas which shoot poison darts and spray green paint, and another whose shaft serves as a rifle barrel while its canopy functions as a bulletproof shield (BM No. 14/4, Dec/Jan '42–'43: "Bargains in Banditry!"); an umbrella with a mirror mounted in its handle, an umbrella which shoots the knob affixed to its handle in the manner of a popgun, a flamethrower umbrella, and a motion-picture-camera umbrella with a telescopic lens mounted in its handle (BM No. 21/4, Feb/Mar '44: "The Three Eccentrics!"); a gas-shooting umbrella with an acetylene torch in the handle, and a "radio umbrella" which enables the Penguin "to direct [his] men in their operations! The ribs act as an aerial, and the person holding it provides the ground connection" (Det No. 87, May '44: "The Man of a Thousand Umbrellas").

In addition to these, the Penguin has employed a "glider umbrella" and a one-man helicopter umbrella (Det No. 87, May '44: "The Man of a Thousand Umbrellas"); umbrellas which shoot a large fishnet lined with fishhooks, "throw a heat ray," or "fire explosive cartridges powerful enough to blow [a man] in half" (Det No. 99, May '45: "The Temporary Murders!"); an umbrella with a glass cutter in its handle, an umbrella which ensnares its victims in "a network of silk and umbrella ribs . . . as effectively as a spider's web," and an umbrella booby-trapped to squirt sleeping gas in the face of anyone trying to fire it (BM No. 33/1, Feb/Mar '46: "Crime on the Wing!"); a pogo-stick umbrella (BM No. 36/1, Aug/Sep '46: "The Penguin's Nest!"); a one-man "umbrella-copter" which releases clouds of tear gas, and an umbrella which shoots bolas (BM No. 38/3, Dec/Jan '46–'47: "The Penguin on Parole!"); an umbrella which releases a wire net (BM No. 41/1, Jun/Jul '47: "The Bird Cage Bandits!"); an umbrella whose tip serves as a "super-flashbulb" to blind the Penguin's victims, a "rocket gun" umbrella, a parachute umbrella, an umbrella equipped with tongs, and an umbrella which administers an electric shock (Det No. 126, Aug '47: "Case of the Silent Songbirds!"); an umbrella which ensnares its victims in coils of wire, and a floating umbrella which, when inverted, functions as a small boat (WF No. 35, Jul/Aug '48: "Crime by the Book!"); an "extension handle umbrella" (BM No. 58/1, Apr/May '50: "The State-Bird Crimes!"); umbrellas with magnetized handles and beach umbrellas which whirl like giant fans (BM No. 70/3, Apr/May '52: "The Parasols of Plunder"); an "umbrella-gun" which fires various kinds of cartridges, such as an "explosive cartridge" and a "sleeping gas cartridge" (BM No. 155/2, May '63: "The Return of the Penguin!"); and, finally, a "jet-umbrella," which the Penguin rides through the air like a flying broomstick (BM No. 169/1, Feb '65: "Partners in Plunder!").

Aliases employed by the Penguin in the course of his larcenous career have included the names Mr. Boniface (Det No. 58, Dec '41) and I. Waddle (Det No. 67, Sep '42: "Crime's Early Bird!").

In the texts, the Penguin is referred to as the Bold Bird of Banditry, the Buccaneer of Birds, the Man of a Thousand Umbrellas, and the Umbrella Rogue. One text describes him as a "grotesque creature of ill-omen" (BM No. 36/1, Aug/Sep '46: "The Penguin's Nest!"). Batman and Robin frequently infuriate the Penguin by referring to him as Pudgy (Det No. 134, Apr '48: "The Umbrellas of Crime!"; and others).

In December 1941, after stealing two valuable Watteau paintings from a public art exhibition as a demonstration of his outstanding criminal abilities, an odd little man with a peculiar waddling walk stands before the big-time racketeer referred to only as "the boss" and begs to be allowed to join his gang. When the boss asks the newcomer's name, the odd little man smiles wryly: "Oh--ah--I have so many!" he replies. "Why not call me the Penguin? It does fit---hee--hee!"

Accepted into the gang, the Penguin launches a spectacular crime wave which soon "threatens to engulf the city," and when the boss, apprehensive over the Penguin's rising underworld ambitions, attempts to put the new recruit in his place, the Penguin calmly murders him and assumes control of the gang.

Not long afterward, the Penguin sets the stage for an elaborate insurance fraud by having his henchmen steal a valuable jade idol which he himself owns. When Batman attempts to intervene, the Penguin — posing as a respectable citizen under the alias of Mr. Boniface — accuses Batman of having stolen the jade idol himself and complains to the police that Batman has been "threatening me for weeks! He said I'd have to pay him for protection--and that he stood in so well with the police, that nobody would believe me if I complained!" Before long, Batman finds himself a fugitive from justice, compelled to establish his own innocence in addition to coping with the Penguin's sinister machinations.

Ultimately, however, Batman and Robin surprise the Penguin and his henchmen in the act of looting a local diamond exchange into which they have tunneled from a nearby flophouse. After a furious battle with Batman atop the city's elevated subway tracks, the Penguin escapes, but Batman recovers the stolen diamonds, surrenders them to POLICE COMMISSIONER GORDON, and is exonerated of the charges against him (Det No. 58).

In January 1942 the Penguin hops aboard a freight train somewhere in the Midwest and finds himself sharing a freight car with wanted criminals Bignose Murphy, Lefty Louie, and Mike the Tramp. Together, the four men concoct a scheme to capitalize on their own notoriety by having the Penguin turn each of them in to the authorities in the states where they are wanted, collect the outstanding rewards for their capture, and then free them from prison soon afterward. Despite repeated attempts by Batman and Robin to apprehend the criminals, the Penguin succeeds in surrendering his three companions to the authorities — each in a different state — and then engineering their escapes as soon as he has collected the reward money. Ultimately, in a desperate attempt to escape from Batman and Robin, the Penguin and his cohorts commandeer an old-fashioned riverboat and flee down the Mississippi River. After a series of brief reverses, however, the Dynamic Duo apprehend the Penguin's accomplices, paving the way for Batman's final battle with the Penguin himself. Sensing that defeat is imminent, however, the Penguin breaks off the fight and leaps over the side of the riverboat into the river (Det No. 59: "The King of the Jungle!").

In June–July 1942 the Penguin journeys southward to Florida with his "old compatriots" Buzzard Benny, Joe Crow, and the lovely blond singer CANARY, and launches a combination nightclub and gambling casino called the Bird House. For the most part, the gambling games at the Bird House are operated honestly, but "electro-magnets" concealed in the metal frames of the gaming tables enable the Penguin and his cohorts to allow certain chosen victims to win large sums of money — presumably to give the Bird House a reputation as a desirable place to gamble — after which the criminals waylay the winners and steal back their winnings.

The villains show decidedly poor judgment, however, when they attempt to victimize BRUCE WAYNE, who, with his ward DICK GRAYSON, is vacationing in Florida aboard a small yacht, and their attack on Wayne shortly after he has left the Bird House succeeds only in embroiling them in a series of dramatic encounters with Batman and Robin. Before long, Buzzard Benny and Joe Crow have been taken into custody, and Canary — who has developed a crush on Batman and who has twice, in the course of the adventure, saved his life — has promised to abandon her life in the rackets in favor of a new career as a Red Cross nurse. The Penguin is also captured, but he manages to escape before Batman and Robin can turn him over to the authorities (BM No. 11/4: "Four Birds of a Feather!").

In September 1942 the Penguin returns — this time as I. Waddle, proprietor of the Gilded Cage Bird Shoppe — and commits a series of ingenious crimes involving the use of avian accomplices. He sells a carefully trained parrot to a wealthy jewel collector named Gemly, waits until the bird has had the opportunity to memorize the combination to Gemly's safe, and then, after acquiring the combination from the parrot, kills both Gemly and the bird — using a special gas containing "the germ of psittacosis . . . parrot fever" so that murder will not be suspected — and calmly loots Gemly's safe. Later, he uses a team of jackdaws to steal some valuable diamonds from a jewelry store, then uses a trained falcon to intercept the jackdaws and return them to his hideout with the gems.

Batman and Robin finally corner the Penguin in a belfry, but the villain summons his team of "trained fighting eagles" and, while the Dynamic Duo are busy fighting them off, escapes (Det No. 67: "Crime's Early Bird!").

In December 1942–January 1943 the Penguin launches a "cut-rate crime business" in which, in return for a fee and a percentage of the loot, the Penguin promises to provide other criminals with foolproof plans for elaborate crimes. In practice, however, the Penguin murders his clients after they commit the crimes and seizes all the loot for himself. He is finally apprehended through the heroic efforts of Batman and Robin (BM No. 14/4: "Bargains in Banditry!").

In June–July 1943 the Penguin attends a lecture on "Today's Greatest Criminals and Their Foes" given by Warden Keyes, the warden of the very prison from which he has only recently escaped.

"Ah," thinks the Penguin as the lecture begins, "--it will be a pleasure to hear myself spoken of in accents of awe by the warden who was so recently my host!"

As the lecture proceeds, however, the Penguin is mortified to discover that his own name is not even being mentioned, while other master criminals are receiving prominent attention.

"What about the Penguin?" he cries finally, unable to withstand the outrage to his reputation any longer.

"The **Penguin** is as mean and lowdown as any of them," replies Warden Keyes coolly, "but not as ingenius [sic] and inventive! The **Penguin** has a one-track mind! Without his trick umbrellas, he'd be just another third-rate chiseler with delusions of grandeur!"

Recognized moments later as the man who has just asked the question, the Penguin manages to escape from the lecture hall, but his ego has been badly bruised by Keyes's disdainful remarks. "My umbrellas are as useful as ever," thinks the Penguin, "but people are beginning to laugh at them--I can't stand being laughed at! In order to win back my reputation, I'll have to startle my public with new weapons, a new technique!"

After a great deal of thought, the villain decides to employ sporting goods as weapons and proceeds to commit a series of spectacular robberies with the aid of such unlikely devices as fishing rods, hunting dogs, and horses trained for jumping. Before long, however, he has been apprehended by Batman and Robin and returned safely to his prison cell.

"Is it true," Dick Grayson asks Bruce Wayne, "that you got the warden to make fun of the **Penguin's** umbrellas, hoping to goad him into overreaching himself?"

"Right, Dick!" replies Wayne with a grin. "You see his tenderest spot is his vanity! He refuses to believe that he's too old a bird to learn new tricks!" (BM No. 17/2: "The Penguin Goes A-Hunting").

In February–March 1944 the Penguin enlists the aid of safecracker Sam Chizzell and a second-story man named Spider to help him victimize three wealthy eccentrics: Ebenezer Flint, who distrusts banks and keeps his entire fortune in a private wall safe; Gladys Puffe, famous for her vow to leave her entire estate to her pet pekingese; and John White, noted for his readiness to give money and shelter to needy persons, but who, unbeknownst to the Penguin, has been dead for more than a year.

The Penguin and his henchmen succeed in robbing Ebenezer Flint despite a valiant attempt by Batman and Robin to apprehend them, but the Dynamic Duo thwart the villains' scheme to kidnap Gladys Puffe's pet pekingese and hold it for ransom. Batman and Robin ultimately apprehend Sam Chizzell and Spider in the act of robbing John White's castle residence, and Batman apprehends the fleeing Penguin soon afterward (BM No. 21/4: "The Three Eccentrics!").

By May 1944 the Penguin has once again escaped from prison, but Batman and Robin finally uncover his whereabouts by posing as umbrella repairmen. When they attempt to apprehend the villain, however, he escapes and sets up a new headquarters in the P. N. Quinn umbrella shop. Batman and Robin finally locate the new hideout, only to be taken prisoner and left to perish in a diabolical deathtrap while the Penguin races off to steal some priceless pearls from wealthy Mrs. Van Voort. By the time the villain completes the theft and returns to his shop, however, Batman and Robin have freed themselves from his trap and opened every umbrella in the shop, enabling them to apprehend him easily when he barges unsuspectingly into the hideout and becomes hopelessly entangled in the morass of rolling umbrellas (Det No. 87: "The Man of a Thousand Umbrellas").

The Penguin, 1944 © NPP 1944

In October–November 1944, behind the high gray walls of Gotham Penitentiary, the Penguin and the JOKER become embroiled in a heated argument over which of them is the most ingenious criminal, an argument which leads ultimately to an incredible crime contest between the two infamous villains (BM No. 25/1: "Knights of Knavery"). (*See* JOKER, THE.)

By February–March 1945 the Penguin has acquired a teen-aged apprentice whose father and grandfather were both criminals. Sometime in the past, the boy's father had saved the Penguin's life, and the Penguin had promised to reciprocate by educating the boy in the ways of the underworld. The apprentice, however, is far more interested in being a writer than a criminal, and instead of browsing through the Penguin's files to familiarize himself with criminal theory, as the Penguin has instructed, he sits down and begins writing a book about the Penguin.

When the egotistical Penguin learns about his young charge's literary endeavor, he becomes eager to have it published to acquaint the entire world with his villainous exploits. A publisher rejects the manuscript immediately, however, on the ground that unless such a book were "properly slanted by an authority on crime" to discourage criminality, underworld elements would inevitably utilize it as a crime manual.

Unwittingly, however, the publisher has provided the Penguin with a valuable inspiration: he now decides to alter the text slightly and publish it himself as *The Penguin's Handy Hold-Up Manual.*

When the book is finally ready for production, the Penguin steals a shipment of paper, captures Batman and Robin when they attempt to apprehend him, and races off to the hideout of counterfeiter Snipe to arrange for the actual printing. Batman and Robin escape from the Penguin's hideout, however, locate Snipe's hideout with the aid of the Penguin's young apprentice, and apprehend the Penguin along with Snipe and his henchmen. The apprentice eventually publishes his biography of the Penguin with an introduction by Batman, which states that although the Penguin brags unceasingly about his criminal genius, he invariably ends up behind bars (BM No. 27/1: "The Penguin's Apprentice!").

By May 1945 the Penguin has escaped from prison and returned to plague Batman and Robin with an elaborate swindle. After kidnapping three people — a shipping executive named Rogers, a young girl named Betty, and a third person, who remains unidentified — and manufacturing three wax statues resembling the kidnapped persons in every detail, he sends the statues to relatives and business associates of the victims along with notes claiming that the statues are the real persons, whom he has frozen, and that the three frozen people will die within forty-eight hours unless he is paid $150,000 for the secret of thawing them out safely.

While searching the meat-packing and storage district for the villain on the theory that freezing human beings would require the use of elaborate freezing facilities, Batman and Robin catch sight of the Penguin, only to be lured into a trap and left to die in a huge freezing locker. "I'll miss the little games of hide-and-seek we used to play," cries the Penguin, as he bids farewell to the Dynamic Duo, "— but I was getting tired of being thrown in prison all the time!"

In the Penguin's absence, however, Batman and Robin escape from the freezer deathtrap and free the Penguin's three prisoners. When the Penguin and his henchmen return after having collected the ransom money, Batman and Robin apprehend them (Det No. 99: "The Temporary Murders!").

By August–September 1945 the Penguin has again escaped from prison and, with the aid of two henchmen, staged the spectacularly successful robbery of an armored truck. In order to lure the Penguin into the open, Batman persuades the mayor to hold a mock coronation ceremony — with real jewels borrowed from a prestigious jewelry firm — in honor of the rare king penguins due to arrive soon at the GOTHAM CITY zoo. The king penguins and the valuable jewels, Batman believes, will be irresistible lures for the Penguin.

Batman's hunch is correct, but he and Robin are unable to prevent the Penguin and his men from successfully fleeing the scene of the mock coronation. The Penguin, in fact, sets a trap for the Dynamic Duo, ties them up, and leaves them to die beneath a pile of burning mattresses. Batman and Robin escape from the fiery deathtrap, however, and apprehend the Penguin and his henchmen in the act of looting a Gotham City department store (BM No. 30/1: "Back to the House!").

In February–March 1946 three Gotham City criminals — Melancholy Mike, Willie the Wag, and Ralph the Rook — down in the dumps over the unceasing crime-fighting vigilance of Batman and Robin, offer to bet the Penguin that he could not possibly commit two successful crimes out of three if he were to give Batman a clue in advance of each robbery. The egotistical Penguin eagerly accepts the wager, unaware that the real motive of the three criminals is to use him as a decoy for Batman and Robin, so that while the Dynamic Duo are busy chasing him, they can stage robberies of their own somewhere else.

In the days that follow, the Penguin sends Batman two clues — both of which include pictures of birds — and commits two crimes. One is entirely successful, while the other is thwarted by Batman and Robin. When the Penguin learns, however, that Melancholy Mike, Willie the Wag, and Ralph the Rook have been pulling virtually risk-free crimes while he has borne the brunt of battling the Dynamic Duo, he becomes furious and determined to double-cross them. After learning the details of the trio's upcoming crime and notifying them that he intends to pull the third of his three wager crimes immediately, the Penguin quietly informs Batman exactly when and where the three criminals intend to strike so that the Dynamic Duo can be on hand to apprehend them.

Robin, meanwhile, has deduced the location of the Penguin's third crime, and he soon apprehends the villain in the act of stealing a valuable collection of ten-dollar gold pieces owned by the local fire chief (BM No. 33/1: "Crime on the Wing!").

In August–September 1946 the Penguin opens The Nest, an exclusive restaurant in Gotham City where patrons are asked to write out their own orders and sign them before they are sent to the kitchen. Unbeknownst to the wealthy people who patronize The Nest, however, the Penguin plans to accumulate a roster of rich people's signatures and then get himself sentenced to a short term in Gotham Penitentiary, where the country's top forger, currently an inmate there, will copy the signatures onto a pile of blank checks for the Penguin to cash upon his release.

Batman and Robin become suspicious of the Penguin when they see him make a series of deliberate attempts to get himself arrested for a variety of petty crimes for which he would be sent to jail, but not for very long. With the cooperation of Police Commissioner Gordon, Batman and Robin are able to see to it that no policeman in the city arrests the Penguin until they have had the opportunity to get to the bottom of his latest scheme.

When Batman realizes exactly what the Penguin's scheme entails, he visits The Nest disguised as well-known billionaire Stickney Withers, signs his name to one of the restaurant's order forms, and afterward allows the Penguin to be arrested on some minor charge. Ecstatic over having obtained what he believes to be Withers's signature, the Penguin dutifully serves a month in prison and then emerges from the penitentiary with a huge check forged for him by the inmate forger. He is unable to cash the check, however, because the signature forged in prison by his convict cohort was Batman's and not that of the real Stickney Withers. To add insult to injury, Batman promptly arrests the Penguin on a forgery charge (BM No. 36/1: "The Penguin's Nest!").

In December 1946–January 1947, while serving a term for robbery in State Prison, the Penguin manufactures some trick umbrellas in the prison umbrella shop with the intention of employing them later in his eventual escape. One afternoon, however, the warden visits the umbrella shop and accidentally starts a dangerous fire with the Penguin's flamethrowing umbrella, although without being aware of exactly what it is that has started the fire. In an effort to capitalize on the situation while at the same time concealing exactly what he has been doing in the umbrella shop, the Penguin rescues the warden from the spreading flames. As a reward for his "heroism," the Penguin receives a medal from the governor and a parole in the custody of Batman and Robin.

For a time, it appears that the Penguin actually intends to go straight, although he does turn down a $25,000-a-year job offer on the ground that "Such a **paltry sum** is unworthy of my talents!" At one point, he bluntly informs some underworld colleagues that he has decided to abandon his criminal career. The Penguin becomes infuriated, however, at the current craze surrounding a clownish animated-cartoon character named Peter Penguin, who resembles the Penguin so closely that children on the street assume he is their cartoon hero. No matter where he goes, the Penguin is unable to escape the dolls, toys, and other Peter Penguin paraphernalia that have flooded the marketplace.

Finally the Penguin can stand it no longer, and he resolves to have his revenge on Peter Penguin. After obtaining a public-relations job portraying Peter Penguin, he appears as Peter Penguin at Gotham City's Peter Penguin Day celebration and releases a flock of toy penguins into the air over the heads of the massive crowd. Many of the toy penguins, however, contain angry hornets, which sting the assembled merrymakers and occupy the attention of the police while other toy penguins, filled with explosives, shatter jewelry-store windows and blast open armored cars so that the Penguin and his men can loot them.

Batman and Robin lure the villain into a trap, however, by letting it become known that his recent Peter Penguin stunt has inspired the production of a new Peter Penguin movie to be filmed at the Gotham Zoo. When, as Batman had hoped, the furious Penguin arrives at the zoo to halt the production, Batman and Robin apprehend him (BM No. 38/3: "The Penguin on Parole!").

In February 1947 the Penguin obtains a job as assistant to Professor Boyd, a noted ornithologist who is compiling data for an encyclopedia on birds. By day, the Penguin works with the professor, accumulating all sorts of specialized information about birds. By night he capitalizes on this knowledge by borrowing exotic birds from the professor's private aviary and using them as accomplices in a series of spectacular crimes. On one occasion, for example, he borrows a saw-whet owl and uses its characteristic rasping cry to cover up the sounds made by himself and his henchmen as they force open a warehouse safe. Subsequently, when he is in danger of being apprehended by Batman and Robin, the Penguin lets loose a covey of New Zealand wood hens — birds which instinctively attack anything red — and then escapes while the Dynamic Duo are preoccupied with the birds' frenzied attack on Robin's red uniform. Batman and Robin finally set a trap for the Penguin with the aid of Professor Boyd and ultimately succeed in apprehending him (Det No. 120: "Fowl Play!").

In June–July 1947 the Penguin, newly released from prison, announces his intention to go straight and, in partnership with a Mr. Buzzard, opens up the Penguin and Buzzard Bird Store. Under the pretext of "giving away special birds to notable people" to publicize the opening of the store, the Penguin presents gifts of exotic birds to selected wealthy citizens of Gotham City. Unbeknownst to the recipients, however, each birdcage has been booby-trapped in some way — with blinding flare bombs, fire bombs, or anesthetic gas bombs — to enable the Penguin and his henchmen to rob the recipient at some later time, as when the villains rob the guests aboard Wallace Norton's yacht after a flare bomb concealed in a birdcage has temporarily blinded them. Ultimately, however, Batman and Robin realize that the Penguin's gift birds are the key to this latest series of robberies, and he and Robin apprehend the criminals as they attempt to flee the scene of one of their crimes (BM No. 41/1: "The Bird Cage Bandits!").

In August 1947 the Penguin reappears in Gotham City, this time as the mastermind behind an elaborate scheme to extort money from famous singers by threatening to destroy their singing voices forever unless they agree to "donate" large sums of money to a bogus bird lovers' organization called the Songbird Society, headed by the Penguin's accomplice Throstle. Whenever a professional singer refuses to meet the Penguin's extortionate demands, Throstle delivers a seemingly innocuous radio lecture under the auspices of the Songbird Society, which notifies the Penguin's henchmen, through a subtle code, that they are to destroy that person's singing voice.

Inside each singer's microphone, the Penguin and his henchmen have concealed "a tiny gas-chamber that emits a choking gas when a remote switch is thrown," thereby totally robbing the singer of his ability to sing.

Shortly after Throstle delivers a radio lecture on the canary, for example, the Penguin's henchmen throw their remote switch and spray their debilitating gas into the throat of the attractive songstress who performs at Gotham City's Canary Cage nightclub.

Although Batman and Robin struggle relentlessly to smash the vicious racket, the Penguin and his henchmen succeed in destroying the singing voices of two more professional singers – crooner Jack Martini and blues singer Tessa King – before the Dynamic Duo finally apprehends the villains in the act of attempting to ruin the singing voice of opera star Milly Long (Det No. 126: "Case of the Silent Songbirds!").

In October–November 1947 the Penguin – enraged because local newspaper headlines have been trumpeting the villainous exploits of the JOKER and the CATWOMAN while virtually ignoring his own – launches a series of spectacular crimes based on the famous birds of fiction. One of the crimes consists of robbing the dinner guests at Captain Flint's Buccaneer, a lavish shipboard restaurant decked out like an old-time pirate ship. The name of the restaurant recalls Captain Flint, the pet parrot belonging to the pirate Long John Silver in Robert Louis Stevenson's *Treasure Island.* "Ah! That's more like it!" exclaims the Penguin soon afterward, pleased that the newspapers have finally begun to take note of his escapades. "Headlines about **me**!"

For a time, the ingenious famous-bird crimes proceed unabated. The fourth such crime is a daring jewel theft inspired by the legendary roc in the adventures of Sinbad the sailor, but Batman and Robin apprehend the Penguin and his henchmen as they attempt to flee the scene in a penguin-shaped blimp (BM No. 43/1: "The Blackbird of Banditry!").

In April 1948, after a bolt of lightning has destroyed the Penguin's umbrella-shop hideaway, and with it his entire arsenal of trick umbrellas, the Penguin embarks on a series of ingenious "umbrella crimes," all of which involve "umbrellas that are not umbrellas." One such crime involves an attempt to steal the gate receipts of the Gotham City Fair, which is partially housed in a group of umbrellalike tents, while another of the crimes involves concealing sleeping gas inside the fair's umbrellalike replica of a famous atomic-bomb explosion and then stealing gold from a nearby exhibit while onlookers are incapacitated by the gas. Not long afterward, however, when the Penguin attempts to terrify a crowd of fairgoers with "a blazing 'umbrella' of fireworks and rockets" so that, in the ensuing panic and confusion, he can make off with the valuable crown scheduled to be awarded to the fair's queen, Batman and Robin appear on the scene and take him into custody (Det No. 134: "The Umbrellas of Crime!").

In July–August 1948 the Penguin concocts an ingenious method of paving the way for a "clever new crime campaign" despite the fact that he is still in prison. After carefully preparing the first ten chapters of a seemingly innocuous book called *Birds and their Habits,* he obtains permission from the warden to send the chapters to his publisher, then dispatches them to his cohorts in Gotham City. Unbeknownst to the warden, however, the ten harmless chapters, each purporting to discuss the habits of a different species of bird, contain coded instructions for breaking the Penguin out of prison and committing a series of spectacular crimes. Soon afterward, the Penguin's henchmen break their leader out of prison by following the coded instructions in the book's first chapter. At large once again, the Penguin launches the series of spectacular crimes for which his henchmen have prepared themselves by reading his book. Following the coded instructions in the chapter dealing purportedly with owls, the Penguin and his gang plunge an entire section of Gotham City into darkness by tampering with the power supply and then, equipped with infrared goggles which enable them to see in the dark, set about looting the blacked-out section. Another crime, based on the chapter about cranes, involves robbing the Riverside Bank by using a heavy-duty construction crane to remove the entire roof of the bank building.

Batman and Robin pursue the Penguin, 1944 © NPP 1944

Fortunately for Batman and Robin, however, the prison warden, who had carefully perused the Penguin's ten chapters prior to allowing them to be sent out of the prison, still recalls the opening sentences of several chapters, thus enabling the Dynamic Duo to deduce where the villain will strike next, and ultimately to apprehend him in the act of looting a charity bazaar (WF No. 35: "Crime by the Book!").

In August–September 1948, when Batman and Robin visit him at State Prison, the Penguin complains bitterly about being cooped up in a prison cell. "You're in jail because of your bird crimes!" replies Batman. "Take a tip from us – mend your ways!"

Later, the Penguin ponders Batman's advice. "They're right!" thinks the Penguin. "It's always been my theory that **birds** could help me commit perfect crimes, yet . . . every time I plan **bird** crimes, I land in jail! Ironically, **birds** have become my nemesis! So – from now on I'll plan crimes – **without** birds!"

After successfully breaking out of jail without once utilizing a bird of any kind, the Penguin congratulates himself on his new strategy. "Haw!" he cries. "For once, I've escaped prison without using birds! A new life opens for me! It's an omen!"

In the days that follow, the Penguin commits a series of spectacular crimes without using any birds, but, ironically, his plans are always thwarted because of them. At the scene of a crime in Gotham City's Chinatown, for example, with Batman and Robin clearly at their mercy, the Penguin and his men flee in near-panic when they hear the sound of approaching police sirens. Actually, however, the shrill sounds they hear come only from the bamboo whistles which the Chinese traditionally attach to their pigeons so that they will make pleasant sounds as they fly about.

After the truth has been made known to him, the Penguin paces the floor in anguish. "I deliberately plan a crime **without** birds," he moans, "yet birds spoiled my crime! Does fate mean for me to be ruined by birds **always?**"

On another occasion, when the Penguin attempts to flee from Batman and Robin after stealing the payroll at a refrigeration plant – which he chose as a robbery target in the belief that birds could not possibly be present there – he is forced to abandon the loot when he stumbles headlong into a huge flock of penguins being housed at the refrigeration plant while they recuperate from an attack of heat-sickness they developed at the Gotham City zoo.

"Betrayed again . . . by penguins . . . my namesake!" cries the Penguin in frustration. "What irony! I must move quickly and outrun relentless fate!"

For their next crime, the Penguin and his henchmen attempt to steal a shipment of diamonds being transported by train, but a horde of baby chickens, inadvertently set loose from their crates during the ensuing battle with Batman and Robin, end up swallowing all the diamonds. The Penguin and his men manage to flee with the chickens, but Batman and Robin easily locate and apprehend the criminals by following the noise of the peeping chickens (BM No. 48/1: "The Fowls of Fate!").

In February–March 1949, after having been released from prison on parole, the Penguin goes into show business with Pee-Wee Penguin, a real penguin, with a small microphone concealed inside the folds of its tiny bowtie, which the Penguin passes off to his audiences as a genuine talking penguin. "Pee-Wee reformed me!" explains the Penguin to Batman and Robin. "He convinced me I could make more money with him in show business than I could in crime!" For a time, the Penguin and his "talking penguin" prosper, and it appears that the Penguin has indeed given up his life of crime.

One day, however, two of the Penguin's former henchmen, Sad-eyes and Mope, pay a call on their former boss to demand that he pay them the $20,000 he owes them from a robbery they pulled together sometime in the past, and the Penguin, unwilling to part with the money he has earned with Pee-Wee Penguin, attempts a bank robbery to pay off the debt.

When the attempted bank robbery fails, however, the Penguin promises to pay Sad-eyes and Mope what he owes them if they will first help him lure Batman and Robin into a deathtrap. To set the plot in motion, the Penguin tells the Dynamic Duo that Sad-eyes and Mope have kidnapped his talking penguin and are holding him captive in a lonely forest-ranger tower. When Batman and Robin visit the tower in an attempt to rescue Pee-Wee from the clutches of his alleged abductors, however, the Penguin takes them prisoner and sends them soaring off a high cliff in a glider with a deadly payload of nitroglycerine attached to its nose. By manipulating the glider so that it lands in the water, however, Batman and Robin are able to prevent the explosion of the nitroglycerine and escape. Before long, the Penguin has been taken into custody by Batman and brought to trial on charges of attempted bank robbery, attempted murder, and staging a bogus kidnapping.

At the trial, Batman summons Pee-Wee Penguin as a prosecution witness and uses the microphone concealed in Pee-Wee's bowtie to make it appear that a flood of incriminating testimony is issuing from the mouth of the so-called talking penguin. Thoroughly flustered, the Penguin is unable to restrain himself from blurting out the truth – that his talking penguin is fraudulent and cannot talk at all – an admission which leads ultimately to his conviction of the charges against him (BM No. 51/1: "Pee-Wee, the Talking Penguin!").

By December 1949–January 1950 the Penguin has obtained a reduction in his prison sentence by providing the authorities with incriminating information concerning gangster "Squeeze" Miller, and Miller is executed in the electric chair soon afterward on the basis of information supplied by the Penguin.

Released from Gotham Penitentiary on parole, the Penguin is flabbergasted to learn that Miller has left him $250,000 in bonds to be paid to him as soon as he has committed seven crimes utilizing birds, the first letters of whose names, taken together, must spell out the name Penguin. In accordance with Miller's will, the Penguin commits seven crimes – utilizing, in the process, a **p**elican, **e**agles, **n**octule bats [sic: not a variety of bird], **g**ulls, **u**mbrella birds, an **I**ndia vulture, and **n**ightingales – only to be apprehended by Batman and Robin while attempting to flee the scene of the final theft. And when the Penguin finally receives the bonds left to him by Miller, he discovers that they are all forgeries which he himself printed sometime in the past.

"Miller must have stolen them from someone you'd defrauded--and decided to use them for revenge when your testimony sent him to the chair!" observes Batman with a smile. "He knew your greed would be stronger than your judgment!" (BM No. 56/2: "The Riddle of the Seven Birds!").

In April–May 1950 the Penguin, released from prison on parole, attends a bird show sponsored by the Birdlovers' Society of Gotham City. The patrons of the society are aghast to discover, however, that the Penguin has added a live penguin to the bird show's colorful exhibit of state birds. The Penguin feels that his contribution to the state birds exhibit should be regarded as representing America's Antarctic possessions, but the patrons insist that a penguin is not a legitimate state bird and demand that he remove it from the exhibit at once. "So you society patrons think the penguin isn't good enough to associate with your fancy state birds!" exclaims the Penguin angrily. "You'll find out differently!"

In retaliation against the Birdlovers' Society's exclusion of the penguin, the Penguin launches a series of spectacular "state bird" crimes, each directed against a different patron of the Birdlovers' Society and each involving some sort of pun on the name of the victim's state bird. In order to steal a valuable emerald statuette from an art auction presided over by Birdlovers' Society patron Mark Jason — an art dealer from the state of Alabama, where the state bird is the yellowhammer — the Penguin secretes a tiny canister of choking gas inside Jason's yellow auctioneer's hammer, then flees with the statuette while the onlookers are incapacitated by the debilitating gas. The ingenious state bird crimes are spectacularly successful for a time, but the Penguin is finally apprehended through the heroic efforts of Batman and Robin (BM No. 58/1: "The State-Bird Crimes!").

In October–November 1950 the Penguin engineers a daring escape from Summit Penitentiary—an allegedly escape-proof prison situated atop a high gray cliff on the outskirts of Gotham City — with the aid of a pair of mechanical wings he has constructed secretly in the prison workshop. "Famed **Icarus**--of Greek legend--was the **first** to fly with man-made wings!" gloats the Penguin, as he soars gracefully over the cliff to freedom. "Now, centuries later, I--the **Penguin**--duplicate his feat, as I glide into a new life of **crime!**"

Back in Gotham City, the Penguin launches a series of spectacular "winged people crimes," each drawing its inspiration from a different winged person of mythology or fiction, such as Cupid, Mercury, or Cinderella's fairy godmother. As a fitting climax to his winged-people crimes, the Penguin hopes to uncover the secret identity of Batman.

At one point, the Penguin and his henchmen kidnap Robin as a means of forcing Batman to come to their hideout. There the Penguin informs Batman that Robin is imprisoned in a nearby room, where a fierce lion — whose loud roaring is clearly audible — is poised to attack him unless Batman agrees to unmask. ". . . I ***could*** shoot you," gloats the Penguin, "but that would be too quick! I'd rather give you the slow, ***mental*** torture of killing ***Batman's*** career by ***exposing your secret identity!*** You have a choice--***unmask . . . or Robin dies!***"

"You know I have no choice, you fiend!" replies Batman. ***"I must unmask!"***

Batman slowly removes his cowl, revealing the angular features of Bruce Wayne, but he has managed to smear some streaks of makeup on his face, leading the Penguin to assume that the face he sees before him is merely a disguise being employed by Batman to avoid revealing his secret.

Now Batman leaps at the Penguin and captures him, apparently indifferent to the fact that the enraged Penguin has already thrown the switch releasing the roaring lion into the room where Robin lies helpless.

Only when the villain is safely in his custody does Batman turn his attention to Robin. Batman had already deduced that the menacing sounds from the adjoining room were not the sounds of a lion at all, but rather those of an angry ostrich — which is known to make a sound almost exactly like that of a roaring lion — and that, in spite of the Penguin's sinister threats, Robin was never actually in any great danger (BM No. 61/2: "The Mystery of the Winged People!").

In December 1950–January 1951 the Penguin, at large in Gotham City after a daring escape from prison, attempts to recruit a new gang, only to discover that criminals are reluctant to join him because of his abysmal record of defeats at the hands of Batman. One hoodlum reads aloud to the Penguin from a newspaper editorial which boldly proclaims that "***Batman*** will recapture the ***Penguin! Batman*** has never shown the white feather to any criminal and never will!"

The words of the newspaper editorial, however, inspire the Penguin with an elaborate scheme for humiliating Batman, as well as with ideas for a series of spectacular "feather crimes" revolving around the use of feathers. After gaining entrance to a wealthy home by posing as a brush salesman, for example, the Penguin shakes a feather duster filled with sneezing powder in his host's face, then loots the wall safe while his victim is incapacitated by a sneezing fit.

The Penguin in prison, 1944 © NPP 1944

After committing two such robberies, the Penguin sends a taunting note to Batman, accompanied by a white feather. "Everyone thinks you're brave, afraid of nothing," begins the message, "--but I believe you only PRETEND to be fearless! It's an old custom to send a WHITE FEATHER to a COWARD--so here's yours in advance, for I intend to prove to the world that you, BATMAN, are really a COWARD!" Batman dismisses the note as empty braggadocio, unaware that the Penguin has impregnated it with the germs of a debilitating bird disease whose symptoms, similar to those of either "pigeon fever" or "parrot fever," include headaches, fever, weakness, nervousness, and fainting spells.

As Batman falls further and further under the influence of the disease, the Penguin sets in motion an elaborate scheme designed to make Batman's disease symptoms appear to be signs of increasing cowardice. One ploy entails sending Batman a barrage of letters containing grave warnings about the potentially fatal hazards of Batman's profession. As the days go by and the disease-stricken Batman becomes increasingly edgy and irritable after reading each new message, Robin and Police Commissioner Gordon begin to believe that Batman may in fact be losing his nerve. During his crime-fighting encounters with the Penguin, Batman frequently behaves in an uncharacteristic way, seemingly confirming the Penguin's allegation of cowardice. On one occasion, for example, he becomes dizzy and falls off the roof of a building while preparing to lasso a nearby flagpole with his silken rope. Robin rescues Batman before he can come to any harm, but the incident creates the impression that Batman has inexplicably developed a fear of heights. As the Penguin's campaign to humiliate Batman continues, the people around Batman become convinced that the once-fearless crime-fighter has become inexplicably transformed into a cringing coward.

Ultimately, however, Batman manages to give Robin the bit of help and encouragement he needs to apprehend the Penguin and his henchmen virtually single-handedly. Although Batman, by now severely stricken, has collapsed from his illness, he has deduced that his uncharacteristic behavior has been induced by a bird disease, not by uncertainty or cowardice, and he instructs Robin to call a doctor and repeat the words *ornithosis* and *psittacosis* when the doctor arrives. Aided by Batman's self-diagnosis, the doctor discovers the precise cause of Batman's disease and begins to administer the appropriate medication. When the doctor explains to Robin and Police Commissioner Gordon that Batman has been suffering from a rare bird disease and that, ". . . naturally, a sick person is ***always uncertain*** about himself and his actions," they realize that Batman has been suffering only from illness, not from cowardice (WF No. 49: "A White Feather for Batman!").

In May 1951 the Penguin, freed from prison on parole, purchases an old estate, decorates it with giant models of birds, and transforms it into a combination bird sanctuary and museum. Then, under the pretense of abandoning his criminal career and making restitution to some of his past victims, he pays a series of calls on various businesses and institutions in order to return whatever loot he stole in the past. He returns some cash to a local bank, a pearl to a jewel importer, a platinum ingot to a metal refinery, some money to a swanky nightclub, and a valuable clock to the House of Treasures. On each of these occasions, Batman and Robin, certain that the Penguin is visiting these places only to rob them, race in to make the arrest, only to end up looking foolish when the proprietor explains that the Penguin was only returning valuables, not stealing them.

Unknown to the Dynamic Duo, however, the Penguin has planted gas bombs in each place he visited, all timed to release their gas at precisely the same moment so that the Penguin and his henchmen can loot all the places simultaneously. When the appointed hour arrives, the Penguin and his cohorts swoop down on their selected crime targets in a fleet of helicopters fashioned from the giant bird models on display at the Penguin's bird sanctuary. By commandeering the Penguin's lead craft, however, Batman succeeds in luring the other bandit helicopters out beyond the city limits, where Robin skillfully forces them to the ground with mighty blasts from the "super-powerful jets" of the BATPLANE. The Penguin has managed to flee, but his henchmen, furious with their leader for having deserted them, provide the Dynamic Duo with the location of his secret hiding place, enabling Batman and Robin to apprehend him soon afterward (Det No. 171: "The Menace of the Giant Birds!").

In December 1951–January 1952, on his birthday, the Penguin receives a number of carefully wrapped gifts from various members of the underworld. "Ahhh," sighs the Penguin, proudly surveying the unopened packages, "--tributes to the ***Penguin*** on his birthday from the elite of gangdom! No doubt they are paying their respects to me as the ***maestro of modern crime*** with invaluable gifts. . . ." When the Penguin unwraps his gifts, however, he finds that they contain only crude insults — stuffed birds accompanied by taunting birthday messages in the form of mocking epigrams about birds — the underworld's way of reminding the Penguin that it considers him a bungler and a has-been because of his numerous defeats at the hands of Batman and Robin.

Outraged over this gangland insult, the Penguin vows to teach his detractors a lesson by committing four spectacular crimes based on well-known sayings about birds. After providing Batman with four carefully conceived picture-clues—each representing a well-known bird saying which in turn provides a clue to one of the Penguin's four upcoming crimes — the Penguin embarks on his ingenious "bird sayings crimes." The first of these crimes, based on the saying "A bird in the hand is worth two in the bush," involves an attempt to smuggle stolen jewels into the United States. After the Penguin has concealed himself inside the torch-bearing hand of the Statue of Liberty, his henchmen, who are sailing into the harbor aboard an incoming ship, attach the bag of gems to a homing pigeon and send it flying into the arms of the Penguin. This crime, which is thwarted by Batman and Robin although the Penguin escapes, is followed by two others, until finally the Penguin is prepared for his fourth crime, the murder of Batman and Robin, to be based on the famous saying about killing two birds with one stone.

After luring the Dynamic Duo to his hideout with a series of clues, the Penguin imprisons them inside a garage with a stonebird. At dawn, gloats the Penguin, the stonebird will obey its instincts and fly out the garage window to seek food, thereby triggering an electric-eye device which will detonate a cache of dynamite and blow Batman and Robin to smithereens. After the Penguin has left the garage, however, Batman uses a common marble to trick the stonebird into believing that it has laid an egg, knowing that its instinct to protect its egg will take precedence over its desire to forage for food. Then, with the threat of the dynamite explosion at least temporarily averted, the Dynamic Duo break free of their bonds, flee the garage, and apprehend the Penguin (WF No. 55: "The Bird Sayings Crimes!").

In April–May 1952 the Penguin, who has been a model prison inmate since his last defeat at the hands of Batman and Robin, obtains a parole by promising to dispose of his entire collection of birds as a sign that he is sincere about wanting to reform. Soon afterward, under the pretext of launching a career in legitimate business, the Penguin establishes an umbrella-manufacturing concern called Penguin Umbrellas, Inc.

For a time, Penguin Umbrellas, Inc., enjoys a brisk business, particularly after Batman, as a gesture of goodwill, gives the Penguin's umbrella line his personal endorsement. Unknown to the public, however, the handle of each Penguin umbrella is a powerful magnet, part of a scheme to enable the Penguin to commit another of his spectacular umbrella crimes. One rainy day, while wealthy citizens are walking through the streets of the financial district with their newly purchased Penguin umbrellas, the Penguin's henchmen electrify a nearby statue, transforming it into a huge electromagnet which draws every holder of a Penguin umbrella through the air to the top of the statue, where they dangle precariously high above the street. Then, from down below, the Penguin warns his astonished captives that his men will demagnetize the statue and send them all hurtling to the pavement unless they toss down their wallets, briefcases, and valuables. Batman and Robin arrive on the scene and attempt to thwart the bizarre robbery, but the Penguin manages to escape.

Not long afterward, the Penguin and his gang visit Oasis Beach Island, a Caribbean resort frequented only by the very wealthy. Posing as beach idlers, the criminals set up a row of special beach umbrellas designed by the Penguin for just this occasion. At a signal from the Penguin, the beach umbrellas, which are linked to motors hidden in the sand, begin to whirl rapidly, like giant fans, blowing a storm of sand across the beach. While the resort guards are blinded by the artificial sandstorm, the Penguin and his men intend to loot the beach club nearby, but Batman and Robin arrive on the scene in the batplane, create a small rainstorm to dampen the whirling sand by seeding the nearby clouds with silver iodide, and then capture the Penguin while the resort guards apprehend the villain's henchmen (BM No. 70/3: "The Parasols of Plunder").

In April–May 1953, following his release from prison, the Penguin returns to Gotham City with the announcement that he has discovered actual living specimens of famous flying creatures — such as the phoenix, roc, thunderbird, basilisk, and winged lion — hitherto believed to be merely legendary, and that he intends to go into the legitimate business of exhibiting his creatures publicly. Actually, however, the Penguin's legendary creatures are no more than cleverly constructed mechanical models, and before long the Penguin has begun to employ them to terrorize the people of Gotham City in order to facilitate the commission of a series of spectacular crimes.

One of the creatures which the Penguin unleashes on the city — his so-called "mystery bird" — is a hideous "man-bat" which the Penguin hopes will prove so terrifying that the citizens of Gotham City will form a psychological association between Batman and the man-bat, and thus force Batman into premature retirement by shunning him whenever he appears in public. For a time, it appears that the diabolical plot may actually succeed, but Batman and Robin ultimately apprehend the Penguin and his henchmen and expose the Penguin's flying creatures as man-made mechanical monsters (BM No. 76/2: "The Penguin's Fabulous Fowls!").

In April 1956, when Batman and Robin stage a raid on the Penguin's hideout, the Penguin is forced to flee to an alternate hideout, taking with him only a small batch of unhatched bird eggs that he has managed to salvage in the confusion. He decides to allow the eggs to hatch, and, as each one hatches, to "hatch" a suitable crime to fit the variety of bird that emerges. When a chimney swift hatches from the first egg, the Penguin attempts to steal the gold dust which has accumulated inside the chimney filter of the Gotham Gold Refinery. When a herring gull — a bird that breaks open clams by carrying them high into the air and dropping them on the rocks below — hatches from the second egg, the Penguin instructs his henchmen to steal a safe from a jewelry store and crack it open on some rocks on the outskirts of Gotham City. When a water ouzel hatches from the third egg, the Penguin and his gang steal the ticket receipts from the Gotham Light and Power Show by pouring a large quantity of bubble-producing chemical into a waterfall exhibit and then staging the theft during the ensuing confusion. This time, however, Batman and Robin trail the Penguin to his hideout and capture him when a baby alligator hatches from the Penguin's last remaining egg and momentarily distracts the villain's attention by biting his ankle (BM No. 99/1: "The Golden Eggs!").

After serving yet another term in prison, the Penguin disappears into an extended period of retirement from which he does not emerge until May 1963, after a humiliating visit to a Gotham City poolroom.

"Will ya look who flew into town for a visit!" exclaims one hoodlum, as the Penguin saunters into the underworld hangout. "That one-time genius--the Penguin!"

"'One-time' genius?" cries the Penguin. "You jest, of course! You know that if I ever came out of retirement I'd be as dazzlingly cunning as ever!"

"Are you kidding?" retorts the hoodlum. "You'd be no competition to ***Batman!*** You been away too long, ***Penguin!*** You're a ***has-been!***"

"The ***Penguin***--a ***has-been?***" cries the Penguin, outraged. "I'll prove otherwise! You'll soon read of my exploits in the newspapers . . . that is, if you ignorant louts ***can*** read! ***Pfah!***"

In the days that follow, the Penguin steals some valuable rubies from the eyes of a dragon statue in

Gotham City's Chinatown, then lands atop the roof of the Tompkins Building in a huge penguin-shaped blimp to loot the office safe of millionaire "Big" John Tompkins. These first two crimes are spectacularly successful, but Batman and Robin apprehend the Penguin soon afterward in the act of stealing a set of original sketches by John J. Audubon from the Friends of Birds Society museum (BM No. 155/2: "The Return of the Penguin!").

By February 1965 the Penguin has served his term in prison and is eager to return to crime, but he is disturbed by his inability to concoct a single crime worthy of his genius. He wants desperately to commit a crime that is "**sensational** . . . [and] seething with the **unexpected**," but his usually fertile brain simply refuses to produce any brilliant new ideas.

Suddenly, however, the Penguin is struck by an inspiration, a scheme designed to trick Batman into selecting a suitable crime and mapping out its details without ever realizing that he has been duped into masterminding a crime for the Penguin. The plan involves creating a series of sensational incidents with various kinds of trick umbrellas throughout Gotham City, and then failing to follow up these incidents with any sort of crime. At one point, for example, outside a jewelry store, the Penguin's henchmen hand out free umbrellas which create billowy smoke and artificial lightning when carried inside the store, but the henchmen make no effort whatever to rob the store during the ensuing pandemonium. Other trick umbrellas wreak havoc inside a bank, but the Penguin and his henchmen make no effort to capitalize on the commotion in order to commit a robbery there.

Because he knows full well that the trick umbrellas are the Penguin's handiwork, Batman is baffled when crimes fail to unfold at the scenes of the various umbrella incidents. Leaping to the wholly erroneous conclusion that the various umbrella incidents are clues pointing the way to some impending major crime, Batman and Robin attempt to deduce exactly what crime the Penguin is planning, unaware that it is their own speculation, and not any grand design on the part of the Penguin, that is gradually providing the details of the Penguin's upcoming crime. They are similarly unaware that one of the trick umbrellas which the Penguin has allowed to fall into their hands contains a tiny hidden microphone that is transmitting their every conversation directly to the Penguin's hideout.

Because one of the Penguin's trick umbrellas is multicolored, Batman and Robin decide that the Penguin must be planning to steal a jeweled meteorite from a museum gem exhibit. In an effort to anticipate exactly how the Penguin will proceed, they discuss the security precautions for the exhibit and map out the specific plan of attack they feel the Penguin is likely to use. In effect, Batman and Robin actually "plan" a crime for the Penguin by attempting to impart rational significance to a series of irrational "clues."

Aided by the crime plan unwittingly provided for him by Batman, the Penguin makes off with the museum's jeweled meterorite despite the Dynamic Duo's efforts to apprehend him, but Batman and Robin capture the Penguin and recover the meterorite soon afterward, as the villain attempts to escape aboard his flying "jet-umbrella." The Penguin is sent to prison, but Batman and Robin never learn that it was actually they who provided him with his ingenious crime strategy (BM No. 169/1: "Partners in Plunder!").

PENGUIN AND BUZZARD BIRD STORE. A bird store which serves as the base of operations for the PENGUIN and his accomplice Mr. Buzzard during June–July 1947 (BM No. 41/1: "The Bird Cage Bandits!").

PENGUIN MANOR. The "palatial penthouse hideout" which serves as the PENGUIN's base of operations during June–July 1943 (BM No. 17/2: "The Penguin Goes A-Hunting") and again during February–March 1945 (BM No. 27/1: "The Penguin's Apprentice!").

PENGUIN UMBRELLAS, INC. An umbrella-manufacturing firm founded by the PENGUIN in April–May 1952, ostensibly to manufacture legitimate umbrellas, but actually to manufacture trick umbrellas to aid him in the commission of crimes (BM No. 70/3: "The Parasols of Plunder").

PENNYWORTH, ALFRED. *See* ALFRED.

PENNYWORTH, WILFRED. The older brother of ALFRED, BRUCE WAYNE's butler. Wilfred Pennyworth is a Shakespearean actor who performs with a traveling repertory company known as the Avon Players. His beautiful blond daughter Daphne Pennyworth, Alfred's niece, is an actress with the same company (BM No. 216, Nov '69: "Angel--or Devil?").

PETERS, JUMPY. One of four condemned murderers — the others are Sailor Roggs, Angles Manson, and Careful Kyle — who become the objects of an intense manhunt by BATMAN and ROBIN when they successfully engineer their own daring escape from a GOTHAM CITY courtroom in May–June 1949 after being brought there from their death cells in various parts of the country to testify against Boss Barry, their former gang chief.

During the violence-filled chase that follows, fate intervenes ironically to snuff out the lives of three of the four killers in ways similar to that which the law has already decreed: Sailor Roggs, sentenced to die by asphyxiation in a North Carolina gas chamber, is killed when he unwittingly steals aboard a vessel being fumigated with cyanide bombs to exterminate plague-carrying rats. Angles Manson, sentenced to die on a Kansas gallows, chokes to death when his necktie gets snarled inside a generator at an electrical generating plant. And Careful Kyle, sentenced to death by electrocution in a New York electric chair, is electrocuted by electric eels when he reaches into an aquarium to retrieve a fallen gun.

Of the four original escapees, only Jumpy Peters, apprehended in a wooded area by Batman and Robin, lives to face his legally decreed execution by firing squad in the state of Utah (WF No. 40: "4 Killers Against Fate!").

PETRI, NICK. A member of a gang of criminals who, having learned that his gangland cohorts — the Slasher, Benny the Gimp, the Nutcracker, and Lop-Ears McGoof — were planning to double-cross and murder him as soon as they met to divide the stolen loot that Petri had in his possession, promptly locked the loot inside a safe in an old abandoned house and then wired the safe door to seven separate switches, one rigged to unlock the door safely and the other six to detonate a bomb which, if triggered, would blow the entire safe, and anyone attempting to open it, to kingdom come.

Knowing, therefore, that he cannot risk opening the safe himself and that Petri will not come out of hiding to do it so long as he believes his former companions are lying in wait for him, the Slasher has cunningly faked his own suicide and betrayed Benny the Gimp, the Nutcracker, and Lop-Ears McGoof into the hands of the police in the hope that Petri, believing his gangland enemies dead or captured, will come out of hiding to retrieve the loot so that the Slasher and his henchmen can take it away from him.

Petri is taken in by the Slasher's ruse and returns to the rigged safe to withdraw the loot, but both he and the Slasher, and all of the Slasher's henchmen, are apprehended by BATMAN and ROBIN within moments after he has opened the safe (Det No. 97, Mar '45: "The Secret of the Switch!").

PHAETON (Mr.). A mysterious, wheelchair-ridden criminal who, in collusion with gangster Stack Hawley, is engaged in a lucrative gem-smuggling racket. Both men are apprehended by BATMAN and ROBIN in June–July 1949. Hurled from a motor launch by an exploding shell and struck on the head by the boat's bow early in the adventure, Batman comes to believe that Mr. Phaeton is in reality a renegade scientist from an undersea civilization, an unscrupulous merman who has fled to the surface world after exchanging his fish tail and gills for legs and lungs by means of an ingenious "converting chamber" of his own invention. At the story's end, however, it remains unclear whether Batman's version is the literal truth or merely a fantasy resulting from the delirium caused by his blow on the head (BM No. 53/3: "Batman Under the Sea!").

PHANTOM, THE. A bizarre criminal, endowed with the incredible ability to walk through walls and levitate objects, who matches wits with BATMAN and ROBIN in September 1960. He is in reality Pol, an honest and well-meaning alien from a distant dimension – recently transported to the earthly dimension by an unscrupulous scientist named Carter Wede with the aid of a machine designed to "probe other dimensions" – who reluctantly agreed to use his extradimensional powers for crime after Wede had falsely informed him that his dimension-probing machine was incapable of transporting Pol back to his home dimension and that Pol would therefore be stranded in the earthly dimension forever unless Pol could accumulate, through theft, the funds necessary for the construction of a special interdimensional transmitter.

Although he goes to great lengths to avoid doing anyone actual physical harm, Pol commits a series of spectacular crimes in GOTHAM CITY, and his incredible extradimensional abilities quickly earn him the name the Phantom. Ultimately, however, when Pol sees that Wede is about to murder a captive Batman and Robin, he rebels against the evil scientist and helps the Dynamic Duo apprehend Wede and his henchmen.

Fortunately, Pol will be able to return to his own dimension after all, for in spite of Wede's claims to the contrary, his machine always was capable of sending Pol back home again (Det No. 283: "The Phantom of Gotham City!").

PHANTOM BANDIT, THE. A cunning criminal who commits a series of spectacular burglaries in GOTHAM CITY, each time by opening complicated locks without ever setting off any of the related burglar alarms. He is in reality "Muggsy" Morton, "one of the cleverest crooks in the country." Under the stage name the Great Swami, he performs a nightly mind-reading act at the Polar Bear Club, a lavish nightclub described as the "newest rage of the Gotham City smart set."

Each evening, the Great Swami's lovely assistant moves among the patrons of the Polar Bear Club, soliciting everyday objects and then holding them aloft, wrapped in a handkerchief, so that the swami can demonstrate his "clairvoyant" powers by identifying the objects concealed in the handkerchief.

The supposed "mind reading" is actually accomplished through the use of hidden microphones, but, in addition, a piece of wax concealed inside the assistant's handkerchief enables the swami to obtain wax impressions of the various keys – safe keys, door keys, keys to safety deposit boxes, and the like – that have been handed to his assistant during the course of the evening's entertainment. From these impressions, the swami is able to create duplicate keys and, as the Phantom Bandit, to open the various locks which match the keys without ever activating any of the related security devices.

In February 1954 VICKI VALE uncovers the Phantom Bandit's true identity and unravels the mystery behind his uncanny ability to open complicated locks, but it is BATMAN who finally appears on the scene to apprehend the Phantom Bandit and his assistant (BM No. 81/3: "The Phantom Bandit of Gotham City!").

PHANTOM BANK BANDIT, THE. An elusive and cunning bank robber who matches wits with BATMAN and ROBIN in April 1958. He is secretly Jim Megan, "an ex-con who changed his name [to Jim Morley] and pretended to go straight" as a legitimate businessman.

In April 1958, in an effort to verify his suspicion that businessman Morley is secretly the Phantom Bank Bandit, Batman joins forces with the GOTHAM CITY police in an elaborate scheme to trick Morley into incriminating himself by revealing the hiding place of his hidden bank loot. Under the pretense of requiring additional funds for Robin's college education and his own eventual retirement, Batman announces the opening of the Batman Private Detective Agency and then arranges for a series of bogus threats on Morley's life so that Morley will come to him for protection.

Ultimately, by demanding an exorbitant fee for his services as Morley's bodyguard, Batman forces Morley to dip into his stolen bank loot, thereby betraying his Phantom Bank Bandit identity and enabling the Dynamic Duo to apprehend him (BM No. 115/2: "Batman for Hire").

PICTURE MAGAZINE. The magazine which employs VICKI VALE as a photographer from October–November 1948 (BM No. 49/2: "The Scoop of the Century!") until at least January 1950 (Det No. 155: "Bruce Wayne, Private Detective!"). For a period of several years thereafter, the texts fail to mention the name of Vicki's employer, but by February–March 1953 she has apparently obtained a position as a photographer for VUE MAGAZINE (BM No. 75/2: "Mr. Roulette's Greatest Gamble").

PIED PIPER, THE. The so-called "man of 1,000 pipes," a "tricky criminal" – headquartered in a recently opened pipe shop in GOTHAM CITY – "who boasted that he could do anything with pipes" and whose spectacular crimes and escapes all revolve around the use of pipes, as when he and his henchmen rob the Farmer's Bank with the aid of corncob pipes which emit blinding smoke, or when he escapes from a rooftop by means of the drainpipe and then scrambles to safety through a network of sewer pipes. After stunning Gotham City with a series of spectacular pipe crimes, however, the Pied Piper is finally apprehended by BATMAN and ROBIN in January 1949 (Det No. 143: "The Pied Piper of Peril!").

PINE, JACK. A member of a three-man gang of criminals who recently robbed an armored car and made off with $2,000,000 in cash and gems, as yet unrecovered. He is the only member of the gangland trio still at large as of September 1962, one accomplice having already been apprehended and the other having died of natural causes. The capture of Pine and a few of his newly acquired underworld cronies, as well as the recovery of the missing loot, by BATMAN and ROBIN in September 1962 comes as the culmination of an elaborate ruse – devised by Batman and carried out with the aid of ALFRED, Robin, and Sgt. Helen Smith of the GOTHAM CITY police force – in which Alfred poses as a white-haired old man who exposes Batman to a whiff of mystic love potion, and Sgt. Smith poses as the pretty French girl with whom Batman falls hopelessly in love under the potion's influence, as part of an overall plan to trick Pine into believing that Batman has become so completely preoccupied with his all-consuming love affair that it is now safe for him to come out of hiding to recover his buried loot (BM No. 150/2: "The Girl Who Stole Batman's Heart").

PLAINVILLE. A small United States town which is renamed Batmantown by its citizens in the belief that the new name will excite the national attention necessary for community expansion and economic growth. Soon afterward, however, when it becomes apparent that the name Batmantown is having the unwanted effect of arousing the underworld to acts of reprisal against the town, its citizens rename it Plainville. However, a nationally televised tour of the town, conducted by BATMAN as a favor to the townspeople, promises to arouse sufficient public interest in the community to ensure its continued prosperity (BM No. 100/1, Jun '56: "Batmantown, U.S.A.").

PLANET-MASTER, THE. A cunning criminal who commits a series of spectacular crimes in October 1961 with the aid of costumes, equipment, and techniques symbolic of the nine planets. Unbeknownst even to himself, the Planet-Master is in reality Professor Norbet, an emminent scientist who unconsciously turned to crime after inhaling the fumes of a strange gas concealed inside a meteorite fragment that he had selected for study.

"That gas was evil," realizes Norbet much later, after he has discovered to his surprise that he and the Planet-Master are one and the same man, "--and under its influence I became a sort of Jekyll-Hyde character . . . creating devices for crimes . . . which I never remembered afterward! And because I inhaled the gas while thinking of the planets, I became the ***Planet-Master!***"

The Dynamic Duo's efforts to apprehend the Planet-Master are complicated by the fact that Norbet's unscrupulous assistant, Edward Burke, has discovered that his employer is the Planet-Master and become determined either to join forces with the villain or to use his special equipment to launch a crime wave of his own. Ultimately, however, Norbet returns to normal as the effects of the strange gas wear off, and he helps BATMAN and ROBIN take Burke into custody (Det No. 296: "The Menace of the Planet Master!").

PLAXIUS. An extradimensional planet to which BATMAN and ROBIN are miraculously transported – along with Gurney, a criminal whom they have been pursuing – when they inadvertently blunder into a mysterious "time-warp" in a cavern outside GOTHAM CITY. On Plaxius, Batman and Robin apprehend Gurney – and thwart the efforts of a villain named Rakk to seize control of the planet by fixing the athletic tournament being held to select a new ruler there – before returning through the time-warp to the earthly dimension (BM No. 125/3, Aug '59: "King Batman the First!").

PNEUMO (Dr.). A cunning criminal who uses blasts of compressed air, fired from an ingenious "air-gun," to aid him in his crimes, as when he drills a hole in the vault door of a local bank and then, inserting the nozzle of his air-gun in the hole, fills the vault so full of compressed air that the vastly increased air pressure literally blows the massive vault door off its hinges.

The Dynamic Duo's efforts to apprehend Dr. Pneumo are severely hampered by the fact that a blow on the head, suffered during an early battle with the villain, has injured BATMAN's optic nerve, perhaps permanently, and made Batman totally blind. Aided by special electronic earplugs, however, one of which alerts him to the presence of obstacles while the other enhances his hearing, Batman bravely continues his fight against crime until finally, after another blow on the head has restored his sight, he and ROBIN apprehend Dr. Pneumo and his henchmen (BM No. 143/2, Oct '61: "The Blind Batman").

P. N. QUINN SHOP. The umbrella shop which serves as the PENGUIN's hideout during May 1944 (Det No. 87: "The Man of a Thousand Umbrellas").

POLKA-DOT (Mr.). A cunning criminal whose crimes revolve around the general theme of dots, as when he steals a black pearl from a foreign dignitary who travels with a spotted leopard.

Mr. Polka-Dot wears a white costume covered with multicolored polka dots, each of which, when torn from its place, instantly transforms itself into some sort of bizarre weapon or escape device: "Inside my costume," explains Mr. Polka-Dot, "are wires connected to each dot! While a dot is ***on*** my costume, the dot is neutral . . . but when I rip ***off*** a dot, it is activated electronically --and then does the job for which it was gimmicked!"

In February 1962 Mr. Polka-Dot and his henchmen commit a series of spectacular "dot crimes" in GOTHAM CITY, only to be apprehended by BATMAN and ROBIN (Det No. 300: "The Bizarre Polka-Dot Man!").

POLO, MARCO (1254–1324). A Venetian traveler who was among the first Europeans in medieval times to enter China and the first man to provide Europeans with an intelligible account of the customs and wonders of the Far East and of the power and extent of China. His remarkable account, *The Book of Marco Polo, Citizen of Venice, Called Million, Wherein Is Recounted the Wonders of the World,* now counted among the significant forerunners of scientific geography, describes his journey from Venice to China and back again, as well as his myriad fascinating experiences in the dominions of KUBLA KHAN, the Great Khan of the Mongol empire.

BATMAN and ROBIN save the life of Marco Polo, and help smash a plot to topple Kubla Khan from the throne of his empire, during a time-journey to China in the year 1275 (WF No. 42, Sep/Oct '49: "The Amazing Adventure of Batman and Marco Polo!").

According to this text, Batman and Robin's meeting with the famed Venetian occurs during a period when Polo is serving as governor of China's Yangchow province at the behest of Kubla Khan. Polo's account of his travels does indeed describe him as having served for a time as governor of Yangchow, but this claim has been strongly disputed by modern scholarship.

PONCE DE LEÓN, JUAN (1460–1521). A Spanish explorer noted for his discovery of Florida and his unsuccessful search for the legendary Fountain of Youth. He is perhaps to be identified with the JOHN DELION encountered by BATMAN and ROBIN in August–September 1949, although this identification is admittedly tenuous (BM No. 54/2: "The Door Without a Key!").

POST (Professor). A renegade scientist who developed "a drug that acts on a man's brain--slows up his reflexes--and makes him--lazy. . . ." Post administered the drug to key members of major brokerage houses, thereby rendering them incapable of conducting their daily business, and then extorted money from the firms in return for providing their employees with the antidote. Post was apprehended by BATMAN and ROBIN sometime prior to March 1942 (Det No. 61: "The Three Racketeers!").

POWELL, MIKE "BULLDOG" (Lieut.). The GOTHAM CITY police detective, a twenty-five-year veteran of the force, who is the father of PATRICIA POWELL. In August 1964 Powell attends his daughter's graduation at the Gotham City Police Academy, then helps her solve the mysterious disappearance of "brilliant chemist" PROFESSOR RALPH SMEDLEY.

Later, Powell and his daughter attend a gala charity affair at the home of BRUCE WAYNE (BM No. 165/2: "The Dilemma of the Detective's Daughter!") and then joins forces with BATMAN and ROBIN to apprehend thieves, disguised as waiters, who have infiltrated the grounds of the estate and stolen a fortune in cash and jewelry from the assembled guests (BM No. 166/2, Sep '64: "A Rendezvous with Robbery!").

POWELL, PATRICIA. A beautiful blond policewoman, the daughter of veteran police detective MIKE "BULLDOG" POWELL, who graduates from the Gotham City Police Academy in August 1964 and moves immediately into plainclothes detective work as the result of having been the first trainee in the academy's history to have "ranked **first** [in her class] in all four categories of training--**academic, physical, firearms**--and **overall!**"

Although Patricia is possessed of "amazing intuitive powers" and incredible deductive abilities, she fears that a single bizarre weakness may hamper her career as a policewoman: she has developed a crush on socialite BRUCE WAYNE, and there are occasional intervals when she appears to have "gone into a trance," when she suffers from short-lived but totally "unexpected lapses" during which she "can think of nothing but ***him!***"

In August 1964 BATMAN appears as guest speaker at the police academy's annual graduation exercises and presents Patricia Powell with a special plaque in recognition of her outstanding achievements at the academy. Because he cannot recall ever having met Patricia before, Batman is astonished to learn of her crush on Bruce Wayne, but Patricia explains that although she has met Wayne on a number of occasions, it has always been while she was wearing some sort of mask — a skin-diving mask at an "aqua-lung party," a face mask at a New Years' Eve masquerade party — so that Wayne has never actually seen her face.

Not long afterward, PROFESSOR RALPH SMEDLEY — a "brilliant chemist" who has been perfecting a "flareless, noiseless explosive" for the U.S. Army — is abducted by two criminals who hope to force him to manufacture the explosive so that they can use it to burglarize safes. Smedley, however, manages to leave behind a series of clues pinpointing the lighthouse where he is being held captive, and although Patricia Powell and her father are assigned the task of locating Smedley, it is Patricia Powell and Batman who ultimately capture the professor's abductors and rescue the professor from their clutches. Later, Patricia and her father receive tickets to a gala charity affair being held at the Wayne mansion, and Patricia is overjoyed at the prospect of actually meeting Bruce Wayne face to face (BM No. 165/2: "The Dilemma of the Detective's Daughter!").

As the charity affair gets under way, it appears that Patricia is finally about to meet Bruce Wayne, when suddenly the festivities are interrupted by a gang of criminals who have infiltrated the gathering disguised as waiters. After relieving the guests of their wallets and jewelry, the criminals flee into the night, having carefully laid mines around the Wayne mansion to discourage pursuit. As soon as the mines have been safely deactivated, Patricia and her father set out after the thieves, and Patricia thus loses her long-awaited opportunity to meet Bruce Wayne.

Patricia and her father trail the criminals to their hideout, only to be taken captive, but Batman and ROBIN arrive on the scene soon afterward, rescue them, and, with their help, pursue the criminals to a nearby petrochemical plant and apprehend them there. Throughout, Patricia proves herself a skilled detective, perhaps as brilliant a deductive thinker as Batman himself (BM No. 166/2, Sep '64: "A Rendezvous with Robbery!").

POWERMAN. A mysterious costumed crime-fighter, his identity concealed by a yellow hood, who functions as the crime-fighting ally of SUPERMAN during May–June 1958, much to the chagrin of BATMAN and ROBIN, who feel that their friend Superman has snubbed them in favor of a new partner.

When renegade scientist LEX LUTHOR breaks out of prison vowing revenge on both Superman and METROPOLIS, Batman and Robin volunteer their services to Superman in helping to reapprehend him, only to be informed, somewhat curtly, that the Man of Steel has acquired a new crime-fighting partner, Powerman, and that Powerman has demanded the exclusion of the Dynamic Duo from their crime-fighting team.

Stung at first by this rejection by their longtime friend and ally, Batman and Robin help apprehend Luthor anyway, only to discover that Powerman is in reality a costumed robot created by Superman as part of a well-meaning ploy to discourage his good friends from risking their lives in the battle against Luthor (WF No. 94: "The Origin of the Superman-Batman Team!").

PRAVHOR (Swami). An unscrupulous GOTHAM CITY fortune-teller who, in collusion with an unnamed "swami" in South Africa, operates an elaborate diamond-smuggling operation in which unsuspecting merchant seamen, sailing from South Africa to the United States, are offered lucky rabbits' feet ostensibly designed to protect them against the hazards of the coming voyage but actually containing contraband diamonds destined for Swami Pravhor in Gotham City. BATMAN and ROBIN apprehend Swami Pravhor and his henchmen — Gouger, Sam, and Muggsy — in Spring 1944 and announce their intention to cable the South African authorities to arrest Swami Pravhor's accomplice in South Africa (WF No. 13: "The Curse of Isis!").

PROFESSOR. The nickname of a "master criminal," otherwise unnamed in the chronicles, who, with the aid of wanted criminals Smite and Bragan, makes off with a collection of fantastic futuristic devices once presented by a space traveler named Odin to the Mayan inhabitants of a remote Mexican village in gratitude for their having nursed him back to health after his spacecraft had crash-landed in the region.

Armed with the stolen devices, the "Professor" and his cohorts launch a spectacular crime wave in GOTHAM CITY until BATMAN finally realizes that another of the alien's gifts, a strangely inscribed medallion with no clearly specified function, has actually been intended as a sort of safety device designed to protect mankind against the misuse of the other gifts. By breaking this medallion, Batman releases an "unknown force" which swiftly renders all of Odin's devices useless, thus enabling him and ROBIN to apprehend the startled criminals (Det No. 263, Jan '59: "The Secret of the Fantastic Weapons!").

PROFESSOR RADIUM. A tragic but nonetheless deadly villain who commits two grisly, albeit unintended, murders before he is finally defeated by BATMAN and ROBIN. He is Professor Henry Ross, a dedicated research scientist who becomes transformed into "a human radium ray" — and ultimately into a homicidal maniac — by the very "radium serum" with which he had hoped to benefit humanity.

In December 1941–January 1942 Professor Henry Ross achieves a major scientific triumph when, working alone in his "hospital laboratory," he administers his new "radium serum" to two dead dogs and miraculously brings them back to life, thus establishing beyond any doubt that doses of radium serum can "repair dead tissue." Ross's exultation quickly turns to bitterness, however, when the director of the institute for which he works refuses to believe his findings and dismisses him from his post for making fanciful scientific claims.

"Bah!" exclaims Ross bitterly. "I'll show him what a true scientist is! . . . A man who is willing to experiment on himself to prove to the world he's right!" Back in his laboratory, Ross deliberately swallows a vial of deadly poison, taking care to leave behind a sample of his miraculous radium serum along with a note containing instructions on how to bring him back to life. Soon afterward, Professor Johnston, Ross's colleague, enters the lab, finds the body, and brings Ross back to life with the radium serum. When Ross inadvertently touches Johnston, however, and Johnston slumps to the floor dead, Ross suddenly realizes the true nature of the horror he has wrought: "I have made myself a monster!" cries Ross. "A human radium ray!" Indeed, when the lights are turned out, Ross finds that his body "glows eerily with a green radiant light."

Setting feverishly to work in the hope of finding an antidote, Ross discovers that the costly drug "Volitell" is successful in reducing the "radium activities" of his blood — so that his touch is no longer lethal — but that the effects of Volitell wear off after twenty-four hours and that a new dose must then be administered.

Desperate to obtain as large a supply of the costly Volitell as possible, but anxious not to harm anyone, Ross "fashions a suit woven from a rubberoid-lead composition--a garb through which the deadly radium rays [emitted by his body] will not pass," and then commits a series of spectacular hospital thefts in quest of the valuable drug. At one point, Ross escapes from Batman and Robin after a brief encounter with them at Gotham Hospital, but in his haste he drops one of his gloves and, by dusting it for fingerprints, the Dynamic Duo soon succeed in establishing the identity of its owner.

Soon afterward, Ross gives himself an injection of Volitell, takes off his protective suit, and pays a call on his girlfriend, Mary Lamont. The drug's stabilizing effects, however, wear off sooner than Ross had anticipated, and suddenly, without realizing it, he begins to glow with an eerie greenish glow. When he touches his girlfriend, he accidentally destroys her. After a horrified maid has reported the murder to the police — and an autopsy has revealed that Mary Lamont died "of internal radium burns" — the police stake out Ross's home in the event he returns there and "the greatest manhunt in the history of crime" is launched in an effort to find him.

Meanwhile, however, Professor Ross — who has by now become known as Professor Radium — has begun to notice a "dreadful change" taking place in his body. "My hair is falling out!" cries Ross. "The radium is beginning to wreak its havoc on my body! I want to murder---wait---what's the matter with me? The radium --it's eating into my body--into my brain — I'm going mad — I'm mad! Ha-ha! **I'm crazy! The cursed radium!**"

In the belief that Professor Radium will return home to retrieve his supply of Volitell, but that he will not show himself if he spies policemen guarding the house, Batman asks the GOTHAM CITY police to call off their stakeout. Indeed, soon afterward, Professor Radium returns home for his precious Volitell. "So strong is the radium-charged body of the professor that he literary [sic] sears his way through the door" of the house, but Batman and Robin have prepared themselves for the coming battle by coating their bodies with a "transparent rubberoid composition" which renders them immune to the lethal radium-rays emitted by the professor's body.

No sooner has Professor Radium recovered his Volitell from its hiding place, than Batman and Robin leap to the attack, but Professor Radium temporarily defeats the Dynamic Duo and flees to a local shipyard with Batman and Robin in hot pursuit. During the ensuing shipyard battle, Professor Radium plummets into the murky waters of the nearby river and is presumed drowned (BM No. 8/2: "The Strange Case of Professor Radium!").

PUNCH AND JUDY. A husband-and-wife swindling team who squabble continually among themselves and who match wits with BATMAN and ROBIN in October–November 1945. The textual narrative introduces them as "that couple so well versed in the art of sarcasm and squabble! But that isn't all! They're past masters in flim-flammery too. . . ."

Punch and Judy are a pair of crooked carnival operators who also put on a live Punch-and-Judy show in which they play the roles traditionally reserved for the comical Punch and Judy puppets.

When Batman discovers that the carnival's concessions are crooked, Punch and Judy self-righteously deny any part in the swindling and promptly fire all their crooked concessionaires in an attempt to allay his suspicions.

Soon afterward, Punch and Judy offer to donate the day's ticket receipts to charity if Batman and Robin will agree to put on an acrobatics display when the carnival opens in Central Park. On the appointed day, however, while Batman is busy putting on a parachute-jumping exhibition in the sky overhead, Punch, Judy, and an unnamed accomplice prepare to skip town with the accumulated gate receipts. Robin intervenes, only to be taken captive.

When Punch and Judy learn that their henchman has sabotaged Batman's parachute, however, they are absolutely furious, for although they regard swindling as a perfectly legitimate activity, they are unalterably opposed to murder. The henchman responds by overpowering Punch and Judy and leaving them tied up alongside Robin while he flees with the carnival money, but Batman, who has had the foresight to carry a spare parachute, reaches the ground safely, captures the fleeing henchman, and rescues the captive Robin. Punch and Judy face a prison term for attempted robbery (BM No. 31/1: "Punch and Judy!").

PUPPET MASTER, THE. A villainous puppeteer and cunning master criminal whose treacherous scheme to "gain [possession of] great inventions to sell to warring nations" involves using a diabolical "thought serum" to transform men like famed atom scientist Dr. Craig into mindless "human puppets" compelled to do his bidding. Aided by this thought serum and the helpless "mental slaves" who have fallen beneath his sway, the Puppet Master steals a top-secret "formula for atomic energy" and attempts to make off with the so-called Voss Rifle, a "newly developed secret army gun," before he is finally apprehended by BATMAN and ROBIN in Fall 1940 (BM No. 3/1: "The Strange Case of the Diabolical Puppet Master").

PURDY, PACK. A ruthless gangland chieftain who has concocted an elaborate scheme to steal $5,000,000 from the hold of the docked ocean liner *Natonic.* To uncover the details of the planned robbery, BATMAN infiltrates Purdy's mob disguised as one of his henchmen, learns the details, and, with ROBIN's help, captures the criminals as they are about to cut their way into the hold of the *Natonic* with underwater torches (BM No. 101/1, Aug '56: "The Vanished Batman").

PURPLE MASK MOB, THE. A gang of criminals, their faces partially concealed by purple bandannas, who commit a series of spectacular crimes in GOTHAM CITY and environs before they are finally apprehended by SUPERMAN and ROBIN in March–April 1955. BATMAN is confined to the BATCAVE throughout much of the adventure, recuperating from the effects of a slow-acting poison, but it is his skillful deduction which reveals the location of the gang's hideout and enables Superman and Robin to make the final capture (WF No. 75: "The New Team of Superman and Robin!").

Q

QUEENIE. A beautiful raven-haired girl who—along with her companions Diamond Jack Deegan and Clubsy—becomes an accomplice of the JOKER in Spring 1941.

When Bruce Wayne pays a visit to the gambling ship which the Joker and his cohorts have recently opened just beyond the three-mile limit, Queenie falls in love with him and ultimately deduces, by matching a shaving nick on Wayne's face with one she sees soon afterward on BATMAN's, that socialite Wayne is secretly Batman.

Later, Queenie saves Batman's life by shooting Diamond Jack Deegan just as Deegan is about to shoot him. In retaliation, the dying Deegan shoots Queenie, mortally wounding her, and Queenie dies in Batman's arms moments later after begging for a final kiss. "This is my finish," gasps Queenie. "I guess I . . . . loved you all the time, Mr. Bruce Wayne. I'm going. . . . Please, kiss me . . . kiss me before it's too late--"

Batman never learns exactly how Queenie discerned his identity. She retains the distinction of being the first criminal ever to learn Batman's secret identity (BM No. 5/1: "The Riddle of the Missing Card!").

QUORK. A "distorted genius" from the planet MARS who, after embarking on a career of evil on his home planet, steals an experimental spacecraft and flees to Earth, where he quickly becomes known as the Stranger, commiting a series of spectacular crimes with the aid of such scientifically advanced devices as a "personal jet-flight unit" and a Martian "invisibility belt." Aided by the Martian lawman ROH KAR—who facilitates the tense manhunt with such ingenious "scientific detection devices" as a "human compass," a special "detectophone device," and personal jet-flight units similar to Quork's—BATMAN finally apprehends Quork in August–September 1953 (BM No. 78/1: "The Manhunter from Mars!").

R

RACER, THE. A cunning thief who flees the scenes of his crimes in a high-speed sports car, which he then drives into the back of a large van to elude the police. The Dynamic Duo's efforts to apprehend the Racer are hampered by the fact that the BATMOBILE's engine is damaged, forcing them to pursue the villain in an ordinary sports car fitted with a batmobile body. Despite this handicap, however, BATMAN and ROBIN finally apprehend the Racer in March 1956 (BM No. 98/3: "Secret of the Batmobile"). (*See also* VALE, VICKI.)

RADBEY. The unscrupulous secretary of the Seven Seas Insurance Co., who has conspired with disreputable shipowners to sink their ships so that they can collect the outstanding insurance from Seven Seas. Radbey, who sinks the ships with the aid of a special submarine camouflaged to resemble a great white whale, and Captain Burly, a cruel sea captain who relentlessly hunts the white whale in hopes of collecting the sizable reward being offered by the insurance company for its capture, ultimately kill each other in a battle over the submarine's only remaining diving helmet (BM No. 9/2, Feb/Mar '42: "The White Whale!").

RADIUM (Professor). *See* PROFESSOR RADIUM.

RADKO, ACE. A European-born mobster, deported from the United States as an undesirable alien and now a powerful gangster in his native country, who concocts an elaborate scheme to lure BATMAN and ROBIN to Europe so that he can kidnap Batman and hold him for $1,000,000 ransom from the U.S. Government. Radko and his henchmen are apprehended in August–September 1950 by Batman, Robin, and a courageous old millionaire named Rogers, a retired big-game hunter, who learns Batman's secret identity in the course of the adventure but who dies of heart failure soon afterward, taking Batman's secret with him (WF No. 47: "Crime Above the Clouds!").

RAFFERTY BROTHERS, THE. A trio of notorious gangsters, all three of them brothers and wearers of bulletproof vests, whose series of violent encounters with BATMAN and ROBIN — described as having taken place during May and June of 1939 — are recalled by Batman and Robin in August–September 1942.

Steve Rafferty perished during an attempted robbery at the Acme Scrap Co. when the scrap yard's electromagnetic crane seized him by his metal vest and buried him beneath tons of metal scrap.

Mike Rafferty died soon afterward when, during a scuffle aboard a boat with Batman and Robin, he fell over the side and was dragged to the bottom by his heavy metal vest.

Pete Rafferty, who had always wanted to go straight but who had been forced into a life of crime by his brothers, ultimately died of a gunshot wound inflicted by one of his slain brothers' disgruntled henchmen, but not before he had courageously endeavored to atone for his criminal acts by joining the two ends of a severed electrical cable to his metal vest during a power failure, thus completing the electrical circuit and bringing light to a nearby house, where a doctor was attempting to perform an emergency appendectomy (BM No. 12/1: "Brothers in Crime!").

RAGLAND, "TIGER." A "notorious thief and gunman" who leaps onto a sightseeing bus in an attempt to flee the scene of a loan company robbery, only to be murdered by other criminals who hijack the bus in order to steal Ragland's loot. The hijackers flee with the loot after leaving the bus passengers to die in a flooded basement, but BATMAN and ROBIN appear on the scene to rescue the passengers and apprehend the escaping criminals (Det No. 93, Nov '44: "One Night of Crime!").

RAINBOW BEAST, THE. A bizarre, rainbow-striped creature — BATMAN describes it as a "freak of nature" spawned by the activity of a local volcano — that wreaks havoc in an unnamed "South American republic" until it is finally destroyed by Batman and ROBIN in September 1960. The rainbow beast can radiate intense heat, shatter objects by "sending out a freezing aura," transform vehicles into a sort of mist, and make people "as thin as leaves," as if they were merely dolls cut out of paper.

When it begins terrorizing native villages near the fiery volcano that gave it birth, an evil band of revolutionaries led by the rebel Diaz attempt to blackmail the government into submission by claiming that they have created the beast and will allow it to rampage across the countryside unless the government capitulates to their demands. Batman and Robin defeat the rebels with the aid of local villagers and finally destroy the rainbow beast by draining it of its powers and permanently sapping its "life-force" (BM No. 134/1: "The Rainbow Creature!").

RANDALL, BILL. An alias employed by BATMAN in April–May 1947 when, after faking BRUCE WAYNE's death in an auto accident as part of his plan to expose HENRY BUSH, he poses as a new recruit for the role of Batman, the so-called Batman II, so that he can continue to function as Batman without allowing ALFRED to learn that Bruce Wayne is not really dead (BM No. 40/2: "The Case of Batman II").

RANGER, THE. An Australian crime-fighter whose methods and techniques are modeled after those of America's BATMAN. In January 1955, in response to Batman's personal invitation, the Ranger and other foreign lawmen — including the GAUCHO, the LEGIONARY, the MUSKETEER, and the KNIGHT and the SQUIRE —

arrive in GOTHAM CITY to study Batman's techniques firsthand, only to find themselves embroiled in a deadly battle of wits with "underworld chieftain" "KNOTS" CARDINE (Det No. 215: "The Batmen of All Nations!"). (*See also* BATMAN (section F, the Batman counterparts].)

RED HOOD, THE. The red-hooded criminal who, according to Detective Comics No. 168, achieved his greatest infamy as the JOKER (Feb '51: "The Man Behind the Red Hood!")

RED MASK MOB, THE. A gang of criminals who are apprehended in April 1959 through the heroic efforts of BATMAN, ROBIN, and ACE THE BAT-HOUND. In order to infiltrate the gang and learn the identity of its secret leader, Batman arranges for an elaborate public charade in which POLICE COMMISSIONER GORDON announces that Batman has become a fugitive from justice and in which Robin and Bat-Hound make a series of apparent attempts to track Batman down and take him into custody. Ultimately, however, after Batman has attained membership in the Red Mask Mob and learned that its leader is LUCKY LANE, he turns on the gang and helps Robin and Bat-Hound take them into custody (BM No. 123/3: "The Fugitive Batman!").

RED RAVEN. The leader of the Red Raven Gang, a gang of criminals whom BATMAN helps apprehend during an unplanned visit to an extradimensional parallel world.

Forced to crash-land the BATPLANE during a violent thunderstorm in September 1963, Batman finds himself on "a twin world" of his own world – on "another Earth" where "evolution has paralleled [his] world's--but with minor variations!" In this dimension, there is no Batman; SUPERMAN is the crime-fighting partner of ROBIN; VICKI VALE is a perfect look-alike for the LOIS LANE who inhabits Batman's world; there is no BATWOMAN; Superman is secretly BRUCE WAYNE, although his features are identical to those of the CLARK KENT Batman knows; and the grotesque face of the JOKER is really the greasepaint mask of television comedian FREDDY FORBES.

Not realizing at first that he has landed on a world other than his own, Batman is taken for a costumed criminal – even a lunatic – until finally he succeeds in demonstrating his goodwill by helping the extradimensional Superman apprehend the Red Raven Gang, whereupon the counterpart Superman helps the bewildered Batman return in the batplane to the familiar Earth he accidentally passed out of in the course of the thunderstorm (WF No. 136: "The Batman Nobody Remembered!").

REED, JULIUS. A greedy, ruthless coal-mine owner who operates a coal mine in the United States town of Gladeville with total disregard for the safety of his miners – and employs a private police force to terrorize his miners into submission – until he is finally made to see the error of his ways by BATMAN and ROBIN, elderly schoolteacher Emma Dodd, his own college-age son Todd, and miner John McGraw, the sole survivor of a recent cave-in whose fatalities could have been avoided if a proper ventilating system had been installed in the mine (Det No. 111, May '46: "Coaltown, U.S.A.").

REKOJ, A. An alias employed by the JOKER in November 1940 when he poses as an elderly music-store proprietor, both to elude the authorities and to conceal from his own henchmen the fact that they are employed by the Joker (Det No. 45: "The Case of the Laughing Death!"). Rekoj is Joker spelled backwards.

REKOJ, I. An alias employed by the JOKER in October-November 1941 (BM No. 7/1). Rekoj is Joker spelled backwards.

RENTER, THE. The proprietor of a secret underworld gun factory, so named because he manufactures guns and then rents them to criminals for use in the commission of crimes. He is in reality Dr. Hagen, a "well-known expert on foreign weapons."

Because the Renter's weapons are returned to him as soon as they have served their purpose, and are privately made and therefore not traceable to any reputable firearms firm, the police have been finding it virtually impossible to recover or identify weapons used to commit crimes. However, by posing as an underworld character with an extensive knowledge of firearms, BATMAN succeeds in obtaining employment at the Renter's clandestine gun factory and ultimately in apprehending the Renter and his leading henchmen (BM No. 73/1, Oct/Nov '52: "Guns for Hire!").

REPP, EDDIE. An ex-convict, once sent to prison by BATMAN and ROBIN, who devises an ingenious "electronic keyboard" to enable him to create and control "television ghost images in three dimensions" – lifelike but apparitional human images which, operated by Repp via remote control, can be made to appear and disappear, to remain visible but insubstantial like ghosts, or even to remain visible but only partly substantial, so that they can inflict powerful blows with their solid fists while remaining otherwise intangible and invulnerable themselves – as part of an elaborate scheme to humiliate and demoralize Batman and Robin as a prelude to letting his so-called "ghost gang" loot the city at will. Although stymied for a time by the ghostly depredations of Repp's "ghost-image gang," Batman and Robin ultimately manage to apprehend Repp in November 1965 (BM No. 175: "The Decline and Fall of Batman!").

REYNOLDS, ROY. A cunning "master criminal" who is renowned both for his brilliantly engineered getaways and for his refusal to be drawn into head-on encounters with BATMAN and ROBIN.

"Far smarter crooks than you or I have tried to capture ***Batman,***" Reynolds reminds his henchmen in March 1965, "--and always they failed! It's the one way to court disaster! I tell you this: if your objective is to get rid of ***Batman*** and ***Robin***--forget it! Their record proves they always manage to escape every trap laid for them! . . . All my efforts are directed to committing a crime and getting away safely! The minute I concentrate on trying to get rid of ***Batman*** and ***Robin***--it'll boomerang on me and cause my own doom!" (BM No. 170/1: "Genius of the Getaway Gimmicks!").

Batman has dubbed Reynolds "the Getaway Genius" (BM No. 174/1, Sep '65: "The Human Punching Bag!").

In March 1965 Reynolds and his henchmen stage a series of spectacular robberies and brilliant getaways, each time assiduously observing Reynolds's strict admonition to avoid conflict with Batman and Robin. As a result, the Dynamic Duo soon arrive at the conclusion that their only hope of apprehending Reynolds and his cohorts lies in luring them into a trap by intentionally placing themselves in such a temptingly helpless position that the criminals will be unable to resist the opportunity to attack them.

Accordingly, Batman and Robin concoct a story for the local newspapers about a fictitious villain called the Hexer who has sworn to use the BAT-SIGNAL in some unspecified way to wreak vengeance on the Dynamic Duo. Soon afterward, as Roy Reynolds and his henchmen flee the scene of a robbery at the home of wealthy Alvin Randall, Batman and Robin – who have donned specially prepared trick costumes for the occasion – dupe the criminals into believing that the light of the bat-signal shining on their uniforms has somehow caused Batman's bat-emblem and Robin's R-emblem to grow drastically in size and wrap around the bodies of the Dynamic Duo as if the emblems had been somehow transformed into living straitjackets. True to his code of a fast robbery followed by a speedy escape, Roy Reynolds hurriedly flees the scene, but his two henchmen, who believe they are witnessing the vengeance of the Hexer taking place before their very eyes, cannot resist the opportunity to attack Batman and Robin while they appear so completely helpless.

Although their arms have been pinned to their bodies by their own trick costumes, Batman and Robin soon succeed in subduing their two attackers with fancy footwork and acrobatic skill, and, aided by information supplied by the captured henchmen, they soon arrive at Reynolds's hideout and capture the villain just as he is preparing to leave town (BM No. 170/1: "Genius of the Getaway Gimmicks!").

By September 1965 Roy Reynolds has been broken out of prison by the BIG GAME HUNTER, a villain who forces Reynolds to plan "a spectacular crime" coupled with "a perfect getaway" as part of an elaborate scheme to capture Batman. Reynolds reluctantly provides the Big Game Hunter with the requested robbery and escape plan, but Batman ultimately apprehends the Big Game Hunter, and Reynolds is returned to prison (BM No. 174/1: "The Human Punching Bag!").

RIDDLER, THE. A wily criminal mastermind whose name derives from his villainous preoccupation with riddles, puzzles, and enigmas of all kinds. His real name is Edward Nigma, and his first initial therefore, coupled with his last name, produces the word *enigma*.

"Because of a quirk in his nature, he never commits a crime without first tipping off ***Batman***--by means of a riddle--where he intends to strike!" (BM No. 171, May '65: "Remarkable Ruse of the Riddler!").

The Riddler wears a green costume decorated with black question marks, a purplish-gray belt, and a narrow mask. The texts refer to him as the Conundrum Champion, the Emir of Enigmas, the King of Conundrums, the Prince of Puzzlers, the Puzzle-Prince of Cryptic Crimes, and the Wizard of Quiz.

Years ago, while Edward Nigma was still a young boy, his history teacher announced a contest to determine which of her students could assemble a certain jigsaw puzzle the fastest. The night before the contest, Nigma pried open his teacher's desk and took a photograph of the assembled puzzle so that the next morning, when the other students were introduced to the puzzle for the first time, he was able to win the contest easily by capitalizing on his knowledge of what the finished puzzle would look like. Having won the puzzle contest, "**E. Nigma** soon became known as a puzzle expert among his friends – who didn't know that he [had] cheated."

Edward Nigma, 1948 © NPP 1948

As an adult, Nigma operated a puzzle booth at a carnival, where customers would compete with him for prize money. If the customer successfully solved Nigma's puzzle, he won a cash prize, but if the customer failed to solve the puzzle, and Nigma succeeded, the customer would pay a fee to Nigma. In each case, Nigma would rig the puzzles in advance to ensure that his customers would always lose.

But the time soon came when "the small pickings of a carnival attraction [did] not satisfy the crooked puzzle master." "I'm clever enough at puzzles to baffle even the police – yes, and **Batman**, too!" muses Nigma to himself in October 1948. "Why don't I commit puzzling crimes? I'll make each crime a duel of wits between myself and the law – and fix the puzzles so I'll always win!" Soon afterward, Nigma dons a bizarre green costume and turns to crime as the Riddler.

In advance of his first crime, the Riddler inscribes a series of baffling word-clues on a huge crossword-puzzle billboard in GOTHAM CITY. After BATMAN and ROBIN have solved the complex word-puzzle and emerged

The Riddler, 1948 © NPP 1948

with the enigmatic message "Basin Street banquet," they race to the scene of the lavish Basin Street civic charity banquet on the assumption the Riddler intends to strike there, only to discover that the Riddler has flooded a nearby bank – the villain's clue should have been translated as "bank-wet" instead of "banquet" – looted the vault with the aid of underwater diving gear, and then fled through the city's labyrinthine sewer system.

The following day, the Riddler sends a gigantic jigsaw puzzle to police headquarters. So large are the individual pieces that it is necessary to transport them to a nearby football field to assemble them. The completed puzzle, however, spells out a clue from the Riddler: "Tonight," reads the clue, "I shall rob the eagle's nest." Acting on this latest clue, Batman instructs Robin to keep a close watch on the Eyrie Nightclub, situated atop one of Gotham City's skyscrapers, while he himself stands guard at the home of millionaire Harrison Eagle. When the Riddler arrives at Eagle's home and attempts to loot it, Batman leaps to the attack. He is forced to abandon the chase, however, in order to rescue Harrison Eagle from a deadly wire puzzle-trap in which the Riddler has imprisoned him, enabling the Riddler to make good his escape.

The Riddler's next clue takes the form of a huge model of an ear of corn, accompanied by the riddle "Why is corn hard to escape from?" The solution to the riddle lies in the fact that corn is also called "maize," that maize sounds exactly like "maze," and that a maze can indeed be "hard to escape from." Soon afterward, the Riddler robs the box office at an amusement pier and then races into a complex maze at one end of the pier. When Batman and Robin give chase, they discover to their horror that the Riddler has fixed the maze so that they cannot get out of it, and hidden a bomb inside which is set to go off at any second. At the last possible instant, Batman and Robin succeed in escaping from the deadly maze, but the Riddler is blown off the pier into the water by the force of the explosion and it is not at all certain whether he has managed to survive it (Det No. 140: "The Riddler").

In December 1948 the Riddler returns. This time, his theft of the prize money from a nationwide puzzle contest provides him with an inspiration for yet another series of spectacular crimes. "I'll run a big puzzle contest of my own!" he exclaims. "One that will make me rich!"

Soon the Riddler launches a spectacular puzzle contest for the benefit of the general public, providing enigmatic clues to the location of prize money and allowing those who find the money to keep it as their prize. The real motive behind the contest, however, is to enable the Riddler to draw huge crowds of money-seekers to various parts of the city, so that the turmoil caused by their presence will enable him to commit a series of crimes there.

At one point, for example, the Riddler lights up the windows of a Gotham City skyscraper in such a way as to form a complex word clue. Before long, in response to the clue, huge crowds of people have converged on a local drive-in to search for the thousand dollars in cash that the Riddler has hidden beneath the movie screen, but the incredible congestion caused by the crowd enables the villain to loot the drive-in box office and escape on a motorcycle, leaving Batman and Robin hopelessly ensnarled in the tumultuous traffic.

The next clue in the Riddler's puzzle contest consists of a huge rebus puzzle drawn through the air behind a large blimp. Soon, in response to the rebus riddle, huge crowds of people surge toward the Rainbow Club, a nightclub situated atop a tall skyscraper, where the Riddler hopes to capitalize on the confusion by robbing the club's safe. Batman and Robin thwart the robbery, but the Riddler escapes by parachuting off the roof. Later, the Riddler provides the public with an elaborate charade clue which draws crowds of people into the Gotham Museum, where the Riddler hopes to steal some priceless Egyptian relics. Batman and Robin arrive on the scene, however, and swiftly apprehend him (Det No. 142: "Crime's Puzzle Contest!").

In May 1965 the Riddler, newly released from the state penitentiary, prepares to match wits with Batman once again, only to learn, to his chagrin, that Batman is presently preoccupied with a gang of criminals known as the Molehill Mob. "I want ***all*** of ***Batman's*** attention when I make my move!" muses the Riddler. "But he can't concentrate on me--if he's out chasing somebody else!"

In order to dispose of the Molehill Mob so that he can enjoy the undivided attention of Batman and Robin, the Riddler uses information he has learned from the prison grapevine to locate the Molehill Mob's hideout and then, under the pretense of having abandoned his life of crime, leads the Dynamic Duo there to apprehend the criminals.

With the members of the Molehill Mob now safely behind bars, the Riddler provides Batman and Robin with a cryptic riddle from which they deduce that he intends to steal the priceless Black Pearl of the Pacific from millionaire "Smiles" Dawson. Batman and Robin apprehend the Riddler in the act of fleeing from Dawson's yacht and find the black pearl in his possession, but the Riddler claims that he has just purchased the pearl with money recently inherited from his uncle Edward, and Dawson promptly corroborates the story.

The Riddler's second riddle-clue leads Batman and Robin to believe that he is about to rob the Peale Art Gallery. When the Riddler emerges from the gallery owner's office with the priceless Cross of the North — a white cross encrusted with rubies — in his possession, Batman and Robin apprehend him, only to learn that the cross represents part of the Riddler's inheritance from his uncle and rightfully belongs to him.

As the Riddler leaves the art gallery, Batman and Robin ask him why he has not yet given them another of his puzzling riddle-clues. The answer to that question, replies the Riddler enigmatically, is that he has already provided them with another riddle-clue, but that it will be up to them to deduce exactly what it is.

The clue of which the Riddler speaks is contained within the circumstances of his two recent encounters with Batman and Robin, the first at "Smiles" Dawson's yacht, and the second at the Peale Art Gallery. Actually, there are two clues: the first reveals the scene of a spectacular crime which the Riddler plans to commit in the near future, while the second is designed only to mislead the Dynamic Duo as to his real intentions.

The misleading clue revolves around the colors of the objects that Batman and Robin mistakenly assumed the Riddler had stolen, i.e., a black pearl and a white and red cross. These colors are in turn suggestive of the old riddle "What is black and white and red [i.e., read] all over?" The answer to this riddle — a newspaper — suggests that the Riddler intends to rob the celebrities attending the 100th anniversary celebration of the Gotham *Times*. Batman and Robin unravel this elaborate riddle-clue, but dismiss it as bogus on the ground that its solution came too easily and was therefore probably intended only to mislead them.

The second clue involves the shape of the two "stolen" objects — a circle and a cross — and refers to the famous riddle "My first is a circle, my second is a cross. Join them together — or be at a loss!" The answer to this old riddle, the word *ox*, suggests that the Riddler intends to stage a robbery at Gotham City's lavish Ox Club. Having solved this elaborate riddle-clue, Batman and Robin race to the Ox Club and apprehend the Riddler and his henchmen in the act of robbing the club's patrons and looting its safe (BM No. 171: "Remarkable Ruse of the Riddler!").

RILEY, NAILS. A GOTHAM CITY gang chief who concocts an elaborate scheme to steal the entire fortune of big-game hunter Byron King. The plot is thwarted in February 1953, and Riley and his henchmen are apprehended, through the heroic efforts of BATMAN and ROBIN (Det No. 192: "The Phantom Eye of Gotham City").

RIVERS, RED. An alias employed by BATMAN in December 1954 when he poses as a member of the underworld as part of his plan to apprehend HERBERT SMIRT, the "scholar with a shady record" who has published *The Batman Encyclopedia* (Det No. 214: "The Batman Encyclopedia").

ROBBER BARON, THE. An "arrogant lordling of the underworld" who stages a series of spectacular robberies of seemingly inaccessible places by firing a grappling hook, with a special cable attached to it, at his objective — e.g., a penthouse — and then riding along the cable, high above the city streets, inside a special cable car designed for the purpose. The Robber Baron and his henchmen are apprehended in May 1943 through the heroic efforts of BATMAN, ROBIN, and ALFRED (Det No. 75: "The Robber Baron!").

ROBIN (the Boy Wonder). The courageous, warm-hearted, hard-fighting, pun-loving teen-ager who, since April 1940, has been the inseparable crime-fighting companion of BATMAN (Det No. 38). Robin is in reality Dick Grayson, the young ward of socialite Bruce Wayne, the man who is secretly Batman.

Robin and Batman, 1957 © NPP 1957

In the texts, Robin is described as Batman's "daredevil young aide" (WB No. 1, Spr '41: "The Witch and the Manuscript of Doom!"), as a "young, laughing Robin Hood of today" (Det No. 40, Jun '40), as an "impatient foolhardy young daredevil" (BM No. 11/1, Jun/Jul '42), as Batman's "reckless, rollicking" companion (BM No. 23/2, Jun/Jul '44: "Damsel in Distress!"), as a "laughing young dare-devil" (Det No. 39, May '40), and as Batman's "grinning, reckless" ally (Det No. 46, Dec '40).

He is a "living hurricane" (BM No. 4/4, Win '41), and a "hard-fisted little scrapper" with a "nimble, wide-awake mind" (BM No. 18/2, Aug/Sep '43: "Robin Studies His Lessons!"). He is "a flashing streak of green and scarlet, a teen-age typhoon in action" (Det No. 226, Dec '55: "When Batman Was Robin!").

"Everyone is familiar with his reckless grin, his devil-may-care courage, his gymnastic skill, yes . . . even his corny puns!" (BM No. 32/2, Dec/Jan '45–'46: "Dick Grayson, Boy Wonder!").

To the denizens of the underworld, he is "tougher to handle than a dozen cops" (BM No. 5/1, Spr '41: "The Riddle of the Missing Card!"), a fighting "wild cat" (BM No. 8/1, Dec/Jan '41–'42: "Stone Walls Do Not a Prison Make") who packs a punch "like a swingin' boom!" (BM No. 24/2, Aug/Sep '44: "Convict Cargo!").

Dick Grayson is the orphaned son of John and Mary Grayson, a husband-and-wife team of circus trapeze artists who, together with their young son Dick, comprised the FLYING GRAYSONS until they were murdered by protection racketeers in April 1940 (Det No. 38). It was Batman who took the young orphan under his wing, helped him avenge the deaths of his parents, trained him for his new life as a crime-fighter, and, as Bruce Wayne, took the legal steps necessary to establish himself as Dick Grayson's "legal guardian" (BM No. 213/1, Jul/Aug '69: "The Origin of Robin!").

It is not possible to establish Dick Grayson's age with any real precision. There were fourteen candles on his birthday cake in April–May 1942, indicating that he turned fourteen during this period, or, if one of these candles was only a "good luck" candle, thirteen. On this same occasion, curiously enough, Bruce Wayne ceremoniously spanks his young ward eight times, plus "one for good measure" and another "to grow on," but it seems absurd to suggest that Grayson was only eight years old at this time (BM No. 10/1: "The Isle That Time Forgot!"). The chronicles, at any rate, treat Grayson as a student of high school age until December 1969, at which time, having apparently attained college age, he leaves GOTHAM CITY to attend his first year of classes at Hudson University (BM No. 217: "One Bullet Too Many!").

Dick Grayson's living relatives include an unscrupulous uncle named GEORGE GRAYSON, who wins legal custody of his young nephew in December 1943–January 1944 as part of an elaborate scheme to extort $1,000,000 from Bruce Wayne (BM No. 20/4: "Bruce Wayne Loses the Guardianship of Dick Grayson!"), and a well-meaning if somewhat overprotective aunt named AUNT HARRIET (Det No. 328, Jun '64: "Gotham Gang Line-Up!"; and others).

For his role as Robin, Grayson wears a green short-sleeved shirt with matching trunks, gloves, and boots that extend only slightly above his ankles. Concealing his green shirt entirely, except for its short sleeves, is a red vestlike garment – referred to both as a "vest" (e.g., in Det No. 41, Jul '40) and a "jerkin" (e.g., in Det No. 50, Apr '41: "The Case of the Three Devils!") – with a Robin insignia, in the form of a yellow "R" inside a small black circle, emblazoned just above the left breast. A yellow cape flows out behind him and fastens at his throat to form a pointed yellow collar at the front of his costume, and a thin black eye-mask conceals the narrow area of his face between his cheekbones and just below his eyebrows.

Around Robin's waist is a black utility belt with a gold buckle which, in function although not in design, is the counterpart of Batman's own. (*See* BATMAN [section C 3, the utility belt].) In two or three early texts, Robin's utility belt is yellow (e.g., in Det No. 38, Apr '40) but from late Summer 1940 onward it is never anything but black.

According to Detective Comics No. 226, the first Robin costume was created by young Bruce Wayne long before he had ever met Robin, or, for that matter, before he had ever embarked upon his own career as Batman. Wayne, then still a teen-ager, had been determined to persuade his idol, police detective HARVEY HARRIS, to train him in the science of crime detection. Realizing that Harris would attempt to discourage him because of his age, and perhaps even notify his parents, Wayne had concealed his identity from Harris by wearing a red, yellow, and green costume almost identical to the one which Robin wears today. Harris had reluctantly agreed to accept Wayne as his pupil, and "since you're brilliant as a robin redbreast in that costume," he had commented, "I'll call you--**Robin!**"

Not long afterward, after his lessons with Harris had come to an end, Wayne had mailed his Robin costume to Harris as his way of assuring the great detective that he would not begin his own crime-fighting career until he had reached manhood (Dec '55: "When Batman Was Robin!"), but many years later, after he had launched his own career as Batman and taken the just-orphaned Dick Grayson under his personal protection, he had created a second Robin costume, modeled directly after the first one, and had given it to Grayson to wear during the coming battle with the racketeers who had murdered his parents (Det No. 38, Apr '40).

In spite of the voluminous information recorded in the chronicles concerning Robin's origin and subsequent career, some confusion remains regarding the origin of the name Robin itself, and some question exists as to whether he was named after ROBIN HOOD or the robin redbreast. The texts provide ample support for either position. Detective Comics No. 38, for example, describes Robin as "an exciting new figure whose incredible gymnastic and athletic feats will astound you . . . a laughing, fighting young daredevil who scoffs at danger like the legendary Robin Hood whose name and spirit he has adopted . . ." (Apr '40). Detective Comics No. 40 describes him as "that young, laughing Robin Hood of today" (Jun '40). And Detective Comics No. 116 describes Robin Hood as Robin's "famous namesake" (Oct '46: "The Rescue of Robin Hood!").

Batman No. 32/2, on the other hand, asserts that Robin was named "after another winged creature" (Dec/Jan '45–'46: "Dick Grayson, Boy Wonder!"), i.e., the robin redbreast, and World's Finest Comics No. 65, in a brief recapitulation of Dick Grayson's early crime-fighting training, pictures Grayson as suggesting that "the partner of ***Batman*** will need to have wings, too--how about me being a ***Robin?***" (Jul/Aug '53: "The Five Different Batmen!").

These conflicting statements and inferences are best reconciled by the lengthy account of Robin's origin which appears in Batman No. 213/1. According to this

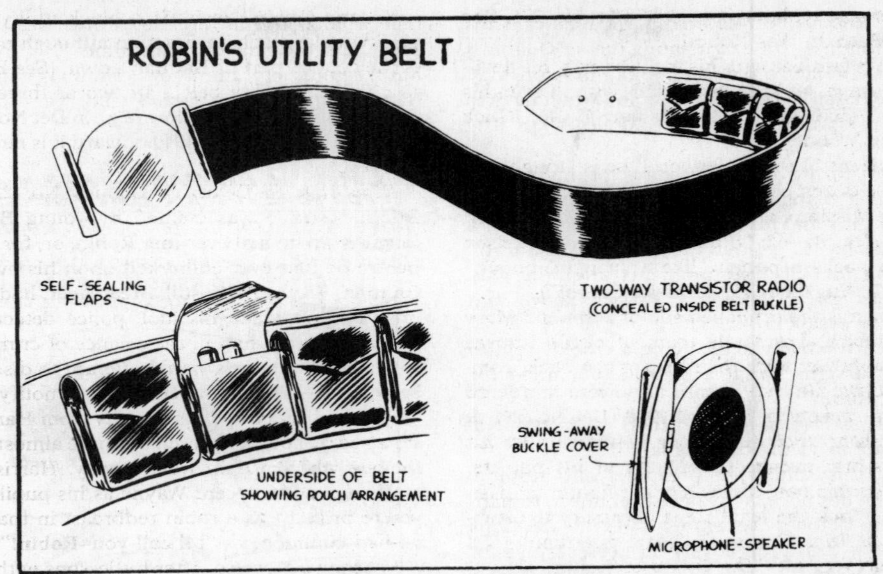

Robin's utility belt © NPP 1968

account, Bruce Wayne first broached the subject of a new name for Dick Grayson as they prepared to set out on their first case together, the tracking down of the killers of Grayson's parents.

"You're almost ready, Dick!" remarked Wayne. "But to operate with ***Batman,*** you'll need another identity . . . a costume . . . and a new name!"

"Since you're ***Batman,*** replied Grayson, "maybe I could take the name of a ***different*** flying creature!"

"I was thinking the same thing!" answered Wayne. "How do you like the name ***Robin?***"

"Swell!" exclaimed Grayson. "***Robin Hood*** was always one of my favorite heroes!" (Jul/Aug '69: "The Origin of Robin!").

The name Robin may well have occurred to Bruce Wayne on this occasion as the result of its prior usage by Harvey Harris many years earlier.

During the early years of his career, Robin carries a slingshot concealed "within his vest" (Det No. 41, Jul '41). Usually it is a simple sling, of the kind used by David against Goliath (Det No. 38, Apr '40; and others), but on occasion it consists of a Y-shaped stick attached to a heavy rubber band (BM No. No. 24/1, Aug/Sep '44: "It Happened in Rome"). Robin's extraordinary proficiency with this simple weapon is amply illustrated by an incident which takes place in August 1940, when he uses a "steel pellet" from his slingshot to knock an arrow out of the air in mid-flight (Det No. 42: "The Case of the Prophetic Pictures!"). By the end of 1944, however, Robin has abandoned the slingshot in favor of the more sophisticated array of crime-fighting apparatus employed by Batman himself. (*See* BATMAN [section E, the extraordinary abilities and the famous crime-fighting equipment].)

Throughout the chronicles, Robin is noted for his love of danger and his eagerness for a good fight. "Gee, Bruce," complains Dick Grayson in Summer 1940, as he and Bruce Wayne pore over a quiet game of chess, "it's too quiet around here. I wish something would happen" (BM No. 2/1).

And in text after text, this basic theme is continually repeated. "Are you all right, Robin?" cries Batman anxiously, as he and Robin plunge into battle with a gang of counterfeiters in July 1940. "Don't worry about me," replies Robin, "--I'm having a swell time!" (Det No. 41).

"Do I detect the eager light of battle in your eyes?" asks Batman, as he and Robin prepare for their coming encounter with the diabolical Clayface (*see* CLAYFACE [BASIL KARLO]). "You do," replies Robin eagerly, "**— and how!**" (Det No. 49, Mar '41: "Clayface Walks Again!").

In March 1944, after Batman has observed that they had better head for the place where trouble is likely to break out next, Robin's eagerness is unmistakable. "That's for me, **Batman!**" he exclaims. "I like to keep company with trouble!" (Det No. 85: "The Joker's Double").

In May 1944 Dick Grayson grows irritable after a period of relative inaction. "Things have been too quiet!" he complains. "I'm so bored I'd welcome a good old-fashioned fist fight!" (Det No. 87: "The Man of a Thousand Umbrellas").

"Careful, fella!" admonishes Batman during a hazardous moment in April 1945. "This is dangerous business!"

"If it wasn't," replies Robin, "it wouldn't be half as much fun!" (Det No. 98: "The King of the Hoboes!").

It is in keeping with this love of danger and excitement that the texts so often speak of Robin as "impetuous" (Det No. 218, Apr '55: "Batman, Junior and Robin, Senior!"), "reckless" (Det No. 46, Dec '40), "impatient," and "foolhardy" (BM No. 11/1, Jun/Jul '42). Indeed, Detective Comics No. 218 observes that "the mature judgment and surpassing detective skill of the **Batman** make him a perfect partner for the more impetuous, reckless courage of young **Robin!**" (Apr '55: "Batman, Junior and Robin, Senior!").

Another of Robin's best-known characteristics is his inexplicable fondness for excruciating puns. "Oohhh! I can't stand it!" moans a defeated JOKER in April–May 1947. "Put me in jail . . . anyplace . . . so I won't have to listen to Robin's puns any more!" (BM No. 40/1: "The 13 Club!").

Particularly during the early days of his career, Robin, like most young boys, exhibits a certain amount of disdain for girls and for romance. ". . . it's too bad a crook like that has to get away, even if she **is** a girl!" grouses Robin in Fall 1940, moments after the wily CATWOMAN has given Batman a sudden shove and made good her escape.

"Yes, and it's too bad she has to be a crook!" replies Batman with a sigh. "What a night! . . . A night for romance, eh, **Robin?**"

"Romance?" exclaims Robin. "**BAH** . . ." (BM No. 3/4: "The Batman vs the Cat-Woman!").

In spite of this somewhat preadolescent attitude, however, Robin has not exactly been immune to romantic feeling. In October–November 1943 he develops something of a crush on lovely Princess Lanya of ATLANTIS (BM No. 19/2: "Atlantis Goes to War!"), and by June–July 1944 he has fallen in love with MARJORY DAVENPORT, a pretty blond classmate – Dick Grayson calls her "the prettiest [girl] in the whole world" – who shuns his affections in favor of the more glamorous Robin. "A fine thing!" thinks Grayson bitterly. "I'm my own rival – and I can't do a thing about it!" (BM No. 23/2: "Damsel in Distress!").

By February 1954 Dick Grayson has developed a crush on a pretty dark-haired classmate named Marcia, but Marcia, like Marjory Davenport before her, is so completely taken with Robin that plain Dick Grayson doesn't stand a chance with her (BM No. 81/2: "The Boy Wonder Confesses!").

In April 1957 Robin launches a serious but short-lived romance with teen-aged ice-skating star VERA LOVELY, but before long he has come to the unhappy conclusion that women simply are not worth the trouble they cause and the time they consume. ". . . from now on, I'm keeping my mind on criminals," he promises Batman finally, "not *girls!*" (BM No. 107/2: "Robin Falls in Love").

Vera Lovely and Robin, 1957 © NPP 1957

Robin and Batman, 1957 © NPP 1957

In April 1961, however, Robin meets Bat-Girl (*see* BAT-GIRL [BETTY KANE]) and begins a sometimes serious relationship with her that is to persist for several years (BM No. 139/3: "Bat-Girl!"). (*See* BAT-GIRL [BETTY KANE].)

Dick Grayson's other romantic interests have included a girl named Edie whom he escorts to a high school dance in June 1963 (BM No. 156/1: "The Secret of the Ant-Man"), and a girl named Nancy whom he escorts to a school prom in June 1965 (Det No. 340: "The Outsider Strikes Again!").

Of all the personal relationships that are dealt with in the Batman chronicles, however, the most important one is the one that exists between Dick Grayson and his legal guardian Bruce Wayne. Batman No. 20/4 observes that "the mutual affection between this man and boy has been as strong as that between father and son" (Dec/Jan '43–'44: "Bruce Wayne Loses the Guardianship of Dick Grayson!"), and Batman No. 156/2 notes that "the friendship of **Batman** and **Robin** is one that has stood steadfast as a rock! To **Batman, Robin** is like his own son--and **Robin** would brave any danger to keep **Batman** from harm!" (Jun '63: "Robin Dies at Dawn!").

Robin has described Batman as "my best friend" (BM No. 3/1, Fall '40: "The Strange Case of the Diabolical Puppet Master") and as "the greatest friend I ever had" (BM No. 118/3, Sep '58: "The Merman Batman!"), and Batman has referred to Robin as "my closest pal" (Det No. 166, Dec '50: "The Man with a Million Faces!") and as "the best friend I've got" (Det No. 49, Mar '41: "Clayface Walks Again!").

"Dick, though you're only my ward," insists Batman in August–September 1951, "I couldn't love you more if you were my own son!" (BM No. 66/3: "Batman II and Robin, Junior!").

The depth of this great relationship is one of the great themes of the Batman chronicles, and the chroniclers have dealt with it extensively, particularly in terms of threats, real and imagined, to its continued existence. In general, threats to the Batman-Robin relationship assume one of three basic forms: (a) an outsider attempts to deprive Bruce Wayne of the legal custody of Dick Grayson; (b) Robin fears, invariably without justification, that Batman intends to replace him with a new crime-fighting partner; and (c) Robin fears that a woman is about to supplant him in Batman's affections, thus destroying his relationship with Batman and bringing an end to their "wonderful life together" (WF No. 110, Jun '60: "The Alien Who Doomed Robin!").

(a) Two attempts have been made to wrest the guardianship of Dick Grayson away from Bruce Wayne, the first by Dick Grayson's unscrupulous uncle George Grayson, who institutes the legal action as part of a scheme to bilk Bruce Wayne out of $1,000,000 (BM No. 20/4, Dec/Jan '43–'44: "Bruce Wayne Loses the Guardianship of Dick Grayson!"), and the second by exconvict Ed Kolum, who hopes to revenge himself on Bruce Wayne for having once exposed him as a charity swindler (BM No. 57/1, Feb/Mar '50: "The Trial of Bruce Wayne!").

(b) There are a number of occasions when Robin becomes convinced that Batman has been training a new partner to take his place in the Dynamic Duo. In December 1948–January 1949 he feels certain that he is about to be replaced by a youngster named Jimmy, only to learn that Jimmy is blind and that Batman has only been training him in criminology to help him fulfill his ambition of becoming a criminologist when he gets older (BM No. 50/3: "The Second Boy Wonder!"). In June–July 1951 Robin becomes intensely jealous of a crime-fighter named WINGMAN, only to discover that, as Batman has insisted all along, Wingman is merely a Northern European crime-fighter whom Batman is training for action in his home country (BM No. 65/1: "A Partner for Batman!"). In May 1956 Robin becomes fearful that he is about to be replaced by JOHN VANCE — a man once known as Batman, Junior — but Vance turns out merely to be someone who helped Batman solve a criminal case many years ago (Det No. 231: "Batman, Junior!").

(c) Robin becomes seized by unhappiness and anxiety whenever it appears that a woman is vying with him for Batman's affections. In February–March 1943, after Bruce Wayne has announced his intention to marry Elva Barr, despite his being fully aware that Elva Barr is secretly the CATWOMAN, Robin is plainly dismayed: "But, **Bruce,** you can't do this! That Elva's the Catwoman! What's got into you? What about Linda [LINDA PAGE]? What about . . us?" (BM No. 15/1: "Your Face Is Your Fortune!").

In October–November 1953, when it appears that Batman may be forced to marry VICKI VALE against his will, Robin becomes decidedly gloomy, but not entirely over the prospect of Batman's acquiring a wife he does not really want: "It looks like we're sunk, ***Batman!***" says Robin dejectedly. "And that means ***everything*** changes! You won't have much time to pal around with me---not with a wife around . . ." (BM No. 79/1: "The Bride of Batman!").

In October 1954 Robin becomes mournful once again, this time over Batman's apparent romance with "international beauty" MAGDA LUVESCU. "***Batman*** hardly has time for me anymore!" complains Robin to Vicki Vale. "I never thought anyone could come between us . . . I see now that I was dead wrong!" (BM No. 87/3: "Batman Falls in Love!").

The true extent of the hostility and resentment which Dick Grayson feels for the women in Bruce Wayne's life is best revealed by a dream which Grayson has in March 1959 after Wayne has left the Wayne mansion for a date with Kathy Kane, the wealthy young heiress who is secretly BATWOMAN. In it, Kathy becomes the wife of Bruce Wayne, and therefore the wife of Batman, and stubbornly pursues her own crime-fighting career in defiance of Batman's admonition that "one crime-fighter in the family is enough" and that "a wife's place is in the home!" The dream reaches a tragic climax when Kathy's recklessness results in the accidental betrayal of Batman's secret identity. Batman remains outwardly calm despite the disclosure, but Robin becomes nearly hysterical with rage: "Kathy, do you know what you've done?" cries Robin, his brow dripping with sweat. "You've wrecked ***Batman's*** career! He's finished, Kathy--and it's all your fault because you wouldn't listen! You did it--you did it. . . ."

Seconds later, Grayson awakens to find Bruce Wayne standing over him, shouting to him to wake up and trying desperately to shake him back to reality. "Fine thing!" cries Wayne. "I come back from a date and instead of finding you in bed, I find you asleep in a chair!"

"Ohh!" moans Grayson, still somewhat dazed. "Then it didn't happen! It was all a ***dream!*** You didn't marry Kathy!"

"I--marry Kathy?" muses Wayne. "I expect some day I will marry! Kathy, eh? Well, she's a nice girl! Who knows--who knows?"

"Golly!" thinks Grayson. "What if Bruce ***does*** marry Kathy some day? Will my dream come ***true?*** Oh, gosh--gosh!" (BM No. 122/3: "The Marriage of Batman and Batwoman!").

There are a number of occasions in the chronicles when Batman and Robin go their separate ways for other reasons. In October–November 1942 Batman parts company with Robin in order to protect him from a gangster known as the Thumb, but Robin, who has not been told the reason for his abrupt dismissal, suffers through a great deal of heartbreak until the Thumb is finally apprehended and the Dynamic Duo are once again reunited (BM No. 13/1: "The Batman Plays a Lone Hand!").

In November 1956, after Bruce Wayne has supposedly been murdered, Bruce Wayne and Dick Grayson are forced to part company so that people will not know that Bruce Wayne is really still alive. During this period, Wayne moves into a furnished room, assumes the name Barney Warren, and becomes a cab driver, but a way is finally found whereby Bruce Wayne can admit his existence once again, and he and Dick Grayson are happily reunited (Det No. 237: "Search for a New Robin!").

In February 1961 an extraterrestrial alien calling himself Mr. Marvel forces Robin to abandon Batman and become his crime-fighting partner by threatening to kill Batman if Robin refuses. Ultimately, Mr. Marvel is defeated and Batman and Robin are reunited, but Batman, who has not been told the reason for Robin's abrupt defection, suffers some anxious moments until he learns that Robin had only pretended to abandon him in order to protect him from Mr. Marvel (BM No. 137/1: "Robin's New Boss!").

From the beginning of their relationship, Bruce Wayne has been studiously protective of his young ward's education, and on more than one occasion he has warned Grayson that "if you don't get good marks in school, you don't go crook-catching!" (BM No. 23/2, Jun/Jul '44: "Damsel in Distress!"; *see also* BM No. 18/2, Aug/Sep '43: "Robin Studies His Lessons!").

"I wish ***Robin*** were here with me," muses Batman in August 1967 as he sets out on his nightly patrol alone, "but he had a book report to work on--and his school work must come first! A good education is one thing not even the cleverest criminal in the world can steal from you!" (Det No. 366: "The Round-Robin Death Threats").

During the greater part of his career as Robin, Dick Grayson has attended classes at Gotham City High School (BM No. 81/2, Feb '54: "The Boy Wonder Confesses!"), popularly known as Gotham High (Det No. 185, Jul '52: "The Secret of Batman's Utility Belt!"). A report card he receives in August–September 1943 indicates that he has taken courses in Latin, chemistry, grammar, physics, algebra, and English (BM No. 18/2: "Robin Studies His Lessons!"), and a remark he makes in August 1960 indicates that he has taken "painting lessons in school" also (WF No. 111: "Superman's Secret Kingdom!").

In addition, Dick Grayson has been active in high school athletics, although he must continually conceal the true extent of his athletic ability in order to safeguard the secret of his dual identity. During his high school years, Grayson pitched for the school baseball team (BM No. 31/1, Oct/Nov '45: "Punch and Judy!"), was "star pole-vaulter on the school track team" (BM No. 32/3, Dec/Jan '45–'46: "All for One, One for All!"), was "the best goal-kicker on [his] high school football squad" (BM No. 56/2, Dec/Jan '49–'50: "The Riddle of the Seven Birds!"), and played on his high school basketball team (BM No. 162/2, Mar '64: "Robin's New Secret Identity!").

If anything can be said to irk Dick Grayson, it is the necessity for continually playing down his remarkable athletic prowess in order to avoid endangering the vital secret of his dual identity. In July–August 1946, for example, Grayson enters Gotham City's all-city high school track meet and intentionally compromises his own performance so that he will not attract undue attention by winning the meet. At one point, after a fellow contestant has made a shot-put throw of 50 feet 6 inches, Grayson muses bitterly that he could easily beat the throw, but that he dare not for fear of betraying his true identity (WF No. 23: "Champions Don't Brag!").

"Gosh, I hate holding myself back like that--not being able to do my **best**!" muses Grayson bitterly in March 1964, after being forced to score fewer baskets than he otherwise might during the Gotham High basketball finals. "But I guess that's one of the drawbacks of being a secret crime-fighter! Ordinary kids have all the fun . . . they can be themselves!"

On this occasion, Grayson even goes so far as to use a wig and theatrical makeup to assume a new identity — that of a red-haired, freckle-faced boy named Danny — just so that he can have the pleasure of going to a downtown recreation center and playing basketball without having to suppress his natural athletic skill (BM No. 162/2: "Robin's New Secret Identity!").

By December 1969 Dick Grayson has apparently graduated from Gotham City High School, for it is then that he departs Gotham City for his first year of classes at Hudson University (BM No. 217: "One Bullet Too Many!").

For Robin, a typical day invariably includes such activities as "a brisk workout in the gym" (BM No. 12/4, Aug/Sep '42: "Around the Clock with the Batman!"), a "daily lesson in the crime lab" on the techniques of scientific crime detection (Det No. 280, Jun '60: "The Menace of the Atomic Man"), testing or improving a piece of crime-fighting equipment, laboratory work in connection with an ongoing criminal investigation, homework for school, entertaining at a hospital or other charitable institution, and battles with one or more gangs of criminals (BM No. 12/4, Aug/Sep '42: "Around the Clock with the Batman!").

Throughout the year, Robin keeps himself in "splendid physical condition" (Det No. 59, Jan '42: "The King of the Jungle!") by boxing (BM No. 1/4, Spr '40), fencing (BM No. 4/2, Win '41: "Blackbeard's Crew and the Yacht Society"), and continually improving his gymnastic and acrobatic skills.

ONE NIGHT IN THE BAT-CAVE, AS DICK GRAYSON (ROBIN, THE BOY WONDER) CHECKS A SCIENTIFIC ANALYSIS WHILE BATMAN IS AWAY...
THE INFLATION OF THE RUBBER BALLOON PROVES THAT THIS POISON GIVES OFF A GAS! HMM! STRANGE-- WHERE'S THAT HUMMING SOUND COMING FROM?
HUMMM-MMMM-MMMMM

Robin, 1951 © NPP 1951

Robin is an honorary member of the Maskers, a club for people who wear masks in their everyday work (BM No. 72/2, Aug/Sep '52: "The Legion of Faceless Men!"), an honorary member of the Folklore Society (WF No. 38, Jan/Feb '49: "The Impossible People!"), and an honorary member of the 50 Fathoms Club, a society for underwater specialists (BM No. 104/3, Dec '56: "The Creature from 20,000 Fathoms!").

As Dick Grayson, he is a member of the Camera Scoops Club, an exclusive photographic society, membership in which is regarded as "the highest photographic honor in Gotham City" (WF No. 21, Mar/Apr '46: "Crime's Cameraman!"). Grayson is also something of a writer, for he has published at least one adventure story in a comics magazine called *Crescent Comics* (BM No. 35/3, Jun/Jul '46: "Dick Grayson, Author!").

In May 1964 Robin and JIMMY OLSEN establish a secret headquarters together in an abandoned observatory which they quickly dub the Eyrie (WF No. 141: "The Olsen-Robin Team versus 'The Superman-Batman Team!' "). The Eyrie is intended to serve as their base of operations on those occasions when they undertake joint adventures as the so-called "Robin and Olsen team" (WF No. 147, Feb '65: "The Doomed Boy Heroes!" pts. 1–2 — "The New Terrific Team!"; "The Doom of Jimmy Olsen and Robin!").

Interestingly, several people in various parts of the world are exact look-alikes for Robin, including EMPEROR TARO of Atlantis (BM No. 19/2, Oct/Nov '43: "Atlantis Goes to War!"), PRINCE STEFAN of Valonia (WF No. 26, Jan/Feb '47: "His Highness, Prince Robin!"), and LITTLE RAVEN, the son of GREAT EAGLE (BM No. 86/3, Sep '54: "Batman--Indian Chief!").

In the texts, Robin is referred to as the Teen-Age Thunderbolt and the Teen Titan. In recent years, in recognition of his having attained college age, he has become known as Robin, the Teen Wonder, in place of the older and better-known Robin, the Boy Wonder.

Since April 1940 Robin has worked and fought with Batman in virtually every one of his amazing adventures. For this reason, the following pages deal exclusively with those events which are central to an understanding of Robin's life and career, as well as with those adventures in which Robin occupies the central role. (*See also* BATMAN and all the other articles dealing with the persons and events of the Batman legend.)

In April 1940 the Haly Circus is playing before capacity crowds in a "rising young town" just outside Batman's resident city. Highlighting the circus are the Flying Graysons, a daring trapeze troupe comprised of John and Mary Grayson and their young son Dick. One night, after circus owner Haly has steadfastly refused to pay the protection money demanded by "Boss" Zucco and his henchmen, the gangsters retaliate by weakening the Graysons' trapeze ropes with acid, and, soon afterward, young Dick watches in horror as a trapeze rope breaks under his parents' combined weight, sending them hurtling helplessly to their doom on the tanbark below.

Not long afterward, on the circus grounds, Dick Grayson overhears Zucco's henchmen warning Haly that the deadly circus "accidents" will continue unless Haly agrees to pay the protection money they have demanded. It is only then that Grayson realizes that the accident which claimed the life of his parents was not an accident at all. He is about to run for the police, when suddenly he finds himself face to face with the mysterious crime-fighter known as Batman, who, in his Bruce Wayne identity, had attended the circus and witnessed the horrifying deaths of John and Mary Grayson.

Batman cautions Grayson that he must not seek help from the police. The entire town, he explains, is under the oppressive thumb of the ruthless "Boss" Zucco, who would order Grayson murdered on the spot if he dared to come forward with what he has overheard. He explains that he too wants the Graysons' murderers brought to justice, but that first hard evidence must be accumulated linking "Boss" Zucco with the vicious crime at the circus. "My parents too were killed by a criminal," explains Batman grimly. "That's why I've devoted my life to exterminate [sic] them."

"Then I want to **also**!" exclaims Grayson. "Take me with you--please!"

"The **Batman** is reluctant," notes the text, "but the troubled face of the boy moves him deeply."

"Well," replies Batman finally, "I guess you and I were both victims of a similar trouble. All right. I'll make you my aide. But I warn you, I lead a perilous life!"

"I'm not afraid--" cries Grayson.

That night, in the yellowed glare of a flickering candle, "two grim figures take an undying oath!"

"And swear," proclaims Batman darkly, "that we two will fight together against crime and corruption and never to swerve from the path of righteousness."

Batman and Dick Grayson, 1940 © NPP 1940

"I swear it!" answers Grayson solemnly.

In the days and weeks which follow, Dick Grayson, the only living person to whom Batman has entrusted the closely guarded secret of his dual identity, undergoes the rigorous physical training – in acrobatics, boxing, and jujitsu – which is to stand him in such good stead throughout his long crime-fighting career. Batman provides him with the stunning red, yellow, and green costume that is to become his trademark and suggests that he assume the name Robin. Finally, "many months later . . . after strenuous work and study," Grayson is ready for the next stage of Batman's plan to destroy "Boss" Zucco. "Well," asks Grayson eagerly, "now that I'm ready, what's our next move?"

The next move brings Batman and Robin back to "Boss" Zucco's stronghold, the small town where the Flying Graysons met their doom. Posing as a newsboy, Grayson stealthily follows some young hoodlums to Zucco's home, where, through a window, he overhears Zucco instructing his henchmen to squeeze even more protection money out of the local merchants before racing away to inform Batman of what he has learned.

Dick Grayson posing as a newsboy, 1940 © NPP 1940

In the hours that follow, Batman swoops vengefully down on "Boss" Zucco's underworld operations in a deliberate attempt to entice the racketeer into overplaying his hand. He beats up several of Zucco's henchmen as they move about the town collecting payoffs and single-handedly demolishes Zucco's lavish illegal gambling casino. Finally, to infuriate the racketeer still further, he sends him a cardboard box containing a live bat and a handwritten note warning him to get out of town and to desist in his efforts to collect protection money from the firm putting up the Canin Building, which, the note asserts, Batman has taken under his personal protection.

Enraged at this brash affront to his power, Zucco personally leads his henchmen to the Canin Building, as Batman had hoped he would, with the intention of dynamiting the building as a warning to other contractors to continue their payoffs or face the destruction of their buildings. Atop the partially constructed Canin Building, however, Robin plunges into battle with the villains before Batman has even arrived, using both his slingshot and his flashing fists. Ultimately, however, the force of numbers begins to tell, and Robin is about to be gunned down by "Boss" Zucco when Batman arrives on the scene, rescues Robin, and hurls himself into the fray.

Robin, 1940 © NPP 1940

At one point in the battle, Batman hurls a silken noose around the neck of one of Zucco's henchmen, dangles the strangling hoodlum over the side of the uncompleted building, and pulls him to safety only after he has indicated his willingness to sign a full confession implicating "Boss" Zucco in the death of the Graysons. Enraged at his henchman for having provided Batman with a confession, Zucco shoves his confederate off a girder, sending him plummeting to a grisly death on the sidewalk far below, but Robin captures the murderous act on film with the aid of a tiny camera, and this photographic evidence, coupled with the dead hireling's hastily dictated confession, ulti-

Robin, 1940 © NPP 1940

mately proves sufficient to convict "Boss" Zucco of murder.

"Well, Dick," asks Bruce Wayne, "now that your parents' deaths have been avenged, are you going back to circus life?"

"No," replies Grayson, "I think mother and dad would like me to go on fighting crime. — And as for me . . . well . . . I love adventure!"

"Okay, you reckless young squirt," replies Wayne, "I ought to whale you for jumping those men alone. Why didn't you wait for me?"

"Aw!" moans Grayson. "I didn't want to miss any of the fun! Say, I can hardly wait till we go on our next case. I bet it'll be a corker!" (Det No. 38).

A number of other texts in the Batman chronicles shed additional light on the events surrounding the emergence of Dick Grayson as Robin, the Boy Wonder. One of these is Batman No. 32/2, which purports to tell the story of "how Dick Grayson won his right to **hold** the title of — **Robin, Boy Wonder,** partner of **Batman!**"

According to this text, Batman had never intended for Dick Grayson to become his permanent partner and had provided him with his costume and special training only so that he could participate in the avenging of his parents' death. Once this task had been completed, explains the text, Bruce Wayne informed Dick Grayson that his life as Robin was over.

"But why?" cried Grayson. "Wasn't I all right? Didn't I even help tackle the big guys?"

"Sure . . . you tackled them," replied Wayne, ". . . because you were mad . . . mad clean through! That motivating force kept you going! But now that your parents' killers have been caught, will you hesitate to fight against terrific odds . . . and will you be **afraid?**"

"Oh! I see what you mean," replied Grayson. "Gee . . . I never thought about that. . . ."

"But **I** have," interjected Wayne abruptly, ". . . and I'm not going to have you on my conscience all my life! I like you too much!"

"But don't you see?" pleaded Grayson. "If I stop being **Robin** now I'll never know whether I'm a coward or not! It'll worry me . . . all my life! You've got to give me a test, Bruce!"

Finally, Wayne relented. In the days that followed, he trained Dick Grayson's mind as he had once so carefully trained his body, teaching him everything he knew about scientific crime detection and modern investigative techniques. One day, when Batman was summoned by POLICE COMMISSIONER GORDON to help solve the Winston Bank robbery case, Robin accompanied him and met Commissioner Gordon for the very first time. "I heard how you helped bring in Boss Zucco!" remarked Gordon. "Keep up the good work, son!"

From a clue provided them by a guard at the Winston Bank, Batman deduced that the leader of the holdup gang was a lisping criminal named Stick-up Sidney, and, with Robin by his side, he invaded the gang's hideout to take the criminals into custody. Stick-up Sidney, however, seized Robin, held a gun to his head, and threatened to kill him unless Batman agreed to surrender. Within moments, Batman had been left tied up in the hideout while the criminals departed to pull another robbery, taking Robin along with them as a hostage. After Stick-up Sidney and his henchmen had staged a successful robbery of a camera company, Robin managed to arouse the attention of the police, but the criminals cut off police pursuit by throwing Robin out of their getaway car into the path of an oncoming police car. Robin was taken to a local hospital, treated for his injuries, and finally released, but by the time he led the police to the gang's hideout, Stick-up Sidney and his cohorts had already abandoned it and taken the captive Batman along with them.

"It's all my fault!" thought Robin, guilt-ridden at having been the cause of Batman's capture. "If I had watched myself **Batman** wouldn't be in a jam! Maybe they've killed him! Oh . . . why did I have to be such a wise guy!"

Then Robin realized that his only hope of rescuing Batman was to apply the detective skills that Batman had taught him. "S'matter with me?" mused Robin. "Got to use my head to think with 'stead of batting it against a wall!"

Ultimately, clues which Robin found in the abandoned hideout led him to a rabbit farm owned by a member of the Stick-up Sidney gang, and before long he had rescued Batman and, with his help, apprehended all the criminals.

Later, back at the Wayne mansion, Dick Grayson sadly presented Bruce Wayne with his Robin costume. "After the boner I pulled I guess you'll want to put it in mothballs! I'm just a fool!"

"You're a fool if you think that!" replied Wayne assuringly. "Why, you did fine! Sure, you made a mistake, but you made up for it! You used your head — and that's what counts! Take good care of this suit! You're going to be using it plenty!" (Dec/Jan '45–'46: "Dick Grayson, Boy Wonder!").

A later text, Batman No. 213/1, contains a lengthy recapitulation of Robin's origin. A number of minor details in this narrative are slightly at variance with details presented previously in Detective Comics No. 38, but by and large the new text represents a well-informed effort to summarize and reconcile details concerning the origin of Robin, his name, and his costume which had never been assembled previously in any one account. Some new facts are also presented: the town where John and Mary Grayson were killed, never before named in the chronicles, was named Newton or, alternately, Newtown; and, Bruce Wayne took steps immediately after his initial meeting with Dick Grayson to establish himself as Grayson's "legal guardian." Wayne's bachelor status, explains the text, made it impossible for him actually to adopt Grayson, and so he was compelled to accept Grayson as his ward rather than as his legally adopted son (Jul/Aug '69: "The Origin of Robin!").

In October–November 1942 Police Commissioner Gordon receives a note from the underworld figure known as the Thumb warning that unless Batman leaves his gang alone, he and his men will kill Robin the next time they see him. Realizing that Robin would only ignore the

Thumb's warning and insist on involving himself in the effort to apprehend him, Batman decides to protect Robin from harm by pretending to dissolve their partnership.

"We're parting company, Dick," explains Bruce Wayne, as he packs his bags and prepares to leave the Wayne mansion to set out on his own. "From now on the **Batman** works alone!" Feigning anger, Wayne complains that it is a nuisance to have to fight criminals while protecting a young boy from harm.

"From now on you can give more time to school work," concludes Wayne. "It isn't right for a kid like you to be chasing around getting into fights!" Then, after assuring Dick Grayson that he has left behind money to care for his needs, Wayne stalks away to continue his crime-fighting career alone.

Grayson is heartbroken. "It isn't true!" he sobs tearfully after Wayne has gone. "I wasn't ever in his way! He just (sob) he just doesn't like me any more!"

After his grief has temporarily subsided, however, Grayson begins to suspect that Wayne's real complaint may have been that Robin was becoming increasingly popular and stealing some of Batman's glory. "I don't want his money and I won't live in this house!" thinks Grayson angrily. "I'll run away and show him I can take care of myself!"

While wandering the streets of Gotham City, Grayson spies Batman in hot pursuit of the Thumb and his henchmen, who have just made an unsuccessful attempt to assassinate the mayor. In the action that follows, Batman uses a Robin dummy to draw the criminals' gunfire, then circles around behind them in an unsuccessful attempt to surprise them from the rear. The criminals escape, but Grayson, who has viewed the action from a distance, is left with the erroneous impression that Batman has acquired a new crime-fighting partner. Convinced that he was summarily dismissed to make way for the newcomer, Grayson sadly carries his two-way belt radio to a pawnshop, where he pawns it for eight dollars in spending money to see himself through the day.

Robin in action, 1940 © NPP 1940

Batman, meanwhile, is lured to the Thumb's hideout, taken prisoner, tied up, and shut away behind a brick wall in the hideout's cellar. He attempts to summon Robin via radio, unaware that Robin has pawned his radio and no longer has it in his possession. Grayson, however, is in a restaurant inquiring about a dishwasher's job when he overhears some of the Thumb's hirelings gloating over their capture of Batman. "His first case without me to help," thinks Grayson grimly, as he follows the hoodlums toward the Thumb's hideout, ". . . and he failed! I'll bet the other kid let him down!"

At the hideout, Robin makes a desperate effort to apprehend the Thumb and his henchmen, only to be taken captive himself. However, when the criminals tear a hole in their new brick wall in order to imprison Robin alongside Batman, Batman, who has managed to undo his bonds, leaps through the opening and, with Robin's help, quickly subdues the Thumb and his henchmen.

"Well . . . you won't be needing me anymore . . ." remarks Robin. "Guess I'll go make a nuisance of myself somewhere else!"

"Wait," cries Batman, "--you know I'd rather lose both arms than you!" He shows Robin the Thumb's threatening letter and explains his reasons for temporarily dissolving their partnership.

"Then you were thinking of me all the time!" exclaims Robin.

"Of course!" replies Batman. "But if you'd known the truth, you'd have insisted on getting into the scrap!"

"Gee, Batman," exclaims Robin happily, "I'm so happy, I-I'm going to BAWL!" (BM No. 13/1: "The Batman Plays a Lone Hand!").

In August–September 1943 Dick Grayson brings home a flunking high school report card and Bruce Wayne lays down an ultimatum. "Your adventures as Robin are temporarily suspended!" announces Wayne sternly. "From now on **Batman** works alone, until . . . until you pass everyone [sic] of those subjects! You are going to study every night . . . and under no circumstances will you leave this house!"

Soon afterward, however, Batman is taken captive by a gang of criminals led by a hoodlum named Spike, and Robin defies Wayne's admonition long enough to rescue Batman and help him apprehend Spike and his henchmen. In the course of the adventure, however, Robin displays an acute knowledge of chemistry that seems strangely inconsistent with the flunking grade he received in that subject on his report card. Sure enough, a visit to Grayson's professor reveals that the flunking card had been issued to Grayson by mistake and that Grayson's "own report is excellent, especially in chemistry!" (BM No. 18/2: "Robin Studies His Lessons!").

In December 1943–January 1944 Dick Grayson's uncle George Grayson arrives at the Wayne mansion — accompanied by a female accomplice calling herself Clara Grayson and claiming, apparently untruthfully, to be George's wife — and announces that he has come to claim legal custody of Dick Grayson. When Dick refuses to go with his uncle, and when Bruce Wayne refuses to surrender Dick into his uncle's custody, George Grayson files a lawsuit alleging that Bruce Wayne is an unfit guardian.

At the custody hearing, ALFRED testifies that he has "never seen Mr. Wayne deny the young lad anything! He fair worships the boy!"

"Dick is like my own son!" pleads Bruce Wayne. ". . . I . . . I love that boy! Please don't take him from me!"

". . . when Mom and Pop died in the circus," testifies a tearful Dick Grayson, "I was all alone! Then Bruce . . . Mr. Wayne took me in! A fella couldn't want a better friend!"

George Grayson's lawyer, however, submits a stack of damaging news clippings, "all reporting Mr. Wayne's activities as a nightclubbing, shiftless, cafe society playboy!"

"What can I do?" agonizes Bruce Wayne silently. "I can't tell the judge that my playboy act is only camouflage for my **Batman** work!"

After all the evidence has been presented, the judge awards George and Clara Grayson custody of young Dick, and Bruce Wayne and his former ward are forced to say tearful good-byes.

"In order to cover up my **Batman** work, I had to pretend to be a playboy," complains an agonized Bruce Wayne to Alfred after Dick Grayson has departed the Wayne mansion to go live with his uncle, ". . . and now it's made me lose the person I love the most! It isn't fair! It isn't fair!"

Soon afterward, however, Wayne learns the real motive behind George Grayson's custody suit when Grayson offers to behave in an unfit and immoral manner, so that the judge will award custody of Dick Grayson back to Bruce Wayne, if Wayne will agree to pay him and his accomplice $1,000,000. Wayne is furious, but Grayson reminds him that if he repeats the story to the authorities, they will assume he has merely made it up in an effort to regain custody of his former ward.

Wayne subsequently confronts George Grayson as Batman in an effort to frighten Grayson into signing a full confession and leaving town, but Grayson responds by contacting gangster Fatso Foley and arranging to lure Batman into a trap.

For a time, things look grim for Batman, but Alfred and Robin learn of Batman's plight and join forces to rescue him. Before long, the Fatso Foley mob has been apprehended and the police have taken George Grayson and his female accomplice into custody. Dick Grayson is unwilling to press charges against his uncle because he does not want to be responsible for sending his father's brother to prison, but the judge is quick to reverse his original custody decision as soon as the full facts have been made known to him.

"Incidentally," the judge tells Bruce Wayne, "I'm inclined to agree with the **Batman!** He visited me before and said, that in spite of your playboy activities, you were really a good man!" (BM No. 20/4: "Bruce Wayne Loses the Guardianship of Dick Grayson!").

In April–May 1944 Dick Grayson takes a part-time job as a telegraph boy, leaving Bruce Wayne thoroughly befuddled. **"A . . A job?"** exclaims Wayne. "You don't need the money! I give you an allowance! Besides, you've got homework to do after school . . . and crook hunting to do in your spare time!"

"Bruce," stammers Grayson, "I . . I just can't explain now!" The reason for the part-time job becomes apparent, however, when Grayson presents Bruce Wayne with a surprise birthday present. He had spent all his allowance money, he explains, on war bonds, thus forcing him to earn extra money if he was to surprise Wayne on his birthday (BM No. 22/2: "Dick Grayson, Telegraph Boy!").

In June–July 1946, after Dick Grayson has complained that comic-book stories often seem untrue to life, Bruce Wayne's friend Jim Hale, the editor of *Crescent Comics,* offers to let Grayson write a story of his own. Grayson is at a loss for a plot, however, until Bruce Wayne suggests that he write about their recent battle with racketeer Duke Ryall. Comic editor Hale is ecstatic about Grayson's finished story and promptly agrees to publish it. "It's the real thing, Dick!" exclaims Hale. "You must have a great imagination to make it so true to life! I'll buy as many like it as you can write!"

"Between you and me," confesses Dick Grayson to Bruce Wayne as they pore over the published version of Grayson's story, "I'll stay a success as long as I write about **Batman** and **Robin** cases, and stick to facts!" (BM No. 35/3: "Dick Grayson, Author!"). (*See also* CONROY, BIG ED.)

By February–March 1950, unscrupulous press agent and ex-convict Ed Kolum has set in motion a vengeful plot to deprive Bruce Wayne of the legal custody of Dick Grayson in retaliation for Wayne's having once exposed him to the authorities as a charity swindler. Two years ago, Kolum had organized a lucrative racket involving the promoting of bogus charity shows. Kolum lent an aura of respectability to his shows by duping prominent citizens into lending the use of their names and reputations to what they believed were legitimate fund-raising enterprises. Wayne, however, had discovered that Kolum was a swindler and had contacted the authorities, and Kolum had been tried, convicted, and sentenced to a term in prison.

Dick Grayson, 1953–1954 © NPP 1954

Upon his release, Kolum had returned to Gotham City and plotted his revenge. ". . . he loves that kid like he was his own son!" thought Kolum. "If the court took the kid away, Wayne would suffer . . . *slow!!* Wayne's got a mild rep as a playboy! I'll exaggerate his playboy routine!"

In the days that followed, Kolum succeeded – by deliberately arranging for Wayne to become embroiled in a fistfight and an auto accident – in creating a public impression of Wayne as an irresponsible playboy unfit to serve as Dick Grayson's guardian. So great is the outcry against Wayne as the result of Kolum's cunningly stage-managed incidents, that Wayne soons finds himself on trial, fighting to retain custody of his ward. Even at the trial, however, Kolum's influence is apparent, for he has bribed witnesses to provide damaging false testimony concerning Bruce Wayne's character.

As Batman, Wayne soon learns that it is Kolum who has masterminded the attempts to make him seem an unfit guardian. Proving Kolum's guilt is difficult, however, since none of the people whom Kolum has bribed has actually seen his face, and none, therefore, can really identify him. Ultimately, however, Batman succeeds in tricking Kolum into making a slip of the tongue in open court which betrays him as the villain behind the plot to besmirch Bruce Wayne's character and deprive him of the custody of his ward.

". . . your honor," pleads Batman, after he has explained the details of Kolum's plot to the presiding judge, ". . . I'd like to testify *for* Bruce Wayne! . . . I tell you I know Wayne as well as I know myself! He is no loose-living playboy, I assure you! In his own quiet way, he has fought injustice and evil as much as I have! Police Commissioner Gordon and other responsible people could tell you of Bruce Wayne's many charities! ***They*** know Wayne's character . . . and now ***you*** know it, too!"

With Kolum's scheme exposed, Bruce Wayne is found innocent of the charges against him and is permitted to retain full custody of young Dick Grayson (BM No. 57/1: "The Trial of Bruce Wayne!").

In November 1951, shortly after suspect MONROE PEEL has been accused of murder by Batman and Robin and then released from police custody due to his apparent innocence, a series of bizarre thefts begin taking place in the BATCAVE, all of them involving pieces of crime-detecting apparatus that had helped the Dynamic Duo build their case against Peel, as well as against other murder suspects, already executed for their crimes, who had gone to their deaths proclaiming their innocence.

Since the location of the batcave is a closely guarded secret and its elaborate alarm system would presumably betray the presence of intruders, the nightly thefts stymie the Dynamic Duo until Batman discovers that Robin has been committing the thefts in his sleep and disposing of the stolen objects by throwing them into the underground river flowing through the batcave.

"The terrible shock of our arresting Peel for murder only to learn he was innocent has upset ***Robin!***" realizes Batman. "His subconscious, working while he slept, expressed his guilt feeling by having him destroy the things which apprehended Peel. . . . Fearing we've made other errors, he's destroyed the objects which solved other murder cases."

Ultimately, however, Batman establishes that Monroe Peel is indeed guilty of the murder, and together with Robin he promptly reapprehends him. Robin, informed finally of his responsibility for the somnambulistic thefts, is able to shed his unconscious guilt at having conceivably helped send innocent men to their doom after a review of the files of the Dynamic Duo's past murder cases has convinced him that the men he and Batman accused of murder were all truly guilty (Det No. 177: "The Robberies in the Bat-Cave!").

In February 1954 Dick Grayson arrives at school late and stuns his classmates with the startling confession that he is secretly Robin, the Boy Wonder. For a time, it appears that the dual identities of Batman and Robin are no longer secret, but Grayson's startling announcement is actually part of an elaborate ploy by Batman to discredit some films, inadvertently taken by a criminal named MR. CAMERA, which purportedly show Bruce Wayne and Dick Grayson changing into their Batman and Robin costumes. Eventually, after the threat posed by Mr. Camera has been dealt with successfully, Grayson's classroom confession is explained away as a boyish attempt to impress Marcia, a dark-haired co-ed (BM No. 81/2: "The Boy Wonder Confesses!").

In April 1955 Robin is transformed into a mature adult – and Batman is transformed into an impulsive teen-ager – when they are inadvertently exposed to the "age-principle and youth-principle gases" developed by "famed scientist" DR. RICHARD MARSTEN. For a time, their traditional roles are reversed, with a wise and deductive Robin holding a tight rein on an eager and reckless Batman. "He--he's like a boy now," thinks Robin silently, "impulsive and reckless, as **I** once was! I've got to restrain him the way he used to restrain **me!**" Ultimately, however, Batman and Robin apprehend "criminal ex-scientist" Wilton Winders, who has stolen the miraculous gases, and use the recovered gases to restore themselves to normal (Det No. 218: "Batman, Junior and Robin, Senior!").

In November 1956, when both Bruce Wayne and Batman are scheduled to appear at a dedication ceremony inaugurating the opening of a new bridge over the Gotham River, Batman appears on the dignitaries' platform with a Bruce Wayne dummy and uses ventriloquism to make it appear that the Bruce Wayne dummy is the real Bruce Wayne. During the ceremony, however, gangsters with a grudge against Bruce Wayne "assassinate" the Bruce Wayne dummy, sending it toppling off the dignitaries' platform into the river to be swept away by the swift-moving tide.

Batman swiftly apprehends the gangsters and turns them over to the authorities, but Bruce Wayne is declared officially dead and Batman finds himself caught on the horns of a cruel dilemma: he cannot admit that the "murdered" man was only a dummy for fear of betraying his dual identity, and with Wayne "dead" he cannot appear as Wayne in public or continue to live at the Wayne mansion. Reluctantly, Batman decides that he will have to leave Wayne Manor, end his partnership with Robin, and assume a new civilian identity, at least until he can find a way to resurrect Bruce Wayne without arousing suspicion.

After saying a tearful good-bye to Robin while carefully avoiding giving Robin any hint that their separation may prove to be permanent, Batman leaves Wayne Manor, moves into a simple furnished room somewhere in Gotham City, and assumes the new civilian identity of Barney Warren, cab driver. "I couldn't tell him [Robin] the real truth," thinks Batman sadly, as he sits alone in his furnished room, ". . . that it might be impossible to work together anymore--ever!"

In the days that follow, Batman meets two young boys about Robin's age – one a rascally mischief-maker, the other a verbose bookworm – and cannot help fantasizing about what a disaster it would be if either of these boys were to become the new Robin. "It surely won't be easy having to battle crime alone," he muses at one point. "I **could** train another boy to take Dick's place, but I'd never dream of it!"

One day, while "Barney Warren" is driving about the city in his cab, Robin pulls alongside him in the BATMOBILE, loudly accuses him of secretly being Bruce Wayne, and escorts him to the office of Police Commissioner Gordon. Gordon explains that members of his department had found pieces of a Bruce Wayne dummy in the Gotham River and that he had launched a citywide search for the real Bruce Wayne as a result. It is then that Bruce Wayne realizes the genius behind Robin's deliberate exposure of his Barney Warren masquerade. "Er--I feared that attack from racketeers trying to force themselves into one of my private businesses," stammers Wayne. "And I played dead for safety till ***Batman*** smoked out the ringleaders!"

The Bruce Wayne dummy, therefore, has now been successfully explained away as part of a ploy by Batman to lure Wayne's would-be assassins into the open while the real Bruce Wayne took refuge temporarily in the identity of cab driver Barney Warren. Since Batman has now apprehended Wayne's would-be killers, the explanation continues, Wayne can now abandon his Barney Warren disguise and resume his normal life at Wayne Manor.

"Luckily that dummy turned up," remarks Bruce Wayne sometime later, when he and Dick Grayson are alone, "though, at first, I thought it would be a giveaway. Then, when you played that trick of finding my cab and calling me Bruce. . . ."

"What really worried me," interjects Dick Grayson, "was that you might decide to break in some other fellow as ***Robin.***"

"Dick," replies Wayne assuringly, "--there's one thing I learned while I was Barney Warren. There'll never be another Robin!" (Det No. 237: "Search for a New Robin!").

In February 1957 Robin adopts a new identity in an effort to prove to Batman that his skill with disguises is as great as Batman's own. After altering his features

Robin © NPP 1976

with a special rubber face mask and adopting the name Freddy Loyd, he tells Batman that Robin is currently recuperating at the Loyd home from injuries he received while battling criminals and that he has asked Freddy to stand in for him as Robin until such time as he is able to return to action himself. The fact that young Freddy is wearing Robin's costume and is privy to the secret of his dual identity seems to corroborate his startling story, and in the hours that follow he even demonstrates sufficient crime-fighting skill to help Batman apprehend notorious criminal Gorilla Hardy.

Later, back at the BATCAVE with Bruce Wayne and Alfred, a triumphant "Freddy" yanks off his rubber face mask to reveal that he is really Robin in disguise. "Yes--it's me, the real **Robin!**" he cries. "I wanted to see if I was as good as you at disguises, Bruce, and it worked! I had you both fooled!"

Suddenly, however, both Wayne and Alfred break into uncontrolled laughter. Robin had given himself away from the very beginning, explains Wayne, by the ease with which he had found a light switch in the darkened batcave, even though, as Freddy Loyd, he was supposedly a stranger there. ". . . so I tipped off Alfred with a wink," concludes Wayne, "and we let you continue your game, to teach you a lesson!"

"And I sure learned it!" replies Robin. "You can't beat the master of disguise at his own game--eh, **Batman?**" (BM No. 105/2: "The Second Boy Wonder!").

In March–April 1957 SUPERMAN narrates the story of his first encounter with the villainous ELTON CRAIG, which evidently took place sometime in the past. In the course of this narrated encounter, Robin becomes endowed with super-powers for the first time in his career, when, at Superman's request, he and Batman swallow a pair of the special "radioactive capsules" developed on the planet KRYPTON by Superman's father JOR-EL (WF No. 87: "The Reversed Heroes!"). (*See* CRAIG, ELTON.)

By April 1957 Superman has discovered a mysterious lead-lined box floating in outer space and has left it with Batman and Robin for temporary safekeeping. When Dick Grayson inadvertently touches the outer surface of the box, it emits a strange gas which knocks him unconscious, and Grayson regains consciousness the following morning to find that he has been transformed overnight into a full-grown man. "That strange gas," exclaims Grayson, "--it causes sudden growth to anyone who breathes it!"

When the time comes to answer the BAT-SIGNAL, Grayson realizes that he can no longer fit into his Robin costume, and Batman instructs him to remain at home so that he will not betray the secret of his dual identity by appearing in public both as a grown-up Dick Grayson and as a grown-up Robin. Robin offers to solve this problem by wearing one of Batman's spare costumes instead of his own, but Batman declines. "No, Dick!" he replies. "You may look like a man, but you'll think like a boy, act like a boy! You've got a lot of 'growing' to do before you're ***really*** a man!"

As Batman prepares to leave, however, Grayson "reacts like an impulsive youngster," hastily dons an owl masquerade costume owned by Bruce Wayne, and secretly hitches a ride aboard the batmobile.

Soon afterward, as Batman plunges into battle with a trio of acrobatic bandits known as the Daredevils, Robin joins the fray as Owlman. "Dick--wearing my masquerade costume!" thinks Batman angrily. "That foolish kid disobeyed my orders! I'd tan his hide--if he wasn't so big now!"

Batman's momentary surprise at Robin's appearance proves a boon for the criminals, who hurl some tear gas in their direction and make good their escape. Robin attempts to give chase, but he has forgotten that he weighs a great deal more than he used to, and Batman is compelled to rescue him when he swings onto a flagpole that will not support his weight. "Still acting like a kid," scolds Batman, "--still rushing ahead without thinking!"

By this time, Grayson has begun to feel a certain amount of regret at having grown up so quickly, particularly since all his school friends are now children by comparison, and he has begun to feel a bit lonely. He is elated, however, about his manly physique. "What muscles!" he thinks happily as he gazes at himself in the mirror. "I'm as big as **Batman** now! And I'll bet I can be as big a crime-buster, too! I'll show **Batman** I'm as good as he is!"

And so, bursting with youthful overconfidence, Robin sets out to capture the Daredevils alone. Clad in his Owlman costume, he overtakes the criminals at the headquarters of Frankie the Fence and moves in to apprehend them, but he fails to take into account his newly acquired adult height, hits his head against a ceiling beam, and is quickly taken prisoner. The Daredevils unmask him, but they do not recognize his features and take him to their hideout intending to force him to tell them who he really is.

Batman, however, trails the criminals to their hideout, frees Robin, and, with his help, takes the Daredevils into custody. Not long afterward, Robin suddenly passes out, and when he revives several hours later, he is back to his normal size and age again, the effects of the strange gas having apparently been only temporary. "Gee," muses Dick Grayson as he rejoins his old schoolmates, "it's good to be a kid again!" (BM No. 107/3: "The Grown-Up Boy Wonder!").

By February 1961 two extraterrestrial aliens have entered into a strange wager: one has bet the other that he can succeed in separating the Dynamic Duo to the extent of making Robin his partner for ten full days, while the other maintains that the Dynamic Duo are inseparable and that any effort to separate them will surely fail. In an effort to win the wager, the first alien dons a hooded costume to conceal the fact that he is an alien, assumes the name Mr. Marvel, and foils an attempted mail robbery in Gotham City with an array of futuristic devices. ". . . I am a scientist who has worked for years on inventions to fight crime!" explains Mr. Marvel to a group of newsmen. "I am a crime-fighter, like ***Batman*** . . . but ***unlike Batman,*** I am no athlete--for I believe that lawmen should not have to use fisticuffs! I think ***Batman*** is outdated . . . ***I*** am the crime-fighter of the future!"

Soon afterward, Mr. Marvel approaches Robin and asks him to abandon Batman and become his partner instead. "I'm sorry, ***Mr. Marvel,*** " replies Robin, "but ***Batman*** and I are partners! I'd never leave him!"

Willing to resort to any tactic to win his wager, the alien tells Robin a cruel lie. "My belt's dial is tuned to ***Batman's*** frequency!" he claims. "If I but touch the button, an electronic beam will be transmitted to ***Batman*** and destroy him!--Unless you team up with me!"

Confronted with what he assumes to be a real threat to Batman's life, Robin agrees to abandon Batman and join forces with Mr. Marvel, intending to turn the tables on Mr. Marvel and defeat him as soon as the opportunity presents itself. He does not, however, confide the truth to Batman. "You taught me all you can about crime-fighting," says Robin to his longtime partner, ". . . ***Mr. Marvel*** can teach me more! He's promised to acquaint me with all his latest inventions!" Batman protests, but Robin remains adamant. "Sorry, ***Batman,*** " he insists, "but I've got my own career--my future--to think about!"

Stunned by Robin's decision to abandon him, Batman continues to fight crime on his own, but his mind is always on Robin. "I've been like a father to that boy!" he thinks to himself as he chases a gang of criminals. "I just can't understand how he could act that way!"

Later, however, after the initial shock of Robin's decision has worn off, he begins to analyze Robin's recent behavior more dispassionately. "I've been so unhappy," he thinks to himself, "I haven't been thinking clearly . . . but now, I wonder if ***Robin*** really did leave me for the reason he gave me?" He resolves to keep a close watch on Robin and Mr. Marvel to see what develops.

In the days that follow, Mr. Marvel and Robin become a spectacularly successful crime-fighting team, and Robin pretends to have abandoned all regret about leaving Batman. "I realize, now, I've got my future to think of!" he assures Mr. Marvel. "With your teaching and your inventions, I can do better with you than I ever could with ***Batman!***"

Finally, however, while Robin and Mr. Marvel are pursuing some criminals at a railroad siding, Robin sees his opportunity, knocks Mr. Marvel unconscious, and seizes the special belt which controls all of Mr. Marvel's miraculous crime-fighting inventions and presumably also the deadly beam which allegedly threatens Batman. With Mr. Marvel's belt removed and his crime-fighting inventions inoperative, Robin is in grave danger of being killed by the criminals at the railroad siding, but Batman, who has been following Robin and Mr. Marvel all this time, leaps to the rescue and helps Robin defeat them.

It is then that Robin tells Batman about Mr. Marvel's threat and the real reason for his apparent defection. Unmasking Mr. Marvel, they see that his maroon hood conceals the white skin and twin antennae of an extraterrestrial alien. Mr. Marvel tells them about his wager with his alien companion and assures Batman that he was never in any actual danger. Then suddenly, a strange beam shoots down from his hovering spaceship and whisks him away, leaving a relieved Batman and Robin happily reunited once again. And, because Robin was the alien's partner for only nine days, and not ten, Mr. Marvel has lost his wager (BM No. 137/1: "Robin's New Boss!").

In March 1964 Dick Grayson, irked over the need to conceal his true ability in sports in order to protect the secret of his dual identity, dons theatrical makeup and a red wig, assumes the name Danny, and dazzles the boys at a downtown recreation center with his incredible skill at basketball. A serious complication develops, however, when "Danny" is knocked accidentally to the ground toward the end of the basketball game and suffers a complete loss of memory. For a time, "Danny" wanders through the city, hoping that something will jog his memory to help him remember who he is and where he comes from, but his efforts are sadly unsuccessful. At one point, he and Batman make a pair of daring rescues at the scene of an apartment-house fire, but Batman does not recognize Dick Grayson in his disguise and so the two friends go their separate ways without becoming aware of their true relationship. Ultimately, however, Batman realizes that the red-headed boy at the fire must have been Dick Grayson, and, after searching the city, he finally locates him and succeeds in restoring his memory (BM No. 162/2: "Robin's New Secret Identity!").

Dick Grayson, 1964 © NPP 1964

In February 1965 the minds of Robin and his friend Jimmy Olsen are "taken over and possessed" by some weirdly glowing jewels from a far-distant planet which Superman has presented to Jimmy as a gift, unaware that the strange gems are really alien "living things with super-telepathic powers." Under the baleful influence of the extraterrestrial gems, Robin and Jimmy turn against Batman and Superman, but the famed crime-fighters soon succeed in freeing their young pals from the jewels' telepathic clutches, thus enabling Superman to return the gems safely to the planet that spawned them (WF No. 147: "The Doomed Boy Heroes!" pts. 1–2 – "The New Terrific Team!"; "The Doom of Jimmy Olsen and Robin!").

In December 1969 Dick Grayson departs Wayne Manor to attend his first year of classes at Hudson University (BM No. 217: "One Bullet Too Many!").

ROBIN HOOD. The hero of a series of popular ballads, the earliest of which date from the fourteenth century or quite possibly even earlier. In the ballads he is a gallant outlaw and master bowman, dwelling in Sherwood Forest with his band of Merry Men, robbing the rich and giving to the poor, and striking out against oppressive authority, usually personified by his most frequent enemy, the ruthless Sheriff of Nottingham. His most noteworthy companions are Little John, Friar Tuck, and the lovely Maid Marian. According to several accounts, BATMAN's young companion, ROBIN, was named after him (Det No. 38, Apr '40; and others).

Dispatched through the time barrier by PROFESSOR CARTER NICHOLS to England in the thirteenth century, Batman and Robin feast with Robin Hood and his Merry Men in the depths of Sherwood Forest; accompany the outlaws to the famous archery tournament sponsored by the Sheriff of Nottingham; and join with them in an action-packed adventure which culminates in the storming of the sheriff's castle and the capture of the sheriff and his henchmen (Det No. 116, Oct '46: "The Rescue of Robin Hood!").

RODDY, JOHN. An innocent man sentenced to die at midnight for a murder he did not commit. Although their investigative efforts are severely hampered by the fact that they have accidentally locked themselves in the BATCAVE, BATMAN and ROBIN manage to deduce the identity of the real murderer, escape from the locked batcave, and apprehend the real killer – criminal Len Paul – in time to rescue Roddy from an undeserved execution (BM No. 108/2, Jun '57: "Prisoners of the Bat-Cave").

RODER, RALPH. The unscrupulous assistant to Arthur Harris, a famous animal trainer who performs at the Gotham City Charity Circus in March 1958 with his "famous educated ape," Mogo. By surreptitiously sending a surge of electrical voltage through Mogo's circus performing platform in the midst of Mogo's act, Roder not only creates a diversion which enables his underworld accomplices, the Vanning brothers, to make off with the circus's ticket receipts, but also casts immediate suspicion on animal trainer Harris for having apparently purposely allowed his ape to run amok while the robbery was taking place.

Later, after the Vanning brothers have fled with their loot and Harris has been wrongfully arrested for the crime, BATMAN intervenes to prevent Roder from cruelly confining the "super-intelligent" Mogo inside a cramped, tiny cage, as the result of which Mogo develops an all-abiding affection for Batman. Eager to be with his newfound friend, Mogo flees the circus, follows Batman to the BATCAVE – where he playfully dons one of Batman's spare capes and cowls, thus earning the nickname Bat-Ape – and ultimately helps the Dynamic Duo apprehend Roder and the Vanning brothers and exonerate Harris of the charges against him (BM No. 114/3: "The Bat-Ape!").

ROG. The Stone Age man who is secretly TIGER MAN (BM No. 93/3, Aug '55: "The Caveman Batman").

ROGAN, "ROCKETS." A notorious "arch-criminal" and leader of a gang of bandits – nicknamed "Rockets" because of his fondness for such rocket-powered equipment as his "rocket-car" and "rocket-copter," as well as for the high-powered rocket launcher with which he blasts open the wall of a GOTHAM CITY bank – who is apprehended in June 1961, along with all his henchmen and a host of underworld big shots, through the heroic efforts of BATMAN, ROBIN, and BATWOMAN.

Batman's efforts to capture the Rogan gang, and indeed all of his activities during this period, are severely hampered by the fact that his accidental exposure to a weird mixture of "upper atmosphere" gas samples in a Gotham City laboratory has temporarily transformed him into a colossal giant, forcing him to go into self-imposed exile outside the city to avoid wreaking fearsome destruction with every giant step, and to take such precautions to protect the secret of his dual identity as having his friend SUPERMAN disguise himself as Bruce Wayne and stand in for him at a community fund dinner (Det No. 292: "The Colossus of Gotham City!").

ROGERS. The pilot of the world's "first manned rocket," which is hurled into moon orbit by SUPERMAN in December 1958 and then caught by Superman when it descends to Earth again. Due to a mysterious "chemical reaction" resulting from his simultaneous exposure to the light of the moon and the eerie glow of a passing comet during his brief journey through space, Rogers soon launches a spectacular career in crime as the MOONMAN (WF No. 98: "The Menace of the Moonman!").

ROGERS, EDDIE. An inmate at State Prison, granted a one-day Christmas parole in recognition of his good behavior, who becomes the target of an apparently motiveless murder attempt almost immediately upon his release. In an effort to apprehend the would-be murderers and uncover the motive for their attack, BATMAN – who happens to be a perfect look-alike for Rogers – impersonates Rogers long enough to thwart an attempt by his attackers to tunnel their way into State Prison to free their leader, Scarface Malone. Rogers, determined to go straight as soon as he had paid his debt to society, had refused to participate in the impending jailbreak, causing convict Malone to order him silenced to prevent his disclosing the existence of the escape tunnel to prison authorities (BM No. 45/2, Feb/Mar '48: "A Parole for Christmas!").

ROGUE'S ROOST. The "palatial sanctuary" shared by the JOKER and the PENGUIN after they join forces in October–November 1944 (BM No. 25/1: "Knights of Knavery").

ROH KAR. The Martian lawman who journeys to Earth in August–September 1953 to help Batman apprehend the villainous QUORK. Roh Kar, the so-called "first lawman of Mars," has described BATMAN as "the greatest lawman of the universe!" (BM No. 78/1: "The Manhunter from Mars!").

ROHTUL. A ruthless villain of the thirtieth century A.D. who is a descendant of the renegade scientist LEX LUTHOR. Rohtul, in fact, is Luthor spelled backwards.

In the year 2957 A.D., Rohtul and his henchmen steal a wide array of scientific apparatus to enable them to build a "destruction-ray projector of tremendous range" with which to terrorize the Earth, but BATMAN, ROBIN, and SUPERMAN track the villains to their stronghold on the moon and ultimately take them into custody (WF No. 91, Nov/Dec '57: "The Three Super-Sleepers!").

ROKEJ (Chief). The police chief of GOTHAM CITY in the twenty-first century A.D. Chief Rokej is a perfect look-alike for the JOKER. "The Joker was my ancestor!" explains Chief Rokej to BATMAN and ROBIN. "But I decided to work ***with*** the law instead of against it . . .!"

In the world of the twenty-first century, Batman and Robin expose an industrial saboteur named Erkham who has been hired by the owners of the Meteor spacecraft company to sabotage the ships built by the competing Comet company, and help Chief Rokej apprehend a band of brutal space pirates (BM No. 59/3, Jun/Jul '50: "Batman in the Future!").

ROLLING, BIG BEN. The leader of a gang of criminals who murder the holders of large life-insurance policies after forcing the victims to sign the death benefits over to them. Big Ben Rolling (also referred to as Big Ben Bolling) and his henchmen are apprehended by BATMAN and ROBIN in October–November 1943 and ultimately executed for their crimes, including the murder of Larry Spade, the crusading newspaperman who first brings Rolling's racket to the attention of the Dynamic Duo (BM No. 19/1: "Batman Makes a Deadline!").

ROSE, "SPECS." A "notorious criminal" who concocts an elaborate scheme to wreck and plunder a train carrying a valuable shipment of bank currency. BATMAN and ROBIN thwart the train robbery and apprehend Rose in December 1949–January 1950 (BM No. 56/3: "A Greater Detective Than Batman!").

ROSS, HENRY (Professor). The research scientist who achieves infamy as PROFESSOR RADIUM (BM No. 8/2, Dec/Jan '41–'42: "The Strange Case of Professor Radium!").

ROULETTE (Mr.). A man seemingly possessed by an insatiable passion for gambling, his true identity concealed by a black hood, who claims to have become so jaded by ordinary gambling that his life's only fulfillment now lies in a daily gamble with death itself. He is secretly Rigger Sims, the partner of renowned gambler Charley Denver in a "fabulous oil well"; the role of Mr. Roulette is part of Sims's elaborate scheme to murder Charley Denver while making it appear that Denver has accidentally killed himself.

First Mr. Roulette allows it to become known that he has deliberately filled his elaborately appointed residence with innumerable death-dealing booby-traps, any one of which might kill him at any time. It is this continual, self-imposed gamble with death, claims Mr. Roulette, that gives his life its meaning and exhilaration. Then, as soon as word of the darkly eccentric Mr. Roulette has spread throughout GOTHAM CITY, Sims murders Charley Denver and dresses his corpse in the hooded costume of Mr. Roulette, intending to make it appear that Charley Denver was Mr. Roulette all along, and that his death was merely the inevitable tragic consequence of one of his own deadly booby-traps. BATMAN deduces the truth, however, after examining the death-scene, and he and ROBIN pursue Rigger Sims, the real Mr. Roulette, and ultimately apprehend him (BM No. 75/2, Feb/Mar '53: "Mr. Roulette's Greatest Gamble").

ROYCE, JOHN. An alias employed by Clayface (*see* CLAYFACE [MATT HAGEN]) in June 1962 when he poses as a new arrival in GOTHAM CITY as part of a scheme to rob the members of the exclusive Pharaoh Club (Det No. 304: "The Return of Clay-Face!").

RUSSO, BIG MIKE. A notorious underworld czar, sentenced to a term in North Island Prison through the unrelenting efforts of BATMAN, who seizes control of the prison, arranges for one of his henchmen to impersonate the warden, and then transforms the prison into an underworld headquarters from which Death Row prisoners make periodic forays into the city to pull robberies before sneaking back to a perfect alibi within the prison walls. Batman and ROBIN expose the prison takeover and apprehend Russo and his henchmen in December 1941–January 1942 (BM No. 8/1: "Stone Walls Do Not a Prison Make").

RYALL, ROGER. A ruthless gangland chieftain, under the care of a psychoanalyst for treatment of his "gatophobia" (abnormal fear of cats), who rifles his analyst's private files, uncovers confidential information concerning the bizarre phobias of some of his analyst's wealthier patients, and then plays on these phobias (e.g., John West's fear of shadows, Hilda Granville's fear of mirrors, and Grant Young's fear of heights) in order to rob the patients of their money and jewelry. BATMAN and ROBIN apprehend Ryall's henchmen during an attempted robbery at the home of big-game hunter Raymond Troxel, but Ryall flees into Troxel's private trophy room and dies of a heart attack when his "gatophobia" is aggravated by the stuffed lions and tigers mounted on display there (BM No. 39/1, Feb/Mar '47: "The Frightened People!").

RYDER, BEN. One of a pair of notorious "international jewel thieves" — the other is Slick Ronson — who commit a series of spectacular robberies while posing as men from the distant past — fifteenth-century knights, Mongol warriers, and the like. When BATMAN and ROBIN discover that their wily adversaries are not men from the past at all, but only ordinary modern-day criminals, they concoct an elaborate ruse to draw them out of hiding and ultimately apprehend them in August 1962 (BM No. 149/2: "The Invaders from the Past!").

S

SABRE, SAMMY. The leader of a gang of bank robbers and the secret owner of a newly opened bank in GOTHAM CITY. Knowing that any losses his bank suffers will be covered by insurance, Sabre blackmails the president of the bank—an honest man who served time in prison on a forgery charge twenty years ago—into helping his gang rob the bank, its payroll deliveries, and its safety deposit boxes, but BATMAN and ROBIN ultimately apprehend Sabre and his henchmen with the aid of a tip provided them by the courageous bank president (Det No. 194, Apr '53: "The Stolen Bank!").

SAMPSON (Dr.). "The most brilliant psychologyst [sic] in Gotham City . . . sentenced to prison for malpractice" sometime in the past, and now the leader of a gang of criminals who employ a potent memory-erasing "amnesia gas" and a wide array of cunning psychological ploys to help them commit spectacular crimes. The Dynamic Duo's efforts to apprehend Sampson and his henchmen are complicated by the fact that BATMAN has become exposed to the amnesia gas and, as a result, completely forgotten his crime-fighting training, but an antidote ultimately restores Batman's memory, enabling him and ROBIN to take the villains into custody (Det No. 190, Dec '52: "How to Be the Batman!").

SATURN. The sixth planet from the sun.

Saturn is the home of the ruthless warlord Fura, who is defeated by BRANE and his young companion Ricky in the year 3000 A.D. (BM No. 26/2, Dec/Jan '44–'45: "The Year 3000!").

SAX GOLA. A respected Martian scientist who, having accidentally developed a diabolical "crime-ray" which warped his brain and transformed him into a criminal, hatches a plot to dominate MARS by seizing control of the great pump station at Canal City which controls the flow of water through the Martian canals. Transported to Mars by the good Martian scientist Thund Dran, BATMAN and ROBIN defeat Sax Gola and his followers before returning safely to the planet Earth (BM No. 41/3, Jun/Jul '47: "Batman, Interplanetary Policeman!").

SCANLON, SCOOP. The ace reporter for *View* magazine, a "picture and true detective magazine" whose publisher assigns Scanlon the task of boosting the magazine's flagging circulation by writing an exclusive story exposing the secret of BATMAN's identity. After poring over files of Batman's past cases, Scanlon deduces correctly that Bruce Wayne is Batman, but Batman tricks the ace reporter into believing he has made an error by enlisting the aid of a dying actor to pose as Batman while he appears in Scanlon's presence simultaneously as millionaire Bruce Wayne (WF No. 6, Sum '42: "The Secret of Bruce Wayne!").

SCARECROW, THE. A fiendish "crime master" (WF No. 3, Fall '41: "The Scarecrow!") who dresses in the ragged garb of an eerie barnyard scarecrow. He is in reality Jonathan Crane, a "renegade college professor and authority on the psychology of terror" who may be

Jonathan Crane, 1943 © NPP 1943

justifiably regarded as "one of the most dangerously brilliant men of our time" (Det No. 73, Mar '43: "The Scarecrow Returns").

"Very often," observes World's Finest Comics No. 3, "an incident in childhood suggests the sort of person that child will be when he has grown up. Such was the case with Jonathan Crane. As a small boy, Jonathan Crane liked to frighten birds!"

By Fall 1941 Crane has established himself as a professor of psychology at a GOTHAM CITY university. Because he is tall and spindly, wears shabby clothing, and spends all his money on books, Crane is regarded as something of an oddball, and behind his back his colleagues on the faculty refer to him derisively as "Scarecrow" Crane.

In the classroom, Crane is no less unconventional. On one occasion, for example, as part of a lecture on the psychology of fear, Crane shatters a flower pot with a bullet from an automatic pistol to impress upon his students a point concerning the nature of fear. It is precisely for this sort of bizarre classroom behavior that Crane is ultimately dismissed from the university—". . . your teachings," explains the university president, "are entirely too fanatical!"—even before BATMAN has unmasked him as the Scarecrow.

While strolling across the campus one afternoon prior to his dismissal, Crane overhears some of his

The Scarecrow, 1967 © NPP 1967

fellow teachers whispering derisively about his shabby clothes and his habit of spending his entire salary on books. "The fools!" snarls Crane angrily. "Do they think I would give up my precious books just to buy clothes? Bah! They think I'm queer and I look like a scarecrow--a scarecrow! They judge human values by money--if I had money they'd respect me – and I could buy more books! Yes---if I only had money---lots of money--"

In school the following day, Crane teaches his students about the methods used by protection racketeers to extort money from their victims. Later, when he is at home, "Crane's distorted brain begins thinking along fantastic lines---along criminal lines--"

"So I look like a scarecrow," muses Crane bitterly, "--that will be my symbol--a symbol of poverty and fear combined! The perfect symbol---the **Scarecrow!**"

In the guise of a grotesque scarecrow, Jonathan Crane soon launches a reign of murder and terror, hiring himself out to unscrupulous businessmen who want their competitors or business associates intimidated. Ultimately, however, Batman deduces that Crane is the Scarecrow, and he and ROBIN lure the villain into a trap and apprehend him (WF No. 3: "The Scarecrow!").

By March 1943 the Scarecrow has escaped from prison, and now, aided by a gang of henchmen, he embarks on a series of spectacular crimes centering around the theme of three-letter words. His "hat" crime, for example, involves the theft of a collection of priceless antique hats. Batman and Robin finally apprehend the Scarecrow and his henchmen, however, in the act of robbing an Oriental curio shop in Gotham City's Chinatown (Det No. 73: "The Scarecrow Returns").

NEVER THOUGHT I'D EVER SEE A FLYING SCARE-CROW!

The Scarecrow and Batman, 1967 © NPP 1967

SCARLET HORDE, THE. A team of four renegade scientists, headed by Prof. Carl Kruger and aided by a ruthless army of 2,000 men, whose diabolical bid for world domination is thwarted by BATMAN in November 1939.

By November 1939 Prof. Carl Kruger, released from an insane asylum after undergoing treatment for a deep-seated "Napoleon complex," has perfected an awesomely hideous "death ray machine" through the successful "fusion of ozone gas and the gamma ray." After mounting the death ray machine aboard a scarlet dirigible, Kruger and his lieutenants – the so-called Scarlet Horde – stage a deadly foray over downtown Manhattan, toppling tall buildings and slaughtering thousands in a diabolical effort to establish himself as "dictator of the world."

Batman ultimately destroys the "dirigible of doom" by ramming it with the BATPLANE. Kruger flees in a small airplane, but Batman climbs aboard the airborne craft, renders Kruger unconscious with a gas pellet, and then bails out seconds before the plane, with the unconscious Kruger still on board, crashes into a nearby bay (Det No. 33: "The Batman Wars Against the Dirigible of Doom").

SCARPIS, BUGS. A wily confidence man who, employing the alias Scorpio, poses as an alchemist and, by means of hypnosis, successfully dupes a number of prominent people into believing that certain magical secrets, which he alone possesses, enable him to transform ordinary substances – such as clay, glass, and coal – into priceless gems and other treasures. For a time, Scarpis bilks his victims of large sums by selling them his magical "secrets," but he and his henchmen are finally apprehended by BATMAN and ROBIN in January 1946 (Det No. 107: "The Mountain of the Moon!").

SCORPIO. An alias employed by confidence man BUGS SCARPIS when he poses as an alchemist as part of an elaborate scheme to bilk the wealthy (Det No. 107, Jan '46: "The Mountain of the Moon!").

SCUTTLER, THE. "The scourge of the West Coast," a ruthless criminal with a long cape and a black moustache who is determined to steal the plans for a priceless new invention by intercepting a registered letter containing the plans which has been mailed to a patent attorney in GOTHAM CITY. BATMAN and ROBIN apprehend the Scuttler and his henchmen in June–July 1945, and the registered letter reaches its destination safely (BM No. 29/3: "The Mails Go Through!").

SEA-FOX, THE. The leader of a gang of criminals, armed with underwater spear guns, who speed through the water on special "underwater sleds" and travel to and from the places they intend to rob via the city's labyrinthine sewer systems and underground rivers. The Sea-Fox and his henchmen commit a series of spectacular crimes in GOTHAM CITY before they are finally tracked to their hideout on an abandoned island army base and apprehended there by BATMAN and ROBIN (BM No. 132/3, Jun '60: "The Lair of the Sea-Fox!").

SECRET STAR, THE. An elite five-man organization, chosen by POLICE COMMISSIONER GORDON and personally trained by BATMAN and ROBIN, whose members are intended to serve as replacements for Batman in the event of his death or long-term disability. The Secret Star's five charter members include Lt. Philip Gray, the U.S. Army's top intelligence agent; Harry Vincent, honors student and all-around athlete at a leading university; Dave Fells and Sam Olson, decorated police officers; and TED BLAKELY, "brightest young man in the FBI" (BM No. 77/2, Jun/Jul '53: "The Secret Star").

SHADOW CITY. A bogus movie-set "city" which is established by the JOKER in a GOTHAM CITY warehouse in April–May 1945 as part of an elaborate scheme to bilk the wealthy (BM No. 28/1: "Shadow City!").

SHARK, THE. A member — along with the Fox and the Vulture — of the TERRIBLE TRIO.

SHARL. A now-extinct planet which was once the fifth planet from the sun in the solar system that includes Earth until "it exploded to form the asteroids between Mars and Jupiter" eons ago.

In May 1961 a monstrous, green, one-eyed "rukk," an awesomely powerful retrieving creature dispatched to Earth by the inhabitants of Sharl as part of an interplanetary treasure hunt millions of years ago, emerges from its state of suspended animation inside its robot-controlled space capsule in the depths of the BATCAVE, where it had landed during Earth's prehistoric age but, through an accident, never awakened as the inhabitants of Sharl had intended. Unaware that Sharl is now extinct and its treasure-hunt mission therefore pointless, it runs amok on the planet Earth, prevented from wreaking death and serious destruction only by the heroic intervention of BATMAN and ROBIN. Finally, its appointed treasure-hunt chore fulfilled, it climbs back into its space capsule and rockets off into the stars, headed back toward a planet that no longer exists.

GOTHAM CITY gang boss Big Ed Bailey and his henchmen attempt to trail the rukk and prevent the Dynamic Duo from destroying it, knowing that eventually it will lead them to the batcave, where its capsule is, thereby betraying the secret identities of Batman and Robin. The famed crime-fighters successfully thwart this scheme, however, and apprehend the criminals after a battle at the Gotham Foundry (Det No. 291: "The Creature from the Bat-Cave!").

SHELLEY, MARY WOLLSTONECRAFT. An English writer who is best remembered as the author of *Frankenstein* (1818), the story of a scientist who creates a monster out of charnel fragments and is ultimately destroyed by it. According to Detective Comics No. 135, however, the grisly story of BARON FRANKENSTEIN and his monster is based upon a set of startling facts which were related to Mary Shelley (1797–1851) by BATMAN during a time-journey he made to nineteenth-century Europe (May '48: "The True Story of Frankenstein!").

SHEPHERD, HARRY. A criminal who kidnaps and then impersonates an inspector from Scotland Yard visiting GOTHAM CITY as part of an elaborate scheme to destroy BATMAN's crime-fighting career by tricking him into revealing his secret identity. The scheme involves tampering with Batman's belt radio in such a way as to enable Shepherd to manipulate Batman's subconscious and force him to have a series of terrifying nightmares culminating in a complete nervous collapse. Ultimately, however, Batman sees through Shepherd's impersonation and, with ROBIN's help, apprehends Shepherd and his henchmen and rescues the real Scotland Yard inspector from the villains' clutches (BM No. 84/3, Jun '54: "Ten Nights of Fear!").

SHINER, THE. A villain in a shining hood who, with the aid of two accomplices and a group of retired airplane pilots whom he has duped into helping him, has been stealing radium from the Ross Radium Company and smuggling it across the United States border into Canada. BATMAN and ROBIN apprehend the radium thieves in May 1947 and unmask the Shiner as Smythe, manager of the Ross Radium Company (Det No. 123: "The Dawn Patrol Crimes!").

SHORT, SKINNER. "A notorious gang leader from the States," now active in Canada, whose gang robs trappers and plunders fur warehouses in quest of valuable animal pelts. Short and his henchmen are ultimately apprehended "in Canada's remote Northwest territories, near Hudson Bay," through the heroic efforts of BATMAN, ROBIN, and members of the Royal Canadian Mounted Police (BM No. 23/3, Jun/Jul '44: "Pelt Plunderers!").

SIGNALMAN. A costumed criminal who brazenly announces his forthcoming crimes by means of elaborate clues — the texts refer to them as "sign-clues" (BM No. 124/2, Jun '59: "The Return of Signalman") — consisting of signs and symbols of various kinds. In June 1959, for example, he announces his intention to loot a showboat box office by sending BATMAN a pair of Janus masks, symbolizing the theater, along with a nautical symbol traditionally used to announce a short voyage (BM No. 124/2: "The Return of Signalman").

Signalman wears a red costume with a white sunburst emblazoned on his chest; black-and-yellow striped trunks; a green belt; a yellow cowl with matching gloves and boots; and a yellow cape embroidered with bright green chemical, astrological, and other symbols.

Phil Cobb, 1957 © NPP 1957

He is in reality Phil Cobb, "a small-time crook with big ideas" who assumes the role of Signalman in the hope of becoming an underworld "big shot" (BM No. 112/1, Dec '57: "The Signalman of Crime"). In April 1961 – approximately three and a half years after his initial appearance as Signalman – Cobb establishes himself in yet another underworld identity, that of the Blue Bowman (BM No. 139/1: "The Blue Bowman").

In December 1957 Phil Cobb arrives in GOTHAM CITY with high hopes of becoming an underworld big shot. To his dismay, however, he discovers that an out-of-town criminal without a prior reputation is hard-pressed to recruit a gang of henchmen in the big city. As the disconsolate Cobb wanders through the streets, he spies the famous BAT-SIGNAL flashing across the sky and is suddenly seized by an inspiration: "A signal," exclaims Cobb, "--that's the answer! Like the **Joker** and the **Penguin**, I'll make a quick reputation as a criminal because I'll be unique! But I'll be smarter than them--**I** won't get caught!"

Cobb assumes the identity of Signalman and embarks on a spectacular series of crimes, each time providing Batman with advance warning in the form of one of his ingenious sign-clues. Batman and ROBIN succeed in thwarting every one of Signalman's crimes, but they are unable to apprehend the villain, and the resulting newspaper headlines soon establish for Signalman the underworld reputation he has been seeking. At one point, Signalman captures Batman and Robin, imprisons them aboard a cabin cruiser, and then makes off with the Dynamic Duo's bat-launch, intending to use it to help him rob the wealthy guests aboard the Van Dorf yacht. Batman and Robin escape from the cabin cruiser, however, pursue Signalman, and, somewhat ironically, apprehend the villain when he runs the bat-launch aground on a shoal after failing to notice a signal-bell buoy afloat in the water (BM No. 112/1: "The Signalman of Crime").

In June 1959 Signalman breaks out of jail and attempts to recruit a gang in Gotham City, only to learn that although he has indeed acquired a substantial underworld reputation, it is as "the guy Batman put in jail," and not as a successful criminal. "I'll show them!" vows Signalman bitterly. "Before I'm through, they'll come crawling, begging me to let them join my gang!"

Signalman, 1959 © NPP 1959

After an unsuccessful attempt to loot a showboat box office, followed by the successful theft of a valuable necklace from a movie actress at Gotham Studios, Signalman attempts to enhance his reputation – and make a fool out of Batman – by stealing a collection of honorary police badges, presented to Batman by police departments throughout the world, which are on display at a Gotham City exhibition hall. Batman and Robin appear on the scene, however, and apprehend Signalman before he can escape (BM No. 124/2: "The Return of Signalman").

By April 1961 Signalman has escaped from prison and returned to Gotham City, this time clad in a blue archer's costume decorated with orange trim and employing the name the Blue Bowman. In prison, Signalman had made the acquaintance of Bulls-eye, a villainous archer who had taught him how to make and use a wide variety of trick arrows to aid him in his crimes. "I failed against him [Batman] as the Signalman," he had remarked, "--but I'll bet I could succeed as a bandit ***bowman!***"

The Blue Bowman © NPP 1961

During a series of colorful encounters, the Blue Bowman attempts to defeat Batman with a bizarre arsenal of trick arrows, including a "buzz-saw arrow," a "boxing-glove arrow," a "boomerang arrow," a "hook arrow," a flame-tipped "incendiary arrow," and a "cobweb arrow" which ensnares its victim in a "net of tough silken rope."

Batman retaliates with his ingenious array of batarangs – he uses his "saw-tooth batarang," for example, to slice apart the silken net released by the Blue Bowman's cobweb arrow, and his "fire-prevention batarang" to counter the incendiary impact of the incendiary arrow – and he and Robin apprehend the villain and his henchmen when they attempt to loot the Gotham Archery Company (BM No. 139/1: "The Blue Bowman"). (*See* BATMAN section E 2 d ii, the batarang.)

SIKES, PAUL "KILLER." An alias employed by BATMAN in December 1941–January 1942 when he enters North Island Prison as an inmate in order to investigate the activities of the infamous BIG MIKE RUSSO (BM No. 8/1: "Stone Walls Do Not a Prison Make").

SIKES, SMILEY. The leader of a gang of criminals who, having framed parking garage attendant Joe Sands on a drunk driving charge to prevent him from telling the police about a stolen car they had parked in his garage overnight, viciously beat ROBIN to the very edge of death when he and BATMAN attempt to investigate the frame-up. Transformed into "a terrible figure of vengeance" by the brutal assault on his young partner, Batman storms enraged into the gangsters' hideout and, ignoring the three bullets that come slamming into his chest in the course of the ensuing battle, beats Smiley Sikes senseless and forces him to sign a full confession before turning both Sikes and his confession over to the authorities (BM No. 5/3, Spr '41: "The Case of the Honest Crook").

SIMAK. The leader of a gang of criminals who, having successfully stolen the blueprints for an awesomely destructive "ultra-sonic weapon" invented by JULES VERNE from the grounds of the Verne Memorial Exhibition on Sunny Island off GOTHAM CITY, threaten to reduce the city to rubble unless they are paid $10,000,000 in extortion money.

Dispatched through the time barrier by PROFESSOR CARTER NICHOLS to Paris, France, in the year 1900, however, BATMAN and ROBIN swiftly locate the famous founder of modern science fiction, tell him of their plight, and persuade him to return with them to the mid-twentieth century to help construct a new weapon capable of countering the effects of the one which has fallen into criminal hands.

Ultimately, with Verne's help, and with the aid of the "reflecto-beam" mechanism which he designs and helps them construct, Batman and Robin defeat Simak and his henchmen and eventually take them into custody (BM No. 98/1, Mar '56: "The Return of Mr. Future!").

SIMMONS, HECTOR. The unscrupulous secretary to Professor Ezra Dorn, the owner of "the world's largest criminal library and collection of historical crime souvenirs" and a scholar widely renowned as "the historian of crime." In April–May 1950 Simmons imprisons Dorn in his own cellar and embarks on a "series of bizarre crimes" using weapons and other items from Dorn's crime collection while clad in garb resembling that of the various famous criminals of history whose exploits he has chosen to emulate. For a time, public suspicion centers on Professor Dorn, since the items used by the villainous "crime historian" are all from Dorn's collection, but BATMAN and ROBIN ultimately apprehend the mysterious bandit and unmask him as the secretary Simmons (WF No. 45: "The Historian of Crime!").

SIMMS (Professor). An evil scientist who, having already perfected a serum designed to "activate [men's] growth glands" and transform them into twelve-foot giants, concocts an elaborate scheme to create an army of powerful giants to help him commit spectacular crimes. Because Simms wants his giants to possess superhuman strength as well as extraordinary size, he dupes researcher Steve Condon – who has been conducting hormone experiments designed to increase people's strength and vitality – into becoming his assistant in the hope that Condon's findings, combined with his own, will enable him to transform his henchmen into powerful giants. Events take a complicated turn, however, when an accident in Simms's laboratory, resulting from the chance combination of Condon's strength formula with Simms's growth formula, transforms Condon into a powerful twelve-foot giant who promptly wanders off into bitter seclusion to escape from the society that has branded him a freak. Simms eventually extracts the strength formula from Condon – now known as the Titanic Man – and uses it, in combination with his own growth formula, to transform his henchmen into powerful giants, but BATMAN, ROBIN, and Condon ultimately apprehend Simms and his henehmen and use an antidote to restore Condon – and presumably the other giants – to their normal size (Det No. 278, Apr '60: "The Man Who Became a Giant!").

SIMPLE SIMON. A tall, lanky criminal with large buckteeth and the locution of a country bumpkin who commits a series of ingenious crimes based on the Simple Simon nursery rhyme until he and his henchmen are finally apprehended by BATMAN and ROBIN in March 1961 (BM No. 138/2: "The Simple Crimes of Simple Simon").

SIMS, RIGGER. The man who is secretly MR. ROULETTE (BM No. 75/2, Feb/Mar '53: "Mr. Roulette's Greatest Gamble").

SINISTER 8, THE. A group of eight ruthless international criminals (Frenchy Le Doix, Singh Dan, Baron Hengler, Ling Chee, Luigi Verona, Aldo Toledano, the Liverpool Kid, and Sumatra Joe), all escapees from the infamous Satan's Island Prison in the South Atlantic until their recent recapture by BATMAN and ROBIN, who are transported safely back to Satan's Island by the Dynamic Duo in August–September 1952 despite determined efforts by the international underworld to destroy the two lawmen and set their captives free (BM No. 72/1: "The Jungle Batman!").

SKIGG (Alderman). A crooked alderman, in cahoots

with a powerful mobster known as Fancy Dan, who is exposed and apprehended in August–September 1941 through the heroic efforts of BATMAN, ROBIN, and a rookie policeman named Jimmy Kelly (BM No. 6/4: "Suicide Beat!").

SKY CREATURE, THE. A weird, orange-colored being of phenomenal powers – BATMAN speculates that it is "a creature from another dimension" – who may be called forth at will, like a magic genii, by whoever possesses "the accursed lantern of Celphus the Sorcerer." In October 1960 a gang of criminals, who have come upon the ancient lantern while looting an antique shop, summon the sky creature and force it to use its unearthly powers to aid them in their crimes. When ROBIN finally smashes the lantern with a stone, however, the sky creature disappears forever, thus enabling Batman and Robin to apprehend the criminals (BM No. 135/3: "The Menace of the Sky Creature!").

SKYBOY. The name given by SUPERMAN to a teen-ager from outer space, endowed with superhuman powers similar to Superman's, who arrives on the planet Earth in January–February 1958 afflicted with total amnesia as the result of a collision between his spacecraft and an oncoming meteor. Skyboy, who ultimately recovers his memory with Superman's help, is in reality Tharn, the son of a lawman on the far-distant planet Kormo who dispatched his son to Earth to alert its inhabitants to the recent arrival on Earth of a band of interplanetary outlaws led by the villainous Rawl. On Earth, Rawl and his bandits stage a series of spectacular thefts of copper, Kormo's most precious metal, before they are finally apprehended through the heroic efforts of Superman, Skyboy, BATMAN, and ROBIN (WF No. 92: "The Boy from Outer Space!").

SKYE, JOHN. The leader of a syndicate of gangland chieftains, including "some of the nation's leading crooks," who are eager to prevent passage of pending national legislation which would appropriate funds for the construction of a small factory to provide much-needed employment for job-seeking ex-convicts. Fearful that such legislation would seriously undermine their ability to recruit and retain henchmen to perform their mobs' dirtiest chores, Skye and his colleagues become determined to murder BATMAN and ROBIN to prevent them from testifying on behalf of the legislation before the United States Senate.

Locked in an airtight vault at Skye's warehouse headquarters on the outskirts of Washington, D.C., Batman and Robin are rescued from seemingly certain death by four reformed ex-convicts who have accompanied them to Washington to help press for passage of the legislation. With their help, the Dynamic Duo apprehend Skye and his confederates, then continue to the Senate to argue the case for the pending bill.

"The great lesson of democracy," Batman had explained in a recent radio address, "is that all men are created equal. Why then should anyone continue to suffer for a mistake after this debt has been paid? . . . for this great nation cannot allow prejudice to deprive it of the badly needed skills of these men!" (BM No. 28/3, Apr/May '45: "Batman Goes to Washington!").

SLICK. An underworld figure who operates a hideout for fugitive criminals in the northern part of the Florida Everglades. BATMAN infiltrates the village hideaway by posing as fugitive gang chieftain Knuckles Donegan and ultimately apprehends Slick and his cohorts with the aid of ROBIN and the Miami police (BM No. 31/2, Oct/Nov '45: "Vanishing Village!").

SLOANE, PAUL. A professional actor, hired to play the role of TWO-FACE on television's "True Crime Playhouse," whose mind snaps after his face is scarred by a vial of acid, and who then turns to crime in the crazed belief that he is the original Two-Face (BM No. 68/3, Dec/Jan '51–'52: "The New Crimes of Two-Face!"). (*See* TWO-FACE.)

SMARTE, CARL. An official of the Marine Construction Corporation and the proprietor of an ingenious pay-by-the-day hideout for fugitive criminals – a hollowed-out artificial island at the bottom of a huge fishtank which Smarte's firm designed for the huge Seaorama aquarium in GOTHAM CITY.

BATMAN's efforts to locate the secret hideaway are severely hampered by the fact that a freak accident – caused by a bolt of lightning interacting with the chemicals in his UTILITY BELT – has radically altered Batman's "physical structure" and temporarily transformed him into a "human fish," forcing him to wear a transparent water-filled helmet in order to provide his lungs with the watery environment he needs to survive. Despite this overwhelming handicap, however, Batman ultimately locates Smarte's secret sanctuary for wanted criminals and, with ROBIN's help, apprehends Smarte and his underworld clientele (BM No. 118/3, Sep '58: "The Merman Batman!").

SMEDLEY, RALPH (Professor). A "brilliant chemist," in the process of perfecting a "flareless, noiseless explosive" for the U.S. Army, who is abducted in August 1964 by two criminals who hope to force him to manufacture the explosive so that they can use it to burglarize safes. Professor Smedley is rescued, and his two abductors are apprehended, through the heroic efforts of BATMAN and PATRICIA POWELL (BM No. 165/2: "The Dilemma of the Detective's Daughter!").

SMILER. The operator of a plush secret hideaway for wanted criminals situated in a heavily guarded subterranean chamber far beneath the surface of Gotham Village, a picturesque area of GOTHAM CITY inhabited by artists, bohemians, and intellectuals and noted for its espresso houses, sidewalk cafés, and colorful Jefferson Square Park. Access to the hideout – which features such luxurious amenities as a poolroom, movie room, and "special travel bureau" for criminals compelled to flee the country – is by means of a hidden stairway originating inside a large closet in an abandoned Gotham Village residence, and sanctuary is available to any fugitive willing to pay Smiler 50 percent of his stolen loot.

In May 1964 the future of Gotham Village is the subject of vigorous public debate between outraged citizens who regard the village as "a festering wound at the heart of the bustling metropolis" – a haven for hoodlums and undesirables which should be completely razed and rebuilt – and those who regard it as "a historical landmark and valuable living area" which should be preserved intact for future generations. Members of the Committee to Preserve Gotham Village – including Roland Meacham, chairman, and BRUCE WAYNE, vice-chairman – are among the chief advocates of preservation.

For some time, however, BATMAN has suspected the existence of a mysterious refuge for fugitive criminals somewhere in Gotham Village, and in May 1964, while he and ROBIN are attempting to locate jewel thief Frank Fenton, they find it. Before long, the Dynamic Duo have apprehended Smiler and his gangland clientele, including Fenton, and have put an end to their use of Gotham Village as an underworld haven. Then, with the criminals safely in custody, Batman discloses that Smiler is none other than Roland Meacham, who had hoped to ensure the preservation of Gotham Village to prevent the discovery of his subterranean underworld sanctuary there. Fortunately for the defenders of Gotham Village, the municipal authorities ultimately decide to preserve the village as a landmark (Det No. 327: "The Mystery of the Menacing Mask!").

SMILTER, JOHN. A cunning criminal who, clad in a flame-resistant asbestos suit, ignites a parked fuel truck with incendiary bullets and then lunges through the resulting flames to steal the priceless Fabian diamonds from a dockside customs office. Smilter and his accomplice are apprehended by BATMAN and SUPERMAN in May–June 1952, however, while attempting to escape by helicopter from the deck of the cruise ship *VARANIA* (S No. 76/1: "The Mightiest Team in the World!").

SMIRT, HERBERT. The unscrupulous "scholar with a shady record" who is the author of *The Batman Encyclopedia,* an illustrated reference work containing "thousands of facts about Batman" – including his exact height, weight, and physical measurements as well as detailed technical descriptions of his BATMOBILE, BATPLANE, and other crime-fighting equipment – intended for sale to criminals, at $5,000 per encyclopedia, so that they may use its vast "storehouse of information gathered by patient research" to help them outwit BATMAN and ROBIN. In December 1954, however, after cleverly misleading Smirt's underworld clientele into believing that the encyclopedia is inaccurate and its data therefore worthless, Batman and Robin apprehend the wily scholar and his gangland cohorts and, except for one copy destined for their trophy room, confiscate and destroy the entire edition of Smirt's encyclopedia (Det No. 214: "The Batman Encyclopedia").

SMITH, ED. The name by which the JOKER becomes known to the citizens of Farr Corners, U.S.A., after he loses his memory in a plane crash, including all recollection of his criminal past (BM No. 16/1, Apr/May '43: "The Joker Reforms!").

SMITH, SUZIE. An employee of the Gotham *Gazette,* described as "one of **Batman's** most enthusiastic, avid admirers," who quits her job to become BATMAN's secretary in June 1955 after the Dynamic Duo have placed an advertisement in the *Gazette* for a temporary full-time employee to answer their voluminous fan mail. Suzie becomes so attached to her new position that she intentionally encourages citizens to write letters to Batman and ROBIN so that the flow of fan mail – and therefore the need for her services – will continue, but the Dynamic Duo finally dispose of the fan-mail problem in its entirety – at least for the time being – by using the BATPLANE to skywrite a general note of thanks to all their fans at once in the skies over GOTHAM CITY (BM No. 92/1: "Fan-Mail of Danger!").

SMITHERS. The man who served as construction boss during the construction of the new Gotham City Museum, and the leader of a gang of criminals who use the museum as a secret hideaway. Capitalizing on his role as construction boss, Smithers honeycombed the new museum with hidden passageways so that his gang would be able to use it as a secret crime headquarters, but he and his henchmen are apprehended by BATMAN and ROBIN in August–September 1950 (BM No. 60/1: "Crime Through the Ages!").

SMYTHE. The man who is secretly the SHINER (Det No. 123, May '47: "The Dawn Patrol Crimes!").

SMYTHE, SIDNEY. A renowned English mountain climber who is impersonated by a member of an international crime cartel as part of an underworld effort to recover a roll of microfilm containing a list of the cartel's members. The film, which was recently jettisoned from a disabled aircraft flying over the Himalayas, landed on the summit of MOUNT K-4, and now both the F.B.I. and the international underworld are determined to recover it.

In August 1955 an unnamed criminal impersonates Smythe and takes his place in a mountain-climbing expedition up the side of K-4 in hopes of recovering the microfilm for the cartel, but BATMAN and ROBIN – who have been assigned the task of recovering the film for the F.B.I. – join the expedition under assumed names, beat the bogus Smythe to the summit, and ultimately locate the canister containing the microfilm. During a battle with the Dynamic Duo atop the craggy summit, the underworld impostor slips and hurtles to his doom thousands of feet below (BM No. 93/1: "Journey to the Top of the World!").

SNEED, RICHARD. The twin brother of the evil Jasper Sneed. In November 1941, anguished over Jasper's shabby treatment of the woman they both once loved, Richard dons an elaborate disguise, obtains employment as his brother's butler, poisons Jasper with an "Oriental poison" designed to kill its victim in twenty-four hours, and then calmly informs his evil brother that he has exactly twenty-four hours to live.

Confronted with the horrifying reality of his own imminent death, Jasper's "already distorted brain loses its last vestiges of sanity," and he vows to spend his last day on earth murdering the various relatives and business associates whom he knows hate him, but who have all been nice to him in hopes of one day inheriting his money. Jasper successfully commits one murder and, with the aid of accomplices, attempts four others before he is finally captured by BATMAN, only to die moments later as the result of the poison. Richard Sneed, his revenge now complete, dies also, having taken a dose of the same poison with which he killed his brother (Det No. 57: "Twenty-Four Hours to Live!").

SONGBIRD SOCIETY, THE. An organization, ostensibly for bird lovers, which is in reality only a front for the PENGUIN's scheme to extort money from famous singers by threatening to ruin their singing voices unless they make sizable "donations" to the society. The Songbird Society is disbanded in August 1947 through the heroic efforts of BATMAN and ROBIN (Det No. 126: "Case of the Silent Songbirds!").

SPADE, JACK. The ex-convict who is secretly HIJACK (BM No. 122/2, Mar '59: "The Cross-Country Crimes!").

SPARROW, THE. A costumed individual, his true identity unknown except to BATMAN and ROBIN, who joins the Dynamic Duo in their efforts to apprehend the MAESTRO. The Sparrow is in reality musicology professor Ambrose Weems, author of *An Encyclopedia of Music,* whose role in the manhunt is to identify the enigmatic musical clues provided by the Maestro, and whose identity-concealing costume is designed to protect him from possible reprisals by the Maestro and his henchmen (BM No. 149/1, Aug '62: "The Maestro of Crime").

SPEED AIRLINES. The airline which employed Selina Kyle as a stewardess prior to her emergence as the CATWOMAN (BM No. 62/1, Dec/Jan '50–'51: "The Secret Life of the Catwoman").

SPENCE (1961). A cunning racketeer on the island of Koba who, fearful that his gangland cohort Albey may be about to inform on their activities to the authorities, concocts a scheme to murder Albey while making it appear that Albey's death has been caused by a legendary sea monster, much feared by the local natives, called "the beast of Koba Bay." Spence finally kills Albey with the aid of a mechanical monster which he operates from controls inside the creature's body, but BATMAN and ROBIN, who have come to Koba Island to apprehend Albey, eventually discover the mechanical monster and take Spence into custody (Det No. 297, Nov '61: "The Beast of Koba Bay!").

SPENCE (1963). An alias employed by BATMAN in September 1963 when he and ROBIN pose as underworld impersonators of Batman and Robin as part of Batman's plan to apprehend BOBO CULLEN and recover his stolen UTILITY BELT (BM No. 158/3: "Batman and Robin --Imposters!").

SPHINX GANG, THE. A gang of criminals who conceal their identities beneath gray hoods resembling the heads of mythical sphinxes. The leader of the gang is gangster Al Regan. The entire Sphinx Gang is apprehended in February 1964 through the heroic efforts of BATMAN, ROBIN, and SUPERMAN (WF No. 139: "The Ghost of Batman!").

SPINNER, THE. A cunning criminal, clad in a bizarre metallic costume and equipped with a diabolical arsenal of spinning weapons – including a weird riflelike weapon which unleashes deadly "spinning buzz saws," and a "giant, glass-impregnated fan" whose whirling blades reflect "dazzling beams of sunlight" to bedazzle would-be pursuers – who commits a series of spectacular crimes in February 1960, each of which reflects his inexplicable preoccupation with spinning objects, as when he robs the headquarters of the Kool Fan Company or the offices of the Gotham Drill Company. The Spinner is in reality Swami Ymar, a GOTHAM CITY fortune-teller.

In an effort to persuade the authorities he is dead so that he can retire safely with his stolen loot, the Spinner tricks small-time criminal "Peanuts" Gilson into donning a Spinner costume, intending to kill Gilson with a time bomb to make it appear that the Spinner has perished in an accidental explosion. Arriving on the scene moments before the explosion, however, BATMAN and ROBIN apprehend Gilson and unravel the details of the Spinner's nefarious scheme. And soon afterward, with BATWOMAN's help, the Dynamic Duo apprehend the Spinner (BM No. 129/1: "The Web of the Spinner!").

SQUIDGE. The leader of a trio of diamond thieves who are apprehended by BATMAN and ROBIN in April–May 1943 (BM No. 16/3: "The Adventures of the Branded Tree!").

SQUIRE, THE. The young Englishman who is the crime-fighting companion of the KNIGHT. The Knight is in reality the Earl of Wordenshire, and the Squire is his young son Cyril (BM No. 62/2, Dec/Jan '50–'51: "The Batman of England!").

STACY. A ruthless professional gambler and owner of the Lions football team who is willing to resort to any means, including murder, to ensure his team's victory over the Panthers in their upcoming game. Stacy and his henchmen are thwarted at every turn, however, and finally apprehended, through the heroic efforts of BATMAN and ROBIN (BM No. 4/4, Win '41).

STACY, "SLANT." The leader of a gang of "platinum bandits" who match wits with BATMAN and ROBIN in September 1954, during a period when, as the result of their having remained underwater too long while salvaging some sunken cans of nitroglycerine in the Gotham City River, Batman and Robin have been warned that they must remain underwater for two full days if they are to avoid being stricken by the bends, that "terrible physical collapse that strikes divers who rise to the surface too rapidly!"

By operating from inside diving suits, however, as well as from inside a small Navy-surplus pocket-sub which they quickly dub the "batmarine," the Dynamic Duo manage to battle the platinum thieves to a standstill – and ultimately to apprehend them – without ever straying from the watery environment that must remain their prison during two full days of underwater exile (BM No. 86/1: "The Voyage of the First Batmarine!").

STAFFORD, "SLANT." The leader of a gang of criminals who, having successfully stolen – from the laboratory of inventor Dr. Philip Winters – special "radio remote-control" apparatus designed to enable BATMAN and ROBIN to operate the BATPLANE and BATMOBILE via remote control from the BATCAVE, attempt to use their newly acquired control over the famous crime-fighting vehicles to make them destroy Batman and Robin. When that fails, the gangsters hijack the batplane and use it to commit a series of spectacular crimes, but they are finally apprehended by Batman and Robin in April 1955 (BM No. 91/1: "The Living Batplane!").

STANNAR, JOHN. A fugitive thief who, pursued by BATMAN and ROBIN into an "unpeopled Northwoods region," comes upon an unmanned spacecraft from the planet Skar containing a cargo of super-scientific inventions – including a rechargeable "energy-radiator" designed to endow its user with temporary super-strength, and "fourth dimensional tongs" capable of reaching through solid objects – intended as gifts for the people of the planet Earth. Seizing the alien inventions and returning to GOTHAM CITY, Stannar uses them to break some of his underworld cronies out of the Gotham Jail and to commit a series of spectacular crimes before he is finally apprehended by Batman and Robin (Det No. 250, Dec '57: "Batman's Super-Enemy!").

STARK, CHARLEY. A riveter at the Gotham Shipyard who has contracted to smuggle gangster Jud Lukins, "Public Enemy Number One," out of GOTHAM CITY to a safe haven in a foreign country by hiding him inside a sealed air-compartment in the hull of one of the shipyard's newest ships. When a shipyard night watchman is found murdered after having inadvertently stumbled upon Lukins's hiding place, Bruce Wayne – the man who is secretly BATMAN – begins working as a shipyard riveter under an assumed name in an effort to flush out the killer. Ultimately, Batman and ROBIN arrest Stark for the night watchman's murder and apprehend Lukins inside the hidden compartment in which he had hoped to be smuggled to safety (WF No. 46, Jun/Jul '50: "Bruce Wayne, Riveter!").

STARK, EDDIE. A wanted criminal who, along with BATMAN and ROBIN, is among the startled passengers on a GOTHAM CITY ferryboat when an "eerie fog" settling over Gotham Bay combines with the effects of a crackling lightning storm to transport the ferry and its occupants through a warp in space and time to the world of the Yllans, an extradimensional race, inhabiting the city of Ylla, who are periodically attacked by the more biologically primitive race of creatures known as the Gruggs.

"Somehow," explains Batman, "the strange fog and electric storm created a freak phenomenon--a ***time warp*** that caused the ferry to burst through our dimension into this one!"

At one point, after Stark and his fellow passengers have been taken captive by the suspicious Yllans, Stark steals a "tele-dome" – a newly developed device designed to enable its wearer both to read minds and to establish mental control over the Gruggs – from the Yllan chief and uses it to establish his own mental dominion over the Gruggs as part of his scheme to conquer Ylla and seize the captive ferryboat so that he can return with the tele-dome to the earthly dimension, where its incredible mind-reading powers will enable him to acquire great wealth.

The Dynamic Duo, however, successfully repel the Grugg assault against Ylla, capture Stark, and restore the tele-dome to the Yllan chief – thus ensuring a lasting peace between the Yllans and the Gruggs – before steering the ferryboat back into the "lightning-lashed fog" and through the time warp to the earthly dimension (Det No. 293, Jul '61: "Prisoners of the Dark World!").

STARMAN. An alternate identity employed by BATMAN in September 1957 after he has become "afraid of anything that resembles a bat" as the result of having been afflicted with an "artificial phobia" by the "renegade scientist" PROFESSOR MILO (Det No. 247: "The Man Who Ended Batman's Career!").

STAR-MAN, THE. A ruthless costumed villain who is determined to possess a fabulous Tibetan belt which, once its three vital parts – a green belt, a gold buckle, and a red star which fits inside the buckle – have been assembled, will endow its wearer with superhuman strength, the ability to defy gravity, immortality, and other incredible powers. Star-Man is defeated in December 1960 through the heroic efforts of BATMAN, ROBIN, and BATWOMAN, who finally decide to destroy the belt because, in Batwoman's words, "It's far too dangerous for a mortal to possess!" (Det No. 286: "The Doomed Batwoman!").

STARR, JOE. A lowly "errand boy" for the Trigger Smith mob with high aspirations who changes his name to Lucky Starr – and soon afterward murders Trigger Smith and assumes control of his gang – after a fortune-teller has assured him that he was born beneath a "lucky star." Clad in a bright maroon costume emblazoned with yellow stars – and superstitiously certain that he cannot possibly die for another whole year – Starr commits a series of spectacular crimes, all characterized by incredibly reckless derring-do, until he and his henchmen are finally apprehended by BATMAN and ROBIN and he is sentenced to the electric chair for Trigger Smith's murder (WF No. 32, Jan/Feb '48: "The Man Who Could Not Die!").

STARR, LUCKY. *See* STARR, JOE.

STEFAN (Prince). The young ruler of Valonia, a perfect look-alike for ROBIN, who visits the United States with his entourage in January–February 1947 and even exchanges places with Robin for a time in order to escape the tedium of his princely life (WF No. 26: "His Highness, Prince Robin!"). (*See* FARRELL, SPARKS.)

STILETTI, MANUEL. A ruthless "international crook" who, with the aid of two accomplices, attempts to steal a set of priceless crown jewels recently transported to America by the exiled Duke of Dorian, who hopes to use them "to establish credits for [his] government-in-exile!" Stiletti and his henchmen are ultimately apprehended through the heroic efforts of BATMAN, ROBIN, and ALFRED, who makes his textual debut in this adventure (BM No. 16/4, Apr/May '43: "Here Comes Alfred!").

STINSON, SPADE. A ruthless swindler, determined to wreak vengeance on BATMAN for having sent him to prison several years ago, who concocts an elaborate scheme to sully Batman's reputation and transform him into a murderer. In February 1956, after Stinson's hired henchmen have waylaid Batman, knocked him unconscious, and fled, Stinson introduces himself as a doctor, escorts the injured Batman to his "office," and prescribes some innocent-looking pills containing, in actuality, a rare Amazon drug designed to make Batman "go temporarily berserk and commit murder!" Fortunately, not even Stinson's drug can "weaken Batman's strong moral character that much," but the pills do have the effect of making Batman rise from his bed during the night and commit a series of thefts, only to awaken the next morning with no recollection of what he has done.

When ROBIN discovers the loot in the BATCAVE and Batman realizes that he has become a thief, his first impulse is to turn himself over to the police. Ultimately, however, he deduces correctly that the physician who treated his recent injuries was not a physician at all, and before long he succeeds in apprehending Stinson and his henchmen and in returning the stolen loot to its rightful owners (Det No. 228: "The Outlaw Batman!").

STONE, PHIL. An alias employed by BATMAN in February–March 1952 when he poses as a movie actor in order to obtain the role of Batman in W. W. HAMMOND's film *The Batman Story* (BM No. 69/1: "The Batman Exposé!").

STORME, PORTIA. The stage name assumed by JULIE MADISON after her excellent performance in the horror movie *Dread Castle* has made her a star (Det No. 49, Mar '41: "Clayface Walks Again!").

STRAIT, MICHAEL. The racketeer who is best known as the COUNT (BM No. 28/2, Apr/May '45: "Shirley Holmes, Policewoman!").

STRANGE, HUGO (Professor). A "crafty, diabolical, arch-criminal" (Det No. 46, Dec '40) with a "brilliant but distorted brain" (Det No. 36, Feb '40).

Bruce Wayne, the man who is secretly BATMAN, has described Professor Hugo Strange as "the most dangerous man in the world! Scientist, philosopher and a criminal genius---little is known of him, yet this man is undoubtly [sic] the greatest organizer of crime in the world---" (Det No. 36, Feb '40).

A MALIGNANT SMILE CROSSES HIS FACE AS HE BROODS OVER THE MANY EVIL SCHEMES THAT SURGE THROUGH HIS BRILLIANT BUT DISTORTED BRAIN---

Professor Hugo Strange © NPP 1940

By February 1940 Professor Strange has kidnapped electrical engineer Henry Jenkins, inventor of a technique for creating "concentrated lightning" artificially, and has forced him to construct a gigantic lightning machine to aid him in his crimes. Sometime in the past, Strange had discovered that "hot lightning [causes] condensed steam in the air, like a sort of natural fog." Now, by using the lightning machine to blanket the city with a heavy night fog, he enables his henchmen to loot two banks virtually undetected. The following night, Professor Strange once again enshrouds the city in a thick artificial fog, but on this night, Batman, who has disguised himself as a night watchman, apprehends six of the villain's henchmen when they attempt to burglarize the Sterling Silver Company.

Enraged at Batman's interference, Professor Strange has his henchmen set a trap for Batman at the Wolf Bros. Fur Company, and Batman soon finds himself a prisoner at Professor Strange's hideout. "I have brought you here alive," snarls the villain, "so that you may know what it means to interfere with Prof. Strange!" Raising his black bullwhip, Strange begins to lash Batman unmercifully, but Batman's "steel muscles suddenly surge with strength and snap his bonds," and within moments he has overpowered Professor Strange and his henchmen, secured the release of Henry Jenkins, and deactivated the diabolical lightning machine. Before long, the evil Professor Strange has been incarcerated in a cell at the state penitentiary. "They can't keep me here, caged like some wild beast!" vows the villain, glaring through the bars. "I'll escape . . . and when I do, I shall devote the rest of my life in [sic] revenging myself upon the **Batman!**" (Det No. 36).

In Spring 1940 Professor Strange breaks out of prison and, with the aid of his henchmen, abducts five mental patients from the Metropolis Insane Asylum. "Criminals, maniacs, and Strange can only add up to one thing," muses Bruce Wayne grimly, after news of the bizarre abduction has been broadcast over the radio, ". . . something new in crime . . . something fantastic and terrible, very terrible!!"

A month later, a powerful fifteen-foot man-monster appears on a crowded street in downtown Manhattan and begins an orgy of apparently purposeless destruction: it lifts a taxicab full of people high into the air, then dashes it angrily to the pavement; seizes two policemen, one in each hand, and hurls them bodily through a store window; and uproots a heavy lamppost and swings it like a scythe through the panic-stricken downtown crowd. Squads of policemen close in, but their bullets have no effect on the angry man-monster, and it finally lumbers into a waiting truck and roars away after hurling a bomb at its would-be pursuers.

A day later, the man-monster appears again, rips down a section of elevated subway track with its bare hands, and then escapes again in a truck after exploding a powerful bomb to forestall pursuit.

This time, however, Batman follows overhead in his BATPLANE and trails the truck to a clifftop hideaway overlooking the ocean. Inside the hideout, however, he is captured by two powerful man-monsters, and moments later he finds himself face to face with his old enemy Professor Strange. "I expected to see your ugly face around here," exclaims Batman defiantly. "I had a hunch you were behind this. We meet again Professor Strange!"

Bullwhip in hand, the villain tells Batman how he has managed to transform the five kidnapped mental patients into terrifying monsters. "I discovered an extract that speeds up the growth glands," he explains. "I inject this fluid into a normal man. The sudden growth not only distorts the body but also the brain--and soon he is a **monster!!** I have sent out a monster in clothes of bulletproof material so that the public and the police may be--er--acquainted with him. Tomorrow I shall send out two **monsters** and while the police are concerned with them my men will loot the banks. Clever, isn't it? You know, at times I am amazed at my own genius!"

Then, while the monsters hold Batman in their iron grip, Professor Strange plunges a hypodermic needle filled with monster serum into Batman's arm. "Done!" gloats Strange triumphantly. "Observe the clock, Batman! It is exactly 6 o'clock at night. The serum takes 18 hours to work. At precisely noon tomorrow the serum will take effect!"

Left unconscious in a barred cell, Batman awakens at 11:45 the following morning, with only fifteen minutes remaining before the villain's serum transforms him into a brutal monster. Professor Strange's henchmen review their day's crime plans and then depart with two of the five monsters — in two separate trucks — to terrorize the city and loot its banks.

With the aid of chemicals concealed inside his bootheels, Batman concocts a powerful explosive and blasts his way out of his barred prison. Within seconds, he has become embroiled in a deadly battle with Professor Strange and a powerful blow from his fist has sent the villain hurtling through an open window and over the edge of the cliff into the murky waters far below. "I wonder," muses Batman quietly, "if this is really the end of Prof. Hugo Strange???"

Now there remain only minutes before the serum in Batman's body begins to wreak its ghastly transformation, but before Batman can set to work concocting an antidote he is attacked by the three man-monsters who have remained behind at the hideout. By using a long pole to jab one monster between the eyes and cause the other two to collide head-on, Batman sets the monsters to fighting among themselves, then hastily uses the equipment in Professor Strange's laboratory to develop an antidote to the hideous monster serum. Within moments the three monsters have destroyed themselves and Batman has administered the vital antidote to himself precisely one minute before the noon deadline.

Now Batman races to his batplane and soars across the city in pursuit of the two trucks carrying the villain's henchmen and the two remaining monsters. The first truck is speeding along the Post Road, presumably in the Bronx, when Batman blazes "out of the sky" in the batplane, "spitting death" with the water-cooled machine gun mounted on the fuselage.

"Much as I hate to take human life," murmurs Batman grimly, as he coolly guides the batplane toward its target, its machine gun crackling with a deadly rat-tat-tat, "I'm afraid **this time** it's necessary!"

Within seconds, the truck, peppered with bullet holes, has lurched out of control and crashed into a tree, apparently killing Professor Strange's henchmen riding in the cab. When the enraged monster emerges alive from the rear of the battered truck, Batman hurls a noose around its neck and then points the batplane skyward, jerking the struggling monster off its feet and high into the air. For a few anguished moments the monster struggles against the ever-tightening rope; then its body goes limp and Batman knows it is finally dead. "He's probably better off this way," says Batman. Then, as the batplane soars high over a wooded area, Batman pulls out a knife and cuts the rope, sending the corpse of the slain monster hurtling toward the ground.

Soon afterward, Batman overtakes the second truck on Daly Avenue and blazes away at it with his machine gun until finally it careens wildly out of control and crashes into the side of a downtown office building. Emerging from the wreckage of the battered truck, the last of Hugo Strange's terrifying monsters stares angrily up at the batplane and then scales the outer wall of a nearby skyscraper — apparently the Empire State Building — in an insane attempt to snatch it from the sky. As the monster stands unsteadily atop the huge skyscraper tower, Batman blazes away at it with his batplane's machine gun, but its bulletproof clothing protects it from harm. In desperation, Batman unleashes a barrage of gas pellets which, breaking open at the monster's feet, send it reeling groggily over the side of the skyscraper to its doom on the pavement below (BM No. 1/3).

In December 1940 Professor Strange returns, this time with a plan to seize control of the United States Government with the aid of his diabolical "fear dust," which, when sprayed on human beings, makes them panicky and fearful. "I can be dictator of America!" gloats the villain. "Under the influence of my **'fear dust'** the **world** will bow!"

Presumably because his bold plan requires the use of many henchmen, Professor Strange has allied himself with a racketeer named Carstairs. At one point, Carstairs's henchmen — who have rendered themselves immune to the fear dust by taking special pills — spray fear dust inside a bank and then rob it while the guards are demoralized by the dust.

Not long afterward, Batman is captured by the criminals and taken to Professor Strange's hideout. ". . . this time," gloats the villain, "I shall vent my full hatred upon you!" At Professor Strange's signal, the assembled hoodlums hurl themselves at Batman and give him a beating so brutal that he soon lapses into unconsciousness. Moments later, with Batman apparently helpless, Professor Strange and his men leave their hideout to set in motion their scheme for using their fear dust to seize control of the city.

The villain, however, has not reckoned on his adversary's amazing recuperative powers, for "years of rigorous athletic training have enabled the **Batman** not only to resist but to recover from the brutal beating that would have mortally injured most men!" Before long, Batman has escaped from his arch-enemy's hideout and set out to apprehend him.

In the hours that follow, ROBIN prevents some of Professor Strange's henchmen from dumping fear dust in the city reservoir, then defeats another hoodlum attempting to spray it onto a crowd of people from atop a movie marquee. Batman stops another group of criminals from spraying fear dust in the Forty-second Street subway station and then, having learned that Professor Strange intends to spray the entire city with fear dust by airplane, races to the villain's secret airplane hangar. In the furious battle that follows, a blow from Batman's fist sends Professor Strange hurtling over the side of a craggy cliff to certain doom on the rocks below. "Well . . ." muses Batman grimly. "This time it really looks as if it is the end of the evil career of Professor Hugo Strange!" (Det No. 46).

STROBE, PAUL. The electrical engineer and former convict who is secretly ATOMIC-MAN (Det No. 280, Jun '60: "The Menace of the Atomic Man").

STRONG, SAM. A rustic mountain minstrel who arrives in GOTHAM CITY in October 1955 and becomes an overnight musical sensation with his lilting musical tribute, the "Ballad of Batman." For a time, Strong remains in Gotham City, adding new verses to his song to commemorate BATMAN's continuing exploits, and at one point he helps Batman and ROBIN apprehend a gang of protection racketeers by publicizing a new verse which successfully misleads the criminals into believing that the Dynamic Duo have temporarily left the city (BM No. 95/3: "The Ballad of Batman!").

STRYKER, ALFRED. A ruthless chemical company executive who has two of his three former partners murdered and then tries unsuccessfully to murder the third in an attempt to establish himself as sole owner of the Apex Chemical Company without having to honor his commitment to compensate the former partners for their shares of the business. Stryker dies when, during a climactic battle with BATMAN, he plummets headlong into a vat of acid. "A fitting end for his kind," murmurs Batman grimly (Det No. 27, May '39: "The Case of the Chemical Syndicate").

Batman and Alfred Stryker, 1939 © NPP 1939

STYX. The underworld figure who operates the Aqua-Lair, an undersea hideaway located beneath the surface of Gotham Bay, where fugitive criminals can hide from the police by paying rent of $1,000 per day or $10,000 per month. Although Styx impresses his underworld clientele by claiming that the Aqua-Lair is situated at a depth of 2,000 fathoms and that only his special "formula" enables them to survive at that depth, the lair is actually located within swimming distance of the surface. Acting on a tip from BATMAN and ROBIN, who have been imprisoned in the Aqua-Lair and managed to escape, the harbor police raid the hideout and apprehend Styx and his cohorts in November 1952 (Det No. 189: "The Undersea Hideout!").

Superman © NPP 1976

SUPERMAN. A world-famous crime-fighter and adventurer, an orphaned native of the exploded planet KRYPTON, who battles crime and injustice with the aid of an awesome array of superhuman powers, including X-ray vision, the power of flight, and strength far beyond that of any ordinary mortal. In his everyday identity, he is secretly Clark Kent, mild-mannered reporter for the METROPOLIS *Daily Planet.* Superman is a close friend of BATMAN and one of the few persons privy to the closely guarded secret of Batman's identity.

From mid-1954 onward, Batman and Superman regularly participate in certain of their adventures together. Wherever Batman and Superman appear together as co-participants, that adventure is treated in this volume. (For a complete account of the life and career of Superman apart from his involvement with Batman, consult *The Encyclopedia of Comic Book Heroes: Volume VI – Superman.*)

SVENSON, JOHN. A member of the Explorers' Club, now deceased, who has been hailed as "the greatest explorer who ever lived." Because Svenson wanted to bequeath his considerable wealth only to great explorers like himself, he locked his fortune inside a safe at the Explorers' Club and made it known that he had hidden the combination numbers, in pairs, in various parts of the world.

In February–March 1945 a club member named Challoner announces that he has deduced the whereabouts of the combination numbers, only to be found murdered soon afterward. BATMAN exposes explorer Felix Landry as Challoner's murderer and locates the combination numbers to the safe containing Svenson's fortune (BM No. 27/2: "Voyage into Villainy!").

SWANE, BARTON. A self-styled military genius and commander of an underworld army who attempts to use the techniques of modern warfare to defeat the crime-fighting team of BATMAN and ROBIN.

"For years, ***Batman*** has won over the underworld!" muses Swane. "But he's never faced an ***underworld army!*** An army commanded by ***Barton Swane!*** After he is defeated, my name will rank with the greatest military men of history! Perhaps even with the greatest of them all--***Napoleon!***"

For a time, Swane's military maneuvering is immensely successful and soon Batman becomes his prisoner. Ultimately, however, Batman escapes and, with Robin's help, apprehends Swane and his gangland army (Det No. 178, Dec '51: "The Defeat of Batman!").

T

TAL-DAR. The law-enforcement officer from the planet Alcor who is chief of the Interplanetary Space Police. Tal-Dar's principal crime-fighting weapon is an incredible "force-gun" with which he can imprison criminals inside an impenetrable "force-bubble" or ensnare them in "loops of crackling energy."

By August 1960 Tal-Dar has arrived on Earth to spend some time with BATMAN, having long observed him from Alcor by means of his planet's "long-range ultra-telescopes." An extremely insecure man with strong feelings of inferiority concerning his abilities as a crime-fighter, Tal-Dar attempts to conceal his lack of self-confidence beneath a facade of arrogance and conceit.

Tal-Dar's real motive in visiting Earth is to observe Batman at close range so that he can later imitate his crime-fighting techniques on Alcor, but he tells inquiring newspaper reporters that he has come "to observe ***Batman's*** crime-fighting technique--and help improve it by teaching him some tricks of my own," and he tells Batman that he has come to offer him membership in the Interplanetary Space Police, to take effect as soon as Earth has successfully mastered the science of interplanetary travel.

At one point, Tal-Dar joins Batman and ROBIN in a battle with some thieves at the Gotham Metals Plant. Tal-Dar's bungling actually prolongs the fighting and threatens the lives of Batman and Robin, but when the criminals have finally been apprehended it is Tal-Dar who loudly claims credit for their capture.

Soon afterward, some GOTHAM CITY gangsters, eager to obtain possession of Tal-Dar's incredible force-gun, abduct the alien crime-fighter by posing as newspaper reporters and playing on his renowned vanity by claiming that they want him to pose for photographs. Later, after Batman and Robin have finally apprehended the criminals and rescued Tal-Dar from their clutches, Tal-Dar makes a long-overdue confession. "I really came here to ***copy*** your techniques," he explains, "--because, actually, I'm not a good lawman at all! People on ***Alcor*** think I'm great, but the only cases I ever solved were by accident! I was too ashamed to tell you---so I pretended to be superior in order to cover up my faults!"

Just as Tal-Dar is about to depart for his home planet, however, he receives word that the ruthless villain Zan-Rak has stolen his planet's miraculous "star-stone" — a gigantic crystalline gem which "pulses with some strange inner life" and whose bizarre ray-emissions are capable of curing Alcorians of all their diseases and illnesses — and is holding it for the Alcorian equivalent of $1,000,000,000 ransom.

Panic-stricken over the theft of "the most important object on [his] planet," and certain that he could never outwit Zan-Rak on his own, Tal-Dar begs the Dynamic Duo to return with him to Alcor to battle Zan-Rak and recover the star-stone. After flying to Alcor in Tal-Dar's spacecraft, the three crime-fighters set out for the nearby asteroid where Zan-Rak has constructed his fortress and locked away the star-stone. When they arrive, however, Batman pretends to have fallen victim to "radji disease," an Alcorian illness which can be cured only by the rays of the star-stone, in an effort to compel Tal-Dar to assume the leadership role in the coming battle and thus, hopefully, regain his self-confidence.

Outside Zan-Rak's fortress, Batman tells his companions that he has become too weakened by the radji disease to go any farther, and Tal-Dar, although he remains apprehensive and uncertain as to his own abilities, is compelled to seize the initiative. With Robin's help, and driven on by thoughts of the stricken Batman, Tal-Dar manages to defeat Zan-Rak and prevent him from carrying out his threat to destroy the star-stone if attacked. Moments later, while Tal-Dar is busy calling in an air-strike against Zan-Rak's fortress by the Alcorian space armada, Zan-Rak attempts to shoot Tal-Dar, but Batman disarms him in the nick of time.

Later, Batman admits to Tal-Dar that he had never been sick at all. "I did it to force you to take command," explains Batman, ". . . force you to plan and fight as you could--and did! I knew you had to be a good fighter and leader if the other members of the ***I.S.P.*** [Interplanetary Space Police] made you their chief! What I had to do was make you ***realize*** it!"

"Thank you, ***Batman,***" replies Tal-Dar gratefully, ". . . because of you, I'll never be afraid to believe in myself again!" (Det No. 282: "Batman's Interplanetary Rival!").

In September 1961 Batman and Robin receive a strange gift from Tal-Dar: a powerful flying robot which, according to the explanatory sound film which has been sent along with it, has been "electronically conditioned to do one thing . . . ***protect your life!***" Wherever Batman and Robin go, the robot bodyguard follows, continually adding new data to its electronic brain to help it protect Batman from any possible harm.

Ironically, however, the ingenious robot soon proves to be more of a burden than a lifesaver. At one point, for example, when Batman attempts a daring swing across a caldron of molten metal at a steel mill in an effort to apprehend a fleeing criminal, the robot prevents Batman from making the swing on the ground that it is too dangerous, thus enabling the criminal to escape.

Back in the BATCAVE, Batman and Robin ponder the

dilemma posed by the robot's recent behavior. "Doesn't it understand," exclaims Robin, "that ***every time*** we go into action against crooks, there's a risk?" This remark however, is recorded by the robot's electronic brain, and, soon afterward, when Batman and Robin prepare to set out after some criminals on the Gotham City waterfront, the robot prevents them from going into action on the ground that they might be in danger if they did. "Your ***robot-guardian*** is so fanatical about keeping you out of danger," moans Robin, "it's stopping you from getting into action even before you get started!"

Finally Batman and Robin devise an elaborate scheme to deceive the robot into thinking that Batman is dead so that, believing its protective mission at an end, it will return to its home planet. Ultimately the ruse succeeds, the robot self-destructs, and Batman and Robin are left free to resume their dangerous crime-fighting careers in peace (BM No. 142/1: "Batman's Robot-Guardian").

TANG. The chief of the Zotos, a primitive but peace-loving people whose civilization flourished somewhere in the Middle East *ca.* 700 A.D. Sent into the past by PROFESSOR CARTER NICHOLS, BATMAN and ROBIN help Chief Tang and his fellow Zotos defend themselves against the depredations of "the terrible river canyon giants," who, "for centuries," have staged periodic forays into the Zotos's valley stronghold in search of slaves for their mills. By performing a series of "magical" feats with the aid of items from his UTILITY BELT, Batman tricks the superstitious giants into believing that he is a powerful costumed genie determined to protect the Zotos from harm, thus ensuring that the Zotos will henceforth be able to live in peace, without further fear of attack (BM No. 115/3, Apr '58: "Batman in the Bottle!").

TARO (Emperor). The boy emperor of ATLANTIS, who is a perfect look-alike for ROBIN. Taro's sister, Empress Lanya, rules Atlantis by his side. Robin develops something of a crush on Lanya during a visit to the sunken continent in October–November 1943 (BM No. 19/2: "Atlantis Goes to War!").

TATE, MARTIN. The owner of the Tate Jewelry Shop and the man who is secretly the GOBLIN (Det No. 152, Oct '49: "The Goblin of Gotham City!").

TAYLOR, AMBROSE. The wealthy GOTHAM CITY businessman – the chairman of a citizens' committee formed to support the vigorous campaign against organized crime being spearheaded by special prosecutor William Kendrick – who is the secret leader of the West Side Mob, the rivals of the notorious East Side Mob for control of the Gotham City underworld. In Summer 1941, after Taylor has brutally murdered Kendrick to prevent the special prosecutor from exposing him as the leader of one of the city's two major crime factions, BATMAN and ROBIN apprehend Taylor and the rival East Side Mob along with the ruthless "political boss" who has been providing the East Side Mob with political protection in return for a share of their loot (WF No. 2: "The Man Who Couldn't Remember!").

TAYLOR, BRANE. A citizen of Earth in the thirty-first century A.D. who, with the aid of his young nephew, has revived the legend of BATMAN and ROBIN in order to battle crime and lawlessness in the technologically advanced world of the distant future.

"I studied micro-films of . . . ***Batman's*** exploits in our museums," explains Taylor, "and I trained myself and my young nephew to duplicate them--and thus another ***'Batman*** and ***Robin'*** team was born--in the thirty-first century!"

Robin and Brane Taylor, 1951 © NPP 1951

Although Brane Taylor and his nephew wear costumes identical to those worn by Batman and Robin in the twentieth century, their arsenal of crime-fighting equipment reflects the scientifically advanced age in which they live. Their headquarters is the "bat-belfry," situated high above the ground, since, in Taylor's words, "we of the future live so much in the sky," and their principal means of transportation is a sleek spacecraft known as the "batship." Their basic equipment includes a time machine shaped like "a globe of gleaming steel," special plastic lassos for binding their opponents (BM No. 67/3, Oct/Nov '51: "The Lost Legion of Space"), "personal jet-motors" for propelling themselves through the air, an "invisibility refractor" for rendering themselves invisible, and a "truth vapor" which compels criminals to answer questions truthfully (Det No. 216, Feb '55: "The Batman of Tomorrow!").

To conceal the fact that he is secretly the Batman of the far future, Taylor assumes the everyday role of a "rich man-about-town" whose business interests include a fleet of interplanetary cargo ships (BM No. 67/3, Oct/Nov '51: "The Lost Legion of Space"). Taylor is six feet two inches tall, has a physique similar to Batman's, and, like his young nephew, who remains unnamed in the chronicles, has thick, curly, blond hair. He is also a charming, gallant man with a flowery tongue and an eye for a pretty face, qualities which arouse the immediate suspicions of VICKI VALE when Taylor attempts to impersonate Batman in February 1955 (Det No. 216: "The Batman of Tomorrow!").

The obvious similarities between Brane Taylor and the thirty-first-century hero BRANE have given rise to speculation that Brane and Brane Taylor are one and the same man, but the textual evidence does not support this view. According to Batman No. 26/2, Brane is a descendant of BRUCE WAYNE and "the twentieth direct descendant of [his] family" to bear Wayne's name. He is called Brane, asserts the text, and not Bruce Wayne, because of a thirty-first-century custom which dictates that individuals be known by contractions of their first and last names. By thirty-first-century tradition, therefore, the name Bruce Wayne has yielded the contraction Brane (Dec/Jan '44–'45: "The Year 3000!").

The Brane Taylor texts make no mention of this custom; indeed, they state quite explicitly that Taylor's first name is Brane and that his last name is Taylor (BM No. 67/3, Oct/Nov '51: "The Lost Legion of Space"; Det No. 216, Feb '55: "The Batman of Tomorrow!"). Furthermore, Brane and his young companion Ricky have black hair, while Brane Taylor and his unnamed nephew have curly blond hair. All in all, it seems safe to conclude that Brane and Brane Taylor are two entirely separate persons, but that it was Brane's appearance in the texts in December 1944–January 1945 (BM No. 26/2: "The Year 3000!") that inspired later chroniclers to introduce Brane Taylor approximately seven years later (BM No. 67/3, Oct/Nov '51: "The Lost Legion of Space").

In October–November 1951 Robin is working alone in the BATCAVE when suddenly a "shimmering outline" appears before him, gradually "takes on form and shape . . . and materializes as a globe of gleaming steel!"

As Robin looks on in amazement, Brane Taylor, the Batman of the distant future, steps from the gleaming sphere and announces that he has come from the thirty-first century to ask Robin's help. Taylor explains that the young boy who normally functions as Robin in the thirty-first century has broken his leg while battling the villain Yerxa, and Taylor would like the real Robin to journey with him to the future to help him apprehend Yerxa until his own young companion is well enough to fight again.

Yerxa, is a ruthless "Solar System bandit" who has somehow found a way to gain possession of large quantities of "vulcanite," a rare element found only on Vulcan, a tiny prison asteroid situated between the planet Mercury and the sun. Vulcan, explains Taylor, is "a place hotter, drier than the Sahara Desert! . . . It is so unbearable that convicted criminals are given a choice--life imprisonment on Earth--or a pardon after mining vulcanite for five years! Those who accept Vulcan are called ***the Lost Legion!***" When combined with common glass, vulcanite "concentrates the sun's heat to an unbelievable degree" and could easily be fashioned into "a terrible weapon" of awesome power. Because all the vulcanite mined on Vulcan is stored securely in the vaults of the Earth Government, Yerxa's vulcanite must have been smuggled directly from Vulcan itself, and Taylor is determined to apprehend Yerxa and halt the smuggling of vulcanite before the rare ore can be put to an evil purpose.

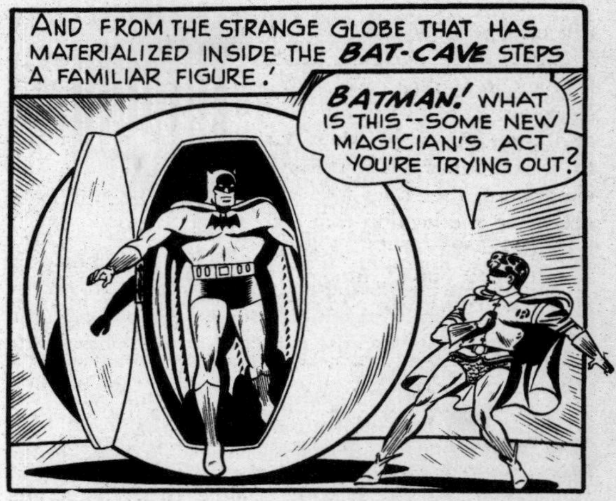

Brane Taylor and Robin, 1951 © NPP 1951

Returning to the future in Taylor's time machine, Robin and Taylor pose as convicted criminals so that they may be shipped to Vulcan to join the Lost Legion. Only in this way, they reason, can they discover exactly how the green vulcanite ore is being smuggled off the asteroid by Yerxa and his henchmen.

One of Vulcan's inmate inhabitants is the Dome, a cunning criminal who "has developed his brain power to such an amazing degree that he ***can read minds!***" Brane Taylor and Robin — who are posing as brothers under the aliases Muscles and Midge McCoy — studiously avoid the Dome, fearing that he will discover their true identities and their real reason for joining the Lost Legion. However, they are forced into open conflict with the Dome, Yerxa, and Yerxa's henchmen when they discover that the Dome has been camouflaging the green vulcanite ore with orange paint, disguising it as ordinary rock and enabling Yerxa and his men to carry it away from the asteroid unhindered.

In the furious battle that follows, Brane Taylor and Robin apprehend Yerxa and his cohorts, but not before Yerxa has accidentally shot and killed the Dome, thus leaving Taylor with the impression that the secret of his dual identity is no longer in jeopardy.

At his trial, however, Yerxa announces that the Dome had succeeded in reading the mind of the thirty-first-century Batman and in discovering the secret of his dual identity. Before dying, Yerxa continues, the Dome informed him that the Batman of the thirty-first-century is none other than Brane Taylor.

Fortunately, however, Robin and his thirty-first-century counterpart — the Robin of the distant future — have been watching Yerxa's trial on television, and Robin promptly travels to the twentieth century in Taylor's time machine and returns to the thirty-first-century with the real Batman. When Batman appears in the courtroom at Brane Taylor's side, the onlookers assume that the Batman in their midst is the thirty-first-century Batman, and that the Batman of the future and Brane Taylor must therefore be two entirely different persons. Then, with the trial over and Yerxa safely under lock and key, Batman and Robin say farewell to their thirty-first-century counterparts and return to GOTHAM CITY in the twentieth century (BM No. 67/3: "The Lost Legion of Space").

By February 1955 Martin Vair, a "theatrical makeup expert" turned criminal, has escaped from prison with the aid of an ingenious disguise and has begun helping criminals gain entrée to the places they intend to rob by making them up to resemble officials, employees, and prominent persons whose presence at the robbery site will not be questioned.

At a charity ball, for example, one of Vair's clients, a criminal who has infiltrated the ball disguised as a prominent banker, knocks a massive scale model of the hospital down a flight of stairs while his cohorts make off with the guests' jewelry in the ensuing commotion. Swift action by socialite Bruce Wayne prevents the gigantic model from hurtling down the stairs and crushing the frightened people on the floor below, but the need to maintain a tight hold on the model prevents Wayne from changing to Batman, and the criminals succeed in escaping.

Vicki Vale, however, on the scene to cover the charity benefit for *VUE MAGAZINE*, has managed to snap a photograph of the well-known banker toppling the massive model, and, when the real banker turns out to have an airtight alibi, Batman and Robin realize that the banker who aided the jewel thieves must have been an impostor. A quick search through their voluminous crime file persuades the Dynamic Duo that "only one man could create such doubles . . . Martin Vair," but the incident at the charity benefit has produced a sticky problem for Batman, because, as Bruce Wayne, he had injured his arm while holding back the giant scale model. ". . . I can't go after Vair with Vicki [Vale] snooping on this case!" complains Batman. "She'd discover my bad arm, and my identity would be exposed!"

Robin suggests that Batman ask Brane Taylor to take his place until his arm heals, and before long Batman has contacted Taylor on the special "super-scientific radio" provided by Taylor for this purpose and Taylor has arrived in the batcave and expressed his willingness to help out. Batman is a bit uneasy about the fact that Taylor is a full inch taller than himself, but he feels fairly confident that no one but he would notice this slight discrepancy between Taylor's description and his own. Before long, in any event, Brane Taylor and Robin have set out in search of Martin Vair.

At a theatrical supply house, where Robin and Taylor have gone in the hope that the proprietor will recognize mug shots of Vair, Taylor encounters Vicki Vale for the first time and arouses her suspicions immediately with his gallant compliments and flowery language. "That doesn't sound like **Batman,**" muses Vicki, "--he never got so romantic before!"

When Brane Taylor and Robin learn that Vair's most recent theatrical purchase was an airline pilot's uniform, they head for the local airport to check the roster of valuable airline cargo shipments. Taylor, however, does not know the way to the airport, and this, coupled with his continuing flattery, convinces Vicki Vale that Batman's place has been usurped by an impostor. Vicki confides her suspicions to Robin, but Robin assures her that this Batman is the real one. "Only I wish he wasn't such a ladies' man right now!" thinks Robin forlornly.

In the hours that follow, Taylor's outgoing personality and relative unfamiliarity with the world of the twentieth century combine to produce one agonizing situation after another for both Taylor and Robin. At one point, for example, having forgotten that the BATMOBILE, unlike thirty-first-century vehicles, has no "jet-assists" to enable it to leap over obstacles, Taylor almost drives the batmobile into the side of a speeding train. In addition, Taylor feels continual frustration at being unable to use the futuristic crime-fighting equipment, so useful in his own time, which would only betray his true identity were he to use it in the twentieth century.

At the airport, Robin and Taylor apprehend a criminal whom Martin Vair has disguised as a pilot, and Taylor surreptitiously uses some of his thirty-first-century "truth vapor" to force the prisoner to reveal the location of Vair's hideout.

When Brane Taylor, Robin, and Vicki Vale arrive at Martin Vair's hideout in an old farmhouse west of Gotham City, Taylor almost betrays his Batman impersonation once again when he uses his "invisibility refractor" to make himself invisible in order to facilitate Vair's capture, and Robin barely manages to warn Taylor in time to restore his visibility before Vicki Vale can realize what has happened.

Inside the farmhouse, the crime-fighters find a man, bound with rope, who looks exactly like a prominent official of the Gotham Bank. When the man claims that Vair used makeup to impersonate him, tied him up, and left the hideout, Taylor, completely taken in by the man's story, begins to untie him, but Robin sees that there are teeth marks on the ropes, indicating that the "captive" tied himself up, and quickly discovers that the self-styled "banker" is actually Martin Vair himself. Robin also discovers some photographs of men wearing special badges which he recognizes immediately as the badges worn by employees of the Gotham Race Track, but the badges mean nothing to Brane Taylor, and his failure to recognize them convinces Vicki Vale that she has been right all along. "That clinches it!" thinks Vicki triumphantly. "***Batman*** wouldn't have missed that--so he ***is*** an imposter! I'll expose him!"

From the farmhouse, Vicki, Brane Taylor, and Robin go to the Gotham Race Track, where they encounter some of Martin Vair's gangland allies attempting to make off with the track's betting receipts while disguised as racetrack employees. When the criminals attempt to escape on horseback, Brane Taylor and Robin mount a pair of horses and pursue them, but Taylor has never ridden a horse, and he barely avoids crashing into a fence by using his thirty-first-century "jet-motors" to lift himself and his horse safely over the top of it. Ultimately, however, Taylor and Robin overtake the criminals and apprehend them.

Meanwhile, Batman has recovered the use of his arm with the aid of a "scientific massage" administered to it earlier by Brane Taylor and, having already been warned by Robin of Vicki Vale's increasing suspicions, he arrives at the racetrack in time to relieve Brane Taylor and help Robin turn the captured criminals over to the authorities.

The Dynamic Duo are still at police headquarters when Vicki Vale arrives to publicly accuse the man playing the role of Batman of being an impostor. To support her contention, she offers photographic evidence that the famous Batman of Gotham City is six feet one inch tall, while the Batman who helped apprehend Martin Vair and his cohorts is a full inch taller. Batman disposes of this discrepancy, however, by explaining that recent electrical experiments he has been conducting have necessitated the wearing of specially insulated boots with inch-thick soles, thus adding one full inch to his apparent height. "Why--then--I guess I was wrong after all!" moans Vicki.

Later, as Brane Taylor prepares to depart for his own time, both he and Robin breathe a sigh of relief that the harrowing impersonation is at an end. "Glad I could help," says Taylor, "--but after trying 1955, I'll be glad to get back to chasing space-pirates in [the year] 3055! It's *easier!*" (Det No..216: "The Batman of Tomorrow!"). (*See also* BATMAN [section F, the Batman counterparts].)

TERLAY, JACQUES. A "famous political prisoner," responsible for the theft of a fortune in gold bullion, who escapes from Devil's Island Prison and comes to GOTHAM CITY, jealously determined to bring an end to the romance between BATMAN and his former girlfriend, "international beauty" Magda Luvescu. Terlay is apprehended by Batman in October 1954 (BM No. 87/3: "Batman Falls in Love!"). (*See* VALE, VICKI.)

TERRIBLE TRIO, THE. "A trio of inventors" — known individually as the Fox, the Shark, and the Vulture — "who utilize fantastic machines to commit crimes on land, sea and air. . . ." Each member of the trio wears a conventional business suit, but conceals his face and head with a mask representing the creature whose name he has adopted. The Fox's job is "to invent machines capable of committing crimes on land"; the Shark's "inventions have mastered the sea"; and the Vulture "has conquered the air!" (Det No. 253, Mar '58: "The Fox, the Shark, and the Vulture!").

The Terrible Trio's inventions include a "burrow machine," invented by the Fox, for burrowing through the earth, brick walls, and steel bank vaults; an elaborate submarine known as the "eel machine," invented by the Shark, for "swallowing up" the burrow machine and escaping with it through the water; a "swordfish machine," invented by the Shark, for boring holes in the sides of ships to make them sink to the bottom, where they can be easily looted; a "pilot fish" machine, invented by the Shark, which attaches itself by suction

The Terrible Trio, 1958 © NPP 1958

to a seagoing vessel, creating an airtight lock between the vessel and the pilot fish, so that loot may be carried from one to the other without suffering water damage (Det No. 253, Mar '58: "The Fox, the Shark, and the Vulture!"); and a powerful aircraft known as the "missile machine," invented by the Vulture (Det No. 321, Nov '63: "The Terrible Trio!").

By March 1958 the Terrible Trio have scuttled and looted a luxury cruise ship with the aid of their swordfish machine and raided the vault of the Gotham City Bank with the aid of their burrow machine. When the Vulture stows away on board the Freedom Plane, loots its cargo of priceless historical exhibits, and then parachutes to safety, BATMAN and ROBIN appear on the scene and recover the loot, but the villains escape underground in their burrow machine. Aided by the "sonic range finder" mounted inside the BATMOBILE, the Dynamic Duo pursue the burrow machine to the GOTHAM CITY coastline, but when the burrow machine and its occupants flee through the water in their eel machine, Batman and Robin are compelled to abandon their pursuit.

Because the villains' first three crimes have fallen into a sea-land-air pattern, Batman reasons that their fourth crime will take place at sea. Accordingly, he and Robin conceal themselves inside mummy cases aboard the S.S. *Cairo*, a ship carrying valuable Egyptian relics from Egypt to the United States. After the Terrible Trio have looted the *Cairo* with the aid of their pilot fish machine and carried the relics back to their lighthouse hideaway, Batman and Robin leap from the mummy cases and, after overcoming a series of diabolical death-weapons — including the Shark's diabolical "flying sting ray"; a mounted fox head, prepared by the Fox, which shoots bullets from its eyes; and "remote controlled vulture robots" directed at them by the Vulture — they apprehend the villains and turn them over to the authorities (Det No. 253: "The Fox, the Shark, and the Vulture!").

In November 1963 the Fox, the Shark, and the Vulture break out of prison and return to Gotham City to plague the Dynamic Duo once again. "If those bizarre criminals have duplicates of their machines cached away," warns Batman, "Gotham will be in for another barrage of **land, sea** and **air** crimes!"

Before long, the Terrible Trio begin devoting their nefarious talents to an elaborate smuggling operation, using homing pigeons to smuggle diamonds into the United States, and later highly trained porpoises to retrieve counterfeit plates dropped from an ocean liner by a confederate so that they may be brought safely aboard the Shark's eel machine.

When Batman becomes convinced that the Terrible Trio's next venture will involve an attempt to smuggle fugitive criminals out of Gotham City, he assumes the fictitious identity of prison inmate Archie Craig, engineers his own escape from a local prison, and then persuades the Fox to smuggle him out of Gotham City inside his burrow machine. After he has been carried as far as the Terrible Trio's hideout, Batman summons Robin to the scene via belt radio and then plunges into battle with the three criminals. However, the Dynamic Duo are taken captive, locked inside two of the Vulture's missile machines with the manual controls rendered inoperative to make it impossible for them to control the direction of their flight, and then launched toward a distant orbit in the farthest reaches of outer space.

Fortunately for Batman and Robin, BATWOMAN has been following the Fox's burrow machine in the hope of apprehending escaped convict Archie Craig, whom she does not realize is actually Batman in disguise. Now, however, Batwoman sneaks into the Terrible Trio's hideout and readjusts the missile machines' ground controls so that Batman and Robin will be able to guide their respective crafts, now already airborne, by means of the manual controls on board. The Terrible Trio discover Batwoman in their presence, however, and are about to overpower her when Batman and Robin, who have in the meantime guided their missile machines back to Earth, invade the hideout and apprehend the villains (Det No. 321: "The Terrible Trio!").

TETCH, JERVIS. The real name of the man who achieves infamy as the MAD HATTER (Det No. 230, Apr '56: "The Mad Hatter of Gotham City!").

THAN-AR. An official of KANDOR and longtime friend of SUPERMAN, sometimes rendered Than-Kar, who agrees to transform himself temporarily into a "metalloid," or metal man — by means of a special "force-radiating instrument" capable of transforming human flesh into "invulnerable metal" — and to embark on a bogus crime rampage in Kandor as part of an elaborate scheme devised by Superman for undoing the serious loss of morale and self-confidence recently suffered by BATMAN as the result of having been wounded by a ricocheting bullet during a battle with criminals. The plot becomes unexpectedly complicated, however, when Jhan-Ar, the evil brother of Than-Ar, steals the force-radiating instrument, manufactures a series of duplicate instruments with which he transforms himself and two accomplices into metalloids, and then unleashes a genuine metalloid menace in Kandor. The villains are ultimately defeated and apprehended by Batman and ROBIN, however, with the aid of Superman and JIMMY OLSEN, who function throughout most of the adventure in their Kandorian identities of NIGHTWING and FLAMEBIRD (WF No. 143, Aug '64: "The Feud between Batman and Superman!" pts. I–II — no title; "The Manhunters from Earth!").

THARN. The boy from the planet Kormo who becomes known as SKYBOY (WF No. 92, Jan/Feb '58: "The Boy from Outer Space!").

THARP, "GUNNER." The leader of a gang of criminals who are apprehended by BATMAN and ROBIN in February 1957 with the aid of a futuristic vehicle — the so-called "bat-missile" — sent to them in the BATCAVE by some mysterious unknown benefactor. The bat-missile — a fantastic land-sea vehicle that "operates by thought-control" and can literally pass through solid matter on its way to any destination — is actually the future-era counterpart of the BATMOBILE belonging to the "Batman of the far future," a crime-fighter from a far-distant era, his career inspired by Batman's own, who learned of Batman and Robin's search for "Gunner" Tharp by peering into the twentieth century through his "time-telescope" and decided to lend them his "batmobile" to aid them in their manhunt (BM No. 105/3: "The Mysterious Bat-Missile").

THATCH. The small-time criminal who achieves infamy as BLACKBEARD (BM No. 4/2, Win '41: "Blackbeard's Crew and the Yacht Society").

THINKER, THE (1947). A diabolical "arch criminal," confined to a motorized wheelchair, "whose wasted body houses a restless, writhing brain!" Somewhere "on the Great Western Desert" of the United States, the Thinker operates a secret factory, manned by well-meaning ex-convicts who have been duped into believing that they are working on a top-secret government project, which produces arms and ammunition for the underworld.

During a climactic battle with BATMAN, the Thinker accidentally kills himself by severing a live electrical cable with a wild gunshot. As "the live cable strikes [the Thinker's wheelchair] . . . the wheelchair becomes an **electric** chair! The murderous **Thinker** has electrocuted himself!" (Det No. 125, Jul '47: "The Citadel of Crime!").

THINKER, THE (1949). "One of the most fiendish criminals of our time. . . ! A man who employs superhuman 'thinking machines' to plan every inch of his crimes — a methodical monster. . . ." The Thinker and his cohorts are apprenhended in April–May 1949 through the heroic efforts of BATMAN, ROBIN, and ALFRED (BM No. 52/1: "The Man with the Automatic Brain!"). (*See* ALFRED.)

THOR. An awesome villain in the image of the Norse thunder god, a man of towering strength who, armed with a mighty hammer capable of toppling lampposts and smashing through a bank's steel doors, commits a series of spectacular robberies — always in the midst of thunderstorms – in October 1959, apparently convinced that he is actually the legendary Thor and that he is amassing his ill-gotten wealth in order to construct a temple to Odin. In reality, however, Thor is Henry Meke, a mild-mannered curator of a small museum of mythological curios whose mind-staggering powers derive from his having touched the replica of Thor's hammer on display at his museum after a meteorite weirdly affected by the "cosmic forces" of space had hurtled through the museum window during a thunderstorm and imparted its "strange powers" to the otherwise ordinary hammer.

Now, his mind somehow hypnotically affected whenever a thunderstorm strikes, Meke takes the hammer from its place of concealment and goes forth to commit his crimes – firmly convinced that he is the fabled god of thunder – returning afterward to the museum, and to his Henry Meke identity, completely unaware of the deeds he committed while under the baleful influence of the meteorite.

While interviewing Meke, BATMAN and ROBIN actually witness his astounding transformation into the villainous Thor, and when the hammer accidentally strikes a fuse box during their ensuing battle with him, the barrage of electricity that courses through it robs it forever of its strange powers, thereby assuring that curator Meke will never again be transformed into the mighty Thor (BM No. 127/3: "The Hammer of Thor!").

THORNE, MATT. The leader of a gang of American criminals who, by December 1950–January 1951, have arrived in England in search of a fortune in gold buried there by Nazi spies during World War II. Thorne and his henchmen are ultimately apprehended, and the Nazi treasure hoard recovered, through the heroic efforts of BATMAN and ROBIN, aided by their English crime-fighting counterparts, the KNIGHT and the SQUIRE (BM No. 62/2: "The Batman of England!").

THORNE, MATTHEW (Dr.). A "brilliant surgeon" (Det No. 77, Jul '43: "The Crime Clinic!") – torn between a love of medicine and a love of crime – who functions as head of an incredible "crime clinic" until his untimely death in August–September 1943 at the hands of an angry gunman (BM No. 18/4: "The Crime Surgeon!"). He is both a "doctor of medicine and [a] doctor of crime," and the story of his life is one of "two strong wills, good and evil, constantly in a tug-of-war for a man's soul!" (BM No. 18/4, Aug/Sep '43: "The Crime Surgeon!").

"I love surgery," explains Dr. Thorne to BATMAN in July 1943, ". . . yet crime excites me! It's like a drug inside my body! I can't help it . . . but I **enjoy** acting criminally!" (Det No. 77: "The Crime Clinic!").

In July 1943 Dr. Matthew Thorne, a brilliant surgeon with a respectable medical practice, opens a special "crime clinic" for criminals who have been experiencing difficulty with their underworld operations. In return for 25 percent of the loot from any given crime, Dr. Thorne promises to "diagnose" a criminal's "ailment" and provide him with a "prescription" for greater success in the future. For 50 percent of the loot, Dr. Thorne will make an actual "house call," appearing on the scene of a crime in progress to remove whatever obstacles exist to the crime's successful completion.

At one point, for example, when a gang of criminals find themselves unable to sneak past an armed guard at the Novelty Rubber Company, they put through a call to Dr. Thorne, who streaks to the scene in his ambulance and swiftly subdues the troublesome guard with knockout gas. On this particular occasion, however, Batman and ROBIN are attracted by the presence of the ambulance and decide to investigate. A battle ensues and, although Dr. Thorne and his underworld clients escape, Batman succeeds in affixing a "tiny, low power short wave transmitter" to the ambulance, which enables him to locate Dr. Thorne's home and headquarters by means of a special "direction finder" mounted in the BATMOBILE.

I LOVE SURGERY... YET CRIME EXCITES ME! IT'S LIKE A DRUG INSIDE MY BODY! I CAN'T HELP IT...BUT I ENJOY ACTING CRIMINALLY!

Dr. Matthew Thorne © NPP 1943

Batman and Robin take Dr. Thorne and his assistant Albert by surprise, but the wily physician momentarily blinds Batman with a powerful beam of light from his head-reflector and is on the verge of escaping when suddenly one of his regular medical patients enters the house suffering from an acute attack of appendicitis.

Ever faithful to his physician's creed, Thorne declares a temporary truce and, with Batman's help, saves the patient's life in a skillful emergency operation. "I love surgery," explains Dr. Thorne to the bewildered Batman, ". . . yet crime excites me! It's like a drug inside my body! I can't help it . . . but I **enjoy** acting criminally!"

Then, with the patient out of danger and the truce therefore at an end, Dr. Thorne captures Batman and Robin, ties them up, and escapes.

Soon afterward, Dr. Thorne and his assistant steal a valuable formula designed "to change the atomic order of objects," and then head for the site of the Eastington Atom Smasher, where Dr. Thorne plans to use the formula to change base metals into solid gold. In the interim, however, Batman and Robin have escaped from their bonds, and, after a brief battle at the atom smasher, they take Dr. Thorne and his assistant into custody (Det No. 77: "The Crime Clinic!").

In August–September 1943 the warden of the prison where Dr. Matthew Thorne has been incarcerated is badly wounded during a jailbreak, and Dr. Thorne is temporarily released from his cell to perform the necessary emergency operation. Applying his extraordinary surgical skill, Dr. Thorne succeeds in saving the warden's life, then promptly capitalizes on his temporary freedom in order to effect his own spectacular escape.

At large once again, Dr. Thorne reestablishes his crime clinic, this time in a mobile trailer in which he travels about the country from city to city. For a fee, Dr. Thorne consults with local criminals and advises them on how to commit crimes effectively.

In an unidentified city somewhere west of GOTHAM CITY, Dr. Thorne appears on the robbery scene in person in order to help local criminal Flopears Bailey stage an elaborate bank heist, but Batman and Robin thwart the robbery and Dr. Thorne is compelled to flee to another city.

Batman and Dr. Matthew Thorne, 1943 © NPP 1943

In the next city that Dr. Thorne visits, Batman impersonates a local criminal and lets it be known that he needs Dr. Thorne's help so that he will be led to the crime doctor's secret hideout. Batman is indeed taken to Dr. Thorne's hideaway, but Robin, who has been following close behind him, is taken captive by the criminals, and Batman and Robin soon find themselves forced into a premature battle with Dr. Thorne and his henchmen.

When, in the course of the fighting, Robin is shot by one of Dr. Thorne's henchmen, however, Dr. Thorne becomes livid with rage: "You trigger mad rat!" he cries. "I told you I wouldn't tolerate any shootings! You're working for a doctor, not a killer!"

Almost inexplicably, all fighting stops, as Dr. Thorne prepares to operate on the wounded Robin. It is, in the words of the textual narrative, "An unbelievable scene! **Robin** under the knife of a crime doctor. . . ! A strange man, Doctor Thorne . . . a doctor first, a criminal last!"

Batman assists the dedicated doctor, and after the operation has been completed and Robin's life has been saved, Dr. Thorne tells Batman that he must now rush Robin to a hospital immediately.

"You . . . you mean you're not going to try to stop us?" exclaims Batman incredulously.

"No," replies Dr. Thorne, "I'm still a doctor even though I'm barred from practice! That boy needs care!"

Batman is blindfolded so that he will not be able to find his way back to the hideout, and then he and Robin are driven to a local hospital by one of Dr. Thorne's henchmen. As soon as Robin has been safely installed in his hospital room, Batman sets out to relocate Thorne's hideout, but by the time he succeeds in finding it, the crime clinic has once again left town.

The next stop for the crime-clinic trailer is California, where Dr. Thorne is scheduled to help a band of local criminals rob the assay office of a lucrative California goldfield. The wife of one of the criminals is seriously ill and Thorne knows she will need an operation, but the night for which he has scheduled the operation is also the only night on which it will be possible to steal the gold from the assay office before it is transported to a different location.

"Oh . . . I just remembered!" exclaims Dr. Thorne, when he belatedly realizes that he must choose between stealing the gold and performing his duty as a physician. "Mocco's wife! But if I operate now I won't be able to perform the gold operation! What'll I do?? All that gold . . . so much of it! No . . . I can't give it up! Besides, Mocco's wife isn't too ill! She can wait! I'll operate later!"

"And so," observes the text, "for the first time, Dr. Thorne betrays his doctor's oath" and allows his love of money to triumph over his devotion to medicine.

When Dr. Thorne and the other criminals set out for the assay office, Mocco remains behind to care for his sick wife, and Dr. Thorne finds himself plagued by his conscience even as he works furiously to open the massive door of the assay-office safe. In the midst of the robbery, however, Batman appears on the scene and hurls himself at the criminals, and, moments later, as Batman trades blows with Dr. Thorne atop the nearby gold dredge, it becomes clear that "the doctor's fear of prison is even greater than his fear of **Batman's** fists! Something snaps in his brain," and he lunges insanely at Batman with a sharpened scalpel.

Suddenly, however, as if from out of nowhere, "a gun thunders . . . and a bullet smashes into the doctor's spine!" It is Mocco, who has raced to the crime scene after suffering the agony of watching his wife die before his very eyes. "You double crossing rat!" screams Mocco. "She died! My wife died! You could have saved her! But you didn't! You didn't!"

"But he's right, you know!" whispers the dying Dr. Thorne as Batman kneels over him. "Any doctor who deserts a patient should be shot! Going to die now . . . glad it's all over! Won't have to go on fighting myself anymore. . . . Don't think too badly of me, **Batman** . . . and . . . tell **Robin** I'm sorry he was hurt . . . tell him . . . ahhhhhh. . . ."

"Yes . . . I'll tell him," murmurs Batman softly, as Dr. Matthew Thorne breathes his last. ". . . I'll tell **Robin** his doctor was asking about him!" (BM No. 18/4: "The Crime Surgeon!").

THORPE, JACK "FIVE STAR." The crusading editor of the Gotham *Gazette,* whose colorful "newspaper exposes of criminal activity in Gotham City have run most of the big-time crooks out of town!" However, unknown to anyone including his own henchmen, Thorpe is the leader of the Artisans, a gang of ruthless criminals made up of "experts in various mechanical fields . . . men who once worked legitimately at their trades but went wrong." Its members include electrician John Slagg, telephone lineman Fred Bower, plumber Peter Hogan, and welder Ed Peters. ". . . whenever some mechanical skill is required for a job," observes the text, "— they've got it!"

In June–July 1951 Thorpe offers to train Bruce Wayne as a crime reporter, ostensibly to win a lighthearted wager, but actually as part of an elaborate scheme to murder a prominent GOTHAM CITY citizen and then trick Wayne into "exposing" the dead man as the secret leader of the Artisans, so that he himself can fade safely into retirement with his accumulated loot. Wayne, however, sees through Thorpe's scheme, exposes him as the leader of the Artisans, and, as BATMAN, apprehends him with some help from ROBIN (BM No. 65/2: "Bruce Wayne — Crime Reporter!").

THREE DEVILS, THE. A trio of former circus acrobats, clad in devil costumes, who use their acrobatic skills to help them stage a series of spectacular jewel robberies. They are apprehended by BATMAN and ROBIN in April 1941 (Det No. 50: "The Case of the Three Devils!").

THREE MUSKETEERS, THE. A trio of swashbuckling swordsmen — melancholy Athos, gigantic Porthos, and quick-witted Aramis — who, with their comrade D'Artagnan, play central roles in a series of famous historical romances by the French novelist Alexandre Dumas (1802–1870).

In Batman No. 32/3, after having been dispatched through the time barrier by PROFESSOR CARTER NICHOLS to early seventeenth-century France during the reign of Louis XIII (1601–1643), BATMAN and ROBIN make the acquaintance of D'Artagnan and the Three Musketeers and join them in safeguarding Anne of Austria and those loyal to her against the sinister machinations of the wily Cardinal Richelieu (Dec/Jan '45–'46: "All for One, One for All!").

Years later, in World's Finest Comics No. 82, Batman and Robin return through the time barrier, this time accompanied by SUPERMAN, to France in the year 1696 during the reign of Louis XIV (1638–1715), where they again encounter D'Artagnan and the Three Musketeers and help bring about the downfall of the king's "evil chancellor" BOURDET (May/Jun '56: "The Three Super-Musketeers!").

THUMB, THE. A "dapper desperado who seeks to spread a reign of terror over Gotham City. . . ." The Thumb and his henchmen are apprehended by BATMAN and ROBIN in October–November 1942 (BM No. 13/1: "The Batman Plays a Lone Hand!"). (*See* ROBIN.)

THURBRIDGE, CASPER. A GOTHAM CITY bank president who, fed up with the hectic and demanding life of a banker, adopts the name Casper the Coaster, hits the road as a hobo, and uses the money he carries with him to rennovate a hobo camp and provide it with a free commissary and other services for hoboes. When three criminals — Silvers Silke, Soapy Waters, and Squint — recognize Thurbridge and attempt to separate him from his bankroll, BATMAN and ROBIN apprehend them, and Thurbridge ultimately comes to realize that his real niche in life is back at the bank, although he still nurses the hope of one day providing hoboes with a nationwide chain of comfortable hobo havens (Det No. 98, Apr '45: "The King of the Hoboes!").

TIGER MAN. A caveman, his true identity concealed by a mask made from the head of a saber-toothed tiger, who battles crime and injustice in the Stone Age much as BATMAN fights crime in the twentieth century. Tiger Man, whom DICK GRAYSON has described as "probably the world's first lawman," is in reality the primitive caveman Rog.

Dispatched through the time barrier to the Stone Age by PROFESSOR CARTER NICHOLS in the hope that they will be able to authenticate an ancient cave painting — depicting the historically improbable scene of cavemen pursued by a tyrannosaurus — recently unearthed by Dr. William Sayre of the Gotham Museum, Batman and ROBIN make the acquaintance of their Stone Age counterpart and help him defeat the ruthless Borr, the leader of a band of brutal cavemen who have been tyrannizing the local cave dwellers by threatening to unleash a gigantic tyrannosaurus frozen in a block of ice in their cavern hideout (BM No. 93/3, Aug '55: "The Caveman Batman").

TIGERMAN. An alias employed by SUPERMAN in August 1961 when he dons a tiger-striped costume and assumes the role of a hopelessly inept crime-fighter as part of an elaborate scheme — devised with the aid of BATMAN and ROBIN — to apprehend GENERAL GRAMBLY and smash his Purple Legion (WF No. 119: "The Secret of Tigerman!").

TIGER SHARK. The leader of a gang of criminals who, operating from their undersea headquarters aboard a sunken ship some 200 miles from shore, commit a series of spectacular crimes at sea and on the waterfront until they are finally apprehended by BATMAN and ROBIN in May 1949. Ironically, the Dynamic Duo capture the criminals with the aid of a special "subbatmarine" designed especially for their use by Dr. Gaige, the famed oceanographer who is secretly Tiger Shark (Det No. 147: "Tiger Shark!").

TIMMINS, WALTER (Dr.). The discoverer of a fabulous "elixir of invisibility." The JOKER kidnaps Dr. Timmins in August 1948 and uses his invisibility elixir for crime, but Timmins is rescued, and the Joker is ultimately apprehended, through the heroic efforts of BATMAN and ROBIN (Det No. 138: "The Invisible Crimes!").

TITUS, JOHN. The GOTHAM CITY millionaire who is secretly the Condor (WF No. 97, Oct '58: "The Day Superman Betrayed Batman!"). (*See* CONDOR GANG, THE [1958].)

TLANO. An alien scientist, an inhabitant of the far-distant planet Zur-en-arrh, who fights crime on Zur-en-arrh much as BATMAN fights crime on the planet Earth. Indeed, it was after viewing Batman's exploits "through a powerful telescope" that Tlano decided to adopt an alternate identity and battle the forces of evil as the Batman of Zur-en-arrh.

For his role as the Batman of Zur-en-arrh, Tlano wears a colorful costume inspired by Batman's own, including a purple cape and bat-eared cowl with matching gloves, trunks, and boots; a sleeveless red vestlike garment fitted over a long-sleeved yellow shirt and emblazoned across the chest with a black bat-insignia on a yellow oval field; close-fitting red tights; and a yellow utility belt with a black bat-insignia on the buckle.

Tlano operates from a secret subterranean headquarters modeled after Batman's BATCAVE, but because the science of Zur-en-arrh is far advanced over that of Earth, Tlano's crime-fighting arsenal is a futuristic version of Batman's own; it includes a saucer-shaped BATMOBILE with an "atomic-powered motor," a BATPLANE in the form of a small spacecraft, a large "teleview screen" for receiving the various BAT-SIGNALS which summon him to action, and such ingenious devices as the "bat-radia," a tiny electronic component which "issues electronic molecules that cause controlled disturbances in the atmosphere."

In February 1958, when Zur-en-arrh faces annihilation at the hands of powerful "invaders from an enemy planet," Tlano teleports Batman to Zur-en-arrh to help him cope with the alien menace. Batman enjoys a unique advantage on Zur-en-arrh, for the "relatively weak gravity" of the planet and certain other of its features combine to give Batman superhuman powers on Zur-en-arrh which are similar, although not entirely identical to, the powers which SUPERMAN enjoys on the planet Earth. Aided by Tlano's scientific ingenuity and his own incredible superhuman strength, Batman drives off the alien invaders before saying farewell to his new friend Tlano and departing for home (BM No. 113/3: "Batman--The Superman of Planet X!"). (*See also* BATMAN [section F, the Batman counterparts].)

TOLMAR, JOHN "SQUINT." A penitentiary inmate who inexplicably attempts to escape the day before he is scheduled to be paroled, and then deliberately injures his hand in the prison shop to assure his temporary transfer to the prison infirmary.

To uncover the explanation behind Tolmar's seemingly irrational behavior, BATMAN — who has been functioning as the prison's temporary warden until a successor to the retiring one can be selected — leaves the prison, ostensibly on official business, and then arranges to be admitted as an inmate under the alias Walter "Slug" Braden.

In his inmate guise, Batman spies on Tolmar and soon uncovers the truth behind Tolmar's bizarre behavior: Tolmar is determined to recover a fortune in stolen loot left behind by executed murderer Big George Howlett. Because Howlett left fragments of information pertaining to the loot's location in various parts of the prison — Death Row, the infirmary, and so on — Tolmar has deliberately behaved in ways calculated to enable him to visit the various parts of the prison in order to assemble the various fragments.

Tolmar ultimately learns the location of Howlett's hidden loot, but so does Batman, thus assuring that Howlett's loot will be recovered and handed over to the authorities (Det No. 169, Mar '51: "Batman--Boss of the Big House!").

TONE, MARGUERITE. An alias employed by the CATWOMAN in April–May 1942 when she establishes herself as a pillar of high society in order to gain entrée to the homes of the wealthy (BM No. 10/3: "The Princess of Plunder!").

TORA. A far-distant planet, revolving about the great star Vega, whose peace-loving, humanoid inhabitants, the Torans, have been conquered, subjugated, and forced into slavery by a ruthless gang of green-skinned, froglike escaped convicts from another planet led by the evil Cafis, who promptly proclaimed himself emperor of Tora. Arriving on the planet Tora in June 1958, BATMAN and ROBIN overthrow Cafis and his fellow convicts and liberate the Torans from slavery with the aid of a courageous band of Toran freedom-fighters and a brave group of volunteer earthlings that includes among its members a reformed ex-convict once sent to prison by Batman (Det No. 256: "The Captive Planet!").

TORG. The commander of a contingent of yellow-skinned aliens from the planet Nakor who journeyed to ancient Egypt during the age of the pharaohs with the intention of invading and conquering Earth. Dispatched through the time barrier to ancient Egypt by PROFESSOR CARTER NICHOLS, BATMAN and ROBIN use a series of elaborate ruses to repel the extraterrestrial invaders and send them scurrying homeward, vowing to warn their leaders never again to attempt to invade this planet (Det No. 295, Sep '61: "The Secret of the Beast Paintings!").

TORREY, TODD. A fanatical lover of books who was employed as a librarian at the Gotham City Public Library until seven years ago, when he was tried for murder and sentenced to be executed after killing a library official who had been on the verge of discharging him "from the job [he] loved!" Somehow, Torrey escaped from the authorities before his death sentence could be carried out, and for seven years he has lived clandestinely in the library, reading books, moving about in the secret passageways he has built in the library's hollow walls, and plotting a twisted vengeance against the men responsible for his arrest and conviction.

In December 1945, however, after making a series of unsuccessful attempts on the lives of the police detective who arrested him and the judge who sentenced him, Torrey confronts BATMAN and ROBIN in the library, loses his balance as he swings through the air on a massive chandelier suspended from a high-vaulted ceiling, and hurtles to his death on the floor far below.

"Strange," murmurs the dying Torrey, ". . . I feel clear-headed — sane! I — I must have been crazy all these years! I'd read so much — thought I was wiser than anybody else — thought I was privileged even to kill. . . . Seven years of living — as a shadow — in darkness! Thinking only of murder! It's just as well — I'm — dying —" (Det No. 106: "The Phantom of the Library!").

TORSON, HAL. An unscrupulous stockbroker, clearly in danger of being prosecuted for a stock swindle, who joins forces with Lester Guinn, an unscrupulous attorney who has embezzled a large trust fund belonging to one of his clients, in an elaborate scheme to make it appear that both of them have died, so that the authorities will abandon all thought of pursuing and prosecuting them. Torson and Guinn construct a huge mechanical sea beast — half lizard, half fish — which, in March 1961, gives the appearance of having destroyed both men in a series of murderous attacks on their yachts in Gotham Bay. For a time, even BATMAN is duped into believing that the sea beast is a living, rampaging sea creature and that Torson and Guinn are actually dead, but ultimately he discovers the true nature of the sea beast, gains access to its innards by impersonating a wanted criminal who has made arrangements with Torson and Guinn for his own sea-beast "death," and finally, with ROBIN's help, apprehends Torson and Guinn inside the sea beast's mechanical body (BM No. 138/3: "The Secret of the Sea Beast!").

TRAPPER, THE. A cunning criminal who uses the arcane lore of animal trapping and an arsenal of complex traps to aid him in his crimes. He is in reality Jason Bard, a man who has been obsessed with the paraphernalia and techniques of trapping since a fateful day, many years ago, when he watched a woman — perhaps his mother — catch a mouse in a tiny mousetrap.

"I'm going to learn every kind of trap," vowed Bard, "and be the greatest trapper of all!" Before long, Bard had achieved his ambition, but he had also become bitter and greedy, and animal trapping no longer offered the rewards he craved. "He knows ***everything*** about trapping," observed one acquaintance, "--but he's a lunatic about it!"

By April 1954 the Trapper has concocted an elaborate scheme to trap the entire GOTHAM CITY police force inside Gotham Square Garden so that he and his henchmen can loot "the unguarded down-town district" unhindered, but the plot is thwarted — and the Trapper and his henchmen are ultimately apprehended — through the heroic efforts of BATMAN and ROBIN (Det No. 206: "The Trapper of Gotham City!").

TRAVERS, BART. The leader of a gang of criminals who successfully dupe an alien creature, recently landed on the planet Earth, into helping them commit a series of crimes by persuading it that BATMAN, ROBIN, and other lawmen are nothing but vicious criminals attempting to seize control of the planet Earth, while they themselves are courageous freedom-fighters determined to deprive the villains of the treasures they possess in order to help save Earth from brutal tyranny. For a time, Travers and his henchmen succeed in persuading the alien to use its extraterrestrial powers for crime, but Batman ultimately convinces the alien that he has been duped, and Travers and his cohorts are swiftly taken into custody (Det No. 270, Aug '59: "The Creature from Planet X!").

TRAVERS, "TRIGGER JOE." A ruthless GOTHAM CITY gang boss who puts his naïve younger brother Steve Travers through medical school, sets him up in a fancy new office immediately after his graduation, and then, by threatening to kill Steve's girlfriend if Steve refuses to cooperate, forces him to become his gang's "official sawbones," treating their gunshot wounds and providing them with new faces and fingerprints through plastic surgery without reporting any of these illicit medical services to the police. When "Trigger Joe" demands plastic surgery on his own face, however, Steve wreaks an ironic vengeance on his villainous older brother by endowing him with the face and fingerprints of a wanted murderer, with the result that "Trigger Joe" is gunned down by policemen within seconds after appearing on the Gotham City streets with his new features. Steve Travers surrenders himself to the authorities and is ultimately exonerated as the result of BATMAN's testimony in his behalf (Det No. 131, Jan '48: "The Underworld Surgeon!").

TREASURE HUNTER, THE. A wily criminal who steals a series of valuable items from private collections belonging to wealthy members of the Hobby Horse, a club for collectors in GOTHAM CITY. The Treasure Hunter is in reality Charles, the club steward, who uses the inside information available to him at the club to help him commit spectacular crimes.

"I only stole because I wasn't rich like the club members!" complains Charles, after he has been apprehended by BATMAN and ROBIN in August–September 1949. "I couldn't buy expensive collectors' items!"

"A **true** collector collects only what he can afford, because he has a genuine love for his hobby!" replies Batman sternly. "***You*** were ***greedy!*** Now ***you're*** going to join a collection — of prison convicts!" (BM No. 54/1: "The Treasure Hunter!").

TREMONT, CAL. A neighbor of BRUCE WAYNE who is suspected by the police of having committed a series of neighborhood burglaries. Tremont is exonerated in June 1955, however, when BATMAN and ROBIN apprehend the real burglar, Tremont's gardener (BM No. 92/2: "Batman's Guilty Neighbor!").

TRENT, TOMMY. A young schoolboy who runs away from home after being scolded for receiving a bad report card, who subsequently helps BATMAN, ROBIN, and a group of firemen capture a gang of criminals known as the Milo gang. "Any boy who can think as clearly in tight spots as you do should be good in school!" exclaims Batman, whereupon Tommy returns home and resolves to study hard from now on (BM No. 10/2, Apr/May '42: "Report Card Blues!").

TRI-STATE GANG, THE. A notorious criminal gang formed by the merger of three separate gangs from three separate states. BATMAN and ROBIN apprehend the Tri-State Gang in June 1964, but only after their butler ALFRED has apparently sacrificed his life to save their own (Det No. 328: "Gotham Gang Line-Up!"). (*See* ALFRED.)

TURG, ELIAS. One of COUNT GRUTT's aliases (Det No. 37, Mar '40).

TWEED, DEEVER. The look-alike cousin of Dumfree Tweed. Deever and Dumfree Tweed are best known as TWEEDLEDUM AND TWEEDLEDEE (BM No. 18/1, Aug/Sep '43: "The Secret of Hunter's Inn!").

TWEED, DUMFREE. The look-alike cousin of Deever Tweed. Dumfree and Deever Tweed are best known as TWEEDLEDUM AND TWEEDLEDEE (BM No. 18/1, Aug/Sep '43: "The Secret of Hunter's Inn!").

TWEEDLEDUM AND TWEEDLEDEE. A pair of rotund but ruthless criminals, cousins, who look so much alike that they are frequently mistaken for identical twins. They are so fat, so lazy, and so eager to avoid exertion of any kind that they usually direct their criminal operations from a car or truck while their hired henchmen do the actual dirty work. Their real names are Deever and Dumfree Tweed, but they are best known to readers of the chronicles as Tweedledum and Tweedledee. The texts call them the Corpulent Duo and the Rotund Rascals, or refer to them simply as the Tweeds. Their appearance is perhaps best described by ROBIN after he has encountered Deever Tweed for the first time in April 1943: "Is he real?" exclaims the Boy Wonder. "He looks like a fat spider!" (Det No. 74: "Tweedledum and Tweedledee!").

In April 1943 Deever Tweed and his henchmen loot a fur company in GOTHAM CITY, capture BATMAN and Robin when they attempt to intervene, and then race off, leaving the Dynamic Duo hopelessly ensnared in a set of powerful wolf traps. Batman and Robin escape from the traps, only to be summoned to another part of the city, where Dumfree Tweed and his cohorts are staging a jewel robbery. When Batman and Robin attempt to intervene, Dumfree Tweed stuns them with a "high-powered electrical gadget" concealed in his cane and easily flees the scene with his henchmen.

Tweedledum and Tweedledee, 1944 © NPP 1944

Not long afterward, Batman and Robin discover the location of the villains' hideout, only to be taken prisoner once again and left frozen motionless in an elaborate electrical trap while the Tweeds, dressed as Tweedledum and Tweedledee from Lewis Carroll's *Alice in Wonderland,* and two of their henchmen, dressed as the Mad Hatter and the March Hare, race off to a costume party being held for the benefit of the Allied war effort, where they hope to steal the thousands of dollars in war bonds which have been collected as admissions fees. Batman and Robin escape from the electrical trap however, outrace the criminals to the costume party, and apprehend the villains as they attempt to make off with the war bonds (Det No. 74: "Tweedledum and Tweedledee!").

In August–September 1943 the Tweeds set up a lodge and restaurant that is identical in nearly every physical respect to a nearby inn owned and operated by reformed ex-convict Soup McConell. Through an elaborate system of camouflage, the Tweeds are able to conceal either the road leading to their own inn or the road leading to McConell's, so that, with the complicity of two of McConell's employees, they can divert McConell's wealthiest guests to their own inn to rob them. The victims invariably complain to the police, but, by concealing the road leading to their own inn, the Tweeds divert all investigating policemen to McConell's inn. Because McConell is an ex-convict, he readily falls under a cloud of suspicion.

When Batman and Robin learn about the series of recent robberies alleged to have taken place at McConell's inn, they decide to pay a visit there as Bruce Wayne and Dick Grayson in order to investigate. Ultimately, they discover the two identical inns and the elaborate camouflaging system, and, with the aid of local police, apprehend the Tweeds and their accomplices (BM No. 18/1: "The Secret of Hunter's Inn!").

In August–September 1944 the Tweeds trick the citizens of the town of Yonville into electing them mayor by concealing the fact that there are actually two of them and cleverly creating the impression of one super-efficient candidate. After being elected, the Tweeds, continuing to conceal the fact that they are really two people, effectively seize control of the entire town by appointing themselves to the heads of virtually every public office and municipal department.

When Batman and Robin come to town and attempt to foil a bank robbery there, one of the Tweeds, in his capacity as local judge, imprisons the Dynamic Duo on the trumped-up charge of having violated a town ordinance by ripping up a sidewalk plank during the fighting at the bank.

With Batman and Robin safely in jail, the Tweeds salt an abandoned gold mine they have purchased with a few gold nuggets and then "selflessly" offer to donate the profits from the mine to those townspeople who agree to contribute money towards the mine's development. Before long, virtually every family in Yonville has scraped together its savings and invested heavily in the mine.

When they learn of the mine swindle, Batman and Robin break out of jail and confront the Tweeds, but the villains leave them trapped inside the mine along with a cache of dynamite set to explode at any moment. Batman and Robin escape from the mine and capture the Tweeds, only to learn that the dynamite explosion with which the Tweeds had attempted to destroy them has unexpectedly uncovered a rich vein of previously undiscovered gold. In gratitude, the people of Yonville elect Batman their mayor. After appointing himself to the position of municipal judge, Batman sentences the Tweeds to jail pending their trial. The Tweeds will go to prison, and the people of Yonville will profit from the rich vein of gold that the Tweeds inadvertently sold them (BM No. 24/3: "The Mayors of Yonville!").

TWO-FACE. A hideous, tormented criminal – half good, half evil; half Jekyll, half Hyde – whose entire life in crime revolves around the numeral two. His name derives from his terrifying face, the right side of which is handsome and whole, while the left side is a gruesome mass of rotted scar. When Two-Face makes a decision, it is by tossing the two-headed silver dollar that has become his personal trademark and most famous symbol, for the coin, shiny and handsome on one side and deliberately scratched and scarred on the other, is both a mocker and a determiner of its owner's twisted criminal career.

Before he launched his bizarre career in crime, Two-Face was Harvey Kent, handsome district attorney. But since the day the left side of his face was left horribly scarred by a vial of acid hurled at him in a GOTHAM CITY courtroom by gangster "Boss" Moroni, Harvey Kent has lived in the shadow of Two-Face, "the most bizarre, the most unpredictable crime-master of all time" (Det No. 66, Aug '42: "The Crimes of Two-Face!"). From December 1948–January 1949 onward, due to what can only be regarded as a chronicler's error, the texts refer to Harvey Kent as Harvey Dent (BM No. 50/2: "The Return of Two-Face!"; and others).

In August 1942 gangster "Boss" Moroni is on trial for murder in a Gotham City courtroom, and BATMAN is on the witness stand, presenting testimony on behalf of the prosecution. Prosecuting the case on behalf of the people of Gotham City is Harvey Kent, a handsome district attorney whose exceptional good looks have earned him the nickname "Apollo" Kent from the newsmen covering the trial.

Under Kent's careful questioning, Batman reaches the climactic point in his testimony when he directly accuses "Boss" Moroni of having perpetrated the gangland murder with which he is charged. When Moroni shouts loudly from the defendant's chair that Batman is a liar, Kent responds by producing a two-headed silver dollar – the lucky piece that "Boss" Moroni has always carried with him everywhere – and then announces to the hushed courtroom that this coin, which the killer accidentally abandoned at the scene of the crime, implicates Moroni in the brutal murder beyond any reasonable doubt.

Enraged at the turn which the trial has taken, Moroni unleashes a hidden vial of concentrated vitriol, a powerful acid, and hurls it directly at the face of the astonished district attorney. Batman instinctively yells a warning and deflects the vial of acid slightly by punch-

Harvey Kent, 1942 © NPP 1942

ing Moroni as it leaves his hand, but the vial strikes the left side of Kent's face nevertheless and splatters its contents over his left hand and the left side of his face, leaving the areas it has touched hideously scarred.

Kent soon learns that his scarred features might yet be repaired through plastic surgery, but Dr. Ekhart, the only man sufficiently skilled and knowledgeable to perform the necessary operation, traveled to Germany to visit his brother sometime prior to the start of World War II and is even now incarcerated in a German concentration camp.

Later, after the bandages have been removed from his hideously scarred face, Kent pays a call on his fiancée Gilda, a brown-haired sculptress. Although she loves Kent, Gilda is sickened and dismayed at his terrifying appearance, and her horrified reaction drives Kent temporarily berserk, causing him to smash the left side of a bust of himself which she herself sculpted.

Later, in the solitude of his own home, Harvey Kent stares into a mirror and ponders the tragedy that has befallen him. "Who . . . what am I?" he cries aloud.

Two-Face, 1952 © NPP 1952

"I'm not a man! **I'm half a man** . . . beauty and beast . . . good and evil! **I'm a living Jekyll and Hyde!**"

Then Kent's gaze falls on the two-headed silver dollar whose presentation in the courtroom had precipitated the awful acid attack. "You . . ." cries Kent at the coin, his mind clearly shaken, "you caused all my trouble!" Seizing a dagger, Kent slashes insanely at one side of the two-headed silver dollar until one side of it is as scarred and disfigured as the left side of his own mutilated face. "Now one [side] is scarred," exclaims Kent with crazed satisfaction, ". . . ugly like **mine!**"

Next Kent turns his maniacal fury on the mirror and smashes it in a burst of tormented emotion. "There!" cries Kent insanely. "I'm all alone now . . . shunned . . . like a shameful thing . . . a criminal! Wouldn't take much to make me one now . . . a trick of fate perhaps . . . a flip of a coin. . . ."

Once again Kent turns his attention to the fateful two-headed coin. "And why not," he muses grimly, ". . . and with the very coin responsible for my trouble! If the good side wins . . . I'll wait till Dr. Ekhart is free! The scarred side . . . and I enter a life of crime!"

Now "Boss" Moroni's weird good-luck piece twirls through the air, and when it lands, it is with the scarred side facing glaringly upward. "CRIME WINS!" cries Kent, maniacally exultant. "From now on I decide everything on a flip of a coin . . . on its two faces that symbolize mine . . . beautiful and ugly . . . good and bad . . . hee hee!"

"And so," observes the text, "is born the most bizarre, the most unpredictable crime-master of all time . . . **Two-Face!**"

From this day forward, the man who achieves infamy as Two-Face adopts the number two as his personal symbol and compulsively orders his life and appearance around it. His suits, divided vertically down the middle to conform with the scarred appearance of his face, are one color on one side and another color on the other. His hideout is either divided down the middle, with handsome, expensive furnishings on one side and shabby, dilapidated furnishings on the other (Det No. 66, Aug '42: "The Crimes of Two-Face!"), or else is deliberately equipped with two of everything, such as two chairs, two telephones, and two pen-and-pencil sets (BM No. 81/1, Feb '54: "Two-Face Strikes Again!"). He drives a two-tone car (BM No. 81/1, Feb '54: "Two-Face Strikes Again!") and pays his henchmen in two-dollar bills (Det No. 80, Oct '43: "The End of Two-Face!"), and each of his bizarre crimes centers around the number two. Typically, Two-Face tosses his lucky coin prior to every robbery: if the good side lands upward, Two-Face and his henchmen commit a daylight robbery and contribute the loot to charity; if the scarred side lands upward, they rob by night and keep the booty for themselves (Det No. 66, Aug '42: "The Crimes of Two-Face!"; and others).

To the bizarre and unpredictable Two-Face, the use of twos is far more than self-conscious posturing, for Two-Face is a man torn in two, a man in whom good and evil play an equal part. At one point, for example, when Two-Face believes, albeit erroneously, that he has killed Batman, he suffers through a period of torturous remorse. "I'm a rat!" he muses grimly. "Once I was the **Batman's** friend . . . today, I killed him. But my bad side made me. If only the good side had won . . ." (Det No. 66, Aug '42: "The Crimes of Two-Face!").

When Harvey Kent makes the fateful decision to become the villain Two-Face, he turns to crime with an unmatched vengeance. He holds up a messenger on a double-decker bus and then robs the patrons of a movie theater showing a double feature. Ultimately, however, Batman trails Two-Face to his bizarre hideaway and confronts him.

"Kent," pleads Batman, "be smart! Give yourself up! The court remembers your fine record as a D.A.! They'll know this is only temporary insanity induced by your terrible misfortune! I'll even speak for you! You'll get a light sentence! By the time your term is up, perhaps Dr. Ekhart will be free. You'll get your face fixed! You can start your life all over again!"

Visibly torn, Two-Face agrees finally to allow his famous coin to decide his fate. If the good side comes up, he will go quietly with Batman. If the scarred side turns up, he will continue to live the life of a criminal.

The coin hurtles through the air and then, incredibly, lands on a crack in the floor and comes to rest on its edge. Batman urges Two-Face to decide the issue with another toss, but Two-Face grimly declines. "No, **Batman!**" replies the villain. ". . . I toss once against chance! And since I can't decide for myself, **it's up to fate to decide what to do with my life now!**" (Det No. 66, Aug '42: "The Crimes of Two-Face!").

As Batman and Two-Face stand confronting one another in Two-Face's hideout, a policeman bursts into the room and fires a bullet at Two-Face, presumably to prevent him from injuring Batman. Two-Face escapes through a window unhurt, but outside he notices that the policeman's bullet had smashed into the scarred side of his silver coin. The two-headed coin had thus saved his life.

"The bullet," exclaims Two-Face, ". . . **it hit the scarred side!** Fate's given me my answer! The scarred side saved my life . . . for **a life of crime!** This is the path destiny's chosen for me . . . goodbye forever to Harvey Kent, D.A. . . . it's **Two-Face,** crime king, from now on!"

In the days that follow, Two-Face and his henchmen rob the spectators at a doubles tennis match and kidnap a look-alike — a double — for an eccentric millionaire who frequently employs his double to stand in for him at boring parties and banquets. Batman and ROBIN rescue the kidnapped look-alike, but Two-Face escapes. "I could kill the **Batman,**" thinks Two-Face at one point in the fighting, ". . . but I'm not a killer yet . . . besides, he was my friend! Well . . . I'll get going before I give in to temptation!"

Later, Two-Face purchases some wax makeup from an old mask maker, transforms his scarred face into the handsome face of Harvey Kent, and then pays a call on his fiancée Gilda, claiming that his face has finally been restored to normal again.

Gilda, overjoyed to see him, sets the table for a romantic candlelight dinner and swears that she will wait for Kent forever if only he will surrender to the authorities for the crimes he has committed as Two-Face. When suddenly the heat from one of the table candles begins to melt the wax makeup on Two-Face's face, however, Gilda, heartbroken, realizes that Kent's face has not really been restored to normal at all. "Oh," cries Gilda, ". . . why did you try deceit? Why couldn't you have come to me with the truth? Oh, Kent . . . Kent . . . even your good side is changing! I can see it in your eyes! **You like being wicked!**"

It is at this moment that Batman, having secretly staked out Gilda's home in the expectation that Two-Face might visit there, bursts into the room. Two-Face manages to escape, but now he feels certain that his sweetheart—who had been completely unaware of Batman's presence—had deliberately attempted to betray him. ". . . he's gone away thinking I betrayed him!" moans Gilda. "He'll never believe me again! Never!"

The scarred two-headed silver dollar used by Two-Face © NPP 1954

Not long afterward, Two-Face wreaks a twisted vengeance on the mask maker who sold him the fragile wax makeup by burning down his store and leaving his family homeless and destitute. In retaliation, the mask maker's son infiltrates Two-Face's gang by posing as a wanted criminal and then tips off Batman and Robin that the gang is planning to steal the ticket receipts from a baseball double-header. Before long, acting on the tip, Batman and Robin have apprehended Two-Face and his entire gang. "Ha!" cries Two-Face. "What irony! I based all my crimes on the number **two** and end up finally being double-crossed by one of my own mob!"

Two-Face is soon safely behind bars, but nevertheless he remains defiant: "I'll escape, **Batman,**" he warns, ". . . and I'll bet you on that, **double** or nothing!" (Det No. 68, Oct '42: "The Man Who Led a Double Life!").

By October 1943, Two-Face has escaped from prison and is once again at large in Gotham City. "Because of his face," observes a troubled BRUCE WAYNE, "Kent thinks everybody shuns him . . . even his girl, Gilda! He's bitter at everything normal, and finds refuge in things abnormal . . . like crime! I've got to save that man before it's too late! I must make him understand we want to help!"

At one point, after Two-Face and his henchmen have attempted to rob the audience attending a performance of Brahms's Double Concerto, Batman and Robin trail the criminals to the two-masted schooner that serves as their hideout. There, after a brief battle, Two-Face pulls out a pistol and aims it at Batman.

"Kent, put away your gun!" urges Batman. "I'm here to help you! I'm still your friend!"

"'Friend' . . . hah!" replies Two-Face contemptuously. "I have no friends! My friends can't look at my face! Not even my sweetheart, Gilda! I'm a freak, now . . . a monster! So I seek the company of other monsters . . . criminals, murderers, thieves! **They** are my friends . . . and you my enemy . . . that's why you must **die!**"

At the instant Two-Face squeezes the trigger, however, Gilda, who has followed Batman and Robin to Two-Face's hideout in the hope of using her influence to end Harvey Kent's maniacal criminal career, bursts into the hideout, cries for Two-Face not to shoot, and leaps into the path of the onrushing bullet.

"**Gilda!**" cries Two-Face, now stricken with remorse. "I've killed the person I love most! She's dead! I did it!"

Gilda, however, is not dead, although she has been gravely wounded. At the hospital, a troubled doctor explains to Batman that she seems to have lost the will to live, and that she keeps murmuring the words "Kent doesn't love me enough! Kent doesn't love me!"

When Batman tells Two-Face that Gilda has lost the will to live because she believes that Kent does not love her enough to abandon his life as a criminal, Two-Face, now in police custody, enters her room and stands by her bedside. "Gilda, darling," pleads Two-Face, ". . . you've got to live! You've got to! I'll do anything you ask! Darling I love you so much!"

"I waited so long for you to say that!" smiles Gilda.

A short while later, as Two Face leaves the hospital in police custody, his henchmen snatch him out of the hands of the authorities and, when they learn that their leader has decided to abandon his criminal career, threaten to murder Gilda unless he provides them with the details of the next robbery he had planned for them. Then, leaving Two-Face tied up in their hideout, they race off to commit the crime, the theft of a shipment of Double-O chewing gum which will bring the criminals a high price on the black market.

Batman and Robin rescue Two-Face from the hideout and then take him to the scene of the chewing-gum robbery. The criminals are ultimately apprehended by the police, but not before Two-Face has risked his life, in the midst of the battle, to rescue Batman from the wheels of an oncoming train.

Indeed, it is a reformed Two-Face who, soon afterward, stands before a judge to be sentenced for his crimes. "Because of new developments in your case based on evidence submitted by **Batman,**" intones the judge, "your sentence is hereby cut to only one year in the state penitentiary!"

In addition, Dr. Ekhart has escaped from Germany and made his way to the United States, and two months later he performs an operation that restores to Harvey Kent the handsome appearance he enjoyed before becoming transformed into the hideous Two-Face.

"I'm thinking I'm glad we turned a criminal into a law abiding, useful citizen!" remarks Batman to Robin. "That's better than merely sending him to prison! Yes, **Robin,** I'm glad . . . and proud!" (Det No. 80: "The End of Two-Face!").

By December 1948–January 1949 Harvey Kent has married Gilda and established himself as a "successful lawyer." During this period, Kent's butler, Wilkins, attempts to capitalize on his employer's previous criminal career by drugging his food to keep him soundly asleep while he commits a series of spectacular crimes disguised as the incredible Two-Face. For a time, the public is duped into believing that Harvey Kent has resumed his maniacal Two-Face career, but Batman and Robin ultimately apprehend Wilkins, rescue Harvey Kent from his clutches, and exonerate Kent of any wrongdoing (BM No. 50/2: "The Return of Two-Face!").

In December 1951–January 1952 professional actor Paul Sloane agrees to reenact the role of Two-Face on television's "True Crime Playhouse," a program which dramatizes the ill-fated careers of notorious criminals.

One scene in the program is a dramatic restaging of the famous courtroom incident in which gangster "Boss" Moroni hurled a vial of acid at District Attorney Harvey Kent. Unknown to Paul Sloane, however, a prop man named Joe, insanely jealous over his girlfriend's crush on the handsome actor, substitutes a vial of real acid for the vial of colored water prepared for use on the program. As the fateful scene unfolds on television before the eyes of millions of viewers, actor Sloane is struck in the face by the vial of acid and horribly transformed into a look-alike for the original Two-Face.

Batman swiftly apprehends the guilty prop man, but, in Batman's words, "The fact that [Sloan has] studied his 'Two-Face' role so long--plus the mental shock--has made Sloane really believe he *is Two-Face!*"

In the days that follow, Paul Sloane, acting under the maniacal delusion that he is actually Two-Face, commits a spectacular series of crimes based upon the number two. Harvey Kent, the original Two-Face, makes an urgent nationwide television appeal to Sloane to surrender to the authorities and undergo plastic surgery, but Sloane, his mind gone, believes that he is Two-Face, that Kent is merely an actor who has been hired to portray him, and that the telecast is part of a plot to lure him into a trap.

Finally, after surreptitiously substituting a specially weighted two-headed coin for the coin that Sloane has been using as Two-Face, Batman deliberately allows Sloane to capture him. When Sloane prepares to toss his coin to decide whether Batman should live or die, as Batman was confident he would, Batman gets Sloane to agree to plastic surgery in the event the coin lands on its edge. Sloane agrees, believing the odds against such an occurrence overwhelming, but the specially weighted coin Batman has slipped into Sloane's pocket is specially designed to land on its edge, and when it does, Sloane, true to his word, abides by the coin's decision (BM No. 68/3: "The New Crimes of Two-Face!").

In September 1952 Harvey Kent, the man who was once Two-Face, agrees to portray his former criminal self at the Gotham Theater's Crusade Against Crime exhibition, featuring such colorful crime-fighting mementoes as Two-Face's own original two-headed coin, provided for the occasion by Batman and Robin.

When Kent arrives at the theater, the manager, George Blake, offers to assist Kent in applying his Two-Face makeup, but when the two men are alone, Blake knocks Kent unconscious, disguises himself as Two-Face, and then appears at the exhibition in Harvey Kent's place. Before the large crowd that has come to view the exhibit, Blake tosses a two-headed silver coin in the manner of the original Two-Face, as if to show the audience how Two-Face used to do it. Then, when the coin lands with its scarred side upward, Blake pretends that the sight of the scarred coin has driven him berserk and re-created the dangerously unbalanced state of mind that had originally led to Harvey Kent's emergence as Two-Face a decade earlier. When Blake seizes a double-edged hatchet from the crime exhibition, roars out of the theater on a twin-cylinder motorcycle, and launches a one-man crime wave based on the number two, the public assumes that the strain of re-creating the role of Two-Face was too much for Harvey Kent and that Kent has resumed his maniacal Two-Face career.

In the days that follow, Blake – who has entered into conspiracies to rob a sightseeing company and an optical company so that the corrupt managements of both firms can collect the outstanding insurance – remains grimly faithful to the Two-Face theme. He steals a payroll from the sightseeing company and escapes aboard one of its double-decker buses, incapacitates Batman and Robin with a gas that makes its victims see double and then robs the Double-Vue Lens Company, and makes a daring escape by climbing aboard a twin-wheeled excursion boat and mingling with a crowd of twins attending a twins' convention in Gotham City.

Despite Blake's clever mimicry of the Two-Face style, however, Batman soon begins to suspect that his cunning adversary is not the original Two-Face. The most telling clue is the new villain's face, which is scarred on the right side instead of the left as the result of Blake's having used a newspaper photograph of Two-Face, printed from a reversed negative, as a guide in preparing his makeup. Batman feels confident that the real Two-Face would never have made such a glaring mistake.

An even more important clue comes later, when Batman comes upon two specially magnetized coins – one designed to land always with the scarred side uppermost, the other designed to land with the good side uppermost – which Blake had had prepared in advance in order to guarantee himself complete control over the various decisions which the real Two-Face had always entrusted to chance. Batman is convinced that the real Two-Face would not have altered his traditional behavior pattern in this way.

Indeed, Batman and Robin soon apprehend the new Two-Face, unmask him as George Blake, and exonerate Harvey Kent of any wrongdoing (Det No. 187: "The Double Crimes of Two-Face!").

In February 1954, while walking through the streets of Gotham City, Harvey Kent comes upon a gang of criminals in the act of robbing a television-store safe and courageously attempts to apprehend them alone. The burglars flee, but Kent is exposed to the full impact of the explosive charge with which the criminals had intended to blow open the safe, and, although he escapes serious injury, he finds to his horror that the force of the explosion has undone the plastic surgery performed by Dr. Ekhart and re-created the hideous appearance that originally led to his emergence as Two-Face. "Look at me!" thinks the anguished Kent. "The explosion has undone all my plastic surgery--I have become **Two-Face!! Two-Face TWO-FACE!!**"

"And now it becomes clear," observes the textual narrative, "that more than Dent's [sic] face has been re-injured! The scar reaches right through to his brain!"

"This settles it!" decides Kent. "This **proves** I was **meant** to be a criminal! Fate has decreed it! My doctor warned me against any future accidents--said plastic surgery couldn't be performed a second time! I'm doomed to look this way for the rest of my life! All right! If that's the way it must be, I'll give it the final test! I had a duplicate made of my famed **two-faced** coin, to keep as a memento! I'll soon see if its decision concurs with that of fate!"

Now the silver coin tumbles through the air, to land seconds later with its scarred side uppermost: "The **evil** side up!" muses Kent. "The criminal career of **Two-Face** begins again!"

In the days that follow, Two-Face, aided occasionally by henchmen, commits a series of robberies of men who, like himself, may be said to possess two faces: the victims include Tarando the clown, who has a real face and his clown face; actor John Benson, famous for his portrayals of Abraham Lincoln, who has his own face and his Lincoln face; big-time gambler "Chicago Al" Garver, who has a regular face and "the one he plays cards with, ***his poker face***"; and a Japanese envoy who has been cited for misconduct — who has "lost face" — thereby becoming endowed with two faces, his regular face and the one he "lost."

Batman and Robin set an ingenious trap for Two-Face and his henchmen and attempt to apprehend them, but the criminals capture the Dynamic Duo and take them to their hideout. There Two-Face straps Batman and Robin to one side of a gigantic coin built to resemble, on a huge scale, the coin he tosses to make each of his decisions. The giant coin is to be flipped over a long bed of sharpened spikes, so that if it lands with Batman and Robin in the "up" position, they will be spared, whereas if it lands with them in the "down" position, they will be impaled on the spikes.

In mid-air, however, Batman and Robin hastily transform their utility-belt radios into small electromagnets and, by hooking them up to the wires which bind them to the coin, create a powerful magnetic field sufficient to repel the metal spikes and thus ensure their landing safely on the upward side of the coin. Then, having landed safely, the Dynamic Duo swiftly free themselves from their bonds and take Two-Face and his henchmen into custody (BM No. 81/1: "Two-Face Strikes Again!").

TYLER, STILTS. A GOTHAM CITY racketeer who, a decade ago, offered to pay small-time criminal Tom Macon $100,000 if Macon would agree to claim that he, and not Tyler, was the head of Gotham City's rackets and thereby serve a ten-year prison term in Tyler's stead. Macon accepted the money, hid it so that Tyler and his men would not be able to steal it in his absence, went to prison in Tyler's stead, and was finally released in December 1948–January 1949, ten years later. In an effort to get back the $100,000, Tyler and his henchmen take Macon captive and attempt to force him to reveal its whereabouts, but Macon dies of a heart attack after confiding the secret only to BATMAN. The criminals make several attempts to wrest the secret from Batman or force him to lead them to the hidden money, but they are ultimately apprehended by Batman and ROBIN with some timely assistance from VICKI VALE (BM No. 50/1: "Lights — Camera — Crime!").

U

UTILITY BELT. The unique belt, specially designed and equipped, which is one of the principal items of crime-fighting apparatus employed by BATMAN. (*See* BATMAN [section C 3, the utility belt].)

V

VALE, VICKI. The lovely photographer who, during the course of her long career, has been linked romantically with both Bruce Wayne and Batman. From October–November 1948 onward, she labors continually to verify her suspicion that Bruce Wayne and Batman are one and the same man (BM No. 49/2: "The Scoop of the Century!").

In her early textual appearances, Vicki is described as a photographer for *Picture Magazine* (BM No. 49/2, Oct/Nov '48: "The Scoop of the Century!"; and others), but from February–March 1953 (BM No. 75/2: "Mr. Roulette's Greatest Gamble") onward she is repeatedly described as working for "a picture weekly" (BM No. 81/3, Feb '54: "The Phantom Bandit of Gotham City!") called *Vue Magazine.* At least one text calls it *View Magazine,* but this rendering may safely be dismissed as a chronicler's error (Det No. 309, Nov '62: "The Mystery of the Mardi Gras Murders!"). Another text describes Vicki as a newspaper photographer for the Gotham *News,* but this may also be dismissed as a chronicler's error (BM No. 119/1, Oct '58: "The Arch-Rivals of Gotham City").

On rare occasions, Vicki Vale's first name has appeared as *Vickie* (e.g., Det No. 316, Jun '63: "Double Batman vs. Double X"), but *Vicki* is by far the most common rendering.

Vicki Vale is indisputably a redhead, but over the years her hair color has been rendered in at least four distinct shades of red — light red (BM No. 157/2, Aug '63: "The Hunt for Batman's Secret Identity!"; and others), red (BM No. 73/2, Oct/Nov '52: "Vicki Vale's Secret!"; and others), dark red (BM No. 75/2, Feb/Mar '53: "Mr. Roulette's Greatest Gamble"; and others), and flame-red (BM No. 49/2, Oct/Nov '48: "The Scoop of the Century!"; and others). Several texts have portrayed Vicki as a blonde (BM No. 56/3, Dec/Jan '49–'50: "A Greater Detective Than Batman!"; and others), but these texts represent infrequent exceptions to the basic red-hair rule.

Vicki Vale, 1957 © NPP 1957

The texts are divided on the question of Vicki's residence: according to one text, she lives in a "cottage" in Gotham Heights, "a suburb of Gotham City" (BM No. 64/1, Apr/May '51: "The Candid Camera Killer!"), but according to at least four others she inhabits an apartment somewhere in Gotham City (BM No. 73/2, Oct/Nov '52: "Vicki Vale's Secret!"; and others). Her sister Anne attends a college somewhere upstate (BM No. 64/1, Apr/May '51: "The Candid Camera Killer!").

In the words of Batman No. 49/2, "Vicki will climb the highest mountain . . . [and] swim the deepest seas . . . just to get a picture!" (Oct/Nov '48: "The Scoop of the Century!"). She is continually risking her life to obtain sensational photographs for her magazine, and a fellow journalist has observed that "she handles the toughest assignments on the staff!" (BM No. 50/1, Dec/Jan '48–'49: "Lights — Camera — Crime!").

The texts describe her as an "ace photographer" (Det No. 152, Oct '49: "The Goblin of Gotham City!"), a "girl crime photographer" (Det No. 167, Jan '51: "Bodyguards to Cleopatra!"), a "cute society photographer with a pert nose for news" (BM No. 73/2, Oct/Nov '52: "Vicki Vale's Secret!"), a "noted news photographer" (BM No. 155/2, May '63: "The Return of the Penguin!"), and a "famed news photographer" (Det No. 320, Oct '63: "Batman and Robin--the Mummy Crime-Fighters!").

Bruce Wayne has described her as a "female camera fiend" (BM No. 49/2, Oct/Nov '48: "The Scoop of the Century!"), Dick Grayson has called her "the town's prettiest photographer" (BM No. 73/2, Oct/Nov '52: "Vicki Vale's Secret!"), and Robin has dismissed her as a "pest" (BM No. 56/3, Dec/Jan '49–'50: "A Greater Detective Than Batman!"). (*See also* Batman [section J 3, the relationship with Vicki Vale].)

In October–November 1948, after Vicki's editor at *Picture Magazine* has examined her recent photograph of Batman fighting the Mad Hatter, he assigns her to prepare "a picture series showing how [Batman] tackles a case from beginning to end." Vicki arrives at police headquarters to discuss the series with Batman just as he is wondering aloud about how would-be criminals might best be discouraged from embarking on a life of crime. Seizing upon this natural opportunity, Vicki suggests that a picture series of Batman in action might help achieve Batman's goal. ". . . once a person sees pictures of who he's up against," insists

Vicki, "he'll hesitate before turning to a life of crime!" "Stopping crime before it starts has always been my hope!" replies Batman. "Okay, Vicki . . . you're now our **official photographer!**"

In the days that follow, Vicki not only accumulates the pictures she needs for her series, but also assists in the final capture of the villainous Mad Hatter. In the course of the adventure, however, Vicki notices that Bruce Wayne invariably disappears from view just before Batman swings into action. Her suspicions are further aroused when she observes that a small cut on Batman's chin also appears on the chin of Bruce Wayne. "Why is it every time Bruce disappears, **Batman** appears?" wonders Vicki. "And there's that cut on Bruce's chin . . . like **Batman's!** I wonder if it's possible Bruce's playboy pose is just an act?"

To verify her suspicion that Bruce Wayne is secretly Batman, Vicki takes closeup photographs of the heads of both men and then carefully superimposes them. "The two heads match perfectly!" exclaims Vicki. "The same shape of the mouth, the jaw and chin! **Bruce Wayne *is* Batman!**"

Realizing that positive proof of this assertion would give her the "scoop of the century," Vicki concocts an elaborate scheme to trick Batman into revealing the secret of his dual identity. After secretly placing some fluorescent powder on the palm of her hand, she obtains Batman's permission to try on one of his gloves. The fluorescent powder, reasons Vicki, will rub off onto the inside of the glove, and from there onto Batman's hand. If, later, Bruce Wayne's hand glows in the dark, then Vicki will know for certain that Bruce Wayne is Batman.

Batman discovers Vicki's plan, however, and ingeniously outwits her. Soon afterward, when, as Bruce Wayne, he picks her up at her home for their evening date, he brings her a bouquet of luminous flowers that glow in the dark. Because luminous substance from the flowers has rubbed off onto the hand in which Wayne has been holding the bouquet, Vicki finds to her dismay that both of Bruce Wayne's hands glow in the dark, leading her to assume that both of Wayne's hands have become fluorescent as a result of carrying the luminous flowers.

"Now that I've fooled her," thinks Wayne to himself, "there'll be no harm in seeing her again!"

Vicki, however, has not been entirely persuaded that her original deductions were incorrect. "I have a feeling he tricked me!" thinks Vicki. "Mr. Bruce Wayne, you'll be seeing more of me!" (BM No. 49/2: "The Scoop of the Century!").

In December 1948–January 1949 Vicki's magazine assigns her the task of taking on-the-spot photographs of various law-enforcement agencies – the F.B.I., the U.S. Coast Guard, and the State Troopers – in action. Finally, with most of her assignment completed, all Vicki requires are some action photographs of Batman and Robin. "Well, I'll help you," promises Batman, ". . . but only because your pictures might stop some would-be crooks from choosing a career of crime!"

Not long afterward, Vicki, Batman, and Robin are taken captive by racketeer STILTS TYLER, but Tyler and his henchmen later allow their captives to escape in the hope that Batman will lead them to a cache of hidden money. Ultimately, however, inside the lighthouse where the money has been hidden, Batman and Robin apprehend the villains with some timely assistance from Vicki Vale (BM No. 50/1: "Lights – Camera – Crime!").

In April–May 1949, on board the pleasure yacht *Carolina* during its gala maiden voyage, Vicki snaps a photograph of Bruce Wayne as he apparently topples over a railing into the sea. Actually, however, the falling figure in Vicki's picture is only a dummy, and the apparent drowning of Bruce Wayne is part of Batman's elaborate plan to defeat the THINKER, "one of the most fiendish criminals of our time" (BM No. 52/1: "The Man with the Automatic Brain!").

In October 1949 Vicki's editor at *Picture Magazine* suggests that Vicki bring together three men whose lives were saved by Batman in the past and prepare a feature story on what has become of each of them since then. Vicki summons the three men to a picture-taking session, completely unaware that one of them, jewelry store owner Martin Tate, is secretly the notorious safecracker known as the GOBLIN. Soon afterward, in the mistaken belief that Vicki has a photograph which, if examined closely, could betray his true identity, the Goblin knocks Batman unconscious and carries Vicki captive to his jewelry store. When Robin attempts to rescue Vicki alone, Tate takes him prisoner and leaves both his captives to suffocate inside an airtight safe. Ultimately, however, Batman arrives on the scene, tricks Tate into blasting open the tightly sealed safe, and then apprehends him with the aid of the Gotham City police (Det No. 152: "The Goblin of Gotham City!").

In December 1949–January 1950 Vicki, who is fiercely loyal to Batman and Robin, becomes infuriated when amateur sleuth Jack Starr begins to receive more publicity for his crime-fighting efforts than Batman himself, and she becomes determined to help Batman recapture the limelight. Vicki's efforts, however, prove more a hindrance than a help. At one point, for example, Batman and Robin are forced to break off their battle with "notorious criminal" "SPECS" ROSE and allow him to escape after the villain has produced a vial of acid and threatened to hurl it at Vicki.

"I knew she'd prove a pest!" mutters Robin (BM No. 56/3: "A Greater Detective Than Batman!").

In January 1950 Vicki takes some photographs in the BATCAVE for an upcoming magazine article on Batman's trophy room. One of the pictures is of a small toy train which once belonged to deceased underworld figure Tracks Carlin. Unbeknownst to Batman and Robin, however, the train contains a secret wire-recording of Carlin's voice detailing the confidential information that Carlin had been using to blackmail hundreds of ostensibly respectable people secretly engaged in underworld activities.

Not long after the picture-taking session, Bruce Wayne takes Vicki to dinner, but Vicki spends the entire evening talking about Batman. "Bruce," exclaims Vicki at one point, "you're hopeless! Now take ***Batman*** . . . there's a **man!**"

"Him?" replies Wayne with a disinterested yawn. "Oh, he's just a glorified detective! I could probably do as well if I had the chance!"

Vicki surprises Wayne, however, by taking him at his word. A private-detective friend of hers is in the hospital, and Vicki arranges for Wayne to substitute for him until he is well enough to return to work. "Hmmm!" mumbles Wayne to himself, after Vicki has installed him in his temporary office and presented him with a book on how to be a detective. "Imagine **Batman** . . . having to study how to be a detective! The things I do to keep my identity a secret!"

In the days that follow, Wayne adequately carries out whatever routine private-detecting chores happen to come his way, and Vicki publishes an article in her magazine about the recent transformation of Bruce Wayne, playboy, into Bruce Wayne, private detective.

Meanwhile, however, Vicki's article on Batman's trophy room has already appeared in print, and Tracks Carlin's former blackmail victims – including a lawyer named Tilley, who is secretly the head of an underworld numbers syndicate, and architect Frank Kelcey, who secretly designs hideouts and gambling dens for mobsters – become aware, for the first time, that the train containing Carlin's potentially damaging wire-recording has found its way into Batman's trophy collection. When Vicki's second article appears, and Tilley and Kelcey realize that Batman's friend Bruce Wayne has become a private detective, they each try independently to hire Wayne to buy or steal the train from Batman's collection, ostensibly because they are model train hobbyists or because they want the train as a souvenir of the deceased gangster, but actually because they hope to use the incriminating information contained on Carlin's wire recording to launch a blackmail racket of their own.

At one point, after Tilley and Kelcey have joined forces to locate the toy train – and after Batman has led them to believe that Bruce Wayne is holding the train at his office – Wayne sits at his desk while Robin hides nearby to surprise the criminals when they come for the train. Vicki, however, arrives at the office ahead of the criminals to keep a dinner date with Wayne, and the villains, who enter seconds later, seize Vicki and threaten to shoot her unless Wayne surrenders the train to them. In the brief scuffle that follows, Vicki is knocked unconscious, enabling Wayne to change to Batman unobserved so that he and Robin can pursue the criminals as they flee with the phony train that Wayne had placed in the office as a decoy. Soon afterward in the batcave, after Batman has captured the criminals and Robin has turned them over to the police, Batman discovers the wire recording hidden inside Carlin's toy train and realizes, for the first time, exactly why Tilley and Kelcey had been so eager to obtain it.

Later, when Bruce Wayne – his stint as a private detective now over – takes Vicki out to dinner, she compliments him on the "quick thinking" he displayed during a scuffle with the villains. "But let's not kid ourselves," adds Vicki, ". . . you're no **Batman!**" (Det No. 155: "Bruce Wayne, Private Detective!").

In October 1950, when ace crime-reporter Dave Purdy of the Gotham City *Gazette* is doing research on the BAT-SIGNAL for an upcoming newspaper article, Vicki tells him about an incident that occurred sometime in the past, when she spotted gangster Big Red and his henchmen making off with the bat-signal. The criminals had seized Vicki and taken her to their hideout on Tracy Hill overlooking Gotham City, but Vicki had resourcefully summoned Batman to the scene by activating the stolen bat-signal on the pretense of wanting to dry some wet clothing on its hot lens, and Batman had responded to the signal, apprehended the criminals, and rescued Vicki from their clutches (Det No. 164: "Untold Tales of the Bat-Signal!").

In October–November 1950, when Vicki hears that Batman has broken his legs while chasing some criminals, she visits the Wayne mansion to see if Bruce Wayne's legs are also broken in an effort to verify her long-held suspicion that Wayne is secretly Batman. Wayne thwarts her for the time being by speaking to her from a steam cabinet which conceals his legs, but he does not succeed in quelling her suspicions.

"So you still think I'm ***Batman,*** eh?" asks Wayne. "Haven't I disproved that notion to you in the past?"

"Maybe," replies Vicki, ". . . but you can disprove it again . . . by ***taking me dancing tonight!*** We had a date . . . and your legs better be in good condition for the rhumba!"

Soon afterward, however, Batman discovers that his legs were never really broken at all (*see* CHUBB [DOCTOR]). When he arrives at Vicki's house that evening as millionaire Bruce Wayne, Vicki is unable to conceal her surprise. Moments later, however, as the couple set out on their date, they hear a newsboy on a street corner shouting the news that Batman's legs were never really broken, leaving Vicki as much in the dark concerning Batman's identity as she was before the entire incident occurred.

"Is Bruce Wayne just a society figure . . . or is he ***Batman,*** too?" she asks herself silently as she dances with Wayne. "I still don't know whether I'm dancing with ***one man or two!***" (BM No. 61/3: "The Wheelchair Crimefighter!").

In April–May 1951 deranged criminal GREGORY BOTA takes refuge in Vicki Vale's cottage in Gotham Heights and forces Vicki to hide him there by threatening to have her sister Anne murdered if she fails to cooperate. Later, after Bota thinks that he has murdered Batman and Robin with his diabolical "camera-gun" – a device designed to shoot Batman and Robin while simultaneously recording the event on film – he returns to Vicki's home to kill her, only to be apprehended there by Batman and Robin (BM No. 64/1: "The Candid Camera Killer!").

By October–November 1952 Vicki has concocted an elaborate scheme to enable her to prove her long-held suspicion that Bruce Wayne and Dick Grayson are secretly Batman and Robin. Recently Vicki snapped a photograph of fugitive criminal "Keys" Bennett sneaking through the stage door of the deserted Bijou Theater in Gotham City, indicating that Bennett and his henchmen have been hiding out there. Now, pretending to be frightened and upset, Vicki rushes to the Wayne mansion and begs Wayne to allow her to hide there for awhile. She tells Wayne that she has gotten herself into serious trouble and that her life has been threatened, but pretends to be too hysterical and overwrought to tell him exactly what has happened. Vicki feels certain that Wayne and Grayson will visit her apartment as Batman and Robin in an effort to uncover some clue to her panicky behavior, and she has cleverly arranged things so that even a chance slip of the tongue will betray the Dynamic Duo's secret identities.

"Tee-hee!" chuckles Vicki to herself, after she has been left alone to "rest" at the Wayne mansion. "Oh, how they fell for it! My long-lived suspicion that ***Bruce*** is ***Batman*** may well be proven ***tonight!*** They went for my bait like two starved fish! Tee-hee!

"If they went to my apartment, as I'm **sure** they have--and made ***one*** slip, their goose is cooked! For there's a nice little ***recording machine*** picking up every word they say!"

Indeed, as Vicki had suspected, Batman and Robin have gone to Vicki's apartment in the hope of finding out exactly what has upset her. When they come upon Vicki's photograph of "Keys" Bennett, they assume that it is Bennett who has been threatening Vicki and swiftly make their way to the abandoned theater. There they are taken captive by Bennett's henchmen, only to free themselves and apprehend Bennett and his cohorts soon afterward.

When Bennett swears that he knows absolutely nothing about Vicki Vale, however, Batman realizes exactly what kind of trap Vicki has set for them. Fortunately, Batman had spotted the recording device at Vicki's apartment and, not realizing who had put it there, had turned on an electric fan in order to drown out his and Robin's conversation with electrical static.

Now Batman instructs Robin to return home while he returns to Vicki's apartment. There Batman alters Vicki's recording to make it appear that Bruce Wayne and Batman are two entirely different persons, then changes to Bruce Wayne and returns to the Wayne mansion.

"Oh, come on boys," crows Vicki, "--the jig's up! Admit you're ***Batman*** and ***Robin!*** And credit Vicki with a neat little ***scoop!*** For instance, how do you explain your absence tonight, ***while Batman was nabbing Bennett?*** And how did ***Batman*** learn of Bennett's hideout, if not from ***my*** picture, left in ***my*** apartment?"

Wayne and Grayson explain that they had informed Batman of Vicki's distraught condition and that he had gone to Vicki's apartment to investigate. Then they accompany Vicki to her apartment to listen to her recording, which, in its altered form, serves only to quell Vicki's suspicions and persuade her that she has been mistaken all along.

"Bruce--how can you ever forgive me!" says Vicki apologetically.

"Forget it, Vicki!" replies Wayne. "Only please--stop playing detective from now on! Just stay as sweet as you are!" (BM No. 73/2: "Vicki Vale's Secret!").

In Batman No. 75/2 — which purports to describe a series of events that transpired "earlier this year" — Vicki Vale visits the home of the incredible MR. ROULETTE and then writes a story about him for *Vue Magazine* (Feb/Mar '53: "Mr. Roulette's Greatest Gamble").

In October–November 1953 the fabulously wealthy Shah of Nairomi, ruler of the country which "contains the single largest source of uranium in the world," arrives in Gotham City for a visit. At a reception in his honor, the shah makes the acquaintance of Vicki Vale and apparently falls in love with her, for the next day members of his entourage arrive at Vicki's apartment with the "happy news" that the shah has decided to marry her. "For years," explains the shah's secretary, "the shah has combed the world searching for the right woman to be his wife! The search is over, Miss Vale! He has selected **you!**"

"Me???" cries Vicki, stunned, **"Vicki Vale??** There must be some mistake!"

"It's no mistake!" replies the secretary calmly. "And now I leave you, to consider his proposal. I shall return this evening for the answer---confident, of course, that you will not anger the shah by refusing him. . . ."

In desperation, Vicki races to her magazine editor for advice, and before long they have been joined by two U.S. State Department officials. "Miss Vale," explains one official, "this is a very delicate situation! We cannot afford to offend the shah! Anything but a very good reason for turning him down . . . would offend him!"

It is at that moment that "a wild idea forms in Vicki's mind!"

"I can't marry him," blurts Vicki, ". . . because I'm ***engaged!*** I'm ***secretly*** engaged to be married!"

"Come, Miss Vale!" replies the State Department official. "These days, a well-known personality such as you could scarcely keep her engagement a secret! You can't ask the shah to believe ***that!***"

"Yes, I can!" insists Vicki. "You see . . . ***my*** engagement has been kept secret because ***I'm engaged to Batman!***"

"Engaged?" cries Batman soon afterward, after Vicki has informed him of what she has done. "Vicki, how could you do such a thing? I'll have to deny it!"

"Please, ***Batman!***" begs Vicki. "It's only for a few weeks, until the shah leaves! It's the only way out for me---and it's for the good of our country, too!"

Reluctantly, Batman agrees to allow Vicki to perpetuate her hoax until the shah has returned to his own country. ". . . I'll do it," promises Batman, "---but only because of the seriousness of the world situation. But remember---it's your hoax! I'll leave the handling of it to you!"

"Oh, thank you, ***Batman!***" exclaims Vicki happily.

Before long, Batman's engagement to Vicki Vale has become the sensation of Gotham City. The shah accepts his defeat gracefully, congratulates the engaged couple, and even hosts a lavish reception in their honor. "Come on, **Batman,**" whispers Vicki, as she hugs Batman tightly and coaxes him around the dance floor, "we've got to make this look good!"

"She's enjoying the whole hoax," muses Batman grimly, "---but I'd be much happier taking on a deadly criminal, any day!"

Sometime afterward, when the gracious shah throws a dinner party for the engaged couple, Vicki insists that Batman bring her flowers. On his way to the party, however, Batman is forced to discard the bouquet long enough to help Robin thwart an attempted museum robbery. When the momentarily discarded bouquet is eaten by a passing pushcart horse, Batman is forced to appear at the shah's party empty-handed.

"Batman," scolds Vicki, "I ***told*** you to bring me flowers! Was that so ***hard*** to do? Now I don't know what to say! I told ***everyone*** you always bring me flowers!"

"Am I glad this engagement is only temporary!" thinks Batman to himself. "I couldn't put up with much more of **this**!"

Both Batman and Vicki, however, have reckoned without the spiteful intervention of Eloise Leach, a photographer who has always disliked Vicki and who has become convinced that the Batman-Vicki Vale betrothal is nothing but a hoax.

"I'll teach Vicki and ***Batman*** a lesson," thinks Eloise to herself, "---I'll embarrass them into admitting the hoax---by forcing ***them into a marriage neither of them wanted!***"

Within a few days, Eloise has hopelessly entangled Vicki and Batman in the already complicated situation by anonymously informing the press that the engaged couple are to be married in only two weeks and by sending bogus wedding invitations "to the most important people in town," including the shah. "Now," gloats Eloise, as she surveys a headline in the Gotham *Gazette* announcing Batman's impending wedding, "won't Vicki squirm!"

Indeed, thanks to Eloise's meddling, Batman and Vicki soon find themselves embroiled in preparations for a wedding that neither of them ever expected to take place. The shah, elated that the wedding is to take place while he is still in Gotham City, assumes complete command of the preparations: he purchases an entire circus to entertain at the wedding party, presents "the priceless ***Matinoor diamond*** . . . the pick of his crown jewels," to the engaged couple as a gift, and announces that he is "flying . . . a staff of special chefs [to Gotham City] to prepare the wedding feast!" Even the President of the United States announces that he is "arranging his schedule so that he can be present at the wedding!"

"You're getting in deeper and deeper!" murmurs Robin to Batman. "I sure hope you can pull yourself out!"

Meanwhile, Eloise Leach has arrived at Vicki's apartment to gloat over her handiwork. "Well, my pet," says Eloise scornfully, "I've done my little dirty work. When are you going to come out now and admit this whole engagement is a **HOAX???**"

"You're right, Eloise," replies Vicki serenely, "---it was a hoax! But you know something? Without meaning to, you've done me a tremendous favor!

"Being ***Batman's*** fiancee was quite something! I ***liked*** it! And I like the idea of ***marrying*** him! Now that ***you've*** put it in the works, I'm going ahead with it! Goodbye now!"

And soon afterward, when Batman arrives at Vicki's apartment in the hope of working out some acceptable way of cancelling the impending wedding, Vicki tells him substantially the same thing: "I didn't send out those invitations and announce our wedding date to the press!" she explains. "Eloise did, hoping to embarrass us into admitting the hoax! But I'll tell you the truth---now that it's gone this far and can't be stopped, I'm glad! I ***want*** to be ***Mrs. Batman!***"

Late that night, "two desperate figures seek an answer in the gloom of the ***batcave. . . .***"

"It looks like we're sunk, ***Batman!***" says Robin grimly. "And that means ***everything*** changes! You won't have much time to pal around with me---not with a wife around. . . ."

"Don't talk like that, ***Robin!***" replies Batman. "You know that nobody can ever separate us!"

Finally, however, Batman conceives of a way to extricate himself from his cruel dilemma.

The next day, as Batman and Vicki pose for photographs at the Gotham *News*, the shah barges in to "demand that this wedding be ***stopped!*** I have been informed," he explains, "that Vicki Vale's ***beauty*** will be lost forever to the world, if she marries ***Batman!*** I will not allow this to happen!"

"Yes," continues the shah's secretary, "the girl who weds ***Batman*** must undergo ***facial surgery*** to change her appearance completely! She must have a new identity to protect her ***husband's*** vital secrets! Remember, he is the famous ***Batman!***"

"Oh, ***Batman,***" shudders Vicki, "you wouldn't ask me to---"

"I'm afraid I must," replies Batman coolly, "for safety's sake!"

The wedding is promptly canceled to avoid offending the shah, and the shah's secretary quickly explains that the shah will not marry Vicki either, since his "ancient royal code prohibits him from marrying a woman once betrothed!"

That night, in the batcave, two old friends celebrate their victory over a bottle of milk. "***Wow*** . . . that was a close call!" exclaims Robin. "I'm sure glad you told Eloise Leach about the plastic surgery ***Batman's*** wife would have to undergo!"

"Yes!" replies Batman with a smile. "I called on her as Bruce Wayne, gave her a scoop! I knew she'd run right to the shah---and I figured he'd take the steps he did when he learned what would happen to the Vicki he so cherished!" (BM No. 79/1: "Bride of Batman!").

In February 1954 Vicki's editor at *Vue Magazine* assigns her the task of covering the activities of Gotham City's incredible PHANTOM BANDIT. Vicki manages to uncover the secret of how the Phantom Bandit has been able to open complicated locks without ever setting off any burglar alarms, and enlists the aid of Dick Grayson in an elaborate plan to lure the villain into a trap. The plan backfires somewhat when the Phantom

Bandit and his accomplice knock Vicki Vale and Dick Grayson unconscious with knockout gas, but Batman, who has been hiding nearby, appears on the scene and takes the criminals into custody (BM No. 81/3: "The Phantom Bandit of Gotham City!").

In August 1954 Vicki obtains permission from her editor at *Vue Magazine* to prepare a feature story about the various men who, at one time or another, have impersonated Batman for some legitimate reason, such as to portray him in a motion picture or serve as his temporary replacement while he was ill. The men in Vicki's story include policeman Jerry Weiler, model Farley Marden, socialite Bruce Wayne, circus acrobat Verreau, and HUBERT HALL, who, unbeknownst to Vicki, is secretly a criminal (BM No. 85/3: "The Costume of Doom!").

In October 1954, when television station GCTV presents the story of Batman's life on its "Your Life Story" program, Vicki appears on the program as one of the guests (BM No. 87/1: "Batman's Greatest Thrills!").

During this same period, Vicki becomes bitter and jealous when Batman launches a whirlwind romance with "international beauty" Magda Luvescu, unaware that it is only part of Batman's plan to lure Magda's former lover – "famous political prisoner" and Devil's Island escapee JACQUES TERLAY – out of hiding and into a trap.

At one point, just after the jealous Terlay has charged into Magda's apartment and Batman has subdued him, the meddlesome Vicki rushes into the apartment and hits Batman over the head with her camera in an effort to "knock some sense into [his] head" and persuade him to abandon the romance. This foolish intervention gives Terlay the opportunity he needs to turn the tables on his captors, and he swiftly ties up Batman, Magda, and Vicki, turns on the gas in the apartment, and flees. Batman, however, helps his companions escape, then apprehends Terlay at Farraday Airport as he is attempting to flee the country (BM No. 87/3, Oct '54: "Batman Falls in Love!").

In February 1955 Vicki becomes convinced that Batman is being impersonated by an impostor and sets out to prove that her suspicions are correct. Unbeknownst to Vicki, however, Batman's impersonator is BRANE TAYLOR, the Batman of the thirty-first century A.D. (Det No. 216: "The Batman of Tomorrow!"). (*See* TAYLOR, BRANE.)

In March 1956, while the BATMOBILE is out of commission with a damaged engine, Batman and Robin fit the shell of the batmobile's body over Bruce Wayne's sports car and use it as a temporary substitute to prevent the underworld from realizing that their crime-fighting efforts will be hampered until they can make the necessary repairs. During this period, however, Vicki Vale – who is emerging from an open manhole after working on a story about Gotham City's underground cable repairmen – inadvertently snaps a picture of the oncoming batmobile at such an angle that, were the picture to be examined closely, it would reveal the motor serial number of Bruce Wayne's sports car underneath the batmobile shell – a potentially damaging clue to the secret of Batman's dual identity.

In order to stall for time so that Vicki will not publish the picture before he can concoct a means of getting it away from her, Batman offers to provide Vicki with sufficient inside information for an entire series of articles on the batmobile, with the stipulation that Vicki's most recent picture not appear in print until the final installment in the series. Although her suspicions have been aroused by this stipulation, Vicki agrees to proceed with the series. Ultimately, however, she discovers the truth – that the batmobile that Batman and Robin have been using recently is not the real batmobile – although she does not notice the all-important engine number in her photograph.

When Vicki confronts Batman with what she has uncovered, he readily admits the truth of her charge and promises to allow her to photograph the real batmobile, which is now once again in service, if only she will return the photograph of the "fake" batmobile along with the negative. Vicki agrees.

"Now that I've given you back that worthless picture of your ***imitation batmobile,***" crows Vicki, completely unaware of the great secret that had lain within her grasp, but nevertheless annoyed at Batman for what she regards as his attempt to trick her with a phony batmobile, "you can pose the real one for me all day! You'll learn you can't fool ***me!***" (BM No. 98/3: "Secret of the Batmobile").

In November–December 1956 Vicki Vale and LOIS LANE become jealous and upset when it appears that both Batman and SUPERMAN have fallen in love with PRINCESS VARINA, the lovely brown-haired ruler of the "faraway kingdom of Balkania." In a meddlesome effort to place Princess Varina out of reach of the men they love, Vicki and Lois offer to help the princess elope with the man she really loves, an "officer of [the] guards" named Captain Stefan. Batman and Superman are compelled to thwart the attempted elopement for the same reason that they have been so zealously courting the princess – because her marriage to the commoner Stefan would precipitate a civil war in her country – but they manage ultimately to make Stefan a hero in the eyes of his countrymen so that the Balkanian parliament will grant him permission to marry the princess (WF No. 85: "The Super-Rivals!").

In July 1957 Vicki becomes determined to uncover the secret identity of the enigmatic crime-fighter known as Mysteryman. Finally she succeeds, but not without some surreptitious help from Batman (Det No. 245: "The Dynamic Trio!"). (*See* GORDON, JAMES W. [POLICE COMMISSIONER].)

In October 1957 Vicki sets out to learn more about mysterious criminal BLAIR GRAEME, only to discover that Blair Graeme is actually Batman (BM No. 111/3: "The Armored Batman!").

In January 1958 Vicki recoils in horror at Batman's touch after she and all the other citizens of Gotham City have been duped into believing that Batman is secretly an extraterrestrial alien (Det No. 251: "The Alien Batman!"). (*See* BALLARD, BRAND.)

In October 1958 Vicki Vale and BATWOMAN are chosen as the finalists in "the annual contest to pick Gotham City's 'Woman of the Year.'" Unable to agree on a final decision, the judges give Vicki and Batwoman six additional hours "in which to prove who is more talented in her chosen field" and therefore most deserving of the contest's prize, a special award plus a date with Batman.

"Those jealous girls are sure to get themselves in trouble, trying to out-do each other, ***Batman!***" observes Robin. Batman agrees, and instructs Robin to follow Batwoman while he keeps an eye on Vicki Vale.

When Vicki learns of an attempt by armed prisoners to break out of Gotham Prison, she flies there by helicopter and parachutes into the prison yard to obtain on-the-spot photographs of the breakout, only to be taken captive by the escaping convicts. Batman races to her rescue, thwarts the prison break, and rescues Vicki from the convicts' clutches, all of which elates Vicki, who feels certain that her spectacular pictures of Batman foiling the prison break will enable her to win the Woman of the Year contest.

Moments afterward, however, Robin warns Batman that Batwoman has donned a skin-diving outfit and set out in search of a gang of harbor pirates who have been looting the Gotham City waterfront. Batwoman finally locates the gang's hideout in a sunken hulk at the bottom of the harbor and plunges into battle with the criminals. Just as the villains are about to overpower her, Batman races to the rescue, and together he and Batwoman subdue the harbor pirates and take them into custody. Batwoman is quite proud of herself, for she feels certain that this feat will win her Gotham City's Woman of the Year award.

Because the judges are still unable to select a winner, however, the contest is extended again. This time, both Vicki and Batwoman, working independently, spy Nick Danton, a member of the Moose Malloy gang, and trail him to the gang's hideout on an old movie lot. Both women are taken prisoner, but Batman streaks to their rescue and, with their help, apprehends the criminals.

This time the contest judges agree to declare the contest a tie, and Vicki and Batwoman set out immediately on their promised date with Batman. "Remember, ***Batman,***" insists Batwoman, "--I get the first dance!"

"Oh, no," replies Vicki, "--he dances with me first!"

"Poor **Batman!**" sighs Robin. "They won--but he lost!" (BM No. 119/1: "The Arch-Rivals of Gotham City").

In November 1962, at a gala Mardi Gras festival, Vicki takes a photograph of a man in a musketeer costume which ultimately enables Batman and Robin to apprehend J. J. ASHLEY.

Later, although Batman has been elected king of the Mardi Gras and Batwoman his queen, Batman suggests that Vicki be allowed to share the queenly honors because of her role in Ashley's capture. "Imagine ***Batman*** choosing ***her*** to share this honor with ***me!***" fumes Batwoman jealously. "Hmmmph!" (Det No. 309: "The Mystery of the Mardi Gras Murders!").

In June 1963, when Vicki's photograph of Double Batman disappearing in a puff of smoke is shown on television, both Doctor X and DOUBLE X are tricked into believing that Double Batman has been destroyed. Actually, however, the destruction of Double Batman was a ruse, achieved with the aid of a smoke pellet (Det No. 316: "Double Batman vs. Double X").

In August 1963 Vicki's meddlesome efforts to ingratiate herself with Batman only further complicate his efforts to apprehend the notorious MIRROR-MAN (BM No. 157/2: "The Hunt for Batman's Secret Identity!").

In October 1963, after the skin coloring of both Bruce Wayne and Dick Grayson has been temporarily transformed into a ghastly green by the explosion of a strange green disc from outer space, Vicki makes a series of attempts to verify her pet suspicion that Bruce Wayne and Dick Grayson are secretly Batman and Robin. The Dynamic Duo outwit Vicki at every turn, however, and she is left with the firm conviction that her suspicions were foolish and unfounded (Det No. 320: "Batman and Robin--the Mummy Crime-Fighters!").

VAN CLEER, CAMERON. The alias employed by the man who is secretly KILLER MOTH (BM No. 63/3, Feb/Mar '51: "The Origin of Killer Moth!").

VANCE, JOHN. A young lad — described in the text as a "star school athlete" — who, in the days before BATMAN had adopted ROBIN as his crime-fighting partner, witnessed a bank robbery committed by Birrel Bintner and an accomplice and afterward informed Batman that he could identify the criminals.

In order to safeguard the young eyewitness against possible gangland reprisal, Batman outfitted the youngster in a boy-sized version of his own Batman costume and bestowed on him the pseudonym of Batman, Junior. It was in this costumed identity that young John Vance ultimately helped Batman identify and apprehend the criminals.

That lone incident had concluded the short-lived crime-fighting career of Batman, Junior, but in May 1956 Birrel Bintner escapes from prison and, having finally deduced the true identity of the youngster who once fingered him for Batman, resolves to track down John Vance — now a full-grown adult employed as a shipbuilding engineer — in the misguided belief that Vance must know the secret of Batman's identity and that he will be able to force him to reveal it. Birrel Bintner and his henchmen are ultimately apprehended by Batman and Robin, with some assistance from John Vance (Det No. 231: "Batman, Junior!").

VANE, VIOLA. An aspiring actress who is prevented from committing suicide and then launched on the road to a successful career in the theater by BATMAN in July 1941 (Det No. 53).

VANNEY, JAY. "A crook with a long record" who invades DR. GREGGSON's laboratory in May 1957 in an attempt to steal the "maximizer" and the "minimizer," two incredible "projectors" capable of enlarging or diminishing either people or objects. When BATMAN attempts to intervene, Vanney drops the maximizer and flees with the minimizer, but Batman is accidentally bathed in the maximizer's ray-beam, which quickly transforms him into a thirty-foot giant. Although he tries his best to overcome the difficulties imposed by his new, gargantuan size, the giant Batman soon becomes such a clumsy, towering menace that POLICE COMMISSIONER GORDON is compelled to banish him from

GOTHAM CITY. Ultimately, however, Batman lures Vanney out of hiding, transforms him into a giant with the aid of the maximizer, and defeats him in a rousing battle. Then, with Vanney unconscious, ROBIN seizes Vanney's minimizer and restores both Batman and Vanney to their normal size (Det No. 243: "Batman the Giant!").

VANNING, COLIN. A renowned operatic tenor, afflicted with a heart ailment that is certain to end his career and force his retirement, who surreptitiously murders two of his fellow singers with poison gas at the Gotham City Opera and makes a series of other attempts, all thwarted by BATMAN and ROBIN, on the lives of several others. Vanning finally commits suicide in spectacular fashion by shattering his own heart with a high-pitched note at the climax of his last performance, much as on previous occasions he had used his voice to shatter goblets.

"He planned to die -- and to take with him those who would continue to get the applause he loved," explains Batman. "He was an egomaniac! He wanted to die spectacularly so that he would be remembered!" (BM No. 40/3, Apr/May '47: "The Grand Opera Murders!").

VARANIA. The name of a coastal cruise-ship on which, while vacationing separately as Bruce Wayne and Clark Kent in May–June 1952, BATMAN and SUPERMAN find themselves forced to share a cabin due to a lack of space. In the course of the cruise, the two heroes learn each other's secret identity completely by accident when the light of a fire coming through a porthole suddenly and unexpectedly illuminates their cabin while they are surreptitiously changing into their costumes in the dark (S No. 76/1: "The Mightiest Team in the World!").

VARDEN, JAY. An ostensibly "respectable engineer" who secretly uses his considerable engineering talents to devise intricate crime plans for a gang of GOTHAM CITY criminals headed by "crime chief" Mack Manchard. Certain that Varden is the mastermind behind a recent rash of carefully planned robberies but unable to obtain a confession incriminating him from any of the gang members he has captured, BATMAN and ROBIN set in motion a complex ruse designed to trick the Manchard gang into confessing Varden's involvement in their escapades by persuading them that Varden is secretly Batman and that he has been engaged for some time in an elaborate scheme to betray his underworld clients into the hands of the authorities. Ultimately, the ruse succeeds, and Batman and Robin apprehend the entire Manchard gang and take Varden into custody (WF No. 70, May/Jun '54: "The Crime Consultant!").

VARDEN, VINCE. A "robber-baron of modern crime" who acquires seven ingenious underworld inventions to aid him in his crimes. The devices – which include a "mechanical forger" capable of duplicating any signature; a "hydraulic jimmy" for prying open safes; a "vacuum thief" for sucking up loose currency and other valuables; a "second-story burglar machine" for scaling the sides of buildings; a "magnetic mobster" which seizes loot with its powerful magnetic hands; a "phantom getaway car" whose entire shape and color can be altered at the touch of a button; and a special gas, ruinous to silk, with which Varden hopes to rot the silken ropes used by the Dynamic Duo so that they fall to their deaths as soon as they attempt to swing through the air on them – are "the products of the greatest criminal inventors used in the world's most famous crimes! . . . The 7 wonders of the underworld!"

Aided by these bizarre devices, Varden and his henchmen launch a spectacular crime wave in GOTHAM CITY, only to be apprehended finally by BATMAN and ROBIN in February 1955 (BM No. 89/2: "The Seven Wonders of the Underworld!").

VARINA (Princess). The lovely brown-haired ruler of the "faraway kingdom" of Balkania, who visits the United States in November–December 1956, accompanied by Count Zitu, Balkania's prime minister, and Captain Stefan, an "officer of [the royal] guards" with whom she is deeply in love.

When BATMAN and SUPERMAN learn that Princess Varina is contemplating abdicating her throne in order to marry the commoner Stefan, and that such a move by the princess would inevitably plunge Balkania into a bloody civil war, they set in motion a complex scheme designed to prevent the princess from marrying Stefan – by pretending to be rivals for her affection themselves – while they search desperately for some means of sufficiently elevating Stefan's status in the eyes of Balkania's parliament to make it possible for the princess to marry him without abdicating her throne.

When the Pete Kaney gang attacks the princess's car in a brazen attempt to steal Balkania's royal jewels, Batman and Superman help Stefan apprehend the criminals while carefully contriving to remain unseen so that Stefan will receive all the credit for the capture. As Batman and Superman had hoped, Stefan's courageous efforts on behalf of the princess make him a hero to his native Balkanians, thus persuading the country's parliament to approve his marriage to the princess (WF No. 85: "The Super-Rivals!").

VARNER, "BLAST." The leader of a gang of criminals who have been assembling a gigantic cache of stolen explosives as part of a scheme to blow up a large ship just offshore of the financial district with sufficient explosive force to blast open the vaults of nearby banks so that the criminals can easily loot them. Inspired, however, by an unfounded rumor that has been circulating recently among the underworld to the effect that BATMAN may actually be a robot operated by ROBIN, Batman constructs a lifelike Batman robot, tricks Varner and his cohorts into stealing it from Robin, and ultimately locates Varner's hideout and apprehends the criminals by concealing himself inside the robot (Det No. 224, Oct '55: "The Batman Machine!").

VARREL MOB, THE. A gang of GOTHAM CITY criminals who are rumored to be setting a deadly trap for BATMAN. In order to distract Batman's attention from the Varrel Mob and keep him safely out of Gotham City while he hunts for the criminals alone, SUPERMAN devises an elaborate ruse to make Batman believe that some unknown person in METROPOLIS has correctly deduced that Clark Kent is Superman, and that Batman must therefore come to Metropolis immediately to help uncover the culprit's identity. Ultimately, however, Batman realizes what his friend Superman has done, and he and ROBIN return to Gotham City in time to help Superman apprehend the Varrel Mob (WF No. 78, Sep/Oct '55: "When Superman's Identity Is Exposed!").

VATHGAR. A ruthless villain on the extradimensional world of Xeron who masterminds a scheme to establish himself as the dictator of Xeron by transforming ordinarily harmless creatures called "skrans" into creatures of awesome destructiveness by feeding them iron ore — a substance which is exceedingly rare on Xeron, but which Vathgar hopes to obtain in quantity from the planet Earth — and then using the skrans to help him establish absolute dominion over Xeron and its people.

In June 1961, with the aid of a special machine designed to facilitate the passage of people or objects through "the space-time barrier," Vathgar transmits a single skran to Earth to ascertain whether Earth contains sufficient iron ore to fulfill the needs of his scheme. Vathgar's dictatorial ambitions are ultimately shattered, however, and his dangerous iron-fed skrans rendered completely harmless, through the heroic efforts of BATMAN, ROBIN, and SUPERMAN (WF No. 118: "The Creature That Was Exchanged for Superman!").

VEKING, LARS. A "notorious modern-day pirate" who, operating from a secret island base somewhere in the mid-Atlantic, preys on merchant shipping with a band of henchmen and a special pirate submarine.

In October–November 1953, while transporting a planeload of hardened convicts — Finch Evers, Bugs Luther, Harry Green, George Jensen, Scar Dudley, Pockets Gray, and Ape Hagger — from Harkness Penitentiary to the Coneida Prison, BATMAN and ROBIN are forced out to sea by a hurricane and compelled to crash-land on Veking's island, where Veking and his henchmen become determined to murder the Dynamic Duo and their cargo of convicts in order to protect the secret location of their hidden pirate base.

Veking is killed, however, during an ensuing battle, and ultimately, aided by the special criminal skills of their seven convict captives, Batman and Robin succeed in overpowering and apprehending Veking's henchmen.

With the Veking gang defeated, the Dynamic Duo's seven captives attempt to kill their captors and escape to the mainland aboard Veking's pirate submarine, but they are all eventually recaptured through the heroic efforts of Batman and Robin (BM No. 79/3: "Batman---Gang Boss!").

VELVET (Mr.). The undisputed ruler of a vast, nationwide crime syndicate, which he operates from a secret nerve center in a plush GOTHAM CITY skyscraper. The text describes Mr. Velvet's lavish headquarters as "the nation's secret crime capital! From it stream the orders which become acts of evil in a dozen distant cities. To it come the lush profits from an underworld empire. . . ."

In October 1951, after a series of unsuccessful attempts to ferret out the police informants whom he knows have infiltrated his organization, Mr. Velvet orders his henchmen to kidnap ROBIN and then, by threatening to kill Robin, attempts to force BATMAN to use his renowned skills of observation and deduction to uncover the identities of the traitors in his midst. For a time, Batman is compelled to cooperate with Mr. Velvet. Ultimately, however, he succeeds in rescuing Robin and, with his help, apprehends Mr. Velvet and his underworld cohorts (Det No. 176: "The Underworld Crime Committee!").

VENABLE, FRED. The onetime impersonator who risks death daily in his hazardous career as the HUMAN TARGET (Det No. 201, Nov '53: "Human Target!").

VENTA, JACQUES. The alias employed by an unnamed Devil's Island escapee who is now residing in GOTHAM CITY in the guise of a prominent botanist and explorer after spending ten years as a prisoner on Devil's Island and additional years in hiding, following his escape, in some far-off jungle haven. He is determined to wreak revenge on socialite BRUCE WAYNE for having prevented his escape many years ago from the scene of the Paris hotel robbery that resulted in his decade-long imprisonment. With the aid of a rare orchid known as the "orchid of madness," Venta succeeds in hypnotizing Bruce Wayne every night at 10:00, thus enabling Venta and his accomplice Perrins to commit a series of crimes every night at that hour while contriving to make it appear that Wayne was the culprit. For a time, even Wayne believes himself guilty of the crimes, but ultimately, as BATMAN, he deduces Venta's involvement and, with ROBIN's help, takes both Venta and Perrins into custody (WF No. 44, Feb/Mar '50: "The Confession of Batman!").

VENTRIS, FLOYD. The escaped convict who achieves infamy as MIRROR-MAN (Det No. 213, Nov '54: "The Mysterious Mirror-Man!").

VENTURA. The "gamblers' planet," a far-distant world whose entire civilization is preoccupied with games of chance and where "everyone is trained from childhood in the art of gambling."

"With our super-science to support us," explains one Venturan, "we've no need to work, so we live for gambling!"

In June 1965 Rokk and Sorban, a pair of utterly unscrupulous gambling addicts described as "the last surviving members of [Ventura's] hereditary ruling class," make a hostage of BATMAN on the planet Ventura in order to force SUPERMAN to compete with them in a world-shattering game of "solar system roulette," a heinously cold-blooded game of chance in which the planets and planetoids of Earth's solar system, including Earth itself, are capriciously moved about like chess pawns with "mighty beams of force" which threaten to jerk them from their orbits and send them hurtling toward the sun.

However, with his friend Batman a captive and the very survival of Earth at stake in the Venturans' diabolical "super-gambling match," Superman manages to outplay his alien opponent decisively, thus winning freedom for Batman and survival for Earth (WF No.

150: Pts. I–II – "The Super-Gamble with Doom!"; "The Duel of the Super-Gamblers!").

VERN, RALPH (Prof.). A State University professor (BM No. 168/2, Dec '64: "How to Solve a Perfect Crime --in Reverse!") – and a member of the MYSTERY ANALYSTS OF GOTHAM CITY – "whose laboratory sleuthing [has] led to the conviction of a score of criminals" (BM No. 164/2, Jun '64: "Batman's Great Face-Saving Feat!").

In December 1964 Prof. Vern turns to crime by stealing the valuable Kashpur Diamond from Mergen's Jewelry Store, and then announces to the assembled Mystery Analysts, via a tape recording, that one of their members is guilty of the crime and challenges them to discover who it is. BATMAN and ROBIN unravel the mystery and unmask Prof. Vern as the jewel thief (BM No. 168/2: "How to Solve a Perfect Crime--in Reverse!").

VERNE, JULES. A French author and pioneer in the field of modern science fiction whose remarkable works – such as *From the Earth to the Moon* (1865), *Twenty Thousand Leagues Under the Sea* (1870), and *Around the World in Eighty Days* (1873) – anticipated interplanetary travel along with such inventions as the airplane, television, and the submarine.

Dispatched through the time barrier by PROFESSOR CARTER NICHOLS to Paris, France, in the year 1900, BATMAN and ROBIN seek out Jules Verne (1828–1905) and persuade him to return with them to the twentieth century to help them construct a weapon capable of defeating the villain SIMAK (BM No. 98/1, Mar '56: "The Return of Mr. Future!").

VERRIL, CARL. An eccentric millionaire who has recently died, leaving behind a bizarre will stipulating that his son Vincent must successfully squander $1,000,000 within four days' time in order to be entitled to inherit his remaining estate of $10,000,000. Verril's motive was to force his heir to experience one whirlwind spending spree to enable him to get any foolish spending notions he might have out of his system, but events become almost hopelessly complicated when Vincent Verril is hospitalized and therefore unable to embark on the spending spree; BATMAN is officially authorized to spend the $1,000,000 in Verril's stead; Vincent's cousin, who stands to inherit the remaining $10,000,000 if Batman fails, hires thugs to see to it that Batman's spending spree is unsuccessful; and SUPERMAN, unaware of the real motive behind Batman's reckless spending, secretly uses his super-powers to make Batman's deliberate wastefulness turn unwantedly profitable. Ultimately, however, Vincent's unscrupulous cousin is thwarted, Superman helps Batman spend the $1,000,000 by selling him some of his personal souvenirs of his own adventures and then contributing the proceeds to charity, and Vincent emerges from the hospital to inherit his father's $10,000,000 (WF No. 99, Feb '59: "Batman's Super-Spending Spree!").

VIEW MAGAZINE. *See* VUE MAGAZINE.

VILMER (Professor). An evil biologist, recently dismissed from his post at Gotham University because of his "experiments with forbidden drugs," who has kidnapped star athlete Johnny Marden, given him an amnesia-producing drug, and persuaded him that he is only a "synthetic man" created from artificial tissues. Professor Vilmer has also told Marden that he is to be known henceforth as Adam Newman and that he must obey Vilmer's every instruction if he does not want Vilmer to withhold the regular doses of a special elixir which, Vilmer falsely claims, are essential to "Newman's" continued survival.

Basically well-intentioned, but convinced that he is a synthetic man whose very existence depends upon regular doses of Vilmer's elixir, Marden – whose strength and speed have been greatly enhanced by another of Vilmer's special drugs – helps Vilmer commit a series of spectacular crimes designed to help Vilmer amass great wealth as well as to avenge himself on the university that dismissed him.

Ultimately, however, BATMAN and ROBIN discover Adam Newman's true identity and apprehend the ruthless Professor Vilmer along with a group of GOTHAM CITY racketeers who have agreed to pay Vilmer $100,000 to have his synthetic man capture Batman (BM No. 87/2, Oct '54: "The Synthetic Crime King!").

VINCENT (Professor). A professor at Gotham College who murders the dean of the college in June–July 1950 and then endeavors to escape prosecution by claiming that evil spirits lurking in a haunted cellar had driven him temporarily berserk and that he was therefore not responsible for his actions at the time he killed the dean. By placing a "rare and deadly mushroom" – "whose fumes strike at the brain and cause homicidal mania for 72 hours" – inside the cellar, Vincent drives two other men temporarily insane, thereby buttressing his claim that the cellar is haunted and that entering it induces temporary insanity. An investigation by BATMAN, however, soon discloses that Vincent and his assistant Perkins had been swindling huge sums of money from Gotham College for some time, that the dean had been on the verge of discovering the thefts, and that his murder was part of a premeditated effort by Vincent to prevent his embezzlements from being exposed (BM No. 59/2: "The Forbidden Cellar!").

VISIO, PAUL (Dr.). A "famous ghost-hunter" and secret leader of a gang of criminals who concocts an elaborate scheme to betray rival gangs to the police, thereby eliminating his own underworld competition, while making it appear that the actual betraying is being done by the ghost of an executed murderer returned from beyond the grave. BATMAN and ROBIN ultimately apprehend Visio and his cohorts, however, and expose the complex trickery behind the so-called ghost of GOTHAM CITY (Det No. 150, Aug '49: "The Ghost of Gotham City!").

VOHR (Professor). The inventor of a "new electronic generator," due to receive its initial testing at the opening of the World Electronics Convention, whose operation will inevitably result in the production of minute "kryptonite rays" capable of paralyzing SUPERMAN if he is present in the immediate vicinity.

Because the convention committee has decided to hold a contest between BATMAN and Superman to determine which of their respective home cities, GOTHAM CITY or METROPOLIS, will receive the honor of hosting the prestigious convention — with the winner of the contest to guard the convention hall while the convention is in session — it becomes essential that Batman win the contest in order to protect Superman from possible exposure to the deadly KRYPTONITE ray-emissions from Professor Vohr's generator.

Ultimately, however, the generator suffers a complete breakdown after only a few moments of operation — thus removing the danger of any inadvertent harm to Superman — and the contest is declared a tie, so that half of the convention sessions will be held in Gotham City, with Batman as host guard, and half in Metropolis, under the watchful eye of Superman (WF No. 76, May/Jun '55: "When Gotham City Challenged Metropolis!").

VON BURITZ (Admiral). The commander of a fleet of Nazi U-boats who, having accidentally stumbled upon the location of sunken ATLANTIS somewhere in the depths of the Atlantic Ocean, has managed to dupe the naïve and peace-loving Atlanteans into allowing his fleet to use their undersea city as a base from which to prey on Allied merchant shipping in the Caribbean. Arriving in Atlantis in October–November 1943, BATMAN and ROBIN awaken the Atlanteans to the Nazis' treachery and, with their help — and that of shipwrecked American seaman Ben Stunsel, who is mortally wounded at the onset of the climactic battle — defeat Admiral Von Buritz and his Nazi cohorts and drive them forever from the sunken continent (BM No. 19/2: "Atlantis Goes to War!").

VON DORT (General). A "brilliant but evil" Nazi general — affiliated with the Afrika Korps during World War II and believed to have perished with Hitler in his Berlin bunker — who recruits an army of underworld followers in GOTHAM CITY in September 1965, ostensibly because he has devised a "daring plan to revolutionize crime by military methods," but actually because he intends to use the spectacular "military-slanted crimes" staged by his henchmen as diversions to enable him to steal a "vital radioactive metal isotope called M-244" from a top-security laboratory, which he needs in order to complete construction of a hideously diabolical "death ray" with which he and a small band of surviving Nazis hope to launch a bloody campaign of world conquest. BATMAN and ROBIN apprehend General Von Dort's underworld hirelings during an attempted art and antique theft in Gotham City, and a short while later, with the aid of the ELONGATED MAN, capture Von Dort and his Nazi cohorts in their secret hideout high in the Andes Mountains (Det No. 343: "The Secret War of the Phantom General").

VON LUGER (Baron). The leader of a Nazi spy ring whose members attempt to sabotage a colorful campaign to promote the sale of war bonds being waged by BATMAN and ROBIN. Their efforts thwarted at every turn, Von Luger and his cohorts are apprehended by the Dynamic Duo in August 1943 (Det No. 78: "The Bond Wagon").

VON PELTZ (Baron). An alias employed by the BLAZE in January 1945 as part of his scheme to lure BATMAN into a deathtrap (Det No. 95).

VOR. A far-distant planet whose evil rulers imprison SUPERMAN and four other super-heroes from other planets in a so-called "prison for heroes" on a barren planet — and subject BATMAN to "super-hypnotism" in order to transform him into the prison's ruthless, merciless warden — as the prelude to launching a campaign of interplanetary conquest against the captive heroes' home worlds. The scheme is ultimately thwarted by Superman and the other imprisoned heroes, who turn the tables on the hypnotized Batman, undo the effects of the super-hypnotism that have made him the Vorians' ally, and, with his help, apprehend the evil aliens and destroy the stockpile of armaments with which they had hoped to subjugate other planets (WF No. 145, Nov '64: "Prison for Heroes!" pt. I–II — no title; "The Revenge of Superman!").

VORDA. The faraway world in a distant solar system which is the home of the Vordians, a race of yellow-skinned aliens who journey to the planet Earth and set up headquarters in an abandoned sulphur-mining town not far from GOTHAM CITY. Disguised as earthmen and aided by gangster Bert Collins, they set about recruiting a loyal army of underworld followers in preparation for the day when they will conquer Earth with their "grav-ray," an awesomely destructive weapon which "magnifies the gravitational pull of an area thousands of times--causing structures within its range to collapse instantly under the terrific strain!"

In December 1960, however, after spotting Collins aboard a ferry in Gotham Bay and pursuing him to the formerly abandoned mining town, BATMAN and ROBIN discover the alien nature of its inhabitants, smash the Vordian plot to conquer Earth, demolish the grav-ray, and apprehend Collins as he attempts to escape.

"We return home in disgrace," murmurs one Vordian as he and his comrades soar away from the planet Earth aboard their saucerlike spacecraft, ". . . an army of invaders defeated by a man and a boy!" (BM No. 136/2: "The Town That Hated Batman").

VORDEN, "LENS." An underworld photographer — a member of a gang of swindlers led by gangster Big Hugo — who, in January 1956, devises a scheme to penetrate the secret of BATMAN's identity by taking a series of photographs of Batman as he demonstrates various disguises for students at the Kean School of Makeup. By carefully creating a photo-composite of Batman's features, Vorden hopes to construct a photographic likeness of Batman's real face, but the scheme is thwarted, and Vorden and the entire Big Hugo gang are apprehended, through the heroic efforts of Batman, ROBIN, and master impersonator BARRETT KEAN, the man who first taught Batman the art of impersonation (Det No. 227: "The 50 Faces of Batman!").

VREEKILL, HUGO (Dr.). The inventor of a diabolical "short wave" device which "can decompose the elements that make up steel so that it is actually disintegrated!"

"With my machine," gloats Vreekill, "I can become the most powerful man in the world! I can hold it as a club over those who deal in steel constructions! . . . I shall become a king – a king of crime!"

Cornered finally in his laboratory by BATMAN and ROBIN, Vreekill commits suicide by electrocution rather than face capture (NYWF, 1940).

VUE MAGAZINE. The "picture weekly" (BM No. 81/3, Feb '54: "The Phantom Bandit of Gotham City!") which employs VICKI VALE as a photographer from February–March 1953 (BM No. 75/2: "Mr. Roulette's Greatest Gamble") onward. In several texts, *Vue Magazine* is erroneously rendered *View Magazine* (e.g., in Det No. 309, Nov '62: "The Mystery of the Mardi Gras Murders!").

From October–November 1948 (BM No. 49/2: "The Scoop of the Century!") through January 1950 (Det No. 155: "Bruce Wayne, Private Detective!"), the texts describe Vicki as a photographer for *Picture Magazine.* Then, for a period of several years, the texts fail to mention Vicki's employer by name. From February–March 1953 (BM No. 75/2: "Mr. Roulette's Greatest Gamble") onward, however, the texts consistently describe Vicki as an employee of *Vue Magazine.*

VULCAN. The tiny prison asteroid, revolving in an orbit between Mercury and the sun, which is the sole source of the rare element known as "vulcanite." Vulcan is the scene of a furious battle pitting ROBIN and BRANE TAYLOR, the BATMAN of the distant future, against the ruthless "Solar System bandit" Yerxa (BM No. 67/3, Oct/Nov '51: "The Lost Legion of Space"). (*See* TAYLOR, BRANE.)

VULTURE, THE. A member – along with the Fox and the Shark – of the TERRIBLE TRIO.

W

WADDLE, I. An alias employed by the PENGUIN in September 1942 when he opens a bird store as part of his scheme to trick Mr. Gemly, a famous jewel collector, into buying a pet parrot that has been specially trained to memorize the combination to Gemly's safe as soon as Gemly utters it aloud (Det No. 67: "Crime's Early Bird!").

WALEY, WALLACE. An ex-convict and former scientist who, having devised an arsenal of ingenious "anti-Batman weapons" designed to sabotage the operation of BATMAN's famous crime-fighting equipment — including a special tailpipe apparatus for getaway cars designed to shoot oil into the path of the oncoming BATMOBILE, and special smoke-screen equipment designed to prevent effective use of the BATPLANE — then proceeds to sell his equipment to members of the underworld. Batman and ROBIN effectively combat the use of the anti-Batman weapons by temporarily adopting a whole new array of crime-fighting apparatus completely invulnerable to the crimesters' weapons — including a tanklike "bat-track," impervious to oil slicks, to substitute for the batmobile, and a flying saucerlike aerodyne to take the place of the batplane — and ultimately apprehend Waley and his gangland cohorts in October 1956 (Det No. 236: "The New-Model Batman!").

WALKER, BRAINY. A cunning criminal, once arrested for counterfeiting by BATMAN and ROBIN and now paroled after serving three years in prison, who promptly resumes his criminal career by hiding thousand-dollar bills in various parts of the city, publicly broadcasting clues to their location, and then committing a series of spectacular robberies while the police are stymied by mobs of citizens surging through the streets in search of the hidden money.

At one point, through a clever ruse, Walker tricks Robin into blurting out the secret location of the BATCAVE, but, with ALFRED's help, Batman ultimately succeeds in persuading Walker that Robin's slip of the tongue was only part of a deliberate attempt by the Dynamic Duo to lead Walker and his henchmen into a trap. Then, with Walker safely convinced that he has not learned the batcave's location after all, Batman and Robin swing into action and take Walker and his cohorts into custody (Det No. 242, Apr '57: "The Underworld Bat-Cave!").

WARD (Mr.). An unscrupulous attorney who murders his client, millionaire Harvey Storme, and two of Storme's heirs as part of an elaborate scheme to acquire possession of Storme's hidden gold mine while casting suspicion for the murders on Storme's longtime enemy Clubfoot Beggs. Ward is exposed and apprehended by BATMAN and ROBIN in Summer 1940 (BM No. 2/3: "The Case of the Clubfoot Murders").

WARNER, ANDREW (Governor). A former college roommate of BRUCE WAYNE, and the governor of the state that includes GOTHAM CITY until, in August 1964, having learned from his doctors that he possesses a "unique gland" near his pituitary that is gradually transforming him into a "future man" — an example of what the rest of mankind will eventually become after millions of years of natural evolution — he resigns his governorship so that, for the benefit of science, he may retire to a medical research center in "an isolated area" and allow the functioning of this special "mutation gland" to be accelerated by "a battery of radioactive ray-lamps" to enable scientists to garner an early glimpse of the evolutionary future of the human race.

Once the weird "mutant-gland" has done its work, however, and his accelerated evolutionary transformation is complete, Warner finds that he is "no longer a member of the human race," but rather a terrifying "mutated man," growing ever more gigantic in size, possessed of "strange and awesome powers" — including the ability to communicate by telepathy, to "teleport" himself from place to place, and to repel his attackers with strange "hoops of pale blue power" — and dominated by "sheer contempt" for mankind and an overwhelming urge to "subjugate" what he now perceives as "inferior beings."

Fortunately, however, a "few traces of humanity" still linger in the hideously mutated mind of Andrew Warner, and it is this overshadowed aspect of Warner's personality that causes him to communicate a series of vital clues to BATMAN and ROBIN which ultimately enable the famed crime-fighters to defeat their mutated opponent and place him in a state of suspended animation, where he will remain until such time as the rest of the human race has attained his level of advanced evolution (BM No. 165/1: "The Man Who Quit the Human Race!").

WARNER, BIFF. An American gangster who is apprehended by BATMAN and ROBIN in "a remote region of the Yucatan jungle" in September 1962. The Dynamic Duo's efforts to capture Warner are complicated for a time by a "freak lightning bolt" which, striking Robin in the midst of an electrical storm, temporarily clouds Robin's memory and endows him with superhuman strength, thus enabling Warner to use Robin as his dupe in an elaborate scheme to turn Robin and the local Indians against Batman and then trick Robin into using his super-strength to mine a fortune in gold for him from a nearby mountainside (BM No. 150/3: "Robin, the Super Boy Wonder!").

WARREN, BARNEY. An alias employed by BATMAN in November 1956 when he becomes a cab driver following the presumed death of BRUCE WAYNE (Det No. 237: "Search for a New Robin!"). (*See* ROBIN.)

WARTS. The leader of a gang of criminals who use the Smith's Fireworks Company in GOTHAM CITY as a front for the manufacture of ammunition for holdup mobs. They are apprehended by BATMAN and ROBIN in February–March 1949 with the aid of a white-haired little man named Mr. Wimble, a handyman at a local amusement-park wax museum who has always idolized the Dynamic Duo and wished that he too could be a great detective (BM No. 51/3: "The Wonderful Mr. Wimble!").

WARWICK, EARL. An alias employed by BATMAN in May 1952 when he joins the Namesake Club in an effort to uncover the identity of the man who has been murdering its members (Det No. 183: "Famous Names Crimes!"). (*See* COOK, JOHN.)

WATERS, BILL. A GOTHAM CITY theatrical producer who murders his two business partners, James Dice and Fred Barker, in order to prevent them from learning that he has been embezzling money from the firm. Waters attempts to place the blame for the killings on former partner Thomas Slade, but BATMAN exposes Waters as the real murderer in July 1950 (Det No. 161: "The Men Who Died on Time!").

WAYNE, BRUCE. The millionaire socialite who is secretly BATMAN.

WAYNE, BRUCE N. A distant cousin of Bruce Wayne, the man who is secretly BATMAN. Bruce N. Wayne lives somewhere "out on the Coast," where he has acquired a reputation as "one of the greatest private detectives in the country." According to Batman No. 111/2, Bruce N. Wayne was a cousin of DR. THOMAS WAYNE, the father of Bruce Wayne. Assuming that the relationship intended here is that of first cousin, GOTHAM CITY's Bruce Wayne is Bruce N. Wayne's first cousin once removed. Bruce Wayne was named after Bruce N. Wayne.

Arriving in Gotham City in October 1957 in pursuit of Varrel – a "cunning thief" specializing in the theft of new inventions – Bruce N. Wayne is introduced to his cousin Bruce Wayne for the very first time and, dismayed that his namesake appears to be nothing but a "useless playboy," resolves to make a man of him by training him to be a detective. Complications arise when Bruce N. Wayne becomes suspicious – and then virtually certain – that Bruce Wayne and his ward are secretly Batman and ROBIN, but Batman manages to apprehend the fugitive Varrel and then, through an elaborate ruse, to convince his cousin that Bruce Wayne and Batman are two separate persons, thereby protecting the secret of his dual identity ("The Other Bruce Wayne").

WAYNE, MARTHA. The wife of DR. THOMAS WAYNE and the mother of Bruce Wayne, the millionaire socialite who is secretly BATMAN. The brutal murder of Martha Wayne and her husband on a city street in 1924 marked a crucial turning point in Bruce Wayne's life and fired him with the grim determination to eradicate evil that led to his emergence as Batman.

The murder of Thomas and Martha Wayne © NPP 1939

In 1924 – or, to quote the text precisely, "some fifteen years" prior to November 1939 – Thomas Wayne and his wife and their young son Bruce were on their way home from a movie when suddenly an unidentified gunman leaped from the shadows, announced a holdup, and reached out to grab the necklace around Martha Wayne's neck. When Thomas Wayne attempted to intervene, the gunman shot him dead with a single bullet, then murdered the shrieking Martha Wayne before fading away into the deepening twilight shadows (Det No. 33: "The Batman Wars Against the Dirigible of Doom"; *reprinted in* BM No. 1/1, Spr '40: "The Legend of the Batman – Who He Is and How He Came to Be!").

Later texts asserted that Thomas Wayne died of a bullet wound while Martha Wayne – whose "weak heart could not stand seeing her husband shot down" – died of a heart attack (Det No. 190, Dec '52: "How to Be the Batman!"; *see also* BM No. 47/3, Jun/Jul '48: "The Origin of Batman!"), but the texts are unanimous in their assertion that it was this dread event that first launched Batman on his fabled crime-fighting career. (*See* BATMAN [section A, Origin].)

In June–July 1948, approximately twenty-four years after the death of his parents, Batman encounters the man who murdered them and grimly sets out to bring him to justice (BM No. 47/3: "The Origin of Batman!"). (*See* CHILL, JOE.)

In September 1956 a text appears which sheds new light on the murder of the Waynes and the origin of Batman. According to this text, Joe Chill, the man who perpetrated the Wayne murder, "only ***pretended*** to be a holdup man" when he waylaid the Waynes in 1924. In reality, explains the text, Chill was a "hired killer" employed by LEW MOXON, a convicted bank robber whom Thomas Wayne had once helped send to the penitentiary (Det No. 235: "The First Batman!").

WAYNE, SILAS (ancestor). An eighteenth-century Philadelphia silversmith and ancestor of BRUCE WAYNE alleged to have been the leader of a band of ruthless highwaymen. Dispatched through the time barrier by PROFESSOR CARTER NICHOLS to Philadelphia in the year 1787, BATMAN and ROBIN meet BENJAMIN FRANKLIN, capture the highwaymen, exonerate Silas Wayne of the ıarges against him, and expose the real leader of the ighwaymen as Philadelphian Henry Gant, who had ttempted to frame Silas Wayne for the crimes he imself had committed (BM No. 44/3, Dec/Jan '47–'48: The First American Detective!").

'AYNE, SILAS (great-uncle). The elderly great-uncle Bruce Wayne, the man who is secretly BATMAN. On s deathbed in December 1958, Silas Wayne becomes ne of the few individuals to be entrusted with the cret of Batman's identity.

In December 1958, after Silas Wayne has repri-anded Bruce Wayne for being a "rich idler" and for iling to measure up to the heroic example set by his ustrious ancestors — all "brave adventurers . . . who ought pride and honor to the family" by performing urageous, valorous deeds — Bruce Wayne becomes termined to prove his worth to his great-uncle, and us earn the privilege of having his portrait hung ongside those of his ancestors in the Wayne family ortrait gallery. He is also determined, however, not to tray the secret of his dual identity.

The result is an elaborate scheme in which Batman d ROBIN, aided by ALFRED, apprehend the "Baby-ce" Muller gang at their carpentry-shop hideout in a anner designed to make it appear that Bruce Wayne s courageously disguised himself as Batman in order help the world's greatest detective capture the crimi-ls. As a result, Batman's portrait is installed in the mily gallery and admired by Wayne's relatives, who lieve it to be merely a picture of Bruce Wayne attired the costume he wore when he courageously dou-ed for the real Batman!" On his deathbed, however, as Wayne learns from Bruce Wayne that his nephew really Batman, and he promises to "die proudly owing a Wayne is actually the greatest hero of our ne. . . !" (BM No. 120/2: "The Failure of Bruce ayne").

AYNE, THOMAS (Dr.). The prominent physician (Det . 235, Sep '56: "The First Batman!") and onetime ny doctor (BM No. 120/2, Dec '58: "The Failure of uce Wayne") who was, until his tragic death, the sband of Martha Wayne and the father of Bruce ayne, the millionaire socialite who is secretly BATMAN. e brutal murder of Thomas Wayne and his wife on a y street in 1924 marked a crucial turning point in uce Wayne's life and fired him with the grim determi-tion to eradicate evil that led to his emergence as tman (Det No. 33, Nov '39: "The Batman Wars ainst the Dirigible of Doom"; *reprinted in* BM No. , Spr '40: "The Legend of the Batman — Who He Is l How He Came to Be!").

Little is actually known about Bruce Wayne's father. netime during his career, perhaps during World War Thomas Wayne served as a U.S. Army doctor, held rank of colonel, and, according to Bruce Wayne's at-uncle Silas (*see* WAYNE, SILAS), performed deeds ich made him one of the many Waynes to have ought pride and honor to the family . . ." (BM No. /2, Dec '58: "The Failure of Bruce Wayne").

When Martha Wayne gave birth to an infant son, the ynes named him Bruce in honor of Thomas Wayne's cousin BRUCE N. WAYNE, a private detective who lives somewhere "out on the Coast" (BM No. 111/2, Oct '57: "The Other Bruce Wayne").

By the time of his death, Thomas Wayne had apparently amassed a sizable fortune, for the income from his estate has left Bruce Wayne financially independent (Det No. 33, Nov '39: "The Batman Wars Against the Dirigible of Doom"), and a notation in Thomas Wayne's private diary, discovered by accident in a desk drawer in September 1956, contains the observation that "I'd invested my savings wisely and became [sic] wealthy!" (Det No. 235: "The First Batman!").

In a sense, Thomas Wayne was the first Batman, for at one point in his career he single-handedly apprehended fugitive bank robber LEW MOXON and two of his henchmen while clad in an eerie "bat-man" costume that he had worn to a masquerade ball. Indeed, it is Bruce Wayne's subconscious recollection of his father's old costume which ultimately leads him to design the famous blue and gray costume that has become Batman's most famous personal trademark (Det No. 235, Sep '56: "The First Batman!").

In 1924 — or, to quote the text precisely, "some fifteen years" prior to November 1939 — Thomas Wayne and his wife and their young son Bruce were on their way home from a movie when suddenly an unidentified gunman leaped from the shadows, announced a holdup, and reached out to grab the necklace around Martha Wayne's neck. When Thomas Wayne attempted to intervene, the gunman shot him dead with a single bullet, then murdered the shrieking Martha Wayne before fading away into the deepening twilight shadows (Det No. 33: "The Batman Wars Against the Dirigible of Doom"; *reprinted in* BM No. 1/1, Spr '40: "The Legend of the Batman — Who He Is and How He Came to Be!").

The murder of Dr. Thomas Wayne © NPP 1939

Later texts asserted that Thomas Wayne died of a bullet wound while Martha Wayne — whose "weak heart could not stand seeing her husband shot down" — died of a heart attack (Det No. 190, Dec '52: "How to Be the Batman!"; *see also* BM No. 47/3, Jun/Jul '48: "The Origin of Batman!"), but the texts are unanimous in their assertion that it was this dread event that first launched Batman on his fabled crime-fighting career. (*See* Batman [section A, Origin].)

In June–July 1948, approximately twenty-four years after the death of his parents, Batman encounters the man who murdered them and grimly sets out to bring him to justice (BM No. 47/3: "The Origin of Batman!"). (*See* Chill, Joe.)

In September 1956 a text appears which sheds new light on the murder of the Waynes and the origin of Batman. According to this text, Joe Chill, the man who perpetrated the Wayne murder, "only ***pretended*** to be a holdup man" when he waylaid the Waynes in 1924. In reality, explains the text, Chill was a "hired killer" employed by Lew Moxon, a convicted bank robber whom Thomas Wayne had helped send to the penitentiary some ten years earlier (Det No. 235: "The First Batman!").

WAYNE, VANDERVEER. A young cousin of Bruce Wayne and a close contemporary of Dick Grayson. The "scion of a super-fashionable family," young Vanderveer is arrogant, boastful, and conceited. Stung when Dick Grayson, fed up with Vanderveer's incessant bragging, shows him up by performing a "series of sparkling acrobatic feats" in the well-equipped Wayne gymnasium, Vanderveer concocts a scheme to one-up Grayson by convincing Grayson that he, Vanderveer, is secretly Robin. Vanderveer's hoax – which involves hiring onetime vaudeville acrobat "Jumpy" Regan to impersonate Batman so that he and the bogus Batman can cope with a manufactured emergency – backfires, however, when Regan decides to continue impersonating Batman long enough to burglarize a safe at the Stuart Ice Cream Plant and takes Vanderveer captive when he refuses to pose as Robin to help the scheme along. Batman and Robin ultimately apprehend the Batman-costumed Regan with some timely assistance from Vanderveer, but the experience has persuaded Vanderveer that it is unwise to be so vain and boastful (BM No. 148/2, Jun '62: "The Boy Who Was Robin").

WEBB, BOLEY. An unscrupulous former racketeer, supposedly now reformed, who entices Judson Field, "America's dean of detectives," into betting Webb $50,000 that he can, through training, transform the next man they see into a first-rate detective. The trainee turns out to be socialite Bruce Wayne, secretly Batman, and although Webb tries time and time again to sabotage Field's training effort to ensure winning the wager, Wayne's real problem lies in concealing his secret identity and awesome detecting skill while he pretends to take lessons in crime detection from the well-intentioned Field. Ultimately, however, Wayne passes the detection test put to him by the bettors, and Boley Webb's efforts to win the bet through chicanery end in well-deserved failure (WF No. 64, May/Jun '53: "Bruce Wayne . . . Amateur Detective!").

WEBB (Colonel). The United States Army colonel who is the inventor of the "vacuum blanket," an experimental device which Batman and Robin install as permanent equipment in the new-model batplane – known as Batplane II – which they construct in October–November 1950. When activated in mid-air, direc over an opposing aircraft, Webb's vacuum blan causes a total engine failure in the target craft, th forcing its pilot to make an immediate emerger landing (BM No. 61/1: "The Birth of Batplane II (*See* Batman [section E 2 b i, the batplane].)

WEEMS, AMBROSE. The professor of musicology w is secretly the Sparrow (BM No. 149/1, Aug '62: "T Maestro of Crime").

WEIR (Mr.). The inventor of an ingenious remote-co trolled "robot cop" which almost forces Batman in premature retirement in April–May 1952 until it is d covered that exposure to X-rays renders the rob totally inoperative, a fact that the Gotham City und world would inevitably turn to its advantage (BM N 70/1: "The Robot Cop of Gotham City"). (*See* Gordo James W. [Police Commissioner].)

WELKEN, "WIRES." "An electrical wizard turn crooked, who cleverly short-circuited bank alarm-wi on the roof so his accomplices could break in." Wh Welken was finally apprehended by Batman, someti in the past, a spool of insulated wire found in his poc was placed on display in the batcave's trophy roo but Batman remained unaware that his innocent-lo ing trophy was in reality a cleverly disguised recordi containing the names of the three members of Welken gang who have successfully managed to elu the authorities.

In October 1955, when Batman and Robin outfi special "bat-train" for a nationwide tour to public Anti-Crime Week, Welken's spool of wire is among trophies on public exhibition in the bat-train's Muse of Justice car, and the three fugitive accomplices, fe ful that Welken's recording will one day lead to th arrest, make a series of daring attempts to steal Ultimately, however, Batman and Robin capture three accomplices and discover the significance of spool of wire that has been in their possession sin Welken's arrest (BM No. 95/2: "The Bat-Train"). (S *also* Batman [section D, the batcave].)

WEST, PORTER. One of a group of Gotham City m lionaires, including Bruce Wayne, who are lured to mysterious house on a lonely island where an unse villain, addressing them periodically over a lou speaker system, attempts to terrorize them into reve ing the secret techniques, formulas, and industrial pr esses which have enabled them to amass great weal With Robin's help, however, Batman exposes West the mysterious criminal mastermind and takes him in custody (BM No. 62/3, Dec/Jan '50–'51: "The Myste of Millionaire Island!").

WEVER, BURT. A well-known television news comme tator and secret leader of a Gotham City crime syn cate who concocts an elaborate scheme to ruin B man's reputation and thus destroy his effectiveness a crime-fighter by framing the famed lawman for a ser of old unsolved crimes. With the manufactured e dence against Batman steadily mounting and Poli Commissioner Gordon – the only man who could stantly exonerate Batman – lost in Africa on safari appears that Batman's career has come to an ignoble end. Ultimately, however, with the aid of Gotham City policemen who refuse to believe he is really guilty, Batman succeeds in establishing his innocence and in bringing Burt Wever to justice (Det No. 240, Feb '57: "The Outlaw Batman!").

WEXLEY, THOMAS. The manager of the Jolly Roger, a multimillion-dollar luxury hotel situated on an island off the coast of GOTHAM CITY on the site of an old pirate fortress. Wexley is secretly the infamous smuggler known as JOLLY ROGER (Det No. 202, Dec '53: "Millionaire Island!").

WHEELER, SLIM. An old-time confidence man who, having spent fifteen years attempting to unravel the secret of BATMAN's identity, has correctly concluded that Bruce Wayne is Batman. Wheeler sells his knowledge for $100,000 to gangster GLENN FARR, who, hoping to utilize the secret as protection against Batman, attempts to verify it by comparing Bruce Wayne's signature with Batman's. Since Batman always signs his name with his right hand as Bruce Wayne, however, and with his left hand as Batman, Farr becomes convinced that both he and Wheeler have made a mistake (WF No. 60, Sep/Oct '52: "The Richest Crook in the World!").

WILKER, JOHN. The original owner of Ace, the courageous canine who achieves renown as Bat-Hound (*see* ACE [THE BAT-HOUND]). Batman No. 92/3 describes Wilker as a "skilled engraver," employed by the Gotham Printing and Engraving Company, who lives alone in a small cottage in "an isolated suburb" of GOTHAM CITY (Jun '55: "Ace, the Bat-Hound!").

In June 1955, when Wilker is abducted by criminals who hope to force him to use his skill as an engraver to counterfeit bonds for them, Ace plays a key role in helping BATMAN and ROBIN apprehend the criminals and rescue Wilker from their clutches (BM No. 92/3: "Ace, the Bat-Hound!"). (*See* ACE [THE BAT-HOUND].)

In February 1956 Wilker lends Ace to Batman and Robin so that they can use him to track down a gang of criminals who are using a trained dog to help them commit crimes (BM No. 97/3: "The Return of the Bat-Hound!"). (*See* MILLEN, ROSS.)

In October 1956 Wilker is in Europe, having left Ace in the temporary care of his friends BRUCE WAYNE and DICK GRAYSON. During this period, in his role as Bat-Hound, Ace helps Batman and Robin solve several cases, including the capture of fugitive criminal Baldy Gore (BM No. 103/3: "Bat-Hound, Movie Star!"). (*See* ACE [THE BAT-HOUND].)

In April 1958, while Wilker is on vacation, Ace is once again left in the custody of Bruce Wayne and Dick Grayson. During this period, in his role as Bat-Hound, Ace helps Batman and Robin recover a vial of powerful explosive stolen from the home of scientist PROFESSOR DI PINA (Det No. 254: "One Ounce of Doom!").

In April 1959, while Wilker is away in Europe, Ace helps Batman and Robin capture the RED MASK MOB (BM No. 123/3: "The Fugitive Batman!").

By August 1959 Wilker has accepted a "new job" which "will keep [him] traveling constantly" and has asked Bruce Wayne to give Ace a permanent home at the Wayne mansion. Both Wayne and Ace are enthusiastic about the new arrangement, for it will enable Ace to become Bat-Hound more often (BM No. 125/1: "The Secret Life of Bat-Hound").

WILKINS. HARVEY KENT's butler. In December 1948–January 1949 Wilkins disguises himself as TWO-FACE and commits a series of spectacular crimes, hoping that Kent, because of his prior career as Two-Face, will be blamed for them. Wilkins is apprehended, however—and Harvey Kent is exonerated of any wrongdoing—through the heroic efforts of BATMAN and ROBIN (BM No. 50/2: "The Return of Two-Face!").

WINGMAN. A costumed crime-fighter who serves as BATMAN's partner during June–July 1951 after ROBIN has been temporarily confined to a wheelchair with a broken leg. A series of ambiguous developments combine to convince Robin that Wingman is being groomed as his permanent replacement, but his fears are put to rest when he learns that Wingman is actually a naturalized American from a Northern European country whom Batman has agreed to train for a crime-fighting career in his native country (BM No. 65/1: "A Partner for Batman!"). (*See also* BATMAN [section F, the Batman counterparts].)

WINNS, HENRY. A noted scientist whose recent "secret discoveries in suspended animation" led him to the invention of two remarkable devices, a cameralike device capable of placing human beings in suspended animation by transforming them into bronze statues, and a second device designed to bring them back to life again. By April 1962, however, an underworld figure named Vulcan, having kidnapped Winns and stolen his inventions, uses the miraculous devices to facilitate a series of elaborate thefts. Posing as a sculptor of bronze statues, Vulcan smuggles his henchmen—whom he has turned to bronze for the occasion by means of one of Winns's inventions—into museums and other places he intends to rob disguised as statues he himself has ostensibly sculpted, and then restores his bronzed cohorts to normal with Winns's second invention so that they can loot the infiltrated places at their leisure. Aided by BATWOMAN, BATMAN and ROBIN apprehend Vulcan and his henchmen and rescue Henry Winns from their clutches (Det No. 302: "The Bronze Menace!").

WINTHROP. The treasurer of the Purity Milk Co. and the secret leader of a gang of criminals who steal jewelry from the city's wealthiest homes in the early morning hours and then make good their escape by posing as milkmen. Winthrop and his henchmen are apprehended by BATMAN and ROBIN in April–May 1943 (BM No. 16/2: "The Grade A Crimes!").

WIST, DAVID. The expert watch repairman and small-time safecracker who achieves infamy as the HUMAN MAGNET (Det No. 181, Mar '52: "The Crimes of the Human Magnet!").

WITTS, JOHNNY. The leader of a gang of criminals who prides himself on his seemingly unerring ability to outwit BATMAN and ROBIN by anticipating, well in advance, what the Dynamic Duo will do in any given situation. Witts and his henchmen are apprehended by Batman and Robin in October 1965 with the aid of the GOTHAM CITY police (Det No. 344: "The Crime-Boss Who Was Always One Step Ahead of Batman!").

WONG. The Chinese-American citizen who functions as "unofficial mayor of Chinatown" (Det No. 35, Jan '40) until he is brutally murdered by agents of a Chinese tong known as the GREEN DRAGON in May 1940 (Det No. 39). According to Detective Comics No. 52, the honest, law-abiding Wong is a direct descendant of the Mongol conqueror Genghis Khan (Jun '41: "The Secret of the Jade Box").

In January 1940, by providing BATMAN with vital information about a Chinese fence named Sin Fang, Wong brings Batman one step closer to defeating the villainous SHELDON LENOX (Det No. 35).

In May 1940 Wong summons Batman to Chinatown by placing a want ad in a local newspaper, and then informs him about the evil Green Dragon tong whose members have begun to "work many wicked enterprises" in the city. A day later, Batman pays another call on Wong, this time in the hope of learning the address of the tong's headquarters, but by the time he arrives Wong has been savagely murdered by the tong's agents. On his desk, however, Wong has managed to scratch the message "Pier 3," a clue which leads ultimately to the smashing of the ruthless tong and the capture of its leader (Det No. 39).

According to a later text, Detective Comics No. 52, Wong had been a direct descendant of Genghis Khan and the owner of an ornate serpent ring – the traditional symbol of the khan's power – which had passed from the Great Khan to his descendants down through the generations.

". . . down the ages," explains the text, each descendant of Genghis Khan "gathered 'round him a group of cutthroats and bandits who plagued the people of small towns" and exacted tribute from them. Wong had been far too honorable to use the ring to exact tribute from his fellows, but LOO CHUNG, his successor as Chinatown's unofficial mayor, gains possession of the ring in June 1941 and uses it to launch a ruthless protection racket among the local Chinese merchants ("The Secret of the Jade Box").

WORDENSHIRE. The quiet English village on whose outskirts Wordenshire Castle is situated. Wordenshire Castle is the home of the Earl of Wordenshire and his young son Cyril, the father and son who are secretly the KNIGHT and the SQUIRE. Wordenshire is apparently a fictitious place, although Batman No. 62/2 places it somewhere in the vicinity of Stonehenge (Dec/Jan '50–'51: "The Batman of England!").

WORDENSHIRE, EARL OF. The British nobleman who is secretly the KNIGHT (BM No. 62/2, Dec/Jan '50–'51: "The Batman of England!").

WRECKER, THE. A mysterious villain – clad in a full-length maroon robe and hood that completely conceal his identity, with a white letter "W" emblazoned on his chest – who appears in GOTHAM CITY in July 1953 and loudly proclaims his intention to avenge the deaths of three brothers allegedly sent to the electric chair by BATMAN by striking out not only at Batman himself, but at all those who have glorified his deeds. In reality, however, the Wrecker is Dwight Forrow, the author of a book entitled *Batman's 10 Greatest Cases* and a man heavily in debt due to his profligate gambling, who has concocted the role of the Wrecker as part of an elaborate scheme to fake his own death at the hands of the Wrecker so that he and his brother, Doug Forrow, can collect the outstanding insurance on Dwight Forrow's life and flee to South America to begin a new life.

In apparent fulfillment of his vow of vengeance, the Wrecker and his henchmen loot and demolish a series of establishments that may be said to have glorified the Batman name – including the Gotham Mechanical Toy Co., makers of Batman statuettes, toy batmobiles, utility belts, and batplanes; the Geo. V. Dewey Co., manufacturers of Batman and Robin electric signs; and the studio of sculptor Rolf Baglund, whose work has included a gigantic World's Fair statue of Batman and Robin – and then carry out the apparent vengeance murder of author Dwight Forrow, ostensibly in retaliation for his book about Batman, but both Dwight Forrow and his brother Doug are ultimately exposed and apprehended by Batman and ROBIN (Det No. 197: "The League Against Batman!").

WRECKERS, THE. "A gang [of criminals] that commits robberies by creating catastrophes and getting away in the midst of the danger and confusion they've caused!" The Wreckers are apprehended by BATMAN and ROBIN in September 1960 (WF No. 112: "The Menace of Superman's Pet!").

WRIGHT. A prominent book publisher who is secretly a ruthless "fifth columnist" engaged in the publication and dissemination of subversive anti-American propaganda "dealing with the greatness of our fatherland's cause." When mystery writer Erik Dorne is murdered in Spring 1941 and an unfinished manuscript stolen from his desk, there are four prime suspects – Joshua Grimm, author of numerous books on witchcraft and demonology; Melissa Brunt, the murdered man's embittered aunt; actress Jane Ware, the murdered man's estranged wife; and Wright, the murdered man's publisher – but BATMAN and ROBIN soon learn of Wright's involvement in anti-American subversion, realize that he killed Dorne in order to prevent Dorne from exposing him as a FIFTH COLUMNIST in his latest novel, and ultimately take Wright and his cohorts into custody (WB No. 1: "The Witch and the Manuscript of Doom!").

WRIGHT (Bill Waters). An alias employed by BILL WATERS when he poses as a jeweler as part of an elaborate scheme to murder his business partners and frame a former partner for the killings (Det No. 161, Jul '50: "The Men Who Died on Time!").

WYRE, ALEC. An "electronic genius . . . turned criminal" – an inventor of sophisticated electronic devices for use by the underworld – whose dead body is discovered in the BATCAVE by BATMAN and ROBIN in

February 1959, leading the Dynamic Duo to the conclusion that Wyre was murdered in the batcave and that the killer, having somehow uncovered the batcave's secret location, must therefore also know their secret identities. The search for the murderer, and the man apparently now privy to their secret, results in the capture by Batman and Robin of three of Wyre's former gangland clients – Jigger Mulane, Dan Dolson, and Hank Purdy – but Wyre, it turns out, was not murdered at all; rather, he had located the batcave on his own with the aid of a special "supersonic transmitter" and had died after slamming his head into a stalactite while stumbling about in the darkness (BM No. 121/1: "The Body in the Bat-Cave").

X

X (Planet). *See* ZUR-EN-ARRH.

X (Planetoid). The "remote and unexplored asteroid" where BATMAN, ROBIN, and the alien lawman Tutian apprehend Earth criminal Eddie Marrow and "the notorious space raider" GARR in August 1958. The planetoid's physical features include a "giant orchard" with fruits fifty to a hundred times the size of their Earth counterparts, a vast "cave area" which is the home of a gigantic dinosaurlike creature, and a large lake, apparently without tides, which is referred to as a "silent sea" (BM No. 117/3: "Manhunt in Outer Space!").

XANU. An evil extradimensional scientist and would-be dictator who inhabits a bizarre world enterable from the earthly dimension by means of an antique mirror, apparently "made centuries ago" by "sorcerers from their world or ours," which serves as "a door between the two worlds." Entering the strange mirror-world with BATMAN and ROBIN in November 1961 in hopes of curing Batman of the freakish qualities he acquired during an earlier visit there, SUPERMAN defeats the evil Xanu and puts an end to his dictatorial ambitions (WF No. 121: "The Mirror Batman!").

XERON. The extradimensional world – referred to also as Xeros – which is the home of the villainous VATHGAR (WF No. 118, Jun '61: "The Creature That Was Exchanged for Superman!").

XLUR. A far-distant planet whose "weird" atmosphere temporarily transforms BATMAN and ROBIN into extraterrestrial aliens, endowing them with the green skin, twin protruding antennae, and other characteristics of the planet's native inhabitants.

Sometime in the recent past, while experimenting with a newly developed "space-warp ray," a group of scientists on the planet Xlur accidentally snatched the BATPLANE out of the skies over GOTHAM CITY and transported it to Xlur, where Batman and Robin found themselves marooned for three full days while the apologetic scientists labored to perfect their space-warp ray so that it could be used to transport the Dynamic Duo and their batplane back to Earth.

During that time, however, Batman and Robin discovered that their bodily structures had miraculously changed to resemble those of Xlur's green-skinned inhabitants. ". . . somehow," exclaimed Batman incredulously, "this weird planet's atmosphere is affecting ***us***--changing us into ***aliens!***"

Even after their successful return to Earth, Batman and Robin retained their alien forms, and they discovered that these same forms endowed them with fantastic powers: they could make gigantic leaps because "their bodies [had become] adapted to the alien planet's greater gravitational pull," and they could exert "an amazing magnetic force" with their antennae which enabled them to exercise a phenomenal control over metal objects. The alien forms were not without their disadvantages, however, since they made it almost impossibly difficult for the Dynamic Duo to maintain the closely guarded secret of their dual identities.

In June 1961, with the aid of their alien powers Batman and Robin battle a notorious gang of criminals known as the Yellow Sweater Gang. Ultimately, the Dynamic Duo's alien characteristics fade away of their own accord, and Batman and Robin apprehend the Yellow Sweater Gang, in their normal human forms moments afterward (BM No. 140/3: "The Eighth Wonder of Space!").

XLYM. A "planet of another star" with a science far advanced over that of Earth. In July–August 1958, after having observed both BATMAN and SUPERMAN through their planet's "ultra-telescopes," two of Xlym's inhabitants become embroiled in a bitter quarrel over which of the two heroes would perform the most impressive feats if both were endowed with the superhuman powers of Superman. In a misguided effort to settle their wager, the two aliens teleport Batman and Superman to Xlym, endow Batman with superhuman powers identical to Superman's by means of a special "super power-ray," transform both men from close friends into bitter rivals by subjecting them to a potent "hate ray," eradicate all memory of their interplanetary visit with a special "amnesia-ray," and then teleport them back to Earth to observe which of them performs the most breathtaking feats now that they are evenly matched.

For a time, Batman and Superman astound the world with their bitter, potentially destructive, and seemingly senseless personal rivalry, but after a time Batman's super-powers suddenly vanish and the personalities of the two men return to normal, apparently bcause the aliens' superior on the planet Xlym became aware of his subordinates' mischief and took the appropriate super-scientific steps to correct it (WF No. 95: "The Battle of the Super-Heroes!").

Y

'BAR. The far-distant planet which is the home of the ·il sorcerer ZERNO (WF No. 127, Aug '62: "The Sorcerer om the Stars!").

ELLOW MASK MOB, THE. A gang of criminals who e captured by BATMAN and ROBIN while attempting to b the purser's office aboard an ocean liner in March 49. The Dynamic Duo's efforts to apprehend the iminals are severely hampered by the fact that an ccidental blow on the head has temporarily afflicted obin with near-total amnesia, causing him to lose all collection of his life following the death of his parents *ee* FLYING GRAYSONS, THE), including his vital crime-fighting training (Det No. 145: "Robin, the Boy Failure!").

YLLA. The extradimensional city to which BATMAN, ROBIN, and wanted criminal EDDIE STARK are transported in July 1961 when an "eerie fog" combines with the effects of a crackling electric storm to thrust the ferryboat on which they are passengers through a warp in space and time (Det No. 293: "Prisoners of the Dark World!").

YMAR (Swami). The GOTHAM CITY fortune-teller who is secretly the SPINNER (BM No. 129/1, Feb '60: "The Web of the Spinner!").

Z

ZEBO. An evil extradimensional scientist whose attempt to establish a dictatorship in his home dimension is thwarted in February 1963 through the heroic efforts of BATMAN, ROBIN, BATWOMAN, and BAT-GIRL (*see* BAT-GIRL [BETTY KANE]) (BM No. 153: chs. 1–3 – "Prisoners of Three Worlds!"; "Death from Beyond"; "Dimension of Doom").

ZEBRA-MAN, THE. A "bizarre criminal" whose entire "body is . . . charged with energy so powerful, it sends lines of force right through [his] costume" and endows him with the eerie, zebra-striped appearance from which his name is derived. When he stretches out his hand, "strange emanations dart from his fingers," enabling him to attract or repel either people or objects as though he were some sort of incredible human electromagnet.

In January 1960 the Zebra-Man uses his incredible powers to commit a series of spectacular crimes in GOTHAM CITY, each time escaping despite the Dynamic Duo's attempts to apprehend him. After a careful investigation, BATMAN and ROBIN finally locate the villain's hideout, only to have their efforts complicated even further when Robin falls against the machine responsible for the Zebra-Man's powers and bathes Batman "in an eerie light," infusing him "with lines of force" and transforming him into an eerily striped "Zebra-Batman" with powers equivalent to those of his adversary. Lacking a special "control belt" of the type worn by the Zebra-Man, however, Batman is unable either to control or neutralize his power, so that people and objects fly away from him in all directions as soon as he approaches them.

Ultimately, however, Batman defeats the Zebra-Man, removes the villain's control belt – thus depriving the Zebra-Man of his awesome powers – and then uses his own repelling powers to drive the Zebra-Man's henchmen directly into the waiting arms of Robin and the Gotham City police. Then Batman dons the Zebra-Man's control belt and uses its complex controls to eradicate his own lines of force and restore himself to normal (Det No. 275: "The Zebra Batman!").

ZERNO. An evil sorcerer from the far-distant planet Y'bar who is able, by means of a "strange crystal" in his possession, to summon instantaneously from distant planets awesome weapons and creatures which he can force to do his bidding. Zerno arrives on Earth in August 1962, determined to "loot and plunder" the planet and to accumulate a large supply of bronze, a metal with the power to rob all inhabitants of Y'bar "completely of [their] physical and mental strength," so that, once back on his native planet, he can "gain complete control over [his] people." Zerno and his henchman Sborg are ultimately defeated and apprehended through the heroic efforts of BATMAN, ROBIN, a SUPERMAN (WF No. 127: "The Sorcerer from t Stars!").

ZERO, THE. A mysterious hooded criminal w matches wits with BATMAN and ROBIN in Novembe December 1953. "His methods of robbery are cunnin varied," observes Robin, ". . . but he always strikes the most ***unusual*** loot!" Batman and Robin ultimat apprehend the Zero and unmask him as ex-conv Willis Gibling (WF No. 67: "The Millionaire Det tive!").

ZERO (Mr.). A cunning criminal who has been doom to dwell in an icy zero-degree environment since t day he was accidentally saturated with an experimen "freezing solution" while working to perfect a diabo cal weapon known as the "ice gun."

"Golly, boss," exclaimed a startled henchman at t time of the accident, "--you've become a--a hum icicle! You gotta live in zero temperature . . . foreve

Undaunted, Mr. Zero "perfected an air-condition costume to help [him] commit [his] crimes" and "bu [a] hidden refrigerated mountain lair" somewh "within a remote mountain outside Gotham City."

In February 1959 Mr. Zero commits a series of sp tacular crimes in GOTHAM CITY with the aid of diabolical ice gun, a bizarre double-barreled handg which fires a frigid "ice gas" from one barrel and blazing "heat ray" from the other. Mr. Zero and henchmen are ultimately apprehended by Batman a Robin, but not before a freak steam accident has tra formed Mr. Zero into a normal man again and made unnecessary for him to dwell any longer in a ze degree environment.

"Yes, Mr. Zero, that steam treatment must ha changed you back to normal!" observes Batman wry "Now we'll see if the law can straighten out your dist ted mind!" (BM No. 121/3: "The Ice Crimes of M Zero!").

ZERO (Professor). An evil scientist who reduces seve prominent citizens to about nine inches in height w his "invisible black light" reducing ray so that he c extort large sums of money from them in return restoring them to normal. BATMAN and ROBIN's effo to apprehend Professor Zero are severely hampered the fact that they too have been shrunk by the diabo cal ray, but the villain accidentally shoots himself w a shotgun while attempting to kill them and the ra effects wear off after only three days (Det No. 148, J '49: "The Experiment of Professor Zero").

ZODIAC MASTER, THE. A cunning criminal w concocts an elaborate scheme to deceive the und world into believing that he is capable of making infal ble astrological predictions so that its members w agree to pay him 25 percent of their loot in return for his predicting the probable success or failure of each impending crime.

The Zodiac Master wears a pale blue costume colorfully emblazoned with the signs of the zodiac, each of which, when torn from its place on the costume, instantly transforms itself into some sort of bizarre weapon, such as the ram's-head symbol of Aries which transforms itself into a powerful battering ram.

For a time, the Zodiac Master succeeds in collecting lucrative fees from the underworld in return for his largely worthless predictions, but, after a lengthy battle, he is finally apprehended by BATMAN and ROBIN in the act of stealing a gem-encrusted golden bull from the Gotham Museum (Det No. 323, Jan '64: "The Zodiac Master!").

ZORN. A "hero-idol" of ancient Babylon whose 3,000-year-old statue, unearthed in September 1956, depicts him wearing a costume almost identical to BATMAN's (BM No. 102/2: "The Batman from Babylon"). (*See* BARTOR, BRAND.)

ZORON. A far-distant planet which is rescued from the cruel domination of CHORN and the Baxians in December 1960 through the heroic efforts of BATMAN, ROBIN, and SUPERMAN (WF No. 114: "Captives of the Space Globes!").

ZUCCO, "BOSS." The corpulent crime czar whose effort to extort protection money from the owner of the Haly Circus in April 1940 sets in motion the chain of events which culminates in the emergence of Dick Grayson as ROBIN. To "Boss" Zucco belongs the distinction of being the first criminal ever apprehended by the newly formed crime-fighting team of BATMAN and Robin (Det No. 38). (*See* ROBIN.)

"Boss" Zucco © NPP 1940

ZUR-EN-ARRH. The far-distant planet which is the home of TLANO, the man who is secretly the BATMAN of Zur-en-arrh. In February 1958, when Zur-en-arrh is attacked by "invaders from an enemy planet," Tlano teleports Batman to Zur-en-arrh to help him defeat the alien menace. In the text, Zur-en-arrh is also referred to as Planet X (BM No. 113/3: "Batman--The Superman of Planet X!").

BIOGRAPHY

BORN IN NEW YORK CITY IN 1942, MICHAEL L. FLEISHER graduated from the Horace Mann School, in Riverdale, New York, in 1960, then completed his freshman year at the University of Chicago before dropping out of college to pursue a career as a writer. In 1969, with the generous cooperation of DC Comics, he began work on *The Encyclopedia of Comic Book Heroes,* which culminated in three exhaustive, meticulously detailed volumes chronicling the comic book exploits of Batman, Wonder Woman, and Superman—the first two of which were published by Macmillan and the third by Warner Books.

In the course of the 22-year period from 1969 to 1991, Fleisher scripted approximately 650 comic book stories, overwhelmingly for DC Comics, but also for Marvel and other comic book publishers. His Spectre revival, featuring tales in which The Spectral Avenger employed his otherworldly powers to dispatch evildoers in grisly fashion—such as when he transformed a villain into a lifelike wooden statue and then ran him through a buzz saw—were controversial in their day and earned Fleisher no small measure of notoriety among the comics fraternity.

The highlight of Fleisher's comic book career, however, and the series for which he is still best known, is the lengthy run, over a 13-year period, of *Jonah Hex* stories, the overwhelming majority of them written under the editorship of Joe Orlando.

In 1991, having earned a B.A. in anthropology from Columbia University, Fleisher left comics, earned a doctorate in anthropology at the University of Michigan, Ann Arbor, in 1997, and now serves as an anthropological consultant to international organizations in Africa and Asia.

In addition to *The Encyclopedia of Comic Book Heroes*, Fleisher is also the author of a novel, *Chasing Hairy* (Macmillan, 1977), and an anthropological treatise on cross-border cattle raiding between the East African countries of Tanzania and Kenya (University of Michigan Press, 2000).

The manuscript of a new novel by Fleisher, set in the New York comic book world of the 1980s, is currently in search of a publisher.

CONFESSIONS OF AN OVERAGE COMIC BOOK FANATIC

IN 1976, MICHAEL FLEISHER informed DC fans of the Encyclopedia of Comic Book Heroes with this article which appeared in the pages of THE AMAZING WORLD OF DC COMICS #12:

Confessions of an Overage Comic Book Fanatic!

Or how I spent seven years of my life reading comic books—and found Nirvana.

By Michael L. Fleisher

What's **that**?! You say you're a dedicated, devoted, hard-core, dyed-in-the-wool superhero **fanatic**? You say you buy every superhero mag you can get your **hands** on and would travel all the way to **Okefenokee Swamp** to attend a comic book convention if **DC Comics** decided to **hold** one there?

You think **you've** got troubles, eh? You think **you're** addicted? **Hah!** Just wait 'til you hear **my** story. I passed through my entire boyhood—in the prehistoric forties and early fifties—relatively **unscathed** by comics. Oh, I **read** them, to be sure. I read every issue of **Batman** and **Superman**. I even read (gasp) **Wonder Woman** when none of my friends was looking. And of course I **ignored** my parents when they warned me that reading too many comic books would turn my mind to moldy Jello.

But then I grew up. I sold all my comic books to a junk lady on New York's Third Avenue for a penny apiece. (Please, don't remind me that if I sold that collection today I'd probably have enough money to buy myself a brand new Jaguar touring car. **I know! I know!**)

I went to **college**. I got an **education**. I forgot all about my parents' warning. I became a thoughtful, hard-working, contributing member of society. I became (shudder) an **adult**!

And I became a **writer**. Not a comic book writer, a **real-world** writer. Then one day, without thinking, I signed a contract with a publisher to write a book about superheroes. It was to be called *The Encyclopedia of Comic Book Heroes*. It was supposed to be one volume long. And I figured it would take about a year to 18 months to write. That was in early 1969.

That's when I first walked into the National offices and asked for permission to do the research for my book. Of course, I had not so much as glanced sideways at a comic book in about 15 years. I dimly recalled that **Batman**, my favorite character, had come out eight or ten times a year. I didn't think I would have that many comic books to read.

When Gerda Gattel, the DC librarian, opened the library door and turned on the light, I nearly died. Here was this room, filled from floor to ceiling with bound copies of DC's back-issue comic books, thousands upon thousands of them. It came to me with a sickening, mind-deadening thud that if I wanted my encyclopedia to be truly **definitive**, I'd have to read (gasp and double gasp) **all** of them, at least all of them that had stories about super-heroes.

So that's what I did. And it didn't take me too long to finish the book either. Just every single day of my life for **seven years**! And the work went a little faster after the first year or so, because I hired a full-time assistant, **Janet Lincoln**, to help me.

Together Janet and I read about 10,000 comic book stories and filled approximately 20,000 5" x 8" index cards with detailed typewritten notes on what we had read. Every now and then some DC staffer would poke his nose in the door to see how the two lunatics in the library were doing. Eventually, the typewritten notes were transformed into the 6,000 articles that make up *The Encyclopedia of Comic Book Heroes.*

My little one-volume encyclopedia, by the way, had turned out a trifle longer than I expected. It grew to 2,000,000 words (that's about 8,000 typewritten pages) and finally had to be divided into eight individual oversized volumes. (Along the way, of course, I ran completely out of money to live on, and when my landlord began threatening me with eviction, I became a **DC** writer to stave off starvation. But that's another story).

Under the auspices of the **Macmillan Publishing Company**, the eight volumes are now being published at the rate of two volumes a year. By the time you read this, the first volume, devoted entirely to **Batman**, should already be in the bookstores. Take it from me, comic fans, *The Encyclopedia of Comic Book Heroes: Volume 1: BATMAN* contains every scrap of information you could possibly want to know about Batman. It consists of 416 double-column, oversized pages and boasts over 200 rare illustrations culled directly from the comics. It answers all those nagging questions that inevitably prey on the mind of any real fan, even while he sleeps – questions such as:

(**1**) Who taught **Batman** the art of makeup and impersonation? (**2**) Who taught **Batman** to throw a boomerang and devised the first batarang? (**3**) Who hired **Joe Chill** to murder **Batman's** parents? (**4**) Who was the first criminal to ever shoot **Batman**? (I'd answer those questions for you here and now, you understand, but then [heh heh] you might not buy the book).

If you do get hold of a copy of the **Batman** volume (Please **buy** one! I am **poor**!), take a long look through it and then drop me a line at **AMAZING WORLD** and let me know what you think of it (No letter-bombs, please!). The second volume, due out in October, is devoted to **Wonder Woman**. Future volumes will immortalize **Superman**, **Green Lantern**, the **Flash**, **Hawkman** and many others. (Many of the heroes were even published by other companies, but we'll keep that that our little secret.)

Now I see that my space is running out, so I would like to direct this final comment to my mom and dad: Hi, Folks! I know that when you sent me away to the University of Chicago you never expected me to use my higher education to become a comic book expert. But look at it this way: if enough people buy my encyclopedia, at least I'll have been paid for reading all those comic books, sort of. **MLF**

P.S. Okay, already! Don't break into loud sobbing! Don't beat your head against the wall! Here are the answers to those four Bat-trivia questions in the above article: (**1**) impersonator Barrett Kean; (**2**) Australian circus performer Lee Collins; (**3**) bank robber Lew Moxon; (**4**) Doctor Death's Indian assistant, Jabah. **MLF**

SHOWCASE PRESENTS

OVER 500 PAGES OF DC'S CLASSIC HEROES AND STORIES PRESENTED IN EACH VOLUME!

GREEN LANTERN VOL. 1

SUPERMAN VOL. 1

SUPERMAN VOL. 2

SUPERMAN FAMILY VOL. 1

JONAH HEX VOL. 1

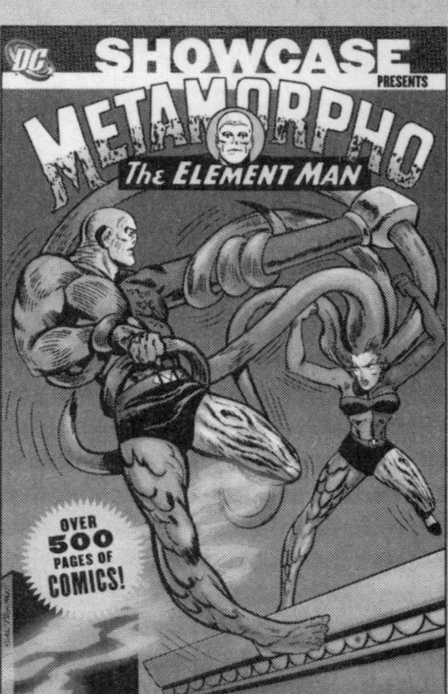

METAMORPHO VOL. 1

SEARCH THE GRAPHIC NOVELS SECTION OF

www.DCCOMICS.com

FOR ART AND INFORMATION ON ALL OF OUR BOOKS!